S0-ADM-214

THE EMC MASTERPIECE SERIES

LITERATURE AND THE LANGUAGE ARTS

Grades 6-8

A truly integrated literature and language arts program

EMCParadigm

Components In Each Level

THE EMC MASTERPIECE SERIES
LITERATURE AND THE LANGUAGE ARTS

The *Experiencing Literature* level components, intended for the ninth grade, are shown above. These same components are available for each level in *The EMC Masterpiece Series* middle school program for grades six through eight. Each level in the middle school series includes the following materials:

- Student Textbook
- Annotated Teacher's Edition
- Essential Skills Practice Books in five language arts subject areas
- Assessment Portfolio
- Reader's Guide and Activity Workbook
- Transparency Set
- CD-ROM containing the Annotated Teacher's Edition for easy access to the selections
- Three Gallery Posters of renowned authors

Multimedia Kit

THE EMC MASTERPIECE SERIES
LITERATURE AND THE LANGUAGE ARTS

The Multimedia Kit for the middle school series includes:

- Three sixty-minute audiocassettes including songs and dramatic readings from the series.
- Videocassette and video laser disc featuring dramatic performances from the series.
- CD-ROM containing an idea generator and a test generator.
- IBM and Macintosh diskettes containing test generators.

Comprehensive Classic and Contemporary Works Collection

THE EMC MASTERPIECE SERIES
LITERATURE AND THE LANGUAGE ARTS

- Integrates literature and the language arts more thoroughly than any other series.
- Contains the most extensive collection of classic literary works available in any series today, as well as engaging contemporary selections.
- Strong representation of culturally diverse authors.
- Strong cross-curricular integration with every selection, including social studies, mathematics, science, art/humanities, music, technology, and applied arts.
- Emphasizes reader response, relating literature to student experiences while enabling the teacher to guide responses to ensure cultural transmission.
- Offers the most comprehensive portfolio assessment program available.
- Includes abundant teacher resources: Essential Skills Practice Books in five language arts subject areas; Assessment Portfolio; Reader's Guide and Activity Workbook; Transparency Set; and exciting, motivational multimedia components such as Audiocassettes, a Videocassette, Computer Software, a Video Laser Disc, two CD-ROM Programs, and the Annotated Teacher's Editions on CD-ROM.

DISCOVERING LITERATURE
REDWOOD LEVEL–GRADE 6

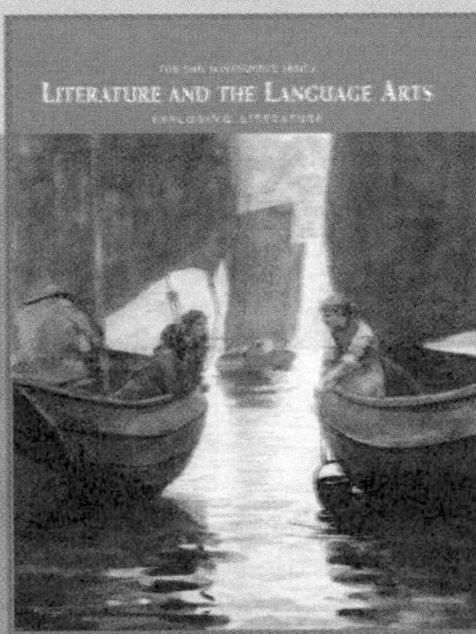

EXPLORING LITERATURE
CEDAR LEVEL–GRADE 7

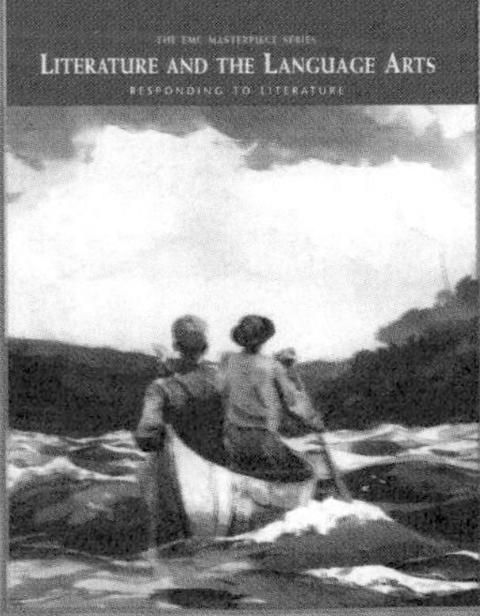

RESPONDING TO LITERATURE
OAK LEVEL–GRADE 8

The EMC Masterpiece Series, Literature and the Language Arts contains the most comprehensive collection of classic literary works available in any series today, as well as current multicultural selections, to captivate your students. In addition, this series thoroughly models the complete range of literary types and genres: poetry, fiction, nonfiction, drama, myth, fairy tale, fable, parable, legend, tall tale, and folk song.

Global Representation of Authors

- Geronimo, from *Geronimo's Story of His Life* (Native American)
- Zlata Filipović, from *Zlata's Diary: A Child's Life in Sarajevo* (Bosnian)
- Seamus Heaney, "Digging" (Northern Irish)
- Sandra Cisneros, from *A House on Mango Street* (Mexican American)
- Pablo Neruda, "Ode to My Socks" (Chilean)
- Rita Dove, "The First Book" (African American)
- Yoshiko Uchida, "Tears of Autumn" (Japanese American)
- Alice Walker, "Women" (African American)

Strong Representation of Culturally Diverse Authors

The EMC Masterpiece Series contains an unequaled representation of works by authors from various cultural backgrounds. The series provides a well-rounded view of literary activity in cultural contexts around the corner and around the world.

Flexible Organization

The EMC Masterpiece Series provides a flexible organization allowing varied approaches to the literature, so teachers can readily adapt the materials to their individual teaching styles and to their students' needs.

Discovering Literature, Exploring Literature, and *Responding to Literature*

The middle school textbook levels are organized into separate sections presenting genres and techniques, themes, and modes (science fiction, fantasy, adventure, mystery, and detective fiction). No other series covers all three in a single volume.

Student Textbook

PREREADING provides **CROSS-CURRICULAR CONNECTIONS** to other academic areas such as social studies, mathematics, and science, tying in intriguing insights from the various disciplines to the selection.

AS YOU READ sections involve students with various activities to help them better understand the selection.

Prereading

SUMMER

"All Summer in a Day"
by Ray Bradbury

Cross-curricular Connections

Science. Venus is the second planet from the sun and the second brightest object in our nighttime sky. (Our moon is the brightest.) Often called Earth's sister planet, Venus is very similar to Earth in size and mass. Venus is covered by a nine-mile-thick layer of clouds. This layer of clouds led early twentieth-century scientists to predict that Venus might be a very wet planet covered with swampy plant life. Now we know that Venus is much too hot for water to form, that its clouds are made of sulfuric acid, and that its atmosphere is made up mostly of carbon dioxide. Life as we know it, even swampy plant life, cannot exist under such conditions. Venus's heavy clouds trap great amounts of solar heat as the result of what is known as "the greenhouse effect." In fact, Venus is so hot that its rocks glow red with heat. One especially curious thing about Venus is its "refraction" effect. Because of the high surface pressure and dense atmosphere, light is refracted, or bent. This means that if you were standing or walking around on Venus it would always appear as if you were standing in a low hollow.

Health. You may have heard about the "wintertime blues" or noticed that some people seem much happier and more energetic in spring, summer, and early fall than they do in winter. All people react to seasonal changes to some degree, but for some, winter and its decreased sunlight can cause serious emotional problems. People affected by Seasonal Affective Disorder, or SAD, feel very depressed and tired in winter. Their self-esteem drops. As a result, they often retreat from family and friends and have trouble concentrating. Doctors have found that controlled exposure to bright light can make people with SAD happier and more productive. In the story you are about to read, the sun seldom shines, and one of the characters experiences the sadness and isolation that those who have Seasonal Affective Disorder feel.

As You Read

"All Summer in a Day" describes the planet Venus as the author imagines it would appear both in rain and in sunshine. Make a comparison-contrast chart like the one below. As you read, record details from the author's imaginary description of Earth's sister planet.

VENUS IN THE RAIN	VENUS IN THE SUNSHINE
constant drumming sound of rain	incredible silence

READER'S JOURNAL

What if you had to describe the sun to someone who had never seen or felt it before? In what way would you describe the sun? To what could you compare it? How would you say that the sun makes you feel?

"All Summer in a Day"

RAY BRADBURY

"Ready?"

"Ready."

"Now?"

"Soon."

"Do the scientists really know? Will it happen today, will it?"

"Look, look; see for yourself!"

The children pressed to each other like so many roses, so many weeds, intermixed, peering out for a look at the hidden sun.

It rained.

It had been raining for seven years; thousands upon thousands of days compounded and filled from one end to the other with rain, with the drum and gush of water, with the sweet crystal fall of showers and the con-cussion of storms so heavy they were tidal waves come over the islands. A thousand forests had been crushed under the rain and grown up a thousand times to be crushed again. And this was the way life was forever on the planet Venus, and this was the schoolroom of the children of the rocket men and women who had come to a raining world to set up civilization and live out their lives.

Where does this story take place?

"It's stopping, it's stopping!"

"Yes, yes!"

Margot stood apart from them, from these children who could never remember a time when there wasn't rain and rain and rain. They were all nine years old, and if there had been a day, seven years ago, when the sun came out for an hour and showed its face to the stunned world, they could not recall. Sometimes, at night, she heard them stir, in remembrance, and she knew they were dreaming and remembering gold or a yellow crayon or a coin large enough to buy the world with. She knew that they thought they remembered a warmness, like a blushing in the face, in

What is the weather like? How long has the weather been this way?

WORDS FOR EVERYDAY USE — con • cus • sion (kən kush´ən) *n.,* strong shaking

"ALL SUMMER IN A DAY" 3

READER'S JOURNAL activities relate the literature to students' feelings and experiences.

GUIDED READING QUESTIONS for each selection point out key elements and encourage critical response reading.

WORDS FOR EVERYDAY USE sections provide the definitions for vocabulary that is underlined in the selection.

RESPONDING TO THE SELECTION activities relate the literature to students' lives and experiences to spark their interest and to stimulate classroom discussion.

The unique pedagogical design of this series virtually guarantees close reading. The novel organization of the **REVIEWING THE SELECTION** questions ensures that interpretations of the literature will be based on evidence from the selections.

Responding to the Selection

How would you feel if you were Margot and had missed the one hour of sunlight that comes only once every seven years? Imagine that you are one of Margot's classmates. How do you feel about your actions? Why?

Reviewing the Selection

RECALLING AND INTERPRETING

1. R What is the weather like on Venus? What is supposed to happen on this particular day?
   I Why are the other children unable to remember the sun? How does Margot feel about the weather on Venus?
2. R What makes Margot different from the other children?
   I Why do the other children dislike Margot?
3. R What do the other children do to Margot? What do the children do when the sun comes out?
   I Why do the other children do what they do to Margot? How do the children feel about the sun?
4. R What do the children remember when it starts to rain again?
   I How do the children feel when it starts to rain again? How do they feel about what they have done to Margot?

SYNTHESIZING

5. Before the children see the sun, they hate Margot "for . . . reasons, of big and little consequence." After the children see the sun, they "could not meet each other's glances" when they think of what they have done to Margot. Has seeing the sun changed the children in any way? If so, how? Do the children better understand and sympathize more with Margot after seeing the sun? Why, or why not?

Understanding Literature (Questions for Discussion)

Science Fiction. Science fiction is imaginative literature based on scientific principles, discoveries, or laws. Science fiction writers often suspend or alter elements of reality to teach the reader something about our planet or ourselves. Review the Cross-curricular Connection about the planet Venus. How does Bradbury's picture of Venus differ from what scientists actually know about that planet? What elements of this story are not strictly realistic? What elements of this story are realistic? What do you think Bradbury is trying to teach us about ourselves? Explain.

"ALL SUMMER IN A DAY" 9

The **RECALLING** questions ask about facts in the selection. Paired with each recalling question is an **INTERPRETING** question that uses these facts as a basis for critical analysis and interpretation.

SYNTHESIZING questions pull together particular parts of the analysis just conducted, enabling students to arrive at a general understanding of each piece.

UNDERSTANDING LITERATURE questions provide instruction in literary movements, types, and techniques.

Unit 10 To Everything There is a Season

Long Leg, Edward Hopper, 1935

Four seasons fill the measure of the year;
There are four seasons in the mind of men.

—John Keats
Four Seasons

401

UNIT OPENERS feature fine art correlated to the themes covered in the unit.

Language Lab

Editing for Usage Errors

When someone confuses one word with another the result is a **usage error.** Many pairs of words are easily confused by writers, so it is always a good idea to check your writing for usage errors. The following chart lists some of the word pairs that students often misuse in writing and speech. For more information, refer to the Language Arts Survey, 2.23–2.24, "Common Usage Problems I and II."

COMMONLY MISUSED WORDS

Word	Meaning	Example
accept	*Accept* means "to receive willingly."	The children did not **accept** Margot's differences.
except	*Except* means "to exclude or leave something out."	The children would **except** Margot from their games.
altogether	*Altogether* is an adverb that means "wholly, all being counted."	I have read eight of Ray Bradbury's stories **altogether.**
all together	*All together* is an adverb that means "all in one group."	**All together** the class made a time capsule.
among	Use *among* when you are talking about a group of three or more.	There was no disagreement **among** the scientists about the sun shining.
between	Use *between* when you are talking about two people or things at a time.	We discovered the difference **between** sunny weather and rainy weather.
can	Use the verb *can* when expressing ability.	**Can** the other students understand Margot's sadness?
may	Use the verb *may* to express permission or possibility.	You **may** go outside in the sun. It **may** rain today.
fewer	Use *fewer* with plural nouns to tell "how many."	Should the teacher have noticed there were **fewer** children in class?
less	Use *less* with singular words to tell "how much."	I wish that there were **less** rain on this planet.

10 UNIT TEN / TO EVERYTHING THERE IS A SEASON

LANGUAGE LABS develop students' language arts skills in the context of literary study. Additional practice can be found in the Essential Skills Practice Books.

Try It Yourself

Exercise A. On your own paper, write the following words in alphabetical order.

daydream	opal	shade
daylight	option	venture
bellow	manual	intimidate
opaque	manufacture	man

Exercise B. The illustration below shows the top of a dictionary page, with its guide words. Decide which of the following words belong on this page of the dictionary.

sudden	task	tear
tattle	tease	tension
taste	tax	tea

just for fun

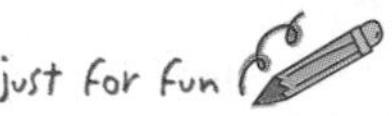

Have you ever tried your hand at making up a word? Now's your chance!

Invent a word that means something specific, and write a dictionary definition for it. Make your definition sound as real as possible. Include the part of speech and word origins for your word.

EXAMPLE **skwashlet** n., [fr. *squash,* to smush, and *chiclet,* a small piece of gum] a small piece of chewed gum stuck to a surface, especially a shoe

STUDY AND RESEARCH SKILLS: USING A DICTIONARY 1

The **JUST FOR FUN** exercises reinforce language skills using the text from the selection.

READER RESPONSE EMPHASIS
The EMC Masterpiece Series motivates students through high-interest affective and cognitive activities that relate literature to students' experiences, followed by teacher-directed activities to ensure cultural transmission.

READER RESPONSE ACTIVITIES
- Reader's Journal
- Guided Reading Questions
- Responding to the Selection

TEACHER DIRECTED ACTIVITIES
- Reviewing the Selection
- Understanding Literature
- Language Arts Survey
- Just for Fun

- **For Your Reading List** section features book reviews from real middle school students complete with their comments on the selection.
- **Cross-curricular Connections** to other academic areas such as social studies, art, mathematics, and science tie in intriguing insights from the various disciplines to the selection.
- **Unit Reviews** reinforce major concepts from the unit and provide Synthesizing questions for writing, discussion, and research.
- **The Handbook of Literary Terms** contains twice as many terms as any other textbook program to promote students' understanding of literary movements, types, and techniques.

Student Textbook

THINKING SKILLS sections help students improve their problem solving, decision making, and analytical skills.

Thinking Skills

Problem Solving and Decision Making

Solving problems and making decisions can be difficult tasks. There are several techniques that can make these activities easier.

All problem solving involves four steps: understanding the problem, making a course of action, taking the action, and evaluating the results. The following four problem solving techniques use these four steps.

Techniques for Problem Solving

For more information about these techniques see the Language Arts Survey, 4.21, "Making Decisions and Problem Solving."

Trial and Error. Sometimes you can make a guess about how to solve a problem and see if it works. Trial and error can be useful if only a few solutions exist.

Represent the Situation. It may be easier to solve some problems if you make a visual representation of the problem such as a diagram or model.

Divide and Conquer. Another way to solve a problem is to divide the problem into parts. Then solve each part in a logical order.

Work Backward. Working backward is another way to face a complex problem. Imagine that you have solved your problem. Describe what you have accomplished. Then think about what would have to happen for you to accomplish that goal. Continue working backward until you get to a situation that you know how to create.

Try It Yourself

Exercise A. Which technique would be most useful for solving each of the problems below? Explain why you would use the technique to solve the problem.

EXAMPLE You are writing a story that takes place in an amusement park and you need to keep track of the action.
Representing the situation would be a good way to plan and track the action, because you will be able to visualize your setting.

1. You need to plan your time so that you can finish your science report by Thursday morning.
2. You have four keys and you are not sure which one opens your front door.

Writing Skills

A Personal Memoir

In "Eleven," the writer has focused on a small but meaningful incident in the life of Rachel, the narrator.

Every person's life is full of small but meaningful events. Because of this, every person is full of interesting stories. A person needs only to tap into his or her personal memories. A **personal memoir** is a person's account of an incident or event in his or her own life.

Try It Yourself

Write your own personal memoir. Your memoir can be about any experience that you consider to be special or important. Review the Language Arts Survey, 1.10, "Freewriting." Then use this technique as a way of coming up with interesting ideas for your memoir.

Student Model

Tanya sat down to write her own personal memoir. She tried freewriting to help her think of an interesting topic.

A personal memoir? What should I write about? My family. The poster on the wall reminds me of Grandma. Watercolors. Grandma taught me to use watercolors when I was just seven years old. We sat at the big wooden table in her kitchen and ate soft, warm blueberry muffins. Sweet. delicious. She pulled out a pad of white paper and a tray of watercolors. Smooth wooden brush handle. Colors on my finger tips. Different pictures of the lake outside her home. Sometimes people were swimming in the lake. Sometimes the lake was still and showed reflections of the trees or the moon. Painting is now something special that I know how to do. My older sister doesn't paint. My parents don't paint. My parents hang my pictures in our kitchen. The picture window in our apartment. The elevator and the row of mailboxes. Long hallways. The yummy smell of the Chinese restaurant next door. My next-door neighbor Marco with the rock collection. The rock collection. quartz. Oh no—I remember looking at the rock collection one day after school. Third grade. There was one piece of quartz I wanted. It would have made a nice necklace. rough. clear. Like a diamond. A tiny castle. He had so many neat rocks. I slipped it into my pocket. Marco didn't think that I took it. I felt so bad that I told him. I was in trouble. I remember trying to apologize. Painted him a picture. Found rocks for him. We were friends again. Hot chocolate after school. Finishing puzzles. Puppet shows. I still don't know what made me take a rock from my very best friend. I learned an important lesson. Should this be my personal memoir?

WRITING SKILLS activities help students relate the basic concept of the selection to real life as well as learn the writing process, enhance their writing skills, and build their writing portfolio.

UNIT PROJECTS featured at the end of each unit allow students to perform multimodel, cross-curricular exercises based on the literature, further connecting it to students' actual lives.

Unit Project

Making a Quilt

People have been making quilts for hundreds, maybe even thousands, of years. Quilts began as covers for beds but now are often hung to decorate walls, too. Some quilts are made from scraps of cloth that are stitched together in beautiful patterns. Other quilts feature cloth shapes sewn together to make one or many pictures. These quilts often tell a story or celebrate the past by showing important people, places, things, and events.

Try It Yourself

Work with your classmates to make a quilt. Have the quilt show people, places, things, or events from stories you have read in Unit 1.

Student Model

Renaldo and Juanita want to make a special quilt for their grandparents' fiftieth wedding anniversary gift. They ask their whole family—parents, aunts, uncles, and cousins—to show their different memories of Grandma and Grandpa's life together as pictures on sixteen squares that will make up the quilt.

People from the family meet to decide what their square will look like. Would it be fun to show Grandma and Grandpa's favorite movies? Could they picture places to which Grandma and Grandpa traveled? What about showing them at a family picnic?

Next, Renaldo and Juanita tell the family how big each square must be to fit well when the squares are sewn together. They choose felt material for the square because it is a heavy fabric and will not need a border.

Some members of the family cut shapes out of felt and then glue them on the squares. Others draw right on the squares and then add special paint. Family members who are good at sewing decorate their square with needlepoint pictures. Each square looks different, but they all show something that is important to Grandma and Grandpa.

Renaldo and Juanita gather the finished squares together, making sure that everyone signs his or her square. They try to arrange the squares in time order. Then their uncle sews the squares together and adds three loops to the quilt's top edge. Renaldo and Juanita slip a thin, round piece of wood through each loop. The colorful, attractive quilt is ready to hang.

Now the whole family meets for a party. The creators of each square explain their pictures and tell why they chose their subject. Later, when Grandma and Grandpa see the quilt hanging on the wall, they remember the good times they had over the years and how everyone worked together to celebrate with them.

Examining the Model

1. What was Renaldo and Juanita's part in creating the quilt? the other family members' part?
2. What did Renaldo and Juanita do to make sure the quilt fits together properly?
3. How did Renaldo and Juanita prepare the quilt for hanging?

APPLIED ENGLISH SKILLS activities give students hands-on experience tying basic English skills to everyday life.

Applied English Skills

Writing a Personal Letter

Panchito and his family cannot stay in the same place for more than a season because their work is to follow the crops and pick the harvest. When the family has to leave a place that has been home to them, they might want to stay in touch with friends there. For example, Panchito might have wanted to write to Mr. Lema to thank him for offering to teach him to play the trumpet.

A personal letter usually includes the following parts:

THE FORM OF A PERSONAL LETTER	
return address	name and address of sender
date	month, day, and year
salutation (followed by a comma)	polite greeting, such as "Dear Marty,"
body	news, questions, and message
closing (followed by a comma)	polite good-bye, such as "Sincerely," or "Yours,"
signature	sender's handwritten name in script
postscript (optional)	an additional note

There are two standard forms for a personal letter: block form and modified block form. In block form, each part of the letter starts at the far left side of the page, as in the following example:

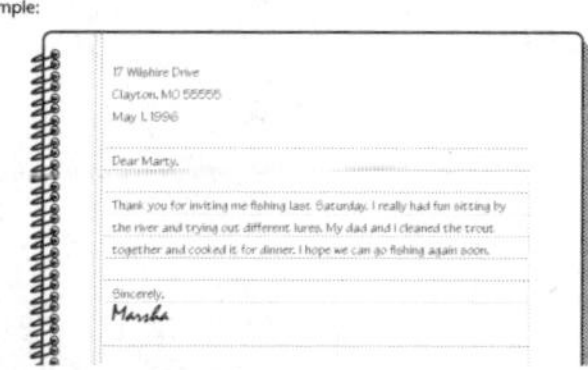

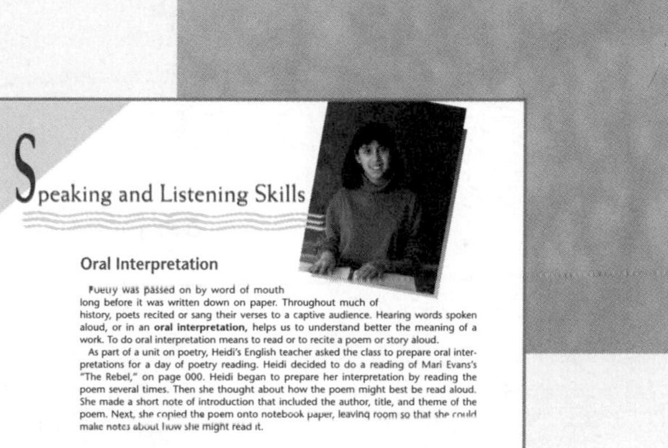

Speaking and Listening Skills

Oral Interpretation

Poetry was passed on by word of mouth long before it was written down on paper. Throughout much of history, poets recited or sang their verses to a captive audience. Hearing words spoken aloud, or in an **oral interpretation,** helps us to understand better the meaning of a work. To do oral interpretation means to read or to recite a poem or story aloud.

As part of a unit on poetry, Heidi's English teacher asked the class to prepare oral interpretations for a day of poetry reading. Heidi decided to do a reading of Mari Evans's "The Rebel," on page 000. Heidi began to prepare her interpretation by reading the poem several times. Then she thought about how the poem might best be read aloud. She made a short note of introduction that included the author, title, and theme of the poem. Next, she copied the poem onto notebook paper, leaving room so that she could make notes about how she might read it.

Try It Yourself

Choose a poem or part of a short story to read aloud to your class. The piece may come from your textbook or from another source.

Student Model

SPEAKING AND LISTENING SKILLS activities provide students with the tools to develop clear and confident speaking skills as well as active and insightful listening skills.

VOCABULARY SKILLS and **PRONUNCIATION AND SPELLING SKILLS** activities ensure basic fundamental teaching in areas that students need most. These skills increase in depth and complexity according to grade level.

Vocabulary Skills

Base Words and Prefixes

Understanding the building blocks of words can make learning new words easier. Many words are formed by adding prefixes to a base. By knowing what the parts of an unfamiliar word mean, you may be able to figure out the meaning of the word. For example, if you do not know what the word *multilingual* means, but you know that the prefix *multi–* means "many" and the base *lingual* means "of language," you can determine that *multilingual* means "of many languages."

The following chart shows some common prefixes, their meanings, and ways to use them. For other examples see the Language Arts Survey, 2.38, "Base Words, Prefixes, and Suffixes."

Prefix	Meaning	Example	Meaning
bi–	two, twice	bicultural	of two cultures
im–	against, not	impossible	not possible
mis–	wrong, badly	misguide	guide badly
pre–	before	preflight	before the flight

Try It Yourself

Exercise A. Complete each sentence with a word from the following list. Explain why the word you chose makes sense in the sentence, using what you know about prefixes.

preview	misjudged	unwashed	impossible	insecurity
reread	uncover	retried	repay	nonbeliever

1. Last night the producers and their guests saw the movie before its release to the public. The _______ was well received.
2. Mark read the instructions again. In other words, he _______ them.
3. If you don't mow the lawn, I'll want my money back. You'll have to _____ me.
4. The modern world doesn't always feel safe and secure. It is full of _______.
5. I could reach the third level only rarely. At other times, finding it was _______.

Exercise B. Combine each of these prefixes with a base word below. Then use your new word correctly in a sentence.

non– im– mis– pre– un– in– bi– counter– dis– post–

1. stop	3. proper	5. clear	7. cover	9. date
2. view	4. finite	6. behave	8. cycle	10. act

Language Arts Survey

***The EMC Masterpiece Series* has the most extensive language arts skills coverage of any program. The coverage of English skills is so comprehensive that an additional English skills textbook isn't needed. The Language Arts Survey sections may be taught as separate units, using the student textbook and ancillary worksheets, or may be taught incidentally in conjunction with study of the literature.**

Stimulating, literature-based activities in this series cover the full range of language arts skills:

- Emotional and critical responses to literature
- The process of writing
- Grammar, usage, mechanics, spelling, and vocabulary
- Varieties of English
- Speaking and listening
- Applied English
- Test-taking
- Critical thinking
- Study and research

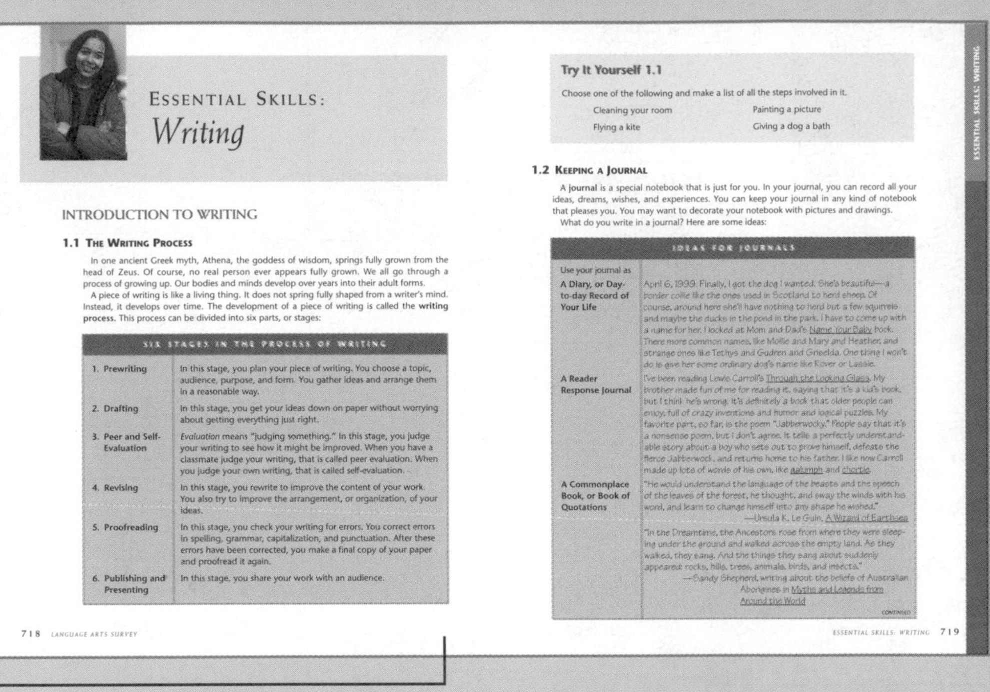

ESSENTIAL SKILLS: *Writing*

INTRODUCTION TO WRITING

1.1 The Writing Process

In one ancient Greek myth, Athena, the goddess of wisdom, springs fully grown from the head of Zeus. Of course, no real person ever appears fully grown. We all go through a process of growing up. Our bodies and minds develop over years into their adult forms.

A piece of writing is like a living thing. It does not spring fully shaped from a writer's mind. Instead, it develops over time. The development of a piece of writing is called the **writing process.** This process can be divided into six parts, or stages:

SIX STAGES IN THE PROCESS OF WRITING	
1. Prewriting	In this stage, you plan your piece of writing. You choose a topic, audience, purpose, and form. You gather ideas and arrange them in a reasonable way.
2. Drafting	In this stage, you get your ideas down on paper without worrying about getting everything just right.
3. Peer and Self-Evaluation	*Evaluation* means "judging something." In this stage, you judge your writing to see how it might be improved. When you have a classmate judge your writing, that is called peer evaluation. When you judge your own writing, that is called self-evaluation.
4. Revising	In this stage, you rewrite to improve the content of your work. You also try to improve the arrangement, or organization, of your ideas.
5. Proofreading	In this stage, you check your writing for errors. You correct errors in spelling, grammar, capitalization, and punctuation. After these errors have been corrected, you make a final copy of your paper and proofread it again.
6. Publishing and Presenting	In this stage, you share your work with an audience.

718 LANGUAGE ARTS SURVEY

Try It Yourself 1.1

Choose one of the following and make a list of all the steps involved in it.

Cleaning your room — Painting a picture
Flying a kite — Giving a dog a bath

1.2 Keeping a Journal

A **journal** is a special notebook that is just for you. In your journal, you can record all your ideas, dreams, wishes, and experiences. You can keep your journal in any kind of notebook that pleases you. You may want to decorate your notebook with pictures and drawings.

What do you write in a journal? Here are some ideas:

IDEAS FOR JOURNALS	
Use your journal as	
A Diary, or Day-to-day Record of Your Life	April 6, 1999. Finally, I got the dog I wanted. She's beautiful—a border collie like the ones used in Scotland to herd sheep. Of course, around here she'll have nothing to herd but a few squirrels and maybe the ducks in the pond in the park. I have to come up with a name for her. I looked at Mom and Dad's Name Your Baby book. There more common names, like Mollie and Mary and Heather, and strange ones like Tethys and Gudren and Griselda. One thing I won't do is give her some ordinary dog's name like Rover or Lassie.
A Reader Response Journal	I've been reading Lewis Carroll's Through the Looking Glass. My brother made fun of me for reading it, saying that it's a kid's book, but I think he's wrong. It's definitely a book that older people can enjoy, full of crazy inventions and humor and logical puzzles. My favorite part, so far, is the poem "Jabberwocky." People say that it's a nonsense poem, but I don't agree. It tells a perfectly understandable story about a boy who sets out to prove himself, defeats the fierce Jabberwock, and returns home to his father. I like how Carroll made up lots of words of his own, like galumph and chortle.
A Commonplace Book, or Book of Quotations	"He would understand the language of the beasts and the speech of the leaves of the forest, he thought, and sway the winds with his word, and learn to change himself into any shape he wished." —Ursula K. Le Guin, A Wizard of Earthsea
	"In the Dreamtime, the Ancestors rose from where they were sleeping under the ground and walked across the empty land. As they walked, they sang. And the things they sang about suddenly appeared: rocks, hills, trees, animals, birds, and insects." —Sandy Shepherd, writing about the beliefs of Australian Aborigines in Myths and Legends from Around the World

CONTINUED

ESSENTIAL SKILLS: WRITING 719

ESSENTIAL SKILLS: WRITING

The **ESSENTIAL SKILLS: WRITING** section surveys the entire process of writing. It includes computer-assisted composition and emphasizes work with writing portfolios.

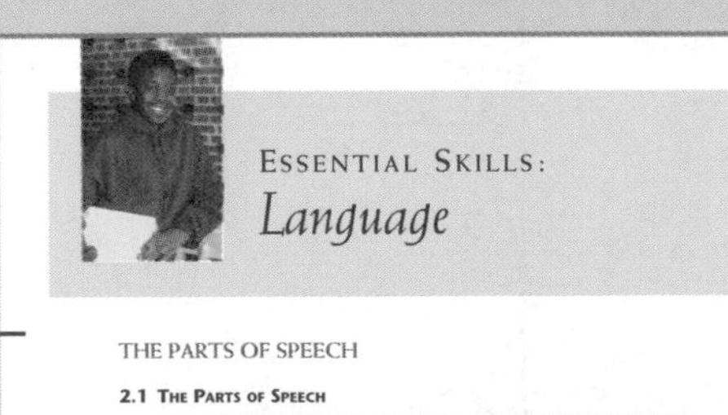

ESSENTIAL SKILLS: *Language*

THE PARTS OF SPEECH

2.1 The Parts of Speech

There are eight parts of speech. Each part of speech is identified in the chart below.

DEFINITION	EXAMPLE(S)
Noun. A **noun** names a person, place, thing, or idea.	sister, Jacob, India, street, car, pizza, love, happiness
Verb. A **verb** expresses action or a state of being.	jump, sing, believe, laugh, think, enjoy, talk
Pronoun. A **pronoun** is used in place of a noun.	Call **Luisa** and tell **Luisa** to meet **Janet and me** at the library. Call **Luisa** and tell **her** to meet **us** at the library.
Adjective. An **adjective** modifies, or changes the meaning of, a noun or pronoun.	**sticky** spoon, **busy** street, **black** cat
Adverb. An **adverb** modifies, or changes the meaning of, a verb, an adjective, or another adverb.	Chandra drove **carefully.** Chiara thought the movie was **very** funny.
Preposition. A **preposition** is used to show how a noun or a pronoun is related to other words in the sentence. Common prepositions are *in, after, among, at, behind, beside, off, through, until, upon,* and *with.*	Raoul walked **through** the woods and collected fallen leaves. Place the jar **in** the cabinet.
Conjunction. A **conjunction** is used to join words or groups of words. Common conjunctions are *and, but, for, nor, or, so,* and *yet.*	I made pasta with sauce, **and** George made salad. We had tickets to the baseball game, **but** the game was canceled.
Interjection. An **interjection** is a word used to express emotion. Common interjections are *oh, ah, well, say,* and *wow.*	**Wow!** Did you see that bolt of lightning? **Oh,** what a long day I have had!

CONTINUED

744 LANGUAGE ARTS SURVEY

Try It Yourself 2.1 — "ELEVEN," PAGE 000

Identify the part of speech of the underlined words in the following sentences.

EXAMPLE We read a story by Sandra Cisneros. **verb**

1. Today Rachel is eleven years old.
2. Rachel sits in her classroom.
3. The teacher finds a red sweater in the closet.
4. She shows the sweater to the class.
5. "Say, I think that sweater belongs to Rachel," one student says.
6. The teacher quickly puts the sweater on Rachel's desk.
7. Rachel argues that the sweater is not hers, but the teacher does not listen.
8. "Oh, I wish I could disappear," Rachel says.
9. Rachel is having a bad day.
10. Rachel wishes that she were a balloon floating in the sky.

2.2 Types of Nouns

A **noun** is a person, place, thing, or idea.

EXAMPLES Maya (person), Chicago (place), bicycle (thing), friendship (idea)

A **compound noun** is made up of two or more nouns joined together.

COMPOUND NOUNS sunlight, firetruck, baseball, toothpaste, apple tree

A **common noun** names any person, place, thing, or idea.
A **proper noun** names a specific person, place, or thing, and begins with a capital letter.

COMMON NOUNS child, country, holiday
PROPER NOUNS Tonya Jackson, Puerto Rico, Hanukah

ESSENTIAL SKILLS: LANGUAGE 745

ESSENTIAL SKILLS: LANGUAGE

The **ESSENTIAL SKILLS: LANGUAGE** section surveys key concepts in grammar, usage, mechanics, spelling, vocabulary development, and language variety. Grammar usage and mechanic instruction focuses on editing and proofreading applications.

ESSENTIAL SKILLS:
Speaking and Listening

3.1 VERBAL AND NONVERBAL COMMUNICATION

When people express themselves through spoken words, they are using **verbal communication.** When they express themselves in other ways, by smiling or by shaking hands, for example, they are using **nonverbal communication.**

ELEMENTS OF VERBAL COMMUNICATION

Element	Description	Guidelines for Speakers
Volume	Loudness or softness	Vary your volume, but make sure that you can be heard.
Melody, Pitch	Highness or lowness	Vary your pitch. Avoid speaking in a **monotone** (at a single pitch).
Pace	Speed	Vary the speed of your delivery to suit what you are saying. Excitement, for example, can be communicated by a fast pace, and seriousness can be communicated by slowing down and saying something forcefully.
Tone	Emotional quality	Suit your tone to your message and vary it appropriately as you speak. For example, you might use a light tone for a happy message and a heavier one for a sad message.

ELEMENTS OF NONVERBAL COMMUNICATION

Element	Description	Guidelines for Speakers
Eye Contact	Looking audience members in the eye	Make eye contact regularly with everyone in your audience.
Facial Expression	Using your face to show emotion	Use your facial expression to emphasize your message—raised eyebrows for a question, pursed lips for concentration, eyebrows lowered for anger, and so on.
Gesture	Meaningful motions of the arms and hands	Use gestures to emphasize points. Be careful, however, not to overuse gestures. Too many can be distracting.
Posture/Body	Position of the body	Keep your spine straight and head high. Stand with your arms and feet slightly apart, except when adopting other postures to express particular emotions.

Try It Yourself 3.1

Exercise A. Choose a short poem from your textbook that you would be willing to read aloud to your classmates. Make a copy of the poem. Write notes in the margins to show places where you might increase or decrease your volume or pace. Also make notes on the tone with which you will read each part of the poem. Finally, practice reading the poem aloud, varying your volume, pitch, pace, and tone.

Exercise B. Work with classmates to communicate various emotions nonverbally. Take turns adopting various facial expressions, gestures, and postures to communicate emotions such as displeasure, sorrow, joy, fear, forgiveness, caring, and awe. Discuss the various ways in which each of these emotions can be expressed without saying a word. Make a chart of your findings. On the chart, list emotions and the ways in which they can be communicated nonverbally. Follow this example:

EXAMPLE

Emotion	Method of Expression
Anger	Clenched fist
	Lowered eyebrows
	Narrowed eyes
	Stamping foot

ESSENTIAL SKILLS: SPEAKING AND LISTENING

The **ESSENTIAL SKILLS: SPEAKING AND LISTENING** section surveys verbal and nonverbal communication, active listening, interpersonal communication, discussion, public speaking, and oral interpretation.

ESSENTIAL SKILLS:
Study and Research

STUDY SKILLS

4.1 DEVELOPING GOOD STUDY HABITS

One of the most important things you can do to be successful in school is to develop good study habits. If you learn how to study effectively, you will be able to complete your assignments more quickly and easily.

Finding a place to work. You will work much better if you have a special study area. Use these guidelines to set up your own study area:

- Choose a quiet location. Distractions such as conversation, television, a ringing telephone, or loud music can hurt your concentration.
- Make sure your work area is well lighted and comfortable. Studying without enough light can cause eyestrain and headaches.
- Keep your study area neat and organized. You can waste a lot of time looking for materials in a messy study area.
- Have all your tools handy. Keep paper, pencils, pens, erasers, notebooks, a dictionary, and other items nearby as you study.
- Make sure that your study area is available at regular times. Set aside a specific time for study each day.

Keeping an assignment notebook. The further you progress in school, the more assignments you will get. At some point, it will become impossible to keep track of them all in your head. Therefore, get into the habit of writing down each assignment as soon as it is given. Keep a special notebook for this purpose, and record the following information about each assignment:

- The name of the subject
- The details of the assignment
- The date the assignment was given
- The date the assignment is due

Learning to set goals. Some of your assignments will be due the following day. Others will be long-term projects. If you organize your time well, you will be able to complete all your assignments by their due dates. The key to planning your time is to set short- and long-term goals.

After school each day, look over your assignment notebook. Determine which assignments need to be completed by the next day, and make them your **short-term goals.** Have a regular time each day to do these assignments.

When you have a big assignment that is not due for several days or weeks, you need to follow the example of the arctic tern. The arctic tern is a small bird that accomplishes a seemingly impossible task—flying from the Arctic Circle to Antarctica and back, a distance of about 25,000 miles. It does not make this journey all at once but divides it up into many short trips. In the same way, you have to break up a big assignment into smaller steps. Finishing the entire project by the due date is your **long-term goal,** and each of the smaller steps is a short-term goal. You will have to identify the smaller steps and plan ahead to be able to complete each one.

Making a study plan. To organize your time so that you can achieve both your short- and long-term goals, learn to make study plans to schedule when you will do the various tasks. Find a regular block of time in your daily schedule to complete your short-term goals. Divide your long-term goals into smaller steps that can be spread out over the time available. You will find it easier to get started on a big project if you begin with a very small step. Try to make yourself do one little task for a big project as soon as the project is assigned. For example, if you are writing a report on volcanoes, you could start by checking a book on volcanoes out of the library. If you have to make a model of a Native American village, you could begin by listing the materials you will need.

Suppose that over the next two weeks you have to write a four-page paper on the United Nations, in addition to doing your regular daily work. You might want to set up a calendar like this one to schedule your tasks:

M	T	W	T	F	S
Read one article on the U.N.	Go to Student Council meeting	Do research, collect notes	Do research, collect notes	Work out in gym	Organize notes
Begin rough draft	Finish rough draft	Study for science test	Revise paper	Attend Carmen's birthday party	Type final copy

Try It Yourself 4.1

Make a study plan for yourself for the next two weeks. Look over your assignment notebook and figure out what you need to accomplish during that time. Break down the ...oals for each day. Include time to work on long-term projects and ... schedule in any meetings or special events coming up. Follow ...ve.

ESSENTIAL SKILLS: STUDY AND RESEARCH

The **ESSENTIAL SKILLS: STUDY AND RESEARCH** section surveys thinking, reading, research, and test-taking skills, including skills for taking standardized tests.

ESSENTIAL SKILLS:
Applied English

5.1 FILLING OUT FORMS AND APPLICATIONS

A form is a way of presenting information about yourself. You may need to fill out a form for a new school or a new doctor. Later on in your life, you will probably fill out job application forms. The form will represent you, so you want it to be neat, accurate, and complete. Here are some guidelines for filling out forms:

GUIDELINES FOR COMPLETING FORMS

- Get an extra copy or make a photocopy of the form so that you can complete a practice form.
- Read through the directions and the form itself.
- Gather the information you will need to complete the form. This information may include former addresses, dates of events, and a social security number.
- Complete the form neatly. Avoid smudges or cross-outs. Use the writing implement requested on the form. Most forms request that you either type or use black or blue ink.
- Do not leave any lines blank. Use N.A. for "not applicable" if a request for information does not apply to you. For example, if you have always lived at the same address, you would write N.A. in the blank following "Previous Addresses."
- Proofread the form for errors in punctuation, spelling, or grammar. Make sure your information is correct.
- Submit the form to the appropriate person or address. Use an envelope or folder to keep the form neat and clean.
- It is a good idea to keep a copy of the form for your own records.

Try It Yourself 5.1

On your own paper, copy down the following new patient form for a doctor's office. Then complete it.

Patient's Name ______________________
Last First Middle Initial

Address ______________________
Street City State ZIP Code

Phone ______________________

Social Security No. ______________________

Reason for Initial Visit ______________________

Referred by ______________________

Health Insurance Company ______________________

Health Insurance Policy No. ______________________

Previous Physician ______________________

Address ______________________

Phone ______________________

5.2 GIVING DIRECTIONS

People often ask others for directions or instruction. Good directions are thorough and concise. They provide all of the information that a person will need in a logical order.

Here are some guidelines to keep in mind when someone asks you for instructions or directions:

1. Think through the process from start to finish before you begin.
2. Remember to tell the person what materials he or she may need.
3. Give directions in the proper order. Assume that the person knows nothing about what you are explaining.

ESSENTIAL SKILLS: APPLIED ENGLISH

The **ESSENTIAL SKILLS: APPLIED ENGLISH** section surveys applications of English skills to the world of work.

Annotated Teacher's Edition

The Annotated Teacher's Edition contains a wealth of materials to enrich your teaching:

A list of suggested affective and cognitive goals for the selection.

A list of worksheets, assessment materials, and multimedia materials to use in teaching the unit.

A list of cross-curricular activities.

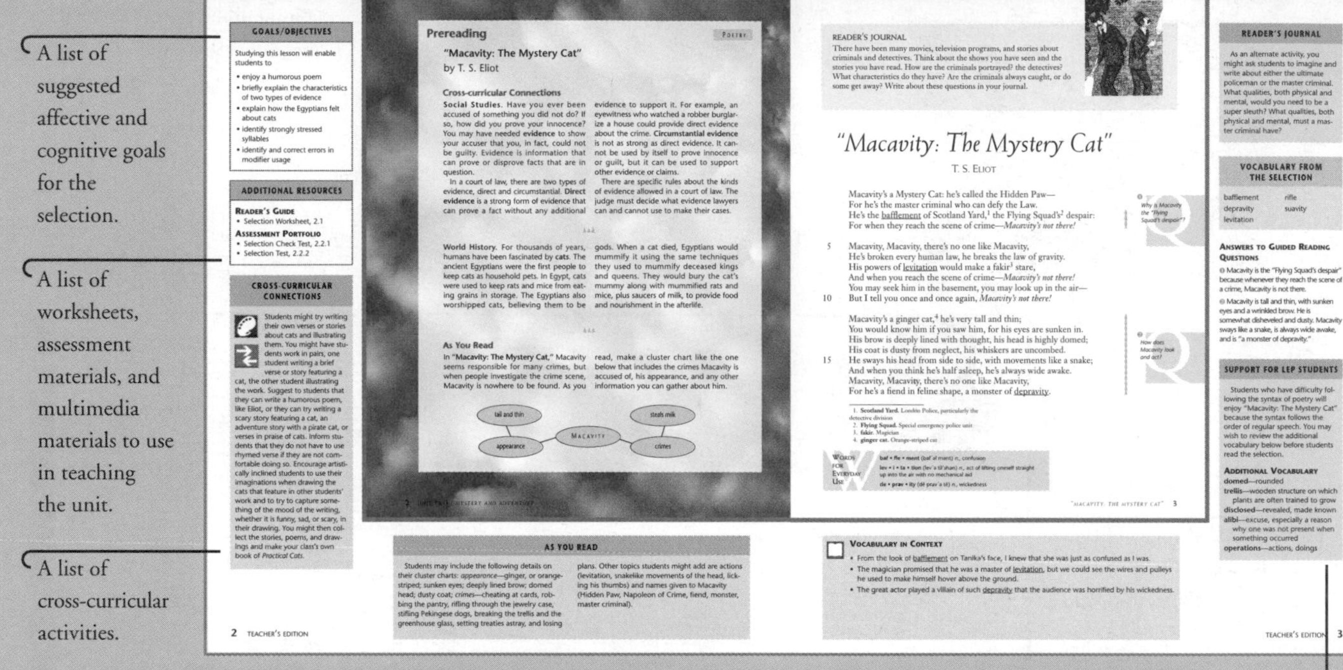

Notes on syntax and semantics plus lists of idioms, colloquialisms, and additional vocabulary for students needing extra help.

Historical and Art Notes providing information on artists, schools, periods, and techniques.

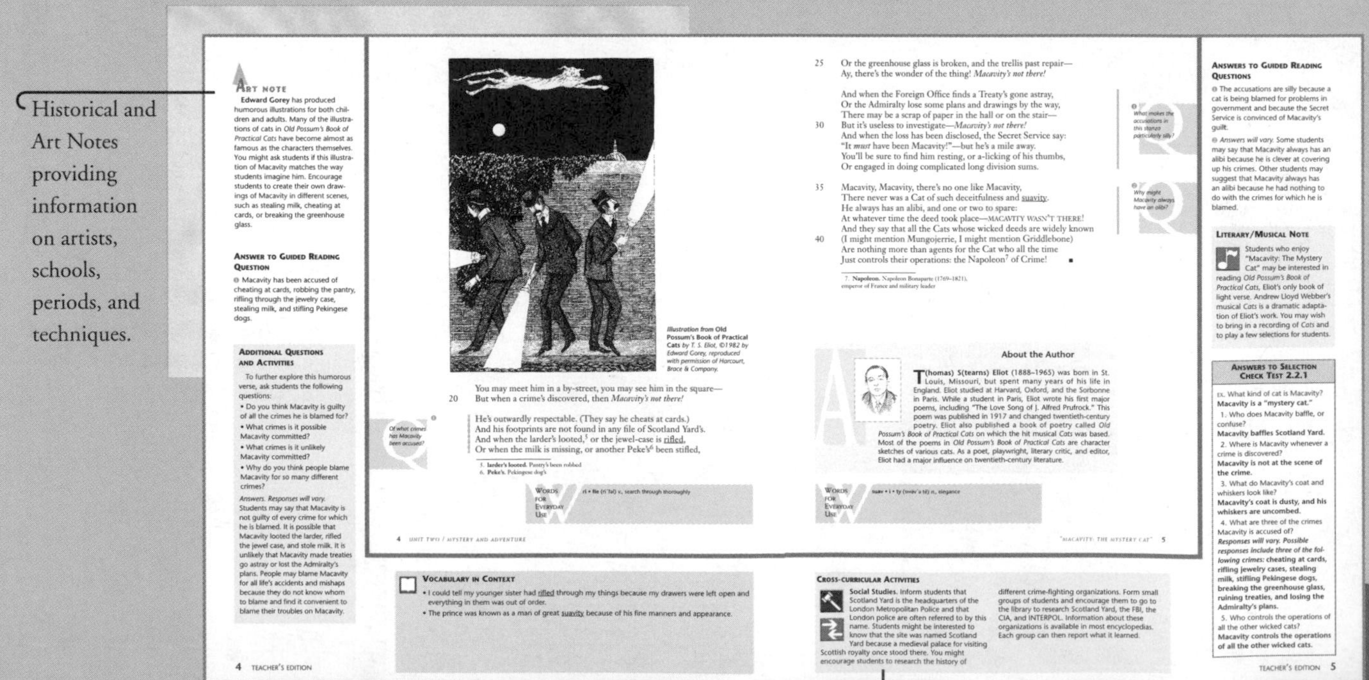

Icons identifying cross-curricular and multiple intelligence activities will help you tailor your instructions to individual students' abilities. Icons identifying SCANS activities will help your students reach Goals 2000.

RESPONDING TO THE SELECTION assignments assist you in helping students relate the topic to their experiences, anticipate questions or difficulties students might have, or suggest alternate formats (such as large or small group discussion, role playing, etc.). These notes give special attention to concerns of diversity.

RESPONDING TO THE SELECTION

You might make two lists on the blackboard titled *Evidence for the Prosecution* and *Evidence for the Defense.* Ask students to suggest evidence for both Macavity's guilt and his innocence. Place students' suggestions in the proper lists, and then ask the class to evaluate, based on their evidence, whether Macavity is guilty or innocent.

ANSWERS FOR REVIEWING THE SELECTION

1. **Recalling.** Scotland Yard is unable to catch Macavity, no matter how hard they try. Macavity is never there when people from Scotland Yard investigate the scene of a crime. **Interpreting.** A cat is able to jump so that it appears it is suspended in air.
2. **Recalling.** Macavity is ginger colored, tall, and thin. His eyes are sunken, and his brow is deeply lined. His head is highly domed. He is dusty, and his whiskers are uncombed. **Interpreting.** *Responses will vary.* Students may say that Macavity sounds like a stray cat.
3. **Recalling.** People think that Macavity has cheated at cards, rifled jewelry cases, stolen milk, stifled Pekingese dogs, broken the greenhouse glass, ruined treaties, and lost the Admiralty's plans. While some of these crimes may have been committed by a cat, it is impossible that a cat could be responsible for others, such as ruining treaties. **Interpreting.** *Answers will vary.* Macavity may be a likely suspect because he is a stray cat and is out roaming at night when crimes are committed.
4. **Recalling.** Eliot compares Macavity to Napoleon. Like Napoleon, Macavity is seemingly unstoppable. **Interpreting.** *Answers will vary.* Eliot might have compared Macavity to Napoleon because both are powerful, clever, and reputed invincible.
5. **Synthesizing.** *Responses will vary. Possible responses are given.* Like Macavity, real cats can leap, move smoothly like a snake, seem half asleep when they are awake, (cont.)

Responding to the Selection

Scotland Yard thinks Macavity is responsible for committing several crimes. Do you think he is guilty? How would you defend Macavity's innocence? What would be necessary to prove his guilt?

Reviewing the Selection

RECALLING AND INTERPRETING

1. R Why is Macavity the "bafflement" of Scotland Yard? Who is never there when people from Scotland Yard investigate the scene of a crime?
   I How does a cat break the law of gravity?
2. R What does Macavity look like?
   I What does the description of Macavity tell you about him?
3. R What crimes do people think that Macavity has committed? Are these crimes likely to have been committed by a cat?
   I Why might Macavity be a likely suspect?
4. R To what famous leader does Eliot compare Macavity?
   I Why does Eliot compare Macavity to this leader?

SYNTHESIZING

5. What characteristics do real cats share with Macavity? What is the speaker of the poem telling us about cats? Explain.

Understanding Literature (Questions for Discussion)

Stress. **Stress,** or accent, is the level of emphasis given to a syllable. If a syllable receives a strong emphasis, it is described as strongly stressed or accented. A weakly stressed or unaccented syllable receives weak emphasis. The words *bafflement, broken,* and *gravity* have strongly stressed first syllables. The words *defy, neglect,* and *asleep* have weakly stressed first syllables. Say the following words and phrases aloud and describe their stress patterns: *Macavity, levitation, criminal, the law of gravity, always wide awake, his whiskers are uncombed.*

6 UNIT TWO / MYSTERY AND ADVENTURE

Language Lab

Editing for Errors in Modifier Usage

Authors like T. S. Eliot use detailed descriptions to make their writing come alive. Using modifiers is a common way to add details to descriptions. A **modifier** is a word or phrase that tells about or describes another word or phrase.

EXAMPLES Macavity is a *mysterious* cat. (The word *mysterious* modifies, or tells about, the word *cat.*)

Macavity disappeared *mysteriously.* (The word *mysteriously* modifies, or tells about, the word *disappeared.*)

Lurking in the shadows, Macavity cased the room. (The phrase *lurking in the shadows* modifies, or tells about, the word *Macavity.*)

Read the following sentence. Notice the modifying phrase in italics.

EXAMPLE *Seeing the overturned plants,* the cat was thought to be responsible.

This sentence sounds as though the cat were seeing the overturned plants. Obviously, that is not so. If not, then who *is* doing the seeing in this sentence? The sentence does not tell us.

LANGUAGE LAB: EDITING FOR ERRORS IN MODIFIER USAGE 7

LANGUAGE LAB

- **Introducing the Skill.** Inform students that they already use modifiers in their everyday speech, both to describe nouns and verbs. You may wish to review with students the Language Arts Survey, 2.5, "Adjectives and Articles," and 2.6, "Adverbs." Then write the following simple sentence on the chalkboard: The cat strolled by me. Ask students if they can think of one word that modifies the noun *cat.* Students should suggest adjectives such as *black, sneaky,* or *striped.* Then ask students if they can think of one word that modifies the verb *strolled.* Students should suggest adverbs such as *casually, slowly,* or *innocently.* Finally, ask students to think of phrases that might modify the noun *cat.* Some students may find this activity more difficult, so you might suggest that many phrases are formed using verbs ending in *ing.* Students should suggest phrases such as *slinking out of the alley* or *purring to himself.*
- **Previewing the Skill.** Have students review the teaching in the Language Lab. Ask students why the second example sentence ("*Meowing, purring, and cleaning its face,* the police officer found the cat.") sounds silly. Emphasize that modifiers should be placed close to the words they modify.
- **Practicing the Skill.** Once students seem familiar with modifiers and common modifier errors, ask them to do the Try It Yourself Exercises.
- **Reviewing the Skill.** Review problematic areas of modifier usage with students as a class. Some students may need individual help in order to use modifiers correctly. You might offer students who need extra help Exercise A in For Additional Practice. Exercise B in For Additional Practice covers more common errors in modifier usage students frequently make.
- ▶ **Teaching Note.** Students who enjoy the Just For Fun activity might like to form small groups and play a MadLibs-type exercise using all the parts of speech.

ANSWERS FOR REVIEWING THE SELECTION (cont.)

mischievously steal milk and food, have minor accidents in which they break things, and lick their paws. The speaker is saying that cats are sometimes mysterious, mischievous creatures who are clever enough always to appear innocent.

ANSWERS FOR UNDERSTANDING LITERATURE

▶ See the evaluation form for collaborative learning, *Assessment Portfolio,* 4.10.

Responses will vary. Possible responses are given.

Stress. The words are stressed as follows

Macavity, levitation, criminal, the law of gravity, always wide awake, his whiskers are uncombed.

6 TEACHER'S EDITION

TEACHER'S EDITION 7

Color-coded answers for exercises are provided on the same page as the exercises themselves.

ANSWERS FOR REVIEWING THE SELECTION give sample responses to Recalling, Interpreting, and Synthesizing questions.

ADDITIONAL PRACTICE EXERCISES offer you the opportunity to provide students with more extensive work on specific skills.

8 TEACHER'S EDITION

TEACHER'S EDITION 9

ALSO INCLUDED IN THE ANNOTATED TEACHER'S EDITION:

- Practical advice and strategies for reader response and portfolio-based language arts instruction.
- Sample lesson cycles.
- Information on thematic and genre approaches.
- Additional resources for language arts teachers.

ANNOTATED TEACHER'S EDITION ALSO AVAILABLE ON CD-ROM

Assessment Portfolio

Name ____________ Class ____________ Date ________

Writing Evaluation Form: Holistic Response 7.5

Short Story

CONTENT AND COHERENCE		
The short story… • does not have a central conflict • does not develop and resolve the conflict • does not depict the setting vividly • does not develop main character(s) amply • does not develop theme clearly	(Circle one.) 1 2 3 4 5 6 7 8 9 10 ×7 = ____	The short story… • has a central conflict • develops and resolves the conflict • depicts the setting vividly • develops main character(s) amply • develops theme clearly
CONVENTIONS		
The short story… • makes errors in spelling • makes errors in grammar • makes errors in usage • makes errors in punctuation • does not follow proper manuscript form	(Circle one.) 1 2 3 4 5 6 7 8 9 10 ×3 = ____	The short story… • uses proper spelling • uses good grammar • avoids errors in usage • uses proper punctuation and capitalization • follows proper manuscript form
CONTENT AND COHERENCE ____ + CONVENTIONS ____ = TOTAL ____		

What I like most about this short story is…

What I like least about this short story is…

What I would do to improve this short story is…

STUDENT'S SIGNATURE ____________
PEER EVALUATOR'S SIGNATURE ____________
TEACHER'S SIGNATURE ____________

© 1996 EMC Corporation

ADDITIONAL EVALUATION FORMS AND WORKSHEETS 5

HOLISTIC EVALUATION FORMS allow for "total effect" peer, self-, and teacher evaluation of student writing.

The EMC Masterpiece Series has the most complete assessment portfolio available today. This ancillary package contains blackline master materials for:

- Unit Study Guides and Tests, including Vocabulary Worksheets
- Selection Check Tests and Comprehensive Tests
- Writing Skills Study Guides and Post-tests
- Other Language Arts Skills Study Guides and Tests
- Worksheets and Forms for Portfolio Assessment
    - Forms for Analytic and Holistic Evaluation for Other Language Arts Activities and Projects
- Worksheets and Forms
- Answer Keys

ANALYTIC EVALUATION FORMS allow for part-by-part, criteria-based peer, self-, and teacher evaluation of student writing.

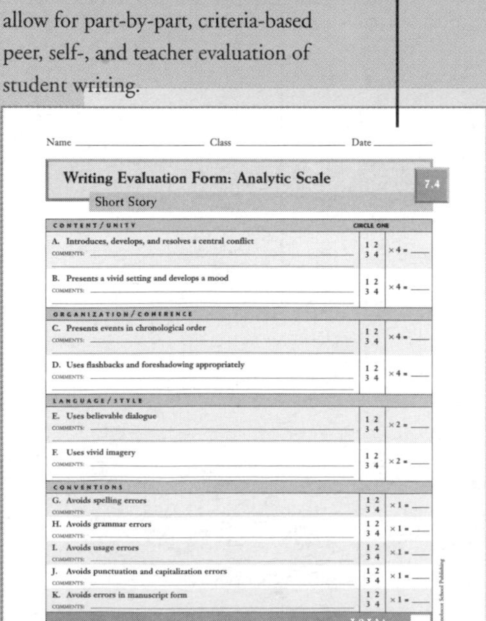

Name ____________ Class ____________ Date ________

Writing Evaluation Form: Analytic Scale 7.4

Short Story

CONTENT/UNITY	CIRCLE ONE	
A. Introduces, develops, and resolves a central conflict COMMENTS:	1 2 3 4	×4 = ____
B. Presents a vivid setting and develops a mood COMMENTS:	1 2 3 4	×4 = ____
ORGANIZATION/COHERENCE		
C. Presents events in chronological order COMMENTS:	1 2 3 4	×4 = ____
D. Uses flashbacks and foreshadowing appropriately COMMENTS:	1 2 3 4	×4 = ____
LANGUAGE/STYLE		
E. Uses believable dialogue COMMENTS:	1 2 3 4	×2 = ____
F. Uses vivid imagery COMMENTS:	1 2 3 4	×2 = ____
CONVENTIONS		
G. Avoids spelling errors COMMENTS:	1 2 3 4	×1 = ____
H. Avoids grammar errors COMMENTS:	1 2 3 4	×1 = ____
I. Avoids usage errors COMMENTS:	1 2 3 4	×1 = ____
J. Avoids punctuation and capitalization errors COMMENTS:	1 2 3 4	×1 = ____
K. Avoids errors in manuscript form COMMENTS:	1 2 3 4	×1 = ____
	TOTAL	

Key: 1 = needs substantial improvement 2 = needs improvement 3 = good 4 = outstanding

STUDENT'S SIGNATURE ____________
PEER EVALUATOR'S SIGNATURE ____________
TEACHER'S SIGNATURE ____________

© 1996 Perfection School Publishing

4 ADDITIONAL EVALUATION FORMS AND WORKSHEETS

PORTFOLIO EVALUATION FORMS allow students and teachers to monitor the development of students' writing over time.

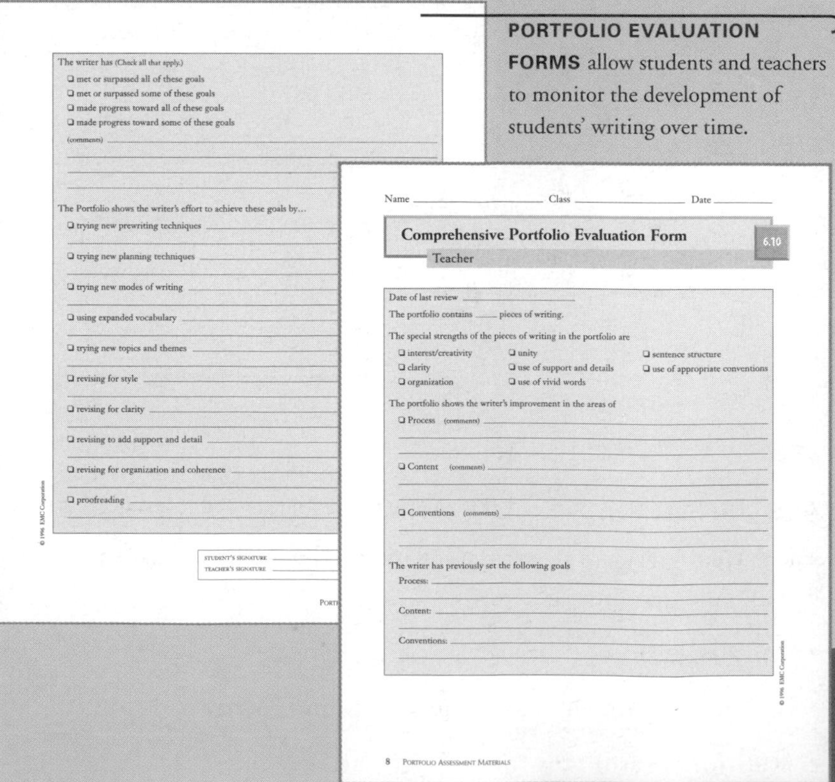

The writer has (Check all that apply.)

- ❑ met or surpassed all of these goals
- ❑ met or surpassed some of these goals
- ❑ made progress toward all of these goals
- ❑ made progress toward some of these goals

(comments)

The Portfolio shows the writer's effort to achieve these goals by…

- ❑ trying new prewriting techniques
- ❑ trying new planning techniques
- ❑ trying new modes of writing
- ❑ using expanded vocabulary
- ❑ trying new topics and themes
- ❑ revising for style
- ❑ revising for clarity
- ❑ revising to add support and detail
- ❑ revising for organization and coherence
- ❑ proofreading

STUDENT'S SIGNATURE ____________
TEACHER'S SIGNATURE ____________

© 1996 EMC Corporation

PORT

Name ____________ Class ____________ Date ________

Comprehensive Portfolio Evaluation Form 6.10

Teacher

Date of last review ____________

The portfolio contains ____ pieces of writing.

The special strengths of the pieces of writing in the portfolio are

- ❑ interest/creativity
- ❑ clarity
- ❑ organization
- ❑ unity
- ❑ use of support and details
- ❑ use of vivid words
- ❑ sentence structure
- ❑ use of appropriate conventions

The portfolio shows the writer's improvement in the areas of

- ❑ Process (comments)
- ❑ Content (comments)
- ❑ Conventions (comments)

The writer has previously set the following goals

Process:

Content:

Conventions:

© 1996 EMC Corporation

8 PORTFOLIO ASSESSMENT MATERIALS

Additional Components

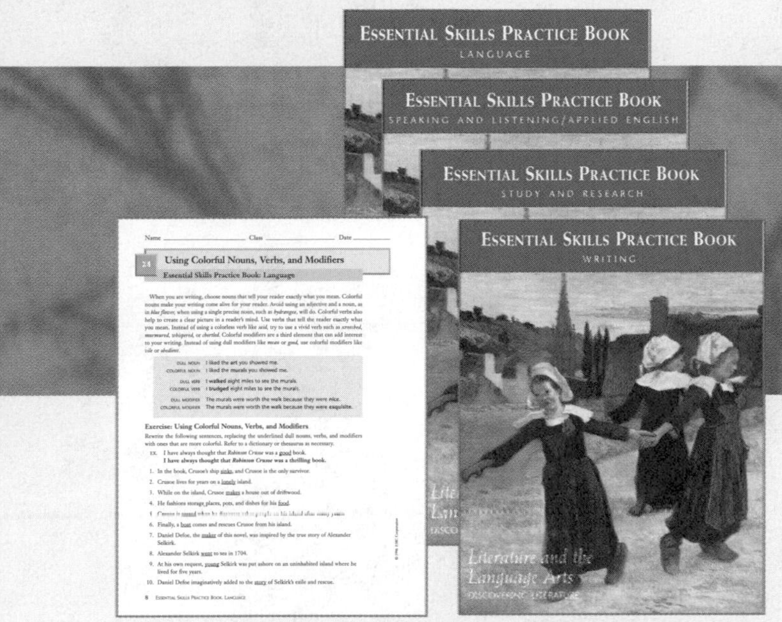

ESSENTIAL SKILLS PRACTICE BOOKS

The four Essential Skills Practice Books–Writing, Language, Study and Research, and Speaking and Listening/Applied English–contain blackline masters of exercises keyed to the Language Arts Survey sections of the student textbooks.

TRANSPARENCY SET

Transparencies guide students through preparation of reader's journals, use of writing portfolios, and peer and self-evaluation of writing.

MULTIMEDIA COMPONENTS

- Three sixty-minute audiocassettes of songs and dramatic readings from the series.
- A videocassette and video laser disc of dramatic performances from the series.
- A CD-ROM containing an idea generator for prewriting and a test generator for creating tests appropriate for six-week, nine-week, twelve-week, and semester-long schedules.
- Test generators also available on IBM and Macintosh diskettes.
- The Annotated Teacher's Edition is available on CD-ROM for easy access to the selections.

READER'S GUIDE

The Reader's Guide and Activity Workbook consists of blackline master worksheets that provide a step-by-step process for completing the student textbook activities.

Contents

Overview

Program Philosophy

The Cognitive Revolution and the Teaching of Literature

Through the 1960s, psychology in America was dominated by behaviorism, a theoretical methodology popularized by the brilliant and irascible B. F. Skinner. Skinner and other behaviorists argued that because we cannot observe mental phenomena directly, we cannot speak scientifically (i.e., intelligibly) of such matters as sensations, intuitions, feelings, thoughts, reasons, motives, imaginings, wishes, beliefs, and dreams. Oddly, some behaviorists went so far as to claim that mental phenomena did not exist. Such peculiar notions were positively reinforced by government grants and academic appointments and found expression in several generations of programmed learning textbooks designed to meet behavioral objectives. Learning theorists working within the behaviorist model encouraged educators to consider their students' observable behaviors without regard to, and indeed in scorn of, underlying mental processes.[1]

Of course, most English teachers knew that something was radically wrong with the behaviorist model of learning. They knew all along that they were teaching young *people*, not young bundles of behaviors, that those "mythical" realms of thought and feeling pooh-poohed by the behaviorists were, in fact, the quite real places that they explored daily with students in discussions of works of literature. In the 1960s and '70s, a revolution occurred in American psychology that brought psychologists to an understanding of what teachers had sensed all along. That revolution was the emergence of the field of cognitive science.[2]

One consequence of the cognitive revolution in psychology is that education theorists now widely accept the idea, advanced by psychologist Lev Vygotsky and championed by Jerome Bruner, that **teaching must begin with what students already know and feel and must build on that foundation.** This idea has often been presented as something altogether new. However, it is something that good English teachers have known all along. To help students to understand and to appreciate literature, one must first

> provide opportunities for students to connect with the literature on their own terms

and then

> build from that place toward higher levels of understanding and appreciation.

***EMC's* Literature and the Language Arts** *is the first literature textbook series specifically designed to accomplish both of those higher-order goals. Each lesson in this series first provides opportunities for*

1. According to the behaviorist theory, learning results from the differential positive or negative reinforcement of spontaneously occurring, preexisting behaviors. A rat turns randomly this way or that way in a maze. By means of positive or negative reinforcements (e.g., food and mild electric shocks), the researcher/teacher reinforces turning one way instead of another, and thus learning takes place.

2. As Thomas Kuhn points out in *The Structure of Scientific Revolutions* (1962), when scientists working in a particular field discover phenomena that cannot be accounted for by extending or modifying the prevailing theoretical paradigm, they are forced to revise that paradigm to come up with a new theory. Kuhn calls the intractable phenomena that force scientists to rethink their theories "anomalies."

The twin anomalies that dealt the death blow to behaviorism were commonplace human behaviors: musical improvisation and speech. Neither could be adequately accounted for by behaviorist theory. Karl Lashley pointed out in a famous paper that musical improvisation, like many other human serial behaviors, cannot be explained without reference to what goes on inside people's minds. Improvisation simply happens too quickly to be explicable as a connected sequence of stimuli and responses. It must involve learned mental constructs, or structures, that are played out. Noam Chomsky, in his review of Skinner's *Verbal Behavior* (1957), explained that stimulus/response or imitation models cannot account for readily observable facts about language such as the production of sentences that, while entirely consistent with the rest of the grammar of the language, are utterly novel in structure (not to mention content).

Cognitive science is a cross-disciplinary study involving work in such fields as artificial intelligence, linguistics, psychology, and neuroscience. The cognitive scientist constructs models of mental processes and then tests these models to see that they yield all the outputs produced by minds and only those outputs. For example, a cognitive scientist might be interested in constructing a model of the mechanism for short-term storage and retrieval of information such as the telephone number of a taxi service. One famous paper in cognitive psychology describes the neurological mechanism for pattern recognition that enables frogs to detect bugs moving across their field of vision. The essential or defining attribute of such studies is that they posit processes that are functionally, or operationally, equivalent to mental processes. See Farnham-Diggory, S. *Cognitive Processes in Education.* New York: Harper, 1992; Bourne, L. E. et al. *Cognitive Processes.* Englewood Cliffs, NJ: Prentice, 1986; and Lindsay, P. H., and D. A. Norman, *Human Information Processing.* New York: Academic Press, 1977.

students to connect to literature through ***reader response*** *activities and then provides materials that teachers can use to assist students in elaborating and refining their responses.*

Reader Response Theory

The Theoretical Foundations of Reader Response Theory. Reader response theory offers a theoretical framework for teaching that enables students to connect to literature on their own terms. The theory springs from a simple observation about the relationship between a literary text and its meaning, or interpretation: this relationship is not as direct as the relationship between text and meaning in, say, a train schedule. Suppose, for example, that a train schedule reads as follows:

> The B train from Marston arrives at Holyoke Station at 12:45.

That statement has one acceptable and correct interpretation. Differing interpretations (e.g., "The B train arrives at 12:55") are simply wrong (and can lead to pointless standing around on railway platforms).

One cannot make such statements about the rightness or wrongness of a literary judgment because literary texts do not function as train schedules do. A literary text provides much more than a report of observable facts about the world: It provides an opportunity for an imaginary experience. If one is reading well, that imaginary experience is every bit as vivid as an actual experience, such as trekking up a mountainside in the Peruvian Andes or shopping in the Ginza district of Tokyo.

When one reads a work of literature, one does not *read about the world*, one *enters a world*, and not *the world as it is*, but *the world as it might be.* That world is an imaginative construct formed partly on the basis of the text and partly on the basis of experiences that the reader brings to the reading.

Imagine, for a moment, that you and some other travelers have just returned from a real-life excursion. There will doubtless be aspects of the trip that you can agree upon (e.g., "The Ginza is crowded"; "The air at high elevations in the Andes is quite thin"). However, the real meaning, or significance, of the trip will differ for each of you depending on what you brought to the journey. The same is true of the journeys that people take when they read. Your experience of Emily Dickinson's "I'm Nobody! Who are you?" or of Jack London's *The Call of the Wild* will differ from another person's depending on what you brought (and continue to bring) to the text.

Literary Works as Worlds. The idea that a literary text offers the reader (or listener) an opportunity to create a world into which he or she can travel is not new. When the Nobel Prize-winning poet Derek Walcott writes

> At the end of this sentence, rain
>   will begin.
> At the end of the rain, a sail.

he evokes the ancient, shamanistic power of the poet to call a world into existence. This power connects Walcott in an unbroken line through Dickinson and Shakespeare and Homer to the first unknown poet who enthralled an audience with the pre-proto-Indo-European equivalent of "Once upon a time. . . ."

In the early twentieth century, the idea that a literary text creates a world of its own was eloquently advanced by the so-called New Critics, such as Cleanth Brooks writing in *The Well-Wrought Urn.* The New Critics insisted on close reading of texts, and this insistence led some to think that the New Criticism was about arriving, through analysis, at one acceptable meaning; however, that is a misinterpretation of New Critical theory. Brooks, Warren, Empson, and other New Critics advanced a much more subtle and powerful idea. They believed that literary texts created worlds and that one had to attend closely to the texts in order to distinguish the nuances of those worlds. In the words of that masterpiece of New Critical theory, Archibald MacLeish's poem "Ars Poetica,"

> A poem should not mean
> But be.

Reader response theory extends this formulation by acknowledging the large role played by the reader, as well as by the text, in the creation of "the world of a reading."

The world of a literary work, like the real world, provides an opportunity to have an experience. Critical faculties and concepts, like a tourist's guidebook, will help to make that experience valuable, but the experience itself has no one meaning, any more than a waterfall or a revolution or any other real-life experience does.

The Construction of Meaning. Different readers will read and interpret a text differently, depending on

what they bring to it. Suppose, for example, that a story begins as follows:

> Isaac opened his lunchbox. It contained the usual sandwich wrapped in brown paper (his father, who made his lunches, thought that plastic wrap constituted a sin against the environment). It also contained what seemed to him an ordinary apple.

If you are reading well, then you will give yourself over imaginatively to the story, creating the scene in your mind's eye. Of course, the scene that you create will depend partly on the text and partly on your experiences. When you read about lunchboxes, perhaps you think of the metal variety found beside construction workers perched on girders, or perhaps you think of the plastic variety decorated with Simbas or Power Rangers. When you think of ordinary apples, you might picture a green Granny Smith or a Golden Delicious or a red Winesap. If you are an environmentalist, you might wonder whether Isaac's observation about his father means that the boy is insensitive about environmental issues. You might recall that a certain famous Isaac is popularly associated with apples and might begin wondering whether the juxtaposition of Isaac and apples in this story constitutes some sort of significant allusion. Perhaps this Isaac is going to make a discovery. The point is that as you begin reading the story, you begin constructing the world of the story based on clues in the text and on your own experience. That world will have its similarities to the world constructed by another reader, but it will have its differences, too. To some extent, large or small, your interpretation, your sense of the meaning of the text, will be unique.

Furthermore, the meaning of a text does not remain the same even for a single person. Robert Frost wrote eloquently about the evolution of his understanding of Emerson's poem "Brahma," advising readers not to be too anxious to come to a single, final interpretation of a poem but rather to carry the poem around in their heads so that its meaning would become enlarged and enriched (and, indeed, changed) by experience.

Reader Response or Cultural Transmission?

Relativism and Reader Response. A text comes to have meaning through a complex transaction between the text and the reader. This idea that the reader helps to create meaning can be dated to Louise Rosenblatt's seminal work *Literature as Exploration.* Recent developments of that idea owe much to Post-Modernist critical theory, in particular to Jacques Derrida's Deconstructionism. The same criticisms that have been directed at Derrida can also be directed against the extreme form of reader response theory that holds that a literary text can mean anything.

One such criticism of reader response theory asks: If literary texts mean different things to different people, what happens to the whole concept of cultural transmission through literature? Surely, the skeptic says, the idea that texts have different meanings for different persons is equivalent to Humpty Dumpty's position on the meanings of words, familiar to readers of *Through the Looking Glass:*

> "I don't know what you mean by 'glory,'" Alice said.
>
> Humpty Dumpty smiled contemptuously. "Of course you don't—till I tell you. I meant 'there's a nice knock-down argument for you!'"
>
> "But 'glory' doesn't mean 'a nice knock-down argument,'" Alice objected.
>
> "When I use a word," Humpty Dumpty said, in a rather scornful tone, "it means just what I choose it to mean—neither more nor less."
>
> "The question is," said Alice, "whether you can make words mean so many different things."
>
> "The question is," said Humpty Dumpty, "which is to be master—that's all."

Some have charged that both Deconstructionism and reader response theory are instances of a Humpty Dumptyish "relativism." Surely, critics of such theories say, "Auld Lang Syne" has a meaning that all Western speakers of English understand. Its meaning is part of the common cultural heritage of English speakers in the West. To deny that Burns's poem has a consensus meaning or interpretation is to ignore that it has become a popular New Year's Eve tune with a cultural significance that is passed from generation to generation in the West. To fail to

teach this meaning to students is to deny them access to their cultural heritage, to deprive them of a small portion of the legacy that binds them to others, making them part of a cultural entity rather than alienated individuals. This attitude forms the core of the argument made eloquently and popularly by E. D. Hirsch and Alan Bloom, among others.[3]

A Nonrelativistic Theory of Reader Response. The charge of relativism holds up only against the radical form of reader response theory that holds that a text can mean anything. To understand what shape a nonrelativistic reader response theory might take, let us return to our guiding metaphor, that of reading as a journey into another place (a journey made possible, as Coleridge pointed out in his *Biographia Literaria*, by "a willing suspension of disbelief"). Imagine that a child from the United States, having learned nothing of ancient Rome, were to stroll through the ruins of the Forum. Most likely, that child would make little sense of the experience, if we read "making sense" as interpreting the experience in grown-up terms. The Forum would be, for the child, a mere pile of rocks. The child's sense of wonder might be aroused by the occasional stray or feral cat or by various trinkets dropped on the ground by tourists. Now imagine that you yourself are walking through the Forum. To make the experience all the more exciting, imagine that you have with you a guide versed in Roman history (Livy or Gibbon would be nice). You wouldn't need a stray cat to arouse your sense of wonder. You are an educated person. You know about ancient Rome (and much of what you don't know can be supplied by your guide).

Reader response theory says that literary texts mean different things to different people, but it does not deny that some readings, like some walks through the Forum, are more informed than others. If one is in the process of becoming educated (and most of us are most of the time), then one's readings will not simply change over time, they will deepen. Furthermore, the process of becoming informed or educated about a text will include coming to understand the consensus interpretations of that text—the interpretations that have become part of our common cultural heritage.

Consider, for example, a line from another famous poem by Burns: "My love is like a red, red rose." One leading reader-response-based literature anthology, after asking students what this comparison might mean, suggests as an answer simply that "answers will vary." However, a red rose, in the context of a love poem, has a definite meaning in a Western cultural context. In the West, a rose is a conventional symbol of beauty and romantic love. Much of the work of a teacher is to pass on the accumulated knowledge, traditions, and symbols of a culture, and any textbook that does not assist teachers in that job does teachers and students a disservice. Such a text undermines the role of the teacher in the transmission of culture and ignores a rather fundamental fact: **the teacher is there because he or she knows much that the students do not as yet know.**

Interpreting literature involves achieving a sort of "equilibrium" among three factors: the reader's background knowledge, experience, and attitudes; the historically developed and culturally recognized canons of meaning; and the text itself.

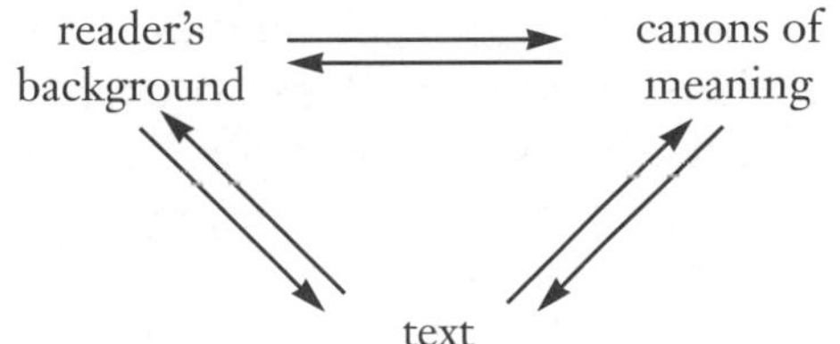

These canons of meaning are part of cultural literacy and include knowledge of literary genres, movements, and techniques as well as familiarity with history, authors' lives, other literary works, and some literary criticism, all part of the special knowledge the professional teacher of literature brings to the classroom. While respecting the student's responses and recognizing that those responses will always be to some large extent unique to that student, the teacher can still guide the student toward fuller, more sophisticated, more informed responses, ones that attend more closely to texts and to culturally transmitted aspects of texts such as conventional symbolism.

3. Preservation of students' unique cultural backgrounds and promotion of a shared cultural literacy need not be, as is often supposed, mutually exclusive goals. To achieve both, educators must expand their definitions of what constitutes the larger shared culture. Long ago, Jean de Crèvecoeur and Alexis de Tocqueville observed that America is strong because that country draws upon its diversity to create a new, larger union. *E pluribus unum*, says the motto on United States coins. The tension, the paradox, in that motto is one that those with literary education will appreciate. Out of such creative tensions new and wonderful syntheses are born.

Reader Response and Cultural Transmission in *Literature and the Language Arts*

What makes *Literature and the Language Arts* unique among available literature programs is that it does not offer teachers an unacceptable choice between reader response and cultural transmission. Instead, it provides ample reader response materials for engaging students on their own terms and then builds on what students already know, refining those responses in light of literary conventions and traditions. The unique design of the study materials in this series enables students to encounter the literature on their own and connect it to their lives, and then enables teachers to correct their students' discoveries to the mainstreams of literary tradition.

The psychologist Lev Vygotsky pointed out that at the outset of any learning situation, the learner has already reached a certain stage in his or her understanding. This stage really has two parts: what the learner can do on his or her own and what the learner can do with some assistance. The area between these two points is what Vygotsky called the **zone of proximal development,** or **ZPD.** The teacher's role is to assign the learner tasks that are within the ZPD and to provide the assistance that the learner needs while allowing the learner to do on his or her own as much as he or she is able. The teacher provides **scaffolding** that supports the learner until he or she reaches a new level. Then the old scaffolding is unnecessary and the learner is ready to move on to new learning.

The study materials in *Literature and the Language Arts* make it possible for students to begin with what they already know—their own lives—and connect what they know to the literature. Once that connection is made, students then explore the literature independently and in collaborative activities that provide a foundation for the teacher-assisted instruction, or scaffolding, that follows.

Partial Bibliography

Bloom, A. *The Closing of the American Mind.* New York: Simon and Schuster, 1987.

Brooks, C. *The Well-Wrought Urn.* New York: Renal and Hitchcock, 1947.

Bruner, J. *Toward a Theory of Instruction.* New York: Norton, 1966.

———. *On Knowing: Essays for the Left Hand.* Expanded ed. Cambridge: Belknap/Harvard UP, 1979.

Chomsky, N. *Language and Mind.* New York: Harcourt, 1968.

———. Review of B. F. Skinner's *Verbal Behavior. Language*, 35 (1959), 26–58.

Derrida, J. *Of Grammatology.* Trans. C. Spivak. Baltimore: Johns Hopkins UP, 1976.

Donaldson, M. *Children's Minds.* New York: Norton, 1978.

Eisner, E. *The Educational Imagination.* 2nd ed. New York: Macmillan, 1985.

Farrell, E. J. *Deciding the Future.* Research Rep. No. 12. Urbana, IL: NCTE, 1971.

Flower, L. S. *Problem-Solving Strategies in Writing.* 2nd ed. Orlando, FL: Harcourt, 1985.

Hirsch, E. D. *Cultural Literacy: What Every American Needs to Know.* New York: Houghton, 1987.

Kempson, R. M. *Semantic Theory.* Cambridge: Cambridge UP, 1977.

Kuhn, T. S. *The Structure of Scientific Revolutions.* 2nd ed. Chicago: U of Chicago P, 1970.

Lashley, K. "The Problem of Serial Order in Behavior." L. Jeffries, ed. *Cerebral Mechanisms in Behavior.*

Lindemann, E. *A Rhetoric for Writing Teachers.* 3rd ed. New York: Oxford UP, 1995.

Novak, J. D. *A Theory of Education.* Ithaca, NY: Cornell UP, 1984.

Resnick, L., and L. Klopfer. *Toward the Thinking Curriculum: Current Cognitive Research.* Alexandria, VA: ASCD, 1989.

Rosenblatt, L. *Literature as Exploration.* 4th ed. New York: MLA, 1983.

———. *The Reader, the Text, the Poem: The Transactional Theory of the Literary Work.* Carbondale, IL: Southern Illinois UP, 1978.

Skinner, B. F. *Science and Human Behavior.* New York: Macmillan, 1953.

———. *Verbal Behavior.* New York: Appleton, 1957.

Strike, K. A. "On the Expressive Potential of Behaviorist Language." *American Educational Research Journal*, 11 (1974), 103–20.

Thorndike, E. L. *The Fundamentals of Learning.* New York: Teacher's College, 1932.

Vygotsky, L. S. *Mind in Society.* Cambridge: Harvard UP, 1978.

———. *Thought and Language.* New York: Wiley, 1962.

Watson, J. B. *Behaviorism.* New York: Norton, 1925.

Weaver, C. *Grammar for Teachers.* Urbana, IL: NCTE, 1979.

Wimsatt, W. K. *The Verbal Icon: Studies in the Meaning of Poetry.* UP of Kentucky, 1954.

Program Components

Student Edition

Twelve Units per Book
- Superlative Texts
- Fine Art and Photographs
- Unit Reviews

Selection Study Materials
- Cross-curricular Connections
- As You Read
- Reader's Journal
- Guided Reading Questions
- Words for Everyday Use
- Notes
- About the Author
- Responding to the Selection (Reader Response)
- Reviewing the Selection
  - Recalling
  - Interpreting
  - Synthesizing
- Understanding Literature

Skills Lessons
- Writing Skills
- Language Labs
- Speaking and Listening Skills
- Study and Research Skills
- Applied English Skills
- Vocabulary Skills
- Reading Skills
- Test-taking Skills

Language Arts Survey
- Writing
- Language
- Speaking and Listening
- Study and Research
- Applied English

Handbook of Literary Terms

Reader's Guide and Activity Workbook*

Selection worksheets providing a step-by-step reader response guide for each selection and prewriting assistance for all writing assignments in the text

Essential Skills Practice Books*

Blackline masters for additional practice

Writing

Language

Speaking and Listening/Study and Research

Applied English

Assessment Portfolio*

Unit Study Guides and Tests
- Including vocabulary worksheets

Selection Tests
- Check tests
- Comprehensive tests

Worksheets and Forms for Writing Evaluation and Portfolio Assessment

Additional Worksheets and Forms

Answer Keys

Transparency Set*

Multimedia Kit

Audiocassette
- Selections from the program

Videocassette
- Selections from the program

*Contained in the Teacher's Resource Kit

CD/ROM
- Idea generator
- Test generator

Diskettes (IBM and Macintosh)
- Test generators

Laser Disc
- Selections from the program

Annotated Teacher's Edition

For Units
- Unit goals and objectives
- List of additional unit materials in the Assessment Portfolio
- List of cross-curricular connections in the unit
- Unit skills outline
- Project notes
- Answers for questions on project models
- Vocabulary check tests
- Spelling check tests

For Selections
- Lesson goals and objectives
- List of additional resources for use with lesson
- Cross-curricular Connections notes
- As You Read notes
- Reader's Journal notes
- Spelling and vocabulary words from the selection
- Answers to Guided Reading Questions
- Support for LEP Students
  - Pronunciation of proper nouns and adjectives
  - Additional Vocabulary
- Art notes
- Additional Questions and Activities
- Bibliographic notes
- Music notes
- Selection check test with answers
- Vocabulary in Context sentences
- Historical notes
- Literary notes
- Literary Technique notes
- Cross-curricular Activities
- Quotables
- Responding to the Selection notes
- Answers for Reviewing the Selection
- Answers for Understanding Literature
- Answers for Language Labs and other skills activities
- Writing Skills notes
- Analytic Scales for Writing Skills

Answer Keys
- Selection check tests with answers
- Answers for all exercises
- Analytic evaluation scales for writing activities and projects

Identifiers for Cross-curricular Activities, Activities Using Multiple Intelligences, and Activities Using SCANS Skills

Themes Chart

Teaching Strategies and Options

Additional Resources for Language Arts Teachers

Organization of the Text

The editors and authors of *Literature and the Language Arts* understand that teachers might want to vary their approaches to the teaching of literature. *Literature and the Language Arts* does not limit teachers to one approach. The literature in this text is organized both thematically and according to genre. Each unit begins with a quote that speaks to the particular genre or theme featured in the unit.

The text is organized into four parts.

Part One: Themes in Literature *presents literature using a thematic approach. It consists of five units organized under fascinating themes in literature—Open a Book, Open a World; Imaginings; Relationships; Discrimination; and Visions of the Future.*

Unit 2 Imaginings

—Joseph Joubert

47

Unit 1 Open a Book, Open a World

Le Moulin de la Galette, Auguste Renoir

There is no Frigate like a Book
To take us Lands away
Nor any Coursers like a Page
Of prancing Poetry

—Emily Dickinson

2 Unit One / Open a Book, Open a World

3

Part Two: Oral Traditions *presents a thorough introduction to the cultures and oral literatures of ancient Mesopotamia, Egypt, India, China, and Japan, as well as to the five major regions of Africa.*

Unit 6 Long Ago and Far Away

—Octavio Paz

221

Unit 7 African Traditions

Let me tell you a story my grandfather told me.

—Fitzgerald Iyamabo

278 Unit Seven / African Traditions

279

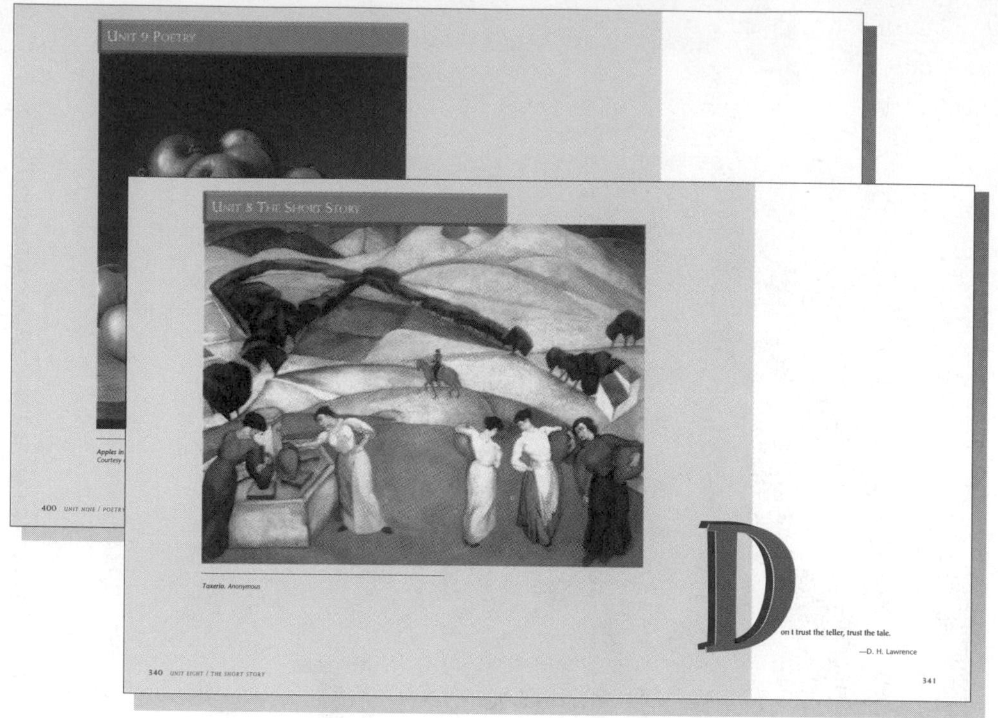

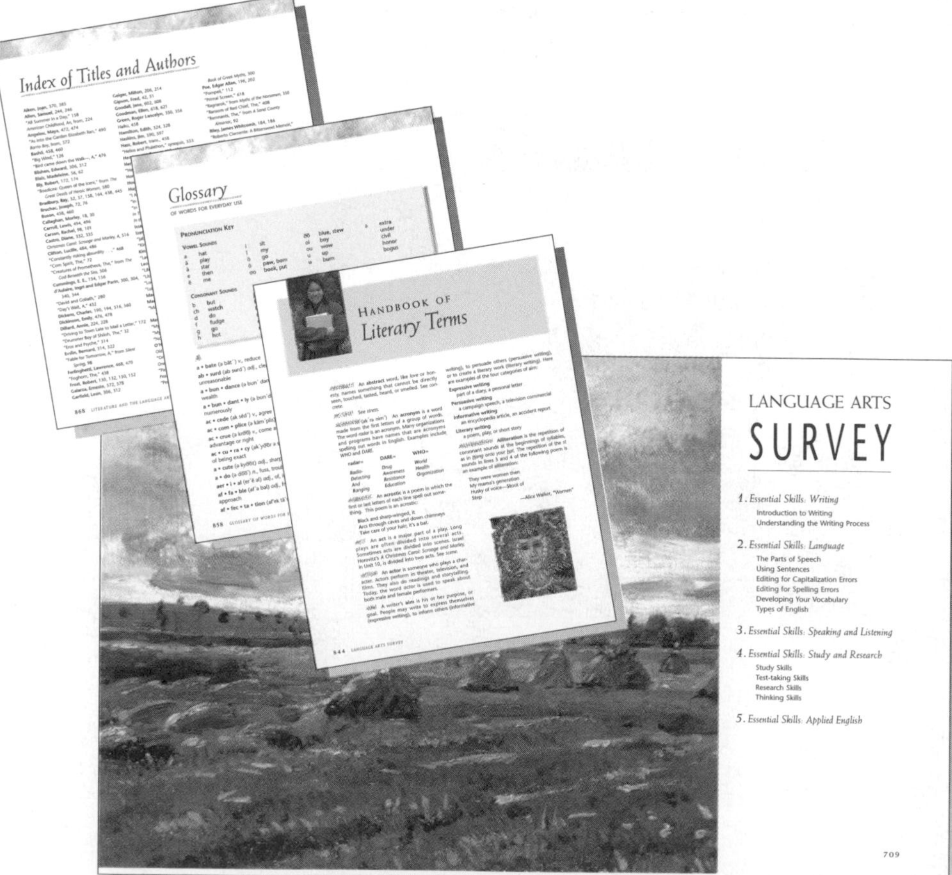

Part Three: Genres of Literature *contains five units overlaying the major literary genres—the short story, poetry, drama, nonfiction, and the novel.*

Each unit teaches vocabulary with **Words for Everyday Use** and is followed by a unit review that offers synthesis questions for discussion or writing. Each unit concludes with an extended **Language Lab** or **Language Arts Workshop,** as well as a **Unit Project** for engaging non-linguistic intelligences. The Language Labs present instruction and practice in grammar, usage, mechanics, spelling, and the varieties of English. The Language Arts Workshops present instruction in speaking and listening, study and research, thinking, and applied English. The labs and workshops often refer students to the Language Arts Survey in the back of the book for additional instruction.

Part Four of this text contains four sections. **The Language Arts Survey** offers comprehensive instruction in the complete range of language arts skills. (Each lesson in the Language Arts Survey is keyed to a worksheet in one of the four *Essential Skills Practice Books* in the Teacher's Resource Kit.) The **Handbook of Literary Terms** defines and provides examples of terms for literary movements and schools of thought, literary techniques, genres of literature, and common allusions. The **Glossary** collects all the Words for Everyday Use and provides both pronunciations and definitions. The text ends with indexes of titles and authors, skills, and fine art.

Part Four *contains*

- *A comprehensive* ***Language Arts Survey***
- *A thorough* ***Handbook of Literary Terms***
- *A* ***Glossary*** *of Words for Everyday Use*
- ***Indexes*** *of Titles and Authors, Skills, and Fine Art*

Lesson Design and Teaching Strategies

Literature Instruction

A typical lesson in *Literature and the Language Arts* contains materials for two phases of instruction, the Reader Response phase and the Teacher-Assisted phase.

The Reader Response Phase. Cognitive theory and common sense tell us that learning is more likely to occur when students are first provided with a context for what they are to learn. As the proverb says, a seed will grow in prepared ground. Each lesson in this book begins with a **Prereading** page that provides essential background information that connects the literary work to one or more other curricular areas and that gives the student an active reading strategy to carry out while reading the selection. The **Cross-curricular Connections** activities explore a wide variety of topics across the entire middle school curriculum. These activities demonstrate that academic subjects, including English, are essentially interrelated. The **As You Read** activities encourage students to read actively by presenting graphic organizers to be completed during reading.

The selection page itself begins with a writing activity to be done in the student's **Reader's Journal.** The Reader's Journal activity raises a central theme from the selection and asks the student to relate that theme to his or her own life. If, for example, a selection deals with a character who fails to exhibit courage, the student might be asked to write about a time when he or she acted courageously or wanted to act courageously but could not. After completing this activity, the student will be thinking about courage

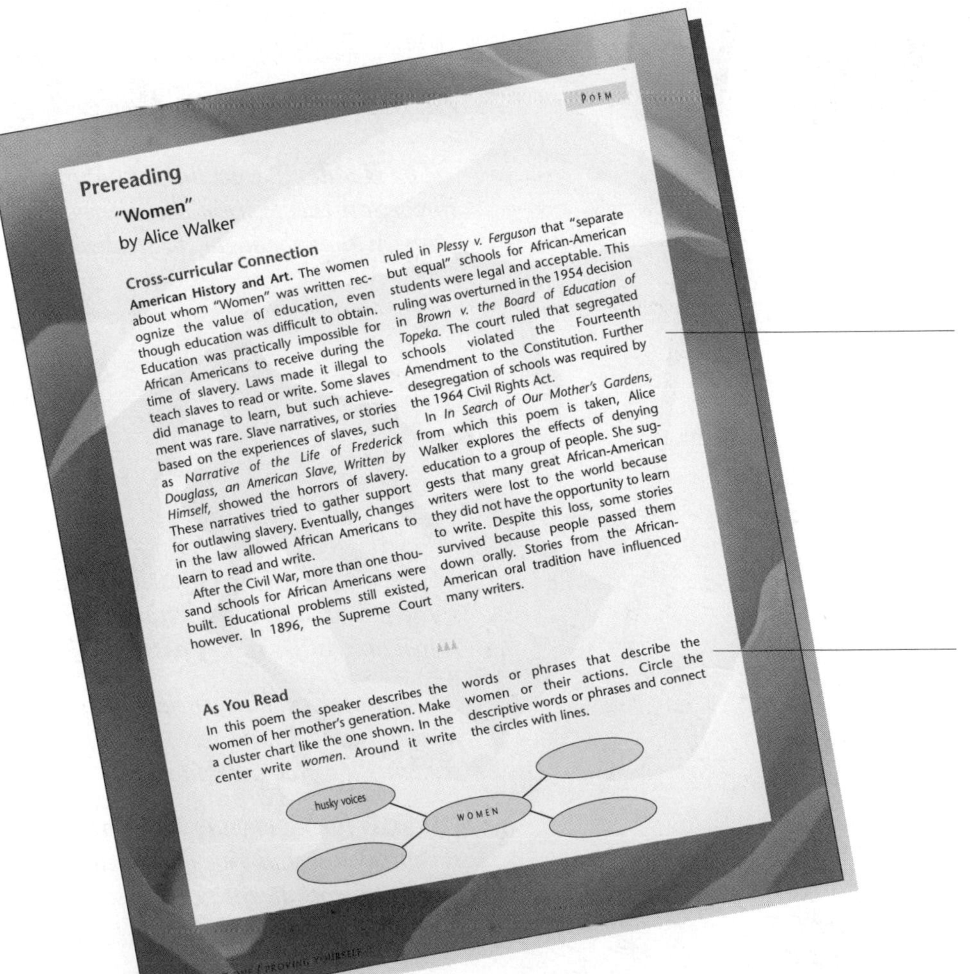

POEM

Prereading

"Women"
by Alice Walker

Cross-curricular Connection

American History and Art. The women about whom "Women" was written recognize the value of education, even though education was difficult to obtain. Education was practically impossible for African Americans to receive during the time of slavery. Laws made it illegal to teach slaves to read or write. Some slaves did manage to learn, but such achievement was rare. Slave narratives, or stories based on the experiences of slaves, such as *Narrative of the Life of Frederick Douglass, an American Slave, Written by Himself,* showed the horrors of slavery. These narratives tried to gather support for outlawing slavery. Eventually, changes in the law allowed African Americans to learn to read and write.

After the Civil War, more than one thousand schools for African Americans were built. Educational problems still existed, however. In 1896, the Supreme Court ruled in *Plessy v. Ferguson* that "separate but equal" schools for African-American students were legal and acceptable. This ruling was overturned in the 1954 decision in *Brown v. the Board of Education of Topeka.* The court ruled that segregated schools violated the Fourteenth Amendment to the Constitution. Further desegregation of schools was required by the 1964 Civil Rights Act.

In *In Search of Our Mother's Gardens,* from which this poem is taken, Alice Walker explores the effects of denying education to a group of people. She suggests that many great African-American writers were lost to the world because they did not have the opportunity to learn to write. Despite this loss, some stories survived because people passed them down orally. Stories from the African-American oral tradition have influenced many writers.

As You Read

In this poem the speaker describes the women of her mother's generation. Make a cluster chart like the one shown. In the center write *women.* Around it write words or phrases that describe the women or their actions. Circle the descriptive words or phrases and connect the circles with lines.

4 UNIT ONE / PROVING YOURSELF

Sample Prereading Page

Cross-curricular Connections *relate literature to subjects across the entire middle-school curriculum.*

As You Read *activities provide graphic organizers to encourage active reading.*

in relation to his or her own life and therefore be more likely to relate the selection to himself or herself and so become emotionally invested in it. This emotional investment in the literature is, of course, key, and that is why the Reader's Journal activities are primarily affective in nature. Responses to these Reader's Journal activities can be made on the **Selection Worksheets** found in the ***Reader's Guide and Activity Workbook***, or they can be made in the student's notebook.

Once the student begins reading the selection, he or she can then take advantage of the **Guided Reading Questions** that appear in the margins. These questions are designed to bring to the student's attention key passages in the selection and issues raised by those passages. Like a guide taking a tourist through the Roman Forum and pointing out important or interesting landmarks, these questions take the student through the selection, ensuring that the most important or interesting aspects of the selection will not be missed. (It would be wonderful if every student could have his or her own private guide to literature. These questions provide the next best thing.)

Again, the student can answer these questions on the Selection Worksheets or in his or her notebook.

After reading the selection, the student can then meet with other students in small **collaborative learning groups** to share responses to the Reader's Journal activity and Guided Reading Questions. In these groups, students can also discuss the questions raised in the **Responding to the Selection** activity that follows the selection. Again, this is an affective-response activity, one designed to connect the student emotionally to the literature.

These three components of the instructional apparatus, the Reader's Journal activity, the Guided Reading

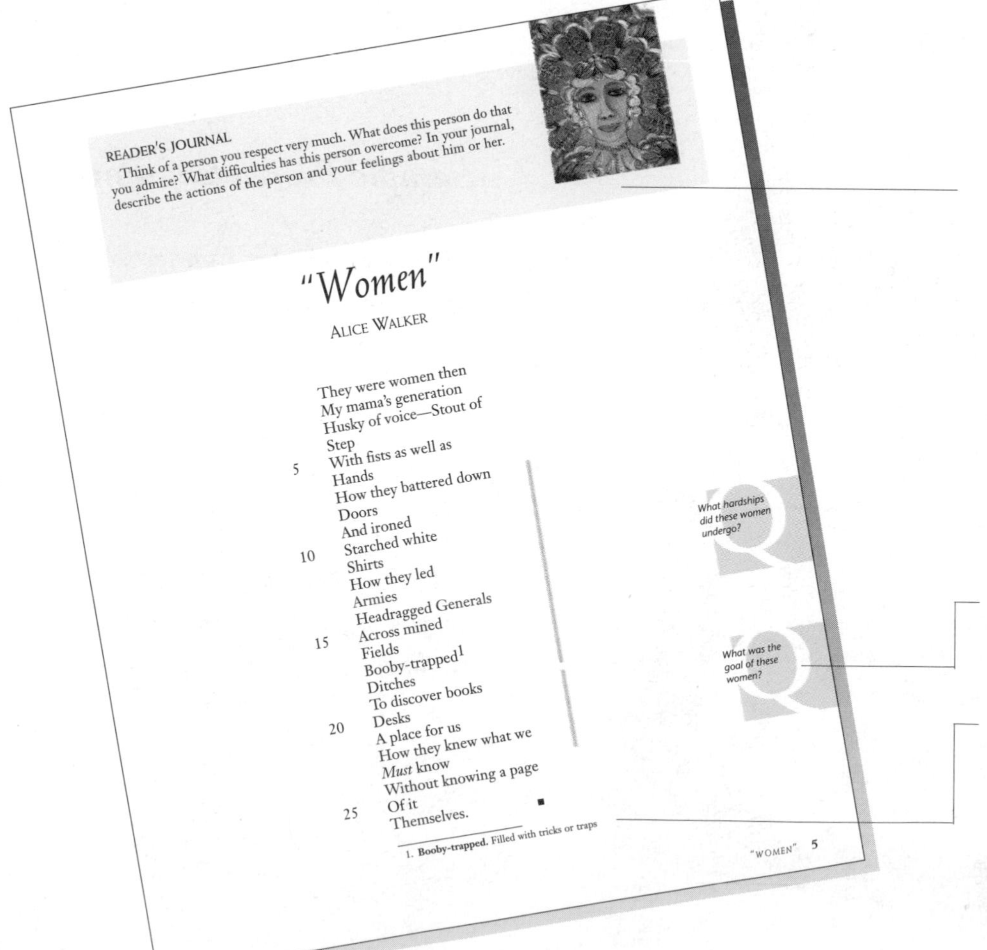

READER'S JOURNAL

Think of a person you respect very much. What does this person do that you admire? What difficulties has this person overcome? In your journal, describe the actions of the person and your feelings about him or her.

"Women"

ALICE WALKER

They were women then
My mama's generation
Husky of voice—Stout of
Step
With fists as well as
Hands
How they battered down
Doors
And ironed
Starched white
Shirts
How they led
Armies
Headragged Generals
Across mined
Fields
Booby-trapped[1]
Ditches
To discover books
Desks
A place for us
How they knew what we
Must know
Without knowing a page
Of it
Themselves. ■

What hardships did these women undergo?

What was the goal of these women?

1. **Booby-trapped.** Filled with tricks or traps

"WOMEN" 5

Sample Selection Page

*The **Reader's Journal** activity raises an important theme from the selection and connects that theme to the student's life.*

***Guided Reading Questions** guide students through the selection by raising important issues in key passages.*

***Footnotes** explain obscure references, unusual usages, and terms meant to enter students' passive vocabularies.*

***Words for Everyday Use notes** (not shown) define and give pronunciations for difficult terms meant to enter students' active vocabularies.*

questions, and the Responding to the Selection activity, connect the student to the selection, guide him or her through it, and then make it possible for the student to share his or her responses with others. Together, these activities ensure that once the teacher-assisted phase of the instruction begins, the student will have a wealth of responses to share in discussions with the whole class.

Additional teaching suggestions for the Reader's Journal, Guided Reading, and Responding to the Selection activities are provided in the ***Annotated Teacher's Edition.***

The Teacher-Assisted Phase. The **Reviewing the Selection** questions that follow the Responding to the Selection activity are designed to take the student through the selection step by step, building upon his or her responses and refining those through questions of successive complexity. These questions are organized by level of cognitive sophistication into three sections:

The **Recalling** questions ensure basic comprehension of key facts from the selection.

The **Interpreting** questions ask students to make interpretations or critical evaluations based on facts from the selection.

The **Synthesizing** questions ask students to draw together what they have gathered through recall and interpretation to make generalizations about the meaning, significance, or value of the selection. Often these questions ask the student to apply what he or she has learned from the selection to some larger context (to larger trends or themes in literature, for example, or to some larger social, cultural, ethical, or political context).

Uniquely, each Interpreting question in Reviewing the Selection is keyed to a Recalling question that provides the facts on which the interpretation can be based. **This keying of interpreta-**

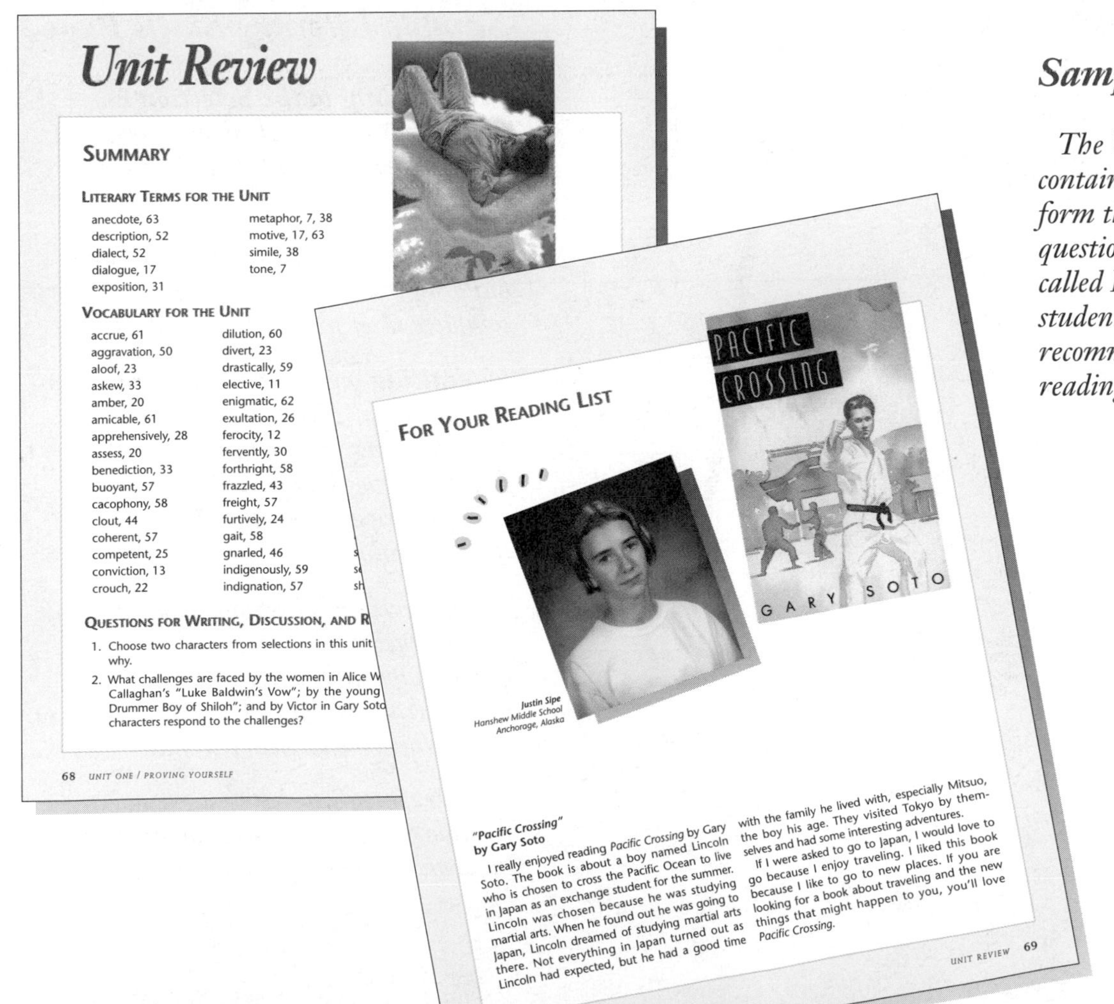

Unit Review

Summary

Literary Terms for the Unit

anecdote, 63
description, 52
dialect, 52
dialogue, 17
exposition, 31
metaphor, 7, 38
motive, 17, 63
simile, 38
tone, 7

Vocabulary for the Unit

accrue, 61
aggravation, 50
aloof, 23
askew, 33
amber, 20
amicable, 61
apprehensively, 28
assess, 20
benediction, 33
buoyant, 57
cacophony, 58
clout, 44
coherent, 57
competent, 25
conviction, 13
crouch, 22
dilution, 60
divert, 23
drastically, 59
elective, 11
enigmatic, 62
exultation, 26
ferocity, 12
fervently, 30
forthright, 58
frazzled, 43
freight, 57
furtively, 24
gait, 58
gnarled, 46
indigenously, 59
indignation, 57

Questions for Writing, Discussion, and R

1. Choose two characters from selections in this unit why.
2. What challenges are faced by the women in Alice W Callaghan's "Luke Baldwin's Vow"; by the young Drummer Boy of Shiloh"; and by Victor in Gary Soto characters respond to the challenges?

68 UNIT ONE / PROVING YOURSELF

For Your Reading List

Justin Sipe
Hanshew Middle School
Anchorage, Alaska

"Pacific Crossing"
by Gary Soto

I really enjoyed reading *Pacific Crossing* by Gary Soto. The book is about a boy named Lincoln who is chosen to cross the Pacific Ocean to live in Japan as an exchange student for the summer. Lincoln was chosen because he was studying martial arts. When he found out he was going to Japan, Lincoln dreamed of studying martial arts there. Not everything in Japan turned out as Lincoln had expected, but he had a good time with the family he lived with, especially Mitsuo, the boy his age. They visited Tokyo by themselves and had some interesting adventures.

If I were asked to go to Japan, I would love to go because I enjoy traveling. I liked this book because I like to go to new places. If you are looking for a book about traveling and the new things that might happen to you, you'll love *Pacific Crossing.*

UNIT REVIEW 69

Sample Unit Review Page

The Unit Review at the end of each unit contains a complete list of literary terms form the unit, writing and discussion questions for the unit, and a special feature called For Your Reading List in which students from around the country make recommendations for enjoyable related reading.

tion to facts from the selection ensures that student responses will be based on evidence from the selection. No other text now available offers this feature.

Because students often are not readily familiar with literary terminology and its applications, such terminology does not appear in the questions for Reviewing the Selection. Literary terminology and techniques are covered in the next part of the instructional apparatus, which is called **Understanding Literature.** Each Understanding Literature activity begins with a boldfaced term that names a literary movement, genre, or technique. The term is followed by its definition and by one or more questions that apply the concept to the selection. Having responded to the selection and having reviewed it in detail, the student can now learn some of the technical details about how the selection worked to achieve its effects. Students needing or desiring additional information about a term introduced in the Understanding Literature activity can refer to the discussion of that term in the **Handbook of Literary Terms** at the back of the book.

Approaches to the teacher-assisted phase of the literature instruction can vary, depending on your teaching style and the needs of your students. Some teachers will prefer to have students answer questions on Reviewing the Selection and Understanding Literature individually or in small groups and then will hold whole-class discussions of these questions. Others will prefer to treat these questions as prompts for whole-class, teacher-directed discussions. Another alternative, especially appropriate in advanced classes, is to assign students to conduct whole-class discussions of these questions.

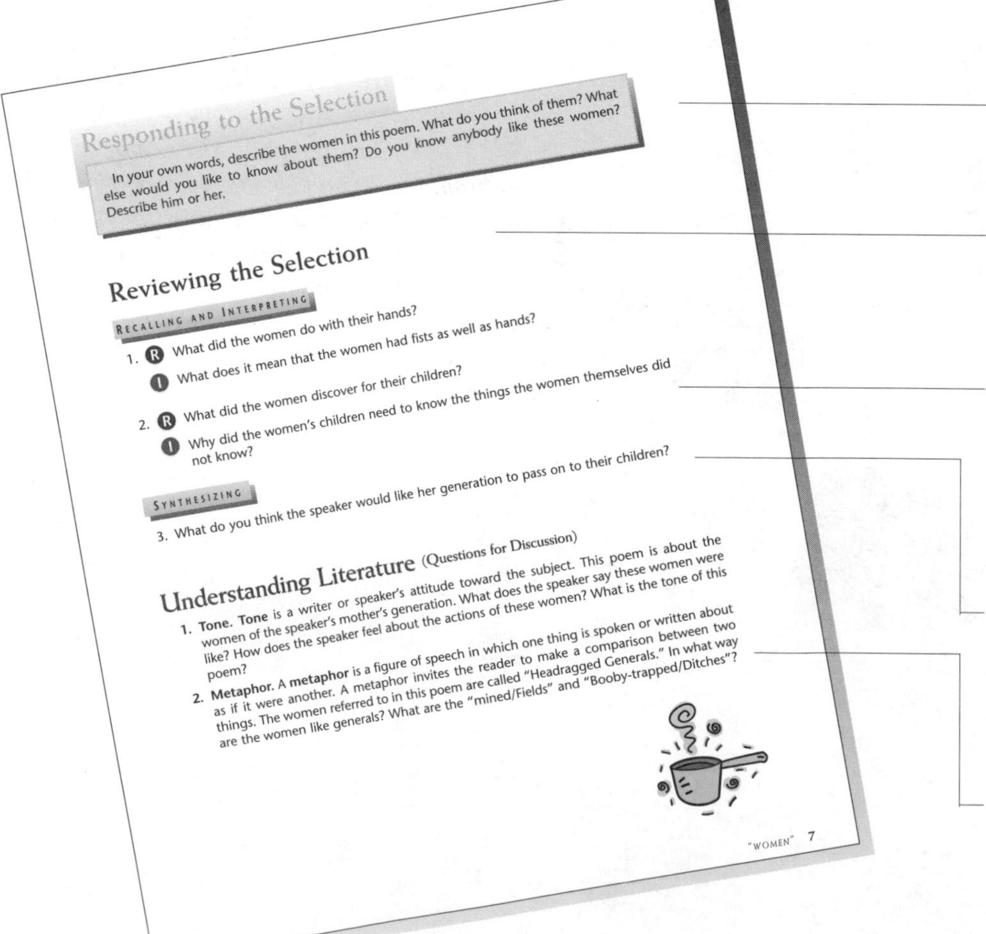

Responding to the Selection

In your own words, describe the women in this poem. What do you think of them? What else would you like to know about them? Do you know anybody like these women? Describe him or her.

Reviewing the Selection

RECALLING AND INTERPRETING

1. R What did the women do with their hands?
   I What does it mean that the women had fists as well as hands?
2. R What did the women discover for their children?
   I Why did the women's children need to know the things the women themselves did not know?

SYNTHESIZING

3. What do you think the speaker would like her generation to pass on to their children?

Understanding Literature (Questions for Discussion)

1. **Tone.** **Tone** is a writer or speaker's attitude toward the subject. This poem is about the women of the speaker's mother's generation. What does the speaker say these women were like? How does the speaker feel about the actions of these women? What is the tone of this poem?
2. **Metaphor.** A **metaphor** is a figure of speech in which one thing is spoken or written about as if it were another. A metaphor invites the reader to make a comparison between two things. The women referred to in this poem are called "Headragged Generals." In what way are the women like generals? What are the "mined/Fields" and "Booby-trapped/Ditches"?

"WOMEN" 7

Sample Literary Skills Page

Responding to the Selection *is a reader response activity designed to elicit an affective response to the selection.*

Reviewing the Selection *takes students through the work step by step, building from their individual responses a complete interpretation of the work.*

Recalling *questions address comprehension of key facts from the selection.* ***Interpreting*** *questions, keyed to the Recalling questions by arrows, evoke interpretations based on evidence from the selection.*

Synthesizing *questions tie together interpretations of parts of the selection and prompt students to make informed generalizations that relate the selection to larger themes or literary trends.*

Understanding Literature *questions provide selection-related study of literary movements, genres, and techniques.*

Instruction in Other Language Arts Skills: An Integrated Approach

It has been shown that a student may demonstrate knowledge in a classroom but be unable to use that knowledge in "real-life" situations. Grammar, usage, mechanics, spelling, and vocabulary skills have traditionally been taught in isolation as independent skills, but just as instruction in the separate concepts of physiology does not make us healthier, neither does instruction in the abstract concepts of speech or grammar make us speak or write better (Hillocks; Braddock). Skills must be taught in ways that enable students to "transfer" them to real contexts, i.e., to use them in their lives. The transferability of knowledge is a function of meaningfulness (Prawat). Teachers can promote meaningfulness by providing (1) a wide variety of examples, (2) practice in a wide variety of contexts, (3) an explanation of the value or uses of the learning, (4) an advance organizer at the beginning of the lesson, and (5) reviews. These five tasks have served as guideposts in the planning and writing of *Literature and the Language Arts.*

The exercises in this text are organized so that instruction in essential skills—those for writing, language, speaking, listening, study and research, thinking, test-taking, and applied English—develops in the context of literature appreciation activities. The study of engaging literature can provide motivation and context for teaching these practical skills.

Following selections in the text are skills activities covering the gamut of language-arts skills. Areas covered include writing, language, speaking and listening, study and research, and applied English. These activities are

Sample Language Arts Skills Activities Page

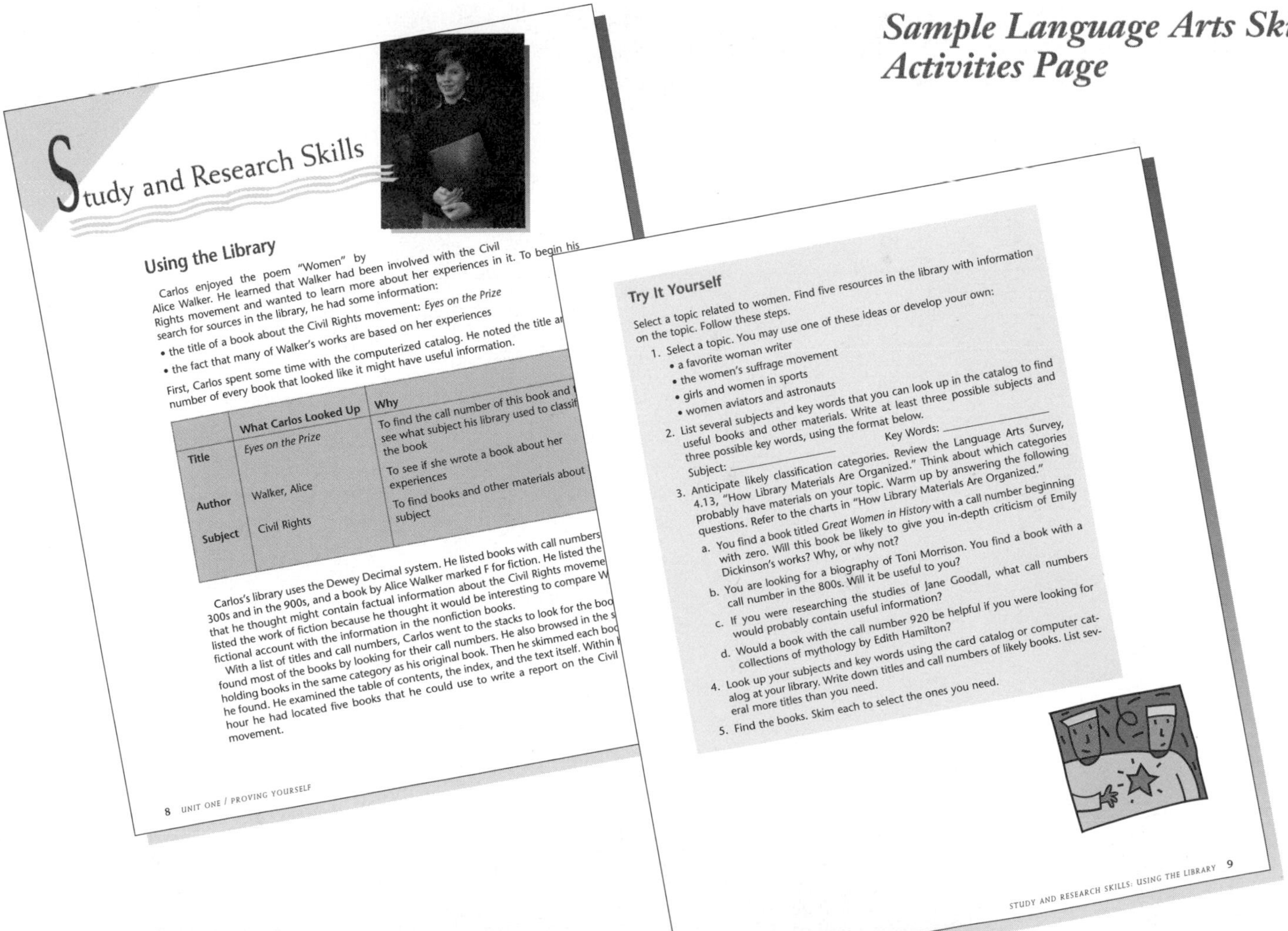

Study and Research Skills

Using the Library

Carlos enjoyed the poem "Women" by Alice Walker. He learned that Walker had been involved with the Civil Rights movement and wanted to learn more about her experiences in it. To begin his search for sources in the library, he had some information:

- the title of a book about the Civil Rights movement: *Eyes on the Prize*
- the fact that many of Walker's works are based on her experiences

First, Carlos spent some time with the computerized catalog. He noted the title ar number of every book that looked like it might have useful information.

	What Carlos Looked Up	Why
Title	*Eyes on the Prize*	To find the call number of this book and see what subject his library used to classif the book
Author	Walker, Alice	To see if she wrote a book about her experiences
Subject	Civil Rights	To find books and other materials about subject

Carlos's library uses the Dewey Decimal system. He listed books with call numbers 300s and in the 900s, and a book by Alice Walker marked F for fiction. He listed the that he thought might contain factual information about the Civil Rights moveme listed the work of fiction because he thought it would be interesting to compare W fictional account with the information in the nonfiction books.

With a list of titles and call numbers, Carlos went to the stacks to look for the boo found most of the books by looking for their call numbers. He also browsed in the s holding books in the same category as his original book. Then he skimmed each boo he found. He examined the table of contents, the index, and the text itself. Within h hour he had located five books that he could use to write a report on the Civil movement.

8 UNIT ONE / PROVING YOURSELF

Try It Yourself

Select a topic related to women. Find five resources in the library with information on the topic. Follow these steps.

1. Select a topic. You may use one of these ideas or develop your own:
   - a favorite woman writer
   - the women's suffrage movement
   - girls and women in sports
   - women aviators and astronauts
2. List several subjects and key words that you can look up in the catalog to find useful books and other materials. Write at least three possible subjects and three possible key words, using the format below.
   Subject: ______ Key Words: ______
3. Anticipate likely classification categories. Review the Language Arts Survey, 4.13, "How Library Materials Are Organized." Think about which categories probably have materials on your topic. Warm up by answering the following questions. Refer to the charts in "How Library Materials Are Organized."
   a. You find a book titled *Great Women in History* with a call number beginning with zero. Will this book be likely to give you in-depth criticism of Emily Dickinson's works? Why, or why not?
   b. You are looking for a biography of Toni Morrison. You find a book with a call number in the 800s. Will it be useful to you?
   c. If you were researching the studies of Jane Goodall, what call numbers would probably contain useful information?
   d. Would a book with the call number 920 be helpful if you were looking for collections of mythology by Edith Hamilton?
4. Look up your subjects and key words using the card catalog or computer catalog at your library. Write down titles and call numbers of likely books. List several more titles than you need.
5. Find the books. Skim each to select the ones you need.

STUDY AND RESEARCH SKILLS: USING THE LIBRARY 9

thematically related to the literature selections in keeping with an integrated approach. Each unit ends with a **Unit Project** that extends the instruction in the lesson in ways that call upon students' multiple intelligences.

The **Language Arts Survey** at the back of the book provides a comprehensive overview of the complete range of language arts skills. The survey is divided into five sections, as follows:

- Essential Skills: Writing
- Essential Skills: Language
- Essential Skills: Speaking and Listening
- Essential Skills: Study and Research
- Essential Skills: Applied English/ Tech Prep

Students may refer to these sections when doing writing or skills activities. Teachers wishing to give their students additional practice in any of these skills areas will find skills instruction and activities for each lesson in the Language Arts Survey, as well as a corresponding worksheet in one of the four ***Essential Skills Practice Books*** in the Teacher's Resource Kit. Teachers wishing to present whole units related to specific skills can have students work through parts of the Language Arts Survey, doing the activities found there and in the *Essential Skills Practice Books*.

Partial Bibliography

Ausubel, D. *Educational Psychology*. 2nd ed. New York: Holt, 1978.

Braddock, R., R. Lloyd-Jones, and L. Schoer. *Research in Written Composition*. Champaign, IL: NCTE, 1963. (ED 003 374)

Bruner, J. *Toward a Theory of Instruction*. New York: Norton, 1966.

Eggen, P., and D. Kauchak. *Educational Psychology: Classroom Connections*. 2nd ed. New York: Merrill, 1994.

Eisner, E. *The Educational Imagination*. 2nd ed. New York: Macmillan, 1985.

Hillocks, G., Jr. *Research on Written Composition: New Directions for Teaching*. Urbana, IL: Natl. Conference on Research in English and ERIC/CRCS, 1986.

Prawat, R. "Promoting Access to Knowledge, Strategy, and Disposition in Students: A Research Synthesis." *Review of Educational Research*, 59 (1989), 1–41.

Novak, J. D. *A Theory of Education*. Ithaca, NY: Cornell UP, 1984.

The EMC Synoptic Approach to Cross-Curricular Studies

The EMC Masterpiece Series Middle School literature program has been specifically designed to exemplify the advantages of cross-curricular study. The program embodies, in its cross-curricular strand, what the great modern historian Will Durant called the "synoptic approach," presenting particular cultures in terms of politics, economics, geography, philosophy, art, and literature. No other program currently available takes such a thorough approach to the integration of literature and the language arts with other ares of study. The EMC Masterpiece Series accomplishes this integration into two ways. First, every selection in the program is preceded by a prereading page that includes, prominently, one or more Cross-curricular Connections features. These features connect the literature selection to be read to information in another curricular area, most often one from the social sciences. Cross-curricular Connections features appear for each of the following curricular areas:

American History
Applied Arts
Art
Geography
Health
Home Economics
Mathematics
Music
Science
Social Studies
World History

Second, and uniquely, selected units throughout the series have a social studies cross-curricular focus. These units deal with major cultures worldwide and provide in-depth historical, cultural, and geographical introductions to literature selections representative of those cultures. The following table describes this Synoptic World Cultures Strand in the EMC Middle School literature program.

EMC Middle School Literature
The Synoptic World Cultures Strand

Africa

African Traditions, in Unit 7, Grade 8, represents a epochal change in how literature textbooks treat African materials. Much of the student population of the United States is of African heritage. Given this fact, one can only be saddened by the poor quality of the coverage of Africa in most literature textbook programs. Most other literature programs, if they include African materials at all, contain only works that have been retold and reinterpreted by Westerners not intimately familiar with African culture. Furthermore, these selections generally come from only one or two regions of the vast African continent. The treatment of Africa in the EMC program is a complete departure from the past in both these regards. The EMC section on Africa begins with a thorough historical, cultural, and geographical introduction. This introduction is followed by five sections, each devoted to one of the major regions of the continent—Northern, Western, Eastern, Central, and Southern Africa. Each section presents pieces from the oral tradition of its region, freshly retold for this series by a native African storyteller. This program is the only one that uses only authentic retellings by native Africans and the only one that covers the entire continent.

The Far East—China and Japan

The Far East, in Unit 6, Grade 8, begins with an introduction that surveys the histories and cultural attainments of China and Japan and presents representative selections dealing with ancient Chinese and Japanese mythologies.

CONTINUED

Greece and Rome

Greek Mythology, in Unit 7, Grade 7, begins with a thorough introduction to the history, politics, arts, philosophy, literature, and mythology of ancient Greece. This introduction includes a map of ancient Greece, Crete, and Asia Minor; photographs and discussions of classic Greek artwork and architecture; and a complete genealogy chart of the Greek and Roman gods. Greek and Roman mythology itself, so important to an understanding of allusions in later literature, is represented by four complete selections from definitive sources and, uniquely, by synopses of many of the major tales from the Greek tradition. No other program provides such a thorough grounding in the Greek mythological tradition.

Israel

Literature from the Bible, in Unit 7, Grade 7, begins with a thorough introduction to Hebrew culture and history, including a map of ancient Israel. Following this introduction are classic selections from the Bible—the story of Noah and the Flood and the story of David and Goliath. Becoming familiar with such selections is, of course, an essential component of cultural literacy in the West.

Native America and the United States

Respecting the Earth, Unit 2, Grade 7, demonstrates the roots of American environmentalism in Native American respect for and love of the land. The unit begins with traditional and contemporary works by Native Americans and then connects these works thematically to the emergence of the environmentalist movement. This movement is represented in classic works by Aldo Leopold and Rachel Carson.

The All-American Game, Unit 6, Grade 7, presents selections and historical backgrounds (in the Cross-Curricular Connections features) enabling students to take a synoptic literary and historical perspective on the most essentially American of sports—baseball. Studying this unit will give students a clear example of how synoptic literary and historical study can illuminate a specific subject.

The Near East—Mesopotamia, Egypt, and India

The Near East, in Unit 6, Grade 8, begins with introductions to Mesopotamia, Egypt, and India. These introductions treat historical events, major cultural attainments, and mythologies and include maps of ancient Mesopotamia, Egypt, and India. Through these introductions and the literature selections that follow, students will come to a comprehensive understanding of these early, foundational cultures—the earliest of human civilizations.

Scandinavia

Norse Mythology, in Unit 7, Grade 7, begins with an introduction to Norse culture and history and a discussion of the pantheon of major Norse gods and goddesses. The breadth of the Norse tradition is represented, from the creation story "Yggdrasil, the World Tree" to the hero tale "The Theft of Thor's Hammer" to the end-of-time story "Ragnarok." The editors and writers have attempted to give students, from a cultural literacy perspective, an overview of the central aspects of the Norse tradition.

Teacher's Edition Annotations

The ***Annotated Teacher's Edition*** is designed for your convenience.

Answers for exercises are usually provided on the same pages as the exercises themselves. All items are color-coded: answers to student edition exercises are on white backgrounds, supplementary notes and activities are on yellow backgrounds, and special items, such as lists of goals, enrichment and remedial notes, and selection check test answers, use distinguishing colors.

Sample Unit Opening Pages

A list of ***Goals/Objectives*** *helps you plan overall intended learning outcomes for teaching the unit. Affective goals, consistent with the program philosophy, emphasize reader involvement. Cognitive goals stress understanding of literary techniques and development of skills in writing and other language arts areas.*

Connections across the Curriculum *lists the cross-curricular activities from the unit.*

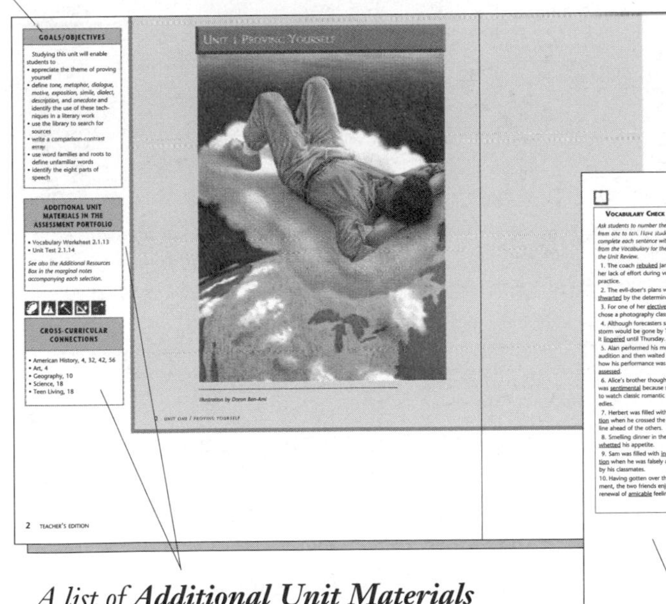

GOALS/OBJECTIVES

Studying this unit will enable students to
- appreciate the theme of proving yourself
- define *tone, metaphor, dialogue, motive, exposition, simile, dialect, description,* and *anecdote* and identify the use of these techniques in a literary work
- use the library to search for sources
- write a comparison-contrast essay
- use word families and roots to define unfamiliar words
- identify the eight parts of speech

ADDITIONAL UNIT MATERIALS IN THE ASSESSMENT PORTFOLIO
- Vocabulary Worksheet 2.1.13
- Unit Test 2.1.14

See also the Additional Resources Box in the marginal notes accompanying each selection.

CROSS-CURRICULAR CONNECTIONS
- American History, 4, 32, 42, 56
- Art, 4
- Geography, 10
- Science, 18
- Teen Living, 18

2 TEACHER'S EDITION

UNIT SKILLS OUTLINE

LITERARY SKILLS AND CONCEPTS
- Anecdote, 63
- Description, 52
- Dialect, 52
- Dialogue, 17
- Exposition, 31
- Metaphor, 7, 38
- Motive, 17, 63
- Simile, 38
- Tone, 7

OTHER LANGUAGE ARTS SKILLS AND CONCEPTS
- The Parts of Speech, 53
- Using the Library, 8

VOCABULARY CHECK TEST

Ask students to number their paper from one to ten. Have students complete each sentence with a word from the Vocabulary for the Unit in the Unit Review.

1. The coach rebuked Janie for her lack of effort during volleyball practice.
2. The evil-doer's plans were thwarted by the determined hero.
3. For one of her electives, Mara chose a photography class.
4. Although forecasters said the storm would be gone by Tuesday, it lingered until Thursday.
5. Alan performed his musical audition and then waited to hear how his performance was assessed.
6. Alice's brother thought she was sentimental because she liked to watch classic romantic comedies.
7. Herbert was filled with exultation when he crossed the finish line ahead of the others.
8. Smelling dinner in the oven whetted his appetite.
9. Sam was filled with indignation when he was falsely accused by his classmates.
10. Having gotten over their argument, the two friends enjoyed the renewal of amicable feeling.

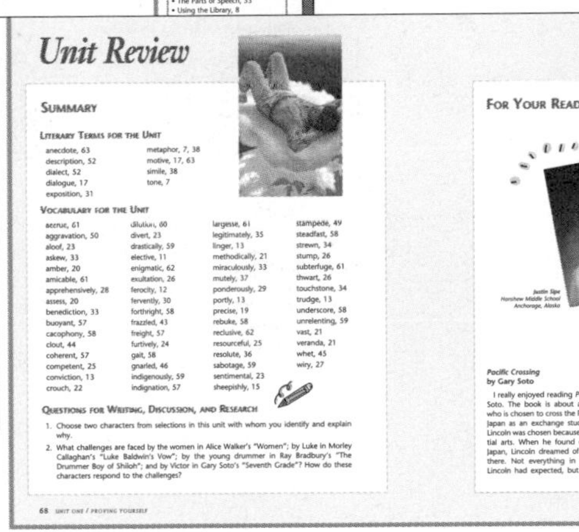

Unit Review

SUMMARY

LITERARY TERMS FOR THE UNIT

anecdote, 63; description, 52; dialect, 52; dialogue, 17; exposition, 31; metaphor, 7, 38; motive, 17, 63; simile, 38; tone, 7

VOCABULARY FOR THE UNIT

accrue, 61; aggravation, 50; aloof, 23; askew, 33; amber, 20; amicable, 61; apprehensively, 28; assess, 20; benediction, 33; buoyant, 57; cacophony, 58; clout, 44; coherent, 57; competent, 25; conviction, 13; crouch, 22; dilution, 60; divert, 23; drastically, 59; elective, 11; enigmatic, 62; exultation, 26; ferocity, 12; fervently, 30; forthright, 58; frazzled, 43; freight, 57; furtively, 24; gait, 58; gnarled, 46; indigenously, 59; indignation, 57; largesse, 61; legitimately, 35; linger, 13; methodically, 21; miraculously, 33; mutely, 37; ponderously, 29; portly, 13; precise, 19; rebuke, 58; reclusive, 62; resourceful, 25; resolute, 36; sabotage, 59; sentimental, 23; sheepishly, 15; stampede, 49; steadfast, 58; strewn, 34; stump, 26; subterfuge, 61; thwart, 26; touchstone, 34; trudge, 13; underscore, 58; unrelenting, 59; vast, 21; veranda, 21; whet, 45; wiry, 27

QUESTIONS FOR WRITING, DISCUSSION, AND RESEARCH

1. Choose two characters from selections in this unit with whom you identify and explain why.
2. What challenges are faced by the women in Alice Walker's "Women"; by Luke in Morley Callaghan's "Luke Baldwin's Vow"; by the young drummer in Ray Bradbury's "The Drummer Boy of Shiloh"; and by Victor in Gary Soto's "Seventh Grade"? How do these characters respond to the challenges?

68 UNIT ONE / PROVING YOURSELF

FOR YOUR READING LIST

Justin Sipe
Hanshew Middle School
Anchorage, Alaska

PACIFIC CROSSING
GARY SOTO

Pacific Crossing
by Gary Soto

I really enjoyed reading *Pacific Crossing* by Gary Soto. The book is about a boy named Lincoln who is chosen to cross the Pacific Ocean to live in Japan as an exchange student for the summer. Lincoln was chosen because he was studying martial arts. When he found out he was going to Japan, Lincoln dreamed of studying martial arts there. Not everything in Japan turned out as Lincoln had expected, but he had a good time with the family he lived with, especially Mitsuo, the boy his age. They visited Tokyo by themselves and had some interesting adventures.

If I were asked to go to Japan, I would love to go because I enjoy traveling. I liked this book because I like to go to new places. If you are looking for a book about traveling and the new things that might happen to you, you'll love *Pacific Crossing*.

UNIT REVIEW 69

SPELLING CHECK TEST

Ask students to number their papers from one to ten. Read each word aloud. Then read aloud the sentence containing the word. Repeat the word. Ask students to write the word on their papers, spelling it correctly.

1. The politician spoke with conviction when he gave his speech about changing the country.
2. We did not want to linger in the dark parking lot after the meeting.
3. My sister and I have to trudge a mile in deep snow every day.
4. Some sentimental people will cry when that store in the center of town goes out of business.
5. Chantel had a feeling of exultation when she won the award.
6. I tried to change Jamie's mind, but he was resolute in his decision.
7. At night, the gnarled tree branches made scary shadows.
8. The crowds and confusion at the grocery store caused Lorenzo a great deal of aggravation.
9. Saying they needed a drink of water was their subterfuge for sneaking to the kitchen and grabbing cookies.
10. Monica's largesse kept her

68 TEACHER'S EDITION

TEACHER'S EDITION 69

A list of ***Additional Unit Materials*** *refers you to a vocabulary worksheet and unit test for use with the unit as a whole.*

A list of ***Cross-curricular Connections*** *indicates instructional materials related to other subject areas.*

A ***Vocabulary Check Test*** *checks students' ability to use vocabulary words from the unit in context.*

A ***Spelling Check Test*** *checks students' ability to spell unit vocabulary words correctly.*

Sample Prereading Page

A list of ***Goals/Objectives*** *helps you to plan overall intended learning outcomes for teaching the selection. The list contains both affective and cognitive goals.*

A list of ***Additional Resources*** *refers you to materials in the Teacher's Resource Box and Multimedia Kit that can be used with the selection.*

Cross-curricular Connections *presents one or more activities for extending the cross-curricular teaching on the Prereading page.*

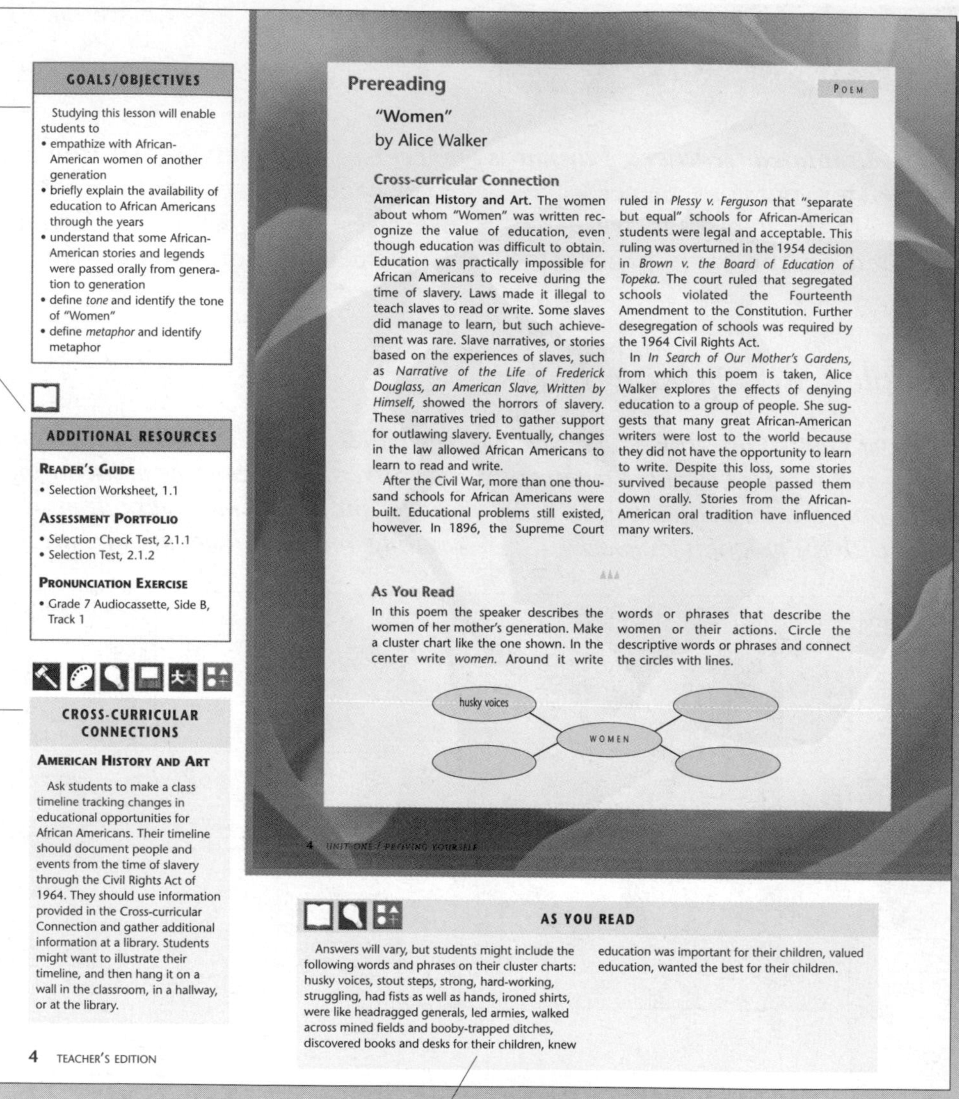

GOALS/OBJECTIVES

Studying this lesson will enable students to
- empathize with African-American women of another generation
- briefly explain the availability of education to African Americans through the years
- understand that some African-American stories and legends were passed orally from generation to generation
- define *tone* and identify the tone of "Women"
- define *metaphor* and identify metaphor

ADDITIONAL RESOURCES

Reader's Guide
- Selection Worksheet, 1.1

Assessment Portfolio
- Selection Check Test, 2.1.1
- Selection Test, 2.1.2

Pronunciation Exercise
- Grade 7 Audiocassette, Side B, Track 1

CROSS-CURRICULAR CONNECTIONS

American History and Art

Ask students to make a class timeline tracking changes in educational opportunities for African Americans. Their timeline should document people and events from the time of slavery through the Civil Rights Act of 1964. They should use information provided in the Cross-curricular Connection and gather additional information at a library. Students might want to illustrate their timeline, and then hang it on a wall in the classroom, in a hallway, or at the library.

Prereading POEM

"Women"
by Alice Walker

Cross-curricular Connection

American History and Art. The women about whom "Women" was written recognize the value of education, even though education was difficult to obtain. Education was practically impossible for African Americans to receive during the time of slavery. Laws made it illegal to teach slaves to read or write. Some slaves did manage to learn, but such achievement was rare. Slave narratives, or stories based on the experiences of slaves, such as *Narrative of the Life of Frederick Douglass, an American Slave, Written by Himself,* showed the horrors of slavery. These narratives tried to gather support for outlawing slavery. Eventually, changes in the law allowed African Americans to learn to read and write.

After the Civil War, more than one thousand schools for African Americans were built. Educational problems still existed, however. In 1896, the Supreme Court ruled in *Plessy v. Ferguson* that "separate but equal" schools for African-American students were legal and acceptable. This ruling was overturned in the 1954 decision in *Brown v. the Board of Education of Topeka.* The court ruled that segregated schools violated the Fourteenth Amendment to the Constitution. Further desegregation of schools was required by the 1964 Civil Rights Act.

In *In Search of Our Mother's Gardens,* from which this poem is taken, Alice Walker explores the effects of denying education to a group of people. She suggests that many great African-American writers were lost to the world because they did not have the opportunity to learn to write. Despite this loss, some stories survived because people passed them down orally. Stories from the African-American oral tradition have influenced many writers.

As You Read

In this poem the speaker describes the women of her mother's generation. Make a cluster chart like the one shown. In the center write *women.* Around it write words or phrases that describe the women or their actions. Circle the descriptive words or phrases and connect the circles with lines.

4 UNIT ONE / PROVING YOURSELF

AS YOU READ

Answers will vary, but students might include the following words and phrases on their cluster charts: husky voices, stout steps, strong, hard-working, struggling, had fists as well as hands, ironed shirts, were like headragged generals, led armies, walked across mined fields and booby-trapped ditches, discovered books and desks for their children, knew education was important for their children, valued education, wanted the best for their children.

4 TEACHER'S EDITION

The ***As You Read*** *note provides suggest responses for the As You Read active reading activity on the Prereading page.*

READER'S JOURNAL

Think of a person you respect very much. What does this person do that you admire? What difficulties has this person overcome? In your journal, describe the actions of the person and your feelings about him or her.

"Women"

ALICE WALKER

They were women then
My mama's generation
Husky of voice—Stout of
Step
With fists as well as
Hands
How they battered down
Doors
And ironed
Starched white
Shirts
How they led
Armies
Headragged Generals
Across mined
Fields
Booby-trapped[1]
Ditches
To discover books
Desks
A place for us
How they knew what we
Must know
Without knowing a page
Of it
Themselves. ■

1. **Booby-trapped.** Filled with tricks or traps

❶ *What hardships did these women undergo?*

❷ *What was the goal of these women?*

READER'S JOURNAL

As an alternate writing activity, you might ask students to think about their own education. What would life be like if they were denied the right to learn to read and write? What basic things would they be unable to do? What everyday activities would be difficult or impossible? What careers would be closed to them?

ANSWERS TO GUIDED READING QUESTIONS

❶ The women of the speaker's mother's generation lived lives of hard work and injustice. They ironed shirts, "battered down doors," led armies "Across mined/Fields/Booby-trapped/Ditches."

❷ The goal of the women was to have their children educated. The women knew that the children must know certain things if they were ever to improve their lives.

SUPPORT FOR LEP STUDENTS

ADDITIONAL VOCABULARY

headragged—having a rag tied as a scarf around a person's head
mined—filled with land mines, or explosives buried underground
starched—treated with a substance that causes fabric to be stiff
stout—strong, sturdy

Sample Selection Page

The Reader's Journal note provides extension or alternate prompts for the Reader's Journal activity.

Possible ***Answers to Guided Reading Questions*** *are keyed to questions in the student edition.*

Support for LEP Students *identifies additional vocabulary words that might cause problems for nonnative speakers of English and other limited English proficiency students. Where appropriate, this section also identifies and provides pronunciations for proper nouns and adjectives in the selection.*

Vocabulary in Context *(not shown) provides sample sentences using the target vocabulary from Words for Everyday Use. For selections of more than one page, a list of all target vocabulary words in the selection is given in* ***Vocabulary from the Selection*** *on the first page of the selection.*

Sample Selection Page

***Literary Notes** provide additional information about literary history, genres, styles, and movements. **Literary Technique** notes (not shown) point out and explain special techniques used in particular passages.*

***Additional Questions and Activities** provide opportunities to extend the lesson.*

***Selection Check Tests** check basic comprehension and allow you to confirm that students have done assigned readings.*

LITERARY NOTE

Alice Walker won a Pulitzer Prize in 1983 for her novel *The Color Purple.* The Pulitzer Prize is an award given each year for outstanding work in literature, journalism, and music.

ADDITIONAL QUESTIONS AND ACTIVITIES

Ask each student to write a letter or design a greeting card from the speaker of the poem to a woman of her mother's generation. What might the speaker want to say directly to her mother, or to another woman of her mother's generation? For what might she thank her?

SELECTION CHECK TEST WITH ANSWERS

EX. Alice Walker writes about the women of whose generation?
She writes about the women of her mother's generation.

1. According to the poem, what were the voices and steps of the women like?
The women had husky voices and were "Stout of Step."

2. What did the woman have as well as hands?
They had fists as well as hands.

3. Where did the women lead their "armies"?
They led their armies across mined fields and booby-trapped ditches.

4. What did the women discover?
The women discovered books, desks, and a "place for us."

5. What did the women know?
The women knew that their children must learn.

***Design Made at Airlie Garden.** Minnie Evans, 1967. National Museum of American Art*

About the Author

Alice Walker (1944–) was born in Eatonton, Georgia. She attended Spelman College and Sarah Lawrence. She writes novels, short stories, poems, and essays. She has also written a biography of Langston Hughes, a poet and writer of the Harlem Renaissance, and edited an anthology of the works of Zora Neale Hurston. Many of Walker's works are based on her experiences growing up in the South, working in the Civil Rights movement, and traveling in Africa. Walker's books include *The Color Purple* and *In Search of Our Mother's Gardens.* The poem "Women" is from Walker's introduction to *In Search of Our Mother's Gardens.*

6 UNIT ONE / PROVING YOURSELF

6 TEACHER'S EDITION

Responding to the Selection

In your own words, describe the women in this poem. What do you think of them? What else would you like to know about them? Do you know anybody like these women? Describe him or her.

Reviewing the Selection

RECALLING AND INTERPRETING

1. R What did the women do with their hands?
   I What does it mean that the women had fists as well as hands?

2. R What did the women discover for their children?
   I Why did the women's children need to know the things the women themselves did not know?

SYNTHESIZING

3. What do you think the speaker would like her generation to pass on to their children?

Understanding Literature (Questions for Discussion)

1. **Tone. Tone** is a writer or speaker's attitude toward the subject. This poem is about the women of the speaker's mother's generation. What does the speaker say these women were like? How does the speaker feel about the actions of these women? What is the tone of this poem?
2. **Metaphor.** A **metaphor** is a figure of speech in which one thing is spoken or written about as if it were another. A metaphor invites the reader to make a comparison between two things. The women referred to in this poem are called "Headragged Generals." In what way are the women like generals? What are the "mined/Fields" and "Booby-trapped/Ditches"?

RESPONDING TO THE SELECTION

You might ask students to write their responses to these questions informally on scrap paper, and then invite them to discuss their responses as a class or in small groups.

ANSWERS FOR REVIEWING THE SELECTION

RECALLING AND INTERPRETING

1. **Recalling.** The women battered down doors, ironed white shirts, and led armies across "mined fields" and "booby-trapped ditches."
Interpreting. The women had strength and were willing to fight for what they and their children deserved.
2. **Recalling.** The women discovered books, desks, and a place for their children.
Interpreting. The children needed to know things that would help them to accomplish goals beyond what their mothers were able to achieve.

SYNTHESIZING

Responses will vary. Possible responses are given.

3. The speaker would like her generation's children to appreciate education and the freedom to learn. She would like them to know how hard the women of her mother's generation had to fight for learning and freedom.

ANSWERS FOR UNDERSTANDING LITERATURE

Responses will vary. Possible responses are given.

1. **Tone.** The speaker portrays the women of her mother's generation as independent and strong. The acts of these women are portrayed as justified and heroic. Overall, the speaker is thankful and grateful for the work the women of the previous generation undertook to secure freedoms for their children.
2. **Metaphor.** The women of this poem are like generals in that they are leading their people into a battle against injustice. The "mined fields" and "booby-trapped ditches" can be seen as just some of the obstacles faced at that time by African Americans, especially women, in their fight to educate their children.

Sample Selection Activity Page

Responding to the Selection *notes give tips on teaching the activity.*

Answers for Reviewing the Selection *gives possible responses for Recalling, Interpreting, and Synthesis questions.*

Answers for Understanding Literature *gives possible responses to questions about literary techniques used in the selection.*

Using Literature and the Language Arts *for Writing Instruction*

Recent Advances in the Theory of Writing Instruction

Let's face it. Learning to write well isn't easy. Simply mastering the conventions of spelling, grammar, usage, and mechanics takes years. Learning to write elegant, balanced sentences takes years more. Then there are all those tricks of the writer's craft—the forms or genres, the methods of organization, the rhetorical techniques and figures of speech, the modulations of tone and register, the subtleties of connotation—all these must be learned and then, in a sense, forgotten so that the writer's words flow from some deep, authentic place, from some uncommon spring, to produce a voice, a style. Little wonder it is then that Yeats should write, "there is no fine thing/Since Adam's fall but needs much laboring," or that Chaucer should remind us of the Latin adage *Ars longa; vita brevis:* "Art is long; life, short."

Given the time and effort that it takes to become a reasonably competent writer, it follows that no one would do so without some powerful motive. Fortunately for English teachers, children come into the world with such a motive. The child, newly arrived, cries out, trying to communicate: it's cold out here, and strange. As children grow, they keep trying to communicate and will keep trying so long as the will to do so isn't drowned in a sea of criticism. Unfortunately, some well-intentioned but unreflective teachers did, in the past, drown their students' attempts at written communication in red ink that would, taken *in toto*, the multitudinous seas incarnadine (to borrow a phrase from *Macbeth*).

One of the most exciting things that has happened in English education in the past few years is the emergence of a new model of writing instruction that respects the student's voice and effort. That model is the process and portfolio approach. Process and portfolio instruction breaks individual acts of writing and the overall business of learning to write into manageable steps, with guidance and feedback at each step. Today, when students are given writing assignments, they no longer have to figure out on their own how to get from the assignment to the completed piece of writing. Instead, they are trained in techniques for prewriting, drafting, evaluating their drafts by themselves and with peers, revising, and publishing. Writing portfolios and evaluation forms are used to track development of pieces of writing over time. Assessment has been expanded from simple marking of papers to include self-evaluation, peer evaluation, and a variety of approaches to assessment that avoid turning teachers into copyeditors. The result of these changes in writing instruction has been that student writing has improved dramatically in recent years.

Literature and the Language Arts contains comprehensive materials for integrated instruction in the process of writing and for management of writing portfolios. The notes that follow describe those materials and how they can be used.

Introducing the Writing Process

Section 1 of the Language Arts Survey, which is called Essential Skills: Writing and begins on page 724, surveys the entire writing process from prewriting through publishing. This section of the Survey is divided into twenty-four lessons, each containing instructional material and a writing activity. Additional practice activities for each lesson in the Language Arts Survey can be found in the *Essential Skills Practice Book: Writing* in the Teacher's Resource Kit.

Teaching the Writing Assignments in the Text

Following many selections in the text are step-by-step writing skills activities keyed to selection. Each activity begins with a writing prompt

and a student model and is followed by questions for examining the model. Have students read the model and answer the questions in small groups or in a whole-class session. Then have them work through the rest of the lesson, which provides instructions divided into parts on Prewriting and Drafting, Evaluation and Revising, and Proofreading and Publishing. Notes for teaching each writing skills activity are given in this annotated teacher's edition, along with responses for Examining the Model questions and an analytic evaluation scale for the activity.

Using Writing Portfolios

The student's Writing Portfolio is a folder in which he or she stores drafts and finished pieces of writing. You can ask your students to keep a portfolio to enable you and the students to assess their progress over time. Portfolios show students' capabilities and progress better than any test or single writing assignment can.

You may wish to ask your students to keep **comprehensive portfolios** that contain all the writing that they do for class, along with Writing Summary Forms and/or evaluation forms for each piece of writing. Alternatively, you can ask your students to keep **selected portfolios** that contain pieces of writing chosen by the students as representative of their best work. Students should be encouraged to choose for their selected portfolios pieces that show the various skills they have developed and the various types of writing that they have done (informative, persuasive, creative, etc.).

When students place works in their portfolios, make sure that they attach their notes and drafts behind these works so that you will be able to see at a glance how each piece of writing was developed. Also have students attach to their works any evaluation forms they have used.

From time to time, you will want to do a comprehensive evaluation of the students' portfolios. A Comprehensive Evaluation Form: Teacher, in the *Assessment Portfolio*, has been provided for this purpose. You should also have each student do his or her own comprehensive evaluation using the Comprehensive Evaluation Form: Student, also in the *Assessment Portfolio*. Once these evaluations are complete, you can meet in a conference with each student to discuss his or her progress, provide praise for work well done, and make plans for improvement in the future.

Assessing Student Writing

(For a more complete treatment of assessment, see the introduction to the *Assessment Portfolio* in the Teacher's Resource Kit.)

Assessment of student writing should not have as its primary purpose meting out rewards or punishments. Instead, assessment should be seen as a development tool allowing the teacher and the student, working in collaboration, to monitor the student's progress toward achieving his or her goals.

Approaches to assessment vary. Two common approaches to assessing writing are analytic evaluation and holistic evaluation.

Analytic Evaluation. An analytic evaluation of a piece of writing begins with an analysis of the several features or qualities desired in the writing. These desired features or qualities are then used as standards or criteria against which the piece is compared. The evaluator merely goes down the list of criteria, giving the piece of writing a score for each criterion. A summary evaluation of the writing is obtained by combining these several scores.

Analytic evaluation is particularly valuable for formative evaluation. A general judgment of a student's work may be daunting, especially for students who do not do as well as they expect to do. Likewise, students who perform well, if given general comments about the writing, find in such general judgments little specific guidance telling them what they might do to write better. An analytic evaluation can show students exactly what their strengths and weaknesses are and where they should concentrate their efforts.

Analytic evaluation is valuable as a measure of either progress or achievement. To evaluate progress, you can evaluate the student's progress in each area by comparing the current work with previous similar writing assignments. To measure raw achievement, you can compare the student's product against some imagined ideal. Of course, in either case you must make sure that your

students are aware of the criteria on which they are being graded.

The Analytic Scales provided next to the writing assignments in this *Annotated Teacher's Edition* provide lists of appropriate criteria for analytic evaluation, along with simple procedures for scoring. In addition, a general Peer and Self-Evaluation Form: Analytic Scale is provided in the *Assessment Portfolio.*

Holistic Evaluation. Holistic evaluation of a piece of writing calls for an overall judgment. Holistic evaluation is most useful as a measure of achievement. It is difficult to score holistic evaluations according to a student's progress. To do a holistic evaluation, simply look over the general analytic criteria and then assign a score that reflects how well the student met those criteria taken as a whole.

Holistic evaluation takes less time than analytic evaluation and in most cases results in the same score. The saved time can be used to make encouraging written comments to the student, pointing out features of the writing that you admire and features of the writing that you would like to see improve in later work by the student. A general Peer and Self-Evaluation Form: Holistic Response is provided in the *Assessment Portfolio.*

Grading. Some teachers prefer to grade each writing assignment. Others feel that grading selected assignments chosen by the teacher and student to reflect the student's best work provides a more realistic assessment of the student's optimal capabilities. If the latter option is chosen, you may wish to provide credit for completion of assignments that are not graded.

Marking Student Papers. A student who receives back from a teacher a paper covered with corrections in red ink is not likely to be encouraged to do more and better writing. Furthermore, such marking of student papers is enormously time consuming and discourages frequent writing practice. A more encouraging approach is to mark one or two consistent problems and to mark three or four successes in each paper or, better yet, to allow students and their peers to do such marking and then to review these evaluations in conferences. Such marking can be done in conjunction with the completion of evaluation forms and/or analytic scales.

Reports and Research Papers

Literature and the Language Arts contains complete materials for instruction in the preparation of reports and research papers. The Research Skills section of Essential Skills: Study and Research in the Language Arts Survey in the student edition contains a complete overview of research procedures from using the library through documenting sources. Of course, these sections of the Language Arts Survey are accompanied by worksheets in the corresponding *Essential Skills Practice Books* in the Teacher's Resource Kit. The Synthesis questions that appear at the end of each Unit Review make excellent topics for reports.

Remedial Exercises in Specific Writing Skills

During your evaluations of students' writing, either of individual pieces or of entire portfolios, you will doubtless discover consistent areas of weakness. One student may have trouble with using transitions, another may consistently use serial commas incorrectly, and another may rely too heavily on the passive voice. The Language Arts Survey in the student edition and the accompanying *Essential Skills Practice Book* worksheets provide ample activities for remediation of particular recurring problems. Most of the instruction and activities in the writing and language sections of the Language Arts Survey are useful for this purpose. Thus if a student has a tendency to write sentence fragments, you can have him or her read the Language Arts Survey section in the student edition on sentence fragments, assign the exercise given there, and assign the corresponding worksheet in the *Essential Skills Practice Book: Language.* Thus the Language Arts Survey and the *Essential Skills Practice Books* can be used to individualize writing instruction and to target it to remediation of particular problem.

Teaching Strategies

Teaching to Develop Students' Multiple Intelligences and to Accommodate Diverse Learning Styles

Activities using multiple intelligences are identified by green icons. See the legend on page T32.

Use the techniques in the chart at right to teach and encourage students with diverse intellectual strengths and learning styles and to help all students use and develop the full range of their abilities.

Teaching Multiple Intelligences

- Use multiple modes of expression: e.g., read aloud selections; read aloud questions; use visual aids—charts, graphs, tables, or other graphics, art, and films; play songs; and perform demonstrations.
- Encourage students to use multiple modes of expression, including nonverbal expressions and performances such as drawing, painting, collage, sculpture, dance and choreography, acting and oral interpretation, photography, filmmaking, video production, and musicianship and singing.
- Ask students to read aloud.
- Precede written work with a related oral activity.
- Teach students to use graphic aids for understanding and for studying.
- Facilitate group work.
- Use cooperative learning.
- Allow students ample thinking time.

Teaching Students Whose Native Language Is Not English

Use the techniques in the chart at right to facilitate learning and participation for students whose native language is not English.

Teaching Students Whose Native Language Is not English

- Ask students to read aloud.
- Precede written work with a related oral activity.
- Use cooperative learning.
- Allow ample thinking time.
- When using small groups, pair with English-proficient students.
- Provide ample opportunity for nongraded, even nonevaluated, writing in English.
- Use multiple modes of expression: e.g., read aloud selections; read aloud questions; use visual aids—charts, graphs, tables, or other graphics, art, and films; play songs; and perform demonstrations.
- Encourage students to use multiple modes of expression, including nonverbal expressions and performances such as drawing, painting, collage, sculpture, dance and choreography, acting and oral interpretation, photography, filmmaking, video production, and musicianship and singing.

Teaching Students with Diverse Cultural Backgrounds

Use the techniques in the chart at right to facilitate learning and participation for students with diverse cultural backgrounds.

Teaching Students with Diverse Cultural Backgrounds

- Encourage discussion of cultural differences; invite students to share contrasting experiences; invite them to share events and characters that strike them as odd. Rely on students for your cultural information; be aware that you are liable to overlook differences unless you can take up a different point of view.
- Use multiple modes of expression: e.g., read aloud selections; read aloud questions; use visual aids—charts, graphs, tables, or other graphics, art, and films; play songs; and perform demonstrations.
- Encourage students to use multiple modes of expression, including nonverbal expressions and performances such as drawing, painting, collage, sculpture, dance and choreography, acting and oral interpretation, photography, filmmaking, video production, and musicianship and singing.
- Ask students to read aloud.
- Precede written work with a related oral activity.
- Use cooperative learning.
- Allow ample thinking time.
- When using small groups, pair with English-proficient students.
- Preview/explain culturally loaded terms and names.
- Discuss idioms and word origins.
- Discuss topics with universal appeal and relevance—for instance, independence versus family ties; independence versus friendship; identity.
- Discuss literature from both an "insider" and an "outsider" perspective.

Teaching Students with Learning Disabilities

Learning disabilities are physical conditions that make it difficult to complete certain types of tasks. Students with learning disabilities are often highly intelligent but lack specific abilities; for instance, one person may lack the ability to discriminate certain sounds, while another person who has that discrimination may be unable to remember certain auditory messages. Use the techniques in the chart at right to help students with learning disabilities succeed in your classroom.

Teaching Students with Learning Disabilities

- Discover the particular effects of each individual's disability and try to fill gaps.
- Allow ample thinking time.
- Seat students in front.
- Repeat important ideas frequently.
- Summarize and check students' bearings frequently.
- Monitor progress frequently.
- On larger projects, provide step-by-step guidance.
- Precede written work with a related oral activity.
- Use cooperative learning.
- Use multiple modes of expression: e.g., read aloud selections; read aloud questions; use visual aids—charts, graphs, tables, or other graphics, art, and films; play songs; and perform demonstrations.
- Encourage students to use multiple modes of expression, including nonverbal expressions and performances such as drawing, painting, collage, sculpture, dance and choreography, acting and oral interpretation, photography, filmmaking, video production, and musicianship and singing.

Teaching Students with Special Academic Gifts and Talents

Just as students who work below grade level may lose interest because tasks are too difficult, students with special academic gifts and talents may lose interest because they complete work quickly or because they are not sufficiently challenged.

Activities involving other curricular areas are identified by red icons. See the legend on page T32.

Teaching Students with Special Academic Gifts and Talents

- Encourage students to use multiple modes of expression, including nonverbal expressions and performances such as drawing, painting, collage, sculpture, dance and choreography, acting and oral interpretation, photography, filmmaking, video production, and musicianship and singing.
- Use cooperative learning.
- Allow ample thinking time.
- Involve students in the planning, preparation, and presentation or conduct of lessons.
- Provide or encourage extension activities once mastery is demonstrated.
- Provide or encourage self-guided activities and independent research.

Achieving Gender Equity

Sexism cannot be combatted subtly (Sadker and Sadker 123). In addition to using the techniques listed at right, make a directed effort to combat gender stereotypes and to treat all students as valued learners.

Achieving Gender Equity

Facts: Boys call out answers eight times as frequently as do girls (Sadker and Sadker 43). Boys receive more evaluative feedback—both positive and negative (Sadker, Sadker, and Klein 300; Sadker and Sadker 55).

Responses:

- Make a special effort to call on girls and to give them specific feedback, both positive and negative. (Note: if you give more than one-third of your attention to girls you may be accused of favoring girls; see Sadker and Sadker 266–267.)
- When intervening in student-student interactions, concentrate on raising girls' confidence rather than criticizing boys' behavior.

Fact: Exposure to gender-biased materials appears to increase gender stereotypes (Sadker, Sadker, and Klein 279; Sadker and Sadker 73–75, 128–135, 266).

Responses:

- Be aware of biases in literature and point them out.
- When appropriate, provide historical context for stereotyping by explaining older attitudes and practices.
- Provide direct lessons about gender stereotypes and gender-related communication styles.

Facts: Girls are more likely than boys to attribute their successes to luck and less likely than boys to attribute their successes to ability (Sadker, Sadker, and Klein 303). Girls are more likely than boys to attribute their failures to lack of ability and less likely than boys to attribute their failures to lack of effort (303). Teachers are more likely to comment on girls' appearance and the neatness of their work, and more likely to comment on the intellectual qualities of boys' work (Sadker and Sadker 57).

Responses:

- Make an effort to avoid commenting on students', especially girls', appearance.
- Make an effort to attribute all success to effort and ability.
- Make an effort to rebut forcefully students' self-deprecating comments.

Facts: Girls have lower expectations of success (Sadker, Sadker, and Klein 302) and are more likely to display signs of "learned helplessness" (303). Teachers are more likely to help boys solve their own problems but to solve problems for girls (Sadker and Sadker 81–83).

Responses:

- Fear of being "too tough" on girls is patronizing and hinders them from developing independence and confidence. Don't be afraid to criticize girls' work and don't let them off easy (Holt; Sizer).
- Make an effort to rebut forcefully students' self-deprecating comments.

Teaching Students to Work Cooperatively

Prepare your students for work in cooperative learning groups by teaching them how to listen actively, how to participate fully in discussions, and how to give one another positive feedback. Refer students to the lessons on listening, interpersonal communication, and discussion, sections 3.4–3.6 of the Language Arts Survey.

Uses for Small Groups. Use these task and project ideas to direct the work of collaborative learning groups.

- brainstorming
- peer tutorial sessions
- learning partners for practice or review and for all stages of the writing process
- inquiry-based concept learning
- multimedia and community-based projects
- topical symposia
- panel discussions
- mock jury trials
- role playing
- dramatizations
- simulations
- Reader's Theater

Teaching Students to Work Cooperatively

Preparing Students for Small Group Work

PARTICIPATION

- Review/preteach vocabulary and cultural concepts for nonnative speakers.
- Begin with a nongraded, fun, get-to-know-one-another activity.
- Take steps to ensure that group members know each other's names.
- Assign tasks that call on multiple intelligences.
- Ask questions that call for personal response and interpretation.
- Value interpretations that differ from your own.
- Have students determine the wording of their topics or questions.

- Don't talk too much.
- Model tentativeness and openness.
- Model courtesy and respect for all.
- Respond only holistically and orally to early drafts and initial products.
- Avoid judging early drafts; discuss ideas rather than expression.
- Discuss anonymous samples.
- Praise students for taking risks.
- Require (only) positive feedback from peers.
- Use joint grading for group work: (1) everyone in the group receives the average among the group; (2) everyone receives the lowest grade among the group; (3) a final product is graded and everyone receives that grade.

Leadership

- Ask students to conduct lessons.
- Rotate leadership assignments in groups.
- Appoint two group leaders—one to learn from the other.
- Model and give direct instruction and practice in asking questions.
- Model and give direct instruction and practice in reporting a summary.
- Model and give direct instruction and practice in involving nonparticipants.
- Model and give direct instruction and practice in restraining dominators.
- Model and give direct instruction and practice in providing positive feedback.
- Model and give direct instruction and practice in providing constructive feedback.

Listening/discussing

- Model, explain, and encourage attentive listening, eye contact, and not interrupting.
- Give practice in paraphrasing students' words and your own.
- Ask students to identify good speaking and listening habits and skills.
- Ask students to evaluate group processes and roles in their groups (use the form in the *Assessment Portfolio*, 5.10).

Forming Groups

- Groups should contain a maximum of six students for a complex task, a maximum of four otherwise.
- For peer writing groups, two may be the ideal size. Require periodically that students change partners.
- In the prewriting stage, it can be good to match those who share a primary language other than English.
- Working groups should contain students of varied abilities.
- Allow groups to vary their seating arrangements (suggest possibilities).

Guiding and Monitoring

- Give specific tasks.
- Explain criteria for success.
- Assign roles in group, or assign groups to distribute roles.
- When assigning roles in groups, divide responsibilities to assure interdependence and cooperation. One workable division of responsibilities is among (1) a discussion leader/facilitator; (2) a recorder; (3) a reporter; (4) a materials manager.
- Specify desired behaviors (see "Preparing Students for Small Group Work," above).
- Monitor group interactions and advise when appropriate.
- Intervene to diffuse conflict and to foster collaborative skills.
- When intervening in group work, ask a question rather than giving advice directly.
- If multiple groups have the same problem, interrupt the process and clarify or reteach.

Closure and Assessment

- Ask for sharing of a product.
- Both students and teacher should assess the quality of the product. Assessment can be among the entire class or only within groups.
- Both students and teacher should assess the quality of the group processes and communication.

References

Herman, J., P. Aschbacher, and L. Winters. *A Practical Guide to Alternative Assessment.* Alexandria, VA: ASCD, 1992.

Eggen, P., and D. Kauchak. *Educational Psychology.* 2nd ed. New York: Merrill, 1994.

Gardner, H. *Frames of Mind: The Theory of Multiple Intelligences.* New York: Basic, 1985.

———. *The Unschooled Mind: How Children Think and How Schools Should Teach.* New York: Basic, 1991.

Holt, J. *How Children Learn.* New York: Putnam, 1967.

Ohrlich, D., et al. *Teaching Strategies.* 4th ed. Lexington, MA: Heath, 1994.

Sadker, M., and D. Sadker. *Failing at Fairness.* New York: Scribner's, 1993.

Sadker, M., D. Sadker, and S. Klein. "The Issue of Gender in Elementary and Secondary Education." *Review of Research in Education,* 17 (1991), 269–334.

Sizer, T. *Horace's Compromise.* Boston: Houghton, 1984.

Slavin, R. *Cooperative Learning: Theory, Research, and Practice.* Englewood Cliffs, NJ: Prentice, 1990.

———. *Educational Psychology.* 3rd ed. Englewood Cliffs, NJ: Prentice, 1991.

Thematic Organization Chart

The chart on these pages lists forty-seven common literary themes and identifies the selections in this book that deal with these themes. Choose the themes you wish to teach in your course, and use the chart to identify selections that deal with those themes.

	AGE	ALIENATION	ART AND ARTISTRY	BEAUTY	BIRTH	CONFUSION	COURAGE AND FEAR	DEATH	DISCOVERING AND LEARNING	DIVERSITY AND PLURALISM	DRAMA AND ACTING	EXILE	FAITH	FAMILY	FREEDOM	FRIENDSHIP	THE FUTURE	GIVING	GOD	GREED AND AMBITION	GROWTH/GROWING UP	HERO/HEROISM	HOME AND COUNTRY	HONESTY	HOPE	IDENTITY	IMAGINATION	INDEPENDENCE	JUSTICE	KNOWLEDGE/WISDOM	LAW AND CUSTOM	LEADERSHIP AND AUTHORITY	LOSS AND REMEMBRANCE	LOVE	NATURE	ORDER/DISORDER	PARENTS AND CHILDREN	PEACE	PRIDE AND VANITY	RELIGION	SCIENCE	STRUGGLE	TECHNOLOGY	TRUTH/REALITY	WAR	WORK	WRITING AND BOOKS
UNIT 1																																															
"The First Book," 4									•																		•																				•
"How to Eat a Poem," 8									•																		•																				•
"The Story-Teller," 24																																					•										•
from *The Autobiography of Malcolm X*, 24									•						•						•									•																	•
from *Fahrenheit 451*, 32																	•													•	•	•	•										•				•
UNIT 2																																															
"Night Clouds," 48																											•								•									•			
"The City Is So Big," 52																											•																	•			
"The Song of Wandering Aengus," 58	•		•																	•							•																	•			•
"A Rabbit as King of the Ghosts," 62																											•			•		•											•	•			
"The Flying Machine," 68																											•																	•			
"Bums in the Attic," from *The House on Mango Street*, 76																					•						•																	•			
"The Cleveland Wrecking Yard," from *Trout Fishing in America*, 80																											•								•									•			
UNIT 3																																															
"My Father's Hands Held Mine," 96	•							•						•							•					•								•			•										
"My Father Is a Simple Man," 100	•						•	•	•					•							•					•								•			•										
"For My Sister Molly Who in the Fifties," 104			•	•					•	•				•				•			•				•	•	•							•													•
"If You Should Go," 112																																	•	•													
"The War of the Wall," 118			•					•	•	•								•			•	•	•								•		•														
"Tears of Autumn," 126		•				•	•		•	•				•									•		•												•										
UNIT 4																																															
"A Dream Deferred," 144																									•	•																•					
"Name Giveaway," 148		•				•				•																•																					
"The Fan Club," 154		•				•	•			•						•					•					•						•										•					
"The Medicine Bag," 162		•				•	•		•	•				•							•					•								•			•		•					•			
UNIT 5																																															
"Earth," 182																	•																								•	•	•		•		
"Humans Are Different," 188								•	•								•													•											•	•	•				

Selection	AGE	ALIENATION	ART AND ARTISTRY	BEAUTY	BIRTH	CONFUSION	COURAGE AND FEAR	DEATH	DISCOVERING AND LEARNING	DIVERSITY AND PLURALISM	DRAMA AND ACTING	EXILE	FAITH	FAMILY	FREEDOM	FRIENDSHIP	THE FUTURE	GIVING	GOD	GREED AND AMBITION	GROWTH/GROWING UP	HERO/HEROISM	HOME AND COUNTRY	HONESTY	HOPE	IDENTITY	IMAGINATION	INDEPENDENCE	JUSTICE	KNOWLEDGE/WISDOM	LAW AND CUSTOM	LEADERSHIP AND AUTHORITY	LOSS AND REMEMBRANCE	LOVE	NATURE	ORDER/DISORDER	PARENTS AND CHILDREN	PEACE	PRIDE AND VANITY	RELIGION	SCIENCE	STRUGGLE	TECHNOLOGY	TRUTH/REALITY	WAR	WORK	WRITING AND BOOKS
“Zoo,” 192								•	•							•			•			•			•															•		•				
“Lose Now, Pay Later,” 196			•													•																					•			•				
“Harrison Bergeron,” 204			•			•			•					•		•									•			•							•						•	•			
UNIT 6																																														
“The Epic of Gilgamesh,” 230	•						•	•			•					•					•			•					•		•	•		•				•			•		•			
“The Secret Name of Ra,” 240								•												•										•		•				•						•					
“The Instruction of Indra” from *The Power of Myth*, 248									•												•										•				•		•			•					•		•	
“P’an Ku and the Great Egg,” 260					•				•																									•	•												
“Amaterasu,” 266																																			•	•			•			•					
UNIT 7																																														
“Goha and His Donkey,” 284						•																																									
“Goha and the Pot,” 288															•		•		•																												
“Yemọja, Queen of the Seas,” 294																					•													•							•					
“Why the Sky Is Far Away from the Earth,” 300																					•												•				•													
“Why the Frog Croaks,” 308			•													•				•															•	•			•									
“How Tortoise Got His Patterned Shell,” 312																					•									•						•				•								
“How the Common Man Married the Princess,” 320																														•	•												•					
“Dingane the Brave Warrior,” 326							•		•				•							•	•	•			•					•						•					•					
UNIT 8																																														
“Rip Van Winkle,” 344	•	•									•			•																															
“The Sniper,” 364														•																															•		
“A Retrieved Reformation,” 372																										•						•																
“Last Cover,” 384			•					•						•							•						•											•					•					
UNIT 9																																														
“The Garden,” 404				•																	•							•								•											
“The Stolen Child,” 408													•	•																									•										
“I do not consider . . .,” 412																										•										•											
“Everyone is asleep . . .,” 412																										•		•							•											
“The Brain—is wider than the Sky,” 418																					•								•			•						•						•						•
“Ode to My Socks,” 422			•												•				•									•																	
“Digging,” 430	•														•																							•							•	•

	AGE	ALIENATION	ART AND ARTISTRY	BEAUTY	BIRTH	CONFUSION	COURAGE AND FEAR	DEATH	DISCOVERING AND LEARNING	DIVERSITY AND PLURALISM	DRAMA AND ACTING	EXILE	FAITH	FAMILY	FREEDOM	FRIENDSHIP	THE FUTURE	GIVING	GOD	GREED AND AMBITION	GROWTH/GROWING UP	HERO/HEROISM	HOME AND COUNTRY	HONESTY	HOPE	IDENTITY	IMAGINATION	INDEPENDENCE	JUSTICE	KNOWLEDGE/WISDOM	LAW AND CUSTOM	LEADERSHIP AND AUTHORITY	LOSS AND REMEMBRANCE	LOVE	NATURE	ORDER/DISORDER	PARENTS AND CHILDREN	PEACE	PRIDE AND VANITY	RELIGION	SCIENCE	STRUGGLE	TECHNOLOGY	TRUTH/REALITY	WAR	WORK	WRITING AND BOOKS
“The Rebel,” 434							•	•																		•																					
“The Pied Piper of Hamelin,” 438												•		•						•				•					•		•						•										
UNIT 10																																															
from *The Diary of Anne Frank,* 460							•					•	•	•	•						•				•	•		•					•				•			•		•			•		•
A Midsummer Night’s Dream, 506				•		•					•										•					•	•				•	•		•	•	•	•					•		•			
UNIT 11																																															
from *Of Men and Mountains,* 530							•						•			•																			•							•					
from *Ishi in Two Worlds,* 544		•					•					•				•															•										•						
“Ships in the Desert,” from *Earth in the Balance,* 554									•																										•	•					•		•				
“The Size of Things,” from *Red Giants and White Dwarfs,* 562																																									•		•	•			
UNIT 12																																															
The War of the Worlds, 576						•	•	•									•					•			•											•					•	•	•	•	•		

Key to Icons in the Annotated Teacher's Edition

Cross-curriculum Icons

Arts and Humanities

Mathematics and Sciences

Social Studies

Applied Arts

Multiple Intelligence Icons

Musical Intelligence

Logical-Mathematical Intelligence

Spatial Intelligence

Kinesthetic Intelligence

Interpersonal/ Intrapersonal Intelligence

SCANS Icons

Managing Resources

Interpersonal Skills

Information Skills

Systems Skills

Technology Skills

Basic Skills

Thinking Skills

Personal Qualities

Staff Credits:

For **EMC/Paradigm Publishing**, St. Paul, Minnesota

Laurie Skiba
Editor

Shannon O'Donnell Taylor
Associate Editor

Eileen Slater
Editorial Consultant

For **Penobscot School Publishing, Inc.**, Danvers, Massachusetts

Editorial

Robert D. Shepherd
President, Executive Editor

Tina Kolb
Managing Editor

Kim Leahy Beaudet
Editor

Sara Hyry
Editor

Marilyn Murphy Shepherd
Editor

Sybil B. Fetter
Senior Copyeditor

Peggy J. Flanagan
Copyeditor

Julie S. Roberts
Copyeditor

Design and Production

Charles Q. Bent
Production Manager

Sara Day
Art Director

Heath P. O'Leary
Design Assistant

Victoria B. Eich
Compositor

Linda Rill
Permissions

Marc D. McCauley
Permissions Assistant

ISBN 0-8219-1364-6

Published by EMC/Paradigm Publishing
300 York Avenue
St. Paul, Minnesota 55101

Printed in the United States of America.
10 9 8 7 6 5 4 3 2 1 XXX 02 01 00 99 98 97

Acknowledgments:

Doubleday. "The Instruction of Indra," from *The Power of Myth,* by Joseph Campbell and Bill Moyers. Copyright © 1988 by Apostrophe S Productions, Inc. and Bill Moyers and Alfred van der Marck Editions for itself and the estate of Joseph Campbell. Used by permission of Doubleday, a division of Bantam Doubleday Dell Publishing Group. **Rita Dove.** "The First Book," copyright © 1994 by Rita Dove. Reprinted by permission of the author. **Farrar, Straus & Giroux, Inc.** "Digging," from *Poems, 1965–1975* by Seamus Heaney. Copyright © 1980 by Seamus Heaney. Reprinted by permission of Farrar, Straus & Giroux, Inc. **Richard Garcia.** "The City Is So Big," by Richard Garcia. Copyright © 1973 by Richard Garcia. Reprinted by permission of the author. **GRM Associates.** "Lose Now, Pay Later," by Carol Farley; copyright © 1991 by Carol Farley, from *2041: Twelve Short Stories About the Future,* edited by Jane Yolen. Reprinted by permission of GRM Associates on behalf of the author. **Washington Irving.** "Rip Van Winkle," by Washington Irving. **Harcourt Brace and Company.** "For My Sister Molly Who in the Fifties," from *Revolutionary Petunias & Other Poems,* by Alice Walker. Copyright © 1972 by Alice Walker, reprinted by permission of Harcourt Brace and Company. **HarperCollins Publishers, Inc.** Excerpt [slightly adapted] from pp. 314–325, *Of Men and Mountains,* by William O. Douglas. Copyright © 1950 by William O. Douglas. Reprinted by permission of HarperCollins Publishers, Inc. "The Garden," from *Where the Sidewalk Ends,* by Shel Silverstein. Copyright © 1974 by Evil Eye Music, Inc. [Reprinted by permission of HarperCollins Publishers, Inc.] **O. Henry.** "A Retrieved Reformation," by O. Henry.

(continued on page 897)

THE EMC MASTERPIECE SERIES

LITERATURE AND THE LANGUAGE ARTS

Responding to Literature

EMC/Paradigm Publishing
St. Paul, Minnesota

Literature and the Language Arts

Oak Level
Responding to Literature

Cedar Level
Exploring Literature

Redwood Level
Discovering Literature

Consultants and Writers

Dr. Edmund J. Farrell
Emeritus Professor of English Education
University of Texas at Austin
Austin, Texas

Wole Alade
Instructor, African-American Studies
Phillips Academy
Andover, Massachusetts
Emerson College
Boston, Massachusetts

Dr. Dael Angelico-Hart
Director of Language Arts
Danvers Public Schools
Danvers, Massachusetts

Janet Battiste
Freelance Education Writer
Chicago, Illinois

Diane Benison
Freelance Education Writer
Northboro, Massachusetts

Diane Castro
Freelance Education Writer
Hamilton, Massachusetts

Ngolela Dibinga
Central African Literature Consultant
Boston, Massachusetts

Corinne DiRusso
Reading Consultant, Literacy Specialist
Lancaster, Massachusetts

Elizabeth Duncan
Freelance Education Writer
Chicago, Illinois

Rebecca Gander
English, Reading Instructor
Sandburg Middle School
Anoka, Minnesota

Aida de Cancio Garcia
Language Arts Department Chair
Madison Middle School
Miami, Florida

Elizabeth Grube
Freelance Education Writer
Cambridge, Massachusetts

Joanne Harder
Director of Language Arts
Shore Country Day School
Beverly, Massachusetts

Fitzgerald Iyamabo
West African Literature Consultant
Winthrop, Massachusetts

Carol Kolb
Teacher of English and Social Studies
Seymour High School
Seymour, Connecticut

Maria Manzola
Director, Navaho Reservation Student Teacher Training Program
Indiana University
Bloomington, Indiana

Angela Shelf Medearis
Author, Multicultural Consultant
Austin, Texas

Michael R. Medearis
Author, Multicultural Consultant
Austin, Texas

Mahmoud Ibrahim Mostafa
North African Literature Consultant
Columbia, South Carolina

Sheila Neylon
Teacher of English
Arlington High School
Arlington, Massachusetts

Tandiwe Njobe
South African Literature Consultant
Boston, Massachusetts

James O'Laughlin
Lecturer
University College
Northwestern University
Evanston, Illinois

Pat Opaskar
President, Opaskar and Trost
Cleveland Heights, Ohio

Connie Plantz
English Education Supervisor
San Diego State University
San Diego, California

Deborah Prato
Freelance Education Writer
Westford, Massachusetts

Nightingale Rukuba-Ngaiza
East African Literature Consultant
Norwood, Massachusetts

Carol Satz
Clinician—Center for Reading and Writing
Rider University
Lawrenceville, New Jersey

Dr. Stuart Shotwell
Freelance Education Writer
Lubec, Maine

Kendra Sisserson
Facilitator, Department of Education
The University of Chicago
Chicago, Illinois

Nancy Sladky
Freelance Education Writer
Augusta, Georgia

Paul David Sladky
Department of Languages and Literature
Augusta College
Augusta, Georgia

Susan Solomon
English Instructor
Hammocks Middle School
Miami, Florida

Lisa S. Torrey
Freelance Education Writer
Kenosha, Wisconsin

Jill Triplett
Special Collections Assistant
Wellesley College Library
Wellesley, Massachusetts

Mary-Ann Trost
Writer, Opaskar and Trost
Cleveland Heights, Ohio

Geraldine Troutman
English Instructor
E. O. Green Junior High School
Oxnard, California

Anita Usmiani
Language Arts Supervisor K–12
Hamilton Township School District
Hamilton Square, New Jersey

Contents

PART 1 THEMES IN LITERATURE

LANGUAGE ARTS SURVEY

1 ESSENTIAL SKILLS: WRITING

2 ESSENTIAL SKILLS: LANGUAGE

To the Student

Reading Literature

Have you ever become so wrapped up in a movie that when the credits started to roll and the lights came up, you felt a kind of shock? One moment you were in the world on the screen, perhaps identifying with some hero and feeling her joys and sorrows. The next moment you were back in your own world again. The art of the filmmaker transported you to another time and place.

When you read a good story, poem, or play, the same sort of transport should take place. The key to reading literature is to use your imagination to take the journey planned for you by the writer. This willingness to extend yourself imaginatively is the most important characteristic that you can have as a reader. Suppose, for example, that you read the following passage in a story:

> Three lions, a male and two females, lay sunning beside what remained of a kill—an eland, perhaps. We approached in the Range Rover. They ignored us. Chico stopped about fifty meters away, and we both took out binoculars for a closer look. The lions lay heavily, dreamily, self-satisfied. A slight breeze ruffled their fur, yellow-brown like the savannah grass in this season between the rains. It was Chico who noticed that the kill wasn't an eland at all, for attached to part of it was, unmistakably, a large black boot.

It is possible to read that passage and understand it, intellectually, without having experienced it. However, reading literature is all about having experiences. To read the passage well, you need to picture three lions, to imagine what it might be like to approach them, to see in your mind's eye the yellow grass, to feel the slight breeze, to notice the boot. If you have done that—if you have imagined the scene vividly—then it will have an impact on you. That impact will be its significance—its meaning for you.

Imagine that you have taken a journey. You have hiked up a mountainside in Peru or have wandered through the Valley of the Kings in Egypt. You have gone shopping in the Ginza district of Tokyo or have bounced in a spacesuit over the surface of the moon. After such an experience, you return home a different person. You think about the experience and what it meant to you.

A work of literature is a chance to take just such an exotic journey. Using your imagination, you take the writer's trip. You have an experience. Then you reflect on the experience that you had. You think about what you thought and felt, about what the experience meant to you. That reflection is called **reader response.**

When you sit down to read a literary work, remember that your task, at that moment, is not to prepare for a quiz or to get ready for a class discussion. Your task is to use your imagination to have the experience that the writer has prepared for you. Think of the writer as a tour guide to interesting times and places. In those times and places, you will meet fascinating people and have powerful, moving experiences, ones that will enrich your life.

Sharing Your Responses with Others

No two people are exactly alike. Because of this wonderful fact, the experience that you have when reading a particular story, poem, or play will be different from the experience had by the student who sits next to you. That's what makes discussing literature with other students interesting. You can share your experiences with others and learn from them. In this course you will have many opportunities to share responses in class discussions and in group projects.

Educating Your Imagination

You might naturally ask, at the beginning of a course such as this, what you stand to gain from it. Two answers to that question have already been suggested: First, reading literature will provide you with many fascinating imaginative experiences. Second, discussing literature and doing group projects will provide opportunities for sharing with others. A third answer is suggested by the first two: reading literature and sharing responses with others will educate your imagination. It will train you to think and feel in new ways.

Life is short, opportunities for real-life experience are limited, and events often happen only once, without your having had the chance to practice, or even think about, how you might react to them. Reading literature is a way around all those difficulties. Through reading, you can find out what it might be like to sail around the globe, to march into battle, to fall in love, to lose a friend, to win a great prize, to live in the rain forest, to be faced with a moral problem, to confront your greatest fear, to travel backward in time or forward into the future. Writers write because they want to share interesting, valuable experiences with you, the reader. In the process of reading literary works and thinking about your own and others' responses to them, you will exercise your imagination and grow in ways that might otherwise have been impossible.

Using This Text

This text is first and foremost a literature anthology. The selections in Units 1–12 have been chosen both for their literary quality and for their interest to students like you. To assist you in understanding the selections, the authors and editors have created activities that appear after the selections. These activities will also help you to develop your abilities in many language arts areas. Most of these activities ask you to refer to the section at the back of the book called the Language Arts Survey. Before doing the activity, you will read a section of the Survey, which will introduce you to some key concepts. Then you will apply what you have learned from the Survey when doing the activity.

Part One

Themes in Literature

GOALS/OBJECTIVES

Studying this unit will enable students to
- gain a greater appreciation for reading
- identify the aim and theme of a piece of literature
- explain metaphors
- understand parallelism and apostrophe
- use the proper reading rate
- recognize the parts of speech
- write a children's story
- use a library for research
- make a book

ADDITIONAL UNIT MATERIALS IN THE ASSESSMENT PORTFOLIO

- Vocabulary Worksheet 2.1.11
- Unit Test 2.1.12

See also the Additional Resources Box in the marginal notes accompanying each selection.

CROSS-CURRICULAR CONNECTIONS

- American History, 24
- Applied Arts, 32
- Science, 8
- Social Studies, 4
- World History, 8, 14, 32

UNIT 1 OPEN A BOOK, OPEN A WORLD

Le Moulin de la Galette. *Auguste Renoir*

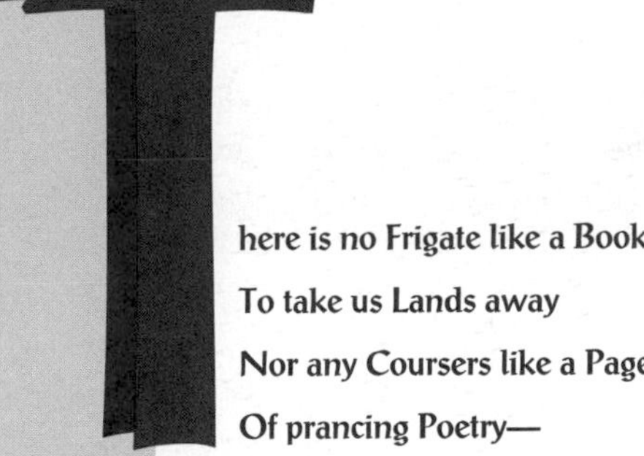

There is no Frigate like a Book
To take us Lands away
Nor any Coursers like a Page
Of prancing Poetry—

—Emily Dickinson

3

UNIT SKILLS OUTLINE

Literary Skills and Concepts

- Aim, 7
- Apostrophe, 7, 11
- Autobiography, 29
- Conflict, 20
- Metaphor, 11
- Parallelism, 11
- Science Fiction, 39
- Theme, 20

Other Language Arts Skills and Concepts

- Parts of Speech, 12
- Reading Rates, 40
- Using a Library, 30
- Writing a Children's Story, 21

Quotables

"Reading is to the mind, what exercise is to the body."

—Joseph Addison

"'Tis the good reader that makes the good book."

—Ralph Waldo Emerson

GOALS/OBJECTIVES

Studying this lesson will enable students to

- enjoy a poem about reading
- identify the aim of a poem
- define *apostrophe*

ADDITIONAL RESOURCES

READER'S GUIDE

- Selection Worksheet, 1.1

ASSESSMENT PORTFOLIO

- Selection Check Test, 2.1.1
- Selection Test, 2.1.2

PRONUNCIATION EXERCISE

- Grade 8 Audiocassette, Side B, Track 1

CROSS-CURRICULAR CONNECTIONS

SOCIAL STUDIES

- Have students learn about reading organizations in your community. These might include literacy classes, book discussion groups, or special library services.
- Ask students to keep a travel and new experiences journal to record the new places they visit and new experiences they have through reading.
- Make a class reading list. Ask all students to recommend to each other their favorite books and magazines. You might organize the list by genres such as science fiction, fantasy, mystery, western, and historical fiction.

Prereading

POEM

"The First Book"
by Rita Dove

Cross-curricular Connection

Social Studies. Reading and writing, like speaking and listening, are ways of employing language to communicate with others. Learning to read can be difficult, but reading is a necessary skill. In the United States, reading is usually taught in the early grades of school. It is a skill that is built upon each year, and it affects a student's ability to study and to research other subjects.

Some people fail to realize that reading can be an enjoyable activity as well. Written words can be a source of information or direction, but they can also be a treat for your imagination. Reading offers the opportunity to expand your experiences beyond the things that you are actually able to do, the places you are able to go, and the people you have the chance to meet. When you read, you are able to visit the city of Pompeii before it was destroyed, climb a mountain, or meet Martians.

Rita Dove understands the power and pleasures of reading. As a child, she was a voracious reader who connected strongly with her reading and realized the effects her readings had on her. As an adult, Dove visited her daughter's school and found that many children did not enjoy reading and seemed frightened of failing at it. Dove wrote "The First Book" to encourage people to enjoy reading.

As You Read

In **"The First Book,"** the speaker offers encouragement to a reluctant reader. In your journal, make a chart like the one below. As you read, record commands, advice, and coaxing phrases the speaker gives in the first column of the chart. In the second column, write a response from a reluctant reader.

SPEAKER'S WORDS	READER'S RESPONSE
Open it	**Why bother?**

AS YOU READ

Students might include the following information in their charts:

Speaker's Words—Go ahead, it won't bite; Well . . . maybe a little; It's pleasurable, really; You may fall in; Sure, it's hard to get started . . . Dig in; It's not like it's the end of the world—just the world as you think you know it; Try it and see.

Reader's Response—Are you sure?; How much?; Well, I don't know. I might not like it; It is kind of interesting; Maybe I'll try; What will I find, then?

READER'S JOURNAL

Do you enjoy reading? Why, or why not? Write about an experience with reading that was especially enjoyable or especially difficult for you. Explore your feelings about reading in your journal.

"The First Book"

RITA DOVE

Open it.

Go ahead, it won't bite.
Well . . . maybe a little.

More a nip, like. A tingle.
It's pleasurable, really.

You see, it keeps on opening.
You may fall in.

Sure, it's hard to get started;
remember learning to use

knife and fork? Dig in:
you'll never reach bottom.

It's not like it's the end of the world—
just the world as you think

you know it. ■

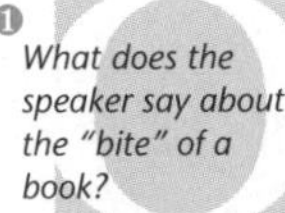

❶ *What does the speaker say about the "bite" of a book?*

❷ *To what does the speaker compare learning to read a book?*

READER'S JOURNAL

As an alternative activity, you might ask students to write a dialogue between two people about reading, including why it is important, what their feelings are about it, and what they think a reader gains through reading.

ANSWERS TO GUIDED READING QUESTIONS

❶ A book will not bite, or if it does, it will only be a little nip or tingle.

❷ The speaker compares learning to read with learning to eat with a knife and fork. The speaker encourages the reader to "Dig in."

ADDITIONAL QUESTIONS AND ACTIVITIES

Designate and celebrate Reading Week at your school. Students might spend extra time reading books of their choice. Students might also read to younger students. Have students make posters promoting the joy of reading or create displays of their favorite books. Students might also decorate a bulletin board on the theme, "Fall into Reading."

QUOTABLES

“Some books are to be tasted, others to be swallowed, and some few to be chewed and digested.”

—Sir Francis Bacon

ADDITIONAL QUESTIONS AND ACTIVITIES

Have a “book tasting.” Each student should choose a book that he or she enjoyed reading. The student should select a short passage from the book and give an oral interpretation of the selection. Refer students to the Language Arts Survey, 3.6, “Oral Interpretation.” This interpretation will serve as a taste of a book that may entice others to take a bite.

SELECTION CHECK TEST WITH ANSWERS

EX. What is the first thing the speaker says to do?
The speaker says to open the book.

1. What will the book’s bite be like?
It will be a nip or a tingle.

2. What may happen as the book keeps opening?
You may fall in.

3. What does the speaker ask if you remember doing?
The speaker asks, “Remember learning to use knife and fork?”

4. What will you never reach?
You will never reach bottom.

5. What does the speaker say the experience is not?
It is not the end of the world.

The Home Lesson. *Albert Anker*

About the Author

Rita Dove (1952–) was born in Akron, Ohio. She was educated at Miami University in Ohio and University at Tubingen in Germany, where she was a Fulbright scholar. Dove has served as writer-in-resident at Tuskegee Institute, as a teacher of creative writing at Arizona State University, and as Commonwealth Professor of English at the University of Virginia. She won the Pulitzer Prize for poetry in 1987 for her collection *Thomas and Beulah.* Her other books of poetry include *The Yellow House on the Corner* and *Grace Notes.* She has also published a collection of short stories entitled *Fifth Sunday* and a novel, *Through the Ivory Gate.* Dove was appointed poet laureate of the United States by President Clinton.

Responding to the Selection

Do you find this poem encouraging? Does it change your feelings about reading? What would you say to convince somebody to try reading?

Reviewing the Selection

Recalling and Interpreting

1. **R** What is the speaker's first command?

   I What feelings does the speaker assume the reader has toward books?

2. **R** What does the book keep doing? What might happen to you?

   I Why might you "fall in" if you begin to read?

3. **R** To what does the speaker compare learning to read?

   I In what way are eating and reading similar?

4. **R** What is reading not like?

   I Why is reading the end of "the world as you think you know it"?

Synthesizing

5. How does the speaker feel about reading? What reasons do you think the speaker has for his or her feelings about reading? Do you share the speaker's feelings? Why, or why not?

Understanding Literature (Questions for Discussion)

1. **Aim.** A writer's **aim** is his or her purpose, or goal. People may write to express themselves (expressive writing), to inform (informative writing), to persuade others (persuasive writing), or to create a literary work (literary writing). What aim or aims did Dove have in writing "The First Book"?
2. **Apostrophe.** An **apostrophe** is a poem that addresses an object or person directly. Who does the speaker address in "The First Book"? What is the speaker's attitude toward the person he or she is addressing?

Responding to the Selection

Students may wish to write their own poems encouraging people to read.

Answers for Reviewing the Selection

RECALLING AND INTERPRETING

1. **Recalling.** The speaker's first command is "Open it." **Interpreting.** *Responses will vary.* The speaker assumes the reader is frightened of the book.

2. **Recalling.** The book keeps opening. You might fall in. **Interpreting.** *Responses will vary.* You might become interested in what you are reading and want to read more.

3. **Recalling.** The speaker compares learning to read with learning to eat with a knife and fork. **Interpreting.** Whether reading or eating, you should dig right in. Both activities feed you: eating feeds your body, while reading feeds your mind or your imagination.

4. **Recalling.** Reading is not like the end of the world. **Interpreting.** *Responses will vary.* Reading is the end of the world as you know it because reading opens many new worlds to you.

SYNTHESIZING

Responses will vary. Possible responses are given.

5. The speaker thinks that reading is an enjoyable activity in which more people should take part. The speaker has probably found that reading awakens his or her imagination and gives him or her many pleasurable hours. The speaker is not afraid of reading, nor does the speaker see reading as a chore. The speaker knows the sense of wonder he or she can find by opening a book and falling into it.

Answers for Understanding Literature

Responses will vary. Possible responses are given.

1. **Aim.** Dove's poem is both literary and persuasive. It is a poem that encourages a person to become a reader—to open a book and enjoy it.

2. **Apostrophe.** The speaker addresses "you" or any reluctant reader. The speaker is encouraging by considering the fears of the person he or she is addressing.

GOALS/OBJECTIVES

Studying this lesson will enable students to
- appreciate a poem about poetry
- understand metaphors
- identify parallelism
- explain apostrophe
- identify parts of speech and use them correctly

ADDITIONAL RESOURCES

READER'S GUIDE
- Selection Worksheet, 1.2

ASSESSMENT PORTFOLIO
- Selection Check Test, 2.1.3
- Selection Test, 2.1.4

PRONUNCIATION EXERCISE
- Grade 7 Audiocassette, Side B, Track 2

CROSS-CURRICULAR CONNECTIONS

WORLD HISTORY

Discuss students' ideas about poetry. Then have students write their own essays or poems about poetry. They may choose to define poetry or to offer suggestions about writing poetry.

SCIENCE

Students can dissect a fruit to find the different parts including the rind or skin, the pit, and the seeds. Students can make a fruit cup out of their dissected fruits. Ask them to compare and contrast the flavors, textures, appearances, and the structures of two different fruits.

Prereading

POEM

"How to Eat a Poem"
by Eve Merriam

Cross-curricular Connections

World History. People have been writing about literature for thousands of years. Aristotle's *Poetics,* written in the fourth century BC, analyzes the nature of poetry, compares the poet to the historian, and defines tragedy. Interestingly, some critics have also been fine writers of literature themselves. Samuel Johnson (1709–1784) wrote poetry as well as the *Dictionary of the English Language,* but he is also known for his brilliant critical essays, including a series of essays on William Shakespeare. Samuel Taylor Coleridge (1772–1834) is primarily known as a Romantic poet, but he also was a great literary critic and theorist.

While people have been writing about literature for a long time, such writing has usually been in the form of the essay. It was not until the twentieth century that poems about writing and reading poems, and fiction about writing and reading fiction, became popular. The poem you are about to read by Eve Merriam is one such poem. Some other poems that discuss poetry are Marianne Moore's "Poetry" and Archibald MacLeish's "Ars Poetica."

Science. Fruit is the ripe, fleshy ovary of a plant, containing the plant's seed or seeds. Apples, peaches, bananas, tomatoes, cucumbers, almonds, and pecans are all fruits; however, when most people think of fruit, they think of sweet, dessert-type fruits. When flowers are fertilized, the ovules become seeds, and the ovaries become the fruits that contain the seeds. Common parts of a fruit include the following: the stem, which connects the fruit to the plant; the rind, or tough outer covering that grows on some fruits such as watermelons and oranges; the skin, a thinner outer covering that grows on fruits such as apples and peaches; the pit, which is a hard stone in the center of some fruits that contains the seed; and the seed, which is the embryo of a new plant. People have cultivated fruits for thousands of years. The term *fruit* has also been used to refer to the result or product of any action, especially something produced by hard work.

As You Read

In **"How to Eat a Poem,"** a poem is described as if it were something else. The poet achieves this effect by describing both the qualities a poem has and the qualities it does not have. Make a chart like the one below. As you read, write the details the author provides about what a poem has and what it lacks.

QUALITIES IT HAS	QUALITIES IT LACKS
can be bitten	

8 UNIT ONE / OPEN A BOOK, OPEN A WORLD

AS YOU READ

Students may include the following information in their charts: *Qualities It Has*—you can pick it up with your fingers; it has juice that may run down your chin; it is ripe; and it is ready. *Qualities It Lacks*—you need no knife, spoon, or fork to eat it; you do not need a plate or napkin or tablecloth to eat it; it has no stem; it has no rind; it has no pit; it has no seed; and it has no skin.

READER'S JOURNAL

What do you think of poetry? What do you like, or dislike, about it? Are you ever nervous or apprehensive when you are assigned a poem to read, or are you eager? Write about these questions in your journal.

"How to Eat a Poem"

EVE MERRIAM

Don't be polite.
Bite in.
Pick it up with your fingers and lick the juice
 that may run down your chin.
It is ready and ripe now, whenever you are.
You do not need a knife or fork or spoon
or plate or napkin or tablecloth.
For there is no core
or stem
or rind
or pit
or seed
or skin
to throw away. ■

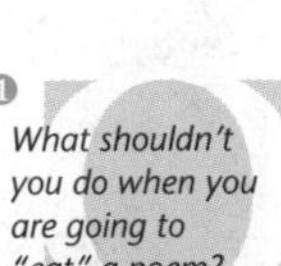

❶ *What shouldn't you do when you are going to "eat" a poem? What should you do?*

❷ *Why doesn't the person who is "eating" a poem need these things?*

READER'S JOURNAL

As an alternative activity, you might ask students to discuss the differences between reading poetry and prose. Which do they prefer to read? Why do they prefer one to the other?

ANSWERS TO GUIDED READING QUESTIONS

❶ You should not be polite. You should bite right in, pick it up with your fingers, and lick the juice that runs down your chin.

❷ The person does not need anything such as utensils because nothing is needed to access or enhance the poem, and no part of the poem is left as waste.

CROSS-CURRICULAR ACTIVITIES

MATHEMATICS

Have students take a poll of their class or of their school to determine students' attitudes toward poetry. Students might ask if students dislike poetry; like poetry, but prefer prose; prefer poetry. Students can graph the results of their poll and answer the following questions. How many students dislike poetry? What percentage of students like poetry? Do more students prefer poetry or prose?

Quotables

"A poem should be palpable
and mute
As a globed fruit."

—Archibald MacLeish

Selection Check Test with Answers

EX. What does this poem tell you how to do?
It tells you how to eat a poem.

1. What should you not do when eating a poem?
You should not be polite.

2. With what should you pick up a poem?
Pick it up with your fingers.

3. What might the juices of the poem do?
The juices might run down your chin.

4. What six things does the speaker say you do not need when eating a poem?
The speaker says you do not need a fork, a spoon, a knife, a plate, a napkin, or a tablecloth.

5. Name three of the six things the speaker says a poem does not have.
Three of the following are acceptable: core, stem, rind, pit, seed, or skin.

Still Life—Fruit. *Vincent van Gogh*

About the Author

Eve Merriam (1916–1992) was an award-winning poet and playwright who wrote more than thirty books. Among her poetry collections are *Family Circle, The Trouble with Love,* and *It Doesn't Have to Rhyme,* from which "How to Eat a Poem" was selected. Her books *After Nora Slammed the Door* and *Growing Up Female in America: Ten Lives* are about women's rights. Merriam also wrote television scripts, advertising copy, song lyrics, and fiction.

Responding to the Selection

What do you think of the speaker's instructions in "How to Eat a Poem"? What does the speaker seem to feel about poetry in general? Do you agree with this opinion? Why, or why not? What do you think of this particular poem? Is it one that you would enjoy "eating"? Why, or why not?

Reviewing the Selection

Recalling and Interpreting

1. **R** What don't you have to do when you eat a poem? In what way does the poem say you should "pick up" a poem?

   I What is the speaker suggesting about the rules for reading poems? Would these rules be followed at a fancy restaurant?

2. **R** What does the speaker say a poem is "whenever you are"?

   I To what are poems being compared?

3. **R** What utensils do you not need while reading a poem?

   I What does not needing special tools or utensils suggest about reading poetry?

4. **R** What don't you have to "throw away" when reading a poem?

   I What does the fact that there is nothing to throw away indicate about the ways in which poems are written or constructed?

Synthesizing

5. Which lines in the poem seem to be extending you, the reader, an invitation? What do you think of the speaker's invitation? Is it one that you would like to accept? Why, or why not?

Understanding Literature (Questions for Discussion)

1. **Metaphor.** A **metaphor** is a figure of speech in which one thing is spoken or written about as if it were another. What activity is spoken of in this poem as something else? As what activity is it described? What does this metaphor suggest about reading poetry?
2. **Parallelism. Parallelism** is the expression of similar ideas in a similar way. For example, both of the first two lines of this poem are instructions for the reader written in the imperative. What other examples of parallelism can you find in this poem? What does the use of parallelism in this poem emphasize?
3. **Apostrophe.** An **apostrophe** is a poem that addresses an object or person directly. Who is the speaker addressing in this poem? Why do you think the speaker chooses to address this person or persons directly?

Responding to the Selection

As an alternative activity, have students consider "The First Book" and "How to Eat a Poem." They both compare reading to eating. Ask students whether they think the comparison works better in one poem than the other. Why? Have students explain which poem they would prefer to eat.

Answers for Reviewing the Selection

RECALLING AND INTERPRETING

1. **Recalling.** You do not have to be polite. Pick up a poem with your fingers. **Interpreting.** *Responses will vary.* The speaker is suggesting that there are no steadfast rules for reading poetry. It is a relaxed activity.
2. **Recalling.** The poem is ripe and ready. **Interpreting.** *Responses will vary.* Poems are being compared to fruits.
3. **Recalling.** You do not need any utensils to read a poem. **Interpreting.** *Responses will vary.* Anybody can read a poem at any time without any special equipment.
4. **Recalling.** You do not have to throw away anything. **Interpreting.** *Responses will vary.* Poems are concise. They contain only what they need.

SYNTHESIZING

Responses will vary. Possible responses are given.

5. Lines 2–5 extend an invitation to the reader. Students may like to try eating poems, if they begin to think of them as easily accessible and trouble free, as the speaker presents them.

Answers for Understanding Literature

Responses will vary. Possible responses are given.

1. **Metaphor.** Reading is spoken of as if it were eating. Perhaps reading poetry nourishes the reader as food does the eater.
2. **Parallelism.** The things that a poem does not have are also expressed in parallel form, suggesting that they are all equally unimportant.
3. **Apostrophe.** The speaker directly addresses the reader because this is the usual form for directions. It also invites the reader to take part in the poem.

Language Lab

Introducing the Skill

Inform students that the words they use everyday can be classified by their function.

Previewing the Skill

Students are probably familiar with the parts of speech. Ask students to name the eight parts of speech and explain the function of each part. Then have students read the material about the parts of speech on pages 12–13.

Practicing the Skill

Have students complete the Try It Yourself exercises on page 13. If students need more practice, refer them to the activity in the Language Arts Survey, 2.1, "The Parts of Speech."

Reviewing the Skill

Review the answers to the Try It Yourself exercises and respond to any questions students have about the parts of speech.

Language Lab

Parts of Speech

Poetry and other written and spoken works are made up of words. Words can be classified by the way they are used. The eight parts of speech are noun, pronoun, verb, adverb, adjective, preposition, conjunction, and interjection. These parts of speech are reviewed below and in the Language Arts Survey, 2.1, "The Parts of Speech." Put what you have learned about the parts of speech to use in the following exercises.

Nouns and Pronouns

A **noun** is a word that names a person, place, thing, or idea. A **pronoun** is a word used as a substitute for a noun.

NOUNS	poem	stem	core	pit
PRONOUNS	she	them	it	

Verbs

A **verb** is a word that expresses action or a state of being.

VERBS	read	are	gobble	remain

Adjectives and Adverbs

An **adjective** is a word that modifies a noun by answering the questions "What kind?" "Which one?" or "How many?" An **adverb** is a word that modifies a verb, an adjective, or another adverb.

ADJECTIVES	**apple** core	**first** book	**only** word
ADVERBS	nibbled **politely**	**extremely** tasty	**very** quickly

Prepositions

A **preposition** is a word that shows how a noun or a pronoun is related to some other word in the sentence.

PREPOSITIONS	after	into	under

Conjunctions and Interjections

A **conjunction** is a word used to join words or groups of words. An **interjection** is a word used to express emotion.

CONJUNCTIONS	and	but	or
INTERJECTIONS	wow	hey	hurray

Try It Yourself

Exercise A. On your own paper, write the nouns and the pronouns in the following sentences. Underline each pronoun that you write.

1. There are shelves and shelves of books in the library.
2. Vanessa is a bookworm; she likes to go and browse among the books of poetry.
3. There are lots of them.
4. She chooses collections of poetry by Rita Dove and Eve Merriam.

Exercise B. On your own paper, write sentences using each of these verbs.

eat open jump is

Exercise C. On your own paper, write an adjective or an adverb that completes each sentence below.

1. Reading is a (adjective) activity.
2. Eve Merriam says to eat a poem (adverb).
3. Poems are (adverb) messy to eat.
4. Rita Dove says books make (adjective) eating also.

Exercise D. On your own paper, write out the prepositions in each of the following sentences.

1. Lucia reads any book in sight.
2. Reading has taken her on many journeys.
3. She has traveled under the sea in a submarine, raced over the prairies on horseback, and skimmed over the mountains in a hot air balloon.
4. She has met people of all ages from all times and gotten to know them well.

Exercise E. On your own paper, write a conjunction or an interjection that completes each sentence below. Use clues in the sentence to help you to choose a word that makes sense.

1. Did you read "The First Book" ____ "How to Eat a Poem"?
2. I read Rita Dove's poem, ____ I really ate up the poem by Eve Merriam.
3. ____! Was it that good?
4. Well, it depends on your taste, ____ I think you would like them both.

ANSWERS FOR TRY IT YOURSELF

EXERCISE A

1. There, shelves, shelves, books, library
2. Vanessa, bookworm, she, books, poetry
3. There, them
4. She, collections, poetry, Rita Dove, Eve Merriam

EXERCISE B

Responses will vary.

EXERCISE C

Responses will vary. Possible responses are given.

1. fun
2. hungrily
3. extremely
4. tasty

EXERCISE D

1. in
2. on
3. under, in, over, on, over, in
4. of, from

EXERCISE E

Responses will vary. Possible responses are given.

1. and
2. but
3. Wow
4. but

GOALS/OBJECTIVES

Studying this lesson will enable students to

- have a positive experience reading a story about storytelling
- identify a conflict
- recognize the theme of a story
- write a children's story

ADDITIONAL RESOURCES

READER'S GUIDE

- Selection Worksheet, 1.3

ASSESSMENT PORTFOLIO

- Selection Check Test, 2.1.5
- Selection Test, 2.1.6

PRONUNCIATION EXERCISE

- Grade 8 Audiocassette, Side B, Track 3

CROSS-CURRICULAR CONNECTIONS

WORLD HISTORY

Hold a storytelling festival. First, have students discuss why they think storytelling has been such a popular activity through the ages. Then ask them to prepare to tell a short story to the class, keeping in mind what they have discussed. Discuss with students ways to keep an audience interested in a story. These techniques might include appropriate body language and gestures, maintaining eye contact, answering questions from the audience, and pacing. Of course, the story itself should be of interest as well.

Prereading

SHORT STORY

"The Story-Teller"
by Saki

Cross-curricular Connections

World History. In cultures throughout history, people have loved to tell stories. Storytelling allows humans to share experiences and emotions, and the human impulse to tell stories led to the development of literature.

Storytelling existed long before people started writing things down. The first forms of storytelling in ancient human societies may have been chants that praised the sun and stars as well as chants that were sung while performing certain tasks such as sharpening weapons or grinding corn. As humans began to wonder about the world they lived in, they composed songs, stories, poems, and mythical tales about their experiences. Myths also help societies to explain where things came from and how the world took the form that it has today.

Before the development of writing, storytellers were also the historians for social groups. Storytellers were responsible for remembering and sharing the history, myths, and stories that defined the social group. In addition, the storyteller was also responsible for entertaining the community.

During the Middle Ages, the troubadour was a poet and musician who traveled about and told stories, reported news, and entertained people. It is reported that at the wedding of Princess Margaret of England in 1290, there were 426 troubadours employed telling stories, singing songs, and entertaining guests.

When movable type was invented in 1440, printed books and pamphlets began to appear. As printing technology grew and books became inexpensive to produce, and as the general population became educated in reading and writing, books replaced professional storytellers. Many people, however, still practice the art of storytelling for their own and for others' enjoyment. In the selection you are about to read, you will encounter a character who is a very skilled storyteller.

As You Read

"The Story-Teller" involves a story within a story. In your journal, make a chart like the one below. As you read, write down the main events in each story.

STORY 1	STORY 2
Event 1: children and aunt are riding on a train. The children ask a lot of questions that annoy adults.	Event 1
	Event 2
	Event 3
Event 2	Event 4

AS YOU READ

Students may include the following events in their charts: *Story 1*—The aunt tries unsuccessfully to distract the children, the man in the compartment shows his displeasure three times, the aunt tells a story, the children say they did not like the story, the man says the story was bad, the man tells a story, the children are interested in the man's story, the aunt disapproves of the story, the man leaves the train.

Story 2—Girl is good, girl is invited to visit park, girl sees wild animal, girl hides, animal finds girl because of clinking medals, animal eats girl.

READER'S JOURNAL

What kinds of stories did you enjoy hearing when you were a small child? What kinds of stories do you enjoy now? What makes a story good? Write about these questions in your journal.

"The Story-Teller"

SAKI

It was a hot afternoon, and the railway carriage was correspondingly sultry, and the next stop was at Templecombe, nearly an hour ahead. The occupants of the carriage were a small girl, and a smaller girl, and a small boy. An aunt belonging to the children occupied one corner seat, and the further corner seat on the opposite side was occupied by a bachelor who was a stranger to their party, but the small girls and the small boy emphatically occupied the compartment. Both the aunt and the children were conversational in a limited, persistent way, reminding one of the attentions of a housefly that refused to be discouraged. Most of the aunt's remarks seemed to begin with "Don't," and nearly all of the children's remarks began with "Why?" The bachelor said nothing out loud.

"Don't, Cyril, don't," exclaimed the aunt, as the small boy began smacking the cushions of the seat, producing a cloud of dust at each blow.

"Come and look out of the window," she added.

The child moved reluctantly to the window. "Why are those sheep being driven out of that field?" he asked.

"I expect they are being driven to another field where there is more grass," said the aunt weakly.

But there is lots of grass in that field," protested the boy; "there's nothing else but grass there. Aunt, there's lots of grass in that field."

"Perhaps the grass in the other field is better," suggested the aunt fatuously."

"Why is it better?" came the swift, inevitable question.

"Oh, look at those cows!" exclaimed the aunt. Nearly every field along the line had contained cows or bullocks, but she spoke as though she were drawing attention to a rarity.

1 *To what are the aunt and the children compared? Why?*

WORDS FOR EVERYDAY USE

sul • try (sul´trē) *adj.*, humid, excessively hot and moist

per • sist • ent (pər sist´ənt) *adj.*, continuing in the face of opposition; unrelenting

fat • u • ous • ly (fach´o͞o əs lē) *adv.*, foolishly; stupidly

READER'S JOURNAL

As an alternative activity, you might ask students if there is a difference between reading a story and being told a story. Are different kinds of stories appropriate for each situation? Explain.

SPELLING AND VOCABULARY WORDS FROM THE SELECTION

assail
dissentient
fatuously
ferocity
listlessly
persistent
petulant
resolute
sultry

ANSWER TO GUIDED READING QUESTION

1 The aunt and the children are compared to a housefly that is very bothersome and will not go away.

SUPPORT FOR LEP STUDENTS

ADDITIONAL VOCABULARY

conviction—certainty
diversion—distraction
emphatically—forcibly
estimation—opinion, judgment
inevitable—unavoidable
novelty—newness
unenterprising—unambitious; unwilling to take on something new

VOCABULARY IN CONTEXT

- Irma longed for snow on the sultry summer day.
- Carmen finally let the secret slip after ten hours of persistent questioning by Jason.
- Mr. Kline answered the questions cleverly, while his opponent replied fatuously to every query.

Additional Questions and Activities

- What is the aunt's opinion of the man in her compartment?
- On what does she base her opinion?
- What opinion do you think the man has of the aunt?
- On what do you think he bases his opinion?

ANSWERS

- The aunt thinks the man is hard and unsympathetic.
- She judges him on his frown and scowl, the looks he gives her, and his thoughts of calling the conductor.
- The man probably thinks the aunt is rather stupid and inept at amusing or controlling the children.
- He judges her on her tactics for distracting the children, the behavior of the children, her answers to the children's questions, and the story she tells the children.

Answers to Guided Reading Questions

❶ The aunt says it is difficult to tell a story that children will both understand and appreciate.

❷ The aunt tells a boring, uninspired, moralistic story. The purpose of the story is to teach the children to be good. The children think the story is stupid and boring.

"Why is the grass in the other field better?" persisted Cyril.

The frown on the bachelor's face was deepening to a scowl. He was a hard, unsympathetic man, the aunt decided in her mind. She was utterly unable to come to any satisfactory decision about the grass in the other field.

The smaller girl created a diversion by beginning to recite "On the Road to Mandalay."[1] She only knew the first line, but she put her limited knowledge to the fullest possible use. She repeated the line over and over again in a dreamy but resolute and very audible voice; it seemed to the bachelor as though someone had had a bet with her that she could not repeat the line aloud two thousand times without stopping. Whoever it was who had made the wager was likely to lose his bet.

❶ *What does the aunt say is difficult about storytelling?*

"Come over here and listen to a story," said the aunt, when the bachelor had looked twice at her and once at the communication cord.[2]

The children moved listlessly toward the aunt's end of the carriage. Evidently her reputation as a story-teller did not rank high in their estimation.

❷ *What type of story does the aunt tell? What is the purpose of the aunt's story? What do the children think of her story?*

In a low, confidential voice, interrupted at frequent intervals by loud, petulant questions from her listeners, she began an unenterprising and deplorably uninteresting story about a little girl who was good, and made friends with everyone on account of her goodness, and was finally saved from a mad bull by a number of rescuers who admired her moral character.

"Wouldn't they have saved her if she hadn't been good?" demanded the bigger of the small girls. It was exactly the question that the bachelor had wanted to ask.

"Well, yes," admitted the aunt lamely, "but I don't think they would have run quite so fast to her help if they had not liked her so much."

"It's the stupidest story I've ever heard," said the bigger of the small girls, with immense conviction.

"I didn't listen after the first bit, it was so stupid," said Cyril.

The smaller girl made no actual comment on the story, but she had long ago recommenced a murmured repetition of her favorite line.

"You don't seem to be a success as a story-teller," said the bachelor suddenly from his corner.

The aunt bristled in instant defense at this unexpected attack.

"It's a very difficult thing to tell stories that children can both understand and appreciate," she said stiffly.

"I don't agree with you," said the bachelor.

"Perhaps *you* would like to tell them a story," was the aunt's retort.

"Tell us a story," demanded the bigger of the small girls.

"Once upon a time," began the bachelor, "there was a little girl called Bertha, who was extraordinarily good."

1. **"On the Road to Mandalay."** Poem by Rudyard Kipling
2. **communication cord.** Switch pulled to call the conductor of the train

Words for Everyday Use

res • o • lute (rez´ ə lo͞ot´) *adj.,* determined; unwavering
list • less • ly (list´lis lē) *adv.,* without interest
pet • u • lant (pech´ə lənt) *adj.,* impatient; irritable

Vocabulary in Context

- Nora's voice was resolute as she demanded her money back.
- Despite attempts to amuse him, Colin stared listlessly out the window.
- The petulant child pouted and stamped his foot.

The children's momentarily aroused interest began at once to flicker; all stories seemed dreadfully alike, no matter who told them.

"She did all that she was told, she was always truthful, she kept her clothes clean, ate milk puddings as though they were jam tarts, learned her lessons perfectly, and was polite in her manners."

"Was she pretty?" asked the bigger of the small girls.

"Not as pretty as any of you," said the bachelor, "but she was horribly good."

There was a wave of reaction in favor of the story; the word horrible in connection with goodness was a novelty that commended itself. It seemed to introduce a ring of truth that was absent from the aunt's tales of infant life.

"She was so good," continued the bachelor, "that she won several medals for goodness, which she always wore, pinned on to her dress. There was a medal for obedience, another medal for punctuality, and a third for good behavior. They were large metal medals and they clinked against one another as she walked. No other child in town where she lived had as many as three medals, so everybody knew that she must be an extra good child."

"Horribly good," quoted Cyril.

"Everybody talked about her goodness, and the Prince of the country got to hear about it, and he said that as she was so very good she might be allowed once a week to walk in his park, which was just outside the town. It was a beautiful park, and no children were ever allowed in it, so it was a great honor for Bertha to be allowed to go there."

Artist's Father. Edward Hopper, 1900

"Were there any sheep in the park?" demanded Cyril.

"No," said the bachelor, "there were no sheep."

"Why weren't there any sheep?" came the inevitable question arising out of that answer.

The aunt permitted herself a smile, which might almost have been described as a grin.

"There were no sheep in the park," said the bachelor, "because the Prince's mother had once had a dream that her son would either be killed by a sheep or else by a clock falling on him. For that reason the Prince never kept a sheep in his park or a clock in his palace."

The aunt suppressed a gasp of admiration.

"Was the Prince killed by a sheep or by a clock?" asked Cyril.

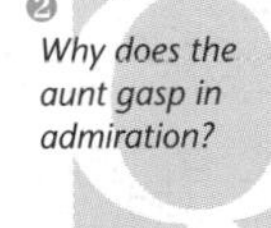

❶ *What does the bachelor say that interests the children in the story?*

❷ *Why does the aunt gasp in admiration?*

Additional Questions and Activities

- How does the man begin his story?
- In what way is the beginning of his story like the beginning of the aunt's story? In what way do the stories differ?
- What is the children's initial reaction to the story? Does their reaction change? Explain.

ANSWERS

- The man begins, "Once upon a time . . ."
- The man, like the aunt, begins his story with a good little girl. In the man's story goodness is not rewarded.
- The children are interested by the new storyteller, but they soon come to think that all stories are the same. When the man says that the girl was horribly good, their attention is captured again.

Answers to Guided Reading Questions

❶ The bachelor says that the girl was not merely good, she was horribly good.

❷ The aunt gasps because the bachelor handles the child's annoying—and almost automatic—question cleverly in a way that satisfies the child and adds interest to the story.

CROSS-CURRICULAR ACTIVITIES

Art

The story the bachelor tells is full of interesting and quirky details, many brought on by the questions of the children. Have students illustrate the episodes in the story that the bachelor tells.

Literary Note

The aim of many early works of literature for children was to instruct children or to teach some moral or lesson. The story the aunt tells falls into this category. Today more children's books aim at entertaining, and the messages are not as pointed. Many of the best examples of children's literature can be enjoyed by adults and children together. Ask students if they think the aunt is enjoying the bachelor's story.

Answers to Guided Reading Questions

❶ The wolf spotted Bertha because her pinafore was so white and clean and visible from a great distance.

❷ Bertha realizes that if she had not been so good, she would be safe in town.

"He is still alive, so we can't tell whether the dream will come true," said the bachelor unconcernedly; "anyway, there were no sheep in the park, but there were lots of little pigs running all over the place."

"What color were they?"

"Black with white faces, white with black spots, black all over, gray with white patches, and some were white all over."

The story-teller paused to let a full idea of the park's treasures sink into the children's imaginations; then he resumed:

"Bertha was rather sorry to find that there were no flowers in the park. She had promised her aunts, with tears in her eyes, that she would not pick any of the kind Prince's flowers, and she had meant to keep her promise, so of course it made her feel silly to find that there were no flowers to pick."

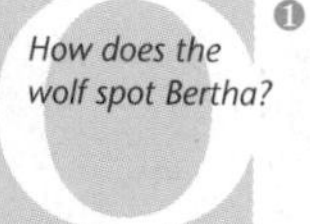

❶ *How does the wolf spot Bertha?*

"Why weren't there any flowers?"

"Because the pigs had eaten them all," said the bachelor promptly. "The gardeners had told the Prince that you couldn't have pigs and flowers, so he decided to have pigs and no flowers."

There was a murmur of approval at the excellence of the Prince's decision; so many people would have decided the other way.

"There were lots of other delightful things in the park. There were ponds with gold and blue and green fish in them, and trees with beautiful parrots that said clever things at a moment's notice, and hummingbirds that hummed all the popular tunes of the day. Bertha walked up and down and enjoyed herself immensely, and thought to herself: 'If I were not so extraordinarily good, I should not have been allowed to come into this beautiful park and enjoy all that there is to be seen in it,' and her three medals clinked against one another as she walked and helped to remind her how very good she really was. Just then an enormous wolf came prowling into the park to see if it could catch a fat little pig for its supper."

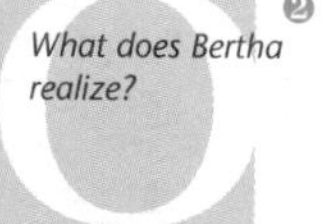

❷ *What does Bertha realize?*

"What color was it?" asked the children, amid an immediate quickening of interest.

"Mud color all over, with a black tongue and pale gray eyes that gleamed with unspeakable ferocity. The first thing that it saw in the park was Bertha; her pinafore[3] was so spotlessly white and clean that it could be seen from a great distance. Bertha saw the wolf and saw that it was stealing toward her, and she began to wish that she had never been allowed to come into the park. She ran as hard as she could, and the wolf came after her with huge leaps and bounds. She managed to reach a shrubbery of myrtle bushes, and she hid herself in one of the thickest of the bushes. The wolf came sniffing among the branches, its black tongue lolling out of its mouth and its pale gray eyes glaring with rage. Bertha was terribly frightened, and thought to herself: 'If I had not been so extraordinarily good, I should have been safe in the town at this

3. **pinafore.** Sleeveless garment worn over a dress

Words for Everyday Use

fe • roc • i • ty (fə räs′ə tē) *n.,* quality of being fierce or savage

Vocabulary in Context

• The ferocity of the guard dog scared the guests as well as would be criminals.

moment.' However, the scent of the myrtle was so strong that the wolf could not sniff out where Bertha was hiding, and the bushes were so thick that he might have hunted about in them for a long time without catching sight of her, so he thought he might as well go off and catch a little pig instead. Bertha was trembling very much at having the wolf prowling and sniffing so near her, and as she trembled the medal for obedience clinked against the medals for good conduct and punctuality. The wolf was just moving away when he heard the sound of the medals clinking and stopped to listen; they clinked again in a bush quite near him. He dashed into the bush, his pale gray eyes gleaming with ferocity and triumph, and dragged Bertha out and devoured her to the last morsel. All that was left of her were her shoes, bits of clothing, and the three medals for goodness."

"Were any of the little pigs killed?"

"No, they all escaped."

"The story began badly," said the smaller of the small girls, "but it had a beautiful ending."

"It is the most beautiful story that I ever heard," said the bigger of the small girls, with immense decision.

"It is the *only* beautiful story I have ever heard," said Cyril.

A dissentient opinion came from the aunt.

"A most improper story to tell to young children! You have undermined the effect of years of careful teaching."

"At any rate," said the bachelor, collecting his belongings preparatory to[4] leaving the carriage, "I kept them quiet for ten minutes, which was more than you were able to do."

"Unhappy woman!" he observed to himself as he walked down the platform of Templecombe station; "for the next six months or so those children will assail her in public with demands for an improper story!" ■

4. **preparatory to.** In preparation for

❶ *What does the aunt think? What do the children think of the story?*

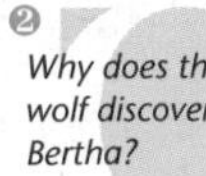

❷ *Why does the wolf discover Bertha?*

About the Author

Saki is the pen name used by Hector Hugh Munro (1870–1916), an English writer known for his witty short stories. Saki was born in Burma. His mother died when he was an infant, and he was sent to England to live with two aunts. He later became a well-known journalist in London. Saki published four collections of short stories and two novels before he was killed in battle in World War I.

Words for Everyday Use

dis • sen • tient (di sen´shent) *adj.,* going against a majority opinion

as • sail (ə sāl´) *v.,* attack with arguments

Answers to Guided Reading Questions

❶ The aunt thinks the story is improper and undoes years of teaching. The children think the story is beautiful.

❷ The wolf is able to find Bertha because it hears her medals clinking together as she trembles in fear.

Selection Check Test with Answers

EX. How many people were in the train compartment?
There were five people in the train compartment.

1. With what word did the aunt's remarks begin?
The aunt's remarks seemed to begin with the word "Don't."

2. What did the aunt point out to distract Cyril from his question about the grass?
She pointed out cows.

3. From what was the good girl saved in the aunt's story?
The good girl was saved from a mad bull.

4. Why is it difficult to tell stories to children according to the aunt?
It is difficult to tell stories that children can both understand and appreciate.

5. What happened to Bertha at the end of the bachelor's story?
She was eaten by a wolf.

Vocabulary in Context

- The decision would have been unanimous, but Ted had a dissentient opinion.
- The students assailed the teacher with requests for less homework, but their cries went unheeded.

Responding to the Selection

If students have differing opinions, have them form two groups and debate the question. Ask students if their response to the story differs from either that of the children or the aunt.

Answers for Reviewing the Selection

RECALLING AND INTERPRETING

1. **Recalling.** The children are hitting the seats, asking a lot of questions, and one child is repeating a line of poetry. The children and the aunt are compared to an annoying fly. **Interpreting.** *Responses will vary.* The children's behavior is typical of that of young children on long trips. The bachelor is annoyed with the aunt for her stupid response to the children, her inability to entertain or control them, and the foolish story she tells the children.

2. **Recalling.** The children think the aunt's story is dull and stupid. **Interpreting.** *Responses will vary.* The point of the aunt's story is that the children should be good. The story is not entertaining, the main character is boring, and the whole thing is just an obvious lesson.

3. **Recalling.** The bachelor says that Bertha was "horribly good." She is eaten by a wolf. **Interpreting.** *Responses will vary.* The phrase delights the children because it expresses their feelings that the girl is too good and rather annoying because of it. The girl's goodness causes her fate. She is in the park where the wolf is because of her goodness, and the wolf is able to find her in the bushes because he hears the clinking of the medals she got for being good. Her fate is unexpected, because good characters are usually saved.

4. **Recalling.** The children think the bachelor's story is great. **Interpreting.** *Responses will vary.* The children have a positive attitude toward the bachelor's story and a negative attitude toward the

(cont.)

Responding to the Selection

After the bachelor finishes telling his story, one of the girls says, "It is the most beautiful story that I ever heard," but the aunt calls it "a most improper story to tell to young children!" Who do you think is right? Why?

Reviewing the Selection

Recalling and Interpreting

1. (R) What are the children doing to disturb the bachelor on the train? To what are the children and the aunt compared?

   (I) What do you think of the children's behavior? With whom is the bachelor more annoyed, the children or the aunt?

2. (R) What is the children's reaction to the story the aunt tells?

   (I) What is the point of the aunt's story? Why do the children react this way to the story?

3. (R) In the bachelor's story, what phrase does the bachelor use to describe the main character? What happens to the little girl at the end of the story?

   (I) Why does this phrase delight the children? What causes the little girl's fate? Why is her fate unexpected?

4. (R) What is the children's reaction to the bachelor's story?

   (I) How does the children's reaction to the bachelor's story differ from their reaction to the aunt's story? Why do you think the children respond in this way to the bachelor's story?

Synthesizing

5. What type of person does the bachelor initially appear to be? What does his story reveal about him? When the aunt voices disapproval of the bachelor's story, the bachelor says that he at least kept the children "quiet for ten minutes, which was more than you were able to do." Do you think that keeping the children quiet was the bachelor's only purpose? Why, or why not?

Understanding Literature (Questions for Discussion)

1. **Conflict.** A **conflict** is a struggle between two people or things in a literary work. A central conflict is the main problem or struggle in the plot of a poem, story, or play. What two characters are involved in the central conflict of this story? What is the basis of their conflict?
2. **Theme.** A **theme** is a central idea in a literary work. What is the theme of this story? In what way does the bachelor's story within a story contribute to this theme?

Answers for Reviewing the Selection (cont.)

aunt's story. They like the bachelor's story because it was not what they expected it to be, and they find the story without a moral more satisfying.

SYNTHESIZING

Responses will vary. Possible responses are given.

5. The bachelor appears to be a hard, unsympathetic man with little patience for children. His story reveals that he has a much better understanding of children than the aunt does. The bachelor probably wanted to counteract the aunt's story, which he thought was as stupid as the children believed it to be.

Writing Skills

A Children's Story

In "The Story-Teller," a bachelor tells children a story that stirs their imaginations and holds their attention, and the children agree that his story is the best that they have ever heard. Telling or writing a good children's story might seem like a difficult task (as it was for the aunt), but you can create a story that captivates your audience if you include imaginative details and unexpected happenings. The children enjoyed the bachelor's tale because it was creative, detailed, and full of unexpected action.

Emma Thomas
Grade 8

"Pretty Susan"

Once upon a time there was a girl named Susan who was very pretty. Every morning when she woke up her mother would say, "Good morning, Susan! You look so pretty, pretty, pretty today." Then Susan would sit in front of the mirror and brush her hair for two hours and thirty-seven minutes, which is exactly the amount of time it takes to make your hair sparkle and float about your head like a fairy princess's. Next Susan would put on a fairy-princess dress which was pink, poofy, and covered with little silver stars. Finally, she would put a diamond tiara upon her head and traipse off to school. (Traipsing is a very fancy way of walking.) On her way to school, she was always very careful not to fall into a puddle or a dust heap, and she kept far away from the other children because they had grubby fingers that might ruin her pretty fairy-princess dress.

At school all the other children would play kickball or jump rope and climb on the monkey bars at recess, but not Susan. During recess, Susan stood on top of a little grass hill, looking very pretty with her diamond tiara sparkling in the sunlight, her hair floating, and her pink dress billowing in the spring breeze. Whenever one of the children would ask Susan if she wanted to play, she would sniff, "I can't play with you because I'm pretty and you're not pretty, so if we played together we would look all mismatched and that wouldn't be very pretty, would it?"

Now everybody knew that Susan was pretty, but finally even the king himself heard about it and invited Susan to come visit him in his castle. This was a great honor because very few people had ever been invited inside and the castle was known far and wide for its loveliness. Susan made sure she looked even

Try It Yourself

Emma and her classmates are writing children's stories. Emma wants her story to be a very unusual kind of fairy tale, like the one that the bachelor tells in "The Story-Teller." Her class plans to read the final versions of the stories to a group of elementary school students.

◄◄ **Student Model**

Writing Skills

Introducing the Skill

Discuss with students why the bachelor's story in "The Story-Teller" was successful. You may also wish to bring in several examples of award-winning or well-loved children's stories for students to read.

Previewing the Skill

Have students read the student model and the steps for writing a children's story on pages 21–23. Students should answer the questions in Examining the Model.

Prewriting and Drafting

Remind students that the plot for a children's story should be relatively simple. They should choose situations and characters that would be interesting to a child. Students might make a story map to organize the elements of their stories. You might refer them to the Language Arts Survey, 1.13, Gathering Ideas," for information on story maps.

Evaluating and Revising

Students should remember that their stories are geared to a younger audience as they evaluate their own and others' stories.

Proofreading and Publishing

Students may wish to illustrate their stories, make covers, and staple them into booklets before sharing them with children.

Answers for Understanding Literature

Responses will vary. Possible responses are given.

1. **Conflict.** The aunt and the bachelor are involved in the central conflict. The aunt believes that children should be taught moral lessons. The bachelor understands children better and does not agree with the aunt's preferred type of story or with the message she sends through her story.
2. **Theme.** The theme is that adults often lose sight of life by trying to live within strict standards. The bachelor's story reflects this theme because the central character's death is caused by perfectly completing all the things adults expected her to do. It also shows that he has not fallen into this trap and understands the interests of children.

ANSWERS FOR EXAMINING THE MODEL

1. Some of the details Emma includes are that Susan brushed her hair for two hours and thirty-seven minutes, the time it takes to make your hair sparkle and float like a fairy princess; Susan's dress was pink, poofy, and covered with silver stars; Susan wore a diamond tiara and traipsed; Susan would not play with the other children because they would be mismatched.
2. Susan is turned into a statue, because she was not a very agreeable little girl.

prettier than usual on the day she went to visit the king. The castle was made of white marble and it had a big oak door.

When Susan knocked on the door, the king himself opened it and said, "My, Susan, aren't you pretty today."

"I'm pretty every day," said Susan.

"Why, of course you are!" chuckled the king, and he showed Susan into the main hall of the castle. The main hall was almost a mile long and it was filled with the most beautiful white marble statues of flowers, animals, and people, for the king was known as a great collector of beautiful things.

"How do you like my castle?" asked the king.

"It sure is pretty, but not as pretty as me," said Susan.

"That's exactly what I thought you would say," said the king. "Now, because you are such a pretty girl, I have a special treat for you," and the king handed her a glass of lemonade.

"I'd rather have some apple juice," said Susan, but she grabbed the glass of lemonade and drank.

As soon as she finished the lemonade, Susan felt funny. She looked down and noticed that the color was fading from her pink dress—it was turning white! She also felt kind of stiff.

"You weren't a very nice little girl, but you will make a lovely statue," said the king, and at that moment Susan turned completely into white marble, another statue for the king's main hall. She still stands there today, not saying much but looking very pretty.

Examining the Model

1. What imaginative details does Emma provide in her story?
2. What unusual, unexpected happenings occur in Emma's story?

Prewriting and Drafting

1. Think of possible topics for your story. Read the Language Arts Survey, 1.13, "Gathering Ideas." Freewrite for several minutes until you come up with a variety of ideas.
2. Read over your ideas. Choose the one that you find most exciting and unusual and that you think your audience would enjoy.
3. Decide who the main character in your story will be. When and where will the story be set?

4. Think about what will happen in your story. How will your main character participate in or react to these events? You may want to make a list describing the story's main events. Try to make sure you include some unusual or unexpected events to keep your audience interested.
5. Review the Language Arts Survey, 1.16, "Drafting." Write your discovery draft, referring to your notes. As you write, try to include imaginative details about your characters, the setting, and the events.

Evaluating and Revising

1. Read the Language Arts Survey, 1.17, "Self-Evaluation." Because you will be reading this story to an audience, read your draft aloud several times. Make notes about parts of your story that might be confusing to a younger audience. Try to locate places where you should add more detail.
2. Read the Language Arts Survey, 1.18, "Peer Evaluation." Read your story to one of your classmates, paying close attention to his or her reaction. Ask your classmate for suggestions about ways in which the story can be improved.
3. Read the Language Arts Survey, 1.19, "Four Types of Revision." Revise your story, referring to your own notes and recalling your classmate's comments.

Proofreading and Publishing

1. Proofread your revised draft. Make a clean copy and proofread it again. Refer to the Language Arts Survey, 1.22, "A Proofreading Checklist."
2. As a class, share your stories with one another and then discuss what age group might enjoy your stories the most. Ask the teacher of a class containing children of this age if you might read your stories to his or her class.

Save your work in your writing portfolio.

ANALYTIC SCALE FOR WRITING SKILLS

Assign a score from 1 to 25 for each grading criterion below.

Children's Story

- **Content/Unity.** The children's story has a simple plot and characters that would be of interest to a child. The story uses details that are related to the main action to add interest.
- **Organization/Coherence.** The story is organized in a logical, easy-to-follow manner.
- **Language/Style.** The story uses vivid and precise nouns, verbs, and modifiers. The language is appropriate for a child.
- **Conventions.** The story avoids errors in spelling, grammar, usage, mechanics, and manuscript form.

GOALS/OBJECTIVES

Studying this lesson will enable students to

- have a positive experience reading an autobiography
- define *autobiography*
- understand the motivations of the subject of the autobiography
- use a library for research

ADDITIONAL RESOURCES

READER'S GUIDE

- Selection Worksheet, 1.4

ASSESSMENT PORTFOLIO

- Selection Check Test, 2.1.7
- Selection Test, 2.1.8

PRONUNCIATION EXERCISE

- Grade 8 Audiocassette, Side B, Track 4

CROSS-CURRICULAR CONNECTIONS

AMERICAN HISTORY

Malcolm X converted to the Black Muslim faith while he was in prison. Late in his life, after a trip to Mecca, he changed his views about black separatism and adapted his views to orthodox religion. Have students research Islam and Nation of Islam, or Black Muslims, and compare and contrast the two. Students might also report on other aspects of the life of Malcolm X. You may wish to refer students to the lesson on using a library on pages 30–31 or to the Language Arts Survey, 4.13, "How Library Materials Are Organized"; 4.14, "Using Catalogs"; and 4.17, "Using Reference Works."

Prereading

AUTOBIOGRAPHY

from *The Autobiography of Malcolm X*
by Malcolm X and Alex Haley

Cross-curricular Connection

American History. Malcolm X was a leader in the Black Muslim religious movement who attracted many followers with his speeches and writings. The Black Muslim movement, also known as Nation of Islam, was established in the United States in the early 1930s by Fard Muhammad, who began as an Orthodox Muslim. The key principle that separated Black Muslims from traditional Muslims was a belief in separation of the black and white races. After the disappearance in 1934 of Fard Muhammad, Elijah Muhammad further developed the movement, which gained popularity by the end of World War II.

Malcolm X, born Malcolm Little, adopted the Black Muslim faith in 1946 while he was serving a prison sentence for burglary in Massachusetts. As part of his conversion, Malcolm Little changed his name to Malcolm X. After his release in 1952, he became a leading spokesperson for the Black Muslim movement, delivering messages such as economic self-sufficiency that inspired many African Americans.

In 1964, Malcolm X had a disagreement with Elijah Muhammad and left the movement. He formed a rival group called the Organization of African-American Unity (OAAU). After a trip to Mecca in 1964, Malcolm X began to modify his ideas about black separatism and to consider the idea of creating one human race. Hostility between the Black Muslims and Malcolm X's followers brought several death threats to the leader, and on February 21, 1965, Malcolm X was assassinated by three men, including two Black Muslims.

As You Read

In this selection from ***The Autobiography of Malcolm X***, Malcolm discusses his self-education while he was in prison. Make a chart like the one below. As you read, fill in the chart with information about Malcolm's motivations, the actions he takes, and the effects that his self-education has on his life.

MOTIVATIONS	ACTIONS	EFFECTS
frustrated at inability to express himself in letters		

AS YOU READ

Students might include the following information in their charts: *Motivation*—frustrated at his inability to express himself in letters; *Actions*—got a dictionary and began copying dictionary entries; *Effects*—learned many words, improved penmanship; *Motivation*—able to use new words; *Actions*—began to read books; *Effects*—freed him in his mind; *Motivation*—read by hall light after hours; *Actions*—stayed up and jumped into bed when the guard came; *Effects*—got little sleep, but spent time well, prepared for life out of prison. Overall his motivations were to educate himself to be able to communicate well. He acted by developing a plan and following through. The results were that he read widely and was able to write and speak well.

READER'S JOURNAL

What do you remember about learning to read and write? What difficulties have you had with reading and writing? What positive or encouraging experiences have you had with reading and writing? Write about these questions in your journal.

FROM

The Autobiography of Malcolm X

MALCOLM X AND ALEX HALEY

It was because of my letters that I happened to stumble upon starting to acquire some kind of a homemade education.

I became increasingly frustrated at not being able to express what I wanted to convey in letters that I wrote, especially those to Mr. Elijah Muhammad. In the street, I had been the most articulate hustler out there—I had commanded attention when I said something. But now, trying to write simple English, I not only wasn't articulate, I wasn't even functional. How would I sound writing in slang,[1] the way I would *say* it, something such as, "Look, daddy, let me pull your coat about a cat, Elijah Muhammad—"

Many who today hear me somewhere in person, or on television, or those who read something I've said, will think I went to school far beyond the eighth grade. This impression is due entirely to my prison studies.

It had really begun back in the Charlestown Prison, when Bimbi first made me feel envy of his stock of knowledge. Bimbi had always taken charge of any conversation he was in, and I had tried to emulate him. But every book I picked up had few sentences which didn't contain anywhere from one to nearly all of the words that might as well have been in Chinese. When I just skipped those words, of course, I really ended up with little idea of what the book said. So I had come to the Norfolk Prison Colony still going through only book-reading motions. Pretty soon, I would have quit even these motions, unless I had received the motivation that I did.

1. **slang.** Informal speech that is outside traditional or standard usage

❶ *Why did Malcolm X have difficulty communicating in letters?*

WORDS FOR EVERYDAY USE

ac • quire (ə kwīr´) *v.*, get or gain by one's own effort

con • vey (kən vā´) *v.*, make known, communicate

ar • tic • u • late (är tik´yo͞o lit) *adj.*, expressing oneself easily and clearly

func • tion • al (fuŋk´ shə nəl) *adj.*, able to perform a task well enough to serve its purpose

en • vy (en´vē) *n.*, ill will or discontent because of another's advantage

em • u • late (em´yo͞o lāt´) *v.*, imitate, copy

READER'S JOURNAL

As an alternative activity, ask students to write about the importance of learning to read and write. In what ways does communicating through writing differ from communicating through speech? Ask them to write about the things they would not be able to do if they did not know how to read or write.

SPELLING AND VOCABULARY WORDS FROM THE SELECTION

acquire	feign
articulate	functional
convey	inevitable
emphasis	isolation
emulate	principally
engross	rehabilitation
envy	riffle

ANSWER TO GUIDED READING QUESTION

❶ He had difficulty communicating in letters because he usually spoke in slang and was unable to express his thoughts in standard written English.

SUPPORT FOR LEP STUDENTS

PRONUNCIATIONS OF PROPER NOUNS AND ADJECTIVES

E • li • jah • Mu • ham • mad (ē lī´jə mo͞o hä´məd) n.

ADDITIONAL VOCABULARY

correspondence—exchange of or communication through letters

devour—take in greedily, absorb

painstaking—very careful

VOCABULARY IN CONTEXT

- By practicing all summer to improve her game, Clarisse acquired a spot on the team.
- Tyler attended the funeral to convey his sympathy to Mr. Miota.
- Kelsey is a very articulate speaker, and he presented the speech with grace.
- The plank and cinderblock bookcases are functional, but they are not very attractive.
- Alyssa was green with envy when Brandon got tickets to the sold-out concert.
- Mr. Wilcox worried when Izzie began to emulate the bully who lived down the street.

ANSWERS TO GUIDED READING QUESTIONS

❶ He learned many words, and he also learned about people, places, and events from history.

❷ Reading worked his mind and offered him new ideas. Once he started reading, he never thought about being in prison. He felt that reading had made him more free than he had ever been before, despite the fact that he was in prison.

ADDITIONAL QUESTIONS AND ACTIVITIES

Have students explore dictionaries to see what else they contain aside from words and definitions. Refer students to Language Arts Survey, 4.15, "Using Dictionaries." Then have students spend time browsing through the dictionary. You might assign each student a letter and have him or her browse the entries under that letter. Have students make a list of people, places, and events they discover. Have students share their most interesting findings with the class.

QUOTABLES

"Stone walls do not a prison make
Nor iron bars a cage;
Minds innocent and quiet take
That for a hermitage."

—Richard Lovelace

❶ *What did Malcolm X learn from copying the dictionary?*

❷ *What effect did reading have for Malcolm X?*

I saw that the best thing I could do was get hold of a dictionary—to study, to learn some words. I was lucky enough to reason also that I should try to improve my penmanship. It was sad. I couldn't even write in a straight line. It was both ideas together that moved me to request a dictionary along with some tablets and pencils from the Norfolk Prison Colony school.

I spent two days just riffling uncertainly through the dictionary's pages. I'd never realized so many words existed! I didn't know *which* words I needed to learn. Finally, just to start some kind of action, I began copying.

In my slow, painstaking, ragged handwriting, I copied into my tablet everything printed on that first page, down to the punctuation marks.

I believe it took me a day. Then, aloud, I read back, to myself, everything I'd written on the tablet. Over and over, aloud, to myself, I read my own handwriting.

I woke up the next morning, thinking about those words—immensely proud to realize that not only had I written so much at one time, but I'd written words that I never knew were in the world. Moreover, with a little effort, I also could remember what many of these words meant. I reviewed the words whose meanings I didn't remember. Funny thing, from the dictionary first page right now, that "aardvark" springs to my mind. The dictionary had a picture of it, a long-tailed, long-eared, burrowing African mammal, which lives off termites caught by sticking out its tongue as an anteater does for ants.

I was so fascinated that I went on—I copied the dictionary's next page. And the same experience came when I studied that. With every succeeding page, I also learned of people and places and events from history. Actually the dictionary is like a miniature encyclopedia. Finally the dictionary's A section had filled a whole tablet—and I went on into the B's. That was the way I started copying what eventually became the entire dictionary. It went a lot faster after so much practice helped me to pick up handwriting speed. Between what I wrote in my tablet, and writing letters, during the rest of my time in prison I would guess I wrote a million words.

I suppose it was inevitable that as my word-base broadened, I could for the first time pick up a book and read and now begin to understand what the book was saying. Anyone who has read a great deal can imagine the new worlds that opened. Let me tell you something: from then until I left that prison, in every free moment I had, if I was not reading in the library, I was reading on my bunk. You couldn't have gotten me out of books with a wedge. Between Mr. Muhammad's teachings, my correspondence, my visitors—usually Ella and Reginald—and my reading of books, months passed without my even thinking about being imprisoned. In fact, up to then, I never had been so truly free in my life.

WORDS FOR EVERYDAY USE

rif • fle (rif´əl) *v.*, leaf or look rapidly through something such as a book

in • ev • i • ta • ble (in´ev´i tə bəl) *adj.*, certain to happen

VOCABULARY IN CONTEXT

- Bianca riffled through the papers on her desk looking for her assignment.
- It was inevitable in the tiny school that Dolores and Chuck would meet.

The Norfolk Prison Colony's library was in the school building. A variety of classes was taught there by instructors who came from such places as Harvard and Boston universities. The weekly debates between inmate teams were also held in the school building. You would be astonished to know how worked up convict debaters and audiences would get over subjects like "Should Babies Be Fed Milk?"

Available on the prison library's shelves were books on just about every general subject. Much of the big private collection that Parkhurst had willed to the prison was still in crates and boxes in the back of the library—thousands of old books. Some of them looked ancient: covers faded, old-time parchment-looking binding. Parkhurst, I've mentioned, seemed to have been principally interested in history and religion. He had the money and the special interest to have a lot of books that you wouldn't have in general circulation. Any college library would have been lucky to get that collection.

Archive Photo, NY

As you can imagine, especially in a prison where there was heavy emphasis on rehabilitation, an inmate was smiled upon if he demonstrated an unusually intense interest in books. There was a sizable number of well-read inmates, especially the popular debaters. Some were said by many to be practically walking encyclopedias. They were almost celebrities. No university would ask any student to devour literature as I did when this new world opened to me, of being able to read and *understand.*

I read more in my room than in the library itself. An inmate who was known to read a lot could check out more than the permitted maximum number of books. I preferred reading in the total isolation of my own room.

When I had progressed to really serious reading, every night at about ten P.M. I would be outraged with the "lights out." It always seemed to catch

Words for Everyday Use

prin • ci • pal • ly (prin´sə pəl lē) *adv.,* most importantly or significantly

em • pha • sis (em´fə sis) *n.,* special attention given to something

re • ha • bil • i • ta • tion (rē´hə bil´ə tā´shən) *n.,* process of restoring physical or mental health; preparation for employment

i • so • la • tion (ī´so la´shən) *n.,* aloneness, solitude

Additional Questions and Activities

Malcolm X says that debates were popular while he was in prison. Divide students into teams and have them debate one of the following questions:

- Should students be required to wear uniforms in schools?
- Should students be required to complete community service hours as part of their schooling?
- Should middle school students be required to study a foreign language?

If there is another issue of interest to students in your class suggest that they debate that issue instead.

Quotables

"All letters, methinks, should be as free and easy as one's discourse, not studied as an oration, nor made up of hard words like a charm."

—Dorothy Osborne, Lady Temple

Additional Questions and Activities

Malcolm X's personal education began with a desire to communicate better through letters. Have students begin their own correspondence. Refer students to the Language Arts Survey, 5.3, "Writing a Personal Letter," and 5.4, "Writing a Business Letter." Suggest that students write one of the following kinds of letters:

- request for information
- thank-you note
- letter to the editor
- personal letter to a friend

You might arrange correspondence between your class and a class in another city, state, or country.

Vocabulary in Context

- Isabel was principally interested in hockey, but she enjoyed watching lacrosse as well.
- One session was dedicated to technique, but the emphasis of the program was on safety.
- After a year of therapy, Ken's rehabilitation was complete.
- Jhourdi works best in isolation, because he is easily distracted by other people.

Answer to Guided Reading Question

❶ He is more educated. He is able to communicate in standard English both verbally and in writing. Although he stays up until all hours reading, he still gets more sleep than he often did on the streets.

Selection Check Test with Answers

EX. Where was Malcolm X when he began to acquire his home-made education?
He was in prison.

1. To whom did Malcolm X wish to write?
He wanted to write to Elijah Muhammad.

2. Whose stock of knowledge did Malcolm envy?
He envied Bimbi's store of knowledge.

3. What did Malcolm do with the dictionary?
He wrote down everything in it.

4. What word springs to Malcolm's mind?
The word *aardvark* springs to his mind.

5. What subjects were especially well represented in the prison library?
History and religion were especially well represented.

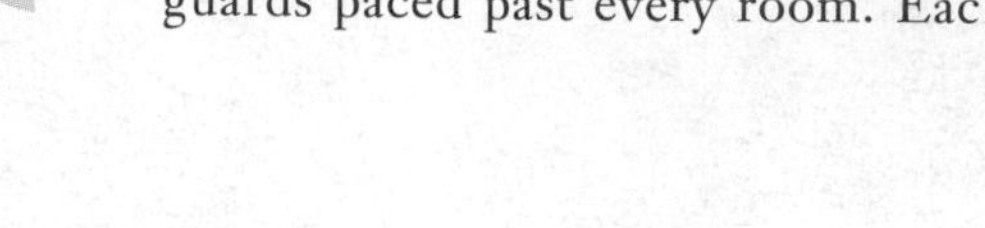

In what ways has Malcolm X's life changed since he was on the streets? ❶

me right in the middle of something engrossing.

Fortunately, right outside my door was a corridor light that cast a glow into my room. The glow was enough to read by, once my eyes adjusted to it. So when "lights out" came, I would sit on the floor where I could continue reading in that glow.

At one-hour intervals the night guards paced past every room. Each time I heard the approaching footsteps, I jumped into bed and feigned sleep. And as soon as the guard passed, I got back out of bed onto the floor area of that light-glow, where I would read for another fifty-eight minutes—until the guard approached again. That went on until three or four every morning. Three or four hours of sleep a night was enough for me. Often in the years in the streets I had slept less than that. ■

About the Author

Malcolm X (1925–1965) was born Malcolm Little in Omaha, Nebraska. In his early years, he lived as a petty criminal. While imprisoned, he adopted the Black Muslim faith and taught himself to read and write. Malcolm X became a strong and influential leader among African Americans. He was the source of much controversy in mainstream America for his willingness to talk about racial issues and the African-American experience. Malcolm X was assassinated in New York City in 1965.

Words for Everyday Use

en • gross (en grōs´) *v.*, take entire attention of, occupy wholly

feign (fān) *v.*, make a false show of, imitate, simulate

Vocabulary in Context

- Chris was so engrossed in his book he did not hear the phone ringing.
- Sadie feigned indifference, but I knew she was upset about the decision.

Responding to the Selection

Why do you think Malcolm was willing to take the time and effort to copy the entire dictionary? Why was he willing to give up sleep to read? What goal would motivate you to sacrifice most of your time? What would you hope to gain from such a venture?

Reviewing the Selection

Recalling and Interpreting

1. **R** Why does Malcolm decide that he must educate himself?

   I Why does he call his education "homemade"?

2. **R** What did Malcolm discover in Charlestown Prison that motivated him to read?

   I Why does he call his early efforts "book-reading motions"?

3. **R** What kind of knowledge did Malcolm gain when he started copying the dictionary?

   I Why would this knowledge help him better understand the books he was reading?

4. **R** How much sleep did Malcolm get each night because of his reading habits?

   I What do these sleep habits suggest about Malcolm's character?

Synthesizing

5. When Malcolm started reading in prison, he says he realized that, until then, he had never been so truly free in his whole life. What were Malcolm's feelings about himself when he gained knowledge from books? Why was reading empowering for Malcolm?

Understanding Literature (Questions for Discussion)

Autobiography. An **autobiography** is the story of a person's life, written by that person. What important event is related in this selection from Malcolm X's autobiography? What else do you learn about the life of Malcolm X in this selection? What do you learn about his motivations and characteristics?

Responding to the Selection

Ask students to describe a goal that they worked toward. What did they have to give up to achieve their goal? Do they think their sacrifices were worthwhile? Why, or why not?

Answers for Reviewing the Selection

RECALLING AND INTERPRETING

1. **Recalling.** He is unable to communicate effectively. **Interpreting.** *Responses will vary.* He calls his education homemade, because he teaches himself through his own methods.

2. **Recalling.** Malcolm was envious of Bimbi's knowledge. Malcolm also realized that he learned little from books, because he skipped over the many words he did not understand. **Interpreting.** *Responses will vary.* He calls his efforts "book-reading motions" because he was only looking at the book, turning the pages, without comprehending what he read.

3. **Recalling.** Malcolm learned new words, and he learned about people, places, and events from history. **Interpreting.** His increased vocabulary allowed him to comprehend better what he read, and he had a greater background of information on which to draw when he read.

4. **Recalling.** He only got three or four hours of sleep a night. **Interpreting.** *Responses will vary.* His actions suggest the he was dedicated to learning and that he was unwilling to let obstacles get in the way of his goals.

SYNTHESIZING

Responses will vary. Possible responses are given.

5. Reading opened new worlds and new ideas for Malcolm, which allowed his mind to roam beyond the walls of the prison. His ability to communicate better allowed him other outlets to the world.

Answers for Understanding Literature

Responses will vary. Possible responses are given.

Autobiography. Malcolm X's self-education is related in this selection. He had been in prison before, he had spent a lot of time on the streets, and he had been respected as a hustler. He had gone to school through the eighth grade. Malcolm X recognized the importance of being able to communicate and his own inability to do so effectively. He was willing to work hard and painstakingly toward a goal.

Language Lab

Introducing the Skill

Malcolm X relied on the prison library for the books he used in his own education. Inform students that libraries hold large collections of books that can be read for information or for pleasure. Libraries have many other resources that provide information of many kinds. It is useful to know how to locate these sources.

Previewing the Skill

Have students read the material on using a library on pages 30–31. Discuss the classification of books and the Dewey Decimal system. If your school or community does not have a computerized catalog, assure students that the process will work as well with a card catalog.

Practicing the Skill

Have students complete the Try It Yourself exercises. Students will need to visit a school or public library to complete this assignment.

Reviewing the Skill

Ask students if they felt their searches were successful. Were they able to find the sources they needed? Respond to any questions or problems students may have encountered while researching the assignment. Remind students that librarians are available to help people find and utilize the library's resources.

Study and Research Skills

Using a Library

Marcus enjoyed reading part of Malcolm X's biography. He wanted to know more about Malcolm X, so he decided to write a research paper on Malcolm X. To begin his search for more sources in the library, he had the following information:

- the selection he had read was taken from *The Autobiography of Malcolm X*
- Alex Haley had been involved in writing *The Autobiography of Malcolm X*
- Malcolm X was a civil rights leader
- Malcolm X had been widely known as a member of the Black Muslims, or Nation of Islam

First, Marcus spent some time with the computerized catalog. He noted the title and call number of every book that looked as if it might have useful information.

WHAT MARCUS LOOKED UP	WHY
Title *The Autobiography of Malcolm X*	To find the call number for a book that he knew was about Malcolm X, and to find out what subjects his library used to classify the book so that he could search for books with similar subjects.
Author Haley, Alex	To see if Haley had written other works about Malcolm X.
Subject Malcolm X Nation of Islam	To find books and other materials about his subject.

Marcus's library uses the Dewey Decimal system. He listed books with call numbers in the 800s, and 900s. He listed the books that he thought might contain information about the life and work of Malcolm X.

With a list of titles and call numbers, Marcus went to the stacks to look for the books. He found most of the books by looking for their call numbers. He also browsed in the shelves holding books in the same category as his original book. Then he skimmed each book that he found. He examined the table of contents, index, and text itself. Within half an hour he had located five books that he could use to write a report on Malcolm X.

Try It Yourself

The selection from *The Autobiography of Malcolm X* shows the importance of being able to read and write. Select a topic related to reading or education. Find five resources in the library with information on the topic. Follow these steps.

1. Select a topic. You may use one of these ideas or develop your own.
   - What writers have to say about reading
   - Fighting a war on illiteracy
2. List several subjects and key words that you can look up in the catalog to uncover useful books and other materials. Write at least three possible subjects and three possible key words, using the format below.

   Subject = ______________ Key Words = ______________
3. Look up your subjects and key words using the card catalog or computer catalog at your library. Write down titles and call numbers of likely books. List several more titles than you will need.
4. Find the books. Skim each to select which ones would be most useful for your topic.

ANSWERS FOR TRY IT YOURSELF

1. Topics should be related to reading or to education.
2. The key words and subjects that students list should be related to their topic.
3. Students should create a sizable list of possible sources of information.
4. Students should select books that are related to their topic.

GOALS/OBJECTIVES

Studying this lesson will enable students to
- enjoy science fiction
- discuss censorship
- recognize the importance of books
- define *science fiction*
- understand different reading rates and use them appropriately

ADDITIONAL RESOURCES

READER'S GUIDE
- Selection Worksheet, 1.5

ASSESSMENT PORTFOLIO
- Selection Check Test, 2.1.9
- Selection Test, 2.1.10

PRONUNCIATION EXERCISE
- Grade 8 Audiocassette, Side B, Track 5

CROSS-CURRICULAR CONNECTIONS

WORLD HISTORY

Discuss censorship with students. Students may be interested to discover some of the books that have been censored in recent history. Have students write editorials expressing their opinions about censorship.

APPLIED ARTS

Books are much more readily available than they once were. Have students collect information about the volume of books available. Students can learn how many books local and school libraries have, poll students in the school about the number of books they own, and contact bookstores to see how many books they stock or sell annually.

Prereading

NOVEL

from *Fahrenheit 451*
by Ray Bradbury

Cross-curricular Connections

World History. Censorship is the suppression of speech or writing that is thought to threaten a society's values. The term *censorship* comes from the Roman office of censor, which was established in 443 BC. The censor conducted a census, or a counting of the Roman people and their property for tax purposes, and was supposed to regulate the morals of the Roman citizens counted. While in ancient times people thought censorship was necessary, today most people feel that censorship is repressive and unjust. People first began to struggle against censorship in the seventeenth and eighteenth centuries. John Milton, an English writer, argued against the government's right to restrain publication in a work called *Areopagitica,* published in 1643.

Adopted in 1791, the First Amendment of the Constitution of the United States guarantees freedom of speech and of the press. While freedom of speech and of the press has been threatened at certain times in the United States, people have fought to protect the rights guaranteed in the First Amendment. Today, countries that censor speech and writing are usually considered to be unenlightened and oppressive. In the selection that you are about to read, the government censors literature.

Applied Arts. The history of printing began in 1456, when Johannes Gutenberg, a German printer, successfully printed a Latin Bible using a system of movable type. For thousands of years prior to Gutenberg's development of the printing press, books had been copied by hand using brushes, reeds, or quills. Because the process of copying books took so long, there were few books in existence. Books were rare and valuable, so they were treasured.

Gutenberg's first printing press was adapted from a device used to press grapes. Gutenberg lined up the raised metal letters, or type, in large wooden forms. The type was then inked and covered with a sheet of paper. By turning a large wooden screw, he lowered a wood block to press against the paper. With this press, Gutenberg could print about three hundred pages a day. Gutenberg printed about two hundred copies of the first printed work, the Latin Bible. About forty or fifty of these Bibles still exist today; fourteen of them are in the United States.

As You Read

In this selection, much is revealed about Montag and Clarisse's society indirectly, through details. Make a chart like the one below. As you read, write details that you discover about this futuristic society and your thoughts about what these details reveal.

DETAIL	WHAT IS REVEALED ABOUT THIS SOCIETY
firemen start fires rather than putting them out	the society must feel that there are many things that should be destroyed

AS YOU READ

Students might include the following information in their charts:

Detail—firemen burn books; Clarisse is not afraid of the fireman, but many people are; reading books is against the law; people move very fast, Clarisse's uncle was arrested for driving slowly; Montag thinks it is strange that Clarisse's family sits around and talks.

What Is Revealed about This Society—the society thinks books should be destroyed; firemen are powerful in the society; the society thinks that there are things people should not know in books; everything must move quickly in this society, it's almost as if they are afraid that somebody will actually see something; people do not communicate much in this society.

ICAL NOTE

mentions three of the
ose work he burns: Edna
Millay, Walt Whitman,
n Faulkner.

Vincent Millay
0) was a noted poet,
, feminist, and political
llay was born in
Maine. She attended
ege. She won a Pulitzer
collection of poetry, *The*
ver.

hitman (1819–1892) left
age eleven and became
boy in a law firm. He
r a doctor and in the
ffice of a newspaper. On
y age fifteen, Whitman
s a printer and later
hool. He eventually
write full time. His rise to
slow and his poetry
w harsh criticism.

n Faulkner (1897–1962)
Nobel Prize for literature
Pulitzer Prizes for his
s fiction often uses stream
ousness and interior
gues. Faulkner wrote
poetry, and screenplays. He
n in New Albany,
pi and spent most of his
xford, Mississippi. Many of
ls are set in the mythical
tawpha County in
opi.

TO GUIDED READING
N

g has not read a book
it is against the law.

hoping that the power might not come on again too soon. . . .

And then Clarisse McClellan said:

"Do you mind if I ask? How long've you worked at being a fireman?"

"Since I was twenty, ten years ago."

"Do you ever *read* any of the books you burn?"

He laughed. "That's against the law!"

"Oh. Of course."

Has Montag ever read a book? Why not?

"It's fine work. Monday burn Millay, Wednesday Whitman, Friday Faulkner, burn 'em to ashes, then burn the ashes. That's our official slogan."

They walked still further and the girl said, "Is it true that long ago firemen put fires *out* instead of going to start them?"

"No. Houses have *always* been fireproof, take my word for it."

"Strange. I heard once that a long time ago houses used to burn by accident and they needed firemen to *stop* the flames."

He laughed.

She glanced quickly over. "Why are you laughing?"

"I don't know." He started to laugh again and stopped. "Why?"

"You laugh when I haven't been funny and you answer right off. You never stop to think what I've asked you."

He stopped walking. "You *are* an odd one," he said, looking at her. "Haven't you any respect?"

"I don't mean to be insulting. It's just I love to watch people too much, I guess."

"Well, doesn't this mean *anything* to you?" He tapped the numerals 451 stitched on his char-colored sleeve.

"Yes," she whispered. She increased her pace. "Have you ever watched the jet cars racing on the boulevards down that way?"

"You're changing the subject!"

"I sometimes think drivers don't know what grass is, or flowers, because they never see them slowly," she said. "If you showed a driver a green blur,

WORDS FOR EVERYDAY USE

bou • le • vard (bool´ə värd´) *n.,* broad, well-made street

READER'S JOURNAL

Is freedom of speech and of the press important to you? Why, or why not? In what ways do you think the United States might be different if freedom of speech and freedom of the press were completely restricted? What types of speech and writing would you miss the most?

FROM

Fahrenheit 451

RAY BRADBURY

The Hearth and the Salamander

IT WAS A PLEASURE TO BURN.

It was a special pleasure to see things eaten, to see things blackened and *changed.* With the brass nozzle in his fists, with this great python spitting its venomous kerosene upon the world, the blood pounded in his head, and his hands were the hands of some amazing conductor playing all the symphonies of blazing and burning to bring down the tatters and charcoal ruins of history. With his symbolic helmet numbered 451 on his stolid head, and his eyes all orange flame with the thought of what came next, he flicked the igniter and the house jumped up in a gorging fire that burned the evening sky red and yellow and black. He strode in a swarm of fireflies. He wanted above all, like the old joke, to shove a marshmallow on a stick in the furnace, while the flapping pigeon-winged books died on the porch and lawn of the house. While the books went up in sparkling whirls and blew away on a wind turned dark with burning.

Montag grinned the fierce grin of all men singed and driven back by flame.

He knew that when he returned to the firehouse, he might wink at himself, a minstrel man, burnt-corked, in the mirror. Later, going to sleep, he would feel the fiery smile still gripped by his face muscles, in the dark. It never went away, that smile, it never ever went away, as long as he remembered.

He hung up his black beetle-colored helmet and shined it; he hung his flameproof jacket neatly; he showered luxuriously, and then, whistling, hands in pockets, walked across the upper floor of the fire station and fell down the hole. At the last moment, when disaster seemed positive, he pulled his hands from his pockets and broke his

What is Montag doing? How does he feel about this activity? What does he want to do "above all"?

WORDS FOR EVERYDAY USE

ven • om • ous (ven´əm əs) *adj.,* poisonous
sym • bol • ic (sim bäl´ik) *adj.,* serving as a representation or suggestion of another thing
stol • id (stäl´id) *adj.,* having or showing little or no emotion or sensitivity
gorge (gôrj´) *v.,* swallow greedily
singe (sinj) *v.,* burn slightly or superficially

READER'S JOURNAL

As an alternative activity, you might ask students if they are aware of attempts at censorship. What happened in these instances? Were materials censored? What reason was given for the censorship? Do students agree or disagree with the decision? How would they feel if something that they wrote was censored?

SPELLING AND VOCABULARY WORDS FROM THE SELECTION

abruptly	infinite
astonishing	intact
awe	lubricated
boulevard	pedestrian
clench	refract
compressed	singe
flue	stolid
gorge	subconscious
hypnotize	symbolic
hysterical	transform
illumination	venomous
imperceptibly	waft

ANSWER TO GUIDED READING QUESTION

Montag is spraying a house with kerosene and lighting it on fire. He enjoys what he is doing. It gives him special pleasure. He wanted above all to roast a marshmallow over the flames of burning books.

SUPPORT FOR LEP STUDENTS

ADDITIONAL VOCABULARY

babbling—speaking constantly and senselessly
immense—large
kerosene—highly flammable oil
vast—great is size or extent

VOCABULARY IN CONTEXT

- It was a relief to turn from the narrow, rutted lanes onto the spacious boulevard.

VOCABULARY IN CONTEXT

- Dirk's leg swelled up after he was bitten by the venomous snake.
- A dove was released as a symbolic gesture of the goodwill between the nations.
- Kara is a very stolid person; I have never seen her weep in sadness or cheer in excitement.
- Gorging yourself on pastries is not healthy.
- The papers were not completely destroyed by the fire, but they were noticeably singed.

Answers to Guided Reading Questions

❶ Montag does not think much at all.

❷ Montag felt that he had said something quite wonderful, although he had only said hello.

Additional Questions and Activities

- What does Montag notice as he reaches the corner?
- In what manner does the girl seem to look at the world?
- In what way is Montag different than the girl?

ANSWERS

- Montag notices a different quality in the air. He feels as though somebody had just been there, though he is not sure what it is that he detects.
- The girl seems to look at the world with an infinite amount of curiosity.
- Montag seems to move through the world, noticing very little.

fall by grasping the golden pole. He slid to a squeaking halt, the heels one inch from the concrete floor downstairs.

He walked out of the fire station and along the midnight street toward the subway where the silent air-propelled train slid soundlessly down its lubricated flue in the earth and let him out with a great puff of warm air onto the cream-tiled escalator rising to the suburb.

❶ *What does this character think about?*

Whistling, he let the escalator waft him into the still night air. He walked toward the corner, thinking little at all about nothing in particular. Before he reached the corner, however, he slowed as if a wind had sprung up from nowhere, as if someone had called his name.

The last few nights he had had the most uncertain feelings about the sidewalk just around the corner here, moving in the starlight toward his house. He had felt that a moment prior to his making the turn, someone had been there. The air seemed charged with a special calm as if someone had waited there, quietly, and only a moment before he came, simply turned to a shadow and let him through. Perhaps his nose detected a faint perfume, perhaps the skin on the backs of his hands, on his face, felt the temperature rise at this one spot where a person's standing might raise the immediate atmosphere ten degrees for an instant. There was no understanding it. Each time he made the turn, he saw only the white, unused, buckling sidewalk, with perhaps, on one night, something vanishing swiftly across a lawn before he could focus his eyes or speak.

But now tonight, he slowed almost to a stop. His inner mind, reaching out to turn the corner for him, had heard the faintest whisper. Breathing? Or was the atmosphere compressed merely by someone standing very quietly there, waiting?

He turned the corner.

The autumn leaves blew over the moonlit pavement in such a way as to make the girl who was moving there seem fixed to a sliding walk, letting the motion of the wind and the leaves carry her forward. Her head was half bent to watch her shoes stir the circling leaves. Her face was slender and milk-white, and in it was a kind of gentle hunger that touched over everything with tireless curiosity. It was a look, almost, of pale surprise; the dark eyes were so fixed to the world that no move escaped them. Her dress was white and it whispered. He almost thought he heard the motion of her hands as she walked, and the infinitely small sound now, the white stir of her face turning when she discovered she was a moment away from a man who stood in the middle of the pavement waiting.

❷ *What does Montag feel when the girl looks at him?*

The trees overhead made a great sound of letting down their dry rain. The girl stopped and looked as if she might pull back in surprise, but instead stood regarding Montag with eyes so dark and shining and alive, that he felt he had said something quite wonderful. But he knew his mouth had only moved to say hello, and then when she

Words for Everyday Use

lu • bri • cat • ed (lo͞o´bri kāt´id) *adj.*, smooth or slippery
flue (flo͞o) *n.*, pipe, tube, or shaft
waft (wäft) *v.*, transport as if through the air
com • pressed (kəm prest´) *adj.*, made more compact
in • fi • nite • ly (in´fə nit lē) *adv.*, beyond measure or comprehension

seemed hypnotized by the salamander on his arm and the phoenix-disc on his chest, he spoke again.

"Of course," he said, "you're our new neighbor, aren't you?"

"And you must be—" she raised her eyes from his professional symbols "—the fireman." Her voice trailed off.

❶ *What is Montag's job?*

"How oddly you say that."

"I'd—I'd have known it with my eyes shut," she said, slowly.

"What—the smell of kerosene? My wife always complains," he laughed. "You never wash it off completely."

"No, you don't," she said, in awe.

He felt she was walking in a circle about him, turning him end for end, shaking him quietly, and emptying his pockets, without once moving herself.

"Kerosene," he said, because the silence had lengthened, "is nothing but perfume to me."

❸ *What does Montag say about the smell of kerosene?*

"Does it seem like that, really?"

"Of course. Why not?"

She gave herself time to think of it. "I don't know." She turned to face the sidewalk going toward their homes.

"Do you mind if I walk back with you? I'm Clarisse McClellan."

"Clarisse. Guy Montag. Come along. What are you doing out so late wandering around? How old are you?"

They walked in the warm-cool blowing night on the silvered pavement and there was the faintest breath of fresh apricots and strawberries in the air, and he looked around and realized this was quite impossible, so late in the year.

There was only the girl walking with him now, her face bright as snow in the moonlight, and he knew she was working his questions around, seeking the best answers she could possibly give.

"Well," she said, "I'm seventeen and I'm crazy. My uncle says the two always go together. When people ask your age, he said, always say seventeen and insane. Isn't this a nice time of night to walk? I like to smell things and look at things, and sometimes stay up all night, walking, and watch the sun rise."

They walked on again in silence and finally she said, thoughtfully, "You know, I'm not afraid of you at all."

❷ *What does Clarisse say about firemen in general? Montag in particular?*

He was surprised. "Why should you be?"

"So many people are. Afraid of firemen, I mean. But you're just a man, after all. . . ."

He saw himself in her eyes, suspended in two shining drops of bright water, himself dark and tiny, in fine detail, the lines about his mouth, everything there, as if her eyes were two miraculous bits of violet amber that might capture and hold him intact. Her face, turned to him now, was fragile milk crystal with a soft and constant light in it. It was not the hysterical light of electricity but—what? But the strangely comfortable and rare and gently flattering light of the candle. One time, as a child, in a power failure, his mother had found and lit a last candle and there had been a brief hour of rediscovery, of such illumination that space lost its vast dimensions and drew comfortably around them, and they, mother and son, alone, transformed,

Words for Everyday Use

hyp • no • tize (hip´nə tīz´) *v.*, put into a trance
awe (ô) *n.*, mixed feeling of reverence and wonder
in • tact (in takt´) *adj.*, whole and uninjured
hys • ter • i • cal (hi ster´i kəl) *adj.*, wild, uncontrolled
il • lu • mi • na • tion (i lo͞o´mə nā´shən) *n.*, lighting up; clarification, explanation
trans • form (trans fôrm´) *v.*, change nature or character of

Vocabulary in Context

- Celeste got out the oil can and lubricated the machine.
- Make sure you open the flue before you light a fire in the fireplace.
- In a while, the smell of baking bread will be wafting through the air.
- We found the compressed loaf of bread on the chair where Marcello had been sitting.
- The number of possibilities is infinitely large; your options are limitless.

Vocabulary in Context

- Diana tried to hypnotize her grandfather by swinging his watch in front of his eyes.
- Halley stared at the great pyramids in awe.
- Zephyr dug up and destroyed the flower garden in front of the house, but the garden on the side was left intact.
- Jeremy had trouble controlling himself after his fit of hysterical laughter.
- After stumbling through problem after problem without understanding, comprehension came in a sudden flash of illumination.
- The new paint will transform the room from a dark dungeon to a cheerful conference center.

Biograph

Montag writers wh St. Vincent and Willian

Edna St. (1892–19 playwright activist. M Rockland, Vassar Col Prize for a *Harp Wea*

Walt W school at an office worked fo printing his own b worked a taught sc began to fame was often dre

William won the and two work. Hi of consc monolog novels, was born Mississip life in O his nove Yoknapa Mississi

Answe Questi

❶ Monta because

Literar

Simile

A simile *like* or *as*. bright as is used to What qual Clarisse's f simile is us describe C

ANSWERS

Clarisse's moonlight eyes are des were two m amber."

Oh yes! he'd say, that's grass! A pink blur? That's a rose garden! White blurs are houses. Brown blurs are cows. My uncle drove slowly on a highway once. He drove forty miles an hour and they jailed him for two days. Isn't that funny, and sad, too?"

"You think too many things," said Montag, uneasily.

"I rarely watch the 'parlor walls' or go to races or Fun Parks. So I've lots of time for crazy thoughts, I guess. Have you seen the two-hundred-foot-long billboards in the country beyond town? Did you know that once billboards were only twenty feet long? But cars started rushing by so quickly they had to stretch the advertising out so it would last."

"I didn't know that!" Montag laughed abruptly.

"Bet I know something else you don't. There's dew on the grass in the morning."

He suddenly couldn't remember if he had known this or not, and it made him quite irritable.

"And if you look—" she nodded at the sky—"there's a man in the moon."

He hadn't looked for a long time.

They walked the rest of the way in silence, hers thoughtful, his a kind of clenching and uncomfortable silence in which he shot her accusing glances. When they reached her house all its lights were blazing.

"What's going on?" Montag had rarely seen that many house lights.

"Oh, just my mother and father and uncle sitting around, talking. It's like being a pedestrian, only rarer. My uncle was arrested another time—did I tell you?—for being a pedestrian. Oh, we're *most* peculiar."

"But what do you *talk* about?"

She laughed at this. "Good night!" She started up her walk. Then she seemed to remember something and came back to look at him with wonder and curiosity. "Are you happy?" she said.

"Am I *what?*" he cried.

But she was gone—running in the moonlight. Her front door shut gently.

"Happy! Of all the nonsense."

He stopped laughing.

He put his hand into the glove hole of his front door and let it know his touch. The front door slid open.

Of course I'm happy. What does she think? I'm *not?* he asked the quiet rooms. He stood looking up at the ventilator grill in the hall and suddenly remembered that something lay hidden behind the grill, something that seemed to peer down at him now. He moved his eyes quickly away.

What a strange meeting on a strange night. He remembered nothing like it save one afternoon a year ago when he had met an old man in the park and *they* had talked. . . .

Montag shook his head. He looked at a blank wall. The girl's face was there, really quite beautiful in memory: astonishing, in fact. She had a very thin face like the dial of a small clock seen faintly in a dark room in the middle of a night when you waken to

❶ *What happened when Clarisse's uncle tried to drive slowly?*

❷ *What does Montag say about Clarisse? What explanation does Clarisse give for her behavior?*

❸ *Of what does Clarisse remind Montag? Why does this annoy him?*

Words for Everyday Use

a • brupt • ly (ə brupt´lē) *adv.*, suddenly, unexpectedly

clench (klench) *v.*, grip tightly

pe • des • tri • an (pi des´trēən) *n.*, walker, one who moves on foot

as • ton • ish • ing (ə stän´ish iŋ) *adj.*, amazing, wonderful

Answers to Guided Reading Questions

❶ Clarisse's uncle was jailed for two days for driving slowly.

❷ Montag says that Clarisse thinks too many things. Her thoughts make him uneasy. Clarisse says she has time to think a lot because she rarely watches the "parlor walls" or goes to the races or Fun Parks.

❸ Clarisse reminds Montag that there is dew on the grass in the morning. Montag is annoyed because he cannot remember if he had known this or not.

Quotables

"Ask yourself whether you are happy, and you cease to be so."

—John Stuart Mill

Additional Questions and Activities

Ask students whether they think Montag is happy. Have them give reasons to support their responses.

Vocabulary in Context

- Tom and Hillary were whispering about Mrs. Olloway, but they stopped abruptly when she entered the room.
- Zeke's hands were clenched into fists as he stormed out of the room.
- The driver failed to yield to the pedestrian in the crosswalk.
- It is astonishing how much work we can get done when everyone cooperates.

Selection Check Test with Answers

EX. What is Montag's profession?
He is a fireman.

1. What does Montag want, above all, to shove into the fire?
He wants to shove a marshmallow on a stick into the fire.

2. Whom does Montag meet on the way home?
He meets Clarisse McClellan.

3. What does Montag smell like?
He smells like kerosene.

4. Why has Montag never read a book?
Montag has never read a book because it is against the law.

5. Why was Clarisse's uncle jailed for two days?
Clarisse's uncle was jailed for two days for driving too slowly on the highway.

Literary Technique

SIMILE

Montag compares Clarisse to most people. He says Clarisse refracts his own light. Then he searches for a simile that reflects most people. What simile does he choose? In what way is the simile related to his line of work? What does the simile say about most people?

ANSWERS

Montag says that most people are "torches, blazing away until they whiffed out." The simile is related to his work because he torches and burns things for a living. The simile says that most people shine brightly during their lives, but their lives are not related or connected to others.

see the time and see the clock telling you the hour and the minute and the second, with a white silence and a glowing, all certainty and knowing what it has to tell of the night passing swiftly on toward further darknesses, but moving also toward a new sun.

"*What?*" asked Montag of that other self, the subconscious idiot that ran babbling at times, quite independent of will, habit, and conscience.

He glanced back at the wall. How like a mirror, too, her face. Impossible; for how many people did you know that refracted your own light to you? People were more often—he searched for a simile, found one in his work—torches, blazing away until they whiffed out. How rarely did other people's faces take of you and throw back to you your own expression, your own innermost trembling thought?

What incredible power of identification the girl had; she was like the eager watcher of a marionette show,[1] anticipating each flicker of an eyelid, each gesture of his hand, each flick of a finger, the moment before it began. How long had they walked together? Three minutes? Five? Yet how large that time seemed now. How immense a figure she was on the stage before him; what a shadow she threw on the wall with her slender body! He felt that if his eye itched, she might blink. And if the muscles of his jaws stretched imperceptibly, she would yawn long before he would. ■

1. **marionette show.** Show or skit using puppets controlled by strings

About the Author

Ray Bradbury (1920–) was born in Waukegan, Illinois. He is best known as a writer of science fiction and fantasy stories. His science fiction stories offer social criticism and warnings against the dangers of uncontrolled technological development. He has published more than twenty books, including novels, collections of short stories, poetry, and plays.

Words for Everyday Use

sub • con • scious (sub kän´shəs) *adj.,* occurring without full knowledge or perception

re • fract (ri frakt´) *v.,* cause a wave of light or sound to bend

im • per • cep • ti • bly (im´pər sep´tə bəl lē) *adv.,* unnoticeably

Vocabulary in Context

- Do you believe dreams reveal subconscious desires?
- The water refracted the light.
- The car was rolling forward almost imperceptibly until it picked up speed on the hill.

Responding to the Selection

When Montag feels uneasy with Clarisse's questions and comments, he says to her, "You think too many things." Is it possible to think too many things? Does Clarisse think too much, or does Montag think too little?

Reviewing the Selection

Recalling and Interpreting

1. **R** What is Montag's job? What duties are a part of Montag's job? What does Montag think about the smell of kerosene?

   I What role do you think people with Montag's job play in his society? Why do you think Montag enjoys his job so much?

2. **R** What reason does Montag give for never reading the books he burns? What is the "official slogan"?

   I What do you think of Montag's society? Why do they burn books? What effect might destroying books have upon the population?

3. **R** Why does Clarisse think that drivers don't know what grass or rose gardens are? What has happened to the billboards?

   I What does Clarisse's concern with grass, rose gardens, and the way society has changed reveal about her character?

4. **R** Of what two natural events does Clarisse remind Montag? What is Montag's response to the fact that Clarisse's family sits around and talks?

   I Why does Clarisse remind Montag of these things? What is revealed about Montag's society by the fact that he thinks talking with your family is unusual?

Synthesizing

5. What effects has the destruction of books had upon Montag's society? Think about the types of things Montag doesn't think about and the types of things he finds unusual. Would Clarisse be considered unusual in our society? Why is she unusual in Montag's society?

Understanding Literature (Questions for Discussion)

Science Fiction. Science fiction is imaginative literature based on scientific principles, discoveries, or laws. This story is filled with details that indicate a future full of new technology. What details in the story show scientific or technical advances? In what ways has this society advanced, and in what ways has it stopped advancing? Do you think the new inventions compensate for what this society has lost? Why, or why not?

Responding to the Selection

Ask students why they think Clarisse's thoughts make Montag uneasy.

Answers for Reviewing the Selection

RECALLING AND INTERPRETING

1. **Recalling.** Montag is a fireman. He burns books. Montag thinks the smell of kerosene is like perfume. **Interpreting.** Firemen are powerful and respected for burning books. Montag enjoys the power of his position and his destructive force.

2. **Recalling.** It is illegal to read. The official slogan is "burn 'em to ashes, then burn the ashes." **Interpreting.** *Responses will vary.* They burn books to suppress ideas. A lot of stories and information will be lost.

3. **Recalling.** She thinks that drivers go so fast that they only see a blur of color. Billboards have gotten larger. **Interpreting.** Clarisse does not travel as fast as most of this society. She is aware of her surroundings, and she thinks. She recognizes the many things that are being lost because of the changes in society.

4. **Recalling.** Clarisse reminds Montag of dew in the morning and the man on the moon. Montag wonders what Clarisse's family talks about. **Interpreting.** Clarisse wants to share the things she knows and pass them on to others. There is little connection or communication between people in this society.

SYNTHESIZING

Responses will vary. Possible responses are given.

5. People do not read at all and they do not think much. People also do not talk with each other very often, so there is very little communication. Clarisse is considered odd because she is aware of things around her, she moves slowly, and she thinks.

Answers for Understanding Literature

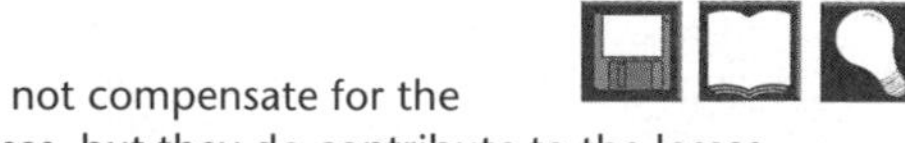

Responses will vary. Possible responses are given.

Science Fiction. People are able to drive faster. Other methods of transportation seem to move faster as well. Society has stopped advancing because information is suppressed and destroyed, people are no longer in touch with each other or with the world around them. The new inventions do not compensate for the losses, but they do contribute to the losses.

Language Lab

Introducing the Skill

Ask students to think about different ways they read. Suggest the following situations as examples: looking for a movie time in the newspaper, trying to see if an article would be a useful source for a particular assignment, enjoying a novel. Reading for these three purposes is very different, and each requires a different reading rate.

Previewing the Skill

Have students read the information about reading rates on page 40. Discuss tips for each reading rate and when each rate would be appropriate.

Practicing the Skill

Have students complete the Try It Yourself exercise on page 41.

Reviewing the Skill

Discuss the answers to the Try It Yourself exercise. Give students several reading assignments and ask them which reading rates they used to complete them.

Reading Skills

Reading Rates

The purpose you have for reading something affects how you read it. Slow and careful reading is required in some situations, scanning and skimming in others.

Scanning is very quickly looking through written material to locate some particular information that you want. For example, if you were looking for an article on local elections in your local paper, you might scan the first few pages of the newspaper until you spot the appropriate headline.

Skimming is glancing quickly through a piece of writing to get the general idea. Skimming is a useful way to preview your reading or to review your reading before taking a test or planning an essay.

Slow and careful reading is the technique you should use when you are reading for pleasure or for instruction. When you are reading a poem, a story, a novel, or an essay, you will read every word from the first to the last, and think about what you have been reading. Another important part of slow and careful reading is looking up any words you do not know in a dictionary. For more information on active reading, see the Language Arts Survey, 4.6, "Reading Actively."

READING TECHNIQUES

Technique	Purpose	Tips
Scanning	Finding specific information quickly	Look for key words; look at chapter and part headings.
Skimming	Getting the general idea of the content of a piece	Ask questions; look at introductions; look at chapter and part headings.
Slow and careful reading	Learning and enjoyment	Read actively.

Try It Yourself

For each situation described below, tell whether you should scan, skim, or read slowly and carefully. Write your answers on your own paper.

EXAMPLE You have found a lost dog. You want to see if someone put an ad for the dog in the Lost and Found section of the classified ads in your paper. **Scan**

1. You have found eight articles for a research report that you are working on. You want to get the general idea of each article to decide if the article will be a good source for your report.
2. The morning paper arrived. You want to see what movies are playing in your local theater.
3. Your teacher assigned you to read chapter 3 of your history textbook.
4. You found another novel by your favorite author. You can't wait to curl up in a chair and start reading.
5. You have done all your reading, but you would like to be further prepared for a test.

ANSWERS FOR TRY IT YOURSELF

1. skim
2. scan
3. skim, then slow and careful
4. slow and careful
5. skim

PROJECT NOTE

- Remind students that when choosing selections, they may draw on stories and poems they have heard or written as well as on those they have read.
- Students might organize the selections by breaking them into chapters by theme or by genre.
- If students decide to give a reading, discuss with them techniques for oral interpretation. Allow time for practicing reading the selections aloud.

Unit Project

MAKING A BOOK

A book is more than just a collection of words and sentences. Through reading books, people can visit different places, meet interesting characters, and learn about new ideas. What are some books that you will never forget? If you were to put together a collection of your favorite pieces of writing, what pieces would you want to include? What special characters, settings, and ideas would you like to share with other people?

TRY IT YOURSELF

Work with your classmates to put together a collection of favorite poems, stories, and essays. Each student should try to find one piece of writing that he or she enjoys. Collect favorite selections from everyone in the class and make a book.

STUDENT MODEL

Diego and his classmates are putting together a collection of their favorite stories, poems, folk tales, and essays. Each student will contribute one piece to the collection. Diego thinks about stories and poems he has heard or read through the years. He remembers enjoying tall tales about characters such as Paul Bunyan, John Henry, and Pecos Bill. His mother used to read these tales to him, and now Diego reads them to his younger sister. Diego chooses a story about Paul Bunyan for the class collection.

Students in Diego's class contribute a variety of selections to the collection. Diego's friend Julia brings in the poem "Casey at the Bat" by Ernest Lawrence Thayer. The poem is about her favorite sport, baseball. His friend Rodney, who loves cats, brings in the poem "The Naming of Cats" by T. S. Eliot. Diego's friend Rodrigo brings in a short tale that his grandmother wrote. When all the selections are in, the class gathers everything together and estimates that the selections will fill about thirty-five pages. Students decide that some selections should be illustrated. They also decide to include five extra pages of art and photos.

The class then begins to put the book together. Tasks are distributed among everyone. Several people retype selections on typewriters and word processors. Then several students proofread selections to make sure that no errors have appeared after the selections were retyped. Some people are in charge of gathering art and illustrating certain selections. Others are in charge of creating the cover.

After everything is neatly typed, proofread, and put in order, pages of art are inserted. Then students attach the cover by punching three holes through the cover and the book and looping string through the holes. They name their collection *Many Worlds* and draw a multicolored globe on the front cover because the selections show readers a variety of places, characters, and ideas. Each student writes his or her name on the back cover of the book. After everyone in the class has a chance to read the collection, the students donate it to a local library.

Examining the Model

1. What different types of selections do students choose for their class book?
2. What different tasks are involved in putting the book together? What do the students do to organize and divide the tasks?

Planning Your Book

1. Think about folk tales, stories, essays, and poems that you have read and enjoyed. Go to the library or flip through books at home to find a special selection. Bring the selection to class.
2. Gather together the class selections. Estimate the number of pages your book will be. If you are in an especially large class, consider splitting the class into two groups and making two books. If you split the class into two groups, each group should be in charge of producing one book.
3. Decide if you would like to use illustrations and photos in your book. If you decide to use art, how many pieces will you use? Where will the art be placed?
4. Distribute tasks among everyone in the class. You will need people to type or handwrite out selections, proofread selections, illustrate, and design and create the book's cover. People can complete more than one task, but be sure that everyone has a job.

Making the Book

1. Type or write out selections for the final copy of the book.
2. Proofread the selections after they have been written or typed out. You are looking only for errors that appear after the typing/writing process. You should not change any original wording or spelling.
3. Place the pages in some kind of order. For example, you might decide to put all short stories together, all poems together, and all folk tales and essays together. Create illustrations and insert art. Some art can probably fit on selection pages, and some might need separate pages.
4. Create the cover of the book. You might use two pieces of cardboard or paper held together by string or yarn, or you might simply staple one corner of the book.

Publishing the Book

1. Keep the book on display in your classroom. Allow students in the class to borrow the book so that they can read all of the selections.
2. Ask if you can place your book in a school or local library. Students and other people in the community might be interested in reading the pieces you have selected.
3. You might plan a reading. At the reading, each person in the class should read his or her favorite selection. Invite teachers, other classes, and your principal to the reading.

Answers for Examining the Model

1. Students choose stories; poems; folk tales, including a tall tale about Paul Bunyan; essays; poems about baseball and cats; and a story by a family member.
2. Tasks include typing selections, proofreading selections, creating illustrations, and designing and creating the book's cover. The tasks are distributed among everyone. Several students work on each task.

ANALYTIC SCALE FOR PROJECT

Assign a score from 1 to 25 for each grading criterion below.

Book

- **Organization.** The group set attainable goals and created a schedule or strategy for achieving those goals.
- **Cooperation.** The group assigned tasks fairly to each member, and each member cooperated toward achieving the group's goals.
- **Goal Achievement.** The group worked steadily toward its goals and did, in fact, achieve them.
- **Presentation.** The group presented a product of high quality that met the initial project description.

Vocabulary Check Test

Ask students to number their papers from one to ten. Have students complete each sentence with a word from the Vocabulary for the Unit in the Unit Review.

1. George played the prank, but feigned innocence when Martha sought the culprit.
2. Riley sat bored in the waiting room and listlessly flipped the pages of the magazine.
3. Every muscle in Gwyneth's body was clenched as she clung to the ledge for dear life.
4. The garter snake is harmless, but watch out for the venomous cobra.
5. The petulant child's sunny disposition returned after his nap.
6. We were frightened by the ferocity of Commando's growl, but Jules said that his bark was worse than his bite.
7. Grandma, in her infinite wisdom, provided us with the perfect solution to the problem.
8. Jules used to nervously stammer his way through speeches, but with practice he became an articulate speaker.
9. Sherry put too much emphasis on studying for her chemistry test and not enough on preparing for her English exam.
10. "It's not the heat; it's the humidity," cried Kirra on one of the many sultry days.

Unit Review

Summary

Literary Terms for the Unit

aim, 7
apostrophe, 7, 11
autobiography, 29
conflict, 20
metaphor, 11
parallelism, 11
science fiction, 39
theme, 20

Vocabulary for the Unit

abruptly, 37
acquire, 25
articulate, 25
assail, 19
astonishing, 37
awe, 35
boulevard, 36
clench, 37
compressed, 34
convey, 25
dissentient, 19
emphasis, 27
emulate, 25
engross, 28
envy, 25
fatuously, 15
feign, 28
ferocity, 18
flue, 34
functional, 25
gorge, 33
hypnotize, 35
hysterical, 35
illumination, 35
imperceptibly, 38
inevitable, 26
infinitely, 34
intact, 35
isolation, 27
listlessly, 16
lubricated, 34
pedestrian, 37
persistent, 15
petulant, 16
principally, 27
refract, 38
rehabilitation, 27
resolute, 16
riffle, 26
singe, 33
stolid, 33
subconscious, 38
sultry, 15
symbolic, 33
transform, 35
venomous, 33
waft, 34

Questions for Writing, Discussion, and Research

1. Compare and contrast the techniques used in each selection to promote the interest and importance of literature.
2. What difficulties facing readers or storytellers are described or implied in the works in this unit?

For Your Reading List

Lance Walters
Colony Middle School
Palmer, Alaska

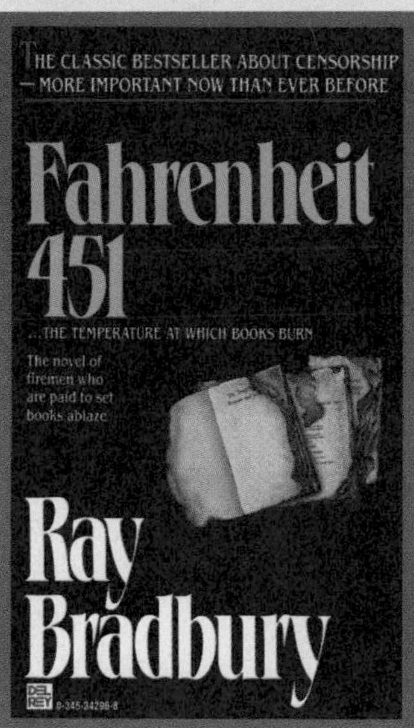

Fahrenheit 451
by Ray Bradbury

Although I am not a fan of science fiction, I thoroughly enjoyed *Fahrenheit 451* by Ray Bradbury. In this book, the government has made it illegal to read books, even though the fire chief has a whole library. The fire chief believes it is legal to have books as long as they are not read. The firemen in *Fahrenheit 451* burn books instead of putting out fires. The main character, Guy Montag, decides to find books and read them to see what they are about. Later, while being chased by police, he meets a group of people who have photographic memories and can memorize the books before they are burnt. These people are able to recall the stories whenever they want.

I think that if the government were able to really keep people from reading, they would have a lot of power over them. People might no longer be imaginative and they might be easier to control. I recommend this book to anyone, even if you don't consider yourself a science fiction fan. *Fahrenheit 451* is interesting and exciting and makes the reader think about how different society would be if reading books were illegal.

Spelling Check Test

Ask students to number their papers from one to ten. Read each word aloud. Then read aloud the sentence containing the word. Repeat the word. Ask students to write the word on their papers, spelling it correctly.

1. **acquired**
By practicing all summer to improve her game, Clarisse acquired a spot on the team.
2. **feigned**
Sadie feigned indifference, but I knew she was upset about the decision.
3. **emulate**
Mr. Wilcox worried when Izzie began to emulate the bully who lived down the street.
4. **dissentient**
The decision would have been unanimous, but Ted had a dissentient opinion.
5. **imperceptibly**
The car was rolling forward almost imperceptibly until it picked up speed on the hill.
6. **abruptly**
Tom and Hillary were whispering about Mrs. Olloway, but they stopped abruptly when she entered the room.
7. **assailed**
The students assailed the teacher with requests for less homework, but their cries went unheeded.
8. **boulevard**
It was a relief to turn from the narrow, rutted lanes onto the spacious boulevard.
9. **hypnotize**
Diana tried to hypnotize her grandfather by swinging his watch in front of his eyes.
10. **fatuously**
Mr. Kline answered the questions cleverly, while his opponent replied fatuously to every query.

GOALS/OBJECTIVES

Studying this unit will enable students to

- enjoy poems and short fiction that explore the imagination
- define *image, speaker, allegory, personification, exposition, irony of situation, motivation, tone,* and *understatement* and recognize these techniques and elements in their reading
- write a dream report
- take both formal and informal notes
- edit for errors in modifier usage
- imagine and make models of creatures from other worlds

ADDITIONAL UNIT MATERIALS IN THE ASSESSMENT PORTFOLIO

- Vocabulary Worksheet 2.2.15
- Unit Test 2.2.16

See also the Additional Resources Box in the marginal notes accompanying each selection.

CROSS-CURRICULAR CONNECTIONS

- American History, 76
- Applied Arts, 68, 80
- Geography, 52
- Health, 58
- Science, 48, 58, 62, 68
- World History, 48, 52

UNIT 2 IMAGININGS

Starry Night. *Vincent van Gogh, 1889*

magination is the eye of the soul.

—Joseph Joubert

UNIT SKILLS OUTLINE

Literary Skills and Concepts

- Allegory, 61
- Exposition, 75
- Image, 51, 55
- Irony of Situation, 75
- Motivation, 79
- Personification, 65
- Speaker, 55
- Tone, 79
- Understatement, 86

Other Language Arts Skills and Concepts

- Editing for Errors in Modifier Usage, 87
- Taking Notes, 66
- Writing a Dream Report, 56

ART NOTE

Vincent van Gogh (1853–1890) was one of the greatest of the Expressionist painters. Expressionism is an artistic style in which the artist makes exaggerated use of his or her medium to express a unique personal vision. Expressionist painters tend to use a lot of paint, heavy brush strokes, and vivid lines. *Starry Night* is an excellent example of Expressionism, for it is not at all a realistic portrayal of the night sky above a village. It is, rather, a portrayal of the artist's feelings about his subject.

GOALS/OBJECTIVES

Studying this lesson will enable students to

- enjoy a poem that uses figurative language
- briefly explain different types of clouds
- describe ancient people's beliefs about the moon
- define *image* and recognize images in works that they read

ADDITIONAL RESOURCES

READER'S GUIDE

- Selection Worksheet, 2.1

ASSESSMENT PORTFOLIO

- Selection Check Test, 2.2.1
- Selection Test, 2.2.2

PRONUNCIATION EXERCISE

- Grade 8 Audiocassette, Side B, Track 6

CROSS-CURRICULAR CONNECTIONS

SCIENCE

You might locate a book on weather to show students what the four different types of clouds look like.

WORLD HISTORY

Some students might enjoy writing their own myths or poems about the moon. If students choose to write a myth, ask them to think about what explanation they might provide for the moon's presence in the nighttime sky. How might they explain the changing phases of the moon? If students choose to write a poem, inform them that their poem need not rhyme nor use meter if they find these techniques to be difficult. Encourage students to think about the feelings the moon evokes in them.

Prereading

POEM

"Night Clouds"

by Amy Lowell

Cross-curricular Connections

Science. Clouds are masses of moisture, either water droplets or ice crystals, that move on air currents. There are four major classifications of clouds.

The highest clouds are thin and feathery. These are cirrus clouds and they are usually found between 45,000 feet and 16,500 feet above the ground. Cirrus clouds that thicken and move lower are called stratus clouds. Stratus clouds, often a sheet of gray cloud, are found from 23,000 feet to 6,500 feet above ground. As stratus clouds descend and produce rain or snow, they become nimbus clouds. The fourth type of cloud is the cumulus cloud. Cumulus clouds are found from 4,000 feet to 6,500 feet above ground and are the puffy white clouds often seen on a fair day. People often see shapes in the clouds. In this poem, the speaker imaginatively describes the night clouds.

World History. Many early societies believed the moon was a powerful god or goddess whose chariot moved across the night sky. In Norse mythology, a god drove the chariot of the moon across the sky every night; his sister drove the chariot of the sun each day. In some versions, they are each chased by a wolf. In the mythology of the ancient Greeks, the goddess of the moon was Selene. The god of the sun was her brother, Helios. Every day, Helios would drive his fiery chariot across the sky, bringing daylight to the world. Every night, Selene would drive her chariot across the sky, lighting the black sky with golden rays from her crown. In Roman mythology, the goddess of the moon was Luna, who closely resembled Selene. The Romans believed that if people offended Luna, she would drive them insane. That is where the word *lunatic* comes from. In Latin, *lunatic* means "moonstruck." In English, it means "insane" or "wildly foolish."

As You Read

"**Night Clouds**" uses figurative language to describe natural objects in the sky. Several vivid images are used to depict the sky and its features. In your journal, make a chart like the one below. Fill in the chart with images related to the senses of sight and sound and with vivid action images from the poem.

SIGHT	SOUND	ACTION
white mares		rushing across the sky

AS YOU READ

Students may include the following details under the heading *Sight*: golden hoofs, glass heavens, mares standing on hind legs, green porcelain doors, milky dust of stars, tiger sun, vermilion tongue.

Students may include the following details under the heading *Sound:* beating upon the glass Heavens, pawing at doors.

Students may include the following details under the heading *Action:* beating their golden hoofs, standing on hind legs, pawing against green doors, flying, straining, scattering, tiger sun leaping and destroying, lick of the sun's tongue.

READER'S JOURNAL

Have you ever looked at the clouds and seen the shapes of other things? Have you ever made up stories about shapes you saw in the clouds? What do you see in the clouds? Write about something you have seen in the clouds or something you imagine clouds might look like.

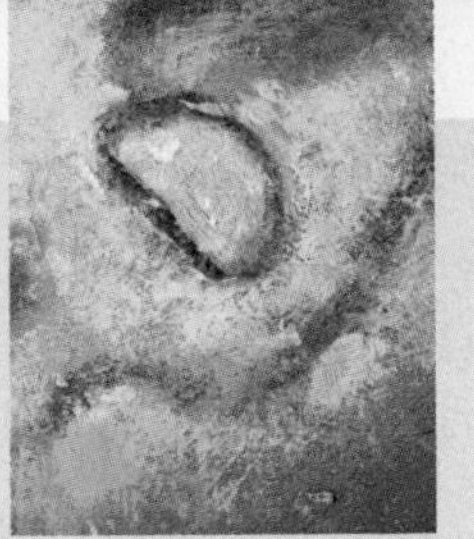

"Night Clouds"

AMY LOWELL

The white mares of the moon rush along the sky
Beating their golden hoofs upon the glass Heavens;
The white mares of the moon are all standing on their hind legs
Pawing at the green porcelain doors of the remote Heavens.
Fly, Mares!
Strain your utmost,
Scatter the milky dust of stars,
Or the tiger sun will leap upon you and destroy you
With one lick of his vermilion tongue. ■

❶ *What might the "white mares of the moon" be?*

❷ *What does the speaker tell the mares to do? What warning does the speaker give?*

WORDS FOR EVERYDAY USE

por • ce • lain (pôr´sə lin) *adj.,* made of or like a hard, translucent ceramic

re • mote (ri mōt´) *adj.,* distant

ver • mil • ion (vər mil´yən) *adj.,* bright red or scarlet

VOCABULARY IN CONTEXT

- The baby's skin was so white and smooth that it looked porcelain.
- The village was remote, located far from civilization.
- The setting sun is sometimes vermilion.

READER'S JOURNAL

If students have difficulty getting started, ask them to think of the different types of clouds they have seen, such as high, white threads of cloud on a summer day, thick puffy clouds, or dark storm clouds. Ask students what different feelings these clouds evoke in them. Of what do these different types of clouds remind them?

SPELLING AND VOCABULARY WORDS FROM THE SELECTION

porcelain
remote
vermilion

ANSWERS TO GUIDED READING QUESTIONS

❶ The "white mares of the moon" might be clouds passing before the moon.

❷ The speaker tells the mares to fly. The speaker warns that the morning sun will destroy the night clouds.

SUPPORT FOR LEP STUDENTS

PRONUNCIATIONS OF PROPER NOUNS AND ADJECTIVES

Low • ell (lō´əl) n.

ADDITIONAL VOCABULARY

mares—female horses
utmost—to the greatest point or degree

Selection Check Test with Answers

EX. What time of day is described in this poem?
Night is described.

1. Where do the mares beat their golden hoofs?
They beat their golden hoofs upon "the glass Heavens."

2. At what do the mares paw?
They paw "at the green porcelain doors of the remote Heavens."

3. What does the speaker tell the mares to do?
The speaker tells the mares to fly.

4. What does the speaker tell the mares to scatter?
The speaker tells the mares to scatter "the milky dust of stars."

5. What does the speaker say the "tiger sun" will do?
The speaker says the "tiger sun" will leap upon the mares and destroy them with "one lick of his vermilion tongue."

About the Author

Amy Lowell (1874–1925) was born into a distinguished New England family in Brookline, Massachusetts, and educated at private schools. Lowell was highly influenced by the poet Ezra Pound. Following Pound's approach to poetry, Lowell became a leading figure in the movement called Imagism. She wrote poetry that is filled with clear, precise images of objects in the world rather than descriptions of her inner feelings. Lowell also wrote a biography of John Keats and several books about the poetry being written in her time.

Responding to the Selection

Which image in this poem did you find most powerful? Why? Can you picture the scene described? How might the speaker describe the actions of the tiger sun during the day?

Reviewing the Selection

RECALLING AND INTERPRETING

1. R What creatures does the speaker describe in lines 1–4?
   I What might these creatures be?
2. R What actions occur in lines 1–4?
   I What emotions are associated with the actions in lines 1–4?
3. R What words does the speaker use to urge on the mares in lines 5–9?
   I What feeling or mood is created in lines 5–9?
4. R What will the "tiger sun" do to the mares of the moon?
   I What characteristics of the sun are portrayed? of the moon?

SYNTHESIZING

5. In what ways is the description in this poem similar to other stories you have heard about the sun and moon? Why do you think people are so fascinated with what they see in the sky?

Understanding Literature (Questions for Discussion)

Image. An **image** is language that describes something that can be seen, heard, touched, tasted, or smelled. What images describe the clouds? To what senses do these images appeal? What image is used to describe the sun? The images in this poem are especially vivid because of the powerful actions described. What actions are attributed to the "mares of the moon"? to the sun? How do these actions add to or change the descriptions of the sun and the moon?

RESPONDING TO THE SELECTION

You might ask students to discuss whether they believe the speaker prefers the daytime or the nighttime. Tell students to support their answers with evidence from the poem.

ANSWERS FOR REVIEWING THE SELECTION

RECALLING AND INTERPRETING

1. **Recalling.** The speaker describes white mares high up in the sky. **Interpreting.** The white mares might be clouds.

2. **Recalling.** The mares rush along the sky, beat their hoofs upon the "glass Heavens," stand on their hind legs, and paw against the "green porcelain doors" of the Heavens. **Interpreting.** These actions are associated with emotions of exuberance, wonder, and joy.

3. **Recalling.** The speaker uses the following words and phrases to urge on the mares: *fly, strain your utmost,* and *scatter.* **Interpreting.** The feeling is one of suspense, excitement, and urgency.

4. **Recalling.** The "tiger sun" will leap upon the mares and destroy them. **Interpreting.** The sun is portrayed as vicious, powerful, and destructive. The moon is portrayed as romantic, mysterious, and awe-inspiring.

SYNTHESIZING

Responses will vary. Possible responses are given.

5. Students may say that the moon is often portrayed as cool, mysterious, and beautiful and that the sun is often portrayed as a powerful force.

ANSWERS FOR UNDERSTANDING LITERATURE

Responses will vary. Possible responses are given.

Image. The images that describe the clouds are white mares, rushing along the sky. These images appeal to the senses of sight and sound. The image used to describe the sun is a tiger with a vermilion tongue that will leap upon the mares. The actions attributed to the mares are rushing, beating their hoofs, standing on their hind legs, and pawing. The sun leaps upon and destroys the mares with one lick of its vermilion tongue. The mares' actions make them seem beautiful and playful. The sun's actions make it seem ferocious and powerful.

GOALS/OBJECTIVES

Studying this lesson will enable students to

- appreciate a poem that imaginatively describes a city
- briefly describe when cities began to develop, the elements necessary to sustain a city, and the characteristics of some modern cities
- define *image* and recognize to which senses different images appeal
- define *speaker* and identify the speaker of a literary work

ADDITIONAL RESOURCES

READER'S GUIDE

- Selection Worksheet, 2.2

ASSESSMENT PORTFOLIO

- Selection Check Test, 2.2.3
- Selection Test, 2.2.4

PRONUNCIATION EXERCISE

- Grade 8 Audiocassette, Side B, Track 7

CROSS-CURRICULAR CONNECTIONS

GEOGRAPHY AND WORLD HISTORY

Encourage students to make pro and con charts listing the benefits and drawbacks of living in the city and living in the country. Students might then share the pros and cons they have listed in their charts. Encourage students to discuss where they would prefer to live when they are older and why.

Prereading

POEM

"The City Is So Big"
by Richard Garcia

Cross-curricular Connection

Geography and World History. People have not always lived in cities. Although human beings have lived on Earth for two-and-a-half million years, they have lived in permanent settlements for only ten thousand years. The first permanent settlements appeared when people started to farm and no longer had to wander from place to place hunting for food and gathering plants. By 3500 BC, settlements had become villages and some villages were developing into small cities.

A city needs four things to establish itself and to grow: a good environment—a safe location, ready food and water supplies, and a suitable climate; technology that helps people improve their way of life—farming, manufacturing, industry, and automobiles, for example; social organization—government and laws to keep order; and a growing population that chooses to live together in a community.

In the selection you are about to read, the speaker feels frightened and intimidated by a city. Modern cities can be intimidating because they are spread out, the buildings are huge, and they are crowded with people. According to a 1990 census, or population count, the largest city in the world was Tokyo, Japan, with a population of over twenty-six million people. In both 1980 and 1990 censuses, New York City was the largest city in the United States, with more than seven million people. There are over twenty thousand people living in each square mile of New York City. In comparison, the population density in the rest of the United States averages less than one hundred people per square mile. Crowds do not seem to bother most Americans, however. The 1990 census showed that over 77 percent of the United States population lives in a metropolitan area.

As You Read

In **"The City Is So Big,"** the speaker gives an imaginative description of a city. In your journal, create a cluster chart like the one below. In each circle around the word *city*, write a detail from the poem. Around each of these circles, write your impression of this detail.

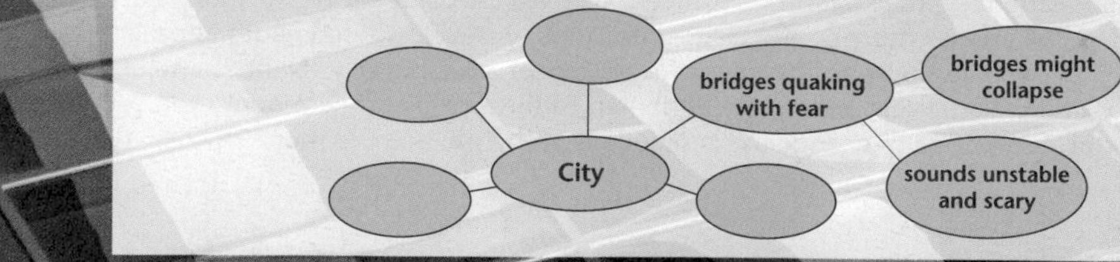

AS YOU READ

Students may include the following details and impressions in their cluster charts: lights slide from house to house—sounds scary, slowly moving headlights; trains passing windows shining like a smile full of teeth—sounds threatening as if it might bite; machines eating houses—sounds like a science fiction story; stairways walking by themselves—sounds creepy; elevators making people disappear—sounds scary and lonely.

READER'S JOURNAL

Have you ever visited or lived in a large city? What did you like best about it? What did you like least? If you could change the city in any way, how would you change it? Do you view yourself as more of a "city" or "country" person? Write about these questions in your journal.

"The City Is So Big"

RICHARD GARCIA

The city is so big
Its bridges quake with fear
I know, I have seen at night

The lights sliding from house to house
And trains pass with windows shining
Like a smile full of teeth

I have seen machines eating houses
And stairways walk all by themselves
And elevator doors opening and closing
And people disappear. ■

❶ *Why do the city's bridges quake?*

❷ *What do the windows of the train look like?*

WORDS FOR EVERYDAY USE

quake (kwāk) *v.*, tremble or shake

READER'S JOURNAL

As an alternative activity, students might write about what frightened them when they were younger. Did they ever imagine monsters under their bed or in their closet? Have students describe their childhood fears and how they conquered them.

SPELLING AND VOCABULARY WORDS FROM THE SELECTION

quake

ANSWERS TO GUIDED READING QUESTIONS

❶ The city's bridges quake because they are afraid.

❷ The windows of the train look like a smile full of teeth.

SUPPORT FOR LEP STUDENTS

PRONUNCIATIONS OF PROPER NOUNS AND ADJECTIVES

Gar • ci • a (gär sē´ə) n.

ADDITIONAL VOCABULARY

elevator—a boxlike structure used to raise people or things in a building

VOCABULARY IN CONTEXT

• After seeing the scary movie, we were all quaking with fear.

Selection Check Test with Answers

EX. What size is the city?
The city is big.

1. What do the bridges in the city do?
The bridges quake with fear.

2. When does the speaker observe these scary images of the city?
The speaker says that he or she has seen these things at night.

3. What do the shining train windows look like?
They look like a smile full of teeth.

4. What do the machines and stairways do?
The machines eat houses and the stairways walk by themselves.

5. What happens when the elevator doors open and close?
People disappear.

Quotables

"Cities, like cats, will reveal themselves at night."

—Rupert Brooke

About the Author

Richard Garcia (1941–) was born in San Francisco, California, and has lived in Mexico and Israel. Garcia has served as the director of the Poets in the Schools program in Marin County, California. He writes poetry for both adults and young people. If you like "The City Is So Big," you may want to read his collection *Selected Poetry* (1973).

Responding to the Selection

Would a city appear more frightening to you if you had never seen a city before? If you could talk to the speaker of this poem, how would you explain the things that the speaker finds so frightening? How would you make the speaker feel more comfortable?

Reviewing the Selection

Recalling and Interpreting

1. **R** What does the speaker say the bridges are doing?

   I Why might the size of the city make the bridges do this?

2. **R** What does the speaker say the passing trains look like?

   I What kind of feeling does this image give you?

3. **R** What does the speaker say the machines in the city do?

   I In what ways might machines actually do these things? What might the speaker be saying about the role of machines and technology in our lives?

4 **R** What does the speaker say about stairways? about elevators?

   I What might this type of stairway be? Why might it seem that elevators have this effect upon people?

Synthesizing

5. What does the speaker seem to dislike most about the city? Why might the city make the speaker feel that people lack control, or are powerless? Do you agree with the speaker's feelings and perceptions about the city? Why, or why not?

Understanding Literature (Questions for Discussion)

1. **Image.** An **image** is language that describes something that can be seen, heard, touched, tasted, or smelled. The poet uses images to describe the city. What images can you find in the poem? To what senses do the images appeal? How do the images contribute to the overall effect of the poem?
2. **Speaker.** The **speaker** is the voice that speaks, or narrates, a poem. Based on this poem, who or what kind of person might the speaker be? Try to think of at least two different people who might see the city in this way.

Responding to the Selection

Students might work in pairs, one student role playing the frightened speaker, and the other student role playing the advisor to the speaker.

Answers for Reviewing the Selection

RECALLING AND INTERPRETING

1. **Recalling.** The speaker says that the bridges are quaking with fear. **Interpreting.** The city might be filled with so much traffic that the passing cars make the bridges shake.
2. **Recalling.** The speaker says the trains look like a smile full of teeth. **Interpreting.** Because the smile is full of teeth, it seems to be more menacing than friendly.
3. **Recalling.** The speaker says that the machines eat houses. **Interpreting.** In the city old building must sometimes be torn down by machine to clear space for newer and bigger buildings. The speaker might be saying that we trust too much in technology—a machine that can tear down a house can also damage people.
4. **Recalling.** The speaker says that stairways walk by themselves and that elevator doors open and close, causing people to disappear. **Interpreting.** The stairway might be an escalator. It might seem that elevators have this effect because the next time the doors open, the people are gone.

SYNTHESIZING

Responses will vary. Possible responses are given.

5. The speaker seems to dislike technology the most. The city may make the speaker feel that people are powerless because the city is so large and full of technological devices.

Answers for Understanding Literature

Responses will vary. Possible responses are given.

1. **Image.** Students may include the following images: quaking bridges, sliding lights, trains like a smile full of teeth, machines eating houses, stairways walking, and elevators making people disappear. Most of these images appeal to the sense of sight, but the first appeals to the sense of touch as well. The images help create a fearful mood and express the anxiety of the speaker.
2. **Speaker.** The speaker might be a small child, an older person who has never seen the city before, or someone who strongly disapproves of city life.

Writing Skills

Introducing the Skill

Inform students that people remember dreams most vividly in the morning, shortly after they have awakened. Over the course of a day, people often find that their memory of a dream fades. Some people keep journals in which they write dream reports, or descriptions of the dreams they have had. They write their reports in the morning, and then read them over again, looking for recurring images, themes, or hidden meanings in their dreams.

Previewing the Skill

Have students read the model dream report. Point out that it is okay if dream reports contain events that do not seem logical or that are difficult to explain. The sequence of events in a dream report may also be unusual.

Prewriting and Drafting

Tell students that it might be easier for them to write a dream report if they keep a pen and paper beside their bed for a few evenings and write down their dreams as soon as they get up in the morning.

Evaluating and Revising

After students receive comments from their peer, they might read over their dream report themselves, noting additional areas that need improvement.

Proofreading and Publishing

Students might also collect their dream reports into an illustrated class anthology of dreams.

Writing Skills

A Dream Report

The dreams we have at night can be wonderful, strange, or frightening. Sometimes your dreams can make great stories. Often you will remember only bits and pieces of a dream at first, but once you start retelling your dream, you will remember more of it. Dreams are often filled with rich and detailed images.

Try It Yourself

Write about a dream you have had, trying to capture all the strange details and images that made it vivid. Many people believe that the best time to write a dream report is first thing in the morning, because the dream is still fresh and clear in your mind.

Student Model ▸▸

Vivienne Taylor
English 8

I had a great dream last night. I think it might have had something to do with the fact that it was so cold outside. In my dream, I woke up, looked out the window, and saw four feet of the most beautiful snow on the ground. It was incredible. I wasn't in my own home. I was in a cabin at the top of a hill in the woods. The snow was so powdery and shiny. I looked out my window and saw picture-perfect pine trees covered with snow. At the bottom of this hill was a large pond shaped like a pear. It was frozen over and covered with snow. Everything was still and smooth.

Then other people started getting up. My family was in the cabin with me, but it felt like we were home, not on vacation. I smelled a fire in a fireplace and coffee brewing. My brothers and sisters got up and went outside. (I only have one of each, but they seem to have multiplied in my dream.) I got dressed and took out two sleds. One was wooden and had runners and the other was a silver saucer. When I walked outside, I smelled pine trees. My good friend Shana suddenly appeared so we each took a sled. It seemed as though Shana appeared out of thin air, and she was wearing a strange silver hat. I took the sled with the runners.

We each pushed off the top of the hill. My sled moved so quickly that it felt as if I were flying. (Maybe I was.) When I got to the bottom of the hill, I floated across the frozen pond. I remember snow flying in my face and into my mouth. I know snow really doesn't have a sweet taste, but in my dream, the snow was sweet. I don't remember getting to the top of the hill, but I remember going down the hill over and over again. I also remember how quiet and soundless the dream was.

Examining the Model

1. What vivid details does Vivienne remember about her dream? What does she remember seeing, hearing, touching, tasting, and smelling?
2. What strange details does Vivienne include that give her dream the unreal quality that many dreams have?

Prewriting and Drafting

1. Review the section on freewriting in the Language Arts Survey, 1.13, "Gathering Ideas." Freewrite for ten to fifteen minutes about a dream you have had. As you write, think about how you felt while you were dreaming. Write down all the details from your dream. Do not worry about putting the events in order or making perfect sense. You may remember things in bits and pieces. One memory may jog another memory.
2. Read the section on sensory detail charts in the Language Arts Survey, 1.13, "Gathering Ideas." Make a sensory detail chart, describing what you remember seeing, hearing, feeling, tasting, and smelling in your dream.
3. Review the chart and your freewriting. Make notes, organizing the details of your dream in the order that they occurred. You may be unsure of the order of some events, so try to place them in as sensible an order as possible.
4. Review the Language Arts Survey, 1.16, "Drafting." Using your freewriting, sensory detail chart, and organizational notes, draft your dream report.

Evaluating and Revising

1. Review the Language Arts Survey, 1.18, "Peer Evaluation." Exchange drafts with a classmate. Evaluate each other's work. Note places where your classmate's dream report becomes too confusing, or the ordering of events is not understandable.
2. Carefully considering your classmate's suggestions, revise your draft. Follow the guidelines in the Language Arts Survey, 1.19, "Four Types of Revision."

Proofreading and Publishing

1. Proofread your revised manuscript. Then make a clean copy of it and proofread it again. Refer to the Language Arts Survey, 1.22, "A Proofreading Checklist."
2. Illustrate your dream report with images from your dream, and share your work with your classmates.

Save your work in your writing portfolio.

Answers for Examining the Model

1. Vivienne remembers the powdery shiny snow, the pear-shaped pond, Shana's strange silver hat, the feeling of flying, and the sweet taste of the snow. She remembers seeing the snow, the pond, the woods, the sled, and Shana's hat. She remembers hearing nothing but quiet. She remembers smelling a fire in a fireplace, coffee, and pine trees. She remembers the snow flying in her face and the feeling of floating. She remembers the sweet taste of the snow.

2. Vivienne includes the following strange details: suddenly living with her family in a cabin in the woods, having more brothers and sisters than she actually does, Shana appearing out of thin air, Shana's strange silver hat, the sweet taste of the snow, and going down, but never up, the hill.

ANALYTIC SCALE FOR WRITING SKILLS

Assign a score from 1 to 25 for each grading criterion below.

Dream Report

- **Content/Unity.** The dream report vividly describes one of the writer's dreams.
- **Organization/Coherence.** The dream report is written in as sensible an order as possible. The reader is informed about inconsistencies in time or place.
- **Language/Style.** The dream report uses vivid and precise nouns, verbs, and modifiers.
- **Conventions.** The dream report avoids errors in spelling, grammar, usage, mechanics, and manuscript form.

GOALS/OBJECTIVES

Studying this lesson will enable students to

- have a positive experience reading a poem about the stages of life
- briefly explain what happens during growth and aging
- explain why imagination is an important function of the human mind
- define *allegory* and recognize allegories in their reading

ADDITIONAL RESOURCES

READER'S GUIDE

- Selection Worksheet, 2.3

ASSESSMENT PORTFOLIO

- Selection Check Test, 2.2.5
- Selection Test, 2.2.6

PRONUNCIATION EXERCISE

- Grade 8 Audiocassette, Side B, Track 8

CROSS-CURRICULAR CONNECTIONS

HEALTH

Encourage students to discuss the positive aspects of aging, such as the wisdom gained with experience, the opportunity of seeing their loved ones grow, and the opportunity to enjoy the fruits of their earlier labors. Students might also interview an older person they know to discover what this person has enjoyed about growing older.

SCIENCE

Students might use their imaginations to draw pictures of themselves when they were younger, as they are now, as they envision themselves as adults, and as they envision themselves when they are older.

Prereading

POEM

"The Song of Wandering Aengus"

by W. B. Yeats

Cross-curricular Connections

Health. Living things undergo two major processes during a lifetime. One is growth and the other is aging. During growth, the organism increases in size and efficiency. During aging, it decreases in size and efficiency. Changes in the makeup of cells, bones, and tissues are part of the aging process.

The processes of growing and aging are not yet fully understood. Some scientists believe that they never will be and, therefore, that aging in humans will never be controlled. Other scientists believe that aging can be controlled. They point out that certain kinds of fish, for example, continue to grow right up until they die. Also, single-celled animals that do not appear to age have been grown in laboratories. So far, however, scientists have been unable to keep human cells alive without aging. In this poem, the speaker talks about the aging process.

Science. Imagination is an important function of the human mind. Through imagination, people are able to expand their experiences, conceive new worlds and products, and bear difficult situations by thinking of alternatives. Imagination is also an important part of literature and other arts. Imagination sparks the minds of writers and other artists. Imagination is also essential to readers because it allows them to create in their minds written images or experiences. In "The Song of Wandering Aengus," the speaker's imagination burns and begins the speaker's journey.

As You Read

"The Song of Wandering Aengus" follows the different periods of the speaker's life. Each stanza represents the speaker's experience at a different age. In your journal, make a chart like the one below. As you read, fill in the chart with the actions and emotions of the speaker at each stage of his life.

	EMOTIONS	ACTIONS
youth		went to a hazel wood
adulthood		
old age		

AS YOU READ

Students may include the following details beside *youth:* emotions—excited and filled with wonder; actions—cut and peel a hazel wand, hook a berry to a thread, drop the berry in the stream, and catch a silver trout. Beside *adulthood* students might write the following details: emotions—restless, eager; actions—lay trout on floor, blow fire aflame, hear something rustling, watch trout turn into a girl who runs away. Beside *old age* students might write the following details: emotions—still determined, filled with love, contented; actions—wandering, searching for lost girl, walking among dappled grass, plucking silver and gold apples.

READER'S JOURNAL

What people and activities or events from your early childhood do you treasure? Have you ever felt a desire to return to previous experiences and relive them? Write your thoughts about these questions in your journal.

"The Song of Wandering Aengus[1]"

W. B. YEATS

I went out to the hazel wood,[2]
Because a fire was in my head,
And cut and peeled a hazel wand,
And hooked a berry to a thread;
And when white moths were on the wing,
And moth-like stars were flickering out,
I dropped the berry in a stream
And caught a little silver trout.

When I had laid it on the floor
I went to blow the fire aflame,
But something rustled on the floor,
And some one called me by my name:
It had become a glimmering girl
With apple blossom in her hair
Who called me by my name and ran
And faded through the brightening air.

Though I am old with wandering
Through hollow lands and hilly lands,
I will find out where she has gone,
And kiss her lips and take her hands;

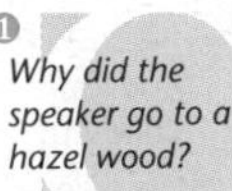
❶ *Why did the speaker go to a hazel wood?*

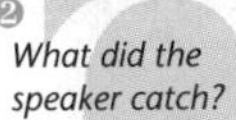
❷ *What did the speaker catch?*

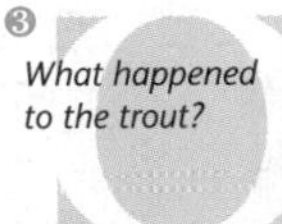
❸ *What happened to the trout?*

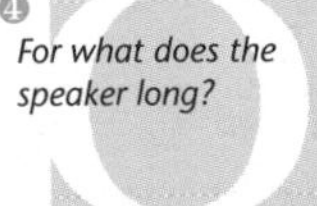
❹ *For what does the speaker long?*

1. **Aengus.** God of love in Celtic mythology
2. **hazel wood.** Woods made up of hazel trees from the birch family

READER'S JOURNAL

You might also encourage students to write about moments from their present lives that they think they might treasure or remember fondly later in life.

SPELLING AND VOCABULARY WORDS FROM THE SELECTION

dappled

ANSWERS TO GUIDED READING QUESTIONS

❶ The speaker went to a hazel wood because he had a fire in his head.

❷ The speaker caught a little silver trout.

❸ The trout rustled and became a glimmering girl with apple blossom in her hair.

❹ The speaker longs to find the girl again.

SUPPORT FOR LEP STUDENTS

PRONUNCIATIONS OF PROPER NOUNS AND ADJECTIVES

Yeats (yāts) n.
Aen • gus (āŋ´gəs) n.

IDIOM

on the wing—flying, or while in flight

ADDITIONAL VOCABULARY

brightening—growing brighter or lighter

Answer to Guided Reading Question

➊ The speaker will pluck the silver apples of the moon and the golden apples of the sun.

Selection Check Test with Answers

EX. Where did the speaker go first?
The speaker went to the hazel wood.

1. What does the speaker say he had in his head?
The speaker says he had a fire in his head.

2. What did the speaker catch?
The speaker caught a little silver trout.

3. What happened to this thing? What did this new thing do?
The trout rustled and became a glimmering girl who called the speaker's name and ran.

4. What is the speaker now determined to do?
The speaker is determined to find the girl.

5. What does the speaker say that he will do "till time and times are done"?
The speaker says that he will pick the silver apples of the moon and the golden apples of the sun.

What will the speaker do "till time and times are done"? ➊

And walk among long dappled grass,
And pluck till time and times are done
The silver apples of the moon,
The golden apples of the sun. ■

About the Author

William Butler (W. B.) Yeats (1865–1939) was an Irish poet and dramatist who won the Nobel Prize for literature in 1923. Yeats was born in Dublin and grew up in London and in County Sligo, Ireland. Yeats studied art before leaving school to pursue his writing. His writing was heavily influenced by traditional legends and myths. He was a leader in the Irish Literary Revival, a movement that helped rekindle the Irish culture by encouraging Irish authors.

Words for Everyday Use

dap • pled (dap´ əld) *adj.,* spotted

Vocabulary in Context

• The cow was white dappled with brown.

Responding to the Selection

How do you think the speaker feels about the actions and feelings of his younger days? How does he feel about the turns his life has taken? Explain your answers.

Reviewing the Selection

RECALLING AND INTERPRETING

1. (R) What reason does the speaker give for going to the hazel wood?

   (I) What does this reason suggest about the speaker's age and character?

2. (R) Into what does the trout change?

   (I) What effect does the trout's transformation have on the speaker's life?

3. (R) What verb tenses are used to open stanzas 1 and 2? What verb tense is used to open stanza 3?

   (I) What conclusion can be drawn about the present age of the speaker?

4. (R) What does the speaker want to do with the girl once he finds her again?

   (I) What is the speaker's attitude toward his search? toward aging?

SYNTHESIZING

5. Do you think the speaker will succeed in his quest? Why, or why not? Why is the speaker's search important to him at this stage in his life?

Understanding Literature (Questions for Discussion)

Allegory. An **allegory** is a literary work in which each part stands for, or symbolizes, something else. This poem is traditionally read as an allegory for a person's aging. How might this poem be an allegory for the creative process? What do you think the fire in the speaker's head symbolizes? What does the transformation of the fish symbolize? What does the quest of the aged speaker symbolize?

RESPONDING TO THE SELECTION

Students might also talk about what the trout symbolizes in a person's life. Might this creature symbolize time? dreams? hope? creativity?

ANSWERS FOR REVIEWING THE SELECTION

RECALLING AND INTERPRETING

1. **Recalling.** The speaker says that he went into a hazel wood because a fire was in his head. **Interpreting.** This reason suggests that the speaker was young and "burning" with youth, vitality, eagerness, and new ideas.
2. **Recalling.** The trout changes into a girl with apple blossom in her hair. **Interpreting.** The trout's transformation sparks the speaker's imagination and sends him on a quest.
3. **Recalling.** Stanzas 1 and 2 are opened by verbs in the past tense. Stanza 3 is opened with a verb in the present tense. **Interpreting.** The speaker is presently old.
4. **Recalling.** The speaker wants to kiss the girl and take her hand. **Interpreting.** The speaker is hopeful and still excited by his search. The speaker seems content to age, having enjoyed his journey through life. He seems to enjoy the thought of plucking silver and gold apples "till time and times are done."

SYNTHESIZING

Responses will vary. Possible responses are given.

5. The speaker's search is important to him because he finds it inspirational.

ANSWERS FOR UNDERSTANDING LITERATURE

Responses will vary. Possible responses are given.

1. **Allegory.** This poem might be an allegory for the creative process because in the creative process one gets a little glimmer of an idea, like the fish; this idea is transformed into something more wonderful, like the girl; and then one follows this creative idea until its completion. The fire in the speaker's head might symbolize sudden inspiration. The transformation of the fish may symbolize the birth of something wonderful from the original creative idea. The quest of the aged speaker might symbolize following through with this creative idea.

GOALS/OBJECTIVES

Studying this lesson will enable students to

- appreciate a poem that celebrates the power of imagination
- briefly explain the characteristics of rabbits
- explain which animals scientists consider the most intelligent
- define *personification* and recognize its use in a poem
- take both formal and informal notes

ADDITIONAL RESOURCES

READER'S GUIDE

- Selection Worksheet, 2.4

ASSESSMENT PORTFOLIO

- Selection Check Test, 2.2.7
- Selection Test, 2.2.8

PRONUNCIATION EXERCISE

- Grade 8 Audiocassette, Side B, Track 9

CROSS-CURRICULAR CONNECTIONS

SCIENCE

Students might choose an animal and write a poem or a brief short story from that animal's point of view. Students should focus on that animal's thoughts, fears, desires, and emotions. If students know little about the animal they have chosen, they should research the characteristics of the animal in an encyclopedia or natural history book. Tell students that it is important that they think of their animal as a speaker, narrator, or character with its own character traits and motives.

Prereading

POEM

"A Rabbit as King of the Ghosts"

by Wallace Stevens

Cross-curricular Connection

Science. Rabbits are a common type of rodent native to Europe, North and South America, Asia, and Africa. The rabbit has been introduced in New Zealand and Australia, where it has become populous enough to be a serious pest, destroying crops and grassland. Rabbits have long ears, short tails, and gray or brown fur. Females can bear many litters of two to eight young each year. Rabbits are hairless, blind, and defenseless at birth.

The rabbit in the selection you are about to read is concerned with a predator. Rabbits, indeed, have an extraordinary number of predators. They are a major source of food for many other animals. Humans hunt and raise rabbits for food and for their fur, which is used to make felt.

Although we see the intelligent and creative imagination of a rabbit in Stevens's poem, rabbits are not very intelligent. Scientists who study animal intelligence have determined that if an animal is highly intelligent, it will quickly learn to solve problems. It will also play with its young and, as an adult, try new experiences. After human beings, the most intelligent animals are apes, monkeys, dolphins, and whales. Next are cats, dogs, and other mammals that eat flesh, such as bears, tigers, and wolves. These predators show an ability to learn and to solve problems. Hoofed animals such as pigs, horses, and elephants can learn commands and signals, but pigs are the best problem solvers among this group. Rodents, such as rabbits, are even less intelligent, although they are able to solve problems that deal with finding pathways. The least intelligent animals are reptiles, fish, and animals without backbones. These creatures can learn to find food or to avoid pain, but not much else.

As You Read

"A Rabbit as King of the Ghosts" is a poem filled with vivid and unusual visual images. In your journal, make a chart like the one below. As you read, record the visual images that are given in the poem. Then in the right-hand column, write any personal responses, reflections, or ideas about the image.

IMAGES FROM THE POEM	PERSONAL RESPONSES
the cat slopping its milk	My cat is a slob when she drinks her milk—it gets all over her whiskers.

AS YOU READ

Students may include the following images in their charts: shapeless shadows covering the sun; fat cat, red tongue, green mind, white milk; monument of cat; grass and trees; red cat hiding away in the fur-light; the rabbit humped up high, black as stone; little green cat is a bug in the grass.

Students' personal responses to these images will vary.

READER'S JOURNAL

Imagine that you have the power to make any animal change in any way that you desire. What things would you change in the animal kingdom if you were in charge? Why would you make these changes? Describe what you would change and why in your journal.

"A Rabbit as King of the Ghosts"

WALLACE STEVENS

The difficulty to think at the end of day,
When the shapeless shadow covers the sun
And nothing is left except light on your fur—

There was the cat slopping its milk all day,
Fat cat, red tongue, green mind, white milk
And August the most peaceful month.

To be, in the grass, in the peacefullest time,
Without that monument of cat,
The cat forgotten in the moon;

And to feel that the light is a rabbit-light,
In which everything is meant for you
and nothing need be explained;

Then there is nothing to think of. It comes of itself;
And east rushes west and west rushes down,
No matter. The grass is full

And full of yourself. The trees around are for you,
The whole of the wideness of night is for you,
A self that touches all edges,

❶ *How might a rabbit feel about cats? Why?*

❷ *What makes this moment peaceful?*

❸ *How does the rabbit start to feel at this time of day?*

WORDS FOR EVERYDAY USE

slop (släp) *v.*, spill or splash
mon • u • ment (män´yo͞o mənt) *n.*, statue or pillar

READER'S JOURNAL

As an alternative activity, you might ask students to write about a time when they were younger and were frightened of something. Of what were they frightened? Was it something real or something in their imaginations? Did they ever try imagining that this frightening thing was conquered or vanquished in some way?

SPELLING AND VOCABULARY WORDS FROM THE SELECTION

monument
slop

ANSWERS TO GUIDED READING QUESTIONS

❶ A rabbit might feel frightened of cats because cats often hunt rabbits.

❷ This moment is peaceful because the "monument of cat" is forgotten in the moon.

❸ The rabbit starts to feel more at ease and confident.

SUPPORT FOR LEP STUDENTS

ADDITIONAL VOCABULARY

rush—hurry

VOCABULARY IN CONTEXT

- After the rainstorm, the children ran outside to slop about in the mud.
- One of the most impressive monuments we saw in Washington, DC, was the Lincoln Memorial.

ANSWER TO GUIDED READING QUESTION

❶ The rabbit imagines that the cat is a bug in the grass.

SELECTION CHECK TEST WITH ANSWERS

EX. What does the cat do all day?
The cat slops its milk all day.

1. According to the rabbit, what does the cat look like?
According to the rabbit, the cat is fat, has a red tongue, a green mind, and is associated with white milk.

2. For the rabbit, what is the most peaceful month?
August is the most peaceful month.

3. What does the rabbit feel about the grass and trees?
The rabbit feels that the grass is full of himself or herself and that the trees belong to it.

4. Where does the red cat hide away?
The red cat hides away in the fur-light.

5. What is the little green cat?
The little green cat is a bug in the grass.

You become a self that fills the four corners of night.
The red cat hides away in the fur-light
And there you are humped high, humped up,

You are humped higher and higher, black as stone—
You sit with your head like a carving in space
And the little green cat is a bug in the grass. ■

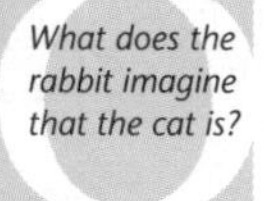

❶ *What does the rabbit imagine that the cat is?*

About the Author

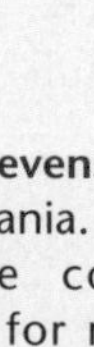

Wallace Stevens (1879–1955) was born in Reading, Pennsylvania. He became a lawyer and worked as an insurance company executive in Hartford, Connecticut, for many years. Although his daily life seemed very conventional and ordinary, Stevens wrote rich, imaginative poetry. Few of his colleagues knew about Stevens's poetic talent. Most of the recognition for Stevens's writing came late in his life and after his death. Many of his poems celebrate the human imagination. In 1955, Stevens won the Pulitzer prize for his *Collected Poems.*

Responding to the Selection

What do you think of the rabbit's imagination? If you were the rabbit, in what way would you imagine the cat? If you were feeling frightened, would you imagine the cat differently than you would when you were feeling self-confident? Describe how your image of the cat would change in different situations.

Reviewing the Selection

Recalling and Interpreting

1. **R** What time of day is it in stanza 1? In what way is the cat described in stanza 2?

   I How do you think the rabbit feels at the end of the day? From the rabbit's description, how do you think the rabbit feels about the cat? What do you think a "green mind" might be like?

2. **R** In stanza 3, what makes this moment in the grass peaceful? What does the speaker say about the light in stanza 4?

   I Why might the rabbit be able to forget about the cat at this time of day? What might a "rabbit-light" be? Why might the rabbit feel so at ease?

3. **R** In stanza 5, what does the speaker say about east? about west?

   I What natural phenomenon might the speaker be describing? What rushes from east to west and then goes down in the west?

4. **R** In stanza 6, what does the speaker say about night? In stanzas 7 and 8, in what way is the rabbit described? In what two ways is the cat described?

   I In what way do the traditional roles of the cat and the rabbit change at night? Why might the rabbit imagine the cat in this way at night?

Synthesizing

5. What message about imagination do you see in this poem? Why might imagining the world in a different way have a positive effect on one's mental and emotional state? Can imagining ever be dangerous? If so, why? If not, why not?

Understanding Literature (Questions for Discussion)

Personification. Personification is a figure of speech in which something not human is described as if it were human. What is being personified in this poem? What human characteristics are used to personify it? What creature is not personified in this poem? Why isn't this thing personified?

Answers for Understanding Literature

Responses will vary. Possible responses are given.

Personification. The rabbit is personified. It is attributed with intelligence and an imagination. The cat is not personified because it is portrayed as the evil-minded but unintelligent enemy of the rabbit.

Responding to the Selection

You might also ask students to think about which images of the cat are the most frightening to the rabbit. Why does the final image of the cat make the rabbit feel most confident?

Answers for Reviewing the Selection

RECALLING AND INTERPRETING

1. **Recalling.** It is the end of the day. The cat is described as slopping white milk. The cat is fat and has a red tongue and a green mind. **Interpreting.** Students may say that the rabbit may be tired after running from the cat all day. The rabbit thinks the cat is evil. A "green mind" might be full of malice.

2. **Recalling.** The moment in the grass is peaceful because the cat is temporarily forgotten. The speaker says that the light is a "rabbit-light,/In which everything is meant for you." **Interpreting.** The rabbit may be able to forget about the cat because the cat is home for the night. A "rabbit-light" might be the time of day when the rabbit feels most at ease.

3. **Recalling.** The speaker says that east rushes west and west rushes down. **Interpreting.** The speaker might be describing the sun, which rushes from east to west and sets in the west.

4. **Recalling.** The speaker says that the "whole wideness of the night is for you." The rabbit is described as humped up high and black as stone. The cat is described as red and hiding in the fur-light. and as a little green bug in the grass. **Interpreting.** The cat is now hiding from the rabbit. The rabbit might imagine the cat as something small and scared and itself as something large like a stone "monument" because the rabbit is feeling at ease and is dreaming of the way it would like things to be.

SYNTHESIZING

Responses will vary. Possible responses are given.

5. Imagination can help people bear difficult situations by offering alternatives. It might make one feel more relaxed and happier about life. Students might say that too much daydreaming can be dangerous. For example, if the rabbit spent all its time daydreaming, the cat might catch it.

STUDY AND RESEARCH SKILLS

INTRODUCING THE SKILL

Inform students that taking good informal notes will aid their comprehension in class. Students will perform better on tests when they take good notes and review them carefully. Tell students that formal note-taking is essential when preparing a research report. If students take good notes as they research, they will be able to keep track of important facts and better organize their report.

PREVIEWING THE SKILL

Have students review the teaching. If necessary, have them review the Language Arts Survey, 4.7, "Taking Notes," and 4.20, "Formal Note-taking," as well. Point out that when taking formal notes students should prepare bibliography cards and number them. These numbers are the ones that they will use to identify the source of their notes. (For more information see the Language Arts Survey, 4.18, "Documenting Sources.")

PRACTICING THE SKILL

Once students seem familiar with the guidelines for taking both formal and informal notes, have students do the Try It Yourself exercises.

REVIEWING THE SKILL

If students need additional practice, have them do the Try It Yourself exercises in the Language Arts Survey, 4.7, "Taking Notes," and 4.20, "Formal Note-taking."

Study and Research Skills

Taking Notes

When you are gathering information it is helpful to take notes. When you take notes in class or when you read a homework assignment, you should take **informal notes.** When you are preparing a research report or a speech, you should take **formal notes,** because you will need to quote from and document your sources. For more information on note-taking, review the Language Arts Survey, 4.7, "Taking Notes," and 4.20, "Formal Note-taking."

Read the paragraph below. Sheila took both informal notes and formal notes on this paragraph. Notice that in her informal notes, she uses a modified outline form, does not use complete sentences, and uses abbreviations whenever possible. In her formal notes, Sheila uses complete sentences, directly quotes sources, and documents her sources. (See the Language Arts Survey, 4.18, "Documenting Sources," and 4.19, "Paraphrasing and Summarizing.") In her formal notes, Sheila uses a separate card for each quotation, fact, or summary.

The Great Wall of China is one of the longest structures ever built. It is about four hundred miles long, stretching over mountains and hills. It was built entirely by hand and is made of brick and stone. It was built as protection against invaders.

(page 137, Julie Doe, *Chinese History*)

Informal

Size of the Great Wall of China
—Longest structure ever built
—Abt. 400 mi. long
—Built entirely by hand
—Made of brick & stone

Formal

The Great Wall of China 4

"The Great Wall of China is one of the longest structures ever built. It is about four hundred miles long, stretching over mountains and hills."

p. 137

The following are some tips for informal note-taking:

TIPS FOR INFORMAL NOTE-TAKING

1. Use a modified outline form like that shown in the student model.
2. Write main ideas beginning at the left margin, introduced by a dash.
3. Write details or lesser ideas beneath the main ideas. Indent these ideas and introduce them with a dash.
4. Write notes as phrases, not complete sentences. Feel free to leave out unnecessary small words such as *a, an,* and *the.*
5. Use symbols and abbreviations. Make sure that the abbreviations are ones that you will be able to interpret later.

The following are some guidelines for formal note-taking:

GUIDELINES FOR FORMAL NOTE-TAKING

1. Identify the source of your note at the top right corner of the card. Use the source number from your bibliography cards. (See the Language Arts Survey, 4.18, "Documenting Sources.")
2. Identify the subject or the topic of the note card on the top line of the card. This will help you to organize the cards later.
3. Use a separate card for each quotation, fact, or summary. (See the Language Arts Survey, 4.19, "Paraphrasing and Summarizing.")
4. Write the page number or numbers after the note.

Try It Yourself

Exercise A. Take informal notes on the following paragraph:

Many protective walls have been built throughout the years in China, starting in about 600 BC. Different rulers would add to these walls and repair those that were damaged. Most of the Great Wall that we see today was built by the Ming dynasty in the 1400s AD as a defense against a Mongol invasion. Although the wall was built as protection against invaders, it was unable to repel major attacks. In the modern day, much repair work has been done on the Great Wall. Today, however, the wall's purpose is not to repel invaders, but to attract tourists.

(page 138, Julie Doe, *Chinese History*)

Exercise B. Using proper form, and remembering to use only one note card for each quotation, fact, or summary, take formal notes on the above paragraph.

ANSWERS FOR TRY IT YOURSELF

EXERCISE A

Responses will vary. Possible responses are given.

The building of the Great Wall
—many walls built from 600 BC on
  —different rulers would add to and repair walls
—most built by Ming dyn. @ 1400 AD
—built to protect agst. invaders
  —unable to repel maj. attacks
—today has been repaired
  —to attract tourists

EXERCISE B

Students' formal notes should include only one fact, summary, or quotation on each note card. Students' note cards should contain the following elements: a number in the upper right corner identifying the source; a subject or topic identified on the top line of the card; and a page number after the note.

GOALS/OBJECTIVES

Studying this lesson will enable students to

- have a positive experience reading an ironic short story
- briefly explain early flying devices
- briefly describe the importance of kites in China
- define *exposition* and recognize the setting, major characters, and mood an exposition introduces
- define *irony of situation* and recognize the use of this technique in works that they read

ADDITIONAL RESOURCES

READER'S GUIDE

- Selection Worksheet, 2.5

ASSESSMENT PORTFOLIO

- Selection Check Test, 2.2.9
- Selection Test, 2.2.10

PRONUNCIATION EXERCISE

- Grade 8 Audiocassette, Side B, Track 10

CROSS-CURRICULAR CONNECTIONS

SCIENCE AND APPLIED ARTS

Students might enjoy one of the following activities:

- Students might research early means of flight, such as hot air balloons and gliders, focusing on how these means of flight worked.
- Students might research historical figures renowned for their contributions to human flight. Possibilities include Orville and Wilbur Wright, Charles Lindbergh, and Amelia Earhart.
- Students might design and create their own kites and display them in class.

Prereading

SHORT FICTION

"The Flying Machine"
by Ray Bradbury

Cross-curricular Connection

Science and Applied Arts. Humans have long been fascinated with flight. Science fiction writers popularized the idea of human flight before the possibility was realistic. The earliest human attempts to fly were based on observations of birds and centered on creating flapping, winglike structures. The first successful human flight was by means of a balloon. Further successes in flight studies were made by people who experimented with models, gliders, and kites.

The kite is a device made of paper or fabric stretched over a light wooden framework. A kite is tied to string and flown in the air. There are two versions of how the kite was invented. One story says that it was invented by an ancient Greek named Archytas sometime between 400 and 300 BC. The other story says that the kite was invented in ancient China in 206 BC by a general named Han Sin for use in war.

People in China still celebrate Kites' Day on the ninth day of the ninth month. Thousands of kites of every imaginable shape, color, and size are flown. Kites shaped like fish, dragons, butterflies, and birds fill the sky. Kites' Day in China comes from an old legend. The legend tells the story of a man who dreamed that something bad was going to happen to him and his family on a certain day. On that day, he took his family out to fly kites. When the family returned, they found that their house had been destroyed. The kite-flying celebration of Kites' Day is in honor of the man's family being saved. Each kite is believed to make evils disappear for the kite flyer.

People in Asian countries like China, Japan, and Korea have been making and flying interesting kites for centuries. The story you are about to read is set in motion by an ancient Chinese kite.

As You Read

"The Flying Machine" is a story with some surprising twists and turns. You may find it helpful to track the major events in the order in which they happen. Make a chart like the one below. As you read, fill in the chart with the events from the story.

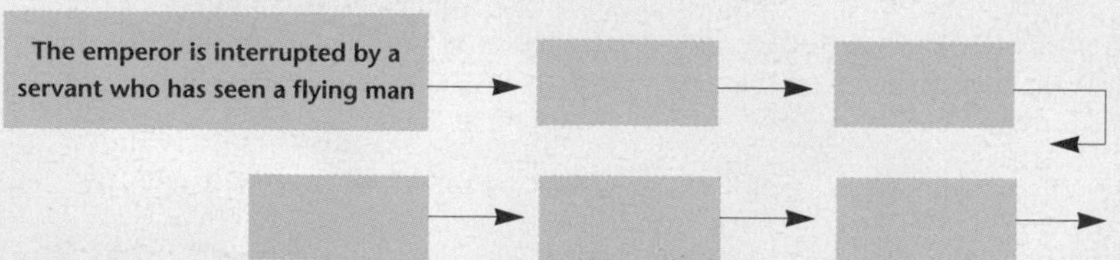

AS YOU READ

Students may include the following events on their charts: the emperor makes the servant sit and have tea with him; the emperor and the servant go to observe the flying man; the emperor orders the flying man to come down; the emperor has the flying man go with him back to the great house; the emperor orders the man executed; the flying man asks why and the emperor explains his reasons; the executioner kills the man; the emperor orders his servant to hold his tongue about the flying machine he has observed; the emperor sits with his mechanical garden and admires the tiny birds.

READER'S JOURNAL

Have you ever imagined what it would be like to fly? How would it feel? What would you want to see? What would be the positive aspects of being able to fly? the negative aspects? Write about these questions in your journal.

"The Flying Machine"

RAY BRADBURY

In the year AD 400, the Emperor Yuan held his throne by the Great Wall of China,[1] and the land was green with rain, readying itself toward the harvest, at peace, the people in his dominion neither too happy nor too sad.

Early on the morning of the first day of the first week of the second month of the new year, the Emperor Yuan was sipping tea and fanning himself against a warm breeze when a servant ran across the scarlet and blue garden tiles, calling, "Oh, Emperor, Emperor, a miracle!"

"Yes," said the Emperor, "the air is sweet this morning."

"No, no, a miracle!" said the servant, bowing quickly.

"And this tea is good in my mouth, surely that is a miracle."

"No, no, Your Excellency."

"Let me guess then—the sun has risen and a new day is upon us. Or the sea is blue. That now is the finest of all miracles."

"Excellency, a man is flying!"

"What?" The Emperor stopped his fan.

"I saw him in the air, a man flying with wings. I heard a voice call out of the sky, and when I looked up, there he was, a dragon in the heavens with a man in its mouth, a dragon of paper and bamboo, colored like the sun and the grass."

"It is early," said the Emperor, "and you have just wakened from a dream."

"It is early, but I have seen what I have seen! Come, and you will see it, too."

"Sit down with me here," said the Emperor. "Drink some tea. It must be a strange thing, if it is true, to see a man fly. You must have time

1. **Great Wall of China.** Stone and earth wall built in the third century BC across northern China to keep out foreign invaders

❶ *What amazing thing has the servant seen?*

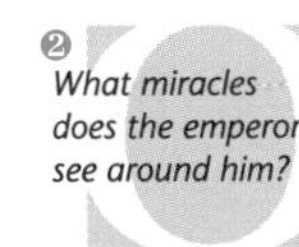

❷ *What miracles does the emperor see around him?*

WORDS FOR EVERYDAY USE

do • min • ion (də min′yən) *n.,* governed territory or country

READER'S JOURNAL

Students also might want to consider whether it would be more interesting to fly in a plane or to be able to fly like a bird does. Why? Which would be more comfortable? more difficult? more rewarding? more exciting?

SPELLING AND VOCABULARY WORDS FROM THE SELECTION

alight	merciful
apparatus	seize
bewilder	solace
dominion	vision
horde	writhe
lope	

ANSWERS TO GUIDED READING QUESTIONS

❶ The servant has seen a man flying.

❷ The emperor sees sweet air, good tea, the rising of the sun and the beginning of a new day, and the blue sea as miracles.

SUPPORT FOR LEP STUDENTS

PRONUNCIATIONS OF PROPER NOUNS AND ADJECTIVES

Yuan (yo͞o än′) n.

ADDITIONAL VOCABULARY

bamboo—light, woody stem of a type of plant
majesty—stateliness, dignity
nestled—settled down comfortably
pelts—skins of fur-bearing animals
serene—calm, peaceful
sorrowful—full of sadness

VOCABULARY IN CONTEXT

• At one time Rome's dominion stretched to the west as far as England.

Answers to Guided Reading Questions

❶ *Responses will vary.* Students might say the Emperor is curious to see if such a thing is possible.

❷ The man says that he has flown in the sky. No, the emperor is not satisfied with this response.

Literary Technique

Image and Simile

An **image** is language that describes something that can be seen, heard, touched, tasted, or smelled. A **simile** is a comparison using *like* or *as*. Ask students the following questions: What images are presented of the man and his apparatus while flying? To what senses do these images appeal? What emotions do these images create? What images are presented of the man and his apparatus once he alights? To what senses do these images appeal? What similes are used to describe the flying man and his apparatus?

Answers

The images of the man while flying are "And in the sky, laughing so high that you could hardly hear him laugh, was a man; and the man was clothed in bright paper and reeds to make wings and a beautiful yellow tail, and he was soaring all about" and "the flying man soared down the morning wind." These images appeal to the senses of sight and sound. These images create emotions of joy and exuberance. The images of the man once he alights are "rustle of paper and creak of bamboo reeds," "he came proudly to the Emperor, clumsy in his rig," and "pretty paper and birdlike keel . . . smelled cool, of the wind." These images appeal to the senses of sight, sound, and smell. The flying man and his apparatus are compared to "the largest bird in a universe of birds" and to "a new dragon in a land of ancient dragons."

to think of it, even as I must have time to prepare myself for the sight."

They drank tea.

"Please," said the servant at last, "or he will be gone."

❶ *Why do you think the emperor wants to see the flier?*

The Emperor rose thoughtfully. "Now you may show me what you have seen."

They walked into a garden, across a meadow of grass, over a small bridge, through a grove of trees, and up a tiny hill.

"There!" said the servant.

The Emperor looked into the sky.

And in the sky, laughing so high that you could hardly hear him laugh, was a man; and the man was clothed in bright papers and reeds to make wings and a beautiful yellow tail, and he was soaring all about like the largest bird in a universe of birds, like a new dragon in a land of ancient dragons.

❷ *What does the man say he has done? Is the emperor satisfied with his response?*

The man called down to them from high in the cool winds of morning, "I fly, I fly!"

The servant waved to him. "Yes, yes!"

The Emperor Yuan did not move. Instead he looked at the Great Wall of China now taking shape out of the farthest mist in the green hills, that splendid snake of stones which writhed with majesty across the entire land. That wonderful wall which had protected them for a timeless time from enemy hordes and preserved peace for years without number. He saw the town, nestled to itself by a river and a road and a hill, beginning to waken.

"Tell me," he said to his servant, "has anyone else seen this flying man?"

"I am the only one, Excellency," said the servant, smiling at the sky, waving.

The Emperor watched the heavens another minute and then said, "Call him down to me."

"Ho, come down, come down! The Emperor wishes to see you!" called the servant, hands cupped to his shouting mouth.

The Emperor glanced in all directions while the flying man soared down the morning wind. He saw a farmer, early in his fields, watching the sky, and he noted where the farmer stood.

The flying man alit with a rustle of paper and a creak of bamboo reeds. He came proudly to the Emperor, clumsy in his rig, at last bowing before the old man.

"What have you done?" demanded the Emperor.

"I have flown in the sky, Your Excellency," replied the man.

"What have you done?" said the Emperor again.

"I have just told you!" cried the flier.

"You have told me nothing at all." The Emperor reached out a thin hand to touch the pretty paper and the birdlike keel[2] of the apparatus. It smelled cool, of the wind.

"Is it not beautiful, Excellency?"

"Yes, too beautiful."

"It is the only one in the world!" smiled the man. "And I am the inventor."

"The only one in the world?"

"I swear it!"

2. **keel.** Assembly of pieces at the bottom of an airship to prevent sagging

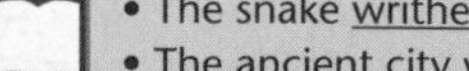

Words for Everyday Use

writhe (rīth) *v.,* twist or turn

horde (hôrd) *n.,* large tribe or group

a • light (ə līt´) *v.,* come down [past tense: alit]

ap • pa • ra • tus (ap´ə rat´əs) *n.,* any complex machine used for a specific purpose

Vocabulary in Context

- The snake writhed through the undergrowth.
- The ancient city was looted by a horde of vandals.
- Through my binoculars, I saw the kingfisher alight on the branch of a tree.
- A loom is a complex and bulky apparatus.

"Who else knows of this?"

"No one. Not even my wife, who would think me mad with the sun. She thought I was making a kite. I rose in the night and walked to the cliffs far away. And when the morning breezes blew and the sun rose, I gathered my courage, Excellency, and leaped from the cliff. I flew! But my wife does not know of it."

"Well for her, then," said the Emperor. "Come along."

They walked back to the great house. The sun was full in the sky now, and the smell of the grass was refreshing. The Emperor, the servant, and the flier paused within the huge garden.

The Emperor clapped his hands. "Ho, guards!"

The guards came running.

"Hold this man."

The guards seized the flier.

"Call the executioner," said the Emperor.

Words for Everyday Use

seize (sēz) *v.,* take by force

Additional Questions and Activities

Ask students the following questions: What do you think the emperor means by his repeated question "What have you done?" Does he really want to know what the man has done, or does he say this for another reason? What does the emperor mean by saying that the apparatus is "too beautiful"? Why do you think the emperor asks if anyone else knows about the flying apparatus? When did you first predict that the emperor is plotting against the flying man?

Answers

Responses will vary. Possible responses are given.

The emperor means how could the man have dared to do such an outrageous thing. No, the emperor is expressing his shock at what the man has done, rather than asking him how he accomplished this feat. The emperor means that it is too beautiful to have been created. The emperor asks if anyone else knows about the flying apparatus to determine whether killing the man alone will be enough or whether he will have to track down others as well.

Vocabulary in Context

- The child seized another child's toy and would not give it back.

Answers to Guided Reading Questions

1 The flying man's invention is similar to the emperor's in that both allow their creators to see a tiny world spread out below them. The flying man's invention, however, shows him the real world and gives him freedom, while the emperor's invention is merely a mechanical miniature of the world.

2 The emperor orders that the flying man be executed because he is concerned that someone evil might see the flying man, create a similar device, and use it for evil purposes.

Quotables

"He who has imagination without learning has wings but no feet."

—Joseph Joubert

"The human race is governed by its imagination."

—Napoleon Bonaparte

Literary Technique

CHARACTER

A **character** is a person or animal who takes part in the action of a literary work. Encourage students to describe the emperor's character in their own words. What do they think of the emperor?

ANSWERS

Students may say that the emperor appreciates beauty and at first seems gracious and civilized, but he acts like a tyrant and ruthlessly orders the flying man killed merely for creating something beautiful.

"What's this!" cried the flier, bewildered. "What have I done?" He began to weep, so that the beautiful paper apparatus rustled.

1 Is the flying man's invention similar to the emperor's invention? Why, or why not?

"Here is the man who has made a certain machine," said the Emperor, "and yet asks us what he has created. He does not know himself. It is only necessary that he create, without knowing why he has done so, or what this thing will do."

The executioner came running with a sharp silver ax. He stood with his naked, large-muscled arms ready, his face covered with a serene white mask.

"One moment," said the Emperor. He turned to a nearby table upon which sat a machine that he himself had created. The Emperor took a tiny golden key from his own neck. He fitted this key to the tiny, delicate machine and wound it up. Then he set the machine going.

The machine was a garden of metal and jewels. Set in motion, birds sang in tiny metal trees, wolves walked through miniature forests, and tiny people ran in and out of sun and shadow, fanning themselves with miniature fans, listening to the tiny emerald birds, and standing by impossibly small but tinkling fountains.

2 Why does the emperor order the flying man to be executed?

"Is it not beautiful?" said the Emperor. "If you asked me what I have done here, I could answer you well. I have made birds sing, I have made forests murmur, I have set people to walking in this woodland, enjoying the leaves and shadows and songs. That is what I have done."

"But, oh, Emperor!" pleaded the flier, on his knees, the tears pouring down his face. "I have done a similar thing! I have found beauty. I have flown on the morning wind. I have looked down on all the sleeping houses and gardens. I have smelled the sea and even seen it, beyond the hills, from my high place. And I have soared like a bird; oh, I cannot say how beautiful it is up there, in the sky, with the wind about me, the wind blowing me here like a feather, there like a fan, the way the sky smells in the morning! And how free one feels! *That* is beautiful, Emperor, that is beautiful, too!"

"Yes," said the Emperor sadly, "I know it must be true. For I felt my heart move with you in the air and I wondered: What is it like? How does it feel? How do the distant pools look from so high? And how my houses and servants? Like ants? And how the distant towns not yet awake?"

"Then spare me!"

"But there are times," said the Emperor, more sadly still, "when one must lose a little beauty if one is to keep what little beauty one already has. I do not fear you, yourself, but I fear another man."

"What man?"

"Some other man who, seeing you, will build a thing of bright papers and bamboo like this. But the other man will have an evil face and an evil heart, and the beauty will be gone. It is this man I fear."

"Why? Why?"

Words for Everyday Use

be • wil • der (bē wil´dər) *v.*, confuse; puzzle

Vocabulary in Context

- The fun house's many different twists and turns bewildered Jimmy.

"Who is to say that someday just such a man, in just such an apparatus of paper and reed, might not fly in the sky and drop huge stones upon the Great Wall of China?" said the Emperor.

No one moved or said a word.

"Off with his head," said the Emperor.

The executioner whirled his silver ax.

"Burn the kite and the inventor's body and bury their ashes together," said the Emperor.

The servants retreated to obey.

The Emperor turned to his hand-servant, who had seen the man flying. "Hold your tongue. It was all a dream, a most sorrowful and beautiful dream. And that farmer in the distant field who saw, tell him it would pay him to consider it only a vision. If ever the word passes around, you and the farmer die within the hour."

"You are merciful, Emperor."

"No, not merciful," said the old man. Beyond the garden wall he saw the guards burning the beautiful machine of paper and reeds that

Words for Everyday Use

vi • sion (vizh´ən) *n.,* something seen in a dream or a trance

mer • ci • ful (mʉr´si fəl) *adj.,* full of mercy; showing or having feeling

Additional Questions and Activities

Ask students the following questions: Which would you prefer to do—look at a miniature, mechanical world or look at the real world from high above as the flying man did? Why might the emperor be jealous of the flying man? What reason does the emperor give for having the flying man killed? Do you think that this is his only reason, or might the emperor have another reason?

ANSWERS

Responses will vary. Possible responses are given.

Students may say that they would prefer to see the real world as the flying man did. The emperor might be jealous because he is a great appreciator of beauty and the flying man has seen a beautiful thing that the emperor will probably never be able to see. The emperor says that he is killing the flying man so that an evil man will not build a similar contraption and drop huge stones on the Great Wall of China. The emperor might also be motivated by jealousy.

Vocabulary in Context

- Having heard about the benefits of positive thinking, Ralph tried to create a mental vision of himself winning the big game.
- The judge was merciful and gave the defendant a light sentence.

Answer to Guided Reading Question

➊ The emperor takes solace in the fact that he has ended one life to save millions of others.

Selection Check Test with Answers

EX. What is Emperor Yuan doing at the beginning of the story?
Emperor Yuan is drinking tea and fanning himself.

1. What does the emperor's servant tell him?
The emperor's servant tells him that a man is flying.

2. After he sees the flying man what does the emperor order his servant to do?
He orders his servant to call the flying man down.

3. What orders does the emperor give about the flying man?
The emperor orders that the executioner kill the flying man.

4. What has the emperor made?
The emperor has made a mechanical garden of metal and jewels.

5. Why does the emperor order the flying man to be killed?
The emperor ordered the flying man to be killed because he is afraid that someone may use the flying man's invention to destroy the Great Wall of China.

smelled of the morning wind. He saw the dark smoke climb into the sky. "No, only very much bewildered and afraid." He saw the guards digging a tiny pit wherein to bury the ashes. "What is the life of one man against those of a million others? I must take solace from that thought."

In what thought does the emperor take solace? Why does this idea comfort him? ➊

He took the key from its chain about his neck and once more wound up the beautiful miniature garden. He stood looking out across the land at the Great Wall, the peaceful town, the green fields, the rivers and streams. He sighed. The tiny garden whirred its hidden and delicate machinery and set itself in motion; tiny people walked in forests, tiny foxes loped through sun-speckled glades in beautiful shining pelts, and among the tiny trees flew little bits of high song and bright blue and yellow color flying, flying, flying in that small sky.

"Oh," said the Emperor, closing his eyes, "look at the birds, look at the birds!" ■

About the Author

Ray Bradbury (1920–) is a highly respected writer of science fiction and fantasy. His short stories and novels are lyrical, poetic, and fanciful but address serious themes. Themes that recur in his works include the value of individuality over conformity and modern society's overdependence on machines and technology. Bradbury was born in Waukegan, Illinois. He has published many collections of short stories, including *The Martian Chronicles* and *The Illustrated Man,* and several novels, including *Fahrenheit 451* and *Something Wicked This Way Comes.*

Words for Everyday Use

so • lace (säl´is) *n.,* something that gives comfort or relief
lope (lōp) *v.,* move along easily and quickly

Vocabulary in Context

- During exam time, John took solace in the fact that everyone else was just as busy as he.
- The deer loped through the tranquil spring glade.

Responding to the Selection

The emperor tells the inventor, "I do not fear you . . . , but I fear another man. . . . the other man will have an evil face and an evil heart, and the beauty will be gone." Do you agree with the emperor's views of humanity? Why, or why not? Do you think the emperor is wise to destroy the flying machine and its creator? Explain your answer.

Reviewing the Selection

RECALLING AND INTERPRETING

1. (R) What things does the emperor consider to be miracles? What is the emperor's response when he learns what the servant has seen?

   (I) Why are the things the emperor mentions miracles? Why do you think the emperor reacts in this way?

2. (R) What has the Great Wall of China done for Emperor Yuan's people?

   (I) What do you think is the emperor's attitude toward the Wall?

3. (R) In the emperor's mind, what requirements does the flying man's invention fail to satisfy?

   (I) In what way does the emperor's own creation satisfy his requirements?

4. (R) What fear causes the emperor to have the flying man executed?

   (I) Will the emperor's actions assure that his fears will not come to pass? Explain.

SYNTHESIZING

5. The emperor winds up his miniature garden and says, "Look at the birds, look at the birds!" Yet, he has his eyes closed. What does this suggest about the emperor's approach to life? What other people or inventions might the emperor fear?

Understanding Literature (Questions for Discussion)

1. **Exposition.** The **exposition** is the part of a plot that introduces the setting and the major characters. What setting is described in the first two paragraphs? What characters are introduced? What is the mood of these two paragraphs?
2. **Irony of Situation.** An event that contradicts the expectations of the characters, the reader, or the audience of a literary work is an example of **irony of situation.** What expectations did you have that were contradicted?

RESPONDING TO THE SELECTION

You might ask students to discuss whether or not the emperor has to take a cautious and negative view of humanity to help protect his people.

ANSWERS FOR REVIEWING THE SELECTION

RECALLING AND INTERPRETING

1. **Recalling.** The emperor considers the sweet air, the good tea, the sunrise and the new day, and the blue sea to be miracles. The emperor asks the servant to sit down and have some tea. **Interpreting.** These things are miracles because they are part of the wonder and beauty of the natural world. The emperor may react this way to give himself time to decide what to do about the flying man.

2. **Recalling.** The Great Wall has protected the emperor's people and preserved peace "for years without number." **Interpreting.** The emperor probably is proud of and thankful for the wall and hopes to preserve it at all costs.

3. **Recalling.** The flying man is unable to explain what he has done by creating his invention. He does not know what the effects of his creation will be in the future. **Interpreting.** The emperor knows what he has done by creating the metal garden.

4. **Recalling.** The emperor has the flying man killed because he is afraid that someone might see the flying man and his apparatus, create a similar device, and use it to drop large stones upon the Great Wall of China. **Interpreting.** No, other people might independently come up with a similar invention because it is impossible to stop humans from imagining and creating things.

SYNTHESIZING

Responses will vary. Possible responses are given.

5. It suggests that the emperor does not look realistically at things and is influenced mainly by his own internal perceptions. The emperor may fear anything that might threaten the tranquility of his realm.

ANSWERS FOR UNDERSTANDING LITERATURE

Responses will vary. Possible responses are given.

1. **Exposition.** The setting is Emperor Yuan's garden in China in the morning of the first day of the first week of the second month of the new year in AD 400. The emperor and the servant are introduced. The mood is one of serenity and tranquility until the servant interrupts this mood.

2. **Irony of Situation.** Students may say that they expected the emperor to admire the flying man and his creation, not destroy them.

GOALS/OBJECTIVES

Studying this lesson will enable students to

- enjoy a piece of short fiction in which a young speaker imagines her future life
- briefly explain who Jane Addams was
- explain the services that Hull House has provided in the past and that it provides today
- define *motivation* and explain a character's motivations
- define *tone* and identify a speaker's attitude toward his or her subject

ADDITIONAL RESOURCES

Reader's Guide

- Selection Worksheet, 2.6

Assessment Portfolio

- Selection Check Test, 2.2.11
- Selection Test, 2.2.12

Pronunciation Exercise

- Grade 8 Audiocassette, Side B, Track 11

CROSS-CURRICULAR CONNECTIONS

American History

Encourage students to discuss ways in which they might help people who are less fortunate. As a class, you might research local volunteer groups to discover what services they provide for the community. Encourage students to volunteer their time at one of these groups or to organize a food drive or clothing drive to help others. Students might also be interested in forming a group to read to children in a local hospital or to people in local convalescent homes.

Prereading

SHORT FICTION

"Bums in the Attic" from *The House on Mango Street* by Sandra Cisneros

Cross-curricular Connection

American History. Many countries around the world have tried to institute government reforms and create laws to help people with no housing and little or no money. However, individuals have also made many noble efforts to help disadvantaged people. One such individual was Jane Addams (1860–1935), an American social worker who won the Nobel Peace Prize in 1931.

In the late 1800s, a large number of people of all races and religions immigrated to the United States. Many of these people arrived in the United States with little money and soon found themselves in terrible living conditions. In 1889, Jane Addams founded Hull House in Chicago to help these immigrants. Known as a settlement house, Hull House was a kind of neighborhood center. Jane Addams's Hull House offered people in Chicago programs that helped to improve their living conditions. Hull House had day nurseries where working parents could leave their children. It also offered classroom instruction to help people improve their English, get jobs, and become American citizens. Hull House continues to serve people in Chicago. Today, there are over twenty Hull House Community Centers that offer child care, counseling, housing, and assistance for people in need.

Helping others was a lifelong project for Jane Addams. In the selection you are about to read, the main character decides to make helping others an important part of her life as well.

As You Read

In **"Bums in the Attic,"** the main character describes what people who live in houses on hills are like and what she hopes to be like when she grows up. Make a Venn diagram like the one below. As you read, write details about the people in houses on hills and the main character. Your details should show how the two are similar and how the two are different. Write the details in the appropriate places on the diagram.

People in Houses on Hills	Both	Main Character
have forgotten those "who live too much on earth"	people own homes, main character wants to own home	will never forget where she came from

AS YOU READ

In the part of the Venn diagram that describes how people in houses on hills are different, students might include the following details: do not look down except to be content to live on hills, have nothing to do with garbage or rats, and are never woken by anything but the wind. In the part of the Venn diagram that shows similarities between people in houses on hills and the main character, students might write that both will sit in front of fires with guests after dinner. In the part of the Venn diagram that describes how the main character is different, students might write that the narrator will offer her attic to bums and tell her guests about the bums.

READER'S JOURNAL

What would you do if you won the lottery or suddenly became very wealthy? Would your life change? Why, or why not? What things that money cannot buy matter to you? Write your thoughts about these questions in your journal.

"Bums in the Attic"

SANDRA CISNEROS

I want a house on a hill like the ones with the gardens where Papa works. We go Sundays, Papa's day off. I used to go. I don't anymore. You don't like to go out with us, Papa says. Getting too old? Getting too stuck-up, says Nenny. I don't tell them I am ashamed—all of us staring out the window like the hungry. I am tired of looking at what we can't have. When we win the lottery . . . Mama begins, and then I stop listening.

People who live on hills sleep so close to the stars they forget those of us who live too much on earth. They don't look down at all except to be content to live on hills. They have nothing to do with last week's garbage or fear of rats. Night comes. Nothing wakes them but the wind.

One day I'll own my own house, but I won't forget who I am or where I came from. Passing bums will ask, Can I come in? I'll offer them the attic, ask them to stay, because I know how it is to be without a house.

Some days after dinner, guests and I will sit in front of a fire. Floorboards will squeak upstairs. The attic grumble.

Rats? they'll ask.

Bums, I'll say, and I'll be happy. ■

❶ *Why does the speaker no longer want to look at the houses on the hill? Why does her family think she no longer wants to look at them?*

READER'S JOURNAL

You might also ask students to consider whether or not they think their personality would change if they suddenly became very wealthy. Why do they believe that sudden wealth might or might not change a person?

ANSWER TO GUIDED READING QUESTION

❶ The speaker no longer wants to look at the houses on the hill because she is ashamed and tired of looking at things her family cannot have. Her family thinks that she is growing too old or becoming stuck-up.

SUPPORT FOR LEP STUDENTS

PRONUNCIATIONS OF PROPER NOUNS AND ADJECTIVES

Cis • ner • os (siz nə´rōs) n.

COLLOQUIALISMS

bum—hobo, tramp, or beggar
stuck-up—snobbish, conceited

QUOTABLES

"We ought not to treat living creatures like shoes or household belongings, which when worn with use we throw away."

—Plutarch

SELECTION CHECK TEST WITH ANSWERS

EX. Where does the speaker's father work?
The speaker's father works at a house on a hill with gardens.

1. Where does the speaker's family go on Sundays?
The speaker's family goes to look at the houses on the hill.

2. Of what is the speaker tired?
The speaker is tired of looking at things that her family cannot have.

3. What have people who live on hills forgotten?
They have forgotten those "who live too much on earth."

4. What will the speaker do one day when she comes across passing bums?
The speaker will offer to let them stay in the attic.

5. What will the speaker say when her guests hear squeaks from upstairs and ask her if she has rats?
The speaker will say that she has bums and will be happy.

About the Author

Sandra Cisneros (1954–), a poet and novelist born in Chicago, is from a large Mexican-American family that includes her mother, her father, and six brothers. Cisneros has worked as a teacher, a college recruiter, and an arts administrator. She has published a volume of poetry and a collection of short stories called *Woman Hollering Creek. The House on Mango Street,* from which "Bums in the Attic" is taken, is about a girl named Esperanza growing up in the Hispanic section of Chicago.

Responding to the Selection

What would happen if the main character in this selection became a United States senator? Do you think she would institute programs to help the homeless? Why, or why not?

Reviewing the Selection

Recalling and Interpreting

1. **R** Where did the speaker's family go on Sundays? What reason does the speaker give for not going with her family on Sundays any longer?

   I Why do you think the speaker feels this way about the Sunday trips?

2. **R** For what does the speaker's mother hope?

   I Why do you think that the speaker stops listening to her mother whenever she speaks of this hope?

3. **R** What effect does sleeping "so close to the stars" have upon "people who live on hills"?

   I What does it mean to "live too much on earth"?

4. **R** Where does the speaker imagine herself in the future? What does the speaker imagine that she and her guests are doing when they hear the floorboards squeak? What is causing the squeaking?

   I Why does the speaker's picture of the future make her so happy?

Synthesizing

5. In her mind, the speaker imagines a future life that is very different from the life she has. What experiences from her present life shape her vision of her future life? Do you think that the speaker's feelings of shame about her family will change as she grows older? Why, or why not?

Understanding Literature (Questions for Discussion)

1. **Motivation.** A **motivation** is a force that moves a character to think, feel, or behave in a certain way. What is the speaker's motivation for treating her family as she does? What is her motivation for dreaming of a different future for herself? What is her motivation for planning her future behavior?
2. **Tone. Tone** is a writer or speaker's attitude toward the subject. What is the speaker's tone in the last line of the story? What do you think the guests' reaction would be to the speaker's words? Does the speaker care about this reaction? Why, or why not? How does the speaker feel about the person she has decided to be?

Answers for Understanding Literature

Responses will vary. Possible responses are given.

1. **Motivation.** The speaker's motivation is shame. Her motivation is to accomplish a dream for both herself and her family. The speaker's motivation is knowing what it is like to be without a house.

2. **Tone.** The speaker's tone is lighthearted and humorous. The guests might be shocked. The speaker does not care about the guests' reaction and finds their surprise amusing. She cares more about helping others than impressing guests. The speaker is proud of and happy with the person she has decided to be.

Responding to the Selection

Students might also discuss what they believe the guests' reactions would be to the main character's announcement.

Answers for Reviewing the Selection

RECALLING AND INTERPRETING

1. **Recalling.** The speaker's family went to look at the houses on the hill. The speaker says that she is ashamed and tired of looking at what her family cannot have. **Interpreting.** The speaker may feel that it is pointless and embarrassing to envy others.

2. **Recalling.** The speaker's mother hopes to win the lottery. **Interpreting.** The speaker believes that her mother's hopes will never be realized so it pains her to hear her mother speak in this way.

3. **Recalling.** It makes the people who live on hills forget about the people "who live too much on earth." **Interpreting.** It may mean that one is too connected with the problems and hardships of daily life.

4. **Recalling.** The speaker imagines herself in her own house. She imagines that she and her guests are sitting in front of a fire after dinner. The bums in the attic are causing the squeaking. **Interpreting.** The speaker's picture of the future makes her happy because in her dream she has accomplished her goals without forgetting who she is or where she came from and she is helping others.

SYNTHESIZING

Responses will vary. Possible responses are given.

5. Her experience of knowing what it is like to be without a house shapes her vision of her future. Students may say that the speaker will probably become more accepting and understanding of her family as she grows older.

GOALS/OBJECTIVES

Studying this lesson will enable students to

- appreciate an imaginative piece of short fiction
- define *conservation* and briefly explain some of the issues of conservation
- define *understatement* and recognize the use of this technique in works that they read
- edit for errors in modifier usage
- identify and correct errors in modifier usage

ADDITIONAL RESOURCES

READER'S GUIDE

- Selection Worksheet, 2.7

ASSESSMENT PORTFOLIO

- Selection Check Test, 2.2.13
- Selection Test, 2.2.14

PRONUNCIATION EXERCISE

- Grade 8 Audiocassette, Side B, Track 12

CROSS-CURRICULAR CONNECTIONS

APPLIED ARTS

Students might create posters that portray the importance of conservation and that urge people to practice conservation. Inform students that in a good poster the image, the design, and the text all work together to create a single message that a casual viewer notices immediately. Students should decide what images best display their messages, choose colors and designs that grab the viewer's attention, and choose for their text a simple slogan that is easy to remember. The text of a poster should be large enough to be read from a distance.

Prereading

SHORT FICTION

"The Cleveland Wrecking Yard" from *Trout Fishing in America*

by Richard Brautigan

Cross-curricular Connection

Applied Arts. Conservation involves managing and protecting the natural resources that support life. The human population keeps growing, but the earth's resources are limited. For that reason, conservationists work to maintain enough water, forests, soil, minerals, plants, and animals to support all forms of life. Major kinds of conservation include energy, soil, wildlife, water, and forest conservation, and the conservation of grazing lands.

Water conservation programs help to make sure that water is available for human needs. These needs include cooking, cleaning, bathing, drinking, washing clothes, irrigating croplands, and producing electric power. One problem is the fact that water supplies are very uneven. One area may get more rainfall than it needs, and another area may not get enough. Drilling wells and building dams on rivers are ways to obtain and conserve water. A dam can be harmful to some wildlife, however, because it changes the flow of water in the river. Downstream from a dam there is decreased water flow, while upstream from a dam, the land is flooded, destroying the homes of the area's wildlife. Balancing the need to protect the environment with the need to maintain industrial and agricultural production is one of the many challenges that conservationists face.

As You Read

In **"The Cleveland Wrecking Yard,"** the speaker finds a trout stream for sale. Make a chart like the one below. Fill in the left column with your ideas of a stream. What would you see in or around a stream? What would you hear? smell? feel? Then, as you read, fill in the second column with the narrator's experiences with the trout stream.

MY IDEAS ABOUT A STREAM	NARRATOR'S EXPERIENCES WITH STREAM
found in woods or field	found at Cleveland Wrecking Yard

AS YOU READ

Students' ideas about streams will vary. In the column headed *Narrator's Experiences with Stream,* students may list the following details: sold by the foot; waterfalls, trees, birds, flowers, grass, and ferns are sold separately; insects given away free with minimum purchase of ten feet; sold for $6.50 a foot for the first hundred feet and $5.00 for each foot after that amount; width varies between five and eleven feet; three deer are left; very clear; came from Colorado; stacked in lengths; trout come with stream; waterfalls in used plumbing department; waterfalls are $19.00 a foot; there are trout in the stream; hundreds of mice left.

READER'S JOURNAL

Think of something that is worth preserving. What effect would the disappearance of this thing have on your life? What reasons can you give for preserving this thing? Write about these questions in your journal.

"The Cleveland Wrecking Yard"

RICHARD BRAUTIGAN

My own experience with the Cleveland Wrecking Yard began two days ago when I heard about a used trout stream they had on sale out at the Yard. So I caught the Number 15 bus on Columbus Avenue and went out there for the first time. . . .

I got off the bus right next to an abandoned Time Gasoline filling station and an abandoned fifty-cent self-service car wash. There was a long field on one side of the filling station. The field had once been covered with a housing project[1] during the war, put there for the shipyard workers.

On the other side of the Time filling station was the Cleveland Wrecking Yard. I walked down there to have a look at the used trout stream. The Cleveland Wrecking Yard has a very long front window filled with signs and merchandise.

There was a sign in the window advertising a laundry marking machine for $65.00. The original cost of the machine was $175.00. Quite a saving.

There was another sign advertising new and used two and three ton hoists.[2] I wondered how many hoists it would take to move a trout stream.

There was another sign that said:

**THE FAMILY GIFT CENTER,
GIFT SUGGESTIONS FOR THE ENTIRE FAMILY**

The window was filled with hundreds of items for the entire family. *Daddy, do you know what I want for Christmas? What, son? A bathroom. Mommy, do you know what I want for Christmas? What, Patricia? Some roofing material.*

1. *What did the Cleveland Wrecking Yard have on sale?*

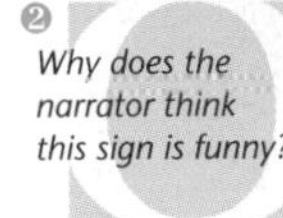

2. *Why does the narrator think this sign is funny?*

1. **housing project.** Housing built by the government for low-income families
2. **hoists.** Machines for raising heavy things

WORDS FOR EVERYDAY USE

a • ban • doned (ə ban′dənd) *adj.,* given up; deserted

READER'S JOURNAL

As an alternative activity, students might write about what they think might happen to Earth if people do not conserve natural resources. What are some ways that they might conserve resources on their own? What are some ways that they might convince others to do so as well?

SPELLING AND VOCABULARY WORDS FROM THE SELECTION

abandoned
abundance
enamel
prefabricate

ANSWERS TO GUIDED READING QUESTIONS

1. The Cleveland Wrecking Yard had a used trout stream on sale.
2. The narrator thinks it is ridiculous that the Wrecking Yard claims that it is a family gift center because children seldom want bathrooms and roofing material for gifts.

SUPPORT FOR LEP STUDENTS

PRONUNCIATIONS OF PROPER NOUNS AND ADJECTIVES

Brau • ti • gan (brä′ti gən) n.
Cleve • land (klēv′lənd) n.
Ger • man (jʉr′mən) adj.

COLLOQUIALISMS

filling station—gasoline station

VOCABULARY IN CONTEXT

• All the children in town were scared to walk past the old, abandoned house.

Answers to Guided Reading Questions

❶ The Cleveland Wrecking Yard sells its trout stream by the foot length.

❷ They are giving the insects away free.

❸ The salesperson says that they cannot guarantee the birds because they are used.

Literary Technique

DIALOGUE

Dialogue is conversation involving two or more people or characters. Point out to students that merely transcribing a conversation between people does not make for good written dialogue because people often communicate through gestures, tone of voice, nods, and sentence fragments. Good writers, however, are skilled at writing dialogue that seems very realistic. Have students examine the dialogue between the narrator and the salesman. Encourage them to note elements of the dialogue that seem particularly realistic. Ask them why they think Brautigan included such a realistic style of dialogue when his characters are talking about such a fantastic subject.

There were jungle hammocks in the window for distant relatives and dollar-ten-cent gallons of earth-brown enamel paint for other loved ones.

There was also a big sign that said:

USED TROUT STREAM FOR SALE.
MUST BE SEEN TO BE APPRECIATED.

I went inside and looked at some ship's lanterns that were for sale next to the door. Then a salesman came up to me and said in a pleasant voice, "Can I help you?"

❶ How does the Cleveland Wrecking Yard sell its trout stream?

"Yes," I said. "I'm curious about the trout stream you have for sale. Can you tell me something about it? How are you selling it?"

"We're selling it by the foot length. You can buy as little as you want or you can buy all we've got left. A man came in here this morning and bought 563 feet. He's going to give it to his niece for a birthday present," the salesman said.

❷ What are they giving away free?

"We're selling the waterfalls separately of course, and the trees and birds, flowers, grass and ferns we're also selling extra. The insects we're giving away free with a minimum purchase of ten feet of stream."

"How much are you selling the stream for?" I asked.

"Six dollars and fifty-cents a foot," he said. "That's for the first hundred feet. After that it's five dollars a foot."

❸ What does the salesperson say about the birds?

"How much are the birds?" I asked.

"Thirty-five cents apiece," he said. "But of course they're used. We can't guarantee anything."

"How wide is the stream?" I asked. "You said you were selling it by the length, didn't you?"

"Yes," he said. "We're selling it by the length. Its width runs between five and eleven feet. You don't have to pay anything extra for width. It's not a big stream, but it's very pleasant."

"What kinds of animals do you have?" I asked.

"We only have three deer left," he said.

"Oh . . . What about flowers?"

"By the dozen," he said.

"Is the stream clear?" I asked.

"Sir," the salesman said. "I wouldn't want you to think that we would ever sell a murky trout stream here. We always make sure they're running crystal clear before we even think about moving them."

"Where did the stream come from?" I asked.

"Colorado," he said. "We moved it with loving care. We've never damaged a trout stream yet. We treat them all as if they were china."

"You're probably asked this all the time, but how's fishing in the stream?" I asked.

"Very good," he said. Mostly German browns, but there are a few rainbows."[3]

"What do the trout cost?" I asked.

"They come with the stream," he said. "Of course it's all luck. You never know how many you're going to get or how big they are. But the fishing's very

3. **German browns . . . rainbows.** Fish in the trout family

Words for Everyday Use

en • am • el (e nam´əl) *n.*, smooth, hard, glossy surface

Vocabulary in Context

• Hetty was painting a dresser and, because she wanted it to be shiny, she chose enamel paint.

good, you might say it's excellent. Both bait and dry fly,"[4] he said smiling.

"Where's the stream at?" I asked. "I'd like to take a look at it."

"It's around in back," he said. "You go straight through that door and then turn right until you're outside. It's stacked in lengths. You can't miss it. The waterfalls are upstairs in the used plumbing department."

"What about the animals?"

"Well, what's left of the animals are straight back from the stream. You'll see a bunch of our trucks parked on a road by the railroad tracks. Turn right on the road and follow it down past the piles of lumber. The animal shed's right at the end of the lot."

"Thanks," I said. "I think I'll look at the waterfalls first. You don't have to come with me. Just tell me how to get there and I'll find my own way."

"All right," he said. "Go up those stairs. You'll see a bunch of doors and windows, turn left and you'll find the used plumbing department. Here's my card if you need any help."

"Okay," I said. "You've been a great help already. Thanks a lot. I'll take a look around."

"Good luck," he said.

I went upstairs and there were thousands of doors there. I'd never seen so many doors before in my life. You could have built an entire city out of those doors. Doorstown. And there were enough windows up there to build a little suburb entirely out of windows. Windowville.

4. **bait and dry fly.** Two different methods of fishing

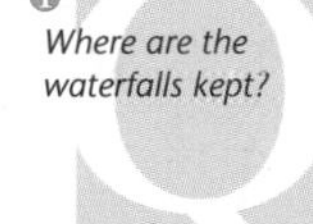

❶ *Where are the waterfalls kept?*

Answer to Guided Reading Question

❶ The waterfalls are kept in the used plumbing department.

Literary Note

Brautigan's writing is filled with whimsy and humor. Some students may have difficulty at first with Brautigan's particular style of humor which is wry, dark, and very unusual. For example, Brautigan wrote of his first novel, *Trout Fishing in America,* from which this selection is excerpted, "Expressing a human need, I always wanted to write a book that ended with the word *Mayonnaise.*"

Answers to Guided Reading Questions

❶ Lumber is usually stacked in this way.

❷ Mice are left. Mice are usually considered to be pests, so it is unlikely that people would buy many of them.

Literary Note

Inform students that in *Trout Fishing in America,* the narrator travels around the country looking for a perfect trout stream. More often than not, his search meets with little success. You might share with students the following misadventure of the narrator.

Quotables

“How beautiful the field looked and the creek that came pouring down in a waterfall off the hill.

But as I got closer to the creek I could see that something was wrong. The creek did not act right. There was a strangeness to it. There was a thing about its motion that was wrong. Finally I got close enough to see what the trouble was.

The waterfall was just a flight of wooden stairs leading up to a house in the trees.”

—Richard Brautigan

What material is usually stacked in this way? ❶

I turned left and went back and saw the faint glow of pearl-colored light. The light got stronger and stronger as I went farther back, and then I was in the used plumbing department, surrounded by hundreds of toilets.

The toilets were stacked on shelves. They were stacked five toilets high. There was a skylight above the toilets that made them glow like the Great Taboo Pearl of the South Sea movies.

Stacked over against the wall were the waterfalls. There were about a dozen of them, ranging from a drop of a few feet to a drop of ten or fifteen feet.

There was one waterfall that was over sixty feet long. There were tags on the pieces of the big falls describing the correct order for putting the falls back together again.

The waterfalls all had price tags on them. They were more expensive than the stream. The waterfalls were selling for $19.00 a foot.

I went into another room where there were piles of sweet-smelling lumber, glowing a soft yellow from a different color skylight above the lumber. In the shadows at the edge of the room under the sloping roof of the building were many sinks and urinals covered with dust, and there was also another waterfall about seventeen feet long, lying there in two lengths and already beginning to gather dust.

What type of animal is left? Why might this be? ❷

I had seen all I wanted of the waterfalls, and now I was very curious about the trout stream, so I followed the salesman's directions and ended up outside the building.

O I had never in my life seen anything like that trout stream. It was stacked in piles of various lengths: ten, fifteen, twenty feet, etc. There was one pile of hundred-foot lengths. There was also a box of scraps. The scraps were in odd sizes ranging from six inches to a couple of feet.

There was a loudspeaker on the side of the building and soft music was coming out. It was a cloudy day and seagulls were circling high overhead.

Behind the stream were big bundles of trees and bushes. They were covered with sheets of patched canvas. You could see the tops and roots sticking out the ends of the bundles.

I went up close and looked at the lengths of stream. I could see some trout in them. I saw one good fish. I saw some crawdads[5] crawling around the rocks at the bottom.

It looked like a fine stream. I put my hand in the water. It was cold and felt good.

I decided to go around to the side and look at the animals. I saw where the trucks were parked beside the railroad tracks. I followed the road down past the piles of lumber, back to the shed where the animals were.

The salesman had been right. They were practically out of animals. About the only thing they had left in any abundance were mice. There were hundreds of mice.

5. **crawdads.** Crayfish; small freshwater animals resembling little lobsters

Words for Everyday Use

a • bun • dance (ə bun´dəns) *n.,* great supply

Vocabulary in Context

• The Pilgrims held the first Thanksgiving in honor of the fact that they had an abundance of crops.

Beside the shed was a huge wire birdcage, maybe fifty feet high, filled with many kinds of birds. The top of the cage had a piece of canvas over it, so the birds wouldn't get wet when it rained. There were woodpeckers and wild canaries and sparrows.

On my way back to where the trout stream was piled, I found the insects. They were inside a prefabricated steel building that was selling for eighty-cents a square foot. There was a sign over the door. It said

INSECTS ■

About the Author

Richard Brautigan (1935–1984) was born in Tacoma, Washington, and lived in San Francisco, Tokyo, and Montana. Brautigan is best known for his first novel, *Trout Fishing in America,* from which this selection is taken. The novel is a darkly humorous work that explores the deterioration of the landscape and the people of America. Brautigan's other novels include *In Watermelon Sugar, A Confederate General from Big Sur,* and *Sombrero Fallout: A Japanese Novel.* Brautigan also published several books of poetry.

WORDS FOR EVERYDAY USE

pre • fab • ri • cate (prē fab´ri kāt´) *v.,* construct in sections for quick assembly

SELECTION CHECK TEST WITH ANSWERS

EX. Where does this selection take place?
It takes place at the Cleveland Wrecking Yard.

1. What does the Cleveland Wrecking Yard have on sale?
The Cleveland Wrecking Yard has a used trout stream on sale.

2. What does the sign outside the Cleveland Wrecking Yard say?
It says, "The Family Gift Center, Gift Suggestions for the Entire Family."

3. How does the Cleveland Wrecking Yard sell the trout stream?
They sell the trout stream by the foot.

4. What is the Cleveland Wrecking Yard "giving away free with a minimum purchase of ten feet of stream"?
They are giving away insects.

5. Where are the waterfalls kept?
The waterfalls are kept in the used plumbing department.

VOCABULARY IN CONTEXT

• Because Bob was not a carpenter, he bought a prefabricated tool shed.

RESPONDING TO THE SELECTION

Students might also discuss whether they think people would be more likely to conserve or exploit these natural resources if they owned them.

ANSWERS FOR REVIEWING THE SELECTION

RECALLING AND INTERPRETING

1. **Recalling.** The narrator sees a sign for a laundry marking machine which originally cost $175 marked down to $65. **Interpreting.** The displayed items are all odds and ends of used goods and surplus items.
2. **Recalling.** The narrator is attracted by a sign that reads "Used Trout Stream for Sale. Must Be Seen to Be Appreciated." **Interpreting.** The sign says this to encourage people to come in and examine the trout stream even though it is "used."
3. **Recalling.** The trout stream is stacked in various lengths and scraps are stored in a box. **Interpreting.** The trout stream is being compared to lumber.
4. **Recalling.** The water feels cold and good. **Interpreting.** The trout stream is real in that it is described as being made of cold water and being full of trout. It is not a stream at all in the fact that it can be divided up and stacked in lengths like lumber and can be moved from its original spot.

SYNTHESIZING

Responses will vary. Possible responses are given.

5. Yes, it is possible to sell parts of nature, but not in the way the narrator describes. People can buy land that contains a lake, a mountain, a forest, or a stream, but the lake, mountain, forest, or stream cannot be picked up and sold separately in a store.

Responding to the Selection

What would you think if you saw a sign advertising a used trout stream for sale? Would you want to buy it? Would you like to buy a mountain? an ocean? If you could visit a place like the Cleveland Wrecking Yard, what items from the natural world would you want to buy? Why?

Reviewing the Selection

RECALLING AND INTERPRETING

1. **R** What does the narrator first see in the window of the Cleveland Wrecking Yard?
   I What quality do the displayed items share?
2. **R** What sign attracts the narrator's attention?
   I Why do you think the sign says "must be seen to be appreciated"?
3. **R** In what manner is the trout stream stored at the Cleveland Wrecking Yard?
   I To what is the trout stream being compared?
4. **R** How does the water feel on the narrator's hand when he puts it in the trout stream?
   I In what ways is the trout stream real? In what ways is it not a stream at all?

SYNTHESIZING

5. Do you think the narrator's experience is real or imagined? Is it possible to sell parts of nature? Can it be done as the narrator describes? Explain your answer.

Understanding Literature (Questions for Discussion)

Understatement. An **understatement** is a statement that treats something important as though it were not important. This story about the relationship between humans and nature may be viewed as an understatement. What is important about our relationship with nature? To what are elements of nature such as streams, animals, and flowers compared in this selection? How does this story use understatement to present the relationship between humans and nature as if it were not important?

ANSWERS FOR UNDERSTANDING LITERATURE

Responses will vary. Possible responses are given.

Understatement. Students may say that our survival depends upon adequate resources provided by the natural world. Elements of nature are compared to merchandise. In the selection, people can casually buy important elements of nature just as if they were roofing material, hammocks, or enamel paint.

Language Lab

Editing for Errors in Modifier Usage

Like most successful authors, Richard Brautigan used detailed description to make his writing come alive. Using modifiers is a common way to add details to descriptions. A modifier is a word or phrase that tells about or describes another word or phrase.

EXAMPLES The salesman was selling a crystal-clear trout stream. (The words *crystal-clear* and *trout* modify, or tell about, the word *stream.*)

The salesman spoke convincingly. (The word *convincingly* modifies, or tells about, the word *spoke.*)

I was in the used plumbing department, looking for the waterfall. (The phrase *looking for the waterfall* modifies, or tells about, the word *I.*)

Try It Yourself

Exercise A. On your own paper, write out the modifiers in the following sentences. Next to each modifer write the word it modifies.

EXAMPLE The curious customer asked about the stream. **curious customer**

1. Pointing to the door, the salesman showed the man where the trout stream was located.
2. He walked slowly outside to where the stream was located.
3. The man listened carefully to the salesman.
4. Walking back, the man found the insects.
5. Filled with all kinds of birds, the bird cage sat beside the shed.
6. I followed the dusty road back to the shed.
7. The cold water felt good.
8. It was a cloudy day.
9. Looking all around, the man saw the trees and bushes.
10. They were covered with sheets of patched canvas.

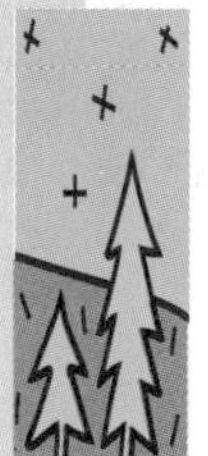

Language Lab

Introducing the Skill

Inform students that they already use modifiers in their everyday speech to describe nouns and verbs. You may wish to review with students the Language Arts Survey, 2.5, "Adjectives and Articles," and 2.6, "Adverbs." Then write the following simple sentence on the chalkboard: *The man bought the stream.* Ask students if they can think of one word that modifies the noun *man.* Students should suggest adjectives such as *young.* Then ask students if they can think of one word that modifies the verb *bought.* Students should suggest adverbs such as *eagerly.* Finally, ask students to think of phrases that might modify the noun *man.* Suggest that many phrases are formed using verbs ending in *–ing.* Students should suggest phrases such as *hoping to do some fishing.*

Previewing the Skill

Have students review the teaching in the Language Lab. Emphasize that modifiers should be placed close to the words they modify.

Practicing the Skill

Once students seem familiar with modifiers and common modifier errors, ask them to do the Try It Yourself exercises.

Reviewing the Skill

Review problematic areas of modifier usage as a class. Some students may need individual help to use modifiers correctly. You might offer students who need extra help Exercise A in For Additional Practice. Exercise B in For Additional Practice covers more common errors in modifier usage.

Answers for Try It Yourself

Exercise A

1. Pointing to the door, the salesman; trout stream
2. slowly walked
3. carefully listened
4. Walking back, the man
5. Filled with all kinds of birds, the bird cage
6. dusty road
7. cold water
8. cloudy day
9. Looking all around, the man
10. patched canvas

Exercise B

Responses will vary. Possible responses are given.

1. After fishing up and down the stream, I thought the trout seemed uncatchable.
2. I could not outsmart the fish, even when the fish was rising for a fly in the calm water.
3. While wading upstream in the rapids, I was completely puzzled by the trout's intelligence.
4. Imagining a trophy fish mounted on my wall, I purchased night crawlers and dry flies at the bait shop.
5. Slipping on the rocks, I dropped my tacklebox into the stream.
6. I spotted three small brook trout feeding in the riffles.
7. Without any actual proof, my friend believed that trout did not live in the stream.
8. I showed her the trout in the shallows.
9. My friend did not see the trout swimming away quickly.
10. My friend was sad that I lost the fish, which snapped my line with a leap.

Read the following sentence and notice the modifying phrase in italics.

EXAMPLE Selling the trout stream by the foot, *the waterfalls were said to be sold separately.*

This sentence sounds as though the waterfalls were selling the trout stream. Obviously, this is not so. If not, then who is selling the trout stream in this sentence? The sentence does not tell us. It contains a mistake that writers sometimes make when using modifying phrases. They fail to include the word that the phrase is actually modifying.

Read this revised version of the previous example:

REVISED The salesperson who was selling the trout stream by the foot said that the waterfalls were to be sold separately.

Read the following sentence. Notice the modifying phrase in italics.

EXAMPLE *Costing nineteen dollars a foot,* the customer found the waterfall located upstairs.

This sentence sounds as though the customer costs nineteen dollars a foot. However, it is the waterfall that costs nineteen dollars a foot. The modifier is placed too far from the word it is modifying *(waterfall).* The phrase *which costs nineteen dollars a foot* should be placed near the word *waterfall.*

Read this revised version of the previous example:

EXAMPLE The customer found the waterfall, which costs nineteen dollars a foot, located upstairs.

Try It Yourself

Exercise B. Rewrite the sentences below, correcting the missing or misplaced modifiers.

EXAMPLE Hiding in the deepest pool, I saw the big brown trout.
I saw the big brown trout hiding in the deepest pool.

1. Fishing up and down the stream, the trout seemed uncatchable.
2. Even when rising for a fly in the calm water, I could not outsmart the fish.

CONTINUED

Try It Yourself (cont.)

3. While wading upstream in the rapids, the trout's intelligence completely puzzled me.
4. Imagining a trophy fish mounted on my wall, night crawlers and dry flies were purchased at the bait shop.
5. Slipping on the rocks, my tackle box fell in the stream.
6. Feeding in the riffles, I spotted three small brook trout.
7. My friend believed that trout did not live in the stream without any actual proof.
8. I showed the trout to her in the shallows.
9. Swimming away quickly, my friend did not see the trout.
10. Snapping my line with a leap, my friend was sad that I lost the fish.

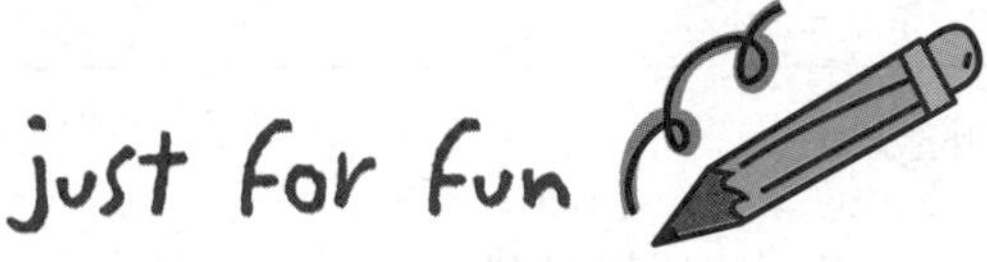

Misplaced modifiers can create humorous pictures in the mind of the reader. Illustrate sentences with misplaced modifiers to show these humorous pictures. You might draw pictures to go with the sentences in the exercise above or you might write your own faulty sentences to illustrate.

For Additional Practice

Exercise A

Rewrite the sentences below, correcting the missing or misplaced modifiers.

1. With a hook in its mouth, I saw the fish.
2. Swimming quickly, I sighed as the trout escaped me.
3. Casting my line, the trout bit my lure.
4. Harold pointed out the trout's hiding spot to me underwater.
5. With a flip of its tail, I saw the fish swim away.

Answers

1. I saw the fish with a hook in its mouth.
2. I sighed as the trout, swimming quickly, escaped me.
3. After casting my line, I saw the trout bite my lure.
4. Harold pointed out the trout's underwater hiding spot to me.
5. I saw the fish swim away with a flip of its tail.

Exercise B

Rewrite the sentences below, correcting the errors in modifier use.

1. I always wanted to catch one of them fish.
2. After I caught the fish I felt badly.
3. My friend George fished good.
4. It was George's turn to feel badly.
5. I let them fish go.

Answers

1. I always wanted to catch one of those fish.
2. After I caught the fish I felt bad.
3. My friend George fished well.
4. It was George's turn to feel bad.
5. I let those fish go.

PROJECT NOTE

To make sure that each student receives an equal opportunity to contribute to the plans and model of the creature, you might choose to form pairs of students. Point out that students should not follow the student model exactly when creating their model of a creature, but should use their imaginations and devise their own way of creating a creature. Tell students that their creations can be as humorous, frightening, or strange as they would desire.

Unit Project

IMAGINING CREATURES FROM OTHER WORLDS

You have just read poems and stories that deal with the imagination. What is in your own imagination? What situations, places, people, or creatures have been in your daydreams or nightmares? Everything in your imagination is unique, and it can be interesting to share your thoughts and ideas with other people.

TRY IT YOURSELF

With your classmates, create a creature that will appeal to young children. Your creature can be from an imaginary country or continent, from a distant planet, or from a hidden place within your own neighborhood or city. Make an outline describing your creature. Then create a model of your creature that will be appropriate for young children.

STUDENT MODEL

Students in Mr. Wu's class are putting together a presentation called "Creatures from Other Worlds" for a local kindergarten class. First, the class forms groups of three. Each group is responsible for creating a creature. Lan, Nicholas, and Selena hold a brainstorming session. Nicholas records the group's ideas on paper. They come up with the following idea:

A snow creature hides in snow drifts along the sides of roads. The snow creature normally lives in the clouds, is made of snow, ice, and crystals, and has the power to dump large quantities of special snow on certain areas. The snow is supposed to wash the area clean of bad luck and hard times.

The three then begin making a rough outline. This outline will help them when they have to describe their creature during the presentation. Part of their outline is provided below.

Drift, the Snow Creature from the Clouds
Appearance
—white and sparkling, like fresh snow
—eyes made of ice crystals
—body dotted with frozen rain drops
Personality
—gentle, likes to observe
—dislikes rude and inconsiderate people. These people slide and fall in the snow, get snow in their socks, or spin their tires in the snow.
—likes kind and considerate people. These people walk safely on snow and ice, and snow blows gently away from their cars.

Using the outline, the group sketches Drift to see what it will look like. Then they gather materials for a model: a large piece of thick, black paper; salt, sugar, and flour; gray construction paper; glue; and two clear beads. On the paper, Lan draws Drift's outline, then Nicholas fills the outline with glue. Over the glue, they sprinkle salt, sugar, and a bit of flour. They make Drift's eyes from the beads, and cut feet from gray paper. Selena creates frozen raindrops all over the body with drops of glue, which will be clear when dry.

A few days later, Lan, Nicholas, Selena, and their classmates present their models to the kindergartners. After the presentation, Mr. Wu's class donates the models to the kindergarten classroom.

Examining the Model

1. What did the three students first do to gather ideas? What did they do to organize their ideas?
2. What did they do before they began to make a model? What kinds of materials did they use in making the model?

Planning and Creating Your Imaginary Creature

1. Get into small groups. Then hold a brainstorming session with your group. Allow each person to share his or her ideas for a creature from another world.
2. As a group, decide which idea is the most interesting and fun.
3. Make your rough outline. Your outline should include important details about your creature.
4. Draw a rough sketch of your creature.
5. Decide what materials you will need to make your model, such as paint, clay, pencils, paper, cardboard, papier-maché, cloth, glue, etc. You might paint the creature, or you might use glued fabric and construction paper. You might also try making something three-dimensional, like a clay, cardboard, or papier-maché sculpture.
6. Create your model. Each person in your group should participate in the creation of the model.

Presenting Your Creatures From Other Worlds

1. Find out if you can visit the classrooms of younger children or invite them to your classroom. Have each group present its creature and talk about its looks, personality, and other characteristics. Talk to the younger children about imagination, and perhaps encourage them to talk about their own imaginings.
2. Find out if you can place your projects in your local or school library. You might want to create a display entitled, "Explore Your Imagination."
3. Find out if there are daycare centers, children's hospitals, or other places in the community that would be interested in seeing or having your projects.

Answers for Examining the Model

1. The group held a brainstorming session. The group made a rough outline to organize their ideas.
2. The group made an outline of their presentation, sketched their creature, and gathered materials before making the model. The group used construction paper, glue, salt, sugar, and flour, and beads.

ANALYTIC SCALE FOR PROJECT

Assign a score from 1 to 25 for each grading criterion below.

Imagining Creatures from Other Worlds

- **Organization.** The group set attainable goals and created a schedule or strategy for achieving those goals.
- **Cooperation.** The group assigned tasks fairly to each member, and each member cooperated toward achieving the group's goals.
- **Goal Achievement.** The group worked steadily toward its goals and did, in fact, achieve them.
- **Presentation.** The group presented a product of high quality that met the initial project description.

Vocabulary Check Test

Ask students to number their papers from one to ten. Have students complete each sentence with a word from Vocabulary for the Unit in the Unit Review.

1. Helena wore a bright vermilion dress to the party.
2. There is not an endless abundance of natural resources.
3. There were so many different items on the menu that Alex was bewildered about what to order.
4. My grandmother kept a collection of fragile, porcelain figurines.
5. His skin was dappled with freckles.
6. The farmhouse was remote from the busy center of town.
7. After hearing the ghost story, the children quaked with fear.
8. The wolves loped across the snowy field.
9. People often find solace in their friendships.
10. They constructed a monument to honor their ruler.

Unit Review

Summary

Literary Terms for the Unit

allegory, 61
exposition, 75
image, 51, 55
irony of situation, 75
motivation, 79
personification, 65
speaker, 55
tone, 79
understatement, 86

Vocabulary for the Unit

abandoned, 81
abundance, 84
alight, 70
apparatus, 70
bewilder, 72
dappled, 60
dominion, 69
enamel, 81
horde, 70
lope, 74
merciful, 73
monument, 63
porcelain, 49
prefabricate, 85
quake, 53
remote, 49
seize, 70
slop, 63
solace, 74
vermilion, 49
vision, 73
writhe, 70

Questions for Writing, Discussion, and Research

1. What is imagined in each poem in this unit? What do you learn about each speaker from the things he or she imagines?
2. What elements of reality are found in each imagining selection? Why might the speaker or narrator of each selection prefer the world created in his or her imagination to reality?

For Your Reading List

Virginia Kendall
Lakeside High School
Atlanta, Georgia

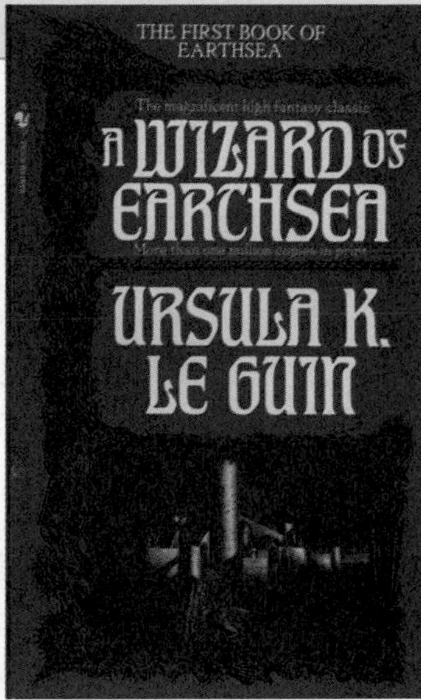

A Wizard of Earthsea
by Ursula K. Le Guin

If you like science fiction and fantastic stories, you will love *A Wizard of Earthsea* by Ursula K. Le Guin. This novel is about a boy named Sparrowhawk. He is born with magical powers, so he studies magic on Roke Knoll, an island in the East Reaches. While he is still young and ego-driven, Sparrowhawk tries to prove his abilities too soon and unleashes a terrible force. Haunted by an evil shadow throughout the story, Sparrowhawk tries to correct the results of his youthful mistake. This riveting story will keep you guessing until the very end.

Spelling Check Test

Ask students to number their papers from one to ten. Read each word aloud. Then read aloud the sentence containing the word. Repeat the word. Ask students to write the word on their papers, spelling it correctly.

1. **porcelain**
The baby's skin was so white and smooth that it looked like porcelain.
2. **dappled**
The cow was white dappled with brown.
3. **writhe**
The snake writhed through the undergrowth.
4. **horde**
The ancient city was looted by a horde of vandals.
5. **seize**
The child seized another child's toy and would not give it back.
6. **abandoned**
All the children in town were scared to walk past the old, abandoned house.
7. **abundance**
The pilgrims held the first Thanksgiving in honor of the fact that for the first time they had an abundance of crops.
8. **vermilion**
The setting sun is sometimes vermilion.
9. **bewildered**
The fun house's many different twists and turns bewildered Jimmy.
10. **merciful**
The judge was merciful and gave the defendant a light sentence.

GOALS/OBJECTIVES

Studying this unit will enable students to

- enjoy four poems and two stories dealing with different types of relationships
- briefly discuss family groups, old age, sisterhood, creativity, romantic love, murals, and marriage and family life in Japan
- define the literary terms *alliteration, anecdote, apostrophe, flashback, irony of situation, motif, repetition, setting,* and *symbol*
- analyze a poem, practice interpersonal skills, and proofread for comma errors

ADDITIONAL UNIT MATERIALS IN THE ASSESSMENT PORTFOLIO

- Vocabulary Worksheet 2.3.13
- Unit Test 2.3.14

See also the Additional Resources Box in the marginal notes accompanying each selection.

CROSS-CURRICULAR CONNECTIONS

- Art, 118
- Science, 104
- Social Studies, 96, 100, 104, 112
- World History, 126

UNIT 3 RELATIONSHIPS

Poets Garden III. *Vincent van Gogh, 1888*

old a true friend with both hands.

—Nigerian proverb

95

UNIT SKILLS OUTLINE

Literary Skills and Concepts

- Alliteration, 115
- Anecdote, 109
- Apostrophe, 115
- Flashback, 134
- Irony of Situation, 125
- Motif, 109
- Repetition, 99
- Setting, 125, 134
- Symbol, 103

Other Language Arts Skills and Concepts

- Proofreading for Comma Errors, 135
- Analyzing a Poem, 110
- Interpersonal Communication, 116

GOALS/OBJECTIVES

Studying this lesson will enable students to

- appreciate a speaker's connection to his or her family
- briefly discuss the different definitions of *family* in different cultures
- define *repetition* and recognize it in a poem

ADDITIONAL RESOURCES

Reader's Guide

- Selection Worksheet, 3.1

Assessment Portfolio

- Selection Check Test, 2.3.1
- Selection Test, 2.3.2

Pronunciation Exercise

- Grade 8 Audiocassette, Side B, Track 13

CROSS-CURRICULAR CONNECTIONS

Social Studies

Ask students to create family tree diagrams of their own family units. Their diagrams can be as detailed as they would like, having several branches or having only a few branches. Encourage students to decorate their family trees.

Prereading

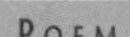

"My Father's Hands Held Mine"
by Norman H. Russell

Cross-curricular Connection

Social Studies. In all cultures there are family groups that range in size from a two-person family to an extended family made up of grandparents, parents, and children. Sometimes, even aunts, uncles, cousins, and other community members are included in an extended family. Such extended family groups sometimes live together in the same house and sometimes live in separate houses.

The word *family* is also used to refer to one's ancestors. Members of your family include those relatives who are no longer living. Families are usually based on what are called kinship relations. This means that family members are connected through marriage, birth, or adoption. In some situations, and in some cultures, kinship is not necessary for a group of people to consider themselves a family. Sharing a home and having emotional ties may be enough. In the United States, for example, foster parents and foster children are not related by kinship, yet they commonly consider themselves a family. Emotional ties are very important in defining a family unit. A family usually shares emotional support, affection, and a sense of belonging.

The functions of the family also differ from culture to culture. In most societies, the family is the basic social unit into which children are born and from which they receive protection and training. Through family life, children are taught the rules and norms of their society, plus social skills such as how to get along with others. Family traditions are based on the family's cultural roots. Since there is such a mix of people with different cultural backgrounds in the United States, we have no single kind of family tradition. Some American families have little contact with extended family members, while others keep close ties with and frequently see members of the extended family. In the poem that you are about to read, a speaker expresses the deep connection he feels with his family members.

As You Read

In **"My Father's Hands Held Mine,"** hands are mentioned several times. In your journal, make a chart like the one below. As you read, list the people whose hands are described in the poem. In the middle column, state what this person did, does, or will do with his or her hands. In the third column, describe what you think the person's action means.

Person	Action with Hands	Meaning
father	**held the speaker's hands when he cut his first flint**	**guidance, love, concern**

AS YOU READ

Possible responses include:

Person	Action with Hands	Meaning
speaker	cuts his own arrows	remembers father's loving lesson
speaker/father	kills deer	was taught basic survival skills
wife's mother	helps wife to sew moccasins	mother served as teacher
father	hands on him	love, guidance, concern

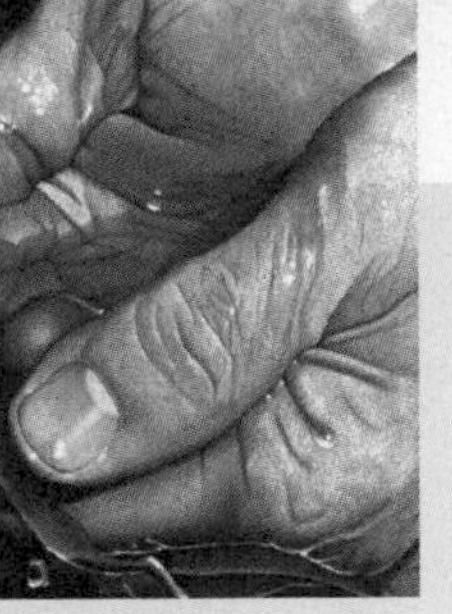

READER'S JOURNAL

What skills or lessons do you appreciate your family members teaching you? Why are these skills or lessons important to you? Do you ever think of these family members when you practice these skills or follow these lessons? Are these skills or lessons that you might want to pass on to your own family members some day?

"My Father's Hands Held Mine"

NORMAN H. RUSSELL

my father's hands held mine
the first flint

now my hands alone
cut our arrows

the deer that dies from them
falls from both our hands

wife of my heart your mother's hands
help you sew my moccasins

my father speaks to me in many ways
i feel his hands on me

he is always with me
i will always touch my sons ■

❶ *With what did the speaker's father help him?*

❷ *What did the wife's mother teach her to do?*

READER'S JOURNAL

Encourage students to make a list of skills or lessons they have learned. Then ask them to focus on just one or two that seem most important. They should describe the circumstances surrounding the one or two important lessons and then explain why they are so important.

ANSWERS TO GUIDED READING QUESTIONS

❶ The speaker's father helped him to cut arrows.

❷ The wife's mother helped her to sew moccasins.

SUPPORT FOR LEP STUDENTS

ADDITIONAL VOCABULARY

flint—a type of rock that breaks into pieces with sharp edges

moccasins—a type of slipper, usually made out of leather

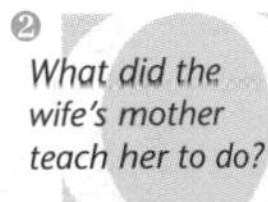

SELECTION CHECK TEST WITH ANSWERS

EX. About what family member does this speaker write?

The speaker writes about his father.

1. What did the father do as the speaker cut his first flint?

The father held the speaker's hands.

2. From whose hands does the deer fall?

The deer falls from the speaker's hands.

3. Who helps the speaker's wife to sew moccasins?

The wife's mother helps her to sew moccasins.

4. Who speaks to the speaker in many ways?

The speaker's father speaks to the speaker in many ways.

5. What will the speaker always do?

The speaker will always touch his sons.

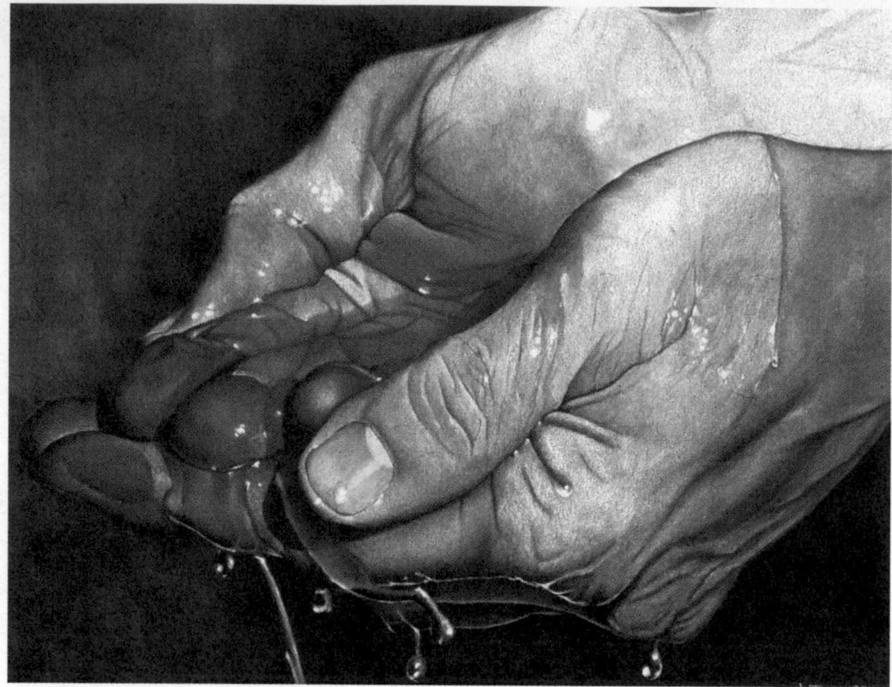

The Anointing. *Bonnie Auten, 1995*

About the Author

Norman H. Russell (1921–) was born in Big Stone Gap, Virginia. He has a Ph.D. in botany and has worked as a professor at many universities. In addition to writing botany textbooks, he has written several collections of poetry, including *At the Zoo* and *I Am Old.* Russell's Cherokee heritage has influenced his poetry.

Responding to the Selection

What is your impression of the relationship between the speaker and his father? Do you think the speaker will be a good father to his own children? Why, or why not?

Reviewing the Selection

Recalling and Interpreting

1. **R** With what do the speaker's father's hands first help him?

   I What does this suggest about the role of the speaker's father in the speaker's life?

2. **R** What do the speaker's hands now do alone? What does the speaker say about the deer?

   I Why does his father no longer guide the speaker in making arrows? What might have happened to the father? In what way does the speaker's father aid him in hunting?

3. **R** What does the speaker call his wife? What does the speaker say his wife's mother's hands do?

   I How does the speaker feel about his wife? In what way is the relationship between the wife and her mother similar to the speaker's relationship with his father?

4. **R** What does the speaker say his father still does? Where is his father "always"? What will the speaker do "always"?

   I In what way is the speaker's father a constant part of his life? In what way does the speaker plan to be a constant part of his sons' lives?

Synthesizing

5. What does this poem suggest about the ways in which our ancestors live on? When the speaker says that he will "always touch" his sons, what two meanings does the phrase have? Why might the speaker want his sons to feel about him as he felt about his own father?

Understanding Literature (Questions for Discussion)

Repetition. Repetition is the use, again, of a sound, word, or group of words. What word is repeated in the first five stanzas? What word is repeated in the last stanza? Why do you think that these words are repeated? Do you think this repetition helps to emphasize the connections between succeeding generations? Why, or why not?

Responding to the Selection

Ask students to be specific about why the speaker's father was probably a good father and why the speaker himself will probably be a good father.

Answers for Reviewing the Selection

RECALLING AND INTERPRETING

1. **Recalling.** The speaker's father's hands first help him to cut flint. **Interpreting.** The speaker's father served as a teacher and role model for the speaker.

2. **Recalling.** The speaker's hands now cut arrows alone. The speaker says that the deer that dies at his hands actually falls from his father's hands as well. **Interpreting.** The speaker has learned to make his own arrows. The father might have passed away. The father's lessons about hunting guide the speaker as he hunts.

3. **Recalling.** The speaker calls his wife "wife of my heart." His wife's mother's hands help the wife to sew moccasins. **Interpreting.** The speaker loves his wife. Just as the speaker learned a great deal from his father, the speaker's wife learned a great deal from her mother. They were both taught valuable life skills.

4. **Recalling.** The speaker says that his father speaks to him in many ways. The father is with the speaker always. The speaker will always touch his son's life in the way that his own father touched his life. **Interpreting.** The speaker's father taught him many things about life, so in that way the father is a constant part of his life. He wants to teach his sons and touch their lives in the same way.

SYNTHESIZING

Responses will vary. Possible responses are given.

5. Ancestors live on through the lessons they teach younger generations. Their lessons are passed on. The speaker means that he will touch his sons when they are

(cont.)

Answers for Understanding Literature

Responses will vary. Possible responses are given.

Repetition. The word *always* is repeated in the last stanza. This word is repeated to emphasize the lasting lessons taught by parents. The repetition of the word *always* does help to emphasize the connections between succeeding generations because the word *always* means forever, or never-ending. It shows that people live on through the lessons they teach their children and other people.

Answers for Reviewing the Selection (cont.)

young by teaching them certain everyday life skills. He will also touch them throughout their lives with his love and lessons. The speaker had positive feelings for his father, and probably hopes that his sons will have positive feelings for him.

GOALS/OBJECTIVES

Studying this lesson will enable students to
- enjoy reading a poem praising a special parent
- briefly explain different views about old age
- define *symbol* and recognize a symbol in a poem

ADDITIONAL RESOURCES

READER'S GUIDE
- Selection Worksheet, 3.2

ASSESSMENT PORTFOLIO
- Selection Check Test, 2.3.3
- Selection Test, 2.3.4

PRONUNCIATION EXERCISE
- Grade 8 Audiocassette, Side B, Track 14

CROSS-CURRICULAR CONNECTIONS

SOCIAL STUDIES

Ask each student to interview one elderly person. Encourage the students to ask their interviewees for advice, simple stories about a time in his or her life, and humorous stories, lessons, or anecdotes. Students might tape record the interview (with the interviewee's permission) or write down the information. Students should write out the information in clear paragraphs and then work together to make a collection of the pieces.

Prereading

POEM

"My Father Is a Simple Man"
by Luis Omar Salinas

Cross-curricular Connection

Social Studies. People's attitudes toward old age vary widely. Some people look forward to old age as a time when they can relax and enjoy leisure activities. Their children will be grown and they will have fewer responsibilities, so they can travel and pursue other interests. Not everyone takes this positive attitude toward old age, however. Some people believe that old age means that they will be less active, less alert, and less open-minded. Even though few old people describe themselves in this way, that is how they describe other old people.

In nonindustrial societies where few books and computers are available to store information, elderly people are highly respected for the wealth of knowledge and life experience they have. In modern industrial societies, elderly people are not always thought of as "older and wiser" sources of knowledge. In "My Father Is a Simple Man," the speaker recognizes the knowledge and experience of his aging father.

As You Read

"My Father Is a Simple Man" is about the relationship between a father and son. In your journal, make a cluster chart like the one below. As you read, fill in the chart with information about the father from the son's point of view. You might include physical descriptions, things the father has said to the son or done for the son, or how the son feels about his father.

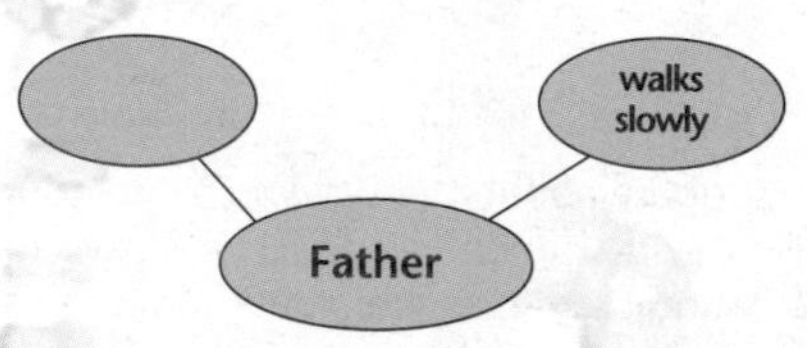

AS YOU READ

Answers will vary, but some students might fill out their cluster charts in the following way:

father—simple, wise, leader of lifelong journey, likes oranges, perpetual values, has sixth grade education, realistic about death, kind, patient, scholarly, hard-working, a provider, learned simple facts in life, lived by simple facts of life, generous, unpretentious, great

READER'S JOURNAL

Think about a person you admire very much. What qualities do you admire in this person? What actions on the part of this person have impressed you? In what ways would you want to be like this person? Write about these questions in your journal.

"My Father Is a Simple Man"

LUIS OMAR SALINAS

I walk to town with my father
to buy a newspaper. He walks slower
than I do so I must slow up.
The street is filled with children.
We argue about the price
of pomegranates, I convince
him it is the fruit of scholars.
He has taken me on this journey
and it's been lifelong.
He's sure I'll be healthy
so long as I eat more oranges,
and tells me the orange
has seeds and so is perpetual;
and we too will come back
like the orange trees.
I ask him what he thinks
about death and he says
he will gladly face it when
it comes but won't jump
out in front of a car.
I'd gladly give my life
for this man with a sixth
grade education, whose kindness
and patience are true . . .
The truth of it is, he's the scholar,
and when the bitter-hard reality
comes at me like a punishing
evil stranger, I can always

❶ *Why does the speaker want his son to eat oranges? What significance do oranges have for the speaker?*

❷ *What does the speaker say about his father's education? In what way is the speaker's father the true scholar?*

READER'S JOURNAL

To get started, students might make a cluster chart like the one they will fill out as they read the poem. In their cluster chart they can include physical descriptions, things the person has said and done, and feelings the student has for the person.

ANSWERS TO GUIDED READING QUESTIONS

❶ The father believes that his son will be healthy if he eats oranges. He also believes that because an orange has seeds it is perpetual, and people who eat oranges will "come back like the orange trees."

❷ The speaker says that his father has a sixth grade education. The speaker's father is the true scholar because he has kindness, patience, holds no pretense, was a worker and provider, and because he learned the simple facts of life and lived by them.

SUPPORT FOR LEP STUDENTS

ADDITIONAL VOCABULARY

fanfare—a showy celebration of someone or something

perpetual—constant, continuing without interruption

pomegranates—round fruit with red skin, filled with seeds covered in sweet, edible flesh

pretense—a false claim, or an overblown claim of intelligence, excellence, or importance

scholar—a person who knows a great deal

Additional Questions and Activities

Students should answer the following questions:

Why will the father leave without "fanfare or applause"? Which people usually get this kind of fanfare? What does society often forget to honor?

ANSWERS

Responses will vary.

Students might say that because the father is not famous, but an ordinary guy in the eyes of many, he will leave without fanfare. Well-known celebrities often get a great deal of fanfare. Often society forgets to honor ordinary people who live important lives that often are not so ordinary.

Selection Check Test with Answers

EX. To where do the speaker and his father walk?

The speaker and his father walk to town to buy a newspaper.

1. Why must the speaker "slow up"?

The speaker must slow up because his father walks slower than he does.

2. About what do the speaker and his father argue?

They argue about the price of pomegranates.

3. What does the speaker's father tell the speaker to eat?

The speaker's father tells the speaker to eat oranges.

4. What does the speaker's father say about death?

The father says that he will gladly face death, but that he won't jump out in front of a car.

5. What will the speaker have learned from his father?

He will have learned what little there is about greatness.

remember that here was a man
who was a worker and provider,
who learned the simple facts
in life and lived by them,
who held no pretense.
And when he leaves without
benefit of fanfare or applause
I shall have learned what little
there is about greatness. ■

About the Author

Luis Omar Salinas (1937–) was born in Robstown, Texas. His family moved to Mexico when he was four years old. His mother died the next year and Salinas returned to the United States with an aunt and uncle who had adopted him. Salinas took classes at many California colleges, including Fresno State University, where he worked as an editor of a literary magazine and took several creative writing classes. Many of the poems that he wrote at this time appeared in the first collection of his work, *Crazy Gypsy.* His poems have been published in several anthologies, journals, and newspapers. Salinas works in California as a translator and continues to write poetry.

Responding to the Selection

The speaker says "And when he leaves . . . I shall have learned what little there is about greatness." About what person in your own life would you say this? From whom can you say that you have learned "what little there is about greatness"? Describe that person and explain his or her greatness.

Reviewing the Selection

Recalling and Interpreting

1. **R** Where does the speaker go with his father? What do they argue about?

   I What does the speaker mean when he says his father has taken him on a lifelong journey?

2. **R** What does the father tell his son to do so he will stay healthy?

   I Why does the father say that the orange is perpetual? In what way is this statement related to his argument about health?

3. **R** What does the father say when the son asks him what he thinks of death?

   I Why do you think the son asks his father about death?

4. **R** Why would the son gladly give his life for his father?

   I In what ways would the son wish to be like his father?

Synthesizing

5. What does the speaker mean when he says that his father is a "simple man"? Does the speaker admire or look down upon his father for being simple? How do you know?

Understanding Literature (Questions for Discussion)

Symbol. A **symbol** is a thing that stands for or represents both itself and something else. What does the father say about the orange and the orange tree? What does the orange tree symbolize in this poem?

Answers for Understanding Literature

Responses will vary. Possible responses are given.

Symbol. The father says that oranges are healthy and perpetual. He believes that because the orange seeds make orange trees and more oranges grow, they also help people to be perpetual and to live on. The orange tree symbolizes life that comes from other life. Just as the orange will live on through the new tree that grows from its seeds, the father's life, or more specifically his values, will live on through his son.

Responding to the Selection

You might have a class discussion about this phrase with students. Ask students to write down and discuss their own definitions of human greatness.

Answers for Reviewing the Selection

RECALLING AND INTERPRETING

1. **Recalling.** The speaker walks into town with his father to buy a newspaper. They argue about the price of pomegranates. **Interpreting.** His father has raised him.
2. **Recalling.** The father tells his son to eat oranges to stay healthy. **Interpreting.** The orange is perpetual because it has seeds, trees grow from those seeds, and more oranges grow from those trees. He believes the oranges, because they are perpetual, give people health and the ability to "come back like the orange trees."
3. **Recalling.** When the son asks him about death, the father says that he will gladly face it but he won't jump out in front of a car. **Interpreting.** The son is worried about death because he knows that his father is getting older and closer to death.
4. **Recalling.** The son loves and admires his father and believes that is father has lived an exemplary life. **Interpreting.** The son wishes that he could be as patient, kind, hard-working, and unpretentious as his father.

SYNTHESIZING

Responses will vary. Possible responses are given.

5. When the speaker says that his father is a simple man, he means that his father has a simple but admirable set of values by which he lives. The speaker admires his father's values, and wishes to be more like his father. The reader knows that the speaker admires his father because the speaker says that he would give his life for the man, that his father is the scholar, and that he often remembers his father's values when he experiences tough times.

GOALS/OBJECTIVES

Studying this lesson will enable students to
- enjoy a poem about a special sister
- briefly discuss ideas about relationships between sisters
- understand creativity
- define *anecdote*
- recognize a motif in a poem
- analyze a poem

ADDITIONAL RESOURCES

READER'S GUIDE
- Selection Worksheet, 3.3

ASSESSMENT PORTFOLIO
- Selection Check Test, 2.3.5
- Selection Test, 2.3.6

PRONUNCIATION EXERCISE
- Grade 8 Audiocassette, Side B, Track 15

CROSS-CURRICULAR CONNECTIONS

SOCIAL STUDIES

Ask students to write reports about sisterhood. A student may write a report on a pair of biological or adoptive sisters that he or she knows, on sisters related by dedication to a certain cause or religion, or on sisters related by marriage. The student might also choose to write about the lives of famous sisters.

SCIENCE

Ask students to do additional research about theories of creativity. Encourage them to make trips to a library to look at resources related to this subject. Students should share their findings with the class and have a class discussion.

Prereading

POEM

"For My Sister Molly Who in the Fifties"
by Alice Walker

Cross-curricular Connections

Social Studies. In the poem that you are about to read, the speaker portrays her sister as an exceptional person and as a profound influence on her life. Many people interested in women's studies are especially interested in the relationship between sisters. While the term *sisters* usually refers to two women who are related by blood and who share the same parents, it also applies to women related by adoption, marriage, religious commitment, or dedication to a cause. Blood sisters traditionally share a close bond, which may be why the term is also used to describe such a wide variety of people who also share a common bond. When they are young, sisters sometimes compete for a parent's affection, but sisters usually identify with each other and deeply sense their connection. When sisters disagree and stop communicating, each usually feels that she has lost an important part of herself. Many famous female writers, including Emily Dickinson, Jane Austen, Christina Rossetti, and Virginia Woolf, have had close relationships with their sisters.

Science. Psychologists have long been interested in what makes certain individuals exceptionally creative. By studying creative individuals, psychologists have determined that creative people are usually very intelligent and capable of meeting the problems of daily life, but usually rely more on intuition than on intellect. Creative people are generally very interested in disorder, contradiction, and the irrational sides of themselves and others. Some people associate creative people with psychological instability, but in actuality many creative people just have different personality traits because they are more open to new experiences and different behavior patterns. Creative people usually have a wide variety of interests and enjoy challenges. Molly, the speaker's sister in the poem you are about to read, is a good example of a creative person.

As You Read

The speaker in **"For My Sister Molly Who in the Fifties"** fondly remembers her older sister Molly. In your journal, make a chart like the one below. As you read, write down all of the things that Molly does for the speaker. In the right column, describe the positive effect each action has on the speaker.

WHAT MOLLY DOES FOR THE SPEAKER	ITS POSITIVE EFFECT ON THE SPEAKER
made a fairy rooster from mashed potatoes	was fun and taught her something about imagination

AS YOU READ

Answers will vary, but students might fill out their charts in the following way:

What Molly Does for the Speaker
- taught the speaker songs of Africa
- told the speaker and other siblings stories
- sent the speaker letters and money for college

Its Positive Effect on the Speaker
- speaker learned to love the songs
- "woke up story buds"
- encouraged the speaker to grow through education

READER'S JOURNAL

Do you have a brother or a sister that you look up to or admire? If not, who do you admire? Describe your feelings about this person. What has this person done for you that you especially appreciate?

"For My Sister Molly Who in the Fifties"

ALICE WALKER

Once made a fairy rooster from
Mashed potatoes
Whose eyes I forget
But green onions were his tail
And his two legs were carrot sticks
A tomato slice his crown.
Who came home on vacation
When the sun was hot
and cooked
and cleaned
And minded least of all
The children's questions
A million or more
Pouring in on her
Who had been to school
And knew (and told us too) that certain
Words were no longer good
And taught me not to say us for we
No matter what "Sonny said" up the
road.

FOR MY SISTER MOLLY WHO IN THE FIFTIES.
Knew Hamlet well and read into the night
And coached me in my songs of Africa
A continent I never knew

❶ *What didn't Molly mind?*

❷ *What did Molly tell the children?*

READER'S JOURNAL

As an alternative activity, ask students if a particular person, book, or poem has ever inspired them to be creative or to work hard toward a goal. Ask them to describe this experience.

ANSWERS TO GUIDED READING QUESTIONS

❶ Molly didn't mind the children's questions.

❷ Molly told the children that certain words were no longer good, or correct to say, such as *us* when they meant *we*.

SUPPORT FOR LEP STUDENTS

PRONUNCIATIONS OF PROPER NOUNS AND ADJECTIVES

Rot • ter • dam (rät´ər dam) n.
Prague (präg) n.
Li • ber • i • a (lī bir´ē ə) n.
Meth • o • dist (meth´ə dist) n.

ADDITIONAL VOCABULARY

cloddish—dull and stupid
extinguished—destroyed, smothered
inexpressible—unable to be shared or made known (especially an idea or feeling)
precise—exact
remote—distant
wearisome—tiresome

Answers to Guided Reading Questions

❶ The speaker learned to love the songs because Molly said that the songs were good and that the people in Africa could carry a tune.

❷ Molly woke up the "story buds" in the children.

❸ Molly brought back news from London, Rotterdam, Prague, and Liberia. The family typically follows news about crops, weather, funerals, Methodist Homecoming, and Easter speeches.

Literary Note

Alice Walker's novel *The Color Purple* was not only made into an award-winning movie—in 1983 the book won a Pulitzer Prize. The Pulitzer Prize is an award given annually for outstanding work in literature, journalism, and music.

Cross-Curricular Connections

Geography

Ask students to get into three groups. Then each of the three groups should create a map showing one of the places to which Molly travels—London, Rotterdam, and Liberia. In addition to making a map, each group should look up information on one of the places. Ask them to find out details about their place and to describe why the place is interesting and might attract a person like Molly. Each group should share its findings with the rest of the class.

❶ *Why does the speaker learn to love these songs of Africa?*

❷ *What did Molly wake up in the children?*

❸ *What type of news does Molly bring back? What type of news does the family typically follow?*

But learned to love
Because "they" she said could carry
A tune
And spoke in accents never heard
In Eatonton.[1]
Who read from *Prose and Poetry*
And loved to read "Sam McGee from Tennessee"
On nights the fire was burning low
And Christmas wrapped in angel hair[2]
And I for one prayed for snow.

WHO IN THE FIFTIES
Knew all the written things that made
Us laugh and stories by
The hour   Waking up the story buds
Like fruit. Who walked among the flowers
And brought them inside the house
And smelled as good as they
And looked as bright.
Who made dresses, braided
Hair. Moved chairs about
Hung things from walls
Ordered baths
Frowned on wasp bites
And seemed to know the endings
Of all the tales
I had forgot.

WHO OFF INTO THE UNIVERSITY
Went exploring To London and
To Rotterdam

Prague and to Liberia[3]
Bringing back the news to us
Who knew none of it
But followed
crops and weather
funerals and
Methodist Homecoming;
easter speeches,
groaning church.

1. **Eatonton.** Town in Georgia
2. **angel hair.** Fine, white, filmy Christmas tree decoration
3. **London . . . Liberia.** London is the capital of England; Rotterdam, the capital of the Netherlands; Prague, the capital of Czechoslovakia; and Liberia, a nation in Africa.

WHO FOUND ANOTHER WORLD
Another life With gentlefolk
Far less trusting
And moved and moved and changed
Her name
And sounded precise
When she spoke And frowned away
Our sloppishness

WHO SAW US SILENT
Cursed with fear A love burning
Inexpressible
And sent me money not for me
But for "College."
Who saw me grow through letters
The words misspelled But not
The longing Stretching
Growth
The tied and twisting

Tongue
Feet no longer bare
Skin no longer burnt against
The cotton

1 *For what does Molly send the speaker money?*

Answer to Guided Reading Question

1 Molly sends the speaker money for college.

Additional Questions and Activities

Ask students to answer the following questions:

In what ways does Molly "leave" her family? Is it only physically, when she travels to school and then to Europe and to Africa, or is it in another way as well?

ANSWERS

Responses will vary.

Students should understand that Molly not only leaves her family physically; she also leaves her family in spirit. She is no longer able to relate to them and their world. Her education and creativity put her in her own world and make her almost judgmental toward her family.

ANSWERS TO GUIDED READING QUESTIONS

❶ The speaker compares Molly to a bright light—bright but also blinding.

❷ According to the speaker, Molly "no doubt" mourned for light that had been extinguished.

SELECTION CHECK TEST WITH ANSWERS

EX. What did Molly once make with her mashed potatoes?
Molly once made a "fairy rooster."

1. What did Molly do while on her school vacation?
She cooked, cleaned, and answered the children's questions.

2. What songs does the speaker remember learning from Molly?
The speaker remembers learning the songs of Africa.

3. What does Molly "wake up" like fruit?
Molly "wakes up story buds."

4. Why does Molly send the speaker money?
Molly sends the speaker money for college.

5. When the speaker says that Molly is "bright and also blinding," to what is she comparing Molly?
The speaker is comparing Molly to a light bulb.

❶ *To what does the speaker compare Molly?*

WHO BECAME SOMEONE OVERHEAD
A light   A thousand watts
Bright and also blinding
And saw my brothers cloddish
And me destined to be
Wayward
My mother remote   My father
A wearisome farmer
With heartbreaking
Nails.

FOR MY SISTER MOLLY WHO IN THE FIFTIES
Found much
Unbearable
Who walked where few had
Understood   And sensed our
Groping after light
And saw some extinguished
And no doubt mourned.

❷ *For what did Molly "no doubt" mourn?*

FOR MY SISTER MOLLY WHO IN THE FIFTIES
Left us. ■

About the Author

Alice Walker (1944–) was born in Eatonton, Georgia, and has written poetry, essays, short stories, and novels. An African-American feminist, Walker explores cultural tradition, race, and gender in her writing. Her novel *The Color Purple* (1982) was made into a movie in 1985. Like "My Sister Molly Who in the Fifties," Walker's other works often emphasize the importance of relationships among women.

Responding to the Selection

If you have a brother or a sister, is your relationship with him or her anything like the relationship between the speaker and her sister Molly? In what ways is it similar? In what ways is it different? If you don't have a sister or a brother, what kind of relationship would you like to have with a sister or brother if you did have one?

Reviewing the Selection

Recalling and Interpreting

1. **R** In stanza 1, what does the speaker remember Molly doing when she came home on vacation?

   I What do these details suggest about Molly's character?

2. **R** What is it that "Sonny said" that Molly says is wrong?

   I Why do you think Molly is concerned with the children's grammar?

3. **R** What kinds of things does Molly read? What songs does Molly teach the speaker?

   I Why does Molly share these things with the speaker? How does the speaker feel about the things that Molly teaches her?

4. **R** In stanza 3, what does Molly do for the children? What does she "wake up" in them? What does she seem to know?

   I What effect do you think Molly's actions have upon the speaker and the other children?

Synthesizing

5. The speaker recalls many details that reveal Molly's character. Some of her actions seem highly imaginative and creative, and some of her actions seem very nurturing and motherly. Which trait do you think is strongest in Molly, the creative or the motherly? Is it possible to have both traits as part of your character at the same time? Explain your answer.

Understanding Literature (Questions for Discussion)

1. **Anecdote.** An **anecdote** is a brief story, usually told to make a point. The speaker opens this poem with an anecdote about Molly creating a rooster from mashed potatoes. What is the main purpose of this anecdote? What does this anecdote reveal about Molly's character?
2. **Motif.** A **motif** is anything that appears repeatedly in one or more works of literature, art, or music. One of the motifs in this poem is books and language. How many different times does the speaker mention books and language? If this poem is primarily about Molly's role in shaping the speaker, why might books and language be such an important part of this poem? What does this motif reveal about the speaker?

Responding to the Selection

You might pair a person who does not have siblings with a person who does have siblings so that they can discuss the poem.

Answers for Reviewing the Selection

RECALLING AND INTERPRETING

1. **Recalling.** The speaker remembers that Molly cooked, cleaned, and answered children's questions. **Interpreting.** The details tell the reader that Molly liked taking care of people and sharing knowledge.
2. **Recalling.** Sonny used the pronoun *us* for the pronoun *we.* **Interpreting.** Molly wants the children to sound educated.
3. **Recalling.** Molly reads *Hamlet,* prose, poetry, and "Sam McGee from Tennessee." Molly teaches the speaker songs of Africa. **Interpreting.** Molly is excited about things she's learned and wants to share everything with her sister. The speaker enjoys the things Molly teaches her.
4. **Recalling.** Molly tells the children stories, she brings flowers into the house, makes dresses, braids hair, decorates, orders baths, and frowns on wasp bites. She "wakes up the story buds" in the children. Molly seems to know the endings of tales that the speaker had forgotten. **Interpreting.** Molly has a positive effect on the children and their lives. She gets them interested in stories and reading and makes the home a cheerful, bright place.

SYNTHESIZING

Responses will vary. Possible responses are given.

5. Ask students to point out which traits they consider to be motherly and which traits they consider to be creative. Encourage students to consider the idea that a person can be whomever he or she wants to be. There should not be rules saying "If you are this way, you cannot be that way."

Answers for Understanding Literature

Responses will vary. Possible responses are given.

1. **Anecdote.** The anecdote about the rooster creates an interesting picture of Molly in the reader's mind. This anecdote reveals that Molly is highly imaginative and creative.
2. **Motif.** The speaker mentions books and language about five different times—she mentions Molly correcting the children's grammar, the books Molly reads, the stories Molly shares with the children, the news from foreign countries that Molly shares, and the speaker's letters to Molly. Molly wanted to help people to grow through books, language, and learning. Molly saw a certain freedom and "light" in reading and learning. The speaker considers Molly's lessons about language and learning valuable.

Writing Skills

Introducing the Skill

Explain to students that organizing an analysis paper is an important skill that they will use in a variety of classes. In English classes they will be called upon from time to time to analyze poems, novels, and stories; and in science, social studies, or history classes they will undoubtedly be called upon to analyze materials, situations, or people.

Previewing the Skill

Ask students to read the model analysis and then complete the Examining the Model questions. Encourage students to ask questions about the model and about setting up an analysis.

Prewriting and Drafting

Tell students to flip through the textbook and choose a poem that they like. Ask students to follow the steps provided in this lesson when they begin to draft their papers. Discuss the importance of creating a rough outline and making sure that they have clear ideas about what they want to say.

Evaluating and Revising

Ask students to get into pairs to do peer evaluations. Remind them that when evaluating, they should use constructive criticism, but they should also comment on aspects of the papers that are good.

Proofreading and Publishing

Encourage students to proofread carefully. Tell them that a paper with great ideas but with many errors can discourage readers.

When students get the chance to read their poems and papers out loud, they can invite other students to ask questions.

Writing Skills

Analyzing a Poem

When you analyze something, you break it down into parts and then study the parts carefully to see how they are related to one another and to the whole. An analysis of a poem considers, for example, the poem's theme, or main idea, and how the poet has conveyed this main idea using special literary techniques such as rhythm, rhyme, alliteration, onomatopoeia, metaphor, simile, and personification.

Try It Yourself

Choose a poem from this textbook and write a three-to-five page analysis of it. Introduce your analysis by describing the major theme, or main idea, of the poem. Then explain how the poet presents this main idea. Conclude by restating the theme and summarizing the major techniques the poet used to get the theme across.

Student Model

Roger Gormann

English 8

In traditional cultures, skills are passed down from generation to generation, from fathers and mothers to their children. This direct training of a child by his or her parents creates a bond between them and ensures the survival of the parents' traditional way of life. The theme of Norman Russell's poem, "My Father's Hands Held Mine," is this passing on of cultural skills from parents to children.

The poem is divided into six two-line stanzas. The first three stanzas describe the relationship between the speaker and his father. The poem opens with a stanza that describes how the speaker's father taught him to make arrows from flint: "my fathers hands held mine/the first flint." The alliteration of f sounds in "father" and "first flint" emphasizes the association of the speaker's father with the task that he teaches. The second stanza provides the additional information that the father is now gone, perhaps dead: "now my hands alone/cut our arrows." However, as the third stanza tells us, there is a sense in which the father still lives on in his son: "the deer that dies from them/falls from both our hands." In other words, what the speaker now does is a direct consequence of what his father taught him.

In the fourth stanza, the subject of the poem changes from the speaker and his father to the speaker's wife and her mother. In the same way that the father taught the speaker to make flint arrows, the speaker's mother taught the speaker's wife how to make moccasins: "wife of my heart your mother's hands/help you sew my moccasins." Again, the poet uses alliteration, in "mother" and "moccasins," to connect the parent and the skill being taught. Alliteration is also used to emphasize the caring connection between the mother and daughter. The mother's "hands help," in the same way that the father's "hands held" the speaker's.

The last two stanzas reassert the connection between the speaker and his father and explain that this connection will continue into the third generation.

my father speaks to me in many ways
i feel his hands on me

he is always with me

i will always touch my sons

In these stanzas, the speaker uses metaphor to compare the teaching of skills that are used by later generations to speaking and touching, two kinds of communication. The main idea of these stanzas is that by teaching a culture's skills, a person communicates with future generations. Using the lowercase i, instead of the conventional uppercase I, emphasizes that the speaker considers himself less important than the whole tradition of which he is part.

In his poem, Russell gives two examples of skills taught by parents to their children, the making of flint arrows and the making of moccasins. He then goes on to explain their importance, how they communicate down through the generations, touching the children. In the final line, the speaker vows to continue this tradition of direct teaching, thus ensuring the survival of part of himself in his sons.

Examining the Model

1. What main idea, or theme, does the poem present, according to this paper?
2. Into what parts does the student divide the poem? What literary techniques does the student identify as important? How does the student support the points that he makes about the poem?

Prewriting and Drafting

1. Read about the techniques of poetry given in the introduction to Unit 8, "Poetry."
2. Read the poem that you chose to identify its theme. Then note the ways the poet supports this theme, including the speaker's statements and literary techniques that support the theme, such as metaphor, onomatopoeia, or personification.
3. Make a rough outline of your analysis. Include an introduction, a body, and a conclusion. Organize the body in one of two ways: You can divide the poem into parts and discuss each part in a separate paragraph, or you can discuss in separate paragraphs two or three main ideas that are related to the overall theme.
4. Using your outline and your notes, write a rough draft of your analysis, including a conclusion that summarizes the main points made in your paper.

Evaluating and Revising

1. Review the Language Arts Survey, 1.17, "Self-Evaluation," and 1.18, "Peer Evaluation." Exchange papers with a classmate and evaluate each other's work. Check to make sure that your classmate's analysis has an introduction, body, and conclusion; that it presents the major theme of the poem, and that it explains how the poem conveys that theme. After reviewing your classmate's comments, evaluate your own paper following the same guidelines that you used for the peer evaluation.
2. Revise your paper, following the guidelines for revision in the Language Arts Survey, 1.19, "Four Types of Revision," and 1.20, "A Revision Checklist."

Proofreading and Publishing

1. Proofread your revised draft. Make a clean copy and proofread it again. Refer to the Language Arts Survey, 1.21, "Using Proofreader's Marks," 1.22, "A Proofreading Checklist," and 1.23, "Proper Manuscript Form."
2. In a small group, read your poem aloud and then your analysis of it.

Save your work in your writing portfolio.

Answers for Examining the Model

1. The theme of the poem is the passing on of cultural skills and values from parents to children.
2. The student divides the poem into six two-line stanzas. The student talks about alliteration and metaphor. The student supports the points he makes about the poem by including lines and details from the poem in his analysis.

Analytic Scale for Writing Skills

Assign a score from 1 to 25 for each grading criterion below.

Analyzing a Poem

- **Content/Unity.** The analysis is thorough and statements about the poem are backed up with details from the poem.
- **Organization/Coherence.** The analysis starts with an introduction describing the major theme, explains how the poet presents the main idea, then ends with a conclusion restating the theme and summarizing how the poet presents the theme.
- **Language/Style.** The analysis uses vivid and precise nouns, verbs, and modifiers.
- **Conventions.** The account avoids errors in spelling, grammar, usage, mechanics, and manuscript form.

GOALS/OBJECTIVES

Studying this lesson will enable students to

- appreciate a lyric poem about the loss of love
- briefly discuss love and the potential difficulties of ending a relationship
- define *apostrophe*
- define *alliteration* and recognize when this technique is being used in a poem
- use techniques of interpersonal communication

ADDITIONAL RESOURCES

READER'S GUIDE

- Selection Worksheet, 3.4

ASSESSMENT PORTFOLIO

- Selection Check Test, 2.3.7
- Selection Test, 2.3.8

PRONUNCIATION EXERCISE

- Grade 7 Audiocassette, Side B, Track 16

CROSS-CURRICULAR CONNECTIONS

SOCIAL STUDIES

Ask students to locate poems, stories, or novels that deal with the ending of a relationship or relationships. Each student should find at least two books and then bring those books to class and share them. The class should have a discussion about the subject. During the discussion, people might mention movies and television shows that they have seen that address this subject.

Prereading

POEM

"If You Should Go"
by Countee Cullen

Cross-curricular Connection

Social Studies. Love is a deep, tender feeling of affection toward someone or something. One kind of love happens when two people get to know each other well. They come to share a deep affection for each other. This is called romantic love. As a couple who is in love spends more time together, they begin to understand each other better and enjoy being together even more. Two people who are in love want to protect each other, share and discuss their feelings, and share their life activities.

When two people who have loved each other find that their relationship no longer meets their individual needs or fails to bring them satisfaction, they can choose to separate or "break up" the relationship. The emotions brought on by separation are often painful and difficult for people to deal with. Past associations of love can be difficult for people to erase. "If You Should Go" is about the difficulty of ending a relationship.

As You Read

"If You Should Go" compares the loss of love to the passing of light at the end of the day and to a fading dream. Make a chart like the one below. As you read, complete the chart with sensory details or descriptive phrases about both the light and the dream.

LIGHT	DREAM
gentle	remembered in bits and pieces

AS YOU READ

Answers will vary, but some students might fill out their charts in the following way:

Light	Dream
gentle	quiet
passing	leaves no trace
slips away without much notice	creates a gleam on the dreamer's face

READER'S JOURNAL

Have you ever ended a relationship with someone you cared for? How did you feel? What did you do? In your journal, write about the experiences you have had with ending relationships. If you have not had this experience, write about the emotions you imagine might accompany this type of experience.

"If You Should Go"

COUNTEE CULLEN

Love, leave me like the light,
  The gently passing day;
We would not know, but for the night,
  When it has slipped away.

Go quietly; a dream,
  When done, should leave no trace
That it has lived, except a gleam
  Across the dreamer's face. ■

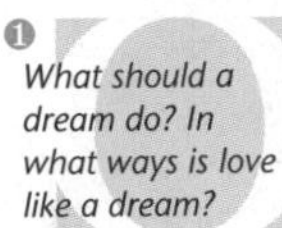

1 *What should a dream do? In what ways is love like a dream?*

READER'S JOURNAL

Students might also write about how it feels to miss someone who has left or moved away—either temporarily or permanently. Ask students to focus on a specific situation and write about how it felt to miss someone and what they missed most.

ANSWER TO GUIDED READING QUESTION

1 A dream should go quietly. Love goes quietly, like a dream.

SUPPORT FOR LEP STUDENTS

ADDITIONAL VOCABULARY

gleam—glow
trace—evidence, sign

SELECTION CHECK TEST WITH ANSWERS

EX. Who wrote the poem "If You Should Go"?

Countee Cullen wrote the poem "If You Should Go."

1. According to the speaker, in what way should love leave?

The speaker wants love to leave like the light of a gently passing day.

2. According to the speaker, when do people realize that day has left?

People realize that day has left when night arrives.

3. How does the speaker want love to sound when it leaves?

The speaker wants love to leave quietly.

4. In the second stanza, to what is love compared?

Love is compared to a dream.

5. What should love leave behind when it leaves?

Love should leave no trace but a gleam across the speaker's face.

About the Author

Countee Cullen (1903–1946) was born in New York City and given the name Countee Leroy Porter. He was adopted by the Reverend Frederick Cullen in 1918. He studied at New York University and at Harvard University. He served as editor of the magazine *Opportunity: Journal of Negro Life,* taught French in a high school, and wrote and published children's books. He also wrote novels and many poems. His works include *Color, Copper Sun, The Ballad of the Brown Girl, One Way to Heaven,* and *On These I Stand.*

Responding to the Selection

Imagine that you are the speaker and that your love is gone. How would you feel? How would your actual experience differ from your hopes for the end of your love?

Reviewing the Selection

Recalling and Interpreting

1. **R** Has the speaker's relationship with his or her beloved ended yet?
   I How do you know?
2. **R** What simile is used in stanza 1 to describe how the speaker would want love to leave?
   I What quality would the speaker like the loss of love to have?
3. **R** In stanza 2, in what manner would the speaker like love to leave?
   I What fears do you think the speaker has about the loss of love?
4. **R** What does the speaker say is the only trace a dream should leave behind?
   I What would the speaker like to have left behind when love is gone?

Synthesizing

5. Do you think it could ever be as easy to end a relationship as the speaker hopes? Why, or why not? Do you think the speaker is being unrealistic? Why, or why not?

Understanding Literature (Questions for Discussion)

1. **Apostrophe.** An **apostrophe** is a poem that addresses an object or person directly. Who or what is addressed in this poem? What requests does the speaker make of the addressee?
2. **Alliteration. Alliteration** is the repetition of consonant sounds at the beginnings of syllables, as in *blind as a bat.* Alliteration creates a unified and pleasing sound in poetry. What examples of alliteration can you find in the first line of this poem? What other examples of alliteration can you find in the poem?

Responding to the Selection

Ask students to get into pairs to discuss feelings that might actually occur when love leaves. They should discuss whether or not the speaker of the poem is being realistic.

Answers for Reviewing the Selection

RECALLING AND INTERPRETING

1. **Recalling.** The speaker's relationship has not ended yet. **Interpreting.** We know that the relationship has not ended because the speaker is addressing someone, telling that person how they might end the relationship.
2. **Recalling.** The speaker wants the love to leave like the light of a passing day. **Interpreting.** The speaker wants the love to pass away quietly, so that its passing is barely noticed.
3. **Recalling.** In stanza 2, the speaker would like love to leave like a dream. **Interpreting.** Answers may vary. The speaker does not want the loss of love to be too painful and difficult.
4. **Recalling.** The only trace a dream should leave behind is a gleam across the dreamer's face. **Interpreting.** The speaker would like to have a "gleam" from having experienced the love, but no pain for having lost the love.

SYNTHESIZING

Responses will vary. Possible responses are given.

5. Students might recognize that a special and important relationship would be difficult to end, regardless of how much the people involved in the relationship want to avoid pain. After people have meant a great deal to one another and have spent a great deal of time together, parting is inevitably difficult.

Answers for Understanding Literature

Responses will vary. Possible responses are given.

1. **Apostrophe.** The speaker's "love" is being addressed. The speaker is requesting that their relationship end quietly and without pain.
2. **Alliteration.** The *l* sound is repeated in the opening line of the poem—*love, leave, like,* and *light.* Alliteration can also be found in the third line of the poem—the *n* sound is repeated with the words *not, know,* and *night.* In the second stanza, there is a repetition of the *d* sound in the words *dream, done,* and *dreamer.*

INTERPERSONAL COMMUNICATION

INTRODUCING THE SKILL

Explain to students that good interpersonal communication skills can help them in their personal lives as well as in school and on the job. Being able to communicate with others and to listen to others are two of the most important skills a person can have.

PREVIEWING THE SKILL

Ask students to read the Student Model and make notes about what they believe are good interpersonal communication skills. Ask students to complete the Examining the Model questions.

PRACTICING THE SKILL

Ask students to complete the Try it Yourself exercise. You might remind them to refer to the model if they are in need of assistance.

REVIEWING THE SKILL

Listen to students' presentations and then offer suggestions. If students do not understand or agree with a certain concept, discuss the concept as a class.

Speaking and Listening Skills

Interpersonal Communication

In this unit you are reading about special relationships between people. For any relationship to be successful, there must be communication. Interpersonal communication is what happens in ordinary, everyday interactions between people. Learning effective interpersonal communication skills can help you to form strong, lasting relationships. Study the model below of effective interpersonal communication.

Student Model

Any relationship has its ups and downs. Carmen is complaining to Anna that her good friend, Sandy, is bothering her. Carmen is upset and needs someone to talk to.

"I'm getting really sick and tired of my friend Sandy. She's making me go nuts! She has to go with me everywhere and know what I'm doing at all times," complains Carmen.

Anna turns to Carmen and says, "I see you with Sandy a lot. You say she's been bothering you lately?"

"A lot! I know we're good friends, but she's been calling me every night! She asks me what my plans are for just about every second of the day. She has to spend all weekend with me, and she gets really upset whenever I tell her that I have plans with other friends," Carmen says. "It never used to bother her when I went to visit other friends. She always did things with other friends, too."

Anna listens and then pauses to think. "Why do you think Sandy has been acting that way? You say she wasn't like that before. When did she start?"

"Hmmm, let me think," says Carmen. "You know, I first noticed her acting this way when her mom went into the hospital about three weeks ago. Her mom was pretty sick there for a while. I spent a lot of time at Sandy's house that first week. Do you think that this has anything to do with the way she's been acting?"

"What do you think?" asks Anna. "Do you think there is some connection?"

Carmen thinks. "The more I think about it, the more I can see the connection. I bet Sandy is really scared. The doctors say her mom's going to be all right, but she's still a little sick. It must be hard on Sandy to see her mom so sick."

"Seems to me you've figured out what has made Sandy change so much lately. What can we do to help her so she doesn't feel so dependent on you?" Anna asks.

"Well, I could be more understanding about her mother. I hardly ever ask Sandy how her mother is doing anymore. Maybe I can talk to Sandy's dad to see if he's noticed how Sandy feels. Maybe he can reassure her that her mom is going to be okay. And I need to call her before she calls me. I don't want her to think that she's losing me as a friend," says Carmen. "Thanks, Anna. You are really a good friend!"

Examining the Model

Read the Language Arts Survey, 3.3, "Communicating with Others." Then examine the model above, keeping in mind the hints for effective interpersonal communication.

1. How does Anna react when Carmen complains to her? How does Anna show that Carmen has her undivided attention?
2. Find a time when Anna mirrors back what Carmen says. Why is mirroring a more effective response than simply giving Carmen advice?
3. Find an example of thinking before speaking. Why is careful speech a good idea in interpersonal communication?
4. What kind of feedback does Anna give Carmen?
5. Who solves Carmen's problem? Does Anna ever seem irritated with Carmen? How do Anna's even-tempered responses help Carmen work through her problem?
6. How do you know that Carmen appreciates the help Anna gives her? What might have been Carmen's reaction toward Anna if Anna had criticized her? If Anna had done so, do you think Carmen would confide in Anna again?

Try It Yourself

Work with a friend to role play a conversation about a difficult situation. One of you will play a person with a problem; the other will play a friend who listens and tries to help. Choose from the situations below or make up one of your own.

Your brother/sister won't leave your things alone.
Your older brother/sister will not let you do anything with him or her.
Your best friend is moving away.

Role play the conversation two ways. One way should show the wrong way to communicate; the other way should show the right way. Get ready to present the conversations to an audience. Follow these steps.

1. Decide on your roles. Decide which of you will be the one with the problem and which of you will try to help. Discuss your relationship with each other for the role play. Decide whether you will switch roles for the right and wrong ways to communicate or keep the same roles.
2. Plan your conversations. Remember what you read in the Language Arts Survey, 3.3, "Communicating with Others." Be sure to follow the rules there for the right way to communicate. Ignore these rules when demonstrating the wrong way to communicate. You may want to jot down some notes for your conversations and use them to plan your lines.
3. Once your conversations are planned, practice each a few times. If possible, tape record or videotape your conversations. Listen to your words and tone of voice. Watch your nonverbal communication. Do you look or sound irritated or bored or helpful?
4. Present your conversations to an audience. Be sure that your posture matches what you are saying. Don't forget to make eye contact when demonstrating the right way to communicate effectively.

Answers for Examining the Model

1. Anna takes Carmen's complaint seriously. Anna turns to face Carmen.

2. Anna is mirroring Carmen when she says, "You say she's been bothering you lately?" and when she says, "You say she wasn't like that before?" Mirroring shows that Anna is trying to understand Carmen's story.

3. Anna stops to think before she asks Carmen why Sandy is acting different. She shows that she is taking seriously Carmen's problem. Thinking also stops her from jumping to conclusions about the situation.

4. Anna asks Carmen if there might be a connection between Sandy's behavior and the fact that Sandy's mother is ill. Anna asks Carmen what she thinks can be done to change Sandy's behavior.

5. Carmen solved her own problem. Anna never seems irritated with Carmen. Carmen never becomes defensive or angry. She is encouraged by Anna to think carefully about the problem.

6. We know that Carmen appreciates the help Anna gives her because she says thank you and tells Anna that she is a good friend. If Anna had criticized her, Carmen might have become defensive and refused to listen. She would probably be reluctant to confide in Anna again.

Answers for Try It Yourself

- To demonstrate the wrong way to communicate, students might role play situations in which people yell, refuse to make eye contact, jump to conclusions, and misunderstand each other.
- To demonstrate the right way to communicate, students should follow rules outlined in the Language Arts Survey, 3.3, "Communicating with Others."

GOALS/OBJECTIVES

Studying this lesson will enable students to
- enjoy a short story about a community and a special wall
- briefly discuss the history of murals
- define *irony of situation*
- define *setting* and understand the importance of it in a story

ADDITIONAL RESOURCES

Reader's Guide
- Selection Worksheet, 3.5

Assessment Portfolio
- Selection Check Test, 2.3.9
- Selection Test, 2.3.10

Pronunciation Exercise
- Grade 8 Audiocassette, Side B, Track 17

CROSS-CURRICULAR CONNECTIONS

Art

Ask students to work together to design a mural. The mural should represent the class, the community, or the city in some way. Students might think of special events, people, buildings, and places that might be interesting and important to include in the mural. Students should first do a rough draft of their mural on a sheet of paper. Then they might try to get permission to do the large, final version on a wall or bulletin board somewhere. If this space is not available, they can create their mural on large sheets of paper taped together, or a large roll of paper. Then they can find a location to hang the mural.

Prereading

SHORT STORY

"The War of the Wall"
by Toni Cade Bambara

Cross-curricular Connection

Art. A mural is a painting or design that is painted on a wall. People paint murals on both indoor and outdoor walls. There is a long history of murals that have been painted inside and outside of churches and other public buildings. Mural painting started with prehistoric artists, who painted pictures on the walls of caves. These pictures often depicted hunting scenes. In ancient Egypt, tombs of the dead were decorated with murals. These murals showed the people and possessions that were known to be important to the dead person. The ancient Romans created murals on the inside walls of their homes and their gardens.

In the United States, there was a period in the 1930s when artists painted murals on government buildings, primarily showing Americans at work and at play. Murals painted on the outside walls of public buildings were again popular in the United States during the 1960s and 1970s. Many of these exterior murals portrayed images of human goodness and community. Many of these murals had social themes. They expressed a deep concern for social problems such as racial discrimination, the rights of women, poverty, and war. In "The War of the Wall," a mural is created on a wall in the narrator's neighborhood.

As You Read

In **"The War of the Wall,"** the narrator is upset by an artist who comes into his or her neighborhood to paint a mural. Make a cluster chart like the one below. As you read, add details about the wall to the cluster chart. You might add sensory details that describe the wall, examples of why the wall is important, or people's feelings about the wall.

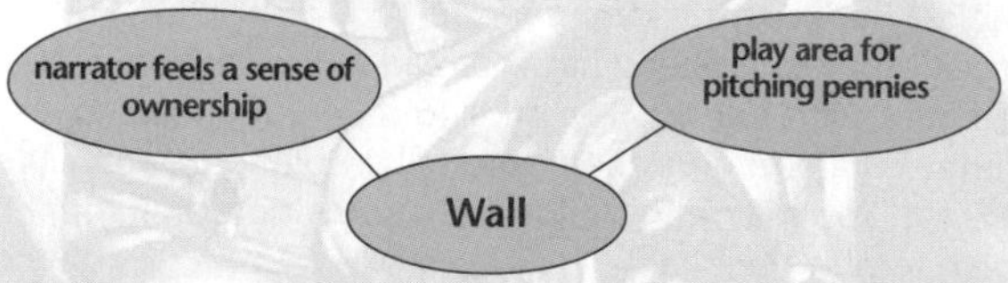

narrator feels a sense of ownership — Wall — play area for pitching pennies

AS YOU READ

Answers may vary, but students might fill out their cluster charts in the following way:

Wall—smells of bubble gum and kids' sweat, provides shade, used for handball, shows the name Jimmy Lyons, stands in center of town, backdrop for the painter's work, causes narrator and Lou to scheme, shows mural of African-American leaders, bright colors, attracts crowd, shows faces of people in the neighborhood, has inscription about Taliaferro Street and Jimmy Lyons

READER'S JOURNAL

Has anyone ever tried to take something from you that you cared about deeply? How did you react? Were you able to stop the person from taking it? How did you feel when the situation had been resolved? Write about these questions in your journal.

"The War of the Wall"

TONI CADE BAMBARA

Me and Lou had no time for courtesies. We were late for school. So we just flat out told the painter lady to quit messing with the wall. It was our wall, and she had no right coming into our neighborhood painting on it. Stirring in the paint bucket and not even looking at us, she mumbled something about Mr. Eubanks, the barber, giving her permission. That had nothing to do with it as far as we were concerned. We've been pitching pennies against that wall since we were little kids. Old folks have been dragging their chairs out to sit in the shade of the wall for years. Big kids have been playing handball against the wall since so-called integration[1] when the crazies 'cross town poured cement in our pool so we couldn't use it. I'd sprained my neck one time boosting my cousin Lou up to chisel Jimmy Lyons's name into the wall when we found out he was never coming home from the war in Vietnam to take us fishing.

"If you lean close," Lou said, leaning hipshot against her beat-up car, "you'll get a whiff of bubble gum and kids' sweat. And that'll tell you something—that this wall belongs to the kids of Taliaferro Street." I thought Lou sounded very convincing. But the painter lady paid us no mind. She just snapped the brim of her straw hat down and hauled her bucket up the ladder.

"You're not even from around here," I hollered up after her. The license plates on her old piece of car said "New York." Lou dragged me away because I was about to grab hold of that ladder and shake it. And then we'd really be late for school.

When we came from school, the wall was slick with white. The painter lady was running string across the wall and taping it here and there. Me and Lou leaned against the gum ball machine outside the pool hall and watched. She had strings up and down and back and forth. Then she began chalking them with a hunk of blue chalk.

The Morris twins crossed the street, hanging back at the curb next to the

1. **integration.** Referring to legislation in the 1960s that outlawed segregation, the separation of the races in public places

❶ *Who owns the wall, according to Lou? What does Lou say is the sign of their ownership?*

❷ *What mark had the narrator and Lou made on the wall? Why had they marked the wall in this way?*

READER'S JOURNAL

If students have never had anything taken away, they might write about something they care about and try to imagine how they would feel if it were ever damaged or destroyed.

Answers to Guided Reading Questions

❶ According to Lou, the kids of Taliaferro Street own the wall. The smell of bubble gum and kids' sweat is the sign of their ownership of the wall.

❷ They carved the name Jimmy Lyons into the wall. They had learned that he was not returning from Vietnam.

SPELLING AND VOCABULARY WORDS FROM THE SELECTION

beckon	satchel
drawl	scheme
hunch	

SUPPORT FOR LEP STUDENTS

Pronunciations of Proper Nouns and Adjectives

Mr. Eu • banks (mis´tər yo͞o´baŋks) n.
Vi • et • nam (vē´et näm´) n.
Tal • i • a • fer • ro (tal´yə fer´ ō) n.
Mal • colm (mal´kəm) n.

Additional Vocabulary

hip—interesting, fashionable
onceover—a looking over or examining to be sure someone or something is acceptable
poncho—a coat that looks like a blanket with a hole in the middle for the head
rap—speech
trance—a state of great concentration when one barely notices the world around him or her

Answers to Guided Reading Questions

❶ Not everyone in the neighborhood shares the narrator's hostile feelings. Two young girls had brought the painter dinner, and Lou said that she had great concentration.

❷ The painter does not pay much attention to the people in the neighborhood. This makes the narrator angry.

Literary Note

In "War of the Wall," Bambara shows readers how a mural can reflect the complexities and the beauty in everyday lives. In another of her popular short stories, "Geraldine Moore the Poet," Bambara shows how poetry can do the same thing. The poet in that story, Geraldine Moore, is actually a young student. Geraldine is having a difficult time—her mother is sick, her family is having financial difficulties, her father never visits anymore, and she and her sister are losing their apartment. When her teacher tells her to write a beautiful poem, Geraldine believes that she can't do it, because "Nothing lovely's been happening in her life." Geraldine's teacher then writes down the exact words Geraldine uses to express her feelings, and then tells her that she just wrote one of the best poems she has ever heard. The teacher changes Geraldine's ideas about what poetry is and what it means to be poetic. The teacher lets Geraldine know that her words make a poem because they are sincere and they paint a picture of her life.

❶ *Do all the people in the neighborhood share the narrator's feelings? How do you know?*

❷ *Describe the painter's interactions with the people of the neighborhood. How do her actions make the narrator feel?*

beat-up car. The twin with the red ribbons was hugging a jug of cloudy lemonade. The one with yellow ribbons was holding a plate of dinner away from her dress. The painter lady began snapping the strings. The blue chalk dust measured off halves and quarters up and down and sideways too. Lou was about to say how hip it all was, but I dropped my book satchel on his toes to remind him we were at war.

Some good aromas were drifting our way from the plate leaking pot likker onto the Morris girl's white socks. I could tell from where I stood that under the tinfoil was baked ham, collard greens, and candied yams. And knowing Mrs. Morris, who sometimes bakes for my mama's restaurant, a slab of buttered cornbread was probably up under there too, sopping up some of the pot likker. Me and Lou rolled our eyes, wishing somebody would send us some dinner. But the painter lady didn't even turn around. She was pulling the strings down and prying bits of tape loose.

Side Pocket came strolling out of the pool hall to see what Lou and me were studying so hard. He gave the painter lady the onceover, checking out her paint-spattered jeans, her chalky T-shirt, her floppy-brimmed straw hat. He hitched up his pants and glided over toward the painter lady, who kept right on with what she was doing.

"Whatcha got there, sweetheart?" he asked the twin with the plate.

"Suppah," she said, all soft and country-like.

"For her," the one with the jug added, jerking her chin toward the painter lady's back.

Still she didn't turn around. She was rearing back on her heels, her hands jammed into her back pockets, her face squinched up like the masterpiece she had in mind was taking shape on the wall by magic. We could have been gophers crawled up into a rotten hollow for all she cared. She didn't even say hello to anybody. Lou was muttering something about how great her concentration was. I butt him with my hip, and his elbow slid off the gum machine.

"Good evening," Side Pocket said in his best ain't-I-fine voice. But the painter lady was moving from the milk crate to the step stool to the ladder, moving up and down fast, scribbling all over the wall like a crazy person. We looked at Side Pocket. He looked at the twins. The twins looked at us. The painter lady was giving a show. It was like those old-timey music movies where the dancer taps on the table top and then starts jumping all over the furniture, kicking chairs over, and not skipping a beat. She didn't even look where she was stepping. And for a minute there, hanging on the ladder to reach a far spot, she looked like she was going to tip right over.

"Ahh," Side Pocket cleared his throat and moved fast to catch the ladder. "These young ladies here have brought you some supper."

Words for Everyday Use

satch • el (sach´əl) *n.*, small bag for carrying belongings, especially clothes or books

Vocabulary in Context

• I dropped my satchel, and my money, gum, and pencils rolled out onto the floor.

"Ma'am?" The twins stepped forward. Finally the painter turned around, her eyes "full of sky," as my grandmama would say. Then she stepped down like she was in a trance. She wiped her hands on her jeans as the Morris twins offered up the plate and the jug. She rolled back the tinfoil, then wagged her head as though something terrible was on the plate.

"Thank your mother very much," she said, sounding like her mouth was full of sky too. "I've brought my own dinner along." And then, without even excusing herself, she went back up the ladder, drawing on the wall in a wild way. Side Pocket whistled one of those oh-brother breathy whistles and went back into the pool hall. The Morris twins shifted their weight from one foot to the other, then crossed the street and went home. Lou had to drag me away, I was so mad. We couldn't wait to get to the firehouse to tell my daddy all about this rude woman who'd stolen our wall.

All the way back to the block to help my mama out at the restaurant, me and Lou kept asking my daddy for ways to run the painter lady out of town. But my daddy was busy talking about the trip to the country and telling Lou he could come too because Grandmama can always use an extra pair of hands on the farm.

Later that night, while me and Lou were in the back doing our chores, we found out that the painter lady was a liar. She came into the restaurant and leaned against the glass of the steam table, talking about how starved she was. I was scrubbing pots and Lou was chopping onions, but we could hear her through the service window. She was asking Mama was that a ham hock in the greens, and was that a neck bone in the pole beans, and were there any vegetables cooked without meat, especially pork.

"I don't care who your spiritual leader is," Mama said in that way of hers. "If you eat in the community, sistuh, you gonna eat pig by-and-by, one way or t'other."

Me and Lou were cracking up in the kitchen, and several customers at the counter were clearing their throats, waiting for Mama to really fix her wagon for not speaking to the elders when she came in. The painter lady took a stool at the counter and went right on with her questions. Was there cheese in the baked macaroni, she wanted to know? Were there eggs in the salad? Was it honey or sugar in the iced tea? Mama was fixing Pop Johnson's plate. And every time the painter lady asked a fool question, Mama would dump another spoonful of rice on the pile. She was tapping her foot and heating up in a dangerous way. But Pop Johnson was happy as he could be. Me and Lou peeked through the service window, wondering what planet the painter lady came from. Who ever heard of baked macaroni without cheese, or potato salad without eggs?

"Do you have any bread made with unbleached flour?" the painter lady asked Mama. There was a long pause, as though everybody in the restaurant was holding their breath, wondering if Mama would dump the next spoonful on the painter lady's head. She didn't. But when she set Pop Johnson's plate down, it came down with a bang.

When Mama finally took her order, the starving lady all of a sudden couldn't make up her mind whether she wanted

❶ *What does the painter do that shows she is not part of the community? What do her actions show about her character?*

❷ *What does the narrator ask his or her father to do about the painter? What is the father's reaction?*

Answers to Guided Reading Questions

❶ The painter will not eat the food that the twins bring her, and she later goes to the restaurant and asks for food without meat, cheese, or eggs. The painter will not eat certain foods even though people are getting annoyed with her. She also does not speak to the elders when she comes into the restaurant. She seems aloof, and almost arrogant, to the people of the community.

❷ They ask the narrator's father if there is a way to run the painter out of town. The father does not seem to pay attention. He changes the subject.

Additional Questions and Activities

Ask students to answer and discuss the following questions:

Is the narrator's mother right to get annoyed, or should she be more tolerant? Should the painter be less open about her eating habits, once she realizes that her habits are different from those of the rest of the community?

ANSWERS

Responses will vary.

Students will most likely not be in agreement on this issue. Some will believe that the narrator's mother should not be so annoyed just because her diet is different. Some will believe that because the painter is the outsider, she should not come into the restaurant and begin criticizing everything. Encourage students to discuss issues of tolerance as they see them in their everyday lives.

Answer to Guided Reading Question

❶ The narrator's mother believes that the woman does not have manners because she is from the North, but she is sorry that she snapped at the painter. She says that the woman is simply trying to stick to a strict diet. She does not feel as strongly about the wall as the narrator does. She believes that the artist wants to paint the wall so that people will look at her work.

Selection Check Test with Answers

EX. Who is "messing" with the wall in the narrator's neighborhood?
A painter is "messing with," or painting, the wall.

1. Whose name is carved into the wall?
Jimmy Lyons's name is carved into the wall.

2. Why are the narrator and Lou "at war" with the painter?
They do not want the painter ruining their wall.

3. Why does the painter seem like an outsider?
She doesn't socialize very much, and she doesn't eat what everyone else eats.

4. What do the narrator and Lou plan to do to the wall?
They plan to spray paint the wall.

5. In what ways does the painter surprise the narrator?
She personalizes the wall for the people of the neighborhood. She also dedicates the wall to her cousin Jimmy Lyons.

The Contribution of the Negro to Democracy in America, 1943. *Charles White. Egg tempra (fresco secco), 11′ 9″ x 17′3″. Hampton University Museum, Hampton, VA*

a vegetable plate or fish and a salad. She finally settled on the broiled trout and a tossed salad. But just when Mama reached for a plate to serve her, the painter lady leaned over the counter with her finger all up in the air.

"Excuse me," she said. "One more thing." Mama was holding the plate like a Frisbee, tapping that foot, one hand on her hip. "Can I get raw beets in that tossed salad?"

"You will get," Mama said, leaning her face close to the painter lady's, "whatever Lou back there tossed. Now sit down." And the painter lady sat back down on her stool and shut right up.

❶ *How does the narrator's mother feel about the painter? Does she feel as strongly about the wall as the narrator does?*

All the way to the country, me and Lou tried to get Mama to open fire on the painter lady. But Mama said that seeing as how she was from the North, you couldn't expect her to have any manners. Then Mama said she was sorry she'd been so impatient with the woman because she seemed like a decent person and was simply trying to stick to a very strict diet. Me and Lou didn't want to hear that. Who did that lady think she was, coming into our neighborhood and taking over our wall?

"Wellllll," Mama drawled, pulling into the filling station so Daddy could take the wheel, "it's hard on an artist, ya know. They can't always get people to look at their work. So she's just doing her work in the open, that's all."

Me and Lou definitely did not want to hear that. Why couldn't she set up an easel downtown or draw on the sidewalk in her own neighborhood? Mama told us to quit fussing so much; she was tired and wanted to rest. She climbed into the back seat and dropped down into the warm hollow Daddy had made in the pillow.

Words for Everyday Use

drawl (drôl) *v.*, speak in a slow way, drawing out the syllables

Vocabulary in Context

- "Noooooo," the man said in a slow drawl.

All weekend long, me and Lou tried to scheme up ways to recapture our wall. Daddy and Mama said they were sick of hearing about it. Grandmama turned up the TV to drown us out. On the late news was a story about the New York subways. When a train came roaring into the station all covered from top to bottom, windows too, with writings and drawings done with spray paint, me and Lou slapped five. Mama said it was too bad kids in New York had nothing better to do than spray paint all over the trains. Daddy said that in the cities, even grown-ups wrote all over the trains and buildings too. Daddy called it "graffiti." Grandmama called it a shame.

We couldn't wait to get out of school on Monday. We couldn't find any black spray paint anywhere. But in a junky hardware store downtown we found a can of white epoxy[2] paint, the kind you touch up old refrigerators with when they get splotchy and peely. We spent our whole allowance on it. And because it was too late to use our bus passes, we had to walk all the way home lugging our book satchels and gym shoes, and the bag with the epoxy.

When we reached the corner of Taliaferro and Fifth, it looked like a block party or something. Half the neighborhood was gathered on the sidewalk in front of the wall. I looked at Lou, he looked at me. We both looked at the bag with the epoxy and wondered how we were going to work our scheme. The painter lady's car was nowhere in sight. But there were too many people standing around to do anything. Side Pocket and his buddies were leaning on their cue sticks, hunching each other. Daddy was there with a lineman[3] he catches a ride with on Mondays. Mrs. Morris had her arms flung around the shoulders of the twins on either side of her. Mama was talking with some of her customers, many of them with napkins still at the throat. Mr. Eubanks came out of the barbershop, followed by a man in a striped poncho, half his face shaved, the other half full of foam.

"She really did it, didn't she?" Mr. Eubanks huffed out his chest. Lots of folks answered right quick that she surely did when they saw the straight razor in his hand.

Mama beckoned us over. And then we saw it. The wall. Reds, greens, figures outlined in black. Swirls of purple and orange. Storms of blues and yellows. It was something. I recognized some of the faces right off. There was Martin Luther King, Jr. And there was a man with glasses on and his mouth open like he was laying down a heavy rap. Daddy came up alongside and reminded us that that was Minister Malcolm X. The serious woman with a rifle I knew was Harriet Tubman because my grandmama has pictures of her all over the house. And I knew Mrs. Fannie Lou Hamer 'cause a signed photograph of her hangs in the restaurant next to the calendar.

2. **epoxy.** Substance used to make glue or tough lacquer

3. **lineman.** Person who works on telephone or electric power lines

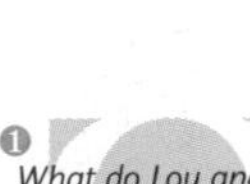

❶ *What do Lou and the narrator plan to do?*

❷ *What has the painter done to the wall? How do you think the narrator feels upon seeing this?*

Words for Everyday Use

scheme (skēm) *v.,* plan in a deceitful way, plot

hunch (hunch) *v.,* push, shove

beck • on (bek´'n) *v.,* call or summon by a silent gesture

Answers to Guided Reading Questions

❶ Lou and the narrator plan to spray paint on the wall and destroy the mural.

❷ The painter has created a mural with bright colors and the faces of several important African-American leaders.

Additional Questions and Activities

Ask students to get into small groups. Each group should do a report and presentation about one of the famous people included on the artist's wall. Students might also choose a famous African-American leader who is not mentioned, but who might have been included on the wall.

Vocabulary in Context

- We must scheme ways to stop them from tearing down our favorite building.
- Do not hunch people out of the way so that you can be first.
- Beckon my brother over here, so that he can see the show.

Answer to Guided Reading Question

❶ The artist had painted people who resemble members of the community. The people of the community might be surprised because they had believed that she was there simply to show off her artistic abilities. They did not think she had any respect for the people of the community, or that she had even noticed them.

CROSS-CURRICULAR ACTIVITIES

Geography

Ask students to work as a class to make a map of Africa, marking the places mentioned by Side Pocket—Ghana, Tanzania, Guinea-Bissau, Angola, and Mozambique. Students should also research to find information about each place. If the class is large, you might want to split the class into groups. Each group would be responsible for completing the assignment.

Selection Check Test with Answers

EX. Who told the painter to "quit messing with the wall"?
Lou and the narrator told her.

1. What happened while the narrator was boosting Lou up to chisel Jimmy Lyon's name into the wall?
The narrator sprained his or her neck.

2. Where had the painter come from according to her license plates?
She came from New York.

3. What do Lou and the narrator decide they will do to the wall?
The decide to spray paint graffiti on the wall.

4. Who is pictured on the wall?
Famous African-Americans and residents of Taliaferro Street are pictured on the wall.

5. The wall is painted in memory of whom?
The wall is painted in memory of the artists cousin Jimmy Lyons.

❶ In what way has the artist personalized the wall for the community? Why might this surprise the people of the community?

Then I let my eyes follow what looked like a vine. It trailed past a man with a horn, a woman with a big white flower in her hair, a handsome dude in a tuxedo seated at a piano, and a man with a goatee holding a book. When I looked more closely, I realized that what had looked like flowers were really faces. One face with yellow petals looked just like Frieda Morris. One with red petals looked just like Hattie Morris. I could hardly believe my eyes.

"Notice," Side Pocket said, stepping close to the wall with his cue stick like a classroom pointer. "These are the flags of liberation," he said in a voice I'd never heard him use before. We all stepped closer while he pointed and spoke. "Red, black, and green," he said, his pointer falling on the leaflike flags of the vine. "Our liberation flag. And here Ghana, there Tanzania. Guinea-Bissau, Angola, Mozambique." Side Pocket sounded very tall, as though he'd been waiting all his life to give this lesson.

Mama tapped us on the shoulder and pointed to a high section of the wall. There was a fierce-looking man with his arms crossed against his chest guarding a bunch of children. His muscles bulged, and he looked a lot like my daddy. One kid was looking at a row of books. Lou hunched me 'cause the kid looked like me. The one that looked like Lou was spinning a globe on the tip of his finger like a basketball. There were other kids there with microscopes and compasses. And the more I looked, the more it looked like the fierce man was not so much guarding the kids as defending their right to do what they were doing.

Then Lou gasped and dropped the paint bag and ran forward, running his hands over a rainbow. He had to tiptoe and stretch to do it, it was so high. I couldn't breathe either. The painter lady had found the chisel marks and had painted Jimmy Lyons's name in a rainbow.

"Read the inscription, honey," Mrs. Morris said, urging little Frieda forward. She didn't have to urge much. Frieda marched right up, bent down, and in a loud voice that made everybody quit oohing and ahhing and listen, she read,

To the People of Taliaferro Street
I Dedicate This Wall of Respect
Painted in Memory of My Cousin
Jimmy Lyons ■

About the Author

Toni Cade Bambara (1939–1995) grew up in Harlem and Brooklyn, New York; and in Jersey City, New Jersey. She studied theater and English at Queens College and the City College of New York. She worked as a film writer and producer and taught college English. During the 1960s and 1970s, she was active in the Civil Rights movement. She published two collections of short stories, *Gorilla, My Love* and *The Sea Birds Are Still Alive;* a novel, *The Salt Eaters;* and several television and film scripts.

Responding to the Selection

In the first paragraph of the story, the narrator explains some of the reasons the wall is important to the neighborhood. How do you think the narrator feels about the wall at the end of the story? Why do you think the narrator feels this way? What role will the painted wall have in the community?

Reviewing the Selection

RECALLING AND INTERPRETING

1. (R) What is the narrator determined to keep the "painter lady" from doing?

   (I) Why is the narrator angry?

2. (R) What is the painter's reaction to the narrator? to Side Pocket? to the twins?

   (I) In what way might the narrator's feelings toward the painter be related to the way she interacts with the people of the narrator's community?

3. (R) What do Lou, the narrator, and the narrator's family see on the news while visiting at the farm?

   (I) What do Lou and the narrator plan to do? Why are they intent on carrying out their plan?

4. (R) What does the inscription on the wall say?

   (I) How do the people of the community feel when they read the inscription on the wall?

SYNTHESIZING

5. Do you think the painter took the wall from the people, as the narrator thought, or gave the people their wall? Explain. Do you think the narrator's opinion changed at the end of the story? Why, or why not?

Understanding Literature (Questions for Discussion)

1. **Irony of Situation.** An event that contradicts the expectations of the characters, the reader, or the audience is an example of **irony of situation.** What opinion do most of the characters have of the painter? What does the narrator expect will happen to the wall? What surprises the narrator about the finished wall? What do the characters and the reader learn from the dedication of the wall? Why is the end of the story an example of irony of situation?
2. **Setting.** The **setting** of a literary work is the time and place in which it happens. Describe the setting of this story. How does the narrator feel about the setting? Why are people important to this setting?

RESPONDING TO THE SELECTION

Ask students what people might say to the painter if she were there when they first viewed the mural. What might the narrator say to her?

ANSWERS FOR REVIEWING THE SELECTION

RECALLING AND INTERPRETING

1. **Recalling.** The narrator is determined to keep the "painter lady" from painting the wall. **Interpreting.** The narrator feels that the painter, a stranger from out of town, is taking a wall that belongs to the children of the neighborhood.

2. **Recalling.** The painter tells the narrator that she has permission to paint the wall. The painter barely acknowledges Side Pocket. She thanks the twins for bringing the food but she does not eat it. **Interpreting.** The painter does not seem to relate to the people. This contributes to the narrator's feelings that the woman is an outsider who has no business taking over the wall.

3. **Recalling.** They see a subway train in New York City covered with graffiti. **Interpreting.** Lou and the narrator plan to spray paint the wall. They are angry with the artist, and they want to prove that the wall belongs to them.

4. **Recalling.** The inscription on the wall dedicates the wall to the people of Taliaferro Street and says that "This Wall of Respect Painted in Memory of My Cousin Jimmy Lyons." **Interpreting.** The people of the community are impressed with the wall, and they feel pride.

SYNTHESIZING

Responses will vary. Possible responses are given.

5. The painter personalized the wall for the people and in a sense "gave them their wall." Students will probably agree that the narrator was pleasantly surprised.

ANSWERS FOR UNDERSTANDING LITERATURE

Responses will vary. Possible responses are given.

1. **Irony of Situation.** At the beginning of the story, most of the characters dislike the painter and feel that the painter is an outsider. The narrator expects that the wall will no longer look like it belongs to the children of her neighborhood. The narrator is surprised to see that the painter has personalized the wall for the people of the neighborhood. The characters and the reader learn that Jimmy Lyons is her cousin. The end of the story is unexpected.

2. **Setting.** This story takes place in a southern city, in a family neighborhood. The time is either during or just after the Vietnam War. The narrator feels protective of the neighborhood. The unique personalities and customs of the people in the neighborhood help to create the setting.

GOALS/OBJECTIVES

Studying this lesson will enable students to
- empathize with a young woman from another time and culture
- briefly explain marriage and family life in Japan
- define *setting* and understand the role setting plays in a story
- define *flashback*

ADDITIONAL RESOURCES

READER'S GUIDE
- Selection Worksheet, 3.6

ASSESSMENT PORTFOLIO
- Selection Check Test, 2.3.11
- Selection Test, 2.3.12

PRONUNCIATION EXERCISE
- Grade 8 Audiocassette, Side B, Track 18

CROSS-CURRICULAR CONNECTIONS

WORLD HISTORY

Encourage students to get into small groups and do additional research on Japan. Ask students to choose a particular area—art, history, current events, religion, family life, or people—and locate information at the library. Each group should put together a presentation for the rest of the class.

Prereading

SHORT STORY

"Tears of Autumn"
by Yoshiko Uchida

Cross-curricular Connection

World History. Marriage and family life in Japan has changed since the end of World War II. Before 1945, many Japanese people lived in large family units that included parents, children, grandparents, and sometimes even uncles or aunts and their families. When a child was old enough to marry, his or her parents would select each child's marriage partner and make all the arrangements for the wedding. The Japanese term for an arranged marriage is *miai-kekkon.* Under this system of arranged marriages, it was not uncommon for a bride and groom to meet for the first time on their wedding day. Once a couple was married, the husband had complete control and authority over his wife. Wives were expected to be dutiful and obedient toward their husbands. Parents expected their children to behave respectfully toward their elders and to obey their wishes.

After World War II, Japan was profoundly altered by the influence of the West, particularly the United States, and family units in Japan grew smaller. Today, a typical Japanese family resembles a typical American family in many ways. Japanese children are given more freedom today, although not as much as American children. Most Japanese children still follow the tradition of respecting their elders. Although some parents still select partners and arrange marriages for their children, most people in Japan now choose their own marriage partner and marry for love. Japanese women now can work outside the home if they so choose. After the war, the Japanese civil code was rewritten to allow for equality between the sexes and women were allowed to vote for the first time. In the selection you are about to read, a young Japanese woman from Japan's traditional culture in which marriages were arranged, is sent to America to marry a man she has never met.

As You Read

In **"Tears of Autumn,"** Hana poses many questions that reflect her doubts about her journey to America and her arranged marriage. In your journal, make a chart like the one below. As you read, record the questions that Hana asks herself. Then, in the right-hand column, write answers to these questions as you discover them or figure them out.

HANA'S QUESTIONS TO HERSELF	ANSWERS TO HER QUESTIONS
Why did I ever leave Japan?	To create a new kind of life for herself and to escape from her family

AS YOU READ

Students might fill out their charts in the following way:

Hana's Questions to Herself

Why did I ever listen to my uncle?

What would she say to Taro when they first meet, and for all the days and years after?

Answers to Her Questions

She actually made the decision to leave because she knows that leaving the village might be a good opportunity for her.

Conversation will come naturally when they get to know each other and begin spending time together.

READER'S JOURNAL

Have you ever been in a situation where you promised someone that you would do something, but later you had second thoughts? Why did you have second thoughts? Did you follow through on your promise, or did you change your mind? If you found yourself in the same situation again, what would you do differently? Write about these questions in your journal.

"Tears of Autumn"

YOSHIKO UCHIDA

Hana Omiya stood at the railing of the small ship that shuddered toward America in a turbulent November sea. She shivered as she pulled the folds of her silk kimono[1] close to her throat and tightened the wool shawl about her shoulders.

She was thin and small, her dark eyes shadowed in her pale face, her black hair piled high in a pompadour[2] that seemed too heavy for so slight a woman. She clung to the moist rail and breathed the damp salt air deep into her lungs. Her body seemed leaden and lifeless, as though it were simply the vehicle transporting her soul to a strange new life, and she longed with childlike intensity to be home again in Oka Village.

She longed to see the bright persimmon dotting the barren trees beside the thatched roofs, to see the fields of golden rice stretching to the mountains where only last fall she had gathered plump white mushrooms, and to see once more the maple trees lacing their flaming colors through the green pine. If only she could see a familiar face, eat a meal without retching, walk on solid ground, and stretch out at night on a tatami mat[3] instead of in a hard narrow bunk. She thought now of seeking the warm shelter of her bunk but could not bear to face the relentless smell of fish that penetrated the lower decks.

Why did I ever leave Japan? she wondered bitterly. Why did I ever listen to my uncle? And yet she knew it was she herself who had begun the chain of events that placed her on this heaving ship. It was she who had first planted in her uncle's mind the thought that she would make a good

1 *Where is Hana going?*

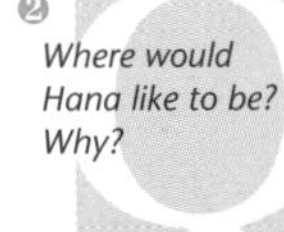

2 *Where would Hana like to be? Why?*

1. **kimono.** Japanese robe with wide sleeves and a sash
2. **pompadour.** Women's hairstyle in which the hair is swept up high into a roll
3. **tatami mat.** Floor mat woven of rice straw

WORDS FOR EVERYDAY USE

tur • bu • lent (tʉr´byo͞o lənt) *adj.,* marked by wildly irregular motion

retch (rech) *v.,* become ill; vomit

VOCABULARY IN CONTEXT

- The turbulent water tossed the tiny boat in all directions.
- She accidentally drank sour milk and began to retch.

READER'S JOURNAL

As an additional journal activity, ask each student to make a list of his or her strong points. What personal qualities does each student value most? What qualities do they want others to see in them?

ANSWERS TO GUIDED READING QUESTIONS

1 Hana is going to America.

2 She longed to be back in Oka Village, her home. She wanted to see the bright persimmon dotting the trees beside thatched roofs and to see the rice fields. She wanted to see a familiar face.

SPELLING AND VOCABULARY WORDS FROM THE SELECTION

affluence	meager
consent	perpetuate
degrade	placid
emigrate	recoil
expanse	retch
lavish	turbulent

SUPPORT FOR LEP STUDENTS

PRONUNCIATIONS OF PROPER NOUNS AND ADJECTIVES

Ha • na O • mi • ya (hä nä ō mē yä) n.

O • ka (ō kä) n.

Ta • ro Ta • ke • da (tä rō tä keh dä) n.

Note: In Japanese, most syllables are equally stressed.

ADDITIONAL VOCABULARY

leaden—heavy

prospect—plan

ventured—expressed at risk of criticism

latitude—freedom

abruptly—suddenly

flustered—nervous and embarrassed

Answer to Guided Reading Question

❶ Her uncle speaks freely of Taro because he's sure Hana would never consider him.

Additional Questions and Activities

Ask students to answer and discuss the following questions:

- How does Hana's mother feel about the fact that Hana isn't married?
- Why do you think Hana's mother feels the way she does?
- Is this attitude about marriage different from, or similar to, the attitude you or your family has?

ANSWERS

Responses will vary.

Students will probably say that Hana's mother is worried and embarrassed that Hana is not married and does not appear interested in marriage. Hana's mother feels the way she does because it is tradition in the village and in her culture for a young woman to be married or close to marriage by the time she is Hana's age. Students will have various responses to the last question. Invite them to discuss their responses.

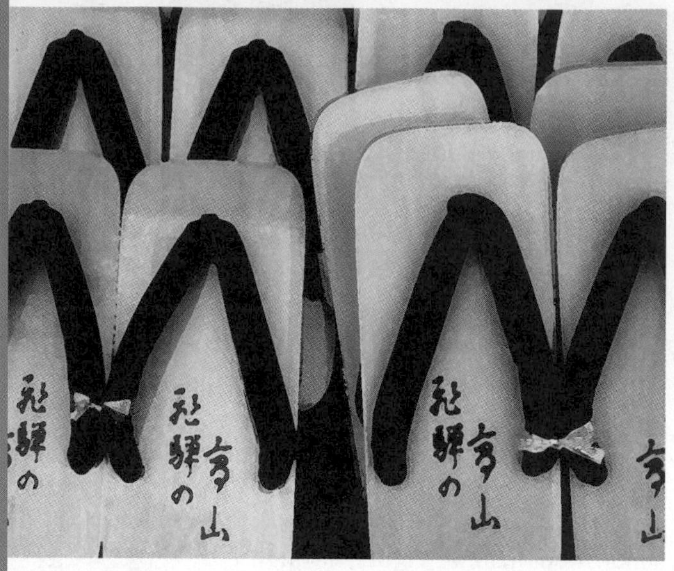

wife for Taro Takeda, the lonely man who had gone to America to make his fortune in Oakland, California.

❶ *Why does Hana's uncle speak "freely" of Taro?*

It all began one day when her uncle had come to visit her mother.

"I must find a nice young bride," he had said, startling Hana with this blunt talk of marriage in her presence. She blushed and was ready to leave the room when her uncle quickly added, "My good friend Takeda has a son in America. I must find someone willing to travel to that far land."

This last remark was intended to indicate to Hana and her mother that he didn't consider this a suitable prospect for Hana, who was the youngest daughter of what once had been a fine family. Her father, until his death fifteen years ago, had been the largest landholder of the village and one of its last samurai.[4] They had once had many servants and field hands, but now all that was changed. Their money was gone. Hana's three older sisters had made good marriages, and the eldest remained in their home with her husband to carry on the Omiya name and perpetuate the homestead. Her other sisters had married merchants in Osaka and Nagoya and were living comfortably.

Now that Hana was twenty-one, finding a proper husband for her had taken on an urgency that produced an embarrassing secretive air over the entire matter. Usually, her mother didn't speak of it until they were lying side by side on their quilts at night. Then, under the protective cover of darkness, she would suggest one name and then another, hoping that Hana would indicate an interest in one of them.

Her uncle spoke freely of Taro Takeda only because he was so sure Hana would never consider him. "He is a conscientious, hardworking man who has been in the United States for almost ten years. He is thirty-one, operates a small shop, and rents some rooms above the shop where he lives." Her uncle rubbed his chin thought-

4. **samurai.** Member of the Japanese military class

Words for Everyday Use

per • pet • u • ate (pər pech´ o͞o āt') *v.,* cause to continue or be remembered

Vocabulary in Context

- They will perpetuate that woman's memory by building a statue in her honor.

fully. "He could provide well for a wife," he added.

"Ah," Hana's mother said softly.

"You say he is successful in this business?" Hana's sister inquired.

"His father tells me he sells many things in his shop—clothing, stockings, needles, thread, and buttons—such things as that. He also sells bean paste, pickled radish, beancake, and soy sauce. A wife of his would not go cold or hungry."

They all nodded, each of them picturing this merchant in varying degrees of success and affluence. There were many Japanese emigrating to America these days, and Hana had heard of the picture brides who went with nothing more than an exchange of photographs to bind them to a strange man. "Taro San is lonely," her uncle continued. "I want to find for him a fine young woman who is strong and brave enough to cross the ocean alone."

"It would certainly be a different kind of life," Hana's sister ventured, and for a moment, Hana thought she glimpsed a longing ordinarily concealed behind her quiet, obedient face. In that same instant, Hana knew she wanted more for herself than her sisters had in their proper, arranged, and loveless marriages. She wanted to escape the smothering strictures of life in her village. She certainly was not going to marry a farmer and spend her life working beside him planting, weeding, and harvesting in the rice paddies until her back became bent from too many years of stooping and her skin was turned to brown leather by the sun and wind. Neither did she particularly relish the idea of marrying a merchant in a big city as her two sisters had done. Since her mother objected to her going to Tokyo to seek employment as a teacher, perhaps she would consent to a flight to America for what seemed a proper and respectable marriage.

Almost before she realized what she was doing, she spoke to her uncle. "Oji San, perhaps I should go to America to make this lonely man a good wife."

"You, Hana Chan?" Her uncle observed her with startled curiosity. "You would go all alone to a foreign land so far away from your mother and family?"

"I would not allow it." Her mother spoke fiercely. Hana was her youngest and she had lavished upon her the attention and latitude that often befall the last child. How could she permit her to travel so far, even to marry the son of Takeda who was known to her brother?

But now, a notion that had seemed quite impossible a moment before was lodged in his receptive mind, and Hana's uncle grasped it with the pleasure that comes from an unexpected discovery.

"You know," he said looking at Hana, "it might be a very good life in America."

Hana felt a faint fluttering in her heart. Perhaps this lonely man in America was her means of escaping

1 *What is Hana's mother's reaction to Hana's decision?*

1 *What does Hana decide in that instant?*

Words for Everyday Use

af • flu • ence (af´lo͞o əns) *n.*, abundance of riches, wealth

em • i • grate (em´i grāt) *v.*, leave one country to live in another

con • sent (kən sent´) *v.*, give permission or approval

lav • ish (lav´ish) *v.*, give or spend generously or liberally

Answers to Guided Reading Questions

1 Hana's mother says that she refuses to allow it.

2 Hana decides that she wants more for herself than the lives her sisters have in their arranged, loveless marriages. She wants to escape her strict village, and she does not want to marry a farmer or a businessman.

Vocabulary in Context

- They tried to show off their affluence by buying fancy clothing and jewelry.
- We will emigrate to India because my favorite cousin got a job there.
- The teacher wants the consent of all parents before he plans the field trip.
- Dana will lavish gifts on her new baby brother.

Answers to Guided Reading Questions

➊ Hana's sister's husband would be happy to be rid of her because he believes that she has radical ideas about life and the role of women.

➋ She does not receive much information about Taro from his letters. She thinks this is fine because they have a lifetime to get to know each other.

Additional Questions and Activities

Ask students to discuss the attitude of Hana's sister's husband. How does his attitude make them feel? What might they say to him about his ideas about life and the role of woman and education?

both the village and the encirclement of her family.

Her uncle spoke with increasing enthusiasm of sending Hana to become Taro's wife. And the husband of Hana's sister, who was head of their household, spoke with equal eagerness. Although he never said so, Hana guessed he would be pleased to be rid of her, the spirited younger sister who stirred up his placid life with what he considered radical ideas about life and the role of women. He often claimed that Hana had too much schooling for a girl. She had graduated from Women's High School in Kyoto, which gave her five more years of schooling than her older sister.

➊ *Why did Hana think her sister's husband would be happy to be rid of her?*

"It has addled her brain—all that learning from those books," he said when he tired of arguing with Hana.

➋ *What does Hana learn about Taro in his letters? How does she feel about this?*

A man's word carried much weight for Hana's mother. Pressed by the two men, she consulted her other daughters and their husbands. She discussed the matter carefully with her brother and asked the village priest. Finally, she agreed to an exchange of family histories and an investigation was begun into Taro Takeda's family, his education, and his health, so they would be assured there was no insanity or tuberculosis or police records concealed in his family's past. Soon Hana's uncle was devoting his energies entirely to serving as go-between for Hana's mother and Taro Takeda's father.

When at last an agreement to the marriage was almost reached, Taro wrote his first letter to Hana. It was brief and proper and gave no more clue to his character than the stiff formal portrait taken at his graduation from middle school. Hana's uncle had given her the picture with apologies from his parents, because it was the only photo they had of him and it was not a flattering likeness.

Hana hid the letter and photograph in the sleeve of her kimono and took them to the outhouse to study in private. Squinting in the dim light and trying to ignore the foul odor, she read and reread Taro's letter, trying to find the real man somewhere in the sparse unbending prose.

By the time he sent her money for her steamship tickets, she had received ten more letters, but none revealed much more of the man than the first. In none did he disclose his loneliness or his need, but Hana understood this. In fact, she would have recoiled from a man who bared his intimate thoughts to her so soon. After all, they would have a lifetime together to get to know one another.

So it was that Hana had left her family and sailed alone to America with a small hope trembling inside of her. Tomorrow, at last, the ship would dock in San Francisco and she would meet face to face the man she was soon to marry. Hana was overcome with excitement at the thought of being in America, and terrified of the meeting about to take place. What would she say to Taro Takeda when they first met, and for all the days and years after?

Words for Everyday Use

plac • id (plas´id) *adj.*, calm; undisturbed; tranquil

re • coil (ri koil´) *v.*, start or shrink back, as in fear, surprise or disgust

Vocabulary in Context

- The placid lake looked like a sheet of ice.
- His scream caused me to recoil and then call for help.

Hana wondered about the flat above the shop. Perhaps it would be luxuriously furnished with the finest of brocades and lacquers,[5] and perhaps there would be a servant, although he had not mentioned it. She worried whether she would be able to manage on the meager English she had learned at Women's High School. The overwhelming anxiety for the day to come and the violent rolling of the ship were more than Hana could bear. Shuddering in the face of the wind, she leaned over the railing and became violently and wretchedly ill.

By five the next morning, Hana was up and dressed in her finest purple silk kimono and coat. She could not eat the bean soup and rice that appeared for breakfast and took only a few bites of the yellow pickled radish. Her bags, which had scarcely been touched since she boarded the ship, were easily packed, for all they contained were her kimonos and some of her favorite books. The large willow basket, tightly secured by a rope, remained under the bunk, untouched since her uncle had placed it there.

She had not befriended the other women in her cabin, for they had lain in their bunks for most of the voyage, too sick to be company to anyone. Each morning Hana had fled the closeness of the sleeping quarters and spent most of the day huddled in a corner of the deck, listening to the lonely songs of some Russians also traveling to an alien land.

As the ship approached land, Hana hurried up to the deck to look out at the gray expanse of ocean and sky, eager for a first glimpse of her new homeland.

"We won't be docking until almost noon," one of the deckhands told her.

Hana nodded. "I can wait," she answered, but the last hours seemed the longest.

About what does Hana wonder? About what does she worry?

5. **brocades and lacquers.** Fancy clothes and furniture, respectively

Words for Everyday Use

mea • ger (mē´gər) *adj.,* of poor quality or small amount

ex • panse (ek spans´) *n.,* large, open area

Answer to Guided Reading Question

❶ Hana wondered what her apartment would look like, and she worried that the English she learned in high school would not be enough to help her get by.

CROSS-CURRICULAR CONNECTIONS

Mathematics

Hana travels from Japan, to Angel Island, to San Francisco, and then across the San Francisco Bay to Oakland.

Ask students to look at maps to figure out how many miles Hana traveled in all.

Students who want an additional challenge might try to figure out how long the journey would take at different speeds. If they want to be more exact, they might do research to find out how fast a large steamship would be traveling. They might want to research how long the trip would be by airplane.

Vocabulary in Context

- We had only a meager amount of food in the cupboard, so we went shopping.
- The expanse of the football field impressed the small child.

Answers to Guided Reading Questions

❶ Hana believes he looks older than thirty-one.

❷ Hana is grateful that he doesn't mention marriage right away.

Additional Questions and Activities

Ask students to write two diary entries from the point of view of Hana.

- The first entry should be one that she writes on her first night in Oakland, and it should describe the end of her journey and her meeting with Taro.
- The second diary entry will be one that Hana writes ten years after her arrival in America. Students must use their imaginations as they address the following questions: What is her marriage like? Does she go to school? Does she have children? Where do they live? Encourage students to be creative, but to also be true to the characters as they are created by the author of the story.

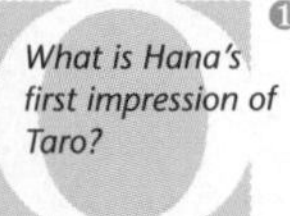

❶ *What is Hana's first impression of Taro?*

❷ *Why is Hana grateful?*

When she set foot on American soil at last, it was not in the city of San Francisco as she had expected, but on Angel Island, where all third-class passengers were taken. She spent two miserable days and nights waiting, as the immigrants were questioned by officials, examined for trachoma[6] and tuberculosis, and tested for hookworm.[7] It was a bewildering, degrading beginning, and Hana was sick with anxiety, wondering if she would ever be released.

On the third day, a Japanese messenger from San Francisco appeared with a letter for her from Taro. He had written it the day of her arrival, but it had not reached her for two days.

Taro welcomed her to America, and told her that the bearer of the letter would inform Taro when she was to be released so he could be at the pier to meet her.

The letter eased her anxiety for a while, but as soon as she was released and boarded the launch for San Francisco, new fears rose up to smother her with a feeling almost of dread.

The early morning mist had become a light chilling rain, and on the pier black umbrellas bobbed here and there, making the task of recognition even harder. Hana searched desperately for a face that resembled the photo she had studied so long and hard. Suppose he hadn't come. What would she do then?

Hana took a deep breath, lifted her head and walked slowly from the launch. The moment she was on the pier, a man in a black coat, wearing a derby and carrying an umbrella, came quickly to her side. He was of slight build, not much taller than she, and his face was sallow and pale. He bowed stiffly and murmured, "You have had a long trip, Miss Omiya. I hope you are well."

Hana caught her breath. "You are Takeda San?" she asked. He removed his hat and Hana was further startled to see that he was already turning bald. "You are Takeda San?" she asked again. He looked older than thirty-one.

"I am afraid I no longer resemble the early photo my parents gave you. I am sorry."

Hana had not meant to begin like this. It was not going well.

"No, no," she said quickly. "It is just that I . . . that is, I am terribly nervous. . . ." Hana stopped abruptly, too flustered to go on.

"I understand," Taro said gently. "You will feel better when you meet my friends and have some tea. Mr. and Mrs. Toda are expecting you in Oakland. You will be staying with them until . . ." He couldn't bring himself to mention the marriage just yet and Hana was grateful he hadn't.

He quickly made arrangements to have her baggage sent to Oakland, then led her carefully along the rain-slick pier toward the streetcar that would take them to the ferry.

6. **trachoma.** Contagious infection of the eye

7. **hookworm.** Disease caused by small worms that attach themselves to the intestines

Words for Everyday Use

de • grade (dē grād´) *v.,* bring into dishonor or contempt; humiliate

Vocabulary in Context

- To bully people or to make fun of people is to degrade them.

Hana shuddered at the sight of another boat, and as they climbed to its upper deck she felt a queasy tightening of her stomach.

"I hope it will not rock too much," she said anxiously. "Is it many hours to your city?"

Taro laughed for the first time since their meeting, revealing the gold fillings of his teeth. "Oakland is just across the bay," he explained. "We will be there in twenty minutes."

Raising a hand to cover her mouth, Hana laughed with him and suddenly felt better. I am in America now, she thought, and this is the man I came to marry. Then she sat down carefully beside Taro, so no part of their clothing touched. ■

❶ *Why is Hana relieved?*

About the Author

Yoshiko Uchida (1921–1992) frequently focused on the experiences of Asian Americans in her writing. Her books for young people include *Picture Bride* and *Desert Exile: The Uprooting of a Japanese American Family.* In this latter work, Uchida wrote from her own experience about the Japanese internment camps in the United States during World War II. When Uchida was a senior at the University of California, Berkeley, the government ordered people of Japanese descent to be incarcerated. Uchida and her family were first sent to a detention center at the Tanforan racetrack in California and were later moved to a guarded camp called Topaz in Utah. Uchida later earned a master's degree in education, but decided not to teach because it took to much time away from her writing.

ANSWER TO GUIDED READING QUESTION

❶ Hana is relieved that the boat trip to Oakland will not take long.

SELECTION CHECK TEST WITH ANSWERS

EX. Where is Hana Omiya going?
Hana is going to America.

1. For what does Hana long when she is on the ship?
Hana longs for her village in Japan.

2. Why is Hana going to America?
Hana is going to America to get married.

3. Why does Hana want to leave her village when she hears that Taro needs a wife?
Hana believes that her village will smother her. She wants a different life.

4. What surprises Hana when she first sees Taro?
Taro does not look like his picture—he looks older than she imagined him to be.

5. What does Taro say that relaxes Hana after her journey?
Taro tells her that the boat ride to Oakland is only twenty minutes long.

Responding to the Selection

You might ask students to get into small groups to discuss the characters and the situation. One person in the group should take notes.

Answers for Reviewing the Selection

RECALLING AND INTERPRETING

1. **Recalling.** Hana is on a ship going to America. She misses her home town. She wonders bitterly why she ever left Japan. **Interpreting.** She feels bitter because she is homesick, frightened, and uncomfortable.

2. **Recalling.** Hana is going to marry Taro Takeda, a lonely man who left Japan to make his fortune in Oakland, California. She knows that he is thirty-one years old, that he operates a small shop and rents some of the rooms above the shop, and that he has been in the United States for almost ten years. **Interpreting.** Hana might have decided to marry because she looked at it as a way to leave her village. She wanted a life different from the lives of her sisters.

3. **Recalling.** Her mother at first says no to the idea. **Interpreting.** Hana is sure that going to America will help her to escape the rigid life in her village.

4. **Recalling.** Hana thinks that Taro looks older than she had expected him to look. Hana feels better when Taro laughs and tells her that Oakland is only twenty minutes away by boat. **Interpreting.** The laughter relieves her tension after her stressful journey, which at that moment she realizes is almost over.

SYNTHESIZING

Responses will vary. Possible responses are given.

5. Students might say that Hana will have feelings of both doubt and happiness as she gets to know Taro. Students might say that the last line shows Hana's nervousness and a wish to take things slowly.

Responding to the Selection

Which character did you like the most in this story? the least? Why? Did your feelings about any character change as the story progressed? If so, which character did you change your feelings about and why?

Reviewing the Selection

Recalling and Interpreting

1. **R** Why is Hana on the ship? What does she miss? What does she wonder "bitterly"?

   I Why do you think Hana feels bitter about her present situation?

2. **R** Who is Hana going to marry? What does she know about this person?

   I Hana has not seemed very interested in getting married. Why do you think she has decided to marry anyway?

3. **R** What is her mother's first response when Hana suggests that she marry Taro?

   I Why does her mother's response make Hana determined to go to America?

4. **R** What does Hana think of Taro when she first sees him? What does Taro do and say that makes Hana feel better about her decision?

   I Why do you think this interaction makes Hana feel better?

Synthesizing

5. Do you think that Hana and Taro will be happy together? Why, or why not? Do you think Hana's feelings of doubt have changed? Why, or why not? In what way do you read the story's last line: "Then she sat down carefully beside Taro, so no part of their clothing touched."

Understanding Literature (Questions for Discussion)

1. **Setting.** The **setting** of a literary work is the time and place in which it happens. When and where is this story set? What details of the setting go along with Hana's state of mind?
2. **Flashback.** A **flashback** is a part of a story, poem, or play that presents events that happened at an earlier time. This story opens with Hana's traveling on a ship from Japan to America and ends with Hana's meeting her future husband. Between these two events, readers are given a flashback that tells how Hana came to make this journey. Identify the sentences that indicate the beginning and the end of the flashback. What does the flashback reveal about Hana and her situation that would otherwise be unknown to the reader?

Answers for Understanding Literature

Responses will vary. Possible responses are given.

1. **Setting.** This story takes place in an earlier time, on a steamship. The details about the moving ship and the sickness Hana feels while on the ship go along with her nervousness about her new adventure.

2. **Flashback.** The flashback begins with the line, "It all began one day when her uncle had come to visit her mother." The flashback ends with the line, "So it was that Hana had left her family and sailed alone to America with a small hope trembling inside of her." The flashback reveals Hana's reasons for marrying Taro, and the events and thoughts that led to her making this important decision.

Language Lab

Proofreading for Comma Errors

Without commas, writing would be confusing to read because words and phrases that should be separated would run together. You should always proofread your work and check to see that you have used commas correctly. Study the guidelines below to learn where commas are necessary in your own writing.

Use commas to separate items in a series. Three or more words make a series.

EXAMPLES Hana frets, worries, and reminisces.

Hana hoped her husband would be successful, affluent, and kind.

Use commas when you combine sentences using *and, but, for, so,* or *or.* Place the comma before these words.

UNCOMBINED	Hana stood at the rail of the ship. She thought about how she would miss Japan.
COMBINED	Hana stood at the rail of the ship, **and** she thought about how she would miss Japan.
UNCOMBINED	Hana was on her way to America. She was no longer sure that she wanted to go.
COMBINED	Hana was on her way to America, **but** she was no longer sure that she wanted to go.
UNCOMBINED	Hana wondered why she had ever left Japan. She thought about the chain of events that had led her to where she was today.
COMBINED	Hana wondered why she had ever left Japan, **so** she thought about the chain of events that had led her to where she was today.

Language Lab

Introducing the Skill

Explain to students that learning to use commas correctly will improve their writing. Readers are less likely to be confused because their sentences will be clearer.

Previewing the Skill

Go over with students the examples provided. Then ask students to review the Language Arts Survey, 2.27, "Commas."

Practicing the Skill

After students seem comfortable with comma usage, ask them to complete the Try it Yourself exercises.

Reviewing the Skill

Go over the correct answers to Try it Yourself. Review areas that seemed to cause the most difficulty. Some students might need individual attention.

Use a comma to set off words or phrases that interrupt sentences. Use two commas, one before and one after the interrupting word or phrase, if the word or phrase falls in the middle of the sentence. Use one comma if the word or phrase comes at the beginning or end of a sentence.

EXAMPLES Wow, I know I would never want to marry someone that I had never met before.

I read "Tears of Autumn," a short story.

Hana, who was well educated, was not content to always listen to the opinions of the men in her family.

Use commas to separate the parts of a date. Do not put a comma between the month and the day of the week.

EXAMPLE The date of their wedding was August 8, 1939.

Please read that story by Thursday, October 29.

Use commas to separate the parts of an address. Do not put a comma between the state and the ZIP Code.

EXAMPLE Hana was traveling to Oakland, California.

Appleville, IA 00100

Try It Yourself

Exercise A. Rewrite the sentences below, adding commas where they are necessary.

EXAMPLE Taro a kind man tried to make Hana feel more comfortable.
Taro, a kind man, tried to make Hana feel more comfortable.

1. My grandmother married my grandfather on February 14 1929.
2. My grandmother had just immigrated from Canton China.
3. My grandmother's parents who were farmers in China arranged the marriage with my grandfather in California.

CONTINUED

Answers for Try It Yourself

Exercise A

1. My grandmother married my grandfather on February 14, 1929.
2. My grandmother had just immigrated from Canton, China.
3. My grandmother's parents, who were farmers in China, arranged the marriage with my grandfather in California.
4. Honestly, I would be nervous traveling all the way to America to marry someone whom I had never met.
5. My grandmother respected her parents' judgment, so she traveled all the way to America on a ship.
6. She recognized my grandfather as soon as she saw him, and they shyly smiled at each other.
7. She was so nervous that her knees were quaking, but her fears disappeared once she realized how kind my grandfather was.
8. I have a picture of my grandmother and grandfather in my locket, the one that you borrowed last week and never returned.
9. Say, do you mind returning that locket sometime soon?
10. The locket reminds me of the story of my grandparents' arranged marriage, and it reminds me that often things work out for the best after all.

Exercise B

Say, did you know marriage customs vary widely in different cultures around the world? Marrying for love, free choice in choosing marriage partners, and romantic love itself are all relatively recent developments in Western culture. Free choice in marriage is usually a sign that a culture is composed of small families, and arranged marriages are usually a sign that the extended family is important in a culture. Matches are formed through an intermediary, or matchmaker, in societies with arranged marriages. The traditions associated with weddings differ depending on time, place, and culture.

Try It Yourself (cont.)

4. Honestly I would be nervous traveling all the way to America to marry someone whom I had never met.
5. My grandmother respected her parents' judgment so she traveled all the way to America on a ship.
6. She recognized my grandfather as soon as she saw him and they shyly smiled at each other.
7. She was so nervous that her knees were quaking but her fears disappeared once she realized how kind my grandfather was.
8. I have a picture of my grandmother and grandfather in my locket the one that you borrowed last week and never returned.
9. Say do you mind returning that locket sometime soon?
10. The locket reminds me of the story of my grandparents' arranged marriage and it reminds me that often things work out for the best after all.

Exercise B. The paragraph below contains errors in comma use. Rewrite the paragraph, correcting errors in comma use where necessary.

Say did you know marriage customs vary widely, in different cultures around the world? Marrying for love free choice in choosing marriage partners and romantic love itself are all relatively recent developments in Western culture. Free choice in marriage, is usually a sign that a culture is composed of small families and arranged marriages are usually a sign that the extended family is important in a culture. Matches are formed through an intermediary or matchmaker in societies, with arranged marriages. The traditions associated with weddings differ depending on time place and, culture.

ANALYTIC SCALE FOR PROJECT

Assign a score from 1 to 25 for each grading criterion below.

PLANNING A FRIENDSHIP HOLIDAY

- **Organization.** The group set attainable goals and created a schedule or strategy for achieving those goals.
- **Cooperation.** The group assigned tasks fairly to each member, and each member cooperated toward achieving the group's goals.
- **Goal Achievement.** The group worked steadily toward its goals and did, in fact, achieve them.
- **Presentation.** The group presented a product of high quality that met the inital project description.

Unit Project

PLANNING A FRIENDSHIP DAY CELEBRATION

Throughout the year, people celebrate certain relationships. Romantic couples celebrate Valentine's Day. Parents usually get presents and special meals on Mother's Day and Father's Day. There are also special days for grandparents, secretaries, and bosses. One important type of relationship that doesn't seem to have its own holiday is friendship. What if a new holiday were invented to celebrate friendship? What rituals and traditions might be a part of this holiday?

TRY IT YOURSELF

Your country is trying to establish a National Friendship Day celebration. Form committees of four or five people. Each committee should come up with a proposal, or plan, for a friendship holiday celebration. Proposals should answer the following questions: When will the holiday take place? What items and traditions will come to be associated with the holiday?

STUDENT MODEL

Students in Mr. Lorenzo's class are trying to organize a National Friendship Day celebration. They decide that people should take time to honor and appreciate good friends on this special day. The class splits into several committees. Each committee is in charge of putting together a proposal filled with ideas for the holiday. One committee has a discussion about friendship and what it means to people. Then the members of the committee talk about rituals, traditions, foods, and gifts that might be popular on this day. The committee then comes up with the following proposal:

National Friendship Day Celebration

Date: May 2

Purpose: This special holiday will encourage people to think about important friends in their lives and how valuable they are. They will spend the morning reflecting on their friends and writing notes to them or calling them.

Activities: The country will be on a two-hour delay. Businesses and schools will open two hours late on Friendship Day. The night before Friendship Day, there will be a special celebration at the White House. People will spend their mornings writing notes or putting together gifts. Then they will deliver them to special friends.

Friendship Day flowers: Wild flowers, particularly dandelions, daisies, and violets

Friendship Day foods: Pizza, because it is something people can share; oranges or tangerines that are split into sections for sharing

Friendship Day rituals: Leaving notes, flowers, or homemade gifts on the doorstep of a friend, or in some other place where the friend will easily find them

When all the proposals are finished, the class discusses them and decides upon the best and most realistic ideas from each proposal. Although the class is not able to put together a national holiday, they do organize a small, local Friendship Day. Students encourage people to participate by handing out fliers explaining the importance of showing appreciation for their friends.

Examining the Model

1. Why do the students want to put together a friendship celebration?
2. What are some of the steps that are taken to complete the project?
3. What ideas in the proposal did you like? What ideas might you change?

Planning the Celebration

1. Split the class into committees of four or five. As a committee, have a discussion about what friendship means to people. What sorts of ideas and activities do you associate with friendship?
2. Name specific traditions, rituals, and activities associated with holidays that are currently popular. Invent two or three traditions for your celebration.
3. What foods, decorations, or colors will be associated with your committee's friendship celebration? Should the celebration take place every year at the same time? If so, when will it take place?
4. Put your ideas in an outline similar to the one shown in the model.
5. You might include illustrations and diagrams with your proposal. Make designs for decorations or greeting cards.

Having and Sharing the Celebration

1. When each committee has come up with a proposal, combine some of the best ideas from each proposal to put together a class celebration.
2. Invite people to participate in the celebration by hanging signs, passing out fliers, or creating greeting cards. Tell people what the celebration is all about, and explain some of the traditions and rituals that you and your classmates have invented.
3. Even if a friendship holiday celebration does not catch on and become a widely honored tradition, you can vow to honor the tradition in your own way. Show your friends that you appreciate them by using some ideas brought up in the class proposals.

Project Note

Give students time to discuss and brainstorm ideas for the holiday. Remind them not to discard ideas until they have thought them through.

You might ask them to make a list of holiday rituals that already exist and then to do variations on those.

Vocabulary Check Test

Ask students to number their papers from one to ten. Have students complete each sentence with a word from the Vocabulary for the Unit in the Unit Review.

1. My kitten will recoil and hide at the sound of that loud noise.
2. Do not lavish gifts on the child—you will spoil him.
3. I just saw Sally beckon us over to her table.
4. We were hungry twenty minutes after eating the meager meal.
5. His small satchel held a wallet and a hairbrush.
6. Do they perpetuate the myth that the house on the hill is haunted?
7. Our canoe floated calmly on the placid lake.
8. Did your sister emigrate to another country?
9. People who get seasick should not boat in rough, turbulent waters.
10. The sight of the dirt and filth made me retch.

Unit Review

Summary

Literary Terms for the Unit

Vocabulary for the Unit

Questions for Writing, Discussion, and Research

1. Compare and contrast the relationships described in the selections in this unit.
2. Which characters from the selections in this unit do you admire? What traits and aspects of their relationships do you admire.

Spelling Check Test

Ask students to number their papers from one to ten. Read each word aloud. Then read aloud the sentence containing the word. Repeat the word. Ask students to write the word on their papers, spelling it correctly.

1. **expanse**

The expanse of the sea is breathtaking.

2. **affluence**

Some people show off affluence by driving fancy cars.

3. **consent**

Parents must give consent before their children may have surgery.

4. **scheme**

My little sister will scheme ways to get cookies.

5. **hunch**

Do not be rough and hunch people in line.

6. **lavish**

I will lavish praise on Samantha for her good work.

7. **drawl**

He speaks with a charming drawl.

8. **perpetuate**

It is wrong to perpetuate rumors about people.

9. **degrade**

Getting a poor grade on a test will degrade him.

10. **turbulent**

Turbulent waters caused our ship to sink.

For Your Reading List

Natassia Rozario
Grice Middle School
Hamilton, New Jersey

The House on Mango Street
by Sandra Cisneros

I found *The House on Mango Street* by Sandra Cisneros to be a heartwarming novel. It is a book with characters that come alive. The story is about a Hispanic girl named Esperanza who has been moving from apartment to apartment all her life. Her parents make promises of a beautiful house, but Esperanza and her family move into 4006 Mango Street, in a run-down neighborhood. She knows in her heart that this isn't the promised house. On Mango Street, she befriends two girls, Rachel and Lucy. With them she meets new people and learns their stories. Despite the people she meets, she feels that no one understands her except four skinny trees that live on her block. These trees are her inspiration and they are just like her. They don't belong on Mango Street. They, like her, have better dreams and must keep reaching for them. If they fail to reach their dreams, they droop in sadness. Esperanza's dream is to leave Mango Street and find out where she belongs in life. I strongly recommend this book. It is written in a unique style that touches the soul. It is the kind of book that is meant to be read over and over and treasured for a lifetime.

GOALS/OBJECTIVES

Studying this unit will enable students to

- enjoy two poems and two stories that focus on diversity
- briefly discuss such topics as the Harlem Renaissance, Native American languages, group thinking, the Sioux, and adolescence
- define the literary terms *alliteration, anecdote, concrete, conflict, irony,* and *motivation*
- proofread for punctuation errors, and write an oral history

ADDITIONAL UNIT MATERIALS IN THE ASSESSMENT PORTFOLIO

- Vocabulary Worksheet 2.4.9
- Unit Test 2.4.10

See also the Additional Resources Box in the marginal notes accompanying each selection.

CROSS-CURRICULAR ACTIVITIES IN THIS UNIT

- American History, 144, 162
- Science, 154
- Social Studies, 148
- Teen Living, 162

UNIT 4 DISCRIMINATION

The Problem We All Live With. Norman Rockwell. *Printed by permission of the Norman Rockwell Family Trust. Copyright © 1995 The Norman Rockwell Family Trust. Photo courtesy of the Norman Rockwell Museum of Stockbridge*

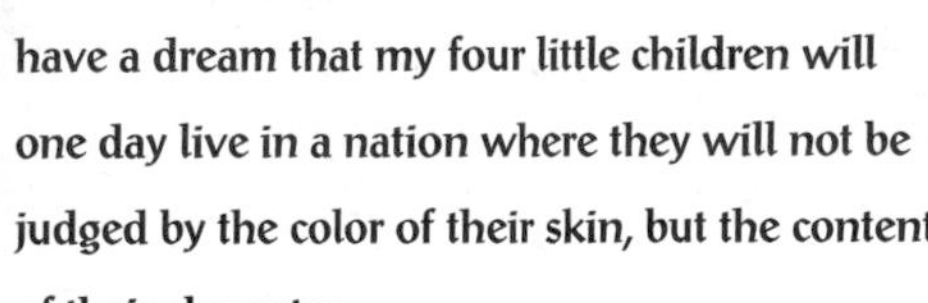

I have a dream that my four little children will one day live in a nation where they will not be judged by the color of their skin, but the content of their character.

—Martin Luther King, Jr.

UNIT SKILLS OUTLINE

Literary Skills and Concepts

- Alliteration, 147
- Anecdote, 172
- Concrete, 147
- Conflict, 161, 172
- Irony, 161
- Motivation, 151

Other Language Arts Skills and Concepts

- Editing for Punctuation Errors, 152
- Writing an Oral History, 173

GOALS/OBJECTIVES

Studying this lesson will enable students to

- enjoy a classic poem about the need to fulfill dreams
- briefly discuss the Harlem Renaissance
- define *alliteration* and find examples of alliteration in a poem
- define *concrete* and locate concrete words in a poem

ADDITIONAL RESOURCES

READER'S GUIDE

- Selection Worksheet, 4.1

ASSESSMENT PORTFOLIO

- Selection Check Test, 2.4.1
- Selection Test, 2.4.2

PRONUNCIATION EXERCISE

- Grade 8 Audiocassette, Side B, Track 19

CROSS-CURRICULAR CONNECTIONS

AMERICAN HISTORY

Ask students to do research on the Harlem Renaissance and then put together a report or project. Students might do a brief overview of the period or of one genre of art, or they might focus on one writer, artist, singer, or musician. Invite students to present their work to the rest of the class.

Prereading

POEM

"A Dream Deferred"
by Langston Hughes

Cross-curricular Connections

American History. The 1920s were known as "The Roaring Twenties" in the United States. This decade marked a period of growth, prosperity, and widespread social change in the country. With World War I just ended, Americans wanted to forget the troubles of warfare and enjoy life.

For many African Americans, the 1920s also marked the beginning of something much greater—an artistic and cultural blossoming. Led by scholar W. E. B. Du Bois, philosopher Alain Locke, and writer James Weldon Johnson, African-American writers, scholars, and artists discovered a wider audience and received much-deserved attention. This creative period later came to be known as the Harlem Renaissance.

Langston Hughes was an African-American poet who became widely known during the 1920s. He is often considered one of the most important poets of the Harlem Renaissance as well as one of the finest American poets. "A Dream Deferred" is one of Hughes's most famous and often-quoted poems. It addresses what happens to a people when prejudice holds their dreams in check for too long.

As You Read

In your journal, make a chart like the one below. As you read, list all the things that the speaker says can happen to a dream that is deferred, or postponed. Then, list your own ideas about what can happen to a dream when it is realized.

DREAM DEFERRED	DREAM REALIZED
dries up like a raisin in the sun	swells with sweetness like ripening strawberries

AS YOU READ

Charts will vary. Here are possible responses:

Dream Deferred	Dream Realized
festers and runs like a sore	glows like good health
stinks like rotten meat	smells like an orchard filled with fruit
crusts and sugars over like a syrupy sweet	rises and fills with warmth like a fresh loaf of bread
sags like a heavy load	a breeze of fresh air carrying a leaf
explodes	blooms

READER'S JOURNAL

What dreams do you have for yourself? How do you see yourself in the future? What do you imagine yourself accomplishing? What would it feel like if your dreams came true? What would it feel like if your dreams never came true? Write about these questions in your journal.

"A Dream Deferred"

LANGSTON HUGHES

Harlem

What happens to a dream deferred?

Does it dry up
like a raisin in the sun?
Or fester like a sore—
And then run?
Does it stink like rotten meat?
Or crust and sugar over—
like a syrupy sweet?

Maybe it just sags
like a heavy load.

Or does it explode? ■

❶ *Which of the options offered by the speaker do you think happens to a dream deferred? Why?*

WORDS FOR EVERYDAY USE

fes • ter (fes´tər) *v.*, form pus, become infected; grow bitter; decay

READER'S JOURNAL

Allow students to freewrite in their journals about their dreams. Then you might encourage them to narrow their list down to three dreams that they think are realistic. They should think of reasons why each dream might be difficult to fulfill, and then think of ways they might deal with and overcome the difficulties.

SPELLING AND VOCABULARY WORDS FROM THE SELECTION

fester

ANSWER TO GUIDED READING QUESTION

❶ Answers will vary. Students should explain why they believe a dream deferred would dry up, fester, rot, crust over, sag, or explode. You might ask them how these figures of speech translate into real human behavior. For example, how might a dream (and the person dreaming it) "explode"?

SUPPORT FOR LEP STUDENTS

ADDITIONAL VOCABULARY

deferred—delayed, postponed, put off,
syrupy—sweet and thick

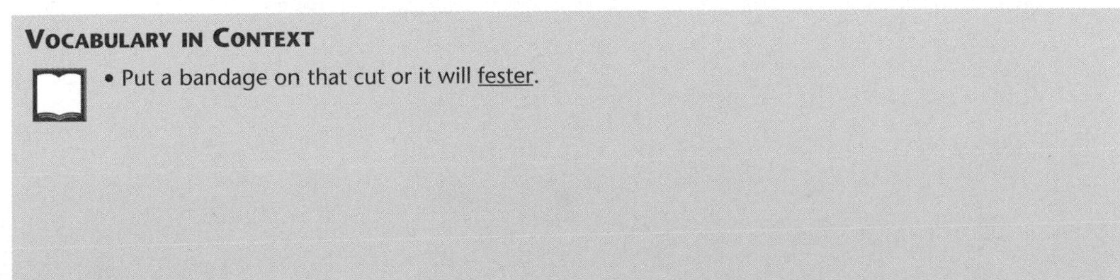

VOCABULARY IN CONTEXT

• Put a bandage on that cut or it will fester.

Selection Check Test with Answers

EX. What community is mentioned in this poem?

Harlem is mentioned in this poem.

1. With what question does the speaker open the poem?

The speaker opens the poem with the question, "What happens to a dream deferred?"

2. According to the speaker, if a dream deferred dries up, what might it look like?

A dream deferred might look like a raisin in the sun.

3. According to the speaker, what might a dream deferred smell like?

A dream deferred might "stink like rotten meat."

4. How might a dream deferred sag?

A dream deferred might sag like a heavy load.

5. What is the speaker's last question?

The speaker asks if a dream deferred might explode.

Photograph: Ricardo Blanc

Rooftops (No. 1, This is Harlem) [Harlem]. *Jacob Lawrence, 1943. Hirshhorn Museum and Sculpture Garden, Smithsonian Institution, Gift of Joseph H. Hirshhorn, 166.*

About the Author

Langston Hughes (1902–1967) was an American poet and short story writer born in Joplin, Missouri. He attended Columbia University for one year and then held many odd jobs until he published his first book of poems, *The Weary Blues* (1926). In this book, Hughes used sharp humor to relieve the despair he felt about economic and social conditions for African Americans. All of his books, including *The Dream Keeper* (1932) and *The Panther and the Lash* (1967), express Hughes's belief in the need for social justice.

Responding to the Selection

How would you respond if you were unable to realize your dreams? What would you wish to say about your dreams? Would you want to tell others why your dreams were important to you? Would you struggle until your dreams were fulfilled?

Reviewing the Selection

Recalling and Interpreting

1. **R** What community is named at the beginning of the poem?

   I What does the presence of this name imply about the poet's subject?

2. **R** What is the main question being asked by the speaker of the poem?

   I What types of dreams do you think the speaker is discussing?

3. **R** What verbs does the speaker use to describe the actions of a dream deferred?

   I What do you think the speaker is suggesting with these verbs?

4. **R** What two lines in the poem are written in italics?

   I Why do you think these two phrases are given special attention? Are they connected in any way? What might the speaker be suggesting by emphasizing these two lines?

Synthesizing

5. In what way does the action verb in the last line of the poem contrast with the action verbs in the previous lines of the poem? What does the presence of this final verb suggest about the need for people to feel like they are fulfilling their dreams?

Understanding Literature (Questions for Discussion)

1. **Alliteration. Alliteration** is the repetition of consonant sounds at the beginnings of syllables, as in *blind as a bat.* Notice that the alliterative consonant used at the beginning of the poem is repeated in the last line. Why do you think the poet made this consonant the last sound in the poem? What other examples of alliteration can you find in this poem?
2. **Concrete.** A **concrete** word, like *kite* or *sour,* refers to something that can be directly seen, tasted, touched, heard, or smelled. What concrete words can you find in this poem? What kinds of feelings and emotions do they call up? Why do you think the poet chose to use concrete examples that call up these feelings and emotions?

Responding to the Selection

Ask students to get into pairs to discuss their dreams. As a pair they should think of things that might stand in the way of their dreams. Then they should discuss ways to deal with these problems.

Answers for Reviewing the Selection

RECALLING AND INTERPRETING

1. **Recalling.** Harlem is named at the beginning of the poem. **Interpreting.** The presence of this name implies that the community of Harlem is the subject of the poem.
2. **Recalling.** The main question being asked is "What happens to a dream deferred?" **Interpreting.** The speaker might be discussing dreams of school, career, travel, or generally living a free, productive, happy life.
3. **Recalling.** The speaker uses the verbs *dry up, fester, run, stink, crust and sugar, sag,* and *explode.* **Interpreting.** The speaker is suggesting that nothing good can come of a dream deferred. Deferring a dream produces negative, unhealthy results.
4. **Recalling.** The lines *"Harlem,"* and *"Or does it explode?"* are written in italics. **Interpreting.** Harlem is populated mostly by African Americans, people whose dreams have often been deferred by social injustice. The speaker is suggesting that when people are not able to fulfill their dreams, the dreams do not simply disappear.

SYNTHESIZING

Responses will vary. Possible responses are given.

5. The verb *explode* is different in that it implies an action that is fast, violent, loud, and powerful. The other verbs imply a slow deterioration. The final verb suggests that the problem is urgent—that the dreams won't simply die with no further consequences.

Answers for Understanding Literature

Responses will vary. Possible responses are given.

1. **Alliteration.** The speaker wanted to relate the phrase "dream deferred" to the word explode. Students might notice sun and sore, run and rotten, and sugar and syrupy sweet as examples of alliteration.
2. **Concrete.** Words like *raisin, sun, dry, fester, sore, run, rotten, meat, crust, sugar, sweet, sag,* and *load* are all concrete. Students might say that most of these words present images of things dying, deteriorating, being heavy, or changing form. They call up feelings of sadness, despair, and loss. The poet wanted to use concrete words that call up these emotions because he wanted his readers to have these feelings about his subject.

GOALS/OBJECTIVES

Studying this lesson will enable students to

- enjoy a brief poem that shows a person from one culture being forced to adapt to the culture of another
- briefly discuss Native American languages
- define and understand *motivation*
- edit for punctuation errors

ADDITIONAL RESOURCES

READER'S GUIDE

- Selection Worksheet, 4.2

ASSESSMENT PORTFOLIO

- Selection Check Test, 2.4.2
- Selection Test, 2.4.3

PRONUNCIATION EXERCISE

- Grade 8 Audiocassette, Side B, Track 20

CROSS-CURRICULAR CONNECTIONS

SOCIAL STUDIES

Ask students to go to the library to do more research on Native American people. In small groups, students can choose to study one particular tribe or group from one particular area. In their research they might focus on language, daily life, art, and/or trade.

Prereading

POEM

"Name Giveaway"
by Phil George

Cross-curricular Connection

Social Studies. When the first European settlers arrived in America, Native American people on the North and South American continents spoke over two thousand different languages. North of Mexico alone, native groups spoke over two hundred languages. Many of these languages are unknown today, lost forever because the peoples who spoke them ceased to exist without leaving a written record of their language.

Scientists have classified ten different groups of Native American languages. Although some of these languages have similar words and grammar, others differ greatly. When members of many different tribes regularly came in contact, they would often choose one language for communication. For example, when other tribes came to trade in Chinook territory, the Chinook tribe did the speaking while trading took place. Chinook eventually became the trade language for tribes along the Columbia River in the Pacific Northwest.

Another way that Native Americans communicated was through a system of commonly understood gestures called sign language. Sign language, however, could not communicate complicated ideas. Smoke signals and drum signals were also used to communicate, although smoke and drum signals could also transmit only limited information such as a warning.

The most highly developed systems of communication were developed by communities in Central and South America. The Mayas developed a system of glyphs, which were symbols carved in stone. Mayan glyphs stood for both ideas and sounds, and were written on bark paper or deer hide. The Aztecs developed a system of writing—pictographs—that used pictures to stand for objects. This system was used mainly for keeping records and not for communicating ideas.

When separate cultures come in contact with each other, one often dominates the other. In the poem "Name Giveaway," the speaker is a Native American who is forced to adapt his language—including his name—to the dominant language of his school.

As You Read

"Name Giveaway" describes experiences of the speaker. In your journal, make a chart like the one below. As you read, fill in the chart with the speaker's experiences. In the second column, write how you think the items in the first column make the speaker feel or think.

SPEAKER'S EXPERIENCES	SPEAKER'S EMOTIONS AND THOUGHTS
teacher gave him or her a new name	confused, angry

AS YOU READ

Charts will vary. Here are possible responses:

Speaker's Experiences	Speaker's Emotions and Thoughts
teacher does not have feasts or a giveaway	upset and offended
speaker does not know what new names mean	confused
speaker believes his original name must be too hard to remember	sad, confused

READER'S JOURNAL

Have you ever asked your parents why they chose your name? Have you ever thought about giving yourself a different name? If you could pick any name for yourself, what would it be? Explain why you think this would be a better name. Write about these questions in your journal.

"Name Giveaway"

PHIL GEORGE

That teacher gave me a new name . . . again.
She never even had feasts or a giveaway!

Still I do not know what "George" means;
and now she calls me: "Phillip."

TWO SWANS ASCENDING FROM STILL WATERS
must be a name too hard to remember. ■

❶ *What is the speaker's name? Why does the teacher change the speaker's name?*

WORDS FOR EVERYDAY USE

as • cend (ə send´) *v.*, move upward, rise

READER'S JOURNAL

As an alternative activity, you might ask students if they have ever felt singled out or mistreated for being different in some way. Why are people sometimes rude or disrespectful to people who are different from themselves? Why are people sometimes afraid of diversity among people? What are some good reasons to enjoy diversity among a group of people?

SPELLING AND VOCABULARY WORDS FROM THE SELECTION

ascending

ANSWER TO GUIDED READING QUESTION

❶ The speaker's name is Two Swans Ascending From Still Waters. According to the speaker, the teacher changes his name to something that's easier for her to remember.

VOCABULARY IN CONTEXT

- Is that a whale ascending from the water?

ADDITIONAL QUESTIONS AND ACTIVITIES

The speaker's Native American name is beautiful and descriptive. It uses a scene from nature to reflect something in the speaker's personality. If you were to give yourself a name like this, what name would you choose for yourself? What in nature might reflect something in your own personality?

SELECTION CHECK TEST WITH ANSWERS

EX. What is the poet's name?

The poet's name is Phil George.

1. What did the teacher give the speaker again?

The teacher gave the speaker a new name.

2. What did the teacher not do?

The speaker did not have feasts or a giveaway.

3. What is the speaker's problem with the new names?

The speaker does not know what the names mean.

4. What is the speaker's original name?

The speaker's original name is Two Swans Ascending From Still Waters.

5. Why does the speaker believe the teacher has changed his name?

The speaker believes that his original name must be too hard for the teacher to remember.

Corn Dancers. *Mural in New Mexico*

About the Author

Phil George is a Nez Percé–Tsimshian poet. His Native American name is Two Swans Ascending From Still Waters. He is the great grandson of Chief Tawatoy. He loves grandmas, war-dancing, and fry-bread. George is a member of the Seven Drum religion.

Responding to the Selection

Is your name important to you? How would you feel if someone changed your name? What would you think of somebody who changed your name the way a teacher changed the speaker's name?

Reviewing the Selection

RECALLING AND INTERPRETING

1. **R** According to the speaker, what has the teacher done again? What does the speaker say the teacher did not have?

   I How does the speaker feel about what the teacher has done and has not done?

2. **R** What does the speaker say he does not understand?

   I Why do you suppose the teacher changed the speaker's name?

SYNTHESIZING

3. How does the teacher feel toward the speaker? Does the teacher respect him? How do you know? What does the teacher do that shows that she does not understand the speaker and his culture?

Understanding Literature (Questions for Discussion)

Motivation. Motivation is a force that moves a character to think, feel, or behave in a certain way. Although the teacher's motivation for calling the speaker Phillip and George is not stated directly, it is central to the meaning of the poem. What does the speaker think is the teacher's motivation for renaming him? What do you think is the teacher's motivation for renaming him?

RESPONDING TO THE SELECTION

You might ask students what they might say to the teacher if they were in the speaker's position. What might they say to the teacher in defense of the speaker keeping his original name?

ANSWERS FOR REVIEWING THE SELECTION

RECALLING AND INTERPRETING

1. **Recalling.** The speaker says that the teacher has given him a new name again. The speaker says that the teacher did not have feasts or a giveaway.

Interpreting. The speaker feels upset that the teacher gave him a new name, and that she did it without having the proper ceremonies.

2. **Recalling.** The speaker does not understand the meaning of his new name.

Interpreting. The teacher probably changed his name so that he would have a European name to which she is more accustomed.

SYNTHESIZING

Responses will vary. Possible responses are given.

3. By changing the speaker's name to a name that he does not like or understand, the teacher is showing disrespect to the speaker and his culture. She obviously does not understand that in the speaker's culture, a name is important and is not simply given without ceremony.

ANSWERS FOR UNDERSTANDING LITERATURE

Responses will vary. Possible responses are given.

1. **Motivation.** The speaker thinks that the teacher renames him because his original name is too hard for her to remember. Students might say that the teacher is motivated by intolerance for a name that is not from her own culture. Students might feel that she gives him an English name to replace his Native American name because she does not want to try to remember a name that is different from what she is used to hearing.

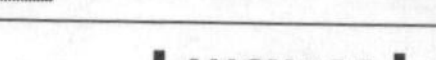

LANGUAGE LAB

INTRODUCING THE SKILL

Be sure that students understand the importance of proofreading. A paper with numerous punctuation errors will be difficult for a reader to enjoy, even if it is well written with excellent ideas.

PREVIEWING THE SKILL

Have the students examine the chart provided. Be sure that they read each of the examples carefully.

PRACTICING THE SKILL

When students seem to understand how to look for punctuation errors, ask them to complete the Try it Yourself exercises.

REVIEWING THE SKILL

Check the students' work. Spend time going over trouble spots. Some students might need individual attention.

Language Lab

Editing for Punctuation Errors

One of the final steps in the writing process before producing a final draft is proofreading your work for punctuation errors. Below you will find some punctuation rules that will help you proofread your writing. For more information on punctuation see the Language Arts Survey, 2.26–2.33, "Editing for Punctuation Errors."

PUNCTUATION

Type of Punctuation	Usage	Example
period	ends a declarative sentence	His name is George**.**
question mark	ends an interrogative sentence	Why do you call me Phillip**?**
exclamation point	ends an exclamatory sentence	She never even had a giveaway**!**
comma	after words like *yes, no, well* at the beginning of a sentence	Well**,** what should I call you?
	before a conjunction in a compound sentence	My name is Two Swans Ascending from Still Water**,** and I would like you to call me by name.
	between items in a list	She called me George**,** Phillip**,** and John.
semicolon	when combining sentences without a conjunction	She changed my name again**;** I do not understand.
	between items in a list that includes commas	She called me George, after a king**;** Phillip, after her brother**;** and John, because she liked the name.
colon	introduces a list	You may choose from the following names**:** Bob, Bill, Brian, or Bert.

CONTINUED

Type of Punctuation	Usage	Example
apostrophe	to form possessives, usually before an *s*	The student's name was not George.
italics	for titles of long works	***Voices of the Rainbow***
underlining	for titles of long works when italic type is not available	Voices of the Rainbow
quotation marks	for direct quotations and dialogue	"Do not call me George," said Two Swans Ascending from Still Water. "Okay, Phillip," replied the teacher.
	for titles of short works	"Name Giveaway"
hyphen	to link words in compound nouns, adjectives, or adverbs	George is an eighth-grade student.
dash	to show a sudden break in thought or to replace a phrase such as *in other words* or *namely*	The teacher thought little about what she did—changing the student's name.
parentheses	to enclose information that is not the main point in a sentence	The teacher (with no regard for my feelings) began to call me Gordon.

Try It Yourself

Rewrite the following sentences to correct any punctuation errors.

1. My family moved recently; and I had to go to a new school.
2. There were a lot of difficult things about going to a new school-making new friends and adjusting to new classes.
3. Introducing myself to the class was a nerve—wracking experience.
4. My name is Floating Like a Feather on the Wind, I said quietly.
5. "You'll have to speak up, Flo!" the teacher said calmly.
6. I repeated my name, everyone just stared at me.
7. "Well take a seat," said the teacher.
8. "We are reading the play "The Diary of Anne Frank."
9. "Have you read it," the teacher asked.
10. I told her I had read it; acted in it, and seen it performed.

Answers for Try It Yourself

1. My family moved recently, and I had to go to a new school.
2. There were a lot of difficult things about going to a new school—making new friends and adjusting to new classes.
3. Introducing myself to the class was a nerve-wracking experience.
4. "My name is Floating Like a Feather on the Wind," I said quietly.
5. *Correct.*
6. I repeated my name; everyone just stared at me.
7. "Well, take a seat," said the teacher.
8. We are reading the play, The Diary of Anne Frank.
9. "Have you read it?" the teacher asked.
10. I told her I had read it, acted in it, and seen it performed.

GOALS/OBJECTIVES

Studying this lesson will enable students to

- appreciate a story about intolerance and group thinking
- briefly discuss the psychology of group behavior
- define *conflict*
- define *irony* and recognize irony in a story

ADDITIONAL RESOURCES

READER'S GUIDE

- Selection Worksheet, 4.3

ASSESSMENT PORTFOLIO

- Selection Check Test, 2.4.5
- Selection Test, 2.4.6

PRONUNCIATION EXERCISE

- Grade 8 Audiocassette, Side B, Track 21

CROSS-CURRICULAR CONNECTIONS

SCIENCE

Ask students to conduct their own human observation experiment. They should go someplace where there is a crowd or more than a few people (hallway, park, supermarket, or library). Students should simply observe and take notes. Do they notice anything interesting? How do people behave with people they know? How do people behave with strangers? Can they make any generalizations based on their observations? Students should share their notes with the rest of the class.

Prereading

SHORT STORY

"The Fan Club"
by Rona Maynard

Cross-curricular Connection

Science. Social psychology is the study of human behavior in social settings. Social psychologists examine social groups and how a person's place within a social group affects the way in which he or she perceives others. They also study the ways in which individual personalities change in different social settings. Like chameleons that change color according to their environment, people can change their personalities according to their social situation. For example, a person might be very quiet when with one group of people but behave more boisterously when with another group.

In the story you are about to read, the main character changes her personality to belong to a certain social group. The main character claims that she has firm beliefs about the need to accept others regardless of their differences, but because of the peer pressure of a social group, she abandons her principles.

Social psychologists have conducted experiments that have given information about people's behavior in groups. One important factor in group behavior is called group cohesiveness. Group cohesiveness is the degree to which the members of a group are attracted to that group. When people are highly motivated to belong to a group, they are more likely to conform to the group's standards of conduct. In groups that are highly cohesive, members of the group also tend to interact and communicate more with each other. Members of a cohesive group also have higher morale and enthusiasm for the group and the group's activities. While group cohesiveness can be positive, it can also have negative consequences. When a group's standards involve making others feel inferior, as they do in "The Fan Club," group cohesiveness can encourage the members of a group to behave in intolerant, or unaccepting, ways.

As You Read

To help keep track of the plot development in this story, make a chart like the one below in your journal. As you read, record the actions and events. At the bottom of your chart, describe the message or lesson of the story.

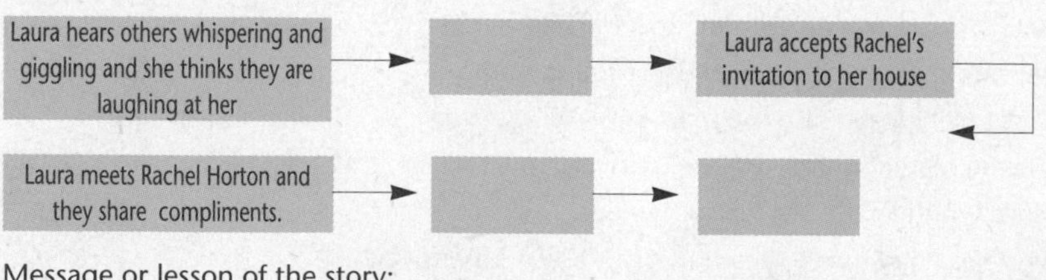

Message or lesson of the story: ______________________________

AS YOU READ

Answers may vary, but students might fill out their charts in the following way:

Laura hears whispering and giggling—Laura assumes people are laughing at her—Laura and Rachel chat—Rachel invites her to her home—Laura accepts the invitation reluctantly—Laura gives her speech about civil rights—Rachel gives a speech about shells—people laugh at Rachel—Laura breaks down and joins the nastiness.

Message or lesson of the story: It is easy to talk about civil rights, but shunning a group to be true to oneself takes courage and a strong character.

READER'S JOURNAL

How important is it to belong to groups? Do you ever feel that there is too much pressure to belong to certain groups? To what groups do you belong? What do you think your life would be like if you did not belong to any group or groups? Write about these questions in your journal.

"The Fan Club"

RONA MAYNARD

It was Monday again. It was Monday and the day was damp and cold. Rain splattered the cover of *Algebra I* as Laura heaved her books higher on her arm and sighed. School was such a bore.

School. It loomed before her now, massive and dark against the sky. In a few minutes, she would have to face them again—Diane Goddard with her sleek blond hair and Terri Pierce in her candy-pink sweater. And Carol and Steve and Bill and Nancy. . . . There were so many of them, so exclusive as they stood in their tight little groups laughing and joking.

Why were they so cold and unkind? Was it because her long stringy hair hung in her eyes instead of dipping in graceful curls? Was it because she wrote poetry in algebra class and got A's in Latin without really trying? Shivering, Laura remembered how they would sit at the back of English class, passing notes and whispering. She thought of their identical brown loafers, their plastic purses, their hostile stares as they passed her in the corridors. She didn't care. They were clods, the whole lot of them.

She shoved her way through the door and there they were. They thronged the hall, streamed in and out of doors, clustered under red and yellow posters advertising the latest dance. Mohair sweaters, madras shirts, pea-green raincoats. They were all alike, all the same. And in the center of the group, as usual, Diane Goddard was saying, "It'll be a riot! I just can't wait to see her face when she finds out."

Laura flushed painfully. Were they talking about her?

"What a scream! Can't wait to hear what she says!"

❶ *Laura thinks this group of students is whispering about and staring at whom?*

❷ *What does Laura think of this group of students?*

❸ *What does Laura say about the group and conformity?*

WORDS FOR EVERYDAY USE

throng (thrôŋ) *v.*, crowd; press upon in large numbers

READER'S JOURNAL

You might also ask students to write about the ways in which being in a group can be negative. How might a group mistreat people or prevent free thinking?

ANSWERS TO GUIDED READING QUESTIONS

❶ Laura thinks that they are whispering about her and staring at her.

❷ Laura thinks that the group is exclusive, cold, and unkind.

❸ According to Laura, they dress, look, and behave the same as one another.

SPELLING AND VOCABULARY WORDS FROM THE SELECTION

billow	gesture
cynical	irrational
distributive	jostling
gaudy	throng

SUPPORT FOR LEP STUDENTS

PRONUNCIATIONS OF PROPER NOUNS AND ADJECTIVES

God • dard (gäd´ərd) n.
Mer • rill (mer´əl) n.
Hor • ten • sky (hôr ten´skē) n.

ADDITIONAL VOCABULARY

district—area of a town; neighborhood
flushed—blushed
hollow—emotionless
liberals—open-minded and tolerant people
madras—a type of cotton cloth
snickers—mean-spirited, nasty laughs
submerged—buried, placed under or below

VOCABULARY IN CONTEXT

• Will people throng the hall, or will it be a quiet day?

Answers to Guided Reading Questions

❶ Laura is flattered by Rachel's compliment. She feels embarrassed and blushes.

❷ Laura has reservations about becoming Rachel's friend and visiting Rachel in her neighborhood.

Additional Questions and Activities

Ask students to answer the following questions:

- Why does Laura not seem excited to have Rachel for a friend?
- How might Rachel feel if she knew what Laura was thinking when Rachel invited her to her house?

ANSWERS

Responses will vary.

Students might say that Laura is so caught up in the idea that Rachel is not part of the popular crowd, that she does not feel completely comfortable with her as a friend. She is afraid of being teased.

Students might recognize that Rachel would probably feel hurt and disappointed if she knew what Laura was thinking.

❶ How does Laura feel about Rachel's compliment?

❷ How does Laura feel about becoming Rachel's friend?

Silently she hurried past and submerged herself in the stream of students heading for the lockers. It was then that she saw Rachel Horton—alone as always, her too-long skirt billowing over the white, heavy columns of her legs, her freckled face ringed with shapeless black curls. She called herself Horton, but everyone knew her father was Jacob Hortensky, the tailor. He ran that greasy little shop where you could always smell the cooked cabbage from the back rooms where the family lived.

"Oh, Laura!" Rachel was calling her. Laura turned, startled.

"Hi, Rachel."

"Laura, did you watch *World of Nature* last night? On Channel 11?"

"No—no, I didn't." Laura hesitated. "I almost never watch that kind of program."

"Well, gee, you missed something—last night, I mean. It was a real good show. Laura, it showed this fly being born!" Rachel was smiling now; she waved her hands as she talked.

"First the feelers and then the wings. And they're sort of wet at first, the wings are. Gosh, it was a good show."

"I bet it was." Laura tried to sound interested. She turned to go, but Rachel still stood there, her mouth half open, her pale, moon-like face strangely urgent. It was as if an invisible hand tugged at Laura's sleeve.

"And Laura," Rachel continued, "that was an awful good poem you read yesterday in English."

Laura remembered how Terri and Diane had laughed and whispered. "You really think so? Well, thanks, Rachel. I mean, not too many people care about poetry."

"Yours was real nice though. I wish I could write like you. I always like those things you write."

Laura blushed. "I'm glad you do."

"Laura, can you come over sometime after school? Tomorrow maybe? It's not very far and you can stay for dinner. I told my parents all about you!"

Laura thought of the narrow, dirty street and the tattered awning in front of the tailor shop. An awful district, the kids said. But she couldn't let that matter. "Okay," she said. And then, faking enthusiasm, "I'd be glad to come."

She turned into the algebra room, sniffing at the smell of chalk and dusty erasers. In the back row, she saw the "in" group, laughing and joking and whispering.

"What a panic!"

"Here, you make the first one."

Diane and Terri had their heads together over a lot of little cards. You could see they were cooking up something.

Fumbling through the pages of her book, she tried to memorize the theorems she hadn't looked at the night before. The laughter at the back of the room rang in her ears. Also those smiles—those heartless smiles. . . .

A bell buzzed in the corridors; students scrambled to their places. "We

Words for Everyday Use

bil • low (bil´ō) *v.*, surge; swell

Vocabulary in Context

- The hot-air balloon will billow as it is filled.

will now have the national anthem," said the voice on the loudspeaker. Laura shifted her weight from one foot to the other. It was so false, so pointless. How could they sing of the land of the free, when there was still discrimination. Smothered laughter behind her. Were they all looking at her?

And then it was over. Slumping in her seat, she shuffled through last week's half-finished homework papers and scribbled flowers in the margins.

"Now this one is just a direct application of the equation." The voice was hollow, distant, an echo beyond the sound of rustling papers and hushed whispers. Laura sketched a guitar on the cover of her notebook. Someday she would live in the Village and there would be no more algebra classes and people would accept her.

She turned towards the back row. Diane was passing around one of her cards. Terri leaned over, smiling. "Hey, can I do the next one?"

". . . by using the distributive law." Would the class never end? Math was so dull, so painfully dull. They made you multiply and cancel and factor, multiply, cancel, and factor. Just like a machine. The steel sound of the bell shattered the silence. Scraping chairs, cries of "Hey, wait!" The crowd moved into the hallway now, a thronging, jostling mass.

Alone in the tide of faces, Laura felt someone nudge her. It was Ellen. "Hey, how's that for a smart outfit?" She pointed to the other side of the hall.

The gaudy flowers of Rachel Horton's blouse stood out among the fluffy sweaters and pleated skirts. What a lumpish, awkward creature Rachel was. Did she have to dress like that? Her socks had fallen untidily around her heavy ankles, and her slip showed a raggedy edge of lace. As she moved into the English room, shoelaces trailing, her books tumbled to the floor.

"Isn't that something?" Terri said. Little waves of mocking laughter swept through the crowd.

The bell rang; the laughter died away. As they hurried to their seats, Diane and Terri exchanged last-minute whispers. "Make one for Steve. He wants one too!"

Then Miss Merrill pushed aside the book she was holding, folded her hands, and beamed. "All right, people, that will be enough. Now, today we have our speeches. Laura, would you begin please?"

So it was her turn. Her throat tightened as she thought of Diane and Carol and Steve grinning and waiting for her to stumble. Perhaps if she was careful they'd never know she hadn't thought out everything beforehand. Careful, careful, she thought. Look confident.

"Let's try to be prompt." Miss Merrill tapped the cover of her book with her fountain pen.

Laura pushed her way to the front of the class. Before her, the room was large and still. Twenty-five round,

1 *How do the other students behave towards Rachel?*

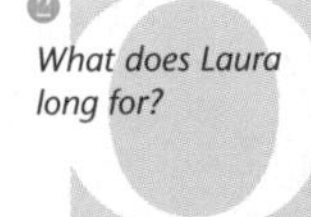

2 *What does Laura long for?*

WORDS FOR EVERYDAY USE	
	dis • trib • u • tive (di strib´yo͞o tiv) *adj.*, administered; furnished
	jos • tling (jäs´liŋ) *adj.*, roughly pushing
	gaudy (gôd´ē) *adj.*, bright and showy, but lacking in good taste

ANSWERS TO GUIDED READING QUESTIONS

1 The other students make fun of Rachel and her clothing. They laugh at her.

2 Laura longs for the day when she can move away and never do algebra again. She wants to move to a place where people will accept her.

CROSS-CURRICULAR CONNECTIONS

SCIENCE

Ask students to find books and articles in the library that address issues of self-esteem in young people. How might Rachel's school experience affect her years from now? Ask them also to consider how the treatment of Rachel by her classmates reflects on the self-esteem of the victimizers.

VOCABULARY IN CONTEXT

- Are you using distributive law to do that math problem?
- The jostling students filled the hallway.
- Do you think that the bright flower pattern is gaudy?

Additional Questions and Activities

Ask students to discuss the ideas expressed in Laura's speech. Do they agree with them? What is the best point that she makes? Do they think that Laura will hold true to these ideals?

blurred faces stared blankly. Was that Diane's laughter? She folded her hands and looked at the wall, strangely distant now, its brown paint cracked and peeling. A dusty portrait of Robert Frost, a card with the seven rules for better paragraphs, last year's calendar, and the steady, hollow ticking of the clock.

Laura cleared her throat. "Well," she began, "my speech is on civil rights." A chorus of snickers rose from the back of the room.

"Most people," Laura continued, "most people don't care enough about others. Here in New England, they think they're pretty far removed from discrimination and violence. Lots of people sit back and fold their hands and wait for somebody else to do the work. But I think we're all responsible for people that haven't had some of the advantages. . . ."

Diane was giggling and gesturing at Steve Becker. All she ever thought about was parties and dates—and such dates! Always the president of the student council or the captain of the football team.

Words for Everyday Use

ges • ture (jes´chər) *v.,* express or emphasize ideas and emotions with physical movement

Vocabulary in Context

• His frantic gesture indicated a serious problem.

"A lot of people think that race prejudice is limited to the South. But most of us are prejudiced—whether we know it or not. It's not just that we don't give other people a chance; we don't give ourselves a chance either. We form narrow opinions and then we don't see the truth. We keep right on believing that we're open-minded liberals when all we're doing is deceiving ourselves."

How many of them cared about truth? Laura looked past the rows of blank, empty faces, past the bored stares and cynical grins.

"But I think we should try to forget our prejudices. We must realize now that we've done too little for too long. We must accept the fact that one person's misfortune is everyone's responsibility. We must defend the natural dignity of people—a dignity that thousands are denied."

None of them knew what it was like to be unwanted, unaccepted. Did Steve know? Did Diane?

"Most of us are proud to say that we live in a free country. But is this really true? Can we call the United States a free country when millions of people face prejudice and discrimination? As long as one person is forbidden to share the basic rights we take for granted, as long as we are still the victims of irrational hatreds, there can be no freedom. Only when every American learns to respect the dignity of every other American can we truly call our country free."

The class was silent. "Very nice, Laura." Things remained quiet as other students droned through their speeches. Then Miss Merrill looked briskly around the room. "Now, Rachel, I believe you're next."

There was a ripple of dry, humorless laughter—almost, Laura thought, like the sound of a rattlesnake. Rachel stood before the class now, her face red, her heavy arms piled with boxes.

Diane Goddard tossed back her head and winked at Steve.

"Well, well, don't we have lots of things to show," said Miss Merrill. "But aren't you going to put those boxes down, Rachel? No, no, not there!"

"Man, that kid's dumb," Steve muttered, and his voice could be clearly heard all through the room.

With a brisk rattle, Miss Merrill's pen tapped the desk for silence.

Rachel's slow smile twitched at the corners. She looked frightened. There was a crash and a clatter as the tower of boxes slid to the floor. Now everyone was giggling.

"Hurry and pick them up," said Miss Merrill sharply.

Rachel crouched on her knees and began very clumsily to gather her scattered treasures. Papers and boxes lay all about, and some of the boxes had broken open, spilling their contents in wild confusion. No one went to help. At last she scrambled to her feet and began fumbling with her notes.

"My—my speech is on shells."

A cold and stony silence had settled upon the room.

❶ *What does Laura say about prejudice?*

❷ *What does the class's laughter sound like?*

❸ *What does Laura think about during her speech?*

❹ *What does Laura wonder about the "in" group?*

❺ *What does Laura say about responsibility? about dignity?*

Words for Everyday Use

cy • ni • cal (sin´i kəl) *adj.*, sarcastic; sneering

ir • ra • tion • al (ir rash´ə nəl) *adj.*, lacking the power to reason; absurd

Answers to Guided Reading Questions

❶ Laura says that most people are prejudiced, whether they know it or not.

❷ The class's laughter has the sound of a rattlesnake.

❸ Laura wonders how many people in the "in" group care about truth.

❹ Laura thinks about how none of the people in the popular group knew what it was like to be unwanted or unaccepted.

❺ Laura says that one person's misfortune is everyone's responsibility, and that the natural dignity of people must be defended.

Additional Questions and Activities

Students might be disturbed by the ending of the story. Invite them to discuss Laura's actions. They should address the following ideas in their discussion.

- What do the students feel is the reason for Laura's behavior?
- Do students totally disrespect Laura? Why, or why not?
- Ask students to write a letter to Rachel, trying to convince her that life will eventually improve. They should try to be positive and give her ways to cope.

Vocabulary in Context

- She thought her speech had been good, but she sensed some cynical laughter coming from the back of the classroom.
- Their dislike for the innocent person was irrational.

Answers to Guided Reading Questions

❶ Laura feels relieved that the group is plotting against Rachel, not her. When she looks at Rachel's face, she feels bad.

❷ The laughter and the comments make Rachel nervous and cause her to forget what she is saying.

Selection Check Test with Answers

EX. Where is Laura going on Monday morning?
Laura is going to school.

1. What kinds of groups does Laura dread seeing?
Laura dreads seeing the popular groups.

2. About whom does Laura think the popular kids whisper?
Laura thinks the popular kids whisper about her.

3. Who invites Laura to her house after school?
Rachel invites Laura to her house.

4. What is the subject of Laura's speech?
Civil rights is the subject of Laura's speech.

5. What does the class do when Rachel gives her speech?
The class laughs and makes fun of Rachel.

"Lots of people collect shells, because they're kind of pretty—sort of, and you just find them on the beach."

"Well, whaddaya know!" It was Steve's voice, softer this time, but all mock amazement. Laura jabbed her notebook with her pencil. Why were they so cruel, so thoughtless? Why did they have to laugh?

"This one," Rachel was saying as she opened one of the boxes, "it's one of the best." Off came the layers of paper and there, at last, smooth and pearly and shimmering, was the shell. Rachel turned it over lovingly in her hands. White, fluted sides, like the close-curled petals of a flower; a scrolled coral back. Laura held her breath. It was beautiful. At the back of the room snickers had begun again.

❶ *How does Laura feel when she realizes the "in" group was plotting against Rachel, not her?*

"Bet she got it at Woolworth's," somebody whispered.

"Or in a trash dump." That was Diane.

Rachel pretended not to hear, but her face was getting very red and Laura could see she was flustered.

❷ *What effect does the students' laughter and comments have upon Rachel?*

"Here's another that's kind of pretty. I found it last summer at Ogunquit." In her outstretched hand there was a small, drab, brownish object. A common snail shell. "It's called a . . . It's called. . . ."

Rachel rustled through her notes. "I—I can't find it. But it was here. It was in here somewhere. I know it was." Her broad face had turned bright pink again. "Just can't find it. . . ." Miss Merrill stood up and strode toward her. "Rachel," she said sharply, "we are supposed to be prepared when we make a speech. Now, I'm sure you remember those rules on page twenty-one. I expect you to know these things. Next time you must have your material organized."

The bell sounded, ending the period. Miss Merrill collected her books.

Then, suddenly, chairs were shoved aside at the back of the room and there was the sound of many voices whispering. They were standing now, whole rows of them, their faces grinning with delight. Choked giggles, shuffling feet—and then applause—wild, sarcastic, malicious applause. That was when Laura saw that they were all wearing little white cards with a fat, frizzy-haired figure drawn on the front. What did it mean? She looked more closely. "HORTENSKY FAN CLUB," said the bright-red letters.

So that was what the whispering had been about all morning. She'd been wrong. They weren't out to get her after all. It was only Rachel.

Diane was nudging her and holding out a card. "Hey, Laura, here's one for you to wear. "

For a moment Laura stared at the card. She looked from Rachel's red, frightened face to Diane's mocking smile, and she heard the pulsing, frenzied rhythm of the claps and the stamping, faster and faster. Her hands trembled as she picked up the card and pinned it to her sweater. And as she turned, she saw Rachel's stricken look.

"She's a creep, isn't she?" Diane's voice was soft and intimate.

And Laura began to clap. ■

Responding to the Selection

If you were Laura, how would you have acted at the end of the story? Would you have put on the pin and clapped? Why, or why not?

Reviewing the Selection

RECALLING AND INTERPRETING

1. **R** What does Laura do in algebra class? What does she do in Latin class "without really trying"?

   I Why might this behavior make other students act "cold and unkind" toward her?

2. **R** What is Rachel Horton's real name? What is Laura's response to Rachel's invitation?

   I Why do you think Rachel chooses to call herself Rachel Horton? What does Laura's response reveal about her character?

3. **R** What is the subject of Laura's speech? In what way does the class respond when Laura finishes the speech?

   I What does Laura's speech reveal about her character? about her anxieties?

4. **R** To what is the class's laughter compared? What does the class do during Rachel's presentation? after her presentation?

   I What does this comparison reveal about the class? What does their treatment of Rachel reveal about the class?

SYNTHESIZING

5. Why do you think Laura joined the "fan club"? Did her action surprise you? Why, or why not? In your opinion, who hurt Rachel more, Laura or Diane? How did you feel about the end of the story? Explain your responses.

Understanding Literature (Questions for Discussion)

1. **Conflict.** A **conflict** is a struggle between two people or things in a literary work. What is the conflict that opens this story? In what ways do Laura and Rachel seem like teammates struggling against the same opposition in this conflict?
2. **Irony. Irony** is a difference between appearance and reality. Explain why Laura's speech on prejudice is ironic, given her later behavior and her relief that "They weren't out to get her after all. It was only Rachel."

RESPONDING TO THE SELECTION

Ask students to discuss what they might say to Laura after class. Would they be understanding, or would they confront her about her cruel act against Rachel?

ANSWERS FOR REVIEWING THE SELECTION

RECALLING AND INTERPRETING

1. **Recalling.** She writes poetry in algebra class and gets A's in Latin without really trying. **Interpreting.** Because the group seems to be against anyone who is different, she feels that her behavior might prompt them to dislike her.

2. **Recalling.** Her real name is Rachel Hortensky. Rachel accepts the invitation, but she has reservations about it. **Interpreting.** Rachel might call herself Rachel Horton so that she will fit in with others at school. Laura's response reveals that she wants to be nice, but that she cares a great deal about what others think.

3. **Recalling.** Laura's speech is about civil rights. The class is silent when she finishes her speech. **Interpreting.** Laura's speech reveals her concern about acceptance. This concern has more to do with her own anxieties and her own wish to fit in than anything else.

4. **Recalling.** The class's laughter is compared to the noise of a rattlesnake. The class laughs at Rachel and her presentation. After the presentation they ridicule her by wearing buttons that say "Hortensky Fan Club." **Interpreting.** The comparison reveals that the class is mean, insensitive, and nasty.

SYNTHESIZING

Responses will vary. Possible responses are given.

5. Laura does not have the strength to stand up for what she believes. Students might say that Laura is more hurtful because Rachel thought of her as a friend.

ANSWERS FOR UNDERSTANDING LITERATURE

Responses will vary. Possible responses are given.

1. **Conflict.** The conflict that opens this story is the conflict between Laura and the popular crowd. Laura and Rachel both seem to be outsiders, with their own interests.

2. **Irony.** Even after she just finished telling people to be more accepting, and that the dignity of people should be defended, Laura takes part in the cruel ridicule of Rachel. She even seems relieved and free of anxiety as soon as she hears that Rachel is the object of the ridicule.

GOALS/OBJECTIVES

Studying this lesson will enable students to

- enjoy a short story about a family's heritage
- briefly discuss the Sioux people
- briefly discuss adolescence
- define and understand *conflict*
- define *anecdote*
- write an oral history

ADDITIONAL RESOURCES

READER'S GUIDE

- Selection Worksheet, 4.4

ASSESSMENT PORTFOLIO

- Selection Check Test, 2.4.7
- Selection Test, 2.4.8

PRONUNCIATION EXERCISE

- Grade 8 Audiocassette, Side B, Track 22

CROSS-CURRICULAR CONNECTIONS

AMERICAN HISTORY

Ask students to do papers or reports about some aspect of the Sioux. They can focus on their daily lives, their art and their crafts, their connection to the natural world, or their struggles against the U.S. Army. They should share their information, pictures, or other materials with the rest of the class.

TEEN LIVING

Ask students to interview teenagers at various stages of their adolescence. People they interview should talk about what is hardest about being an adolescent, and what they have learned about their personal identities. Students can share their findings with the rest of the class.

Prereading

SHORT STORY

"The Medicine Bag"
by Virginia Driving Hawk Sneve

Cross-curricular Connections

American History. Long before the arrival of Europeans in North America, the Sioux, or Dakota, built one of the proudest of all Native American cultures. The Sioux originally lived near Lake Superior but migrated to the Great Plains in the middle of the seventeenth century. On the prairies of this region, they gained fame as skilled hunters of buffalo. They also created beautiful beaded embroidery.

The Sioux felt a strong spiritual connection to the land that supported them. Their religion shows respect for the natural world and all its creatures. It is not surprising that people who felt such a connection to the land were determined not to let settlers take it away. The U.S. Army and the Sioux fought a series of wars over land. At first, the Sioux succeeded in their struggle. Red Cloud led warriors to victory, and the Treaty of Fort Laramie in 1868 protected Sioux rights. The treaty, however, was broken, and leaders such as Sitting Bull and Crazy Horse engaged in further battles. One of the most famous was the Battle of Little Bighorn in which Lieutenant Colonel George Armstrong Custer was defeated. Despite such victories, the Sioux could not stop the tide of incoming settlers. Sioux chiefs surrendered, were captured, or were killed. When innocent Sioux men, women, and children were massacred at the Battle of Wounded Knee in 1890, Sioux resistance died with them. The people who had once traveled the wide prairies were confined to reservations. Today, some forty thousand Sioux live on reservations in North and South Dakota, Montana, and Nebraska.

Teen Living. During adolescence, the period from roughly age thirteen to age nineteen, a young person begins to create his or her own identity, or self-definition. Thinking about such matters as family history and cultural heritage can be an important part of the search for a concept of the self. In "The Medicine Bag," the narrator realizes that his heritage is an important part of his identity. He begins to see himself as deeply connected to a larger community—to his cultural heritage and to his people.

As You Read

"The Medicine Bag" contains many words describing parts of Native American culture. In your journal, make a chart like the one below. As you read, list Native American terms and write definitions for them, based on what you know and on clues in the story.

NATIVE AMERICAN TERM	DEFINITION
moccasins	soft leather slippers

162 UNIT FOUR / DISCRIMINATION

AS YOU READ

Answers may vary, but students might complete their charts in the following way:

rawhide—animal skin

Hau, Takoza—a greeting

Wicincala—greeting

medicine bag—leather pouch in which important items are kept. Bag is passed from generation to generation.

READER'S JOURNAL

What is your ethnic heritage? Do you think that your ethnic heritage is important? Is your heritage a source of pride for you or something that you rarely consider? What do you know about your ancestors? Do you have any family traditions or stories? Write about these questions in your journal. If you know little about your ethnic heritage, write about whether finding out about your ethnic heritage is important to you.

"The Medicine Bag"

VIRGINIA DRIVING HAWK SNEVE

My kid sister Cheryl and I always bragged about our Sioux grandpa, Joe Iron Shell. Our friends, who had always lived in the city and knew about Indians only from movies and TV, were impressed by our stories. Maybe we exaggerated and made Grandpa and the reservation sound glamorous, but when we'd return home to Iowa after our yearly summer visit to Grandpa, we always had some exciting tale to tell.

We always had some authentic Sioux article to show our listeners. One year Cheryl had new moccasins that Grandpa had made. On another visit he gave me a small, round, flat rawhide drum that was decorated with a painting of a warrior riding a horse. He taught me a real Sioux chant to sing while I beat the drum with a leather-covered stick that had a feather on the end. Man, that really made an impression.

We never showed our friends Grandpa's picture. Not that we were ashamed of him, but because we knew that the glamorous tales we told didn't go with the real thing. Our friends would have laughed at the picture because Grandpa wasn't tall and stately like TV Indians. His hair wasn't in braids but hung in stringy gray strands on his neck, and he was old. He was our great-grandfather, and he didn't live in a tepee but all by himself in a part log, part tar-paper shack on the Rosebud Reservation[1] in South Dakota. So when Grandpa came to visit us, I was so ashamed and embarrassed I could've died.

There are a lot of yippy poodles and other fancy little dogs in our neighborhood, but they usually barked singly at the mailman from the safety of their own yards. Now it sounded as

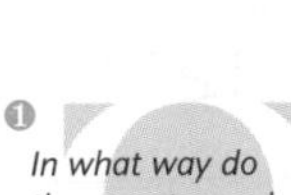

❶ *In what way do the narrator and his sister impress their friends?*

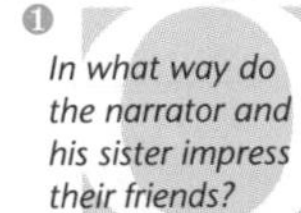

❷ *How does the narrator feel when Grandpa comes to visit?*

1. **Rosebud Reservation.** Land set aside for the Sioux; has a population of eighteen thousand

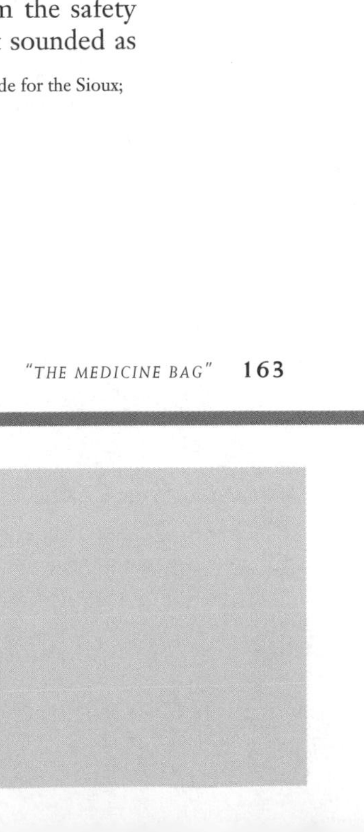

WORDS FOR EVERYDAY USE

state • ly (stāt´lē) *adj.*, dignified

READER'S JOURNAL

Students might choose to focus on one or two of the questions provided. They should answer the questions that they find most interesting.

SPELLING AND VOCABULARY WORDS FROM THE SELECTION

basin	reluctantly
commotion	rouse
confine	sheepishly
descendant	stately
fatigue	thong
purifying	unseemly
reinforce	

ANSWERS TO GUIDED READING QUESTIONS

❶ The narrator and his sister impress their friends with stories about their grandfather and the reservation. They also show off genuine Sioux articles.

❷ The narrator feels ashamed and embarrassed when Grandpa comes to visit.

SUPPORT FOR LEP STUDENTS

PRONUNCIATIONS OF PROPER NOUNS AND ADJECTIVES

Sioux (so͞o) n.

ADDITIONAL VOCABULARY

awed—fascinated
burden—bother, difficult problem
embrace—hug

VOCABULARY IN CONTEXT

• His stately manner often impressed people.

Answers to Guided Reading Questions

1 The narrator is angry that the dogs are bothering his grandfather. He feels protective of his grandfather.

2 Grandpa does not believe in displays of affection. They embarrass him.

Additional Questions and Activities

Ask students the following question:

What conflicting feelings does the narrator have for his great-grandfather when he sees him in the street with dogs nipping at his legs, and then when he must help him to the house?

ANSWERS

Responses will vary.

Students might say that the narrator feels protective and compassionate for his great-grandfather, but that he is also embarrassed by him.

if a whole pack of mutts were barking together in one place.

I got up and walked to the curb to see what the commotion was. About a block away I saw a crowd of little kids yelling, with the dogs yipping and growling around someone who was walking down the middle of the street.

I watched the group as it slowly came closer and saw that in the center of the strange procession was a man wearing a tall black hat. He'd pause now and then to peer at something in his hand and then at the houses on either side of the street. I felt cold and hot at the same time as I recognized the man. "Oh, no!" I whispered. "It's Grandpa!'

How does the narrator feel when he sees Grandpa surrounded by dogs? Why does the narrator feel this way? 1

I stood on the curb, unable to move, even though I wanted to run and hide. Then I got mad when I saw how the yippy dogs were growling and nipping at the old man's baggy pant legs and how wearily he poked them away with his cane. "Stupid mutts," I said as I ran to rescue Grandpa.

When I kicked and hollered at the dogs to get away, they put their tails between their legs and scattered. The kids ran to the curb where they watched me and the old man.

What does Grandpa think about displays of affection? 2

"Grandpa," I said and felt pretty dumb when my voice cracked. I reached for his beat-up old tin suitcase, which was tied shut with a rope. But he set it down right in the street and shook my hand.

"*Hau, Takoza,* Grandchild," he greeted me formally in Sioux.

All I could do was stand there with the whole neighborhood watching and shake the hand of the leather-brown old man. I saw how his gray hair straggled from under his big black hat, which had a drooping feather in its crown. His rumpled black suit hung like a sack over his stooped frame. As he shook my hand, his coat fell open to expose a bright red satin shirt with a beaded bolo tie[2] under the collar. His get-up wasn't out of place on the reservation, but it sure was here, and I wanted to sink right through the pavement.

"Hi," I muttered with my head down. I tried to pull my hand away when I felt his bony hand trembling and looked up to see fatigue in his face. I felt like crying. I couldn't think of anything to say, so I picked up Grandpa's suitcase, took his arm, and guided him up the driveway to our house.

Mom was standing on the steps. I don't know how long she'd been watching, but her hand was over her mouth, and she looked as if she couldn't believe what she saw. Then she ran to us.

"Grandpa," she gasped. "How in the world did you get here?"

She checked her move to embrace Grandpa, and I remembered that such a display of affection is unseemly to the Sioux and would embarrass him.

"*Hau,* Marie," he said as he shook Mom's hand. She smiled and took his other arm.

2. **bolo tie.** Cord with ornamental fastening, worn as a necktie

Words for Everyday Use

com • mo • tion (kə mō´shən) *n.,* noisy rushing about
fa • tigue (fə tēg´) *n.,* extreme weariness or exhaustion
un • seem • ly (un sēm´lē) *adj.,* not decent or proper

Vocabulary in Context

- What is all that noise and commotion about?
- My fatigue following my illness kept me from attending the windsurfing race.
- Chewing with your mouth open is unseemly behavior.

Grandpa Stones. *Illustration by Marvin Toddy. Courtesy of the artist.*

As we supported him up the steps, the door banged open and Cheryl came bursting out of the house. She was all smiles and was so obviously glad to see Grandpa that I was ashamed of how I felt.

"Grandpa!" She yelled happily. "You came to see us!"

Grandpa smiled, and Mom and I let go of him as he stretched out his arms to my ten-year-old sister, who was still young enough to be hugged.

"*Wicincala*, little girl," he greeted her and then collapsed.

He had fainted. Mom and I carried him into her sewing room, where we had a spare bed.

After we had Grandpa on the bed, Mom stood there helplessly patting his shoulder.

"Shouldn't we call the doctor, Mom?" I suggested, since she didn't seem to know what to do.

"Yes," she agreed with a sigh. "You make Grandpa comfortable, Martin."

I reluctantly moved to the bed. I knew Grandpa wouldn't want to have Mom undress him, but I didn't want

1 *How does Cheryl feel about Grandpa's visit? How does her attitude make the narrator feel?*

Words for Everyday Use

re • luc • tant • ly (ri luk´tənt lē) *adv.*, unwillingly

Answer to Guided Reading Question

1 Cheryl is excited to see her grandfather. Cheryl's unrestrained excitement makes the narrator feel ashamed.

CROSS-CURRICULAR ACTIVITIES

Art

- Ask students to look at the illustration on this page called *Grandpa Stones*. Who do they think the people are in the illustration? What kind of story might they imagine for this family?
- Ask students to look through magazines and books to find other pictures depicting families. As a class, students should gather examples of as many types of families as possible. They may also bring in their own family pictures. Ask students to discuss how teenage family members are portrayed. Is the overall image positive or negative?

Vocabulary in Context

- We didn't want to leave; we reluctantly packed our bags.

Answer to Guided Reading Question

➊ The narrator notices a small leather pouch that hangs from a thong around Grandpa's neck.

Additional Questions and Activities

• Ask students if they can relate to the narrator's conflicting feelings about having his great-grandfather visit. Have they ever felt embarrassment because of a particular family member? Who was the family member? What was the reason for the embarrassment? How did they deal with these feelings?

• Ask students to write their answers. Students who feel comfortable doing so might share their work.

Biographical Note

Crazy Horse was a Sioux chief in the nineteenth century. He was one of the leaders who led Native American forces to victory at the Battle of Little Big Horn.

What does the narrator notice around Grandpa's neck? ➊

to, either. He was so skinny and frail that his coat slipped off easily. When I loosened his tie and opened his shirt collar, I felt a small leather pouch that hung from a thong around his neck. I left it alone and moved to remove his boots. The scuffed old cowboy boots were tight, and he moaned as I put pressure on his legs to jerk them off.

I put the boots on the floor and saw why they fit so tight. Each one was stuffed with money. I looked at the bills that lined the boots and started to ask about them, but Grandpa's eyes were closed again.

Mom came back with a basin of water. "The doctor thinks Grandpa is suffering from heat exhaustion," she explained as she bathed Grandpa's face. Mom gave a big sigh, "*Oh, hinh,* Martin. How do you suppose he got here?"

We found out after the doctor's visit. Grandpa was angrily sitting up in bed while Mom tried to feed him some soup.

"Tonight you let Marie feed you, Grandpa," spoke my dad, who had gotten home from work just as the doctor was leaving. "You're not really sick," he said as he gently pushed Grandpa back against the pillows. "The doctor said you just got too tired and hot after your long trip."

Grandpa relaxed, and between sips of soup, he told us of his journey. Soon after our visit to him, Grandpa decided that he would like to see where his only living descendants lived and what our home was like. Besides, he admitted sheepishly, he was lonesome after we left.

I knew that everybody felt as guilty as I did—especially Mom. Mom was all Grandpa had left. So even after she married my dad, who's a white man and teaches in the college in our city, and after Cheryl and I were born, Mom made sure that every summer we spent a week with Grandpa.

I never thought that Grandpa would be lonely after our visits, and none of us noticed how old and weak he had become. But Grandpa knew, and so he came to us. He had ridden on buses for two and a half days. When he arrived in the city, tired and stiff from sitting so long, he set out, walking, to find us.

He had stopped to rest on the steps of some building downtown, and a policeman found him. The cop, according to Grandpa, was a good man who took him to the bus stop and waited until the bus came and told the driver to let Grandpa out at Bell View Drive. After Grandpa got off the bus, he started walking again. But he couldn't see the house numbers on the other side when he walked on the sidewalk, so he walked in the middle of the street. That's when all the little kids and dogs followed him.

I knew everybody felt as bad as I did. Yet I was so proud of this eighty-six-year-old man who had never been away from the reservation, having the courage to travel so far alone.

"You found the money in my boots?" he asked Mom.

Words for Everyday Use

thong (thôŋ) *n.,* narrow strip of leather

bas • in (bās´ən) *n.,* round, shallow container for holding water

de • scend • ant (dē sen´dənt) *n.,* immediate or remote offspring of a person

sheep • ish • ly (shēp´ish lē) *adv.,* in an awkwardly shy or embarrassed manner

Vocabulary in Context

- I made a necklace by hanging beads from a thong.
- We washed after we filled a basin with warm, soapy water.
- I am a descendant of Native Americans.
- Carla admitted sheepishly that she would like us to stay.

"Martin did," she answered, and roused herself to scold. "Grandpa, you shouldn't have carried so much money. What if someone had stolen it from you?"

Grandpa laughed. "I would've known if anyone had tried to take the boots off my feet. The money is what I've saved for a long time—a hundred dollars—for my funeral. But you take it now to buy groceries so that I won't be a burden to you while I am here."

"That won't be necessary, Grandpa," Dad said. "We are honored to have you with us, and you will never be a burden. I am only sorry that we never thought to bring you home with us this summer and spare you the discomfort of a long trip."

Grandpa was pleased. "Thank you," he answered. "But do not feel bad that you didn't bring me with you, for I would not have come then. It was not time." He said this in such a way that no one could argue with him. To Grandpa and the Sioux, he once told me, a thing would be done when it was the right time to do it, and that's the way it was.

"Also," Grandpa went on, looking at me. "I have come because it is soon time for Martin to have the medicine bag."

We all knew what that meant. Grandpa thought he was going to die, and he had to follow the tradition of his family to pass the medicine bag, along with its history, to the oldest male child.

"Even though the boy," he said, still looking at me, "bears a white man's name, the medicine bag will be his."

I didn't know what to say. I had the same hot and cold feeling that I had when I first saw Grandpa in the street. The medicine bag was the dirty leather pouch I had found around his neck. "I could never wear such a thing," I almost said aloud. I thought of having my friends see it in gym class or at the swimming pool and could imagine the smart things they would say. But I just swallowed hard and took a step toward the bed. I knew I would have to take it.

But Grandpa was tired. "Not now, Martin," he said, waving his hand in dismissal. "It is not time. Now I will sleep."

So that's how Grandpa came to be with us for two months. My friends kept asking to come see the old man, but I put them off. I told myself that I didn't want them laughing at Grandpa. But even as I made excuses, I knew it wasn't Grandpa that I was afraid they'd laugh at.

Nothing bothered Cheryl about bringing her friends to see Grandpa. Every day after school started, there'd be a crew of giggling little girls or round-eyed little boys crowded around the old man on the patio, where he'd gotten in the habit of sitting every afternoon.

Grandpa would smile in his gentle way and patiently answer their questions, or he'd tell them stories of brave warriors, ghosts, and animals; and the kids listened in awed silence. Those little guys thought Grandpa was great.

❶ How does the narrator feel about wearing the medicine bag?

❷ Why didn't Grandpa come to visit earlier?

❸ What do Cheryl's friends think of Grandpa?

WORDS FOR EVERYDAY USE

rouse (rouz) *v.*, stir up, as to anger or action

ANSWERS TO GUIDED READING QUESTIONS

❶ The narrator does not want to wear the medicine bag. He feels that it would be embarrassing.

❷ Grandpa didn't come to visit earlier because it was not the right time.

❸ Cheryl's friends think that Grandpa is great.

VOCABULARY IN CONTEXT

- Marty tried to rouse sympathy by whining and pouting.

Additional Questions and Activities

Ask students to answer the following questions:

- Why might Grandpa have dressed up?
- Do you think that he senses the narrator's feelings of embarrassment?

ANSWERS

Responses will vary.

Students might believe that Grandpa dressed up out of consideration for the narrator's feelings. Because he is a wise man, he probably senses the narrator's feelings of discomfort.

Biographical Note

Sitting Bull was a leader of the Sioux tribe in the late nineteenth century. He was a chief and a medicine man. A medicine man was a person believed to have the powers to cure disease and control spirits of all kinds. The medicine man was always a highly respected member of the community.

Sitting Bull was the medicine man of the Sioux when they fought against settlers in the northern Great Plains.

Plateau or Plains medicine bag

Finally, one day after school, my friends came home with me because nothing I said stopped them. "We're going to see the great Indian of Bell View Drive," said Hank, who was supposed to be my best friend. "My brother has seen him three times, so he oughta be well enough to see us."

When we got to my house, Grandpa was sitting on the patio. He had on his red shirt, but today he also wore a fringed leather vest that was decorated with beads. Instead of his usual cowboy boots, he had solidly beaded moccasins on his feet that stuck out of his black trousers. Of course, he had his old black hat on—he was seldom without it. But it had been brushed, and the feather in the beaded headband was proudly erect, its tip a brighter white. His hair lay in silver strands over the red shirt collar.

I stared just as my friends did, and I heard one of them murmur, "Wow!"

Grandpa looked up, and when his eyes met mine, they twinkled as if he were laughing inside. He nodded to me, and my face got all hot. I could tell that he had known all along I was afraid he'd embarrass me in front of my friends.

"*Hau, hoksilas,* boys," he greeted and held out his hand.

My buddies passed in a single file and shook his hand as I introduced them. They were so polite I almost laughed. "How, there, Grandpa," and even a "How-do-you-do, sir."

"You look fine, Grandpa," I said as the guys sat on the lawn chairs or on the patio floor.

"*Hanh*, yes," he agreed. "When I woke up this morning, it seemed the right time to dress in the good clothes. I knew that my grandson would be bringing his friends."

"You guys want some lemonade or something?" I offered. No one answered. They were listening to Grandpa as he started telling how he'd killed the deer from which his vest was made.

Grandpa did most of the talking while my friends were there. I was so proud of him and amazed at how respectfully quiet my buddies were. Mom had to chase them home at supper time. As they left, they shook Grandpa's hand again and said to me,

"Martin, he's really great!"

"Yeah, man! Don't blame you for keeping him to yourself."

"Can we come back?"

But after they left, Mom said, "No more visitors for a while, Martin. Grandpa won't admit it, but his strength hasn't returned. He likes having company, but it tires him."

That evening Grandpa called me to his room before he went to sleep. "Tomorrow," he said, "when you come home, it will be time to give you the medicine bag."

I felt a hard squeeze from where my heart is supposed to be and was scared, but I answered, "OK, Grandpa."

All night I had weird dreams about thunder and lightning on a high hill. From a distance I heard the slow beat of a drum. When I woke up in the morning, I felt as if I hadn't slept at all. At school it seemed as if the day would never end, and when it finally did, I ran home.

Grandpa was in his room, sitting on the bed. The shades were down, and the place was dim and cool. I sat on the floor in front of Grandpa, but he didn't even look at me. After what seemed a long time, he spoke.

"I sent your mother and sister away. What you will hear today is only for a man's ears. What you will receive is only for a man's hands." He fell silent, and I felt shivers down my back.

"My father in his early manhood," Grandpa began, "made a vision quest[3] to find a spirit guide for his life. You cannot understand how it was in that time when the great Teton Sioux[4] were first made to stay on the reservation. There was a strong need for guidance from Wakantanka, the Great Spirit. But too many of the young men were filled with despair and hatred. They thought it was hopeless to search for a vision when the glorious life was gone and only the hated confines of a

3. **vision quest.** Spiritual journey
4. **Teton Sioux.** One of the three major divisions of the Sioux people; the Teton Sioux are also called Western Sioux

❶ *Why do you think the narrator has these "weird dreams"? What is on his mind?*

❷ *In what way do the narrator's friends react to Grandpa?*

❸ *In what way did Grandpa's father find his spirit guide?*

Words for Everyday Use

con • fine (kän´fīn) *n.*, limit or boundary

Answers to Guided Reading Questions

❶ The narrator is nervous and stressed about getting the medicine bag.

❷ The narrator's friends think that Grandpa is great. That are quiet and respectful as they listen to him.

❸ Grandpa's father found his spiritual guide by going on a vision quest, or spiritual journey.

Vocabulary in Context

• Being limited to the confines of the living room is frustrating to the little dog.

ANSWERS TO GUIDED READING QUESTIONS

❶ Grandpa's father's medicine brought him to a blacksmith house, where he could learn and work with the white man's iron.

❷ His dream was about finding the white man's iron after a long journey. He did not understand because at the time white people were the enemy.

HISTORICAL NOTE

The Battle of Wounded Knee, at which two hundred Sioux were killed, was the last major military conflict between whites and Native Americans. The conflict began when soldiers were disarming warriors in an army camp at Wounded Knee. A rifle was fired and alarmed soldiers, who began the brutal massacre. The battle took place on December 29, 1890.

Wounded Knee is a small village and creek in South Dakota.

❶ *What did Grandpa's father's medicine do for him?*

❷ *What was Grandpa's father's sacred dream? Why didn't he understand this dream?*

reservation lay ahead. But my father held to the old ways.

"He carefully prepared for his quest with a purifying sweat bath, and then he went alone to a high butte[5] top to fast and pray. After three days he received his sacred dream—in which he found, after long searching, the white man's iron. He did not understand his vision of finding something belonging to the white people, for in that time they were the enemy. When he came down from the butte to cleanse himself at the stream below, he found the remains of a campfire and the broken shell of an iron kettle. This was a sign that reinforced his dream. He took a piece of the iron for his medicine bag, which he had made of elk skin years before, to prepare for his quest.

"He returned to his village, where he told his dream to the wise old men of the tribe. They gave him the name Iron Shell, but neither did they understand the meaning of the dream. The first Iron Shell kept the piece of iron with him at all times and believed it gave him protection from the evils of those unhappy days.

"Then a terrible thing happened to Iron Shell. He and several other young men were taken from their homes by the soldiers and sent far away to a white man's boarding school. He was angry and lonesome for his parents and the young girl he had wed before he was taken away. At first Iron Shell resisted the teacher's attempts to change him, and he did not try to learn. One day it was his turn to work in the school's blacksmith shop. As he walked into the place, he knew that his medicine had brought him there to learn and work with the white man's iron.

"Iron Shell became a blacksmith and worked at the trade when he returned to the reservation. All of his life he treasured the medicine bag. When he was old and I was a man, he gave it to me, for no one made the vision quest any more."

Grandpa quit talking, and I stared in disbelief as he covered his face with his hands. His shoulders were shaking with quiet sobs, and I looked away until he began to speak again.

"I kept the bag until my son, your mother's father, was a man and had to leave us to fight in the war across the ocean. I gave him the bag, for I believed it would protect him in battle, but he did not take it with him. He was afraid that he would lose it. He died in a faraway place."

Again Grandpa was still, and I felt his grief around me.

"My son," he went on after clearing his throat, "had only a daughter, and it is not proper for her to know of these things."

He unbuttoned his shirt, pulled out the leather pouch, and lifted it over his head. He held it in his hand, turning it over and over as if memorizing how it looked.

5. **butte.** Flat-topped hill

WORDS FOR EVERYDAY USE

pu • ri • fy • ing (pyoor´ ə fī´ ŋ) *adj.,* cleansing
re • in • force (rē´in fôrs´) *v.,* strengthen

VOCABULARY IN CONTEXT

- The clean water was purifying to my face.
- Mia tried to reinforce the wobbling table by adding another leg.

"In the bag," he said as he opened it and removed two objects, "is the broken shell of the iron kettle, a pebble from the butte, and a piece of the sacred sage."[6] He held the pouch upside down and dust drifted down.

"After the bag is yours, you must put a piece of prairie sage within and never open it again until you pass it on to your son." He replaced the pebble and the piece of iron and tied the bag.

I stood up, somehow knowing I should. Grandpa slowly rose from the bed and stood upright in front of me holding the bag before my face. I closed my eyes and waited for him to slip it over my head. But he spoke.

"No, you need not wear it." He placed the soft leather bag in my right hand and closed my other hand over it. "It would not be right to wear it in this time and place where no one will understand. Put it safely away until you are again on the reservation. Wear it then, when you replace the sacred sage."

Grandpa turned and sat again on the bed. Wearily he leaned his head against the pillow. "Go," he said. "I will sleep now."

"Thank you, Grandpa," I said softly, and left with the bag in my hands.

That night Mom and Dad took Grandpa to the hospital. Two weeks later I stood alone on the lonely prairie of the reservation and put the sacred sage in my medicine bag. ■

6. **sage.** A type of fragrant plant

What is in the bag? What must the narrator do with the medicine bag?

About the Author

Virginia Driving Hawk Sneve (1933–) often writes about her Sioux ancestry. Born on the Rosebud Reservation in South Dakota, she studied at South Dakota University. In addition to writing, she works as a counselor at Rapid City Central High School in South Dakota. "The Medicine Bag" was inspired by the personal experience of one of Sneve's friends. If you liked "The Medicine Bag," you might want to read Sneve's award-winning novel *Jimmy Yellow Hawk*.

ANSWER TO GUIDED READING QUESTION

❶ In the bag is the broken shell of an iron kettle, a pebble from the butte, and a piece of the sacred sage. The narrator must go to the reservation, find some prairie sage, put the prairie sage into the bag, and then never open the bag again until he passes it on to his own son.

SELECTION CHECK TEST WITH ANSWERS

EX. About what does the narrator always brag?
The narrator always brags about his Sioux grandpa.

1. Where does Grandpa live?
Grandpa lives on a reservation.

2. Why does Grandpa come to visit one day?
He feels he must pass the family medicine bag on to the narrator.

3. Why doesn't the narrator want the medicine bag at first?
The narrator is afraid that people at school will laugh at it.

4. How do the narrator's friends feel about Grandpa?
The narrator's friends love Grandpa.

5. What must the narrator do with the medicine bag?
The narrator must fill it with sacred sage from the reservation, and then pass it along to his own son or grandson some day.

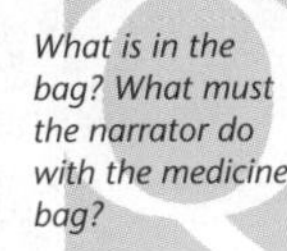

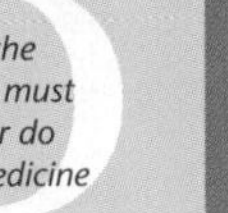

Responding to the Selection

Invite students to discuss as a class Martin and his great-grandfather. Do they understand Martin's various feelings toward the man?

Answers for Reviewing the Selection

RECALLING AND INTERPRETING

1. **Recalling.** Their friends know only what they've seen in movies and on television. Martin and Cheryl show their friends genuine Sioux articles and impress them with stories. **Interpreting.** They are afraid that their Grandpa's picture would not live up to the image they've created by telling stories.

2. **Recalling.** Grandpa comes to visit so that he might give Martin the medicine bag before he dies. **Interpreting.** At first Martin is nervous about his friends meeting Grandpa. Martin at first does not want the medicine bag. He's afraid it might embarrass him.

3. **Recalling.** It surprises Martin that his friends are so polite and respectful as they listen to Grandpa. **Interpreting.** Friends of both Martin and Cheryl love Grandpa. Martin is proud of Grandpa.

4. **Recalling.** The bag contains the broken shell of an iron kettle, a pebble from the butte, and a piece of the sacred sage. Grandpa's father gave the medicine bag to him. Grandpa asks Martin to take the bag to the reservation and find some sacred prairie sage. **Interpreting.** A "vision quest" is a spiritual journey. After Martin puts the sage in the bag, he must not open the bag until his son becomes a man.

SYNTHESIZING

Responses will vary. Possible responses are given.

5. Martin gains a new respect for his grandfather because he is able to see him through the eyes of others.

Responding to the Selection

How do you feel about Martin's great-grandfather? How would you feel if he were your great-grandfather? Would your reactions be similar to or different from Martin's?

Reviewing the Selection

RECALLING AND INTERPRETING

1. **R** What do Martin and Cheryl's friends know about Native Americans? What do Martin and Cheryl show their friends? What do they say to impress them?

   I Why don't Martin and Cheryl show their friends a picture of Grandpa?

2. **R** Why does Grandpa come to visit? What does he wish to give to Martin?

   I How does Martin feel at first when his friends meet Grandpa? How does Martin feel at first about receiving the medicine bag?

3. **R** What surprises Martin about his friends' behavior when they meet Grandpa?

   I How do Cheryl and Martin's friends feel about Grandpa? How does Martin feel about Grandpa after Grandpa meets Martin's friends?

4. **R** What does the medicine bag contain? Who gave the medicine bag to Grandpa? What does Grandpa ask Martin to do with the medicine bag?

   I What is a "vision quest"? At what point in a person's life does he pass the medicine bag on to the next generation? Why does Grandpa say that Martin need not wear the bag?

SYNTHESIZING

5. Why does Martin put the sacred sage in his medicine bag? How have Martin's feelings changed? Why has carrying on Grandpa's tradition become important to Martin?

Understanding Literature (Questions for Discussion)

1. **Conflict.** A **conflict** is a struggle between two people or things in a literary work. An **internal conflict** is a struggle that takes place inside the mind of a character. What conflicting feelings does the narrator have about his great-grandfather at the beginning of this story? How is this conflict finally ended, or resolved? How have the narrator's feelings about his heritage changed at the end of the story? How do you know?
2. **Anecdote.** An **anecdote** is a brief story, usually told to make a point. At the end of this story, the narrator's great-grandfather tells him an anecdote. The anecdote is about a vision quest. What do you suppose is the point of this anecdote? What is a vision quest? Why did Sioux men go on such a quest? In what ways did going on a vision quest help the narrator's grandfather to achieve his adult identity?

Answers for Understanding Literature

Responses will vary. Possible responses are given.

1. **Conflict.** The narrator loves his great-grandfather, but he is also worried that people might think he is strange. The narrator's feelings have changed about his great-grandpa and about the medicine bag. He is proud of his heritage and its traditions.

2. **Anecdote.** Grandpa shares the anecdote about his father so that Martin might appreciate his struggles and the origin of the medicine bag.

Writing Skills

An Oral History

Long before writing was invented, people told one another stories from the past. In that way, they kept the memories of their families and clans alive. A true story that is passed down by word of mouth is known as an **oral history.**

"Granny Gaskins's Story"
by Lynette Carter

Granny Gaskins is seventy-three years old and lives with her son on a farm in Russell Springs, Kentucky. I interviewed her in her home, and she told me an interesting story that happened during the Korean War.

Lynnette: Ms. Gaskins, you told me that you were living with your daughter-in-law during the Korean War and that your son, Ed, was in the army.

Granny Gaskins: That's right, child. Edvert—that's his full name—was a sergeant in the infantry, and his wife, Pearl, was staying with me during that time. We were mighty afraid that something was going to happen to Ed because the fighting in Korea was just terrible.

Lynnette: When was this? I'm ashamed to say I don't know when the Korean War took place.

Granny Gaskins: Well, it must have been about 1948. Yes, that's right. 1948.

Lynnette: And you say that you were afraid for Ed.

Granny Gaskins: Pearl and I both were. We got letters from him sometimes. And, of course, we listened to the radio for reports about the war.

Lynnette: Did Ed come through OK? I mean, did he manage to get through the war without being hurt?

Granny Gaskins: That's just what I was going to tell you about. One night, I had the strangest dream. I dreamed I saw Ed coming up over the top of a hill. Just as clear as day, he said, "Mom, I was hit on the 14th. But I'll be all right. I'm coming home." Then he just fell to the ground and I woke up.

Lynnette: Sounds like a scary dream.

Granny Gaskins: Yes. And the next morning, I told Pearl about it. Maybe I shouldn't have, but it had me worried, that dream. Well, as I was standing

Try It Yourself

Interview an older person and ask him or her to tell you an interesting or amusing story about a personal experience or about an experience that happened to a family member. Write down the story in a question-and-answer format with a brief introduction and conclusion.

◀◀**Student Model** 

Writing Skills

Introducing the Skill

Explain to students that older people can hold a wealth of knowledge, and that it can be exciting to conduct an interview.

Previewing the Skill

Ask students to read the model and then to answer the Examining the Model questions. Ask them to decide what they like or do not like about this interview.

Prewriting and Drafting

Be sure that students complete a prewriting activity to try to find possible interview subjects.

Remind students to be polite and gracious at the interview. They should also be prompt.

Evaluating and Revising

Remind students to give one another constructive criticism, but also to be positive with one another.

Proofreading and Publishing

Students should be encouraged to share their work. You might suggest that they share the finished oral history with the person they interviewed.

Answers for Examining the Model

1. Lynette keeps the conversation moving with questions. She also refers to things that her interviewee had mentioned earlier, or things she already knew about the situation.

2. Lynette did remember to thank her interviewee and to ask permission to use material in her school report.

there telling her about my dream, a car pulled up in the driveway, and a fellow got out with a telegram in his hand. When Pearl saw that, she screamed, "He's dead" and fainted right away.

Lynnette: But Ed obviously didn't die. I met him just a few minutes ago.

Granny Gaskins: That's right. He didn't die. He had stepped on a land mine behind enemy lines. A soldier in his platoon picked him up and carried him, under fire, to a helicopter. Saved his life. Of course, he lost his leg from the knee down.

Lynnette: That's terrible.

Granny Gaskins: Well, yes and no. I'm mighty proud of Ed. Losing that leg didn't slow him down any. He got fitted with an artificial leg, and then he went to school and learned to be a dental technician. In a few years, he built himself a lab where he makes false teeth. Would you like to see it? It's right across the patio there.

Lynnette: Sure. Ms. Gaskins, thank you for speaking with me. Would it be OK for me to use the story you just told me in my report for school?

Granny Gaskins: Sure it would.

Examining the Model

1. How did Lynnette keep the conversation moving? What did she do to draw information from the subject of her interview?
2. Did Lynnette remember to thank her interviewee? Did she remember to get permission to use material from the interview?

Prewriting and Drafting

1. Make a list of possible subjects for interviews. These subjects should be older people whom you know. They may be family members, neighbors, or acquaintances. You may want to complete a cluster chart like this one:

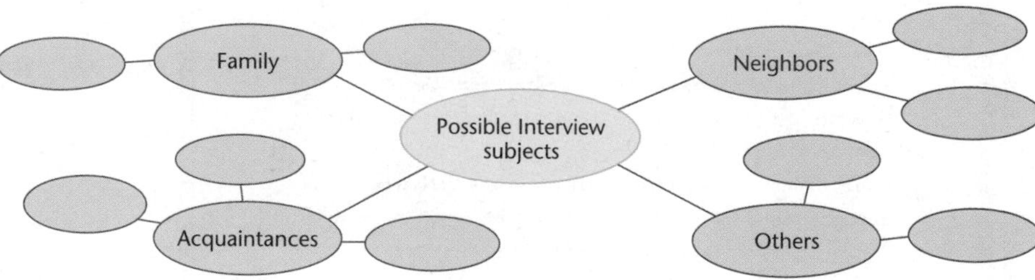

2. Choose a subject from your list and contact him or her to set up an interview. Explain that you are writing a paper for class and need to interview people to gather oral histories, which are interesting or amusing stories from people's personal experiences.

3. Before going to the interview, read about interviewing in the Language Arts Survey, 1.13, "Gathering Ideas." Make a list of questions that you might ask your subject. These should be questions that will prompt the interviewee to tell stories. Begin your questions with the words *who, what, where, when, why,* and *how.*
4. Show up on time for the interview. If possible, tape the interview, but be sure to ask permission before doing so. If you cannot locate a tape recorder, or if you cannot get permission to record the interview, take careful notes so that you can reconstruct the conversation after the interview.
5. Choose some part of the interview that contains an interesting story and transcribe it, word for word, from your notes or from your recording.
6. Write a brief introduction and conclusion for the interview. Your introduction should state the name of the interviewee and provide some information about him or her. It should also mention the subject of the oral history. Your conclusion may comment on the story or draw a lesson from it, relate the story to your readers' lives, or summarize the main idea or theme of the story. The introduction and conclusion should be separate paragraphs.

Evaluating and Revising

1. Review the Language Arts Survey, 1.17, "Self-Evaluation" and 1.18, "Peer Evaluation." Exchange drafts with a classmate and evaluate each other's work. Consider the following questions:
   a. Does the oral history have an introduction and a conclusion?
   b. Does the introduction state the name of the interviewee and provide some information about him or her?
   c. Does the body of the oral history present a story? Does the body present questions and answers in proper form as in the model?
   d. Does the conclusion comment on the story or draw a lesson from it, relate the story to the reader's life, or summarize the main idea or theme of the story?
2. Revise your draft. Follow the guidelines in the Language Arts Survey, 1.19, "Four Types of Revision," and 1.20, "A Revision Checklist."

Proofreading and Publishing

1. Proofread your revised manuscript. Then make a clean, final copy of it and proofread it again. Refer to the Language Arts Survey, 1.22, "A Proofreading Checklist," and 1.23, "Proper Manuscript Form."
2. Share your work with your classmates in one of these ways:
   a. Work with your classmates to compile a booklet of oral histories.
   b. Join with two other classmates to hold readings for the class of the oral histories. Have one person in your group read aloud the introduction and conclusion of the oral history. Have the other two people in your group take the parts of the interviewer and the interviewee. In this manner, each group should read to the class the three oral histories prepared by members of the group.

Save your work in your writing portfolio.

ANALYTIC SCALE FOR WRITING SKILLS

Assign a score from 1 to 25 for each grading criterion below.

AN ORAL HISTORY

- **Content/Unity.** The oral history contains interesting information. The reader is able to learn something about the subject.
- **Organization/Coherence.** The oral history is organized in a way that makes sense. The writer included a brief introduction and conclusion.
- **Language/Style.** The account uses vivid and precise nouns, verbs, and modifiers.
- **Conventions.** The account avoids errors in spelling, grammar, usage, mechanics, and manuscript form.

Project Note

Encourage students to be creative in gathering materials for the collage. Ask them to pay special attention to the items collected in the student model. It is important to have photos and pictures in a collage, but other items, such as menus, speeches, poetry, or drawings add a special touch.

Unit Project

Making a Diversity Collage

Diversity means "variety," or "difference." Look around you. You can see diversity in your school, in your neighborhood, at a local supermarket, or on television. People have diverse interests, and they are diverse in the way they look, speak, dress, and behave. Diversity is what makes the world exciting and interesting. A collage is a collection of pictures or objects pasted together. Seen individually, the pictures may seem random, but they work together to give meaning to the collage as a whole. What pictures or objects might you gather for a collage entitled "Diversity"?

Try It Yourself

Work with your classmates to make a diversity collage. Your collage can be made up of personal photographs, magazine photographs, original drawings or paintings, and objects. You might also include favorite quotations or a favorite poem related to the subject of diversity.

Student Model

Members of Ms. Santo's class are putting together a diversity collage. They decide to create their collage on pieces of black poster board. Before they begin working on the actual collage, the students have a discussion about diversity. They think about pictures, objects, and poems that relate to this subject. After having the discussion the students have a clearer idea about what items they should try to find on their own for the collage.

A few days later, each student comes to class with different items for the collage. Chantel has a photograph she took of people sitting in a park outside her home. She also has a picture of her grandmother standing outside her childhood home in Jamaica. Wesley has several magazine pictures, and a copy of the "I Have a Dream" speech by Martin Luther King, Jr. Wesley decided to use this speech because in it, King talks about diversity in the United States and how he wishes that all people would live together peacefully and respect one another. Yun brings in a picture she painted of several different types of trees, and a picture of her family. Anita brings in magazine pictures and photographs of different types of families. Other students bring in magazine photos of older people, young people, people in business suits, people in uniforms, and people in jeans. There are also photos of people and art from several different countries. One student gets permission to use copies of menus from a Chinese restaurant, a Japanese restaurant, an Indian restaurant, a Mexican restaurant, and an Italian restaurant.

After sorting through everything, students arrange the items on the poster board. They leave space in the middle of the collage so that they can write the word *diversity* in big letters. After everyone is satisfied with the arrangement, students fasten items to the poster board with glue.

When the glue is dry, the collage is ready to be displayed. They hang the collage in a hallway near the front entrance of the school. All parents, teachers, students, and visitors can see the work of Ms. Santo's class and know that diversity is appreciated in the school.

Examining the Model

1. What do the students first discuss? Why do they have this discussion?
2. What are some of the items brought in by the students?

Planning Your Collage

1. Have a class discussion about diversity. Discuss examples of diversity in your school, neighborhood, town, and country.
2. Decide what materials you want to use in making your collage. Do you want to use only photographs, or do you want to use poems, quotations, and certain objects? How many items will each student be asked to add to the collage? To attach items to poster board, you will need tape, glue, or rubber cement. If you choose to attach items to a bulletin board, you should use staples or small tacks and pins.
3. Decide how big you want the entire collage to be and how big you want individual items to be. You might simply paste pictures in a random order, or you might try to create patterns within the collage.

Making the Collage

1. Each student should bring in a certain number of items for the collage.
2. When all items are in, arrange everything on a clean surface. Figure out what looks best in what position, and in which part of the collage.
3. Fasten items, one at a time, to the background. Don't use too much glue, tape, or rubber cement on the backs of pictures. You don't want them to appear lumpy. If you are placing items onto a bulletin board, use tacks or pins that aren't too large or showy. Putting your collage onto a bulletin board can be a good idea. Pins or staples are not as messy as glue, and you can stand back and change things as you work.

Showing the Collage

1. You might want to find out if you can hang your collage in a public place. Maybe you can hang it in the school hallway, the school library, or somewhere in your town.
2. If you have access to a bulletin board in a public place, you might want to put your collage directly onto the bulletin board. If the bulletin board is large, find out if you can fill the entire space.
3. Let friends, family, and teachers know where your collage is. Invite them to look at it.

Answers for Examining the Model

1. Students have a discussion about diversity. They decide what pictures, objects, or poems relate to diversity. They have this discussion so that they will all have a clearer idea about what items they should try to find for their collage.
2. The students bring in photographs, a speech, magazine pictures, and menus.

ANALYTIC SCALE FOR PROJECT

Assign a score from 1 to 25 for each grading criterion below.

Making a Diversity Collage

- **Organization.** The group set attainable goals and created a schedule or strategy for achieving those goals.
- **Cooperation.** The group assigned tasks fairly to each member, and each member cooperated toward achieving the group's goals.
- **Goal Achievement.** The group worked steadily toward its goals and did, in fact, achieve them.
- **Presentation.** The group presented a product of high quality that met the inital project description.

Vocabulary Check Test

Ask students to number their papers from one to ten. Have students complete each sentence with a word from the Vocabulary for the Unit in the Unit Review.

1. Do you see the flag billow in the breeze?
2. We could not hear anything over the commotion.
3. The large, gaudy gemstone was ugly.
4. Dora said no at first, but then she reluctantly gave away the secret.
5. The shy child smiled sheepishly as she entered the room.
6. I am a proud descendant of that tribe.
7. She waved and Martin saw this friendly gesture.
8. Please try not to rouse my anger today.
9. People were appalled at the unseemly behavior.
10. Please fill the basin and wash the dishes.

Unit Review

Summary

Literary Terms for the Unit

alliteration, 147
anecdote, 172
concrete, 147
conflict, 161, 172
irony, 161
motivation, 151

Vocabulary for the Unit

ascend, 149
basin, 166
billow, 156
commotion, 164
confine, 169
cynical, 159
descendant, 166
distributive, 157
fatigue, 164
fester, 145
gaudy, 157
gesture, 158
irrational, 159
jostling, 157
purifying, 170
reinforce, 170
reluctantly, 165
rouse, 167
sheepishly, 166
stately, 163
thong, 166
throng, 155
unseemly, 164

Questions for Writing, Discussion, and Research

1. What different types of discrimination are portrayed in the selections in this unit? What do the different types of discrimination have in common? What are the negative consequences of discrimination?
2. Compare and contrast the main characters in Rona Maynard's "The Fan Club" and Virginia Driving Hawk Sneve's "The Medicine Bag."

SPELLING CHECK TEST

Ask students to number their papers from one to ten. Read each word aloud. Then read aloud the sentence containing the word. Repeat the word. Ask students to write the word on their papers, spelling it correctly.

1. **ascend**

The balloon will ascend into the air.

2. **fatigue**

His fatigue kept him from being fast in the race.

3. **stately**

The old horse looked stately as he stood in the winner's circle.

4. **reinforce**

I want to reinforce the roof with additional beams.

5. **purifying**

We will be purifying the water to make it drinkable.

6. **jostling**

The jostling crowd entered the theater.

7. **fester**

Cover the wound so that it does not fester.

8. **confine**

We have to confine the dog to our yard.

9. **cynical**

Jackson is cynical about the politician's plan.

10. **descendant**

We are descendants of our grandparents.

FOR YOUR READING LIST

Erin O'Donnell
Rosemount Middle School
Rosemount, Minnesota

Roll of Thunder, Hear My Cry
by Mildred D. Taylor

Mildred D. Taylor wrote the book *Roll of Thunder, Hear My Cry,* which is now one of my favorite books. She really held my interest in the book by expressing everything in an exciting way. This novel is narrated by Cassie Logan, a nine-year-old girl. The story takes place in a small town in Spokane County, Mississippi, in the 1930s. Racism deeply affects Cassie and her family. They hear about racial violence toward people they know, and Cassie and her brothers are forced to walk to school in every type of weather, while white children ride on school busses. Cassie is frustrated by the situation and does not understand why nobody does anything to stop these things from happening. When the problems become dangerously worse, Cassie's father comes up with a plan. This book shows what it is like to face racism. It is an interesting book that challenged my imagination. I think that once you begin reading *Roll of Thunder, Hear My Cry,* you won't want to put it down.

GOALS/OBJECTIVES

Studying this unit will enable students to
- appreciate poems and short stories that portray a vision of the future
- define *science fiction* and recognize and provide examples of works of science fiction
- recognize a shifting point of view
- define *satire, irony, dramatic irony, irony of situation,* and *simile* and recognize the use of these techniques in works that they read
- edit for spelling errors
- classify information
- plan a time travelers' club

ADDITIONAL UNIT MATERIALS IN THE ASSESSMENT PORTFOLIO

- Vocabulary Worksheet 2.5.11
- Unit Test 2.5.12

See also the Additional Resources Box in the marginal notes accompanying each selection.

CROSS-CURRICULAR CONNECTIONS

- Health, 196
- Science, 182, 188, 204
- Social Studies, 188, 196
- World History, 188, 192

UNIT 5 VISIONS OF THE FUTURE

Lemons. *Diego Rivera, 1916*

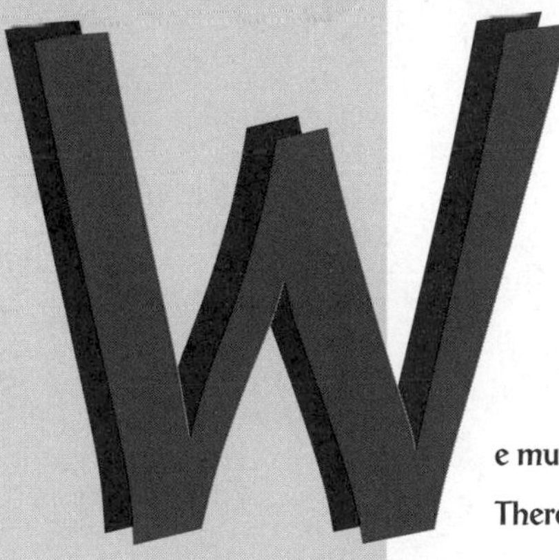

e must not think our world is the only one.

There are worlds outside our experience.

—Anonymous

UNIT SKILLS OUTLINE

Literary Skills and Concepts

- Dramatic Irony, 191
- Irony, 185
- Irony of Situation, 195
- Point of View, 195
- Satire, 185, 212
- Science Fiction, 191, 203
- Simile, 212

Other Language Arts Skills and Concepts

- Classifying, 213
- Editing for Spelling Errors, 186

ART NOTE

Diego Rivera (1886–1957) was a Mexican painter who painted large murals with simplified forms and bold colors. These murals became very popular in Latin America and the United States. Rivera often painted the people of Mexico and their society, history, and economy. In Mexico, he painted murals for the National Preparatory School, the Ministry of Education, and the National Agricultural School. He also held exhibitions and painted in the United States.

GOALS/OBJECTIVES

Studying this lesson will enable students to

- enjoy a satirical poem
- briefly explain the characteristics of Mars
- explain arguments for and against the existence of life on Mars
- define *satire* and *irony* and recognize the use of these techniques in works that they read
- edit for spelling errors

ADDITIONAL RESOURCES

READER'S GUIDE

- Selection Worksheet, 5.1

ASSESSMENT PORTFOLIO

- Selection Check Test, 2.5.1
- Selection Test, 2.5.2

PRONUNCIATION EXERCISE

- Grade 8 Audiocassette, Side B, Track 23

CROSS-CURRICULAR CONNECTIONS

SCIENCE

Students might enjoy one of the following activities:

- Students might draw or paint pictures of the Martian landscape. Students' pictures may be highly imaginative or they may be realistic. If students want to draw realistic pictures, have them look for photographs of the surface of Mars in encyclopedias or books.
- Students might draw or paint what they imagine Martians would look like if they did exist. Encourage students to think about what type of creature could survive in Mars's very cold temperatures.

Prereading

POETRY

"Earth"

by John Hall Wheelock

Cross-curricular Connection

Science. Of the nine planets in our solar system, Mars is the fourth closest to the sun. Its orbit lies between the orbits of Earth and Jupiter. Mars is the only planet with a surface that can be observed in detail from Earth. The surface of Mars is more like that of Earth than any other planet in the solar system. Mars resembles the desert terrain of the southwestern United States with its windblown sand dunes and jagged rocks. The temperature on Mars ranges from –191 degrees Farenheit at night during the winter season to –24 degrees Farenheit in the day during the summer season.

Astronomers have used powerful telescopes and photographs taken by unmanned spacecraft to examine closely the geography and climate of Mars. They have found evidence that millions of years ago large amounts of surface water covered Mars. Today, this water may be frozen in polar caps. The evidence of liquid water, plus the scant traces of oxygen found in the atmosphere have led a few scientists to believe that some form of life may exist, or did exist at one time, on Mars. Scientific tests have not been able either to prove or to disprove that life exists, or existed, on Mars in some form. However, most scientists believe that the possibility of life on Mars is very slim. We do know that no highly developed species lives on Mars.

In 1877, an Italian astronomer named Giovanni Schiaparelli identified a series of dark lines on the surface of Mars that he called "channels" or "canals." This discovery led some scientists to believe that the channels might be waterways that were constructed by some kind of intelligent creature. Today, astronomers have determined that these canals are an optical illusion. Despite the lack of scientific evidence, scientists, writers, and moviemakers alike have been excited by the idea of intelligent life on Mars.

As You Read

In your journal make two cluster charts like the ones below. In the first, write your thoughts about Martians. Then, as you read, fill in the second cluster chart with what the Martian thinks about people.

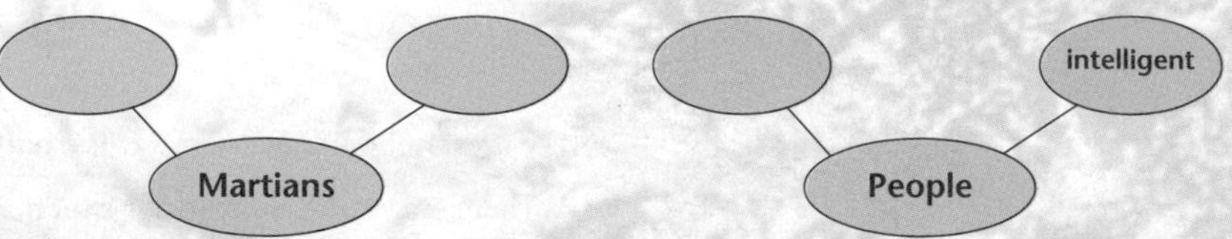

AS YOU READ

Students' cluster charts about Martians will vary. Student's cluster charts about what the Martian thinks of people might include the following details: intelligent, can explode planets, advanced civilization, people are now all deceased.

READER'S JOURNAL

Have you ever wondered whether there is life on other planets? What do you think this form of life might look like? Would it be "intelligent" life? Would it have language? music? transportation? What kind of lifestyle might a creature on another planet lead? Write about these questions in your journal.

"Earth"

JOHN HALL WHEELOCK

"A planet doesn't explode of itself," said drily
The Martian astronomer, gazing off into the air—
"That they were able to do it is proof that highly
Intelligent beings must have been living there." ■

WORDS FOR EVERYDAY USE

dri • ly (drī´lē) *adv.,* without emotion, in a matter-of-fact way

READER'S JOURNAL

As an alternative activity, you might ask students to imagine what a creature from another planet might think of people on Earth. Do you think the creature would admire how advanced we are or find our culture very primitive? Why? How do you think a creature from another world would feel about the way we treat our own planet? the way we treat other people?

SPELLING AND VOCABULARY WORDS FROM THE SELECTION

drily

SUPPORT FOR LEP STUDENTS

PRONUNCIATIONS OF PROPER NOUNS AND ADJECTIVES

Whee • lock (wē´läk) n.
Mar • tian (mär´shən) adj.

ADDITIONAL VOCABULARY

astronomer—expert in the science of the universe in which stars, planets, etc. are studied

VOCABULARY IN CONTEXT

• The speaker gave his lecture so drily that it was hard to pay attention to his emotionless voice.

Selection Check Test with Answers

ex. Who wrote "Earth"?
The selection was written by John Hall Wheelock.

1. Who is speaking in this poem?
A Martian astronomer is speaking.

2. What does the speaker say that planets do not do?
The speaker says that planets do not explode of themselves.

3. What tone of voice does the speaker use?
The speaker speaks "drily," or without emotion.

4. What does the speaker say this occurrence proves about the beings of Earth?
The speaker says that this occurrence proves the beings of Earth were intelligent.

5. In what tense does the speaker speak of the beings of Earth?
The speaker speaks of them in the past tense.

Courtesy of National Aeronautics and Space Administration (NASA)

A

About the Author

John Hall Wheelock (1886–1978) was born in Far Rockaway, New York. He was educated at Harvard, where he published his first book of poems, *Verses of Two Undergraduates,* with a classmate, Van Wyck Brooks. Wheelock later worked as an editor, director, and treasurer at Charles Scribner's Sons, a publishing house.

Responding to the Selection

Do you think it would be possible for human beings to explode Earth? Why, or why not? Do you think the ability to explode Earth is related to intelligence in any way? In what way would you respond to the Martian astronomer if you could?

Reviewing the Selection

RECALLING AND INTERPRETING

1. **R** What does the Martian astronomer say about the planet he or she is observing?

   I Why might the Martian say this remark "drily"? What does the Martian's "gazing off into the air" reveal about how this event has affected the Martian emotionally?

2. **R** What does the Martian say is proven by the event he or she has witnessed?

   I Why does the Martian speak of the residents of this planet in the past tense? Why does this event prove this theory?

SYNTHESIZING

3. How does the Martian astronomer seem to feel about what he or she has observed? What does the Martian seem to be missing? How intelligent is a being that will destroy itself and its habitat? What do the residents of planet Earth seem to be missing?

Understanding Literature (Questions for Discussion)

1. **Satire. Satire** is humorous writing that points out errors or failings in people, things, or ideas. The aim of satire is to reform human behavior or institutions. Do you think the destruction of Earth, as described by the Martian astronomer, is proof of high intelligence on Earth? To qualify as satire, the poem must be humorous. What about this poem is humorous? What errors or failings does the poem point out? What behaviors and institutions does the poem aim to reform? Is the poem a successful satire?
2. **Irony. Irony** is a difference between appearance and reality. Dramatic irony happens when something is known by the reader or audience of a literary work but is not known by the characters. A statement that says one thing but means the opposite is an example of verbal irony. In this poem, do you see dramatic irony, verbal irony, or both? Explain where the irony exists and what makes this situation or statement ironic.

RESPONDING TO THE SELECTION

Students might also discuss why the Martian takes an emotionless attitude toward the destruction of Earth. What does this reveal about the Martian?

ANSWERS FOR REVIEWING THE SELECTION

RECALLING AND INTERPRETING

1. **Recalling.** The Martian says that a planet does not explode of itself. **Interpreting.** The Martian might make this remark "drily" because he or she believes his or her statement is a well-known fact. It reveals that while the Martian finds the destruction of Earth scientifically interesting, he or she is not at all concerned with the loss of Earth and all its inhabitants.

2. **Recalling.** The Martian says that the event proves that intelligent beings must have been living on Earth. **Interpreting.** The Martian speaks of the residents of this planet in the past tense because they are now all dead, having destroyed themselves. The beings of Earth must have possessed enough intelligence to build technological devices capable of destroying a planet.

SYNTHESIZING

Responses will vary. Possible responses are given.

3. The speaker does not seem emotionally involved with what he or she has observed. Students may say that the Martian seems to be missing emotions or that the Martian is missing empathy or sympathy with the beings of Earth. A being that will destroy itself and its habitat is not very intelligent. The residents of Earth seemed to be missing concern with their own fate and that of their planet.

ANSWERS FOR UNDERSTANDING LITERATURE

Responses will vary. Possible responses are given.

1. **Satire.** Students might say that the destruction of Earth by its inhabitants is proof of the inhabitants' lack of intelligence. The Martian's assumption that the ability to destroy something is a sign of intelligence is humorous. This poem points out that humans see their technological developments as a sign of their intelligence, when it is really the ability to use technology wisely that is a sign of intelligence. The poem aims to reform humans' use of technology for destructive purposes.

2. **Irony.** Students might say that verbal irony as well as dramatic irony exists in the Martian's statement that the beings of Earth must have been intelligent because they destroyed themselves.

Language Lab

Introducing the Skill

Inform students that before they present or publish a piece of writing, they should always edit their work for errors in spelling. Tell students that even the best writers make spelling errors occasionally, so if they are unsure of the spelling of a word they should look it up in the dictionary. Memorizing a few basic spelling rules, as outlined in the Language Lab, can help them to recognize an incorrect spelling of a word more easily.

Previewing the Skill

Have students review the Language Lab.

Practicing the Skill

Once students seem familiar with the spelling rules outlined in the Language Lab, have them do the Try It Yourself exercise.

Reviewing the Skill

If students still have difficulty with spelling errors, have them do the Try It Yourself exercises in the Language Arts Survey, 2.39–2.41, "Editing for Spelling Errors." If students still have difficulty spelling certain words, have the class as a whole come up with different mnemonic aids for remembering the correct spellings of certain words, such as "there is *a rat* in *separate.*"

Language Lab

Editing for Spelling Errors

Below are some tips to help you avoid some common spelling errors. For a list of common spelling errors, see the Language Arts Survey, 2.39–2.41, "Editing for Spelling Errors." If you are uncertain of the spelling of a word, consult a dictionary.

Avoiding Common Spelling Errors

Use *i* before *e* except after *c* or in words that have the long *a* sound (ā).

IE SOUNDED AS LONG *E*	thief, believe, yield
EI AFTER *C*	ceiling, receipt
LONG *A*	weight, sleigh, eight

To spell words with a syllable that is pronounced like the word *seed,* use one of three spellings.

CEDE	concede, precede, recede, secede
CEED	exceed, proceed, succeed
SEDE	supersede (This is the only word in English spelled with the *–sede* ending.)

To form plurals of nouns ending in *s, x, z, ch,* or *sh,* add *es.*

EXAMPLE	kiss + es = kisses	branch + es = branches
	box + es = boxes	bush + es = bushes
	buzz + es = buzzes	

When adding a prefix, do not change the word itself.

EXAMPLE un + done = undone re + finish = refinish

Before adding a suffix to a word ending in *y,* with more than one syllable, change the *y* to *i.*

EXAMPLE easy + er = easier
rely + able = reliable

Before adding a suffix to a word ending in *e,* drop the *e* before adding the suffix if the suffix begins with a vowel.

EXAMPLE interfere + ence = interference
believe + able = believable

When a suffix begins with a consonant, do not drop the final *e* from the root word.

EXAMPLE arrange + ment = arrangement
care + less = careless

Before adding a suffix beginning with a vowel, double the final consonant when the word has one syllable or the accent is on the last syllable, and the word ends in a single consonant preceded by a single vowel.

EXAMPLE drop + er = dropper
forget + ing = forgetting
remit + ance = remittance
pig + ish = piggish
plan + er = planner

Try It Yourself

Proofread the following paragraph for spelling errors. Write correct spellings on a separate sheet of paper.

It was an unbeleivable night. We were campping high in the mountains of Colorado when a terrible storm blew up. We had planed for rain, but not for the kind of poundding we recieved. We were all tucked in our tents when the high winds started. The wind blew dirt and sand up into the air. Small bushs looked as though they would be uprrooted. We all rushed around trying to secure everything to prevent it from being blown away. We were terribely woryed not only for our equipment but for our own safty. The rain began, but the winds died down. We all huddled into one tent, hopping the lineing of the tent would not leak. No one could sleep under these conditions. After what seemed like forever, the rains began to stop. We all happyly went to our own tents and fell fast asleep. This was an expereince we would not soon forget.

Answers for Try It Yourself

It was an unbelievable night. We were camping high in the mountains of Colorado when a terrible storm blew up. We had planned for rain, but not for the kind of pounding we received. We were all tucked in our tents when the high winds started. The wind blew dirt and sand up into the air. Small bushes looked as though they would be uprooted. We all rushed around trying to secure everything to prevent it from being blown away. We were terribly worried not only for our equipment but for our own safety. The rain began, but the winds died down. We all huddled into one tent, hoping the lining of the tent would not leak. No one could sleep under these conditions. After what seemed like forever, the rains began to stop. We all happily went to our own tents and fell fast asleep. This was an experience we would not soon forget.

GOALS/OBJECTIVES

Studying this lesson will enable students to
- enjoy a brief science fiction story
- briefly define *robot* and explain how the word and popular ideas about robots entered our culture
- define and recognize *science fiction* and *irony*

ADDITIONAL RESOURCES

READER'S GUIDE
- Selection Worksheet, 5.2

ASSESSMENT PORTFOLIO
- Selection Check Test, 2.5.3
- Selection Test, 2.5.4

PRONUNCIATION EXERCISE
- Grade 8 Audiocassette, Side B, Track 24

CROSS-CURRICULAR CONNECTIONS

SCIENCE AND WORLD HISTORY

Encourage students to think of a task that they do not like to perform. Have each student write a description of a robot that would perform this task for them. Students might then sketch what these robots would look like. Tell students that they should consider the tasks a robot will have to perform when they design what it would look like. For example, a robot that has to take trash down the stairs will need a clamp of some kind to hold the trash, a means of getting down the stairs, and a mechanism to open the trash can.

SOCIAL STUDIES

Students might discuss what periods of human history they would be interested in studying if they were to become archaeologists.

Prereading

SHORT STORY

"Humans Are Different"

by Alan Bloch

Cross-curricular Connections

Science and World History. A robot is a machine or device that works automatically, or by remote control. Examples of robots include a mechanical arm in an auto assembly plant, a device that takes photographs or samples on the moon or deep underwater, and a nurse's helper cart in a hospital that follows a wired path from room to room. Robots follow instructions stored in their control centers to perform specific tasks. They vary widely in appearance, but few have the android, or humanlike appearance that commonly appears in science fiction books and movies. Many popular ideas about robots as well as the word *robot* have entered our culture because of a Czech playwright named Karl Capek (pronounced CHOP-ek).

In 1921, Capek first produced the play *R. U. R.* The initials in the title stand for Rossum's Universal Robots. Capek derived the word *robot* from the Czech term *robota,* which means "servile labor" or "drudgery." In the play, Rossum's Universal Robots manufactures machines that resemble people. The robots perform work that people no longer wish to do. These machines work well until their creators give them feelings. The robots then rebel and destroy their creators. In the selection you are about to read, robots try to piece together the nature and history of humans.

Social Studies. People have always been interested in the way that humans lived in the past. Anthropology is the science that studies humans and their cultures. One branch of anthropology is called archaeology. Archaeologists study objects such as buildings, tools, artwork, and clothing left behind by earlier peoples. By examining these objects, archaeologists can determine how people once lived. In the selection you are about to read, an archaeologist studies humans and wonders exactly what made humans different from robots.

As You Read

The main character in "**Humans Are Different**" notes similarities and differences between humans and robots. Make a Venn diagram like the one below. As you read, fill in the diagram with similarities and differences between humans and robots.

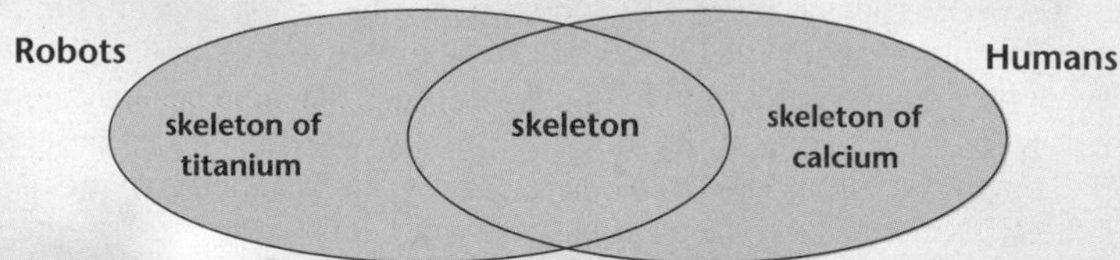

AS YOU READ

In the part of the Venn diagram that describes robots' differences, students might write the following details: not from Earth, have no "divine" flame, have thermostat circuits, can be turned on and off, do not decay. In the part of the diagram that shows similarities, students might write that both can become archaeologists, both go to school, both speak languages, both can get too hot, and both stop moving when "switched off." In the part that describes humans' differences, students might write the following details: from Earth, have disappeared, have "divine" flame, can get sick with fever, have different organs, cannot be made to run once dead, decay.

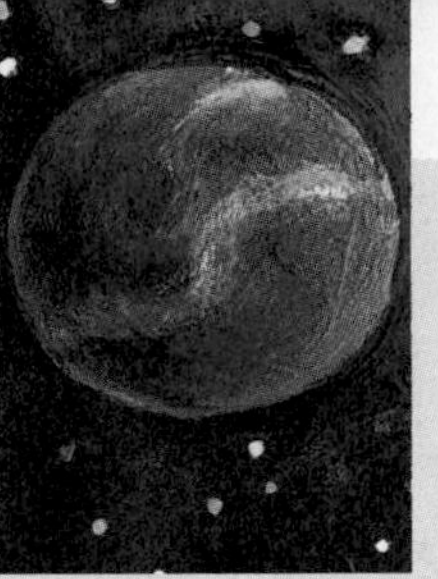

READER'S JOURNAL

What qualities do you have that make you different from a machine? Think about both your physical and mental characteristics. What characteristics of a machine would you like to have? What characteristics would you not like to have? Write about these questions in your journal.

"Humans Are Different"

ALAN BLOCH

I'm an archaeologist, and Humans are my business. Just the same I wonder if we'll ever find out what made Humans different from us Robots—by digging around on the dead planets. You see, I lived with a Human once, and I know it isn't as simple as they told us back in school.

We have a few records, of course, and Robots like me are filling in some of the gaps; but I think now that we aren't really getting anywhere. We know, or at least the historians say we know, that Humans came from a planet called Earth. We know, too, that they rode out bravely from star to star and wherever they stopped, they left colonies—Humans, Robots, and sometimes both—against their return. But they never came back.

Those were the shining days of the world. But are we so old now? Humans had a bright flame—the old word is "divine," I think—that flung them far across the night skies, and we have lost the strands of the web they wove.

Our scientists tell us that Humans were very much like us—and the skeleton of a Human is, to be sure, almost the same as the skeleton of a Robot, except that it's made of some calcium compound instead of titanium. They speak learnedly of "population pressure" as a "driving force toward the stars." Just the same, though, there are other differences.

It was on my last field trip, to one of the inner planets, that I met the Human. He must have been the Last Human in this system and he'd forgotten how to talk—he'd been alone so long. Once he learned our language we got along fine together, and I planned to bring him back with me. Something happened to him, though.

One day, for no reason at all, he complained of the heat. I checked his temperature and decided that his thermostat circuits were shot. I had a kit of field spares with me, and he was obviously out of order, so I went to work. I turned him off without any trouble. I pushed the needle into his neck to operate the cut-off switch, and he stopped moving, just like a Robot. But when I opened him up he wasn't the same inside. And when I put him back together I couldn't get him running

1 *What isn't as simple as the robot was told in school?*

2 *Why had the human forgotten how to talk?*

3 *Why did humans explore the universe?*

READER'S JOURNAL

As an alternative activity, you might ask students to imagine and write about what machines might think of humans if they were able to think. What would they admire about us? What would they find flawed in us?

SPELLING AND VOCABULARY WORDS FROM THE SELECTION

weather

ANSWERS TO GUIDED READING QUESTIONS

1 What makes humans different from robots isn't as simple as the robot was told in school.

2 The human had forgotten how to talk because he had been alone so long.

3 The humans explored the universe because they possessed a "divine" flame that made them travel far across the night skies.

SUPPORT FOR LEP STUDENTS

PRONUNCIATIONS OF PROPER NOUNS AND ADJECTIVES

Bloch (bläk) n.

ADDITIONAL VOCABULARY

colonies—groups of people who settle in a distant land but remain under the authority of their native land
field—area where practical work is done
spares—extra parts or things
thermostat—apparatus or device for regulating temperature

Selection Check Test with Answers

ex. Who is the narrator of the selection?
The narrator is a robot.

1. What is the robot's profession?
The robot is an archaeologist.

2. What is the difference between a robot skeleton and a human skeleton?
A robot skeleton is made of titanium and a human skeleton is made of a calcium compound.

3. What did the robot discover on his last field trip?
The robot discovered "the Last Human in this system."

4. What did the robot do when the human complained of the heat?
The robot took the human's temperature, decided that his thermostat circuits were shot, and tried to repair him.

5. What had happened to the human by the time the robot was ready to come home?
The human had weathered until only his bones remained.

again. Then he sort of weathered away—and by the time I was ready to come home, about a year later, there was nothing left of him but bones. Yes, Humans are indeed different. ■

About the Author

Alan Bloch (1915–) brings to his writing a strong background in physics and mathematics. Born in New York City, Bloch attended Swarthmore College and Oberlin College before beginning a career in engineering, physics, and computer development. Later he became a science consultant, a writer of nonfiction (usually about science and computers), and an award-winning science fiction writer.

Words for Everyday Use

weath • er (weth´ər) *v.,* become discolored or disintegrated from exposure to the elements

Vocabulary in Context

• When wood weathers, it often becomes gray in color.

Responding to the Selection

How did you feel about the way the robot described humans and what happened to them? Did you find this story shocking? scary? funny? something different? Explain why you felt as you did.

Reviewing the Selection

RECALLING AND INTERPRETING

1. **R** Who or what is the narrator of the story? What is his job?

   I What do you think has happened to all the humans?

2. **R** What does the robot say is already known about humans?

   I What does the robot mean when he says "we have lost the strands of the web they wove"?

3. **R** What did the robot discover during a field trip to "one of the inner planets"? What differences did the robot discover in this creature?

   I Does the robot seem to feel any particular emotion toward the creature? If so, what? If not, why not? What do you think it would be like to be the last surviving member of your species?

4. **R** What was wrong with the human? What did the robot think was wrong? How did the robot treat the human?

   I What happened to the human? Why did the robot find this occurrence so baffling?

SYNTHESIZING

5. Does the narrator recognize that robots were the creations of humans, or does he consider robots to be superior to humans? What do humans possess that the robots are lacking?

Understanding Literature (Questions for Discussion)

1. **Science Fiction. Science fiction** is imaginative literature based on scientific principles, discoveries, or laws. What scientific principles, discoveries, or laws make this work seem realistic, or like a possible reality? What elements of this story are unrealistic?
2. **Dramatic Irony. Dramatic irony** happens when something is known by the reader or audience of a literary work but is not known by the characters. What is ironic about the narrator's attempt to fix the human? What other examples of irony do you see in this story?

RESPONDING TO THE SELECTION

Students might also discuss what they would say to the robot to explain how humans are different.

ANSWERS FOR REVIEWING THE SELECTION

RECALLING AND INTERPRETING

1. **Recalling.** The narrator is a robot who works as an archaeologist. **Interpreting.** All the humans seem to have died.

2. **Recalling.** The robot says it is known that humans came from Earth, explored space, colonized other planets with humans and robots, never came back to the colonies, and have skeletons made of a calcium compound. **Interpreting.** The robot means that he cannot understand the reasons humans had for exploring space.

3. **Recalling.** The robot discovered the last human. The robot discovered that humans are different than robots inside; that once a human is "turned off," it is impossible to turn him or her back on again; and that humans decay once they have died. **Interpreting.** The robot does not seem to feel any particular emotion toward the human, nor toward his discovery, merely saying "we got along fine together." The robot may not be able to feel emotions. Being the last surviving member of a species would probably be terribly lonely and frightening.

4. **Recalling.** The human was sick with a fever. The robot thought that the human's thermostat circuits were shot. The robot treated the human by sticking a needle in his neck and then taking him apart. **Interpreting.** The human died. The robot found this baffling because robots do not die.

SYNTHESIZING

Responses will vary. Possible responses are given.

5. The narrator does not recognize that humans created robots. The robot believes that humans are superior in ways and inferior in ways. Humans possess emotions.

ANSWERS FOR UNDERSTANDING LITERATURE

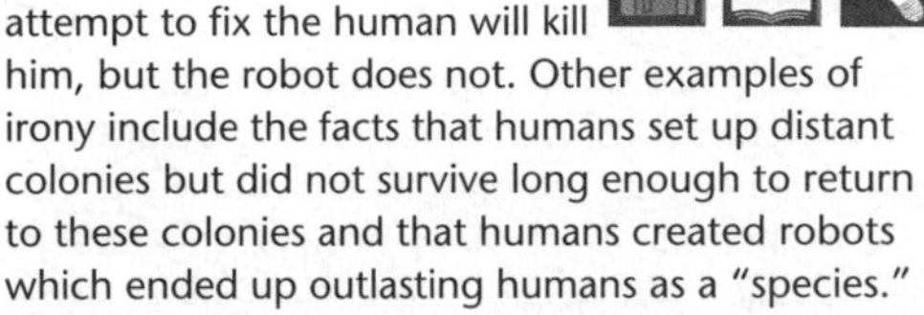

Responses will vary. Possible responses are given.

1. **Science Fiction.** Our increasing technological advances in space travel and in robotics makes this work seem like a possible reality. Unrealistic elements include the ability to travel to other solar systems and the colonies on other planets as well as robots that can think.

2. **Dramatic Irony.** The reader knows that this attempt to fix the human will kill him, but the robot does not. Other examples of irony include the facts that humans set up distant colonies but did not survive long enough to return to these colonies and that humans created robots which ended up outlasting humans as a "species."

GOALS/OBJECTIVES

Studying this lesson will enable students to

- appreciate a story with a shifting point of view
- briefly explain how modern zoos differ from zoos in the past
- define *point of view* and identify the points of view in a story
- define *irony of situation* and recognize the use of this technique

ADDITIONAL RESOURCES

READER'S GUIDE

- Selection Worksheet, 5.3

ASSESSMENT PORTFOLIO

- Selection Check Test, 2.5.5
- Selection Test, 2.5.6

PRONUNCIATION EXERCISE

- Grade 8 Audiocassette, Side B, Track 25

CROSS-CURRICULAR CONNECTIONS

WORLD HISTORY

Encourage students to write to famous zoos or zoos in their area to discover what educational programs the zoos offer or what research programs they support. If students have specific questions to ask about zoos, they might pose these questions in their letters as well. This might be a good opportunity to introduce the proper form of a business letter. Refer students to the Language Arts Survey, 5.4, "Writing a Business Letter." Inform students that their business letters should be brief and to the point.

Prereading

SHORT STORY

"Zoo"

by Edward D. Hoch

Cross-curricular Connection

World History. Most of us have visited a zoo or have at least seen pictures of wild animals kept in zoos. The earliest known zoo dates back to 1500 BC. Throughout history, zoos have been places where wild animals are displayed. However, the purposes, or reasons, for creating a zoo have changed over time.

Today, zoos have three primary purposes. The first is to entertain and to educate. People come to zoos to look at animals that they would not otherwise see. Zoos often contain beautiful gardens for people to walk through as they watch rare and not-so-rare creatures. Zoos offer information about their animals and often provide guided tours.

The second purpose of today's zoos is to protect and conserve different species of wildlife. Zoos breed endangered animals with the hope of returning them to their natural habitats and preventing their extinction.

The third purpose of zoos is to study the animals. Scientists study animal habitats, disease, and behavior with the hope of learning how to better care for and protect animals.

These three purposes of present-day zoos differ from the purposes of zoos in the past. Early zoos were created so rulers could display their wealth and power. The first known zoo displayed the wealth and power of Egypt. Another large zoo was established by a Chinese emperor around 1000 BC. The ancient Greeks and Romans also kept zoos. The Greeks had public zoos that students could visit to study animals. The Romans had private zoos and displayed wild animals that were later used cruelly in the Colosseum for entertainment.

In the 1700s, zoos became popular in Europe. Many were very small with extremely poor conditions for the animals. In fact, many people refused to visit these zoos because the owners were unwilling or unable to care for their animals properly. Eventually, new zoos were developed that protected the animals and used them for education and research of animal behavior, not just for profit.

As You Read

In "Zoo" the author uses many vivid phrases that help you to visualize how the scenes look and sound. In your journal, make a chart like the one below. As you read, fill in the chart with words and phrases that appeal to your sense of sight and sound.

WORD OR PHRASE	SENSE
silver spaceship	sight
constantly chattered in a high-pitched tone	sound

AS YOU READ

Students might include the following details in their charts: crowds, long lines clutching a dollar—sight; three legged creatures, tall thin men, snakelike horrors—sight; small, horse-like animals moving quickly and jerkily—sight; chattering in a high-pitched tongue—sound; Professor's rainbow cape and top hat—sight; crowd's noise—sound; creatures running up walls of cages like spiders—sight; familiar jagged rocks—sight, touch; horse-like people scurrying—sight; babbled greeting in strange tongue—sound.

READER'S JOURNAL

Have you ever wondered what the creatures in a zoo think of the people watching them? Imagine that you are a creature in a zoo. What type of animal are you? What do you think about the humans who come to watch you? What have you observed about humans?

"Zoo"

EDWARD D. HOCH

The children were always good during the month of August, especially when it began to get near the twenty-third. It was on this day that the great silver spaceship carrying Professor Hugo's Interplanetary[1] Zoo settled down for its annual six-hour visit to the Chicago area.

Before daybreak the crowds would form, long lines of children and adults both, each one clutching his or her dollar, and waiting with wonderment to see what race of strange creatures the Professor had brought this year.

In the past they had sometimes been treated to three-legged creatures from Venus, or tall, thin men from Mars, or even snakelike horrors from somewhere more distant. This year, as the great round ship settled slowly to earth in the huge tri-city parking area just outside of Chicago, they watched with awe as the sides slowly slid up to reveal the familiar barred cages. In them were some wild breed of nightmare—small, horse-like, animals that moved with quick, jerking motions and constantly chattered in a high-pitched tongue. The citizens of Earth clustered around as Professor Hugo's crew quickly collected the waiting dollars, and soon the good Professor himself made an appearance, wearing his many-colored rainbow cape and top hat. "Peoples of Earth," he called into his microphone.

The crowd's noise died down and he continued. "Peoples of Earth, this year you see a real treat for your single dollar—the little-known horse-spider people of Kaan—brought to you across a million miles of space at great expense. Gather around, see them, study them, listen to them, tell your friends about them. But hurry! My ship can remain here only six hours!"

❶ *Why are the children good during the month of August?*

❷ *Why is this year's Zoo a special treat? Why is it a "bargain"?*

1. **interplanetary.** Between different planets

WORDS FOR EVERYDAY USE

awe (ô) *n.*, feeling of fear and wonder

chat • ter (chat´ər) *v.*, talk fast

READER'S JOURNAL

If students have never been to a zoo before, tell them to write using what they know about zoos from books, movies, and television. If students are having difficulty with this assignment, they might write instead about what they imagine pets might think of their owners.

SPELLING AND VOCABULARY WORDS FROM THE SELECTION

awe
babble
chatter
garment
scurry

ANSWERS TO GUIDED READING QUESTIONS

❶ The children are good during the month of August because they know the Interplanetary Zoo is coming and they wish to be allowed to go.

❷ This year's Zoo is a special treat because people will get to see "the little-known horse spider people of Kaan." It is a "bargain" because it only costs one dollar per person.

SUPPORT FOR LEP STUDENTS

PRONUNCIATIONS OF PROPER NOUNS AND ADJECTIVES

Hoch (häk) n.
Hu • go (hyo͞o´gō) n.
Lon • don (lun´dən) n.
Par • is (par´is) n.
Rome (rōm) n.
Hong Kong (häŋ kaŋ) n.
To • ky • o (tō´kē ō') n.

ADDITIONAL VOCABULARY

horrors—frightening or shocking things
offspring—child or descendant

VOCABULARY IN CONTEXT

- The tourists were overcome with awe as they gazed at the majesty of the Grand Canyon.
- At first Katie found it difficult to understand French, but after a few months she was chattering away in the language.

Answers to Guided Reading Questions

❶ The creatures enjoyed Earth because the creatures there were so strange.

❷ The Earth people agree that it was the best Zoo yet.

❸ The young horse-spider says that his trip was the best Zoo ever.

Selection Check Test with Answers

EX. In what month in Chicago are the children always good?
The children are always good in August.

1. What type of zoo comes to visit Chicago?
Professor Hugo's Interplanetary Zoo comes to visit Chicago.

2. How much does it cost to view the creatures in the Zoo?
It costs one dollar.

3. What creatures have come to Earth this year?
The horse-spider people of Kaan.

4. What do the people of Earth think about the Zoo?
They think that it was the best Zoo ever.

5. What was the young horse-spider's favorite place that he visited?
His favorite place was Earth.

And the crowds slowly filed by, at once horrified and fascinated by these strange creatures that looked like horses but ran up the walls of their cages like spiders. "This is certainly worth a dollar," one man remarked, hurrying away. "I'm going home to get the wife."

All day long it went like that, until ten thousand people had filed by the barred cages set into the side of the spaceship. Then, as the six-hour limit ran out, Professor Hugo once more took the microphone in hand. "We must go now, but we will return next year on this date. And if you enjoyed our zoo this year, telephone your friends in other cities about it. We will land in New York tomorrow, and next week in London, Paris, Rome, Hong Kong, and Tokyo. Then on to other worlds!"

❶ *What do creatures in the Zoo think of Earth?*

❷ *What do the Earth people agree?*

❸ *What does the young horse-spider say about his trip?*

He waved farewell to them, and as the ship rose from the ground, the Earth peoples agreed that this had been the very best Zoo yet. . . .

Some two months and three planets later, the silver ship of Professor Hugo settled at last onto the familiar jagged rocks of Kaan, and the odd horse-spider creatures filed quickly out of their cages. Professor Hugo was there to say a few parting words, and then they scurried away in a hundred different directions, seeking their homes among the rocks.

In one house, the she-creature was happy to see the return of her mate and offspring. She babbled a greeting in the strange tongue and hurried to embrace them. "It was a long time you were gone. Was it good?"

And the he-creature nodded. "The little one enjoyed it especially. We visited eight worlds and saw many things."

The little one ran up the wall of the cave. "On the place called Earth it was the best. The creatures there wear garments over their skins, and they walk on two legs."

"But isn't it dangerous?" asked the she-creature.

"No," her mate answered. "There are bars to protect us from them. We remain right in the ship. Next time you must come with us. It is well worth the nineteen commocs it costs."

And the little one nodded. "It was the very best Zoo ever. . . ." ■

About the Author

Edward D. Hoch (1930–) was born in Rochester, New York. He graduated from the University of Rochester and worked for the Rochester Public Library. He also has worked as a copywriter for an advertising company. Hoch has written many mysteries, as well as science fiction stories and novels. He won an award from the Mystery Writers of America for a short story, "The Oblong Room." Some of his stories have been adapted for television.

Words for Everyday Use

scur • ry (skʉr´ē) *v.,* run quickly

bab • ble (bab´əl) *v.,* talk foolishly or too much

gar • ment (gär´mənt) *n.,* any article of clothing

Vocabulary in Context

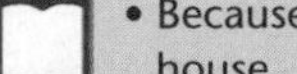

- Because the children did not want to be late for dinner, they scurried home from their friend's house.
- Roger always babbles nonsensically about too many subjects at once.
- My sister raids my closet every morning for garments to wear to school.

Responding to the Selection

How would you feel about being observed by other creatures? Would it make you uncomfortable? Would it not bother you? Would you be happier if you did or did not know you were being observed?

Reviewing the Selection

RECALLING AND INTERPRETING

1. **R** For what are the children of Earth anxiously waiting? What types of creatures have people on Earth seen in the past?

   I What mood does the description of former visits create in the reader?

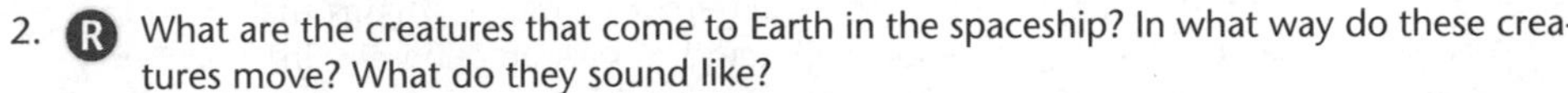

2. **R** What are the creatures that come to Earth in the spaceship? In what way do these creatures move? What do they sound like?

   I Why do you suppose the Professor refers to these creatures as "people"?

3. **R** What does the he-creature say about their travels? What does the young creature say he or she liked best about Earth? What does the he-creature say about the bars?

   I In what way are the creatures of Kaan like humans?

4. **R** What does Professor Hugo do to make money from both the people of Earth and other creatures?

   I What does Professor Hugo's scheme suggest about his character?

SYNTHESIZING

5. In what way are the reactions of the humans and the people of Kaan similar? In what way does each group regard the other? In what way does each group regard themselves? In the Professor's Zoo, is one group really the "creatures" and the other group the true "observers"? Explain your answer.

Understanding Literature (Questions for Discussion)

1. **Point of View. Point of view** is the vantage point from which a story is told. The point of view in this story changes from one group to another. From whose points of view is this story told? Why did the author shift the point of view? How would the story have been different if it were told only from the point of view of the Earthlings? of the people of Kaan?
2. **Irony of Situation.** An event that contradicts the expectations of the characters, the reader, or the audience of a literary work is an example of irony of situation. What contradicts your expectations in this story?

RESPONDING TO THE SELECTION

Students might discuss whether either group (humans or the horse-spiders) knew that they were being observed.

ANSWERS FOR REVIEWING THE SELECTION

RECALLING AND INTERPRETING

1. **Recalling.** The children of Earth are anxiously awaiting the arrival of Professor Hugo's Interplanetary Zoo. People on Earth have seen three-legged creatures from Venus, tall thin men from Mars, and snakelike horrors. **Interpreting.** The description creates a mood of suspense and expectation.
2. **Recalling.** The creatures are the horse-spider people of Kaan. They move in quick, jerking motions and can climb up walls. They chatter in a high-pitched tongue. **Interpreting.** The Professor may refer to the creatures of Kaan as people because they are as intelligent and as highly developed as humans.
3. **Recalling.** The he-creature says that they visited eight worlds and saw many things. The young creature liked Earth because the creatures there wore garments and walked on two legs. **Interpreting.** The creatures of Kaan are like humans in that both enjoy seeing strange creatures from far away places.
4. **Recalling.** Professor Hugo charges creatures to take them aboard his Zoo and charges other creatures to look at these creatures. **Interpreting.** Professor Hugo is a shrewd business person who understands that many creatures love strangeness and variety.

SYNTHESIZING

Responses will vary. Possible responses are given.

5. The humans and the people of Kaan are both horrified and entertained by what they have seen. Each group regards the other group as strange and themselves as normal. Both groups are both "creatures" and "observers."

ANSWERS FOR UNDERSTANDING LITERATURE

Responses will vary. Possible responses are given.

1. **Point of View.** The story is told from humans' point of view and from the people of Kaan's point of view. The author shifts point of view to show how similar these different groups actually are. In either case, only differences instead of similarities would be illustrated.
2. **Irony of Situation.** The fact that the horse-spider people of Kaan also paid money to see strange creatures from other worlds contradicts the reader's expectations as does Professor Hugo's shrewd business deal.

GOALS/OBJECTIVES

Studying this lesson will enable students to
- enjoy a science fiction story set on Earth in the future
- explain how advertisements often make use of propaganda
- explain what a healthy body requires
- define *science fiction* and recognize realistic elements in science fiction

ADDITIONAL RESOURCES

Reader's Guide
- Selection Worksheet, 5.4

Assessment Portfolio
- Selection Check Test, 2.5.7
- Selection Test, 2.5.8

Pronunciation Exercise
- Grade 8 Audiocassette, Side B, Track 26

CROSS-CURRICULAR CONNECTIONS

Social Studies

Have students locate advertisements in magazines or take notes about advertisements on television. Students should bring these magazine advertisements and their notes into class. Encourage a class discussion on the different types of propaganda students can identify in these advertisements.

Health

As a class have students create two collages—one of unhealthy foods and images and one of healthy foods and images.

Prereading

SHORT STORY

"Lose Now, Pay Later"

by Carol Farley

Cross-curricular Connections

Social Studies. At some time we have all been convinced to act or think a certain way when there is little or no evidence to support that action or way of thinking. Often, these situations involve propaganda, or the use of misleading language to influence people's thoughts and actions. Propaganda appeals to people's emotions rather than to logic.

Advertisements often use forms of propaganda. For example, seeing a superstar use a product in an advertisement is a form of propaganda. The advertisers hope that the good feelings you have about the star will transfer to their product. Another type of propaganda, bandwagon appeal, appeals to our desire to belong to a group. Advertisements are often created to give the impression that "everyone" is buying the product. If you want to be a part of the group, you should buy the product, too.

Statements or arguments that initially seem sound and logical may be addressing your emotions. Things that seem too good to be true often are. In "Lose Now, Pay Later," two new products appeal to people's emotions, although few facts are known about them.

Health. Advertising can affect the way we perceive and feel about our own bodies. Many people feel that they should be thin like the models in the advertisements, or they associate being thin with being rich, popular, or happy. For many people the ideal body is unnaturally thin. People are constantly searching for new, easy ways to reach low body weights. There are thousands of diets, pills, drinks, and plans designed to make people lose weight quickly. Unfortunately, too many people are concerned with weight loss rather than with healthy bodies and lifestyles. A healthy body requires a diet that provides vitamins and other nutrients to maintain the body as well as to energize it. Moderate exercise is also important to a healthy body. Healthy foods and activities lead to a healthy body.

As You Read

"Lose Now, Pay Later" uses many details that appeal to the five senses. Make a sensory detail chart like the one below. As you read, fill in the chart with details that appeal to each sense.

Sight	Sound	Smell	Taste	Touch
dim and dingy			peanut-butter-fudge-crunch	

AS YOU READ

Students might include the following details in their charts: *Sight*—bright and glaring; five or six gold-colored machines; bare and bright, so empty and clean; tall, white plastic box; deeply tanned, thin woman in a green turban and jumpsuit; empty, stark white; coffinlike structure as bare and bright as an old microwave oven; little blue marks; delicate tattooed bracelet. *Sound*—loud humming sound; strange voice. *Smell*—terrific aroma of flavors; wonderful spurt of air that rushes out of expensive box of candy. *Taste*—butter-rum-pecan; chocolate-nut-mint; coconut-almond-marshmallow. *Touch*—cold like ice cream; warm like cooked pudding; warm beach.

READER'S JOURNAL

Think about a favorite food. Write about the way it tastes and smells. What emotions or memories do you associate with this food? Freewrite about this food and the experiences it brings to mind.

"Lose Now, Pay Later"

CAROL FARLEY

I think my little brother is crazy. At least I hope he is. Because if his looney idea is right, then all of us are being used like a flock of sheep, and that's a pretty gruesome thought. Humans just can't be that stupid. My brother has a dumb idea, that's all. It's just a dumb idea.

This whole situation started about eight months ago. That's when I first knew anything about it, I mean. My best friend, Trinja, and I were shopping when we noticed a new store where an old insurance office used to be. It was a cubbyhole, really, at the far end of the mall where hardly anybody ever goes. We were there because we'd used that entrance as we came home from school.

"Swoodies!" Trinja said, pointing at the letters written across the display window. "What do you think they are, Deb?"

I stared through the glass. The place had always looked dim and dingy before, full of desks, half-dead plants, and bored-looking people; but now it was as bright and glaring as a Health Brigade Corp office. There weren't any people inside at all, but there were five or six gold-colored machines lining the walls. Signs were hung everywhere.

SWEETS PLUS GOODIES = SWOODIES, one said. Flavors were posted by each machine; peanut-butter-fudge-crunch . . . butter-rum-pecan . . . chocolate-nut-mint . . . Things like that. The biggest sign of all simply said FREE.

I have to admit that the place gave me the creeps that first time I saw it. I don't know why. It just looked so bare and bright, so empty and clean, without any people or movement. The glare almost hurt my eyes. And I guess I was suspicious about anything

❶ *What was the narrator's initial reaction to the swoodie shop? What caused these feelings?*

WORDS FOR EVERYDAY USE

din • gy (din´je) *adj.*, not bright or clean; shabby

READER'S JOURNAL

As an alternative activity, you might ask students to write about advertisements or offers that seem too good to be true. What is promised in these advertisements or offers? Why do students believe that these deals or products cannot deliver what is promised?

SPELLING AND VOCABULARY WORDS FROM THE SELECTION

binge	placid
consumption	ravage
cubicle	scarf
cull	stark
dingy	unnerve
gullible	

ANSWER TO GUIDED READING QUESTION

❶ The narrator's initial reaction was that the swoodie shop was creepy. She felt this way because the swoodie shop was unnaturally bare, bright, empty, clean, and devoid of people.

SUPPORT FOR LEP STUDENTS

PRONUNCIATIONS OF PROPER NOUNS AND ADJECTIVES

Far • ley (fär´lē) n.
Trin • ja (trin ´jə) n.

ADDITIONAL VOCABULARY

dignity—quality of being worthy of esteem or honor
gruesome—causing horror or disgust
sacrifice—give up
yen—basic monetary unit of Japan

VOCABULARY IN CONTEXT

- The windows of the old house were dingy until we gave them a good cleaning.

Answers to Guided Reading Questions

❶ Deb's "brain burst into memories associated with each flavor."

❷ Deb and Trinja found it odd that everything was free. They believed that it might be a publicity stunt.

that was completely free. Still, though, there was a terrific aroma drifting out of there—sort of a combination of all those flavors that were listed on the signs.

"Let's go in," Trinja said, grabbing my arm. I could see that the smell was getting to her too. She's always on a diet, so she thinks about food a lot.

What happened when Deb tried her first swoodie? ❶

"But it's so empty in there," I said, drawing away.

"They've just opened, that's all," she told me, yanking my arm again. "Besides, machines and robots run lots of the stores. Let's go inside and see what's in there."

Do you know that wonderful spurt of air that rushes out when you first open an expensive box of candy? The inside of that store smelled just like the inside of one of those boxes. For a few seconds we just stood there sniffing and grinning. My salivary glands[1] started swimming.

Trinja turned toward the nearest machine. "Coconut-almond marshmallow." She was almost drooling. "I've got to try one, Deb." She pressed the button, and a chocolate cone dropped down, like a coffee cup from a kitcho machine. Then a mixture, similar to the look of soft ice cream, filled it. "Want to try it with me?" she asked, reaching for the cone. We both took a taste.

What did Deb and Trinja find odd about the shop? What explanation did they offer? ❷

It was absolutely the neatest sensation I've had in my whole life. Swoodies aren't cold like ice cream or warm like cooked pudding, but they're a blending of both in temperature and texture. The flavor melts instantly, and your whole mouth and brain are flooded with tastes and impressions. Like that first swoodie I tried, coconut-almond-marshmallow; suddenly, as my mouth separated the individual tastes, my brain burst into memories associated with each flavor. I felt as if I were lying on a warm beach, all covered with coconut suntan oil—then I heard myself giggling and singing as a group of us roasted marshmallows around a campfire—then I relived the long-ago moments of biting into the special Christmas cookies my grandmother made with almonds when I was little.

"Wow!" Trinja looked at me, and I could see that she had just experienced the same kind of reactions. We scarfed up the rest of that swoodie in just a few more bites, and we moved on to another flavor. With each one it was the same. I felt a combination of marvelous tastes and joyous thoughts. We tried every flavor before we finally staggered out into the mall again.

"I'll have to diet for a whole year now," Trinja said, patting her stomach.

"I'll feel like a blimp myself," I told her, but neither one of us cared. We both felt terrific. "Go ahead in there," I called to some grade-school kids who were looking at the store. "You'll love those swoodies."

"It's a publicity stunt, we think," Trinja told them. "Everything is free in there."

1. **salivary glands.** Glands in the mouth that make saliva or spit

Words for Everyday Use

scarf (skärf) *v.,* consume greedily; eat quickly

Vocabulary in Context

• The hungry dog scarfed his bowl of food as soon as we placed it before him.

In no time at all the news about the swoodie shop had spread all over town. But days passed, and still everything was absolutely free. Nobody knew who the new owners were or why they were giving away their product. Nobody cared. The mall directors said a check arrived to pay for the rent, and that was all they were concerned about. The Health Brigade Corp said swoodies were absolutely safe for human consumption.

Swoodies were still being offered free a month later, but the shop owners had still not appeared. By then nobody cared. There were always long lines of people in front of the place, but the swoodies tasted so good nobody minded waiting for them. And the supply was endless. Soon more shops like the first one began opening in other places around the city, with machines running in the same quiet, efficient way. And everything was still absolutely free.

Soon all of us were gaining weight like crazy.

"It's those darn swoodies," Trinja told me as we left the mall after our daily binge. "I can't leave them alone. Each one must have a thousand calories, but I still pig out on them."

I sighed as I walked out into the sunshine. "Me too. If only there was some easy way to eat all the swoodies we want and still not gain any weight!"

The words were hardly out of my mouth when I noticed a new feature in the mall parking lot. Among all the usual heliobiles there was a tall white plastic box, sort of like those big telephone booths you see in old pictures. A flashing sign near the booth said THE SLIMMER. A short, thin woman was standing beside it. She was deeply tanned, and her head was covered with a green turban almost the same color as the jumpsuit she was wearing.

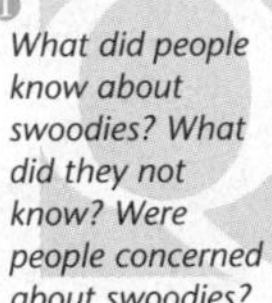

❶ *What did people know about swoodies? What did they not know? Were people concerned about swoodies?*

Trinja looked at the sign, then glanced at the woman. "What's that mean?"

"It means that this machine can make you slimmer," the woman answered. She had a deep, strange-sounding voice. "Just step inside, and you'll lose unwanted fat."

She seemed so serious and confident that I was startled. In the old days people thought they could lose weight in a hurry, but those of us who live in 2041 aren't that gullible. No pills or packs or wraps or special twenty-four-hour diets can work. There isn't any easy way to get rid of fat, and that's all there is to it. I knew this booth was a scam or a joke of some kind, but the woman acted as if it were a perfectly respectable thing. Her seriousness sort of unnerved me. I looked into the booth half expecting someone to jump out laughing. But it was empty, stark white, and, except for some overhead grill work, it was completely smooth and bare.

❷ *What is Deb's reaction to the new machine that appears in the mall parking lot?*

"How can a thing like this make you slimmer?" I asked.

The woman shrugged. "A new process. Do you care to try? Twenty-five yen to lose one pound of body fat."

Words for Everyday Use

con • sump • tion (kən sump´shən) *n.*, act of eating and drinking

binge (binj) *v.*, spree of unrestrained eating

gul • li • ble (gul´ə bəl) *adj.*, easily cheated or tricked

un • nerve (un nʉrv´) *v.*, cause to lose one's courage or self-confidence

stark (stärk) *adj.*, bleak; desolate; barren

Answers to Guided Reading Questions

❶ People knew that swoodies were free and that the rent for the shop was paid by check. People did not know who the owners were or why they were giving away their product. People were not concerned about swoodies because the Health Brigade Corp said that swoodies were safe for human consumption.

❷ Deb thinks that the new machine is a scam or a joke.

Additional Questions and Activities

Ask students the following questions: What is unusual about the appearance of the woman who runs the slimmer? What is unusual about her actions? What do you think the woman's unusual qualities indicate about her?

ANSWERS

Students might say that the woman is extremely thin and that she is wearing an unusual costume. Students might say that her voice is unusual as well. The woman is very serious and does not seem to care whether the girls try the slimmer. Students might predict that the woman is an alien.

Vocabulary in Context

- It was determined that the water in the reservoir was unfit for human consumption.
- Martha is so health conscious that the only food she ever binges on is salad.
- Henry was so gullible that he would believe almost anything people would tell him.
- The thought of jumping into the cold water of the lake unnerved me.
- The desert landscape is stark but beautiful.

Quotables

"The future is called 'perhaps,' which is the only possible thing to call the future. And the important thing is not to allow that to scare you."

—Tennessee Williams

"We should all be concerned with the future because we will have to spend the rest of our lives there."

—C. F. Kettering

Additional Questions and Activities

Read students the above quotations and ask them to discuss the vision of the future presented in "Lose Now, Pay Later." Ask students what is appealing about this vision of the future. What is unappealing about this vision of the future?

Sherberts. Tamayo, 1938

Trinja and I both burst into laughter. "And how long is it before the pound disappears?" she asked.

The woman never even cracked a smile. "Instantly. Body fat is gone instantly." She gestured to a small lever on the side nearest to her. "I regulate the power flow according to your payment."

My mouth dropped open. "But that's impossible! No exercise? No chemicals? No starving on a retreat week?"

"No." The woman folded her arms and leaned against the smooth white sides of her cubicle, as if she didn't much care whether we tried her new process or not. Trinja and I stared at each other. I was wondering if the woman had tried her machine herself—she didn't have an ounce of fat.

"You got any money?" I asked Trinja. As she was shaking her head, I was rummaging through my pack. "I've got a hundred and thirty yen."

"Five pounds then," the woman said, taking my money with one hand and setting her lever with the other. She literally pushed me into the booth, and the door slammed behind me.

At first I wanted to scream because I was so scared. The whole thing had happened too fast. I wanted to prove that this woman and her slimmer were a big joke, but suddenly I was trapped in a coffinlike structure as bare and as bright as an old microwave oven. My heart was hammering, and the hair on the back of my neck stood up straight. I opened my mouth, but before I could scream, there was a loud humming sound, and instantly the door flew open again. I saw Trinja's frightened face peering in at me.

"Are you all right, Deb? Are you okay? I guess she decided not to do anything after all. You ought to get your money back."

"Five pounds are gone," the woman said in her strange voice.

Trinja pulled me away. "I'll just bet!" she shouted back at the woman.

Words for Everyday Use

cu • bi • cle (kyo͞o´bi kəl) *n.*, small compartment

Vocabulary in Context

• The office was arranged into a series of tiny cubicles in which people worked.

"Somebody ought to report you and that phony machine! We might even call the Health Brigade Corp!" She leaned closer to me. "Are you really okay, Deb?"

I took a deep breath. "My jeans feel loose."

Frowning, Trinja shook her head. "It's just your imagination, that's all. What a fake! I think that woman was wacko, Debbie, really weird. The only thing slimmer after a treatment like that is your bank account. Nobody but nobody can lose weight that easily. We'll go to my house, and you can weigh yourself. You haven't lost an ounce."

But Trinja was wrong. I really *was* five pounds lighter. I know it sounds impossible, but Trinja's calshow is never wrong. The two of us hopped and howled with joy. Then we ravaged her bedroom trying to find some more money. We ran all the way back to the mall, worrying all the way that the woman and her miracle machine might have disappeared. But the slimmer was still there. Within minutes Trinja had used up her three hundred yen, and she looked terrific.

"I can't believe it! I just can't believe it!" she kept saying as she notched her belt tighter. "Twelve pounds gone in seconds!"

"For safety's sake I'll have to prick your wrist, my dear," the woman said. "For every ten pounds you lose we give a tiny little mark. Nobody will ever notice it."

"It didn't even hurt," Trinja said as we walked home. And neither of us could see the tiny blue pinprick unless we looked closely. We were both so happy about the weight loss that we almost floated. All our worries and problems about calories and fat and diets were over forever.

In no time at all the slimmers were all over the city, near all the swoodie stores. They've been a real blessing. Everybody says so. Now there's hardly a fat person left on the streets. A few people have so many blue marks on their wrists that you can see them, but most have just four or five pinpricks.

Nobody really understands how these slimmers work. The attendants, all just as strange sounding as the woman in our mall, get so technical in their explanations that none of us can follow the principles they're talking about, so we don't much worry about it. The process has something to do with invisible waves that can change fat cells into energy, which then radiates away from the body.

"I don't care how the slimmers work," Trinja says happily. "Now I can eat swoodies all day long if I want, and I never gain an ounce. That's all I care about."

Everybody feels that way, I guess. We're too happy to want to upset anything by asking questions. Maybe that's why you don't hear about the swoodies or slimmers on the fax or the bodivision or read about them anywhere. Nobody understands them well enough to sound very intelligent about

❶ *Do the people understand how the slimmers work? Are they concerned about the new machines?*

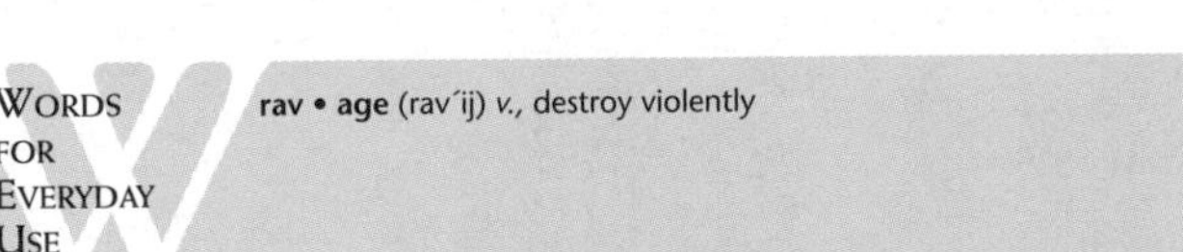

Words for Everyday Use

rav • age (rav´ij) *v.,* destroy violently

Answer to Guided Reading Question

❶ People do not understand how the slimmers work. They are not, however, concerned about the new machines.

Vocabulary in Context

• The forest was ravaged by fire.

Answers to Guided Reading Questions

❶ Trevor believes that the swoodies and the slimmers are run by aliens from outer space.

❷ Deb says that she does not believe that Trevor's idea is possible, but she seems unsure.

Selection Check Test with Answers

EX. What does the narrator think of her little brother?
The narrator thinks that her brother has a dumb idea.

1. What opens one day in the mall?
A swoodie shop opens.

2. What happens when you eat a swoodie?
When you eat a swoodie, you have wonderful memories associated with each flavor.

3. What opens in the mall parking lot?
"The Slimmer," a machine that can make you shed unwanted pounds, opens.

4. What does the narrator think of the slimmer at first?
At first, the narrator thinks it is a scam or a joke.

5. What does the narrator's brother think of the swoodies and the slimmers?
The narrator's brother thinks that they are run by aliens from outer space.

them. But people all over Earth are beginning to use them. My cousin in Tokyo faxed to say that they have them in her area now and people there are just as happy as we are.

Except for my brother, Trevor. He's not the least bit happy, he says. Of course, few ten-year-olds worry about weight, so he doesn't know the joy of being able to eat everything in sight and still stay thin.

What is Trevor's idea about the swoodies and slimmers?

Does Deb believe Trevor's idea is possible?

"Suppose the swoodies and the slimmers are run by aliens from outer space," he says. "From lots farther than we've been able to go. Maybe they have big starships posted around Earth, and they're gathering up the energy from human fat that's sent up from the slimmers. Maybe the swoodies are here so people will get fat quicker so that there'll be more to harvest through the slimmer machines. Then they'll take the fat back to their planet and use it as fuel."

"That's the dumbest thing I ever heard of!" Trinja has told him. "Why don't we hear about the spaceships, then? Why doesn't the Health Brigade Corp tell us to stop doing this if it isn't good for us?"

Trevor thinks he has the answers. He says the spaceships are invisible to human detection, and he says the aliens have hypnotized our leaders into being as calm and placid as we all are. The blue marks on our wrists play a big role. He says maybe after each of us has had so many blue marks, we'll be culled from the flock because our fat content won't be as good anymore.

He's crazy, isn't he? He must think we all have the brains of sheep. Ten-year-old brothers can be a real pain. He simply doesn't know people yet, that's all. Humans would never sacrifice their freedom and dignity just so they could eat and still be thin. Even aliens ought to know that.

I could quit eating swoodies and using those slimmers any time I want to.

But all those little blue marks Trinja and I have are beginning to look like delicate tattooed bracelets, and we both think they look really neat on our wrists. ■

About the Author

Carol Farley (1936–) has worked as a fruit picker, a clothing salesperson, and a schoolteacher, as well as a writer. While in school, her favorite classes were literature classes because she enjoyed discussing what she had read. Farley believes that children often perceive the obvious, even when it eludes the adults around them.

Words for Everyday Use

plac • id (plas´id) *adj.*, tranquil; calm

cull (kul) *v.*, pick out; select

Vocabulary in Context

- It was a beautiful summer day and the water of the bay was placid and still.
- Annie culled the bad apples from the bushel.

Responding to the Selection

What reasons do Deb and Trinja have for continuing to use the slimmer? Do you think Deb and Trinja have made a wise decision to keep eating the swoodies and using the slimmer? Why, or why not? Do you think that they will encounter problems from the swoodies and the slimmer? Explain.

Reviewing the Selection

Recalling and Interpreting

1. **R** What do Deb and Trinja discover at the far end of the mall?

   I What makes swoodies different from sweets or goodies? Why are swoodies so popular?

2. **R** What appears in the mall parking lot soon after the swoodie shops become well known?

   I Why does Deb decide to try the new machine? In what way is her decision to try the new machine similar to her decision to try the swoodies?

3. **R** What indicates the growing popularity of the slimmers? How do the slimmers work?

   I Why are people so eager to use the slimmers? Why are people content with knowing so little about the slimmers?

4. **R** What explanation does Deb's little brother have for the swoodie shops and the slimmers?

   I Does her brother's idea make sense? Why might people be unwilling to believe such an idea?

Synthesizing

5. Deb says, "Humans would never sacrifice their freedom and dignity just so they could eat and still be thin." Do you agree with Deb's assessment of humans? Why, or why not? Use examples of human behavior from the story and from your own experience to support your answer.

Understanding Literature (Questions for Discussion)

Science Fiction. Science fiction is imaginative literature based on scientific principles, discoveries, or laws. Science fiction allows writers to change certain elements of reality in order to create interesting and instructive alternatives. In what year does this story take place? What clues indicate that the story has a futuristic setting? What has the writer altered in the world? Why could a story like this take place just about any time? What point might the writer be trying to make in this story?

Answers for Understanding Literature

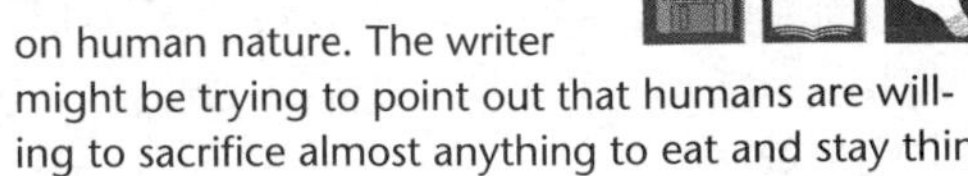

Responses will vary. Possible responses are given.

Science Fiction. This story takes place in the year 2041. Clues indicating the futuristic setting are that "heliobiles" instead of cars are in the parking lot and that microwaves are called "old." The writer alters the world by creating machines that can instantly make people thin. A story like this could take place at any time because it is mostly focused on human nature. The writer might be trying to point out that humans are willing to sacrifice almost anything to eat and stay thin.

Responding to the Selection

Also ask students what they think of Deb's brother. How might he try to get others to take his idea seriously?

Answers for Reviewing the Selection

RECALLING AND INTERPRETING

1. **Recalling.** Deb and Trinja discover a new shop that gives away a type of dessert called swoodies. **Interpreting.** Swoodies cause the eater to relive memories associated with different flavors. They become popular because they taste good, evoke wonderful memories, and make people happy.

2. **Recalling.** A new machine called "The Slimmer" appears. **Interpreting.** Deb decides to try the new machine to prove that it is a hoax or a joke. Both decisions are impulsive.

3. **Recalling.** The growing popularity of the slimmers is indicated by the fewer fat people and the many tiny blue dots on people's wrists. No one knows exactly how the slimmers work, but they transform excess fat into energy which radiates away. **Interpreting.** People are eager to use the slimmers because they are gaining weight from eating swoodies. People are content to know little about the slimmers because they allow people to eat as many swoodies as they want without gaining weight.

4. **Recalling.** Deb's little brother says that the swoodie shops and slimmers are both run by aliens who are trying to fatten people so that they can harvest their fat and convert it to energy. **Interpreting.** Her brother's idea does make sense. People might be unwilling to believe such an idea because it implies that people lack self-control.

SYNTHESIZING

Responses will vary. Possible responses are given.

5. Students may disagree with Deb's statement and point to the excessive behavior of the characters in the story.

GOALS/OBJECTIVES

Studying this lesson will enable students to

- appreciate a short story about why differences are important
- briefly explain different types of intelligence
- define *satire* and explain what errors or failings a satire points out
- define *simile* and identify similes
- classify information

ADDITIONAL RESOURCES

READER'S GUIDE

- Selection Worksheet, 5.5

ASSESSMENT PORTFOLIO

- Selection Check Test, 2.5.9
- Selection Test, 2.5.10

PRONUNCIATION EXERCISE

- Grade 8 Audiocassette, Side B, Track 27

CROSS-CURRICULAR CONNECTIONS

SCIENCE

Students might want to write short personal essays in which they analyze their own intelligence. Encourage them to focus on all the different types of intelligence that they possess.

Prereading

SHORT STORY

"Harrison Bergeron"

by Kurt Vonnegut, Jr.

Cross-curricular Connection

Science. Intelligence is difficult to define, but it involves the speed and ability to understand ideas and use them to solve problems and create new ideas. Traditionally, logical/mathematical abilities and verbal/linguistic abilities have been used to measure intelligence; but today, many scientists believe that humans have more than just these two types of intelligences. Other types of intelligence include visual/spatial, or the ability to understand and manipulate space and objects; bodily/ kinesthetic, or the ability to use the body in motion; musical/rhythmic, or the ability to work with pitch and rhythm; and interpersonal and intrapersonal, or the ability to understand oneself and work with other people.

In the past, intelligence was viewed as static and fixed, that is, it never changed. It was believed that people were born with certain intelligence. Today, however, many people believe that intelligence is influenced by one's environment. It is also believed that a person can improve his or her intelligence.

Because much of the information about intelligence is theoretical, our understanding of the mind and its abilities will continue to grow and change as we discover new things about the human mind and how it works. We do recognize that abilities vary within each person. For example, a person may have high ability in some areas, such as mechanics, and lower ability in other areas, such as geometry. Every person has some areas in which they are stronger than others. It is important to recognize the intelligences and abilities that each person has. In "Harrison Bergeron," different abilities are not appreciated.

As You Read

"**Harrison Bergeron**" portrays a society whose goal is to make everyone equal. Special talents and characteristics are squelched. Make a chart like the one below. As you read, note the special skills or characteristics of the characters and what handicaps they are given to put them on a level plane with others.

CHARACTERISTIC	HANDICAP
above-average intelligence	noise transmitter

AS YOU READ

Students may include the following details on their charts: *characteristic*—grace and strength, *handicap*—sashweights and bags of birdshot; *characteristic*—beauty, *handicap*—masks; *characteristic*—nice voices, *handicap*—must speak in a squawk; *characteristic*— Harrison's super intelligence, *handicap*—earphones and spectacles with wavy lenses; *characteristic*—Harrison's tremendous strength, *handicap*—scrap metal weights; *characteristic*—Harrison's good looks, *handicap*—red rubber ball nose, shaved eyebrows, black teeth caps.

READER'S JOURNAL

What abilities and talents do you have that you think might not be recognized by others? What do you think could be done at school to better recognize everyone's special abilities and intelligence? Write about these questions in your journal.

"Harrison Bergeron"

KURT VONNEGUT, JR.

The year was 2081, and everybody was finally equal. They weren't only equal before God and the law. They were equal every which way. Nobody was smarter than anybody else. Nobody was better looking than anybody else. Nobody was stronger or quicker than anybody else. All this equality was due to the 211th, 212th, and 213th Amendments to the Constitution, and to the unceasing vigilance of agents of the United States Handicapper General.

Some things about living still weren't quite right, though. April, for instance, still drove people crazy by not being springtime. And it was in that clammy month that the H-G men took George and Hazel Bergeron's fourteen-year-old son, Harrison, away.

It was tragic all right, but George and Hazel couldn't think about it very hard. Hazel had a perfectly average intelligence, which meant she couldn't think about anything except in short bursts. And George, while his intelligence was way above normal, had a little mental handicap radio in his ear. He was required by law to wear it at all times. It was tuned to a government transmitter.[1] Every twenty seconds or so, the transmitter would send out some sharp noise to keep people like George from taking unfair advantage of their brains.

George and Hazel were watching television. There were tears on Hazel's cheeks, but she'd forgotten for the moment what they were about.

On the television screen were ballerinas.

A buzzer sounded in George's head. His thoughts fled in panic, like bandits from a burglar alarm.

"That was a real pretty dance, that dance they just did." said Hazel.

1. **transmitter.** Mechanism that can generate and send out radio waves

❶ *What tragedy have George and Hazel Bergeron experienced? Why are they not upset about this event?*

WORDS FOR EVERYDAY USE

un • ceas • ing (un sēs´ŋ) *adj.*, not ending

vig • i • lance (vij´ə ləns) *n.*, the quality of being watchful and alert to danger and trouble

READER'S JOURNAL

As an alternative activity, you might ask students to write about special abilities and talents they have and others they would like to develop. Why are these talents and abilities important to them?

SPELLING AND VOCABULARY WORDS FROM THE SELECTION

bellow	luminous
consternation	neutralize
cower	symmetry
envious	synchronize
gambol	unceasing
glimmering	vague
gravely	vigilance
hindrance	wince
impediment	

ANSWER TO GUIDED READING QUESTION

❶ George and Hazel's son Harrison has been taken away by the H-G men. They are not upset about it because they are not able to think about anything except in short bursts.

SUPPORT FOR LEP STUDENTS

PRONUNCIATIONS OF PROPER NOUNS AND ADJECTIVES

Kurt Von • ne • gut (kurt vän´ə gut') n.

Har • ri • son Ber •ger •on (har´ə s'n bur´jur ôn') n.

ADDITIONAL VOCABULARY

birdshot—small metal pellets

resemblance—likeness

COLLOQUIALISMS

doozy—anything outstanding of its kind

VOCABULARY IN CONTEXT

- The fire alarm let off an unceasing clamor.
- The citizens' vigilance deterred crime in their neighborhood.

Additional Questions and Activities

Ask students the following questions: What does George think about the ballerinas' dance? What "vague notion" does George have before his thoughts are interrupted by the radio? Do you think people occasionally have thoughts like this in this futuristic society? Why, or why not? Why don't people ever use these ideas to reform their society?

Answers

George thinks the ballerinas' dance isn't very good. George thinks that maybe dancers should not be handicapped so that they could do better dances. Students may say that people occasionally have thoughts like this in this society because the extreme "equality" leads to mediocrity in all areas of life. People do not use these ideas to reform society because they are distracted from these thoughts by the radio transmitters in their ears.

Quotables

"It is dangerous to be right in matters on which the established authorities are wrong."

—Voltaire

"Huh?" said George.

"That dance—it was nice," said Hazel.

"Yup," said George. He tried to think a little about the ballerinas. They weren't really very good—no better than anybody else would have been, anyway. They were burdened with sashweights[2] and bags of birdshot, and their faces were masked, so that no one, seeing a free and graceful gesture or a pretty face, would feel like something the cat drug in. George was toying with the vague notion that maybe dancers shouldn't be handicapped. But he didn't get very far with it before another noise in his ear radio scattered his thoughts.

George winced. So did two out of the eight ballerinas.

Hazel saw him wince. Having no mental handicap herself, she had to ask George what the latest sound had been.

"Sounded like somebody hitting a milk bottle with a ball peen hammer," said George.

"I'd think it would be real interesting, hearing all the different sounds," said Hazel, a little envious. "All the things they think up."

"Um," said George.

"Only, if I was Handicapper General, you know what I would do?" said Hazel. Hazel, as a matter of fact, bore a strong resemblance to the Handicapper General, a woman named Diana Moon Glampers. "If I was Diana Moon

2. **sashweights.** Weights attached to a cord

Words for Everyday Use

vague (vāg) *adj.*, not sharp, certain or precise in thought, feeling or expression

wince (wins) *v.*, shrink or draw back slightly, usually with a grimace

en • vi • ous (en´ve əs) *adj.*, showing or feeling discontent and ill will because of another's advantages or possessions

Vocabulary in Context

- Because she had been asleep most of the time, her memories of being sick were vague.
- Johnny stubbed his toe on the stairway and winced.
- Julie had always been envious of her older sister.

Glampers," said Hazel, "I'd have chimes on Sunday—just chimes. Kind of in honor of religion."

"I could think, if it was just chimes," said George.

"Well—maybe make 'em real loud," said Hazel. "I think I'd make a good Handicapper General."

"Good as anybody else," said George.

"Who knows better'n I do what normal is?" said Hazel.

"Right," said George. He began to think glimmeringly about his abnormal son who was now in jail, about Harrison, but a twenty-one-gun salute in his head stopped that.

"Boy!" said Hazel, "that was a doozy, wasn't it?"

It was such a doozy that George was white and trembling, and tears stood on the rims of his red eyes. Two of the eight ballerinas had collapsed to the studio floor, were holding their temples.[3]

"All of a sudden you look so tired," said Hazel. "Why don't you stretch out on the sofa, so's you can rest your handicap bag on the pillows, honeybunch." She was referring to the forty-seven pounds of birdshot in a canvas bag, which was padlocked around George's neck. "Go on and rest the bag for a little while," she said. "I don't care if you're not equal to me for a while."

George weighed the bag with his hands. "I don't mind it," he said. "I don't notice it any more. It's just a part of me."

"You been so tired lately—kind of wore out," said Hazel. "If there was just some way we could make a little hole in the bottom of the bag, and just take out a few of them lead balls. Just a few."

"Two years in prison and two thousand dollars fine for every ball I took out," said George. "I don't call that a bargain."

"If you could just take a few out when you came home from work," said Hazel. "I mean—you don't compete with anybody around here. You just set around."

"If I tried to get away with it," said George, "then other people'd get away with it—and pretty soon we'd be right back to the dark ages again, with everybody competing against everybody else. You wouldn't like that, would you?"

❶ *Why is George unwilling to risk bending the rules?*

"I'd hate it," said Hazel.

"There you are," said George. "The minute people start cheating on laws, what do you think happens to society?"

If Hazel hadn't been able to come up with an answer to this question, George couldn't have supplied one. A siren was going off in his head.

"Reckon it'd fall all apart," said Hazel.

"What would?" said George blankly.

"Society," said Hazel uncertainly. "Wasn't that what you just said?"

"Who knows?" said George.

3. **temples.** Sides of the forehead

Words for Everyday Use

glim • mer • ing • ly (glim´ər ing lē) *adv.*, faintly, dimly

Answer to Guided Reading Question

❶ George is unwilling to risk bending the rules because other people might also try to get away with it, and soon society would be right back in the "dark ages," when people competed with one another.

Cross-Curricular Activities

Arts and Humanities

You might ask students to draw or paint their own pictures of the ballerinas. Encourage students to focus upon the ballerinas' lack of grace and their "handicaps" to create a humorous picture of life in the year 2081.

Vocabulary in Context

• The distant star shone glimmeringly in the evening sky.

Answers to Guided Reading Questions

❶ Harrison Bergeron wears a red rubber ball as a nose, has shaved eyebrows and black caps on his teeth, wears earphones and a pair of spectacles with thick wavy lenses, and is covered in scrap metal. His handicaps suggest that he is very intelligent, strong, and good-looking.

❷ The dancer must apologize for her wonderful voice. She has to squawk to make her voice "uncompetitive."

Quotables

"Resistance to the organized mass can be effected only by the man who is as well organized in his individuality as the mass itself."

—Carl Jung

The television program was suddenly interrupted for a news bulletin. It wasn't clear at first as to what the bulletin was about, since the announcer, like all announcers, had a serious speech impediment. For about half a minute, and in a state of high excitement, the announcer tried to say, "Ladies and gentlemen—"

He finally gave up, handed the bulletin to a ballerina to read.

"That's all right—" Hazel said of the announcer, "he tried. That's the big thing. He tried to do the best he could with what God gave him. He should get a nice raise for trying so hard."

"Ladies and gentlemen—" said the ballerina, reading the bulletin. She must have been extraordinarily beautiful, because the mask she wore was hideous. And it was easy to see that she was the strongest and most graceful of all the dancers, for her handicap bags were as big as those worn by two-hundred-pound men.

❶ *What does Harrison Bergeron look like? What do his handicaps suggest about his natural appearance and abilities?*

❷ *For what must the dancer apologize? What does she do to remedy the situation?*

And she had to apologize at once for her voice, which was a very unfair voice for a woman to use. Her voice was a warm, luminous, timeless melody. "Excuse me—" she said, and she began again, making her voice absolutely uncompetitive.

"Harrison Bergeron, age fourteen," she said in a grackle squawk, "has just escaped from jail, where he was held on suspicion of plotting to overthrow the government. He is a genius and an athlete, is under-handicapped, and should be regarded as extremely dangerous."

A police photograph of Harrison Bergeron was flashed on the screen—upside down, then sideways, upside down again, then right side up. The picture showed the full length of Harrison against a background calibrated in feet and inches. He was exactly seven feet tall.

The rest of Harrison's appearance was Halloween and hardware. Nobody had ever born heavier handicaps. He had outgrown hindrances faster than the H-G men could think them up. Instead of a little ear radio for a mental handicap, he wore a tremendous pair of earphones, and spectacles with thick wavy lenses. The spectacles were intended to make him not only half blind, but to give him whanging headaches besides.

Scrap metal was hung all over him. Ordinarily, there was a certain symmetry, a military neatness to the handicaps issued to strong people, but Harrison looked like a walking junkyard. In the race of life, Harrison carried three hundred pounds.

And to offset his good looks, the H-G men required that he wear at all times a red rubber ball for a nose, keep his eyebrows shaved off, and cover his even white teeth with black caps at snaggle-tooth random.

"If you see this boy," said the ballerina, "do not—I repeat, do not—try to reason with him."

There was the shriek of a door being torn from its hinges.

Screams and barking cries of consternation came from the television

Words for Everyday Use

im • ped • i • ment (im ped´ə mənt) *n.*, something that delays or obstructs
lu • mi • nous (lo͞o´mə nəs) *adj.*, clear, bright
hin • drance (hin´drəns) *n.*, obstacle
sym • me • try (sim´ə tre) *n.*, balance, proportion
con • ster • na • tion (kän´ster na´shən) *n.*, great fear or shock

Vocabulary in Context

- Although Rachel had a sprained wrist, she found it no impediment to her rollerblading.
- The moon shone with a luminous glow over the lake.
- Ray was never stopped by hindrances but always strived onward to achieve his goals.
- If you fold a paper in half before you cut a shape, that shape will have symmetry.
- Much to his consternation, Jason found that his dog had chewed a hole in the sofa.

set. The photograph of Harrison Bergeron on the screen jumped again and again, as though dancing to the tune of an earthquake.

George Bergeron correctly identified the earthquake, and well he might have—for many was the time his own home had danced to the same crashing tune. "My God—" said George, "that must be Harrison!"

The realization was blasted from his mind instantly by the sound of an automobile collision in his head.

When George could open his eyes again, the photograph of Harrison was gone. A living, breathing Harrison filled the screen.

Clanking, clownish, and huge, Harrison stood in the center of the studio. The knob of the uprooted studio door was still in his hand. Ballerinas, technicians, musicians, and announcers cowered on their knees before him, expecting to die.

"I am the Emperor!" cried Harrison. "Do you hear? I am the Emperor! Everybody must do what I say at once!" He stamped his foot and the studio shook.

"Even as I stand here—" he bellowed, "crippled, hobbled, sickened—I am a greater ruler than any man who ever lived! Now watch me become what I *can* become!"

Harrison tore the straps of his handicap harness like wet tissue paper, tore straps guaranteed to support five thousand pounds.

Harrison's scrap-iron handicaps crashed to the floor.

Harrison thrust his thumbs under the bar of the padlock that secured his head harness. The bar snapped like celery. Harrison smashed his headphones and spectacles against the wall.

He flung away his rubber-ball nose, revealed a man that would have awed Thor, the god of thunder.

"I shall now select my Empress!" he said, looking down on the cowering

Words for Everyday Use

cow • er (kou′ər) *v.,* crouch or huddle, as from fear

bel • low (bel′ō) *v.,* utter loudly or powerfully

Additional Questions and Activities

Ask students the following questions: What has happened at the television station? What does Harrison want to announce on television? What does he say he wants to show others? Why do you think Harrison says that he is "sickened"? Why do you think he wants to show himself without his handicaps on television?

ANSWERS

Harrison has broken into the television station and taken control. Harrison wants to announce that he is the Emperor. He says that he wants to show others what he can become without his handicaps. Harrison is probably sickened because he has not been allowed to live up to his full potential his entire life. Harrison probably wants to encourage others to take off their handicaps and enjoy their differences.

Vocabulary in Context

- The little kitten saw the big dog outside the window and cowered.
- The bull bellowed angrily.

Answers to Guided Reading Questions

❶ He takes the handicaps off the ballerina so that they can dance.

❷ Diana Moon Glampers shoots and kills Harrison Bergeron and the ballerina and orders the musicians at gunpoint to get their handicaps back on. She does this because she is in charge of making sure that everyone is equal and that no one has an unfair advantage over anyone else.

Quotables

"Courage is almost a contradiction in terms. It means a strong desire to live taking the form of a readiness to die."

—G. K. Chesterton

Additional Questions and Activities

Encourage students to discuss their feelings about Harrison's actions and what happens to him. To stimulate students' thinking, ask them the following questions: Was what Harrison did worth its cost? Why was being free to express himself worth so much to him? Why was excellence and difference something Harrison felt that he had to show the world?

people. "Let the first woman who dares rise to her feet claim her mate and her throne!"

A moment passed, and then a ballerina arose, swaying like a willow.

❶ *What does Harrison do after freeing himself of his handicaps?*

Harrison plucked the mental handicap from her ear, snapped off her physical handicaps with marvelous delicacy. Last of all, he removed her mask.

She was blindingly beautiful.

"Now—" said Harrison, taking her hand, "shall we show the people the meaning of the word dance? Music!" he commanded.

The musicians scrambled back into their chairs, and Harrison stripped them of their handicaps, too. "Play your best," he told them, "and I'll make you barons and dukes and earls."

❷ *What does Diana Moon Glampers do? Why does she perform this action?*

The music began. It was normal at first—cheap, silly, false. But Harrison snatched two musicians from their chairs, waved them like batons as he sang the music as he wanted it played. He slammed them back into their chairs. The music began again and was much improved.

Harrison and his Empress merely listened to the music for a while—listened gravely, as though synchronizing their heartbeats with it.

They shifted their weights to their toes.

Harrison placed his big hands on the girl's tiny waist, letting her sense the weightlessness that would soon be hers.

And then, in an explosion of joy and grace, into the air they sprang!

Not only were the laws of the land abandoned, but the law of gravity and the laws of motion as well.

They reeled, whirled, swiveled, flounced, capered, gamboled, and spun.

They leaped like deer on the moon.

The studio ceiling was thirty feet high, but each leap brought the dancers nearer to it.

It became their obvious intention to kiss the ceiling.

They kissed it.

And then, neutralizing gravity with love and pure will, they remained suspended in air inches below the ceiling, and they kissed each other for a long, long time.

It was then that Diana Moon Glampers, the Handicapper General, came into the studio with a double-barreled ten-gauge shotgun. She fired twice, and the Emperor and the Empress were dead before they hit the floor.

Diana Moon Glampers loaded the gun again. She aimed it at the musicians and told them they had ten seconds to get their handicaps back on.

It was then that the Bergerons' television tube burned out.

Hazel turned to comment about the blackout to George. But George had gone out into the kitchen for a can of beer.

George came back in with the beer, paused while a handicap signal shook

Words for Everyday Use

grave • ly (grāv lē) *adj.,* seriously, solemnly; with dignity

syn • chro • nize (sing´krə nīz´) *v.,* cause to agree in time or rate of speed

gam • bol (gam´bəl) *v.,* jump and skip about in play, frolic

neu • tral • ize (no͞o´trə līz´) *v.,* make ineffective

Vocabulary in Context

- As the judge considered the case, he frowned gravely in concentration.
- The dancers carefully synchronized their movements so that they moved in unison.
- The tiny young fawn gamboled through the spring glade.
- Acids can be neutralized with an alkaline substance.

him up. And then he sat down again. "You been crying?" he said to Hazel.

"Yup," she said.

"What about?" he said.

"I forget," she said. "Something real sad on television."

"What was it?" he said.

"It's all kind of mixed up in my mind," said Hazel.

"Forget sad things," said George.

"I always do," said Hazel.

"That's my girl," said George. He winced. There was the sound of a rivetting gun[4] in his head.

"Gee—I could tell that one was a doozy," said Hazel.

"You can say that again," said George.

"Gee—" said Hazel, "I could tell that one was a doozy." ■

4. **rivetting gun.** Instrument used to place rivets or bolts into steel beams

About the Author

Kurt Vonnegut, Jr. (1922–) has written many novels including *Slaughterhouse Five, Player Piano*, and *Cat's Cradle*. His experiences in World War II had a deep effect on his writing. He was captured by the Germans and put in prison in Dresden, Germany, where he witnessed the fire bombing of Dresden. Vonnegut's writing is often playful, but he says he is a moralizing writer with a gloomy outlook. Vonnegut thinks that our only hope for survival is with a sad, but comic, awareness of human folly.

Selection Check Test with Answers

EX. In what year does this story take place?
The story takes place in the year 2081.

1. Why aren't George and Hazel Bergeron upset about what has happened to their son?
They aren't upset because they are only able to think in short bursts.

2. What handicap does George wear because of his intelligence?
He wears a radio transmitter in his ear that regularly sends out sharp noises.

3. What are George and Hazel watching on television?
They are watching ballerinas.

4. Who bursts into the television station? What shocking thing does this person do?
Harrison Bergeron bursts into the television station, takes off his handicaps and those of a ballerina, and proclaims himself Emperor and the ballerina Empress. They begin to dance.

5. What does Diana Moon Glampers do?
She shoots Harrison and the ballerina.

Responding to the Selection

Students might also discuss the positive and negative sides of living in a society like that described in the story.

Answers for Reviewing the Selection

RECALLING AND INTERPRETING

1. **Recalling.** People who have unfair advantages over others, such as intelligence, beauty, or strength, are made to wear handicaps. **Interpreting.** The author thinks that the equalizing process is ridiculous, terrible, and has a negative effect because it encourages mediocrity—people strive to be less than what they can be.
2. **Recalling.** A radio transmitter in his ear that sends out sharp noises keeps George from "taking unfair advantage" of his brain. **Interpreting.** Because people cannot think, they do not realize how ridiculous the equalizing process is and do not try to change it.
3. **Recalling.** The Handicapper General, Diana Moon Glampers, and her department are in charge of keeping everyone equal. The fine for removing the lead balls in George's bag is two thousand dollars and two years in prison for each ball removed. **Interpreting.** The people in charge of equalizing are not handicapped themselves. Tampering with a handicap is dangerous according to the government because it encourages others to do the same and then society would go back to "the dark ages," when people were unequal and competed with one another.
4. **Recalling.** Harrison takes off his handicaps and those of a ballerina and dances a wonderful dance. Harrison is killed by the Handicapper General. **Interpreting.** Harrison's parents do not respond to their son's death because they are unable to think about it or remember it.

SYNTHESIZING

Responses will vary. Possible responses are given.

5. Students might say that people should have equal opportunities and should be governed by equal laws. Students may mention many differences that should be embraced.

Responding to the Selection

George says, "Pretty soon we'd be right back to the dark ages again, with everybody competing against everybody else." Do you think that difference always leads to competition? Is competition always a negative thing? What benefits are there to differences?

Reviewing the Selection

Recalling and Interpreting

1. **R** What is done to make people equal?

   I What is the author's attitude toward the equalizing process? Why does the equalizing process have a negative effect on all of this society?

2. **R** What keeps George from "taking unfair advantage" of his brain?

   I In what way does the handicapping rule maintain itself?

3. **R** Who is in charge of keeping everyone equal? What is the fine for removing any of the lead balls in George's handicap bag?

   I Are the people in charge of equalizing everyone equal themselves? Why is tampering with a handicap such a dangerous action in the minds of the government?

4. **R** What does Harrison do that upsets how the country views equality? What happens to Harrison?

   I Why do Harrison's parents not respond in any meaningful way to what happens to their son?

Synthesizing

5. In what ways do you think all people are, or should be, equal? What types of differences should we embrace? Do you think the government can dictate equality?

Understanding Literature (Questions for Discussion)

1. **Satire. Satire** is humorous writing that points out errors or failings in people, things, or ideas. What people and ideas are satirized in this story? Has the author's satire changed your attitudes or beliefs in any way? Explain.
2. **Simile.** A **simile** is a comparison using *like* or *as*. Identify four similes from this selection. Explain what the two things being compared in each simile have in common.

Answers for Understanding Literature

Responses will vary. Possible responses are given.

1. **Satire.** The idea that the government should create laws to make people equal in every way is satirized.
2. **Simile.** Students may identify the following similes: "His thought fled in panic, like bandits from a burglar alarm." Both George's thoughts and burglars flee quickly at a noise. "Harrison tore the straps of his handicap harness like wet tissue paper." The straps are compared to tissue paper because Harrison tore them easily. "The bar snapped like celery." Both the bar and celery snap in two easily. "They leaped like deer on the moon." Both the dancers and deer on the moon could leap to great heights.

Thinking Skills

Classifying

Classifying is a thinking skill in which information is organized by dividing it into groups. The groups used to classify information are called classes. A class consists of members that have some similar quality or characteristic. When you classify items, you separate them into groups, called categories or sets, based on the qualities or characteristics that they have. You can classify just about any kind of information. For example, you can classify animals by species, books by authors, words by parts of speech, numbers by patterns, or people by periods in their lives.

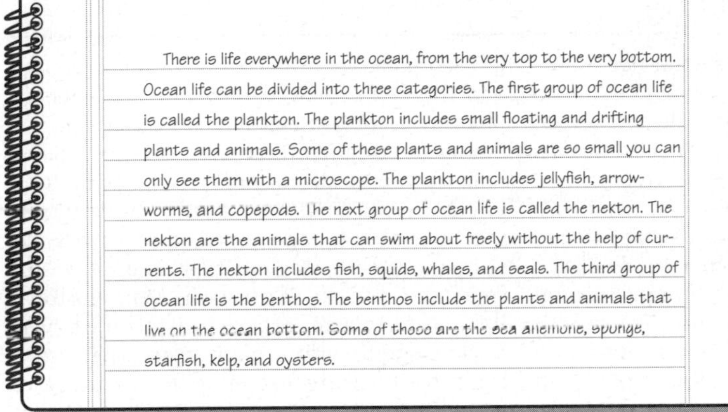
There is life everywhere in the ocean, from the very top to the very bottom. Ocean life can be divided into three categories. The first group of ocean life is called the plankton. The plankton includes small floating and drifting plants and animals. Some of these plants and animals are so small you can only see them with a microscope. The plankton includes jellyfish, arrow-worms, and copepods. The next group of ocean life is called the nekton. The nekton are the animals that can swim about freely without the help of currents. The nekton includes fish, squids, whales, and seals. The third group of ocean life is the benthos. The benthos include the plants and animals that live on the ocean bottom. Some of those are the sea anemone, sponge, starfish, kelp, and oysters.

Student Model

Caitlin's science class has been studying the ocean for the past two weeks. As her final project, she decided to research types of ocean life. She discovered that ocean life can be divided into three main groups: plankton, nekton, and benthos. Caitlin wrote a paragraph about her findings. Here is Caitlin's paragraph.

Examining the Model

1. Into what three groups, or classes, does Caitlin divide ocean life?
2. What characteristics does each of the three groups have?
3. What examples does Caitlin give for each group?

Try It Yourself

Choose ten pieces of writing you have read this year. Identify some characteristics or qualities that you can use to group the materials. Classify the pieces you have selected into two or three groups. Write a short essay that identifies and explains the determining characteristics of the groups you chose and gives examples for each class.

Thinking Skills

Introducing the Skill

Inform students that they identify the qualities and characteristics of things and place them in categories all the time. They identify pieces of music by their genre, identify different food groups, etc.

Previewing the Skill

Have students review the teaching in the Thinking Skills lesson. Have them answer the questions in Examining the Model.

Practicing the Skill

Have students do the Try It Yourself exercise.

Reviewing the Skill

If students need additional practice, refer them to the Language Arts Survey, 4.23, "Classifying." Have them do the Try It Yourself exercise in that section.

Answers for Examining the Model

1. Caitlin divides ocean life into plankton, nekton, and benthos.
2. Plankton are floating and drifting animals, nekton can swim freely on their own, and benthos are plants and animals on the ocean bottom.
3. Caitlin's examples for plankton are jellyfish, arrow-worms, and copepods; for nekton, fish, squids, whales, and seals; and for benthos, sea anemones, sponges, starfish, kelp, and oysters.

Answers for Try It Yourself

Responses will vary. Student essays should identify classes, explain characteristics of a class, and provide examples of a class.

PROJECT NOTE

Inform students that they should each research the people or places they are most interested in visiting and use the results of this research when writing their paragraphs.

Students' maps will be excellent starting places for science fiction stories about time travel. Each student might write a brief story about going back in time and meeting particular people or visiting specific places.

Unit Project

PLANNING A TIME TRAVELERS' CLUB

Imagine that it is the twenty-eighth century and technology is available for time travel. Instead of reading about famous people, places, and events in books for school, students are routinely taken on field trips through time. If you could go on a time trip to any year and place in history, when and where would you go? If you could meet anyone from your history book, whom would you want to meet?

TRY IT YOURSELF

With a small group of your classmates, form a time travelers' club. Make a map of people, places, or events that your club plans to visit if time travel becomes available. Illustrate your map, and briefly explain why each person or place interests you.

STUDENT MODEL

Max, Ariel, and Fernando have formed a time travelers' club. They think it would be fun to travel through time, visiting people and places. Max would like to meet Queen Elizabeth I, who ruled England in the late sixteenth and early seventeenth centuries. Max likes to paint, so he would watch sixteenth-century Italian painter Michelangelo work. Ariel would like to meet the nineteenth-century American poet Emily Dickinson. She would also like to visit some of her ancestors in Poland. Fernando would like to attend the 1963 March on Washington for civil rights and hear Martin Luther King, Jr., give his "I Have a Dream" speech at the Lincoln Memorial. He would also like to meet the nineteenth-century Sioux leader Sitting Bull and ride on horseback through the northern Great Plains.

After they discuss the stops that they will make on their journey through time, the three go to the library to research the people, places, and events that are of special interest to them. They take notes and later write one paragraph on an index card about each planned stop on their trip. In each paragraph, they give two or three facts and then explain why they think the person, place, or event is interesting and important.

After the paragraphs are finished, the group is ready to create a map of their journey. Ariel traces a world map onto a piece of paper and then pastes the paper onto some cardboard. They mark each stop on their journey with a small star and an illustration. Max illustrates Italy, where the group will stop to visit Michelangelo, with a paintbrush. Ariel uses a book to illustrate Amherst, Massachusetts, where they will stop to visit Emily Dickinson. Fernando illustrates Washington, DC, with pictures of the Lincoln Memorial, the Washington Monument, and a crowd of people. When they have finished illustrating the map, the club members paste onto it their destination description cards. The next day, they present their map to the class, sharing their ideas and special interests with the rest of the class. They also have the opportunity to learn about other important people, places, and events from other time travelers' clubs.

Examining the Model

1. How did the club members decide what to include on their map?
2. What did they do to learn more about the people, places, and events on their map?
3. What steps did they follow to create their map?

Starting Your Club

1. Form small groups of three or four. Discuss places and times that you would like to visit. Each person in your club should name at least two places, events, or people that he or she would like to visit.
2. Gather some facts about each stop on your trip. Go to your school or local library, or use reference materials that might be in your classroom. Divide this research among the members of your club. People should research the places and times that are of special interest to them.
3. Write a one-paragraph description of each destination. In each, briefly describe the time period, person, place, or event, and then share why it is interesting and important to you.

Making Your Map

1. Decide if you want your map and your illustrations to be bright, colorful, and whimsical, or plain and subtle. Your drawings can be cartoonlike, or they can be serious. You may even display a variety of styles—one for each member of your club.
2. On a large piece of paper or cardboard, draw a rough sketch of your map. You might create a traditional world map, or you might draw illustrations of only the places you plan to visit. Your map should be some type of diagram showing your trip. Beyond that, the format is up to you.
3. One of the brief descriptions that you wrote should be next to each destination marked on your map. You might write your description on the map itself, or you might type or write it on a separate sheet of paper or index card to paste onto the map.

Reporting Your Club Activities

1. Plan a class presentation day. On this day, each club in the class will present its map and describe the people, places, and events indicated. Club members will talk about why particular places marked on the map are interesting and important. Encourage people to ask questions about your choices.
2. Leave your map on display in the classroom after the presentation so that people can take a closer look at your work.

Answers for Examining the Model

1. The group discussed what to include and each member decided to include one or more places and times.
2. The group members went to the library to research the people, places, and events that were of interest to them.
3. They traced a world map, pasted it on cardboard, marked each stop on their journey with a star and an illustration, and pasted their destination descriptions on the map.

Analytic Scale for Project

Assign a score from 1 to 25 for each grading criterion below.

Planning a Time Travelers' Club

- **Organization.** The group set attainable goals and created a schedule or strategy for achieving those goals.
- **Cooperation.** The group assigned tasks fairly to each member, and each member cooperated toward achieving the group's goals.
- **Goal Achievement.** The group worked steadily toward its goals and did, in fact, achieve them.
- **Presentation.** The group presented a product of high quality that met the initial project description.

Vocabulary Check Test

Ask students to number their papers from one to ten. Have students complete each sentence with a word from Vocabulary for the Unit in the Unit Review.

1. The speaker lectured on drily, but it was difficult to pay attention.
2. The old canoe was weathered from continual exposure to the elements.
3. At first, Alan found learning Spanish to be difficult, but soon he was chattering away with others in the language.
4. Because moths eat wool, Annie put all her wool garments into storage.
5. She was sleepy, so her thoughts were cloudy and vague.
6. Far in the distance, we saw a light shining glimmeringly.
7. When Lisa saw the tornado headed her way, her face showed her consternation.
8. The doctor listened gravely to his patient's heartbeat.
9. The canned food was not appetizing, but it was fit for human consumption.
10. The landscape of the moon is covered with craters, but other than that, it is stark and empty.

Unit Review

Summary

Literary Terms for the Unit

dramatic irony, 191
irony, 185
irony of situation, 195
point of view, 195
satire, 185, 212
science fiction, 191, 203
simile, 212

Vocabulary for the Unit

awe, 193
babble, 194
bellow, 209
binge, 199
chatter, 193
consternation, 208
consumption, 199
cower, 209
cubicle, 200
cull, 202
dingy, 197
drily, 183
envious, 206
gambol, 210
garment, 194
glimmeringly, 207
gravely, 210
gullible, 199
hindrance, 208
impediment, 208
luminous, 208
neutralize, 210
placid, 202
ravage, 201
scarf, 198
scurry, 194
stark, 199
symmetry, 208
synchronize, 210
unceasing, 205
unnerve, 199
vague, 206
vigilance, 205
weather, 190
wince, 206

Questions for Writing, Discussion, and Research

1. In what way has the world been modified in each selection? What problems of human society are pointed out through the creation of modified worlds?
2. Science fiction is highly imaginative literature based on scientific principles, discoveries, or laws. On what scientific theories or discoveries is each selection in this unit based? Which of the selections seem most plausible to you? Why?

For Your Reading List

Rob Pfeil
Meramec Valley Middle School
Pacific, Missouri

The Time Machine
by H. G. Wells

I really enjoyed reading the novel *The Time Machine* by H. G. Wells. I highly recommend reading it. In this book, The Time Traveler is making a time machine, but all of his friends think it's impossible. When he is done making his time machine, he travels to the year 802,701, where he discovers creatures from the future and befriends a creature named Weena. A few days later, he goes back to where he had left his time machine, but it has disappeared. That night he discovers small, white, ratlike creatures called morlocks. He gets a hint that the morlocks have his time machine, so he goes on a big adventure to get it back. When he returns to the present day, none of his friends believe the story he tells them. I think you will like this book, especially if you like to read about strange creatures and time travel.

Spelling Check Test

Ask students to number their papers from one to ten. Read each word aloud. Then read aloud the sentence containing the word. Repeat the word. Ask students to write the word on their papers, spelling it correctly.

1. **drily**

The speaker gave his lecture so drily that it was hard to pay attention to his emotionless voice.

2. **weather**

When wood weathers, it often becomes gray in color.

3. **awe**

The tourists were overcome with awe as they gazed at the majesty of the Grand Canyon.

4. **babble**

Roger always babbles nonsensically about too many subjects at once.

5. **consumption**

It was determined that the water in the reservoir was unfit for human consumption.

6. **gullible**

Henry was so gullible that he would believe almost anything that people would tell him.

7. **ravage**

The forest was ravaged by fire.

8. **unceasing**

The fire alarm let off an unceasing clamor.

9. **vigilance**

The citizens' vigilance deterred crime in their neighborhood.

10. **symmetry**

If you fold a paper in half before you cut a shape, that shape will have symmetry.

Part Two

The Oral Tradition

GOALS/OBJECTIVES

Studying this unit will enable students to

- appreciate the literature of the ancient Near East and the ancient Far East
- define and identify examples of *central conflict, inciting incident, irony, motive, simile, symbol, internal conflict, myth, characterization*
- write an adventure story
- use dictionaries
- understand the ways that words enter a language
- document sources
- read actively
- make masks

ADDITIONAL UNIT MATERIALS IN THE ASSESSMENT PORTFOLIO

- Vocabulary Worksheet, 2.6.11
- Unit Test, 2.6.12

See also the Additional Resources Box in the marginal notes accompanying each selection.

CROSS-CURRICULAR CONNECTIONS

- Applied Arts, 266
- Geography, 230, 240
- Science, 266
- Social Studies, 230, 240, 248, 260
- World History, 230

UNIT 6 LONG AGO AND FAR AWAY

Roman Temple. *Bellotto D. Canaletto*

ontemporary man has rationalized the myths, but he has not been able to destroy them.

—Octavio Paz

221

UNIT SKILLS OUTLINE

Literary Skills and Concepts

- Central Conflict, 236
- Characterization, 270
- Inciting Incident, 245
- Internal Conflict, 253
- Irony, 236
- Motive, 245
- Myth, 263
- Simile, 253
- Symbol, 253

Other Language Arts Skills and Concepts

- Documenting Sources, 264
- Reading Actively, 271
- Using Dictionaries, 246
- Word Origins, 254
- Writing an Adventure Story, 237

Art Note

Bernardo Belloto (1720–1780) was also called Belloto Canaletto or Canaletto the Younger. He was born in Venice, Italy, and studied painting under his uncle Giovanni Antonio Canaletto who was a successful topographical painter of scenes in Venice and London. Belloto painted urban scenes of Venice and later became a court painter in Dresden, Germany, and Warsaw, Poland.

LITERARY NOTE

Some students might be interested in reading the Mesopotamian creation myth, the *Enuma elish*, or "When on High." This creation myth was written in Akkadian in the middle of the second millennium BC. In the Akkadian version of the text, the hero is Marduk, the city-god of Babylon, reflecting Babylon's importance during that time. A later version of the text exists in Assyrian, and in this version the Assyrian god Assur replaces Marduk as the hero. Some scholars believe that the *Enuma elish* was based on an earlier tale in which Enlil, the storm god, played the central role. The myth describes how the basic features of the universe were formed and how the present world came to be.

A reading of the *Enuma elish* might enhance students' readings of "The Epic of Gilgamesh." In the *Enuma elish* an older race of gods becomes disturbed by the clamor of a new race of gods. The older gods decide (but fail) to destroy the younger gods so that their rest will not be disturbed. This is remarkably similar to the scene in "The Epic of Gilgamesh" in which the gods become disturbed by the noise raised by humans and decide to release a terrible flood to wash humans from the Earth. The *Enuma elish* might also be valuable to students because in this work many gods, their domains, and their relations to other gods are described.

Cultures of the Ancient Near East

The History and Mythology of Ancient Mesopotamia

Long before the Greeks and Romans developed their influential cultures, another ancient people, the **Mesopotamians**, developed a great civilization in the country that we now call Iraq. The word *Mesopotamia* comes from Greek words meaning "between rivers." Indeed, life in the region that we know as Mesopotamia was made possible by the **Tigris and Euphrates Rivers,** which carved a narrow, fertile region from a land that can be quite hot and dry.

Mesopotamia is surrounded by land that is much less hospitable to its occupants. Mountains lie to the east of Mesopotamia, and the Arabian and Syrian Deserts lie to the south and west. Life, however, was still not easy in Mesopotamia. The rivers flooded unpredictably, ruining crops, and at other times drought settled over the land. To survive, people had to work together to build irrigation canals and drainage ditches. Because people needed to work together, they formed small communities which later evolved into the powerful **city-states** of ancient Mesopotamia.

Unlike Egypt, which essentially had one culture and one language, ancient Mesopotamia had many. Two of the most important languages spoken and written in ancient Mesopotamia were **Sumerian** and **Akkadian,** although **Assyrian** was also widely used for a time. Ancient Mesopotamians also contributed greatly to astronomy and mathematics.

The Beginnings of Civilization and the Invention of Writing

The oldest cities yet to be discovered by archaeologists lie to the west and north of Mesopotamia. **Jericho,** near the Jordan River, dates from 9000 to 8000 BC, and **Çatal Hüyük,** in modern-day Turkey, from around 7000 BC. By the fourth millennium BC, the first cities had developed in the Fertile Crescent. Irrigation of fields on a large scale led to steady increases in population. Some of Mesopotamia's earliest cities were **Eridu, Uruk, Nippur,** and **Kish.**

Along with the development of cities, government, and a more complex economy, writing was invented some time between the fourth and the third millenniums. The Sumerians were the first people to use writing in the Middle East. Their system of writing, called **cuneiform,** involved making wedge-shaped impressions with a wooden rod into wet clay tablets. Writing was not developed for literary purposes but for economic ones. Early Mesopotamian temples were both religious and economic centers, and scribes within these temples created writing to keep track of transactions and inventories. Only later was writing used for religious, legal, and literary purposes.

Sumer and Akkad

Throughout the third millennium BC, the Sumerians developed city-states which kept up active trade with foreign lands. Each city-state had a patron god or goddess. Ancient peoples believed that this god or goddess protected their city and made life possible there. However, the people of each city-state also believed in a variety of other gods; there are more than two thousand gods in the Mesopotamian pantheon.

Frequently city-states fought against each other, and Mesopotamian history is filled with many such battles. The Mesopotamians believed that if their city suffered, their god suffered, and if their city triumphed and prospered, so did their god. Thus, many of their battles had religious significance as well and many mythological stories were rewritten with the city-god of the victor replacing as hero in a myth the city-god of the defeated. The most famous of all Sumerian literary works, ***The Epic of Gilgamesh,*** is the story of a legendary warrior king of Uruk.

Around 2350 BC, a ruler named **Sargon** united the cities of **Akkad,** north of Sumer. He then conquered the city-states of Sumer itself and established an empire. Around 2100 BC, the city of **Ur** emerged as the greatest power in the region, controlling southern Mesopotamia. The king of this empire, **Ur-Nammu,** built impressive **ziggurats**—pyramid-like structures—at Ur and Uruk.

The Rise of Babylon

One of the city-states ruled by Ur was **Babylon**. In the early part of the second millennium, Ur declined in power, and Babylon asserted its independence. One of the rulers of Babylon, **Hammurabi the Great,** established the first Babylonian Empire, conquering all of Sumer and Akkad. He also created a set of laws, the **Code of Hammurabi,** one of the most famous of surviving cuneiform works. This code deals with many topics, from theft and libel to bride prices and adoption. The code describes extremely harsh penalties for wrongdoing.

Assyrian bas-relief sculpture

The Assyrians and the Later History of Babylon

Between 1600 and 1450 BC, the power of Babylon declined due to invasions by other peoples, the Hurrians and the Kassites. By 1350 BC, the city of **Ashur,** in northern Mesopotamia, had extended its dominion over Mesopotamia, creating what we now call the **Assyrian Empire**. At its height, under the ruler **Ashurbanipal,** in the seventh century BC, Assyria ruled all of Mesopotamia, modern-day Israel, and Egypt. Babylon had one last period of glory under **King Nebuchadrezzar II,** who ruled from 605 to 562 BC. Nebuchadrezzar conquered Syria, Phoenicia, Judah, and Assyria; sacked Jerusalem; brought many Israelites into captivity in Babylon; and built famous structures, including the Tower of Babel, the Ishtar Gate, and the Hanging Gardens of Babylon.

HISTORICAL NOTE

Inform students that the Code of Hammurabi is a collection of two hundred and eighty-two legal decisions that Hammurabi made during his reign. The code was written on a stela, or upright stone slab, and placed in Babylon's temple to Marduk. The stela also shows a relief of Hammurabi and the god Shamash, who was god of the sun and of justice. Many of the laws in the code are based upon much older laws, such as the law that called for an eye for an eye. Penalties in the code varied depending on the social status of the offender, with slaves being the class that was punished most harshly for crimes. Despite the code's severity, it did establish some laws protecting widows and orphans. This indicated that rulers were concerned, at least to some degree, with the welfare of less fortunate members of the populace.

Historical Note

Inform students that the Mesopotamians believed in a vast number of gods. Many of these gods were representative of things in the natural world. Mesopotamians believed that natural phenomena such as reeds and salt all had individual personalities and wills. Although there were many gods, the Mesopotamians saw some as being more powerful than others. The most powerful gods met in an assembly to discuss different issues in the universe and to decide upon a course of action. Anu, sky god, was the leader of the assembly and Enlil, second-highest of gods and storm god, often carried out the will of the assembly. Ninhursaga and Enki were third in importance, representing different aspects of the Earth. Early Mesopotamian government was modeled upon this assembly of gods. In early settlements, decisions were made by an assembly of adult freedmen. Gradually, however, city states developed and more power was claimed by one ruler who was at first known as an *ensi,* or manager of a god's estate, and later as a *lugal,* or king. Some of the most important gods in Mesopotamian literature are described on page 224.

GODS AND GODDESSES IN MESOPOTAMIAN MYTHOLOGY

Anu, the god of the sky and of heaven, was the highest of all the gods.

Dumuzi, also known as **Tammuz,** was the god of shepherds.

Enki, also known as **Ea,** was god of the earth, drinkable water, and crafts, and he frequently helped human beings.

Enlil was the god of storms and led the gods in war.

Erishkigal, also known as **Erkalla,** was queen of the underworld.

Inanna, also known as **Ishtar,** was goddess of love and war and was associated with the evening and morning stars.

Nintu, also known as **Ninmah** or **Ninhursaga,** was the queen of the gods and goddess of the soil and of childbirth.

Sin was the moon god.

Uttu was goddess of cloth and of weaving.

Utu, also known as **Shamash,** was the sun god and the god of justice invoked by Hammurabi.

Mesopotamian Civilization

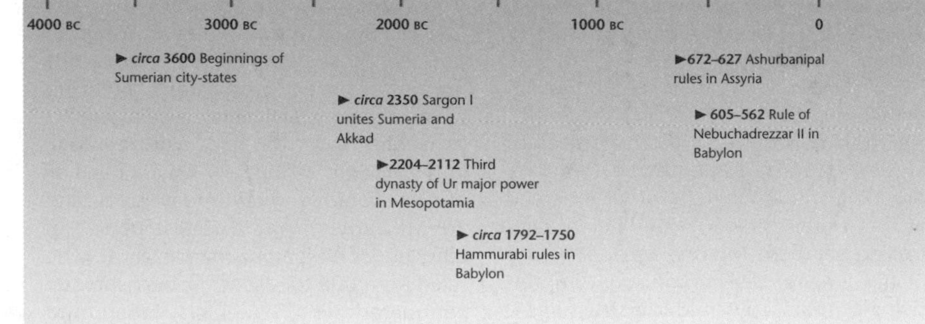

Rock Temples of Ramses II, Egypt

The History and Mythology of Ancient Egypt

Located in northeastern Africa, **Egypt** is a desert country bounded by the **Mediterranean Sea** and the **Red Sea.** The **Nile River** flows north through the country, dividing the desert into unequal parts. Throughout its history, almost all the life to be found in Egypt has been in the valley and delta of the Nile. The floodplains of the river made the land fertile for crop growing, allowing the area to sustain human life. It was along this great river that the civilization of ancient Egypt flourished in an almost unbroken record from about 3100 BC to 30 BC.

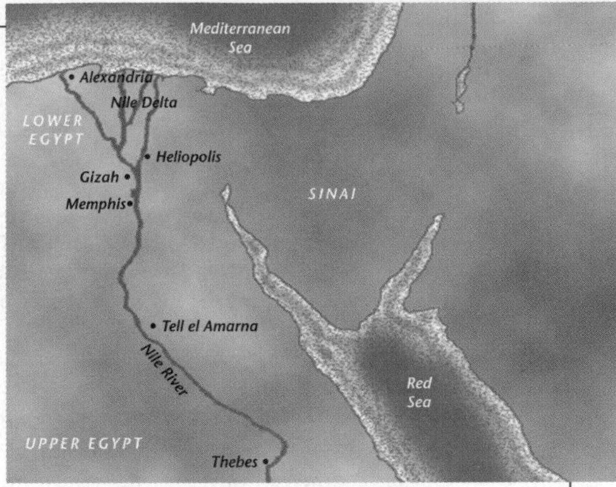

Egyptian History

Two separate communities, Lower Egypt and Upper Egypt, were formed along the Nile during the early 3000s BC. The two kingdoms were joined around 3100 BC, traditionally by **King Menes** of Upper Egypt, though possibly by a former king named **Aha.** The history of ancient Egypt following Menes's conquest is usually divided into thirty or thirty-one dynasties. These dynasties are in turn grouped into four major periods. The most important of these periods were

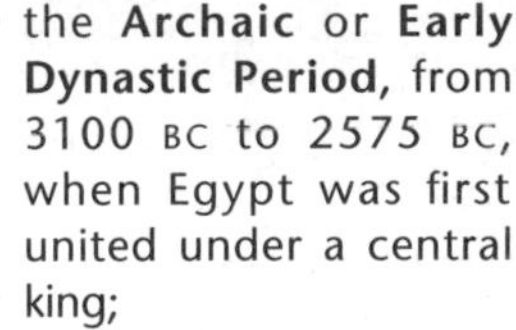

Coffin of King Tutankhamen

- the **Archaic** or **Early Dynastic Period,** from 3100 BC to 2575 BC, when Egypt was first united under a central king;
- the **Old Kingdom,** lasting from 2575 BC to 2040 BC, the period of the great pyramid builders such as **Khufu** and **Khafre**;
- the **Middle Kingdom,** which existed from roughly 2040 BC to 1550 BC and saw the development of the cult of the god Osiris; and
- the **New Kingdom,** or **Golden Age of Egypt,** which extended from about 1532 BC to 1070 BC, a time when powerful rulers such as **Tutankhamen** and **Ramses the Great** oversaw a vast empire extending into Mesopotamia.

Between these great periods of Egyptian history were intermediate periods of social and political upheaval. Nonetheless, Egyptian history shows a remarkable continuity over its three-thousand-year span.

Egyptian Government and Economy

Throughout most of its history, Egypt was ruled by an all-powerful king. The king was believed to be a god. For the first thirty years of his reign, he was identified with the falcon god **Horus.** After reigning for thirty years, or after his death, he was identified with the god of fertility and the underworld, Osiris. As the representative of the gods on Earth, the king had the responsibility to establish *ma'at,* divine

QUOTABLES

"Were the Egyptian to come back today, he would undoubtedly take heart from the endurance of his pyramids, for he accorded to man and to man's tangible achievements more basic significance than most civilizations have been willing to do."

—Thorkild Jacobsen

HISTORICAL NOTE

Inform students that during the First Intermediate Period, Asiatic peoples invaded the Egyptian delta. During the Second Intermediate Period the Hyksos conquered Egypt. Point out that ancient Egyptian historians very seldom make any mention of these two periods of Egyptian history. The concept of *ma'at*, or order, was very important to the ancient Egyptians, so they preferred to present their history as if it had never been interrupted by a period of disorder. Egyptians looked unkindly on foreigners, so having been conquered by a foreign people was a shocking disruption of order that they preferred to forget.

Historical Note

Inform students that the ancient Egyptians also believed that their king was the son of Re, the supreme god, and that the land had been entrusted to the king by Re. However, in Egyptian mythology Re's only son is Shu, god of the air. Tell students that Egyptians were not disturbed by apparent inconsistencies in their system of belief. They believed both that Re only had one son Shu and that the king was the son of Re.

Just as Egyptians willingly accepted more than one explanation of phenomena or occurrences, they also believed that their gods had more than one appearance. Thus Re could appear as a crowned man, a falcon-headed man, a falcon, or a scarab. Students might enjoy drawing or painting some of the Egyptian gods, combining their human and their animal qualities.

order on earth. Beneath the king was a small class of officials, a very large class of common people, and especially in later periods, slaves. A powerful, centralized authority was necessary to run the large-scale irrigation and farming of lands adjacent to the Nile. The wealth of the country was based on its production of crops, mostly wheat and barley.

Ancient Egyptian Writing

The use of writing helped the ancient Egyptians to form and administer a powerful, centralized government. Two forms of writing were invented near the beginning of the Early Dynastic Period. **Hieroglyphs,** which combined pictures and representations of sounds, were used for inscriptions on monuments. A simpler cursive form of writing, **hieratic,** was used for documents. Modern scholars were able to decipher ancient Egyptian after the discovery of the **Rosetta Stone,** on which was carved a single passage in three different languages: hieroglyphics, a late form of Egyptian known as demotic, and the well-known European language Greek. As early as the first dynasty, Egyptians wrote documents on sheets made from the **papyrus** plant.

Ancient hieroglyphics

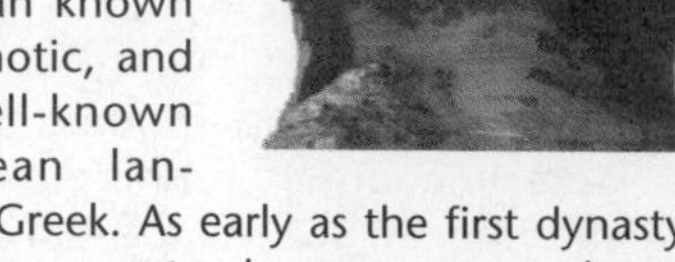

Sphinx

Egyptian Religion

The Egyptians worshiped many gods. When the first centralized state was formed, local gods became absorbed into a single pantheon.

Key to Egyptian religion were the concepts of *ma'at,* discussed above, and of the ***ka,*** or soul, which was believed to live on after death. Most of the great monumental sculpture of ancient Egypt is concerned with preparing for the existence of the king's *ka* in the afterlife. Great tombs, including the pyramids, were built and stocked with goods for use by the dead king. The bodies of royal persons and of some great officials were embalmed in a process called **mummification** so that the

MAJOR GODS AND GODDESSES IN EGYPTIAN MYTHOLOGY

Amon-Re, also known as **Re, Ra, Atum,** and **Ra-Horakhty,** was the sun god, considered the greatest of all the gods.

Anubis was a jackal-headed god, associated with mummification, who judged the dead in the underworld.

Hathor was the cow-headed goddess of love, dance, and music.

Horus was the falcon-headed son of Isis and Osiris associated with the living king.

Isis, the wife and sister of Osiris, was, among other things, the protector of children.

Osiris was a fertility god, the god of the earth, vegetation, the underworld, and the annual rebirth of vegetation following the flooding of the Nile.

Seth was the donkey-headed god of Upper Egypt, deserts, and storms.

Thoth was the ibis or baboon-headed god of wisdom and the moon.

Historical Note

During the period of the Old Kingdom, ancient Egyptians believed that the king became the god Osiris after his death. However, beginning in the Middle Kingdom, ancient Egyptians believed that common people might also continue with their *ka* and become Osiris after death. The ancient Egyptians believed that when a person died, Osiris weighed the person's heart against a symbol of *ma'at.* Those whose good deeds made their heart as light as *ma'at* could pass into the next world and become gods. Those whose hearts were heavier than *ma'at* because of bad deeds would be tortured and destroyed. The gods Re and Anubis were often associated with the judgment of the dead as well.

The Great Pyramids at Giza, Egypt

ka might inhabit the preserved body after death. In addition, elaborate ceremonies were performed to ensure the king's successful journey into the next life.

The History and Religions of Ancient India

The Indus Valley Civilization, 2500–1750 BC

In India, as in Mesopotamia and Egypt, civilization was the gift of a river. Around 2500 BC, in Northwest India, a great civilization developed when people discovered the possibilities of farming the well-watered, fertile lands on the banks of the Indus River. The so-called **Indus Valley Civilization** covered an area larger than present-day Pakistan and included over seventy villages, as well as the large cities of **Mohenjo-daro** and **Harappa,** constructed largely of bricks. Mohenjo-daro and Harappa both contained large citadel mounds suggestive of but cruder than Mesopotamian ziggurats. These citadels included central storehouses, or granaries, and may have been operated, as in Egypt and Mesopotamia, by a powerful priesthood.

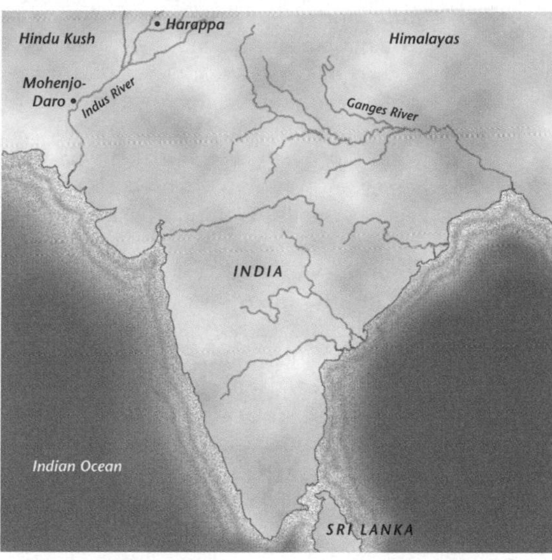

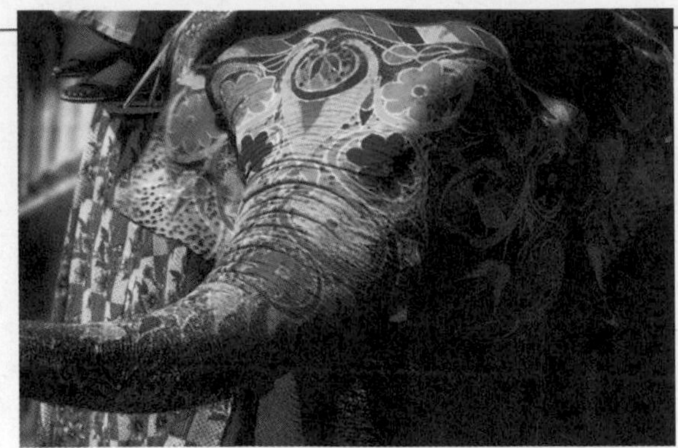

In Hindu belief, writing was the gift of the elephant-headed god Ganesh.

Aryan Civilization, Hinduism, and Buddhism

Aryan Culture. Beginning around 2000 BC, India was invaded by people from the north, perhaps originally from the Steppes region of southern Russia. These people called themselves the **Aryans,** or "noble ones," and brought with them the **Sanskrit** language and a religion that developed into **Hinduism**. Sanskrit is an **Indo-European language,** related to later European languages such as Greek, Latin, French, German, and English. The words *India* and *Hinduism* come from the Sanskrit name for the Indus River, *Sindhu.*

Much of what we know of the Aryans comes from collections of early Sanskrit religious writings, the **Vedas.** These books tell of a people skilled in battle who used horses and chariots, herded cattle, and lived in small agricultural villages. Their society was organized hierarchically according to a caste system into five groups: **Brahmans,** or priests; **Kshatriyas,** or nobles and warriors; **Vaisyas,** or farmers and merchants; **Sudras,** or servants; and **Dasas,** descendants of the peoples whom the Aryans displaced. The Aryans established communities along the Indus River and spread across the whole of northern India, especially along the banks of India's other great river, the **Ganges.**

Hinduism. Based on the Vedas and other later religious texts, scholars have determined that the early Aryan invaders worshiped many gods, one of whom was **Indra,** a sky god associated with war, thunder, and lightning. Eventually, early Aryan **polytheism,** or worship of many gods, developed into a form of **monotheism**, or worship of one god, **Brahma,** and of many lesser gods who were viewed as different aspects, or manifestations, of this god. Indeed, in traditional Hindu belief, all things in the universe are part of Brahma, who created the universe and is one with it. The Hindus believe that the universe Brahma created lasts for 432,000 years, during which time it is sustained by **Vishnu,** the preserver god. Eventually, **Shiva,** the destroyer god, brings the universe to an end, and the cycle of creation begins again.

In times of crisis, Vishnu is born into the world to bring about order, peace, justice, or understanding. The most famous of these appearances of Vishnu was as the cowherd and charioteer **Krishna,** who in the Hindu scripture called the ***Bhagavad Gita*** teaches the warrior Arjuna such principles of proper living as selflessness and detachment from the world.

Just as the universe, in Hindu belief, goes through cycles of death and rebirth, so do individual people. Today, traditional Hindus believe that people are born over and over, in a process called **reincarnation,** until they are able to lead lives of such perfection that they reach a state of oneness with Brahma called **nirvana,** at which point they escape the cycle of rebirth. In older traditional belief, a person who led a bad life might be reincarnated in a lower caste or even as an animal. To achieve oneness with Brahma, Hindus developed many spiritual

Mural, Jaipur, India

disciplines, or **yogas.** Some involved extreme asceticism, or denial of bodily needs; some involved physical training and meditation.

Buddhism. In the sixth century BC, a new religion emerged in India that was to have profound effects on later developments throughout Asia. This religion, called **Buddhism,** was founded by **Siddhartha Gautama,** who later came to be known as the **Buddha,** or "Enlightened One." Born around 560 BC to a royal family in northern India, Gautama left his princely wealth behind at the age of twenty-nine to seek spiritual truth. After trying many paths, he received enlightenment by meditating for forty-nine days under a Bo tree near modern-day Benares. After this experience, he gave a sermon that laid the foundations for the Buddhist religion.

The Buddha taught what he called the **Three Noble Truths:**

1. All suffering is caused by the frustration of desire.
2. People can therefore escape pain by ridding themselves of desires.
3. People can rid themselves of desires by following the **Eightfold Path,** which involves right belief, thought, speech, and action.

After the conversion of the emperor **Asoka** in the third century BC, Buddhism became a powerful religion in India. Thereafter, however, Hinduism regained its former strength in India, while Buddhism traveled to Tibet, China, Japan, and other parts of the Far East, where it developed several major branches and became a major religious force.

Statue of the Buddah, Jaisemer, India

Early Indian Civilization

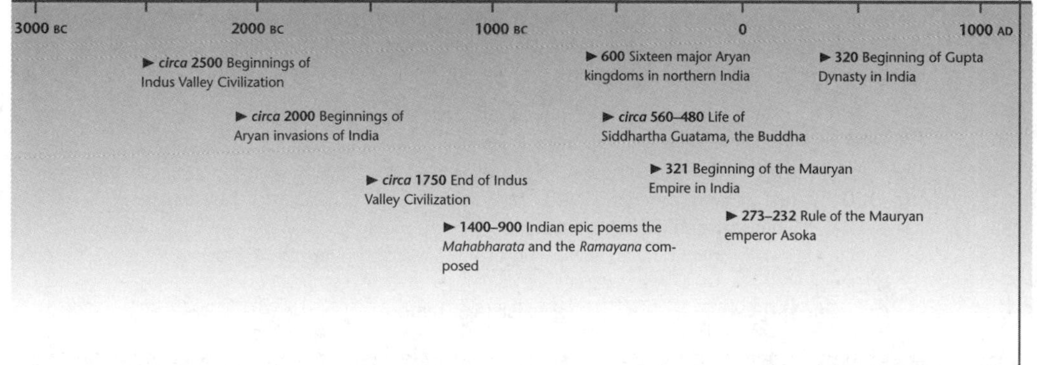

GOALS/OBJECTIVES

Studying this lesson will enable students to

- appreciate an ancient Mesopotamian story
- briefly explain in what way the geography of Mesopotamia shaped the world view of its people
- briefly describe the characteristics of Ishtar
- define *central conflict* and recognize a central conflict in a literary work
- define and recognize *irony*
- write an adventure story

ADDITIONAL RESOURCES

READER'S GUIDE

- Selection Worksheet, 6.1

ASSESSMENT PORTFOLIO

- Selection Check Test, 2.6.1
- Selection Test, 2.6.2

PRONUNCIATION EXERCISE

- Grade 7 Audiocassette, Side B, Track 28

CROSS-CURRICULAR CONNECTIONS

GEOGRAPHY AND SOCIAL STUDIES

Encourage students to discuss the ways in which geography affects their own lives and views of the world. In what way would students look at the world differently if they lived in another place, such as the mountains of Tibet, along the Yangze river in China, or on a remote island in Indonesia?

WORLD HISTORY

Encourage students to draw or paint pictures of Ishtar as they imagine her.

Prereading

MESOPOTAMIA

"The Epic of Gilgamesh"

Anonymous, retold by Christina Kolb

Cross-curricular Connections

Geography and Social Studies. The selection you are about to read was first written down by Mesopotamian peoples around 1800 BC, although the story is much older and was probably composed and told in the oral tradition hundreds of years before this time. It is an epic tale about a hero's struggle against death. The epic of Gilgamesh is pessimistic, or dark and gloomy, in its view of the world. Although Gilgamesh is the greatest of heroes, he cannot give the gift of immortality to his fellow mortals and he must accept death as a part of human life. Throughout the epic, humans are plagued by floods, drought, and earthquakes.

The world view of any culture is strongly shaped by that culture's geography. Some scholars say that the ancient Egyptians were confident about human accomplishments because of the predictability of the Nile River, which would flood at the same time every year, providing rich soil for bountiful crops. The land of ancient Mesopotamia was not as predictable as that of Egypt. The Tigris and the Euphrates Rivers would flood without warning and ruin crops. There were dust storms and periods of drought in which no rain would fall and crops would wither. There were periods of torrential rain in which the land would turn to mud.

The Mesopotamian view of the world reflects the often hostile natural environment. Mesopotamian people saw nature as a collection of individual powers, each of which must be respected. Rivers, grain, and even rocks were all seen as individual personalities each with its own set of characteristics.

World History. Ishtar, or Inanna as the ancient Mesopotamian people originally called her, was the Queen of Heaven and the goddess of the storehouse, rain, war, love, and the morning and the evening star. Ishtar was a fertility goddess who reflected the unique geography of Mesopotamia—at times she brought fertility and bountiful harvests, and at times she brought disaster and war to her people. The Mesopotamians longed for stability. In their mythology, they gradually stripped the unpredictable Ishtar of power and gave more power to more benevolent male gods like Anu, Shamash, Enlil, and Ea.

As You Read

The unpredictable nature of the Mesopotamian region is described in **"The Epic of Gilgamesh."** Make a chart like the one below. As you read, list the disasters that occur and their causes.

DISASTER	CAUSE
earthquake	Ishtar's jealousy

AS YOU READ

Students may include the following details in their charts: *disaster*—drought, *cause*—Bull of Heaven; *disaster*—earthquake, *cause*—Bull of Heaven or Ishtar's jealousy; *disaster*—sickness, *cause*—the gods; *disaster*—flood, *cause*—anger of Enlil; *disaster*—death, *cause*—Gilgamesh's losing the plant.

READER'S JOURNAL

Do you think people should be able to live forever? What would life be like if they did? What would the advantages be? What would the disadvantages be? If you had the opportunity to live forever, would you take it? Why, or why not? Write about these questions in your journal.

"The Epic of Gilgamesh"

ANONYMOUS, RETOLD BY CHRISTINA KOLB

Gilgamesh, king of Uruk in southern Babylonia, was two-thirds divine and one-third human. He himself built the great city of Uruk. He was like a wild bull—powerful, bold, and able to best any man in combat. Perhaps because he was so very powerful, Gilgamesh was also arrogant. He drove the people of Uruk too hard, oppressing even the weak. Eventually the people of Uruk, weighed down by their heavy burdens, prayed to the gods for relief. The gods granted the people's prayers and created Enkidu.

Enkidu was a wild man, all covered with hair, and he dwelled with the animals. Enkidu was tamed by a priestess who then urged him to strive against Gilgamesh. Enkidu challenged Gilgamesh and the two wrestled like bulls. Their fight was long and terrible, but in the end Gilgamesh conquered Enkidu the wild man. From this contest and struggle of bodies emerged the bond of friendship. Together the two brave companions set out seeking adventure. In the cedar forest to the west, they killed Huwawa, a terrible monster who guarded the forest for Enlil, Lord of the Storm.

Ishtar saw Gilgamesh's strength and courage, fell in love with him, and asked him to marry her. Gilgamesh, however, slighted the advances of the tempestuous goddess of love and war, saying that Ishtar was never loyal and faithful to those whom she loved. Enraged, Ishtar flew to the heavens to see her father, Anu. She demanded that Anu make a Bull of Heaven to destroy Gilgamesh. Anu demurred, saying that the Bull of Heaven would cause a seven-year period of drought. Ishtar replied, "If you will not make the Bull of Heaven, I will smash the gates to the underworld, and the dead will devour the living."

Knowing that Ishtar did not make vain threats, Anu created the Bull of

❶ *Why do the people of Uruk pray to the gods? For what do they pray?*

❷ *Why is Ishtar angry with Gilgamesh?*

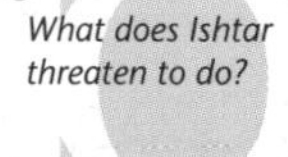

❸ *What does Ishtar threaten to do?*

WORDS FOR EVERYDAY USE

op • press (ə pres´) *v.*, keep down by cruel or unjust use or power

dwell (dwel) *v.*, live; make one's home

e • merge (ē murj´) *v.*, come forth; develop

tem • pes • tu • ous (tem pes´cho͞o əs) *adj.*, violent; stormy

de • mur (dē mur´) *v.*, hesitate because of doubts

vain (vān) *adj.*, without force or effect

VOCABULARY IN CONTEXT

- The cruel tyrant oppressed his people, making them labor long hours without rest.
- Isabel dwelled in New York before she moved to New Mexico.
- The wonderful smell of fresh-baked bread emerged from the oven.
- The boat was tossed about by the tempestuous sea.
- We asked him to state his opinion, but he demurred saying that he had not decided how he felt about the issue yet.
- Because Suzanne did not help Jeremy as she had promised, Jeremy wondered if all Suzanne's promises were vain.

READER'S JOURNAL

You might ask students to think about all the knowledge and experiences they would gain over time. What different things might they see and experience? How would they feel about seeing and experiencing so many things? What do they think society would be like if its members possessed eternal life?

SPELLING AND VOCABULARY WORDS FROM THE SELECTION

chasm	oppress
cower	strewn
demur	talon
dwell	tempestuous
ebb	transgressor
emerge	vain
intolerable	wrest

ANSWERS TO GUIDED READING QUESTIONS

❶ The people of Uruk pray to the gods because Gilgamesh has driven them too hard. They pray for relief from Gilgamesh's oppression.

❷ Ishtar is angry with Gilgamesh because when she asked him to marry her he insulted her.

❸ Ishtar threatens to smash the gates of the underworld and allow the dead to devour the living.

SUPPORT FOR LEP STUDENTS

PRONUNCIATIONS OF PROPER NOUNS AND ADJECTIVES

Gil • ga • mesh (gil´gə mesh´) n.
En • ki • du (eŋ´kē do͞o) n.
Ut • na • pish • tim (o͞ot nə pēsh´ təm) n.
Sha • mash (shä´mäsh) n.
En • lil (en lil´) n.
Si • du • ri (sē do͞o´rē) n.

Answers to Guided Reading Questions

❶ Gilgamesh is grieved, enraged, and terrified by Enkidu's death.

❷ The gods decree that one of the heroes must die because they have killed Huwawa and the Bull of Heaven.

Literary Note

Hubris is wanton insolence or arrogance resulting from excessive pride. In ancient literature, a human hero often commits an act of hubris thereby offending the gods who punish the hero and send the hero's fate on a downward spiral. This theme was commonly explored in Greek mythology (in the stories of Niobe and Arachne, for example) and in Greek tragedy.

You might point out to students that Gilgamesh and Enkidu commit acts of hubris by killing monsters created by the gods. Gilgamesh commits an enormous act of hubris by insulting the goddess Ishtar. Enkidu's death and Gilgamesh's painful and ultimately unsuccessful journey can be seen as punishments for the heroes' acts of hubris. Inform students that tales such as "The Epic of Gilgamesh" pointed out to ancient peoples the importance of accepting, and never striving against, their positions as servants to the gods.

❶ How does Gilgamesh feel about Enkidu's death?

❷ Why do the gods decree that one of the heros must die?

Heaven. Ishtar drove the Bull of Heaven down to Uruk. At the river near the city, the bull snorted, and a hole in the earth opened up and swallowed two hundred men. The bull snorted again, and another two hundred men fell into a chasm in the earth. The bull snorted a third time, and Enkidu seized the horns of the Bull of Heaven. Gilgamesh took his sword and struck the Bull of Heaven in the neck. He slew the bull and then made of it an offering to Shamash.

Ishtar mourned the death of the Bull of Heaven and cursed Gilgamesh. Enkidu seized the thigh bone of the bull and threw it in Ishtar's face. Ishtar and the women of her temple gathered to wail over the thigh bone of the Bull of Heaven.[1]

The next day, Enkidu told Gilgamesh that he had a dream. He said, "I dreamed that the gods were in council and Anu said that because we two have killed Huwawa and the Bull of Heaven, one of us must die. Enlil then said, 'Enkidu must die. Gilgamesh shall not die.' Shamash tried to save me, but in vain."

Then Enkidu fell down in sickness. Gilgamesh sat by his sick friend's side. Enkidu's sickness was long. Finally, he told Gilgamesh, "I dreamed Anzu,[2] who has the paws of a lion and the talons of an eagle, seized me and overpowered me. He carried me down to Erkalla's[3] house of darkness, the house where one goes in and never comes back out, the house of death. I won't die gloriously in battle but in sickness and in shame." Soon after this dream, Enkidu died.

Gilgamesh wept over Enkidu. Before this time Gilgamesh had not worried about death, but the passing of Enkidu made death real and terrifying for him. Gilgamesh cried out, "My friend, my younger brother, what sleep is this that has seized you? You have become dark, and you cannot hear me."

Gilgamesh touched his friend's heart, but it was still. Gently, Gilgamesh covered his friend's face as if he were a bride. Then Gilgamesh roared with rage, tearing off his finery. Gilgamesh was like a madman in his grief. He wept by Enkidu's side for seven days and nights, but his mourning could not bring Enkidu back to life.

Finally, Gilgamesh got up and began wandering. He longed to speak with Utnapishtim, his ancestor who survived the flood and death itself, Utnapishtim who had been granted eternal life by the gods. Gilgamesh wandered to the mountains where the sun sets, followed the passage between the mountains where the sun travels at night, and came at last to a gate. There stood two terrible scorpions.

One scorpion said to the other, "This one is two-thirds god."

His mate answered, "But one-third man."

1. **Ishtar . . . Bull of Heaven.** Ishtar was also sometimes portrayed as a goddess of mourning.
2. **Anzu.** In Mesopotamian mythology, a terrifying monster
3. **Erkalla.** Another name for Ereshkigal, the queen of the underworld

Words for Everyday Use

chasm (kaz´əm) *n.,* deep crack in the earth's surface

tal • on (tal´ən) *n.,* claw of a bird of prey

Vocabulary in Context

- The earthquake caused a great chasm to open up in the earth.
- The eagle seized its prey with its talons.

The first scorpion asked Gilgamesh, "Why have you journeyed thus far to us?"

Gilgamesh said, "I have come to see my ancestor Utnapishtim. My friend Enkidu has died, the common lot[4] of man has claimed him. Men say that Utnapishtim has found everlasting life."

The scorpion said, "No mortal man has journeyed beyond these mountains. There is only death and darkness beyond—you will learn nothing and only come to grief."

"I have already known grief," Gilgamesh said. "I will go on. Open the gate to the mountains!"

The scorpions opened the gate, and Gilgamesh entered the dark. At long last, he came to the valley of the gods. It was lovely, full of fruit and strewn with jewels, and Gilgamesh was overcome by pain, wishing that Enkidu could see what he was seeing. There, Gilgamesh wept, crying "Enkidu, Enkidu."

Shamash came to Gilgamesh and said, "You will never find the eternal life for which you are searching." Gilgamesh, however, would not give up.

Siduri came to Gilgamesh and said, "Gilgamesh, where are you wandering? You will never find the life you seek. When the gods created humans, they let death be man's share and kept life for themselves. Gilgamesh, fill your belly. Make merry. Dance and feast by day and night. Wear fresh clothes and bathe in sweet water. Look at the child who holds your hand, and make your wife happy in your embrace. This is the fitting concern of man."

Gilgamesh said, "How can I give up when Enkidu is dust and I too shall die and be laid in the ground?"

Siduri then sent Gilgamesh to Urshanabit, the boatman, who carried Gilgamesh across the sea to Utnapishtim.

"Utnapishtim, my ancestor, I have crossed mountains and seas to see you. In my heart, my friend has died many times, but he still seems alive to me. He became dust so suddenly. Is there something more than death? I am so tired, so very tired."

Utnapishtim touched Gilgamesh's shoulder. "There is nothing everlasting. Houses fall and floods ebb. The sleeping and the dead are alike—death comes to all, master and servant alike. Only the day of a human's death is unknown."

❶ *Why is Gilgamesh journeying to see Utnapishtim?*

❷ *What does Utnapishtim say about the chances of Gilgamesh achieving eternal life?*

4. **lot.** One's fortune in life

Words for Everyday Use

strewn (strōōn) *adj.*, sprinkled; scattered

ebb (eb) *v.*, flow back; recede

Answers to Guided Reading Questions

❶ Gilgamesh is journeying to see Utnapishtim because he wishes to discover how Utnapishtim gained everlasting life.

❷ Utnapishtim tells Gilgamesh that like all humans he must die one day.

Quotables

"Show me a hero and I will write you a tragedy."

—F. Scott Fitzgerald

"We are not now that strength which in old days

Moved earth and heaven, that which we are, we are—

One equal temper of heroic hearts,

Made weak by time and fate, but strong in will

To strive, to seek, to find, and not to yield."

—Alfred, Lord Tennyson

Additional Questions and Activities

Encourage students to discuss what they think of Gilgamesh's determination to continue on his journey. Ask them to discuss why he continues on his journey, what is at risk on his journey, and whether or not they would consider Gilgamesh a hero.

Vocabulary in Context

- Because the side of the highway was strewn with litter, the students organized a clean-up campaign.
- When the tide ebbs, we can hunt for shells along the shore.

Answers to Guided Reading Questions

1. The gods want to cause a flood to rid the land of the noisy humans who disturbed their rest.
2. Utnapishtim says that his being granted eternal life was a one-time occurrence that will not be repeated.

Literary Note

Inform students that many cultures around the world have flood stories. While students may be most familiar with the biblical story of Noah and the flood, there are also stories of floods in ancient India, China, and Greece. Encourage students to go to the library and locate other traditional flood stories to bring into class. You might have a class reading of these flood stories and then encourage a discussion on the similarities and differences among these tales. Ask students to think about why flood stories were common among the ancient peoples of many different lands.

Gilgamesh then asked, "If this is so, how did you come to gain eternal life?"

Utnapishtim began his story. "I lived in Shurrupak, on the banks of the Euphrates.[5] The city was old, and its gods grew old—Anu, the father; Enlil; Ishtar; Ea; and the rest. People were numerous, and they raised noise that disturbed the gods. The gods met in council. Enlil, Lord of the Storm, said, 'The noise raised by these humans is intolerable. Sleep is no longer possible.' Enlil planned to release a mighty flood, and the other gods consented.

1 Why do the gods want to cause a flood?

"Ea could not warn mankind, but he whispered to the reeds of the river, and the reeds whispered to me in my sleep. In my dreams, I heard Ea's voice, saying, 'Tear down your house and build a ship. Into the ship, bring the seed of all living creatures.'

"Who am I to disobey a god? I built an enormous ship, according to Ea's measurements. After six days of working, I completed my ship on the seventh day. I took my family, the seeds of all living animals, and my possessions, and went into the ship. Soon, the tempest roared, and the land was shattered. Even the gods cowered and wept at the storm's fury. Ishtar cried out, 'Why did I cry out for battle in the council of the gods? I have cried out for the destruction of my people, the people to whom I myself gave birth.' The gods sat together and wept, but still the storm raged for six days and seven nights.

"On the seventh day, I opened the window of the ship, and light fell on my face. The world was covered with water, and humanity was dust. There, for a time, I wept. Then I looked for shore. Finally, the ship ran aground against the mountain Nisir. To see if the waters were receding, I sent a dove which returned to me, seeing no place to stand. Then I sent a swallow out to fly. It also returned. Finally, I sent a crow, which saw that the waters had receded and did not return. In gratitude, I made sacrifice to the gods. Ishtar and the other gods approached the offering.

"When Enlil came, he was furious, saying, 'Has life escaped? No humans were to live through this devastation!' Ninurta then blamed Ea for my escape.

"Ea said, 'You sent the flood senselessly, without thinking it through. You should punish evildoers alone. Let the punishment fit the crime. Do not drive the transgressor too hard. Rather than the flood, you should have let lions, wolves, famine, or plague strike down the people. I did not reveal the secret of our council. Utnapishtim received a vision.'

"Then Enlil picked up my wife and me, touched our foreheads, and blessed us, saying, 'Before now these have been humans. Now, Utnapishtim and his wife are transformed, being like us gods.' Enlil took us away to live here at the source of the rivers.

2 What does Utnapishtim say about the fact that he was given eternal life?

"So, Gilgamesh," Utnapishtim concluded. "Who will assemble the gods for you, to grant you eternal life? It is not to be repeated."

Gilgamesh bowed his head.

5. **Euphrates.** River flowing from Turkey southward to Syria and Iraq

Words for Everyday Use

in • tol • er • a • ble (in täl´ər ə bəl) *adj.*, unbearable; too severe or painful to be endured

cow • er (kou´ər) *v.*, crouch or huddle

trans • gres • sor (trans gres´sər) *n.*, one who breaks a law or commandment

Vocabulary in Context

- We thought that Jessica's rudeness to the new students was intolerable.
- The tiny kitten cowered before the big barking dog.
- The Code of Hammurabi calls for harsh punishments for transgressors of Mesopotamian laws.

"If you wish," Utnapishtim said, "You may test yourself. Prevail against sleep for six days and nights." While Gilgamesh sat there, sleep immediately drifted over him like wet fog. Utnapishtim laughed to his wife, "Look at this hero who seeks everlasting life! Sleep steals over him like mist even now!"

Each day that Gilgamesh slept, Utnapishtim's wife placed a fresh loaf of bread by his side. On the seventh day, Utnapishtim touched Gilgamesh and he came alive. Gilgamesh protested, "I was barely asleep when you woke me!"

Utnapishtim said, "Come on, Gilgamesh. Count these loaves and discover how many days you have slept. Your first loaf is dry, the second leathery, the third soggy, the fourth white with mold, the fifth gray with mildew, the sixth rotten, and the seventh—you woke."

Gilgamesh said, "What shall I do? Where shall I go? Death is a thief that steals over me. Death is wherever I set my feet."

Utnapishtim took Gilgamesh to Urshanabi, the boatman, to lead him back to his own land. Just as Gilgamesh was leaving, Utnapishtim called out, "You have toiled and worn yourself out, so I will give you a gift to carry back to your own country. I shall reveal to you a great secret. Under the water there grows a plant with deep roots. It will prick your hand like a thorn, but hold on to it. If you succeed in getting that plant, you will have eternal life."

Gilgamesh dove under the waters for the plant and wrested it from the bottom of the sea. Gilgamesh called the plant "The-Old-Man-Will-Be-Made-Young," and he planned to give it to the elders of Uruk and then eat it himself. Once on land, Gilgamesh journeyed for several leagues,[6] making his way toward Uruk. He saw a pool of cool water, and he went down to the water to bathe. A snake smelled the plant and rose out of the water and carried the plant away to eat it. As the snake turned to go back to the water, it shed its skin. Ever since that time, snakes have been able to cast off their skin and become young again, but death has remained the lot of humans.

Gilgamesh cried, "For whom have I labored? For whom has my heart's blood dried? I have not brought a blessing on myself. I did the lowly snake a good service."

Gilgamesh sat down and wept bitter tears. ■

6. **league.** Unit of measure

❶ *What happens when Gilgamesh tries to keep from sleeping? Why does Utnapishtim laugh?*

Words for Everyday Use

wrest (rest´) *v.*, pull or force away violently with a twisting motion

Answer to Guided Reading Question

❶ As soon as Gilgamesh is told he must strive against sleep for six days and nights, he falls asleep. Utnapishtim laughs because Gilgamesh is seeking eternal life but cannot fend off sleep.

Selection Check Test with Answers

EX. Of what city was Gilgamesh king?
Gilgamesh was king of Uruk.

1. What did Gilgamesh and Enkidu do before they became friends?
Before they became friends, Gilgamesh and Enkidu fought each other in a wrestling competition.

2. What does Ishtar ask Gilgamesh? What is Gilgamesh's response?
Ishtar asks Gilgamesh to marry her. Gilgamesh refuses, saying that Ishtar was never faithful to those whom she loved.

3. What happens to Enkidu?
Enkidu falls sick and dies.

4. To whom does Gilgamesh journey? Through what disaster did this person live?
Gilgamesh journeys to Utnapishtim who survived a great flood.

5. What happens to the plant that Gilgamesh retrieves from the bottom of the sea?
A snake eats the plant.

Vocabulary in Context

• The small child finally wrested his favorite toy free from another child.

RESPONDING TO THE SELECTION

You might also ask students to discuss what they think of the Mesopotamian gods, given their portrayal in this selection.

ANSWERS FOR REVIEWING THE SELECTION

RECALLING AND INTERPRETING

1. **Recalling.** Gilgamesh is powerful, bold, strong, and arrogant. Enkidu was created because the people of Uruk prayed for relief from Gilgamesh's oppression. Enkidu is a "wild man" who is covered with hair and lives with the animals. **Interpreting.** Gilgamesh and Enkidu fight each other because a priestess urged Enkidu to fight Gilgamesh to prove that he is more powerful. They develop such a strong friendship because they impressed each other with their strength and determination during their wrestling match.

2. **Recalling.** Ishtar asks Gilgamesh to marry her. Gilgamesh refuses, saying that Ishtar is never loyal or faithful. Ishtar is enraged and she flies to her father Anu to ask him to make the Bull of Heaven. **Interpreting.** Ishtar is impulsive and easily overcome by feelings of love and hate.

3. **Recalling.** Enkidu becomes sick and then dies. Gilgamesh decides to search for Utnapishtim. Utnapishtim is Gilgamesh's ancestor who survived the flood. He possesses eternal life. **Interpreting.** Gilgamesh is upset and terrified by Enkidu's death. Gilgamesh may decide to search for Utnapishtim because he wants to bring Enkidu back to life or so that he can achieve eternal life for himself.

4. **Recalling.** Utnapishtim tells Gilgamesh that he must prevail against sleep for six days and nights. Gilgamesh falls asleep immediately. Utnapishtim tells Gilgamesh about a plant that provides eternal life. Gilgamesh gets the plant but it is eaten by a snake. **Interpreting.** Gilgamesh's failure signifies that humans will never gain eternal life and must die. Gilgamesh is heart broken by his failure.

Responding to the Selection

With which characters in this selection did you sympathize? Why? Which characters did you admire? Did you dislike any characters? If so, whom did you dislike and why?

Reviewing the Selection

RECALLING AND INTERPRETING

1. **R** What characteristics does Gilgamesh possess? Why was Enkidu created? What characteristics does Enkidu possess?

   I Why do Gilgamesh and Enkidu fight each other? Why do you think Gilgamesh and Enkidu develop such a strong friendship?

2. **R** What does Ishtar ask Gilgamesh to do? What is his response? What is Ishtar's reaction?

   I What do Ishtar's actions tell you about her character?

3. **R** What happens to Enkidu? What does Gilgamesh decide to do after this happens? Who is Utnapishtim, and what unusual quality does he possess?

   I How does Gilgamesh feel about what happens to Enkidu? Why does Gilgamesh decide to search for Utnapishtim? Why was Utnapishtim granted this unusual quality?

4. **R** What does Utnapishtim tell Gilgamesh that he must do? What does Gilgamesh do? What does Utnapishtim give Gilgamesh as a prize? What happens to the prize?

   I What does Gilgamesh's failure signify for humans? How do you think Gilgamesh feels about failing in this endeavor?

SYNTHESIZING

5. What events in nature does this story explain? What view of humans does this story express? What view of the gods does this story express?

Understanding Literature (Questions for Discussion)

1. **Central Conflict.** A **central conflict** is the main problem or struggle in the plot of a poem, story, or play. What is the central conflict of "The Epic of Gilgamesh"? What did you find to be the most dramatic part of this conflict? What event introduces this conflict? How is this conflict resolved?
2. **Irony. Irony** is a difference between appearance and reality. An event that contradicts the expectations of the characters, the reader, or the audience of a literary work is an example of irony of situation. Although Gilgamesh is not entirely successful in his quest, Utnapishtim gives Gilgamesh the prize he desired. Why is what happens to this prize ironic? Whose expectations were contradicted?

ANSWERS FOR REVIEWING THE SELECTION (CONT.)

SYNTHESIZING

Responses will vary. Possible responses are given.

5. This story explains why snakes shed their skin and why people die. Humans can accomplish great things but they are fated to die. The gods are sometimes vengeful and have retained eternal life only for themselves.

ANSWERS FOR UNDERSTANDING LITERATURE

Responses will vary. Possible responses are given.

1. **Central Conflict.** The central conflict is Gilgamesh's struggle against death to gain eternal life for humans. *Responses will vary.* Enkidu's death introduces this conflict. The conflict is resolved when the snake eats the plant and eternal life is lost for humans.

2. **Irony.** What happens to the prize is ironic because a lowly animal reaps the benefits of Gilgamesh's struggle. Gilgamesh's and the reader's expectations were contradicted.

Writing Skills

Writing an Adventure Story

Adventure stories are tales that are full of action, suspense, and danger. The emphasis in an adventure story is on the plot. The beginning of a plot introduces the characters and the setting. The characters then become involved in a central conflict, or struggle. In an adventure story, the conflict is usually a struggle between characters or a struggle between characters and some outside force, such as a blizzard or a shipwreck at sea. The event that introduces the central conflict is known as the inciting incident. The conflict eventually reaches its climax, or its highest point of interest and suspense. Shortly after the climax is the resolution. The resolution brings the conflict to a conclusion and the story to its ending. Writers have created an enormous variety of exciting adventure stories using these standard elements of plot.

Damion Wilson

Grade 8

Jon and his brother Philip had been planning a camping trip all spring. They would take a canoe down the river to a small island, spend the night, and then canoe further downstream until they reached a point where their dad would pick them up.

At last the day they had scheduled for their trip arrived! The boys put their canoe into the river. The water was calm and not very deep. Jon was at the bow and Philip took the stern. As they pushed the boat into the gentle flow of water, they waved good-bye to their dad. They were on their own.

The boys paddled for three hours before they spotted the island. They were glad to see it because dark clouds had begun to roll in. The temperature was dropping and the wind was picking up. The boys knew they had to get their tents up and their cookfire built in a hurry. Even though it was only two o'clock in the afternoon, it looked as dark as midnight, and they knew a terrible storm was brewing.

Jon and Philip pulled their canoe on land and started to unload gear. They pitched their tent under some pine trees and started hunting for firewood. While gathering wood, Philip yelled, "Jon, our canoe. It's gone!"

Jon came running through the trees to the beach. Sure enough, there was no canoe. "It probably got swept down river," Jon said. "The wind and the

Try It Yourself

Write a short adventure story full of action, suspense, and danger. Introduce your characters and the setting in the beginning of the story. Next, introduce the central conflict with an inciting incident, and build the action up to a suspenseful climax. Finally, put an end to the struggle in a resolution. The student model shows you one student's adventure story.

◄◄ **Student Model**

Writing Skills

Introducing the Skill

Inform students that many of the world's great epics, such as *The Epic of Gilgamesh,* the *Iliad,* and the *Odyssey* focus on adventure. Point out that adventure stories allow the writer to stretch his or her imagination and provide excitement and suspense for the reader.

Previewing the Skill

Have students read the student model. Tell them that, although brief, the story contains all the major plot elements. See if students are able to identify all the major plot elements in the story.

Prewriting and Drafting

Students might also create time lines in which they write the major events of the story in the order in which they will occur. Refer students to the section on time lines in the Language Arts Survey, 1.13, "Gathering Ideas."

Evaluating and Revising

Encourage students to use all four types of revision when they are revising. Remind them to add details, examples, or transitions; to cut unnecessary or unrelated material; to replace weak parts in their writing; and to move parts of their writing to improve its organization.

Proofreading and Publishing

Students might also try exchanging stories with a partner and proofreading each other's work.

ANSWERS FOR EXAMINING THE MODEL

1. John, Philip, and their father are introduced as is the small island down river where the boys plan to camp.
2. The inciting incident is the weather turning bad. The central conflict is the boys' struggle with the weather. The climax of the story is when they discover that the canoe has been swept away.
3. The central conflict is suspenseful because the reader is concerned about the fate of the boys. The story's resolution is the forest ranger's rescue of the two boys.

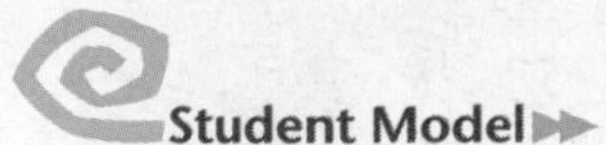

current are so much stronger with this storm coming."

"What are we going to do?" Philip asked.

"We have to make a fire to signal for help," Jon said.

Together, the boys struggled to collect enough dry wood to make a fire. The fire smoldered at first, but eventually it burned.

"No one will ever notice us way out here," Philip said. "We're doomed."

Just then, they heard the roar of an outboard motor.

"You two boys look like you're in a bit of a jam," they heard a hearty voice say.

Two hours later, the forest ranger escorted the wet and shivering boys home. "You have raised some smart and lucky sons," the forest ranger told Jon and Philip's father. "Smart, to have gotten a signal fire going. Lucky, because I happened to be in the area patrolling. That island is a popular camping site, and I was worried that someone might be stuck out there in the storm. Still, I never would have noticed you two boys if it weren't for that signal fire. Next time you plan a camping trip, watch the weather more closely."

"We will," said the boys, but they didn't think they would plan another adventure right away. For now, they were just happy to be home.

Examining the Model

1. What characters and setting are introduced in the beginning of the story?
2. What is the inciting incident of the story? What is the central conflict? What is the story's climax?
3. What made the central conflict suspenseful? What is the story's resolution?

Prewriting and Drafting

1. Think of possible characters and situations for your adventure. Read the Language Arts Survey, 1.13, "Gathering Ideas." Freewrite for several minutes until you come up with a variety of ideas.
2. Read over your ideas. Choose the one that you think will be most exciting and suspenseful for your audience.
3. Decide on your characters and a setting. Who will be involved, and how will they respond in a difficult situation? What setting will be most exciting and interesting to your audience?
4. Think about what will happen in your story. Make a story map in which you list the inciting incident, central conflict, climax, and resolution to your story.
5. Review the Language Arts Survey, 1.16, "Drafting." Write a discovery draft, referring to your story notes.

Evaluating and Revising

1. Review the Language Arts Survey, 1.17, "Self-Evaluation." Read your story silently. Are all the plot elements present? Do you feel there is enough tension? Is there a lot of action? Make notes about what might be improved in your story.
2. Review the Language Arts Survey, 1.18, "Peer Evaluation." Exchange adventure stories with a classmate. As you read each other's work ask yourselves the following questions:
   a. Is the story easy to follow?
   b. Are all the plot elements present? Does one event follow logically from the previous event?
   c. Does the story contain enough action? enough suspense?
3. Review the Language Arts Survey, 1.19, "Four Types of Revision." Using your notes and those of your classmate, revise your draft. If you make major revisions, read your story through again to make sure that it still makes sense.

Proofreading and Publishing

1. Proofread your revised draft. Make a clean copy and proofread again. Refer to the Language Arts Survey, 1.22, "A Proofreading Checklist."
2. Share your adventure story with your classmates in one of these ways:
   a. Hold a storytelling session in which you read aloud your adventure stories. Discuss which adventure stories were most exciting, most action-packed, most suspenseful, and most creative. Discuss how the writers achieved these effects.
   b. Make copies of the adventure stories and bind them as an anthology to share with other classes.

Save your work in your writing portfolio.

ANALYTIC SCALE FOR WRITING SKILLS

Assign a score from 1 to 25 for each grading criterion below.

ADVENTURE STORY

- **Content/Unity.** The adventure story is full of action, danger, and suspense, and it contains an introduction, a central conflict, an inciting incident, a climax, and a resolution.
- **Organization/Coherence.** The adventure story should be written in a logical and sensible order such as chronological order.
- **Language/Style.** The adventure story uses vivid and precise nouns, verbs, and modifiers.
- **Conventions.** The adventure story avoids errors in spelling, grammar, usage, mechanics, and manuscript form.

GOALS/OBJECTIVES

Studying this lesson will enable students to
- enjoy an Egyptian myth
- briefly explain how the geography of Egypt affected ancient Egyptians' world view
- explain how the Egyptians felt about inconsistencies in their mythology
- define *inciting incident* and *motive* and identify these techniques in works that they read
- use dictionaries to find information

ADDITIONAL RESOURCES

READER'S GUIDE
- Selection Worksheet, 6.2

ASSESSMENT PORTFOLIO
- Selection Check Test, 2.6.3
- Selection Test, 2.6.4

PRONUNCIATION EXERCISE
- Grade 7 Audiocassette, Side B, Track 29

CROSS-CURRICULAR CONNECTIONS

GEOGRAPHY AND SOCIAL STUDIES

Students might find photographs or illustrations of the Egyptian landscape in encyclopedias, books, or magazines, and bring them into class to share. Other students might locate photographs of Egyptian artifacts and monuments to share with the class.

SOCIAL STUDIES

Students might draw or paint pictures of the different Egyptian explanations of how the heavens are held apart from the earth.

Prereading

EGYPT

"The Secret Name of Ra"

Anonymous, retold by Geraldine Harris

Cross-curricular Connections

Geography and Social Studies. The landscape of Egypt is one of remarkable contrast. Along the banks of the Nile River, the land is rich, green, and teeming with life. Beyond this narrow green strip lies a wasteland of sand and rock. The Nile floods at regular intervals, covering the land that lies alongside the river with rich silt and mud in which crops thrive. This annual flooding that made life possible in Egypt also gave ancient Egyptians a heightened awareness of the cycle of life and death. When the river was at its annual low point, it seemed that life along the river was coming to an end. When the river flooded, life was renewed.

Egyptians believed that the sun was born each day as it rose in the east and died each day as it set in the west. Then the sun traveled into the underworld during the night. Accordingly, Egyptians believed that the contrast between day and night was like the contrast between life and death. The Egyptians buried their dead to the west of the Nile, in the land of the setting sun, and believed that the souls of the dead then traveled, like the sun, to the underworld. Many gods in Egyptian myth die or come close to death even though they are immortal. In the selection you are about to read, Ra, the sun god, comes close to death.

Social Studies. Ancient Egyptians accepted many different explanations of things as equally true and possible. For example, they believed three different explanations of heaven all at the same time: that it was held up by four pillars, that it was the goddess Nut who crouched over the earth, and that it was a cow. Similarly, they believed that the Pharaoh was the son of Ra. They also believed, however, that he was the living incarnation of Horus, the son of Isis and Osiris. When the Pharaoh died, he became the incarnation of Osiris, god of the underworld.

As You Read

"The Secret Name of Ra" is about many gods with unusual appearances. In your journal, make a chart like the one below. As you read, write the names of the gods, describe their appearances, and add other details that you learn about them, such as where they live or what their special powers or weaknesses are.

GOD	APPEARANCE	OTHER DETAILS
Ra	crowned man	many names

AS YOU READ

Students may include the following details in their charts: Ra, scarab pushing a ball of dung, sole creator, has secret name; Isis, Mistress of Magic, very wise; Horus, falcon-headed, son of Isis, will have Ra's throne; Wadjet, cobra goddess; Sobek, crocodile-headed; Selkis, scorpion goddess; Anubis, the jackal, guardian of the dead; Nekhbet, vulture goddess; Neith, warlike; Bastet, cat-headed, gentle; Sekhmet, lion-headed, fierce; Ptah, god of crafts; Onuris, divine huntsman; Khnum, ram-headed, his wife is Anukis, Satis is his daughter; Thoth, cunning; Seshat, goddess of writing, wise; Renenutet, snake-headed, goddess of the harvest; Taweret, monstrous, goddess of birth.

READER'S JOURNAL

What kinds of tricks have you played on others? Were your tricks used to get something from someone? What kinds of tricks have others played on you? How does it feel to be tricked? Is tricking someone a good way to get something you want? Why, or why not? Write about these questions in your journal.

"The Secret Name of Ra"

ANONYMOUS, RETOLD BY GERALDINE HARRIS

Ra, the Sole Creator was visible to the people of Egypt as the disc of the sun, but they knew him in many other forms. He could appear as a crowned man, a falcon or a man with a falcon's head and, as the scarab beetle,[1] pushes a round ball of dung in front of it, the Egyptians pictured Ra as a scarab pushing the sun across the sky. In caverns deep below the earth were hidden another seventy-five forms of Ra: mysterious beings with mummified bodies[2] and heads consisting of birds or snakes, feathers or flowers. The names of Ra were as numerous as his forms; he was the Shining One, The Hidden One, The Renewer of the Earth, The Wind in the Souls, The Exalted One, but there was one name of the Sun God which had not been spoken since time began. To know this secret name of Ra was to have power over him and over the world that he had created.

Isis longed for such a power. She had dreamed that one day she would have a marvellous falcon-headed son called Horus and she wanted the throne of Ra to give to her child. Isis was the Mistress of Magic, wiser than millions of men, but she knew that nothing in creation was powerful enough to harm its creator. Her only chance was to turn the power of Ra against himself and at last Isis thought of a cruel and cunning plan. Every day the Sun God walked through his kingdom, attended by a crowd of spirits and lesser deities, but Ra was growing old. His eyes were dim, his step no longer firm and he had even begun to drivel.

One morning Isis mingled with a group of minor goddesses and followed behind the King of the Gods.

1. **scarab beetle.** Black-winged beetle held sacred by ancient Egyptians

2. **mummified bodies.** Bodies that have been preserved by removing the internal organs and adding a special substance to keep the body from disintegrating

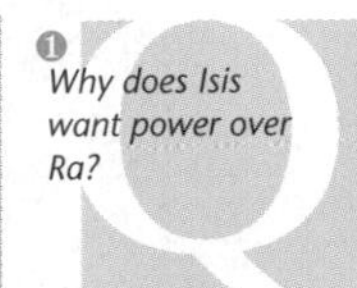

❶ *Why does Isis want power over Ra?*

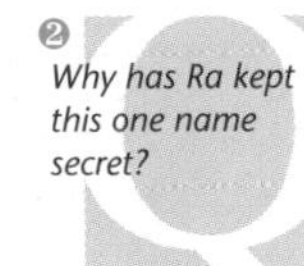

❷ *Why has Ra kept this one name secret?*

WORDS FOR EVERYDAY USE

sole (sōl) *adj.*, only
disc (disk) *n.*, circle-shaped object
cav • ern (kav´ərn) *n.*, large cave
ex • alt (eg zôlt´) *v.*, praise; glorify; worship
cun •ning (kun´iŋ) *adj.*, clever; sly; crafty
de • i • ty (dē´ə tē) *n.*, god or goddess
driv • el (driv´əl) *v.*, drool

READER'S JOURNAL

You might also ask students to consider how they feel about people who trick others to get what they want. Ask them the following questions: If a person tricks someone to get something from him or her, does this person have a right to what he or she gets? Why, or why not?

SPELLING AND VOCABULARY WORDS FROM THE SELECTION

abyss	envoy
betray	exalt
cavern	quiver
cunning	sole
deity	summon
disc	virile
drivel	

ANSWERS TO GUIDED READING QUESTIONS

❶ Isis wants power over Ra because she wants to give his throne to the son, Horus, that she dreams she will have.

❷ Ra has kept this one name a secret because if someone discovers this name that person will have power over Ra and the world he created.

SUPPORT FOR LEP STUDENTS

PRONUNCIATIONS OF PROPER NOUNS AND ADJECTIVES

I • sis (ī´sis) n.
Ho • rus (hō´rəs) n.
O • si •ris (ō si´ris) n.
A • nu •bis (ə no͞o´bis) n.
Sekh • met (sek´met) n.
Ptah (p´tä) n.

ADDITIONAL VOCABULARY

clod—lump
wretched—very inferior

VOCABULARY IN CONTEXT

- Fishing was Lucrecia's sole interest.
- The full moon appeared to be a luminous disc in the sky.
- During the winter the bear hibernated in a cavern.
- People in ancient Babylon exalted their city-god Marduk.
- Foxes are known for their cunning ability to escape from hunters.
- Isis was one of the deities worshiped by the ancient Egyptians.
- When our dog knows it is dinner time it hungrily drivels.

Additional Questions and Activities

Ask students the following questions: Why does Isis use Ra's saliva to create the serpent? What does Ra say about the thing that has wounded him? What emotions does Ra express about being injured?

ANSWERS

Isis used Ra's saliva because nothing in creation is powerful enough to harm Ra, the creator, so Isis must use Ra's own power against him. Ra says that the thing that has wounded him is deadly, that he knows that he did not create it, and that he does not think any of the gods would do such a thing to him. Ra expresses great surprise.

She watched the face of Ra until she saw his saliva drip onto a clod of earth. When she was sure that no-one was taking any notice of her, she scooped up the earth and carried it away. Isis mixed the earth with the saliva of Ra to form clay and modelled a wicked-looking serpent. Through the hours of darkness she whispered spells over the clay serpent as it lay lifeless in her hands. Then the cunning goddess carried it to a crossroads on the route which the Sun God always took. She hid the serpent in the long grass and returned to her palace.

The next day Ra came walking through his kingdom with the spirits and lesser deities crowding behind him. When he approached the crossroads, the spells of Isis began to work and the clay serpent quivered into life. As the Sun God passed, it bit him in the ankle and crumbled back into earth. Ra gave a scream that was heard through all creation.

His jaws chattered and his limbs shook as the poison flooded through him like a rising Nile. "I have been wounded by something deadly" whispered Ra. "I know that in my heart, though my eyes cannot see it. Whatever it was, I, the Lord of Creation, did not make it. I am sure that none of you would have done such a terrible thing to me, but I have never felt such pain! How can this have happened to me? I am the Sole Creator, the child of the watery abyss. I am the god with a thousand names, but my secret name was only spoken

Words for Everyday Use

qui • ver (kwiv´ər) *v.,* shake or tremble

a • byss (ə bis´) *n.,* anything too deep for measurement; ocean depths

Vocabulary in Context

- The thought of going up to the attic alone made the small child quiver with fear.
- The hole was so deep that it almost seemed as if it were a bottomless abyss.

once, before time began. Then it was hidden in my body so that no-one should ever learn it and be able to work spells against me. Yet as I walked through my kingdom something struck at me and now my heart is on fire and my limbs shake. Send for the Ennead! Send for my children! They are wise in magic and their knowledge pierces heaven."

Messengers hurried to the great gods and from the four pillars of the world came the Ennead: Shu and Tefenet, Geb and Nut, Seth and Osiris, Isis and Nephthys. Envoys traveled the land and the sky and the watery abyss to summon all the deities created by Ra. From the marshes came frog-headed Heket, Wadjet the cobra goddess and the fearsome god, crocodile-headed Sobek. From the deserts came fiery Selkis, the scorpion goddess, Anubis the jackal, the guardian of the dead and Nekhbet the vulture goddess. From the cities of the north came war-like Neith, gentle cat-headed Bastet, fierce lion headed Sekhmet and Ptah the god of crafts. From the cities of the south came Onuris, the divine huntsman and ram-headed Khnum with Anukis his wife and Satis his daughter. Cunning Thoth and wise Seshat, goddess of writing; virile Min and snake-headed Renenutet, goddess of the harvest, kindly Meskhenet and monstrous Taweret, goddesses of birth—all of them were summoned to the side of Ra.

The gods and goddesses gathered around the Sun God, weeping and wailing, afraid that he was going to die. Isis stood among them beating her breast and pretending to be as distressed and bewildered as all the other frightened deities.

"Father of All," she began, "whatever is the matter? Has some snake bitten you? Has some wretched creature dared to strike at his Creator? Few of the gods can compare with me in wisdom and I am the Mistress of Magic. If you will let me help you, I'm sure that I can cure you."

Ra was grateful to Isis and told her all that had happened. "Now I am colder than water and hotter than fire," complained the Sun God. "My eyes darken. I cannot see the sky and my body is soaked by the sweat of fever."

"Tell me your full name," said cunning Isis. "Then I can use it in my spells. Without that knowledge the greatest of magicians cannot help you."

"I am the maker of heaven and earth," said Ra. "I made the heights and the depths, I set horizons at east and west and established the gods in their glory. When I open my eyes it is light; when I close them it is dark. The mighty Nile floods at my command. The gods do not know my true name but I am the maker of time, the giver of festivals. I spark the fire of life. At dawn I rise as Khepri, the scarab and sail across the sky in the Boat of Millions of Years. At noon I blaze in the heavens as Ra and at evening I am Ra-atum, the setting sun."

"We know all that," said Isis. "If I am to find a spell to drive out this poi-

1 How do the gods and goddesses act when their creator is injured? How does Isis act?

2 Why does Isis say she needs to know Ra's secret name?

Words for Everyday Use

- **en • voy** (än´voi´) *n.,* messenger
- **sum • mon** (sum´ən) *v.,* call together; order to appear
- **vir • ile** (vir´əl) *adj.,* having stength; forceful
- **be • tray** (bē trā´) *v.,* disclose secret information

Answers to Guided Reading Questions

1 The gods weep and wail with concern when their creator is injured. Isis pretends to be distressed and bewildered.

2 Isis says that she needs to know Ra's secret name to use in her spells to cure him.

Historical Note

Inform students that the Ennead were the supreme council of gods and the family of the sun god Ra. There were nine members of the Ennead: the sun god and four couples—Shu, the god of air; Tefnut, goddess of moisture; Geb, the god of earth; Nut, the goddess of the sky; Osiris, god of the underworld and fertility; Isis, goddess of fertility and children; Seth, god of Upper Egypt, deserts, and storms; and Nephthys, Seth's wife.

You might also point out to students that Isis is not always a mischievous, scheming figure in Egyptian mythology. Egyptian gods seldom have consistent roles. For example, while Seth is often depicted as the evil enemy of Osiris and Horus, he also appears as a good god. In other myths, Isis appears as a loving wife who goes to great lengths to save her husband. Just like humans, the Egyptian gods had many different sides to their characters.

Vocabulary in Context

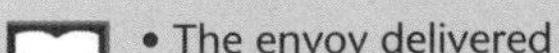

- The envoy delivered the king's message to the ruler of the distant land.
- The sick man summoned a doctor to his home.
- Michelangelo's "David" represents the neoclassic ideal of perfect, virile young manhood.
- Raymond was angry with Andrea for betraying the secret he had shared with her.

Answer to Guided Reading Question

❶ Isis is filled with joy by her success. She knows that her son Horus will one day sit on the throne of Egypt and wield the power of Ra.

Selection Check Test with Answers

EX. In this myth, who is the "Sole Creator"?
In this myth, Ra is the Sole Creator.

1. In what way could someone gain power over Ra?
Someone could gain power over Ra by discovering his secret name.

2. Who wants to gain power over Ra?
Isis wants to gain power over Ra.

3. What creature bites Ra? Of what is this creature made?
A serpent bites Ra. The creature is made of Ra's saliva and earth.

4. What does Isis say she needs to know to cure Ra?
Isis says that she needs to know Ra's secret name.

5. With whom does Ra say that Isis can share his secret name?
Ra says that in time Isis can share his secret name with her son.

son, I will have to use your secret name. Say your name and live."

"My secret name was given to me so that I could sit at ease," moaned Ra, "and fear no living creature. How can I give it away?"

Isis said nothing and knelt beside the Sun God while his pain mounted. When it became unbearable, Ra ordered the other gods to stand back while he whispered his secret name to Isis. "Now the power of the secret name has passed from my heart to your heart," said Ra wearily. "In time you can give it to your son, but warn him never to betray the secret!"

How does Isis feel about her success? What does she know will happen? ❶

Isis nodded and began to chant a great spell that drove the poison out of the limbs of Ra and he rose up stronger than before. The Sun God returned to the Boat of Millions of Years and Isis shouted for joy at the success of her plan. She knew now that one day Horus her son would sit on the throne of Egypt and wield the power of Ra. ■

About the Author

Geraldine Harris has a strong interest in ancient Egypt. She studied Egyptology at Cambridge University in England and has written a book on Egyptian religion. She has written two novels for young people, *White Cranes Castle* and *The Prince of the Godborn.* She has also given lectures on the folklore and mythology of various cultures.

Responding to the Selection

How do you feel about the way Isis went about discovering Ra's secret name? Do you admire her? Why, or why not? Would you have behaved differently if you had been Isis? How do you think Ra would have responded if Isis had asked him for his secret name and told him why she wanted it?

Reviewing the Selection

Recalling and Interpreting

1. **R** What are some of the forms and names Ra took? What is the one thing that could take away this god's power? What is beginning to happen to Ra?

   I Is Ra omnipotent, or all-powerful? Why, or why not? Does Ra seem to be a powerful god, or a figure of fun in this myth?

2. **R** Who is Isis? What dream has she had? What does she want from Ra?

   I What does Isis's plan reveal about her character? Why? What will succeeding at this plan do for her?

3. **R** What does Isis create to harm Ra? From what does she create it? What does Isis say Ra must do in order to be cured?

   I What does the fact that the gods strive against each other make you think of them? Which god seems to be most powerful? most clever? What effect do you think seeing a god at his or her weakest, or most human, had on his or her worshippers?

4. **R** What happens when Ra reveals his secret name? What reaction does Isis have?

   I Do you think that this myth marks a shifting of the balance of power among the gods? Why, or why not?

Synthesizing

5. The gods and goddesses of ancient Egypt possessed both human and divine qualities. What human qualities do Ra and Isis have? What god-like qualities do they have? With which qualities do you most identify? Which qualities do you most admire?

Understanding Literature (Questions for Discussion)

1. **Inciting Incident.** The **inciting incident** is the event that introduces the central conflict, or struggle, in a poem, story, or play. What is the inciting incident in "The Secret Name of Ra"? Does the inciting incident make you sympathize with one character more than another? If so, with which character do you sympathize and why?
2. **Motive.** A **motive** is a reason for acting in a certain way. What is Isis's motive for harming Ra? Do you think her motive can be justified? Why, or why not?

Responding to the Selection

Encourage students to talk about ambition. When is ambition good? When can it lead to wrongdoing?

Answers for Reviewing the Selection

RECALLING AND INTERPRETING

1. **Recalling.** Ra took the form of a crowned man, a falcon, a falcon-headed man, and a scarab. He took the names the Shining One, the Hidden One, The Renewer of the Earth, The Wind in the Souls, and the Exalted One. Knowing Ra's secret name could take away his power. Ra is beginning to grow old. **Interpreting.** Students may say that Ra is not omnipotent because he can grow old and he has a secret weakness. Students may say he seems to be a figure of fun to a certain extent.
2. **Recalling.** Isis is the wise Mistress of Magic. She has dreamed that she will have a falcon-headed son called Horus. She wants to know Ra's secret name so that she can give the throne of Ra to Horus. **Interpreting.** Students may say that Isis's plan reveals her ambition and her ruthlessness because she is willing to trick Ra and inflict pain on him to get her way. Her son will be the most powerful god.
3. **Recalling.** Isis creates a serpent from Ra's saliva and earth. Isis says that Ra must reveal his secret name to her to be cured. **Interpreting.** Students may say that the gods seem similar to ambitious people. *Responses will vary.* Students may say that Isis seems most clever. Students may say that human worshippers could identify with these gods that shared human weakness but that such a view probably did not promote fear or awe of the gods.
4. **Recalling.** Isis chants a spell and Ra is cured and is "stronger than before." Isis shouts with triumphant joy. **Interpreting.** *Responses will vary.* Students may say that Isis and her future son seem to have gained power and Ra seems to have lost power.

SYNTHESIZING

Responses will vary. Possible responses are given.

5. Ra can grow old and is foolish enough to be tricked. Isis is ruthless and ambitious. They are both very powerful.

Answers for Understanding Literature

Responses will vary. Possible responses are given.

1. **Inciting Incident.** The inciting incident is Isis's creating a serpent to harm Ra. Students may say that this action made them sympathize with Ra because he was the victim of a scheme.
2. **Motive.** Isis's motive is to gain power for her future son Horus. Students may say that ambition is not an adequate motive for harming another.

Study and Research Skills

Introducing the Skill

Remind students that dictionaries can help them with pronunciation, grammar, and word history, as well as with definitions of words. Have students review the Language Arts Survey, 4.15, "Using a Dictionary."

Previewing the Skill

Have students read the teaching in the Study and Research Skills lesson. Show students an example of a pronunciation key in a dictionary, as well as a chart that explains abbreviations in a dictionary. You might review both charts with students to make sure they understand how to use them.

Practicing the Skill

After students are familiar with the parts of a dictionary entry, have them do the Try It Yourself exercise.

Reviewing the Skill

Review the answers to the Try It Yourself exercise as a class. If students need additional practice have them do the Try It Yourself exercise in the Language Arts Survey, 4.15, "Using a Dictionary."

Study and Research Skills

Using Dictionaries

Of all the reference works, the one you will probably use most often is the dictionary. While a dictionary is a good tool for finding the meanings of words, a dictionary can also tell you other things about the English language, such as how to pronounce each word, where each word comes from, and what part of speech each word is. Knowing how to use a dictionary can help you to locate information about words quickly and easily.

A dictionary lists words in alphabetical order. Guide words are found at the top of each entry page in the dictionary. They are the first and last words on the page. All the words on the page will be listed alphabetically between the two guide words. The parts of a dictionary entry are described below.

PARTS OF A DICTIONARY ENTRY	
entry word	The words defined in a dictionary are called the entry words. Entry words are divided into syllables.
pronunciation	The pronunciation for each word is indicated by symbols that show how letters are pronounced. You will find a short key to these symbols at the bottom of each page in the dictionary. You will find a complete pronunciation key at the beginning of the dictionary.
part of speech	A dictionary entry also tells a word's part of speech. You will find the part of speech abbreviated after the pronunciation. Some common abbreviations for the parts of speech are adj. = adjective, n. = noun, adv. = adverb, prep. = preposition, conj. = conjunction, v. = verb, interj. = interjection.
origin and history	The origin and history of a word may be included in a dictionary entry. Most dictionaries include word origins in brackets after the part of speech. These word origins often include abbreviations. A chart explaining the abbreviations can be found at the beginning of the dictionary.
definitions	Definitions, or meanings, for the entry word follow the pronunciation, part of speech, and origin. All of a word's definitions will be included and listed by number, often with the most common usage first.

Review the dictionary entries below, paying close attention to all the parts of the entries.

mull[1] (mul) ***vt., vi.*** [ME *mullen,* to grind < *mul,* dust < OE *myl,* dust: for IE base see MOLD[3]] to cogitate or ponder: usually with *over*

mull[2] (mul) ***vt.*** [< ?] to heat, sweeten, and flavor with spices (a beverage)

mul•lein (mul'in) ***n.*** [ME *moleyne* < OFr *moleine* < *mol,* soft < L *mollis:* see MOLLIFY] any of a genus of tall plants of the figwort family, with spikes of yellow, lavender, or white flowers

mul•let (mul'it) ***n.,*** pl. **-lets** or **-let** [ME *molet* < OFr *mulet,* dim. < L *mullus,* red mullet < Gr *myllos,* kind of fish] **1** Any of a family (Mugilidae) of edible, spiny-finned percoid fishes, both freshwater and marine, having a small mouth and feeble teeth; esp. a striped species (*Mugil cephalus*) **2** any goatfish; esp., a species (*Mullus auratus*) with reddish or golden scales

mul•li•gan stew (mul'i-gən) [prob. after pers. name *Mulligan*] ***n.*** a stew made of odd bits of meat and vegetables, esp. as prepared by hobos: also **mulligan**

mum•ble (mum'bəl) ***vt., vi.*** **-bled, -bling** [ME *momelen,* like Ger *mummeln,* Du *mommelen,* of echoic orig.] **1** to speak or say indistinctly and in a low voice, as with the mouth partly closed; mutter **2** [Rare] to chew gently and ineffectively, as with toothless gums —**n.,** a mumbled sound or utterance —SYN. murmur —**mum'bler** ***n.*** —**mumblingly** ***adv.***

Try It Yourself

Answer these questions using the information provided in the dictionary entries above.

1. What inflected forms (or changed forms of a verb or noun) are given for *mumble*?
2. How many syllables are there in *mullein*?
3. What part of speech is *mullein*?
4. From what language did *mullet* originally come?
5. From what language did *mull*[1] come?
6. What is the meaning of *mull*[2]?
7. What is the meaning of *mull*[1]?
8. What is the meaning of *mulligan stew*?
9. What is the etymology of the word *mumble*?
10. From where does the word *mulligan* come?

Answers for Try It Yourself

1. The inflected forms are *mumbled, mumbling.*
2. There are two syllables in *mullein.*
3. *Mullein* is a noun.
4. *Mullet* came from the Greek word *myllos.*
5. *Mull*[1] came from Old English.
6. *Mull*[2] means "to hear, sweeten, and flavor with spices (a beverage)."
7. *Mull*[1] means "to cogitate or ponder."
8. *Mulligan stew* means "a stew made of odd bits of meat and vegetables."
9. The word *mumble* comes from the Middle English word *momelen,* which is similar to the German word *mummeln* and the Dutch word *mommelen.* These words were of echoic origin.
10. The word *mulligan* probably comes from the personal name *Mulligan.*

GOALS/OBJECTIVES

Studying this lesson will enable students to

- enjoy a traditional Hindu story
- briefly explain some traditional Hindu beliefs
- define *simile* and *symbol* and recognize the use of these techniques in works that they read
- define *internal conflict* and identify the internal conflict in a story
- understand the different ways words enter the English language

ADDITIONAL RESOURCES

READER'S GUIDE

- Selection Worksheet, 6.3

ASSESSMENT PORTFOLIO

- Selection Check Test, 2.6.5
- Selection Test, 2.6.6

PRONUNCIATION EXERCISE

- Grade 7 Audiocassette, Side B, Track 30

CROSS-CURRICULAR CONNECTIONS

SOCIAL STUDIES

Ask students to write two paragraphs. The first should be written from the point of view of a person of a high caste. Students should imagine that they are members of one of the highest castes and write about how they feel about karma, or fate, and darma, or duty. The second paragraph should be written from the point of view of a person of the lowest, or "untouchable," caste. Students should imagine that they are members of this less fortunate caste and write about how they feel about fate and their duties.

Prereading

INDIA

"The Instruction of Indra," from *The Power of Myth*

Anonymous, retold by Joseph Campbell (with Bill Moyers)

Cross-curricular Connection

Social Studies. In traditional Hindu belief, the material world is viewed as the goddess Maya, whose name can be understood as meaning "the world illusion." All worldly goods and possessions are illusions that soon pass away. What does not pass away is the soul, which is part of Brahma, creator of the universe. Hinduism teaches that one should cultivate detachment from the things of this world to gain oneness with Brahma and escape the cycle of rebirth. Westerners have often criticized this Hindu theory of detachment, viewing the poverty that has beset India for centuries as a consequence of a theology that asks people to turn away from the world.

Closely connected to the Hindu ideal of detachment is the concept of karma, or fate. Hindus view all things as interconnected. The actions that one takes in one life create consequences that must be lived out in later lives. In the past, many Hindus believed that if one were born into a low caste, this was a matter of one's karma, an inescapable destiny. Therefore, people in India could not rise in caste as a person in the West might, through industriousness, rise from the lower class to the middle class.

Balancing the concept of karma is the Hindu idea of darma, or duty. Krishna, in the *Bhagavad-Gita,* taught that a proper life did not involve withdrawal from action in the world. Instead, according to Krishna, one should practice one's darma. One should continue to act in the world, carrying out one's duties, without becoming emotionally dependent on the worldly outcomes of one's actions. This is the lesson taught to Indra in the following myth, retold by Joseph Campbell, a famous scholar of world mythologies.

As You Read

In **"The Instruction of Indra,"** the god Indra learns several lessons. In each case, he acts differently after he learns the lesson. Make a chart like the one below. As you read, list the lessons that Indra learns and the actions that he decides to take as a result.

LESSON LEARNED	CONSEQUENCE
that he, Indra is very powerful	**decides to build a palace worthy of such a great creature as he**

AS YOU READ

Students may include the following details in their charts: *lesson learned*—that there have been Indras before him, *consequence*—knows that he is not as powerful as he had thought; *lesson learned*—that Indras are reincarnated as lowly ants when they become too prideful, *consequence*—knows that he shall not be powerful forever; *lesson learned*—that many Indras have been destroyed and that life is short, *consequence*—realizes there is no point to building a palace and decides to become a yogi; *lesson learned*—that he should accept his position and be happy with his life, *consequence*—realizes that his job is important and that he must live his life.

READER'S JOURNAL

Have you ever known someone who was terribly vain or boastful? What makes vanity and boastfulness so unpleasant? How should one feel and act, instead, about one's own positive qualities or accomplishments? Write about these questions in your journal.

"The Instruction of Indra"

ANONYMOUS, RETOLD BY JOSEPH CAMPBELL

There is a wonderful story in one of the Upanishads[1] about the god Indra.[2] Now, it happened at this time that a great monster had enclosed all the waters of the earth, so there was a terrible drought, and the world was in a very bad condition. It took Indra quite a while to realize that he had a box of thunderbolts and that all he had to do was drop a thunderbolt on the monster and blow him up. When he did that, the waters flowed, and the world was refreshed and Indra said, "What a great boy am I."

So, thinking, "What a great boy am I," Indra goes up to the cosmic mountain, which is the central mountain of the world, and decides to build a palace worthy of such as he. The main carpenter of the gods goes to work on it, and in very quick order he gets the palace into pretty good condition.

But every time Indra comes to inspect it, he has bigger ideas about how splendid and grandiose the palace should be. Finally, the carpenter says, "My god, we are both immortal, and there is no end to his desires. I am caught for eternity." So he decides to go to Brahma, the creator god, and complain.

Brahma sits on a lotus,[3] the symbol of divine energy and divine grace. The lotus grows from the navel of Vishnu, who is the sleeping god, whose dream is the universe. So the carpenter comes to the edge of the great lotus pond of the universe and tells his story to Brahma. Brahma says, "You go home. I will fix this up." Brahma gets off his lotus and kneels down to address sleeping Vishnu. Vishnu just makes a gesture and says something

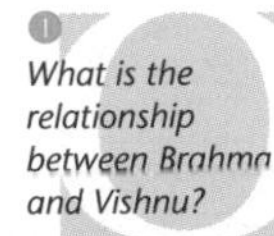

❶ *What is the relationship between Brahma and Vishnu?*

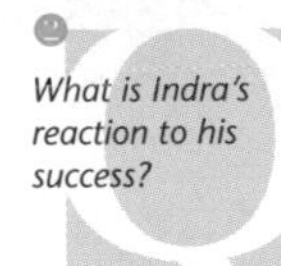

❷ *What is Indra's reaction to his success?*

1. **Upanishads.** Indian philosophical and religious writings
2. **Indra.** Chief god of the early Aryan religion, later absorbed into Hinduism
3. **lotus.** Pink or white waterlily used as a religious symbol in Hinduism

WORDS FOR EVERYDAY USE

drought (drout) *n.*, period of dry weather; lack of rain
cos • mic (käz´mik) *adj.*, relating to the universe as a whole
gran • di • ose (gran´dē ōs´) *adj.*, magnificent; grand
e • ter • ni • ty (ē tʉr´nə tē) *n.*, time without beginning or end

READER'S JOURNAL

Encourage students to describe their own reactions to boastful or vain people. Ask them to think about a time when they behaved boastfully or vainly. In what way did people react to their behavior? In what way might they behave if they were in the same situation again?

SPELLING AND VOCABULARY WORDS FROM THE SELECTION

constellation	illumination
cosmic	infinite
crotchety	manifestation
disillusion	mediate
drought	mission
eternity	privilege
grandiose	radiantly

ANSWERS TO GUIDED READING QUESTIONS

❶ Brahma is the symbol of divine energy and grace who sits on a lotus which comes from the navel of the sleeping god Vishnu who is dreaming of the universe.

❷ Indra thinks "What a great boy am I" and decides to a build a palace worthy of his magnificence.

SUPPORT FOR LEP STUDENTS

PRONUNCIATIONS OF PROPER NOUNS AND ADJECTIVES

In • dra (in´ drə) n
Brah • ma (brä´ mə) n
Vish • nu (vish´ nōō) n
Shi • va (shē´ və) n

ADDITIONAL VOCABULARY

parasol—lightweight umbrella
splendid—magnificent; gorgeous

COLLOQUIALISMS

shot—ruined or worn out

VOCABULARY IN CONTEXT

- There was a period of drought and the crops withered in the sun.
- In ancient Greek mythology, the cosmic center of the gods was Mt. Olympus.
- The eccentric millionaire planned to build a sprawling, grandiose pink mansion.
- The hour spent waiting in the doctor's office seemed to drag on for an eternity.

Answer to Guided Reading Question

❶ The boy says "Indras before you," and Indra was not aware that there were any Indras before him.

Additional Questions and Activities

Ask students the following questions: What does Vishnu say when Brahma tells him about the problem with Indra? Why do you think Vishnu calls Brahma "fly?" What does this comparison indicate about the relationship between Vishnu and Brahma? How long does the life of a Brahma last?

ANSWERS

Vishnu says, "Listen, fly, something is going to happen." Students may say that Vishnu calls Brahma "fly" because Brahma is insignificant compared to Vishnu. This comparison indicates that a Brahma is just a small part of Vishnu's universe. The life of a Brahma lasts four hundred and thirty-two thousand years.

like, "Listen, fly, something is going to happen."

Next morning, at the gate of the palace that is being built, there appears a beautiful blue-black boy with a lot of children around him, just admiring his beauty. The porter at the gate of the new palace goes running to Indra, and Indra says, "Well, bring in the boy." The boy is brought in, and Indra, the king god, sitting on his throne, says, "Young man, welcome. And what brings you to my palace?"

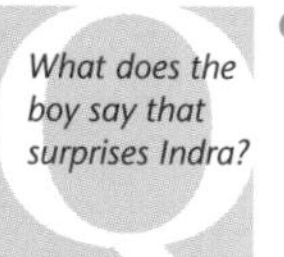

What does the boy say that surprises Indra?

❶ "Well," says the boy with a voice like thunder rolling on the horizon, "I have been told that you are building such a palace as no Indra before you ever built."

And Indra says, "Indras before me, young man—what are you talking about?"

The boy says, "Indras before you. I have seen them come and go, come and go. Just think, Vishnu sleeps in the cosmic ocean, and the lotus of the universe grows from his navel. On the lotus sits Brahma, the creator. Brahma opens his eyes, and a world comes into being, governed by an Indra. Brahma closes his eyes, and a world goes out of being. The life of a Brahma is four hundred and thirty-two thousand years. When he dies, the lotus goes back, and another lotus is formed, and another Brahma. Then think of the galaxies beyond galaxies in infinite

Words for Everyday Use

in • fi • nite (in′fə nit) *adj.,* endless

Vocabulary in Context

• Some people treat our natural resources as if they were infinite, when in actuality our resources are quite limited.

space, each a lotus, with a Brahma sitting on it, opening his eyes, closing his eyes. And Indras? There may be wise men in your court who would volunteer to count the drops of water in the oceans of the world or the grains of sand on the beaches, but no one would count those Brahmin, let alone those Indras."

While the boy is talking, an army of ants parades across the floor. The boy laughs when he sees them, and Indra's hair stands on end, and he says to the boy, "Why do you laugh?"

The boy answers, "Don't ask unless you are willing to be hurt."

Indra says, "I ask. Teach." (That, by the way, is a good Oriental idea: you don't teach until you are asked. You don't force your mission down people's throats.)

And so the boy points to the ants and says, "Former Indras all. Through many lifetimes they rise from the lowest conditions to highest illumination. And then they drop their thunderbolt on a monster, and they think, 'What a good boy am I.' And down they go again."

While the boy is talking, a crotchety old yogi[4] comes into the palace with a banana leaf parasol. He is naked except for a loincloth,[5] and on his chest is a little disk of hair, and half the hairs in the middle have all dropped out.

The boy greets him and asks him just what Indra was about to ask. "Old man, what is your name? Where do you come from? Where is your family? Where is your house? And what is the meaning of this curious constellation of hair on your chest?"

"Well," says the old fella, "my name is Hairy. I don't have a house. Life is too short for that. I just have this parasol. I don't have a family. I just meditate on Vishnu's feet, and think of eternity, and how passing time is. You know, every time an Indra dies, a world disappears—these things just flash by like that. Every time an Indra dies, one hair drops out of this circle on my chest. Half the hairs are gone now. Pretty soon they will all be gone. Life is short. Why build a house?"

Then the two disappear. The boy was Vishnu, the Lord Protector,[6] and the old yogi was Shiva, the creator and destroyer of the world, who had just come for the instruction of Indra, who is simply a god of history but thinks he is the whole show.

Indra is sitting there on the throne, and he is completely disillusioned, completely shot. He calls the carpenter and says, "I'm quitting the building of this palace. You are dismissed." So the carpenter got his intention. He is dismissed from the job, and there is no more house building going on.

Indra decides to go out and be a yogi and just meditate on the lotus feet of Vishnu. But he has a beautiful queen

4. **yogi.** A Hindu holy man, one who practices a spiritual path, or yoga

5. **loincloth.** Cloth worn about the waist and upper thighs

6. **Vishnu, the Lord Protector.** In Hindu belief, one of the appearances of Vishnu on earth was as Krishna, frequently pictured as a beautiful blue-black youth

❶ *Why does the older man say he doesn't have a house?*

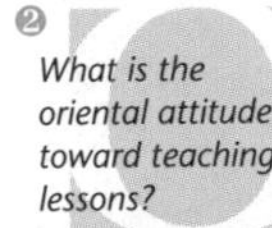

❷ *What is the oriental attitude toward teaching lessons?*

❸ *What does the boy say Indras do throughout many lifetimes?*

Words for Everyday Use

mis • sion (mish´ən) *n.*, belief or purpose

il • lu • mi • na • tion (i lo͞o´mə nā´shən) *n.*, highest spiritual understanding

crotch • et • y (kräch´it ē) *adj.*, grouchy; stubborn

con • stel • la • tion (kän´stə lā´shən) *n.*, cluster; gathering

med • i • tate (med´ə tāt´) *v.*, think deeply

dis • il • lu • sion (dis´i lo͞o´zhen) *v.*, disappointed

Answers to Guided Reading Questions

❶ The older man says that he doesn't have a house because life is too short.

❷ The oriental attitude is that you do not teach until you are asked.

❸ The boy says that Indras rise to the highest illumination and then drop to the lowest throughout many lifetimes.

Vocabulary in Context

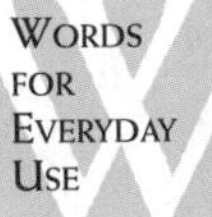

- She decided that her mission was to help others, so she joined several volunteer groups.
- Buddha received illumination after meditating for forty-nine days.
- Very early in the morning many people behave in a crotchety manner.
- That constellation of stars is known as Orion.
- When Gwen was feeling great stress, she would meditate to regain her composure.
- The small child was completely disillusioned to discover that there is no such thing as the Tooth Fairy.

Answers to Guided Reading Questions

❶ The lesson is that each of us is the Indra of his or her own life and we can throw worldly life away to meditate or can stay in the world of politics, achievement, and love.

❷ The priest says that Indra should appreciate and honor his position and "deal with life as though you were what you really are."

Selection Check Test with Answers

EX. In what writing was this story told?
This story was told in one of the Upanishads.

1. What does Indra think after he destroys the monster?
Indra thinks "What a great boy am I."

2. What does Indra decide to build?
He decides to build a palace "worthy of such as he."

3. To whom does the carpenter complain?
The carpenter complains to Brahma, the creator god.

4. What does the boy say that the ants are?
The boy says the ants are former Indras.

5. Who is Hairy, the old yogi, really?
Hairy is really Shiva, the creator and the destroyer of the world.

named Indrani. And when Indrani hears of Indra's plan, she goes to the priest of the gods and says, "Now he has got the idea in his head of going out to become a yogi."

What lesson is there for all people in this myth? ❶

"Well," says the priest, "come in with me, darling, and we will sit down, and I will fix this up."

What attitude does the priest say Indra should take toward his position? ❷

So they sit down before the king's throne, and the priest says, "Now, I wrote a book for you many years ago on the art of politics. You are in the position of the king of the gods. You are a <u>manifestation</u> of the mystery of Brahma in the field of time. This is a high <u>privilege</u>. Appreciate it, honor it, and deal with life as though you were what you really are. And besides, now I am going to write you a book on the art of love so that you and your wife will know that in the wonderful mystery of the two that are one, the Brahma is <u>radiantly</u> present also."

And with this set of instructions, Indra gives up his idea of going out and becoming a yogi and finds that, in life, he can represent the eternal as a symbol, you might say, of the Brahma.

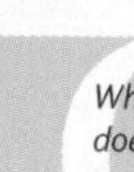

So each of us is, in a way, the Indra of his own life. You can make a choice, either to throw it all off and go into the forest to meditate, or to stay in the world, both in the life of your job, which is the kingly job of politics and achievement, and in the love life with your wife and family. Now, this is a very nice myth, it seems to me. ■

About the Author

Joseph Campbell (1904–1987) gained an international reputation as a scholar of mythology and comparative religion. As a young man, Campbell became interested in mythology after reading about Native American beliefs. He studied at Columbia University and at universities in Paris, France, and Munich, Germany. Campbells's wide-ranging scholarship included thorough knowledge of medieval French, the language of much romance literature about knights in shining armor, and of Sanskrit, the language of the religious texts of early India. Campbell's books include a study of hero myths, *The Hero with a Thousand Faces,* and a multivolume comparative study of mythologies around the world, *The Masks of God.* Shortly before Campbell's death, broadcast journalist **Bill Moyers** interviewed him and followed up by producing a television series and a book based on these interviews called *The Power of Myth.*

Words for Everyday Use

man • i • fes • ta • tion (man´ə fes tā´shən) *n.,* example, instance
priv • i • lege (priv´ə lij) *n.,* right or favor
ra • di • ant • ly (rā´dē ənt lē) *adv.,* brightly

Vocabulary in Context

- Her smile was a <u>manifestation</u> of joy.
- Because Hannah missed her curfew, her parents took away her phone <u>privileges</u>.
- The sun shone <u>radiantly</u> upon the sea.

Responding to the Selection

What does this myth teach about pride? about concern for and involvement in worldly matters? Which do you think is the better course for Indra, withdrawing from the world to become a holy man or remaining active in the world? Why?

Reviewing the Selection

RECALLING AND INTERPRETING

1. **R** After blowing up the monster, what does Indra think of himself? What does Indra decide to build to demonstrate his greatness?

   I How do you feel about Indra at this point in the story?

2. **R** What does the beautiful blue-black boy tell Indra that surprises him?

   I How does the boy's teaching affect Indra? How does Indra change?

3. **R** Who is the blue-black boy? Who is the old yogi? What happens to the old yogi's chest every time an Indra dies?

   I What does Hairy mean when he asks Indra, "Why build a house?"

4. **R** What does Indra decide to do after giving up plans to finish building his palace?

   I Why does Indrani bring the priest to see Indra? What does Indra learn from the priest?

SYNTHESIZING

5. What does this myth teach us about how we should live our lives? How does the story reflect Hindu beliefs?

Understanding Literature (Questions for Discussion)

1. **Simile.** A **simile** is a comparison using *like* or *as*. How is the blue-black boy's voice described early in the story? To what is his voice compared? What does this simile tell you about his voice?
2. **Symbol.** A **symbol** is something that stands for or represents both itself and something else. What do the ants in this story symbolize?
3. **Internal Conflict.** An **internal conflict** is a struggle that takes place inside the mind of the character. In this story, Indra struggles between pridefulness and concern with worldly matters, on the one hand, and humility and concern with spiritual matters, on the other hand. How is the struggle finally ended, or resolved? What middle course does the priest suggest to Indra?

RESPONDING TO THE SELECTION

Students should focus their discussion on whether or not they agree with the advice the priest gives to Indra.

ANSWERS FOR REVIEWING THE SELECTION

RECALLING AND INTERPRETING

1. **Recalling.** Indra thinks very highly of himself. Indra decides to build a palace on the cosmic mountain to demonstrate his greatness. **Interpreting.** Students may say that Indra seems very conceited.

2. **Recalling.** The beautiful blue-black boy tells Indra that there have been Indras before him and that there will be Indras after him. The boy also says that ants are former prideful Indras. **Interpreting.** The boy's teaching surprises and humbles Indra. Indra becomes less conceited and stops the construction of his palace.

3. **Recalling.** The blue-black boy is Vishnu, the Lord Protector. The old yogi is Shiva, the creator and destroyer of the world. Every time an Indra dies a hair drops out of the circle on the yogi's chest. **Interpreting.** Hairy, the old yogi, means that there is no point in focusing your energies on worldly matters because life is so short.

4. **Recalling.** Indra decides to become a yogi and meditate on the lotus feet of Vishnu. **Interpreting.** Indrani brings the priest to see Indra because she feels that Indra's decision to turn over his life to meditation is selfish and foolish. Indra learns that his position is a privilege and that he should appreciate and honor it, and not retreat from the world.

SYNTHESIZING

Responses will vary. Possible responses are given.

5. The myth tells us that we should accepts who we are and carry out our fate in life. This story shows the Hindu belief in rebirth; says that one should accepts one's karma, or fate; and stresses that it is important to carry out one's darma, or duty.

ANSWERS FOR UNDERSTANDING LITERATURE

Responses will vary. Possible responses are given.

1. **Simile.** The boy's voice is described "like thunder rolling on the horizon." His voice is compared to thunder. This simile tells you that his voice is unnaturally loud and powerful.

2. **Symbol.** Ants symbolize former Indras who have to begin the cycle of rebirth again from the bottom.

3. **Internal Conflict.** The struggle is resolved by Indra's losing his pride and paying more attention to spiritual matters, but still carrying out his worldly duties. The middle course is to find spiritual satisfaction in carrying out one's duties.

Vocabulary Skills

Introducing the Skill

Inform students that English is primarily a Germanic language. However, many of the English words students use are based on Greek, Latin, French, and many other languages. Tell students that the English language is dynamic, or constantly changing. The English that students speak now is not the same as the English spoken during the Renaissance period in England and is quite different than the English spoken in England around the year 1000 AD. English has evolved and changed over time through the introduction of new words.

Previewing the Skill

Have students read the teaching in the Vocabulary Skills lesson. Ask students if they can think of more borrowed words, compound words, clipped words, blended words, and words from names that have entered the English language.

Practicing the Skill

Once students seem familiar with the ways that words enter the English language and with dictionary etymologies, have them do the Try It Yourself exercises.

Reviewing the Skill

Review the answers to the Try It Yourself exercises as a class. If students need additional practice, have them do the Try It Yourself exercise in the Language Arts Survey, 2.44, "Word Origins."

Vocabulary Skills

Word Origins

In the Hindu religion, the term *karma* means "the totality of a person's actions in any one of the successive states of that person's existence, thought of as determining the fate of the next stage." However, the term *karma* has also entered the English language in a more simple way, as a synonym for the word *fate* or *destiny*. The study of **word origins** is the investigation of where words come from and how they develop. Words enter our language in many different ways. A language grows and changes through the addition and creation of new words. Here are some ways in which new words enter English.

Borrowed Words

Sometimes speakers borrow words from another language. For example, English speakers borrowed *rendezvous, ensemble,* and *déjà vu* from French.

Compound Words

Sometimes new words are created by joining together old ones. *Daybreak, driveway,* and *outlook* all entered the language in this way.

Clipped Words

People sometimes create new words by shortening words that already exist. For example, *memorandum* became *memo. Omnibus* gave us *bus. Stereophonic receiver* was shortened to *stereo.*

Blended Words

Sometimes words are blended together to make new ones. Thus *smoke* and *fog* became *smog*, and *whale* and *horse* became *walrus.*

Words from Names

Words sometimes come from the names of people or places. If someone calls you "Spartan," it means that you are thought to be like the ancient residents of Sparta, Greece, who were known for their rigorous self-discipline and self-restraint.

Try It Yourself

Exercise A. Match each word on the left with the correct description of its origin on the right.

EXAMPLE Shakespearean
from the name of an English poet and dramatist who lived during the Renaissance

1. limo
2. Machiavellian
3. puerile
4. earring
5. pixel

a. from the Latin word *puer,* meaning boy
b. a blend of the words *picture* and *element*
c. compound word
d. clipped form of a longer word
e. from the name of an Italian political writer who wrote a famous book, *The Prince,* in 1513 that described the maneuvers of a calculating and morally unscrupulous ruler

Most dictionaries provide information about the origins of words. Usually, dictionaries place the history, or **etymology,** of a word in brackets or parentheses. The meanings of the abbreviations used in a word's etymology can usually be found in a chart at the beginning or end of the dictionary.

blithe (blī*th*, blīth) ***adj.*** [ME < OE; ult. < IE base **bhlei-,* to shine, gleam] showing a gay, cheerful disposition; carefree **—blithe'|ly *adv.* —blithe'|ness *n.***

In the etymology in brackets above; *ME* stands for *Middle English,* < stands for *derived from, OE* stands for *Old English, ult.* stands for *ultimately, IE* stands for *Indo-European,* and * means *not attested.* Thus, *blithe* is a Middle English word that comes from an Old English word. The Old English word came from an older Indo-European base, probably *bhlei-*, which meant "to shine or gleam." This Indo-European base, however, has not been verified.

Try It Yourself

Exercise B. Look up the following words in a dictionary. Write the whole etymology, or history, of each word. List all the abbreviations used in each etymology, along with the meanings of these abbreviations.

EXAMPLE blithe
[ME < OE; ult. < IE base **bhlei-,* to shine, gleam]
ME = Middle English; < = derived from; OE = Old English; ult. = ultimately; IE = Indo-European; * = not attested

1. bid
2. insipid
3. cook
4. bodhisattva
5. Seattle

Answers for Try It Yourself

Exercise A

1. d
2. e
3. a
4. c
5. b

Exercise B

1. [ME *bidden,* to ask, plead, pray < OE *biddan* < IE base **bheidh-,* to urge, compel; meaning and form merged with ME *beden,* to offer, present < OE *beodan,* to command, decree < IE base **bheudh-,* to be alert, announce] ME=Middle English; <-derived from; OE=Old English; IE=Indo-European; *=not attested.
2. [<Fr & LL: Fr *insipide* < LL *insipidus* < L *in-,* not + *sapidus,* savory < *sapere,* to taste] Fr=French; &=and; LL=Late Latin; <=derived from; L=classical Latin; +=plus.
3. [ME *cok* < OE *coc* < VL *cocus* < L *coquus* < *coquere,* to cook < IE base **pekw-,* to cook] ME=Middle English; <=derived from; OE=Old English; VL=Vulgar Latin; L=classical Latin; IE=Indo-European; *=not attested.
4. [Sans, lit., one enlightened in essence < *bodhi,* enlightenment (< IE base **bheudh-,* to be alert, recognize > OE *beodan,* to command: see BID1) + *sattva,* being, existence (< IE **sent-,* part, stem of base **es-,* BE > IS)] Sans=Sanskrit; lit.=literally; <=derived from; IE=Indo-European; *=not attested; > whence is derived; +=plus; part.=participial.
5. [after *Seathl,* an Indian chief]

CROSS-CURRICULAR ACTIVITIES

GEOGRAPHY

The map on page 256 focuses on China and Japan. Students can make their own maps of Asia including other countries of this continent. Have students identify countries, capital cities, seas, major rivers, mountain chains, and other major land formations and bodies of water.

WORLD HISTORY

Have students research the voyages of Marco Polo. They might map his route and indicate some of the things he brought back from his voyages.

HISTORICAL NOTE

In 1974, workers digging a well near Xian, discovered an underground chamber which was determined to be part of the grave of the emperor Shih Huang-ti of Ch'in. His grave site is a twenty-square-mile compound. Within this area, archeologists have discovered an army of more than six thousand terracotta figures. The figures are life-sized and include both soldiers and horses. No two figures in the group are alike. Many other objects of leather, jade, metal, and bone were found with the figures. Additional small chambers have been found with other figures. The burial complex is still being excavated.

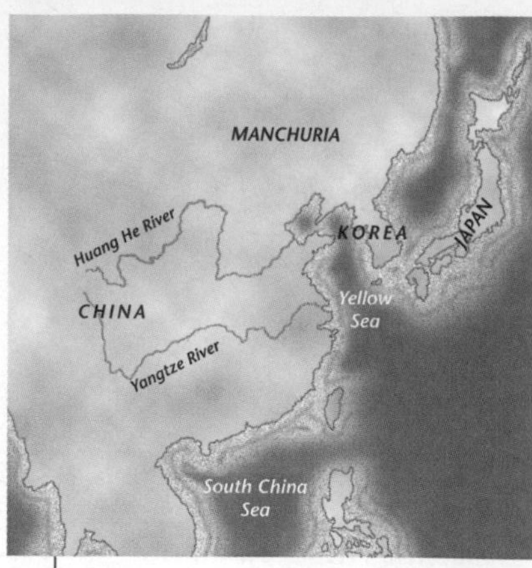

Cultures of the Ancient Far East

Ancient China

The Shang Dynasty and the Emergence of Writing. One of the oldest civilizations of the world is that of China. Archaeologists have found evidence of Chinese agricultural communities along the Huang He, or Yellow River, dating to 6000 BC. In 1726 BC, the first of the historical Chinese empires, the **Shang Dynasty,** developed in northern China. By this time, the Chinese were practicing ancestor worship, cultivating millet and rice, using bronze, harvesting silk from silkworms, and making carvings in the semiprecious stone known as jade. They had also, by this time, developed a system of writing.

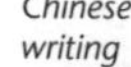

Chinese writing

Chinese writing, unlike Western alphabetical systems, is **ideographic**. In other words, it uses pictures to represent ideas, and every word is represented by a unique character. Abstract ideas are expressed by combining these pictures. For example, the character for *east* combines the characters for *sun* and *tree,* thus representing the idea of the sun seen rising through a tree's branches. Many other cultures in Asia, including those of Japan and Korea, adapted the Chinese writing system.

Later Chinese History. During the millennia that followed, until the Communist Revolution in 1949, China was ruled by a succession of empires organized according to a system of government known as the **feudal system.** In a feudal government, all land ultimately belongs to the emperor, who gives up parts of it to powerful nobles in exchange for loyalty and service. The lands of the nobles are farmed by peasants and slaves. The emperor was himself considered a god, capable of demoting or promoting the other gods and of making people into gods after their deaths. When the European **Marco Polo** visited China in the thirteenth century, he found a vast, wealthy, highly developed civilization, led from **Peking** (now known as **Beijing**) by the most powerful ruler in the world, **Kublai Khan,** the son of the Mongol conqueror **Genghis Khan.** For most of its history, China's various ruling dynasties were supported by vast bureaucracies of scholars who gained their positions through competitive examinations in traditional Chinese philosophy, poetry, and art.

Portion of the Great Wall of China

The Three Doctrines. The fifth century BC was an important period in the development of Chinese culture, for during this time two great religions gained a foothold in the land. Of these, the most important in its consequences for Chinese thought was **Confucianism,** founded by **K'ung Fu-tsu,** known in the West as **Confucius,** a philosopher who lived from 551 to 479 BC. Confucius's teachings, compiled by his followers in a book called the ***Analects***, were more ethical than religious. They stressed achieving a harmonious life through following faithfully one's duties toward family members and toward people above and below one in the social hierarchy. The teachings of Confucius provided a philosophical basis for rigid Chinese feudalism and bureaucracy, but they also called for people to be promoted to positions of authority based on their abilities rather than on their status at birth.

In contrast to the systematic, authority-based, socially-oriented teachings of Confucius were those of **Lao-tse,** the founder of the religion known as **Taoism,** or the Way. Lao-tse taught that one should turn from the artificiality of social life to a simple life in contact with the natural world. Much Chinese philosophy, poetry, and art was inspired by Taoist ideals of simplicity, peacefulness, and harmony with nature.

Dragon vase from Huaching Hot Springs, Sian, China

Buddhism, founded in India by **Siddhartha Gautama,** came to China at a later date. The Buddhists stressed giving up desire, which they considered the source of all suffering, and living a life of virtue. (For more information on Buddhism, see page 229 of this text.) Together, Confucianism, Taoism, and Buddhism, known as **The Three Doctrines,** shaped much of China's intellectual history.

Chinese Contributions to Culture. The rich, varied civilization of China gave much to the cultures of the world. The Chinese invented silk manufacture, porcelain, paper, printing, stirrups, fireworks, and gunpowder. They also created art and poetry of extraordinary delicacy and beauty.

Historical Note

The Great Wall of China runs about 4,000 miles from the easternmost point at Po Hai to the westernmost point in central Asia. The wall is built of masonry and earth and stands thirty feet high. In 214 BC Shih Huang-ti had many existing defensive walls connected. Watch towers were built to guard the fortifications. The towers stand about forty feet high. From them, signals could be sent, by smoke or by fire, to the capital. The wall was built as protection against enemies, principally the Hsiung-nu, nomadic tribes from the north.

Quotables

"For one word a man is often deemed to be wise, and for one word he is often deemed to be foolish. We should be careful indeed of what we say."

—Confucius

"Our theories of the eternal are as valuable as are those which a chick which has not broken its way through its shell might form of the outside world."

—Gautama the Buddha

"To remain whole,
be twisted!
To become straight,
let yourself be bent.
To become full,
be hollow.
Be tattered, that you may be
renewed."

—Lao Tzu

LITERARY NOTE

You may wish to refer students to the For Your Reading List review at the end of Unit 6. The review is of *The Haunted Flute and Other Japanese Stories,* a collection of Japanese folktales.

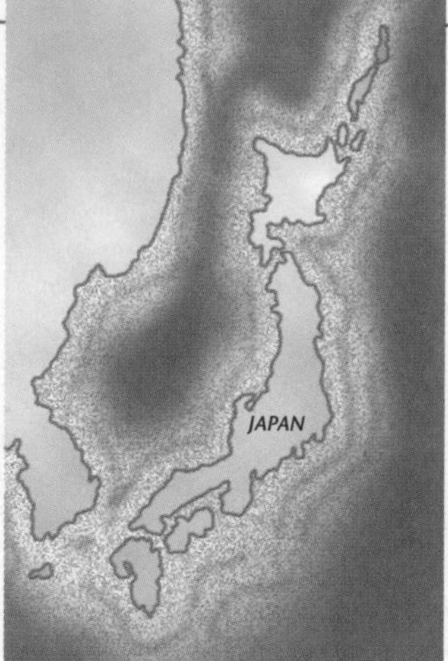

Ancient Japan

The Earliest Japanese Cultures. Eastward from China lies the group of islands that make up Japan. The earliest Japanese culture known clearly from archeological evidence, the **Jomon**, may date from as long ago as 10,000 BC. They lived by hunting and fishing and created a distinctive pottery made from coiled clay. The people of the Jomon culture may have come from mainland Asia, displacing an existing people, the **Ainu,** the descendants of whom still live today on the island of **Hokkaido** in the north. By 300 BC, a new culture had emerged in Japan, based on the cultivation of rice and barley. The people of this **Yayoi** culture used weapons and tools made of bronze and iron.

Shinto. The original religion of Japan, still practiced in much modified form, originated during Yayoi times. Called **Shinto,** a name meaning "the way of the gods," this religion involved worship of the spirits of nature and of departed ancestors. Originally, these spirits were conceived of as invisible forces, but later, under the influence of Buddhism, Japanese gods came to be represented in physical form.

The Yamato Culture. Japan is a mountainous country, and its geography led to the development of small, independent villages. In the second half of the second century AD, however, a priestess named **Himiko** united many of these villages under her rule and established contact and trade with China. This contact had enormous influence on Japan, which eventually adopted and adopted Chinese characters for writing the Japanese language. Around AD 200, the **Yamato** people of central Japan established control over much of the country. The Yamato rulers claimed to be descended from the sun goddess, Amaterasu, a claim that was continued by Japanese emperors into the twentieth century.

Later Japanese History. A detailed account of later Japanese history is beyond the scope of this text. In brief,

Kendoka, or practitioner of the Japanese martial art known as Kendo

however, Japan went through two subsequent stages of development, a long period of imperial government followed by a long period of feudalism characterized by struggle between rival warlords. Japanese contributions to culture, like those of China, have been enormous and include distinctive styles of poetry such as haiku, the philosophical doctrines of Zen Buddhism, the varieties of theater known as Noh drama and Kabuki, and a unique approach to art and design characterized by minimalism, delicacy, and a balancing of order and disorder. The latter can be seen, especially, in the Zen art of flower arranging, known as *ikebana*; in the sparse and beautiful Japanese Zen gardens; in traditional fabric and clothing design; and in contemporary Japanese graphic design, which has had enormous impact worldwide during the concluding decades of the twentieth century.

The gravel of a Japanese Zen garden is carefully raked to represent flowing water.

Japanese woman in formal traditional costume

Ancient China and Japan

2000 BC — 1500 BC — 1000 BC — 500 BC — 0 — AD 500

- ►**1726** Beginnings of Shang Dynasty in China
- ►***circa* 1122** Beginnings of Zhou Dynasty in China
- ►***circa* 604** Birth of Lao-tse, founder of Taoism
- ►**551** Birth of Chinese philosopher K'ung Fu-tsu, also known as Confucius
- ►***circa* 300** Cultivation of rice and barley in Japan
- ►***circa* 220** Beginnings of Qin Dynasty in China
- ►**214** Chinese begin building the Great Wall to protect against invaders
- ►***circa* 202** Beginnings of Han Dynasty in China
- ►***circa* 167** Uniting of Japanese states by Himiko
- ►**67** Introduction of Buddhism to China
- ►**100** Invention of paper in China
- ►***circa* 200** Beginnings of Yamato period in Japan
- ***circa* 522**► Introduction of Buddhism to Japan

CROSS-CURRICULAR CONNECTIONS

Social Studies

Have students work in groups to research the history of Japan. Students might create a display about Japan that offers information, photographs, and objects about the history and culture of Japan.

Literary Note

Have students read the two poems, "I do not consider . . ." and "Everyone is asleep," by Japanese writers in Unit 9. You may wish to have students read several haiku. Then students can try their own hands at writing haiku.

Additional Questions and Activities

Students may enjoy visiting a Japanese garden or an Asian art exhibit. Suggest that students research the arts of Japan and present their findings to the class.

GOALS/OBJECTIVES

Studying this lesson will enable students to

- enjoy a creation myth
- summarize a story
- describe the forces of yin and yang
- define *myth*
- document sources in a research report

ADDITIONAL RESOURCES

Reader's Guide

- Selection Worksheet, 6.4

Assessment Portfolio

- Selection Check Test, 2.6.7
- Selection Test, 2.6.8

Pronunciation Exercise

- Grade 8 Audiocassette, Side B, Track 31

CROSS-CURRICULAR CONNECTIONS

Social Studies

Confucianism encourages people to lead well-disciplined lives and stresses duty and public service. Taoism encourages a simple life and stresses meditation and connection to nature. Ask students which of these two beliefs is closer to their own way of life. Ask students to describe their own philosophies of life.

Prereading

CHINA

"P'an Ku and the Great Egg"

Anonymous, retold by Sara Hyry

Cross-curricular Connection

Social Studies. Taoism is an ancient Chinese philosophy and religion that stresses spontaneity and the freedom of the individual. Taoism probably developed as a reaction to an earlier philosophy. Earlier thinking was guided by Confucius, a philosopher in ancient China. Confucianism stated that people must live well-disciplined lives that stress duty and public service. Taoism, on the other hand, encourages people to lead simple, meditative lives close to nature.

The symbol for Taoism is the yin-yang. Yin and yang represent the opposing and yet complementary forces at work within all life. The yin-yang is depicted as a circle that is half dark and half light, with a small circle of the opposite color in each side. Yin is dark, cold, negative, and feminine. Yang is light, warm, positive, and masculine. "P'an Ku and the Great Egg" is a myth that explains the role of the yin-yang in the creation of Earth.

As You Read

"P'an Ku and the Great Egg" contains two stories about the creation of the world. In your journal, make a chart like the one below. As you read, briefly summarize each tale in your own words.

STORY SUMMARY CHART	
How P'an Ku was created	Long ago there was an egg that split apart and P'an Ku came forth.
How Earth and humans were formed	
How Earth was formed and how people learned about it	

AS YOU READ

Wording of student summaries may vary, but student summaries should contain the points indicated in the responses below.

How Earth and humans were formed: The Earth, the Sun, and the Moon were formed from P'an Ku's body when he died. The vermin who lived on P'an Ku became the first humans.

How Earth was formed and how people learned about it: P'an Ku chiseled out the earth and taught people about it.

READER'S JOURNAL

How have you learned about Earth, the Moon, and the Sun? Think about some of the questions you had as a young child. What explanations were you given? What ideas did you come up with on your own? What did you later learn about Earth, the Moon, or the Sun? From what sources did you draw your knowledge?

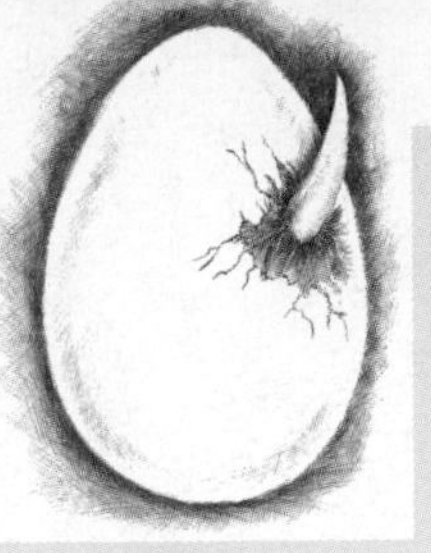

"P'an Ku and the Great Egg"

ANONYMOUS, RETOLD BY SARA HYRY

In the time before time, there was nothing. From nothing came something—a giant egg, and within the egg were two forces—yin and yang. Yin and yang are at odds and at peace; they contrast with and complement each other, and both are found in all things. Yin and yang were in the great egg before the world was formed. From this great egg came forth P'an Ku, who had in him both yin and yang. He had two horns and two tusks, and his body was covered with fur. The stories told about P'an Ku are told widely, but they are not all told the same.

Some say that when the great egg split open and P'an Ku emerged, the yin and yang from within the egg floated apart, and the heavens and Earth were created and separated with P'an Ku in between. It has been told that P'an Ku was wearied by the effort of keeping the two forces apart, and that he died. Upon his death, his body became the world. His head, two arms, body, and feet became five great mountains. His blood gushed out as rivers and oceans. His hair sprang up as plants. The sun was born of one of his eyes, and of the other eye was born the moon. The mighty breath of P'an Ku became the wind, and his voice became the thunder. The pests and vermin who lived upon P'an Ku became the first people.

This is one story of P'an Ku. Others say Earth was formed by the living P'an Ku. When he sprang from the great egg, P'an Ku immediately went to work with a chisel and hammer to carve out valleys and river beds, and pile up the earth he removed to form

❶ *What was inside the great egg? Describe these two forces.*

WORDS FOR EVERYDAY USE

com • ple • ment (käm´plə mənt) *v.,* add to; make complete

READER'S JOURNAL

Ask students to write an explanation for the beginning of the world that they might give to a young child. Inform students that their stories can be imaginative.

SPELLING AND VOCABULARY WORDS FROM THE SELECTION

complement

ANSWER TO GUIDED READING QUESTION

❶ Yin and yang, two opposite forces that complement each other, were inside the great egg. The two forces are found in all things.

SUPPORT FOR LEP STUDENTS

PRONUNCIATIONS OF PROPER NOUNS AND ADJECTIVES

P'an Ku (pän ko͞o) n.

ADDITIONAL VOCABULARY

emerged—came out
vermin—animals or bugs seen as pests
wearied—tired, exhausted

VOCABULARY IN CONTEXT

• Harry's new shoes complemented his new suit.

Answer to Guided Reading Question

❶ *Responses will vary.* P'an Ku may have decided that he had done his job completely. He may have decided it was time to let humans try things on their own.

Selection Check Test with Answers

EX. From what country's oral tradition is this myth taken?
The myth is taken from the oral tradition of China.

1. What two forces were inside the giant egg?
The forces of yin and yang were inside the giant egg.

2. In the first story of the creation of the world, from what is the earth created?
The earth is created from the body of the dead P'an Ku.

3. In the first creation story from what are humans created?
Humans are created from the pests and vermin on P'an Ku's body.

4. How is the earth formed in the second story of the creation of the world?
P'an Ku chisels out the world.

5. What does P'an Ku teach humans?
P'an Ku teaches humans about the sun and the moon, about the oceans and the rivers, and how to build boats and bridges.

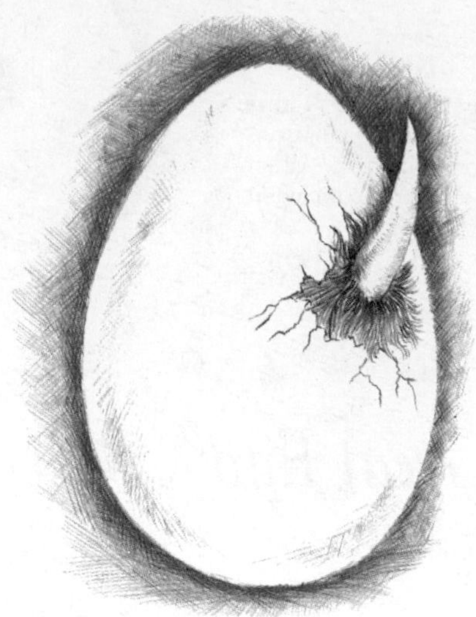

❶ *Why do you think P'an Ku disappears?*

mountains. He placed the Sun, the Moon, and the stars in the sky. When he had done this work, P'an Ku set out to instruct the people. He taught them about the Sun and the Moon. He taught them about the oceans and rivers and how to build boats and bridges to cross the waters. When he had done all this, P'an Ku disappeared to be seen no more. ■

About the Author

Sara Hyry (1972–) was born in Rockport, Massachusetts. She studied English and Romance Languages at Mount Holyoke College. Hyry loves mythology from all parts of the world. She now lives in Boston.

Responding to the Selection

Which story about P'an Ku and the creation of the world do you prefer? Why do you prefer it?

Reviewing the Selection

RECALLING AND INTERPRETING

1. **R** What two forces were inside the egg?
   I What happened to the two forces that were inside the egg?
2. **R** What does P'an Ku become in the first tale?
   I What relationship is formed between humans and the creator or humans and nature in the first tale?
3. **R** From what are the first humans formed in the first tale?
   I In what way is the relationship between P'an Ku and the first humans different in the two tales?
4. **R** How does P'an Ku form the world in the second tale?
   I How do you think the people feel about P'an Ku as their creator and instructor? How do you think they feel when P'an Ku leaves?

SYNTHESIZING

5. Describe the forces of yin and yang. In what way does the myth of "P'an Ku and the Great Egg" reflect Taoist beliefs about the yin-yang?

Understanding Literature (Questions for Discussion)

Myth. A **myth** is a story that explains the beginnings of things in the natural world. Why do you think there are different versions of how P'an Ku created the world? What natural objects or phenomena are explained by each story?

RESPONDING TO THE SELECTION

As an alternative activity, invite students to compare and contrast the story of P'an Ku with other creation myths they know.

ANSWERS FOR REVIEWING THE SELECTION

RECALLING AND INTERPRETING

1. **Recalling.** Yin and yang were inside the egg. **Interpreting.** *Responses will vary.* The two forces floated apart and became the heavens and the Earth. Yin and yang are both present in all things.
2. **Recalling.** P'an Ku becomes the Earth. His eyes become the Sun and the Moon, and his breath becomes the wind. **Interpreting.** *Responses will vary.* Humans are dependent on, almost as parasites, nature and the creator.
3. **Recalling.** The humans in the first tale are formed from the vermin and pests that lived on P'an Ku's body. **Interpreting.** *Responses will vary.* In the first tale, humans are dependent upon P'an Ku but do not know him as P'an Ku, only as the Earth. In the second story, the people know and learn from P'an Ku.
4. **Recalling.** In the second story, P'an Ku chisels out the world. **Interpreting.** *Responses will vary.* The people are probably grateful to learn from P'an Ku. They are probably sad that he leaves them.

SYNTHESIZING

Responses will vary. Possible responses are given.

5. Yin is dark, cold, and negative. Yang is light, warm, and positive. The world was created when the two forces sprang out of the egg. The two freed forces are now found in everything in the world.

ANSWERS FOR UNDERSTANDING LITERATURE

Responses will vary. Possible responses are given.

Myth. There are different versions of the story because the story is part of the oral tradition. As people retold the story and passed it on orally, variations were made. Parts of the story might be taken out and others added. The two stories related here have the great egg and P'an Ku in common, but explanations of how the Earth and other objects were formed differ. Both stories explain the creation of the Earth and its features such as mountains and rivers. Both stories also explain the creation of the Sun and the Moon. The first story explains the creation of the wind, plants, and people.

Study and Research Skills

Introducing the Skill

Discuss the idea of plagiarism with students. Ask them if they have ever done, said, or written something only to have somebody else take credit for it. Remind students that they must always give credit to their sources when borrowing words or ideas.

Previewing the Skill

Have students read through the material about documenting sources on pages 264 and 265. Go over in detail the the forms for entries in a bibliography with them.

Practicing the Skill

You may wish to have students try writing one entry of each kind for practice. Then have students complete the Try It Yourself activity.

Reviewing the Skill

Review students' papers for correct use of documentation and proper bibliographic form. Remind students that they should document sources that they use for any reports or papers they produce.

Study and Research Skills

Documenting Sources

Plagiarism is using someone else's words or thoughts without giving credit to that person. Whenever you use someone else's writing to help you in a paper or a speech, you must be very careful either to put the ideas into your own words or, if you use the exact words of your source, to use quotation marks. In either case, you must give credit to the person whose ideas you are using. Giving such credit to others is called documenting your sources. In a paper or report, sources are documented in a bibliography. Review the Language Arts Survey, 4.18, "Documenting Sources."

A **bibliography** is a list of the sources that you used for your writing. A source is a book, a magazine, a film, or any other written or audiovisual material from which you get information. Entries in a bibliography are entered in alphabetical order by the author's last name. The chart below shows the correct form for different types of bibliography entries.

FORMS FOR ENTRIES IN A BIBLIOGRAPHY

A. Book

Hamilton, Edith. Mythology. New York: Penguin, 1969.

B. Magazine article

Boslough, John. "The Enigma of Time." National Geographic March 1990: 109-132.

C. Encyclopedia article

"China." Encyclopedia Britannica. Chicago: University of Chicago, 1992: Volume 3, 221-230.

D. Interview

Chen, Mei. Personal interview. 29 February 1996.

To keep track of your sources as you work on your paper, write the information that you will need on a bibliography card. Use a separate 3" x 5" index card for each source. Include the name of the author or editor, the title of the work, the title of the article if there is one, the publisher, the place and date of publication, where you found the book, and the call number, if you found it in a library. You should also number each source in the order you found it. For more information, see the Language Arts Survey, 4.20, "Formal Note-taking."

SAMPLE BIBLIOGRAPHY CARD

①

Campbell, Joseph. The Power of Myth: Joseph Campbell, with Bill Moyers. Ed. Betty Sue Flowers. New York: Anchor Books, 1988.

Westerly Public Library
BL304/C36/1988

Try It Yourself

Write a short report and document your sources correctly. Follow the steps below.

1. Choose one of the topics below or one of your own to research.
   China
   creation myths
   Japanese art
   the pyramids of Egypt
2. Find at least three sources of information about your topic. At least one of your sources should be a book, and at least one should be an article.
3. Create a bibliography card for each source.
4. Take notes from your sources. Make sure you paraphrase the work you are using, or indicate with quotation marks that it is a direct quotation.
5. Write your report. Include a complete bibliography of all the sources you used. Use the correct form for a bibliography entry according to the models on the previous page.

ANSWERS FOR TRY IT YOURSELF

Reports should included proper documentation of sources used. You may wish to check bibliography cards before the final report is due to help students correct errors in form.

GOALS/OBJECTIVES

Studying this lesson will enable students to

- enjoy a myth from Japan
- understand the importance of the sun to human life
- identify techniques of characterization
- use techniques to read actively

ADDITIONAL RESOURCES

READER'S GUIDE

- Selection Worksheet, 6.5

ASSESSMENT PORTFOLIO

- Selection Check Test, 2.6.9
- Selection Test, 2.6.10

PRONUNCIATION EXERCISE

- Grade 8 Audiocassette, Side B, Track 32

CROSS-CURRICULAR CONNECTIONS

SCIENCE

- Photosynthesis is a process by which plants convert light into energy. Ask students to research and explain this process.
- Ask students to find and share other myths about sun gods and goddesses.

APPLIED ARTS

- Have students work in pairs in a mirroring activity. Students can take turns mirroring each other's actions.
- Have students brainstorm a list of ways in which mirrors are used. Some examples might be to aid drivers, by a dentist to examine teeth, for amusement at a fun house, and in stores to create attractive displays for merchandise.

Prereading

JAPAN

"Amaterasu"

Anonymous, retold by Carolyn Swift

Cross-curricular Connections

Science. In Japanese mythology, Amaterasu is the goddess of the Sun. Many cultures have powerful gods or goddesses of the Sun because of the importance of the Sun to life on Earth. The Sun is the star around which Earth revolves. The Sun is not an exceptionally large star, although from Earth it appears to dwarf other stars. The Sun appears large from Earth only because it is by far the closest star to Earth at a distance of about 92,957,000 miles. The core of the Sun reaches temperatures hot enough to trigger nuclear reactions. These nuclear reactions generate the energy of the Sun, part of which is transmitted to Earth. The Sun is of vital importance to Earth because it provides the heat and light that are needed to support life.

Applied Arts. A mirror is a surface that reflects images by diverting light in a certain way. The surface of a mirror must be perfectly smooth. A mirror must reflect most of the light that hits it and absorb or transmit very little of the light. Mirrors are used in instruments such as telescopes, as decorations, and for personal viewing.

Before people learned to make mirrors, they noticed that smooth bodies of water, such as still lakes, reflected the objects near them. Early human-made mirrors were polished pieces of metal, usually bronze, tin, or silver. In Venice in the sixteenth century, people began to attach a thin sheet of metal to glass to create a mirroring surface. New techniques in the nineteenth century allowed mirrors to be created at a lower cost and the use of mirrors became more common. A mirror has an important role in the selection you are about to read.

As You Read

In **"Amaterasu"** you will learn about the Sun goddess, Amaterasu. You will discover things about the goddess from her actions and from what others say about her. Make a cluster chart like the one below. As you read, add details about Amaterasu to the cluster chart.

daughter of Lord of the Heavens and Lady of the Underworld

brother of Susanoo

Amaterasu

READER'S JOURNAL

When you are angry or afraid, do you like to be alone or do you prefer to be with others? Write about a time when you spent a great deal of time by yourself. How did your feel when you rejoined your friends? Write about these questions in your journal.

"Amaterasu"

ANONYMOUS, RETOLD BY CAROLYN SWIFT

Back in the mists of time there lived a boy called Susanoo. His father and mother were the first people on earth, but then his father became Lord of the Heavens and his mother Lady of the Underworld.

Susanoo himself lived with his brothers and sisters on the bridge which linked heaven and earth, but he was always complaining. He complained about not being able to visit his mother, even though his father explained to him that if he once went to the underworld he would never be able to come back, and he complained even more when his sister Amaterasu was given the jewelled necklace of heaven and made goddess of the sun, while he was given only corals and made god of the sea. Finally his father became sick of his constant moanings and groanings.

"I don't want to see your face around Heaven any more," he told him. "You have the whole earth and sea to play around in so there's no need for you to make all our lives a misery up here."

"Oh, all right," Susanoo grumbled, "but first I must say goodbye to Amaterasu."

So off he stumped to look for her. Being in a bad mood, he shook every mountain he passed so that rocks crashed down the slopes, and he stamped his feet so that the earth quaked. Hearing all the noise, Amaterasu was frightened. She took up her bow and arrow so that, when her younger brother arrived, he found himself facing the drawn bow of a fierce-looking warrior.

"You can put that thing down," he told her. "I come in peace."

"Prove it," she said suspiciously, not taking her eyes off him.

Susanoo handed her his sword. She took it from him and broke it into three pieces. Then, before he could complain, she blew on them and turned them into three beautiful little girls.

"One day these three little daughters of mine will bring new life into the world," she told him, "while your sword could only have brought death."

1 *Do you think Susanoo would be content if he were able to go to the underworld or rule the sky? Why, or why not?*

READER'S JOURNAL

As an alternative activity ask students to write about how they feel when somebody tricks them. Have them respond to the following questions and prompts: Is it ever pleasant to be tricked? Why, or why not? Write about a specific time when you were tricked. How did it make you feel? What reasons did people have for tricking you?

ANSWER TO GUIDED READING QUESTION

1 Susanoo would probably not be content if he were allowed to go to the underworld. If he were there he would probably complain about not being able to return. If he ruled the sky, he would probably find something else about which to complain. He seems as though he is often unhappy or dissatisfied.

SUPPORT FOR LEP STUDENTS

PRONUNCIATIONS OF PROPER NOUNS AND ADJECTIVES

A • ma • te • ra • su (ä mä tē rä so͞o) n.
Su • sa • noo (so͞o sā nō) n.
A • ma • no U • zu • me (ä mä nō o͞o zo͞o mē) n.
Note: Most syllables in Japanese are stressed equally.

ADDITIONAL VOCABULARY

snapped—spoke irritably or angrily
tempt—persuade by offering something desired
upturned—turned over

Literary Technique

MYTH

A myth is a story that explains the beginnings of things in the natural world. What natural events might the story of Susanoo losing his temper and Amaterasu hiding in a cave explain?

ANSWERS

Susanoo's tantrum might explain a powerful storm that destroyed the rice fields. Amaterasu's disappearance might explain an eclipse, the sun not being seen because of a storm, or the warmth and light of the sun being hidden by heavy covers of smoke and ash from a volcanic eruption.

"I can do better than that!" Susanoo boasted. "Give me the necklaces you're wearing."

So Amaterasu unclasped the five necklaces and gave them to her brother. Then he blew on them and turned them into five little boys.

"Now I have five sons," he said.

"They were made out of my necklaces so they should be my sons!" Amaterasu snapped.

"But your daughters were made from my sword," Susanoo argued.

"That's different!" Amaterasu told him.

At that Susanoo lost his temper. He tore up all the rice fields that Amaterasu had been carefully ripening and caused such destruction that the frightened goddess ran and hid in a cave, blocking the entrance with a large stone.

Because Amaterasu was the sun goddess, this meant that the world was suddenly plunged into darkness. Without the sun's heat the land became very cold and nothing grew in field or forest. Worse still, the evil spirits took advantage of the darkness to get up to all sorts of wickedness. It was a disaster. Something had to be done, so all the good spirits gathered together in a dry river bed to try to decide what to do.

"We must tempt Amaterasu to come out of the cave," said one.

"And block up the entrance the minute she does, so she can't go back into it again," added another.

"But what would tempt her to come out?" asked a third.

"We must put everything she likes most outside," replied the first.

"And what does she like most?" the third asked.

"Seeing her sunny face reflected in the lake," answered a fourth.

"But we can't bring the lake up to the cave!" objected the third.

"Then we must make something that will reflect her face the way the lake does and put that outside the cave," suggested a fifth.

"I don't know what we could make that would do that," the third grumbled, "and anyway, how will she know it's there unless we can get her to come out of the cave in the first place?"

At that they all looked thoughtful. No one spoke for a while.

"I know!" the second suddenly shouted in triumph. "She always used to come out every morning as soon as she heard the cock crow. We must get all the cocks to crow outside the cave."

So they all put their heads together to try to think what would reflect the sun like the waters of the lake. After trying all sort of things in vain, they finally managed to invent a mirror, or looking-glass. This they hung from the branch of a japonica tree[1] immediately opposite the cave and, knowing Amaterasu's fondness for jewellery, they hung jewelled necklaces from the other branches.

When all was ready, they gathered outside the cave with every cock they could find. First they chanted prayers. Then they gave the signal and all the cocks began to crow. Not satisfied with that, everyone present began to sing and dance, led by the goddess Ama no Uzume[2] doing a tap-dance on an upturned tub.

Wondering what all the noise was about, Amaterasu peeped out of the cave and at once saw her own face reflected in the mirror. She had never seen a looking-glass before, so she thought the people must have found another sun to replace her and ran from the cave in a rage. The others immediately stretched ropes across the mouth of the cave to stop her from going back into it again, but there was no need. By then she had discovered that it was her own shining face looking back at her. She was delighted by this and by the necklaces, as well as the singing and dancing for, truth to tell, she had begun to feel lonely in her cave. So once more the sun's bright rays lit the earth and the trees and flowers and rice began to grow again in its heat. Then everyone suddenly remembered the cause of all the trouble.

❶ *What did Amaterasu think when she saw her reflection? Why did she leave the cave?*

"If Susanoo had stayed out of heaven when his father told him to, this would never have happened!" they shouted angrily, and went off in a body to look for him. When they found him, they cut off his pigtail as punishment and threw him out of heaven by force. ■

❷ *Who was blamed for the trouble? Do you think the blame was justly placed? Why, or why not?*

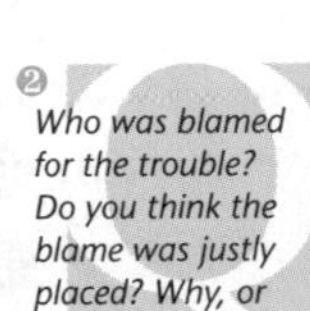

1. **japonica tree.** Any tree, shrub, or plant associated with the far East
2. **Ama no Uzume.** Goddess of dawn and mirth

About the Author

Carolyn Swift lives in Ireland and has written many books for young people. Her retellings of myths include *Irish Myths and Tales.* She has also written two series of novels known as the Bugsy and Robbers series. Swift has a love for the theater. Before she began writing full time, she worked as an actor and a stage manager.

Answers to Guided Reading Questions

❶ Amaterasu thought the people must have found a new sun to replace her. She left the cave in anger to reclaim her position.

❷ Susanoo was blamed for the trouble. *Responses will vary.* Students may say that Susanoo was to blame because his outburst frightened Amaterasu into the cave.

Selection Check Test with Answers

EX. What is Amaterasu's brother's name?
Susanoo is Amaterasu's brother.

1. Over what does Susanoo rule?
Susanoo rules over the seas.
2. What does Amaterasu do with Susanoo's sword?
She breaks it into three pieces and turns them into three little girls.
3. Where does Amaterasu hide when Susanoo loses his temper?
Amaterasu hides in a cave.
4. What does Amaterasu like more than anything else?
She likes to see her face reflected in the lake.
5. What do the people do to get Amaterasu to come out of hiding?
They have all of the cocks crow and they sing and dance.

Responding to the Selection

Students might have a mock trial in which they try Susanoo for the destruction he caused and for making Amaterasu go in the cave. If students find him guilty, they can determine his sentence.

Answers for Reviewing the Selection

RECALLING AND INTERPRETING

1. **Recalling.** Susanoo complains that he cannot visit his mother and that he was only given the seas to rule. Susanoo's father tells him to stay out of heaven because all Susanoo does is complain. **Interpreting.** *Responses will vary.* Students may not want to meet Susanoo because he is whiny.

2. **Recalling.** Amaterasu breaks Susanoo's sword and makes it into three daughters. Susanoo makes five sons out of her necklace. Susanoo becomes destructive. **Interpreting.** *Responses will vary.* Susanoo is competitive and has a quick temper. He is destructive when he is angry.

3. **Recalling.** Amaterasu is frightened by Susanoo's anger. **Interpreting.** *Responses will vary.* Without the sun, the earth is cold and dark, plants do not grow, and evil spirits cause trouble. They would probably be happy if Susanoo were in the cave.

4. **Recalling.** They will get her attention by having cocks crow outside. They will have a mirror outside to draw her out of the cave. **Interpreting.** *Responses will vary.* The plan suggests that Amaterasu is vain. She is happy about the trick because she had been getting lonely.

SYNTHESIZING

Responses will vary. Possible responses are given.

5. Susanoo destroys crops. The earth is plunged into cold darkness. A storm might cause these results. The story explains a time when crops were destroyed and the sun was not seen for a while.

Responding to the Selection

Do you think Susanoo's father's reaction to him was fair? Do you think the reaction of the spirits after Amaterasu had reemerged was fair? Why, or why not? What do you think should have happened to Susanoo?

Reviewing the Selection

Recalling and Interpreting

1. **R** About what things does Susanoo complain? What does Susanoo's father say to him?

   I Do you think Susanoo is somebody you would like to meet? Why, or why not?

2. **R** What does Amaterasu do with Susanoo's sword? What does he do with her necklace? What does Susanoo do after their argument?

   I What do you know about Susanoo's character from this incident? Do you think he was justified in his actions?

3. **R** Why does Amaterasu hide in the cave?

   I Why are the good spirits concerned about Amaterasu staying in the cave? How do you think they would feel if Susanoo were in the cave instead?

4. **R** What plan do the good spirits develop to draw Amaterasu out of the cave?

   I What does the plan suggest about Amaterasu's character? Does she mind being tricked? Why, or why not?

Synthesizing

5. What does Susanoo do when he is angry? What happens when Amaterasu goes into the cave? What natural occurrences might cause these results? What might this story be trying to explain?

Understanding Literature (Questions for Discussion)

Characterization. Characterization is the act of creating a character. Writers create characters by direct description, words and actions of the character, and the character's internal states. What means are used to create the character of Amaterasu? What do you learn about Amaterasu from other characters? What do you learn about her from her actions and her discussion with her brother?

Answers for Understanding Literature

Responses will vary. Possible responses are given.

Characterization. Amaterasu is characterized by her actions and by direct description. Other characters know that Amaterasu likes to look at her own reflection, that she comes out when the cock crows, and that she likes song and dance. Their observations suggest that Amaterasu is vain and that she enjoys celebrations and being with other people. Amaterasu is strong as she demonstrates by her warrior stance when Susanoo comes stomping up, and by breaking his sword. She retreats in the face of anger. She does not like to spend a lot of time alone.

Reading Skills

Reading Actively

Reading actively means interacting with the text as you read. Reading actively helps you to comprehend better what you are reading. The following suggestions will help you to read actively.

SUGGESTIONS FOR ACTIVE READING	
Keep your journal on hand when you read to jot down questions, ideas, or feelings you have while reading.	
Respond to your reading	Pause during your reading to ask questions such as: Do I agree with the author's points? or How would I feel if I were a character?
Question	Use *who, what, where, when, why,* and *how* questions as you read.
	Ask questions about characters, the author, events, motivations, possibilities, or actions.
Predict	Try to guess what will happen next. Consider why you think an event will come to pass
Summarize	In your own words, identify the main points in what you are reading.
	Try to identify the main idea of each paragraph you read.
Identify relationships	What connections are there between ideas in the story?
	What relationships exist between characters?
	What connections can you make between your reading and other things you have read?

Reading Skills

Introducing the Skill

You may wish to compare passive and active reading to passive and active listening. Ask students to think about the difference between just listening to what somebody says and responding as you listen by asking questions, summarizing and repeating what the person has said, and sharing your own thoughts.

Previewing the Skill

Have students preview the chart on page 271. Then go over each suggestion with them in detail.

Practicing the Skill

Have students follow the steps outlined and use active reading techniques while reading the story, "Old Man Coyote and the Beginning." Remind students that these skills are useful when reading any material.

Reviewing the Skill

Using the notes from their reading, students can discuss the story in small groups. Ask students to apply these techniques to another selection.

Answers for Try It Yourself

1. *Responses will vary.*
2. In paragraph 1, Old Man Coyote is lonely and searches for something besides water. In paragraph 2, a duck discovers earth at the bottom of the water. In paragraph 3, Old Man Coyote creates the earth. In paragraph 4, Old Man Coyote makes companions for himself and the ducks. In paragraph 5, Old Man Coyote makes other animals. In paragraph 6, the greedy bear is forced to hibernate because he was not fit to live with the other animals.
3. *Responses will vary.*
4. *Responses will vary.*
5. *Responses will vary.*
6. *Responses will vary.*

Try It Yourself

Use the following suggestions for active reading as you read the story "Old Man Coyote and the Beginning." Make notes in your journal about your predictions and questions.

1. Before you begin reading, make a prediction about the story. As you read, determine whether or not your prediction is right. Reevaluate your prediction or make new predictions as you learn more of the story. Think about the reasons behind the predictons you make.
2. Summarize what happens in each paragraph. What are the main events? In what ways are the events related to previous events?
3. Pose questions about the selection throughout your reading. Begin by jotting down any questions you have before you read the story. As you read, you may find answers to some of your questions and you will raise new questions.
4. As you read, think about how you would feel if you were Old Man Coyote. How would your feelings change over the course of the story? What would you think of the bear?
5. What connections can you make between this story and other myths and tales you have read?
6. When you have finished reading the selection, review your predictions, questions, and summaries. Use your notes to discuss the story with your classmates.

Old Man Coyote and the Beginning

In the beginning there was only water and Old Man Coyote. No one knows where they came from. Old Man Coyote was lonely and thought he needed something more than water. As he was looking around, he saw two red-eyed ducks. Old Man Coyote asked the ducks if they knew of anything else that existed in the world. They told him that they thought there might be something deep under the water. Old Man Coyote asked one of the ducks to dive down to see what was there.

The duck dove down and Old Man Coyote and the other duck waited anxiously. Finally, the duck surfaced. He said that he had bumped into something with his head, so surely there must be something there besides water. The duck dove down again and after some time, he surfaced with a root in his bill. Old Man Coyote thought that where there are roots, there must be earth. He ordered the duck to dive again. This time the duck came up with a lump of soft earth.

CONTINUED

With the small lump of earth, Old Man Coyote said he would make the earth. He blew on the lump of earth and it began to grow. It spread all around. The ducks were surprised and pleased. Old Man Coyote planted the small root and things began to grow. He dug out some earth and made hills and mountains. Then he made rivers, streams, and springs so there would be fresh water and food everywhere.

Old Man Coyote and the ducks thought the earth was beautiful, but Old Man Coyote still felt alone. He knew something was missing—companions. He took some mud and with it he made humans. The ducks wanted companions too. So Old Man Coyote made all kinds of ducks. Everyone was happy.

Old Man Coyote ran into Cirape, the coyote. No one knew where Cirape came from. He was pleased with the earth and its creatures, but he felt there should be some different animals, as well. So Old Man Coyote made buffalo, elk, deer, antelopes, and a bear. All was well until the bear told Old Man Coyote that he was bored. He had nothing to do. Old Man Coyote thought, and then he made a special bird. From the bear's claws, some buffalo sinew, and some leaves, Old Man Coyote formed a prairie chicken. The chicken provided entertainment by dancing for the other animals. The animals all watched the chicken dance, and they too wanted to dance.

Old Man Coyote gave the animals a special dance, but the bear wanted his own dance. (The bear was not easily satisfied.) The bear got his own dance, but he felt something was still missing. He wanted some music to dance to. Old Man Coyote created a grouse and gave him a song, but the bear now felt that he alone should have the power to dance. After all, according to the bear, he was big and important. Old Man Coyote was tired of this impolite bear. He told the bear he was not fit to live with the rest of the animals. He ordered the bear to stay in his den by himself. He would sleep all winter so that the others would see him less often

Project Note

- Students might make masks that represent characters in the myths in this unit. Students might work in groups to represent the stories from the five different cultures.
- Students may wish to wear their masks with or without other costuming the first time they display the masks.
- papier-maché and paints can be messy. Students may wish to wear smocks while working on the project. Newspapers can be used to cover the work space.

Unit Project

Making Masks

Masks have been been made and worn in most cultures throughout history. They have been used in celebrations, dances, and in theatrical performances. Masks have also been used in serious religious events such as healing ceremonies and funeral rituals. Through the years, masks have been made out of any material that can be carved and molded. They are recognized as an important form of art.

Try It Yourself

As a class, put together an exhibit of masks. Agree upon a theme for the exhibit. Each student in the class should create an original papier-maché mask that somehow relates to this theme.

Student Model

It is the anniversary of the opening of the school, and Veronica and her classmates want to do a special project in honor of the occasion. They decide to put together an exhibit of papier-maché masks entitled "Celebration!" Students will make masks and then decorate the masks to match the celebration theme.

First, students collect old newspapers from their own homes and from friends and neighbors. The teacher provides some poster board, and the class gets started. Students cut the poster board into strips, one strip for each person. Veronica takes her strip and staples together the two ends so that she has an oval loop. The oval loop is large enough to encircle her face, so she knows that it is the right size for a mask. Then she builds a base for the mask, by stuffing newspaper into the loop. The papier-maché will be placed over the newspaper. Veronica would like her mask to have a nose, so she tapes a small ball of newspaper to the foundation. This will create a bulge beneath the papier-maché.

The class tears thin strips of newspaper for the making of the papier-maché. Each person has a bowl of warm water and either a bowl of glue or a bowl of flour paste. Strips are dipped in water, then dipped in one of the other mixtures, and then placed over the newspaper. Veronica uses four layers of papier-maché. She and her classmates allow the masks to dry for several days. When her mask is completely dry, Veronica pulls the newspaper out of it. The papier-maché is stiff, and her creation looks like a real mask. With a pair of sharp scissors she cuts out eyes and a small hole for the mouth. Then she begins decorating. She paints the mask half white and half purple, to give it a festive look. She also paints stars on the cheeks, glues glitter all over the mask, and outlines the mouth in pink. Most students paint their masks, and some create detailed designs, with hats and hair made from yarn. When all masks are completed, the class puts the masks on display in the hallway of the school under a sign that reads "Celebration!"

Examining the Model

1. What did Veronica and her classmates do to make sure the masks would fit?
2. What did Veronica do to decorate her mask?

Planning Your Masks

1. As a class, decide what theme your class exhibit should have. Think about feelings, celebrations, and holidays.
2. Gather materials for making mask foundations. For a foundation, each person should have crumpled newspaper and a strip of poster board or corrugated cardboard. The strip should have a width of about two inches, and it should be long enough to encircle your face when the two ends are held together.
3. Gather materials for making the papier-maché. For papier-maché you will need strips of newspaper, warm water, and white glue or a paste made from flour and water.
4. Think about materials for decorating the mask. You might use paint, yarn, cloth, buttons, construction paper, leaves, or twigs. Search for materials that will make your mask interesting and original.

Making Your Masks

1. Begin by making the foundation of your mask. Hold the two ends of the strip together and staple them. This should form an oval ring.
2. Crumple newspaper and stuff it inside of the oval ring. If you would like your mask to have a nose, create a bulge by taping a small ball of crumpled paper to the surface of the newspaper foundation.
3. Tear the newspaper into strips, then dip the strips one at a time into a bowl of warm water. Then dip them into a bowl of glue, or flour paste.
4. Place the strips one at a time over the newspaper, fastening each end to the cardboard ring. Your strips should slightly overlap as you lay them down over the newspaper, and you should smooth them down with your hands as you work. For your mask, you should have four or five layers. You might allow the first two layers to dry before continuing with the last two or three layers.
5. It is very important to allow the mask to dry completely. When the papier-maché is hard and dry, pull out the crumpled newspaper. The dried papier-maché can now stay together without the newspaper. Leave the cardboard ring in place.
6. You might want to use sharp scissors to cut holes in the mask for eyes and a mouth.
7. Have fun decorating your mask. You can paint and/or glue paper, buttons, feathers, sparkles, or anything you'd like, to your mask. Remember to follow the theme that your class has chosen.

Showing Your Masks

1. Hang your masks on a wall in your classroom and invite other teachers and students to look at them. You might invite people to guess the theme behind the masks.
2. Find out if your school or local library would be interested in placing your masks on display. You might also place your masks in the hallway of your school. Make a sign stating the theme of your exhibit.

Answers for Examining the Model

1. Veronica and her classmates used strips of posterboard that they made into circles the size of their heads to make sure the masks would fit.
2. Veronica painted her mask white and purple. She painted stars on the cheeks, glued glitter all over the mask, and outlined the mouth in pink.

ANALYTIC SCALE FOR PROJECT

Assign a score from 1 to 25 for each grading criterion below.

Masks

- **Organization.** The group set attainable goals and created a schedule or strategy for achieving those goals.
- **Cooperation.** The group assigned tasks fairly to each member, and each member cooperated toward achieving the group's goals.
- **Goal Achievement.** The group worked steadily toward its goals and did, in fact, achieve them.
- **Presentation.** The group presented a product of high quality that met the initial project description.

Vocabulary Check Test

Ask students to number their papers from one to ten. Have students complete each sentence with a word from the Vocabulary for the Unit in the Unit Review.

1. The crops withered and died as a result of the drought.
2. Dave had grandiose ideas, but he lacked the gumption to see them through.
3. The fox is often considered a cunning animal.
4. The eagle clutched the snake firmly in its talons.
5. The infinite size of the universe boggles my mind.
6. Elise smiled radiantly in her moment of triumph.
7. Asha's voice quivered in fear.
8. We found impressive examples of stalagmites in the cavern.
9. Everyone died in the crash except Darnell, the sole survivor.
10. After a month of cloudy days, the sun finally emerged.

Unit Review

Summary

Literary Terms for the Unit

central conflict, 236
characterization, 270
irony, 236
inciting incident, 245
internal conflict, 253
motive, 245
myth, 263
simile, 253
symbol, 253

Vocabulary for the Unit

abyss, 242
betray, 243
cavern, 241
chasm, 232
complement, 261
constellation, 251
cosmic, 249
cower, 234
crotchety, 251
cunning, 241
deity, 241
demur, 231
disc, 241
disillusion, 251
drivel, 241
drought, 249
dwell, 231
ebb, 233
emerge, 231
envoy, 243
eternity, 249
exalt, 241
grandiose, 249
illumination, 251
infinite, 250
intolerable, 234
manifestation, 252
meditate, 251
mission, 251
oppress, 231
privilege, 252
quiver, 242
radiantly, 252
sole, 241
strewn, 233
summon, 243
talon, 232
tempestuous, 231
transgressor, 234
vain, 231
virile, 243
wrest, 234

Questions for Writing, Discussion, and Research

1. What values are expressed in the literature of the five cultures represented in this unit?
2. Which culture did you find most intriguing? Why?

Spelling Check Test

Ask students to number their papers from one to ten. Read each word aloud. Then read aloud the sentence containing the word. Repeat the word. Ask students to write the word on their papers, spelling it correctly.

- The full moon appeared to be a luminous disc in the sky.
- Isis was one of the deities worshiped by the ancient Egyptians.
- The eccentric millionaire planned to build a sprawling, grandiose pink mansion.
- Harry's new shoes complemented his new suit.
- There was a period of drought and the crops withered in the sun.
- In ancient Greek mythology, the cosmic center of the gods was Mt. Olympus.
- The thought of going up to the attic alone made the small child quiver with fear.
- The hole was so deep that it almost seemed as if it were a bottomless abyss.
- The envoy delivered the king's message to the ruler of the distant land.
- Raymond was angry with Andrea for betraying the secret he had shared with her.

For Your Reading List

Alejandro Castro
Buker Middle School
Wenham, Massachusetts

The Haunted Flute and Other Japanese Stories
edited by Nina Rosenstein

I read *The Haunted Flute and Other Japanese Stories.* It is a collection of stories from Japan with a moral to each one. The story I liked most was "Reflection." A man who lived on the outskirts of town went into the city for the first time. There he saw a mirror, an object that he had never seen before. When he looked into it he thought he saw his deceased father. He quickly bought the mirror and brought it home and put it in the cupboard. Each night he would go to the closet and converse with his father. His wife saw him and went to take a look. She opened the cupboard and saw her reflection. She was enraged. She thought he was cheating on her with another woman. In the end the problem was resolved by a wise man. To find out how the wise man resolved the problem, you will have to read the book. If you like this story, there is another story about a mirror called "The Matsuyama Mirror." There are also many other interesting stories in *The Haunted Flute* that are just as good.

GOALS/OBJECTIVES

Studying this unit will enable students to

- enjoy contemporary retellings of traditional oral materials from across the entire continent of Africa
- explain and give examples of common types of oral stories, including myths and trickster tales
- briefly describe the geography, resources, and history of Africa
- define and give examples of *setting, folk tale, aim, personification, oral tradition, fable, myth, motif,* and *legend*
- identify sentences by function (declarative, interrogative, imperative, and exclamatory) and by structure (simple, compound, complex, and compound-complex)
- dramatize a traditional tale
- identify base words, prefixes, and suffixes
- distinguish between formal and informal English and use each in its proper context
- write a business letter
- create a time line of African history

ADDITIONAL UNIT MATERIALS IN THE ASSESSMENT PORTFOLIO

- Vocabulary Worksheet, 2.7.17
- Unit Test, 2.7.18

See also the Additional Resources Box in the marginal notes accompanying each selection.

CROSS-CURRICULAR CONNECTIONS

- Geography, 284, 294, 300, 308
- Science, 312
- Social Studies, 308, 320, 326
- World History, 288, 294, 300, 320, 326

UNIT 7 AFRICAN TRADITIONS

Let me tell you a story my grandfather told me.

—Fitzgerald Iyamabo

279

UNIT SKILLS OUTLINE

Literary Skills and Concepts

- Aim, 291, 324
- Fable, 311, 316
- Folk Tale, 291
- Legend, 331
- Motif, 304
- Myth, 304, 311, 316
- Oral Tradition, 299, 304
- Personification, 291
- Setting, 287

Other Language Arts Skills and Concepts

- Base Words, Prefixes, and Suffixes, 317
- Dramatizing a Traditional Tale, 305
- Formal and Informal English, 325
- Sentence Types, 292
- Writing a Business Letter, 332

Additional Questions and Activities

Have your students research topics related to Africa for oral reports to the rest of the class. Interesting topics for oral reports include the following:

the natural history of the Nile River

ancient Egyptian religion

life in a particular African city (Cairo, Lagos, Casablanca, Algiers, Addis Ababa, Johannesburg)

African empires (Kush, Meroë, Axum, Ghana, Mali, Songhay, Kanem-Bornu, Benin, Oyo, the Kongo kingdom)

Roman Africa

African independence movements in the 1960s

the African slave trade

exploration of Africa by Europeans

the languages of Africa

African game parks and reserves

religion in Africa

life in a traditional African village (students should choose a particular culture, such as the Masai or the Bushmen)

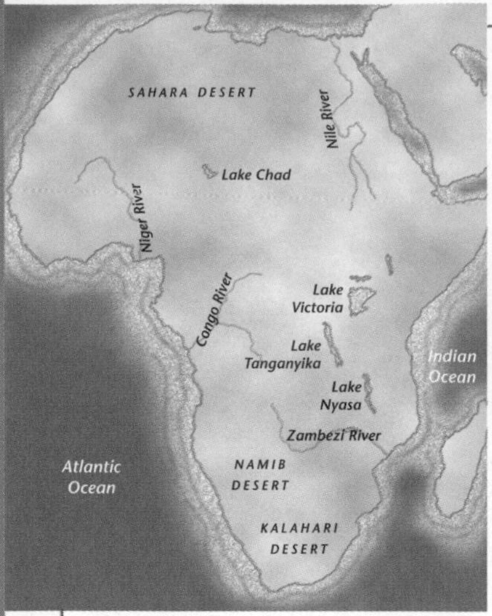

The Geography, History, and Oral Literatures of Africa

No brief introduction can do justice to the richness and variety of Africa. The second largest continent on Earth, Africa has been continually inhabited by humans for over three and a half million years, and during that time, many thousands of fascinating cultures have arisen there. Today, over a thousand languages are spoken on the continent by peoples living in ways that represent the whole range of human experience.

In Africa today one can find modern urbanites living in large cities such as Cairo, Lagos, Casablanca, Algiers, Addis Ababa, and Johannesburg; nomadic Islamic traders eking harsh existences from the vast, arid wasteland of the Sahara Desert; hunting and gathering peoples, the Bambusi, living lives relatively untouched by western civilization in the rain forests of the Congo River Basin; and hundreds of other groups with distinct ways of life. **Northern Africa** has been strongly influenced by Arabia, is largely Islamic, and has many people of Arab and Berber heritage. **Sub-Saharan Africa,** or the part of the African continent south of the Sahara Desert, is inhabited primarily by black Africans who follow Christian, Islamic, or traditional religions. Arabic and related languages are widely spoken in the north, while languages of the Bantu and Khoisan families predominate in Sub-Saharan Africa.

Physical Geography

Africa's cultural richness is paralleled by the vastness and variety of its physical geography. A massive **plateau**, the continent is bounded by the Mediterranean and Red Seas to the north, the Atlantic Ocean to the west, and the Indian Ocean to the east. The equator divides the continent, although the greater area of land lies to the north. The northernmost coast has a typically Mediterranean climate, characterized by warm, dry summers and rainy winters, but most of the rest of the continent is tropical

Nigerian Mask

and quite warm. Much of the north is taken up by the world's largest desert, the **Sahara,** which covers a quarter of the continent. From east to west below the Sahara lies the Sudan, site of many of the earliest black African empires. Along the equator runs a strip of well-watered, lush tropical rain forest. Below the equator are areas of acacia trees and brush, vast grasslands known as savannas, and two smaller deserts, the Namib and the Kalahari. East Africa has several large mountain ranges. The highest peak is **Mount Kilimanjaro,** in Tanzania, at over nineteen thousand feet. Also in East Africa are several large lakes, including Rudolf, Nyasa, Tanganyika, and the largest, **Lake Victoria,** which is the source of the world's longest river, the **Nile.** The Nile flows northward, through Egypt, and empties into the Mediterranean. Another large lake, Chad, is located in north central Africa. Other important rivers include the Niger, the Congo, and the Zambesi.

Mount Kilimanjaro

African Wildlife and Parks

In the popular Western understanding, Africa is associated primarily with its animal life, and especially with large hoofed mammals such as camels, antelope, zebras, giraffes, African elephants, wildebeests, and rhinoceroses. Also fascinating are Africa's species of great apes, the gorillas and the chimpanzees, and its varied birdlife, which includes almost two thousand native species. Many of the larger creatures—the mammals, especially—are threatened by poaching, destruction of habitats, and other consequences of human intervention. For example, the African elephant, represented by some two million individuals in the early 1900s, has declined to a few hundred thousand. Fortunately, a number of African states—notably Botswana, Kenya, Malawi, Namibia, South Africa, Tanzania, Uganda, Zaire, Zambia, and Zimbabwe—have established large game preserves and national parks for the protection of their wildlife. The most famous such parks include the **Serengeti National Park** in Tanzania, the **Tsavo Park** in Kenya, and the **Kalahari Gemsbok National Park** in Botswana and South Africa.

HISTORICAL NOTE

You might wish to share with your students some specific information about one great early African culture. Here are some notes to share on ancient Egypt: Located in northeastern Africa, **Egypt** is a desert country bounded by the **Mediterranean Sea** and the **Red Sea.** The **Nile River** flows north through the country, dividing the desert into unequal parts.Throughout its history, almost all the life to be found in Egypt has been in the valley and delta of the Nile. The floodplains of the river made the land fertile for crop growing, allowing the area to sustain human life. It was along this great river that the civilization of ancient Egypt flourished in an almost unbroken record from about 3100 BC to 30 BC.

Two separate communities, Lower Egypt and Upper Egypt, were formed along the Nile during the early 3000s BC. The two kingdoms were joined around 3100 BC, traditionally by **King Menes** of Upper Egypt, though possibly by a former king named **Aha.** The history of ancient Egypt following Menes's conquest is usually divided into thirty or thirty-one dynasties. These dynasties are in turn grouped into four major periods. The most important of these periods were

- the **Archaic** or **Early Dynastic Period,** from 3100 BC to 2575 BC, when Egypt was first united under a central king;
- the **Old Kingdom,** lasting from 2575 BC to 2040 BC, the period of the great pyramid builders such as **Khufu** and **Khafre;**
- the **Middle Kingdom,** which existed from roughly 2040 BC to 1550 BC and saw the development of the cult of the god Osiris; and
- the **New Kingdom,** or **Golden Age of Egypt,** which extended from about 1532 BC to 1070 BC, a time when powerful rulers such as **Tutankhamen** and **Ramses the Great** oversaw a vast empire extending into Mesopotamia.

Between these great periods of Egyptian history were intermediate periods of social and political upheaval. Nonetheless, Egyptian history shows a remarkable continuity over its three-thousand-year span.

Throughout most of its history, Egypt was ruled by an all-powerful king. The king was believed to be a god. For the first thirty years of his reign, he was identified with the falcon god Horus. After reigning for thirty years, or after his death, he was identified with the god of fertility and the underworld, Osiris. As the representative of the gods on earth, the king had the responsibility to establish ma'at, divine order on earth. Beneath the king was a small class of officials, a very large class of common people, and especially in later periods, slaves. A powerful, centralized authority was necessary to run the large-scale irrigation and farming of lands adjacent to the Nile. The wealth of the country was based on its production of crops, mostly wheat and barley.

The use of writing helped the ancient Egyptians to form and administer a powerful, centralized government. Two forms of writing were invented near the beginning of the Early Dynastic Period. Hieroglyphs, which combined pictures and representations of sounds, were used for inscriptions on monuments. A simpler cursive form of writing, hieratic, was used for documents. Modern scholars were able to decipher ancient Egyptian after the discovery of the Rosetta Stone, on which was carved a single passage in three different languages: hieroglyphics, a late form of Egyptian known as demotic, and the well-knownGreek language. As early as the first dynasty, Egyptians wrote documents on sheets made from the papyrus plant.

Women's farming co-op

History

Africa gave rise to one of the earliest and greatest of cultures, that of ancient **Egypt,** which lasted for approximately three thousand years, from 3000 BC to 30 BC. (See the introduction to Egyptian civilization on pages 225–227). The **Phoenicians** arrived in Africa around 1000 BC and built one of the great cities of the ancient world, **Carthage.** Later, the Romans conquered the northern part of the continent, creating the Roman colony called Africa, from which the current name of the continent comes.

Egypt was not the only major empire in early northeastern Africa. **Kush** and **Meroë,** in the middle of the Nile Valley, lasted for over a thousand years and were important trading centers. The succeeding empire of Axum, itself derived from Arabia, across the Red Sea, developed into the Christian Empire of Ethiopia. Several great African empires emerged in the Sudan, including Ghana, Mali, Songhay, Kanem-Bornu, Benin, Oyo, and the Kongo kingdom. In the southern part of the continent were the empires of Great Zimbabwe and Monomatapa. In the fifteenth century, the Portuguese began to explore the Atlantic coast of Africa, and during the following centuries, the African slave trade developed. It is estimated that as many as ten million Africans were brutally stolen away from their homelands and forced into menial servitude in Europe, the Americas, and elsewhere, before this evil traffic in humans was ended. In the second half of the nineteenth century, European powers divided up the African continent into colonial empires. In the second half of the twentieth century, these colonial governments fell, one by one, becoming independent African states. In 1994, **Nelson Mandela** became the first black president of South Africa. (For information about specific cultures and regions of Africa, see the Cross-curricular Connections introducing the tales in this unit.)

African Oral Literatures

The stories told in this unit are retellings by contemporary Africans of tales from **oral traditions** in each of the five major regions of the continent: North Africa, West Africa, East Africa, Central Africa, and Southern Africa.

Young Masai girl

Especially in Sub-Saharan Africa, oral traditions have been and remain to this day extremely rich and varied. Much of the vast African literature of oral myths, poetry, praise songs, legends, tales, theater, children's rhymes, proverbs, riddles, and spells is unknown outside Africa itself, and much is in danger of extinction as traditional cultures yield to modern, westernized ways of life. Fortunately, in many African universities, scholars are now busily attempting to capture this oral literature in writing and so to preserve the heritage for future generations. In the past, western audiences have often had to depend on watered-down, distorted versions of African tales retold by Europeans who had little familiarity with the cultures in which these tales originated. The editors of this text are therefore proud to present, in this unit, a collection of authentic retellings from original African sources.

Stool from the Ivory Coast

African Civilization

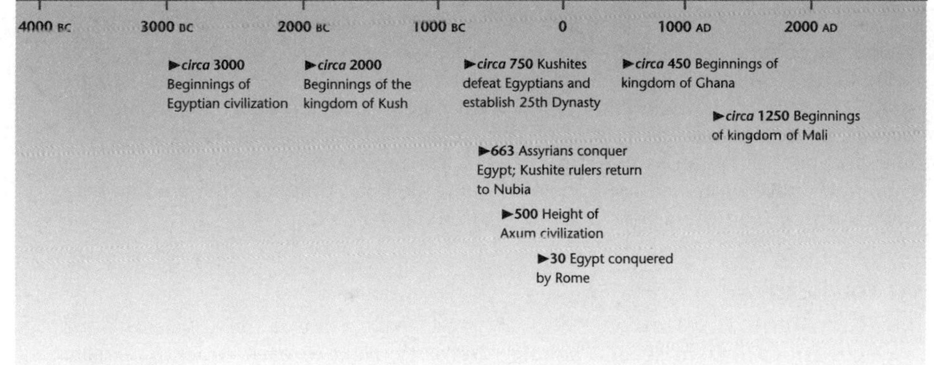

The Egyptians worshiped many gods. When the first centralized state was formed, local gods became absorbed into a single pantheon.

The keys to Egyptian religion were the concepts of ma'at, discussed above, and of the ka, or soul, which was believed to live on after death. Most of the great monumental sculpture of ancient Egypt is concerned with preparing for the existence of the king's ka in the afterlife. Great tombs, including the pyramids, were built and stocked with goods for use by the dead king. The bodies of royal persons and of some great officials were embalmed in a process called mummification so that the ka might inhabit the preserved body after death. In addition, elaborate ceremonies were performed to ensure the king's successful journey into the next life.

QUOTABLES

"Do not look where you fell, but where you slipped."

—African proverb

GOALS/OBJECTIVES

Studying this lesson will enable students to
- enjoy a comic folk tale from North Africa
- briefly describe the geography of North Africa
- explain the term *setting* and use it to analyze a tale

ADDITIONAL RESOURCES

READER'S GUIDE
- Selection Worksheet, 7.1

ASSESSMENT PORTFOLIO
- Selection Check Test, 2.7.1
- Selection Test, 2.7.2

PRONUNCIATION EXERCISE
- Grade 7 Audiocassette, Side B, Track 33

CROSS-CURRICULAR CONNECTIONS

GEOGRAPHY

Have your students locate the countries of Morocco, Algeria, Tunisia, Libya, and Egypt on a map of North Africa.

Prereading

NORTHERN AFRICA

"Goha and His Donkey"

Anonymous, retold by Mahmoud Ibrahim Mostafa

Cross-curricular Connection

Geography. The region of North Africa encompasses the countries of Morocco, Algeria, Tunisia, Libya, and Egypt. The area is bounded to the north and west by the Mediterranean Sea and the Atlantic Ocean, to the east by the Red Sea, and to the south by Western Sahara, Mauritania, Mali, Niger, Chad, Ethiopia, and Sudan. The coastal areas generally enjoy a Mediterranean climate, characterized by rainy winters and long, dry summers. The area around the Atlantic coast tends to experience lower temperatures because of the cool current from the Canary Islands. The southern area of the region is a vast desert called the Sahara. The Atlas Mountains rise between the coastal zone and the desert. Most of the population of North Africa is located in the coastal zone.

The population of the region can be divided according to lifestyle—nomadic or sedentary—or by culture—Berber or Arab. The region has been inhabited by Berbers probably since the Paleolithic or Neolithic periods. To an extent, the Atlas Mountains have protected the people of North Africa from invasions from the south, but over the years they have been invaded from the north by Phoenicians, Romans, Arabs, and French. The Arabs brought the Islamic religion to the region with their victorious conquests during the seventh and eighth centuries. North Africa was colonized by Europeans during the 1800s. Since 1962, when Algeria achieved its independence, all of the countries of North Africa have been independent.

The natural resources and economies of the countries in this region vary considerably. Algeria and Libya have economies based largely on the export of oil and natural gas. Tourism, foreign investments, and the exportation of phosphates are important to Morocco's economic growth. Tunisia has few natural resources and relies mainly on agriculture, although crop yields are generally poor. Egypt produces oil and hydroelectric power and exports many agricultural products, including livestock, citrus fruits, and cotton.

"Goha and His Donkey" and "Goha and the Pot," on page 288, are folk tales from North Africa.

As You Read

In **"Goha and His Donkey,"** Goha receives criticism from several people. Make a chart like the one below. As you read, make a list of the criticisms Goha receives. Next to each criticism, explain how you would respond to it.

CRITICISM	RESPONSE
Goha should not make his son walk on a hot day	When I was a boy, my father made me walk

AS YOU READ

Second criticism: It is disrespectful of the son to let his father walk while the son rides a donkey. Responses of students to this criticism will vary.

Third criticism: Goha and his son should not both be walking when they could be riding the strong donkey and getting to their destination more quickly. Responses of students to this criticism will vary.

Fourth criticism: Both should not ride the donkey on such a hot day, as this is hard on the animal. Responses of students to this criticism will vary.

READER'S JOURNAL

Have you ever had somebody tell you that the way you were doing something was not the best way? What was your response to his or her advice? Did you change your ways? Why, or why not?

"Goha and His Donkey"

ANONYMOUS, RETOLD BY MAHMOUD IBRAHIM MOSTAFA

One summer morning Goha took his son out to work in his cotton field. He was riding his donkey while his son walked next to him, when they came upon some neighbors sitting by the side of the road. One of them called Goha aside and scolded him for riding the donkey and letting his young son walk on a hot summer day. So Goha got off the donkey, and put his son on the donkey's back, and he continued on his way.

A few minutes later he passed by some people from his village and greeted them, and one of them replied, "Goha, don't you think it is disrespectful of the son to let his father walk while he rides a donkey?" Goha thought about it for a minute, and with a smile on his face he decided what he should do.

The next day, Goha and his son walked along with the beast in the dusty and hot afternoon, and they met a friend doing ablution[1] in preparation for a prayer. The friend suddenly shouted at Goha for putting himself and his son through such a difficult walk, when they could have been riding the strong donkey, and getting to their destination more quickly. Goha looked up and began to wonder how he could really solve this problem, especially since only yesterday he had thought he knew exactly what to do.

A few days later Goha decided to have both himself and his son ride on the donkey. It was a very hot day, when yet again he came across one of his neighbors, shaking his head and saying, "Goha, don't you have any pity for the donkey? How can the two of you, father and son alike, be riding a donkey on such a hot day?" And the neighbor left them, shaking his head in disgust. Goha had a very puzzled look on his face, "What am I to do now? One never seems to be able to satisfy anyone in this world. What will I do now?"

❶ For what is Goha scolded? What does he do?

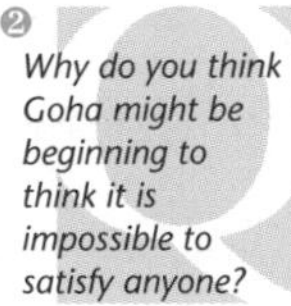

❷ Why do you think Goha might be beginning to think it is impossible to satisfy anyone?

1. **ablution.** Washing the body as part of a religious ceremony

READER'S JOURNAL

As an alternative activity, you might ask students to imagine being a friend of Goha's and advising him on not taking others' criticisms too seriously.

ANSWERS TO GUIDED READING QUESTIONS

❶ Goha is scolded for riding the donkey and letting his young son walk on such a hot day. Goha decides to let his son ride while he walks.

❷ Every time Goha follows someone's advice, he gets scolded for doing so.

SUPPORT FOR LEP STUDENTS

PRONUNCIATIONS OF PROPER NOUNS AND ADJECTIVES

Mah • moud Ib • ra • him Mos • ta • fa (mä´məd ē´bra him´ məs ta´fə) n.
Go • ha (gō´hə) n.

ADDITIONAL VOCABULARY

amiss—wrong

ANSWER TO GUIDED READING QUESTION

❶ Goha solved his problem by enlisting the help of his son to carry the donkey to work.

SELECTION CHECK TEST WITH ANSWERS

EX. Where was Goha going with his son?
They were going to work in the cotton fields.

1. For what is Goha first scolded?
He is scolded for making his son walk on such a hot day.

2. What does Goha's neighbor say when he sees Goha's son riding the donkey?
He says it is disrespectful for the son to ride while the father walks.

3. Who is riding on the donkey when the friend doing ablutions shouts at Goha?
Nobody is riding on the donkey.

4. Why does a neighbor criticize Goha when both he and his son ride the donkey?
The neighbor criticizes Goha for not having pity for the donkey.

5. What solution to Goha's problem does the village meet with disbelief?
The village sees Goha and his son carrying the donkey.

Leather bag. *Morocco*

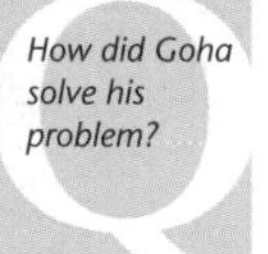

How did Goha solve his problem?

He went home that day not knowing what to do. His wife noticed that something was amiss, but he wouldn't tell her what it was. He could barely eat, and he gave a big portion of his dinner to his son. The son was very happy, but he thought to himself, "Why is father so troubled? I wish him well; my father is a good man." Later, he went to his room, and as he passed through his father's room, he noticed that his father was still sitting on his mat deep in thought.

The very next day, the whole village came out and gathered at the square in the center of the village, looking in disbelief at Goha and his son carrying the donkey on their way to work. ■

About the Author

Mahmoud Ibrahim Mostafa (1943–) was born in Shubra, Cairo, Egypt. He is a physician and has practiced in Columbia, South Carolina, for many years.

Responding to the Selection

What do you think the people of the village might say when they see Goha's latest solution to his problem? What other solutions do you think Goha might try? What would you tell Goha to do?

Reviewing the Selection

Recalling and Interpreting

1. **R** What did one of Goha's neighbors say upon seeing Goha ride a donkey while his son walked?

   I What attitudes does this neighbor have toward youth and age? Do you agree with the neighbor? Why, or why not?

2. **R** What does a person from Goha's village tell him later that day?

   I What attitudes does this person have toward youth and age? Why might this person's ideas be confusing to Goha?

3. **R** What solution does Goha try the next day? Why does Goha's friend shout at Goha? Why does one neighbor think it is wrong for Goha and his son to ride the donkey together?

   I What opinions do these two people have about the rights of animals? What is Goha's opinion?

4. **R** What does Goha try after a night of deep thought?

   I What opinion do you think the people of Goha's village have of him at the end of the story? Explain.

Synthesizing

5. What is your opinion of Goha? Why do you think he has difficulty solving his problem? Is the advice he receives good advice? Why, or why not?

Understanding Literature (Questions for Discussion)

Setting. The **setting** of a literary work is the time and place in which it happens. What is the setting of this tale? In what ways do the time and place relate to the events of the story?

Responding to the Selection

As an alternative activity, you might have students think about which piece of advice they most agree with and why.

Answers for Reviewing the Selection

RECALLING AND INTERPRETING

1. **Recalling.** The neighbor said that Goha should not ride while his young son walks. **Interpreting.** The neighbor seems to think that older people should take care of younger ones by making sure that they do not have to undergo strenuous activity.

2. **Recalling.** The person tells Goha that it shows disrespect for the boy to ride while his father walks. **Interpreting.** This person seems to think that young people should revere older ones. This person's advice directly contradicts the first person's advice.

3. **Recalling.** The next day Goha tries walking with the donkey. A friend shouts at Goha for putting himself and his son through a difficult walk when they could be riding. A few days later, a neighbor castigates Goha for riding with his son on the donkey's back, feeling that this is too difficult for the donkey. **Interpreting.** The first person seems not to care about the rights of animals, whereas the second person cares a great deal. Goha is simply puzzled by the contradictory advice.

4. **Recalling.** Goha tries carrying the donkey. **Interpreting.** The people probably think that Goha is foolish.

SYNTHESIZING

Responses will vary. Possible responses are given.

5. Goha's real problem, of course, is that he takes people's criticisms too seriously and tries to please everyone. He should learn to live more on his own terms. The advice that he receives cannot all be correct, for it is contradictory.

Answers for Understanding Literature

Responses will vary. Possible responses are given.

Setting. This tale is set in a very small town. The small town setting is important to the story because, in such a town, people know one another and feel free to make personal remarks such as those made by Goha's neighbors make.

GOALS/OBJECTIVES

Studying this lesson will enable students to
- enjoy a comic folk tale from North Africa
- name some important events from the history of North Africa
- explain the terms *trickster tale, folk tale, aim,* and *personification* and give examples of each
- identify sentences by function (declarative, interrogative, imperative, and exclamatory) and by structure (simple, compound, complex, and compound-complex)

ADDITIONAL RESOURCES

READER'S GUIDE
- Selection Worksheet, 7.2

ASSESSMENT PORTFOLIO
- Selection Check Test, 2.7.3
- Selection Test, 2.7.4

PRONUNCIATION EXERCISE
- Grade 7 Audiocassette, Side B, Track 34

CROSS-CURRICULAR CONNECTIONS

WORLD HISTORY

Have a student do an oral report on Hannibal and the Punic Wars as an extra credit assignment.

SOCIAL STUDIES

For extra credit, have students research and report to the class on other trickster tales, such as the African tales of Anansi the spider and the Native American coyote tales.

Prereading

"Goha and the Pot"

Anonymous, retold by Mahmoud Ibrahim Mostafa

Cross-curricular Connections

World History. While many people are familiar with the great ancient Egyptian civilization that flourished in North Africa, they are often unaware of the other great empires that gained power in this region. The Phoenicians, a people who originally came from the area of Lebanon, Syria, and Palestine, founded a settlement at Carthage, in modern-day Tunisia, in the eighth century BC. Carthage exerted its influence over the entire North African coast, traded widely, and came to be known in its time as the richest city in the world. In the third and second centuries BC, Carthage fought a series of wars with Rome known as the Punic Wars. Led by Hannibal Barca, Carthaginian forces crossed the Alps and invaded Italy, winning two major battles. Rome later defeated Carthage, and in 149 BC, Romans destroyed the city. Between the fall of Carthage and the establishment of firm Roman control over North Africa, several native kingdoms flourished, such as that of King Masinissa of Numidia who encouraged an increase in agriculture, built a city at Cirta, and issued coins.

Arab writers refer to the area of Northern Africa as Maghrib, which means "setting sun," or "the West." Beginning in AD 643, Arab peoples invaded North Africa, spreading the Arabic language and the Islamic religion. Today, North African culture is largely the result of the mingling of the native Berber culture and the Arabic Islamic culture. In the nineteenth century, North Africa was again occupied by Europeans—the French in Algiers and Tunisia, the Italians in Libya, and the French and the Spanish in Morocco. It was not until 1962 that Algeria achieved independence, the last state in North Africa to do so. In some regions of North Africa, French, or, less commonly, Spanish, is spoken and used in some types of writing.

Social Studies. Trickster tales are traditional stories that are passed on by word of mouth. The tales usually involve deceit, or a trick of some kind. The trickster figure, who is usually a clever underdog, typically outwits a slower-witted character. Trickster tales have been told around the world, especially in native North and South American cultures and in Africa. In Africa, common trickster animals include the hare, the spider, and the tortoise. Many African cultures also have tales about human tricksters.

As You Read

In **"Goha and the Pot,"** Goha tricks his neighbor. As you read, keep track of the interactions between Goha and his neighbor. Make a chart like the one below, noting Goha's actions and his neighbor's reactions.

GOHA'S ACTIONS	NEIGHBOR'S REACTIONS
asks neighbor for loan of a big brass pot	reluctantly lets Goha borrow the pot

AS YOU READ

Goha's action: returns with a big pot and a small one; tells neighbor that the big pot had a baby

Neighbor's reaction: accepts the pots

Goha's action: asks to borrow another pot

Neighbor's reaction: loans Goha two pots

Goha's action: knocks on neighbor's door

Neighbor's reaction: gives Goha all the pots in his possession

Goha's action: does not bring pots back

Neighbor's reaction: waits, hoping for lots of pots, but then gets nervous and goes to Goha to inquire

READER'S JOURNAL

Have you ever seen people behave foolishly because of greed? If so, explain what you have observed. If not, imagine some foolish actions that greed might inspire. Why do you think people behave differently when they are influenced by greed?

"Goha and the Pot"

MAHMOUD IBRAHIM MOSTAFA

One day, many, many years ago, Goha wanted to fix a meal for his family. He found that he needed a big pot, so he went to his next door neighbor to ask if he might borrow a big brass pot. The neighbor was reluctant to lend him the pot, but Goha promised that he would return it to his neighbor the following day.

To the surprise of his neighbor, Goha returned the next day with the big brass pot that he had borrowed and another one, smaller than the first. The neighbor felt that Goha must have made a mistake since he had lent Goha one pot, but Goha said that there was no mistake at all. He explained that overnight the pot he had borrowed went into labor and gave birth to this nice, shiny, little pot, and Goha insisted that the small pot also belonged to his neighbor!

A few days later, Goha returned to the same neighbor and asked if he could borrow another pot. This time the neighbor did not have any trouble giving him two big pots, thinking that Goha would return with more pots anyway. And indeed, when Goha returned the two big pots, he also brought two smaller, shining pots, much to the delight of his neighbor.

The next time Goha knocked on his neighbor's door, before he could even say a word, the neighbor gave him a basket full of big pots. In fact he gave Goha all the pots he had in his possession. His neighbor did not stop there, however; he even helped to carry the pots to Goha's house.

Days passed, then weeks, and the neighbor began to worry, but he did not mention his concern to Goha, hoping that Goha would come by

❶ *Why is the neighbor not reluctant to lend Goha a pot the second time?*

❷ *Why does the neighbor believe that Goha must have made a mistake? What explanation does Goha offer?*

❸ *Why doesn't the neighbor mention his concern to Goha at first?*

READER'S JOURNAL

As an alternative activity, you might have students write in their journals about other folk tales or fairy tales that they know in which someone learns a lesson.

ANSWERS TO GUIDED READING QUESTIONS

❶ The neighbor is not reluctant to lend Goha pots a second time because he believes Goha will bring him more pots.

❷ The neighbor knows that he lent Goha only one pot, but Goha tells his neighbor that over the night, the large pot gave birth to a smaller pot, and that both of them belonged to the neighbor.

❸ The neighbor was probably hoping that the longer he waited, the more pots Goha would eventually bring to him.

SUPPORT FOR LEP STUDENTS

ADDITIONAL VOCABULARY

inquire—ask

Literary Technique

PERSONIFICATION

Personification is the technique of speaking of a nonhuman thing as though it were human. This entire story hinges on examples of personification.

Selection Check Test with Answers

EX. What does Goha discover that he needs when he wants to fix a meal for his family?
Goha discovers that he needs a big pot.

1. From whom does Goha borrow a pot?
Goha borrows a pot from his neighbor.

2. What does Goha return to his neighbor the next day?
Goha returns the big brass pot that he had borrowed and another, smaller pot.

3. What does Goha say has happened to the big brass pot?
Goha says the big brass pot gave birth to the smaller pot.

4. How many pots does Goha's neighbor give him the third time he comes to borrow pots?
Goha's neighbor gives him all his pots.

5. What does Goha say has happened to his neighbor's pots when his neighbor asks Goha about them?
Goha says that all his neighbor's pots have died.

Tuareg altar bowl with stand. Algeria

some day soon with a whole room full of pots. After three whole months had gone by, the neighbor decided to go to Goha to inquire about his pots. Upon his inquiry, Goha with a very sad face said to his neighbor, "My dear neighbor, I'm saddened to tell you that your pots are all dead!"

The neighbor was furious, and he shouted, "Are you a madman? Pots don't die!"

Then Goha quietly said, "My dear neighbor, you were very willing to accept the fact that pots can have babies, weren't you? Why for goodness' sake don't you accept that they can also die?" ■

About the Author

A biography of **Mahmoud Ibrahim Mostafa** appears on page 286.

Responding to the Selection

What do you think of Goha's behavior? Is he clever or cruel? Does his neighbor deserve to be tricked? Why, or why not?

Reviewing the Selection

RECALLING AND INTERPRETING

1. **R** What does Goha ask to borrow from his neighbor? What is his neighbor's reaction to this request?

   I What does the neighbor's reaction reveal about his character?

2. **R** What "surprise" does Goha give his neighbor when he returns the next day? What explanation does Goha provide for this surprise?

   I Do you think the neighbor really believes Goha's explanation? Why is the neighbor willing to accept this explanation?

3. **R** What happens when Goha asks to borrow a pot the second time? the third time? How many pots does the neighbor give Goha the third time?

   I Why does the neighbor give Goha so many pots? Why do you think that Goha returns with more pots the first two times he borrows a pot?

4. **R** How long does the neighbor wait before asking Goha about his pots? What does Goha say has happened to the neighbor's pots? What does Goha say when the neighbor becomes angry?

   I Why does the neighbor wait so long before asking Goha about his pots? Do you think Goha is really "saddened" to tell the neighbor what has happened to the pots? What do you think has really happened to the pots?

SYNTHESIZING

5. Why do you think that Goha tricks his neighbor? What lesson, or moral, does this tale teach?

Understanding Literature (Questions for Discussion)

1. **Folk Tale and Aim.** A **folk tale** is a story passed by word of mouth from generation to generation. A writer's **aim** is his or her purpose, or goal. Why do you think this story was passed on among the people of North Africa? What was the aim in passing on this tale?
2. **Personification. Personification** is a figure of speech in which something not human is described as if it were human. What is personified in this story? What human qualities are given to this object or objects? What events does personification explain in this story? What is suggested about personification by the story's outcome?

ANSWERS FOR UNDERSTANDING LITERATURE

Responses will vary. Possible responses are given.

1. **Folk Tale and Aim.** The story is amusing, and it also teaches an important lesson—not to be greedy or dishonest.

2. **Personification.** Pots are personified in this story. They are described as having babies and as dying. Personification is used in the story to explain Goha's returning more pots than he borrowed and to explain Goha's not returning any pots at the end of the story. The outcome of the story suggests that personfication is merely a figure of speech and not to be taken literally. The neighbor has chosen to look the other way and to take the personfication literally out of greed.

RESPONDING TO THE SELECTION

Most students will agree that the neighbor is greedy and deserves to be tricked. Some, however, will point out that Goha is dishonest.

ANSWERS FOR REVIEWING THE SELECTION

RECALLING AND INTERPRETING

1. **Recalling.** Goha asks to borrow a pot. His neighbor is at first reluctant. **Interpreting.** The neighbor is not a generous person.

2. **Recalling.** Goha brings a second, smaller pot and says that the large pot had a baby. **Interpreting.** Doubtless the neighbor does not believe the story but is willing to accept it because he greedily wants the smaller pot.

3. **Recalling.** After the first time, the neighbor readily lends pots to Goha. The third time, the neighbor lends Goha all the pots that he has. **Interpreting.** The neighbor gives Goha so many pots because he hopes to receive many more pots back. Goha returns more pots than he borrowed the first two times so that he can trick the neighbor into lending him all his pots.

4. **Recalling.** The neighbor waits for three months before asking. Goha tells the neighbor that the pots all died. When the neighbor becomes angry, Goha says that if the neighbor were willing to believe that pots could have babies, he should be willing to believe that they can die. **Interpreting.** The neighbor waits in hopes of getting many pots back. Goha is not really saddened. He has played a trick and has kept the pots.

SYNTHESIZING

Responses will vary. Possible responses are given.

5. Goha tricks his neighbor to teach him a lesson. The lesson is that one should not allow one's greed to sway one from absolute honesty.

LANGUAGE LAB

INTRODUCING THE SKILL

Explain that this lesson deals with the classification of sentences. Explain that classification is the process of putting like things into groups, or classes.

PREVIEWING THE SKILL

Have students read the example sentences in the charts on pages 292 and 293. Ask them to come up with their own examples of declarative, interrogative, imperative, exclamatory, simple, compound, complex, and compound-complex sentences.

PRACTICING THE SKILL

Assign the Try It Yourself exercises on pages 292 and 293.

REVIEWING THE SKILL

If you wish to do so, assign the exercises on types of sentences in the Language Arts Survey. You might also choose to have students do the corresponding worksheet in the Essential Skills Practice Book: Language.

Language Lab

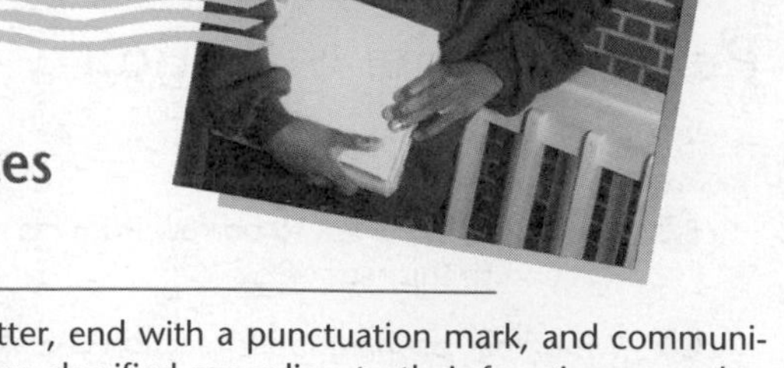

Understanding Sentences

Functions of Sentences

All sentences begin with a capital letter, end with a punctuation mark, and communicate a complete thought. Sentences are classified according to their functions, or roles. Sentences may be declarative, interrogative, imperative, or exclamatory.

FUNCTIONS OF SENTENCES

Function	Definition	Example
Declarative	A declarative sentence is a statement that provides information. It ends with a period.	Goha needed a pot.
Interrogative	An interrogative sentence asks a question. It ends with a question mark.	Why did Goha need a pot?
Imperative	An imperative sentence makes a command or a request. It ends with a period or an exclamation point.	Give Goha the pot. Don't give Goha my favorite pot!
Exclamatory	An exclamatory sentence expresses strong feeling. It ends with an exclamation point.	I love this shiny little pot!

Try It Yourself

Exercise A. On your own paper, tell whether each sentence is declarative, interrogative, imperative, or exclamatory. Indicate the correct punctuation.

EXAMPLE Goha promised that he would return the pot **declarative, period**

1. Goha brought his neighbor two pots when he had borrowed only one
2. What has happened to the pots
3. Why, the pots seem to have multiplied
4. You might believe that the larger pot gave birth to the smaller

Types of Sentences

A complete sentence contains both a subject and a verb. The most basic form of the sentence includes only these two elements. In the sentences below, the subject is italicized and the verb is printed in boldface.

EXAMPLES *Goha* **triumphed.** *To deceive* **angers.**

Sentences would be very dull if they always followed this simple form. The following chart will show you four different types of sentences. For more information, see the Language Arts Survey, 2.10, "Types of Sentences."

TYPES OF SENTENCES

Function	Definition	Example
simple sentence	has one subject and one verb	The pots died.
compound sentence	made up of two or more sentences that are usually combined by a connecting word such as *and, but, for, nor, or, so,* or *yet* and a comma.	Goha explained, but the neighbor became angry anyway.
complex sentence	contains an independent clause and at least one subordinate clause. An independent clause can stand by itself as a sentence. A subordinate clause contains a subject and a verb but cannot stand by itself as a sentence.	The neighbor was angry because Goha had tricked him.
compound-complex	combines a compound sentence and a complex sentence. It must have two or more independent clauses and at least one subordinate clause.	Goha, who was a trickster, explained his reasoning to his neighbor, so he taught his neighbor a valuable lesson.

Try It Yourself

Exercise B. Write a sentence of the type indicated, using the phrase in parentheses.

EXAMPLE simple (*I*)
I enjoyed the tale.

1. simple (*tricked*)
2. compound (*Goha returned the pot*)
3. complex (*there was one more pot than he had borrowed*)
4. compound-complex (*although he lost all of his pots*)

ANSWERS FOR TRY IT YOURSELF

EXERCISE A

1. declarative, period
2. interrogative, question
3. exclamatory, exclamation mark
4. imperative, period

EXERCISE B

Responses will vary. Possible responses are given.

1. Goha tricked his neighbor.
2. Goha returned the pot, and he brought a smaller one, too.
3. When Goha returned the pot, there was one more pot than he had borrowed.
4. Although he lost all of his pots, the neighbor learned a lesson, and perhaps he will be honest in the future.

GOALS/OBJECTIVES

Studying this lesson will enable students to

- enjoy a comic folk tale from Western Africa
- Describe important elements of the geography and history of Western Africa
- explain the term *oral tradition* and explain how oral traditions are used to pass along values to the young

ADDITIONAL RESOURCES

READER'S GUIDE

- Selection Worksheet, 7.3

ASSESSMENT PORTFOLIO

- Selection Check Test, 2.7.5
- Selection Test, 2.7.6

PRONUNCIATION EXERCISE

- Grade 7 Audiocassette, Side B, Track 35

CROSS-CURRICULAR CONNECTIONS

GEOGRAPHY AND WORLD HISTORY

Have students locate Nigeria on a map, along with the course of the Niger River.

Nigeria is a fascinating country with a rich history, a greatly varied population, and many wonderful oral traditions. You may wish to have students do some research and present reports on the geography, history, art, oral traditions, religions, and lifestyles of Nigeria.

Prereading

WESTERN AFRICA

"Yemoja, Queen of the Seas"

Yoruba Tale, retold by Fitzgerald Iyamabo

Cross-curricular Connection

Geography and World History. On the west coast of Africa, bordered by Benin, Niger, Chad, and Cameroon, lies Nigeria, named after the mighty Niger River. With more than 119 million inhabitants, Nigeria is the most populous country in Africa.

The peoples and cultures of Nigeria are extremely varied. Modern cities like Lagos, the capital, exist alongside ancient villages where people live traditional lives. Major groups living in the country include the Ibo in the east, the Hausa and Fulani in the north, and the Yoruba in the west. Altogether, Nigeria has more than 250 different ethnic groups, each with its own customs, traditions, and language. The official language of the country is English, a legacy of British colonial rule, which ended when Nigeria achieved its independence in 1960. Most Nigerians today are Christians or Muslims, although many still practice traditional religions. Often these traditional religions are practiced alongside Christianity or Islam.

Many African Americans can trace their ancestry to Nigeria, which was one of the major sites of the slave trade that began in the fifteenth century and lasted for over two hundred years. The traditional Yoruba people of Nigeria, from whom the two tales in this section come, are a primarily agricultural people with one of the most complex and beautiful oral literatures in the world.

As You Read

The story **"Yemoja, Queen of the Seas"** can be read as having three parts. The first part describes an action taken by the main character, Tunde. The second part tells what happens as a consequence of Tunde's action. The third part tells what Tunde learns from his experience. As you read the story, describe in your journal what happens in each of these three parts.

WHAT TUNDE DOES AT THE BEGINNING OF THE STORY	WHAT HAPPENS TO TUNDE AS A RESULT	WHAT TUNDE LEARNS

AS YOU READ

The three-part dialectic structure of the story is as follows: Part 1—At the beginning of the story, Tunde offends the Maker by hitting a frog with a stone. Part 2—While washing himself in the sea, Tunde either dies or goes into a trance. He awakens in the land of Yemoja, Queen of the Seas. Part 3—While in the kingdom of Yemoja, Tunde learns to have respect for all creatures, and at the end of the story he carries this knowledge with him back to Earth.

READER'S JOURNAL

In your journal, describe an action that you consider offensive to the earth or to the natural world. Tell why this action is offensive and what negative consequences could come from it.

"Yemoja, Queen of the Seas"

YORUBA TALE, RETOLD BY FITZGERALD IYAMABO

Once upon a time, in a remote village by the sea in West Africa, there lived an eleven-year-old boy named Tunde. He lived alone with his mother because his father was dead. He was named Tunde (short for Babatunde) because his father had died just before he was born. It was believed that the spirit of the father had returned as the child, which is what the name says.[1]

One day Tunde went to the riverbank to swim and play with his friends. After a while, the young people began to play a cruel game. The object of this game was to try to hit a frog from a distance with a stone. Being the good-hearted boy that he was, Tunde did not want at first to play. But it is sometimes tempting to do wrong. The other young people seemed to be having fun, and finally Tunde could resist no longer. He picked up a little rock and aimed carefully at a frog on a tree about twenty yards away. The others clapped excitedly as the rock smashed into the frog. Tunde and his friend ran toward the frog, but what they saw when they got there made them sick. The dying frog was still there on the tree, on a low branch, horribly mutilated. Its eyes, still open, appeared to be looking directly at Tunde. Tunde felt dizzy, for he knew he had offended the Maker of that little creature, the same One who made him.

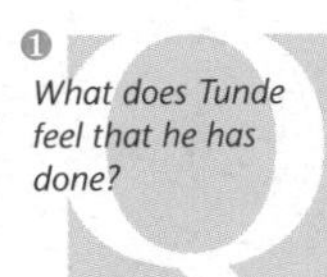

❶ *What does Tunde feel that he has done?*

You can imagine, then, how Tunde felt when the frog slid off the branch and landed on his shoulder! He shook his shoulder hard, and the frog fell off immediately. Scared, Tunde's friends ran away as fast as their legs would carry them, but Tunde felt so filthy that he started running toward the river. He ran and ran and ran until he reached the bank. Then he jumped into the water. He did not even hear the sound of his friends running away. In the water, he splashed around, trying to rid himself of the filth of the frog, but try as he might, he still felt as though the frog were on his shoulder. Then his head started swimming and he soon felt himself slipping away gently, as if he were going to sleep.

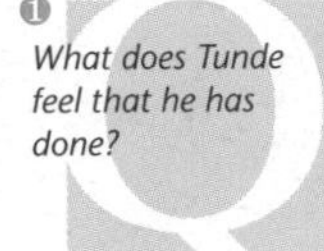

❷ *What happens to Tunde?*

1. **It was believed . . . says.** In many cultures around the world, people believe that a person returns to live again and again on Earth.

READER'S JOURNAL

Contemporary examples include destruction of habitats for animals and plants; killing of animals and plants that are endangered; and pollution of the air, land, and water.

ANSWERS TO GUIDED READING QUESTIONS

❶ Tunde has offended the one who made the frog and who made him.

❷ Tunde either dies or goes into a sleeplike trance. At any rate, he passes into a different place.

SUPPORT FOR LEP STUDENTS

PRONUNCIATIONS OF PROPER NOUNS AND ADJECTIVES

Ye • mo • ja (ye´mō jä′) n.
Yo • ru • ba (yō´ro͞o bä′) n.
I • ya • ma • bo (ē yä ma´bō) n.
Tun • de (to͞on´dā) n.

ADDITIONAL VOCABULARY

remote—distant

Answer to Guided Reading Question

➊ For everything that a person does, there is a fitting consequence. Good comes of good. Bad comes of bad.

Yoruba Ibeji Statuetes. *Nigeria*

When Tunde woke up, he could not believe his eyes. He was in the most beautiful land he had ever seen, a place with wonderful buildings and lovely gardens as far as the eye could see. The colors were brighter, the sounds were purer, and the air (although he knew it was not air) was sweeter than any he had ever known. He could hear *agidigbo*[2] music playing softly in the background. Tunde thought he had died and gone to Paradise, but he was not afraid because everything in that place was so light and pure.

What comes of people's actions, according to Yemoja? ➊

Looking around, Tunde saw two dignified elderly men approach him. They asked him to follow and led him to a beautiful palace. He was taken to the steps of a throne. The sound of the great *bembe*[3] drum announced the arrival of the most wonderful queen. She was unbelievably beautiful and queenly yet she had the kindest face Tunde had ever seen. She told him she was Yemoja, Queen of the Seas. Tunde fell in love with her immediately.

He was brought back to earth when she reminded him of what he had just done. He hung his head in shame and asked if he were going to be punished. Yemoja replied, "For everything you do, there is a consequence. If you do something good, good will return to you. If you do something bad, bad will return to you. So, Tunde, it is right for you to expect that any deed will have

2. **agidigbo.** Thumb piano
3. **bembe.** Large drum, often played with a stick

its fitting consequences." She told him never to think of these consequences as punishments or rewards but as lessons to be learned. In this case, however, Tunde had already learned that what he did was wrong, so he would not be "punished," though, he would have to remain in the kingdom for a long time because there was so much more for him to learn. Tunde was quite relieved at this. He had been worried that he would receive a terrible punishment for killing the frog, but staying in the kingdom was something he actually wanted to do.

Time passed. Tunde stayed in Yemoja's kingdom for ten years and grew into a fine young man. Under the instruction of an old *babalawo*,[4] he learned about the great goodness of Olodumare,[5] who created all things, great and small. Until his arrival in this land, Tunde had had no idea that there was another world under the sea. From the *babalawo*, Tunde learned that there are many other worlds, too many to imagine, each with its own inhabitants. Among these are the *orisha*[6] that Tunde knew so well. Even on earth, there are other beings that exist alongside men and women. Some of these everybody knows, such as fairies, elves, and gnomes. Tunde knew these by Yoruba names, such as *imale*, *oro*, *egbere*, and so on. In addition to these, Tunde learned, there are spirits of the dead who still wander the earth and reside among the living, and there are other beings about whom few, if any, know. Eventually Tunde came to realize that people are not the only guests in the Great House of Olodumare and that we should respect all the other creatures who live in this great universe with us.

As much as Tunde loved the kingdom beneath the sea, he still could not help thinking about his own mother. He wondered how she was coping without him. He finally went to Yemoja and asked for permission to return to the earth. Yemoja was sad because she had grown to love the boy. She told him that if he returned to the earth, he could never come back. Tunde was very unhappy at this because he loved Yemoja's kingdom, but still wanted to go back to see how his mother was doing.

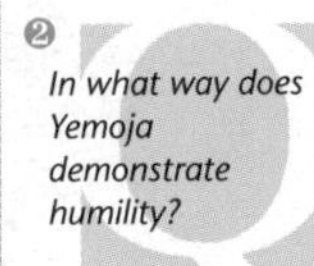
❶ *Why does Tunde want to return?*

Yemoja then gave him permission to return home. He cried at the thought of never seeing her again, but she scolded him: "Didn't you learn that there are lots of other kingdoms in the universe? You will meet many other queens, much greater than I. But the most wonderful of all, the Queen of Orun,[7] you will never be able to see. Even I have never seen Her. Just be grateful that you are allowed to enjoy Her blessings everyday."

❷ *In what way does Yemoja demonstrate humility?*

As soon as she finished speaking these words, Tunde found himself on the riverbank. He began running home as fast as his legs would carry him. His heart was pounding when he knocked on the door of his house. His mother opened the door, and he flew into her arms, but she did not look a day older! She also did not seem particularly surprised to see him. Then Tunde looked at himself again. He could not believe his eyes. He was a young boy once more. He asked his mother how long he had been away, and she said it was only for a few

4. **babalawo.** Medicine man
5. **Olodumare.** God, the creator
6. **orisha.** Deified being in nature
7. **Orun.** Heaven

ANSWERS TO GUIDED READING QUESTIONS

❶ Tunde wants to return because he misses his mother.

❷ Yemoja demonstrates humility by saying that there are many other queens greater than she is and by implying that she herself is too lowly to have seen the Queen of Orun.

Answer to Guided Reading Question

❶ Tunde now has respect for all creatures and believes that they should be protected.

Selection Check Test with Answers

EX. What does Tunde hit with a rock?
He hits a frog.

1. Where does Tunde go to wash himself?
He goes to the ocean.

2. In whose kingdom does Tunde awaken?
He awakens in the kingdom of Yemoja, Queen of the Seas.

3. What, according to Yemoja, are lessons to be learned?
Punishments and rewards are lessons to be learned.

4. Why does Tunde want to return to Earth?
He wants to return to see his mother.

5. How much time has passed when Tunde returns to Earth?
Only a few hours have passed.

hours. He did not understand this at first, until he remembered what the *babalawo* taught him about other worlds. Wouldn't it make sense that their time would also be different? Maybe ten years here would only be a few hours there.

Q ❶ *How do Tunde's experiences change him?*

He went to see all his friends, and none of them had changed from the last time he had seen them. They talked about the frog incident as if it had just happened. He told them that after they left, he went into the sea and saw Yemoja. Other villagers heard him talking about this and took him to the town *babalawo*. After talking to Tunde and asking several questions, the *babalawo* realized that Tunde was telling the truth. He had seen Yemoja, Queen of the Seas. Prayers were offered in thanks for the great blessing. People talked of nothing else for weeks.

And Tunde? As long as he lived he was careful to respect and protect every creature of Olodumare, and he always taught people to do the same. ■

About the Author

Fitzgerald Iyamabo was Director of Culture of Ife Students' Union in Ile-Ife, Nigeria (the cradle of Yoruba culture), where he obtained a degree in English. He later earned a master's degree in business at Boston University. Iyamabo is a keen student of history and of cultural differences. He now lives in Boston, Massachusetts.

Responding to the Selection

Do you agree with the teachings that Tunde receives from Yemoja about punishment and rewards? Why, or why not? Are there parts of the teachings of the *babalawo* with which you agree? Are there parts with which you do not agree? Explain what these parts are and why you do or do not agree with them.

Reviewing the Selection

Recalling and Interpreting

1. (R) What "game" is being played by the children at the beginning of the selection? What wrong action is Tunde tempted to take?

   (I) Why is Tunde "sick" and "dizzy" after the action that he takes?

2. (R) Where does Tunde go to attempt to wash himself? Where does he find himself when he awakens?

   (I) What is unusual about the place in which Tunde finds himself on awakening?

3. (R) Who is Yemoja? According to her, how should Tunde view punishments and rewards?

   (I) Do you agree with Yemoja's views about the consequences of actions? Explain.

4. (R) What does Tunde learn while in the kingdom beneath the sea? Why does he want to return to earth?

   (I) What is "the Great House of Olodumare?" What does it mean to be "only guests" in this house? Who are some of the other "guests"? How should one act toward these guests?

Synthesizing

5. What is the major lesson that Tunde learns from his experiences? How is this lesson related to the wrong action that Tunde takes at the beginning of the story?

Understanding Literature (Questions for Discussion)

Oral Tradition. An **oral tradition** is works, ideas, or customs passed by word of mouth from generation to generation. Many works in the oral tradition embody the traditional values of the people who tell them. They are told to the young to communicate these values. What values are communicated by "Yemoja, Queen of the Seas"?

RESPONDING TO THE SELECTION

If students have difficulty thinking about a secret name for themselves, have them begin by listing things about themselves that nobody knows about them.

ANSWERS FOR REVIEWING THE SELECTION

RECALLING AND INTERPRETING

1. **Recalling.** The children are throwing rocks at frogs. Tunde is tempted to join them in this activity. **Interpreting.** He realizes that what he has done is wrong, that it is offensive to the creator who made both him and the frog.
2. **Recalling.** Tunde goes to the ocean. When he awakens, he finds himself in the realm of Yemoja, the Queen of the Seas. **Interpreting.** The place is very beautiful. The air smells sweet, and there is music playing.
3. **Recalling.** Yemoja is Queen of the Seas. She says that Tunde should view punishments and rewards as lessons to be learned. **Interpreting.** Answers will vary.
4. **Recalling.** Tunde learns to respect all creatures. He wants to return to see his mother. **Interpreting.** The Great House of Olodumane is the creation. Creatures live and then die. They are ephemeral. Like guests, they stay only for a while. All creatures, visible and invisible, are guests (people, frogs, elves, spirits, etc). One should treat all of these with respect.

SYNTHESIZING

Responses will vary. Possible responses are given.

5. Tunde learns to respect all creatures. He needs to learn this lesson because his action at the beginning of the story shows disrespect for a fellow creature.

ANSWERS FOR UNDERSTANDING LITERATURE

Responses will vary. Possible responses are given.

Oral Tradition. This story teaches respect for the creator and for all other creatures who share this world with us.

GOALS/OBJECTIVES

Studying this lesson will enable students to

- enjoy a myth from Western Africa
- Describe important elements of Yoruba culture
- explain the terms *oral tradition* and *motif* and give examples of each
- dramatize a traditional tale

ADDITIONAL RESOURCES

Reader's Guide

- Selection Worksheet, 7.4

Assessment Portfolio

- Selection Check Test, 2.7.7
- Selection Test, 2.7.8

Pronunciation Exercise

- Grade 7 Audiocassette, Side B, Track 36

CROSS-CURRICULAR CONNECTIONS

Geography and World History

Review with students the different kinds of works to be found in the oral tradition. Ask them to give examples of proverbs, tall tales, fables, folk songs, nursery rhymes, and myths. Here are some examples for you to share:

Proverb: "You can lead a horse to water, but you can't make it drink."

Tall Tale: "Paul Bunyan and Babe the Blue Ox"

Fable: "The Fox and the Grapes"

Folk Song: "Barbara Allen"

Nursery Rhyme: Rock a Bye Baby"

Myth: "Thor's Hammer"

Prereading

WESTERN AFRICA

"Why the Sky Is Far Away from the Earth"

Yoruba tale, retold by Fitzgerald Iyamabo

Cross-curricular Connection

Geography and World History. After the Ibo, the Yoruba are the largest ethnic group in Nigeria. Most Yoruba live in the southwestern part of the country, and some live in neighboring Benin and Togo. For the most part, the traditional Yoruba live an agricultural existence, growing crops such as corn, millet, yams, beans, peanuts, and plantains. Yoruba men do the farming, and women market the crops. Yoruba towns were traditionally organized around the palace of the local *oba,* or king, which was surrounded by compounds belonging to extended families, each with its own elder male as its leader.

The Yoruba are famed for their magnificent craftsmanship and for their marvelous, complex oral literature. Among the finest products of Yoruba crafts are woven goods, leather goods, carvings in ivory and wood, and works in bronze.

The Yoruba people have one of the most sophisticated and elaborate bodies of oral poetry in the world, which includes poetry describing ancestries and the histories of towns, songs, incantations, works of praise, hunters' songs, and improvisations. The Yoruba, like many African peoples, have a large body of traditional proverbs, one of which is "If the earthworm does not dance in front of the rooster, he will still be eaten, but at least the rooster cannot say that he was provoked."

In addition to traditional oral literature, the Yoruba have produced several fine contemporary novelists, including Daniel Olorunfemi Fagunwa, author of *The Forest of God*; Femi Jeboda, author of *Mr. People-Rally-Only-around-the-Well-to-Do*; Afolabi Olabimtan, author of *Predestination*; and Akinwunmi Isola, author of *Heart-Rending Incidents Occurred.*

As You Read

In **"Why the Sky Is Far Away from the Earth,"** the people of the ancient kingdom of Benin receive several warnings but fail to heed them. As you read, record what the people do in each case and what happens as a result.

WHAT THE PEOPLE DO WRONG	WHAT HAPPENS AS A RESULT
cut off more of the sky than they can eat	**the elves and fairies that tend the sky warn them that if they continue wasting food, the Owner of the sky will take back His gift**

AS YOU READ

Wrong: The peope kill the innocent animals that live in the forest and waste the meat. **Result:** The gnomes of the forest warn them.

Wrong: The hunter wants a cricket in addition to the other game that he has caught. **Result:** the hunter is crushed under an elephant.

Wrong: Woman cuts off more sky than she can eat and the people conspire to hid the excess. **Result:** The sky is moved far away, and people thereafter have to work to eat.

READER'S JOURNAL

What is greed? How would you define it? Write a definition of *greed* in your journal and give some examples. Explain why greed is considered a terrible quality for a person to have.

"Why the Sky Is Far Away from the Earth"

YORUBA TALE, RETOLD BY FITZGERALD IYAMABO

Let me tell you a story my grandfather told me. It is a story his grandfather told him, and his own grandfather before him. Back in those days, in the ancient kingdom of Benin in present-day Nigeria, the sky wasn't far away from the earth. If an adult stood up straight and stretched his hand, he could touch the sky. Why, you ask? Well, the sky was made of the sweetest food you ever imagined. It tasted something like the sweetest croissant with honey baked into it, only better. And it was very light and fluffy.

Anyway, people did not need to go looking for food every day because the sky was there, so of course there were no hunters or farmers back then. Then, however, people started to get greedy and wasteful. Often they cut off more of the sky than they needed. The sylphs and fairies that tended the sky warned them not to do so, but no one listened. They warned them that if they kept wasting the food, a day would come when the Owner of the sky would take back His gift. But still no one listened.

Even worse, people also started to kill the innocent animals that lived in the forest. They had gotten tired of eating the sky every day, and they decided that they wanted meat. The gnomes that worked in the forest were distressed. They warned the people to stop killing Osanobua's[1] creatures, but they continued killing and eating the animals. Worse yet, they also wasted the meat. They would kill an antelope, for instance, eat a little bit of it, and throw the rest away or let it go bad. So the poor creature would lose its life for nothing.

One day a hunter (and there were now hunters among the Binis[2]) was returning from a hunt. Listen to this. He had an elephant on his back, an antelope in his bag, and a rabbit in

1. **Osanobua.** Almighty God
2. **Binis.** Traditional name for Edo people

❶ *From whom did the narrator learn this story?*

❷ *Of what do the sylphs and fairies warn the people?*

READER'S JOURNAL

Examples of greed that you might share with your students include overcharging for goods or services and conspicuous consumption with others who are in need.

ANSWERS TO GUIDED READING QUESTIONS

❶ The narrator learned the story from his grandfather, who learned it from his grandfather.

❷ They warn the people that the Owner of the sky will take back his gift if they continue to abuse it.

SUPPORT FOR LEP STUDENTS

PRONUNCIATIONS OF PROPER NOUNS AND ADJECTIVES

Be • nin (be nēn´) n.

Ni • ger • i • a (nī jir´ē ə) n.

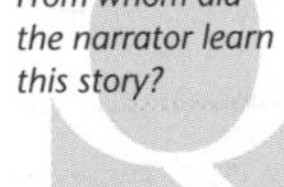

Literary Technique

EPITHET

An **epithet** is a descriptive word or phrase used in place of a proper noun. Epithets are common in oral literature. Notice, in this myth, the use of epithets to describe the gods:

Eshu, *the mischievous one*

Osanobua, *the patient One*

(Notice, also, that the capitalization of the pronoun referring to Osanobua is a recognition of his status as the supreme deity in Yoruba religion.)

Yoruba Gangan (talking drum). *Nigeria*

each hand. When he heard a small cricket chirping in the sand, he wanted that as well! He started digging for it with his big toe. This was too much for Eshu,[3] the mischievous one. He caused the hunter to stumble and fall under the weight of the elephant. He was crushed by the elephant and died immediately. The people were frightened by this, which was a lesson that greed can get you in trouble.

But you see, people forget things quickly. Very soon, they had gone back to their old ways. Osanobua, the patient One, watched sadly as the people continued to disobey Him. But even the patient will one day lose his patience. One day a pregnant woman cut off a large piece of the sky. When she took it into her house, her husband warned her that she might not be able to eat the whole thing, but she reminded him that she was pregnant and eating for two. After a while, she realized that she would not be able to eat everything. She called her husband, and he started to help, but they still couldn't finish it. Frightened, they called their neighbors to help. It seemed that the more food they ate, the more remained. Very soon the whole village was eating, but they soon knew it would be impossible to finish the food.

By this time it was night, so they went into the bush and quietly buried

3. **Eshu.** Yoruba deity

what was left. They thought that in this way they would not be found out, as if you can hide from the all-seeing Eye of Osanobua! Anyway, they woke up the next morning relieved that nothing seemed to have gone wrong. The pregnant woman was the first to go outside her house. Her husband was still inside when he heard her shriek loudly. He rushed outside, and what he saw made his heart start pounding in fear. The sky was no longer there. Then he looked upward, and many, many miles away, he saw the sky. They both started crying loudly, along with the other people who had gathered there, but it was too late.

Then a loud Voice boomed from above: "For years you have enjoyed the many gifts that I gave to you, but you did not think you had to obey my instructions on how to enjoy these gifts. I will still bless you with food, but now you will have to work for it. Because you did the opposite of my will, instead of getting food from above, you will get it from below. You will till the ground until your body aches, before I permit any food to appear. So shall it be from this day forth."

The people cried bitterly, but it was too late. And from that day forth, my friends, the sky has remained far from us, and we have had to depend on the soil for our food. So now you know. Greed will always bring grief, whether it concerns food, riches, attention from others, or anything else. We are allowed only our fair share and no more. ■

❶ *Why is it ridiculous that the people should try to bury the food?*

❷ *What are the consequences of the people's greed?*

About the Author

A biography of **Fitzgerald Iyamabo** appears on page 298.

ANSWERS TO GUIDED READING QUESTIONS

❶ It is ridiculous to try to bury the food because Osanobua sees all things. One cannot hide anything from Him.

❷ As a result of their greed, the people have to work the soil in order to eat.

SELECTION CHECK TEST WITH ANSWERS

EX. Who told the narrator this story?
His grandfather told him the story.

1. What do the people eat at first?
They eat pieces of the sky.

2. Of what do the fairies warn the people?
They warn them that if they keep wasting food, the Owner of the sky will take back his gift.

3. What do people start to do to animals?
They start to kill and eat them.

4. What falls on the hunter and kills him?
An elephant falls on him.

5. What do the people do to try to hide the food?
They bury it.

RESPONDING TO THE SELECTION

As an alternate activity, you might ask students to compare this story to other similar ones that they know.

ANSWERS FOR REVIEWING THE SELECTION

RECALLING AND INTERPRETING

1. **Recalling.** The narrator learned this story from his grandfather, who learned it from his grandfather. That is a way of saying that this is a traditional tale. **Interpreting.** The story comes from the oral tradition because it has been passed down by word of mouth.
2. **Recalling.** In ancient Benin, people did not have to work. They got their food by breaking off pieces of the sky, which was close to the earth. The elves and other creatures warn the people when they start being wasteful. The gnomes are distressed at the killing of animals. **Interpreting.** The story says that people got tired of eating sky every day and decided that they wanted meat. It is shocking that the people waste what they kill, causing animals to die for nothing.
3. **Recalling.** The hunter is so greedy that he wants a cricket as well, and he is punished when an elephant falls on him and crushes him. **Interpreting.** The hunter is terribly greedy because he wants the cricket even though he already has far more than he can eat.
4. **Recalling.** The woman takes the piece home and tries to eat it. She tells her husband that she is eating for two. She realizes that she cannot possible eat it all. She, her husband, and the neighbors try to eat it and then try to hide it. **Interpreting.** Osanobua is the supreme god in the Yoruba religion. The narrator thinks that it is absurd to try to hide anything from Osanobua.

Responding to the Selection

Do you feel that the people in this story get what they deserve? Why, or why not?

Reviewing the Selection

RECALLING AND INTERPRETING

1. **R** According to the narrator, who told him this story? Who told the story to the person who told it to him?

   I How do you know that this is a tale out of the oral tradition?

2. **R** According to this story, how was life different in ancient Benin? What did people do for food? Who warns the people when they start being wasteful? Who is distressed when the people start killing animals?

   I What explanation does this story offer of the origins of hunting? What is particularly shocking about the people's use of the animals that they kill?

3. **R** What happens to the hunter and why?

   I What sort of person is the hunter? How do you know?

4. **R** What does the woman do after cutting off a large piece of the sky? What does she tell her husband? What does she realize? What do the woman, her husband, and their neighbors try to do?

   I Who is Osanobua? How does the narrator feel about trying to hide things from Osanobua? How do you know?

SYNTHESIZING

5. What do the actions of the people in this story reveal about them? What consequence do they suffer? Do you consider this consequence just? Why, or why not?

Understanding Literature (Questions for Discussion)

1. **Oral Tradition and Myth.** An **oral tradition** is works, ideas, or customs passed by word of mouth from generation to generation. A **myth** is a story that explains the beginnings of things in the natural world. Myths are common in the oral tradition. What aspect of the natural world is explained by this myth?
2. **Motif.** A **motif** is anything that appears repeatedly in one or more works of literature, art, or music. One of the most common motifs in the world's mythologies is of a golden age ruined by human wickedness. What golden age is described in this Yoruba myth? What wickedness brings an end to this golden age? What lesson does this story teach?

ANSWERS FOR REVIEWING THE SELECTION (CONT.)

SYNTHESIZING

Responses will vary. Possible responses are given.

5. The people are greedy and wasteful. As a result, they are made to work for their livings. Responses to the last questions will vary, although most students will probably consider the punishment just.

Writing Skills

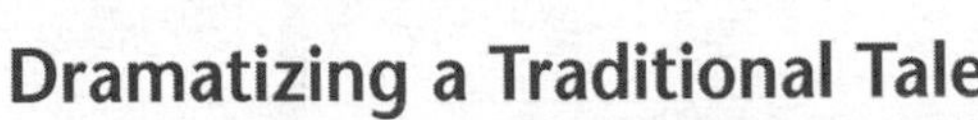

Dramatizing a Traditional Tale

A **drama** is a story told by means of actors who play the parts of the characters. The written text performed by the actors is called the **script.** Scripts contain two kinds of material, **dialogue** and **stage directions.** The dialogue is the words to be said by the actors. The stage directions, often placed in parentheses and written in italics, describe the setting, music, special effects, lighting, costumes, and properties (small, movable pieces carried by the actors). They can also describe actors' movements and emotions.

Often the authors of plays, known as playwrights, take their material from traditional stories or from works of fiction. The act of rewriting a prose tale in the form of a drama is called **adapting** or **dramatizing** it.

Jeri Capelli

English 8

"Why the Sky Is Far Away from the Earth," a Dramatization of a Traditional Yoruba Tale

Scene 1

(The curtain opens and a spotlight reveals an elderly man, downstage center, dressed in traditional West African costume. This is the STORYELLER.)

STORYTELLER *(As the STORYTELLER speaks, the lights slowly rise on the stage behind him, revealing a backdrop showing mud houses and exotic vegetation. Covering the entire stage and hung low within reach of the actors is a vast blue canopy made of painted Styrofoam. An elf sits on a rock downstage left.)* Listen and I will tell you a story. It is a story that my grandfather told me and that his grandfather told him. Long, long ago, in the ancient kingdom of Benin in present-day Nigeria, the sky wasn't far away from the earth. Yes. It's true, what I'm telling you. If an adult stood straight and stretched his hand, he could touch the sky. *(As the speaks the next lines, the STORYTELLER reaches up and tears a small piece from the blue canopy.)* Why, you ask? Well, the sky was made of the sweetest food you ever imagined. It tasted something like the sweetest croissant with honey baked into it, only better. And it was very light and fluffy. Well, I'm going to go eat my little piece of sky, while our masqueraders tell you the rest of the story (*Exits, stage left*).

Try It Yourself

Choose a traditional story or myth from this book. The story can be from this unit or from Unit 6, "Long Ago and Far Away." Write an adaptation, or dramatization, of a scene from this story. In other words, rewrite it in the form of a drama that could be performed by actors.

◀◀ **Student Model** 

Writing Skills

Introducing the Skill

Explain that a dramatization is simply a rewriting of a narrative in the form of a script that can be performed.

Previewing the Skill

Have students read aloud the student model, taking the parts of the Storyteller, the Elf, and the Boy. Then have them answer the Examining the Model questions.

Prewriting and Drafting

Empahsize that students need not dramatize an entire story. They simply may do a single scene.

Evaluating and Revising

Give students the Analytic Scale In the margin of the next page and have them use this scale for evaluating their rough drafts.

Proofreading and Publishing

In the interest of saving time, you might choose to have students stage only one or two dramatizations from the class.

Answers for Understanding Literature

Responses will vary. Possible responses are given.

1. **Oral Tradition and Myth.** This story explains why people have to work and why the sky is for from the earth.
2. **Motif.** The story describes a golden age in which people do not have to work. Greed and gluttony bring an end to this age. The story teaches people no to be greedy and gluttonous.

ANSWERS FOR EXAMINING THE MODEL

1. The scene dramatizes the opening of the story and the warning given by the elves. The second of these parts has been expanded considerably. These additions are necessary in order to make the scene playable.
2. The boy and the elf are introduced. The writer introduces these characters to make a general comment in the original story into a specific, playable scene.
3. The writer indicates what the stage should look like by using stage directions.

(A BOY enters stage right, tears a large piece from the sky canopy, and proceeds to cross right. The ELF, who has pointed ears and blue skin, stops him.)

ELF: Excuse me.

BOY: What? Who's that?

ELF: Oh, I'm sorry, you can't see me (There is a puff of smoke and a jingling sound.) There, now you can see me. I forget sometimes how blind you human creatures can be.

BOY: Who . . . who are you?

ELF: I'm an elf, silly.

BOY: An elf? Why are you all blue?

ELF: Because I'm an elf of the sky, of course. If I were an elf of the grass, I would be green or brown.

BOY: Oh. Gee, I've never met an elf before.

ELF: Glad to make your acquaintance. I see you have a bit of food there.

BOY: Yes, indeed. Can't wait to eat it.

ELF: Actually, you have a lot more than a bit. You must be planning to feed a very large family.

BOY: No, not really. This is for me. Don't get any ideas. You can't have any. If you want some sky to eat, you'll have to get it yourself.

ELF: My goodness! Aren't you being a little bit selfish? I mean, you can't possibly eat all of that yourself, can you? What will you do with the leftovers?

BOY: Well, I'll throw them away, of course, like everyone else. *(There is a roll of thunder and a flickering of the lights across the entire stage. The boy looks shocked.)*

ELF: Throw them away! That is terrible! What a waste of the gifts you are given! I want you to go to your people and tell them that the elves of the sky are very angry about this wastefulness, and it has to stop. If not, the Owner of the Sky will take it back. Do you understand me?

BOY: Sure. Uh, I guess so.

ELF: OK, then. Run along and tell them what I've said. *(Boy drops piece of sky and runs offstage left.)*

Examining the Model

1. What parts of the original story are dramatized in this scene? Which part is very close to the original story? Which part has been added to considerably? Why are these additions necessary?
2. What characters not in the original story were introduced into the dramatized version of the beginning of the story? Why do you think that the writer introduced these characters?
3. How does the writer indicate what the stage should look like?

Prewriting and Drafting

1. Read the information on the techniques of drama given in the introduction to Unit 10, "Drama."
2. Choose a scene that you would like to dramatize. Make a drawing of the setting for your scene and a stage diagram like the one below.
3. List the characters who will appear in your scene. Also list all the events that will occur in it.

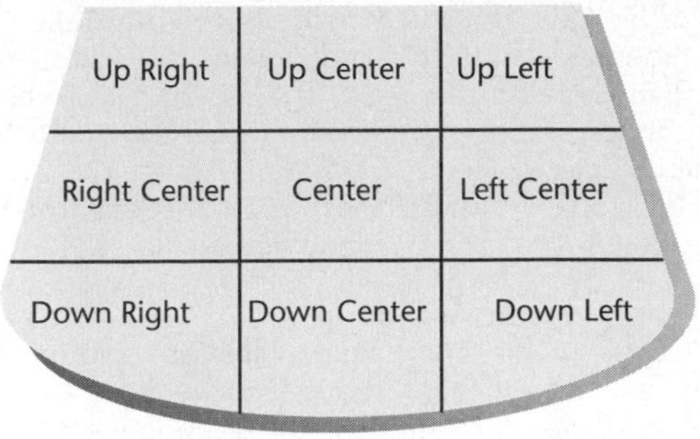

Up Right	Up Center	Up Left
Right Center	Center	Left Center
Down Right	Down Center	Down Left

5. Make a draft of your scene, communicating its ideas, descriptions, and events entirely through dialogue and stage directions.

Evaluating and Revising

1. Review the Language Arts Survey, 1.17, "Self-Evaluation," and 1.18, "Peer Evaluation." Make copies of your rough draft and distribute them to a small group of your classmates. With those classmates, read the rough draft aloud. Then discuss ways in which it might be improved.
2. Based on your classmates' suggestions and your own evaluation, revise your paper. Follow the guidelines for revision in the Language Arts Survey, 1.19, "Four Types of Revision," and 1.20, "A Revision Checklist." Make sure that your characters sound realistic and natural and that everything you have included could actually appear on a stage. Also make sure that the scene follows the formats for dialogue and stage directions given in the student model.

Proofreading and Publishing

1. Proofread your revised draft. Make a clean copy and proofread it again. Refer to the Language Arts Survey, 1.21, "Using Proofreader's Marks," 1.22, "A Proofreading Checklist," and 1.23, "Proper Manuscript Form."
2. Work with other students to stage your scene for the class.

Save your work in your writing portfolio.

ANALYTIC SCALE FOR WRITING SKILLS

Assign a score from 1 to 25 for each grading criterion below.

Historical Account

- **Content/Unity.** The dramatization successfully translates a scene from the original work to the stage.
- **Organization/Coherence.** The dramatization presents a complete scene in a way that does not leave the audience confused.
- **Language/Style.** The dramatization uses natural sounding language.
- **Conventions.** The dramatization avoids errors in spelling, grammar, usage, mechanics, and manuscript form.

GOALS/OBJECTIVES

Studying this lesson will enable students to

- enjoy a folk tale from Eastern Africa
- Describe important elements of Ugandan geography and culture
- explain the terms *fable* and *myth* and give examples of each

ADDITIONAL RESOURCES

Reader's Guide

- Selection Worksheet, 7.5

Assessment Portfolio

- Selection Check Test, 2.7.9
- Selection Test, 2.7.10

Pronunciation Exercise

- Grade 7 Audiocassette, Side B, Track 37

CROSS-CURRICULAR CONNECTIONS

Geography

Have your students locate Uganda on a map, along with the Ruwenzoris, Margherita Peak, Lake Victoria, the Victoria Nile, and the Alberta Nile.

Social Studies

Have students do library research on the arts, history, and peoples of Uganda.

Prereading

EASTERN AFRICA

"Why the Frog Croaks"

Anonymous, retold by Nightingale Rukuba-Ngaiza

Cross-curricular Connections

Geography. Uganda is an East African country that is full of mountains, valleys, and lakes. Its highest mountains, the Ruwenzoris, are snow-capped and rise to 16,763 feet at Margherita Peak. Uganda lies to the south of Lake Victoria, which is the second largest freshwater lake in the world, following Lake Superior. The land's major rivers are the Victoria Nile and the Alberta Nile, which flow northward and contribute to the Nile basin. Uganda is cooler than many countries that lie on the equator because of its mountains and lakes.

Social Studies. Many diverse peoples live in Uganda. The first people who inhabited the region were Bantu-speaking people, such as the Ganda, Soga, Nyoro, and Nkole. Nilotic-speaking peoples who live in Uganda include the Acholi, Lango, and Karamojong. Nilotic-Hamitic speaking peoples moved into Uganda in the seventeenth century.

Certain groups of peoples in Uganda traditionally relied on agriculture, including the cultivation of plantains, which are similar to bananas, while other peoples traditionally relied on raising cattle, sheep, and goats. Many farmers also kept cattle, sheep, and goats.

The Ganda, who compose the largest percentage of Uganda's population, recognized a number of totem animals, animals that are spiritual symbols of the descent or ancestry of certain groups. The Ganda believed that they could approach both the spirits of their ancestors and the gods through a medium, or spiritual channel.

The traditional culture of the Ugandan people changed, however, beginning in the nineteenth century. Arabs came to Uganda in the 1840s to trade ivory and slaves. Uganda was formally declared a British protectorate in 1894 and regained its independence in 1962. Because of these various influences, about four- fifths of Uganda's population practices Christianity (although a third of these people also hold traditional beliefs) and a portion of the population is Muslim as well.

As You Read

In **"Why the Frog Croaks,"** a rat named Wamese seeks his revenge upon a frog named Wakikere. Make a chart like the one below. As you read, keep track of the conflict between the two characters by noting Wakikere's actions, how Wamese feels about Wakikere's actions, and Wakikere's plan for revenge.

WAKIKERE'S ACTIONS	WAMESE'S FEELINGS
Wakikere sings and becomes popular	Wamese wants to better his own reputation by becoming friends with Wakikere

AS YOU READ

Wakikere's Action: He becomes friends with Wamese. **Wamese's Feelings:** He has a grand time.

Wakikere's Action: He continues his act without Wamese. **Wamese's Feelings:** Wamese becomes jealous.

READER'S JOURNAL

What do you think of revenge? Is revenge ever good or necessary, or is it always bad? What do you see as some of the negative consequences of focusing on revenge? Think of a situation in which you wanted revenge. How did you deal with the situation? Would you behave differently now if given the chance? Why, or why not?

"Why the Frog Croaks"

ANONYMOUS, RETOLD BY NIGHTINGALE RUKUBA-NGAIZA

Once upon a time in a small village in Uganda, East Africa, there lived a frog named Wakikere. Wakikere had a very beautiful voice. He sang to little children, animals, and anyone else who would ask him to sing. Many traveled miles from faraway places just to hear him sing. He sang at the king's palace and was popular at the royal court. He sang at the market square, and the local villagers loved to hear him sing. His beautiful voice was the first thing heard in the morning and the last thing heard at night.

Wakikere became famous and popular. Unknown to Wakikere, he had aroused the jealousy of a rat named Wamese who lived in the farmer's house. Farmers disliked Wamese because he destroyed their crops, and children disliked him because he was unsightly. Wamese decided that if he and Wakikere became friends, then he would become acceptable to children and to farmers alike. They would both be welcome in the village. So Wamese the rat became friends with Wakikere the frog. They spent a lot of time in one another's company, often taking long walks together in the woods. Wakikere sang, and Wamese danced. Wamese thought that this was a great act, and soon he and Wakikere were visiting friends and singing to the villagers and having a grand time.

Wamese was disappointed to discover that he was not welcome in the village in spite of his dancing. At the village market, the farmers chased after Wamese, while the children ran away frightened and screaming.

Wamese was very disappointed to discover that his newfound friend, Wakikere, would not stick by him. To add insult to injury, Wakikere continued on with his act without Wamese. This made Wamese jealous and he decided to put an end to Wakikere's fame and popularity. He plotted until he devised a devious scheme to ruin Wakikere.

One fine day, Wamese decided to call on Wakikere, inviting him to come visit with him at the house of Mklima the farmer where Wamese lived. Wakikere was hungry and Wamese told him that there was a pot of stew at

❶ *What quality did the frog possess that it does not possess now?*

❷ *Why do people dislike Wamese?*

READER'S JOURNAL

Explain that the desire for revenge is almost entirely negative. Ask students to think of other ways in which people might deal with hurt, anger, or disappointment.

ANSWERS TO GUIDED READING QUESTIONS

❶ The frog once had a very beautiful voice.

❷ Farmers dislike him because he destroys crops. Children dislike him because he is unsightly.

SUPPORT FOR LEP STUDENTS

PRONUNCIATIONS OF PROPER NOUNS AND ADJECTIVES

Ru • ku • ba-Ngai • za (ro͞o´ko͞o bə-ŋgī´zə) n.
U • gan • da (yo͞o gän´də) n.
Wa • ki • ke • re (wä ki'kär´ə) n.
Wa • me • se (wä mā´sə) n.

ADDITIONAL VOCABULARY

scalding—extremely hot

ANSWERS TO GUIDED READING QUESTIONS

❶ Wakikere is afraid of the farmer.

❷ He got a piece of hot meat stuck in his throat, and this meat scalded him.

SELECTION CHECK TEST WITH ANSWERS

EX. Who are Wakikere and Wamese?
Wakikere is a frog, and Wamese is a rat.

1. What extraordinary quality does Wakikere have?
Wakikere has a beautiful voice.

2. How do people feel about Wakikere?
People admire Wakikere's voice, and he becomes very popular.

3. Why don't people like Wamese?
Farmers don't like Wamese because he destroys their crops, and children don't like him because he is unsightly.

4. What does Wamese tell Wakikere can be found at Mklima the farmer's house?
Wamese tells Wakikere that there is a big pot of stew at Mklima the farmer's house.

5. What happens to Wakikere after the meat burns his throat?
Wakikere can only croak and can no longer sing.

❶ *Why was Wakikere nervous about taking the stew?*

❷ *What happened to Wakikere to make him lose his voice?*

the farmer's house which Wakikere would find quite tasty. Wamese assured Wakikere, who was nervous about the plan, that the farmer would never notice and promised, "We will only take a little bit." Reluctantly, the frog agreed to go inside the house and taste the food which the farmer had prepared.

Wamese opened the door and they both tiptoed into the kitchen where they found a stew cooking in the pot.

"You taste it first and I will watch for Mklima and give you a signal to run if I see him," Wamese said. Being hungry, Wakikere reached into the pot and pulled out a hot piece of meat. Wakikere opened his mouth and quickly shoved the steaming stew meat down his throat. Suddenly Wamese heard footsteps and noticed the farmer was approaching the door so he ran and hid without a word of warning to Wakikere. Wakikere had no warning and almost no time to escape. To remain unnoticed, he had to remain very still, with the hot piece of meat caught in his throat. Unfortunately, Wakikere's throat was badly burnt by the scalding meat.

That evening Wakikere tried to sing to his friends, but he could only croak. He tried again in the morning when it was bright and early, but to his dismay only croaks came from his burnt throat. Wakikere had been invited to sing at a marriage ceremony and meet with other talented animals, but he did not attend the ceremony because he had lost his beautiful voice. Wakikere moved out of the village and moved into the swamps. To this day the frog has never regained his beautiful voice, and that is why the frog croaks. ■

About the Author

Nightingale Rukuba-Ngaiza is an attorney licensed to practice law in both New York State and Uganda. She is also a Ph.D. candidate at Northeastern University in Boston, Massachusetts, where she is specializing in environmental law and policy in developing countries. Rukuba-Ngaiza is Ugandan, and she spent the early part of her childhood with her grandmother in a village called Ihari in the Tooro district of Uganda. The evenings in the village, when people gathered to sit by a fire and cook, were precious moments to Rukuba-Ngaiza, for it was then that traditional stories about war, love, and success were told. Rukuba-Ngaiza learned proverbs, folklore, and beautiful tales about her culture.

Responding to the Selection

What do you think of Wamese's actions? How do you feel about what happens to Wakikere? Does Wakikere deserve what happens to him? Why, or why not?

Responding to the Selection

Most students will probably agree that Wamese is mean-spirited and that Wakikere does not deserve his fate.

Reviewing the Selection

Recalling and Interpreting

1. **R** What special talent does Wakikere have? What do other people think of Wakikere because of this talent?

   I Why might Wakikere's talent make people react to him in this way? How do you think Wakikere feels about his talent?

2. **R** What reaction do people have to Wamese? Why?

   I Why might Wamese want to become friends with Wakikere? How does Wamese feel about Wakikere?

3. **R** What happens when Wakikere and Wamese decide to perform together? What type of scheme does Wamese come up with after this performance?

   I Why would the events in the village make Wamese angry with Wakikere? Is what happened Wakikere's fault? Why, or why not?

4. **R** What is Wamese's revenge upon Wakikere? What does Wakikere do once Wamese has carried out his plan?

   I What makes this revenge especially terrible and painful for Wakikere?

Synthesizing

5. Do you think Wamese meant to carry his revenge as far as it went? Why, or why not? In what way is Wakikere's situation at the end of the story similar to Wamese's at the beginning? Do you think that bringing Wakikere closer to his own level is what Wamese meant to achieve?

Answers for Reviewing the Selection

RECALLING AND INTERPRETING

1. **Recalling.** Wakikere has a beautiful singing voice. People like him because of his talent. **Interpreting.** Wakikere's singing makes people feel good, and they transfer these positive feelings to him. Wakikere doubtless feels good about his own singing.
2. **Recalling.** People dislike Wamese. The farmers do not like him because he eats crops. The children do not like him because they think that he is ugly. **Interpreting.** Wamese wants to become friends with Wakikere so that he, too, can be popular. Wamese is jealous of Wakikere.
3. **Recalling.** The performances do not make Wamese any more popular. After he learns this, Wamese plots to put an end to Wakikere's fame and popularity. **Interpreting.** Wamese is angry because of Wakikere's popularity. However, this popularity is not Wakikere's fault. He cannot help the fact that others are attracted to his singing and dancing.
4. **Recalling.** Wamese's revenge is to cause Wakikere to lose his voice. After losing his voice, Wakikere moves out to a swamp, where he croaks instead of singing. **Interpreting.** Wakikere could not but feel the contrast between the way things are and the way they were.

SYNTHESIZING

5. Responses will vary.

Understanding Literature (Questions for Discussion)

Fable and Myth. A **fable** is a brief story with animal characters and a moral. A **myth** is a story that explains the beginnings of things in the natural world. Who are the main characters in this story? Does this story have a moral? What does this story explain? Is this story a myth or a fable? Explain your response.

Answers for Understanding Literature

Responses will vary. Possible responses are given.

Fable and Myth. The main characters are Wakikere the frog and Wamese the rat. The story is not told to teach a moral lesson, but one can draw from it the moral that jealousy can have terribly negative consequences. The story explains why frogs croak. The story is a myth in the sense that it explains a natural phenomenon and a fable in the sense that it is a simple tale with animal characters who have human characteristics.

GOALS/OBJECTIVES

Studying this lesson will enable students to
- enjoy a folk tale from Eastern Africa
- describe briefly the wildlife of Eastern Africa
- define *myth* and *fable* and give examples of each

ADDITIONAL RESOURCES

READER'S GUIDE
- Selection Worksheet, 2.6

ASSESSMENT PORTFOLIO
- Selection Check Test, 2.7.11
- Selection Test, 2.2.12

PRONUNCIATION EXERCISE
- Grade 7 Audiocassette, Side B, Track 37

CROSS-CURRICULAR CONNECTIONS

SCIENCE

The wildlife of Eastern Africa is one of the most amazing treasures of the world. You may wish to have your students do research in the library and bring to class pictures illustrating the diversity of the wildlife to be found in the parks of Eastern Africa.

Prereading

EASTERN AFRICA

"How Tortoise Got His Patterned Shell"

Ugandan Tale, retold by Samali N. Kajubi

Cross-curricular Connection

Science. Much of eastern Africa is known for its abundance of wildlife. When Europeans began to colonize Africa in the nineteenth century, hunting expeditions, or safaris, became very popular. Game in Africa seemed limitless and was hunted indiscriminately. Many species were killed off entirely or were in danger of becoming extinct. Around the beginning of the twentieth century, game management plans were put into effect. Game management restricts hunters. While people still go on hunting safaris, many people now take photographic safaris in which animals are captured only on film.

National parks, such as Mount Kenya National Park in Kenya and Ruwenzori National Park in Uganda, are the home to many creatures. Kenya is especially known for its wildlife including lions, leopards, wild dogs, elephants, buffaloes, rhinoceroses, zebras, antelopes, gazelles, hippopotamuses, and crocodiles. Mount Kenya National Park covers areas of sparse vegetation and forest above 10,800 feet on Mount Kenya, which is located in central Kenya. Elephants, buffaloes, and other big game can be found in the park. Ruwenzori National park is located in southwestern Uganda. The park land covers 764 square miles of plains and foothills of the Ruwenzori Mountains. Within the park, vegetation varies from rain forest to savannah grasslands, but thickets of acacia trees and evergreens are most common. The park's wildlife is very diverse, including chimpanzees, leopards, lions, elephants, hippopotamuses, and water buffaloes. Several types of antelope including duikers, reedbucks, and topis also make their home in the park. Ruwenzori National Park has an especially rich variety of bird life.

The story "How Tortoise Got His Patterned Shell" takes place in a forest in eastern Africa that hosts a variety of wildlife and many birds.

As You Read

Animals are featured in many folk tales and myths. In this Ugandan tale, Tortoise is the main character. Make a cluster chart like the one below. As you read, fill in the chart with details about Tortoise's appearance, his actions, his character traits, and how other animals feel toward him.

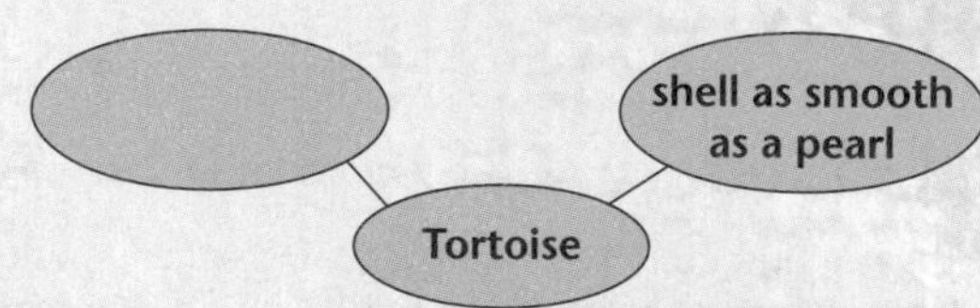

READER'S JOURNAL

Think about a time you acted selfishly. Why did you act that way? How did others react to your actions? Did you regret your actions? Why, or why not? What would you do if one of your friends was acting selfishly?

"How Tortoise Got His Patterned Shell"

ANONYMOUS, RETOLD BY SAMALI N. KAJUBI

There was a time when Tortoise's back was as smooth and beautiful as a pearl. Each day the animals of Kibira forest would visit Tortoise to admire and stroke his beautiful shell. At that time, Tortoise worked hard for his food, but he was growing tired of digging for worms day in and day out among the rocks in Kibira forest. One day, however, while lying on his favorite rock by Lake Nalubaale,[1] Tortoise came up with an idea. If the forest animals admired and loved to stroke Tortoise's shell so much, why not make the other animals provide him with food for the privilege?

The following day, Monkey arrived at Lake Nalubaale with his family after a long journey. "What a beautiful shell!" Monkey cried, seeing Tortoise. Monkey drew closer to stroke Tortoise's smooth shell, but Tortoise was eager to try out his scheme.

"You must feed me if you want to stroke my shell!" Tortoise demanded. Monkey was surprised, but gladly gave Tortoise some food. When Tortoise had eaten and Monkey was about to stroke Tortoise's shell, Tortoise cried, "Give me more food! Your food was not enough!" Every time Tortoise demanded more food, Monkey would feed him, until, at last Monkey ran out of food.

Each day, the animals of Kibira forest came to stroke Tortoise's smooth back. After Monkey, the next who came was Leeya the Leopard who gave Tortoise the juicy piece of meat she was carrying home to feed her family. Tortoise demanded more meat and would not let her stroke his smooth shell as he had promised. Next Timba the Snake gave Tortoise some crocodile eggs. Tortoise gobbled the eggs without a word of thanks and then cried out, "I want more eggs!" Timba the Snake, who was eager to slide across Tortoise's smooth back rushed into his hole in the ground and returned with more eggs. Still, Tortoise was not satisfied. Disappointed, Timba slithered away in disgust. One by one, the animals of Kibira forest came to stroke

1. **Lake Nalubaale.** Luganda name for Lake Victoria

❶ *Of what was Tortoise growing tired? What does he decide to do?*

❷ *In what way is Tortoise behaving toward the other animals in the forest?*

READER'S JOURNAL

As an alternative activity, you might ask students to write in their journals about other myths that explain the origins of phenomena in nature. Some students will be familiar with a few such myths from the Greek and Roman traditions, such as the tale of Echo and Narcissus or the tale of Arachne.

ANSWERS TO GUIDED READING QUESTIONS

❶ Tortoise grows tired of digging for worms day in and day out. He decides to charge the other animals for admiring his shell.

❷ Tortoise is becoming greedy and demanding.

SUPPORT FOR LEP STUDENTS

PRONUNCIATIONS OF PROPER NOUNS AND ADJECTIVES

Sa • ma • li Ka • ju • bi (sə mä´lē kə jo͞o´bē) n.
Ki • bi • ra (kə bē´rə) n.
Na • lu • baa • le(nä'lo͞o bä´lə) n.

Answers to Guided Reading Questions

➊ Tortoise comes up with a clever plan to get more food. He says that his name is "All of you."

➋ Ggulu says that the food is for "all of you," and that is the name that Tortoise has taken.

➌ The birds are patient. They wait as Tortoise eats.

➊ *Why does Tortoise alone eat the food?*

➋ *What does Tortoise devise? What does he say his name is?*

➌ *How would you describe the song birds' behavior?*

Tortoise's smooth back, and all were turned away by Tortoise. After many days of this unkind treatment, word spread about Tortoise's greed, and all the animals of the forest avoided him.

Tortoise continued lying on his favorite rock waiting for the animals to come wanting to stroke his beautiful shell. He could not believe that the other animals no longer found his smooth shell beautiful. Tortoise had also become too lazy to dig for worms among the rocks. A week passed and Tortoise grew thin and weak from hunger. Finally, he was forced to leave his favorite rock in search of food.

As Tortoise crawled off the rock, a flock of song birds who were on their way to attend a feast held by Ggulu, King of the Skies, flew down to wash themselves at Lake Nalubaale. When Tortoise saw the birds, he thought of another clever plan. He smiled and introduced himself. "My name is All of You! Welcome to Kibira forest," he said. When the birds saw Tortoise's smooth beautiful shell, they burst into song.

"Please let us stroke your shell," they sang. But Tortoise had planned for this. "Where are you going?" he demanded.

"If you let us stroke your beautiful shell, we will tell you," the birds cried in chorus.

"Will you take me along with you wherever you are going if I let you stroke my beautiful shell?" Tortoise asked. The song birds agreed to allow Tortoise to accompany them, and Tortoise allowed the birds to stroke his beautiful shell.

The following day, Tortoise rose early and met the song birds by the edge of Lake Nalubaale. The birds lifted Tortoise, whom they knew as "All of You" with their claws and carried him up to the skies. Higher and higher they rose until Kibira forest became a small dot beside Lake Nalubaale. When they arrived in the skies, Ggulu greeted them. His servants brought large baskets of food. There were matooke bananas, lumonde potatoes, and groundnut stew.[2] Ggulu said, "The food is for all of you." Tortoise stepped forward and began eating the food. The song birds waited politely for their turn to eat.

Next, Ggulu's sons brought gourds of delicious beverages for "All of you." Once more Tortoise alone stepped forward and he drank every drop. Seven baskets of fruit were brought before the guests and it was announced that they were for "all of you." There were yellow-ripe mangoes, sweet pineapples, and pawpaws.[3] The birds wished that Tortoise would become full and finish eating so that they could eat too, but Tortoise was hungry and in no hurry. The birds watched, their mouths watering, as Tortoise picked through the fruits for the juiciest ones. When he had eaten the last fruit, Tortoise rubbed his big stomach and belched loudly. The birds watched in anger and disbelief as Ggulu's servants carried away the empty baskets and gourds.

Finally, Ggulu's servants brought sheepskins for his guests to rest upon. The servants announced that the hides were for "all of you." Before they could hand the hides to each guest, Tortoise seized all the sheepskins. Tired and uncomfortable from all the

2. **matooke bananas . . . groundnut stew.** *Matooke banana*—type of banana like a plantain; *lumonde potatoes*—sweet pototoes; *groundnut stew*—edible root

3. **pawpaws.** papayas

food he had eaten, Tortoise lay down and fell asleep.

The feast over, Ggulu bade his guests farewell. The song birds were hungry and furious at Tortoise for eating all the food. They decided to teach him a lesson.

"Why not leave Tortoise in the skies so Ggulu can teach him some manners?" cried one of the birds.

"That would not be punishment enough," another answered. Finally, the birds agreed that it would not be proper to punish Tortoise in Ggulu's presence. It would be best to wait until they got back to earth to teach Tortoise a lesson.

When dawn came, the birds prepared for their homeward flight. First the eagles swooped off the clouds, their mighty wings flapping violently. Next, the swallows and doves took to the skies, followed by the crows, crested cranes, and storks in flying formation. Last, the song birds picked Tortoise up by the edges of his beautiful smooth shell and began their journey homeward.

Lower and lower they flew until Kibira forest came into view beside Lake Nalubaale. When they arrived at Lake Nalubaale, the song birds hovered above Tortoise's favorite rock.

"Please, oh, please, don't let me fall," Tortoise cried out, but the song birds were still angry. They dropped Tortoise upon his favorite rock and his beautiful shell smashed to pieces.

Weeks later, when Monkey saw Tortoise, Tortoise looked very different. Alas, his shell was no longer smooth and beautiful as a pearl. Instead, it was rough and patterned as it is today. ■

❶ *Why don't the song birds leave Tortoise in the skies?*

About the Author

Samali Nakato Kajubi was born and raised in Uganda, East Africa. Kajubi's interest in African folklore stems from early childhood experiences in Uganda. Kajubi received an M.A. in education from Boston University and now works as a technical writer.

Answer to Guided Reading Question

❶ They think that doing so would not be punishment enough for Tortoise.

Selection Check Test with Answers

EX. What was Tortoise's shell once like?
It was once smooth and beautiful as a pearl.

1. What was Tortoise tired of doing?
Tortoise was tired of digging for worms.

2. What did Tortoise demand from Monkey?
Tortoise demanded food in exchange for touching his shell.

3. Why did the animals stop coming to Tortoise?
Tortoise was greedy and kept demanding more food without allowing the animals to touch his shell.

4. For whom is the food that Ggulu's servants distribute meant?
It is meant for all of the animals.

5. What causes Tortoise's shell to shatter?
Tortoise is dropped on a rock by the angry birds.

Responding to the Selection

As an alternate activity, have the students devise a moral for the story.

Answers for Reviewing the Selection

RECALLING AND INTERPRETING

1. **Recalling.** The shell was smooth and beautiful like a pearl. The other animals liked to admire and stroke the shell. **Interpreting.** Tortoise is not very nice to the other animals. He abuses their admiration.

2. **Recalling.** Tortoise tells Monkey that he must give him food in exchange for stroking the shell. **Interpreting.** Monkey probably agrees out of admiration for Tortoise. When Tortoise does not let him touch the shell, Monkey probably feels used.

3. **Recalling.** Tortoise deides to trick the birds. Tortoise says that his name is "All of you." **Interpreting.** When Ggulu offers food to "all of you," he is, unknowningly, offering it to Tortoise, who has assumed that name.

4. **Recalling.** The birds drop Tortoise, thus breaking his shell into pieces. **Interpreting.** The other animals probably will not now admire Tortoise as they did before.

SYNTHESIZING

Responses will vary. Possible responses are given.

5. Pride, gluttony, and lack of concern for others are all flaws that lead to Tortoise's downfall. Perhaps Tortoise will learn a lesson from the consequences of his

Responding to the Selection

Do you think Tortoise deserved what happened to him? Why, or why not? If you were Monkey seeing Tortoise's new look, how would you feel? What would you say to Tortoise?

Reviewing the Selection

Recalling and Interpreting

1. **R** What was Tortoise's shell like long ago? Why did Tortoise's shell make him popular among the animals of Kibira forest?

   I What is Tortoise's attitude toward the other animals of Kibira forest?

2. **R** What does Tortoise tell Monkey he must do if he wants to stroke Tortoise's shell?

   I Why does Monkey agree to Tortoise's demands? How do you think Monkey feels when Tortoise does not let Monkey touch his shell?

3. **R** Whom does Tortoise decide to trick after the animals of Kibira forest stop bringing him food? What does Tortoise say his name is?

   I Why is Tortoise's name important to his trick?

4. **R** What do the birds do to punish Tortoise?

   I How do you think the other animals of Kibira forest will treat Tortoise now?

Synthesizing

5. What character flaws lead to Tortoise's downfall? Do you think Tortoise's character changed after his shell was broken? Explain.

Understanding Literature (Questions for Discussion)

1. **Myth.** A **myth** is a story that explains the beginnings of things in the natural world. What does this story explain? Could this story have really happened? What unnatural elements does it involve?
2. **Fable.** A **fable** is a brief story with animal characters and a moral. Who are the characters in this story? What moral do you think this story teaches? Write one sentence that tells the moral of this story.

Answers for Understanding Literature

Responses will vary. Possible responses are given.

1. **Myth.** This story explains the pattern on the shells of tortoises. The story coud not, of course, really have happened because it involves animals that behave as humans do.

2. **Fable.** The characters in this story include Tortoise, Monkey, Snake, and many birds. The story teaches that pride, gluttony, and lack of concern for others are all wrong. A possible moral is that "Pride cometh before a fall."

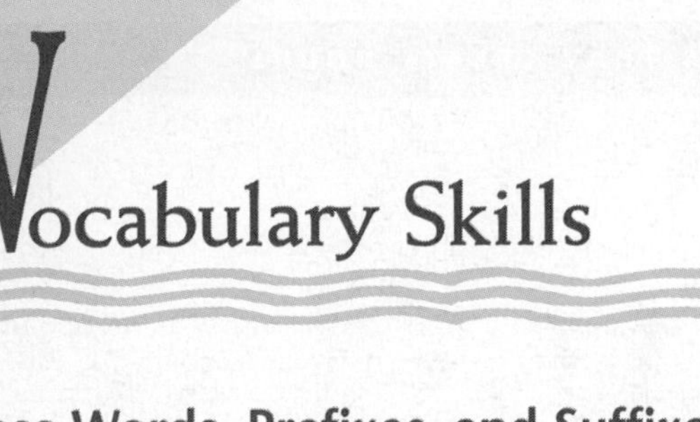

Vocabulary Skills

Base Words, Prefixes, and Suffixes

Building vocabulary is easier if you know the building blocks of words. Many words are formed by adding prefixes or suffixes to a base word. If you know what the parts of an unfamiliar word mean, you will be more likely to figure out the meaning of the word. For example, if you do not know what the word *counteract* means, but you know that the prefix *counter–* means "against," you can deduce that *counteract* means "act against."

The following charts show some common prefixes and suffixes, their meanings, and ways to use them. For other examples, see the Language Arts Survey, 2.43, "Base Words, Prefixes, and Suffixes."

COMMON PREFIXES

Prefix	Meaning	Example	Meaning
bi–	two, twice	bilingual	speaking two languages
dis–	away, opposite of, fail, stop, refuse to, deprive of	disobey	opposite of obey
en–	put into or on, make, make into	entangle	to make tangled
trans–	over, across, beyond	transatlantic	across the Atlantic
un–, in–	not	unfair	not fair

Language Lab

Introducing the Skill

Introduce the skill by writing the word *unmoveable.* Draw lines through its parts as follows: *un* | *move* | *able.* Explain that the prefix *un–* means "not," that the suffix *–able* means "capable of" or "able to be," and that the entire word therefore means "not able to be moved." Explain that prefixes are parts added to the beginnings of words and that suffixes are parts added to the ends of words.

Previewing the Skill

Have students read the lesson material on pages 317 and 318 and ask them to find other examples of words using the prefixes and suffixes on the charts.

Practicing the Skill

Assign the Try It Yourself activities on pages 318 and 319.

Reviewing the Skill

You might also have students read the Language Arts Survey, 2.43, "Base Words, Prefixes, and Suffixes," and do the exercise given there. Students might also do the exercise on the corresponding worksheet in the Essential Skills Practice Book: Language.

Answers for Try It Yourself

Exercise A

1. disappear, opposite of appear
2. remarkable, able to be remarked on
3. inedible, not able to be eaten
4. encourage, put courage into
5. biweekly, twice a week

Exercise B

1. made themselves feel joy
2. full of thought
3. times ten
4. noun form of clever
5. not daunted
6. opposite of taste for
7. deprived of its cover (revealed)
8. not having friends
9. noun form of lazy
10. sent or moved beyond
11. not polite
12. not able to be appeased
13. noun form of punish
14. formed (or changed) over
15. full of regret

SUFFIXES THAT CREATE NOUNS

Suffix	Example
–er, or	create (verb) + –or = creator (noun) paint (verb) + –er = painter (noun)
–ism	Romantic (adjective) + –ism = Romanticism (noun) natural (adjective) + –ism = naturalism (noun)
–ist	final (adjective) + –ist = finalist (noun)
–ment	govern (verb) + –ment = government (noun) entitle (verb) + –ment = entitlement (noun)
–ness	green (adjective) + –ness = greenness (noun) greedy (adjective) + –ness = greediness

SUFFIXES THAT CREATE ADJECTIVES

Suffix	Example
–al	nature (noun) + –al = natural (adjective) series (noun) + –al = serial (adjective)
–istic	future (noun) + istic = futuristic (adjective) natural (noun) + istic = naturalistic (adjective)

When you use a suffix in your writing, check a dictionary, if necessary, to see how the word is spelled.

Try It Yourself

Exercise A. Create new words by joining together each pair of base words and prefixes or base words and suffixes given below. On your own paper, tell what each new word means.

EXAMPLE cheer + ful

cheerful, full of cheer

1. dis + appear
2. remark + able
3. in + edible
4. en + courage
5. bi + weekly

Try It Yourself

Exercise B. Each sentence below contains an underlined word that uses a prefix or a suffix. On your own paper, define the underlined word, using the meaning of the prefix or suffix, the base word, and the context of the sentence.

EXAMPLE Tortoise's shell used to be as <u>beautiful</u> as a pearl.

Beautiful means "showing the quality of beauty," or showing qualities pleasing to the eye.

1. The other animals <u>enjoyed</u> stroking Tortoise's smooth shell.
2. Tired of digging for worms, Tortoise grew <u>thoughtful</u>.
3. "I could increase my resting time <u>tenfold</u> if I did not have to dig for worms," said Tortoise.
4. "Ah," thought Tortoise, "in my <u>cleverness</u> I have thought of a plan."
5. <u>Undaunted</u> Monkey gave Tortoise food, but Tortoise did not let Monkey touch his shell.
6. Monkey developed a <u>distaste</u> for Tortoise's attitude.
7. Tortoise <u>discovered</u> that the animals no longer brought him food.
8. He did not mind his <u>friendless</u> state, but he grew very hungry.
9. His <u>laziness</u> had grown even more intense.
10. Tortoise thought of a new plan that <u>transcended</u> his last plan in its cleverness.
11. Tortoise was taken to a banquet by the birds, but he was a very <u>impolite</u> guest.
12. Tortoise's appetite was <u>unappeasable</u>, and he did not leave any food for the birds.
13. The birds dropped Tortoise on his favorite rock as <u>punishment</u>.
14. Tortoise's shell was <u>transformed</u> from its former smooth state to the broken pattern we know today.
15. Do you think Tortoise is <u>regretful</u> of his actions?

GOALS/OBJECTIVES

Studying this lesson will enable students to
- enjoy an interesting, amusing tale from Central Africa
- briefly describe the Luba culture
- define *aim* and use this term to ananalyze a folk tale
- distingush between formal and informal English and use each in its appropriate context

ADDITIONAL RESOURCES

Reader's Guide
- Selection Worksheet, 2.7

Assessment Portfolio
- Selection Check Test, 2.7.13
- Selection Test, 2.7.14

Pronunciation Exercise
- Grade 7 Audiocassette, Side B, Track 39

CROSS-CURRICULAR CONNECTIONS

Social Studies and World History

Have your students locate Zaire on a map of Africa. You may wish to ask some students to research the history, geography, art, culture, and peoples of Zaire.

Prereading

Central Africa

"How the Common Man Married the Princess"

Luba Tale, retold by Ngolela Dibinga

Cross-curricular Connection

Social Studies and World History. The Luba are a people who live in the tropical forests and savannas of south-central Zaire, and presently number over five and a half million. The Luba are one of the Bantu-speaking people. Many Luba still live traditionally, dwelling in small villages which are composed of a single street lined with thatched-roof huts on either side. There, the Luba hunt, gather food, cultivate corn and cassava (a type of edible root), and keep livestock such as cattle, goats, pigs, and chickens.

Between the fifteenth and seventeenth centuries AD, the Luba developed an empire. This empire, ruled by a king, or *bulopwe,* was a significant military power. Later, foreigners—first Arabs and then Europeans—tried to control the region around the Congo River to gain wealth through the ivory and slave trades. This foreign influence weakened the Luba empire. The empire finally broke down completely when it was colonized by the British in the nineteenth century. The Luba people then formed smaller chiefdoms or kinship groups.

The Luba believe in a supreme being, or creator god. They also worship ancestors and natural spirits. The Luba have a complex and highly evolved literature which includes epic cycles, or series of poems that express the ideals of a people. Women are very important in Luba society, and the Luba practice women's initiation rites. Luba art also reflects the strong influence of women upon their culture. Many of their carved wooden statues feature images of motherhood. The selection you are about to read is a tale about how a common man marries a Luba princess.

As You Read

In **"How the Common Man Married the Princess,"** setting, character, and elements of plot are all important. To help you keep track of these elements, make a story map like the one below. As you read, fill in the story map. If you need help with the definitions of any of the elements of the story map, refer to the Handbook of Literary Terms.

Story Map		
Setting:	**the Luba kingdom**	
Conflict:	☐ **internal**	☐ **external**
Major Characters:		
Plot:	**Inciting incident**	
	Climax	
	Resolution	
Themes:		

AS YOU READ

Setting: the Luba kingdom

Conflict: External (The common man wants to marry the princess must must solve a difficult problem to do so.)

Major Characters: The common man (Malu); the Luba king (Simba)

Inciting incident: The common man is told by the king that, in order to marry the princess, he must give as dowry a goat that is neither male nor female.

Climax: The common man presents his problem to the elders.

Resolution: The king, impressed by the common man's reply, grants his daughter's hand in marriage.

READER'S JOURNAL

Think about a time when someone asked you to accomplish what seemed like an impossible feat or task. What was it? Why did it seem impossible to you at the time? In what way did you handle the situation? Were you successful, or not? If so, what did you do to succeed? Write about these questions in your journal.

"How the Common Man Married the Princess"

LUBA TALE, RETOLD BY NGOLELA DIBINGA

Once upon a time, there was a great king in the Luba kingdom. His name was Simba, and he was a very wealthy person who owned a lot of cattle. His fame went beyond the boundaries of his kingdom because, as a warrior, he had been in constant conflict with neighboring villages.

King Simba had three children, two princes and one princess. The princess's name was Diba, which means "the sun." She was the last of King Simba's three children. Being the last of his children and the only daughter, Diba was a spoiled child. Diba was admired by all the people who met her inside or outside the royal compound because she was attractive and gentle. She was a very beautiful woman in the kingdom of eight thousand souls, and soon her beauty became the story of the land. Diba was so popular that King Simba became worried about her safety.

Like any parent, the king decided to take extreme measures to ensure the safety of his daughter. One of the measures was to ground her from playing or walking outside the royal compound. This way, he could protect her from any danger, as well as from the many men who bothered the king daily to ask for the princess's hand in marriage.

Then, one day, a common man from a distant village who had seen Diba several times came to see the king. His purpose was to convince the king that he was the right person to marry the princess. His name was Malu, which means, in this particular situation, "trouble."

Upon his arrival at the king's compound, Malu was not allowed to enter into the royal court because he came alone. For, to enter for this purpose, tradition required that a suitor be accompanied by an elder person from his family. Because Malu insisted, the king allowed his men to let Malu in. Malu was warmly received by the king and his royal council. As is the custom, they offered Malu good food, and the king gave him a place to sleep until the next day. For, according to tradition, when you have a guest, you must give him something to eat and a place to rest before dealing with the matter of the meeting.

❶ *How do you think King Simba feels about his daughter?*

❷ *How do guests seem to be treated in this culture?*

READER'S JOURNAL

As an alternative activity, you might ask students to think about a difficult goal that they want to achieve and to write about what they might do to achieve it.

ANSWERS TO GUIDED READING QUESTIONS

❶ King Simba must think highly of his daughter given the name that he has given to her and given the fact that he has spoiled her.

❷ In this culture, guests are treated very well. They are given top priority.

SUPPORT FOR LEP STUDENTS

PRONUNCIATIONS OF PROPER NOUNS AND ADJECTIVES

Lu • ba (lo͞o´bä′) n.
Ngo • le • la Di • bin • ga (ŋgō lā´lə də biŋ´gä) n.

Answers to Guided Reading Questions

❶ Malu asks the elders of his village for advice.

❷ The king asks for a goat that is neither male nor female. This request is confusing because no such goat exists.

Whom does Malu ask for advice? ❶

What dowry does the king require? Why does this confuse Malu? ❷

Next morning, Malu was summoned to the royal council chamber. King Simba was on his throne. All his male and female councilors were present. Malu, the guest, was given a special seat.

"My son Malu, welcome. I am very happy to meet you," said the king. "I do not need your presentation because my informants told me all about you and your family. Just tell us the reason for your visit," added King Simba.

"As you already know, I guess, the reason for my being here is to ask for your daughter, Diba, in marriage," said Malu, and he added, "I have seen her several times. I love her."

Now comes the crunch!

"Our investigations on you have concluded that you are a good person and that our daughter, Diba, has high esteem for you. However, before I accept your proposal and make it official," said the king with a smile, "go back to your people and bring me the dowry."[1]

"But what kind of dowry? Gold, gunpowder, copper currency, or what?" asked Malu. The king asked one of his head advisers to explain to the young man what he meant.

The royal adviser stood up and said, "Young man, go back home. Get a goat. Bring it to us. But note this very carefully: do not bring either a female or a male goat. Just a goat."

"My lord, tell me where I can find that goat which is neither male nor female, for I have not seen such a goat!" responded the confused young man. He did not get any reply. He then added, "I thank you, my lord and my king for this royal hospitality expressed on my humble behalf. I am very grateful to you and to the royal family for all that you have done for me. I will report all of this to my folks, including the nature of the dowry requested. Hopefully, we will return."

Very troubled, the young man went back home. There, he remained in his hut for three days. He refused to talk to anyone. On the fourth day, he informed his elders that he had to go away for a few days before he told them about his encounter with King Simba. He traveled throughout the land, visiting markets, consulting with magicians and priests, seeking a goat that was neither female nor male. His search was unsuccessful.

Malu then said to himself, "Let me go back to report the whole story to my own folks. Hopefully, somebody will know the solution to the royal problem." It took him three days to reach his village. He was tired and confused, but he did not want to lose Diba, the royal beauty, the princess of the Luba kingdom.

Malu arrived in the village. He summoned his elders. They all came quickly, anxious to know the state of mind of the young man who, in their view, was acting crazily. Malu stood before the council of the elders and told them, "My honorable elders, women and men, you have seen me a little bit confused and worried. The reason is the nature of the dowry requested by King Simba. The king, after accepting my proposal to marry the princess Diba, asked his head adviser to tell me the nature of the dowry. This advisor told me that the dowry requested is a goat—but not a female or male goat, just a goat."

After hearing Malu's report, the chief of the council of elders stood up and said, "The council is adjourned. We

1. **dowry.** Property brought by one spouse to another upon marriage

will meet again this evening. Let each one of you go and search for the solution to this problem."

At the evening meeting all the elders were excited because they had the solution. Malu was very quiet. He was confused and worried. The chief elder stood up and asked for permission to speak. He said, "We know that Nzambi the Creator has made animals—males and females. King Simba should know better. Listen, young man. King Simba did not want to embarrass you by telling you in public that you were not a suitable candidate for marriage to his daughter."

After a long silence, he went on, "Young man, do not be discouraged. We have the solution." He told the worried and confused young man, "Send a messenger to King Simba to tell him that the goat has been found and it is neither female nor male. The messenger will give King Simba these instructions: King Simba, send your messenger to pick up the goat in our village. However, note this, your messenger should arrive in our village neither in daytime nor in nighttime."

Malu was very happy that a solution was found, although he was not sure he would be accepted by the king as a future son-in-law.

The messenger was sent to the royal court. He told the sovereign about the goat and when it should be picked up. King Simba was extremely surprised by the wisdom of Malu. He told Malu's messenger, "Tell the young man to bring me a male goat and my daughter will be his wife, for there are only female and male in the animal kingdom, and there is no other time division beside daytime and nighttime. Tell Malu that Diba, the princess of Luba, is his wife."

That is how Malu got married to the princess of the Luba kingdom.

Moral: Young people, listen to and seek the wisdom of your elders, for that is where your strength and success reside. ■

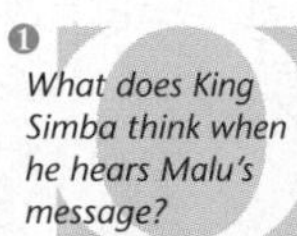

❶ *What does King Simba think when he hears Malu's message?*

❷ *What does the elder say is the reason King Simba made this peculiar dowry request?*

About the Author

Ngolela Dibinga is a teacher and a writer. She has a Ph.D. from Harvard University. Dibinga's stories come from the Luba people of the Kasai Province in central Zaire.

Answers to Guided Reading Questions

❶ King Simba is impressed by Malu's wisdom, which, of course, he has received by heeding the counsel of the village elders.

❷ The elder says that the king made this request because he did not want to embarrass Malu by telling him that a common person is not a suitable candidate for marriage to a princess.

Selection Check Test with Answers

EX. Why was Diba admired?
She was admired because she was attractive and gentle.

1. What does Malu's name mean?
It means trouble.

2. What dowry is demanded by the king?
The king demands a goat that is neither male nor female.

3. What does Malu do after his unsuccessful search?
He presents his problem to the council of elders.

4. When does Malu say the messenger should pick up the dowry?
The messenger should come neither in the daytime nor in the nighttime.

5. What is the moral of this story?
The moral is that young people should listen to their elders because that is where their strength and success lies.

RESPONDING TO THE SELECTION

Most students will probably be impressed by Malu's persistence in finding a solution to the problem. He wisely presents the problem to the elders of his village and heeds their advice.

ANSWERS FOR REVIEWING THE SELECTION

RECALLING AND INTERPRETING

1. **Recalling.** Diba is beautiful and spoiled. Her father is the Luba king, Simba. The king protects her by keeping her from walking outside the royal compound. **Interpreting.** King Simba must love his daughter very much. That is why he attempts to protect her.

2. **Recalling.** Malu is a common man who wishes to marry the king's daughter. The king says that he will agree if Malu can offer as dowry a goat that is neither male nor female. **Interpreting.** It is not possible for Malu to follow the king's commands. Malu accepts these commands anyway because Simba is a king. The elders of Malu's village suggest that the king has given such an order to save Malu from embarrassment.

3. **Recalling.** Malu asks the elders for advice. They tell him to say that the king's people can come get the goat at a time that is neither day nor night. **Interpreting.** The elders' interpretation of the king's command is reasonable, and their response is ingenious.

4. **Recalling.** The king is impressed by Malu's wisdom. The king tells Malu that he may marry the princess in exchange for a dowry of a single male goat. **Interpreting.** The king allows Malu to marry the princess because he is impressed by the man's intelligence.

SYNTHESIZING

Responses will vary. Possible responses are given.

5. One lesson we all can learn from traditional cultures is to honor the wisdom of our elders.

Responding to the Selection

What do you think of Malu? Has he caused "trouble," or has he admirably accomplished a difficult task? What would you have done if you had been in Malu's situation? How would you feel about the elders who helped you through this situation?

Reviewing the Selection

Recalling and Interpreting

1. **R** What is Diba like? Who is her father? What does her father do to protect her?

   I How do you think Diba's father feels about his daughter? Why might he be so concerned with protecting her?

2. **R** Who is Malu? Why does he go to see the king? What does the king say to Malu's proposal?

   I Is it possible for Malu to follow the king's commands? Why does Malu accept these commands? Why does the king give such an order?

3. **R** Whom does Malu ask for advice? What do these people say?

   I Do you agree with this interpretation of the reason for the king's difficult command? What do you think of the plan to circumvent the king's command?

4. **R** What does the king think after he has heard Malu's messenger? What does the king tell Malu to do?

   I Why do you think the king allows Malu to marry the princess?

Synthesizing

5. The moral of this tale is "Young people, listen to and seek the wisdom of your elders, for that is where your strength and success reside." In what way does the action of the story prove this moral? What experiences or knowledge do your elders have that you lack? Do you have anything your elders lack? Does Malu possess any qualities his elders lack? What do you think of the moral of this story? Is it convincing? Why, or why not?

Understanding Literature (Questions for Discussion)

Aim. A writer's **aim** is his or her purpose, or goal. People may write to express themselves (expressive writing), to inform others (informative writing), to persuade others (persuasive writing), or to create a literary work (literary writing). Some works are created with more than one aim, or purpose. What do you think was the aim of this tale? Who do you think might have told this tale? To whom might the tale have been told? Why do you think this tale was passed on from one generation to the next?

ANSWERS FOR UNDERSTANDING LITERATURE

Responses will vary. Possible responses are given.

Aim. This tale can be seen to have two aims: to teach people to persist in adversity and to teach them to respect the wisdom and experience of their elders. This tale might be told to young people to teach them to respect their elders. It is the sort of tale that older people might tell to young people to convince them to show such respect.

Varieties of English

Formal and Informal English

Compare the following two statements:

"How the Common Man Married the Princess" is a really old story that these people called the Luba tell. It teaches a lesson about listening to older folks. I bet you'll like it and maybe even learn something.

"How the Common Man Married the Princess" is a traditional folk tale of the Luba culture. The tale presents a moral about respecting the wisdom of one's elders. I think you will find it both intriguing and instructive.

These statements say much the same thing, but they are written in very different styles. The first is an example of informal English. Informal English uses short, simple words and contractions, such as *you'll* for *you will.* It is appropriate for ordinary, everyday use, as in conversations or letters to friends. The second is an example of formal English. Formal English uses more sophisticated words and usually does not contain contractions. It is appropriate for special uses such as speeches on formal occasions or reports that are done for school. When you write and speak, try to use the kind of English that is appropriate for your occasion, subject, audience, and purpose. For more information, see the Language Arts Survey, 2.45, "Formal and Informal English."

Try It Yourself

Read each sentence and decide whether it is written in formal English or in informal English. On your own paper, indicate your choice and explain which clues led you to your decision.

1. Malu longed to be joined in matrimony with the lovely Diba, princess of the Luba.
2. The king was a really important guy, and he didn't want a common Joe like Malu to marry his daughter.
3. It was a lucky break for Malu that he had all those really wise counselor-types to help!
4. Many traditional societies rely upon a council of elders to inform their decisions.
5. Malu outsmarted the king at his own game.

Language Lab

Introducing the Skill

Have students read aloud the two examples given at the top of this page. Discuss the differences between these examples.

Previewing the Skill

Ask students to give other examples of formal and informal English.

Practicing the Skill

Assign the Try It Yourself exercise. This exercise could be done as an oral activity in class.

Reviewing the Skill

Ask students to read the Language Arts Survey, 2.45, "Formal and Informal English" and assign the activity that accompanies that lesson. You might also have your students do the corresponding worksheet in the Essential Skills Practice Book: Language.

Answers for Try It Yourself

Exercise A

1. formal. The sentence uses sophisticated words (*longed, joined, matrimony*).
2. informal. The sentence uses colloquial words (*really, guy, common Joe*). It also uses contractions.
3. informal. The sentence uses colloquial phrases and constructions (*lucky break, really wise, counselor-types*).
4. formal. The sentence uses sophisticated words (*traditional, rely, council, elders, inform*)
5. informal. The sentence uses colloquial words and phrases (*outsmarted, his own game*).

GOALS/OBJECTIVES

Studying this lesson will enable students to

- enjoy a legend from the Zulu culture of Southern Africa
- explain, briefly, some important events in the history of the Zulu
- define *legend* and give examples of the term
- write a business letter in proper form
- create a time line of African history

ADDITIONAL RESOURCES

Reader's Guide

- Selection Worksheet, 7.8

Assessment Portfolio

- Selection Check Test, 2.7.15
- Selection Test, 2.7.16

Pronunciation Exercise

- Grade 7 Audiocassette, Side B, Track 40

CROSS-CURRICULAR CONNECTIONS

World History and Social Studies

The history of South Africa and that of the Zulu in particular is fascinating. Have your students research this history and present oral reports in class.

Prereading

SOUTHERN AFRICA

"Dingane the Brave Warrior"

Zulu Tale, retold by Tandiwe Njobe

Cross-curricular Connection

World History and Social Studies. The Zulu are a people who live in an area called KwaZululand in the province of Natal, South Africa. The Zulu are grain farmers who also herd cattle. The Zulu have a patriarchal society, and they practice polygyny. That is, a Zulu man may marry more than one woman. The wives are carefully ranked; the mother of a man's heir, or firstborn, has most status. Traditional Zulu beliefs involve ancestor worship as well as the belief in a creator god. The king of the Zulu is thought to have magical powers as well.

The Zulu are composed of many clans. Each clan is ruled by a chief, who owes allegiance to the king. Zulu chiefs are usually advised by a council. Zulu society is very focused on its military. Boys join the Zulu army at adolescence.

Before the early nineteenth century, the Zulu were only one of many peoples in Natal. A leader called Shaka (*circa* 1787–1828), however, transformed his small group into the Zulu Empire. In 1816, Shaka was asked to take over the Zulu, a small group of about fifteen hundred people. He reorganized the Zulu army and taught them military tactics. Within a year, Shaka's army had destroyed neighboring peoples, absorbing the survivors into the Zulu. By 1823, Shaka had conquered all nearby peoples, and terrified clans fled from the mighty Zulu Empire.

Europeans first came to Natal in 1824, and Shaka allowed them to stay and study the Zulu language. Shaka's mother died in 1827, and he went mad with grief. He died in 1828. Shaka's successor was a king named Dingane. Dingane was succeeded by Mpande, who saw much of his territory taken over by Europeans. Mpande's successor, Cetshwayo, refused to place himself under British control and went to war with the European invaders in 1878. *Isandhlwana* was a battle that took place around and near the Isandhlwana River between the Zulu and the British in 1879. The British failed to defend their camp, and an army of twenty thousand Zulu warriors claimed the lives of nearly seventeen hundred British.

In the tale you are about to read, Shaka is described as leading the Zulu into the battle of *Isandhlwana.* This battle occurred after Shaka's death. However, the Zulu have traditionally believed their kings were gods who transcended normal limitations of time and place. The Zulu created rich mythologies around their kings.

As You Read

In the following selection you will learn much about the Zulu culture through details that the author provides. Make a chart like the one below. As you read, keep track of these details, and write what you think these details indicate about Zulu society.

DETAILS	ZULU SOCIETY
Dingane has "responsibility" of being the firstborn son	society is probably patriarchal

AS YOU READ

Answers will vary. Sample respones are given.

Detail: Father lives in separate hut. Zulu Society: More separation between men and women than in Western society.

Detail: Council of Elders mediates disputes. Zulu Society: Elders are treated with respect and honor.

Detail: Bongane has fought in several battles. Zulu Society: The Zulus have been involved in many wars and have a martial tradition.

READER'S JOURNAL

Think about a time when you had to give a presentation, hold a recital, or play in a game, and you felt very nervous and unsure about doing so. What did you have to do? Why do you think you felt nervous and unsure? Did you share your fears with anyone? If so, what did he or she say? What did you do to overcome your fears? Write about these questions in your journal.

"Dingane the Brave Warrior"

ZULU TALE, RETOLD BY TANDIWE NJOBE

In a village located in the province of KwaZululand in South Africa, there lived a young boy by the name of Dingane. Dingane lived with his mother Nandi and his sister Sibusisiwe in a large hut near the center of the village. His father, Bongane, lived in a separate hut close by. Dingane's father had four wives. Each wife had her own hut where she and her children lived. Dingane's mother was Bongane's first wife, and Dingane was their first child. This meant that Dingane bore the great responsibility of being the first born of all Bongane's children.

Bongane was a very important man in the village. He was an advisor to the chief of the village and he sat on the Council of Elders. When there were disputes or problems in the village a meeting was called to discuss the problem. The Council of Elders would mediate between the two disputing parties and try to settle these arguments in the fairest way possible. If the village were in any kind of trouble, the Council of Elders would meet to try to solve the problem. In this way the Council of Elders acted as the court of the village.

Dingane was very proud of his father and wanted to be like him when he grew up. Bongane had also been a warrior when he was a young man, and he had fought for the village in several battles. He often sat for hours with Dingane telling him stories about the battles the Zulu people had fought and won. Bongane told Dingane how brave and strong the Zulu warriors were when they went into battle and how they wore colorful animal skins on their bodies. He also told Dingane about how the people in the village would prepare for these battles by singing songs and dancing the *Indlamu*[1] in

1. **Indlamu.** Traditional Zulu dance using spears and shields

❶ *What role does the Council of Elders play in the village?*

❷ *What are the Zulu like when they go into battle?*

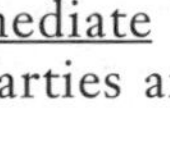

WORDS FOR EVERYDAY USE

me • di • ate (mē´dē āt´) *v.,* bring about an agreement, result, or solution between disputing parties

READER'S JOURNAL

As an alternative activity, you might ask students to write in their journals about actions that they believe demonstrate courage. Based on these examples, they can then attempt to define the term *courage.*

ANSWERS TO GUIDED READING QUESTIONS

❶ The Council of Elders settles disputes and major problems faced by the village. It is a kind of court.

❷ In battle, the Zulu are strong and brave. They wear colorful animal skins.

SUPPORT FOR LEP STUDENTS

PRONUNCIATIONS OF PROPER NOUNS AND ADJECTIVES

Din • ga • ne (diŋ gä´nā) n.
Zu • lu (zo͞o´lo͞o) n.
Tan • di • we • Njo • be (tan di´wə njō´bə) n.

ADDITIONAL VOCABULARY

disputing—arguing; in disagreement

Answers to Guided Reading Questions

❶ People from other parts of the world came to South Africa. These people tried to take over the lands and homes of the Zulu people. This made the Zulu very angry.

❷ Dingane admires Shaka and wants to be like him.

❸ The prospect of leading other boys in the traditional *Indlamu* dance makes Dingane nervous.

praise of their young fighters. Dingane often asked his father why the Zulu people had fought so many wars. Bongane told him that the Zulu fought for their land.

❶ *Who came to South Africa? What did these people try to do? How did the Zulu feel about this?*

Bongane explained to Dingane that a long time ago people had come to South Africa from other parts of the world to build a new home for themselves. The people of KwaZululand welcomed these strangers into their homes and gave them gifts of food and drink. After a while it seemed that these people wanted to take over the land and the homes of the Zulu people for themselves, and this made the Zulu very angry. In those days, the leader of the Zulu people was called Shaka. Shaka was a very strong and brave man. He did not like to see the homes and the land of the Zulu being taken away, so he fought back and he won.

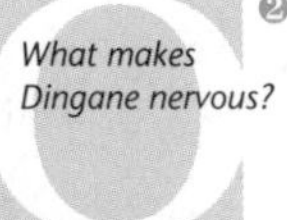

❷ *What makes Dingane nervous?*

❸ *How does Dingane feel about Shaka?*

Dingane loved to hear his father tell these stories. He especially like the story about *Isandhlwana.* The *Isandhlwana* was a battle led by the great Shaka in which the Zulu people were victorious. Dingane often wished he could have lived when Shaka was the king of the Zulu people. He admired Shaka's strength and courage and wanted to be the same way when he grew up.

One morning Dingane woke up a little earlier than usual. It was a special day because the village was going to celebrate the anniversary of the battle of *Isandhlwana.* This meant that there was going to be a lot of dancing and eating. Nandi, Dingane's mother, had been up most of the night with the other women of the village preparing the food and drink for the festivities. In the morning, the women and girls of the village were painting their faces and bodies and putting on the colorful skirts and beads of the Zulu people. Meanwhile, the men of the village were preparing themselves by wearing their best skins, brushing their shields, and polishing their spears and *knopkiris.*[3] Bongane told Dingane that during the wars the men had used spears, shields, and *knopkiris* to fight. Now the men used them when they danced the *Indlamu.*

Dingane could already hear the sound of the drums, which meant that the drummers were practicing for the afternoon's activities. He rose from his bed on the floor and went to greet his mother. "*Sawu-bona mama,*"[4] he said, greeting his mother in Zulu. She smiled and handed him his bowl of porridge. Dingane always ate his porridge with lots of milk. The people of the village said that this made young boys grow into men.

As he ate, Dingane began to think of the events to come later that day. He thought of how he would be leading some of the other boys his age in the traditional *Indlamu* in front of the entire village. Even people from surrounding villages would be coming to share in the celebration. The thought made him nervous, but Dingane was afraid to share his lack of confidence with his mother for fear that she might laugh at him. He had already told his younger sister Sibusisiwe, and she had laughed at him and called him a coward. Dingane was ashamed of his fears because he wanted to be a brave strong man, like King Shaka in the battle of *Isandhlwana.*

3. **knopkiris.** Traditional weapon: a long stick with a solid wooden ball at the top

4. **sawu-bona mama.** "Hello Mama" (literally, "we see you, Mama")

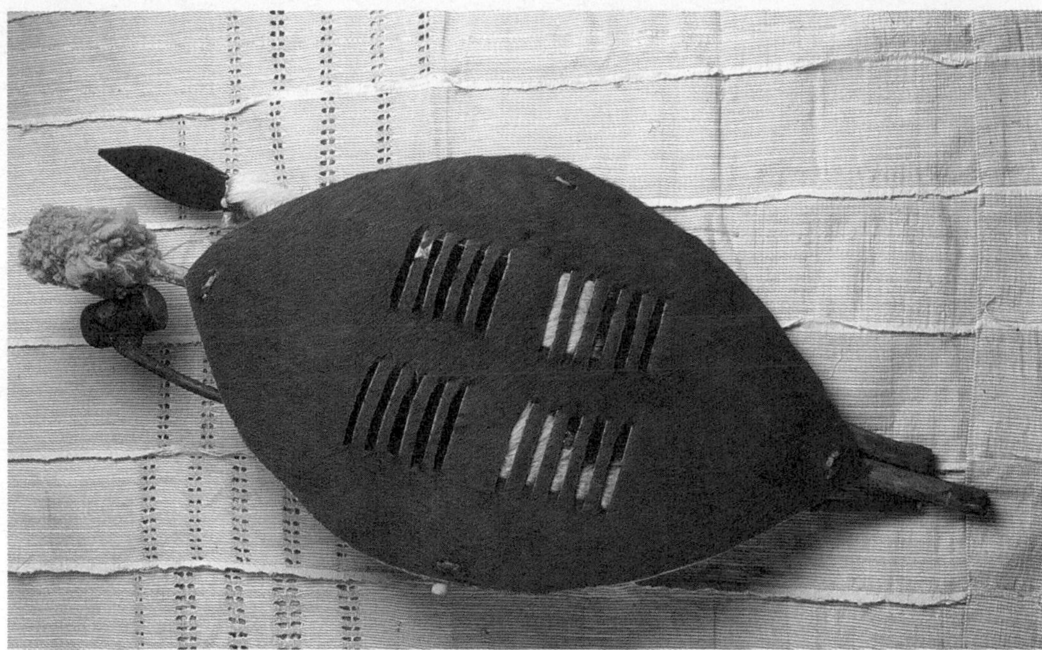

Zulu shield and spear. South Africa

Dingane decided to go down to the river to wash himself and to prepare for the celebration. On his way he thought again of how he would have to lead the *Indlamu*, and once again he felt a twinge of fear. He again wished that he had the bravery and courage of Shaka. When he got down to the river, he began to wash his face and body. Suddenly, he felt the presence of another person. He looked up at the sky and saw nothing. He looked behind him toward the village and still saw nothing. Then he heard a voice calling him, and he looked out to the middle of the river.

Dingane could not believe his eyes. Standing in the middle of the river was the image of Shaka, and he was calling out to Dingane. "*Yebo Inkosi*,"[5] Dingane said to Shaka. This was the respectful way to greet chiefs and kings in the Zulu custom. Dingane dropped to his knees in the respectful manner.

Shaka said in his deep, strong voice, "Dingane, named after the great Dingane who was my father, king of all kings and warrior of all warriors, you carry the name Dingane well. It is a name of dignity and respect. You are growing up to be a fine young man—a Zulu man with the strength and courage of former Zulu warriors who won the battle of *Isandhlwana*. I want you to know that your ancestors are watching over you. We are proud of what we see. We know that you will become a great leader of the Zulu people one day, just like your father and

❶ *What does Shaka say to inspire Dingane?*

5. **Yebo Inkosi.** Formal greeting to a chief or king

Answer to Guided Reading Question

❶ Shaka says that Dingane is named after a great warrior, that the boy carries this great name well, and that the boy's ancestors have been watching him and are proud of him.

Answer to Guided Reading Question

➊ The Zulu feel that such visions are real and occasionally occur to chosen people from the village.

Selection Check Test with Answers

EX. Where does Dingane live?
Dingane lives in a village in KwaZululand in South Africa.

1. Who is Dingane's father?
Dingane's father is Bongane, an important man in the village.

2. What type of stories does Bongane tell Dingane?
Bongane tells Dingane stories about the battles the Zulu people had fought and won.

3. What was *Isandhlwana*?
***Isandhlwana* was a battle led by Shaka in which the Zulu people were victorious.**

4. How does Dingane feel about leading the other boys in the traditional *Indlamu?*
Dingane feels very nervous.

5. What image does Dingane see in the middle of a river?
Dingane sees the great Zulu leader Shaka.

How do the Zulu feel about such visions? ➊

grandfather. That is why you were given the name Dingane."

Just as quickly as the image appeared, it disappeared. Dingane stood up somewhat shaken. He had heard of these visits that the ancestors occasionally paid to chosen people of the village. Realizing the greatness of what had just happened, Dingane began to feel great pride in himself and in his responsibilities. As the firstborn child of Bongane, he knew that he had to set an example, not only for his brothers and sisters, but for the many other young boys and girls in the village. He felt brave and courageous enough to go back to the village and lead the dance of *Indlamu.*

As Dingane walked back to the village, he felt excited. He realized that fear could be overcome. The words of the great King Shaka had strengthened his resolve to gain strength and bravery and to become a great Zulu warrior—just like his father Bongane and the great King Shaka himself. ■

About the Author

Tandiwe Njobe was born in Lusaka, Zambia, to South African parents. Her father's village is called Nxolo. Njobe has lived in Tanzania and has worked as a fourth-grade teacher. She has been living in the United States since 1988.

Words for Everyday Use

re • solve (ri zälv´) *n.,* firm determination; fixed purpose

Vocabulary in Context

• No temptation could shake Karl's resolve to stop eating sweets.

Responding to the Selection

How do you think Dingane feels about receiving his vision? Do you think it indicates his future greatness? Why, or why not? Do you agree with Shaka that an individual's name reveals much about him or her? Why, or why not?

Reviewing the Selection

Recalling and Interpreting

1. **R** What is Dingane's "great responsibility"? What role does Dingane's father Bongane play in the village? What did Bongane do when he was a young man?

   I Why does Dingane want to be just like Bongane when he grows up? What qualities does Bongane possess that are valued among the Zulu?

2. **R** What stories does Bongane share with Dingane? What does Bongane say Shaka did?

   I Why does Bongane tells these stories to Dingane?

3. **R** What was *Isandhlwana?* What does Dingane's village do to celebrate *Isandhlwana?* What part is Dingane supposed to play in the celebration?

   I Why do the villagers celebrate *Isandhlwana?* Why do they use weapons in their celebration? Why is Dingane nervous about participating in this event?

4. **R** Where does Shaka appear to Dingane? What does Shaka say about Dingane's name? about his future?

   I Why does this vision give Dingane confidence?

Synthesizing

5. What lesson does this story teach about the way the lives of ancestors influence the present generation? Do you think Dingane had to have a vision of Shaka, or would the memory of Shaka have been enough to encourage him? Do you think that the Zulu believed that such visions often occurred? Explain your response.

Understanding Literature (Questions for Discussion)

Legend. A **legend** is a story based on important real events or characters, often from the distant past. What elements of this story are based on real events and characters? What elements of this story are imaginative additions to this legendary material?

Answers for Understanding Literature

Responses will vary. Possible responses are given.

Legend. All of the characters are, presumably, real. The appearance of the dead Shaka to the boy is, of course, an imaginative addition.

Responding to the Selection

The vision does indicate future greatness. Names may or may not be significant, depending on whether people consider them to be so.

Answers for Reviewing the Selection

RECALLING AND INTERPRETING

1. **Recalling.** His great responsibility is that he is Bongane's oldest son and heir. Bongane is advisor to the chief and sits on the Council of Elders. When he was a young man, Bongane was a warrior and fought in many battles. **Interpreting.** Dingane is proud of his father's martial exploits and history.
2. **Recalling.** Bongane tells Dingane about battles. He tells him the story of the battle of *Isandhlwana,* which was won under the leadership of the great Shaka. **Interpreting.** These stories cause the boy to become interested in martial matters and in the history of his people.
3. **Recalling.** This was a great battle won by the Zulu. To celebrate *Isandhlwana,* the village holds a festival on its anniversary. Dingane is expected to lead other boys in the traditional *Indlamu* dance. **Interpreting.** They are proud of having won this battle. Weapons commemorate the battle. Dingane is nervous because he has to perform in front of others.
4. **Recalling.** Shaka is standing in the middle of a river when he appears to Dingane. Shaka says that Dingane is a proud name, one belonging to his own warrior father. Shaka says that Dingane will become a great leader. **Interpreting.** Dingane must have a great future ahead of him if something as miraculous as the appearance of an ancestor occurs.

SYNTHESIZING

Responses will vary. Possible responses are given.

5. People in the Zulu culture seem to be strongly influenced by their ancestors. A strong memory would be enough to encourage a person. The story indicates that the Zulu believe that such appearances occur from time to time.

Writing Skills

Introducing the Skill

Explain that business letter form is used whenever one writes a letter that is not of a personal nature. Further explain that using proper form in business letters will impress people and help one to accomplish one's goals.

Previewing the Skill

Have students read the sample business letter on page 333. Point out the parts, in order: the return address, the inside address, the salutation, the body, and the closing, including the complementary close and the signature.

Prewriting and Drafting

Alternatively, you could have students write letters to some local organization (a museum, for example), or to a local or state politician.

Evaluating and Revising

Have students use the Analytic Scale on the next page to evaluate the drafts of their letters.

Proofreading and Publishing

Refer students to the information on proofreading in the Language Arts Survey.

Applied English Skills

Writing a Business Letter

Many letters that you will write in your life will be addressed to people that you do not know personally. Whenever you write such a letter, known as a business letter, you should use a formal tone and the appropriate form. (For more on formal tone, see the Language Arts Survey, 2.45, "Formal and Informal English." One common form is the block form. In the block form, each part of the letter begins at the left margin. The parts are separated by line spaces. See the Language Arts Survey, 5.4, "Writing a Business Letter," for more information about the proper form of a business letter. It is especially important when you write a business letter to avoid errors in spelling, grammar, usage, and mechanics. You should also keep your letter brief and informative. Long, rambling business letters will lose the reader's attention. A business letter should contain the following parts:

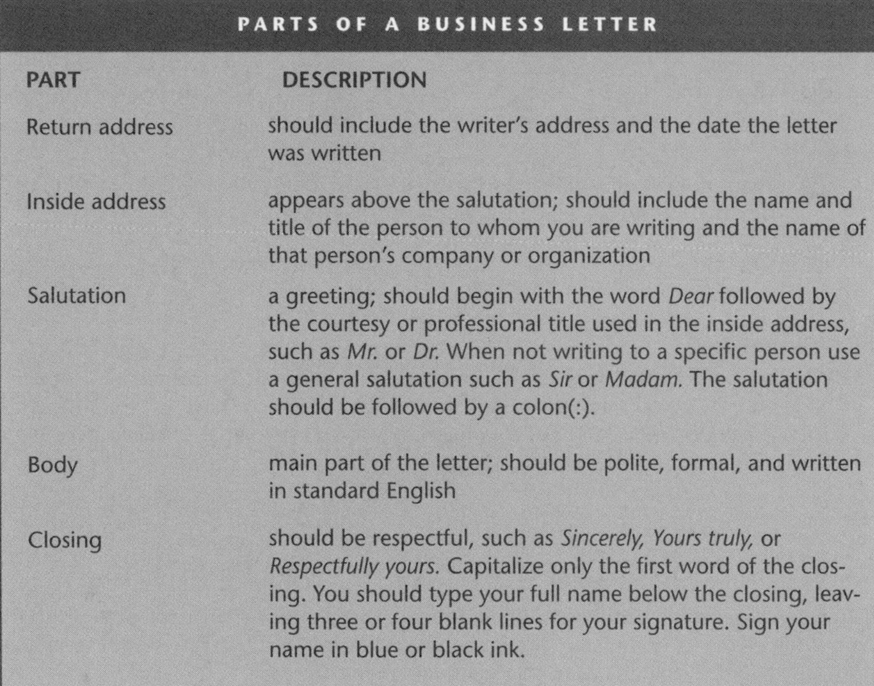

PARTS OF A BUSINESS LETTER

PART	DESCRIPTION
Return address	should include the writer's address and the date the letter was written
Inside address	appears above the salutation; should include the name and title of the person to whom you are writing and the name of that person's company or organization
Salutation	a greeting; should begin with the word *Dear* followed by the courtesy or professional title used in the inside address, such as *Mr.* or *Dr.* When not writing to a specific person use a general salutation such as *Sir* or *Madam.* The salutation should be followed by a colon(:).
Body	main part of the letter; should be polite, formal, and written in standard English
Closing	should be respectful, such as *Sincerely, Yours truly,* or *Respectfully yours.* Capitalize only the first word of the closing. You should type your full name below the closing, leaving three or four blank lines for your signature. Sign your name in blue or black ink.

SAMPLE

498 Blue Key Rd.
Charleston, SC 89943
May 3, 1999

Mr. Davy Jones
Owner
Deep Sea Divers, Inc.
73 Ocean St.
Charleston, SC 89943

Dear Mr. Jones:

Please consider me for a position as a part-time clerk in your store for the coming summer. I understand that in the summer your business increases considerably and that you might have need for a conscientious, reliable, hardworking clerk. I can offer you considerable knowledge of snorkeling and diving equipment and experience working in a retail shop.

I will be available for work three days per week between June 1 and August 12. I am enclosing a résumé and references. Please contact me if you wish to set up an interview.

Sincerely,

Jorge Alvarez
Jorge Alvarez

Try It Yourself

Imagine that you would like to learn more about a particular African culture's mythology and traditional tales. You would like to know what some good sources might be, or if the group to whom you are writing has any information that they can send you. Write a letter to Ms. Sibongile Gikandi, Director of the African Culture and Literature Society, at 239 York Street, New York, New York 00030. Specify which culture you are interested in studying.

ANALYTIC SCALE FOR WRITING SKILLS

Assign a score from 1 to 25 for each grading criterion below.

Business Letter

- **Content/Unity.** The business letter is concise and to the point.
- **Organization/Coherence.** The letter follows proper business letter form as shown in the model on page 333.
- **Language/Style.** The letter is written in formal English.
- **Conventions.** The letter avoids errors in spelling, grammar, usage, mechanics, and manuscript form.

Project Note

Time lines produced by students, especially if illustrated, can make excellent classroom decorations and teaching aids. In addition, preparing a time line is a valuable learning experience. The guidelines provided in this lesson include complete directions for having students prepare their own time lines. You may wish to do this project as a collaborative.

Unit Project

Making an Illustrated Time Line of African History

African history is a fascinating topic. A time line is a simple way of arranging events in chronological order. History is more than a list of dates and events, however. An illustrated time line focuses on major events, but includes pictures and illustrations that help make the progression of events seem more lively.

Try It Yourself

Research major events in African history, then work with your classmates to create an illustrated time line of African history.

Student Model

Mr. Kagazi's class was studying Africa, so they made a time line of African history. First, as a group, they decided they would mark off time in centuries. Then the class divided into five groups. Each group was responsible for a region of Africa. Each group would use the same measurement when dividing their time line, and then the five segments could be pasted together. This way it would be clear what was happening at a given time in different parts of the continent.

Kim, Donta, Manny, Lia, and Claudio were covering eastern Africa. They found some information about their region as a whole. Then each person chose one country to research in depth. They used the encyclopedia, chronologies, and other books about Africa. Major historical events were recorded with a brief description. Each event was recorded on a note card with the date at the top. Then to organize the notes, the cards were put in order by date. When the group decided they had enough information, they were ready to put the information together as a time line.

They gathered a long roll of paper, a yardstick, markers, and paints. Kim marked off the time line using the measurements the class had decided upon. She marked dates at the top and bottom of the page. Then the group reviewed their notes. They chose several major events to illustrate. They would list the other events in smaller print without pictures. Manny and Lia blocked out the areas for the illustrations and captions. Then Donta and Claudio wrote the other events in pencil. The group decided that one area looked empty so they chose to illustrate another event. When they were satisfied with the plan, they copied over the events in black marker. Then they illustrated the events they had chosen. Kim and Manny did the illustrations. Donta, Lia, and Claudio worked with them to create the ideas for the illustrations.

When all the time lines were finished, they were mounted on the wall one over another, creating a time line that reflected the history of all of Africa. Mr. Kagazi's class presented their time line to another class. Each group described the events that they had illustrated on the time line.

Examining the Model

1. How does the class divide the task of researching African history?
2. What does the class do as a whole to make the time line?

Planning Your Time Line

1. First decide how you will divide periods of time on your time line. For example, you might mark off every hundred years. Decide on a standard amount of space for the period of time (one foot might equal one hundred years). You may wish to use a different measurement for very early history in which there are few events that can be dated.
2. Divide into five groups and decide which group will cover each region (northern, eastern, western, central, and southern).
3. Each group should research their region and the histories of specific countries in each region. Take notes on important events. For each event, make a note card with the date, the event, and a brief description.
4. Combine the notes of the people in the group and organize them by date. Choose several events to illustrate.

Making Your Time Line

1. Gather the materials you will need, such as a long roll of paper or several sheets that can be taped together, a yardstick or other straightedge for drawing lines, a dark pen or marker for writing dates and events, markers or other materials for illustrating, and a pencil.
2. Mark the divisions of time on your paper. Then block space within the divisions for the illustrations you will make. Pencil in the other events you will include. Make additions or deletions as necessary.
3. Write the events and dates with a dark pen.
4. Illustrate the major events.

African Civilization

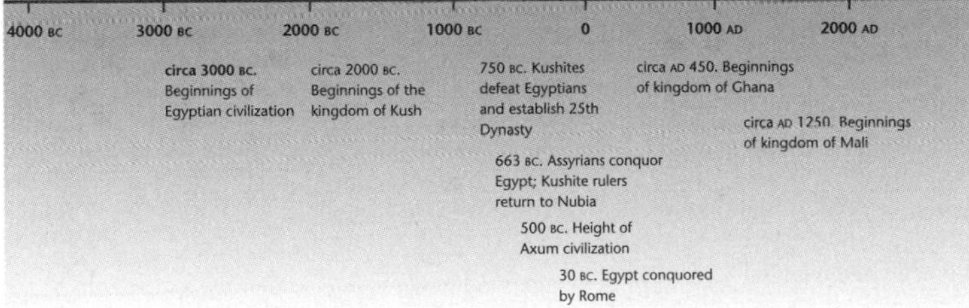

Showing Your Time Line

1. Post the five time lines on a wall, perhaps someplace where others can see it, such as the library.
2. Invite other classes to view your time line. Each group can present information about the events they illustrated.

Answers for Examining the Model

1. They divide the continent of Africa into five regions. Each group researches one of these regions.
2. The five time lines are mounted together on a wall.

ANALYTIC SCALE FOR PROJECT

Assign a score from 1 to 25 for each grading criterion below.

Diorama

- **Organization.** The group set attainable goals and created a schedule or strategy for achieving those goals.
- **Cooperation.** The group assigned tasks fairly to each member, and each member cooperated toward achieving the group's goals.
- **Goal Achievement.** The group worked steadily toward its goals and did, in fact, achieve them.
- **Presentation.** The group presented a product of high quality that met the inital project description.

Spelling Check Test

Read each word aloud. Then read aloud the sentence containing the word. Repeat the word. Ask students to write the word on their papers, spelling it correctly.

1. **mediate**

A lawyer was chosen to mediate the agreement between the company and the striking workers.

2. **resolve**

No temptation could shake Karl's resolve to stop eating sweets.

Unit Review

Summary

Literary Terms for the Unit

aim, 291, 324
fable, 311, 316
folk tale, 291
legend,331
motif, 304
myth, 304, 311, 316
oral tradition, 299, 304
personification, 291
setting, 287

Vocabulary for the Unit

mediate, 327
resolve, 330

Questions for Writing, Discussion, and Research

1. Compare and contrast "Goha and His Donkey" to "Goha and the Pot." In what ways does the character of Goha change?
2. What do you learn about the values of each of the cultures represented in this unit?

For Your Reading List

Jaclyn Hoggard
E. O. Green Middle School
Oxnard, California

West African Trickster Tales
retold by Martin Bennett

I just read a fun collection of short stories called *West African Trickster Tales.* The tales are folk tales from Africa retold by Martin Bennett. The main characters in the stories are Hare, Tortoise, and Ananse the spider. They are all tricksters, and the best trickster is Ananse. The stories tell about all the ways the animals get in and out of scrapes by using trickery. One of the stories tells about how Shark wants to eat Monkey, but Monkey saves himself by tricking Shark. Another story tells how Ananse the spider tricks everyone into thinking he is dead, and then everyone plays a trick on him to teach him a lesson. There are many more fun stories about learning and teaching for you to read. One nice thing about the stories is that they are short, so you can read one every day, even if you don't have a lot of time. I would recommend this exciting collection of short stories to anybody who likes stories and storytelling.

Vocabulary Check Test

Have students complete each sentence with a word from the Vocabulary for the Unit in the Unit Review.

1. The teacher offered to <u>mediate</u> the dispute between the two students.
2. I was impressed by Angela's <u>resolve</u> to get into shape for the marathon.

Part Three

Genres of Literature

GOALS/OBJECTIVES

Studying this unit will enable students to

- enjoy four short stories and understand elements of setting, character, plot, and theme
- describe the Hudson River and its surrounding area
- briefly discuss changes that occurred after the American Revolution, the history of conflicts between Ireland and England, burglary, and the cleverness of foxes
- define the literary terms *setting, concrete, irony of situation, resolution, verbal irony, antagonist,* and *understatement*
- use context clues, reference works, elements of verbal or nonverbal communication, and problem-solving and decision-making skills

ADDITIONAL UNIT MATERIALS IN THE ASSESSMENT PORTFOLIO

- Vocabulary Worksheet 2.8.9
- Unit Test 2.8.10

See also the Additional Resources Box in each selection.

CROSS-CURRICULAR CONNECTIONS

- American History, 344
- Geography, 344, 355
- Science, 384
- Social Studies, 372
- World History, 364

UNIT 8 THE SHORT STORY

Taxeria. *Anonymous*

D on't trust the teller, trust the tale.

—D. H. Lawrence

UNIT SKILLS OUTLINE

Literary Skills and Concepts

- Antagonist, 392
- Concrete, 360
- Irony of Situation, 369
- Resolution, 380
- Setting, 360
- Understatement, 392
- Verbal Irony, 380

Other Language Arts Skills and Concepts

- Elements of Verbal and Nonverbal Communication, 381
- Problem Solving and Decision Making, 393
- Using Context Clues, 361
- Using Reference Works, 370

Elements of Fiction

Fiction is prose writing about imagined events or characters. A **novel** is a long work of prose fiction. Short works of fiction are **short stories**. Long short stories are sometimes called **novellas**. Works of prose fiction usually have the following elements: character, setting, mood, conflict, plot, and theme.

Character. A **character** is a person or animal who takes part in the action of a literary work. The following terms are useful for describing characters:

A **protagonist** is the main character in a story.

An **antagonist** is a character who struggles against the main character.

A **major character** is one who plays an important role in a literary work.

A **minor character** is one who plays a lesser role.

Setting. The **setting** of a literary work is the time and place in which it happens. In fiction, setting is often revealed by description of landscape, scenery, buildings, furniture, seasons, or weather.

Mood. Mood, or **atmosphere,** is the emotion created in the reader by a piece of writing. Mood is created through descriptions of the setting, characters, and events.

Conflict. A **conflict** is a struggle between two people or things in a literary work. One side of the central conflict in a work of fiction is usually taken by the main character. The main character might struggle against another character, against the forces of nature, against society, or against a part of himself or herself.

Plot. A **plot** is a series of events related to a central conflict, or struggle. A typical plot involves the following elements:

The **inciting incident** is the event that introduces the central conflict, or struggle.

The **climax** is the point of highest interest and suspense.

The **resolution** is the point at which the central conflict, or struggle, is ended.

Plots are often illustrated using the following diagram, known as "Freytag's Pyramid" for its creator, Gustav Freytag:

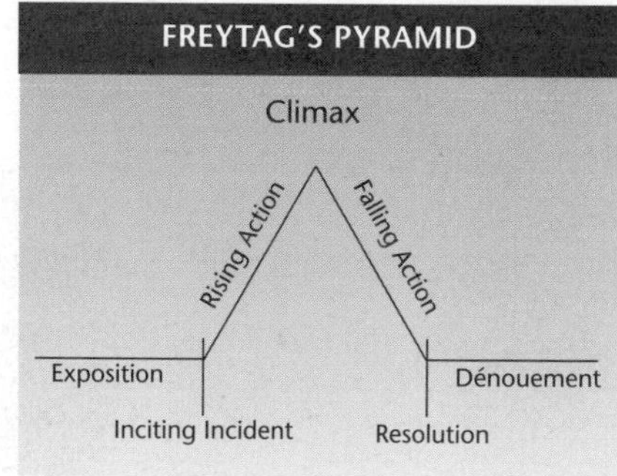

Theme. A **theme** is a central idea in a literary work.

Landscape with Peacocks. *Paul Gauguin*

GOALS/OBJECTIVES

Studying this lesson will enable students to
- enjoy a classic tale about a man who falls asleep for twenty years
- briefly describe the Hudson River and surrounding areas
- briefly describe changes that took place after the American Revolution
- define *setting* and and *concrete*
- use context clues

ADDITIONAL RESOURCES

Reader's Guide
- Selection Worksheet, 8.1

Assessment Portfolio
- Selection Check Test, 2.8.1
- Selection Test, 2.8.2

Pronunciation Exercise
- Grade 8 Audiocassette, Side B, Track 41

CROSS-CURRICULAR CONNECTIONS

Geography

Ask students to get into small groups to create original maps of the Hudson River and Catskill Mountain area of New York. Their maps should be colorful and creative. Students might even choose to create three-dimensional maps. To find out more about what should be included on the maps, they should refer to maps at the library.

American History

Ask students to research the American Revolution. Each student should focus on one aspect of the war and report his or her findings.

Prereading

SETTING

"Rip Van Winkle"
by Washington Irving

Cross-curricular Connections

Geography. The Hudson River is the largest river that begins, ends, and flows entirely in the state of New York. It is 306 miles long. The Hudson River begins in the Adirondack Mountains in upstate New York and empties into the Atlantic Ocean at New York City. In the Highlands region, south of Albany, the Hudson widens and begins to move more slowly. At one point, it passes through a narrow valley with high, rocky shores and beautiful cliffs.

"Rip Van Winkle" is set in a village bounded by the Hudson River and the Catskill Mountains. The Catskills, which reach more than three thousand feet high, are located in southeastern New York. The area was made famous by Irving's story, and its natural beauty is still appreciated.

American History. "Rip Van Winkle" is set in New York shortly before the American Revolution. Before the American Revolution, the American colonies were ruled by the king of England, George III. When Rip leaves his village, he is still a subject of the king. When he returns, the revolution has taken place. He hears of Bunker Hill, the heroes of seventy-six, rights of citizens, and members of Congress, but these terms mean nothing to him. The Battle of Bunker Hill and the heroes of seventy-six refer to important battles during the revolution. Rights of citizens and the Congress were established after the revolution had succeeded. These are among the many changes to which Rip must accustom himself.

As You Read

In **"Rip Van Winkle,"** the main character falls asleep on a mountain and finds things very different when he wakes up. Make a chart like the one below. As you read, fill in the chart with details about the town Rip lives in and about his life before and after his long sleep.

Before	After
Rip: lazy young man	Rip: old man, not expected to work hard

AS YOU READ

Answers may vary, but students might fill out their charts in the following way:

Before
- village is a small province of England
- sign shows King George
- Rip: friendly, helpful man
- Rip: in an unhappy marriage

After
- village is no longer a province of England
- sign shows George Washington
- Rip: town patriarch and story-teller
- Rip: no longer has wife, lives with daughter

READER'S JOURNAL

How do you respond when parents, teachers, or friends frequently remind you to do things? What do you say or do? Is what you say or do different from what you would like to say or do? Why, or why not? Write your thoughts and feelings about these questions in your journal.

"Rip Van Winkle"

WASHINGTON IRVING

Whoever has made a voyage up the Hudson must remember the Catskill[1] mountains. They are a branch of the great Appalachian family,[2] and are seen away to the west of the river, swelling up to a noble height, and lording it over the surrounding country. Every change of season, every change of weather, indeed every hour of the day, produces some change in the magical hues and shapes of these mountains, and they are regarded by all the good wives, far and near, as perfect barometers. When the weather is fair and settled, they are clothed in blue and purple, and print their bold outlines on the clear evening sky; but sometimes, when the rest of the landscape is cloudless, they will gather a hood of gray vapors about their summits, which, in the last rays of the setting sun, will glow and light up like a crown of glory.

At the foot of these fairy mountains, the voyager may have seen the light smoke curling up from a village, whose shingle roofs gleam among the trees, just where the blue tints of the upland melt away into the fresh green of the nearer landscape. It is a little village, of great antiquity, having been founded by some of the Dutch colonists, in the early times of the province, just about the beginning of the government of the good Peter Stuyvesant,[3] (may he rest in peace!) and there were some of the houses of the original settlers standing within a few years, built of small yellow bricks brought from Holland, having

1 *What adjectives does the narrator use to describe the mountains?*

1. **Hudson, Catskill.** River and mountain range, respectively, in upstate New York
2. **Appalachian family.** Mountain range extending from southern Quebec, Canada, to northern Alabama
3. **Peter Stuyvesant.** Last governor of the Dutch colony that was renamed New York when acquired by the British

WORDS FOR EVERYDAY USE

hue (hyo͞o) *n.,* color

ba • rom • e • ter (bə räm´ət ər) *n.,* instrument that forecasts changes in weather

prov • ince (präv´ins) *n.,* territorial district

READER'S JOURNAL

You might also ask students to describe their favorite ways of escaping stresses of daily life. What activities make them feel happy?

ANSWER TO GUIDED READING QUESTION

1 The narrator describes the mountains with the adjectives *noble, magical, blue, purple, bold.*

SPELLING AND VOCABULARY WORDS FROM THE SELECTION

addle	frolic
adherent	gambol
alacrity	hue
approbation	impunity
august	incessantly
austere	metamorphose
aversion	obsequious
azure	persecution
barometer	pestilent
bewilderment	precipice
comely	precipitation
corroborate	province
countenance	quaff
crony	reciprocate
daunt	scoff
disposition	smite
disputatious	surmount
eloquence	termagant
evince	tranquility
fain	transient
fancy	virago
flagon	visage
forlorn	

SUPPORT FOR LEP STUDENTS

PRONUNCIATIONS OF PROPER NOUNS AND ADJECTIVES

Ap • pa • la • chian (ap´ə lā´chən) n.
Stuy • ve • sant (stī´və sənt) n.

ADDITIONAL VOCABULARY

naught—nothing
perplexed—confused
perseverance—the drive to work hard and not give up

VOCABULARY IN CONTEXT

- I do not like that shade of green so let's choose another hue.
- The weather forecaster will look at his barometer before the evening news.
- From what province in Italy is your great grandmother?

Answers to Guided Reading Questions

❶ Rip's main flaw is that he does not not like to work hard.

❷ People liked Rip. He was a favorite among members of the community.

Historical Note

The Netherlands is a country in western Europe bordered by the North Sea, Germany, and Belgium. Amsterdam is the capital. Another name for this area is Holland, and people, places, and things from The Netherlands are often called *Dutch*.

During the sixteenth and seventeenth centuries, The Netherlands had a strong empire. One of the settlements was New Amsterdam, which later became the state of New York.

latticed windows[4] and gable fronts,[5] surmounted with weathercocks.

In that same village, and in one of these very houses (which, to tell the precise truth, was sadly timeworn and weather-beaten), there lived many years since, while the country was yet a province of Great Britain, a simple good-natured fellow, of the name of Rip Van Winkle. He was a descendant of the Van Winkles who figured so gallantly in the chivalrous days of Peter Stuyvesant, and accompanied him to the siege of Fort Christina. He inherited, however, but little of the martial character of his ancestors. I have observed that he was a simple good-natured man; he was, moreover, a kind neighbor, and an obedient henpecked husband. Indeed, to the latter circumstance might be owing that meekness of spirit which gained him such universal popularity; for those men are most apt to be obsequious and conciliating abroad, who are under the discipline of shrews at home. Their tempers, doubtless, are rendered pliant and malleable in the fiery furnace of domestic tribulation which is worth all the sermons in the world for teaching the virtues of patience and long-suffering. A termagant wife may, therefore, in some respects, be considered a tolerable blessing; and if so, Rip Van Winkle was thrice blessed.

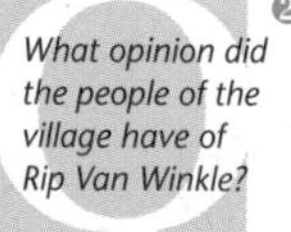

❶ What is Rip's main flaw?

❷ What opinion did the people of the village have of Rip Van Winkle?

Certain it is, that he was a great favorite among all the good wives of the village, who, as usual with the amiable sex, took his part in all family squabbles; and never failed, whenever they talked those matters over in their evening gossipings, to lay all the blame on Dame Van Winkle. The children of the village, too, would shout with joy whenever he approached. He assisted at their sports, made their playthings, taught them to fly kites and shoot marbles, and told them long stories of ghosts, witches, and Indians. Whenever he went dodging about the village, he was surrounded by a troop of them, hanging on his skirts, clambering on his back and playing a thousand tricks on him with impunity; and not a dog would bark at him throughout the neighborhood.

The great error in Rip's composition was an insuperable aversion to all kinds of profitable labor. It could not be from the want of perseverance; for he would sit on a wet rock, with a rod as long and heavy as a Tartar's lance,[6] and fish all day without a murmur, even though he should not be encouraged by a single nibble. He would carry a fowling piece[7] on his shoulder for hours together, trudging through woods and swamps, and up hill and down dale, to shoot a few squirrels or wild pigeons. He would never refuse to assist a neighbor even in the roughest toil, and was a foremost man at all country frolics for husking Indian corn, or building

4. **latticed windows.** Windows with crossed wood strips or bars

5. **gable fronts.** Triangular wall shapes where the slopes of two roofs meet

6. **Tartar's lance.** Long, heavy spear used by members of the Mongolian tribes, which invaded Europe in the thirteenth century

7. **fowling piece.** Type of shotgun used for hunting wild birds

Words for Everyday Use

sur • mount (sər mount´) *v.*, be at the top of
ob • se • qui • ous (əb sē´kwē əs) *adj.*, showing too great a willingness to serve or obey
ter • ma • gant (tʉr mə gənt) *adj.*, quarrelsome
im • pu • ni • ty (im pyo͞o´ni tē) *n.*, freedom from punishment or penalty
a • ver • sion (ə vʉr´zhən) *n.*, definite dislike
frol • ic (fräl´ik) *n.*, lively party or game

Vocabulary in Context

- We will surmount the ski slope.
- Sometimes people take unfair advantage of Martin's obsequious nature.
- The termagant person was difficult and unpleasant.
- He thought he had impunity, but he was caught and punished for his actions.
- Jordan has an aversion to driving a car, so he rides a bike.
- We took part in the frolic in the freshly fallen snow.

stone fences; the women of the village, too, used to employ him to run their errands, and to do such little odd jobs as their less obliging husbands would not do for them. In a word, Rip was ready to attend to anybody's business but his own; but as to doing family duty, and keeping his farm in order, he found it impossible.

In fact, he declared it was of no use to work on his farm; it was the most pestilent little piece of ground in the whole country; everything about it went wrong, and would go wrong, in spite of him. His fences were continually falling to pieces; his cow would either go astray, or get among the cabbages; weeds were sure to grow quicker in his fields than anywhere else; the rain always made a point of setting in just as he had some outdoor work to do; so that though his estate had dwindled away under his management, acre by acre, until there was little more left than a mere patch of Indian corn and potatoes, yet it was the worst conditioned farm in the neighborhood.

His children, too, were as ragged and wild as if they belonged to nobody. His son Rip, an urchin begotten in his own likeness, promised to inherit the habits, with the old clothes of his father. He was generally seen trooping like a colt at his mother's heels, equipped in a pair of his father's cast-off galligaskins,[8] which he had much ado to hold up with one hand, as a fine lady does her train[9] in bad weather.

Rip Van Winkle, however, was one of those happy mortals, of foolish, well-oiled dispositions, who take the world easy, eat white bread or brown, whichever can be got with least thought or trouble, and would rather starve on a penny than work for a pound.[10] If left to himself, he would have whistled life away in perfect contentment; but his wife kept continually dinning in his ears about his idleness, his carelessness, and the ruin he was bringing on his family. Morning, noon, and night, her tongue was incessantly going, and everything he said or did was sure to produce a torrent of household eloquence. Rip had but one way of replying to all lectures of the kind, and that, by frequent use, had grown into a habit. He shrugged his shoulders, shook his head, cast up his eyes, but said nothing. This, however, always provoked a fresh volley from his wife; so that he was fain to draw off his forces, and take to the outside of the house—the only side which, in truth, belongs to a henpecked husband.

Rip's sole domestic adherent was his dog Wolf, who was as much henpecked as his master; for Dame Van Winkle regarded them as companions in idleness, and even looked upon Wolf with an evil eye, as the cause of his master's going so often astray. True it is, in all points of spirit befitting an honorable dog, he was as courageous an animal as ever scoured the woods—but what courage can withstand the

1 *Who is Rip's companion? Why are they so close?*

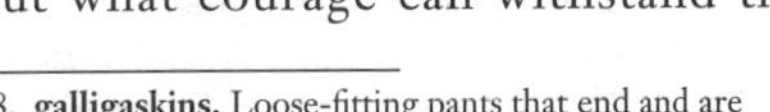

8. **galligaskins.** Loose-fitting pants that end and are tapered at the knee
9. **train.** Part of a dress or skirt that trails behind
10. **pound.** British unit of money

Words for Everyday Use

pes • ti • lent (pes´tə lənt) *adj.*, annoying; troublesome

dis • po • si • tion (dis'pə zish´ən) *n.*, temperament; general frame of mind

in • ces • sant • ly (in ses´ənt lē) *adv.*, never stopping

el • o • quence (el´ə kwəns) *n.*, speech that is powerful, vivid, and persuasive

fain (fān) *adj.*, glad

ad • her • ent (ad hir´ənt) *n.*, supporter or follower

Answer to Guided Reading Question

1 Rip's companion is his dog Wolf. Rip and his dog are close because they are both henpecked by Dame Van Winkle.

Literary Technique

Stereotype

A stereotype is an unexamined, false idea about a type of person or group of people. Point out to students that the personality of Rip's wife reflects a popular stereotype concerning women and marriage. Some stories, television shows, and movies center around meek, unassertive males and super-assertive, controlling wives. People are supposed to find this stereotype humorous because in actuality women have often been denied power and control over their own lives. Explain to students that this story is old, written at a time when the balance of power was tipped toward males even more dramatically than it is today. It is important that students understand this stereotype for what it is and discuss the stereotype. Does it bother them?

Vocabulary in Context

- Their home was full of pestilent fleas this summer.
- To do that job, you need a calm, easygoing disposition.
- The incessantly screaming car alarm woke everyone in the neighborhood.
- The leader spoke to the crowd with eloquence.
- We were fain to see our friends after all these years.
- Mario is an adherent of that popular candidate.

Answer to Guided Reading Question

❶ Rip liked to spend his time at a club for sages, philosophers, and other idle people in the village. He would sit through long days telling stories and discussing village gossip.

Additional Questions and Activities

To deal with the idea of stereotype in this story further, ask students to discuss the following questions:

- If Rip's wife were to describe her marriage to Rip what might she say?
- In what way would it be difficult to have a marriage and raise children with a person like Rip?

ANSWERS

Responses will vary.

- Students are likely to say that Rip's wife would describe her life with Rip in a negative, angry, and sad way.
- Some students might say that Rip is simply a fun-loving guy who deserves to be treated better. Some students, however, might feel that Rip is lazy and does not take care of his responsibilities. He seems to expect his wife to do all the work of raising the children and maintaining the household.

ever-enduring and all-besetting terrors of a woman's tongue? The moment Wolf entered the house his crest fell, his tail drooped to the ground or curled between his legs, he sneaked about with a gallows air, casting many a sidelong glance at Dame Van Winkle, and at the least flourish of a broomstick or ladle, he would fly to the door with yelping precipitation.

Times grew worse and worse with Rip Van Winkle as years of matrimony rolled on; a tart temper never mellows with age, and a sharp tongue is the only edged tool that grows keener with constant use. For a long while he used to console himself, when driven from home, by frequenting a kind of perpetual club of the sages, philosophers, and other idle personages of the village; which held its sessions on a bench before a small inn, designated by a portrait of His Majesty George the Third. Here they used to sit in the shade through a long, lazy summer's day, talking listlessly over village gossip, or telling endless sleepy stories about nothing. But it would have been worth any statesman's money to have heard the profound discussions that sometimes took place when by chance an old newspaper fell into their hands from some passing traveler. How solemnly they would listen to the contents, as drawled out by Derrick Van Bummel, the schoolmaster, a dapper, learned little man, who was not to be daunted by the most gigantic word in the dictionary; and how sagely they would deliberate upon public events some months after they had taken place.

❶ *Where did Rip like to spend his time? What did he do there?*

The opinions of this group were completely controlled by Nicholas Vedder, a patriarch of the village, and landlord of the inn, at the door of which he took his seat from morning till night, just moving sufficiently to avoid the sun and keep in the shade of a large tree; so that the neighbors could tell by the hour by his movements as accurately as by a sundial. It is true, he was rarely heard to speak, but smoked his pipe incessantly. His adherents, however (for every great man has his adherents), perfectly understood him, and knew how to gather his opinions. When anything that was read or related displeased him, he was observed to smoke his pipe vehemently, and to send forth short, frequent, and angry puffs; but when pleased, he would inhale the smoke slowly and tranquilly, and emit it in light and placid clouds; and sometimes, taking the pipe from his mouth, and letting the fragrant vapor curl about his nose, would gravely nod his head in token of perfect approbation.

From even this stronghold the unlucky Rip was at length routed by his termagant wife, who would suddenly break in upon the tranquility of the assemblage and call the members all to naught; nor was that august personage, Nicholas Vedder himself, sacred from the daring tongue of this terrible virago, who charged him outright with encouraging her husband in habits of idleness.

Words for Everyday Use

pre • cip • i • ta • tion (prē sip´ə tā shən) *n.,* rush; haste
daunt (dônt) *v.,* make afraid; discourage
ap • pro • ba • tion (ap´rə bā shən) *n.,* official approval or sanction
tran • quil • i • ty (tran kwil´ə tē) *n.,* calmness
au • gust (ô gust´) *adj.,* worthy of respect
vi • ra • go (vi rā´gō) *n.,* quarrelsome woman

Vocabulary in Context

- They ran from the burning house with precipitation.
- Even a long list of tasks did not daunt the hard-working young woman.
- They needed the principal's approbation before they could go on the field trip.
- Jenna was upset and in need of tranquility.
- People gladly accepted the advice of the august citizen.
- Ignorant people call her a virago, but I say that she is a natural leader with strong opinions.

Hills. Edward Hopper, 1930

Poor Rip was at last reduced almost to despair; and his only alternative, to escape from the labor of the farm and clamor of his wife, was to take gun in hand and stroll away into the woods. Here he would sometimes seat himself at the foot of a tree, and share the contents of his wallet[11] with Wolf, with whom he sympathized as a fellow-sufferer in persecution. "Poor Wolf," he would say, "thy mistress leads thee a dog's life of it; but never mind, my lad, whilst I live thou shalt never want a friend to stand by thee!" Wolf would wag his tail, look wistfully in his master's face, and if dogs can feel pity I verily believe he reciprocated the sentiment with all his heart.

In a long ramble of the kind on a fine autumnal day, Rip had unconsciously scrambled to one of the highest parts of the Catskill Mountains. He was after his favorite sport of squirrel shooting, and the still solitudes had echoed and re-echoed with the reports of his gun. Panting and fatigued, he threw himself, late in the afternoon, on a green knoll, covered with mountain herbage, that crowned the brow of a precipice. From an opening between the trees he could overlook all the lower country for many a mile of rich woodland. He saw at a distance the lordly Hudson, far, far below him, moving on its silent but

11. **wallet.** Bag for carrying provisions

WORDS FOR EVERYDAY USE

per • se • cu • tion (pər´si kyo͞o´shən) *n.*, affliction or constant harassing
re • cip • ro • cate (ri sip´rə kāt´) *v.*, return
prec • i • pice (pres´i pis) *n.*, steep cliff

ART NOTE

Edward Hopper (1882–1967) was an American painter of the twentieth century. He is best known for using bright colors and for creating serious, melancholy moods in his paintings.

Hopper was born in Nyack, New York on July 22. He trained at the New York School of Art in New York City. Hopper often depicted simple scenes from everyday life, particularly city life. His subjects included streets, empty apartments, diners, cottages, and theaters.

Ask any student who is interested in drawing or painting to create a picture in the Hopper style depicting an everyday scene from his or her life.

VOCABULARY IN CONTEXT

- We will not take part in the persecution of another person.
- They made a lovely dinner for us, and now we must reciprocate the favor.
- The mountain climber stood on the precipice and sang a song.

Answers to Guided Reading Questions

❶ Rip helps the stranger because it is in his nature to be eager and willing to help.

❷ At first Rip feels that he must be imagining that he hears his name. When he hears his name for the second time, he begins to feel worried and nervous.

majestic course, with the reflection of a purple cloud, or the sail of a lagging bark,[12] here and there sleeping on its glassy bosom, and at last losing itself in the blue highlands.

On the other side he looked down into a deep mountain glen, wild, lonely, and shagged, the bottom filled with fragments from the impending cliffs, and scarcely lighted by the reflected rays of the setting sun. For some time Rip lay musing on this scene; evening was gradually advancing; the mountains began to throw their long blue shadows over the valleys; he saw that it would be dark long before he could reach the village, and he heaved a heavy sigh when he thought of encountering the terrors of Dame Van Winkle.

❶ Why do you think Rip helps the stranger?

As he was about to descend, he heard a voice from a distance hallooing, "Rip Van Winkle! Rip Van Winkle!" He looked round, but could see nothing but a crow winging its solitary flight across the mountain. He thought his fancy must have deceived him, and turned again to descend, when he heard the same cry ring through the still evening air: "Rip Van Winkle! Rip Van Winkle!"—at the same time Wolf bristled up his back, and giving a low growl, skulked to his master's side, looking fearfully down into the glen. Rip now felt a vague apprehension stealing over him; he looked anxiously in the same direction, and perceived a strange figure slowly toiling up the rocks, and bending under the weight of something he carried on his back. He was surprised to see any human being in this lonely and unfrequented place, but supposing it to be some one of the neighborhood in need of his assistance, he hastened down to yield it.

❷ How does Rip feel when he hears his name called?

On nearer approach he was still more surprised at the singularity of the stranger's appearance. He was a short, square-built old fellow, with thick bushy hair, and a grizzled beard. His dress was of the antique Dutch fashion—a cloth jerkin[13] strapped round the waist—several pairs of breeches, the outer one of ample volume, decorated with rows of buttons down the sides and bunches at the knees. He bore on his shoulder a stout keg, that seemed full of liquor, and made signs for Rip to approach and assist him with the load. Though rather shy and distrustful of this new acquaintance, Rip complied with his usual alacrity; and mutually relieving one another, they clambered up a narrow gully, apparently the dry bed of a mountain torrent. As they ascended, Rip every now and then heard long rolling peals, like distant thunder, that seemed to issue out of a deep ravine, or rather cleft, between lofty rocks, toward which their rugged path conducted. He paused for an instant, but supposing it to be the muttering of one of these transient thundershowers which often take place in mountain heights, he proceeded. Passing through the ravine, they came to a hollow, like a small amphitheater,

12. **bark.** Small sailing boat
13. **jerkin.** Short, close-fitting jacket

Words for Everyday Use

fan • cy (fan´sē) *n.,* imagination
a • lac • ri • ty (ə lak´rə tē) *n.,* eager willingness or readiness
tran • si • ent (tran´zē ənt) *adj.,* temporary; passing quickly

Vocabulary in Context

- Is that story fact or fancy?
- Her alacrity was appreciated by all who knew her.
- The cold weather is only transient—next week will be warmer.

surrounded by perpendicular precipices, over the brinks of which impending trees shot their branches, so that you only caught glimpses of the azure sky and the bright evening cloud. During the whole time, Rip and his companion had labored on in silence; for though the former marvelled greatly what could be the object of carrying a keg of liquor up this wild mountain, yet there was something strange and incomprehensible about the unknown that inspired awe and checked familiarity.

On entering the amphitheater, new objects of wonder presented themselves. On a level spot in the center was a company of odd-looking personages playing at ninepins.[14] They were dressed in a quaint outlandish fashion; some wore short doublets,[15] others jerkins, with long knives in their belts, and most of them had enormous breeches, of similar style with that of the guide's. Their visages, too, were peculiar; one had a large beard, broad face, and small piggish eyes; the face of another seemed to consist entirely of nose, and was surmounted by a white sugar-loaf hat,[16] set off with a little red cock's tail. They all had beards, of various shapes and colors. There was one who seemed to be the commander. He was a stout old gentleman, with a weather-beaten countenance, he wore a laced doublet, broad belt and hanger,[17] high-crowned hat and feather, red stockings, and high-heeled shoes, with roses in them. The whole group reminded Rip of the figures in an old Flemish painting, in the parlor of Dominie Van Shaick, the village parson, and which had been brought over from Holland at the time of the settlement.

What seemed particularly odd to Rip was, that though these folks were evidently amusing themselves, yet they maintained the gravest face, the most mysterious silence, and were, withal, the most melancholy party of pleasure he had ever witnessed. Nothing interrupted the stillness of the scene but the noise of the balls, which, whenever they were rolled, echoed along the mountains like rumbling peals of thunder.

As Rip and his companion approached them, they suddenly desisted from their play, and stared at him with such fixed, statuelike gaze, and such strange, lackluster countenances, that his heart turned within him, and his knees smote together. His companion now emptied the contents of the keg into large flagons, and made signs to him to wait upon the company. He obeyed with fear and trembling; they quaffed the liquor in profound silence, and then returned to their game.

By degrees Rip's awe and apprehension subsided. He even ventured, when no eye was fixed upon him, to taste the beverage, which he found had much of the flavor of excellent

❶ What are the people Rip encounters in the amphitheater wearing? Of what do they remind Rip?

14. **ninepins.** Form of the game bowling
15. **doublets.** Close-fitting jackets
16. **sugar-loaf hat.** Hat shaped like a cone
17. **hanger.** Short sword that hangs from one's belt

WORDS FOR EVERYDAY USE

- **az • ure** (azh´ər) *adj.*, blue colored
- **vis • age** (viz´ij) *n.*, face
- **coun • te • nance** (koun´tə nəns) *n.*, face
- **smite** (smīt) *v.*, hit or strike hard
- **flag • on** (flag´ən) *n.*, container for liquids with a handle, narrow neck, spout, and sometimes a lid
- **quaff** (kwäf) *v.*, drink heartily in a thirsty way

ANSWER TO GUIDED READING QUESTION

❶ The people Rip encounters are wearing short doublets, jerkins, long knives in their belts, and breeches. One person is wearing a high-crown hat and feather, red stockings, and high-heeled shoes with roses in them. They remind Rip of the figures in an old Flemish painting in the parlor of the village parson.

ADDITIONAL QUESTIONS AND ACTIVITIES

Ask students to answer the following questions:

- What are some positive aspects of Rip and his personality?
- What are some negative aspects of Rip and his personality?
- Would you like to know a person like Rip? Why, or why not?

ANSWERS

Responses will vary.

Students might say that his relaxed attitude about life is refreshing. He also seems to have a big heart.

Students might say that his laziness and his disdain for his wife are two negative aspects of his personality. He is also influencing his son with his bad habits.

VOCABULARY IN CONTEXT

- We hiked beneath the bright sun and the azure sky.
- His visage showed a great deal of stress.
- Ben's countenance glowed with happiness.
- She will smite that baseball over the fence.
- I drank juice from a ceramic flagon.
- The dog, after running around for an hour, will quaff the bowl of water within seconds.

Answer to Guided Reading Question

➊ Rip falls asleep after drinking too much of the liquid from the flagon.

Additional Questions and Activities

Ask students to study the painting on this page, and then to illustrate their own favorite scenes from the story. Students may use pencils, pens, paints, crayons—whatever materials they choose.

The Return of Rip Van Winkle. *John Quidor, 1849, Andrew W. Mellon Collection, © Board of Trustees, National Gallery of Art, Washington*

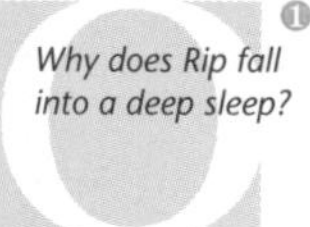

➊ *Why does Rip fall into a deep sleep?*

Hollands.[18] He was naturally a thirsty soul, and was soon tempted to repeat the draft. One taste provoked another; and he reiterated his visits to the flagon so often that at length his senses were overpowered, his eyes swam in his head, his head gradually declined, and he fell into a deep sleep.

On waking, he found himself on the green knoll whence he had first seen the old man of the glen. He rubbed his eyes—it was a bright sunny morning. The birds were hopping and twittering among the bushes, and the eagle was wheeling aloft, and breasting the pure mountain breeze. "Surely," thought Rip, "I have not slept here all night." He recalled the occurrences before he fell asleep. The strange man with a keg of liquor—the mountain ravine—the wild retreat among the rocks—the woe-begone party at ninepins—the flagon—"Oh! that flagon! that wicked flagon!" thought Rip—"what excuse shall I make to Dame Van Winkle?"

18. **Hollands.** Gin made in The Netherlands

He looked round for his gun, but in place of the clean, well-oiled fowling piece, he found an old firelock lying by him, the barrel incrusted with rust, the lock falling off, and the stock worm-eaten. He now suspected that the grave roysters[19] of the mountain had put a trick upon him, and having dosed him with liquor, had robbed him of his gun. Wolf, too, had disappeared, but he might have strayed away after a squirrel or partridge. He whistled after him and shouted his name, but all in vain; the echoes repeated his whistle and shout, but no dog was to be seen.

He determined to revisit the scene of the last evening's gambol, and if he met with any of the party, to demand his dog and gun. As he rose to walk, he found himself stiff in the joints, and wanting in his usual activity. "These mountain beds do not agree with me," thought Rip, "and if this frolic should lay me up with a fit of the rheumatism,[20] I shall have a blessed time with Dame Van Winkle." With some difficulty he got down into the glen; he found the gully up which he and his companion had ascended the preceding evening; but to his astonishment a mountain stream was now foaming down it, leaping from rock to rock, and filling the glen with babbling murmurs. He, however, made shift to scramble up its sides, working his toilsome way through thickets of birch, sassafras, and witch hazel, and sometimes tripped up or entangled by the wild grapevines that twisted their coils or tendrils from tree to tree, and spread a kind of network in his path.

At length he reached to where the ravine had opened through the cliffs to the amphitheater; but no traces of such opening remained. The rocks presented a high impenetrable wall, over which the torrent came tumbling in a sheet of feathery foam, and fell into a broad deep basin, black from the shadows of the surrounding forest. Here, then, poor Rip was brought to a stand. He again called and whistled after his dog; he was only answered by the cawing of a flock of idle crows, sporting high in air about a dry tree that overhung a sunny precipice; and who, secure in their elevation, seemed to look down and scoff at the poor man's perplexities. What was to be done? The morning was passing away, and Rip felt famished for want of his breakfast. He grieved to give up his dog and gun; he dreaded to meet his wife; but it would not do to starve among the mountains. He shook his head, shouldered the rusty firelock, and with a heart full of trouble and anxiety, turned his steps homeward.

As he approached the village he met a number of people, but none whom he knew, which somewhat surprised him, for he had thought himself acquainted with everyone in the country round. Their dress, too, was of a different fashion from that to which he was accustomed. They all stared at him

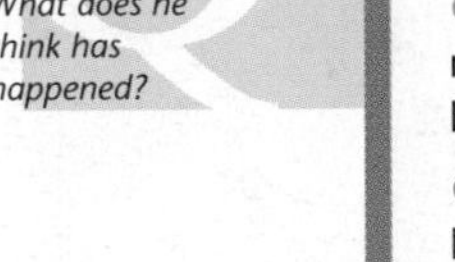

❶ *What does Rip find beside him when he awakes? What does he think has happened?*

❷ *Why is Rip surprised as he nears the village? Why are the people who see him surprised?*

19. **roysters.** Partyers
20. **rheumatism.** Any of various painful conditions of the joints and muscles, characterized by inflammation, stiffness, etc.

Words for Everyday Use

gam • bol (gam´bəl) *n.,* play or frolic
scoff (skôf) *v.,* mock; show contempt

Answers to Guided Reading Questions

❶ Rip finds an old firelock with a rusty barrel. He thinks that he has been robbed.

❷ Rip is surprised that he does not know anyone in the village. The villagers are surprised at the sight of him because he is wearing clothing that is different from everyone else's and because his beard is over a foot long.

Literary Note

Washington Irving is said to be the first American to earn an international literary reputation.

"Rip Van Winkle" and "The Legend of Sleepy Hollow" are considered his most important literary works.

Vocabulary in Context

- The children will gambol in the park for several hours.
- I know he will scoff at my idea, but I will share it with him anyway.

Answer to Guided Reading Question

❶ Rip sees a sign on the front of the inn showing the face of General George Washington. The sign used to show the face of King George. Rip is unaware that the American Revolution has taken place.

Historical Note

When Rip claims to be a loyal subject of the king, people shout at him and call him a "tory." The tories are a political party in Great Britain, also known as the conservative party. Tories were defenders of the king. Cautious about social and political change, the Tories wanted to maintain Great Britain's established interests. After the American Revolution, these people were not popular in the former British colonies.

with equal marks of surprise, and whenever they cast their eyes upon him, invariably stroked their chins. The constant recurrence of this gesture induced Rip, involuntarily, to do the same, when, to his astonishment, he found his beard had grown a foot long!

He had now entered the outskirts of the village. A troop of strange children ran at his heels, hooting after him, and pointing at his gray beard. The dogs, too, not one of which he recognized for an old acquaintance, barked at him as he passed. The very village was altered; it was larger and more populous. There were rows of houses which he had never seen before, and those which had been his familiar haunts had disappeared. Strange names were over the doors—strange faces at the windows—every thing was strange. His mind now misgave him; he began to doubt whether both he and the world around him were not bewitched. Surely this was his native village, which he had left but the day before. There stood the Catskill Mountains—there ran the silver Hudson at a distance—there was every hill and dale precisely as it had always been—Rip was sorely perplexed—"That flagon last night," thought he; "has addled my poor head sadly!"

❶ What does Rip see in front of the inn? What used to be there? Of what change is Rip unaware?

It was with some difficulty that he found the way to his own house, which he approached with silent awe, expecting every moment to hear the shrill voice of Dame Van Winkle. He found the house gone to decay—the roof fallen in, the windows shattered, and the doors off the hinges. A half-starved dog that looked like Wolf was skulking about it. Rip called him by name, but the cur snarled, showed his teeth, and passed on. This was an unkind cut indeed—"My very dog," sighed poor Rip, "has forgotten me!"

He entered the house, which, to tell the truth, Dame Van Winkle had always kept in neat order. It was empty, forlorn, and apparently abandoned. This desolateness overcame all his fears—he called loudly for his wife and children—the lonely chambers rang for a moment with his voice, and then all again was silence.

He now hurried forth, and hastened to his old resort, the village inn—but it too was gone. A large rickety wooden building stood in its place, with great gaping windows, some of them broken and mended with old hats and petticoats, and over the door was painted, "The Union Hotel, by Jonathan Doolittle." Instead of the great tree that used to shelter the quiet little Dutch inn of yore, there now was reared a tall, naked pole, with something on the top that looked like a red nightcap,[21] and from it was fluttering a flag, on which was a singular assemblage of stars and stripes—all this was strange and incomprehensible. He recognized on the sign, however, the ruby face of King George, under which he had smoked so many a peaceful pipe; but even this was singularly metamorphosed. The red coat

21. **red nightcap.** Reference to the liberty cap which was worn by colonists to symbolize their freedom from Great Britain

Words for Everyday Use

ad • dle (ad´'l) *v.,* make muddled or confused
for • lorn (fôr lôrn´) *adj.,* abandoned; in pitiful condition
met • a • mor • phose (met´ə môr´fōs´) *v.,* change

Vocabulary in Context

- Try not to addle Lorna while she gives her speech.
- Why does the puppy look sad and forlorn?
- We will metamorphose the building so that it will look brand new.

was changed for one of blue and buff, a sword was held in the hand instead of a scepter, the head was decorated with a cocked hat, and underneath was painted in large characters, GENERAL WASHINGTON.

There was, as usual, a crowd of folk about the door, but none that Rip recollected. The very character of the people seemed changed. There was a busy, bustling, disputatious tone about it, instead of the accustomed drowsy tranquility. He looked in vain for the sage Nicholas Vedder, with his broad face, double chin, and fair long pipe, uttering clouds of tobacco smoke instead of idle speeches; or Van Bummel, the school-master, doling forth the contents of an ancient newspaper. In places of these, a lean, bilious-looking[22] fellow, with his pockets full of handbills, was speaking vehemently about rights of citizens—elections—members of Congress—liberty—Bunker's Hill—heroes of seventy-six—and other words, which were a perfect Babylonish jargon[23] to the bewildered Van Winkle.

The appearance of Rip, with his long grizzled beard, his rusty fowling piece, his uncouth dress, and an army of women and children at his heels, soon attracted the attention of the tavern politicians. They crowded round him, eyeing him from head to foot with great curiosity. The orator bustled up to him, and, drawing him partly aside, inquired "on which side he voted?" Rip stared in vacant stupidity. Another short but busy little fellow pulled him by the arm, and, rising on tiptoe, inquired in his ear, "whether he was Federal or Democrat?"[24] Rip was equally at a loss to comprehend the question; when a knowing, self-important old gentleman in a sharp cocked hat made his way through the crowd, putting them to the right and left with his elbows as he passed, and planting himself before Van Winkle, with one arm akimbo,[25] the other resting on his cane, his keen eyes and sharp hat penetrating, as it were, into his very soul, demanded, in an austere tone, "what brought him to the election with a gun on his shoulder, and a mob at his heels, and whether he meant to breed a riot in the village?" "Alas! gentlemen," cried Rip, somewhat dismayed, "I am a poor, quiet man, a native of the place, and a loyal subject of the king, God bless him!"

Here a general shout burst from the bystanders—"A tory! a tory! a spy! a refugee! hustle him! away with him!" It was with great difficulty that the self-important man in the cocked hat restored order; and, having assumed a tenfold austerity of brow, demanded again of the unknown culprit, what he came there for, and whom he was seeking. The poor man humbly assured him that he meant no harm, but merely came there in search of some of his

22. **bilious-looking.** Looking cross or bad-tempered
23. **Babylonish jargon.** A language he could not understand
24. **Federal or Democrat.** Two large political parties of that time
25. **akimbo.** Hand on hip, with elbow pointing outward

WORDS FOR EVERYDAY USE

dis • pu • ta • tious (dis′pyo͞o tā′shəs) *adj.,* fond of arguing
aus • tere (ô stir′) *adj.,* severe; forbidding

CROSS-CURRICULAR ACTIVITIES

GEOGRAPHY

The Battle of Bunker Hill was the first great battle of the Revolutionary War. The British drove the Americans from their fort at Breed's Hill to Bunker Hill.

Because Americans killed many British soldiers, this battle was encouraging to the American troops. They realized that even though they didn't have as many supplies as the British soldiers, they could still do well in battle.

- Ask students to go to the library and find out in what city and state the Battle of Bunker Hill was fought. Then ask them to draw a map of the area. Tell them that a monument now stands on Breed's Hill, in honor of the American troops who fought in this battle.

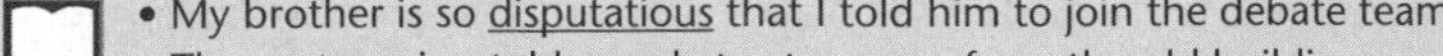

VOCABULARY IN CONTEXT

- My brother is so disputatious that I told him to join the debate team.
- The austere sign told people to stay away from the old building.

Answers to Guided Reading Questions

❶ The people know Rip Van Winkle's son as Rip Van Winkle.

❷ The bystanders don't believe Rip.

Quotables

"The dominant spirit, however, that haunts this enchanted region, and seems to be commander of all the powers of the air, is the apparition of a figure on horseback without a head. It is said by some to be the ghost of a Hessian trooper whose head had been carried away by a cannon-ball, in some nameless battle during the Revolutionary War, and who is ever and and anon seen by various of the country people, hurrying along in the gloom of night, as if on the wings of the wind. His haunts are not confined to the valley, but extend at times to the adjacent roads, and especially to the vicinity of the church that is at no great distance. Indeed, certain of the most authentic historians of those parts, who have been careful in collecting and collating the floating facts concerning this specter, allege, that the body of the trooper having been buried in the churchyard, the ghost rides forth to the scene of battle in nightly quest of his head, and the rushing speed with which he sometimes passes along the hollow, like a midnight blast, is owing to his being belated, and in a hurry to get back to the churchyard before daybreak.

Such is the general purport of this legendary superstition, which has furnished materials for many a wild story in that region of shadows; and the specter is known, at all the country firesides, by The Headless Horseman of Sleepy Hollow."

—Washington Irving
"The Legend of Sleepy Hollow"

neighbors, who used to keep about the tavern.

❶ *Whom do the people know as Rip Van Winkle?*

"Well, who are they? Name them."

Rip bethought himself a moment, and inquired, "Where's Nicholas Vedder?"

There was a silence for a little while, when an old man replied, in a thin, piping voice, "Nicholas Vedder! why, he is dead and gone these eighteen years! There was a wooden tombstone in the churchyard that used to tell all about him, but that's rotten and gone too."

"Where's Brom Dutcher?"

"Oh, he went off to the army in the beginning of the war; some say he was killed at the storming of Stony Point—others say he was drowned in a squall at the foot of Antony's Nose.[26] I don't know—he never came back again."

❷ *What do the bystanders think when Rip begins to explain what happened to him?*

"Where's Van Bummel, the schoolmaster?"

"He went off to the wars, too, was a great militia general, and is now in Congress."

Rip's heart died away at hearing of these sad changes in his home and friends, and finding himself thus alone in the world. Every answer puzzled him too, by treating of such enormous lapses of time, and of matters which he could not understand; war—Congress—Stony Point—he had no courage to ask after any more friends, but cried out in despair, "Does nobody here know Rip Van Winkle?"

"Oh, Rip Van Winkle!" exclaimed two or three. "Oh, to be sure! that's Rip Van Winkle yonder, leaning against the tree."

Rip looked, and beheld a precise counterpart of himself, as he went up the mountain: apparently as lazy, and certainly as ragged. The poor fellow was now completely confounded. He doubted his own identity, and whether he was himself or another man. In the midst of his bewilderment, the man in the cocked hat demanded who he was, and what was his name.

"Goodness knows," exclaimed he, at his wit's end; "I'm not myself—I'm somebody else—that's me yonder—no—that's somebody else got into my shoes—I was myself last night, but I fell asleep on the mountain, and they've changed my gun, and everything's changed, and I'm changed, and I can't tell what's my name, or who I am!"

The bystanders began now to look at each other, nod, wink significantly, and tap their fingers against their foreheads. There was a whisper, also, about securing the gun, and keeping the old fellow from doing mischief, at the very suggestion of which the self-important man in the cocked hat retired with some precipitation. At this critical moment a fresh, comely woman pressed through the throng to get a peep at the gray-bearded man. She had a chubby child in her arms, which, frightened at his looks, began to cry. "Hush, Rip," cried she, "hush, you little fool; the old man won't hurt you." The name of the child, the air of the mother, the tone of her voice, all awak-

26. **Stony Point, Antony's Nose.** Town and mountain on the Hudson River, respectively

Words for Everyday Use

be • wil • der • ment (bē wil´dər mənt) *n.*, condition of being hopelessly confused

come • ly (kum´lē) *adj.*, attractive

Vocabulary in Context

- I could not hide my bewilderment when a group of people sitting next to me at the bus station jumped up and screamed.
- Anyone could see that the freshly groomed West Highland White Terrier knew just how comely she was.

ened a train of recollections in his mind. "What is your name, my good woman?" asked he.

"Judith Gardenier."

"And your father's name?"

"Ah! poor man, Rip Van Winkle was his name, but it's twenty years since he went away from home with his gun and never has been heard of since—his dog came home without him; but whether he shot himself, or was carried away by the Indians, nobody can tell. I was then but a little girl."

Rip had but one question more to ask; but he put it with a faltering voice:

"Where's your mother?"

"Oh, she too had died but a short time since; she broke a blood vessel in a fit of passion at a New England peddler."

There was a drop of comfort, at least, in this intelligence.[27] The honest man could contain himself no longer. He caught his daughter and her child in his arms. "I am your father!" cried he—"Young Rip Van Winkle once—old Rip Van Winkle now! Does nobody know poor Rip Van Winkle?"

All stood amazed, until an old woman, tottering out from among the crowd, put her hand to her brow, and peering under it in his face for a moment, exclaimed, "Sure enough! it is Rip Van Winkle—it is himself! Welcome home again, old neighbor. Why, where have you been these twenty long years?"

Rip's story was soon told, for the whole twenty long years had been to him but as one night. The neighbors stared when they heard it; some were seen to wink at each other, and put their tongues in their cheeks: and the self-important man in the cocked hat, who, when the alarm was over, had returned to the field, screwed down the corners of his mouth, and shook his head—upon which there was a general shaking of the head throughout the assemblage.

It was determined, however, to take the opinion of old Peter Vanderdonk, who was seen slowly advancing up the road. He was a descendant of the historian of that name, who wrote one of the earliest accounts of the province. Peter was the most ancient inhabitant of the village, and well versed in all the wonderful events and traditions of the neighborhood. He recollected Rip at once, and <u>corroborated</u> his story in the most satisfactory manner. He assured the company that it was a fact, handed down from his ancestor the historian, that the Catskill mountains had always been haunted by strange beings. That it was affirmed that the great Henry Hudson, the first discoverer of the river and country, kept a kind of vigil there every twenty years, with his crew of the *Half-Moon;* being permitted in this way to revisit the scenes of his enterprise, and keep a guardian eye upon the river, and the great city called by his name. That his father had once seen them in their old Dutch dresses playing at ninepins in a hollow of the mountain; and that he himself had heard, one summer afternoon, the

❶ *How does Peter Vanderdonk validate Rip's experience?*

27. **intelligence.** In this case, "news"

WORDS FOR EVERYDAY USE

cor • rob • o • rate (kə räb´ə rāt') *v.,* confirm; support; bolster

ANSWER TO GUIDED READING QUESTION

❶ Peter Vanderdonk confirms that the mountains are haunted by strange beings.

VOCABULARY IN CONTEXT

• The defense attorney asked the witness to <u>corroborate</u> her client's testimony.

Answers to Guided Reading Questions

➊ Rip's son is lazy like his father.

➋ Rip loves his new life because he is at an age where it is acceptable to be idle. He feels that he has more freedom.

Additional Questions and Activities

People in Rip's village try to explain summer thunderstorms by saying that Henry Hudson and his crew are playing ninepins. Ask students to invent their own legends to explain certain occurrences in nature. How might students explain lightning? an earthquake? clouds in the sky?

Students who like to draw might illustrate their legends.

➊ *In what ways is young Rip like his father?*

➋ *How does Rip feel about his new life?*

sound of their balls, like distant peals of thunder.

To make a long story short, the company broke up, and returned to the more important concerns of the election. Rip's daughter took him home to live with her; she had a snug, well-furnished house, and a stout, cheery farmer for a husband, whom Rip recollected for one of the urchins that used to climb upon his back. As to Rip's son and heir, who was the ditto of himself, seen leaning against the tree, he was employed to work on the farm; but evinced an hereditary disposition to attend to anything else but his business.

Rip now resumed his old walks and habits; he soon found many of his former cronies, though all rather the worse for the wear and tear of time; and preferred making friends among the rising generation, with whom he soon grew into great favor.

Having nothing to do at home, and being arrived at that happy age when a man can be idle with impunity, he took his place once more on the bench at the inn door, and was reverenced as one of the patriarchs of the village, and a chronicle of the old times "before the war." It was some time before he could get into the regular track of gossip, or could be made to comprehend the strange events that had taken place during his torpor. How that there had been a revolutionary war—that the country had thrown off the yoke of old England—and that, instead of being a subject of his Majesty George the Third, he was now a free citizen of the United States. Rip, in fact, was no politician; the changes of states and empires made but little impression on him; but there was one species of despotism under which he had long groaned, and that was—petticoat government.[28] Happily, that was at an end; he had got his neck out of the yoke of matrimony, and could go in and out whenever he pleased, without dreading the tyranny of Dame Van Winkle. Whenever her name was mentioned, however, he shook his head, shrugged his shoulders, and cast up his eyes; which might pass either for an expression of resignation to his fate, or joy at his deliverance.

He used to tell his story to every stranger that arrived at Mr. Doolittle's hotel. He was observed, at first, to vary on some points every time he told it, which was, doubtless, owing to his having so recently awaked. It at last settled down precisely to the tale I have related, and not a man, woman, or child in the neighborhood, but knew it by heart. Some always pretended to doubt the reality of it, and insisted that Rip had been out of his head, and that this was one point on which he always remained flighty. The old Dutch inhabitants, however, almost universally gave it full credit. Even to this

28. **petticoat government.** Marriage

Words for Everyday Use:

e • vince (ē vins´) *v.,* show plainly

cro • ny (krō´nē) *n.,* close companion

Vocabulary in Context

- Her actions evince kindness to many people.
- Hank is my father's old crony from his boyhood days.

day they never hear a thunderstorm of a summer afternoon about the Catskills, but they say Henry Hudson and his crew are at their game of ninepins; and it is a common wish of all henpecked husbands in the neighborhood, when life hangs heavy on their hands, that they might have a quieting draft out of Rip Van Winkle's flagon. ■

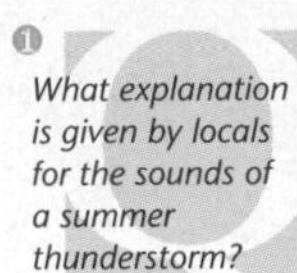

1 *What explanation is given by locals for the sounds of a summer thunderstorm?*

About the Author

Washington Irving (1783–1853) lived during a period when America was beginning to develop an artistic culture and tradition of its own. Irving helped to establish the short story as a popular form of literature with stories such as "Rip Van Winkle" and "The Legend of Sleepy Hollow." Irving was born and educated in New York City, but traveled widely in the United States and in Europe. He worked first as a lawyer but turned eventually to writing full time. Irving wrote stories, essays, histories, and dramas.

Answer to Guided Reading Question

1 People say that the sounds of a summer thunderstorm come from Henry Hudson and his crew at a game of ninepins.

Selection Check Test with Answers

EX. Near what mountains does "Rip Van Winkle" take place?
The story takes place near the Catskill Mountains.

1. How did villagers feel about Rip Van Winkle?
Villagers liked Rip very much.
2. How did Rip feel about work?
Rip did not like work.
3. Why was Rip's wife often angry with him?
Rip's wife thought that he was lazy.
4. Why does Rip fall asleep?
He drinks from a flagon.
5. For how long does Rip sleep?
Rip sleeps for twenty years.

RESPONDING TO THE SELECTION

Ask students to discuss this question in small groups. What about the world do they think might be different twenty years from now?

ANSWERS FOR REVIEWING THE SELECTION

RECALLING AND INTERPRETING

1. **Recalling.** Rip is friendly, kind-hearted, and quite lazy. **Interpreting.** Rip is popular because he takes the time to socialize with and help people.

2. **Recalling.** Rip spends most of his time at a club talking about town gossip and funny stories. He spends more time in the woods to escape from work and from his wife. **Interpreting.** Rip feels that his wife picks on him and never allows him to relax. His wife feels that he is lazy and useless.

3. **Recalling.** Rip tries to figure out who is calling him. He wanders around and finds an odd stranger who leads him to people playing a game called ninepins. Rip falls asleep after he drinks from a flagon. **Interpreting.** Rip accepts the situation so readily because it is in his nature to accept new people and new situations.

4. **Recalling.** People look at Rip strangely because he is dressed in outdated clothing and because his beard is one foot long. **Interpreting.** People pretend to doubt the reality of his story. The old Dutch inhabitants believe the story, and when they hear thunder they say that it is Henry Hudson and the crew playing ninepins. They like to think that people who are trying to escape unhappy lives can take a sip out of Rip's flagon.

SYNTHESIZING

Responses will vary. Possible responses are given.

5. Rip likes his new life because it is more relaxed. As an older man, his relaxed, idle lifestyle is more socially acceptable.

Responding to the Selection

How would you feel if you fell asleep and woke up twenty years later? What benefits might there be to such a situation? What difficulties do you think you would face?

Reviewing the Selection

RECALLING AND INTERPRETING

1. (R) What are Rip's main personality traits?
   (I) Why is Rip so popular?
2. (R) Where does Rip spend most of his time? Why does he begin to spend more and more time in the woods?
   (I) How does Rip feel about his wife? How does Dame Van Winkle feel about Rip?
3. (R) What happens after Rip hears his name being called? What causes Rip to fall asleep?
   (I) Why does Rip accept the strange situation so readily?
4. (R) Why do people look at Rip strangely as he returns to the village?
   (I) What do people think when Rip begins to explain what has happened to him? Why do they come to accept his story?

SYNTHESIZING

5. How do you think Rip feels about his life after his long sleep? Do you think he prefers his new life to his earlier life? Why, or why not?

Understanding Literature (Questions for Discussion)

1. **Setting.** The **setting** of a literary work is the time and place in which it happens. Describe the setting before Rip's long sleep. The events that occur after his sleep are set twenty years later than the events at the beginning of the story. What changes have occurred in Rip's village during the time he was sleeping?
2. **Concrete.** A **concrete** word, like *kite* or *sour,* is something that can be directly seen, tasted, touched, heard, or smelled. The mountain glen where Rip took a long ramble before falling asleep is presented in descriptive concrete detail. What details are used? What is your general impression of the glen? Do its occupants seem real? How would you feel if you were Rip arriving in the glen?

ANSWERS FOR UNDERSTANDING LITERATURE

Responses will vary. Possible responses are given.

1. **Setting.** Before Rip falls asleep, the village is small, with a strong Dutch influence. The village is still under English rule. When Rip awakens, he discovers that the village has more people and is no longer under English rule.

2. **Concrete.** The glen is described as wild, lonely, and shagged. The bottom is filled with fragments from the cliffs, and the area is lighted only slightly by the sun. The glen is lonely and isolated and surrounded by rocks and cliffs. Students might say that the occupants seem a bit too strange and fantastic to be real. They might guess that Rip feels confused, worried, and shocked as he views the people in the glen.

Vocabulary Skills

Using Context Clues

As you read, you may find that you do not know the meaning of every word that you encounter. One way to find out the meaning of an unknown word is to look up the word in the dictionary. Another way is to figure out the word's meaning from its context, or clues in the sentence surrounding the word. Consider the following sentence:

EXAMPLE With *trepidation,* she climbed down the creaky, dark stairway that led to a shadowy basement full of cobwebs.

You may be able to figure out the meaning of the italicized word *trepidation* by thinking about its context. In the above sentence, the person described is going down a dark stairway toward a scary-sounding basement. Therefore, the word *trepidation* must have a negative meaning, probably having something to do with fear. Using context clues alone, you can come fairly close to the dictionary definition of *trepidation,* which is "fearful uncertainty or anxiety." Such an educated guess, based on evidence, is called an inference.

Often context clues will enable you to figure out precisely what a word means. Such context clues include restatements, synonyms, antonyms, and examples.

TYPES OF CONTEXT CLUES

Definition	Example
A **restatement** simply tells what a word means using other words.	Her favorite animal was the marmoset, a very small monkey of South and Central America. (The phrase *a very small monkey of South and Central America* restates the meaning of *marmoset.*)
A **synonym** is another word that is similar in meaning.	That elephant is gargantuan, or huge. (The word *huge* is a synonym for the word *gargantuan.*)

CONTINUED

Using Context Clues

Introducing the Skill

Tell students that being able to figure out the meanings of words by studying their contexts in sentences is a valuable skill. This skill will help them to be better readers and to enjoy reading more.

Previewing the Skill

Ask students to look over the chart provided and study the different types of context clues.

Practicing the Skill

When students seem comfortable using context clues, ask them to complete the Try It Yourself exercise.

Reviewing the Skill

Go over students' work. Hold a discussion during which you ask students what gave them the most trouble when trying to complete the assignment. Some students might need additional practice. Ask students to practice creating their own context clues in the Just for Fun exercise.

ANSWERS FOR TRY IT YOURSELF

EXERCISE A

1. Definition: steep
2. Definition: disagreement
3. Definition: unusual, special
4. Definition: pay
5. Definition: a machine for shaping wood
6. Definition: animals that are out during the daylight hours
7. Definition: restored
8. Definition: a legal order to testify in court
9. Definition: people of high rank or position
10. Definition: feeling of thankfulness
11. Definition: strong-smelling
12. Definition: stubborn
13. Definition: a type of weasel
14. Definition: numbers that help show order, such as *first, second, third*
15. Definition: having a jagged, saw-like edge

TYPES OF CONTEXT CLUES (CONT.)

An **antonym** is another word that is opposite in meaning.	While the gazelle is a svelte creature, the hippopotamus can appear rather chubby. (The word *chubby* is an antonym of the word *svelte.*)
Examples are instances or illustrations of something.	Carnivorous animals, including lions, tigers, and wolves, usually have very sharp teeth. (From the examples given, you can determine that carnivorous animals are those that eat flesh.)

Try It Yourself

Use context clues and inferences to determine the meaning of the italicized word in each sentence below.

EXAMPLE After receiving first prize, Maria was *elated,* or felt great joy.
Definition: great joy

1. That *sheer,* or steep, hill is very dangerous in the winter.
2. Our group came to an agreement right away because there was no *dissension* among the group members.
3. Emily performed a very common dance routine, but Ashton's was *unique.*
4. You must *remit,* or pay, your balance if you wish to buy anything else.
5. Lin used a *lathe,* a machine for shaping wood, to create the table legs.
6. *Diurnal* animals are easy to spot; however, nocturnal animals are harder to see.
7. The neighborhood was fully *renovated,* or restored, to its original condition.
8. The witness was handed a *subpoena,* a legal order to testify in court.
9. Many *dignitaries,* including presidents, prime ministers, kings, and queens, all attended the funeral.
10. After all the help she received, Emily expressed her *gratitude,* a feeling of thankful appreciation.
11. Like a strong-smelling onion, that *pungent* odor made my eyes water.
12. They are right when they say that mules are *obstinate,* that is, stubborn.
13. That is a picture of an *ermine,* a weasel whose fur is brown in summer but white with a black-tipped tail in winter.
14. *Ordinal* numbers, such as first, second, and third, are helpful when showing someone how to do something.
15. I used a smooth knife to slice the banana, but I needed a *serrated* knife to slice the bread.

Just for Fun

Students should have fun with the assignment. Tell them that they might want to make a list of the words and their definitions first, and then create the sentences with good context clues.

Students might want to get into pairs or small groups to exchange sentences.

just for fun

Now that you are familiar with determining the meanings of words from context, try this game with your classmates. Below is a list of nonsense words. Create a definition for each word. Then write a sentence that will allow somebody else to guess from context what the word means. See if others can guess the meanings you gave each word.

EXAMPLE gamel
When visiting the Nabab desert Rudi rode a *gamel,* an animal that shares features of a goat and a camel.
A *gamel* is an animal that lives in the desert that is similar both to a camel and to a goat.

azalene
bennicut
coppilious
dinzle
ebile
fowtissimous
gorple
hankle
ird
jarston
kabloo
loing
mousting
nikean
overtenapolis
priggle
quagular
rooti-tutti
swimper
thrix
ud
vability
wixit
xelion
yogger
zindalist

GOALS/OBJECTIVES

Studying this lesson will enable students to

- empathize with a character caught in a frightening situation
- briefly discuss the history of conflict between England and Ireland
- define *irony of situation*
- use reference works

ADDITIONAL RESOURCES

READER'S GUIDE

- Selection Worksheet, 8.2

ASSESSMENT PORTFOLIO

- Selection Check Test, 2.8.3
- Selection Test, 2.4.4

PRONUNCIATION EXERCISE

- Grade 8 Audiocassette, Side B, Track 42

CROSS-CURRICULAR CONNECTIONS

WORLD HISTORY

Ask students to continue their study of Northern Ireland and England. How have relations been since the settlement of 1921? In what way have people continued to battle in opposition to the situation? What are the latest developments? Ask students to consult newspapers and weekly news magazines.

Prereading

CHARACTER

"The Sniper"

by Liam O'Flaherty

Cross-curricular Connection

World History. Conflict between Ireland and England has existed since 1534, when English King Henry VIII started a policy of direct control of Ireland. He established English laws and the Protestant religion in Ireland, in what is known as English Rule. This policy was difficult because many Irish people were Roman Catholic. They resented any attempt to change their beliefs. Henry VIII's daughter, Queen Elizabeth, went a step further and outlawed Roman Catholic church services altogether. As a result, Irish Catholics united and anti-English feelings were strengthened.

During the late 1800s, after three hundred years of English Rule, some Irish people started to demand Home Rule. This meant that Ireland would remain part of Great Britain but would have its own government and laws. The British government defeated Home Rule bills in 1886 and 1892. As a result, the Irish became more insistent on the right to govern themselves. A political party called *Sinn Fein,* meaning "We Ourselves," was established in 1905. The Irish Republican Brotherhood, whose members were known as Republicans, was also established. The Republicans wanted complete independence from England.

The British government finally passed a Home Rule bill in 1914, but the outbreak of World War I prevented it from taking effect. The Irish Republicans thought that the war offered the chance that Ireland needed to gain independence from England. On the Monday after Easter in 1916, the Republicans started a rebellion against the English, called the Easter Uprising. Fighting lasted for one week before British troops defeated the Republicans and kept control of Ireland. Political and military battles continued for the next five years. Then, in 1921, a settlement was reached between the English and the Irish. The settlement established self-government in southern Ireland (called the Irish Free State) but kept six counties in Northern Ireland (those with a Protestant majority) under British rule.

As You Read

"The Sniper" includes many details about the main character, the sniper. Make a cluster chart like the one below. As you read, fill in the chart with information about the sniper's appearance, actions, and emotions.

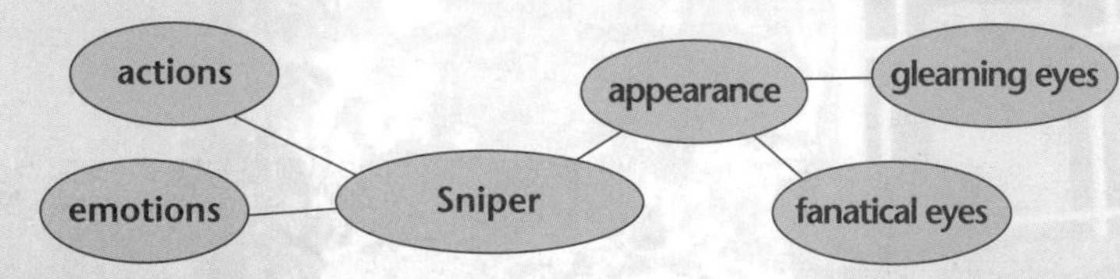

AS YOU READ

Answers may vary, but students might fill out their charts in the following way:

appearance—face of a student, cold gleam in his eyes

actions—watches carefully, eats hungrily, hides behind a chimney, fires at informer, tries to remove bullet from his arm, fires at enemy sniper

emotions—hunger, fear, panic, excitement, anger, horror

READER'S JOURNAL

What images of war have you seen or heard? What images have had the most powerful effect on you? What feelings did these images evoke in you? Write about these questions in your journal.

"The Sniper"

LIAM O'FLAHERTY

The long June twilight faded into night. Dublin lay enveloped in darkness but for the dim light of the moon that shone through fleecy clouds, casting a pale light as of approaching dawn over the streets and the dark waters of the Liffey. Around the beleaguered Four Courts the heavy guns roared. Here and there through the city, machine-guns and rifles broke the silence of the night, spasmodically, like dogs barking on lone farms. Republicans and Free Staters[1] were waging civil war.

On a roof-top near O'Connell Bridge, a Republican sniper lay watching. Beside him lay his rifle and over his shoulders were slung a pair of field glasses. His face was the face of a student, thin and ascetic, but his eyes had the cold gleam of the fanatic. They were deep and thoughtful, the eyes of a man who is used to looking at death.

He was eating a sandwich hungrily. He had eaten nothing since morning. He had been too excited to eat. He finished the sandwich, and, taking a flask from his pocket, he took a short draught. Then he returned the flask to his pocket. He paused for a moment, considering whether he should risk a smoke. It was dangerous. The flash might be seen in the darkness and there were enemies watching. He decided to take the risk.

Placing a cigarette between his lips, he struck a match. There was a flash and a bullet whizzed over his head. He dropped immediately. He had seen the flash. It came from the opposite side of the street.

1. **Republicans and Free Staters.** Republicans wished Ireland to be completely independent of England, while Free Staters wanted Ireland to have self-governing, Dominion status within the British Commonwealth

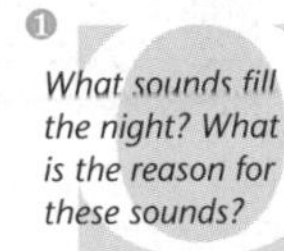

1 *What sounds fill the night? What is the reason for these sounds?*

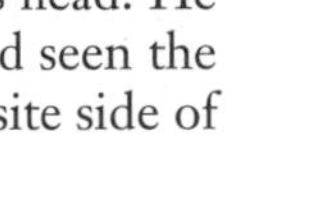

WORDS FOR EVERYDAY USE

be • lea • guer (bē lē´gər) *v.*, beset with difficulties

spas • mod • i • cal • ly (spaz mäd´ik lē) *adv.*, suddenly, violently, and intermittently

as • cet • ic (ə set´ik) *adj.*, characteristic of anyone who lives with strict self-discipline

fa • nat • ic (fə nat´ik) *n.*, person who holds extreme and unreasonable views; zealot

draught (draft) *n.*, drink

READER'S JOURNAL

Ask students to write down everything that comes to their minds when they think of war. Then ask them to write about why people fight in this way.

SPELLING AND VOCABULARY WORDS FROM THE SELECTION

ascetic	gibber
beleaguer	paroxysm
concussion	remorse
draught	ruse
fanatic	spasmodically

ANSWER TO GUIDED READING QUESTION

1 The sounds of machine guns and rifles could be heard. A civil war was going on.

SUPPORT FOR LEP STUDENTS

PRONUNCIATIONS OF PROPER NOUNS AND ADJECTIVES

Dub • lin (dub´lən) n.

O • Con • nell (ō´kän´'l) n.

ADDITIONAL VOCABULARY

flask—small metal container for holding liquids

revolted—taken back with horror and disgust

revolver—type of gun

VOCABULARY IN CONTEXT

- Difficulties continue to beleaguer Stephanie.
- During the earthquake, the ground shook spasmodically.
- He was ascetic and worked long hours without stopping.
- Paul was a fanatic about his political beliefs.
- She took a draught of lemonade on the hot summer day.

ANSWERS TO GUIDED READING QUESTIONS

❶ The old woman points to the sniper on the roof. The sniper fires at the woman.

❷ The sniper takes a bullet in his arm. Sensation in his arm is totally cut off.

LITERARY TECHNIQUE

TONE

Tone is a writer or speaker's attitude toward the subject. Ask students to notice the tone of suspense in the story when the sniper knows people see him and he scrambles to hide behind the chimney. Short sentences such as "His heart beat faster. It was an enemy car. He wanted to fire, but he knew it was useless." help to create tension in the scene. Ask students to find other sentences and descriptions that help to create a tone of tension and suspense.

❶ *What does the old woman do? What happens to the old woman?*

❷ *Where does the sniper take a bullet? In what way will this shot affect him?*

He rolled over the roof to a chimney stack in the rear, and slowly drew himself up behind it, until his eyes were level with the top of the parapet.[2] There was nothing to be seen—just the dim outline of the opposite housetop against the blue sky. His enemy was under cover.

Just then an armored car came across the bridge and advanced slowly up the street. It stopped on the opposite side of the street, fifty yards ahead. The sniper could hear the dull panting of the motor. His heart beat faster. It was an enemy car. He wanted to fire, but he knew it was useless. His bullets would never pierce the steel that covered the gray monster.

Then round the corner of a side street came an old woman, her head covered by a tattered shawl. She began to talk to the man in the turret[3] of the car. She was pointing to the roof where the sniper lay. An informer.

The turret opened. A man's head and shoulders appeared, looking toward the sniper. The sniper raised his rifle and fired. The head fell heavily on the turret wall. The woman darted toward the side street. The sniper fired again. The woman whirled round and fell with a shriek into the gutter.

Suddenly from the opposite roof a shot rang out and the sniper dropped his rifle with a curse. The rifle clattered to the roof. The sniper thought the noise would wake the dead. He stooped to pick the rifle up. He couldn't lift it. His forearm was dead.

"Blast!" he muttered, "I'm hit."

Dropping flat onto the roof, he crawled back to the parapet. With his left hand he felt the injured right forearm. There was no pain—just a deadened sensation, as if the arm had been cut off.

Quickly he drew his knife from his pocket, opened it on the breastwork of the parapet, and ripped open the sleeve. There was a small hole where the bullet had entered. On the other side there was no hole. The bullet had lodged in the bone. It must have fractured it. He bent the arm below the wound. The arm bent back easily. He ground his teeth to overcome the pain.

2. **parapet.** Low wall or railing, as along a balcony; or wall used to screen troops from frontal fire

3. **turret.** Armored, usually revolving, structure on the top of tanks and armored cars used to hold a gun or guns

Then, taking out a field dressing, he ripped open the packet with his knife. He broke the neck of the iodine bottle and let the bitter fluid drip into the wound. A paroxysm of pain swept through him. He placed the cotton wadding over the wound and wrapped the dressing over it. He tied the ends with his teeth.

Then he lay against the parapet, and, closing his eyes, he made an effort of will to overcome the pain.

In the street beneath all was still. The armored car had retired speedily over the bridge, with the machine-gunner's head hanging lifelessly over the turret. The woman's corpse lay still in the gutter.

The sniper lay still for a long time nursing his wounded arm and planning escape. Morning must not find him wounded on the roof. The enemy on the opposite roof covered his escape. He must kill that enemy and he could not use his rifle. He had only a revolver to do it. Then he thought of a plan.

Taking off his cap, he placed it over the muzzle of his rifle. Then he pushed the rifle slowly over the parapet, until the cap was visible from the opposite side of the street. Almost immediately there was a report, and a bullet pierced the center of the cap. The sniper slanted the rifle forward. The cap slipped down into the street. Then, catching the rifle in the middle, the sniper dropped his left hand over the roof and let it hang, lifelessly. After a few moments he let the rifle drop to the street. Then he sank to the roof, dragging his hand with him.

Crawling quickly to the left, he peered up at the corner of the roof. His ruse had succeeded. The other sniper, seeing the cap and rifle fall, thought he had killed his man. He was now standing before a row of chimney pots, looking across, with his head clearly silhouetted against the western sky.

The Republican sniper smiled and lifted his revolver above the edge of the parapet. The distance was about fifty yards—a hard shot in the dim light, and his right arm was paining him like a thousand devils. He took a steady aim. His hand trembled with eagerness. Pressing his lips together, he took a deep breath through his nostrils and fired. He was almost deafened with the report and his arm shook with the recoil.[4]

Then when the smoke cleared, he peered across and uttered a cry of joy. His enemy had been hit. He was reeling over the parapet in his death agony. He struggled to keep his feet, but he was slowly falling forward, as if in a dream. The rifle fell from his grasp, hit the parapet, fell over, bounded off the pole of a barber's shop beneath, and then clattered on the pavement.

Then the dying man on the roof crumpled up and fell forward. The body turned over and over in space and hit the ground with a dull thud. Then it lay still.

4. **recoil.** The backward kick when a gun is fired

❶ *What plan does the sniper use to trick his enemy?*

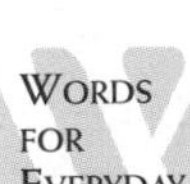

Words for Everyday Use

par • ox • ysm (par´ək siz´əm) *n.*, sudden attack or convulsion
ruse (ro͞oz) *n.*, trick

Answer to Guided Reading Question

❶ The sniper puts his hat on his rifle, holds it up, and makes the enemy believe that it is him. The enemy shoots at the hat and rifle, and then the sniper pretends to lay dead. When the enemy, believing that the sniper is dead, gets up to leave, the sniper takes a clear shot at him with his revolver and kills him.

Additional Questions and Activities

Ask students to discuss the character of the sniper. What kind of a person is he? Is he someone that they admire? Why, or why not?

ANSWERS

Responses will vary.

Some students will believe that he is someone to be admired because he seems to be bright, full of common sense, and able to think on his feet. He also seems dedicated to what he is doing. They might also feel for him as he views the body of his brother. Some students, however, might be opposed to the violence and to anyone who participates in such violence.

Vocabulary in Context

- Leo hunched over in a sudden paroxysm of pain.
- They wanted to surprise Tia with the party, so they needed to think of a ruse to get her there.

Answers to Guided Reading Questions

❶ The sniper feels remorse and then disgust.

❷ The sniper suddenly becomes curious as to the identity of the man he has shot. He is curious because he wonders if he knows him. Something might have drawn him to this particular sniper, who turns out to be his brother.

Selection Check Test with Answers

EX. In what city is the sniper?
The sniper is in Dublin, Ireland.

1. Where does the sniper lie watching?
The sniper lies watching on a rooftop.

2. What is the role of the old woman who points at the roof?
The old woman is an informer.

3. What does the sniper do with his cap and his rifle to trick the enemy?
The sniper places his cap on his rifle to give the enemy a phony target.

4. What happens to the enemy?
The sniper shoots him, and he dies.

5. When the sniper turns the body over, whose face does he see?
He sees his brother's face.

❶ *After his initial joy, what is the sniper's reaction to seeing his dead enemy?*

❷ *About what is the sniper curious? Why do you think he is curious?*

The sniper looked at his enemy falling, and he shuddered. The lust of battle died in him. He became bitten by remorse. The sweat stood out in beads on his forehead. Weakened by his wound and the long summer day of fasting and watching on the roof, he revolted from the sight of the shattered mass of his dead enemy. His teeth chattered, he began to gibber to himself, cursing the war, cursing himself, cursing everybody.

He looked at the smoking revolver in his hand, and with an oath he hurled it to the roof at his feet. The revolver went off with the concussion and the bullet whizzed past the sniper's head. He was frightened back to his senses by the shock. His nerves steadied. The cloud of fear scattered from his mind, and he laughed.

Taking the flask from his pocket, he emptied it at a draught. He felt reckless under the influence of the spirit. He decided to leave the roof now and look for his company commander, to report. Everywhere around was quiet. There was not much danger in going through the streets. He picked up his revolver and put it in his pocket. Then he crawled down through the skylight to the house underneath.

When the sniper reached the laneway on the street level, he felt a sudden curiosity as to the identity of the enemy sniper whom he had killed. He decided that he was a good shot, whoever he was. He wondered did he know him. Perhaps he had been in his own company before the split in the army. He decided to risk going over to have a look at him. He peered around the corner into O'Connell Street. In the upper part of the street there was heavy firing, but around here all was quiet.

The sniper darted across the street. A machine-gun tore up the ground around him with a hail of bullets, but he escaped. He threw himself face downward beside the corpse. The machine-gun stopped.

Then the sniper turned over the dead body and looked into his brother's face. ■

About the Author

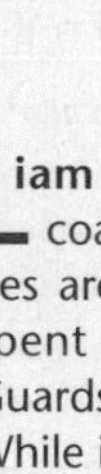

Liam O'Flaherty (1896–1984) grew up off the west coast of Ireland on the Aran Islands. Many of his stories are set on the Aran Islands or in Dublin. O'Flaherty spent time in Dublin after a brief stint with the Irish Guards which ended when he suffered severe shellshock. While in Dublin, O'Flaherty joined in the Irish struggle for independence. O'Flaherty's compassion for the common man is reflected in his psychological novels, including *The Informer* (1925), *Famine* (1937), and *Insurrection* (1951).

Words for Everyday Use

re • morse (ri môrs´) *n.,* deep, torturing sense of guilt
gib • ber (jib´ər) *v.,* speak or utter rapidly and incoherently
con • cus • sion (kən kush´ən) *n.,* shock from impact

Vocabulary in Context

- After the terrible car accident, Tyrone felt remorse.
- The baby began to gibber to herself.
- The thick glass broke from the concussion.

Responding to the Selection

Imagine you are the main character. How would you feel at the end of the story? What would you do next? What effect might this event have on your future actions?

Reviewing the Selection

RECALLING AND INTERPRETING

1. (R) What does the Republican sniper look like? Where is he and what is he doing at the beginning of the story?

   (I) How does the sniper feel about his situation?

2. (R) What does the sniper want to do when he sees the armored car? What does he do to the informer?

   (I) What mind-set might allow the sniper to kill so easily?

3. (R) Where is the sniper wounded? What difficulties does he face as a result of this wound?

   (I) Characterize the sniper's actions after being shot. Why is his ability to react in this way necessary?

4. (R) What trick does the sniper play on his enemy? Is the trick successful?

   (I) Why do you think the sniper's "lust of battle died in him"?

SYNTHESIZING

5. What conclusions about war can you draw from the events related in this selection? What message do you think the author was trying to make about war?

Understanding Literature (Questions for Discussion)

Irony of Situation. An event that contradicts the expectations of the characters, the reader, or the audience of a literary work is an example of **irony of situation.** At the end of the story, what surprised the sniper? What do you think the sniper expected to find? In what way does this ironic situation add to the impact of the story?

Answers for Understanding Literature

Responses will vary. Possible responses are given.

1. **Irony of Situation.** The sniper is surprised to learn that the person he has killed is his brother. The sniper expects to see a stranger, but he instead sees a face he recognizes and about which he cares. It adds to the horror of the scene and to the idea that war destroys lives and makes people almost inhuman.

Responding to the Selection

Ask students to get into small groups to discuss the ending of the story. They should decide how the sniper must feel, and what he might do after the ending of the story.

Answers for Reviewing the Selection

RECALLING AND INTERPRETING

1. **Recalling.** The sniper is young and ascetic looking. He has eyes that are used to looking at death. He is on a roof eating at the beginning of the story. **Interpreting.** The sniper is feeling tense and excited.

2. **Recalling.** The sniper wants to fire when he sees the armored car. He fires at the informer. **Interpreting.** Somebody who has killed many times before, and who has killed to protect himself, would probably be able to shoot easily.

3. **Recalling.** The sniper is wounded in his arm. He has trouble feeling anything in his arm and moving his arm. **Interpreting.** His actions are calculated and clear-headed. He must be able to think clearly and not feel stress or terror if he is to stay alive.

4. **Recalling.** The sniper puts a hat on his rifle and gets the enemy to shoot at his hat. When the enemy believes that the sniper is dead, he gets up to leave. The sniper shoots at him. His trick is successful, and the enemy falls to his death. **Interpreting.** Watching the person fall is difficult. He is tired of the pain and the killing.

SYNTHESIZING

Responses will vary. Possible responses are given.

5. War hardens people to the suffering and the "humanness" of the enemy. The writer is trying to show how war can rip people apart and turn brother against brother. People begin to see one another only as "enemies" and "informers." They forget that the enemy feels pain and has a human face.

Language Lab

Introducing the Skill

Explain to students that learning to use the library is an important research skill that they will find helpful to have for school and for other areas of their lives. The library holds the answers to many of their questions and can open many new doors for them.

Previewing the Skill

Go over the chart provided. Ask students if they have ever used any of the materials described in the chart. You might discuss with them where particular things are in their own school or local library.

Practicing the Skill

Ask students to do the Try It Yourself exercise. Give them plenty of time to get to the library and to familiarize themselves with the sources.

Reviewing the Skill

Review with students the answers to the questions. Ask students what answers they were able to locate, and then ask them if some sources were more difficult to use than others. Invite them to explain why.

Study and Research Skills

Using Reference Works

You can find information of all kinds in the reference books found in any library. Some of the most common reference works include encyclopedias, atlases, and the *Readers' Guide to Periodical Literature*. The information below will help you to use these sources to find the information you need.

TYPES OF REFERENCE WORKS	
Encyclopedia	**Encyclopedias** usually come in many volumes. Each volume contains articles of information about numerous subjects. Encyclopedias are arranged alphabetically. Each volume contains the letter or range of topics covered and the volume number on the book's spine. There are encyclopedias of general knowledge as well as encyclopedias that focus on a particular subject such as sports. The **index**, which is usually in the last volume of the encyclopedia, provides an alphabetical listing of all the subjects in the encyclopedia.
Atlas	An **atlas** is a book of maps. An atlas may also provide factual information such as an area's annual rainfall, natural resources, and population.
Readers' Guide to Periodical Literature	The ***Readers' Guide to Periodical Literature*** is an index of all articles found in over a hundred journals and magazines, or periodicals. The articles are arranged by subject. Each entry provides information for locating the article in the journal or magazine in which it appears. The *Readers' Guide* is printed monthly. After you locate the information on an article, you will need to find the article itself. First see if your library carries the periodical in question. Then, if it is a recent article, you may find a copy of the magazine or newspaper in the library's periodical section. If it is from an older issue, the periodical may be stored, either bound into a book containing many issues or on film. Ask your librarian for assistance finding the article you need.

There are many other reference works available in libraries. You may discover some of them as you search for materials in the catalog, or you can ask the librarian to assist you. Many reference works are now available on computers as well as in printed materials.

Try It Yourself

Use reference works to answer the following questions and find the information requested.

1. What is the current population of Ireland? Where is the population the densest?
2. How far is it from Dublin to Belfast?
3. Name five counties of Ireland.
4. Who is the Prime Minister of Ireland?
5. Name an article written about travel in Ireland. Give the source, issue, and page number where it can be located.
6. What bodies of water surround Ireland?
7. Identify an article about Northern Ireland and give its source.
8. When did the Great Potato Famine occur and what caused it?
9. What are the official languages of Ireland?
10. What is the *Book of Kells?*

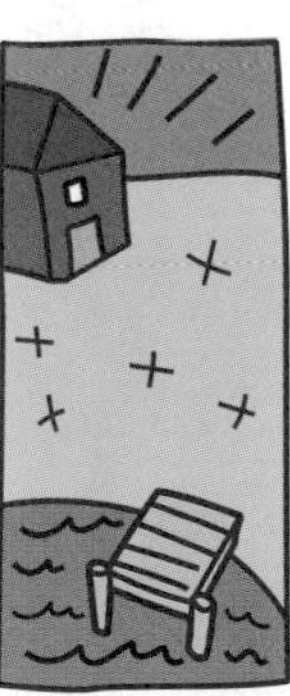

Answers for Try It Yourself

- Ask students to use a variety of reference works as they search for the answers to the questions provided.
- They should mark down what reference work they used, and then say a word or two about whether it was helpful and convenient to use.
- Students might want to share with the class their process for finding answers to the questions.

GOALS/OBJECTIVES

Studying this lesson will enable students to

- enjoy a short story with a plot twist
- briefly discuss crime and punishment in the United States
- define *resolution,* and find the resolution of a story
- define *verbal irony* and find verbal irony in a piece of writing
- use elements of verbal and nonverbal communication

ADDITIONAL RESOURCES

READER'S GUIDE

- Selection Worksheet, 8.3

ASSESSMENT PORTFOLIO

- Selection Check Test, 2.8.5
- Selection Test, 2.8.6

PRONUNCIATION EXERCISE

- Grade 8 Audiocassette, Side B, Track 43

CROSS-CURRICULAR CONNECTIONS

SOCIAL STUDIES

Ask students to research possible careers in law enforcement. Ask them to find one career that sounds particularly interesting to them, then focus on what a typical workday is like in that career. Students might look into police work, law, and social work.

Prereading

PLOT

"A Retrieved Reformation"

by O. Henry

Cross-curricular Connection

Social Studies. Burglary is a crime in which a person enters another person's house or place of business without permission intending to commit a crime. (Usually the crime in burglary is theft.) People often confuse the crime of burglary with the crime of robbery. Robbery involves direct contact between the criminal and the victim. One person, the robber, takes something from another person, the victim, either by force or by threatening violence. Burglary does not involve contact between the criminal and the victim. The burglar enters a person's house or place of business secretly and illegally for the purpose of stealing. Robbery is classified as a crime against a person. Burglary is classified as a crime against property; a criminal robs a person, but burglarizes a house.

Burglary is considered a felony rather than a misdemeanor. Other felonies include murder, robbery, kidnapping, and treason. A felony is a more serious crime than a misdemeanor and is punishable by either death (in some states) or imprisonment. Imprisonment for a felony is more than a year and can include any number of years up to a full life sentence. Misdemeanors include assault and battery, thefts of small sums of money, and traffic offenses. A misdemeanor is punishable by a fine or imprisonment of less than a year. Those imprisoned for a felony usually serve the sentence in a state or federal prison, while those imprisoned for a misdemeanor usually serve the sentence in a city or county jail.

In "A Retrieved Reformation" you will read about a burglar named Jimmy Valentine.

As You Read

"A Retrieved Reformation" is a story about Jimmy Valentine's attempt to change his life. In your journal, make a prediction log like the one below. Make a prediction about Jimmy's first move when he gets out of prison. Then when you have read far enough to see if your prediction was true or not, make a prediction about the next step in Jimmy's life. As you read, continue to make predictions and mark on the chart whether they were correct or not and cite evidence to prove your conclusions.

PREDICTION LOG

Prediction	Confirmed/Rejected
When Jimmy gets out of prison he will . . .	

AS YOU READ

Answers may vary. Below are examples of possible predictions and outcomes:

Prediction	Confirmed/Rejected
• Jimmy immediately dusts his tools off and cracks more safes.	• Confirmed. He dusts his tools off and cracks more safes.
• Jimmy goes back to jail.	• Rejected. Jimmy falls in love and turns his life around.

READER'S JOURNAL

Think of any bad habits that you have had (or things other people considered to be bad habits). What were they? Describe the difficulties you faced trying to break yourself of these habits. Were you successful? What setbacks did you have? Write about these questions in your journal.

"A Retrieved Reformation"

O. HENRY

A guard came to the prison shoe-shop, where Jimmy Valentine was assiduously stitching uppers, and escorted him to the front office. There the warden handed Jimmy his pardon, which had been signed that morning by the governor. Jimmy took it in a tired kind of way. He had served nearly ten months of a four-year sentence. He had expected to stay only about three months, at the longest. When a man with as many friends on the outside as Jimmy Valentine had is received in the "stir" it is hardly worthwhile to cut his hair.

"Now, Valentine," said the warden, "you'll go out in the morning. Brace up, and make a man of yourself. You're not a bad fellow at heart. Stop cracking safes, and live straight."

"Me?" said Jimmy, in surprise. "Why, I never cracked a safe in my life."

"Oh, no," laughed the warden. "Of course not. Let's see, now. How was it you happened to get sent up on that Springfield job? Was it because you wouldn't prove an alibi for fear of compromising somebody in extremely high-toned society? Or was it simply a case of a mean old jury that had it in for you? It's always one or the other with you innocent victims."

"Me?" said Jimmy, still blankly virtuous. "Why, warden, I never was in Springfield in my life!"

"Take him back, Cronin," smiled the warden. "and fix him up with outgoing clothes. Unlock him at seven in the morning, and let him come to the bullpen.[1] Better think over my advice, Valentine."

At a quarter past seven on the next morning Jimmy stood in the warden's

❶ *Why does Jimmy expect to get out of prison before he does?*

❷ *What does the warden tell Jimmy to do? Does he believe Jimmy's response?*

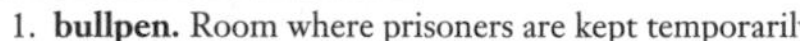

1. **bullpen.** Room where prisoners are kept temporarily

WORDS FOR EVERYDAY USE

as • sid • u • ous • ly (ə sij´o͞o əs lē) *adv.*, carefully; diligently

VOCABULARY IN CONTEXT

• Paula assiduously organized the files.

READER'S JOURNAL

As an alternative activity, ask students to describe how hard it is for a person to shake a particular image, especially if the image is negative.

SPELLING AND VOCABULARY WORDS FROM THE SELECTION

assiduously	genially
clemency	platform
confederate	retribution
convulsion	unobtrusively
eminent	

ANSWERS TO GUIDED READING QUESTIONS

❶ Jimmy had expected to get out sooner because he has many friends on the outside.

❷ The warden tells Jimmy that he is a good man, and that he should make a new man of himself and stop cracking safes. Jimmy acts surprised and tells the warden that he has never cracked a safe. The warden does not believe him.

SUPPORT FOR LEP STUDENTS

PRONUNCIATIONS OF PROPER NOUNS AND ADJECTIVES

Val • en • tine (val´ən tīn´) n.
Cro • nin (krō´nin) n.

ADDITIONAL VOCABULARY

commotion—noise and confusion
elusive—not easily caught
implements—instruments
novelties—special items
pardon—paper allowing a criminal to leave prison

Answers to Guided Reading Questions

❶ Mike asks Jimmy, "Got anything on?" He wants to know if Jimmy is planning any burglaries. Jimmy responds by acting innocent.

❷ After Jimmy's release, a chain of safe-crackings occurs.

Additional Questions and Activities

Ask students to answer the following questions:

- What seems to be Jimmy's most prized possession?
- Judging from his most prized possession, to what sort of life does Jimmy seem to be returning?

ANSWERS

Responses will vary.

Jimmy's most prized possession seems to be his briefcase full of tools. At this point in the story, he seems to want to return to a life of crime.

outer office. He had on a suit of the villainously fitting, ready-made clothes and a pair of the stiff, squeaky shoes that the state furnishes to its discharged compulsory guests.

The clerk handed him a railroad ticket and the five-dollar bill with which the law expected him to rehabilitate himself into good citizenship and prosperity. The warden gave him a cigar, and shook hands. Valentine, 9762, was chronicled on the books "Pardoned by Governor," and Mr. James Valentine walked out into the sunshine.

Disregarding the song of the birds, the waving green trees, and the smell of the flowers, Jimmy headed straight for a restaurant. There he tasted the first sweet joys of liberty in the shape of a chicken dinner. From there he proceeded leisurely to the depot and boarded his train. Three hours set him down in a little town near the state line. He went to the café of one Mike Dolan and shook hands with Mike, who was alone behind the bar.

❶ *What does Mike mean by his question? What is Jimmy's reaction to the question?*

"Sorry we couldn't make it sooner, Jimmy, me boy," said Mike. "But we had that protest from Springfield to buck against, and the governor nearly balked. Feeling all right?"

"Fine," said Jimmy. "Got my key?"

He got his key and went upstairs, unlocking the door of a room at the rear. Everything was just as he had left it. There on the floor was still Ben Price's collar-button that had been torn from that eminent detective's shirt-band when they had overpowered Jimmy to arrest him.

❷ *What happened shortly after Jimmy Valentine was released from prison?*

Pulling out from the wall a folding-bed, Jimmy slid back a panel in the wall and dragged out a dust-covered suitcase. He opened this and gazed fondly at the finest set of burglar's tools in the East. It was a complete set, made of specially tempered steel, the latest designs in drills, punches, braces and bits, jimmies, clamps, and augers, with two or three novelties invented by Jimmy himself, in which he took pride. Over nine hundred dollars they had cost him to have made at——, a place where they make such things for the profession.

In half an hour Jimmy went downstairs and through the café. He was now dressed in tasteful and well-fitting clothes, and carried his dusted and cleaned suitcase in his hand.

"Got anything on?" asked Mike Dolan, genially.

"Me?" said Jimmy, in a puzzled tone. "I don't understand. I'm representing the New York Amalgamated Short Snap Biscuit Cracker and Frazzled Wheat Company."

This statement delighted Mike to such an extent that Jimmy had to take a seltzer-and-milk on the spot. He never touched "hard" drinks.

A week after the release of Valentine, 9762, there was a neat job of safe-burglary done in Richmond, Indiana, with no clue to the author. A scant eight hundred dollars was all that was secured. Two weeks after that a patented, improved, burglar-proof safe in Logansport was opened like a cheese to the tune of fifteen hundred

Words for Everyday Use

em • i • nent (em´ə nənt) *adj.*, renowned; distinguished

gen • i • al • ly (jēn´yəl ē) *adv.*, cheerfully

Vocabulary in Context

- The eminent lawyer is going to run for president.
- The nurse entered my room, smiled genially, and took my temperature.

dollars, currency; securities and silver untouched. That began to interest the rogue-catchers.[2] Then an old-fashioned bank-safe in Jefferson City became active and threw out of its crater an eruption of bank-notes amounting to five thousand dollars. The losses were now high enough to bring the matter up into Ben Price's class of work. By comparing notes, a remarkable similarity in the methods of the burglaries was noticed. Ben Price investigated the scenes of the robberies, and was heard to remark:

"That's Dandy Jim Valentine's autograph. He's resumed business. Look at that combination knob—jerked out as easy as pulling up a radish in wet weather. He's got the only clamps that can do it. And look how clean those tumblers were punched out! Jimmy never has to drill but one hole. Yes, I guess I want Mr. Valentine. He'll do his bit next time without any short-time or clemency foolishness."

Ben Price knew Jimmy's habits. He had learned them while working up the Springfield case. Long jumps, quick getaways, no confederates, and a taste for good society—these ways had helped Mr. Valentine to become noted as a successful dodger of retribution. It was given out that Ben Price had taken up the trail of the elusive cracksman, and other people with burglar-proof safes felt more at ease.

One afternoon, Jimmy Valentine and his suitcase climbed out of the mail hack[3] in Elmore, a little town five miles off the railroad down in the blackjack country of Arkansas. Jimmy, looking like an athletic young senior just home from college, went down the board sidewalk toward the hotel.

A young lady crossed the street, passed him at the corner and entered a door over which was the sign "The Elmore Bank." Jimmy Valentine looked into her eyes, forgot what he was, and became another man. She lowered her eyes and colored slightly. Young men of Jimmy's style and looks were scarce in Elmore.

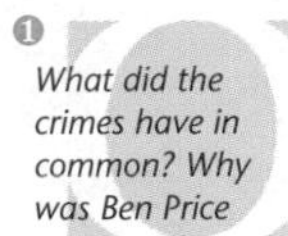

❶ *What did the crimes have in common? Why was Ben Price interested?*

Jimmy collared a boy that was loafing on the steps of the bank as if he were one of the stockholders, and began to ask him questions about the town, feeding him dimes at intervals. By and by the young lady came out, looking royally unconscious of the young man with the suitcase, and went her way.

"Isn't that young lady Miss Polly Simpson?" asked Jimmy, with specious guile.[4]

"Naw," said the boy. "She's Annabel Adams. Her pa owns this bank. What'd you come to Elmore for? Is that a gold watch chain? I'm going to get a bulldog. Got any more dimes?"

Jimmy went to the Planters' Hotel, registered as Ralph D. Spencer, and engaged a room. He leaned on the desk and declared his platform to the clerk. He said he had come to Elmore to look for a location to go into business. How was the shoe business, now,

2. **rogue-catchers.** Police
3. **mail hack.** Horse and carriage used to deliver mail
4. **specious guile.** Cunning that seems to be innocence, but is not

Words for Everyday Use

clem • en • cy (klem´ən sē) *n.,* forgiveness; leniency

con • fed • er • ate (kən fed´ər it) *n.,* partner, accomplice

ret • ri • bu • tion (re´trə byo͞o´shən) *n.,* punishment for a specific act

plat • form (plat´fôrm) *n.,* statement of principles, usually by a political party or candidate

Answer to Guided Reading Question

❶ The crimes were all done neatly and professionally. They resembled the work of Jimmy Valentine. Ben Price was interested in catching Jimmy because Jimmy had never had to pay for his crimes.

Literary Note

O. Henry's stories are famous for their surprise endings. His story "The Gift of the Magi" contains one of his most famous surprise endings.

"The Gift of the Magi" is widely anthologized, but the story was originally published in the 1906 short story collection *The Four Million.* The twenty-five stories in this collection are set in O. Henry's favorite area, New York City. O. Henry enjoys writing about the lower middle class, the unemployed, the homeless, and the forgotten.

Ask students to locate a copy of "The Gift of the Magi." After students have read the story, they should compare it with "A Retrieved Reformation." Encourage students who enjoy O. Henry's work to read some of his other stories.

Vocabulary in Context

- The governor gave that prisoner clemency because of her special situation.
- Not only did the crook get arrested, but so did his close confederate.
- What will be the retribution for the theft of the bicycle?
- That politician's platform is one of good morals and social justice.

Answer to Guided Reading Question

1 Jimmy becomes a prosperous shoe-store owner. A sudden attack of love causes this change of behavior.

Additional Questions and Activities

Ask students to answer the following questions:

- What sort of effect does Miss Annabel Adams have on Jimmy?
- Why does he write to his old friend in St. Louis?

ANSWERS

Responses will vary.

Because he is so taken by Annabel Adams, Jimmy turns his life around.

He writes to his old pal to let him know that he has turned his life around, and to tell him that he is donating his safe-cracking tools to him.

in the town? He had thought of the shoe business. Was there an opening?

The clerk was impressed by the clothes and manner of Jimmy. He, himself, was something of a pattern of fashion to the thinly gilded[5] youth of Elmore, but he now perceived his shortcomings. While trying to figure out Jimmy's manner of tying his four-in-hand,[6] he cordially gave information.

Yes, there ought to be a good opening in the shoe line. There wasn't an exclusive shoe store in the place. The dry-goods and general stores handled them. Business in all lines was fairly good. Hoped Mr. Spencer would decide to locate in Elmore. He would find it a pleasant town to live in, and the people very sociable.

Mr. Spencer thought he would stop over in the town a few days and look over the situation. No, the clerk needn't call the boy. He would carry up his suitcase, himself; it was rather heavy.

1 *In what way does Jimmy change? What cause these changes in his life?*

Mr. Ralph Spencer, the phoenix[7] that arose from Jimmy Valentine's ashes—ashes left by the flame of a sudden and alterative[8] attack of love—remained in Elmore, and prospered. He opened a shoe store and secured a good run of trade.

Socially he was also a success, and made many friends. And he accomplished the wish of his heart. He met Miss Annabel Adams, and became more and more captivated by her charms.

At the end of a year the situation of Mr. Ralph Spencer was this: he had won the respect of the community, his shoe store was flourishing, and he and Annabel were engaged to be married in two weeks. Mr. Adams, the typical, plodding, country banker, approved of Spencer. Annabel's pride in him almost equalled her affection. He was as much at home in the family of Mr. Adams and that of Annabel's married sister as if he were already a member.

One day Jimmy sat down in his room and wrote this letter, which he mailed to the safe address of one of his old friends in St. Louis:

> Dear Old Pal:
>
> I want you to be at Sullivan's place, in Little Rock, next Wednesday night, at nine o'clock. I want you to wind up some little matters for me. And, also, I want to make you a present of my kit of tools. I know you'll be glad to get them—you couldn't duplicate the lot for a thousand dollars. Say, Billy, I've quit the old business—a year ago. I've got a nice store. I'm making an honest living, and I'm going to marry the finest girl on earth two weeks from now. It's the only life, Billy—the straight one. I wouldn't touch a dollar of another man's money now for a million. After I get married I'm going to sell out and go West, where there won't be so much danger of having old scores brought up against me. I tell you, Billy, she's an angel. She believes in me; and I wouldn't do another crooked thing for the whole world. Be sure to be at Sully's, for I must see you. I'll bring along the tools with me.
>
> Your old friend,
>
> Jimmy.

5. **thinly gilded.** In this context, appearing well dressed
6. **four-in-hand.** Necktie
7. **phoenix.** Egyptian mythological bird that bursts into flames and resurrects itself from its own ashes
8. **alterative.** Causing a change or modification

On the Monday night after Jimmy wrote this letter, Ben Price jogged unobtrusively into Elmore in a livery buggy.[9] He lounged about town in his quiet way until he found out what he wanted to know. From the drugstore across the street from Spencer's shoe store he got a good look at Ralph D. Spencer.

"Going to marry the banker's daughter are you, Jimmy?" said Ben to himself, softly. "Well, I don't know!"

The next morning Jimmy took breakfast at the Adamses. He was going to Little Rock that day to order his wedding suit and buy something nice for Annabel. That would be the first time he had left town since he came to Elmore. It had been more than a year now since those last professional "jobs," and he thought he could safely venture out.

After breakfast quite a family party went downtown together—Mr. Adams, Annabel, Jimmy, and Annabel's married sister with her two little girls, aged five and nine. They came by the hotel where Jimmy still boarded, and he ran up to his room and brought along his suitcase. Then they went on

9. **livery buggy.** Horse and carriage taxi

❶ *Does Ben think Jimmy will marry the banker's daughter? Why, or why not?*

WORDS FOR EVERYDAY USE

un • ob • tru • sive • ly (un əb tro͞o´siv lē) *adv.*, without calling attention to oneself

ANSWER TO GUIDED READING QUESTION

❶ Ben doesn't know if Jimmy will marry the banker's daughter. Perhaps Ben will have an effect on whether the marriage takes place.

BIBLIOGRAPHIC NOTE

You might give students the following list of some of O. Henry's short story collections:

Cabbages and Kings (1904)

The Four Million (1906)

The Trimmed Lamp (1907)

Whirligigs (1910)

The Voice of the City (1908)

Strictly Business (1910)

Sixes and Sevens (1911)

QUOTABLES

"And here I have lamely related to you the uneventful chronicle of two foolish children in a flat who most unwisely sacrificed for each other the greatest treasures of their house. But in the last word to the wise of these days let it be said that of all who give gifts these two were the wisest."

—O. Henry

"The Gift of the Magi"

VOCABULARY IN CONTEXT

- The maid unobtrusively vacuumed and dusted while we worked.

ANSWERS TO GUIDED READING QUESTIONS

1 While the family views the safe, one of the children, Agatha, accidentally gets locked inside.

2 Mr. Spencer shows a courteous but "not too intelligent" interest in the safe. Because of his past, Jimmy wants to act as though the safe does not interest him. He does not want to arouse suspicion.

ADDITIONAL QUESTIONS AND ACTIVITIES

Ask students to answer the following questions:

- What sort of bind is Jimmy in when Agatha gets locked in the vault?
- Were you surprised at what Jimmy decides to do?
- If Jimmy had decided to stay still and not pull out his tools, what might have happened, and how would he feel?

ANSWERS

Answers will vary.

Jimmy must decide if he should reveal his past life in order to save the girl's life. Students might feel that if the girl died, Jimmy would feel guilty knowing that he could have saved her.

to the bank. There stood Jimmy's horse and buggy and Dolph Gibson, who was going to drive him over to the railroad station.

All went inside the high, carved oak railings into the banking-room—Jimmy included, for Mr. Adam's future son-in-law was welcome anywhere. The clerks were pleased to be greeted by the good-looking, agreeable young man who was going to marry Miss Annabel. Jimmy set his suitcase down. Annabel, whose heart was bubbling with happiness and lively youth, put on Jimmy's hat, and picked up the suitcase. "Wouldn't I make a nice drummer?"[10] said Annabel. "My! Ralph, how heavy it is! Feels like it was full of gold bricks."

1 *What happens while the family is viewing the new safe?*

"Lot of nickel-plated shoehorns in there," said Jimmy, coolly, "that I'm going to return. Thought I'd save express charges by taking them up. I'm getting awfully economical."

The Elmore Bank had just put in a new safe and vault. Mr. Adams was very proud of it, and insisted on an inspection by everyone. The vault was a small one, but it had a new, patented door. It fastened with three solid steel bolts thrown simultaneously with a single handle, and had a time lock. Mr. Adams beamingly explained its workings to Mr. Spencer, who showed a courteous but not too intelligent interest. The two children, May and Agatha, were delighted by the shining metal and funny clock and knobs.

2 *What is Mr. Spencer's reaction to seeing the new safe? Why do you think he acts this way?*

While they were thus engaged Ben Price sauntered in and leaned on his elbow, looking casually inside between the railings. He told the teller that he didn't want anything; he was just waiting for a man he knew.

Suddenly there was a scream or two from the women, and a commotion. Unperceived by the elders, May, the nine-year-old girl, in a spirit of play, had shut Agatha in the vault. She had then shot the bolts and turned the knob of the combination as she had seen Mr. Adams do.

The old banker sprang to the handle and tugged at it for a moment. "The door can't be opened," he groaned. "The clock hasn't been wound nor the combination set."

Agatha's mother screamed again, hysterically.

"Hush!" said Mr. Adams, raising his trembling hand. "All be quiet for a moment. Agatha!" he called as loudly as he could. "Listen to me." During the following silence they could just hear the faint sound of the child wildly shrieking in the dark vault in a panic of terror.

"My precious darling!" wailed the mother. "She will die of fright! Open the door! Oh, break it open! Can't you men do something?"

"There isn't a man nearer than Little Rock who can open that door," said Mr. Adams, in a shaky voice. "My God! Spencer, what shall we do? That child—she can't stand it long in there. There isn't enough air, and, besides, she'll go into convulsions from fright."

10. **drummer.** Traveling salesman

WORDS FOR EVERYDAY USE

con • vul • sion (kən vul´shən) *n.*, violent, involuntary spasm of the muscles

VOCABULARY IN CONTEXT

- A high fever might cause a convulsion.

Agatha's mother, frantic now, beat the door of the vault with her hands. Somebody wildly suggested dynamite. Annabel turned to Jimmy, her large eyes full of anguish, but not yet despairing. To a woman nothing seems quite impossible to the powers of the man she worships.

"Can't you do something, Ralph—*try*, won't you?"

He looked at her with a queer, soft smile on his lips and in his keen eyes.

"Annabel," he said, "give me that rose you are wearing, will you?"

Hardly believing that she heard him aright, she unpinned the bud from the bosom of her dress, and placed it in his hand. Jimmy stuffed it into his vest pocket, threw off his coat and pulled up his shirt sleeves. With that act Ralph D. Spencer passed away and Jimmy Valentine took his place.

"Get away from the door, all of you," he commanded, shortly.

He set his suitcase on the table, and opened it out flat. From that time on he seemed to be unconscious of the presence of anyone else. He laid out the shining, queer implements swiftly and orderly, whistling softly to himself as he always did when at work. In a deep silence and immovable, the others watched him as if under a spell.

In a minute Jimmy's pet drill was biting smoothly into the steel door. In ten minutes—breaking his own burglarious record—he threw back the bolts and opened the door.

Agatha, almost collapsed, but safe, was gathered into her mother's arms.

Jimmy Valentine put on his coat, and walked outside the railings toward the front door. As he went he thought he heard a far-away voice that he once knew call "Ralph!" But he never hesitated.

At the door a big man stood somewhat in his way.

"Hello, Ben!" said Jimmy, still with his strange smile. "Got around at last, have you? Well, let's go. I don't know that it makes much difference, now."

And then Ben Price acted rather strangely.

"Guess you're mistaken, Mr. Spencer," he said. "Don't believe I recognize you. Your buggy's waiting for you, ain't it?"

And Ben Price turned and strolled down the street. ■

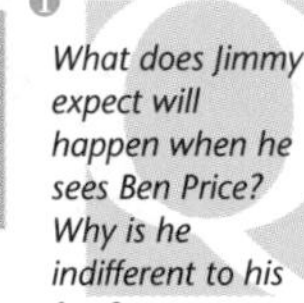

❶ *What does Jimmy expect will happen when he sees Ben Price? Why is he indifferent to his fate?*

About the Author

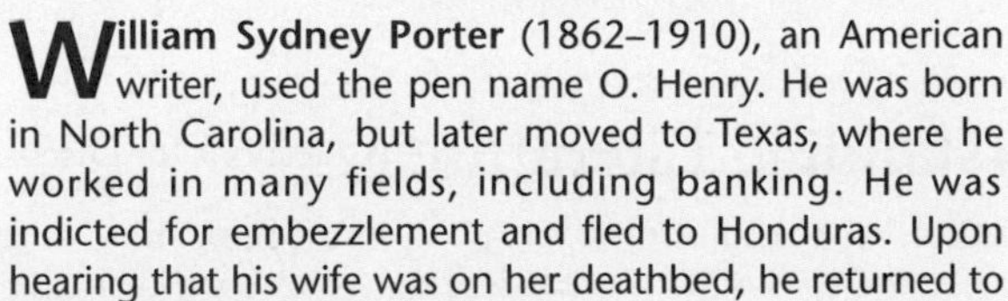

William Sydney Porter (1862–1910), an American writer, used the pen name O. Henry. He was born in North Carolina, but later moved to Texas, where he worked in many fields, including banking. He was indicted for embezzlement and fled to Honduras. Upon hearing that his wife was on her deathbed, he returned to Texas to see her and turned himself in to the authorities. He was tried, found guilty, and sent to prison. During his three years in prison he began to write short stories. O. Henry published fourteen volumes of stories in his lifetime. He is recognized as a master of mechanical plots and is known for his surprise twist endings.

Answer to Guided Reading Question

❶ Jimmy expects that Ben will try to arrest him. Jimmy is indifferent to his fate because he feels that he has probably been caught, and that now he would never get away with being Ralph D. Spencer.

Selection Check Test with Answers

EX. Why does Jimmy get out of jail?
Jimmy gets out of jail because the governor grants him a pardon.

1. What does Jimmy keep in his briefcase?
He keeps tools for opening safes.

2. Why is Ben Price interested in Jimmy?
Ben wants to catch Jimmy and get him back into jail.

3. Why does Jimmy decide to change his life?
Jimmy falls in love.

4. What business does Jimmy go into?
Jimmy goes into the shoe business.

5. Why does Jimmy take out his tools in front of the Adamses?
The little girl becomes trapped in the safe and Jimmy knows that he is the only one who can save her.

RESPONDING TO THE SELECTION

You might ask students to discuss why Jimmy opened the safe, even though he knew it might get him into trouble.

ANSWERS FOR REVIEWING THE SELECTION

RECALLING AND INTERPRETING

1. **Recalling.** Jimmy tells the warden that he has never cracked a safe in his entire life. **Interpreting.** *Responses will vary.* Students might say that Jimmy seems too calm and almost bored with his situation to be an innocent person wrongly accused of a crime and jailed unfairly.
2. **Recalling.** Jimmy first goes to a restaurant and has a chicken dinner. **Interpreting.** *Responses will vary.* Students will probably say that Jimmy has not changed because he goes to his old room to get his tools. He feels pride when he looks at his tools.
3. **Recalling.** Jimmy decides to go into the shoe business. **Interpreting.** Jimmy decides to "quit the old business" because he falls in love with a banker's daughter.
4. **Recalling.** Jimmy brings his tools to the bank in Elmore because he plans to go to Little Rock later in the day to deliver his tools to his friend. Ben Price waits for Jimmy at the bank. **Interpreting.** Ben assumes that Jimmy is involved with the banker's daughter so that he can have access to the bank's money.

SYNTHESIZING

Responses will vary. Possible responses are given.

5. Students might be surprised by Ben Price's behavior and the twist ending and some might have suspected that Jimmy might get himself out of any new binds.

Responding to the Selection

At the end of the story Ben Price says, "Guess you're mistaken, Mr. Spencer. Don't believe I recognize you." How would you have responded if you were Jimmy Valentine? Do you think Jimmy Valentine's life changed again after that experience? If so, in what ways? If not, why not?

Reviewing the Selection

Recalling and Interpreting

1. (R) How does Jimmy Valentine respond when the warden tells him to stop cracking safes?
   (I) Do you believe Jimmy? Why, or why not?
2. (R) Where does Jimmy go as soon as he is released from prison?
   (I) Do you think Jimmy has changed while he was in prison? Why, or why not?
3. (R) What business does Jimmy start in Elmore?
   (I) Why does Jimmy decide to "quit the old business"?
4. (R) Why does Jimmy bring his tools to the bank in Elmore? Who waits for Jimmy in the bank?
   (I) What suspicion does Ben Price have concerning Jimmy and his marriage?

Synthesizing

5. Did you expect Ben Price to act as he did at the end of the story or was it a surprise? What events or information in the story led to your expectations for the end of the story?

Understanding Literature (Questions for Discussion)

1. **Resolution.** The **resolution** is the point in a poem, story, or play in which the central conflict, or struggle, is ended. What is the central conflict in this story? At what point in the story is the conflict resolved? What ends the central conflict?
2. **Verbal Irony.** A statement that says one thing but means the opposite is an example of **verbal irony**. At the end of paragraph 7, the reference to prison inmates as "compulsory guests" is an example of verbal irony. Identify an example of verbal irony in paragraph 8. Why is this statement ironic?

ANSWERS FOR UNDERSTANDING LITERATURE

Responses will vary. Possible responses are given.

1. **Resolution.** The central conflict is the conflict between Jimmy and his past life. Jimmy's past life is always threatening to destroy his new life. The conflict is resolved when Ben allows Jimmy to go free in his new life. The incident in the bank solves the central conflict.
2. **Verbal Irony.** The line that reads, "The clerk handed him a railroad ticket and the five-dollar bill with which the law expected him to rehabilitate himself into good citizenship and prosperity" is an example of verbal irony. This statement is ironic because a person probably cannot completely turn his or her life around with a railroad ticket and five dollars.

Speaking and Listening Skills

Elements of Verbal and Nonverbal Communication

When you think about communication you probably think of conversations, announcements, speeches, letters, and newspapers—all means of communication that involve words. While **verbal communication** is important, good communication involves more than just words. In everyday conversation, as well as in speeches and announcements, people use **nonverbal communication.** Pointing, smiling, raising your eyebrows, and crossing your arms all communicate a message. To learn more about verbal and nonverbal communication, review the charts below.

ELEMENTS OF VERBAL COMMUNICATION		
Element	**Description**	**Guidelines for Speakers**
Volume	Loudness or softness	Vary your volume, but make sure that you can be heard.
Melody, Pitch	Highness or lowness	Vary your pitch. Avoid speaking in a **monotone** (at a single pitch).
Pace	Speed	Vary the speed of your delivery to suit what you are saying. Excitement, for example, can be communicated by a fast pace, and seriousness can be communicated by slowing down and saying something forcefully.
Tone	Emotional quality	Suit your tone to your message, and vary it appropriately as you speak. For example, you might use a light tone for a happy message and a heavier one for a sad message.

Elements of Verbal and Nonverbal Communication

Introducing the Skill

Explain to students that using elements of verbal and nonverbal communication will help them not only to give speeches or present information but to be better communicators in everyday conversations and interactions.

Previewing the Skill

Ask students to read the charts provided. Be sure that they understand each element described in the charts.

Practicing the Skill

Ask students to complete the Try It Yourself exercises.

Reviewing the Skill

When students have completed the activities, discuss with them what they found most challenging about using the elements of verbal and nonverbal communication. Ask them which activity they found most enjoyable and why.

Answers for Try It Yourself

Exercise A

Students should critique one another as they pantomime the emotions. Ask them to notice what was skilled and accurate about each pantomime.

Exercise B

Give students a few days to make their observations. Ask them to try to gather a variety of examples of effective and ineffective communication from live situations and from television or video.

ELEMENTS OF NONVERBAL COMMUNICATION		
Element	**Description**	**Guidelines for Speakers**
Eye Contact	Looking audience members in the eye	Make eye contact regularly with people in your audience.
Facial Expression	Using your face to show emotion	Use your facial expression to emphasize your message—raised eyebrows for a question, pursed lips for concentration, eyebrows lowered for anger, and so on.
Gesture	Meaningful motions of the arms and hands	Use gestures to emphasize points. Be careful, however, not to overuse gestures. Too many can be distracting.
Posture/Body	Position of the body	Keep your spine straight and head high. Stand with your arms and legs slightly open, except when adopting other postures to express particular emotions.

Try It Yourself

Exercise A. Choose one of the following emotions:

joy
anger
sorrow
anxiety
fear
excitement

Pantomime the emotion using only facial expressions and gestures. Have your classmates guess what emotion you are pantomiming.

Exercise B. Observe people communicating. This can be in a live situation or on television or video. Write down all the examples of verbal and nonverbal communication that you notice. Share your notes with your classmates. Discuss how effective the communication you observed was. Tell what made it effective or ineffective.

Try It Yourself (cont.)

Exercise C. With a partner, write a script for a conversation. Include all the verbal and nonverbal elements in your script. Choose from the topics below or decide on one of your own:

1. A conversation between a parent and child about a poor report card.
2. A conversation between a teacher and student about the student winning a statewide writing contest.
3. A conversation between two friends trying to decide which movie to see.
4. A conversation between a student and the play director who is evaluating the student's performance in the school play.

Enact your conversations in front of the class. Use all the verbal and nonverbal elements that you included in your script.

Answers for Try It Yourself

Exercise C

Students should make notes right on their scripts about which elements of verbal and nonverbal communication they should use in the conversation.

Give them time to rehearse their scripts before they demonstrate them in front of the class.

GOALS/OBJECTIVES

Studying this lesson will enable students to

- enjoy a short story about family members' feelings toward a special pet and toward one another
- briefly discuss foxes
- define *antagonist* and identify the antagonist in a story
- define *understatement*
- use problem-solving and decision-making skills

ADDITIONAL RESOURCES

Reader's Guide

- Selection Worksheet, 8.4

Assessment Portfolio

- Selection Check Test, 2.8.7
- Selection Test, 2.8.8

Pronunciation Exercise

- Grade 8 Audiocassette, Side B, Track 44

CROSS-CURRICULAR CONNECTIONS

Science

Ask students to write papers and give presentations on other interesting mammals. Each student should choose one mammal that particularly interests him or her. Then the student should go to the library and research the animal. Students should present their information to the class.

Prereading

THEME

"Last Cover"

by Paul Annixter

Cross-curricular Connections

Science. The fox is a member of the dog family. Foxes are small animals, usually about three feet long (including their tails which make up about a third of their length) and weighing between eight and fifteen pounds. They have bushy tails, long fur, and pointed ears. Foxes are known as quick and skillful hunters with keen senses of smell and hearing. A fox is capable of hearing a mouse squeak at a distance of one hundred feet. Foxes mostly hunt mice and small rodents, but they will eat almost any animal, including the remains of dead animals. Foxes bury the uneaten parts of their prey and return to them later.

Humans are the fox's major enemy. Many poultry farmers find foxes to be pests because they prey on domestic fowl, such as chickens and ducks, and their eggs. However, foxes also help farmers by eating mice, rats, and other unwelcome rodents. Many farmers have experienced a sharp increase in rats and mice when foxes in their area were killed off. As a result, some of them have brought in other foxes for the purpose of controlling the rodent population.

Many people hunt foxes for sport because foxes are skilled at avoiding capture. Hunters use hounds to track the scent of the fox. Foxes are not easy to catch, however. They are well known for their ability to circle, backtrack, and double back on their own trail. They also create false trails and run into water to make their scent difficult for dogs to follow. Because of the fox's ability to outwit its hunters, the fox often appears as a clever character in fables and other traditional stories. In the short story you are about to read, the author has portrayed a fox's skill in evading its hunters.

As You Read

In **"Last Cover,"** the major characters' feelings about a fox and its hunters reveal much about the characters' motivations and their development. In your journal, make a chart like the one below. As you read, write down the name of each major character and add details about how each character feels about both the fox and the hunters. You might then note what the characters' feelings reveal about them.

Character	Feelings	What The Feelings Reveal
Mom	likes the fox and believes it is a good companion for her children	cares deeply about what is best for her children, very warm-hearted

AS YOU READ

Answers may vary. The following are examples of what might be typical chart entries:

Character	Feelings	What The Feelings Reveal
• Father	• Father believes fox is a nuisance	• Father is practical
• Colin	• loves Bandit as a friend	• Colin is warm-hearted, emotional, not as practical

READER'S JOURNAL

Have you ever lost something that you deeply loved? What were the circumstances? What was your response? How did you come to terms with your loss? If you cannot think of such a situation, how would you feel if you lost something that was very important to you and to which you had an emotional attachment?

"Last Cover"

PAUL ANNIXTER

I'm not sure I can tell you what you want to know about my brother; but everything about the pet fox is important, so I'll tell all that from the beginning.

It goes back to a winter afternoon after I'd hunted the woods all day for a sign of our lost pet. I remember the way my mother looked up as I came into the kitchen. Without my speaking, she knew what had happened. For six hours I had walked, reading signs, looking for a delicate print in the damp soil or even a hair that might have told of a red fox passing that way—but I had found nothing.

"Did you go up in the foothills?" Mom asked.

I nodded. My face was stiff from held-back tears. My brother, Colin, who was going on twelve, got it all from one look at me and went into a heartbroken, almost silent, crying.

Three weeks before, Bandit, the pet fox Colin and I had raised from a tiny kit, had disappeared, and not even a rumor had been heard of him since.

"He'd have had to go off soon anyway," Mom comforted. "A big, lolloping fellow like him, he's got to live his life same as us. But he may come back. That fox set a lot of store by you boys in spite of his wild ways."

"He set a lot of store by our food, anyway," Father said. He sat in a chair by the kitchen window, mending a piece of harness. "We'll be seeing a lot more of that fellow, never fear. That fox learned to pine for table scraps and young chickens. He was getting to be an egg thief, too, and he's not likely to forget that."

"That was only pranking when he was little," Colin said desperately.

From the first, the tame fox had made tension in the family. It was Father who said we'd better name him Bandit, after he'd made away with his first young chicken.

"Maybe you know," Father said shortly. "But when an animal turns to egg sucking, he's usually incurable. He'd better not come pranking around my chicken run again."

It was late February, and I remember the bleak, dead cold that had set in, cold that was a rare thing for our Carolina hills. Flocks of sparrows and snowbirds had appeared, to peck hungrily at all that the pigs and chickens didn't eat.

❶ What prediction does Father make about Bandit?

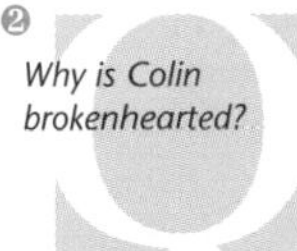

❷ Why is Colin brokenhearted?

READER'S JOURNAL

As an alternative activity, you might ask students to write about a special pet. Each student may describe a pet, his or her relationship with the pet, and why this relationship was or is special.

SPELLING AND VOCABULARY WORDS FROM THE SELECTION

confound	sanction
incredulous	sanctuary
invalid	thicket
rouse	

ANSWERS TO GUIDED READING QUESTIONS

❶ Father predicts that they would see more of Bandit, because he would come around looking for table scraps, chickens, and eggs.

❷ Colin is brokenhearted because his pet fox is missing.

SUPPORT FOR LEP STUDENTS

PRONUNCIATIONS OF PROPER NOUNS AND ADJECTIVES

An • nix • ter (a´nik stər) n.
Col • in (kä´lin) n.

ADDITIONAL VOCABULARY

foothills—low hills near the bottom of mountains
lolloping—full of clumsy movement
mounted—riding horses
pox—a disease, or like a disease

Answers to Guided Reading Questions

❶ The narrator says that he is ordinary, tough, and strong. The narrator says that Colin is special—small for his age, delicate, blond, and often sick.

❷ Colin's father says that making a frame before making a picture is like cutting a man's suit for a twelve-year-old. Colin's mother says that Colin has real talent, and that it is time Colin's father realized it. Colin's father says that all kids have talents, but that they eventually get over them.

Additional Questions and Activities

Ask students to answer the following question:

- According to the father, what would humans do if they had more sense?

Answers

Responses will vary.

Father says that humans would hibernate like forest animals during cold winter weather if they had more sense.

"This one's a killer," Father would say of a morning, looking out at the whitened barn roof. "This one will make the shoats[1] squeal."

A fire snapped all day in our cookstove and another in the stone fireplace in the living room, but still the farmhouse was never warm. The leafless woods were bleak and empty, and I spoke of that to Father when I came back from my search.

"It's always a sad time in the woods when the seven sleepers are under cover," he said.

❶ "What sleepers are they?" I asked. Father was full of woods lore.

What does the narrator say about himself? about Colin?

"Why, all the animals that have got sense enough to hole up and stay hid in weather like this. Let's see, how was it the old rhyme named them?

Surly bear and sooty bat,
Brown chuck and masked coon
Chippy-munk and sly skunk,
And all the mouses
'Cept in men's houses.

"And man would have joined them and made it eight," Granther Yeary always said, "if he'd had a little more ❷ sense."

What does Father say about Colin making a frame before he makes a picture? What does Mom say about Colin's talent? What does Father say about children's talent in general?

"I was wondering if the red fox mightn't make it eight," Mom said.

Father shook his head. "Late winter's a high time for foxes. Time when they're out deviling, not sleeping."

My chest felt hollow. I wanted to cry like Colin over our lost fox, but at fourteen a boy doesn't cry. Colin had squatted down on the floor and got out his small hammer and nails to start another new frame for a new picture.

Maybe then he'd make a drawing for the frame and be able to forget his misery. It had been that way with him since he was five.

I thought of the new dress Mom had brought home a few days before in a heavy cardboard box. That box cover would be fine for Colin to draw on. I spoke of it, and Mom's glance thanked me as she went to get it. She and I worried a lot about Colin. He was small for his age, delicate and blond, his hair much lighter and softer than mine, his eyes deep and wide and blue. He was often sick, and I knew the fear Mom had that he might be predestined. I'm just ordinary, like Father. I'm the sort of stuff that can take it—tough and strong—but Colin was always sort of special.

Mom lighted the lamp. Colin began cutting his white cardboard carefully, fitting it into his frame. Father's sharp glance turned on him now and again.

"There goes the boy making another frame before there's a picture for it," he said. "It's too much like cutting out a man's suit for a fellow that's say, twelve years old. Who knows whether he'll grow into it? "

Mom was into him then, quick. "Not a single frame of Colin's has ever gone to waste. The boy has real talent, Sumter, and it's time you realized it."

"Of course he has," Father said. "All kids have 'em. But they get over 'em."

"It isn't the pox we're talking of," Mom sniffed.

"In a way it is. Ever since you started talking up Colin's art, I've had an invalid for help around the place."

1. **shoats.** Young hogs

Words for Everyday Use

in • val • id (in′və lid) *n.*, weak, sickly person

Vocabulary in Context

- She wanted her illness to go away—she was tired of being an invalid.

Father wasn't as hard as he made out, I knew, but he had to hold a balance against all Mom's frothing.[2] For him the thing was the land and all that pertained to it. I was following in Father's footsteps, true to form, but Colin threatened to break the family tradition with his leaning toward art, with Mom "aiding and abetting him," as Father liked to put it. For the past two years she had had dreams of my brother becoming a real artist and going away to the city to study.

It wasn't that Father had no understanding of such things. I could remember, through the years, Colin lying on his stomach in the front room making pencil sketches, and how a good drawing would catch Father's eye halfway across the room; and how he would sometimes gather up two or three of them to study, frowning and muttering, one hand in his beard, while a great pride rose in Colin, and in me too. Most of Colin's drawings were of the woods and wild things, and there Father was a master critic. He made out to scorn what seemed to him a passive "white-livered" interpretation of nature through brush and pencil instead of rod and rifle.

At supper that night, Colin could scarcely eat. Ever since he'd been able to walk, my brother had had a growing love of wild things; but Bandit had been like his very own, a gift of the woods. One afternoon a year and a half before, Father and Laban Small had been running a vixen through the hills with their dogs. With the last of her strength the she-fox had made for her den, not far from our house. The dogs had overtaken her and killed her just before she reached it. When Father and Laban came up, they'd found Colin crouched nearby holding her cub in his arms.

Father had been for killing the cub, which was still too young to shift for itself, but Colin's grief had brought Mom into it. We'd taken the young fox into the kitchen, all of us, except Father, gone a bit silly over the little thing.

Colin had held it in his arms and fed it warm milk from a spoon.

"Watch out with all your soft ways," Father had warned, standing in the doorway. "You'll make too much of him. Remember, you can't make a dog out of a fox. Half of that little critter has to love, but the other half is a wild hunter. You boys will mean a whole lot to him while he's kit, but there'll come a day when you won't mean a thing to him, and he'll leave you shorn."[3]

For two weeks after that, Colin had nursed the cub, weaning it from milk to bits of meat. For a year they were always together. The cub grew fast. It was soon following Colin and me about the barnyard. It turned out to be a patch fox, with a saddle of darker fur across its shoulders.

I haven't the words to tell you what the fox meant to us. It was far more wonderful owning him than owning my dog. There was something rare and secret, like the spirit of the woods about him; and back of his calm, straw-gold eyes was the sense of a brain the equal of a man's. The fox became Colin's whole life.

Each day, going and coming from school, Colin and I took long side trips through the woods, looking for Bandit. Wild things' memories were short, we new; we'd have to find him soon, or the old bond would be broken.

2. **frothing.** In this context, to speak of trivial ideas
3. **shorn.** Cheated or stripped of power

1 *What is most important to Father? How might Colin "break the family tradition"?*

What warning does Father give about taking care of the fox?

What does Colin like to draw? What does Father think of such drawings?

Answers to Guided Reading Questions

1 The land they live and work on is most important to Father. Colin might break the family tradition by becoming an artist and moving to the city.

2 Father warns the children not to become too attached to the fox.

3 Colin likes to draw scenes from the woods and wild things. Father thinks such drawings are passive interpretations and are wastes of time.

CROSS-CURRICULAR ACTIVITIES

Science

Ask students to research animals who hibernate. Ask them to answer the following questions: What is hibernation? Why do certain animals do it? What happens physically to an animal who hibernates? Which animals hibernate?

Students might decide to focus on one animal, or to focus on a variety of animals. They should put together papers or presentations. You might encourage them to draw pictures and diagrams.

Answers to Guided Reading Questions

1 Colin knows the woods and wild things by instinct.

2 The narrator knows that the fox has been up to no good because the fox has a chicken feather on his chin. The chicken feather means that the fox has been killing chickens.

Additional Questions and Activities

Ask students to answer the following questions:

- Why does Colin believe that they haven't "lost" Bandit, even though Bandit now lives in the wild?
- Why must they keep their contact with the fox a secret from their father?

ANSWERS

Responses will vary.

When Colin approaches Bandit in the woods, Bandit allows Colin to get near him and even to put his arm around him. Bandit seems drawn to them, but then becomes distracted by his new life.

Father believes that the fox is a wild animal and should be kept that way. They can also see that Bandit has been eating chickens, and they know their father would not be pleased by this.

1 In what way does Colin know the woods?

2 How does the narrator know that Bandit has been up to no good? What has Bandit been doing?

Ever since I was ten I'd been allowed to hunt with Father, so I was good at reading signs. But, in a way, Colin knew more about the woods and wild things than Father or me. What came to me from long observation, Colin seemed to know by instinct.

It was Colin who felt out, like an Indian, the stretch of woods where Bandit had his den, who found the first slim, small fox-print in the damp earth. And then, on an afternoon in March, we saw him. I remember the day well, the racing clouds, the wind rattling the tops of the pine trees and swaying the Spanish moss. Bandit had just come out of a clump of laurel;[4] in the maze of leaves behind him we caught a glimpse of a slim red vixen, so we knew he had found a mate. She melted from sight like a shadow, but Bandit turned to watch us, his mouth open, his tongue lolling as he smiled his old foxy smile. On his thin chops, I saw a tell-tale chicken feather.

Colin moved silently forward, his movements so quiet and casual he seemed to be standing still. He called Bandit's name, and the fox held his ground, drawn to us with all his senses. For a few moments he let Colin actually put an arm about him. It was then I knew that he loved us still, for all of Father's warnings. He really loved us back, with a fierce, secret love no tame thing ever gave. But the urge of his life just then was toward his new mate. Suddenly, he whirled about and disappeared in the laurels.

Colin looked at me with glowing eyes. "We haven't really lost him, Stan. When he gets through with his spring sparking he may come back. But we've got to show ourselves to him a lot, so he won't forget."

"It's a go," I said.

"Promise not to say a word to Father," Colin said, and I agreed. For I knew by the chicken feather that Bandit had been up to no good.

A week later the woods were budding, and the <u>thickets</u> were rustling with all manner of wild things scurrying on the love scent. Colin managed to get a glimpse of Bandit every few days. He couldn't get close though, for the spring running was a lot more important to a fox than any human beings were.

Every now and then Colin got out his framed box cover and looked at it, but he never drew anything on it; he never even picked up his pencil. I remember wondering if what Father had said about framing a picture before you had one had spoiled something for him.

I was helping Father with the planting now, but Colin managed to be in the woods every day. By degrees, he learned Bandit's range, where he drank and rested, and where he was likely to be according to the time of day One day he told me how he had petted Bandit again, and how they had walked together a long way in the woods. All this time we had kept his secret from Father.

As summer came on, Bandit began to live up to the prediction Father had

4. **laurel.** Evergreen trees and shrubs

Words for Everyday Use

thick • et (thik´it) *n.,* thick growth of shrubs, underbrush, or small trees

Vocabulary in Context

- The rabbit tried to hide by running into the <u>thicket</u>.

made. Accustomed to human beings he moved without fear about the scattered farms of the region, raiding barns and hen runs that other foxes wouldn't have dared go near. And he taught his wild mate to do the same. Almost every night they got into some poultry house, and by late June, Bandit was not only killing chickens and ducks but feeding on eggs and young chicks whenever he got the chance.

Stories of his doings came to us from many sources, for he was still easily recognized by the dark patch on his shoulders. Many a farmer took a shot at him as he fled, and some of them set out on his trail with dogs, but they always returned home without even sighting him. Bandit was familiar with all the dogs in the region, and he knew a hundred tricks to <u>confound</u> them. He got a reputation that year beyond that of any fox our hills had known.

His confidence grew, and he gave up wild hunting altogether and lived entirely off the poultry farmers. By September, the hill farmers banded together to hunt him down.

It was Father who brought home that news one night. All time honored rules of the fox chase were to be broken in this hunt; if the dogs couldn't bring Bandit down, he was to be shot on sight. I was stricken and furious. I remember the misery of Colin's face in the lamplight. Father, who took pride in all the ritual of the hunt, had refused to be a party to such an affair, though in justice he could do nothing but <u>sanction</u> any sort of hunt; for Bandit, as old Sam Wetherwax put it, had been "purely getting in the Lord's hair."

The hunt began next morning, and it was the biggest turnout our hills had known. There were at least twenty mounted men in the party and as many dogs. Father and I were working in the lower field as they passed along the river road. Most of the hunters carried rifles, and they looked ugly.

Twice during the morning I went up to the house to find Colin, but he was nowhere around. As we worked, Father and I could follow the progress of the hunt by the distant hound music on the breeze. We could tell just where the hunters first caught sight of the fox and where Bandit was leading the dogs during the first hour. We knew as well as if we'd seen it how Bandit <u>roused</u> another fox along Turkey Branch and forced it to run for him, and how the dogs swept after it for twenty minutes before they sensed their mistake.

1 *Why do the farmers want to hunt down Bandit?*

Words for Everyday Use

con • found (kən found´) *v.,* confuse; bewilder
sanc • tion (saŋk´shən) *v.,* support, permit, authorize
rouse (rouz) *v.,* stir up to flight; cause to rise from cover

Answer to Guided Reading Question

1 The farmers want to hunt down Bandit because he eats their chickens and their eggs.

Additional Questions and Activities

Ask students to answer the following questions:

- What sort of character does Colin's father have? Do you agree with his ideas about the fox? Do you understand Colin's position?
- Even though Father is annoyed with Bandit, why does he refuse to take part in the fox hunt? What two different feelings must he have?

ANSWERS

Responses will vary.

Colin's father seems to be a practical man who doesn't want to let emotional issues cloud his judgment. Some students will agree that Bandit should live in the wild, while at the same time they might be sympathetic to Colin's feelings of attachment to the animal.

Students will probably say that although Father understands the plight of the other farmers, he feels for his own son.

Vocabulary in Context

- This riddle is sure to <u>confound</u> you.
- The town will <u>sanction</u> our idea to start a youth softball league.
- Singing the team song and clapping will <u>rouse</u> the team's spirit.

Answers to Guided Reading Questions

❶ The notes of the hunting horn mean that the dogs had lost the trail or found another.

❷ The narrator communicated silently when he met Bandit and Colin.

Additional Questions and Activities

Ask students to respond to the following:

- Creating a picture frame and a picture helps Colin to deal with his sadness and to communicate with his father. Explain how Colin's artwork helps him to resolve these issues.

ANSWERS

Responses will vary.

Students might say that Colin is able to give permanence to the pet he loves and admires by creating the picture. He was able to communicate with his father by picturing something in his art that only a hunter such as his father could see.

What do the notes of the hunting horn mean?

In what way is the narrator's meeting with Bandit and his meeting with Colin similar?

Noon came, and Colin had not come in to eat. After dinner Father didn't go back to the field. He moped about, listening to the hound talk. He didn't like what was on any more than I did, ❶ and now and again I caught his smile of satisfaction when we heard the broken, angry notes of the hunting horn, telling that the dogs had lost the trail or had run another fox.

I was restless, and I went up into the ❷ hills in midafternoon. I ranged the woods for miles, thinking all the time of Colin. Time lost all meaning for me, and the short day was nearing an end, when I heard the horn talking again, telling that the fox had put over another trick. All day he had deviled the dogs and mocked the hunters. This new trick and the coming night would work to save him. I was wildly glad, as I moved down toward Turkey Branch and stood listening for a time by the deep, shaded pool where for years we boys had gone swimming, sailed boats, and dreamed summer dreams.

Suddenly, out of the corner of my eye, I saw the sharp ears and thin, pointed mask of a fox—in the water almost beneath me. It was Bandit, craftily submerged there, all but his head, resting in the cool water of the pool and the shadow of the two big beeches that spread above it. He must have run forty miles or more since morning. And he must have hidden in this place before. His knowing, crafty mask blended perfectly with the shadows and a mass of drift and branches that had collected by the bank of the pool. He was so still that a pair of thrushes flew up from the spot as I came up, not knowing he was there.

Bandit's bright, harried eyes were looking right at me. But I did not look at him direct. Some woods instinct, swifter than thought, kept me from it. So he and I met as in another world, indirectly, with feeling but without sign or greeting.

Suddenly I saw that Colin was standing almost beside me. Silently as a water snake, he had come out of the bushes and stood there. Our eyes met, and a quick and secret smile passed between us. It was a rare moment in which I really "met" my brother, when something of his essence flowed into me, and I knew all of him. I've never lost it since.

My eyes still turned from the fox, my heart pounding, I moved quietly away, and Colin moved with me. We whistled softly as we went, pretending to busy ourselves along the bank of the stream. There was magic in it, as if by will we wove a web of protection about the fox, a ring-pass-not that none might penetrate. It was so, too, we felt, in the brain of Bandit, and that doubled the charm. To us he was still our little pet that we had carried about in our arms on countless summer afternoons.

Two hundred yards upstream, we stopped beside slim, fresh tracks in the mud where Bandit had entered the branch. The tracks angled upstream. But in the water the wily creature had turned down.

We climbed the far bank of wait, and Colin told me how Bandit's secret had been his secret ever since an afternoon three months before, when he'd watched the fox swim downstream to hide in the deep pool. Today he'd waited on the bank, feeling that Bandit,

5. **thrushes.** Any of a large family of birds, including the robin

hard pressed by the dogs, might again seek the pool for sanctuary.

We looked back once as we turned homeward. He still had not moved. We didn't know until later that he was killed that same night by a chance hunter, as he crept out from his hiding place.

That evening Colin worked a long time on his framed box cover that had lain about the house untouched all summer. He kept at it all the next day too. I had never seen him work so hard. I seemed to sense in the air the feeling he was putting into it, how he was *believing* his picture into being. It was evening before he finished it. Without a word he handed it to Father. Mom and I went and looked over his shoulder.

It was a delicate and intricate pencil drawing of the deep branch pool; and there was Bandit's head and watching, fear-filled eyes hiding there amid the leaves and shadows, woven craftily into the maze of twigs and branches, as if by nature's art itself. Hardly a fox there at all, but the place where he was—or should have been. I recognized it instantly, but Mom gave a sort of incredulous sniff.

"I'll declare," she said, "it's mazy as a puzzle. It just looks like a lot of sticks and leaves to me."

Long minutes of study passed before Father's eye picked out the picture's secret, as few men's could have done. I laid that to Father's being a born hunter. That was a picture that might have been done especially for him. In fact, I guess it was.

Finally he turned to Colin with his deep, slow smile. "So that's how Bandit fooled them all," he said. He sat holding the picture with a sort of tenderness for a long time, while we glowed in the warmth of the shared secret. That was Colin's moment. Colin's art stopped being a pox to Father right there. And later, when the time came for Colin to go to art school, it was Father who was his solid backer. ■

❶ *What didn't the narrator and his brother know until later?*

❷ *How does Father feel about the picture? about Colin's art now?*

About the Author

Paul Annixter is the pen name of Howard Sturtzel, a writer who published over five hundred stories. He grew up in Minnesota and later staked a timber claim there. The natural landscape of Minnesota influenced his writing. Many of his stories are about the land and its animals. If you enjoyed "Last Cover," you might also enjoy some of his short story collections, such as *Pride of Lions* and *Devil in the Woods.*

Words for Everyday Use

sanc • tu • ar • y (saŋk´cho̅o̅ er´ē) *n.,* place of refuge or protection, asylum

in • cred • u • lous (in krej´o͞o ləs) *adj.,* skeptical, unwilling or unable to believe

Answers to Guided Reading Questions

❶ The narrator and his brother didn't know that Bandit was killed that same night by a hunter.

❷ Father is impressed by the picture, and he is deeply moved that Colin would share Bandit's secret with him. Father is supportive of Colin's art.

Selection Check Test with Answers

EX. What kind of animal did Colin raise?
Colin raised a fox.

1. Why did Bandit first cause tension in the family?
Bandit killed a chicken.

2. What does Colin like to make?
Colin likes to make picture frames.

3. Why do the hunters go after Bandit?
He had been stealing eggs and killing chickens.

4. What picture does Colin show his father?
Colin shows his father a picture of the place where Bandit was hiding.

5. Of what does Colin's father finally become supportive?
Colin's father finally becomes supportive of Colin's art.

Vocabulary in Context

- Those rare birds are safe in the sanctuary down the street.
- Larry had an incredulous look on his face as he sniffed the strange-looking casserole.

Responding to the Selection

What might Colin tell a hunter to try to convince the hunter not to kill Bandit? What might the hunter say in response?

Answers for Reviewing the Selection

RECALLING AND INTERPRETING

1. **Recalling.** The narrator says that the tame fox causes tension in the family. The fox eats chickens and eggs, and Father feels it should be in the wild. **Interpreting.** Father is practical and feels the animal does not make a good pet. *Responses will vary.* Students might feel that Father could have something to do with Bandit's disappearance because Father is so practical and feels he knows better than anyone what is right.
2. **Recalling.** Colin's talent is art. Colin makes picture frames before he has pictures. Father says that making a frame before making a picture is like cutting a man's suit for a young person. Father feels that making the frame is a waste of time. **Interpreting.** Father feels that Colin's talent is a pox. He feels it is only something that keeps Colin from his chores.
3. **Recalling.** Father feels that it is wrong to coddle Bandit because nothing can change the fact that he is a wild animal. **Interpreting.** Father feels that Colin and his special interest in art should not be coddled because it is not practical.
4. **Recalling.** Father's prediction that Bandit would grow up to kill chickens and steal eggs comes true. **Interpreting.** Father decides that Colin's art is important.

SYNTHESIZING

Responses will vary. Possible responses are given.

5. Colin is like the fox in that he is bright, secretive, and a survivor. Colin finally wins his father's respect by drawing a picture of Bandit's hiding place.

Responding to the Selection

What if Bandit had been your pet fox? How would you feel when the hunters were looking for Bandit? How would you feel when you saw Bandit's hiding place? How would you feel when you later discovered what happened to Bandit?

Reviewing the Selection

Recalling and Interpreting

1. **R** What does the narrator say caused tension in the family from the beginning? What did this thing do to cause tension?

   I What does Father's feelings about Bandit reveal about his character? Do you think he might have had something to do with Bandit's disappearance? Why, or why not?

2. **R** What is Colin's talent? What does Colin do in an unusual order? What does Father say about this action?

   I How does Father feel about Colin's talent? Why might he feel this way?

3. **R** What is Father's attitude toward coddling Bandit when they first take him?

   I In what way is Father's attitude toward Bandit similar to his attitude toward Colin?

4. **R** What "prediction" of Father's does Bandit "live up to"?

   I In what way were Father's predictions about Colin proved wrong?

Synthesizing

5. In what ways was Colin like the fox? In what way does Colin finally win his father's respect and support? Why do you think that it was only in this way that Colin could finally communicate with his father?

Understanding Literature (Questions for Discussion)

1. **Antagonist.** In a story, a character who struggles with the main character is called an **antagonist**. Who is the main character in this story? Which character is struggling with the main character? What relationship does the narrator have with the main character and the antagonist? In the end, how does the relationship between the main character and the antagonist change?
2. **Understatement.** An **understatement** is a statement that treats something important as though it were not important. Looking at Colin's drawing at the end of the story, Father says, "So that's how Bandit fooled them all." Why is this statement an example of understatement? What feelings do you think Father really meant to communicate?

Answers for Understanding Literature

Responses will vary. Possible responses are given.

1. **Antagonist.** Colin is the main character of the story. Father is struggling with Colin, the main character. The narrator is Colin's brother and Father's other son. He understands the practical side of his father, but also understands and feels for Colin.
2. **Understatement.** Father is deeply moved by and impressed with Colin's picture of the hiding place. He realizes in an instant that there is more to Colin and his art than he had previously thought.

Thinking Skills

Problem Solving and Decision Making

In "Last Cover" the father makes a decision to accept his son's artistic abilities. You probably solve many problems and make many decisions over the course of the day. Sometimes our decisions involve simple things like what to have for lunch, which movie to see, or which brand of toothpaste to use. Other decisions, however, involve more serious questions and issues. There are several techniques that can make problem solving and decision making much easier.

All problem solving involves four steps: understanding the problem, planning a course of action, taking the action, and evaluating the results. You will use each of these four steps when you follow any of the problem-solving techniques discussed below. For more information about these techniques see the Language Arts Survey, 4.21, "Making Decisions and Solving Problems."

TECHNIQUES FOR PROBLEM SOLVING

Trial and Error. Sometimes you make a guess about how to solve a problem and see if your guess works. Trial and error can be useful if only a few solutions exist. It is also a way to familiarize yourself with a problem to help you decide how to solve it.

Represent the Situation. It may be easier to solve some problems if you make a visual representation of the problem such as a diagram or model.

Divide and Conquer. Another way to solve problems is to divide the problem into parts. Then solve each part in a logical order.

Work Backward. Working backward is another way to face a complex problem. Imagine that you have solved your problem. Describe what you have accomplished. Then think about what would have to happen for you to accomplish that goal. Continue working backward until you get to a situation that you know how to create.

PROBLEM SOLVING AND DECISION MAKING

INTRODUCING THE SKILL

Tell students that strategies for solving problems and making decisions will help them in school and in other areas of their lives. You might discuss with students times when frameworks for solving problems or making decisions might be useful. For example, when choosing research topics, when trying to decide whether or not to join a club or a team, or when solving any other school-related or personal dilemmas.

PREVIEWING THE SKILL

Ask students to read the lessons and sample charts provided. Ask them to name the advantages of each method shown.

PRACTICING THE SKILL

Ask students to complete the Try It Yourself exercises.

REVIEWING THE SKILL

Look over each student's work. Have a discussion of the different problem-solving and decision-making techniques. Ask students to name which techniques they found to be most helpful and which they found to be difficult or least helpful.

Answers for Try It Yourself

Exercise A

Answers will vary. Encourage students to pay close attention to the models and the lessons as they work. When they are finished, they might exchange work with a partner and offer suggestions to each other.

Try It Yourself

Exercise A. Write the name of the technique that would be most useful for solving each of the problems below. Explain why you believe this technique would help you solve this problem.

EXAMPLE: You are designing a set for a play and you do not know how the scenery should be placed.
Representing the situation would allow you to visualize the stage and better plan where the scenery should be placed.

1. You want to run for class president but do not know how to organize a successful campaign.
2. You are planning a party and have many tasks to complete before the event can take place.
3. You are delivering papers and you are unsure if a house on your delivery route is up the street or down the street.
4. You are on a committee and must plan the best place to put the locker rooms, the pool, and the basketball courts in a new recreation center.

Decision-Making Strategies

Pros and Cons. When you have to make a decision, it may be helpful to consider the pros and cons of each option. Make a list of all your options. Then for each option list the pros, or reasons for choosing it, and the cons, or reasons against choosing it.

PROS AND CONS: CHOOSING A PET

	Hamster	Fox
Pros	easy to care for inexpensive will beg for seeds	good company very clever and beautiful
Cons	not very responsive can be noisy at night	might run back to the wild might be dangerous must eat meat almost impossible to locate and domesticate

Criteria Analysis. Criteria are standards. To use criteria analysis in decision making, you will evaluate how each of your options meets your criteria. To make a criteria chart, list your options across the top. Down the side list your criteria. Then decide how well an option will meet a criteria and assign it a score from 1 to 5. Add the points under each option, and choose the option with the most points.

CRITERIA ANALYSIS: CHOOSING WHAT TO DO FOR SUMMER VACATION

	Babysitting at Home	Camp	Visiting Uncle's Farm
scenic	1	4	5
profitable	5	1	1
challenging	3	4	5
fun	2	4	4
TOTAL	11	13	15

Try It Yourself

Exercise B. Make a pro and con chart or a criteria analysis chart to help you make one of the following decisions.

1. You want to get a job to earn money for a new mountain bike. What kind of job should you get?
2. You would like to participate in an after-school sport. Which one should you choose?
3. Your family is going to take a family vacation? Where should you go?

ANSWERS FOR TRY IT YOURSELF

EXERCISE B

Answers will vary.

Students who seem to need additional practice might do a chart for more than one of the options. Students might also choose to make a chart about a real decision that they need to make. Ask students to exchange charts with a partner. They can read each other's work and offer suggestions to each other.

Project Note

- Be sure to give students plenty of time to think about their stories. Some students might need more time than other students.
- Students who are nervous about telling stories to the class should write down their stories. The more prepared they are, the less nervous they are likely to be.

Unit Project

Playing a Storytelling Game

Apple tree, sweet, bowling ball, screech, and *feathery* are all examples of concrete language. A concrete word names something that can be directly seen, tasted, touched, heard, or smelled. Concrete words help make fiction come alive. If a story is told with many colorful, concrete words, it is more likely to seem interesting and real to a reader.

Try It Yourself

Form pairs, and organize a class storytelling game. Each pair should tell two brief stories—a true story and a fictional story. The other members of the class must decide which story is true and which story is fictional. It is up to the storytellers to make the fictional story sound as believable and real as possible. Using concrete, colorful words, they must try to convince the class that the events in the fictional story, as well as those in the true story, really happened.

Student Model

Miguel and Anna are playing a storytelling game with their class. They must tell a true story and a fictional story, and the class must decide which is true and which is fictional. They brainstorm and come up with the following two ideas:

Story A (True)

My little sister and I were out for a walk one day and we found a stray dog that needed food and a bath. We took the frightened dog home and called the local newspaper to place an ad in the lost-and-found section. Then we scrubbed the dog's matted fur and placed a bowl of food in front of him. After two weeks, nobody claimed the dog, so we decided to keep him. We named him Bart, and my sister and I tried to teach him tricks. We soon discovered that this dog was very smart. He learned his name right away, and we taught him the usual dog tricks like fetching and rolling over. Then we were able to teach him to pick up clothes and toys in our bedrooms, to play hide-and-seek, and to put out his paw to shake hands with guests. We entered Bart in a local dog show. At the show, Bart managed to land a job on a dog-food commercial because he was so friendly and easy to train. We were proud of our little stray dog.

Story B (Fictional)

Two years ago my grandfather learned that he was going to lose his job. He worked in a factory that was going out of business. My grandmother had a job as a clerk in a flower shop, but she and my grandfather really needed two incomes. Grandpa spent weeks searching the want ads. One day my mom and I drove three hours to cheer Grandma and Grandpa up and to have Sunday dinner at their home. Grandma had made a delicious roast with vegetables. Grandpa had made a strawberry-rhubarb pie with homemade whipped cream. There was something about my grandparents' cooking that was extra special. I told them, "Too bad you can't open a restaurant. There aren't any really great restaurants around here." Everyone laughed and continued eating. What I didn't know was that opening a restaurant was a dream that Grandpa had always had. Several weeks later, Grandma and Grandpa decided to take a chance and follow this dream. They had some savings, and my parents and my aunt offered to contribute some money. They live right near a highway exit, so they put up a large sign to attract travelers. Before too long, my grandparents were serving delicious meals and desserts to people from all over their county.

Student Model (cont.)

Anna tells the first story, and Miguel tells the second story. When they are done, the teacher asks, "How many people think story A is fiction and story B is nonfiction?" Over half their classmates raise their hands. Anna and Miguel had succeeded in making people believe that story B was true. The teacher tells Anna and Miguel, "Because you used such specific details in your story, it seemed very real and people believed that it must be true." Then Anna and Miguel take their seats to listen to other students' stories and to guess which stories are true and which are fictional.

Examining the Model

1. What did Miguel and Anna do to come up with story ideas?
2. According to the teacher, why was the class convinced that story B was true?

Organizing the Game

1. Form teams of two. Consult the Language Arts Survey, 1.18, "Brainstorming." Then brainstorm to come up with ideas for a simple fictional story. Choose one idea.
2. Discuss with your partner how you might make your fictional story sound true to your classmates. You might start with a true story and then turn it into fiction.
3. Choose a true story to tell. Think about experiences that you, friends, or relatives have had. Be sure that nobody in your class already knows about the incident.
4. You do not need to read your story word-for-word from a paper, but you might want to make notes for yourself on notecards or a piece of paper.

Playing the Storytelling Game

1. Organize chairs in a circle. If the class is large, you might consider splitting the class in half and making two circles.
2. Decide which pair will go first. One person in the pair should tell the fictional story, and the other person should tell the true story.
3. After both stories have been told, ask the class to decide which story is true and which story is fiction.

Answers for Examining the Model

1. Miguel and Anna brainstorm to come up with story ideas.
2. According to the teacher, the class was convinced that story B was true because Miguel and Anna used so many specific details in telling the story.

Analytic Scale for Project

Assign a score from 1 to 25 for each grading criterion below.

Playing a Storytelling Game

- **Organization.** The group set attainable goals and created a schedule or strategy for achieving those goals.
- **Cooperation.** The group assigned tasks fairly to each member, and each member cooperated toward achieving the group's goals.
- **Goal Achievement.** The group worked steadily toward its goals and did, in fact, achieve them.
- **Presentation.** The group presented a product of high quality that met the initial project description.

Vocabulary Check Test

Ask students to number their paper from one to ten. Have students complete each sentence with a word from the Vocabulary for the Unit in the Unit Review.

1. My brother, who has an aversion to meat, turned away from the plate of steak tips.
2. We were happy and enjoyed the frolic in the snow.
3. Is that a transient business, or do you think it will be around for a long time?
4. Sheila's visage was one of sadness.
5. Is the story about the haunted house fact or fancy?
6. The red kite looked stunning against the clear azure sky.
7. We will corroborate her story about getting lost in the woods.
8. Do not continue to scoff at Roger's good ideas.
9. The thirsty pig will quaff that water from the trough in no time.
10. Wanda, who dusts her room twice per day, is a cleanliness fanatic.

Unit Review

Summary

Literary Terms for the Unit

antagonist, 392
concrete, 360
irony of situation, 369
resolution, 380
setting, 360
understatement, 392
verbal irony, 380

Vocabulary for the Unit

addle, 354
adherent, 347
alacrity, 350
approbation, 348
ascetic, 365
assiduously, 373
august, 348
austere, 355
aversion, 346
azure, 351
barometer, 345
beleaguer, 365
bewilderment, 356
clemency, 375
comely, 356
concussion, 368
confederate, 375
confound, 389
convulsion, 378
corroborate, 357
countenance, 351
crony, 358
daunt, 348
disposition, 347
disputatious, 355
draught, 365
eloquence, 347
eminent, 374
evince, 358
fain, 347
fanatic, 365
fancy, 350
flagon, 351
forlorn, 354
frolic, 346
gambol, 353
genially, 374
gibber, 368
hue, 345
impunity, 346
incessantly, 347
incredulous, 391
invalid, 386
metamorphose, 354
obsequious, 346
paroxysm, 367
persecution, 349
pestilent, 347
platform, 375
precipice, 349
precipitation, 348
province, 345
quaff, 351
reciprocate, 349
remorse, 368
retribution, 375
rouse, 389
ruse, 367
sanction, 389
sanctuary, 391
scoff, 353
smite, 351
spasmodically , 365
surmount, 346
termagant, 346
thicket, 388
tranquility, 348
transient, 350
unobtrusively, 377
virago, 348
visage, 351

Questions for Writing, Discussion, and Research

1. What is the central conflict in each of the stories in this unit, and how is each conflict resolved?
2. Identify the major theme of each story in this unit.

For Your Reading List

Lindsay Hyde
Glades Middle School
Miami, Florida

The Illustrated Man
by Ray Bradbury

I recently read a book by author Ray Bradbury entitled "The Illustrated Man." This science fiction book is a work of art, combining an interesting beginning with excellent writing throughout. The book begins with one man meeting another man. From the beginning, the first man knows that the second man is different, but he can't explain why until the man begins to tell his tale. The man explains how he had wanted a tattoo, but instead, he was "illustrated" by a witch, who enchanted the drawings so they move in the night, each telling a different tale. These tales make up the rest of the book. Some of the stories are amazingly touching and others are totally spine-chilling. This book takes you everywhere you've ever dreamed of and beyond, from Mars to Main Street, enchanted hills to cursed cities. Take yourself on the journey of a lifetime; read *The Illustrated Man.*

Spelling Check Test

Ask students to number their papers from one to ten. Read each word aloud. Then read aloud the sentence containing the word. Repeat the word. Ask students to write the word on their papers, spelling it correctly.

1. **barometer**
The weather forecaster will look at his barometer before the evening news.
2. **termagant**
The termagant person was difficult and unpleasant.
3. **eloquence**
The leader spoke to the crowd with eloquence.
4. **comely**
Anyone could see that the freshly groomed West Highland White Terrier knew just how comely he was.
5. **purifying**
We will be purifying the water to make it drinkable.
6. **spasmodically**
During the earthquake, the ground shook spasmodically.
7. **fatigue**
My fatigue following my illness kept me from attending the athletic event.
8. **genially**
The nurse entered my room, smiled genially, and took my temperature
9. **retribution**
What will be the retribution for the theft of the bicycle?

GOALS/OBJECTIVES

Studying this unit will enable students to

- enjoy and appreciate lyric and narrative poetry
- identify and describe the speaker of a poem
- identify, explain, and create similes and metaphors
- edit sentences for sentence fragments, run-ons, wordiness, and passiveness
- give an oral interpretation of a poem
- plan and take part in a poetry reading
- use a library for research
- make a book

ADDITIONAL UNIT MATERIALS IN THE ASSESSMENT PORTFOLIO

- Vocabulary Worksheet 2.9.17
- Unit Test 2.9.18

See also the Additional Resources Box in the marginal notes accompanying each selection.

CROSS-CURRICULAR CONNECTIONS

- Applied Arts, 404
- Arts and Humanities, 422
- Geography, 430
- Science, 418, 438
- Social Studies, 412, 422, 434
- Teen Living, 430
- World History, 404, 408, 438

UNIT 9 POETRY

Apples in a Tin Pail. *Levi Wells Prentice, 1892. Charles H. Hayden Fund, Courtesy of Museum of Fine Arts, Boston*

P

oetry is the record of the best and happiest moments of the happiest and best minds.

—Percy Bysshe Shelley

UNIT SKILLS OUTLINE

Literary Skills and Concepts

- Couplet, 421
- Flashback, 433
- Image, 407
- Irony of Situation, 407
- Metaphor, 427, 450
- Quatrain, 421
- Refrain, 411
- Repetition, 411
- Simile, 427, 449, 450
- Speaker, 415, 437
- Stanza, 421
- Tercet, 421
- Theme, 433

Other Language Arts Skills and Concepts

- Editing Sentences, 416
- Oral Interpretation, 428
- Using Metaphors and Similes, 450

Quotables

"Poetry is the spontaneous overflow of powerful feelings: it takes its origins from emotion recollected in tranquility."

—William Wordsworth

"Poetry lifts the veil from the hidden beauty of the world, and makes familiar objects as if they were not familiar."

—Percy Bysshe Shelley

Elements of Poetry

Most of the stories in magazines and newspapers are told in **prose,** a type of writing similar to speech. Some of the oldest stories, however, are told in **poetry,** not prose. Ancient storytellers created special **literary techniques** to make their language beautiful and interesting. In this way, the forms that came to be known as poetry emerged.

Types of Poems. The earliest poems, and many poems written today, are **narratives,** that tell stories. Many poems, however, are **lyrics,** that tell the emotions of a speaker and do not tell a story.

Poetic Techniques. Poets choose words carefully to create certain effects. The special techniques that poets use, many of which are borrowed as well by prose writers and playwrights, involve the shapes, sounds, and meanings of words.

Techniques of Shape. When a poet places words on a page in a shape that imitates his or her subject, the result is a **concrete poem.** Other poets use shape in less obvious ways. Often poems are divided into groups of lines, called stanzas, that are separated by spaces. A stanza usually deals with a single idea.

Techniques of Sound. Techniques of sound that poets use include rhythm, rhyme, alliteration, and onomatopoeia. **Rhythm** is the pattern of beats, or stresses, in a poem. **Rhyme** is the repetition of sounds at the ends of words, as in "the moon in June." **Alliteration** is the repetition of consonant sounds at the beginnings of syllables, as in "Peter Piper picked a peck of pickled peppers." **Onomatopoeia** is the use of words like *meow* or *beep* that sound like what they mean.

Techniques of Meaning. Techniques of meaning poets use include images and figures of speech. An image is a concrete word or phrase, one that names something that can be seen, heard, touched, tasted, or smelled. A figure of speech is a statement that has more than a straightforward, literal meaning. The chart below describes some common figures of speech.

	MEANING	EXAMPLE
Metaphor	a figure of speech in which one thing is spoken or written about as if it were another.	Juliet is the sun.
Simile	a comparison using *like* or *as*	Juliet's eyes are like stars.
Symbol	a thing that stands for or represents both itself and something else	doves for peace, snakes for evil, roses for beauty
Personification	a description of something not human as though it were human	The sun smiled on Juliet.

A Boy Bringing Pomegranates. *Pieter de Hooch*

GOALS/OBJECTIVES

Studying this lesson will enable students to

- appreciate the imagery of a poem
- identify images and the senses to which they appeal
- identify and explain an example of irony of situation
- recognize a character created upon the tradition of Simple Simon

ADDITIONAL RESOURCES

Reader's Guide

- Selection Worksheet, 9.1

Assessment Portfolio

- Selection Check Test, 2.9.1
- Selection Test, 2.9.2

Pronunciation Exercise

- Grade 8 Audiocassette, Side B, Track 45

CROSS-CURRICULAR CONNECTIONS

Applied Arts

Students might contact a jeweler to arrange a demonstration of stone cutting techniques.

Students can research their birthstones or other gemstones to determine where they are most likely to be found, what their characteristics are, how valuable they can be, and what traditional properties are attributed to them.

World History

Ask students to think of examples of nursery rhymes, stories and poems that feature Simple Simon or Simple Simon-like characters.

Prereading

IMAGERY

"The Garden"

by Shel Silverstein

Cross-curricular Connections

Applied Arts. Creating the gemstones that you see in jewelry stores is an involved process. Gemstones such as diamonds, rubies, sapphires, emeralds, and garnet start out as rough, uncut stones, or minerals. However, not all gems are minerals. Pearls are produced by oysters, amber comes from the resin of fossil trees, and coral comes from tiny sea animals.

Before they are cut and polished, gem minerals are looked at by experts and judged for such qualities as the shape of the uncut crystals, luster, color, and hardness. Then, using special tools, extra material is cut away until the desired shape appears. When a ray of light passes through a cut diamond, it reflects flashes of the color spectrum. For this reason, diamonds and other transparent gems are cut with many sides or facets. If the stone is cut properly, light that enters the stone at one facet is reflected to others. Light bouncing back and forth across the many cut surfaces creates the twinkling effect of a diamond.

World History. In English, the term *Simple Simon* is an old name for a silly, or foolish, fellow. The first nursery rhymes about Simple Simon were introduced in a chapbook, or small book of poems and ballads, published in 1764. Over the years scholars have tried to find political significance in the Simple Simon nursery rhymes. One scholar has suggested that the rhymes might refer to James I, a seventeenth-century king of England. In the United States in the 1930s, the term *Simple Simon* also became a slang term for "diamond."

Much literature has been written featuring Simple Simon, or characters noticeably like Simon, as a fool. In these poems and stories, Simon is often portrayed as a "wise fool," or someone who is judged as foolish by his society but who turns out to have insight or wisdom, usually revealing that something is wrong with his society's values. In the poem that you are about to read, the author draws upon the Simple Simon tradition to create a character who creates a fantastic garden only to long for an ordinary one again.

As You Read

"The Garden" tells about a special kind of garden. In your journal, make a chart like the one below. As you read, list the unusual fruits of the garden and the words and phrases the author uses to make these fruits seem similar to real fruits.

GARDEN FRUITS	WORDS AND PHRASES THAT MAKE THE FRUITS SEEM REAL
diamonds	planted
sapphires and rubies	on ivory vines

AS YOU READ

Students may include the following fruits and details in their charts: jade/grapes of jade ripen in the shade; amethyst/crow nibbles on it; platinum/weeds; pink pearl/berries to be put in a bushel and hauled into town; opal/nuts up in a tree; silver/potato; emerald/tomato; and coral/melons hanging in reach.

READER'S JOURNAL

Imagine that you are given magical seeds that will grow into anything you want. What would you want to grow? Be imaginative. Would you be satisfied with your garden? What do you think other people would think of it?

"The Garden"

SHEL SILVERSTEIN

Ol' man Simon, planted a diamond,
Grew hisself a garden the likes of none.
Sprouts all growin', comin' up glowin',
Fruit of jewels all shinin' in the sun.
Colors of the rainbow,
See the sun and rain grow
Sapphires[1] and rubies[2] on ivory[3] vines,
Grapes of jade,[4] just
Ripenin' in the shade, just
Ready for the squeezin' into green jade wine.
Pure gold corn there,
Blowin' in the warm air,
Ol' crow nibblin' on the amnythyst[5] seeds.
In between the diamonds, ol' man Simon
Crawls about pullin' out platinum[6] weeds.
Pink pearl berries,
All you can carry,
Put 'em in a bushel and

1 What unusual type of garden does Simon grow?

2 What type of weeds grow in this garden?

1. **sapphires.** Clear, deep blue precious stones
2. **rubies.** Clear, deep red precious stones
3. **ivory.** Hard, white substance that makes up the tusks of elephants
4. **jade.** Hard, greenish gemstone used in jewelry
5. **amnythyst.** Misspelling of amethyst, purple gemstone
6. **platinum.** Silvery precious metal

WORDS FOR EVERYDAY USE

bush • el (bo͞osh´əl) *n.,* unit of measure for grain or fruit

READER'S JOURNAL

As an alternative activity, you might ask students if they have ever planted a real garden. Did they enjoy working in a garden? Why, or why not? Did they enjoy the fruits of their labors?

SPELLING AND VOCABULARY WORDS FROM THE SELECTION

bushel

ANSWERS TO GUIDED READING QUESTIONS

1 Simon grows a garden of jewels.

2 Platinum weeds, or weeds of precious metal grow in Simon's garden.

SUPPORT FOR LEP STUDENTS

ADDITIONAL VOCABULARY

'em—them
hisself—himself
ol'—old

VOCABULARY IN CONTEXT

- We picked a bushel of apples and used them all for pies.

CROSS-CURRICULAR ACTIVITIES

ART

There are many vivid images of the things that grow in Simon's garden. Have students draw, paint, or create models of Simon's garden. Students might also draw or paint pictures of the imaginative gardens they described in the Reader's Journal activity.

ANSWER TO GUIDED READING QUESTION

❶ Simon dreams of a real peach. He is not satisfied with the jewels that surround him. He would like a nice piece of fruit to eat.

SELECTION CHECK TEST WITH ANSWERS

EX. What are the fruits in Simon's garden made of?
The fruits are made of jewels.

1. What kind of jewels are ready for squeezing?
Grapes of jade are ready for squeezing.

2. What does the crow nibble?
The crow nibbles on amethyst seeds.

3. What kind of weeds does Simon pull?
He pulls platinum weeds.

4. What grows in the trees?
Opal nuts and gold pears grow in the trees.

5. What does Simon dream about while working in his garden?
He dreams of one real peach.

Haul 'em into town.
Up in the tree there's
Opal[7] nuts and gold pears—
Hurry quick, grab a stick
And shake some down.
Take a silver tater,[8]
Emerald[9] tomater,
Fresh plump coral[10] melons
Hangin' in reach.
Ol' man Simon,
Diggin' in his diamonds,
Stops and rests and dreams about
One . . . real . . . peach. ■

❶ *What does Simon dream about while digging?*

7. **opal.** Milky white stone that reflects light
8. **tater.** Potato
9. **emerald.** Green precious stone
10. **coral.** Colorful, bony deposits that form in tropical seas. The pink or red variety is often harvested and used in jewelry.

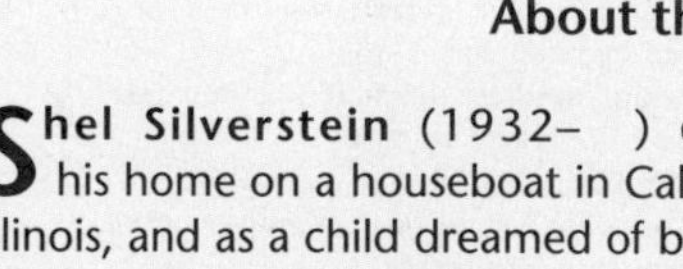

About the Author

Shel Silverstein (1932–) enjoys traveling and makes his home on a houseboat in California. He was born in Chicago, Illinois, and as a child dreamed of becoming a basketball player or a dancer. Instead, his talents led him to write stories, poems, and songs and to draw cartoons. Many of his books, such as *Where the Sidewalk Ends, A Light in the Attic,* and *The Giving Tree,* are popular with both adults and children.

Responding to the Selection

What do you think about Simon's garden? How would you feel if it were your garden? What would you do with your harvest?

Reviewing the Selection

RECALLING AND INTERPRETING

1. **R** What does Simon do to begin his garden? What do the sun and rain do for the garden?

   I What makes this garden seem more beautiful than an ordinary garden at first?

2. **R** What does Simon do with his grapes of jade? What do the crows do?

   I In what ways is this garden like a real garden?

3. **R** What does Simon do with the pink pearl berries? What does the speaker tell the reader to take?

   I Why might Simon do this? Do you suppose Simon would share willingly?

4. **R** What does Simon dream about while "diggin' in his diamonds"?

   I Why might he dream about this thing?

SYNTHESIZING

5. What message do you see in this poem about worldly riches? about human nature? Does it seem that Simon has everything he could desire? Why is he not satisfied? In what ways might real fruit be better than golden or jeweled fruit?

Understanding Literature (Questions for Discussion)

1. **Image.** An **image** is language that describes something that can be seen, heard, touched, tasted, or smelled. In this poem, the garden is described with vivid images. To which senses do the images appeal? To which senses do the images not appeal? Think about the subject of the poem. Can you explain why the author chose to have his images appeal to some senses and not to others?
2. **Irony of Situation.** An event that contradicts the expectations of the characters, the reader, or the audience of a literary work is an example of **irony of situation**. The last two lines of the poem stand out from the rest. What is the irony in these lines? In what way do they contradict your expectations as a reader?

RESPONDING TO THE SELECTION

Simon dreams of a real peach while working in his garden. Ask students what they might dream about if they own Simon's garden.

ANSWERS FOR REVIEWING THE SELECTION

RECALLING AND INTERPRETING

1. **Recalling.** Simon plants a diamond. The sun and rain make the garden grow and shine. **Interpreting.** *Responses will vary.* The fruits are gleaming in the sun. The colors of the fruits are brilliant and show all the colors of the rainbow.

2. **Recalling.** Simon squeezes his grapes of jade to make jade wine. The crows nibble on amethyst seeds. **Interpreting.** *Responses will vary.* The garden is real in that it produces a crop, it has pests that eat the crops, and it has weeds that must be plucked out.

3. **Recalling.** Simon puts the pink pearl berries in a bushel basket and takes them to town. The speaker tells the reader to take opal nuts and gold pears. **Interpreting.** *Responses will vary.* Simon takes the berries to town to sell them.

4. **Recalling.** He dreams of one real peach. **Interpreting.** *Responses will vary.* Simon might dream of a peach because he is working hard yet his labors give him nothing to eat. A peach would taste good after his efforts in the garden. Although his garden is full of riches, it is unable to sustain him.

SYNTHESIZING

Responses will vary. Possible responses are given.

5. Worldly riches do not grant happiness or contentment. It is human nature to want what you do not have. Simon has great riches and a beautiful garden, yet he dreams of what he does not have. Real fruit satisfies the human need to eat.

ANSWERS FOR UNDERSTANDING LITERATURE

Responses will vary. Possible responses are given.

1. **Image.** The images appeal mainly to the sense of sight. Because of all the fruits mentioned, there should be more images that appeal to the sense of taste. The author probably chose not to include images of taste because the fruits of the garden are jewels, so they are not edible.

2. **Irony of Situation.** It seems that Simon has the garden he has dreamed of creating. He has untold riches growing there. The reader might expect that Simon would be satisfied or happy with his garden, yet Simon is not content. The last two lines of the poem surprise the reader, because they contradict the expectations created in the earlier part of the poem.

GOALS/OBJECTIVES

Studying this lesson will enable students to

- enjoy a poem about fairies
- recognize the influence of folklore on a poem
- define *refrain* and identify a refrain in a poem
- discuss the effect of repetition

ADDITIONAL RESOURCES

Reader's Guide

- Selection Worksheet, 9.2

Assessment Portfolio

- Selection Check Test, 2.9.3
- Selection Test, 2.9.4

Pronunciation Exercise

- Grade 8 Audiocassette, Side B, Track 46

CROSS-CURRICULAR CONNECTIONS

World History

Have students work in three groups to research the following topics: William Butler Yeats's life; the geography, climate, and history of county Sligo, Ireland; and Irish folklore. Each group can present its findings to the rest of the class. Students might present their information as oral reports with visual aids such as maps or pictures, in an informative bulletin board, or in a short skit.

Prereading

IMAGERY

"The Stolen Child"

by W. B. Yeats

Cross-curricular Connection

World History. William Butler Yeats was born in Ireland. As he was growing up he often spent his holidays in the county of Sligo, Ireland. One of Yeats's ancestors in Sligo was rector, or minister, of a church that stood near Ben Bulben Mountain, where the *sidhe*, or *sid*, were believed to make their home.

According to Irish folk tradition, the *sidhe* were "little people," or fairies, who made their homes under mounds of earth. The belief in *sidhe* is related to an earlier belief in a race of gods called the Tuatha De Danann who were conquered by another race of gods and then were forced to establish kingdoms under the earth. Folk tradition held that, like the Tuatha De Danann, the *sidhe* worked magic and lived in rich underground kingdoms full of gold and jewels. The *sidhe* could emerge from their mounds, usually at night, and interact with humans in both positive and mischievous or cruel ways. A few humans could visit the underground kingdoms of the *sidhe,* but once there it was difficult to return to the human world, except for short visits on horseback or by boat. If a human who had been to the kingdom of the *sidhe* touched the earth of the human world, he or she would turn to dust.

Yeats was intrigued by Irish folklore and mythology and it influenced much of his writing. In the selection you are about to read a "faery" tries to lure a child away to the fairy world. Yeats may have had in mind stories about the *sidhe* that he heard in Sligo as a young person.

As You Read

"**The Stolen Child**" is a poem about fairies. In your journal, make a chart like the one below. As you read, record in the left column details that describe what the fairies do and how fairies live. In the right column, write what each detail makes you think about the fairies as a group.

Fairies' Actions and Activities	My Opinion of the Fairies
they steal cherries and berries and hide them in vats	they are sneaky, secretive, and mysterious

AS YOU READ

Students may include the following actions of the fairies in their charts: Fairies tell human child to come away; they dance in the moonlight; they chase bubbles while the world is troubled; they seek trout, and whisper things that give the trout bad dreams; they lure the child away from the earthly world of humans. Students' opinions for each fairy action may vary. Possible responses to the fairies include: they are mean spirited, they are devious, they are light-hearted and uncaring of others.

READER'S JOURNAL

In your early childhood, what happened when you lost a tooth? Did you ever get a visit from the sandman in your sleep? What imaginary, fairy-like creatures do you remember from your childhood? Describe them. When did you stop believing in such creatures? Why? Write about these questions in your journal.

"The Stolen Child"

W. B. YEATS

Where dips the rocky highland
Of Sleuth Wood in the lake,
There lies a leafy island
Where flapping herons[1] wake
The drowsy water-rats;
There we've hid our faery vats,
Full of berries
And of reddest stolen cherries.
Come away, O human child!
To the waters and the wild
With a faery, hand in hand,
For the world's more full of weeping than you
can understand.

Where the wave of moonlight glosses
The dim grey sands with light,
Far off by furthest Rosses
We foot it all the night,
Weaving olden dances,
Mingling hands and mingling glances
Till the moon has taken flight;
To and fro we leap
And chase the frothy bubbles,
While the world is full of troubles
And is anxious in its sleep.
Come away, O human child!
To the waters and the wild
With a faery, hand in hand,
For the world's more full of weeping than you
can understand.

1. **heron.** Wading bird with a long neck, long legs, and a long, tapered bill that lives along marshes and riverbanks

❶ *Who is the speaker of this poem? What does the speaker ask the human child to do? Why?*

❷ *What do the speaker and his or her companions do all night? What does the world do?*

READER'S JOURNAL

Ask students to classify the fairy-like creatures they know as good or bad. Were they frightened or delighted by the fairies? Why might these ideas of fairies have been created?

SPELLING AND VOCABULARY WORDS FROM THE SELECTION

low
solemn
scarce

ANSWERS TO GUIDED READING QUESTIONS

❶ The speaker is a fairy. The fairy asks the human child to leave the world and go with the fairy to the fairies' land.

❷ The speaker and his or her companions dance in the moonlight while the world lies troubled in anxious sleep.

SUPPORT FOR LEP STUDENTS

PRONUNCIATIONS OF PROPER NOUNS AND ADJECTIVES

Glen • Car (glen kär) n.
Sleuth Wood (sloo͞th wo͝od) n.

ADDITIONAL VOCABULARY

anxious—full or fear or worry
foot—dance, walk, or run
rushes—thick-stemmed plants that grow in wet places
vats—large container

Literary Note

If students have not already done so, you may wish to have them read Yeats's "The Song of the Wandering Aengus," which appears in Unit 2 of this text.

Answers to Guided Reading Questions

❶ The speaker and his or her companions whisper in the ears of sleeping trout and cause them to have bad dreams.

❷ The child follows the fairy. He will never again hear the lowing of the calves or the kettle on the hob, and he will never again see the brown mice bob around the oatmeal chest.

Selection Check Test with Answers

EX. What do the fairies tell the human child to do?
They tell the human child to come away.

1. How did the fairies get their cherries?
The fairies stole the cherries.

2. What do the fairies do until the moon has taken flight?
The fairies dance.

3. What reason do the fairies give the child for coming away with them?
The fairies say the world is more full of weeping than the child can understand.

4. What do the fairies do to the trout?
The fairies whisper things in the ears of the trout that disturb their dreams.

5. What words are used to describe the child?
The human child is described as solemn-eyed.

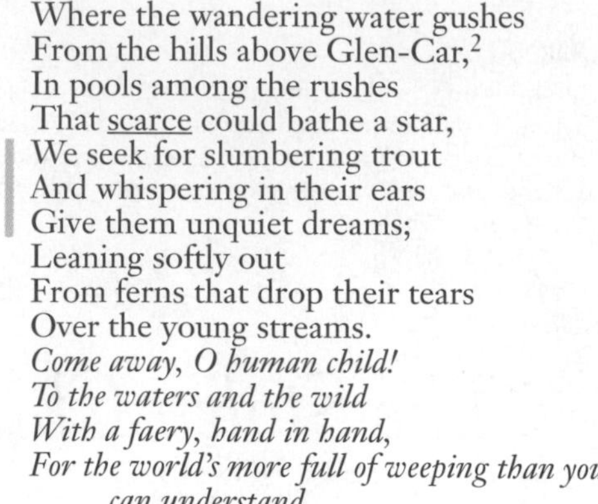

Where the wandering water gushes
From the hills above Glen-Car,[2]
In pools among the rushes
That scarce could bathe a star,
We seek for slumbering trout
And whispering in their ears
Give them unquiet dreams;
Leaning softly out
From ferns that drop their tears
Over the young streams.
Come away, O human child!
To the waters and the wild
With a faery, hand in hand,
For the world's more full of weeping than you can understand.

Away with us he's going,
The solemn-eyed:
He'll hear no more the lowing
Of the calves on the warm hillside
Or the kettle on the hob[3]
Sing peace into his breast,
Or see the brown mice bob
Round and round the oatmeal-chest.
For he comes, the human child,
To the waters and the wild
With a faery, hand in hand,
From a world more full of weeping than he can understand. ■

❶ *What do the speaker and his or her companions do to the sleeping trout?*

❷ *What does the child do? What will he never experience again?*

2. **Glen-Car.** Valley in Scotland
3. **hob.** Shelf by the fireplace or stove

About the Author

William Butler (W. B.) Yeats (1865–1939) was an Irish poet and dramatist who won the Nobel Prize for literature in 1923. Yeats was born in Dublin and lived in London during his childhood. He also made frequent visits to the countryside of Sligo, Ireland, where he absorbed Irish folklore and legend. Many of Yeats's early poems reveal his love for traditional Irish legends and myths. Yeats was a leader in the Irish Literary Revival, a movement that helped rekindle the Irish culture by encouraging Irish authors.

Words for Everyday Use

scarce (skers) *adv.,* hardly
sol • emn (säl´əm) *adj.,* serious
low (lō) *v.,* moo; make the sound of a cow

Vocabulary in Context

- Tara could scarce believe her eyes when she saw snow on the ground during the first week of June.
- The solemn silence at the table could not stop Chandler from telling his new joke.
- We heard the low of a cow and the bark of a dog as we drove down the country lane.

Responding to the Selection

What do you think about the fairies in "The Stolen Child"? If you were the child in the poem, would you have wanted to go with the fairies? What do you find appealing about the fairy world? What do you find unappealing about the fairy world?

Reviewing the Selection

Recalling and Interpreting

1. **R** Where have the fairies hidden their vat of cherries? How did they get the cherries?
   I What do the hidden cherries reveal about the fairies' characters?
2. **R** What do the fairies do until the "moon has taken flight"?
   I What is appealing about the fairy world?
3. **R** What do the fairies do to slumbering trout?
   I What does this action reveal about the nature of the fairies? Are they trustworthy or untrustworthy?
4. **R** What does the human child do? What will the human child see and hear no more?
   I What does the fact that the child is "solemn-eyed" reveal about his feelings about the fairies and their world?

Synthesizing

5. Why does the child go with the fairies in the end? Have the fairies carried off the child? Have they mesmerized or hypnotized the child? Does the child go with them of his own free will? Do you think that the child is going to a better world or a worse one? Explain your answers, basing your response on evidence in the poem.

Understanding Literature (Questions for Discussion)

Refrain and Repetition. A **refrain** is one or more lines repeated in a poem or song. **Repetition** is the use, again, of a sound, word, or group of words. What refrain recurs in each stanza of the poem? In what way is this refrain changed in the final stanza of the poem? Why is the refrain changed in this stanza? What attitude is expressed in the refrain toward the fairy world? toward the human world? What word is repeated at the beginning of the first three stanzas? What word opens the last stanza? Why do you think the poet made this change in his final stanza?

Responding to the Selection

Ask students why they think the fairies wanted to have the children come to their world. What do they think will happen to the child there?

Answers for Reviewing the Selection

RECALLING AND INTERPRETING

1. **Recalling.** They have hidden the vat on a leafy island in a lake in Sleuth Wood. They stole the cherries. **Interpreting.** *Responses will vary.* The hidden cherries reveal that the fairies think nothing of taking what does not belong to them.
2. **Recalling.** They dance. **Interpreting.** *Responses will vary.* The fairies' world is mysterious and lacks anxiety.
3. **Recalling.** The fairies whisper things in the ears of trout and disturb their dreams. **Interpreting.** *Responses will vary.* The action shows that the fairies are mischievous or even mean spirited. The fairies are untrustworthy.
4. **Recalling.** The human child goes with the fairies to the fairies' world. The child will never again hear "the lowing/Of the calves" or "the kettle on the hob," and he will never again see the brown mice bob around the oatmeal chest. **Interpreting.** *Responses will vary.* The child is very serious about where he is going. He does not act as if he is going to a wondrous place.

SYNTHESIZING

Responses will vary. Possible responses are given.

5. The child may be mesmerized by the fairies, or lulled into a half-asleep state to follow them. The world the child leaves is a troubled one, but the actions of the fairies do not suggest that they are the kindest creatures with whom the child could live. The child may also miss things from his life in the human world.

Answers for Understanding Literature

Responses will vary. Possible responses are given.

Refrain and Repetition. The refrain is *"Come away, O human child!/To the waters and the wild/With a faery, hand in hand,/For the world's more full of weeping than you can understand."* In the first three stanzas, the refrain addresses the child. In the last stanza the refrain speaks of the child in the third person. The child is coming with the fairies, and the fairies announce that their calls to the child have been heeded. The fairy land is a wild place free of the weeping of the human world. The human world is a place of unhappiness. In the final stanza, the refrain begins with the words "For he comes" instead of "Come away." The words of the refrain are changed in the final stanza because the child has decided to go with the fairies.

GOALS/OBJECTIVES

Studying this lesson will enable students to

- enjoy two poems rich in images
- recount major events in the development of Japanese literature
- identify relationships
- describe the speakers of the poems

ADDITIONAL RESOURCES

READER'S GUIDE

- Selection Worksheet, 9.3

ASSESSMENT PORTFOLIO

- Selection Check Test, 2.9.5
- Selection Test, 2.9.6

PRONUNCIATION EXERCISE

- Grade 8 Audiocassette, Side B, Track 47

CROSS-CURRICULAR CONNECTIONS

SOCIAL STUDIES

If possible, have somebody who speaks and writes Japanese visit your class to discuss Japanese language and writing. Show your students examples of Japanese writing. Discuss the role of the translator in the version of these works that your students are reading.

Prereading

IMAGERY

"I do not consider . . ."

by Kujō Takeko, translated by Kenneth Rexroth and Ikuko Atsumi

"Everyone is asleep"

by Enomoto Seifu-Jo, translated by Kenneth Rexroth and Ikuko Atsumi

Cross-curricular Connection

Social Studies. Before the tenth century, Japan did not have a written language of its own. Chinese characters were used to represent ideas or sounds, but Japanese is a vastly different language from Chinese. During the tenth century, two systems of writing Japanese were developed. The two types of script are *hiragana* and *katakana.* Both forms were based on Chinese but were adapted to meet the different needs of people writing in Japanese. Each system includes fifty major characters and over one hundred symbols in all. Each character represents a syllable, all but one ending in a vowel.

The introduction of *hiragana* ushered in one of the greatest periods for women writers in Japan because Japanese women had not traditionally learned Chinese characters. Hiragana was sometimes called "women's writing." One of the important early works of this period is Murasaki Shikibu's *The Tale of Genji,* often considered the first novel. Poetry was further developed in this period as well. The major forms were waka, also called tanka, and later haiku.

Modern written Japanese consists of *Kanji,* characters that represent concepts; *hiragana,* used to spell out words that are originally Japanese; and *katakana,* used for young children and to spell out words derived from other languages.

As You Read

Both **"I do not consider . . ."** and **"Everyone is asleep"** deal with the relationship between an individual and society, as well as with the relationship between an individual and nature. In your journal, make a chart like the one below. As you read, make notes about these relationships in the chart.

	"I do not consider . . ."	"Everyone is asleep"
Society	individual sometimes seems insignificant	
Nature		

AS YOU READ

Students may include the following notes about the relationships in "I do not consider": heaven and earth are sometimes too small for the speaker. Students may include the following notes about the relationships in "Everyone is asleep": the speaker enjoys time away from other people, and the speaker has a close relationship with nature as seen by the speaker's enjoyment of time alone with the moon.

READER'S JOURNAL

Have you ever felt that people expected too much of you? that you don't get to decide enough things for yourself? If you had the freedom to decide, what would you do differently? What keeps you from doing those things differently? Write about these questions in your journal.

"I do not consider . . ."

KUJŌ TAKEKO

I do not consider myself worth counting,
but sometimes even for me
heaven and earth are too small. ■

1 How does the speaker feel about himself or herself?

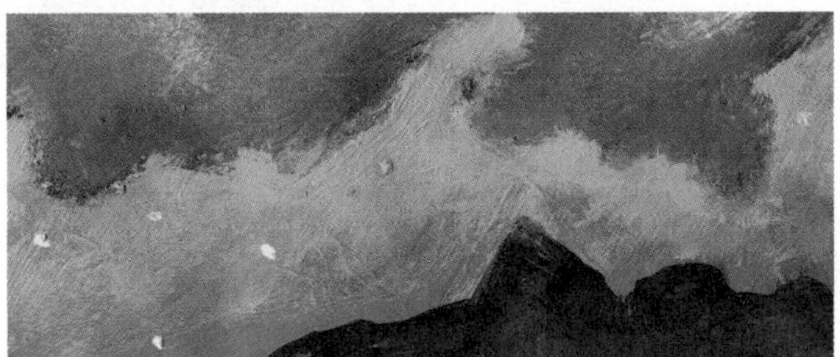

READER'S JOURNAL

As an alternative activity, ask students whether they think the world is large or small. How do they think they fit into the world? How do they feel they fit in with other people in the world?

ANSWER TO GUIDED READING QUESTION

1 The speaker sometimes feels that he or she is insignificant, but at times, the speaker is confined by the size of the world.

SUPPORT FOR LEP STUDENTS

PRONUNCIATIONS OF PROPER NOUNS AND ADJECTIVES

Ku • jō Ta • ke • ko (kōō jō tä keh kō) n.

E • no • mo • to Sei • fu - Jo (eh nō mō tō sā fōō jō) n.

Note: Most syllables in the Japanese language are given equal emphasis.

ADDITIONAL VOCABULARY

consider—regard as; believe

Answer to Guided Reading Question

❶ The speaker enjoys being the only person awake and having time to himself or herself with the moon.

Selection Check Test with Answers

EX. Who is the author of "Everyone is asleep"?
Enomoto Seifu-Jo is the author of "Everyone is asleep."

1. What does the speaker of "I do not consider . . . " think of himself or herself?
The speaker does not consider himself or herself worth counting.

2. What are sometimes too small for the speaker?
Heaven and earth are sometimes too small for the speaker.

3. When is the poem by Seifu-Jo set?
It is set at night.

4. Who is asleep?
Everyone except the speaker is asleep.

5. What comes between the speaker and the moon?
Nothing comes between the speaker and the moon.

Biographical Note

Kobayashi Issa (1763–1827) was born in a small village in the mountains of Japan. He was raised by his grandmother. Issa's poetry is filled with images of tiny creatures, especially mice, lice, fleas, and ticks. These subjects are the result of his close observations of his natural surroundings.

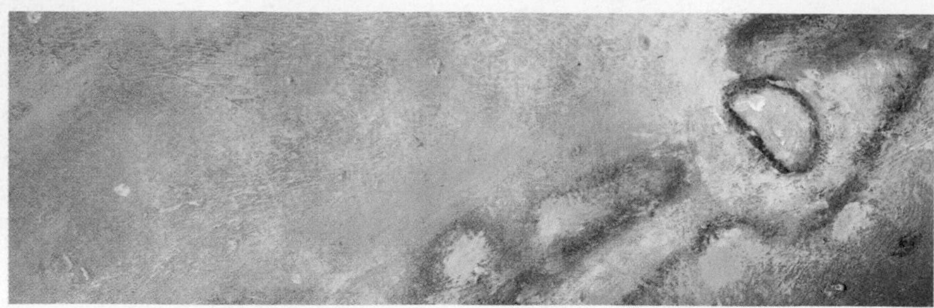

"Everyone is asleep"

Enomoto Seifu-Jo

Q ❶ *How does the speaker feel about being the only person awake?*

Everyone is asleep
There is nothing to come between the moon and me. ■

About the Authors

Kujo Takeko (1877–1928) was the daughter of an abbot, the head of a group of monks, at a temple in Kyoto. She married at age twenty-two and traveled with her husband, a diplomat, to Europe. She returned to Japan and lived alone until her husband returned. Loneliness is a major theme in many of her poems.

Enomoto Seifu-Jo (1731–1814) was a haiku poet who studied under the poet Shiro, a follower of Issa, one of the great haiku artists.

Responding to the Selection

How do you feel about your own relationship to society? to nature? Do you agree with the feelings expressed by either speaker? Explain.

Reviewing the Selection

Recalling and Interpreting

1. **R** What places does the speaker say are sometimes too small in "I do not consider . . . "?

   I How could places like this be too small for a single human being?

2. **R** What does the speaker say happens when everyone is asleep?

   I What impression do you get of the speaker's life when everyone is not asleep?

Synthesizing

3. What is the main idea or feeling expressed by each speaker? Are the two themes similar? Explain.

Understanding Literature (Questions for Discussion)

Speaker. The **speaker** is the voice that speaks, or narrates, the poem. How do you think each speaker feels about himself or herself? What words might each speaker use to describe his or her life?

Responding to the Selection

Ask students what role they think nature should play in the lives of humans. Should nature be an important influence in our lives? in what ways?

Answers for Reviewing the Selection

RECALLING AND INTERPRETING

1. **Recalling.** The speaker says that even heaven and earth can be too small. **Interpreting.** *Responses will vary.* The speaker may feel confined by his or her life or by the people who surround him or her. If the speaker is unable to find relief from these feelings, he or she may feel that the world needs to be bigger.

2. **Recalling.** The speaker says that there is no one to come between him or her and the moon. **Interpreting.** *Responses will vary.* The speaker often has to face the demands of others. The speaker does not often have time to himself or herself.

SYNTHESIZING

Responses will vary. Possible responses are given.

3. The speaker of "I do not consider . . . " suggests that the world can be too small. The speaker of "Everyone is asleep" suggests that people can interfere with the connection between himself or herself and nature. Both selections suggest that people need to have time and space to themselves.

Answers for Understanding Literature

Responses will vary. Possible responses are given.

Speaker. The speaker of "I do not consider . . . " has mixed feelings about himself or herself. The speaker often finds himself or herself insignificant, or not "worth counting." Other times, the speaker feels that he or she is too much for heaven and earth. The speaker might describe his or her life as insignificant, unworthy, or confining. The speaker in "Everyone is asleep" thinks he or she deserves time to be alone. The speaker enjoys solitude though he or she does not often experience it. The speaker might describe his or her life as hectic, dedicated to others, or overwhelming.

Language Lab

Introducing the Skill

Remind students that a sentence expresses a complete thought and includes a subject and a verb. Discuss the difference between active and passive voice.

Previewing the Skill

Students should read the material about editing sentences. Respond to any question students may have about editing sentences.

Practicing the Skill

Have students complete the Try It Yourself exercise. Students can also practice this skill by editing a writing assignment for errors in sentences.

Reviewing the Skill

Review the answers to the Try It Yourself exercise. If students need more practice, refer them to the exercises in the Language Arts Survey, 2.12, "Correcting Sentence Fragments and Run-ons," 2.13, "Correcting Wordy Sentences," and 2.14, "Correcting Passive Sentences."

Language Lab

Editing Sentences

Run-ons and sentence fragments are common errors made in writing, especially during a first draft. These errors can cause confusion for readers. Editing to correct run-ons and sentence fragments will help make your writing clear for your readers.

A sentence should express a complete thought and contain both a subject and a verb. A sentence fragment is a phrase or clause that does not express a complete thought but is punctuated as if it did.

INCORRECT Running a health club.
My aunt June, the former mayor of our town.

To correct a fragment, you must first identify the part of the sentence that is missing. Then add the missing part, either a subject or a predicate, to make the sentence complete, or attach the fragment to another related sentence.

CORRECT Running a health club is a rewarding job for Alexi.
My aunt June, the former mayor of our town, is now running a health club.

A run-on is formed by two or more sentences written as if they were one complete thought.

INCORRECT I should be able to finish my homework I plan on going to the game when I'm done.
It is difficult to study at my house I go to the library.
The library is a quiet place to work there are no distractions.

To correct a run-on, use end punctuation to separate the sentences, or join the two related sentences by using a conjunction and a comma, or a semicolon.

CORRECT WITH END PUNCTUATION	I should be able to finish my homework. I plan on gong to the game when I'm done.
CORRECT WITH A COMMA AND CONJUNCTION	It is difficult to study at my house, so I go to the library.
CORRECT WITH A SEMICOLON	The library is a quiet place to work; there are no distractions.

Try It Yourself

On your own paper, rewrite the following run-ons and sentence fragments as properly punctuated sentences.

EXAMPLE: There is an exhibit of Asian art at the museum do you want to see it?
There is an exhibit of Asian art at the museum. Do you want to see it?

1. The exhibit includes mainly Chinese and Japanese paintings. Including many ancient anonymous works.
2. Chinese painting focused on nature, Japanese painting often focused on nature because it was influenced by Chinese painting.
3. Paintings of birds, flowers, sea, and sky.
4. The Chinese believed that inner harmony and balance existed among all things. That humans and nature were closely related.
5. For many years. Japanese art imitated this tradition.
6. The brush strokes in Chinese paintings have always been delicate and light Chinese painting was related to calligraphy, the art of fine handwriting.
7. This quality also applied to Japanese painting. Until the fourteenth century.
8. Around 1300 AD, Japanese painters began to paint things from their surroundings other than nature they were able to express different ideas about the time and places in which they lived.
9. The use of color. Styles began to emphasize new aspects of painting.
10. Between 1500 and 1800, Japanese painters were called decorators. Because they focused on color and design.

Answers for Try It Yourself

1. The exhibit includes mainly Chinese and Japanese paintings, many of which are ancient, anonymous works.
2. Chinese painting focused on nature. Japanese painting often focused on nature because it was influenced by Chinese painting.
3. In the exhibit, there are many paintings of birds, flowers, sea, and sky.
4. The Chinese believed that inner harmony and balance existed among all things and that humans and nature were closely related.
5. For many years, Japanese art imitated this tradition.
6. The brush strokes of Chinese painting have always been delicate and light, because Chinese painting was related to calligraphy, the art of fine handwriting.
7. Until the fourteenth century, this quality also applied to Japanese painting.
8. Around 1300 AD, Japanese painters began to paint things from their surroundings other than nature. They were able to express different ideas about the time and places in which they lived.
9. Styles began to emphasize new aspects of painting, such as the use of color.
10. Between 1500 and 1800, Japanese painters were called decorators because they focused on color and design.

GOALS/OBJECTIVES

Studying this lesson will enable students to

- have a positive experience reading a lyric poem
- identify attributes and descriptions of the human brain
- make comparisons
- identify stanza types

ADDITIONAL RESOURCES

READER'S GUIDE

- Selection Worksheet, 9.4

ASSESSMENT PORTFOLIO

- Selection Check Test, 2.9.7
- Selection Test, 2.9.8

PRONUNCIATION EXERCISE

- Grade 8 Audiocassette, Side B, Track 48

CROSS-CURRICULAR CONNECTIONS

SCIENCE

- Have students draw maps of the three sections of the brain. If possible, obtain a model of the brain from the science department to show students the different parts.
- Memory is one of the least understood functions of the brain. Ask students to share some of their oldest or most striking memories. Why do they think they have retained these particular memories?

Prereading

FIGURATIVE LANGUAGE

"The Brain—is wider than the Sky—"

by Emily Dickinson

Cross-curricular Connection

Science. The human brain is the master control center of the human body. It receives and analyzes sensory information about conditions inside and outside the body and, responding to these conditions, sends signals that guide responses and actions. The brain stores vast amounts of information from past and present experience that enables human beings to learn and remember. Without such information-storage and processing abilities, humans could not have produced the thoughts, emotions, languages, music, and art that they have produced.

An adult human brain weighs about three pounds and consists of three main divisions: the cerebrum, which makes up about 85 percent of brain tissue; the cerebellum, which is located behind and below the cerebrum; and the brain stem, which connects the cerebrum to the spinal cord. Neurosurgeons have mapped brain functions into these three specific brain areas. The six primary brain functions are sending, receiving, and interpreting sensory messages; controlling body movements; language functions; controlling functions such as heartbeat and breathing; producing emotions; and thinking and remembering. Thinking and remembering constitute the most complex and least understood human brain functions. The cerebrum contains the circuitry that stores, retrieves, and connects the nerve impulses that combine information from the senses and memory to produce human thought.

As You Read

There are still many things we do not understand about the workings of the brain, but it is clear that the brain has astounding capabilities. Make a cluster chart like the one below. As you read **"The Brain—is wider than the Sky—"** fill in the chart with descriptions or attributes of the human brain.

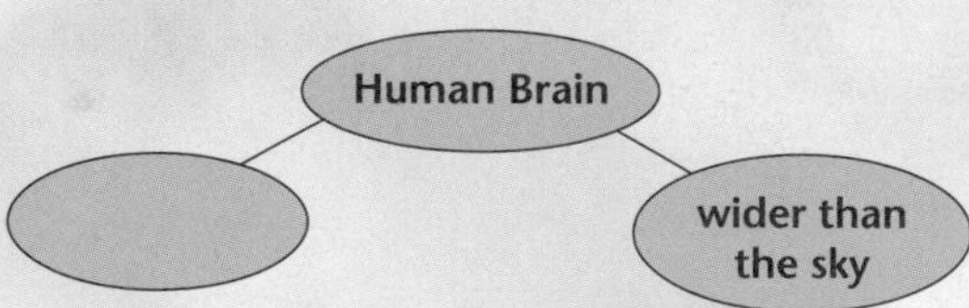

AS YOU READ

Students may include the following descriptions or attributes of the human brain in their cluster charts: can contain the sky; deeper than the sea; can absorb the sea; weight of God.

Ask students to add their own descriptions or attributes to the chart. Some of these may be scientific data about the human brain, information they can obtain from the Cross-curricular Connection material or from other sources; or functions of the brain.

READER'S JOURNAL

Think about the most immense or most powerful parts of nature. What is the biggest thing you can think of? the strongest? the heaviest? In your journal, describe these things and how they make you feel.

READER'S JOURNAL

Suggest to students that they think of natural features, such as oceans or mountains; creatures, such as whales; and forces, such as hurricanes, earthquakes, and tidal waves.

"The Brain—is wider than the Sky—"

EMILY DICKINSON

The Brain—is wider than the Sky—
For—put them side by side—
The one the other will contain
With ease—and You—beside—

The Brain is deeper than the sea—
For—hold them—Blue to Blue—
The one the other will absorb—
As Sponges—Buckets—do—

The Brain is just the weight of God—
For—Heft them—Pound for Pound—
And they will differ—if they do—
As Syllable from Sound— ■

❶ *What does the speaker claim about the brain in line 1? What evidence does the speaker provide to support this claim?*

❷ *What connection is there between a syllable and its sound? What is the speaker saying about the relationship between the Brain and God?*

SPELLING AND VOCABULARY WORDS FROM THE SELECTION

absorb heft

ANSWERS TO GUIDED READING QUESTIONS

❶ The speaker claims that the brain is wider than the sky. The speaker says that if you put them side by side the brain would contain the sky and you as well.

❷ A syllable is a sound. There is not a great difference between a syllable and a sound.

SUPPORT FOR LEP STUDENTS

ADDITIONAL VOCABULARY

syllable—word or part of a word consisting of a single sound

WORDS FOR EVERYDAY USE

ab • sorb (ab sôrb´) *v.,* soak up; take in

heft (heft) *v.,* lift; try to determine the weight of by lifting

VOCABULARY IN CONTEXT

- We used towels to absorb the puddles of water on the floor.
- If you heft the two bags, you will see that they are not too heavy.

SELECTION CHECK TEST WITH ANSWERS

EX. What does the speaker say about the brain in comparison with the sky?
The speaker says the brain is wider than the sky.

1. What will happen if you put the brain and the sky side by side?
The brain will contain the sky and you.

2. What does the speaker say about the brain in relation to the sea?
The brain is deeper than the sea.

3. What will happen if you hold the brain and the sea "Blue to Blue"?
The brain will absorb the sea.

4. What is the weight of the brain?
The brain is the "weight of God."

5. In what way do the weight of God and the brain differ?
They differ as syllable from sound.

About the Author

Emily Dickinson (1830–1886) is considered one of America's great poets. She was born and died in Amherst, Massachusetts, where she spent most of her life in seclusion. Dickinson wrote secretly; only seven of her poems were published while she was living, and those without her consent. After Dickinson's death, her sister discovered more than 1,700 poems that she had written. Four years later, the first book of Dickinson's poetry was published.

Responding to the Selection

What feelings does the speaker have toward the human brain? Do you share the speaker's feelings? Why, or why not?

Reviewing the Selection

RECALLING AND INTERPRETING

1. R Stanza 1 refers to the brain and the sky. Which would contain the other if they were laid side by side?

   I What does stanza 1 suggest about human beings and nature?

2. R What comparison is made between the brain and the sea in stanza 2?

   I What does this comparison suggest about the abilities of the brain?

3. R How does the speaker determine that the brain is equal to the weight of God?

   I Why is it impossible to compare the weights of the brain and of God?

4. R According to the speaker, in what way will the weight of the brain differ from the weight of God?

   I How does a syllable differ from a sound? What light does this difference cast on human beings?

SYNTHESIZING

5. What point does the speaker make by saying the brain differs from the weight of God no more than syllable differs from sound? What do you think this statement suggests about poetry itself?

Understanding Literature (Questions for Discussion)

Stanza. A **stanza** is a group of lines in a poem. Stanzas are usually separated by spaces from other groups of lines. A **couplet** is a two-line stanza. A **tercet** is a three-line stanza. A **quatrain** is a four-line stanza. Which type of stanza is used in this poem? What is the main idea presented in each stanza?

RESPONDING TO THE SELECTION

Ask students to come up with their own comparisons that demonstrate their feelings about the human brain and its powers.

ANSWERS FOR REVIEWING THE SELECTION

RECALLING AND INTERPRETING

1. **Recalling.** The brain would contain the sky. **Interpreting.** *Responses will vary.* Stanza 1 suggests that although humans seem to be a small part of nature, they have the ability to encompass all of nature.
2. **Recalling.** The brain is deeper than the sea. **Interpreting.** *Responses will vary.* The brain has unknown depth and ability to absorb things from the outside world.
3. **Recalling.** The speaker would heft the brain and God to determine their weights. **Interpreting.** *Responses will vary.* It impossible to hold God so it impossible to heft God. The physical brain can be weighed, but the human mind cannot be measured.
4. **Recalling.** The weight of the human brain and God will not differ, except as syllable differs from sound. **Interpreting.** *Responses will vary.* A syllable is a single sound. This difference suggests that human beings have many wonderful qualities.

SYNTHESIZING

Responses will vary. Possible responses are given.

5. There is little difference. The act of creating poetry becomes almost a divine act.

ANSWERS FOR UNDERSTANDING LITERATURE

Responses will vary. Possible responses are given.

Stanza. Quatrains are used in this poem. The main idea of the first stanza is that the brain is large enough to encompass many great things. The main idea of the second stanza is that the brain is able to absorb and understand many things. The main idea of the third stanza is that the human mind has amazing abilities.

GOALS/OBJECTIVES

Studying this lesson will enable students to

- enjoy an unconventional ode
- understand gift giving customs
- compare ordinary and extraordinary objects
- define *metaphor* and *simile*
- identify metaphors and similes
- give an oral interpretation

ADDITIONAL RESOURCES

Reader's Guide

- Selection Worksheet, 9.5

Assessment Portfolio

- Selection Check Test, 2.9.9
- Selection Test, 2.9.10

Pronunciation Exercise

- Grade 8 Audiocassette, Side B, Track 49

CROSS-CURRICULAR CONNECTIONS

Social Studies

Students can describe a gift they would like to give to someone. The gift can be a costly item, a homemade treasure, or an action on the part of the giver. If the gift is within the student's means, the student might decide to bestow his or her gift on the intended recipient.

Arts and Humanities

Ask student to write their own odes. Students might choose lofty subjects such as those of traditional odes, or they might choose simple subjects that have great meaning to them.

Prereading

FIGURATIVE LANGUAGE

"Ode to My Socks"

by Pablo Neruda

Cross-curricular Connections

Social Studies. One of the reasons that the speaker in the poem you are about to read takes so much delight in his socks is that they are a handmade gift, requiring much time and labor on the part of the giver. Gift-giving is an ancient custom that people have practiced all over the world. In modern American culture, people typically exchange or give gifts on certain holidays and birthdays. However, in other cultures, exchanging gifts is an important part of all social relationships.

In these cultures, although gift-giving is seen as voluntary, it is also a part of expected social behavior. Not accepting a gift may be seen as a social rejection. When giving a gift in return, one's prestige is enhanced if one gives a gift of equal or greater value.

Some cultures are almost entirely based upon gift-giving. The Native Americans of the Pacific Northwest practice a ceremonial distribution of gifts to affirm or reaffirm their social status. Known as potlatches, these ceremonial events involve giving away numerous gifts and holding elaborate feasts. A potlatch may be held for important events, but they are often held for trivial reasons because their purpose is mainly to enhance social status. The potlatch can be so costly that individuals essentially bankrupt themselves by giving elaborate gifts.

Arts and Humanities. An ode is a lofty lyric poem on a serious theme. The first odes were parts of ancient Greek dramatic poetry that were meant to be sung by a chorus. Modern odes are rhymed and are usually written as an address to someone or something. Two of the most famous odes are John Keats's "Ode on a Grecian Urn," which discusses art, love, beauty, and truth, and Percy Bysshe Shelley's "Ode to the West Wind," which discusses the power of nature and human hopes and creativity. Pablo Neruda's odes are like traditional odes in that they are long lyrical poems. Like traditional odes, Neruda's odes also exalt their subject matter. Their shape on the page, however, is unconventional, and they are not written in a lofty style.

As You Read

In **"Ode to My Socks,"** many ordinary objects and events are compared to more fantastic ones. In your journal, make a chart like the one below. As you read, write down the ordinary objects and events in the poem. Then describe the extraordinary images that the poet uses to transform these ordinary objects and events.

ORDINARY OBJECT AND EVENT	EXTRAORDINARY IMAGES
socks	jewel cases woven with threads of dusk and sheep's wool

AS YOU READ

Students may include the following comparisons between ordinary objects and events, and extraordinary objects and events: feet became fish, long sharks, two mammoth black birds, two cannons, tired old firefighters; save socks as students save fireflies, scholars save sacred documents; save socks by placing them in a cage of gold and feeding them birdseed and melon; surrender feet to socks as explorers surrender a rare and tender deer to the spit.

Reader's Journal

What gifts have you received that you really love? Did you love the gift immediately, or did your love for it grow over time? Did you ever love something so much that you could not bring yourself to wear it or use it? What happened? Write about these questions in your journal.

"Ode to My Socks"

Pablo Neruda

Maru Mori brought me
a pair
of socks
knitted with her own
shepherd's hands,
two socks soft
as rabbits.
I slipped
my feet into them
as if
into
jewel cases
woven
with threads of
dusk
and sheep's wool.

Audacious socks,
my feet became
two woolen
fish,
two long sharks
of lapis blue

❶ *What makes these socks special?*

❷ *In what way does wearing the socks transform the speaker's feet?*

Words for Everyday Use

au • da • cious (ô dā´shəs) *adj.*, bold or daring
lap • is (lā´pis) *n.*, blue, semiprecious stone

Reader's Journal

As an alternative activity, students might describe a gift they gave to someone. Ask students why they chose the gift for the recipient and how the recipient reacted to the gift.

Spelling and Vocabulary Words from the Selection

audacious	luminous
celestial	mammoth
hoard	ode
impulse	remorse
lapis	sacred

Answers to Guided Reading Questions

❶ The socks were knit by Maru Mori with her own hands.

❷ The bold socks turn the speaker's feet into woolen fish or sharks. The speaker imagines all kinds of things about his feet in the new socks.

Support for LEP Students

Pronunciations of Proper Nouns and Adjectives

Ma • ru Mo • ri (mä´ ro͞o mō´ rē) n.

Additional Vocabulary

spit—thin, pointed rod on which meat is roasted over an open fire
surrender—give over to

Vocabulary in Context

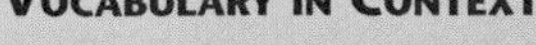

- Everyone was stunned by Pablo's audacious actions.
- The blue stone in the ring is lapis.

Additional Questions and Activities

Ask students to describe their favorite piece of clothing. What does it look like? What does it feel like? How do they feel when wearing this article of clothing? Is it practical? Is it warm or protective? Does it allow for easy movement? Do students worry about keeping this clothing clean? How would they feel if this item of clothing was destroyed or outgrown? Is the clothing something that will go out of style or is it something that reflects the student's own personal style?

shot
with a golden thread,
two <u>mammoth</u> blackbirds,
two cannons,
thus honored
were
my feet
by
these
<u>celestial</u>
socks.
They were
so beautiful
that for the first time
my feet seemed
unacceptable to me,
two tired old
fire fighters
not worthy
of the woven
fire
of those <u>luminous</u>
socks.

Nonetheless,
I resisted
the strong temptation
to save them
the way schoolboys
bottle
fireflies,
the way scholars
<u>hoard</u>
<u>sacred</u> documents.
I resisted
the wild <u>impulse</u>
to place them
in a cage
of gold
and daily feed them
birdseed

❶ *What do the socks make the speaker think of his feet?*

❷ *What temptation did the speaker have to resist?*

Words for Everyday Use

mam • moth (mam´əth) *adj.*, very big
ce • les • tial (sə les´chəl) *adj.*, of the highest kind; perfect
lu • mi • nous (lo͞o´mə nəs) *adj.*, giving off light; shining; bright
hoard (hôrd) *v.*, hide or keep away
sa • cred (sā´krid) *adj.*, holy or special
im • pulse (im´puls´) *n.*, sudden force or action

Answers to Guided Reading Questions

❶ The socks make the speaker think his feet are unacceptable, like two old fire fighters unworthy of the fire.

❷ The speaker resisted the temptation to save the socks the way schoolboys would save fireflies or the way scholars would hoard sacred documents.

Vocabulary in Context

- The <u>mammoth</u> meal was too much for the lone diner.
- Lara's lyrics and Jaime's music were a <u>celestial</u> combination.
- The moon shed a <u>luminous</u> reflection on the water.
- We thought we were out of cereal until we looked in Walter's room and found he had <u>hoarded</u> three boxes.
- The church is a <u>sacred</u> building.
- Pino had not been planning on buying a boat; he did it on an <u>impulse</u>.

ANSWER TO GUIDED READING QUESTION

❶ The speaker's moral is "twice beautiful/is beauty/and what is good doubly/good/when it is a case of two/woolen socks/in wintertime."

SELECTION CHECK TEST WITH ANSWERS

EX. To what is this ode written?
This ode is written to a pair of socks.

1. Who made the socks for the speaker?
Maru Mori made the socks for the speaker.
2. What color are the socks?
The socks are blue.
3. To what does the speaker compare his feet when he looks at them in comparison with the socks?
The speaker compares his feet to two tired old fire fighters.
4. What impulse did the speaker resist?
The speaker resisted the impulse to put the socks in a golden cage and feed them birdseed and melon.
5. What is the moral of the ode?
The moral is that what is beautiful is twice beautiful and what is good is doubly good when it is a case of two woolen socks in winter.

and rosy melon flesh.
Like explorers
who in the forest
surrender a rare
and tender deer
to the spit
and eat it
with remorse,
I stuck out
my feet
and pulled on
the
handsome
socks,
and
then my shoes.

So this is
the moral of my ode:
twice beautiful
is beauty
and what is good doubly
good
when it is a case of two
woolen socks
in wintertime. ■

❶ *What is the speaker's moral?*

About the Author

Pablo Neruda (1904–1973) is considered by many to be the finest Latin-American poet of the twentieth century. He was born Ricardo Eliecer Neftalí Reyes in Parral, Chile. He later adopted the pen name Pablo Neruda and joined a group of experimental poets, publishing several volumes of his poetry before he turned twenty. He later served as a government consul and ambassador in the Chilean diplomatic service. In 1971, Neruda won the Nobel Prize for literature. His books of poetry include *Twenty Love Poems and a Song of Despair* (1924), *Elemental Odes* (1954), and *A New Decade: Poems* (1958–1967).

WORDS FOR EVERYDAY USE

re • morse (ri môrs´) *n.,* deep sense of guilt over a wrong that one has done

ode (ōd) *n.,* poem or song

VOCABULARY IN CONTEXT

- Lena showed no remorse for breaking her promise to Nathan.
- Keats wrote "Ode on a Grecian Urn."

Responding to the Selection

What do you think about the speaker's reaction to his socks? What type of person does the speaker seem to be? What do you learn more about in this poem—the speaker or his socks?

Reviewing the Selection

Recalling and Interpreting

1. **R** What is the reader told about the person who brought socks to the speaker?
   I From this information, what can the reader infer about this person?
2. **R** What does the speaker say his feet turned into when he put on the socks?
   I Why did the speaker's feet suddenly seem unacceptable to him?
3. **R** What strong temptation does the speaker resist?
   I What do you think motivates such a temptation? Why did the speaker not submit to this temptation?
4. **R** What does the speaker announce in the final stanza?
   I What do you think of the speaker's announcement? Is it really a lesson? Why, or why not?

Synthesizing

5. John Keats ended his "Ode on a Grecian Urn" with the following "moral": " 'Beauty is truth, truth beauty,'—that is all/Ye know on earth, and all ye need to know." In what way is this moral similar to Neruda's moral? In what way is it different? What is the subject of each of these morals? What does each speaker say about his subject? What is the tone of each of these morals? What can you infer about each of the speakers from his moral?

Understanding Literature (Questions for Discussion)

Metaphor and Simile. A **metaphor** is a figure of speech in which one thing is spoken or written about as if it were another. A **simile** is a comparison using *like* or *as.* Neruda uses both metaphors and similes throughout his poem. Identify as many examples as you can of each. Why do you think the speaker used so many different similes and metaphors to describe one thing? What does this say about the speaker's imagination?

Responding to the Selection

Ask students what they learn about both the speaker and his or her socks.

Answers for Reviewing the Selection

RECALLING AND INTERPRETING

1. **Recalling.** The person is a shepherd who knitted the socks herself. **Interpreting.** *Responses will vary.* The reader can infer that the speaker cares enough to spend time making gifts for the speaker. The person uses the materials at hand to make gifts.
2. **Recalling.** His feet turned into fish or sharks. **Interpreting.** *Responses will vary.* The speaker feels his feet are unworthy of the wonderful socks.
3. **Recalling.** The speaker resists the temptation to save the socks. **Interpreting.** *Responses will vary.* The speaker is so impressed by the socks, he feels that they should be cherished and not put to use. He realizes the socks were meant to be worn, and he needs the wool socks in the cold weather.
4. **Recalling.** The speaker announces the moral of the ode. **Interpreting.** *Responses will vary.* The speaker's announcement is not really a lesson. It simply states that warm, beautiful clothes are wonderful in the wintertime.

SYNTHESIZING

Responses will vary. Possible responses are given.

5. The end of Neruda's ode also speaks of beauty. Keats likens beauty to the lofty ideal of truth while Neruda connects beauty with the simple object of a pair of socks. The tone of Keats's moral is serious while Neruda's is comical. Neruda's moral is fitting because he chose to write an ode, which is a lofty form of poetry, about a simple subject. His moral reflects the light nature of his subject.

Answers for Understanding Literature

Responses will vary. Possible responses are given.

Metaphor and Simile. Metaphors include *my feet became two woolen fish, two long sharks of lapis blue, two mammoth blackbirds, two cannons,* and *two tired old fire fighters not worthy of the woven fire.*

Similes include *soft as rabbits, I slipped my feet into them* [the socks] *as if into jewel cases,* and *like explorers who in the forest surrender a deer to the spit and eat it with remorse, I stuck out my feet and pulled on the handsome socks.* The many metaphors and similes show the speaker to have a vivid imagination even about mundane things like socks.

Speaking and Listening Skills

Introducing the Skill

Remind students of the oral history of literature. Ask them to think about their own experiences with oral presentations of literature: were they read to when they were younger? Have they seen a play performed? taken part in a poetry reading? If they have done any of these things, they are familiar with the effects hearing literature can have. Giving an oral interpretation is another way of experiencing literature.

Previewing the Skill

To do an oral interpretation simply means to read or recite a poem or story aloud. An oral interpretation should display the mood or tone of the piece or pieces being presented through physical and verbal cues. Have students read the introduction and student model of the Speaking and Listening Skills activity.

Preparing for an Oral Interpretation

Review with students the suggestions in the Language Arts Survey, 3.6, "Dramatic Interpretation of Poetry." Students can apply the same techniques to prose. Then have students follow the guidelines for preparing oral interpretations given in the Oral Interpretation lesson.

Delivering an Oral Interpretation

Many students do not enjoy speaking or performing for groups. Suggest to students who fall into this category that they might practice giving their oral interpretations for a small group of people first. While presenting their oral interpretations, students should be relaxed and maintain good posture. Remind students to make eye contact with their audience throughout the presentation.

Reviewing an Oral Interpretation

You might hold student-teacher conferences with each student to review his or her oral presentation.

Speaking and Listening Skills

Oral Interpretation

Poetry was passed on by word of mouth long before it was written down on paper. Throughout much of history, poets recited or sang their verses to a captive audience. Hearing words spoken aloud, or in an **oral interpretation,** helps us to understand better the meaning of a work. To do oral interpretation means to read or to recite a poem or story aloud.

As part of a unit on poetry, Heidi's English teacher asked the class to prepare oral interpretations for a day of poetry reading. Heidi decided to do a reading of Mari Evans's "The Rebel," on page 000. Heidi began to prepare her interpretation by reading the poem several times. Then she thought about how the poem might best be read aloud. She made a short note of introduction that included the author, title, and theme of the poem. Next, she copied the poem onto notebook paper, leaving room so that she could make notes about how she might read it.

Try It Yourself

Choose a poem or part of a short story to read aloud to your class. The piece may come from your textbook or from another source.

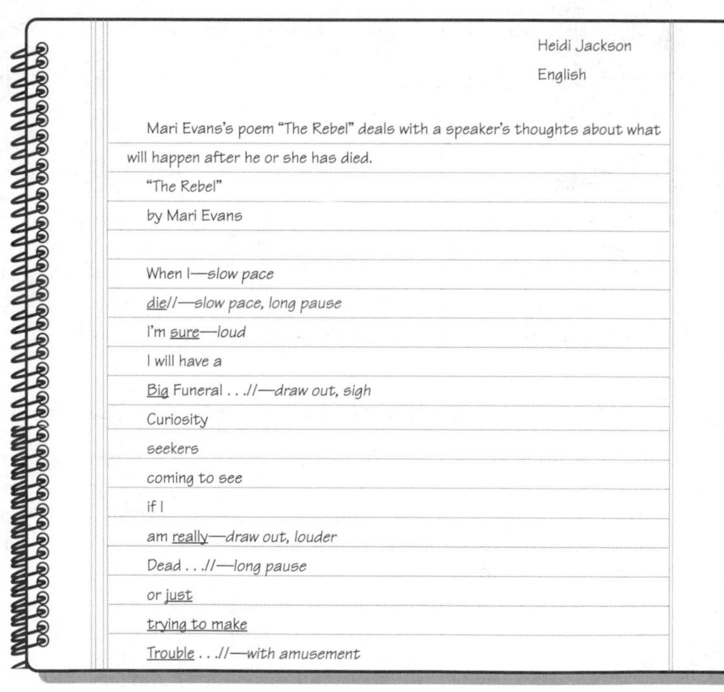
Heidi Jackson
English

Mari Evans's poem "The Rebel" deals with a speaker's thoughts about what will happen after he or she has died.

"The Rebel"
by Mari Evans

When I—slow pace
die//—slow pace, long pause
I'm sure—loud
I will have a
Big Funeral . . .//—draw out, sigh
Curiosity
seekers
coming to see
if I
am really—draw out, louder
Dead . . .//—long pause
or just
trying to make
Trouble . . .//—with amusement

Heidi drew double slashes to show places where she would pause while reading the poem. She underlined words that she would stress, or emphasize. She also made notes about the tone, or emotion, that she would show when reading particular lines, and about the pace, or speed, with which some lines would be read. Before giving her oral interpretation, Heidi practiced reading the poem aloud into a tape recorder. She listened to the recording and then practiced some more. Finally she read the poem to the class, making sure to keep eye contact with her listeners.

Examining the Model

1. What line did Heidi mark to be read with a particular emotion? What emotion did she choose for this line?
2. What words did Heidi mark to be read with special emphasis?
3. Where did she mark that she should change the pace, or speed, of her reading?

Preparing for Your Oral Interpretation

1. Choose a poem or a passage from a short story. Read the poem or passage several times. Look up in a dictionary any words in the piece that are unfamiliar to you. Make sure that you know how every word in the piece is pronounced and what every word means.
2. On a piece of notebook paper, write the author, the title, and the theme of the piece. Write a one- or two-sentence introduction.
3. Copy the poem or passage onto notebook paper. Leave a wide margin so that you will have room to make notes on how the poem should be read.
4. Mark the poem for reading. Underline words or phrases that you want to emphasize. Draw two slashes (//) to show places where you will pause briefly while reading. Make notes about the tone, or emotion, that you will use when reading particular lines. Also note places where you will read faster or slower.
5. Practice reading the poem aloud. If possible, record your reading with a tape recorder or a videotape recorder. Review your reading and practice it until it matches your marked-up script. When you feel that your interpretation is ready, you might try delivering it to a practice audience of family members or friends.

Delivering Your Oral Interpretation

1. Present your interpretation to your classmates. Read from your notes, but be sure to know the piece well enough that you can simply glance at the notes and then look back out at your audience. Keep eye contact with your audience as you read.
2. Stay relaxed and maintain good posture.

Reviewing Your Oral Interpretation

1. After you and your classmates have delivered your oral interpretations, meet in small groups.
2. Discuss these questions:
   a. What did you like and not like about doing an oral interpretation?
   b. What did you learn from the experience?
   c. What would you do differently in a future oral interpretation?

Answers for Examining the Model

1. Heidi marked the last line to be read with amusement.
2. Heidi marked *sure* to be read loudly, *Big* to be drawn out, *really* to be drawn out. She also intended to emphasize *die* and *just trying to make Trouble.*
3. She would read the first two lines slowly, followed by a long pause. She would draw out the line "Big funeral." She would pause after "Dead."

GOALS/OBJECTIVES

Studying this lesson will enable students to

- empathize with the feelings of the speaker about his heritage
- define *flashback* and recognize a flashback
- identify the theme of a poem
- recognize a metaphor

ADDITIONAL RESOURCES

Reader's Guide

- Selection Worksheet, 9.6

Assessment Portfolio

- Selection Check Test, 2.9.11
- Selection Test, 2.9.12

Pronunciation Exercise

- Grade 8 Audiocassette, Side B, Track 50

CROSS-CURRICULAR CONNECTIONS

Geography

Have students make a topographical map of Ireland marking mountains, hills, and bodies of water.

Students can also research the economy of Ireland or the Irish Potato Famine and present their findings to the class.

Teen Living

Ask students to write about the things they honor from their heritage. These things might be values they have learned from parents or grandparents or family traditions they would like to see continue.

Prereading

Theme

"Digging"

by Seamus Heaney

Cross-curricular Connections

Geography. Ireland is an island to the west of Great Britain. The center of Ireland has low, rolling hills, but there are mountains along the island's coast. One of the most notable features of the island is its peat bogs. Peat is partially carbonized vegetable matter that can be burned as fuel. It is found in areas of wet, spongy ground known as bogs. Throughout most of Ireland's history, peat was one of the only sources of fuel for rural people.

Ireland's economy is primarily agricultural, although industry has rapidly become more important in the twentieth century. Most Irish farms are family farms, and potatoes are one of their staple crops. In the nineteenth century, potatoes were so important to Ireland that when a potato blight attacked the crop in 1845, people were left with nothing to eat. The Irish Potato Famine, which lasted from 1845 to 1847, claimed the lives of 750,000 people through starvation and disease. The speaker of the poem that you are about to read shares his memories of his father and grandfather digging potatoes and peat in Ireland.

The southern portion of Ireland is an independent state known as the Irish Republic, or Eire. This state achieved independence from the United Kingdom in 1922. The author of this poem comes from Northern Ireland, or Ulster, which is still part of the United Kingdom.

Teen Living. As children get older they often have conflicting feelings about their parents and the preceding generation. Many young people want to be like their parents, but they also long to establish their own identities. Ultimately, most people realize that you can honor and respect your parents and your heritage and be yourself at the same time. The speaker of the poem you are about to read achieves a balance between striking out on his own and remaining connected to his past.

As You Read

In **"Digging,"** the poet "digs" through memories of his father and grandfather, just as his father and grandfather dug potatoes and peat. In your journal, make cluster charts like the ones below. In each cluster chart, write details of the poet's memories of his father and grandfather.

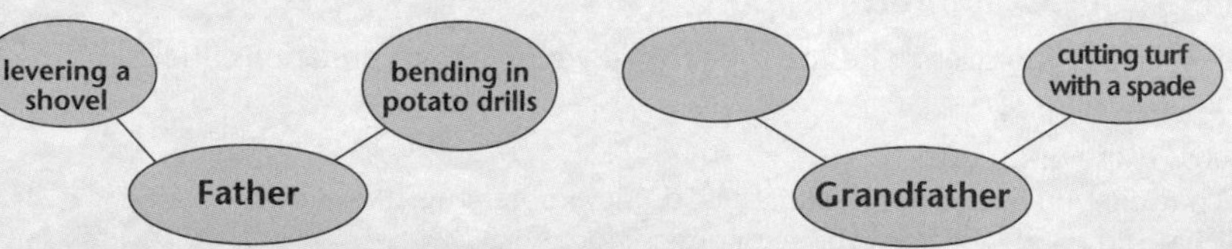

AS YOU READ

Students may include the following information in their cluster charts about the speaker's father: could handle a shovel, like his father, stoops in rhythm, rooted out tops, and scattered new potatoes. Students may include the following information in their cluster charts about the speaker's grandfather: cut more turf in a day than any other; drank milk and returned immediately to work; nicked, sliced, and heaved sods, digging deeper for the good turf.

READER'S JOURNAL

Think about someone who was important to you in your childhood. What images come to your mind when you think of this person? What activities do you remember this person doing? In what way has this person and his or her activities shaped who you are today? Write about these questions in your journal.

"Digging"

SEAMUS HEANEY

Between my finger and my thumb
The squat pen rests; snug as a gun.
Under my window, a clean rasping sound
When the spade sinks into gravelly ground:
My father, digging. I look down

Till his straining rump among the flowerbeds
Bends low, comes up twenty years away
Stooping in rhythm through potato drills[1]
Where he was digging.

The coarse boot nestled on the lug, the shaft[2]
Against the inside knee was levered firmly.
He rooted out tall tops, buried the bright edge deep
To scatter new potatoes that we picked
Loving their cool hardness in our hands.

By God, the old man could handle a spade.
Just like his old man.

My grandfather cut more turf[3] in a day
Than any other man on Toner's bog.[4]

1 What is the speaker doing?

2 Does the speaker's father remain in the same bend for twenty years? What is the speaker's point?

3 How does the speaker feel toward his father? How do you know?

---

1. **potato drills.** Small furrows in which potato seeds are planted
2. **lug, the shaft.** *Lug*—top of the blade (in this case, of the spade); *shaft*—long, slender part of an object (the spade)
3. **turf.** Slabs of peat (partly decayed plant matter) used as heating fuel in Ireland
4. **bog.** Wet, spongy ground as in a swamp

READER'S JOURNAL

Students might write about these questions in the form of a letter to the person telling him or her of his or her impact on the writer's life. Tell students that they are not obligated to share the letter if they choose not to do so.

ANSWERS TO GUIDED READING QUESTIONS

1 The speaker is writing in front of a window.

2 The speaker's father seems to be bending in the same way he has for twenty years. The speaker's point is that his father has worked this way for many years. Seeing his father at work reminds him of his father twenty years ago.

3 The speaker is impressed and respectful of his father. You can tell by his tone when he speaks of his father's skill.

SUPPORT FOR LEP STUDENTS

PRONUNCIATIONS OF PROPER NOUNS AND ADJECTIVES

Sea • mus Hea • ney (shām´əs hā´ nē) n.

ADDITIONAL VOCABULARY

mould—British spelling of mold
nicking—notching, making small cuts
old man—father
rasping—scraping, grating

Answer to Guided Reading Question

❶ The speaker says that he will continue the family tradition of digging, but he will do so with a pen rather than with a shovel.

Selection Check Test with Answers

EX. What is the speaker holding?
The speaker is holding a pen.

1. What does the speaker see out the window?
He sees his father digging.

2. What does the speaker's father dig?
He digs potatoes.

3. What does the speaker's grandfather cut?
He cuts turf.

4. Where does the speaker's grandfather's work exceed that of all others?
The speaker's grandfather cuts more turf than any man on Toner's bog.

5. What does the speaker say he does not have?
The speaker does not have a spade.

Once I carried him milk in a bottle
Corked sloppily with paper. He straightened up
To drink it, then fell to right away
Nicking and slicing neatly, heaving sods[5]
Over his shoulder, going down and down
For the good turf. Digging.

The cold smell of potato mould, the squelch and slap
Of soggy peat, the curt cuts of an edge
Through living roots awaken in my head.
But I've no spade to follow men like them.

❶ *What comparison does the speaker make between himself and his father and grandfather?*

Between my finger and my thumb
The squat pen rests.
I'll dig with it. ■

5. **sods.** Clumps of the surface layer of earth containing grass plants and their roots

About the Author

Seamus Heaney (1939–) was born in Northern Ireland and often writes about Ireland. Many people believe that he is one of the greatest living poets. His volumes of poetry include *Death of a Naturalist, Wintering Out, North, Field Work,* and *Station Island.* Heaney won the Nobel Prize for literature in 1995. Currently, he spends half of his year in the Irish Republic and half in the United States, where he teaches at Harvard University in Cambridge, Massachusetts.

Responding to the Selection

Does the poet convince you that it is possible to "dig" with a pen? Have you ever found it helpful to "dig" through your memories and emotions by writing? Are there any other ways in which you can explore your memories and emotions?

Reviewing the Selection

RECALLING AND INTERPRETING

1. **R** What is the speaker doing when he hears a sound? What does the speaker hear beneath his window? Where is the speaker's father when the speaker looks down?

   I How do you think the speaker feels about this interruption?

2. **R** What does the sight of his father digging make the speaker think of "twenty years ago"? Of what does the thought of his father's actions twenty years ago remind the speaker?

   I Why might the sight of his father digging make the speaker think of increasingly distant memories?

3. **R** What does the grandfather do almost immediately after drinking the bottle of milk?

   I What does this action suggest about the grandfather's character?

4. **R** What does the speaker say he lacks? What does the speaker decide to do?

   I What do you think the speaker means by his decision? In what ways does the speaker decide to be like his father and grandfather? In what ways does he decide to be different?

SYNTHESIZING

5. Why does the poet declare that he will dig with his pen? What do you think digging has come to mean to the poet?

Understanding Literature (Questions for Discussion)

1. **Flashback.** A **flashback** is a part of a story, poem, or play that presents events that happened at an earlier time. Where does the flashback in line 7 send the reader? Where do lines 15–16 send the reader? What information do these flashbacks provide? What do you learn about the speaker through these flashbacks?
2. **Theme.** A **theme** is a central idea in a literary work. This poem discusses three different people and three different periods of time, but there is still one major theme to the poem. What do you think this theme is? In what way do the three different people and periods of time add to, or enhance, this theme?

RESPONDING TO THE SELECTION

Ask students to think of things that their families have done for generations. Ask students if they plan to contribute to these traditions, and if so, how? If not, why not?

ANSWERS FOR REVIEWING THE SELECTION

RECALLING AND INTERPRETING

1. **Recalling.** The speaker is writing. The speaker hears the scrape of a shovel. The speaker's father is in the flowerbeds. **Interpreting.** *Responses will vary.* The speaker does not seem to mind the interruption.

2. **Recalling.** The speaker is reminded of his father digging potatoes twenty years ago. The memory of his father digging potatoes reminds him of his grandfather digging peat. **Interpreting.** *Responses will vary.* One thought of digging leads to another. The digging suggests pulling up layers in the speaker's memory.

3. **Recalling.** The speaker's grandfather goes back to work almost immediately. **Interpreting.** *Responses will vary.* It suggests that the speaker's grandfather is a hard worker.

4. **Recalling.** The speaker lacks a shovel or spade. He decides to dig with his pen. **Interpreting.** *Responses will vary.* He might mean that he will uncover thoughts, ideas, and memories with his pen. He will support himself with his pen. The speaker will dig like his father and his grandfather, but he will be different because his digging will be a mental rather than physical action.

SYNTHESIZING

Responses will vary. Possible responses are given.

5. Digging has come to mean working and following the family ways. The poet will be part of this tradition, although he will modify it to fit his skills.

ANSWERS FOR UNDERSTANDING LITERATURE

Responses will vary. Possible responses are given.

1. **Flashback.** The flashback in line 7 sends the speaker back twenty years to another time his father was digging. The flashback in lines 15 and 16 remind the speaker of a time when his grandfather was digging. Both flashbacks provide insight into the speaker's feelings about his father and grandfather. The speaker respects the two men and the family tradition of digging.

2. **Theme.** The theme is the respect for the past and the continuance of traditions. The speaker shows his respect for his grandfather and his father, and for their work ethics, by deciding to follow in their paths. By choosing to work with a pen, the speaker allows himself to be an individual while maintaining the past ways of his family.

GOALS/OBJECTIVES

Studying this lesson will enable students to

- interpret and appreciate a poem
- discuss funeral customs
- respond to a poem
- identify and describe the speaker of the poem

ADDITIONAL RESOURCES

Reader's Guide

- Selection Worksheet, 9.7

Assessment Portfolio

- Selection Check Test, 2.9.13
- Selection Test, 2.9.14

Pronunciation Exercise

- Grade 8 Audiocassette, Side B, Track 51

CROSS-CURRICULAR CONNECTIONS

Social Studies

Have students research further the funeral customs described in the Cross-curricular Connection.

If students would like to do so, have them discuss funerals they have attended.

Prereading

THEME

"The Rebel"

by Mari Evans

Cross-curricular Connection

Social Studies. Archaeologists have found evidence that prehistoric people had special customs for burying their dead over sixty thousand years ago. Neanderthal grave sites have been found, complete with evidence of flowers, that suggest early human beings mourned for their dead. Although mourning and expressing grief after a death is common to all humans, funeral customs vary widely among social and cultural groups.

The ancient Egyptians embalmed and mummified the bodies of their dead, because they believed the spirit would return to the body in the afterlife. Other cultures are known to prepare dead bodies by painting the body, by anointing it with oils, or by wrapping it in a cloth called a shroud. In Christian, Jewish, and Muslim countries, burial is the most common method for disposing of the body. In Buddhist and Hindu countries, cremation, or burning the dead person's body, is customary. In Tibet, the body of the dead person is sunk in water, while in Australia, some Aboriginal peoples place their dead in trees. The Sioux in North America place their dead on burial platforms.

In the United States, a body is often embalmed by funeral directors. There is often a period when friends and relatives can view the body and mourn the loss. The funeral itself is a service that may include prayers, hymns, music, and eulogies, short speeches that memorialize the deceased. After the funeral service, the body is transported in a hearse to a cemetery or crematory where a final brief ceremony may be held before the body is buried or cremated. After the funeral, mourners often share food and drink with the bereaved family. In "The Rebel," the speaker describes what he or she expects at his or her funeral.

As You Read

In your journal, make a chart like the one below. As you read, copy words or phrases from **"The Rebel"** that intrigue you. In the right column, write questions, opinions, or other comments you may have in response to the words or phrases from the poem.

Word or Phrase	Your Response
Big Funeral	**Why would a big funeral matter? You're not going to be there.**

AS YOU READ

Students may include the following words or phrases from the poem. Possible responses to the words or phases are given.

"Curiosity seekers"/Who are the curiosity seekers? What do they think will happen?

"if I am really Dead"/How could there be a funeral for somebody who is not dead?

"or just trying to make Trouble"/What kind of trouble would the speaker make? I wonder what he or she did in his or her life to make people so curious about his or her funeral.

READER'S JOURNAL

What would you like to be known for during your lifetime and remembered for when you die? How would you like other people to recognize you? Write about these questions in your journal.

"The Rebel"

MARI EVANS

When I
die
I'm sure
I will have a
Big Funeral . . .
Curiosity
seekers . . .[1]
coming to see
if I
am really
Dead . . .
or just
trying to make
Trouble . . . ■

1. **curiosity seekers.** People who come to an event for no reason other than curiosity

❶ *About what subject is the speaker thinking?*

❷ *What reasons will people have for coming to the speaker's funeral?*

READER'S JOURNAL

Explain that a eulogy is speech or writing in praise of someone, especially a person who has just died. Suggest that students write their responses in the form of eulogies about themselves.

ANSWERS TO GUIDED READING QUESTIONS

❶ The speaker is thinking about his or her funeral.

❷ People will come out of curiosity to see if the speaker is really dead or if he or she is just trying to make trouble.

SUPPORT FOR LEP STUDENTS

ADDITIONAL VOCABULARY

curiosity—eagerness to learn things that do not concern you

SELECTION CHECK TEST WITH ANSWERS

EX. Who is the author of this poem?
Mari Evans wrote this poem.

1. What is the speaker called in the title of the poem?
The speaker is called the rebel.

2. What kind of funeral will the speaker have?
The speaker will have a big funeral.

3. Who would come to the speaker's funeral?
Curiosity seekers would come to the speaker's funeral.

4. What do the people who come to the funeral want to see about the speaker?
They want to see if the speaker is really dead.

5. What might people who come to the funeral think the speaker might be instead?
The speaker might be trying to cause trouble.

QUOTABLES

"The only reason I might go to the funeral is to make sure that he's dead."

—Anonymous, quoted by Anthony Sampson

Portrait Woman.
Diego Rivera, 1927

About the Author

Mari Evans has worked as a university professor, editor, poet, playwright, and children's book writer. She has also published several collections of poetry, including *Where Is All the Music, I Am a Black Woman, Nightstar: 1973–1978,* and *A Dark Splendid Mass.* Evans credits the writings of Langston Hughes and the encouragement of her father as major influences on her decision to become a professional writer. Evans is an advocate of building pride in the African-American community. She wrote, directed, and produced a television program, *The Black Experience,* that was praised by critics.

Responding to the Selection

Imagine you are at the speaker's funeral. What might you say about the speaker if you were giving a eulogy? What might you say if you were a curiosity seeker?

Reviewing the Selection

RECALLING AND INTERPRETING

1. **R** What prediction does the speaker make about his or her funeral?

   I How does the speaker feel about the type of funeral he or she will have?

2. **R** Who does the speaker think will come to her funeral?

   I Why do you think the speaker describes the people who will come to his or her funeral this way?

3. **R** What is the first reason the speaker gives for people coming to his or her funeral?

   I Why would people come for the first reason?

4. **R** What is the second reason the speaker gives for people coming to his or her funeral?

   I Why would people come for the second reason? What does that reason tell you about the speaker's character?

SYNTHESIZING

5. Why do you think people will come to the speaker's funeral? Would anyone come to mourn the speaker's death out of love or a genuine sense of loss? Explain.

Understanding Literature (Questions for Discussion)

Speaker. The **speaker** is the voice that speaks, or narrates, a poem. Describe the speaker of this poem. What do you know about the speaker's life by the expectations he or she has for his or her funeral? What does the title of the poem suggest about the speaker?

RESPONDING TO THE SELECTION

Students might role play this scene in small groups. Some students should play curiosity seekers and some should play people truly mourning the death of the speaker.

ANSWERS FOR REVIEWING THE SELECTION

RECALLING AND INTERPRETING

1. **Recalling.** The speaker predicts that his or her funeral will be big. **Interpreting.** *Responses will vary.* The speaker seems to think that his or her funeral will be large, but not necessarily full of mourners.

2. **Recalling.** The speaker thinks curiosity seekers will come to his or her funeral. **Interpreting.** *Responses will vary.* The speaker has caught the interest of many people during his or her life. He or she expects to continue to attract interest at his or her funeral.

3. **Recalling.** People will come to see if he or she is really dead. **Interpreting.** *Responses will vary.* People might wonder if the funeral is just a trick or publicity stunt on the part of the speaker.

4. **Recalling.** People might come to see if he or she were trying to make trouble. **Interpreting.** *Responses will vary.* The speaker is a rebel, so he or she often broke the rules and may have caused trouble. People might wonder if this is not just another troublemaking act on the part of the speaker. The speaker often did things that got attention and was considered a troublemaker by many people. The speaker seems to enjoy his or her notoriety.

SYNTHESIZING

Responses will vary. Possible responses are given.

5. The speaker may be correct that there will be many curiosity seekers at his or her funeral. There would probably also be many people who admired the speaker for his or her courage and daring actions.

ANSWERS FOR UNDERSTANDING LITERATURE

Responses will vary. Possible responses are given.

Speaker. The speaker is a rebel. The speaker has broken rules and done the unexpected. He or she has attracted attention and probably controversy during his or her lifetime. The speaker is aware that he or she attracts a lot of attention and enjoys his or her notoriety. The speaker expects that his or her death will attract as much attention as many of the events of his or her life did.

GOALS/OBJECTIVES

Studying this lesson will enable students to

- enjoy a narrative poem
- discuss people's fear of rats
- identify and summarize main ideas
- identify and understand similes
- write metaphors and similes

ADDITIONAL RESOURCES

READER'S GUIDE

- Selection Worksheet, 9.8

ASSESSMENT PORTFOLIO

- Selection Check Test, 2.9.15
- Selection Test, 2.9.16

PRONUNCIATION EXERCISE

- Grade 8 Audiocassette, Side B, Track 52

CROSS-CURRICULAR CONNECTIONS

SCIENCE AND WORLD HISTORY

The Black Death brought on an intense preoccupation with death throughout much of Europe. An interesting topic of research might be the dance of death or the *danse macabre,* a portrayal of Death whirling away the dead in dance that flourished in the years after the Black Death. Students might make their own representations either through dance and motion or in a model, painting, or drawing of the dance of death.

Prereading

THEME

"The Pied Piper of Hamelin"
by Robert Browning

Cross-curricular Connection

Science and World History. Rats are small rodents with naked feet and tails and dark hair. The two major breeds of rats are black rats and Norway rats. Black rats grow to about eight inches long, not including their long tail. They are skilled at climbing and jumping. Norway rats are also known as barn rats, sewer rats, and wharf rats, and are roughly the same size as black rats. Norway rats can swim and dig burrows. Laboratory rats are an albino strain of Norway rats. Both breeds of rats have followed humans throughout the world, and they adapt readily to new environments. Rats eat almost any type of food, behave aggressively, and can bear up to seven litters of young a year, each litter containing between six and twenty-two young rats.

In the selection you are about to read, some townspeople are very concerned with an infestation of rats. People's concern with rats is well founded. They have carried and transmitted more than twenty different types of disease. One type of disease that rats carry is plague. Rats are infected with the plague by fleas. Usually this disease is only present in a small number of rats, but occasionally the disease spreads throughout a large rat population, killing many rats. When rats that have been killed by the plague live near humans, the fleas that carry the plague and that have left the dead rodent hosts begin to infest humans, infecting them with the disease. There are three types of plague—bubonic (affecting the lymph nodes), pneumonic (affecting the lungs), and septicemic (affecting the bloodstream). All forms of the plague can be fatal, although pneumonic and septicemic are the most deadly. During the fourteenth century the plague was called the Black Death, an appropriate name given that the disease claimed one-fourth of the European population, or about twenty-five million people. During a plague epidemic, people must take special sanitary measures and take action against rats and their fleas. Vaccines are also available for people who come in contact with rats.

As You Read

"The Pied Piper of Hamelin" is a long poem that tells a story. To help keep the story straight, create a chart like the one below in your journal. For each stanza (1–15) write a sentence that summarizes the central action or main idea of the stanza.

Stanza 1	Five hundred years ago, the town of Hamelin was overrun with vermin.
Stanza 2	
Stanza 3	

AS YOU READ

Stanza 2—rats ruin life in the town in many ways; 3—people are angry because elected officials are not fixing the problem; 4—officials meet, but are unable to come up with a solution; 5—strange man comes to the council; 6—pied piper offers to free the town of rats for a fee; 7—piper leads away the rats; 8—celebration begins; 9—mayor refuses to pay the piper; 10—piper makes a threat; 11—mayor does not take the threat seriously; 12—piper begins to lead children away; 13—children disappear with the piper; 14—loss of the children is commemorated in the town and a possible explanation of their whereabouts is given; 15—moral of the story is given

READER'S JOURNAL

Think of a time when a person promised you something and then broke the promise. How did it make you feel? Have you ever promised someone something and then not kept your word? How did you feel? How do you think the other person felt? Why is it important to keep your word? Write about these questions in your journal.

"The Pied Piper of Hamelin"

ROBERT BROWNING

I

Hamelin Town's in Brunswick,
By famous Hanover city;
The river Weser, deep and wide,
Washes its wall on the southern side;
A pleasanter spot you never spied;
But, when begins my ditty,
Almost five hundred years ago,
To see the townsfolk suffer so
From vermin, was a pity.

II

Rats!
They fought the dogs and killed the cats,
And bit the babies in the cradles,
And ate the cheeses out of the vats,
And licked the soup from the cooks' own ladles,
Split open the kegs of salted sprats,
Made nests inside men's Sunday hats,
And even spoiled the women's chats
By drowning their speaking
With shrieking and squeaking
In fifty different sharps and flats.

❶ *In what ways had rats overtaken Hamelin?*

WORDS FOR EVERYDAY USE

spy (spī) *v.*, see; catch sight of; perceive

dit • ty (dit´ē) *n.*, short, simple song

ver • min (vʉr´mən) *n.*, various insects or small animals seen as pests

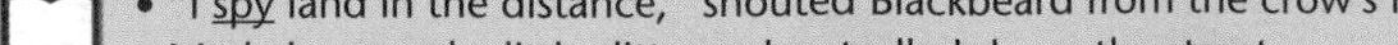

READER'S JOURNAL

As an alternative activity, ask students if they have ever done a job for which they expected to be compensated. Did they think their payment was fair? Why, or why not?

SPELLING AND VOCABULARY WORDS FROM THE SELECTION

bereave	paunch
brook	portal
consternation	replenish
ditty	ribald
endeavor	spy
havoc	stout
hue	subterraneous
mirth	swarthy
obese	vermin

ANSWER TO GUIDED READING QUESTION

❶ The rats fight dogs, kill cats, bite babies, eat people's food, nest in people's clothes, and drown out people's conversation.

SUPPORT FOR LEP STUDENTS

PRONUNCIATIONS OF PROPER NOUNS AND ADJECTIVES

Ham • e • lin (ham´ə lin) n.
We • ser (vā´zer) n.
Ni • zam (ni zäm´) n.
Cae • sar (sē´zer) n.
Tran • syl • va • ni • a (tran´sil vā´nē ə) n.

ADDITIONAL VOCABULARY

decree—official order
flocking—traveling in a group
mutinous—rebellious
old-fangled—old fashioned
perished—died
poke—bag or pocket
sprats—herring, a type of fish

VOCABULARY IN CONTEXT

- "I spy land in the distance," shouted Blackbeard from the crow's nest.
- Marla hummed a little ditty as she strolled down the street.
- "Vermin are eating my grain," complained Farmer Jones.

Additional Questions and Activities

Rats are not always seen as pests. Rats are sometimes sold as pets and they are also used for many scientific experiments. If students have had rats as pets, have them describe these creatures. Students can also research rats to see why they are used for so many studies. Remind students that domesticated rats and laboratory rats differ from wild rats. Wild rats may bite or carry disease.

Answer to Guided Reading Question

➊ The people are angry at their government officials because the officials just want an easy life and are unwilling to deal with the problem of the rats.

III

At last the people in a body
    To the Town Hall came flocking:
"'T is clear," cried they, "our Mayor 's noddy;
    And as for our Corporation—shocking
To think we buy gowns lined with ermine[1]
For dolts that can't or won't determine
What's best to rid us of our vermin!
You hope, because you're old and obese,
To find in the furry civic robe ease?
Rouse up, sirs! Give your brains a racking
To find the remedy we're lacking,
Or, sure as fate, we'll send you packing!"
At this the Mayor and Corporation
Quaked with a mighty consternation.

➊ *How do the people of Hamelin feel about their government officials? Why do they feel this way?*

IV

An hour they sat in council;
    At length the Mayor broke silence:
"For a guilder[2] I'd my ermine gown sell,
    I wish I were a mile hence!
It's easy to bid one rack one's brain—
I'm sure my poor head aches again,
I've scratched it so, and all in vain.
Oh for a trap, a trap, a trap!"
Just as he said this, what should hap
At the chamber-door but a gentle tap?
"Bless us," cried the Mayor, "what's that?"
(With the Corporation as he sat,
Looking little though wondrous fat;
Nor brighter was his eye, nor moister
Than a too-long-opened oyster,
Save when at noon his paunch grew mutinous

1. **ermine.** Soft, white fur of a weasel
2. **guilder.** Unit of money in the Netherlands

Words for Everyday Use

o • bese (ō bēs´) *adj.*, very fat
con • ster • na • tion (kän´stər nā´shən) *n.*, great fear or shock
paunch (pônch) *n.*, large, protruding belly; potbelly

Vocabulary in Context

- The doctor put the obese man on a diet.
- When Eli heard the news of the flood in Riverville, he was filled with consternation for his cousins who lived there.
- The troll's great paunch hung over his belt.

For a plate of turtle green and glutinous)
"Only a scraping of shoes on the mat?
Anything like the sound of a rat
Makes my heart go pit-a-pat!"

V

"Come in!"—the Mayor cried, looking bigger:
And in did come the strangest figure!
His queer long coat from heel to head
Was half of yellow and half of red,
And he himself was tall and thin,
With sharp blue eyes, each like a pin,
And light loose hair, yet swarthy skin,
No tuft on cheek nor beard on chin,
But lips where smiles went out and in;
There was no guessing his kith and kin:[3]
And nobody could enough admire
The tall man and his quaint attire.
Quoth one: "It's as my great-grandsire,
Starting up at the Trump of Doom's tone,
Had walked this way from his painted tombstone!"

VI

He advanced to the council-table:
And, "Please your honors," said he, "I'm able,
By means of a secret charm, to draw
All creatures living beneath the sun,
That creep or swim or fly or run,
After me so as you never saw!
And I chiefly use my charm
On creatures that do people harm,
The mole and toad and newt and viper;
And people call me the Pied Piper."
(And here they noticed round his neck
A scarf of red and yellow stripe,
To match with his coat of the self-same cheque;
And at the scarf's end hung a pipe;
And his fingers, they noticed, were ever straying
As if impatient to be playing

3. **kith and kin.** Friends and relatives

❶ *What is the Piper able to do with his charm?*

Words for Everyday Use

swarth • y (swôr´thē) *adj.,* having a dark complexion

Answer to Guided Reading Question

❶ The pied piper is able to draw any living creatures with his piping. He usually uses his piping to draw away harmful or annoying pests.

Additional Questions and Activities

Students can research different methods people have created to get rid of pests. Some examples might include using other animals as predators, using traps, or using poisons. Students might also speak to an exterminator about his or her job. What pest do people most often need to get rid of?

Vocabulary in Context

• Jim has a light complexion, but Oscar is swarthy.

CROSS-CURRICULAR ACTIVITIES

Art

Have students create a mural of the piper leading away the rats. Students should use information from the text about the piper's appearance.

Music

Students who are musically inclined might make up a tune for a recorder, flute, or other wind instrument that reflects the tone and mood of the Pied Piper's song.

Upon this pipe, as low it dangled
Over his vesture[4] so old-fangled.)
"Yet," said he, "poor piper as I am,
In Tartary I freed the Cham,
Last June, from his huge swarms of gnats;
I eased in Asia the Nizam
Of a monstrous brood of vampire-bats:
And as for what your brain bewilders,
If I can rid your town of rats
Will you give me a thousand guilders?"
"One? fifty thousand!"—was the
exclamation
Of the astonished Mayor and Corporation.

VII

Into the street the Piper stept,
Smiling first a little smile,
As if he knew what magic slept
In his quiet pipe the while;
Then, like a musical adept,
To blow the pipe his lips he wrinkled,
And green and blue his sharp eyes
twinkled,
Like a candle-flame where salt is sprinkled;
And ere three shrill notes the pipe uttered,
You heard as if an army muttered;
And the muttering grew to a grumbling;
And the grumbling grew to a mighty
rumbling;
And out of the houses the rats came
tumbling.
Great rats, small rats, lean rats, brawny rats,
Brown rats, black rats, gray rats, tawny rats.
Grave old plodders, gay young friskers,
Fathers, mothers, uncles, cousins,
Cocking tails and pricking whiskers,
Families by tens and dozens,
Brothers, sisters, husbands, wives—
Followed the Piper for their lives.
From street to street he piped advancing,
And step for step they followed dancing,
Until they came to the river Weser,

4. **vesture.** Clothing or apparel

Wherein all plunged and perished!
—Save one who, stout as Julius Cæsar,
Swam across and lived to carry
(As he, the manuscript he cherished)
To Rat-land home his commentary:
Which was, "At the first shrill notes of the pipe,
I heard a sound as of scraping tripe,
And putting apples, wondrous ripe,
Into a cider-press's gripe:
And a moving away of pickle-tub-boards,
And a leaving ajar of conserve-cupboards,
And a drawing the corks of train-oil-flasks,
And a breaking the hoops of butter-casks:
And it seemed as if a voice
(Sweeter far than by harp or by psaltery
Is breathed) called out, 'Oh rats, rejoice!
The world is grown to one vast drysaltery!
So munch on, crunch on, take your nuncheon,
Breakfast, supper, dinner, luncheon!'
And just as a bulky sugar-puncheon,
All ready staved, like a great sun shone
Glorious scarce an inch before me,
Just as methought it said, 'Come, bore me!'
—I found the Weser rolling o'er me."

❶ *How do the rats die?*

VIII

You should have heard the Hamelin people
Ringing the bells till they rocked the steeple.
"Go," cried the Mayor, "and get long poles,
Poke out the nests and block up the holes!
Consult with carpenters and builders,
And leave in our town not even a trace
Of the rats!"—when suddenly, up the face
Of the Piper perked in the market-place,
With a, "First, if you please, my thousand guilders !"

❷ *What is the people's first reaction to the removal of the rats? What have they forgotten?*

IX

A thousand guilders! The Mayor looked blue;
So did the Corporation too.

Words for Everyday Use

stout (stout) *adj.,* brave; courageous

Answers to Guided Reading Questions

❶ The rats die when they fall into the river. Only one rat swims across and lives.

❷ The people celebrate being freed from the rats. They ring the bells. The mayor calls them to poke out rats' nests and block up rat holes. They have forgotten to pay the piper.

Additional Questions and Activities

Why might it be surprising that the rats died in the river? What did the rat who survived do on the other side?

Answers

Many rats can swim, so it might surprise students that the rats died by drowning. The rat who survived wrote a commentary about the event.

Vocabulary in Context

- The stout-hearted firefighter never wavered in the face of a blazing inferno.

Answers to Guided Reading Questions

❶ The mayor does not want to pay the piper because he wants to keep the money for his own comforts. He does not fear breaking the deal, because the rats are dead and cannot come back.

❷ The piper threatens to pipe in another fashion. *Responses will vary.* Students may have heard the story of the pied piper and be aware that he will pipe the children away. Other students may suggest that the piper will pipe the dead rats back or that he will pipe pests from elsewhere to Hamelin.

❶ *Why is the Mayor reluctant to pay the Piper? Why does he not fear breaking the deal?*

For council dinners made rare havoc
With Claret, Moselle, Vin-de-Grave, Hock;
And half the money would replenish
Their cellar's biggest butt with Rhenish.
To pay this sum to a wandering fellow
With a gypsy coat of red and yellow!
"Beside," quoth the Mayor with a knowing wink,
"Our business was done at the river's brink;
We saw with our eyes the vermin sink,
And what's dead can't come to life, I think.
So, friend, we're not the folks to shrink
From the duty of giving you something for drink,
And a matter of money to put in your poke;
But as for the guilders, what we spoke
Of them, as you very well know, was in joke.
Beside, our losses have made us thrifty.
A thousand guilders! Come, take fifty!"

X

The Piper's face fell, and he cried,
"No trifling! I can't wait, beside!
I've promised to visit by dinner time
Bagdat, and accept the prime
Of the Head-Cook's pottage, all he's rich in,
For having left, in the Caliph's kitchen,
Of a nest of scorpions no survivor:
With him I proved no bargain-driver,
With you, don't think I'll bate[5] a stiver![6]
And folks who put me in a passion
May find me pipe after another fashion."

❷ *What does the Piper threaten? What do you think he might do?*

XI

"How?" cried the Mayor, "d' ye think I brook
Being worse treated than a Cook?
Insulted by a lazy ribald
With idle pipe and vesture piebald?
You threaten us, fellow? Do your worst,
Blow your pipe there till you burst!"

5. **bate.** Lower, lessen
6. **stiver.** Former Dutch coin, equal to one-twentieth of a guilder

Words for Everyday Use

hav • oc (hav´ək) *n.,* great destruction and devastation

re • plen • ish (ri plen´ish) *v.,* make full or complete again; resupply

brook (brook) *v.,* put up with

rib • ald (rib´əld) *n.,* person characterized by coarse or vulgar joking or mocking

Vocabulary in Context

- The hurricane caused havoc on the tiny island.
- The waiter replenished our glasses with water.
- Omar brooked Shelby's criticism for an hour before snapping that he had heard enough.
- Yancy was known as a ribald, but he cleaned up his act and became a master of decorum.

XII

Once more he stept into the street,
And to his lips again
Laid his long pipe of smooth straight cane;
And ere he blew three notes (such sweet
Soft notes as yet musician's cunning
Never gave the enraptured air)
There was a rustling that seemed like a bustling
Of merry crowds justling at pitching and hustling;
Small feet were pattering, wooden shoes clattering,
Little hands clapping and little tongues chattering,
And, like fowls in a farm-yard when barley is scattering,
Out came the children running.
All the little boys and girls,
With rosy cheeks and flaxen curls,
And sparkling eyes and teeth like pearls,
Tripping and skipping, ran merrily after
The wonderful music with shouting and laughter.

XIII

The Mayor was dumb, and the Council stood
As if they were changed into blocks of wood,
Unable to move a step, or cry
To the children merrily skipping by,
—Could only follow with the eye
That joyous crowd at the Piper's back.
But how the Mayor was on the rack,
And the wretched Council's bosoms beat,

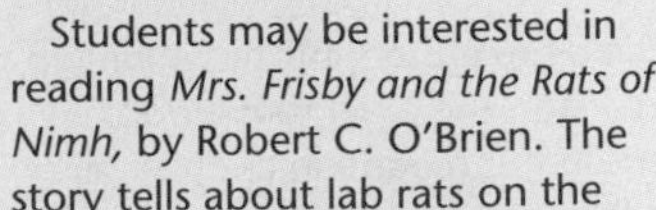

Literary Note

Students may be interested in reading *Mrs. Frisby and the Rats of Nimh,* by Robert C. O'Brien. The story tells about lab rats on the loose who help a widowed mouse.

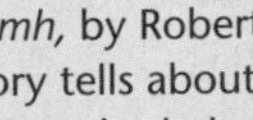

CROSS-CURRICULAR ACTIVITIES

Art

Students might make a mural showing this scene of the piper leading the children away from Hamelin Town. The mural might be posted with the mural the students made of the piper leading away the rats.

Answers to Guided Reading Questions

❶ The people thought the mountain would stop the piper, but a door opens in the mountain and the piper and the children disappear through it.

❷ The child who was left behind regrets that he did not get to go with the other children. He misses his playmates and is sorry he does not get to take part in the wondrous world the piper had promised.

Additional Questions and Activities

- Who escapes the fate of the rats when the piper pipes away the rats?
- Who is left behind when the piper pipes away the children?
- Do you think the piper left the two behind deliberately?
- What information do the two who were left behind share?
- Would you want to go to the world the piper described to the children?

Answers

One stout-hearted rat escapes. One lame child is left behind. The piper may have let the rat escape and left the child behind as reminders of his power. The rat describes the pull of the piper's song. The child describes the wonderful, joyous world the piper promised the children. Students may say that the piper's world sounds tempting. They may say, however, that they would not want to leave their homes and families and the lives they know. Others may suggest that the children had no choice in the matter.

❶ Is anything able to stop the Piper? Where do the Piper and the children disappear?

❷ How does the one child who was left behind feel?

As the Piper turned from the High Street
To where the Weser rolled its waters
Right in the way of their sons and daughters!
However, he turned from South to West,
And to Koppelberg Hill his steps addressed,
And after him the children pressed;
Great was the joy in every breast.
"He never can cross that mighty top!
He's forced to let the piping drop,
And we shall see our children stop!"
When, lo, as they reached the mountain-side,
A wondrous portal opened wide,
As if a cavern was suddenly hollowed;
And the Piper advanced and the children followed,
And when all were in to the very last
The door in the mountain-side shut fast.
Did I say, all? No! One was lame,
And could not dance the whole of the way;
And in after years, if you would blame
His sadness, he was used to say,—
"It's dull in our town since my playmates left;
I can't forget that I'm bereft
Of all the pleasant sights they see,
Which the Piper also promised me.
For he led us, he said, to a joyous land,
Joining the town and just at hand,
Where waters gushed and fruit-trees grew
And flowers put forth a fairer hue,
And everything was strange and new;
The sparrows were brighter than peacocks here,
And their dogs outran our fallow deer,
And honey-bees had lost their stings,
And horses were born with eagles' wings:
And just as I became assured
My lame foot would be speedily cured,
The music stopped and I stood still,
And found myself outside the hill,
Left alone against my will,
To go now limping as before,
And never hear of that country more!"

Words for Everyday Use

por • tal (pôrt´'l) *n.*, doorway, gate, or entrance

be • reave (bē rēv´) *v.*, rob, deprive

hue (hyo͞o) *n.*, color

Vocabulary in Context

- We passed through the portal to the old city.
- Lorna thought the search party might find her buried in the rubble, but she was bereft of hope when she heard the voices retreating.
- The strange hue of the sky suggests that a storm is approaching.

XIV

Alas, alas for Hamelin!
There came into many a burgher's[7] pate[8]
A text which says that heaven's gate
Opes to the rich at as easy rate
As the needle's eye takes a camel in!
The Mayor sent East, West, North and South
To offer the Piper, by word of mouth,
Wherever it was men's lot to find him,
Silver and gold to his heart's content,
If he'd only return the way he went,
And bring the children behind him.
But when they saw 't was a lost endeavor,
And Piper and dancers were gone forever,
They made a decree that lawyers never
Should think their records dated duly
If, after the day of the month and year,
These words did not as well appear,
"And so long after what happened here
On the Twenty-second of July,
Thirteen hundred and seventy-six:"
And the better in memory to fix
The place of the children's last retreat,
They called it, the Pied Piper's Street—
Where any one playing on pipe or tabor
Was sure for the future to lose his labor.
Nor suffered they hostelry or tavern
To shock with mirth a street so solemn
But opposite the place of the cavern
They wrote the story on a column.
And on the great church-window painted
The same, to make the world acquainted
How their children were stolen away,
And there it stands to this very day.
And I must not omit to say

❶ *What was done to commemorate the loss of the children?*

7. **burgher.** Townsperson, often one who is relatively affluent

8. **pate.** Brain or intellect

Words for Everyday Use

en • deav • or (en dev´ər) *n.*, earnest attempt or effort

mirth (murth) *n.*, joyfulness, merriment

Answer to Guided Reading Question

❶ A decree was made that lawyers should record the event every time they noted the date; the place where the children had left town was called Pied Piper's Street; it was illegal to play a pipe or tabor; the story was written on a column.

Additional Questions and Activities

Ask students to compare and contrast the piper and the fairies in "The Stolen Child." What reasons do they have for leading the child or children to another world? Are the fairies kind and caring toward children? Is the piper kind and caring toward children? What are the worlds like to which these beings draw the children? In each situation, do the children choose to go to a new land or are they charmed away?

Vocabulary in Context

- Helvi's endeavors to revive the club were in vain because nobody was interested.
- The room was full of mirth, as indicated by the laughter and broad smiles of everyone in it.

ANSWER TO GUIDED READING QUESTION

❶ The speaker advises Willy to wipe out his scores with others, especially the pipers, and to keep his promises.

SELECTION CHECK TEST WITH ANSWERS

EX. The story of what town is told in this poem?
The story of Hamelin is told.

1. What creatures were overrunning the town?
The town was overrun by rats.

2. What colors does the pied piper wear?
He wears red and yellow.

3. After the piper has completed his job, how much money does the mayor say he will pay the piper?
He says he will give the piper fifty thousand guilders.

4. Who follows the piper into the mountainside?
The boys and girls of Hamelin follow the piper.

5. Where is there a tribe of people who dress outlandishly and come from mothers and fathers in a subterraneous prison?
These people can be found in Transylvania.

That in Transylvania there's a tribe
Of alien people who ascribe
The outlandish ways and dress
On which their neighbors lay such stress,
To their fathers and mothers having risen
Out of some subterraneous prison
Into which they were trepanned[9]
Long time ago in a mighty band
Out of Hamelin town in Brunswick land,
But how or why, they don't understand.

XV

What advice is give in stanza 15? ❶

So, Willy, let me and you be wipers
Of scores out with all men—especially pipers!
And, whether they pipe us free from rats or from mice,
If we've promised them aught, let us keep our promise! ■

9. **trepanned.** Tricked, trapped, or lured

About the Author

Robert Browning (1812–1889) was one of the great poets of Victorian England. Born in London, Browning spent his childhood exploring and reading in his father's extensive private library that contained over six thousand volumes written in several languages. Browning's best-known poetry was written as dramatic monologue, with Browning writing in the voice of imaginary and historical characters. Two of his best-known books are *Men and Women* (1855) and *The Ring and the Book* (1868).

WORDS FOR EVERYDAY USE

sub • ter • ra • ne • ous (sub´tə rā´nē əs) *adj.,* underground

VOCABULARY IN CONTEXT

• We have to go down several flights of stairs to get to the subterraneous station.

Responding to the Selection

Imagine you were one of the inhabitants of Hamelin. How would you feel about seeing the rats led away? How would you feel upon learning the piper had not been paid? Would you think the little boy who did not make it into the mountain was fortunate or unfortunate? Why?

Reviewing the Selection

Recalling and Interpreting

1. **R** What do the people threaten to do to the Mayor if he does not find a remedy to the problem?

   I Why are the people of Hamelin so upset with the town's officials?

2. **R** What does the Pied Piper claim his "secret charm" enables him to do? How much money does he ask to be paid to solve the town's problem? What is the Mayor's response?

   I How does the Piper interpret the Mayor's response?

3. **R** Once the rats are drowned, how much does the Mayor offer to pay the Pied Piper? What does the Piper say happens when people make him angry?

   I Does the Mayor take the Piper's response seriously? Why, or why not? How do you know?

4. **R** What does the Mayor offer the Piper in return for the children? Why is the great church-window painted?

   I Who is blamed for the loss of the children? Who should be held responsible?

Synthesizing

5. What advice is given in the last stanza? Do you think this is good advice? Why, or why not? Do you think the story of the Pied Piper is a good reason to follow this advice? Why, or why not?

Understanding Literature (Questions for Discussion)

Simile. A **simile** is a comparison using *like* or *as.* To what are the Piper's eyes compared in stanza 7? In what way are these things similar? To what sound is the sound of the rats moving compared? In what way are the two things similar? What simile is used in stanza 12 to describe the way the children followed the Piper? In what way are the scenes of the Piper leading the children and the Piper leading the rats similar? different?

RESPONDING TO THE SELECTION

As an alternative activity, have students imagine they were led away by the piper. How might they feel?

ANSWERS FOR REVIEWING THE SELECTION

RECALLING AND INTERPRETING

1. **Recalling.** The people threaten to send the mayor packing. **Interpreting.** *Responses will vary.* The people are upset because the officials of the town are living well off the money of the town but doing nothing to take care of the town's problems.
2. **Recalling.** His charm enables him to lure any living creature. He asks for 1,000 guilders. The mayor says the service is worth 50,000 guilders. **Interpreting.** *Responses will vary.* The piper takes the mayor's response to mean that he will be paid for his services.
3. **Recalling.** The mayor offers to pay the piper fifty guilders. The piper threatens to pipe in another fashion. **Interpreting.** *Responses will vary.* The mayor is not worried about the piper's threat, because he saw the rats die. He tells the piper to pipe as he will.
4. **Recalling.** The mayor offers the piper silver and gold to his heart's content. The window is painted so other people will know what happened. **Interpreting.** *Responses will vary.* The piper is blamed for the loss of the children. The mayor should be blamed for being greedy and not paying the piper.

SYNTHESIZING

Responses will vary. Possible responses are given.

5. The speaker advises keeping promises. It is good advice. If you say you will do something, you should do it. The story is fanciful, but very often people do have to pay in some way for breaking their word.

ANSWERS FOR UNDERSTANDING LITERATURE

Responses will vary. Possible responses are given.

Simile. The twinkle of the piper's eyes is compared to a candle flame where salt is sprinkled. The sound of the rats moving is compared to the noise of an army moving. Both sounds are loud and indicate many bodies moving as one. The children come running like fowls in a farmyard when barley is scattered. The sound of the rats is a muttering or rumbling. The sound of the children is a pattering and clattering. The children are a much happier group. Both groups dance after the piper and in each case, one individual is spared the fate of the group following the piper.

Writing Skills

Introducing the Skill

Define *simile* and *metaphor* for students. A **simile** is a comparison using *like* or *as*. A **metaphor** is a figure of speech in which one thing is spoken or written about as if it were another.

Previewing the Skill

Have students read "Writing Skills: Using Metaphors and Similes." Go over the examples. Have students identify examples of both similes and metaphors from poems in Unit 9.

Practicing the Skill

Have students brainstorm a list of similes and metaphors. Some of these may be clichés, such as "he was as mad as a wet hen." Discuss with students the difference between clichés and original comparisons. Then have students complete the Try It Yourself exercises.

Reviewing the Skill

Review the answers to Try It Yourself, Exercise A. Ask students to share their responses to Exercise B.

Writing Skills

Using Metaphors and Similes

Writers create vivid images in their writing by using **figures of speech**, statements that have more than a straightforward, literal meaning. Two figures of speech that are commonly used are **metaphors** and **similes.**

A metaphor is a figure of speech in which one thing is spoken or written about as if it were another.

METAPHOR The rats were a crawling carpet on the floor.

The rats are being compared to a carpet. The rats and a carpet can be compared because both cover the floor.

METAPHOR The old mayor tapped his hair of snow and wished for a trap.

The mayor's hair is being compared to snow. The hair, like snow, must be white.

A simile is a comparison using *like* or *as*. A simile is a type of metaphor.

SIMILE Behind the Piper, the rats marched as orderly as an army.

The rats are compared to an army. Both march in an orderly fashion.

SIMILE The children tumbled after the Piper like a spring stream rushes down a mountain.

The children are compared to a stream. The children and the stream can be compared because both things move in a haphazard fashion with an excess of energy.

Try It Yourself

Exercise A. On your own paper, list the two things being compared in each sentence. Then tell whether the sentence uses a simile or a metaphor.

1. The rats swarmed around the garbage can like bees around a honey pot.
2. That rat is as big as a truck!
3. The rats are the rulers of the town.
4. When the rats appeared, the cat hissed like a snake.
5. To the agile rat, the trap was a toy.
6. When the townspeople threw rocks, the rats screeched like a thousand cars coming to sudden stops.
7. The people searched for any means to get rid of the rats; the invaders had conquered every inch of the town.
8. The hungry rat burrowed through the cheese like a miner through the ground.
9. The rat swaggered into the room like a boxer ready for a fight.
10. At night, my bed was the rat's dance hall.

Exercise B. Try writing your own metaphors and similes. Complete the following phrases on your own paper.

1. The dripping faucet is
2. I always seem to forget something. I feel like
3. My locker is
4. Time is
5. The sound of the trees in the wind is like
6. Lydia dances like
7. The book was as heavy as
8. Her dog is
9. Climbing to the top floor is like
10. Running is

Answers for Try It Yourself

Exercise A

1. Swarming rats are being compared to bees around a honey pot in this simile.
2. Rats are being compared to a truck in this metaphor.
3. Rats are being compared to rulers in this metaphor.
4. The sound the cat made is compared to the hiss of a snake in this simile.
5. The trap is compared to a toy in this metaphor.
6. The sound of rats is compared to the sound of cars screeching to a halt in this simile.
7. Rats are compared to invaders in this metaphor.
8. A rat is compared to a miner and cheese is compared to the ground in this simile.
9. A rat is compared to a boxer in this simile.
10. A bed is compared to a dance hall in this metaphor.

Exercise B

Responses will vary.

PROJECT NOTE

- Students may wish to create costumes for their presentations.
- Remind students that many people are nervous when speaking before groups. They will be more comfortable if they are properly prepared. Review with students the Language Arts Survey, 3.6, "Oral Interpretation."
- Students may wish to invite others to attend their reading.

Unit Project

PRESENTING A CELEBRITY POETRY READING

Poetry is meant not only to be read, but also to be heard. For this reason, writers and readers of poetry often attend public poetry readings. At a poetry reading, a person stands before an audience and reads his or her own poetry or the work of another poet. Poetry readings have been held in auditoriums, theaters, libraries, bookstores, coffee shops, classrooms, and parks. At some readings, people enjoy hearing and seeing favorite poets read their work. A reading can also be an event at which unknown or unpublished poets have a chance to share their work with others.

TRY IT YOURSELF

Participate in a celebrity poetry reading. Each student should choose one favorite poem from this textbook or another book, look up information about its author, and then prepare to attend the reading as the author of the poem. As the famous poet, share some information about your life, then read the poem. Invite your principal, other classes, teachers, and anyone else you would like to attend the reading.

STUDENT MODEL

Today is the day of the celebrity poetry reading being held at the Grove School. The event is taking place in Ms. Vasquez's classroom, and her students have worked hard to organize the event. Colorful programs, created by the students, sit on a table by the door. The programs list the names of the poets reading and the poems being read. A podium, borrowed from the principal, sits at the head of the classroom. Two large potted plants, which were borrowed from another teacher, sit on either side of the podium. The school principal and a class from down the hall are in the audience. Tammy Rashad is the first person to stand at the podium. Tammy is participating in the reading as Emily Dickinson. She will be reading the poem "The Brain—is wider than the Sky." Tammy is nervous, but she has read her poem aloud in front of a mirror several times. She begins by saying, "My name is Emily Dickinson. I was born in Amherst, Massachusetts, in 1830. I have spent most of my life there. I attended Mt. Holyoke Female Seminary for one year, but I am happiest when I am home writing poetry, reading, thinking, and writing letters to family and close friends. I usually prefer not to attend public readings. I like my private time, and I like to keep most of my writing to myself. Some of my friends and family, however, have been encouraging me to share my work." Tammy, as Emily, then reads her poem. When she is done, the audience claps and watches as Emily Dickinson leaves and Jamie Franco takes the podium as Shel Silverstein. People enjoy the reading because they are able to hear some interesting poetry and learn a bit about the lives of famous poets.

Examining the Model

1. What items did students gather and prepare for the reading?
2. How does Tammy feel when she stands at the podium? What did she do to rehearse for the reading?
3. When each "poet" stands at the podium, what will he or she say?

Choosing Poetry for the Reading

1. Each student should choose one poem to read. Flip through your textbook or look through some books at the library to find a poem that you enjoy. To avoid duplication, have your teacher or one student keep a master list of the poems that are chosen.
2. Gather some information about the life of the author of your poem. "Become" that poet. What will you tell the audience about your life? If your poet had a distinctive appearance or dress, you might try to imitate his or her appearance as well.
3. Practice reading your poem aloud several times in front of a mirror.

Planning the Poetry Reading

1. As a class, decide where your poetry reading will be held. You might hold it in your classroom, the library, the auditorium, or the gymnasium. You might contact a nursing home in your community to see if you may present your reading to the residents. Make the reading a special event, even if your audience is made up only of members of your own class.
2. Design a program. In the program, list the poems and their authors. If you are not able to create and copy programs, make a large poster that provides the audience with this information. Display the poster so that it is in clear view of the audience.
3. Decide if readers should stand in front of a podium or music stand, or sit on a desk or on a stool. If you like, decorate the area for the reading. Plants, posters, and drawings make nice decorations.

Presenting the Poetry Reading

1. Your teacher or a student should welcome the audience and introduce each "poet."
2. When it is your turn, speaking as the poet, give the audience some information about your life. Then introduce and read your poem.
3. When you read the poem, speak loudly and clearly. Look up at your audience occasionally. For more information about speaking before an audience, you might consult the Language Arts Survey, 3.1, "Verbal and Nonverbal Communication."

Answers for Examining the Model

1. The students gathered a podium and two potted plants. They made colorful programs.
2. Tammy feels nervous, but she knows she is well prepared. She rehearsed in front of a mirror.
3. Each student will take on the role of a poet. He or she will introduce himself or herself as the poet and give a brief biography. Then the student will read the poem.

ANALYTIC SCALE FOR PROJECT

Assign a score from 1 to 25 for each grading criterion below.

Celebrity Poetry Reading

- **Organization.** The group set attainable goals and created a schedule or strategy for achieving those goals.
- **Cooperation.** The group assigned tasks fairly to each member, and each member cooperated toward achieving the group's goals.
- **Goal Achievement.** The group worked steadily toward its goals and did, in fact, achieve them.
- **Presentation.** The group presented a product of high quality that met the initial project description.

Vocabulary Check Test

Ask students to number their papers from one to ten. Have students complete each sentence with a word from the Vocabulary for the Unit in the Unit Review.

1. The audacious rat scampered over the table in the middle of dinner.
2. We filled seven washers with the mammoth load of laundry.
3. Juanita hired an exterminator to get rid of the vermin in her house.
4. Havoc and shambles were left behind when the storm finally roared out to sea.
5. The heavy rains replenished the lakes and streams.
6. The chipmunk hoarded seeds in its bulging cheeks.
7. We almost missed the trail, but Bill spied the telltale signs of a broken branch.
8. Katya never does anything on an impulse; she always thinks everything through.
9. The luminous face of the clock on the tower glowed like a full moon.
10. The sponge swelled as it absorbed the water.

Unit Review

Summary

Literary Terms for the Unit

flashback, 433
image, 407
irony of situation, 407
metaphor, 427
refrain, 411
repetition, 411
simile, 427, 449
speaker, 415, 437
stanza, 421
theme, 433

Vocabulary for the Unit

absorb, 419
audacious, 423
bereave, 446
brook, 444
bushel, 405
celestial, 425
consternation, 440
ditty, 439
endeavor, 447
havoc, 444
heft, 419
hoard, 425
hue, 446
impulse, 425
lapis, 423
low, 410
luminous, 425
mammoth, 425
mirth, 447
obese, 440
ode, 426
paunch, 440
portal, 446
remorse, 426
replenish, 444
ribald, 444
sacred, 425
scarce, 410
solemn, 410
spy, 439
stout, 443
subterraneous, 448
swarthy, 441
vermin, 439

Questions for Writing, Discussion, and Research

1. Which images from the poems in this unit did you find most striking? What effect did these images have on you?
2. Which poems would you classify as narrative and which would you classify as lyric? Use evidence from the poems to support your answers.

Spelling Check Test

Ask students to number their papers from one to ten. Read each word aloud. Then read aloud the sentence containing the word. Repeat the word. Ask students to write the word on their papers, spelling it correctly.

1. **celestial**

Lara's lyrics and Jaime's music were a celestial combination.

2. **paunch**

The troll's great paunch hung over his belt.

3. **bereft**

Lorna thought the search party might find her buried in the rubble, but she was bereft of hope when she heard the voices retreating.

4. **audacious**

Everyone was stunned by Pablo's audacious actions.

5. **subterraneous**

We have to go down several flights of stairs to get to the subterraneous station.

6. **lapis**

The blue stone in the ring is lapis.

7. **mirth**

The room was full of mirth, as indicated by the laughter and broad smiles of everyone in it.

8. **ribald**

Yancy was known as a ribald, but he cleaned up his act and became a master of decorum.

9. **consternation**

When Eli heard the news of the flood in Riverville, he was filled with consternation for his cousins who lived there.

10. **bushel**

We picked a bushel of apples and used them all for pies.

For Your Reading List

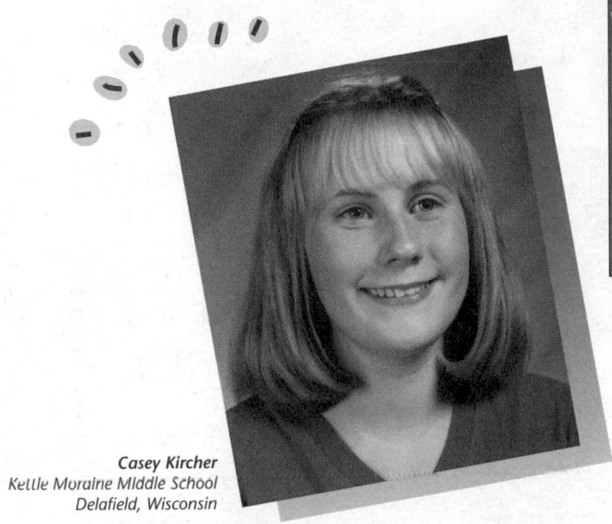

Casey Kircher
Kettle Moraine Middle School
Delafield, Wisconsin

Archy and Mehitabel
by Don Marquis

Archy and Mehitabel is an original book by Don Marquis. I was intrigued by his outstanding creativity with words. The main character, Archy the cockroach, types poems on a typewriter at night. He can't hit the shift key, so he uses only lowercase letters. Archy writes fascinating poems about how he comes face to face with unbelievable characters. Many of the poems Archy writes have to do with one of his good friends, Mehitabel the cat, who believes she was famous women from history in her past lives. Mehitabel has many stories to tell Archy that are filled with excitement and humor. I think that you will have fun reading this book because of the entertaining stories and the clever variety that will keep you guessing what will happen next.

GOALS/OBJECTIVES

Studying this unit will enable students to

- appreciate drama
- name and describe the elements of drama and interpret these in a script
- recognize an adaptation
- define *suspense, dialogue,* and *character* and identify the use of these devices in works that they read
- edit for errors in verbs
- write a dialogue
- design a set and costumes

ADDITIONAL UNIT MATERIALS IN THE ASSESSMENT PORTFOLIO

- Vocabulary Worksheet 2.10.5
- Unit Test 2.10.6

See also the Additional Resources Box in the marginal notes accompanying each selection.

CROSS-CURRICULAR CONNECTIONS

- World History, 460, 506

UNIT 10 DRAMA

The Cliff Walk. *Claude Monet*

Playing, whose end, both at the first and now, was and is to hold, as 'twere the mirror up to nature.

—William Shakespeare

UNIT SKILLS OUTLINE

Literary Skills and Concepts

- Character, 518
- Dialogue, 502
- Suspense, 502

Other Language Arts Skills and Concepts

- Editing for Errors in Verbs, 503
- Writing a Dialogue, 519

Art Note

Claude Monet (1840–1926) was a French painter known for creating the Impressionist style, which represented the play and movement of light upon the surface of objects. Monet's family lived by the sea, and Monet spent much of his childhood along the beaches, where he observed nature closely. Later in life, Monet painted several beach and sea pictures. Monet painted mostly natural scenes, and he insisted on working outdoors, as close to nature as possible.

Elements of Drama

A **drama**, or **play**, is a story told through characters played by actors. Early groups of people around the world enacted ritual scenes related to hunting, warfare, or religion. From these drama arose. Western drama as we know it first began in ancient Greece.

The Playwright and the Script

The author of a play is the **playwright.** A playwright has limited control in deciding how his or her work is presented. Producers, directors, set designers, and actors all interpret a playwright's work and present their interpretations to the audience.

A **script** is the written text from which a drama is produced. Scripts are made up of stage directions and dialogue. Scripts may be divided into long parts called acts and short parts called scenes.

Stage directions are notes included in a play to describe how something should look, sound, or be performed. Stage directions can describe lighting, costumes, music, sound effects, or other elements of a play. They can also describe entrances and exits, gestures, tone of voice, or other elements related to the acting of a play. Stage directions sometimes provide historical or background information. In stage directions, the parts of the stage are described from the actors' point of view.

The speech of the actors in a play is called **dialogue.** A speech given by one character is called a **monologue.**

An **act** is a major part of a play. One-act, three-act, and five-act plays are all common. A **scene** is a short section of a literary work, one that happens in a single place and time. There may be any number of scenes in each act, and the number of scenes may vary from act to act.

The Spectacle

The **spectacle** includes all the elements of the drama that are presented to the audience's senses. The following chart describes some common parts of the spectacle.

ELEMENT	DESCRIPTION
set	A **set** is a collection of objects on a stage that create a scene. Furniture, painted backdrops, and walls all help to create a set.
properties	**Properties** are items that can be carried on and off the stage by actors. Examples of properties include swords, packages, and dinner trays.
special effects	**Special effects** are special audio or visual elements used in a play. Common **sound effects** include rain, telephones, and police sirens. **Visual special effects** can be simple or elaborate, depending on the production.
lighting	The **lighting** of a drama helps to set its **mood** and **setting.** Soft lighting might be used for romantic scenes and bright lighting to indicate sunlight.
costumes	**Costumes** are the clothing and accessories actors wear. Costumes often indicate historical period, occupation, or social status.

Fields. *Vincent van Gogh, 1884*

GOALS/OBJECTIVES

Studying this lesson will enable students to
- enjoy a drama
- appreciate an adaptation
- discuss the impact of the Holocaust
- recognize elements of suspense
- analyze relationships between characters
- edit for errors in verbs

ADDITIONAL RESOURCES

Reader's Guide
- Selection Worksheet, 10.1

Assessment Portfolio
- Selection Check Test, 2.10.1
- Selection Test, 2.10.2

Pronunciation Exercise
- Grade 8 Audiocassette, Side B, Track 53

CROSS-CURRICULAR CONNECTIONS

World History

Have students research the history of the Holocaust to better understand the events described in the Cross-curricular Connection material. Discuss with students why Anne Frank's family left Germany for Holland. Discuss why the Frank family had to go into hiding.

Prereading

PLAY

from *The Diary of Anne Frank*
by Frances Goodrich and Albert Hackett

Cross-curricular Connections

World History. The Holocaust refers to the mass murder of European Jews by German Nazis during World War II. Part of Nazi dictator Adolf Hitler's plan to conquer the world included wiping out the entire Jewish population. The Nazis killed over six million Jewish people in Europe between 1938 and 1945. In addition, Hitler was responsible for the murder of another five million Europeans, including Gypsies, Poles, and Slavs.

The Holocaust began when the Nazis came to power in Germany in 1933 and started to persecute Jewish members of the population. Laws and regulations prevented Jews from attending universities and, in many cases, from owning businesses or property. In 1938, the Nazis began sending German Jews to concentration camps as political prisoners. Concentration camps were places with horrible conditions where Jewish people were used as slave labor. Many people were worked to death, starved, or died from disease. Those who were not able to do hard labor—mostly women, children, the sick, and the elderly—were murdered in gas chambers. In 1939, Germany invaded Poland and forced Jews to leave their homes and live in special areas called ghettos. In 1940 many other countries, including France and the Netherlands, fell to Germany.

Anne Frank was a Jew born in Frankfurt, Germany, in 1929. In 1933 she and her family moved to the Netherlands to escape persecution. There, they were safe until 1940, when the Germans invaded Holland and put anti-Jewish laws into practice. In 1942, when Anne's sister was called for deportation to a concentration camp, the family went into hiding. The Franks hid with another family, the Van Daans, in a few rooms in the upper story of the building where Otto Frank had worked. They were later joined by a dentist named Mr. Dussel. During the two years they were in the "secret annex," as they called their hiding place, Anne kept a diary on which the play *The Diary of Anne Frank* is based.

As You Read

The close quarters and tense situation put a strain on many of the relationships among the residents of the hiding spot. Anne's spirited words and actions often drew strong reactions from others. Make a chart like the one below. As you read, fill in the chart with what Anne said or did and the reaction of one of the others.

Anne's Words/Actions	Reaction of Others
hides Peter's shoes	Peter wrestles her and becomes self-conscious

AS YOU READ

The following list contains some of the words/actions and reactions students that might include in their charts: Anne makes fun of Peter/Peter calls Anne Mrs. Quack Quack; Anne tells Mr. Van Daan she has never heard grownups quarrel/he tells her she is rude; Anne, pretending to dance, spills milk on Mrs. Van Daan's fur coat; Mrs. Van Daan is very upset and calls Anne a clumsy fool; Anne storms to her room after her mother asks her to try to be more like Margot/Anne's mother is upset by her difficulty to communicate with Anne; Anne has a nightmare and screams/Mr. Dussel and Mr. Van Daan are upset and worry that her screams will give them away.

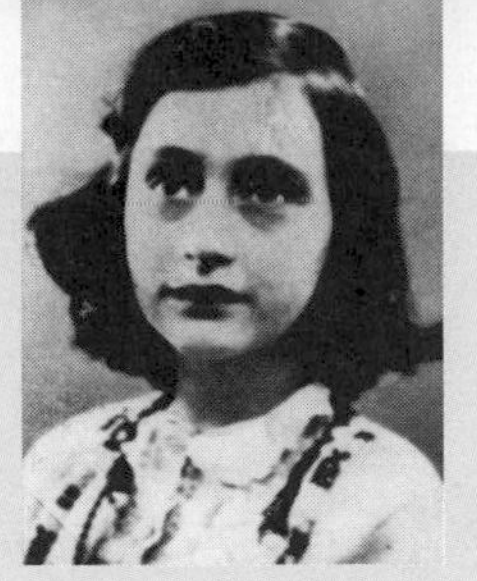

READER'S JOURNAL

Think about a time when you tried to be still and quiet so nobody would know of your presence. Was it difficult? How did you feel as people got closer to your hiding space? How did you feel if you accidentally made a noise or movement? Imagine that you are hiding for your life. How do you think you would react to the tension of this situation?

The Diary of Anne Frank

FRANCES GOODRICH AND ALBERT HACKETT

CHARACTERS

MR. FRANK	MR. VAN DAAN	MARGOT FRANK	MR. KRALER
MIEP	PETER VAN DAAN	ANNE FRANK	MR. DUSSEL
MRS. VAN DAAN	MRS. FRANK		

ACT I

SCENE 1

[The scene remains the same throughout the play. It is the top floor of a warehouse and office building in Amsterdam, Holland. The sharply peaked roof of the building is outlined against a sea of other rooftops, stretching away into the distance. Nearby is the belfry[1] *of a church tower, the Westertoren, whose carillon*[2] *rings out the hours. Occasionally faint sounds float up from below: the voices of children playing in the street, the tramp of marching feet, a boat whistle from the canal.*

The three rooms of the top floor and a small attic space above are exposed to our view. The largest of the rooms is in the center, with two small rooms, slightly raised on either side. On the right is a bathroom, out of sight. A narrow steep flight of stairs at the back leads up to the attic. The rooms are sparsely furnished with a few chairs, cots, a table or two. The windows are painted over, or covered with makeshift blackout curtains.[3] *In the main room there is a sink, a gas ring for cooking and a woodburning stove for warmth.*

The room on the left is hardly more than a closet. There is a skylight in the sloping

1. **belfry.** Bell tower
2. **carillon.** Set of stationary bells, each producing one note of the musical scale
3. **blackout curtains.** Sheets placed over windows to conceal light and reduce the visibility of enemy air bombers

WORDS FOR EVERYDAY USE

sparse • ly (spärs´lē) *adv.*, thinly; not densely

VOCABULARY IN CONTEXT

- We planted trees in the sparsely forested area.

READER'S JOURNAL

As an alternate activity, you might ask students to think about what happens when people are confined together in a small space, for example on an airplane or a long car trip. Have students describe how people react to each other in these situations.

SPELLING AND VOCABULARY WORDS FROM THE SELECTION

capitulation	mercurial
coeducational	meticulous
conspicuous	mimic
extravagant	ostentatiously
falteringly	pantomime
fatalist	portly
gratitude	quarrel
grave	satchel
improvise	scoffingly
indignantly	sparsely
intolerable	threadbare
leisure	vile

SUPPORT FOR LEP STUDENTS

PRONUNCIATIONS OF PROPER NOUNS AND ADJECTIVES

Miep (mēp) n.
Van • Daan (vän dän) n.
Dus • sel (do͞os´əl) n.
West • er • tor • en (vest´ər tôr´n) n.
Zur • ich (zo͞or´ik) n.

ADDITIONAL VOCABULARY

asthma—chronic condition characterized by wheezing or difficulty breathing
branded—identifying mark of disgrace
compassionate—showing sympathy or pity
consult—talk things over to decide something
insufferable—unbearable
interval—period of time
loathe—hate
sustenance—food, nourishment

Answers to Guided Reading Questions

① The beginning of the play is set in late afternoon, November 1945.

② Finding a woman's white glove on the floor in the apartment makes Mr. Frank lose control. Perhaps he recognizes the glove as belonging to someone important to him.

Literary Technique

ADAPTATION

An **adaptation** is a rewriting of a literary work in another form. Frances Goodrich and Albert Hackett's *The Diary of Anne Frank* is an adaptation of Anne Frank's diary, which was published after her death. The diary was published by Mr. Frank under the title *Het Achterhuis* in 1947. The first English translation, *The Diary of a Young Girl,* was published in 1953.

Ask students to read *The Diary of a Young Girl.* Ask them to compare and contrast the events, relationships between characters, and emotions of Anne depicted in each work.

ceiling. Directly under this room is a small steep stairwell, with steps leading down to a door. This is the only entrance from the building below. When the door is opened we see that it has been concealed on the outer side by a bookcase attached to it.

When is the beginning of the play set? ①

The curtain rises on an empty stage. It is late afternoon, November 1945.

The rooms are dusty, the curtains in rags. Chairs and tables are overturned.

The door at the foot of the small stairwell swings open. MR. FRANK *comes up the steps into view. He is a gentle, cultured European in his middle years. There is still a trace of a German accent in his speech.*

He stands looking slowly around, making a supreme effort at self-control. He is weak, ill. His clothes are threadbare.

After a second he drops his rucksack[4] *on the couch and moves slowly about. He opens the door to one of the smaller rooms, and then abruptly closes it again, turning away. He goes to the window at the back, looking off at the Westertoren as its carillon strikes the hour of six, then he moves restlessly on.*

What makes Mr. Frank lose control? Why do you think this object has such an effect on him? ②

From the street below we hear the sound of a barrel organ[5] *and children's voices at play. There is a many-colored scarf hanging from a nail.* MR. FRANK *takes it, putting it around his neck. As he starts back for his rucksack, his eye is caught by something lying on the floor. It is a woman's white glove. He holds it in his hand and suddenly all of his self-control is gone. He breaks down, crying.*

We hear footsteps on the stairs. MIEP GIES *comes up, looking for* MR. FRANK. MIEP *is a Dutch girl of about twenty-two. She wears a coat and hat, ready to go home. She is pregnant. Her attitude toward* MR. FRANK *is protective, compassionate.]*

MIEP. Are you all right, Mr. Frank?

MR. FRANK. [*Quickly controlling himself*] Yes, Miep, yes.

MIEP. Everyone in the office has gone home . . . It's after six. [*Then pleading*] Don't stay up here, Mr. Frank. What's the use of torturing yourself like this?

MR. FRANK. I've come to say good-bye . . . I'm leaving here, Miep.

MIEP. What do you mean? Where are you going? Where?

MR. FRANK. I don't know yet. I haven't decided.

MIEP. Mr. Frank, you can't leave here! This is your home! Amsterdam is your home. Your business is here, waiting for you . . . You're needed here . . . Now that the war is over, there are things that . . .

MR. FRANK. I can't stay in Amsterdam, Miep. It has too many memories for me. Everywhere there's something. . . the house we lived in . . . the school . . . that street organ playing out there . . . I'm not the person you used to know, Miep. I'm a bitter old

4. **rucksack.** Knapsack, backpack
5. **barrel organ.** Hand organ, or an instrument played by turning a crank

Words for Everyday Use

thread • bare (thred´ ber´) *adj.,* worn down so that the threads show

Vocabulary in Context

• Dennis got plush, wall-to-wall carpeting to replace his old threadbare rug.

man. [*Breaking off*] Forgive me. I shouldn't speak to you like this . . . after all that you did for us . . . the suffering . . .

MIEP. No. No. It wasn't suffering. You can't say we suffered. [*As she speaks, she straightens a chair which is overturned.*]

MR. FRANK. I know what you went through, you and Mr. Kraler. I'll remember it as long as I live. [*He gives one last look around.*] Come, Miep. [*He starts for the steps, then remembers his rucksack, going back to get it.*]

MIEP. [*Hurrying up to a cupboard*] Mr. Frank, did you see? There are some of your papers here. [*She brings a bundle of papers to him.*] We found them in a heap of rubbish on the floor after . . . after you left.

MR. FRANK. Burn them. [*He opens his rucksack to put the glove in it.*]

MIEP. But, Mr. Frank, there are letters, notes . . .

MR. FRANK. Burn them. All of them.

MIEP. Burn this? [*She hands him a paperbound notebook.*]

MR. FRANK. [*Quietly*] Anne's diary. [*He opens the diary and begins to read.*] "Monday, the sixth of July, nineteen forty-two." [*To* MIEP] Nineteen forty-two. Is it possible, Miep? . . . Only three years ago. [*As he continues his reading, he sits down on the couch.*] "Dear Diary, since you and I are going to be great friends, I will start by telling you about myself. My name is Anne Frank. I am thirteen years old. I was born in Germany the twelfth of June, nineteen twenty-nine. As my family is Jewish, we emigrated to Holland when Hitler came to power."

[*As* MR. FRANK *reads on, another voice joins his, as if coming from the air. It is* ANNE'S VOICE.]

MR. FRANK AND ANNE. "My father started a business, importing spice and herbs. Things went well for us until nineteen forty. Then the war came, and the Dutch capitulation, followed by the arrival of the Germans. Then things got very bad for the Jews."

[MR. FRANK'S VOICE *dies out.* ANNE'S VOICE *continues alone. The lights dim slowly to darkness. The curtain falls on the scene.*]

ANNE'S VOICE. You could not do this and you could not do that. They forced Father out of his business. We had to wear yellow stars.[6] I had to turn in my bike. I couldn't go to a Dutch school any more. I couldn't go to the movies, or ride in an automobile, or even on a streetcar, and a million other things. But somehow we children still managed to have fun. Yesterday Father told me were going into hiding. Where, he wouldn't say. At five o'clock this morning Mother woke me and told me to hurry and get dressed. I was to put on as many clothes as I could. It would look too suspicious if we walked

6. **yellow stars.** Star of David, placed on the clothes of Jewish persons in German-controlled areas of Europe so that Jews could be more easily identified

1 What does Miep give to Mr. Frank? Why is he not interested in them? What catches his attention?

2 What happened to the Jews after the arrival of the Germans? What step does Anne's family take?

WORDS FOR EVERYDAY USE

ca • pit • u • la • tion (kə pich´yoo lā´shən) *n.,* conditional surrender, act of giving up under prearranged terms

ANSWERS TO GUIDED READING QUESTIONS

1 Miep gives papers, letters, and a notebook that she had found on the floor to Mr. Frank. He does not want them because they might bring back memories he is trying to escape. Anne's diary catches his attention.

2 Many rules were imposed that segregated Jews. Jews could not go to regular schools, ride in cars or on street cars, and they were forced to wear the Star of David for identification. Anne's family goes into hiding.

BIOGRAPHICAL NOTE

Anne Frank (1929–1945) was born in Frankfurt, Germany. She and her family moved to Amsterdam, Holland, in 1933 to escape the Nazi persecution of the Jews. In Amsterdam, Anne Frank attended school, made friends, and lived a normal life. Her life and the lives of thousands of Jews in Holland began to change in 1940 when the Germans invaded Holland. Frank had to leave her school and attend a special school for Jewish students. Roundups of Jews began. Otto Frank, Anne's father, feared for the safety of his family and made arrangements for them to go into hiding in some rooms in the building where his former business was housed. When Margot, Anne's sister, was called to report for deportation on July 5, 1942, the family went into hiding with the Van Daan family. They were later joined by a dentist named Dussel. Loyal friends in the building helped the two families by bringing them food, news, and other necessities.

VOCABULARY IN CONTEXT

• The victorious general accepted the capitulation of the defeated armies.

Answers to Guided Reading Questions

1 The Van Daans are nervous because the Franks are late. They are afraid the Franks have been picked up by the Green Police.

2 The Franks were late because there were too many Green Police on the streets and they had to go around the long way.

Additional Questions and Activities

Point out to students the descriptions of the Van Daans. Have students make a character chart for each character in the play. In the chart they should list details about appearance, habits, and character traits. Students can also describe the character's interactions with other characters. Point out to students that they can learn about each character through stage directions and also through the dialogue of the play. They can learn about a character though what he or she says and through what others say about him or her.

Why are the Van Daans nervous? What do they fear has happened? 1

along carrying suitcases. It wasn't until we were on our way that I learned where we were going. Our hiding place was to be upstairs in the building where Father used to have his business. Three other people were coming in with us . . . the Van Daans and their son Peter . . . Father knew the Van Daans but we had never met them . . .

[*During the last lines the curtain rises on the scene. The lights dim on,* ANNE'S VOICE *fades out.*]

Scene 2

[*It is early morning, July 1942. The rooms are bare, as before, but they are now clean and orderly.*

MR. VAN DAAN, *a tall, portly man in his late forties, is in the main room, pacing up and down, nervously smoking a cigarette. His clothes and overcoat are expensive and well cut.*

Why were the Franks late? 2

MRS. VAN DAAN *sits on the couch, clutching her possessions, a hatbox, bags, etc. She is a pretty woman in her early forties. She wears a fur coat over her other clothes.*

PETER VAN DAAN *is standing at the window of the room on the right, looking down at the street below. He is a shy, awkward boy of sixteen. He wears a cap, a raincoat, and long Dutch trousers, like "plus fours."*[7] *At his feet is a black case, a carrier for his cat.*

The yellow Star of David is conspicuous on all of their clothes.]

Mrs. Van Daan. [*Rising, nervous, excited*] Something's happened to them! I know it!

Mr. Van Daan. Now, Kerli!

Mrs. Van Daan. Mr. Frank said they'd be here at seven o'clock. He said . . .

Mr. Van Daan. They've two miles to walk. You can't expect . . .

Mrs. Van Daan. They've been picked up. That's what's happened. They've been taken . . .

[MR. VAN DAAN *indicates that he hears someone coming.*]

Mr. Van Daan. You see?

[PETER *takes up his carrier and his schoolbag, etc., and goes into the main room as* MR. FRANK *comes up the stairwell from below.* MR. FRANK *looks much younger now. His movements are brisk, his manner confident. He wears an overcoat and carries his hat and a small cardboard box. He crosses to the* VAN DAANS, *shaking hands with each of them.*]

Mr. Frank. Mrs. Van Daan, Mr. Van Daan, Peter. [*Then, in explanation of their lateness*] There were too many of the Green Police[8] on the streets . . . we had to take the long way around.

[*Up the steps come* MARGOT FRANK, MRS. FRANK, MIEP, *(not pregnant now) and* MR. KRALER. *All of them carry bags, packages, and so forth. The Star of David is conspicuous on all of the* FRANKS' *clothing.* MARGOT *is eighteen, beautiful, quiet, shy.* MRS. FRANK *is a young mother, gently bred, reserved. She, like* MR. FRANK, *has a slight German accent.* MR. KRALER *is a Dutchman, dependable, kindly.*

7. **plus fours.** Loose knickers, or short pants
8. **Green Police.** Nazi police who wore green uniforms

Words for Everyday Use

port • ly (pôrt´lē) *adj.,* large and heavy in a dignified way

con • spic • u • ous (kən spik´ yo͞o əs) *adj.,* obvious; attracting attention by being unusual or unexpected

Vocabulary in Context

- Mr. Meyer is rather portly, and his wife, while also dignified, is rather slender.
- Lisette's jeans were conspicuous at the semi-formal dance.

As MR. KRALER *and* MIEP *go upstage to put down their parcels,* MRS. FRANK *turns back to call* ANNE.]

MRS. FRANK. Anne?

[ANNE comes *running up the stairs. She is thirteen, quick in her movements, interested in everything, mercurial in her emotions. She wears a cape, long wool socks and carries a schoolbag.*]

MR. FRANK. [*Introducing them*] My wife, Edith. Mr. and Mrs. Van Daan . . . their son, Peter . . . my daughters, Margot and Anne.

[MRS. FRANK *hurries over, shaking hands with them.*]

[ANNE *gives a polite little curtsy as she shakes* MR. VAN DAAN'S *hand. Then she immediately starts off on a tour of investigation of her new home, going upstairs to the attic room.*]

[MIEP *and* MR. KRALER *are putting the various things they have brought on the shelves.*]

MR. KRALER. I'm sorry there is still so much confusion.

MR. FRANK. Please. Don't think of it. After all, we'll have plenty of leisure to arrange everything ourselves.

MIEP. [*To* MRS. FRANK] We put the stores of food you sent in here. Your drugs are here . . . soap, linen here.

MRS. FRANK. Thank you, Miep.

MIEP. I made up the beds . . . the way Mr. Frank and Mr. Kraler said. [*She starts out.*] Forgive me. I have to hurry. I've got to go to the other side of town to get some ration books[9] for you.

MRS. VAN DAAN. Ration books? If they see our names on ration books, they'll know we're here.

MR. KRALER. There isn't anything . . .

MIEP. Don't worry. Your names won't be on them. [*As she hurries out*] I'll be up later.

MR. FRANK. Thank you, Miep.

MRS. FRANK. [*To* MR. KRALER] It's illegal, then, the ration books? We've never done anything illegal.

MR. FRANK. We won't be living here exactly according to regulations.

[*As* MR. KRALER *reassures* MRS. FRANK, *he takes various small things, such as matches, soap, etc., from his pockets, handing them to her.*]

MR. KRALER. This isn't the black market,[10] Mrs. Frank. This is what we call the white market . . . helping all of the hundreds and hundreds who are hiding out in Amsterdam.

[*The carillon is heard playing the quarter-hour before eight.* MR. KRALER *looks at his watch.* ANNE *stops at the window as she comes down the stairs.*]

ANNE. It's the Westertoren!

MR. KRALER. I must go. I must be out of here and downstairs in the

9. **ration books.** Books of coupons, often distributed during wartime, that limit the amount of scarce items one family can buy

10. **black market.** System for selling illegal or scarce items

❶ *What does Anne do as soon as she is in her new home?*

❷ *What does Mr. Kraler say to reassure Mrs. Frank? In what way does the white market differ from the black market?*

WORDS FOR EVERYDAY USE

mer • cu • ri • al (mər kyo͝or´ē əl) *adj.,* volatile; frequently and unexpectedly changing

lei • sure (lē´zhər) *n.,* free, unoccupied time

ANSWERS TO GUIDED READING QUESTIONS

❶ Anne starts off on a tour of investigation of her new home.

❷ Mr. Kraler tells Mrs. Frank that they are not dealing on the black market, but rather on the white market, a system of obtaining food and other necessary materials for the hundreds and hundreds of people who are hiding in Amsterdam.

VOCABULARY IN CONTEXT

- Jemma is so mercurial that I never know what to expect from her from one minute to the next.
- Alan likes to construct models during his leisure time.

Answers to Guided Reading Questions

❶ Mrs. Van Daan's fur coat, which she was wearing in the middle of July, and Peter's cat, which was making a lot of noise, were two things that might have drawn attention to the Van Daans and made them look suspicious.

❷ It is essential that the people in the hiding place make no noise during the hours the workers are in the building. They must move, in stockinged feet, only when necessary. They must speak in a whisper and must not run any water. They must never throw out trash. There cannot be any signs that there are people living in the building if the two families are to survive.

Literary Technique

Sound Effects

Sound effects are sounds introduced to create a mood or to indicate the presence of something. Ask students to read the stage direction that begins, "Mr. Frank stops abruptly." What sound effect is called for in this direction? What is indicated by this sound? Why does this sound create tension in the group?

Answers

The stage direction calls for the sound of marching feet. It indicates soldiers on the street. The family is afraid of being heard and discovered.

❶ *What two things brought by the Van Daans might have made them seem suspicious?*

office before the workmen get here. [*He starts for the stairs leading out.*] Miep or I, or both of us, will be up each day to bring you food and news and find out what your needs are. Tomorrow I'll get you a better bolt for the door at the foot of the stairs. It needs a bolt that you can throw yourself and open only at our signal. [*To* MR. FRANK] Oh . . . You'll tell them about the noise?

Mr. Frank. I'll tell them.

Mr. Kraler. Good-bye then for the moment. I'll come up again, after the workmen leave.

Mr. Frank. Good-bye, Mr. Kraler.

❷ *What rules are essential to keeping the hiding place a secret?*

Mrs. Frank. [*Shaking his hand*] How can we thank you?

[*The others murmur their good-byes.*]

Mr. Kraler. I never thought I'd live to see the day when a man like Mr. Frank would have to go into hiding. When you think—

[*He breaks off, going out.* MR. FRANK *follows him down the steps, bolting the door after him. In the interval before he returns,* PETER *goes over to* MARGOT, *shaking hands with her. As* MR. FRANK *comes back up the steps,* MRS. FRANK *questions him anxiously.*]

Mrs. Frank. What did he mean, about the noise?

Mr. Frank. First let us take off some of these clothes.

[*They all start to take off garment after garment. On each of their coats, sweaters, blouses, suits, dresses, is another yellow Star of David.* MR. *and* MRS. FRANK *are underdressed quite simply. The others wear several things, sweaters, extra dresses, bathrobes, aprons, nightgowns, etc.*]

Mr. Van Daan. It's a wonder we weren't arrested, walking along the streets . . . Petronella with a fur coat in July . . . and that cat of Peter's crying all the way.

Anne. A cat?

[*Finally, as they have all removed their surplus clothes, they look to* MR. FRANK, *waiting for him to speak.*]

Mr. Frank. Now. About the noise. While the men are in the building below, we must have complete quiet. Every sound can be heard down there. not only in the workrooms, but in the offices too. The men come at about eight-thirty, and leave at about five-thirty. So, to be perfectly safe, from eight in the morning until six in the evening we must move only when it is necessary, and then in stockinged feet. We must not speak above a whisper. We must not run any water. We cannot use the sink, or even, forgive me, the w.c.[11] The pipes go down through the workrooms. It would be heard. No trash . . .

[MR. FRANK *stops abruptly as he hears the sound of marching feet from the street below. Everyone is motionless, paralyzed with fear.* MR. FRANK *goes quietly into the room on the right to look down out of the window.* ANNE *runs after him, peering out with him. The tramping feet pass without stopping. The tension is relieved.* MR. FRANK, *followed by* ANNE, *returns to the main room and resumes his instructions to the group.*]

. . . No trash must ever be thrown out which might reveal that someone is living up here . . . not even a potato paring. We must burn everything in the stove at night. This is the way we

11. **w.c.** Abbreviation for water closet, meaning toilet

Anne Frank

must live until it is over, if we are to survive.

[*There is silence for a second.*]

MRS. FRANK. Until it is over.

MR. FRANK. [*Reassuringly*] After six we can move about . . . we can talk and laugh and have our supper and read and play games . . . just as we would at home. [*He looks at his watch.*] And now I think it would be wise if we all went to our rooms, and were settled before eight o'clock. Mrs. Van Daan, you and your husband will be upstairs. I regret that there's no place up there for Peter. But he will be here, near us. This will be our common room, where we'll meet to talk and eat and read, like one family.

MR. VAN DAAN. And where do you and Mrs. Frank sleep?

MR. FRANK. This room is also our bedroom.

MRS. VAN DAAN. That isn't right. We'll sleep here and you take the room upstairs.

MR. VAN DAAN. It's your place.

MR. FRANK. Please. I've thought this out for weeks. It's the best arrangement. The only arrangement.

MRS. VAN DAAN. [*To* MR. FRANK] Never, never can we thank you. [*Then to* MRS. FRANK] I don't know what would have happened to us, if it hadn't been for Mr. Frank.

MR. FRANK. You don't know how your husband helped me when I came to this country . . . knowing no one . . . not able to speak the language. I can never repay him for that. [*Going to* VAN DAAN] May I help you with your things?

❶ *What will they do after six?*

❷ *Why has Mr. Frank invited the Van Daans to hide with them?*

BIOGRAPHICAL NOTE

Anne Frank wrote of the picture of herself shown on this page that she wished to look like this all the time and that perhaps she would have a chance to go to Hollywood. She dated her words October 10, 1942.

ANSWERS TO GUIDED READING QUESTIONS

❶ After six, they will move around, talk, laugh, have supper, read, play games, and act as they would if they were at home.

❷ Mr. Frank has invited the Van Daans into hiding with them because Mr. Van Daan helped Mr. Frank when he first came to Amsterdam, knowing no one and not even speaking the language.

ANSWERS TO GUIDED READING QUESTIONS

➊ Anne had to leave her cat behind. She is happy to find that Peter has brought his cat. Although she will miss her own cat, she is happy to see that there will be a pet in her new home.

➋ Anne is outgoing and popular. She always seems to be in the middle of a crowd. Peter is shy and a loner.

HISTORICAL NOTE

Holland has a long history of accepting persecuted people. It is the country to which Otto Frank decided to relocate his family in 1933. He recognized the growing danger of the Nazi party, which gained a growing audience in the face of worldwide depression in the 1920s.

Adolf Hitler became the leader, or *fuhrer,* of the Nazi party in 1921. In 1933, he became chancellor of Germany and gained absolute power over the country. He quickly put anti-Jewish programs into effect. The new laws barred Jews from civil service, teaching, and work in the media. More Jews lost jobs and businesses as further restrictions were placed on them. The Gestapo, or secret police, raided homes and businesses and made life increasingly difficult and dangerous for Jews.

➊ *What did Anne have to leave behind that she will miss? What does she find at the hiding place that makes her happy?*

➋ *What difference between Anne and Peter is shown here?*

MR. VAN DAAN. No. No. [*To* MRS. VAN DAAN] Come along, liefje.[12]

MRS. VAN DAAN. You'll be all right, Peter? You're not afraid?

PETER. [*Embarrassed*] Please, Mother.

[*They start up the stairs to the attic room above.* MR. FRANK *turns to* MRS. FRANK]

MR. FRANK. You too must have some rest, Edith. You didn't close your eyes last night. Nor you, Margot.

ANNE. I slept, Father. Wasn't that funny? I knew it was the last night in my own bed, and yet I slept soundly.

MR. FRANK. I'm glad, Anne. Now you'll be able to help me straighten things in here. [*To* MRS. FRANK *and* MARGOT] Come with me . . . You and Margot rest in this room for the time being.

[*He picks up their clothes, starting for the room on the right.*]

MRS. FRANK. You're sure . . . ? I could help . . . And Anne hasn't had her milk . . .

MR. FRANK. I'll give it to her. [*To* ANNE and PETER] Anne, Peter . . . it's best that you take off your shoes now, before you forget.

[*He leads the way to the room, followed by* MARGOT.]

MRS. FRANK. You're sure you're not tired, Anne?

ANNE. I feel fine. I'm going to help Father.

MRS. FRANK. Peter. I'm glad you are to be with us.

PETER. Yes, Mrs. Frank.

[MRS. FRANK *goes to join* MR. FRANK and MARGOT.]

[*During the following scene* MR. FRANK *helps* MARGOT *and* MRS. FRANK *to hang up their clothes. Then he persuades them both to lie down and rest. The* VAN DAANS *in their room above settle themselves. In the main room* ANNE *and* PETER *remove their shoes.* PETER *takes his cat out of the carrier.*]

ANNE. What's your cat's name?

PETER. Mouschi.

ANNE. Mouschi! Mouschi! Mouschi! [*She picks up the cat, walking away with it. To* PETER] I love cats. I have one . . . a darling little cat. But they made me leave her behind. I left some food and a note for the neighbors to take care of her . . . I'm going to miss her terribly. What is yours? A him or a her?

PETER. He's a tom. He doesn't like strangers. [*He takes the cat from her, putting it back in its carrier.*]

ANNE. [*Unabashed*] Then I'll have to stop being a stranger, won't I? Where did you go to school?

PETER. Jewish Secondary.

ANNE. But that's where Margot and I go! I never saw you around.

PETER. I used to see you . . . sometimes . . .

ANNE. You did?

PETER. . . . in the school yard. You were always in the middle of a bunch of kids. [*He takes a penknife from his pocket.*]

ANNE. Why didn't you ever come over?

PETER. I'm sort of a lone wolf. [*He starts to rip off his Star of David.*]

12. **liefje.** (lēf hyə) Dutch for "little love"

ANNE. What are you doing?

PETER. Taking it off.

ANNE. But you can't do that. They'll arrest you if you go out without your star.

[*He tosses his knife on the table.*]

PETER. Who's going out?

ANNE. Why, of course! You're right! Of course we don't need them any more. [*She picks up his knife and starts to take her star off.*] I wonder what our friends will think when we don't show up today?

PETER. I didn't have any dates with anyone.

ANNE. Oh, I did. I had a date with Jopie to go and play ping-pong at her house. Do you know Jopie de Waal?

PETER. No.

ANNE. Jopie's my best friend. I wonder what she'll think when she telephones and there's no answer? . . . Probably she'll go over to the house . . . I wonder what she'll think . . . we left everything as if we'd suddenly been called away . . . breakfast dishes in the sink . . . beds not made . . . [*As she pulls off her star, the cloth underneath shows clearly the color and form of the star.*] Look! It's still there!

[PETER *goes over to the stove with his star.*]

What're you going to do with yours?

PETER. Burn it.

ANNE. [*She starts to throw hers in and cannot.*] It's funny, I can't throw mine away. I don't know why.

PETER. You can't throw . . . ? Something they branded you with . . . ? That they made you wear so they could spit on you?

ANNE. I know. I know. But after all, it *is* the Star of David, isn't it?

[*In the bedroom, right,* MARGOT *and* MRS. FRANK *are lying down.* MR. FRANK *starts quietly out.*]

PETER. Maybe it's different for a girl.

[MR. FRANK *comes into the main room.*]

MR. FRANK. Forgive me, Peter. Now let me see. We must find a bed for your cat. [*He goes to a cupboard.*] I'm glad you brought your cat. Anne was feeling so badly about hers. [*Getting a used small washtub*] Here we are. Will it be comfortable in that?

PETER. [*Gathering up his things*] Thanks.

MR. FRANK. [*Opening the door of the room on the left*] And here is your room. But I warn you, Peter, you can't grow any more. Not an inch, or you'll have to sleep with your feet out of the skylight. Are you hungry?

PETER. No.

MR. FRANK. We have some bread and butter.

PETER. No, thank you.

MR. FRANK. You can have it for luncheon then. And tonight we will have a real supper . . . our first supper together.

PETER. Thanks. Thanks. [*He goes into his room. During the following scene he arranges his possessions in his new room.*]

MR. FRANK. That's a nice boy, Peter.

ANNE. He's awfully shy, isn't he?

MR. FRANK. You'll like him, I know.

ANNE. I certainly hope so, since he's the only boy I'm likely to see for months and months.

❶ *How did the Franks leave their house? What do they expect people to think?*

ANSWER TO GUIDED READING QUESTION

❶ The Franks left everything as if they had been called away suddenly. They left the beds unmade and the dishes unwashed. They expect people to think that they had suddenly been called away.

LITERARY TECHNIQUE

SYMBOL

A symbol is a thing that stands for and represents both itself and something else. The Star of David is a symbol of Judaism. Jews were forced to wear the Star of David on all their clothes to make it easier to identify them. Peter tears the star off his clothes and says he will burn it. Anne is unable to burn hers. She sees it as a symbol of her faith, while Peter sees it as a brand, or a symbol of oppression.

Answers to Guided Reading Questions

❶ Mr. Frank says their minds cannot be imprisoned. Miep will bring them books, and they will read history, poetry, mythology, and anything they can get.

❷ Mr. Frank grabs her arm and pulls her back quickly. He reacts so strongly because he wants to impress on her that she must never go beyond the door. Anne realizes what "going into hiding" means.

Quotables

"Stone walls do not a prison make
Nor iron bars a cage;
Minds innocent and quiet take
That for a hermitage."

—Richard Lovelace

Literary Note

Mr. Frank tells Anne that her mind cannot be imprisoned although she is physically unable to leave the hiding place. The idea of freedom of the mind is expressed by Richard Lovelace in the above quotation. Malcolm X expresses a similar idea in his autobiography when he writes, "You couldn't have gotten me out of books with a wedge. . . . Months passed without my even thinking about being imprisoned. In fact, up to then, I never had been so truly free in my life."

[MR. FRANK *sits down, taking off his shoes.*]

MR. FRANK. Annele, there's a box there. Will you open it?

[*He indicates a carton on the couch.* ANNE *brings it to the center table. In the street below there is the sound of children playing.*]

❶ In what way does Mr. Frank say they cannot be imprisoned? What will they do to remain "free"?

ANNE. [*As she opens the carton*] You know the way I'm going to think of it here? I'm going to think of it as a boarding house. A peculiar summer boarding house, like the one that we— [*She breaks off as she pulls out some photographs.*] Father! My movie stars! I was wondering where they were! I was looking for them this morning . . . and Queen Wilhelmina![13] How wonderful!

MR. FRANK. There's something more. Go on. Look further. [*He goes over to the sink, pouring a glass of milk from a thermos bottle.*]

ANNE. [*Pulling out a pasteboard-bound book*] A diary! [*She throws her arms around her father.*] I've never had a diary. And I've always longed for one. [*She looks around the room.*] Pencil, pencil, pencil, pencil. [*She starts down the stairs.*] I'm going down to the office to get a pencil.

MR. FRANK. Anne! No! [*He goes after her, catching her by the arm and pulling her back.*]

❷ What does Mr. Frank do when Anne goes in search of a pencil? Why does he react so strongly? What realization does Anne have?

ANNE. [*Startled*] But there's no one in the building now.

MR. FRANK. It doesn't matter. I don't want you ever to go beyond that door.

ANNE. [*Sobered*] Never . . . ? Not even at nighttime, when everyone is gone? Or on Sundays? Can't I go down to listen to the radio?

MR. FRANK. Never. I am sorry, Anneke. It isn't safe. No, you must never go beyond that door.

[*For the first time* ANNE *realizes what "going into hiding" means.*]

ANNE. I see.

MR. FRANK. It'll be hard, I know. But always remember this, Anneke. There are no walls, there are no bolts, no locks that anyone can put on your mind. Miep will bring us books. We will read history, poetry, mythology. [*He gives her the glass of milk.*] Here's your milk. [*With his arm about her, they go over to the couch, sitting down side by side.*] As a matter of fact, between us, Anne, being here has certain advantages for you. For instance, you remember the battle you had with your mother the other day on the subject of overshoes? You said you'd rather die than wear overshoes? But in the end you had to wear them? Well now, you see, for as long as we are here you will never have to wear overshoes! Isn't that good? And the coat that you inherited from Margot, you won't have to wear that any more. And the piano! You won't have to practice on the piano. I tell you, this is going to be a fine life for you!

[ANNE'S *panic is gone.* PETER *appears in the doorway of his room with a saucer in his hand. He is carrying his cat.*]

PETER. I . . . I . . . I thought I'd better get some water for Mouschi before . . .

13. **Queen Wilhelmina.** Queen of Holland from 1890 to 1948

MR. FRANK. Of course.

[As he starts toward the sink the carillon begins to chime the hour of eight. He tiptoes to the window at the back and looks down at the street below. He turns to PETER *indicating in* *pantomime* *that it is too late.* PETER *starts back for his room. He steps on a creaking board. The three of them are frozen for a minute in fear. As* PETER *starts away again,* ANNE *tiptoes over to him and pours some of the milk from her glass into the saucer for the cat.* PETER *squats on the floor, putting the milk before the cat.* MR. FRANK *gives* ANNE *his fountain pen and then goes into the room at the right. For a second* ANNE *watches the cat, then she goes over to the center table, and opens her diary.*

In the room at the right, MRS. FRANK *has sat up quickly at the sound of the carillon.* MR. FRANK *comes in and sits down beside her on the settee,*[14] *his arm comfortingly around her.*

Upstairs, in the attic room, MR. *and* MRS. VAN DAAN *have hung their clothes in the closet and are now seated on the iron bed.* MRS. VAN DAAN *leans back exhausted.* MR. VAN DAAN *fans her with a newspaper.*

ANNE *starts to write in her diary. The lights dim out, the curtain falls.*

In the darkness ANNE'S VOICE *comes to us again, faintly at first, and then with growing strength.]*

ANNE'S VOICE. I expect I should be describing what it feels like to go into hiding. But I really don't know yet myself. I only know it's funny never to be able to go outdoors . . . never to breathe fresh air . . . never to run and shout and jump. It's the silence in the nights that frightens me most. Every time I hear a creak in the house, or a step on the street outside, I'm sure they're coming for us. The days aren't so bad. At least we know that Miep and Mr. Kraler are down there below us in the office. Our protectors, we call them. I asked Father what would happen to them if the Nazis found out they were hiding us. Pim said that they would suffer the same fate that we would . . . Imagine! They know this, and yet when they come up here, they're always cheerful and gay as if there were nothing in the world to bother them . . . Friday, the twenty-first of August, nineteen forty-two. Today I'm going to tell you our general news. Mother is unbearable. She insists on treating me like a baby, which I loathe. Otherwise things are going better. The weather is . . .

[As ANNE'S VOICE *is fading out, the curtain rises on the scene.]*

SCENE 3

[It is a little after six o'clock in the evening, two months later. MARGOT *is in the bedroom at the right, studying.* MR. VAN DAAN *is lying down in the attic room above. The rest of the "family" is in the main room.* ANNE *and* PETER *sit opposite each other at the center table, where they have been doing their lessons.* MRS. FRANK *is on the couch.* MRS. VAN DAAN *is seated*

14. **settee.** Small couch or sofa

1 *What activities does Anne miss? What is the most frightening thing to her? Why?*

WORDS FOR EVERYDAY USE

pan • to • mime (pan´tə mīm´) *n.,* dramatic presentation given without words, using only action and gestures

ANSWER TO GUIDED READING QUESTION

1 Anne misses being outdoors, breathing fresh air, running, shouting, and jumping. The silence at night is the most frightening thing for her, because every noise that she hears—creaks in the house or footsteps outside—she imagines to be people coming to get them.

BIOGRAPHICAL NOTE

Queen Wilhelmina, or Wilhelmina Helena Pauline Maria (1880–1962), was queen of the Netherlands from 1890 to 1948. She was influential in the neutrality of the Netherlands during World War I. The Netherlands were invaded by Germany on May 10, 1940. Wilhelmina issued a proclamation of protest to her people. She left shortly thereafter for England. Throughout the war, she issued radio broadcasts from London encouraging her people to maintain their spirits. Seen as a symbol of the Dutch resistance to German occupation, she was welcomed back to the Netherlands when the German occupation ended in 1945.

VOCABULARY IN CONTEXT

- When Jolene lost her voice, she tried to pantomime in order to communicate.

Historical Note

Adolf Hitler had a plan, often referred to as the "final solution," to rid Europe of Jews. Jews were confined to ghettos until they could be transported to death camps where mass executions took place.

By 1942, fifty thousand Jews had been forced into the Warsaw Ghetto in Warsaw, Poland. Many of them were without housing, and those who did have housing often lived as many as thirteen to a room. Thousands died each month of starvation or disease. In July of that year, more than five thousand Jews were taken to Treblinka each day. The official word was that people were being transported to forced labor camps, but inmates of the ghetto soon learned that people being deported were sent to gas chambers.

When the Nazis tried to assemble their next shipment on January 18, 1943, they were surprised by an armed resistance. Fighting continued for four days. About fifty Germans and many more Jews were left dead at the end of the fighting. The Germans stopped the death-camp transports until April 19. On that date Heinrich Himmler began putting into action a plan to clear the ghetto in honor of Hitler's birthday, April 20. That day also marked the beginning of Passover, a Jewish holiday celebrating their freedom from slavery in Egypt.

The Nazis moved into the area heavily armed with tanks and large supplies of ammunition. Most of the Jews hid in bunkers, but about fifteen hundred lightly armed resisters opened fire on the Nazis. They were able to damage some equipment, kill some of the German troops, and hold off reinforcements. The revolt lasted for four weeks. During that time fifty-six thousand Jews were killed or deported to death camps.

Anne Frank house, Amsterdam *Archive Photos*

with her fur coat, on which she has been sewing, in her lap. None of them are wearing their shoes.

Their eyes are on MR. FRANK, *waiting for him to give them the signal which will release them from their day-long quiet.* MR. FRANK, *his shoes in his hand, stands looking down out of the window at the back, watching to be sure that all of the workmen have left the building below.*

After a few seconds of motionless silence, MR. FRANK *turns from the window.*]

Mr. Frank. [*Quietly, to the group*] It's safe now. The last workman has left.

[*There is an immediate stir of relief.*]

Anne. [*Her pent-up energy explodes.*] WHEE!

Mrs. Frank. [*Startled, amused*] Anne!

Mrs. Van Daan. I'm first for the w.c.

[*She hurries off to the bathroom.* MRS. FRANK *puts on her shoes and starts up to the sink to prepare supper.* ANNE *sneaks* PETER'S *shoes from under the table and hides them behind her back.* MR. FRANK *goes in to* MARGOT'S *room.*]

Mr. Frank. [*To* MARGOT] Six o' clock. School's over.

[MARGOT *gets up, stretching.* MR. FRANK *sits down to put on his shoes. In the main room* PETER *tries to find his.*]

Peter. [*To* ANNE] Have you seen my shoes?

Anne. [*Innocently*] Your shoes?

Peter. You've taken them, haven't you?

Anne. I don't know what you're talking about.

Peter. You're going to be sorry!

Anne. Am I? [PETER *goes after her.* ANNE *with his shoes in her hand, runs from him, dodging behind her mother.*]

Mrs. Frank. [*Protesting*] Anne, dear!

Peter. Wait till I get you!

Anne. I'm waiting!

[PETER *makes a lunge for her. They both fall to the floor.* PETER *pins her down, wrestling with her to get the shoes.*]

Don't! Don't! Peter, stop it. Ouch!

MRS. FRANK. Anne! . . . Peter!

[*Suddenly* PETER *becomes self-conscious. He grabs his shoes roughly and starts for his room.*]

ANNE. [*Following him*] Peter, where are you going? Come dance with me.

PETER. I tell you I don't know how.

ANNE. I'll teach you.

PETER. I'm going to give Mouschi his dinner.

ANNE. Can I watch?

PETER. He doesn't like people around while he eats.

ANNE. Peter, please.

PETER. No! [*He goes into his room.* ANNE *slams his door after him.*]

MRS. FRANK. Anne, dear, I think you shouldn't play like that with Peter. It's not dignified.

ANNE. Who cares if it's dignified? I don't want to be dignified.

[MR. FRANK *and* MARGOT *come from the room on the right.* MARGOT *goes to help her mother.* MR. FRANK *starts for the center table to correct* MARGOT'S *school papers.*]

MRS. FRANK. [*To* ANNE] You complain that I don't treat you like a grownup. But when I do, you resent it.

ANNE. I only want some fun . . . someone to laugh and clown with . . . After you've sat still all day and hardly moved, you've got to have some fun. I don't know what's the matter with that boy.

MR. FRANK. He isn't used to girls. Give him a little time.

ANNE. Time? Isn't two months time? I could cry. [*Catching hold of* MARGOT] Come on, Margot . . . dance with me. Come on, please.

MARGOT. I have to help with supper.

ANNE. You know we're going to forget how to dance . . . When we get out we won't remember a thing.

[*She starts to sing and dance by herself.* MR. FRANK *takes her in his arms, waltzing with her.* MRS. VAN DAAN *comes in from the bathroom.*]

MRS. VAN DAAN. Next? [*She looks around as she starts putting on her shoes.*] Where is Peter?

ANNE. [*As they are dancing*] Where would he be!

MRS. VAN DAAN. He hasn't finished his lessons, has he? His father'll kill him if he catches him in there with that cat and his work not done.

[MR. FRANK *and* ANNE *finish their dance. They bow to each other with* extravagant *formality.*]

Anne, get him out of there, will you?

ANNE. [*At* PETER'S door] Peter? Peter?

PETER. [*Opening the door a crack*] What is it?

ANNE. Your mother says to come out.

PETER. I'm giving Mouschi his dinner.

❶ What advice does Mrs. Frank give Anne? What is Anne's reaction?

WORDS FOR EVERYDAY USE

ex • trav • a • gant (ek strav´ə gənt) *adj.*, excessive; beyond reasonable limits

ANSWER TO GUIDED READING QUESTION

❶ Mrs. Frank tells Anne that she should not play with Peter in the way that she does because it is not dignified. Anne replies that she does not care if it is dignified because she does not want to be dignified.

HISTORICAL NOTE

The Holocaust is memorialized at the United States Holocaust Memorial Museum, which opened in April 1993. This permanent exhibition tells the story of Jews and other victims of the Nazis. The exhibit includes text panels, artifacts, audiovisual displays, photographs, documents, and eyewitness testimonies. The museum aims to provide information about the tragedy of the Holocaust, to preserve the memory of those who suffered, and to encourage visitors to reflect on these events and on the question of personal responsibility in preventing human suffering.

For additional information, contact:

Office of Education
United States Holocaust Memorial Council
Suite 588
2000 L Street NW
Washington, DC 20036

VOCABULARY IN CONTEXT

• The fifteen-course dinner was extravagant, but Marcella always likes to do things bigger and better than everyone else.

Answers to Guided Reading Questions

❶ The families are frightened by the sound of an automobile coming to a screeching halt in the street below. They fear the car has come for them.

❷ Anne was called Mrs. Quack Quack at school because she talked so much. She pretends to be outraged when Peter calls her this name.

CROSS-CURRICULAR ACTIVITIES

Arts and Humanities

Students may wish to perform *The Diary of Anne Frank.* All students should be involved in the production. Students who do not act can work on costuming, lighting, set design and construction, and other aspects of the production.

❶ *What sound frightens the families? What do they fear is happening?*

❷ *Why was Anne called Mrs. Quack Quack? How does she feel when Peter calls her this name?*

Mrs. Van Daan. You know what your father says. *[She sits on the couch, sewing on the lining of her fur coat.]*

Peter. For heavens sake. I haven't even looked at him since lunch.

Mrs. Van Daan. I'm just telling you, that's all.

Anne. I'll feed him.

Peter. I don't want you in there.

Mrs. Van Daan. Peter!

Peter. *[To* ANNE*]* Then give him his dinner and come right out, you hear?

[He comes back to the table. ANNE *shuts the door of* PETER'S *room after her and disappears behind the curtain covering his closet.]*

Mrs. Van Daan. *[To* PETER*]* Now is that any way to talk to your little girl friend?

Peter. Mother . . . for heaven's sake . . . will you please stop saying that?

Mrs. Van Daan. Look at him blush! Look at him!

Peter. Please! I'm not . . . anyway . . . let me alone, will you?

Mrs. Van Daan. He acts like it was something to be ashamed of. It's nothing to be ashamed of, to have a little girl friend.

Peter. You're crazy. She's only thirteen.

Mrs. Van Daan. So what? And you're sixteen. Just perfect. Your father's ten years older than I am. *[To* MR. FRANK*]* I warn you, Mr. Frank, if this war lasts much longer, we're going to be related and then . . .

Mr. Frank. Mazeltov![15]

Mrs. Frank. *[Deliberately changing the conversation]* I wonder where Miep is. She's usually so prompt.

[Suddenly everything else is forgotten as they hear the sound of an automobile coming to a screeching stop in the street below. They are tense, motionless in their terror. The car starts away. A wave of relief sweeps over them. They pick up their occupations again. ANNE *flings open the door of* PETER'S *room, making a dramatic entrance. She is dressed in* PETER'S *clothes.* PETER *looks at her in fury. The others are amused.]*

Anne. Good evening, everyone. Forgive me if I don't stay. *[She jumps up on a chair.]* I have a friend waiting for me in there. My friend Tom. Tom Cat. Some people say that we look alike. But Tom has the most beautiful whiskers, and I have only a little fuzz. I am hoping . . . in time . . .

Peter. All right, Mrs. Quack Quack!

Anne. *[Outraged—jumping down]* Peter!

Peter. I heard about you . . . How you talked so much in class they called you Mrs. Quack Quack. How Mr. Smitter made you write a composition . . . "'Quack, quack,' said Mrs. Quack Quack."

Anne. Well, go on. Tell them the rest. How it was so good he read it out loud to the class and then read it to all his other classes!

Peter. Quack! Quack! Quack . . . Quack . . . Quack . . .

[ANNE *pulls off the coat and trousers.]*

15. **Mazeltov.** (mä´zəl tōv´) Yiddish for good luck or congratulations, often yelled at the end of a wedding ceremony

PETER. You are the most intolerable, insufferable boy I've ever met!

[*She throws the clothes down the stairwell.* PETER *goes down after them.*]

PETER. Quack. Quack. Quack!

MRS. VAN DAAN. [*To* ANNE] That's right, Anneke! Give it to him!

ANNE. With all the boys in the world . . . Why I had to get locked up with one like you! . . .

PETER. Quack, Quack, Quack, and from now on stay out of my room!

[*As* PETER *passes her,* ANNE *puts out her foot, tripping him. He picks himself up, and goes on into his room.*]

MRS. FRANK. [*Quietly*] Anne, dear . . . your hair. [*She feels* ANNE'S *forehead.*] You're warm. Are you feeling all right?

ANNE. Please. Mother. [*She goes over to the center table, slipping into her shoes.*]

MRS. FRANK. [*Following her*] You haven't a fever, have you?

ANNE. [*Pulling away*] No. No.

MRS. FRANK. You know we can't call a doctor here, ever. There's only one thing to do . . . watch carefully. Prevent an illness before it comes. Let me see your tongue.

ANNE. Mother, this is perfectly absurd.

MRS. FRANK. Anne, dear, don't be such a baby. Let me see your tongue. [*As* ANNE *refuses,* MRS. FRANK *appeals to* MR. FRANK.] Otto . . . ?

MR. FRANK. You hear your mother, Anne.

[ANNE *flicks her tongue for a second, then turns away.*]

MRS. FRANK. Come on—open up! [*As* ANNE *opens her mouth very wide*] You seem all right . . . but perhaps an aspirin . . .

MRS. VAN DAAN. For heaven's sake. don't give that child any pills. I waited for fifteen minutes this morning for her to come out of the w.c.

ANNE. I was washing my hair!

MR. FRANK. I think there's nothing the matter with our Anne that a ride on her bike, or a visit with her friend Jopie de Waal wouldn't cure. Isn't that so, Anne?

❶ *What does Mr. Frank suggest is the problem when Mrs. Frank thinks Anne is sick?*

[MR. VAN DAAN *comes down into the room. From outside we hear faint sounds of bombers going over and a burst of ack-ack.*[16]]

MR. VAN DAAN. Miep not come yet?

MRS. VAN DAAN. The workmen just left, a little while ago.

MR. VAN DAAN. What's for dinner tonight?

MRS. VAN DAAN. Beans.

MR. VAN DAAN. Not again!

MRS. VAN DAAN. Poor Putti! I know. But what can we do? That's all that Miep brought us.

[MR. VAN DAAN *starts to pace, his hands behind his back.* ANNE *follows behind him, imitating him.*]

16. **ack-ack.** Term to describe an antiaircraft gun's fire

WORDS FOR EVERYDAY USE

in • tol • er • a • ble (in täl´ər ə bəl) *adj.,* unbearable

ANSWER TO GUIDED READING QUESTION

❶ Mr. Frank suggests that Anne needs to ride her bike or visit her friend. Anne is sick of being cooped up inside with the same people day after day.

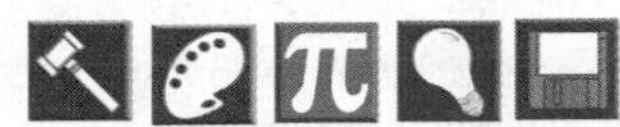

CROSS-CURRICULAR ACTIVITIES

SOCIAL STUDIES

Holocaust Day, observed on April 15th, is a day of commemoration of the beginning of the Warsaw Ghetto Uprising. Ask your students to plan their own Holocaust memorial.

Students might observe the day by sharing information about the Holocaust, speaking with survivors, or sharing published accounts of survivors' experiences. Ask students to respond to what they have learned about the Holocaust. Their responses might be in the form of writing, drawing, sculpture, music, dance, or theatrical performance. Have students share these responses during their Holocaust memorial.

VOCABULARY IN CONTEXT

• We jumped in the pool to cool off when the heat became intolerable.

Answers to Guided Reading Questions

❶ Mrs. Van Daan is concerned with her fur coat because her father bought it for her the year before he died, and because it cost a lot of money. It might also be important to her as a reminder of what her life used to be like.

❷ Anne asks Mrs. Van Daan if she had a lot of boyfriends before she was married. Mrs. Frank thinks the question is impolite because it is too personal. Mrs. Van Daan does not mind answering the question. She is proud to admit that she had many suitors.

Literary Technique

SIMILE

A **simile** is a comparison using *like* or *as.* Ask students to identify the simile Mrs. Van Daan uses when she is discussing the number of boyfriends she had. What does Mrs. Van Daan think of her appearance? How does she treat Mr. Frank?

ANSWERS

She uses the simile "The boys came buzzing round like bees around a jam pot." Mrs. Van Daan thinks she used to be very pretty. She says that even though she may not be as pretty as she used to be, she still has nice legs. She flirts shamelessly with Mr. Frank.

❶ *Why is Mrs. Van Daan so concerned with her fur coat?*

❷ *What question does Anne ask Mrs. Van Daan? Why is Mrs. Frank displeased by the question? Why does Mrs. Van Daan want to answer Anne's question?*

ANNE. We are now in what is known as the "bean cycle." Beans boiled, beans en casserole, beans with strings, beans without strings . . .

[PETER *has come out of his room. He slides into his place at the table, becoming immediately absorbed in his studies.*]

MR. VAN DAAN. [*To* PETER] I saw you . . . in there, playing with your cat.

MRS. VAN DAAN. He just went in for a second, putting his coat away. He's been out here all the time, doing his lessons.

MR. FRANK. [*Looking up from the papers*] Anne, you got an excellent in your history paper today . . . and very good in Latin.

ANNE. [*Sitting beside him*] How about algebra?

MR. FRANK. I'll have to make a confession. Up until now I've managed to stay ahead of you in algebra. Today you caught up with me. We'll leave it to Margot to correct.

ANNE. Isn't algebra vile, Pim!

MARGOT. [*To* MR. FRANK] How did I do?

ANNE. [*Getting up*] Excellent, excellent, excellent, excellent!

MR. FRANK. [*To* MARGOT] You should have used the subjunctive[17] here . . .

MARGOT. Should I? . . . I thought . . . look here . . . I didn't use it here . . .

[*The two become absorbed in the papers.*]

ANNE. Mrs. Van Daan, may I try on your coat?

MRS. FRANK. No, Anne.

MRS. VAN DAAN. [*Giving it to* ANNE] It's all right . . . but careful with it.

[ANNE *puts it on and struts with it.*]

My father gave me that the year before he died. He always bought the best that money could buy.

ANNE. Mrs. Van Daan, did you have a lot of boy friends before you were married?

MRS. FRANK. Anne, that's a personal question. It's not courteous to ask personal questions.

MRS. VAN DAAN. Oh I don't mind. [*To* ANNE] Our house was always swarming with boys. When I was a girl we had . . .

MR. VAN DAAN. Oh, no. Not again!

MRS. VAN DAAN. [*Good-humored*] Shut up!

[*Without a pause, to* ANNE, MR. VAN DAAN *mimics* MRS. VAN DAAN, *speaking the first few words in unison with her.*]

One summer we had a big house in Hilversum. The boys came buzzing round like bees around a jam pot. And when I was sixteen! . . . We were wearing our skirts very short those days and I had good-looking legs. [*She pulls up her skirt, going to* MR. FRANK.] I still have 'em. I may not be as pretty as I

17. **subjunctive.** Form of a verb

Words for Everyday Use

vile (vīl) *adj.,* disgusting; repulsive

Vocabulary in Context

- The rancid meat smelled so vile that we were unable to eat anything at the dinner.

used to be, but I still have my legs. How about it, Mr. Frank?

MR. VAN DAAN. All right. All right. We see them.

MRS. VAN DAAN. I'm not asking you. I'm asking Mr. Frank.

PETER. Mother, for heaven's sake.

MRS. VAN DAAN. Oh, I embarrass you, do I? Well, I just hope the girl you marry has as good. [*Then to* ANNE] My father used to worry about me, with so many boys hanging round. He told me, if any of them gets fresh, you say to him . . . "Remember, Mr. So-and-So, remember I'm a lady."

ANNE. "Remember. Mr. So-and-So, remember I'm a lady. [*She gives* MRS. VAN DAAN *her coat.*]

MR. VAN DAAN. Look at you, talking that way in front of her! Don't you know she puts it all down in that diary?

MRS. VAN DAAN. So, if she does? I'm only telling the truth!

[ANNE *stretches out, putting her ear to the floor, listening to what is going on below. The sound of the bombers fades away.*]

MRS. FRANK. [*Setting the table*] Would you mind, Peter, if I moved you over to the couch?

ANNE. [*Listening*] Miep must have the radio on.

[PETER *picks up his papers, going over to the couch beside* MRS. VAN DAAN.]

MR. VAN DAAN. [*Accusingly, to* PETER.] Haven't you finished yet?

PETER. No.

MR. VAN DAAN. You ought to be ashamed of yourself.

PETER. All right. All right. I'm a dunce. I'm a hopeless case. Why do I go on?

MRS. VAN DAAN. You're not hopeless. Don't talk that way. It's just that you haven't anyone to help you, like the girls have. [*To* MR. FRANK] Maybe you could help him, Mr. Frank?

MR. FRANK I'm sure that his father . . . ?

MR. VAN DAAN. Not me. I can't do anything with him. He won't listen to me. You go ahead . . . if you want.

MR. FRANK [Going to PETER] What about it, Peter? Shall we make our school <u>coeducational</u>?

MRS. VAN DAAN. [*Kissing* MR. FRANK] You're an angel, Mr. Frank. An angel. I don't know why I didn't meet you before I met that one there. Here, sit down. Mr. Frank . . . [*She forces him down on the couch beside* PETER] Now, Peter, you listen to Mr. Frank.

MR. FRANK It might be better for us to go into Peter's room.

[PETER *jumps up eagerly, leading the way.*]

MR. VAN DAAN. That's right. You go in there, Peter. You listen to Mr. Frank. Mr. Frank is a highly educated man.

[*As* MR. FRANK *is about to follow* PETER *into his room,* MRS. FRANK *stops him and*

1 *What does Mrs. Van Daan tell Anne to say to a boy if he gets too "fresh"? Why does Mr. Van Daan think his wife shouldn't talk that way in front of Anne?*

WORDS FOR EVERYDAY USE

co • ed • u • ca • tion • al (kō´ej ə kā´shən əl) *adj.,* having students of both sexes attend classes together

ANSWER TO GUIDED READING QUESTION

1 Mrs. Van Daan tells Anne to say, "Remember, Mr. So-and-So, remember I'm a lady." Mr. Van Daan does not like some of the things his wife is saying to Anne because he thinks that Anne writes everything down in her diary.

ADDITIONAL QUESTIONS AND ACTIVITIES

Ask students what opinion they think Anne held about Mr. and Mrs. Van Daan. Have students support their responses with evidence from the play.

VOCABULARY IN CONTEXT

- Thomas attended an all boys high school, but he went to a <u>coeducational</u> college.

Answer to Guided Reading Question

❶ Mrs. Frank and Margo keep their eyes down and ignore the quarrel between the Van Daans. Anne watches the whole thing with interest. She tells Mr. Van Daan that she did not know that grownups quarreled.

Literary Technique

MOTIVATION

A **motivation** is a force that moves a character to think, feel, or behave in a certain way.

Anne says "It's a wonder that Miep has a life of her own, the way we make her run errands for us." Miep and Mr. Kraler face as great a danger as the hiding families if they are caught. What might be Miep's motivation to sacrifice her time and risk her life?

wipes the lipstick from his lips. Then she closes the door after them.]

Anne. [*On the floor, listening.*] Shh! I can hear a man's voice talking.

Mr. Van Daan. [*To* ANNE] Isn't it bad enough without your sprawling all over the place?

[ANNE *sits up.*]

Mrs. Van Daan. [*To* MR. VAN DAAN] If you didn't smoke so much, you wouldn't be so bad-tempered.

Mr. Van Daan. Am I smoking? Do you see me smoking?

Mrs. Van Daan. Don't tell me you've used up all those cigarettes.

Mr. Van Daan. One package. Miep only brought me one package.

Mrs. Van Daan. It's a filthy habit anyway. It's a good time to break yourself.

Mr. Van Daan. Oh, stop it, please.

Mrs. Van Daan. You're smoking up all our money. You know that, don't you?

Mr. Van Daan. Will you shut up?

❶ [*During this,* MRS. FRANK *and* MARGOT *have studiously kept their eyes down. But* ANNE, *seated on the floor, has been following the discussion interestedly.* MR. VAN DAAN *turns to see her staring up at him.*]

How do Mrs. Frank and Margot react to the quarrel between Mr. and Mrs. Van Daan? What does Anne do?

And what are you staring at?

Anne. I never heard grownups quarrel before. I thought only children quarreled.

Mr. Van Daan. This isn't a quarrel! It's a discussion. And I never heard children so rude before.

Anne. [*Rising indignantly*] *I*, rude!

Mr. Van Daan. Yes!

Mrs. Frank. [*Quickly*] Anne, will you get me my knitting?

[ANNE *goes to get it.*]

I must remember, when Miep comes, to ask her to bring me some more wool.

Margot. [*Going to her room*] I need some hairpins and some soap. I made a list. [*She goes into her bedroom to get the list.*]

Mrs. Frank. [*To* ANNE] Have you some library books for Miep when she comes?

Anne. It's a wonder that Miep has a life of her own, the way we make her run errands for us. Please, Miep, get me some starch. Please take my hair out and have it cut. Tell me all the latest news, Miep. [*She goes over, kneeling on the couch beside* MRS. VAN DAAN.] Did you know she was engaged? His name is Dirk, and Miep's afraid the Nazis will ship him off to Germany to work in one of their war plants. That's what they're doing with some of the young Dutchmen . . . they pick them up off the streets—

Mr. Van Daan. [*Interrupting*] Don't you ever get tired of talking? Suppose you try keeping still for five minutes. Just five minutes.

Words for Everyday Use

quar • rel (kwôr´əl) *v.*, fight; dispute heatedly

in • dig • nant • ly (in dig´nənt lē) *adv.*, angrily; scornfully

Vocabulary in Context

- Mick and Vick quarreled over who would sing first at the concert.
- "I never acted like a fool," said Niles indignantly.

Anne Frank house, Amsterdam

Archive Photos

[*He starts to pace again. Again* ANNE *follows him, mimicking him.* MRS. FRANK *jumps up and takes her by the arm up to the sink, and gives her a glass of milk.*]

MRS. FRANK. Come here, Anne. It's time for your glass of milk.

MR. VAN DAAN. Talk, talk, talk. I never heard such a child. Where is my . . . ? Every evening it's the same talk, talk, talk. [*He looks around.*] Where is my . . . ?

MRS. VAN DAAN. What're you looking for?

MR. VAN DAAN. My pipe. Have you seen my pipe?

MRS. VAN DAAN. What good's a pipe? You haven't got any tobacco.

MR. VAN DAAN. At least I'll have something to hold in my mouth! [*Opening* MARGOT'S *bedroom door*] Margot, have you seen my pipe?

MARGOT. It was on the table last night.

[ANNE *puts her glass of milk on the table and picks up his pipe, hiding it behind her back.*]

WORDS FOR EVERYDAY USE

mim • ic (mim´ik) *v.*, imitate in speech or action

HISTORICAL NOTE

Heroic national efforts were made to save the Jewish population of Denmark in spite of the German occupation. Many Danish Jews were sent to Sweden, a neutral country, to live out the war.

Swedish businessman-diplomat Raoul Wallenberg used his position as a neutral Swedish citizen to help about 100,000 Hungarian Jews escape being sent to Nazi death camps. For his selfless work he was granted honorary United States citizenship.

VOCABULARY IN CONTEXT

- Uma got sick of Theo mimicking everything she said and did.

Answers to Guided Reading Questions

❶ Mrs. Frank tells Anne that she must not answer back. She must show courtesy toward the Van Daans. This will be difficult for Anne because she thinks the Van Daans walk all over Margot and her mother and she does not want this to happen to her. Anne is naturally inquisitive and spirited so it will be difficult for her to hold her tongue.

❷ Anne accidentally spills milk on Mrs. Van Daan's fur coat. Mrs. Van Daan gets very upset and calls Anne a clumsy little fool. She says she could kill Anne for what she has done. Then she storms out of the room.

Bibliographic Note

Students may be interested in reading the following works by Anne Frank:

Frank, Anne. *Tales from the Secret Annex.* New York: Washington Square Press, 1983.

The Diary of a Young Girl. New York: Doubleday, 1952.

Mr. Van Daan. I know, I know. Anne, did you see my pipe? . . . Anne!

Mrs. Frank. Anne, Mr. Van Daan is speaking to you.

Anne. Am I allowed to talk now?

Mr. Van Daan. You're the most aggravating . . . The trouble with you is, you've been spoiled. What you need is a good old-fashioned spanking.

Anne. [*Mimicking* MRS. VAN DAAN] "Remember, Mr. So-and-So, remember I'm a lady." [*She thrusts the pipe into his mouth, then picks up her glass of milk.*]

Mr. Van Daan. [*Restraining himself with difficulty*] Why aren't you nice and quiet like your sister Margot? Why do you have to show off all the time? Let me give you a little advice, young lady. Men don't like that kind of thing in a girl. You know that? A man likes a girl who'll listen to him once in a while . . . a domestic girl, who'll keep her house shining for her husband . . . who loves to cook and sew and . . .

❶ *What does Mrs. Frank tell Anne she must not do? Why will this be difficult for Anne?*

Anne. I'd cut my throat first! I'd open my veins! I'm going to be remarkable! I'm going to Paris . . .

Mr. Van Daan. [Scoffingly] Paris!

Anne. . . . to study music and art.

Mr. Van Daan. Yeah! Yeah!

Anne. I'm going to be a famous dancer or singer . . . or something wonderful.

❷ *What does Anne do accidentally? What is Mrs. Van Daan's reaction?*

[*She makes a wide gesture, spilling the glass of milk on the fur coat in* MRS. VAN DAAN'S *lap.* MARGOT *rushes quickly over with a towel.* ANNE *tries to brush the milk off with her skirt.*]

Mrs. Van Daan. Now look what you've done . . . you clumsy little fool! My beautiful fur coat my father gave me . . .

Anne. I'm so sorry.

Mrs. Van Daan. What do you care? It isn't yours . . . So go on, ruin it! Do you know what that coat cost? Do you? And now look at it! Look at it!

Anne. I'm very, very sorry.

Mrs. Van Daan. I could kill you for this. I could just kill you!

[MRS. VAN DAAN *goes up the stairs. clutching the coat.* MR. VAN DAAN *starts after her.*]

Mr. Van Daan. Petronella . . . liefje! Liefje! . . . Come back . . . the supper . . . come back!

Mrs. Frank. Anne, you must not behave in that way.

Anne. It was an accident. Anyone can have an accident.

Mrs. Frank. I don't mean that. I mean the answering back. You must not answer back. They are our guests. We must always show the greatest courtesy to them. We're all living under terrible tension.

[*She stops as* MARGOT *indicates that* VAN DAAN *can hear. When he is gone, she continues.*]

That's why we must control ourselves . . . You don't hear Margot getting into

Words for Everyday Use

scoff • ing • ly (skäf´iŋ lē) *adv.*, making fun of; in mockery of

Vocabulary in Context

• When Nina told Jake about her dream to be an actress, he said scoffingly, "As if you could make it on Broadway."

arguments with them, do you? Watch Margot. She's always courteous with them. Never familiar. She keeps her distance. And they respect her for it. Try to be like Margot.

ANNE. And have them walk all over me, the way they do her? No thanks!

MRS. FRANK. I'm not afraid that anyone is going to walk all over you, Anne. I'm afraid for other people, that you'll walk on them. I don't know what happens to you, Anne. You are wild, self-willed. If I had ever talked to my mother as you talk to me . . .

ANNE. Things have changed. People aren't like that any more. "Yes, Mother." "No, Mother." "Anything you say, Mother." I've got to fight things out for myself! Make something of myself!

MRS. FRANK. It isn't necessary to fight to do it. Margot doesn't fight, and isn't she . . . ?

ANNE. [*Violently rebellious*] Margot! Margot! Margot! That's all I hear from everyone . . . how wonderful Margot is. . . "Why aren't you like Margot?"

MARGOT. [*Protesting*] Oh, come on, Anne, don't be so . . .

ANNE. [*Paying no attention*] Everything she does is right, and everything I do is wrong! I'm the goat around here! . . . You're all against me! . . . And you worst of all!

[*She rushes off into her room and throws herself down on the settee, stifling her sobs.* MRS. FRANK *sighs and starts toward the stove.*]

MRS. FRANK. [*To* MARGOT] Let's put the soup on the stove . . . If there's anyone who cares to eat. Margot, will you take the bread out?

[MARGOT *gets the bread from the cupboard.*]

I don't know how we can go on living this way . . . I can't say a word to Anne . . . she flies at me . . .

MARGOT. You know Anne. In half an hour she'll be out here, laughing and joking.

MRS. FRANK. And. . . [*She makes a motion upward, indicating the* VAN DAANS] I told your father it wouldn't work . . . but no . . . no . . . he had to ask them, he said . . . he owed it to him, he said. Well, he knows now that I was right! These quarrels! . . . This bickering!

❶ *How does Mrs. Frank feel about the Van Daans?*

MARGOT. [*With a warning look*] Shush. Shush.

[*The buzzer for the door sounds.* MRS. FRANK *gasps, startled.*]

MRS. FRANK. Every time I hear that sound, my heart stops!

MARGOT. [*Starting for* PETER'S *door*] It's Miep. [*She knocks at the door.*] Father?

[MR. FRANK *comes quickly from* PETER'S *room.*]

MR. FRANK. Thank you, Margot. [*As he goes down the steps to open the outer door*] Has everyone his list?

MARGOT. I'll get my books. [*Giving her mother a list*] Here's your list.

[MARGOT *goes into her and* ANNE'S *bedroom on the right.* ANNE *sits up, hiding her tears, as* MARGOT *comes in.*]

Miep's here.

[MARGOT *picks up her books and goes back.* ANNE *hurries over to the mirror, smoothing her hair.*]

MR. VAN DAAN. [*Coming down the stairs*] Is it Miep?

ANSWER TO GUIDED READING QUESTION

❶ Mrs. Frank does not like the Van Daans. She had not wanted Mr. Frank to invite them to share the Franks' hiding place. She is disturbed by their constant bickering.

ADDITIONAL QUESTIONS AND ACTIVITIES

- Why had Mr. Frank invited the Van Daans to share their hiding place?
- Do you think Mr. Frank was right to invite them or is Mrs. Frank right that they would have been better off without the Van Daans?

ANSWERS

Mr. Frank invited the Van Daans to share their hiding place because he felt he owed it to Mr. Van Daan, who had helped him when he first moved to Amsterdam. *Responses to the second question will vary.* Students may say Mr. Frank was right to help others in need. They might say that it would be difficult to live with anybody in close quarters and under an enormous amount of stress without having problems.

Answer to Guided Reading Question

➊ Mr. Kraler has come to ask them to take another person into their hiding place.

Margot. Yes. Father's gone down to let her in.

Mr. Van Daan. At last I'll have some cigarettes!

Mrs. Frank. [*To* MR. VAN DAAN] I can't tell you how unhappy I am about Mrs. Van Daan's coat. Anne should never have touched it.

Mr. Van Daan. She'll be all right.

Mrs. Frank. Is there anything I can do?

Why has Mr. Kraler come?

➊ **Mr. Van Daan.** Don't worry.

[*He turns to meet* MIEP. *But it is not* MIEP *who comes up the steps. It is* MR. KRALER *followed by* MR. FRANK. *Their faces are* *grave*. ANNE *comes from the bedroom.* PETER *comes from his room.*]

Mrs. Frank. Mr. Kraler!

Mr. Van Daan. How are you, Mr. Kraler?

Margot. This is a surprise.

Mrs. Frank. When Mr. Kraler comes, the sun begins to shine.

Mr. Van Daan. Miep is coming?

Mr. Kraler. Not tonight.

[KRALER *goes to* MARGOT *and* MRS. FRANK *and* ANNE, *shaking hands with them.*]

Mrs. Frank. Wouldn't you like a cup of coffee . . . Or, better still, will you have supper with us?

Mr. Frank. Mr. Kraler has something to talk over with us. Something has happened, he says, which demands an immediate decision.

Mrs. Frank. [*Fearful*] What is it?

[MR. KRALER *sits down on the couch. As he talks he takes bread, cabbages, milk, etc., from his briefcase, giving them to* MARGOT *and* ANNE *to put away.*]

Mr. Kraler. Usually, when I come up here, I try to bring you some bit of good news. What's the use of telling you the bad news when there's nothing that you can do about it? But today something has happened . . . Dirk . . . Miep's Dirk, you know, came to me just now. He tells me that he has a Jewish friend living near him. A dentist. He says he's in trouble. He begged me, could I do anything for this man? Could I find him a hiding place? . . . So I've come to you . . . I know it's a terrible thing to ask of you, living as you are, but would you take him in with you?

Mr. Frank. Of course we will.

Mr. Kraler. [*Rising*] It'll be just for a night or two. . . until I find some other place. This happened so suddenly that I didn't know where to turn.

Mr. Frank. Where is he?

Mr. Kraler. Downstairs in the office.

Mr. Frank. Good. Bring him up.

Mr. Kraler. His name is Dussel . . . Jan Dussel.

Mr. Frank. Dussel . . . I think I know him.

Mr. Kraler. I'll get him. [*He goes quickly down the steps and out.* MR.

Words for Everyday Use

grave (grāv) *adj.*, somber; serious

Vocabulary in Context

- The doctor's face was grave when she gave Gordon the results of his test.

FRANK *suddenly becomes conscious of the others.*]

MR. FRANK. Forgive me. I spoke without consulting you. But I knew you'd feel as I do.

MR. VAN DAAN. There's no reason for you to consult anyone. This is your place. You have a right to do exactly as you please. The only thing I feel . . . there's so little food as it is . . . and to take in another person . . .

[PETER *turns away, ashamed of his father.*]

MR. FRANK. We can stretch the food a little. It's only for a few days.

MR. VAN DAAN. You want to make a bet?

MRS. FRANK. I think it's fine to have him. But, Otto, where are you going to put him? Where?

PETER. He can have my bed. I can sleep on the floor. I wouldn't mind.

MR. FRANK. That's good of you. Peter. But your room's too small . . . even for *you.*

ANNE. I have a much better idea. I'll come in here with you and Mother, and Margot can take Peter's room and Peter can go in our room with Mr. Dussel.

MARGOT. That's right. We could do that.

MR. FRANK. No, Margot. You mustn't sleep in that room . . . neither you nor Anne. Mouschi has caught some rats in there. Peter's brave. He doesn't mind.

ANNE. Then how about *this?* I'll come in here with you and Mother, and Mr. Dussel can have my bed.

MRS. FRANK. No. No. *No!* Margot will come in here with us and he can have her bed. It's the only way. Margot, bring your things in here. Help her, Anne.

[MARGOT *hurries into her room to get her things.*]

ANNE. [*To her mother*] Why Margot? Why can't I come in here?

MRS. FRANK. Because it wouldn't be proper for Margot to sleep with a . . . Please, Anne. Don't argue. Please.

[ANNE *starts slowly away.*]

MR. FRANK. [*To* ANNE] You don't mind sharing your room with Mr. Dussel, do you, Anne?

ANNE. No. No, of course not.

MR. FRANK. Good.

[ANNE *goes off into her bedroom, helping* MARGOT. MR. FRANK *starts to search in the cupboards.*]

Where's the cognac?[18]

MRS. FRANK. It's there. But, Otto, I was saving it in case of illness.

MR. FRANK. I think we couldn't find a better time to use it. Peter, will you get five glasses for me?

[PETER *goes for the glasses.* MARGOT *comes out of her bedroom, carrying her possessions, which she hangs behind a curtain in the main room.* MR. FRANK *finds the cognac and pours it into the five glasses that* PETER *brings him.* MR. VAN DAAN *stands looking on sourly.* MRS. VAN DAAN *comes downstairs and looks around at all the bustle.*]

MRS. VAN DAAN. What's happening? What's going on?

MR. VAN DAAN. Someone's moving in with us.

---

18. **cognac.** French brandy

1 *Does Mr. Van Daan want to allow Mr. Dussel to join them? Why not? How does Peter feel about his father?*

ANSWER TO GUIDED READING QUESTION

1 Mr. Van Daan does not want Mr. Dussel to join them. Mr. Van Daan thinks they are crowded enough, and their food supply is already too small. If it were up to him to decide, he would have not have allowed Mr. Dussel to stay with them. Peter is embarrassed by his father's reaction.

ADDITIONAL QUESTIONS AND ACTIVITIES

- What does Mr. Frank assume about the feelings of the others about allowing Mr. Dussel to join them?
- Is his assumption correct?
- How do the others feel?

ANSWERS

Mr. Frank assumes that everyone joins him in accepting Mr. Dussel to their hiding place. His assumption is not correct. Mr. Van Daan does not agree with Mr. Frank, but he says that it is Mr. Frank's right to make the decision. Peter is embarrassed by his father's actions. He knows that helping Mr. Dussel is the right thing to do. Mrs. Van Daan seems to agree with her husband. The Franks seem to agree that they should extend the help that they have received to help Mr. Dussel.

ANSWER TO GUIDED READING QUESTION

❶ Mr. Dussel is a childless bachelor. He is used to living alone. He is meticulous, finicky, and very set in his ways. He will probably have great difficulty adapting to his new living arrangements, especially to sharing a room with Anne.

CROSS-CURRICULAR ACTIVITIES

ART

Have students create drawings or models of the interior of the hiding place of the Franks and the Van Daans. Student works might be created as plans for sets for the play.

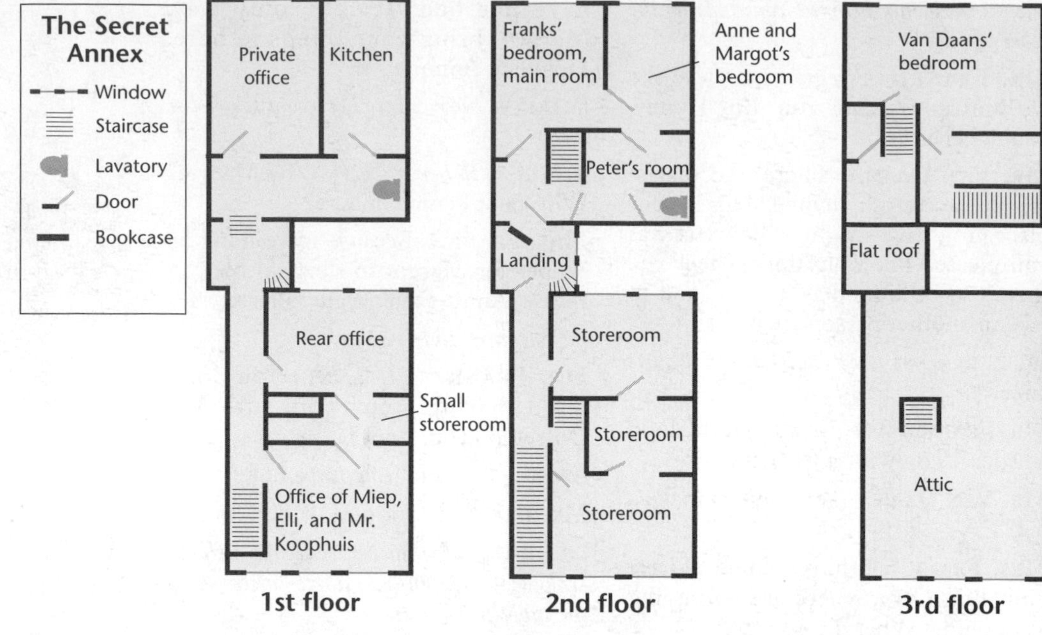

MRS. VAN DAAN. In here? You're joking.

MARGOT. It's only for a night or two . . . until Mr. Kraler finds him another place.

MR. VAN DAAN. Yeah! Yeah!

What kind of man is Mr. Dussel? How do you think he will feel about the secret annex and its inhabitants?

❶ [MR. FRANK *hurries over as* MR. KRALER *and* DUSSEL *come up.* DUSSEL *is a man in his late fifties, meticulous, finicky . . . bewildered now. He wears a raincoat. He carries a briefcase, stuffed full, and a small medicine case.*]

MR. FRANK. Come in, Mr. Dussel.

MR. KRALER. This is Mr. Frank.

MR. DUSSEL. Mr. Otto Frank?

MR. FRANK. Yes. Let me take your things. [*He takes the hat and briefcase, but* DUSSEL *clings to his medicine case.*] This is my wife Edith . . . Mr. and Mrs. Van Daan . . . their son, Peter . . . and my daughters, Margot and Anne.

[DUSSEL *shakes hands with everyone.*]

MR. KRALER. Thank you, Mr. Frank. Thank you all. Mr. Dussel, I leave you in good hands. Oh . . . Dirk's coat.

[DUSSEL *hurriedly takes off the raincoat, giving it to* MR. KRALER. *Underneath is his white dentist's jacket, with a yellow Star of David on it.*]

WORDS FOR EVERYDAY USE

me • tic • u • lous (mə tik´yo͞o ləs) *adj.*, extremely careful about details

VOCABULARY IN CONTEXT

• Sampson was meticulous about checking for errors in his papers.

DUSSEL. [*To* MR. KRALER] What can I say to thank you . . . ?

MRS. FRANK. [*To* DUSSEL] Mr. Kraler and Miep . . . They're our life line. Without them we couldn't live.

MR. KRALER. Please. Please. You make us seem very heroic. It isn't that at all. We simply don't like the Nazis. [*To* MR. FRANK, *who offers him a drink.*] No, thanks. [*Then going on*] We don't like their methods. We don't like . . .

MR. FRANK. [*Smiling*] I know. I know. "No one's going to tell us Dutchmen what to do with our Jews!"

MR. KRALER. [*To* DUSSEL] Pay no attention to Mr. Frank. I'll be up tomorrow to see that they're treating you right. [*To* MR. FRANK] Don't trouble to come down again. Peter will bolt the door after me, won't you, Peter?

PETER. Yes, sir.

MR. FRANK. Thank you, Peter. I'll do it.

MR. KRALER. Good night. Good night.

GROUP. Good night, Mr. Kraler. We'll see you tomorrow, etc., etc.

[MR. KRALER *goes out with* MR. FRANK. MRS. FRANK *gives each one of the "grownups" a glass of cognac.*]

MRS. FRANK. Please, Mr. Dussel, sit down.

[MR. DUSSEL *sinks into a chair.* MRS. FRANK *gives him a glass of cognac.*]

DUSSEL. I'm dreaming. I know it. I can't believe my eyes. Mr. Otto Frank here! [*To* MRS. FRANK] You're not in Switzerland then? A woman told me . . . She said she'd gone to your house . . . the door was open, everything was in disorder, dishes in the sink. She said she found a piece of paper in the wastebasket with an address scribbled on it . . . an address in Zurich. She said you must have escaped to Zurich.

ANNE. Father put that there purposely . . . Just so people would think that very thing!

DUSSEL. And you've been *here* all the time?

MRS. FRANK. All the time . . . ever since July.

[ANNE *speaks to her father as he comes back.*]

ANNE. It worked. Pim . . . the address you left! Mr. Dussel says that people believe we escaped to Switzerland.

MR. FRANK. I'm glad . . . And now let's have a little drink to welcome Mr. Dussel.

[*Before they can drink,* MR. DUSSEL *bolts his drink.* MR. FRANK *smiles and raises his glass.*]

To Mr. Dussel. Welcome. We're very honored to have you with us.

MRS. FRANK. To Mr. Dussel, welcome.

[*The* VAN DAANS *murmur a welcome. The "grownups" drink.*]

MRS. VAN DAAN. Um. That was good.

MR. VAN DAAN. Did Mr. Kraler warn you that you won't get much to eat here? You can imagine . . . three ration books among the seven of us . . . and now you make eight.

[PETER *walks away, humiliated. Outside a street organ is heard dimly.*]

DUSSEL. [*Rising*] Mr. Van Daan, you don't realize what is happening outside that you should warn me of a thing

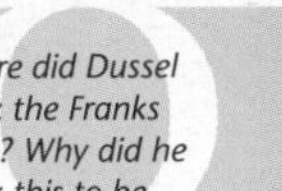

1 *Where did Dussel think the Franks were? Why did he think this to be true?*

ANSWER TO GUIDED READING QUESTION

1 Dussel thought the Franks were in Zurich, Switzerland. He thought they were there because a woman had told him that she had gone to the Franks' house and found a piece of paper in the trash with an address in Zurich scribbled on it. Mr. Frank had done this purposely to make people think they had left for Switzerland.

ADDITIONAL QUESTIONS AND ACTIVITIES

Ask students to discuss what additional or increased difficulties the families will face now that Mr. Dussel has joined them. How do students think he will get along with the other inhabitants of the "secret annex"?

Answer to Guided Reading Question

➊ Mr. Dussel says that hundreds of Jews disappear every day. Blocks are searched house by house. Children come home from school to find their parents gone. People that they know are being deported. Hundreds of people are getting call-up notices, and people who refuse the call-ups are dragged from their homes and sent to Mauthausen. Miep and Mr. Kraler usually bring cheerful news. They have told the Franks and the Van Daans that things were getting better.

Historical Note

Mauthausen was one of many German concentration and extermination camps. Others included Auschwitz, where the Franks and Van Daans were sent after being discovered; Bergen-Belson, where Margot and Anne Frank died; Buchenwald; and Treblinka.

Six million Jews were killed during the Holocaust. It has been said of the concentration camps that death seem to guard all exits.

like that. You don't realize what's going on . . .

[*As* MR. VAN DAAN *starts his characteristic pacing,* DUSSEL *turns to speak to the others.*]

Right here in Amsterdam every day hundreds of Jews disappear . . . They surround a block and search house by house. Children come home from school to find their parents gone. Hundreds are being deported . . . people that you and I know . . . the Hallensteins . . . the Wessels . . .

What news does Dussel bring of the outside world? In what way does this differ from the news Miep and Mr. Kraler usually bring? ➊

Mrs. Frank. [*In tears*] Oh, no. No!

Dussel. They get their call-up notice . . . come to the Jewish theater on such and such a day and hour . . . bring only what you can carry in a rucksack. And if you refuse the call-up notice, then they come and drag you from your home and ship you off to Mauthausen.[19] The death camp!

Mrs. Frank. We didn't know that things had got so much worse.

Dussel. Forgive me for speaking so.

Anne. [Coming to DUSSEL] Do you know the de Waals? . . . What's become of them? Their daughter Jopie and I are in the same class. Jopie's my best friend.

Dussel. They are gone.

Anne. Gone?

Dussel. With all the others.

Anne. Oh, no. Not Jopie!

[*She turns away, in tears.* MRS. FRANK *motions to* MARGOT *to comfort her.* MARGOT *goes to* ANNE, *putting her arms comfortingly around her.*]

Mrs. Van Daan. There were some people called Wagner. They lived near us . . . ?

Mr. Frank. [*Interrupting, with a glance at* ANNE] I think we should put this off until later. We all have many questions we want to ask . . . But I'm sure that Mr. Dussel would like to get settled before supper.

Dussel. Thank you. I would. I brought very little with me.

Mr. Frank. [*Giving him his hat and briefcase*] I'm sorry we can't give you a room alone. But I hope you won't be too uncomfortable. We've had to make strict rules here . . . a schedule of hours . . . We'll tell you after supper. Anne, would you like to take Mr. Dussel to his room?

Anne. [*Controlling her tears*] If you'll come with me, Mr. Dussel? [*She starts for her room.*]

Dussel. [*Shaking hands with each in turn*] Forgive me if I haven't really expressed my gratitude to all of you. This has been such a shock to me. I'd always thought of myself as Dutch. I was born in Holland, My father was born in Holland, and my grandfather. And now . . . after all these years . . . [*He breaks off.*] If you'll excuse me.

[DUSSEL *gives a little bow and hurries off after* ANNE. MR. FRANK *and the others are subdued.*]

19. **Mauthausen.** (mou tou´zən), Village in Austria that was the site of a Nazi concentration camp

Words for Everyday Use

grat • i • tude (grat´ i to͞od´) *n.,* feeling of appreciation; thankfulness

Vocabulary in Context

• I really appreciate everything you have done for me, and I do not know how I can ever show my gratitude.

ANNE. [*Turning on the light*] Well, here we are.

[DUSSEL *looks around the room. In the main room* MARGOT *speaks to her mother.*]

MARGOT. The news sounds pretty bad, doesn't it? It's so different from what Mr. Kraler tells us. Mr. Kraler says things are improving.

MR. VAN DAAN. I like it better the way Kraler tells it.

[*They resume their occupations, quietly.* PETER *goes off into his room. In* ANNE*'s room,* ANNE *turns to* DUSSEL.]

ANNE. You're going to share the room with me.

DUSSEL. I'm a man who's always lived alone. I haven't had to adjust myself to others. I hope you'll bear with me until I learn.

ANNE. Let me help you. [*She takes his briefcase.*] Do you always live all alone? Have you no family at all?

DUSSEL. No one. [*He opens his medicine case and spreads his bottles on the dressing table.*]

ANNE. How dreadful. You must be terribly lonely.

DUSSEL. I'm used to it.

ANNE. I don't think I could ever get used to it. Didn't you even have a pet? A cat, or a dog?

DUSSEL. I have an allergy for fur-bearing animals. They give me asthma.

ANNE. Oh, dear. Peter has a cat.

DUSSEL. Here? He has it here?

ANNE. Yes. But we hardly ever see it. He keeps it in his room all the time. I'm sure it will be all right.

DUSSEL. Let us hope so. [*He takes some pills to fortify himself.*]

ANNE. That's Margot's bed, where you're going to sleep. I sleep on the sofa there. [*Indicating the clothes hooks on the wall*] We cleared these off for your things. [*She goes over to the window.*] The best part about this room . . . you can look down and see a bit of the street and the canal. There's a houseboat . . . you can see the end of it . . . a bargeman lives there with his family . . . They have a baby and he's just beginning to walk and I'm so afraid he's going to fall into the canal some day. I watch him. . . .

DUSSEL. [*Interrupting*] Your father spoke of a schedule.

ANNE. [*Coming away from the window*] Oh, yes. It's mostly about the times we have to be quiet. And times for the w.c. You can use it now if you like.

DUSSEL. [*Stiffly*] No, thank you.

ANNE. I suppose you think it's awful, my talking about a thing like that. But you don't know how important it can get to be, especially when you're frightened . . . About this room, the way Margot and I did . . . she had it to herself in the afternoons for studying, reading. . . lessons, you know . . . and I took the mornings. Would that be all right with you?

DUSSEL. I'm not at my best in the morning.

ANNE. You stay here in the mornings then. I'll take the room in the afternoons.

DUSSEL. Tell me, when you're in here, what happens to me? Where am I spending my time? In there, with all the people?

ANNE. Yes.

DUSSEL. I see. I see.

❶ What does Anne like about her room?

❷ Do you think Anne and Dussel will make good roommates? Why, or why not?

ANSWERS TO GUIDED READING QUESTIONS

❶ Anne likes the window in her room. She likes to watch the family that lives on a houseboat in the canal.

❷ *Responses may vary.* Students are likely to say that Anne and Dussel are not likely to make good roommates. Dussel is not used to living with other people, so he will probably have a difficult time adjusting to living with Anne. Anne will probably get tired of Dussel's finicky ways.

Answer to Guided Reading Question

❶ Dussel says that nothing is right about Anne: her appearance, her manners, or her character. Anne wants to smack him so hard he'll fly up to the ceiling. Anne says that every grownup thinks that he or she knows the best way to bring up children, and grownups who have never had children think they have the best ideas.

Literary Technique

STAGE DIRECTIONS

Stage directions are notes included in a play to describe how something should look, sound, or be performed. Have students read the stage directions at the beginning of scene 4 and answer the following questions:

- What lighting should be used?
- What sound effects are described? What do the sound effects indicate?
- What does Mr. Van Daan do? What might be the significance of his actions?

ANSWERS

The stage should be dark, except for a little light from the skylight in Peter's room. There are sounds of two soldiers singing, a girl's giggle, running feet, and the sound of airplanes. The sounds indicate that there are soldiers and other people on the street. Mr. Van Daan lights a match, moves to the food cupboard, lights a match again and quickly blows it out. He is probably stealing food, which will make matters even more tense if he is discovered.

ANNE. We have supper at half past six.

DUSSEL. [*Going over to the sofa*] Then, if you don't mind . . . I like to lie down quietly for ten minutes before eating. I find it helps the digestion.

ANNE. Of course. I hope I'm not going to be too much of a bother to you. I seem to be able to get everyone's back up.

[DUSSEL *lies down on the sofa, curled up, his back to her.*]

DUSSEL. I always get along very well with children. My patients all bring their children to me, because they know I get on well with them. So don't you worry about that.

[ANNE *leans over him, taking his hand and shaking it gratefully.*]

ANNE. Thank you. Thank you. Mr. Dussel.

[*The lights dim to darkness. The curtain falls on the scene.* ANNE'S VOICE *comes to us faintly at first, and then with increasing power.*]

ANNE'S VOICE. . . . And yesterday I finished Cissy Van Marxvelt's latest book. I think she is a first-class writer. I shall definitely let my children read her. Monday the twenty-first of September, nineteen forty-two. Mr. Dussel and I had another battle yesterday. Yes, Mr. Dussel! According to him, nothing, I repeat . . . nothing, is right about me . . . my appearance, my character, my manners. While he was going on at me I thought . . . sometime I'll give you such a smack that you'll fly right up to the ceiling! Why is it that every grownup thinks he knows the way to bring up children? Particularly the grownups that never had any. I keep wishing that Peter was a girl instead of a boy. Then I would have someone to talk to. Margot's a darling, but she takes everything too seriously. To pause for a moment on the subject of Mrs. Van Daan. I must tell you that her attempts to flirt with father are getting her nowhere. Pim, thank goodness, won't play.

❶ *Why do Anne and Dussel argue? What does Anne say about grownups?*

[*As she is saying the last lines, the curtain rises on the darkened scene.* ANNE'S VOICE *fades out.*]

Scene 4

[*It is the middle of the night, several months later. The stage is dark except for a little light which comes through the skylight in* PETER'S *room.*

Everyone is in bed. MR. *and* MRS. FRANK *lie on the couch in the main room, which has been pulled out to serve as a makeshift double bed.*

MARGOT *is sleeping on a mattress on the floor in the main room, behind a curtain stretched across for privacy. The others are all in their accustomed rooms.*

From outside we hear two soldiers singing "Lili Marlene." A girl's high giggle is heard. The sound of running feet is heard coming closer and then fading in the distance. Throughout the scene there is the distant sound of airplanes passing overhead.

A match suddenly flares up in the attic. We dimly see MR. VAN DAAN. *He is getting his bearings. He comes quickly down the stairs, and goes to the cupboard where the food is stored. Again the match flares up, and is as quickly blown out. The dim figure is seen to steal back up the stairs.*

There is quiet for a second or two, broken only by the sound of airplanes, and running feet on the street below.

Suddenly, out of the silence and the dark, we hear ANNE *scream.*]

ANNE. [*Screaming*] No! No! Don't . . . don't take me!

[*She moans, tossing and crying in her sleep. The other people wake, terrified.* DUSSEL *sits up in bed, furious.*]

DUSSEL. Shush! Anne! Anne, for God's sake, shush!

ANNE. [*Still in her nightmare*] Save me! Save me!

[*She screams and screams.* DUSSEL *gets out of bed, going over to her, trying to wake her.*]

DUSSEL Quiet! Quiet! You want someone to hear?

[*In the main room* MRS. FRANK *grabs a shawl and pulls it around her. She rushes in to* ANNE, *taking her in her arms.* MR. FRANK *hurriedly gets up, putting on his overcoat.*

MARGOT *sits up, terrified.* PETER'S *light goes on in his room.*]

MRS. FRANK. [*To* ANNE *in her room*] Hush. It's all right. It's all right. [*Over her shoulder to* DUSSEL] Will you be kind enough to turn on the light, Mr. Dussel? [*Back to* ANNE] It's nothing, my darling. It was just a dream.

[DUSSEL *turns on the light in the bedroom.* MRS. FRANK *holds* ANNE *in her arms. Gradually* ANNE *comes out of her nightmare still trembling with horror.* MR. FRANK *comes into the room, and goes quickly to the window, looking out to be sure that no one outside has heard* ANNE'S *screams.* MRS. FRANK *holds* ANNE, *talking softly to her. In the main room* MARGOT *stands on a chair, turning on the center hanging lamp. A light goes on in the* VAN DAANS' *room overhead.* PETER *puts his robe on, coming out of his room.*]

DUSSEL. [*To* MRS. FRANK, *blowing his nose*] Something must be done about that child, Mrs. Frank. Yelling like that! Who knows but there's somebody on the streets? She's endangering all our lives.

MRS. FRANK. Anne, darling.

DUSSEL. Every night she twists and turns. I don't sleep. I spend half my night shushing her. And now it's nightmares!

MARGOT *comes to the door of* ANNE'S *room, followed by* PETER. MR. FRANK *goes to them, indicating that everything is all right.* PETER *takes* MARGOT *back.*]

MRS. FRANK. [*To* ANNE] You're here, safe, you see? Nothing has happened. [*To* DUSSEL] Please, Mr. Dussel, go back to bed. She'll be herself in a minute or two. Won't you, Anne?

DUSSEL. [*Picking up a book and a pillow*] Thank you, but I'm going to the w.c. The one place where there's peace!

[*He stalks out.* MR. VAN DAAN, *in underwear and trousers, comes down the stairs.*]

MR. VAN DAAN. [*To* DUSSEL] What is it? What happened?

DUSSEL. A nightmare. She was having a nightmare!

MR. VAN DAAN. I thought someone was murdering her.

DUSSEL. Unfortunately, no.

[*He goes into the bathroom.* MR. VAN DAAN *goes back up the stairs.* MR. FRANK, *in the main room, sends* PETER *back to his own bedroom.*]

MR. FRANK. Thank you, Peter. Go back to bed.

[PETER *goes back to his room.* MR. FRANK *follows him, turning out the light and looking out the window. Then he goes back*

❶ *What is Anne's nightmare about? What does Dussel fear?*

ANSWER TO GUIDED READING QUESTION

❶ Anne dreams that she is being taken away. Mr. Dussel worries that somebody on the street will hear Anne's screams and find thier hiding place.

Answer to Guided Reading Question

❶ The relationship between Anne and her mother is strained. Anne feels that her mother nags her and tries to turn her into a person she is not. Anne's relationship with her mother is similar to that of many teenagers with their parents. Mrs. Frank is hurt by Anne's feelings toward her.

❶ *Describe the relationship between Anne and her mother. How does Mrs. Frank feel about Anne's attitude toward her?*

to the main room, and gets up on a chair, turning out the center hanging lamp.]

Mrs. Frank. [*To* ANNE] Would you like some water? [ANNE *shakes her head.*] Was it a very bad dream? Perhaps if you told me . . . ?

Anne. I'd rather not talk about it.

Mrs. Frank. Poor darling. Try to sleep then. I'll sit right here beside you until you fall asleep. [*She brings a stool over, sitting there.*]

Anne. You don't have to.

Mrs. Frank. But I'd like to stay with you . . . very much. Really.

Anne. I'd rather you didn't.

Mrs. Frank. Good night, then.

[*She leans down to kiss* ANNE. ANNE *throws her arm up over her face, turning away.* MRS. FRANK, *hiding her hurt, kisses* ANNE'S *arm.*]

You'll be all right? There's nothing that you want?

Anne. Will you please ask Father to come.

Mrs. Frank. [*After a second*] Of course, Anne dear.

[*She hurries out into the other room.* MR. FRANK *comes to her as she comes in.*]

Sie verlangt nach Dir! [20]

Mr. Frank. [*Sensing her hurt*] Edith, *Liebe, schau . . .* [21]

Mrs. Frank. *Es macht nichts! Ich danke dem lieben Herrgott, dass sie sich wenigstens an Dich wendet, wenn sie Trost braucht! Geh hinein, Otto, sie ist ganz hysterisch vor Angst*[22] [As MR. FRANK *hesitates*] *Geh zu ihr.*[23]

[*He looks at her for a second and then goes to get a cup of water for* ANNE. MRS. FRANK *sinks down on the bed, her face in her hands, trying to keep from sobbing aloud.* MARGOT *comes over to her, putting her arms around her.*]

She wants nothing of me. She pulled away when I leaned down to kiss her.

Margot. It's a phase . . . You heard Father . . . Most girls go through it . . . they turn to their fathers at this age . . . they give all their love to their fathers.

Mrs. Frank. You weren't like this. You didn't shut me out.

Margot. She'll get over it . . .

[*She smooths the bed for* MRS. FRANK *and sits beside her a moment as* MRS. FRANK *lies down. In* ANNE'S *room* MR. FRANK *comes in, sitting down by* ANNE. ANNE *flings her arms around him, clinging to him. In the distance we hear the sound of ack-ack.*]

Anne. Oh, Pim. I dreamed that they came to get us! The Green Police! They broke down the door and grabbed me and started to drag me out the way they did Jopie.

Mr. Frank. I want you to take this pill.

Anne. What is it?

Mr. Frank. Something to quiet you.

[*She takes it and drinks the water. In the main room* MARGOT *turns out the light and goes back to her bed.*]

Mr. Frank. [*To* ANNE] Do you want me to read to you for a while?

20. **Sie verlangt nach Dir.** (sē fer´ läŋt´näk dir´), German for "She is asking for you."
21. **Liebe, schau.** (le´ bə´ shou), German for "Dear, look."
22. **Es macht . . . vor Angst.** (es mäkt nichts ich dän´ kə dəm le´ bən har´ gôt däs sē sich ven ig stəns än dish ven´ dət ven sē träst broukt gē hē nīn ät tō sē ist gänz hi ste´ rik fär äŋst), German for "It's all right. I thank dear God that at least she turns to you when she needs comfort. Go in, Otto, she is hysterical because of fear."
23. **Geh zu ihr.** (gē tsoo ēr), German for "Go to her."

ANNE. No. Just sit with me for a minute. Was I awful? Did I yell terribly loud? Do you think anyone outside could have heard?

MR. FRANK. No. No. Lie quietly now. Try to sleep.

ANNE. I'm a terrible coward. I'm so disappointed in myself. I think I've conquered my fear . . . I think I'm really grown-up . . . and then something happens . . . and I run to you like a baby . . . I love you, Father, I don't love anyone but you.

MR. FRANK. [*Reproachfully*] Annele!

ANNE. It's true. I've been thinking about it for a long time. You're the only one I love.

MR. FRANK. It's fine to hear you tell me that you love me. But I'd be happier if you said you loved your mother as well . . . She needs your help so much . . . your love . . .

ANNE. We have nothing in common. She doesn't understand me. Whenever I try to explain my views on life to her she asks me if I'm constipated.

MR. FRANK. You hurt her very much just now. She's crying. She's in there crying.

ANNE. I can't help it. I only told the truth. I didn't want her here . . . [*Then, with sudden change*] Oh, Pim, I was horrible, wasn't I? And the worst of it is, I can stand off and look at myself doing it and know it's cruel and yet I can't stop doing it. What's the matter with me? Tell me. Don't say it's just a phase! Help me.

MR. FRANK. There is so little that we parents can do to help our children. We can only try to set a good example . . . point the way. The rest you must do yourself. You must build your own character.

ANNE. I'm trying. Really I am. Every night I think back over all of the things I did that day that were wrong . . . like putting the wet mop in Mr. Dussel's bed . . . and this thing now with Mother. I say to myself, that was wrong. I make up my mind, I'm never going to do that again. Never! Of course I may do something worse . . . but at least I'll never do that again! . . . I have a nicer side, Father . . . a sweeter, nicer side. But I'm scared to show it. I'm afraid that people are going to laugh at me if I'm serious. So the mean Anne comes to the outside and the good Anne stays on the inside, and I keep on trying to switch them around and have the good Anne outside and the bad Anne inside and be what I'd like to be . . . and might be . . . if only . . . only . . .

❶ *What thoughts does Anne have about building her own character?*

[She is asleep. MR. FRANK *watches her for a moment and then turns off the light, and starts out. The lights dim out. The curtain falls on the scene.* ANNE'S VOICE *is heard dimly at first, and then with growing strength.*]

ANNE'S VOICE. . . . The air raids are getting worse. They come over day and night. The noise is terrifying. Pim says it should be music to our ears. The more planes, the sooner will come the end of the war. Mrs. Van Daan pretends to be a fatalist.

WORDS FOR EVERYDAY USE

fa • tal • ist (fat´'l ist) *n.,* one who believes all events are determined by fate and are therefore inevitable

ANSWER TO GUIDED READING QUESTION

❶ Anne is trying to build her own character. She notes when she does things wrong and tries not to make similar mistakes in the future, but she often does. She says she has a sweeter, nicer side, but that she is afraid to show it. Anne is afraid that people will laugh at her if she is serious.

ADDITIONAL QUESTIONS AND ACTIVITIES

Have students discuss their opinions of Anne. Ask if they have ever had mixed feelings about their own characters such as Anne is having.

VOCABULARY IN CONTEXT

• "Que sera, sera. Whatever will be, will be," said Leon, the fatalist.

Answer to Guided Reading Question

1 Mrs. Van Daan wants to be at home with her own things. Peter wants to go to the movies. Mr. Dussel wants to get back to his dentist drill. Anne wants to do many things—ride a bike, laugh until her belly aches, wear new clothes, have a long, hot bath, and be back at school with her friends.

Additional Questions and Activities

Ask students to think of the many objects and activities they take for granted. If they were confined as the Franks and Van Daans were, what things would they miss doing?

Historical Note

The secret annex where Anne and her family hid from the Nazis is today a museum in Amsterdam, preserved in her honor. Thousands of people from all over the world visit each year. The Anne Frank Foundation, which maintains the house, has also established an International Youth Center, which acts as a meeting place and offers lectures and conferences about many topics of international concern.

Anne Frank house, Amsterdam Archive Photos

What will be, will be. But when the planes come over, who is the most frightened? No one else but Petronella! . . . Monday, the ninth of November, nineteen forty-two. Wonderful news! The Allies have landed in Africa. Pim says that we can look for an early finish to the war. Just for fun he asked each of us what was the first thing we wanted to do when we got out of here. Mrs. Van Daan longs to be home with her own things, her needle-point chairs, the Beckstein piano her father gave her . . . the best that money could buy. Peter would like to go to a movie. Mr. Dussel wants to get back to his dentist's drill. He's afraid he is losing his touch. For myself, there are so many things . . . to ride a bike again . . . to laugh till my belly aches . . . to have new clothes from the skin out . . . to have a hot tub filled to overflowing and wallow in it for hours . . . to be back in school with my friends . . .

1 *What does each person want to do when he or she gets out of the secret annex?*

[*As the last lines are being said, the curtain rises on the scene. The lights dim on as* ANNE'S VOICE *fades away.*]

Scene 5

[*It is the first night of the Hanukkah*[24] *celebration.* MR. FRANK *is standing at the head of the table on which is the Menorah.*[25] *He lights the Shamos,*[26] *or servant candle, and holds it as he says the blessing. Seated listening is all of the "family," dressed in their best. The men wear hats,* PETER *wears his cap.*]

Mr. Frank. [*Reading from a prayer book*] "Praised be Thou, oh Lord our God, Ruler of the universe, who has sanctified us with Thy commandments and bidden us kindle the Hanukkah lights. Praised be Thou, oh Lord our God, Ruler of the universe, who has wrought wondrous deliverances for our fathers in days of old. Praised be Thou, oh Lord our God, Ruler of the universe, that Thou has given us life and sustenance and brought us to this happy season." [MR. FRANK *lights the one candle of the*

24. **Hanukkah.** (hä´ noo kä´) *n.,* Jewish celebration that lasts eight days
25. **Menorah.** (mə nō´ rə) *n.,* Candleholder with nine candles used during Hanukkah
26. **Shamos.** (shä´ məs) *n.,* Candle used to light the others in a menorah

Menorah as he continues.] "We kindle this Hanukkah light to celebrate the great and wonderful deeds wrought through the zeal with which God filled the hearts of the heroic Maccabees,[27] two thousand years ago. They fought against indifference, against tyranny and oppression, and they restored our Temple to us. May these lights remind us that we should ever look to God, whence cometh our help." Amen.

ALL. Amen.

[MR. FRANK *hands* MRS. FRANK *the prayer book.*]

MRS. FRANK. [*Reading*] "I lift up mine eyes unto the mountains, from whence cometh my help. My help cometh from the Lord who made heaven and earth. He will not suffer thy foot to be moved. He that keepeth thee will not slumber. He that keepeth Israel doth neither slumber nor sleep. The Lord is thy keeper. The Lord is thy shade upon thy right hand. The sun shall not smite thee by day, nor the moon by night. The Lord shall keep thee from all evil. He shall keep thy soul. The Lord shall guard thy going out and thy coming in, from this time forth and forevermore." Amen.

ALL. Amen.

[MRS. FRANK *puts down the prayer book and goes to get the food and wine.* MARGOT *helps her.* MR. FRANK *takes the men's hats and puts them aside.*]

DUSSEL. [*Rising*] That was very moving.

ANNE. [*Pulling him back*] It isn't over yet!

MRS. VAN DAAN. Sit down! Sit down!

ANNE. There's a lot more, songs and presents.

DUSSEL. Presents?

MRS. FRANK. Not this year, unfortunately.

MRS. VAN DAAN. But always on Hanukkah . . . everyone gives presents . . . everyone!

DUSSEL. Like our St. Nicholas' Day.[28]

[*There is a chorus of "no's" from the group.*]

MRS. VAN DAAN. No! Not like St. Nicholas! What kind of a Jew are you that you don't know Hanukkah?

MRS. FRANK. [*As she brings the food*] I remember particularly the candles . . . First one, as we have tonight. Then the second night you light two candles, the next night three . . . and so on until you have eight candles burning. When there are eight candles it is truly beautiful.

MRS. VAN DAAN. And the potato pancakes.

MR. VAN DAAN. Don't talk about them!

MRS. VAN DAAN. I make the best *latkes* you ever tasted!

MRS. FRANK. Invite us all next year . . . In your own home.

MR. FRANK. God willing!

MRS. VAN DAAN. God willing.

MARGOT. What I remember best is the presents we used to get when we were little . . . eight days of presents . . . and each day they got better and better.

27. **Maccabees.** Followers of Judas Maccabaeus, whose rededication of the Temple in 165 BC is the origin of Hanukkah
28. **St. Nicholas' Day.** December 6, day Christian children in Holland receive gifts

❶ *What are some of the group's favorite Hanukkah traditions?*

ANSWER TO GUIDED READING QUESTION

❶ Their favorite Hanukkah traditions are songs, presents, candles, and potato pancakes.

CROSS-CURRICULAR ACTIVITIES

SOCIAL STUDIES

Hanukkah and St. Nicholas's Day are two holidays celebrated in the winter. Ask students to research these two holidays. Then have students explain the traditions of each holiday based on their research or on their own experience.

APPLIED ARTS

Students may wish to find a recipe for *latkes*, or potato pancakes. Students might make potato pancakes to taste in class.

ANSWER TO GUIDED READING QUESTION

❶ Anne has made or obtained Hanukkah presents for everyone in the hiding place. Her actions show that she thinks of others and that she is creative and innovative.

ADDITIONAL QUESTIONS AND ACTIVITIES

Ask students to discuss gift giving. Have they ever made a gift for somebody? Have they ever received a homemade gift? Does the meaning of a handmade gift differ from that of a bought gift? You may wish to have students read Pablo Neruda's "Ode to My Socks" and the Social Studies Cross-curricular Connection on page 422 to further explore the theme of gift giving.

What has Anne done for Hanukkah? What qualities does this action demonstrate? ❶

MRS. FRANK. [*Sitting down*] We are all here, alive. That is present enough.

ANNE. No, it isn't. I've got something . . . [*She rushes into her room, hurriedly puts on a little hat* improvised *from the lamp shade, grabs a* satchel *bulging with parcels and comes running back.*]

MRS. FRANK. What is it?

ANNE. Presents!

MRS. VAN DAAN. Presents!

DUSSEL. Look!

MR. VAN DAAN. What's she got on her head?

PETER. A lamp shade!

ANNE. [*She picks out one at random.*] This is for Margot. [*She hands it to* MARGOT, *pulling her to her feet.*] Read it out loud.

MARGOT. [*Reading*]
"You have never lost your temper.
You never will, I fear,
You are so good.
But if you should,
Put all your cross words here."

[*She tears open the package.*] A new crossword puzzle book! Where did you get it?

ANNE. It isn't new. It's one that you've done. But I rubbed it all out, and if you wait a little and forget, you can do it all over again.

MARGOT. [*Sitting*] It's wonderful, Anne. Thank you. You'd never know it wasn't new.

[*From outside we hear the sound of a streetcar passing.*]

ANNE. [*With another gift*] Mrs. Van Daan.

MRS. VAN DAAN. [*Taking it*] This is awful . . . I haven't anything for anyone . . . I never thought . . .

MR. FRANK. This is all Anne's idea.

MRS. VAN DAAN. [*Holding up a bottle*] What is it?

ANNE. It's hair shampoo. I took all the odds and ends of soap and mixed them with the last of my toilet water.

MRS. VAN DAAN. Oh, Anneke!

ANNE. I wanted to write a poem for all of them, but I didn't have time. [*Offering a large box to* MR. VAN DAAN] Yours, Mr. Van Daan, is *really* something . . . something you want more than anything. [*As she waits for him to open it*] Look! Cigarettes!

MR. VAN DAAN. Cigarettes!

ANNE. Two of them! Pim found some old pipe tobacco in the pocket lining of his coat . . . and we made them . . . or rather, Pim did.

MRS. VAN DAAN. Let me see . . . Well, look at that! Light it, Putti! Light it.

[MR. VAN DAAN *hesitates.*]

ANNE. It's tobacco, really it is! There's a little fluff in it, but not much.

[*Everyone watches intently as* MR. VAN DAAN *cautiously lights it. The cigarette flares up. Everyone laughs.*]

PETER. It works!

MRS. VAN DAAN. Look at him.

WORDS FOR EVERYDAY USE

im • pro • vise (im´ prə vīz´) *v.*, make with the materials at hand, usually to fill an unforeseen need

satch • el (sach´əl) *n.*, small bag for carrying clothes, books, etc.

VOCABULARY IN CONTEXT

- We did not have enough chairs for everyone, so we improvised a bench with boxes and planks.
- Kayla packed her books in her satchel in preparation for school the next day.

MR. VAN DAAN. [*Spluttering*] Thank you, Anne. Thank you.

[ANNE *rushes back to her satchel for another present.*]

ANNE. [*Handing her mother a piece of paper*] For Mother, Hanukkah greeting.

[*She pulls her mother to her feet.*]

MRS. FRANK. [*She reads*] "Here's an I.O.U. that I promise to pay. Ten hours of doing whatever you say. Signed, Anne Frank." [MRS. FRANK, *touched, takes* ANNE *in her arms, holding her close.*]

DUSSEL. [*To* ANNE] Ten hours of doing what you're told? *Anything* you're told?

ANNE. That's right.

DUSSEL. You wouldn't want to sell that, Mrs. Frank?

MRS. FRANK. Never! This is the most precious gift I've ever had!

[*She sits, showing her present to the others.* ANNE *hurries back to the satchel and pulls out a scarf, the scarf that* MR. FRANK *found in the first scene.*]

ANNE. [*Offering it to her father*] For Pim.

MR. FRANK. Anneke . . . I wasn't supposed to have a present! [*He takes it, unfolding it and showing it to the others.*]

ANNE. It's a muffler . . . to put round your neck . . . like an ascot, you know. I made it myself out of odds and ends . . . I knitted it in the dark each night, after I'd gone to bed. I'm afraid it looks better in the dark!

MR. FRANK. [*Putting it on*] It's fine. It fits me perfectly. Thank you, Annele.

[ANNE *hands* PETER *a ball of paper with a string attached to it.*]

ANNE. That's for Mouschi.

PETER. [*Rising to bow*] On behalf of Mouschi, I thank you.

ANNE. [*Hesitant, handing him a gift*] And . . . this is yours . . . from Mrs. Quack Quack. [*As he holds it gingerly in his hands*] Well . . . open it . . . Aren't you going to open it?

PETER. I'm scared to. I know something's going to jump out and hit me.

ANNE. No. It's nothing like that, really.

MRS. VAN DAAN. [*As he is opening it*] What is it, Peter? Go on. Show it.

ANNE. [*Excitedly*] It's a safety razor!

DUSSEL. A what?

ANNE. A razor!

MRS. VAN DAAN. [*Looking at it*] You didn't make that out of odds and ends.

ANNE. [To PETER] Miep got it for me. It's not new. It's second-hand. But you really do need a razor now.

DUSSEL. For what?

ANNE. Look on his upper lip . . . you can see the beginning of a mustache.

DUSSEL. He wants to get rid of that? Put a little milk on it and let the cat lick it off.

PETER. [*Starting for his room*] Think you're funny, don't you.

DUSSEL. Look! He can't wait! He's going in to try it!

PETER. I'm going to give Mouschi his present!

[*He goes into his room, slamming the door behind him.*]

❶ *What gift does Anne give to her mother? How does her mother react?*

ANSWER TO GUIDED READING QUESTION

❶ Anne gives her mother an I.O.U. saying that she will do ten hours of whatever her mother asks. Mrs. Frank is touched by Anne's gesture and hugs Anne.

QUOTABLES

"Give of yourself, give as much as you can! And you can always, always give something, even if it is only kindness."

—Anne Frank

Answer to Guided Reading Question

➊ Mr. Frank does not think they should sing the Hanukkah song because it is a song of jubilation and they are likely to get carried away and be too loud.

Literary Technique

MOOD

Mood, or atmosphere, is the emotion created in the reader by a piece of writing. Ask students to describe the mood of the gift-giving scene. Ask them to contrast this mood with the mood after the lamp is knocked over and Peter falls.

Mr. Van Daan. [*Disgustedly*] Mouschi, Mouschi, Mouschi.

[*In the distance we hear a dog persistently barking.* ANNE *brings a gift to* DUSSEL]

Anne. And last but never least, my roommate, Mr. Dussel.

Dussel. For me? You have something for me?

[*He opens the small box she gives him.*]

Anne. I made them myself.

Why doesn't Mr. Frank think they should sing the Hanukkah song? ➊

Dussel. [*Puzzled*] Capsules! Two capsules!

Anne. They're ear-plugs!

Dussel. Ear-plugs?

Anne. To put in your ears so you won't hear me when I thrash around at night. I saw them advertised in a magazine. They're not real ones . . . I made them out of cotton and candle wax. Try them . . . See if they don't work . . . see if you can hear me talk . . .

Dussel. [*Putting them in his ears*] Wait until I get them in . . . so.

Anne. Are you ready?

Dussel. Huh?

Anne. Are you ready?

Dussel. Oh! They've gone inside! I can't get them out! [*They laugh as* MR. DUSSEL *jumps about, trying to shake the plugs out of his ears. Finally he gets them out. Putting them away*] Thank you, Anne! Thank you!

[*Together*]

Mr. Van Daan. A real Hanukkah!

Mrs. Van Daan. Wasn't it cute of her?

Mrs. Frank. I don't know when she did it.

Margot. I love my present.

Anne. [*Sitting at the table*] And now let's have the song, Father . . . please . . . [*To* DUSSEL] Have you heard the Hanukkah song, Mr. Dussel? The song is the whole thing! [*She sings.*] "Oh, Hanukkah! Oh, Hanukkah! The sweet celebration . . ."

Mr. Frank. [*Quieting her*] I'm afraid, Anne, we shouldn't sing that song tonight. [*To* DUSSEL] It's a song of jubilation, of rejoicing. One is apt to become too enthusiastic.

Anne. Oh, please, please. Let's sing the song. I promise not to shout!

Mr. Frank. Very well. But quietly now . . . I'll keep an eye on you and when . . .

[*As* ANNE *starts to sing, she is interrupted by* DUSSEL *who is snorting and wheezing.*]

Dussel. [*Pointing to* PETER] You . . . You!

[PETER *is coming from his bedroom,* <u>*ostentatiously*</u> *holding a bulge in his coat as if he were holding his cat, and dangling* ANNE'S *present before it.*]

How many times . . . I told you . . . Out! Out!

Mr. Van Daan. [*Going to* PETER] What's the matter with you? Haven't you any sense? Get that cat out of here.

Peter. [*Innocently*] Cat?

Mr. Van Daan. You heard me. Get it out of here!

Words for Everyday Use

os • ten • ta • tious • ly (äs´tən tā´shəs lē) *adv.*, with a showy display; obviously proud or boastful

Vocabulary in Context

• Milo swaggered <u>ostentatiously</u> around the field holding the trophy high.

PETER. I have no cat. [*Delighted with his joke, he opens his coat and pulls out a bath towel. The group at the table laugh, enjoying the joke.*]

DUSSEL. [*Still wheezing*] It doesn't need to be the cat . . . his clothes are enough . . . when he comes out of that room . . .

MR. VAN DAAN. Don't worry. You won't be bothered any more. We're getting rid of it.

DUSSEL. At last you listen to me. [*He goes off into his bedroom.*]

MR. VAN DAAN. [*Calling after him*] I'm not doing it for you. That's all in your mind . . . all of it! [*He starts back to his place at the table.*] I'm doing it because I'm sick of seeing that cat eat all our food.

PETER. That's not true! I only give him bones . . . scraps . . .

MR. VAN DAAN. Don't tell me! He gets fatter every day! That cat looks better than any of us. Out he goes tonight!

PETER. No! No!

ANNE. Mr. Van Daan, you can't do that! That's Peter's cat. Peter loves that cat.

MRS. FRANK. [*Quietly*] Anne.

PETER. [*To* MR. VAN DAAN] If he goes. I go.

MR. VAN DAAN. Go! Go!

MRS. VAN DAAN. You're not going and the cat's not going! Now please . . . this is Hanukkah . . . Hanukkah . . . this is the time to celebrate . . . What's the matter with all of you? Come on, Anne. Let's have the song.

ANNE. [*Singing*] "Oh, Hanukkah! Oh, Hanukkah! The sweet celebration."

MR. FRANK. [*Rising*] I think we should first blow out the candle . . . then we'll have something for tomorrow night.

MARGOT. But, Father, you're supposed to let it burn itself out.

MR. FRANK. I'm sure that God understands shortages. [*Before blowing it out*] "Praised be Thou, oh Lord our God, who hast sustained us and permitted us to celebrate this joyous festival."

[*He is about to blow out the candle when suddenly there is a crash of something falling below. They all freeze in horror, motionless. For a few seconds there is complete silence.* MR. FRANK *slips off his shoes. The others noiselessly follow his example.* MR. FRANK *turns out a light near him. He motions to* PETER *to turn off the center lamp.* PETER *tries to reach it, realizes he cannot and gets up on a chair. Just as he is touching the lamp he loses his balance. The chair goes out from under him. He falls. The iron lamp shade crashes to the floor. There is a sound of feet below, running down the stairs.*]

❶ *What sound is heard below? What happens in the fear following the sound?*

MR. VAN DAAN. [*Under his breath*] Oh, oh!

[*The only light left comes from the Hanukkah candle.* DUSSEL *comes from his room.* MR. FRANK *creeps over to the stairwell and stands listening. The dog is heard barking excitedly.*]

Do you hear anything?

MR. FRANK. [*In a whisper*] No. I think they've gone.

MRS. VAN DAAN. It's the Green Police. They've found us.

ANSWER TO GUIDED READING QUESTION

❶ There is a crash below. In the fear following the sound they try to turn out the light. As Peter reaches to turn off the light, he loses his balance and the iron lampshade crashes to the ground. They hear the sound of someone running down the stairs.

Answer to Guided Reading Question

❶ Mr. Frank leaves the hidden rooms because he thinks they need to know what happened. It is a Saturday, so they will receive no news from Miep or Mr. Kraler until Monday.

Historical Note

In 1944, the Gestapo, tipped off by a Dutch informer, arrived at the hiding place and took the eight residents to Gestapo headquarters. In 1963, Karl Silberbauer was identified as the Gestapo sergeant who had arrested the Franks. In 1966, Wilhelm Harster, who had been the police chief in the Netherlands during World War II, was arrested in Munich and charged with the deportation of about 100,000 Jews from the Netherlands to Auschwitz. At the trial, a witness testified that the informant who had turned in the Franks had received the usual reward of five gulden—at the time about $1.40—for each of the eight people taken from the hiding place.

Mr. Frank. If they had, they wouldn't have left. They'd be up here by now.

Mrs. Van Daan. I know it's the Green Police They've gone to get help. That's all. They'll be back!

Mr. Van Daan. Or it may have been the Gestapo,[29] looking for papers . . .

Mr. Frank. [*interrupting*] Or a thief, looking for money.

Mrs. Van Daan. We've got to do something . . . Quick! Quick! Before they come back.

Mr. Van Daan. There isn't anything to do. Just wait.

[MR. FRANK *holds up his hand for them to be quiet. He is listening intently. There is complete silence as they all strain to hear any sound from below. Suddenly* ANNE *begins to sway. With a low cry she falls to the floor in a faint.* MRS. FRANK *goes to her quickly, sitting beside her on the floor and taking her in her arms.*]

Mrs. Frank. Get some water, please! Get some water!

[MARGOT *starts for the sink.*]

Mr. Van Daan. [*Grabbing* MARGOT] No! No! No one's going to run water!

Mr. Frank. If they've found us, they've found us. Get the water. [MARGOT *starts again for the sink.* MR. FRANK, *getting a flashlight*] I'm going down.

[MARGOT *rushes to him, clinging to him.* ANNE *struggles to consciousness.*]

Margot. No, Father, no! There may be someone there, waiting . . . It may be a trap!

Why does Mr. Frank leave the hidden rooms? ❶

Mr. Frank. This is Saturday. There is no way for us to know what has happened until Miep or Mr. Kraler comes on Monday morning. We cannot live with this uncertainty.

Margot. Don't go, Father!

Mrs. Frank. Hush, darling, hush.

[MR. FRANK *slips quietly out, down the steps and out through the door below.*]

Margot! Stay close to me.

[MARGOT *goes to her mother.*]

Mr. Van Daan. Shush! Shush!

[MRS. FRANK *whispers to* MARGOT *to get the water,* MARGOT *goes for it.*]

Mrs. Van Daan. Putti, where's our money? Get our money. I hear you can buy the Green Police off, so much a head. Go upstairs quick! Get the money!

Mr. Van Daan. Keep still!

Mrs. Van Daan. [*Kneeling before him, pleading*] Do you want to be dragged off to a concentration camp? Are you going to stand there and wait for them to come up and get you? Do something, I tell you!

Mr. Van Daan. [*Pushing her aside*] Will you keep still!

[*He goes over to the stairwell to listen.* PETER *goes to his mother, helping her up onto the sofa. There is second of silence, then* ANNE *can stand it no longer.*]

Anne. Someone go after Father! Make Father come back!

Peter. [*Starting for the door*] I'll go.

Mr. Van Daan. Haven't you done enough?

[*He pushes* PETER *roughly away. In his anger against his father* PETER *grabs a chair as if to hit him with it, then puts it*

29. **Gestapo.** (gə stä´pō), Nazi secret police, infamous for their cruelty and terrorism

down, burying his face in his hands. MRS. FRANK *begins to pray softly.*]

ANNE. Please, please, Mr. Van Daan. Get Father.

MR. VAN DAAN. Quiet! Quiet!

[ANNE *is shocked into silence.* MRS. FRANK *pulls her closer, holding her protectively in her arms.*]

MRS. FRANK. [*Softly, praying*] "I lift up mine eyes unto the mountains, from whence cometh my help. My help cometh from the Lord who made heaven and earth. He will not suffer they foot to be moved . . . He that keepeth thee will not slumber . . . "

[*She stops as she hears someone coming. They all watch the door tensely.* MR. FRANK *comes quietly in.* ANNE *rushes to him, holding him tight.*]

MR. FRANK. It was a thief. That noise must have scared him away.

MRS. VAN DAAN. Thank goodness.

MR. FRANK. He took the cash box. And the radio. He ran away in such a hurry that he didn't stop to shut the street door. It was swinging wide open. [*A breath of relief sweeps over them.*] I think it would be good to have some light.

MARGOT. Are you sure it's all right?

MR. FRANK. The danger has passed.

[MARGOT *goes to light the small lamp.*]

Don't be so terrified, Anne. We're safe.

DUSSEL. Who says the danger has passed? Don't you realize we are in greater danger than ever?

MR. FRANK. Mr. Dussel, will you be still!

[MR. FRANK *takes* ANNE *back to the table, making her sit down with him, trying to calm her.*]

DUSSEL. [Pointing to PETER] Thanks to this clumsy fool, there's someone now who knows we're up here! Someone now knows we're up here, hiding!

MRS. VAN DAAN. [*Going to* DUSSEL] Someone knows we're here, yes. But who is the someone? A thief! A thief! You think a thief is going to go to the Green Police and say . . . I was robbing a place the other night and I heard a noise up over my head? You think a thief is going to do that?

DUSSEL. Yes. I think he will.

MRS. VAN DAAN. [*hysterically*] You're crazy!

[*She stumbles back to her seat at the table.* PETER *follows protectively, pushing* DUSSEL *aside.*]

DUSSEL. I think some day he'll be caught and then he'll make a bargain with the Green Police . . . if they'll let him off, he'll tell them where some Jews are hiding!

[*He goes off into the bedroom. There is a second of appalled silence.*]

MR. VAN DAAN. He's right.

ANNE. Father, let's get out of here! We can't stay here now . . . Let's go . . .

MR. VAN DAAN. Go! Where?

MRS. FRANK. [*sinking into her chair at the table*] Yes. Where?

MR. FRANK. [*Rising, to them all*] Have we lost all faith? All courage? A moment ago we thought that they'd come for us. We were sure it was the end. But it wasn't the end. We're alive, safe.

[MR. VAN DAAN *goes to the table and sits.* MR. FRANK *prays.*]

"We thank Thee, oh Lord our God. that in Thy infinite mercy Thou hast

❶ *Does everyone agree that the danger has passed? Why, or why not?*

❷ *Why might this prayer have special meaning under the circumstances?*

ANSWERS TO GUIDED READING QUESTIONS

❶ Mr. Dussel thinks that the danger is not over. Although the person has left, somebody is now aware that there are people in the building.

❷ The hiding families have just been spared. They thought they were discovered, but it appears that for the time being they are safe.

ADDITIONAL QUESTIONS AND ACTIVITIES

Suggest that students read the second act of *The Diary of Anne Frank.* Ask students to discuss or write about changes in character and mood that occur in act 2. Several elements of suspense in act 1 are related to events of act 2. Students can discuss or write about the use of suspense in act 2.

SELECTION CHECK TEST WITH ANSWERS

EX. In what city do the events of the play take place?
They take place in Amsterdam.

1. How many people originally share the hiding space?
There are originally seven people who share the hiding place.

2. What is the occupation of Mr. Dussel?
Mr. Dussel is a dentist.

3. Who brings Mr. Dussel to the hiding place?
Mr. Kraler brings Mr. Dussel to the hiding place.

4. What does Anne do to Mrs. Van Daan's fur coat?
Anne spills milk on the coat.

5. What holiday is being celebrated in the last scene?
Hanukkah is being celebrated.

again seen fit to spare us." [*He blows out the candle, then turns to* ANNE.] Come on, Anne. The song! Let's have the song!

[*He starts to sing.* ANNE *finally starts* *falteringly* *to sing, as* MR. FRANK *urges her on. Her voice is hardly audible at first.*]

ANNE. [*Singing*]

"Oh, Hanukkah! Oh, Hanukkah!
The sweet . . . celebration . . ."

[*As she goes on singing, the others gradually join in, their voices still shaking with fear.* MRS. VAN DAAN *sobs as she sings.*]

GROUP.
"Around the feast . . . we . . . gather
In complete . . . jubilation . . .
Happiest of sea . . . sons
Now is here.
Many are the reasons for good cheer."

[DUSSEL *comes from the bedroom. He comes over to the table, standing beside* MARGOT, *listening to them as they sing.*]

"Together
We'll weather
Whatever tomorrow may bring."

[*As they sing on with growing courage, the lights start to dim.*]

"So hear us rejoicing
And merrily voicing
The Hanukkah song that we sing.
Hoy!"

[*The lights are out. The curtain starts slowly to fall.*]

"Hear us rejoicing
And merrily voicing
The Hanukkah song that we sing."

[*They are still singing as the curtain falls.*] ■

WORDS FOR EVERYDAY USE

fal • ter • ing • ly (fôl´tər iŋ lē) *adv.*, unsteadily; uncertainly; haltingly

VOCABULARY IN CONTEXT

• Candy falteringly admitted that she had broken the window.

Editor's Note: The Franks, the Van Daans, and Mr. Dussel continued to live in hiding until August 1944. Food shortages, the length of their stay in cramped quarters, and constantly fearing for their lives led to increased tensions within the group. A sense of despair settled in, but hopes were revived by news of the Normandy invasion, which the families hoped would end German control and the necessity for their stay in the hiding space. About two months later, their worst fears came true. Cars came to a screeching halt outside, and pounding was heard on the doors. The Gestapo, or secret police, had been tipped off by an informer, probably the thief that they had heard below. The families were taken to Auschwitz, where Mrs. Frank died. Later, Mrs. Van Daan, Margot, and Anne were sent to Bergen-Belsen, another concentration camp, where they would all die. Anne died in March 1945. Otto Frank was the only survivor of the eight members of his hiding group. After the war he made his way back to Amsterdam, where Miep Gies gave him Anne's diary and writings. He published Anne's diary as a tribute to his family.

About the Authors

Frances Goodrich (1890–1984) and **Albert Hackett** (1900–) both worked as actors before beginning their careers as scriptwriters. They began working together in 1927 and were married in 1931. Goodrich and Hackett worked for two years on *The Diary of Anne Frank*. During this time, they visited with Anne's father, Otto Frank. The play won a Pulitzer Prize, the Drama Critics Circle Award, and a Tony award for the best play of 1955–1956. In 1962, Goodrich and Hackett adapted their drama as a screenplay.

Quotables

"It is too late to save yesterday's victims. . . . But it is not too late to save ourselves. The next time we truly hear the word *Holocaust,* it will be preceded by the word atomic. We had better learn from whom we can, while we can."

—Elie Wiesel

Bibliographic Note

The following sources may be useful in further exploring the Holocaust with your students.

Chartock, Roselle, and Jack Spender, ed. *The Holocaust Years: Society on Trial.*

Dawidowicz, Lucy. *The War against the Jews.*

Gilbert, Martin. *Atlas of the Holocaust.*

Spiegleman, Art. *Maus* and *Maus II.*

Wiesel, Elie. *Night.*

Literary Note

The Diary of Anne Frank opened in 1955 at the Cort Theater in New York. The play opened in seven German cities on October 1, 1956, and was greeted with stunned silence. The play opened a wave of guilt and shame about what had been done to the Jews. The play, opened on November 27, 1956 in Amsterdam, the city in which the events of the play took place. Many people in the audience had lost Jewish family and friends to Nazi exterminators, and the play was met with sobs and cries.

The Diary of Anne Frank was also adapted as a motion picture and for television. Students might try to view one of these versions.

Responding to the Selection

Ask students to discuss a time when they were in a dangerous or frightening situation. Ask them to describe how they felt about facing the situation with others.

Answers for Reviewing the Selection

RECALLING AND INTERPRETING

1. **Recalling.** Mr. Frank does not want to burn Anne's diary. **Interpreting.** The document leads to a flashback of the time described in the journal. The play shows events depicted in the diary. The diary preserves Anne's spirit.

2. **Recalling.** The families must be absolutely silent. Anne realizes what going into hiding means when her father tells her that she cannot go beyond the door even when there is no one in the building. **Interpreting.** Mr. Frank says that they will be able to act normally in the evenings. Their minds cannot be imprisoned because they are still able to think and learn.

3. **Recalling.** Mr. Kraler asks the hiding families to accept another person into their hiding spot. Mr. Frank agrees immediately. Mr. Van Daan complains that they are too crowded and that they do not have enough food. **Interpreting.** They accept Mr. Dussel because they know the horrible fate he might suffer. They are also indebted to Mr. Kraler for saving their lives.

4. **Recalling.** They hear a sound below. Peter and a lamp fall. Somebody is heard running away. **Interpreting.** This incident makes them all very nervous and tense. They will fear noises more now, because somebody knows of their existence.

SYNTHESIZING

Responses will vary. Possible responses are given.

5. Anne has changed. She has matured and become more introspective. She tries to think of others. Everyone thinks that Anne is thoughtful when she gives them their Hanukkah gifts. Students' opinions of Anne will vary.

Responding to the Selection

At the end of Act I, the families sing, "Together/We'll weather/Whatever tomorrow may bring." Imagine that you are part of the group. What might you have to face tomorrow? What would you do to keep your spirits up? Why might it help to face things together?

Reviewing the Selection

Recalling and Interpreting

1. **R** What is the one document that Mr. Frank does not want to burn at the beginning of the play?
   I What role does this document have in the play? Why do you think he chooses not to burn this document?

2. **R** What must the family do during the day? What makes Anne realize what going into hiding really means?
   I How does Mr. Frank lighten the gravity of the situation? Although they are in hiding, he says that their minds cannot be imprisoned. What does he mean by this statement?

3. **R** What request does Mr. Kraler make of the hiding families? What different reactions do people have to this request?
   I Why, despite the already cramped quarters and limited food supply, do the two families accept Mr. Dussel into their hiding place?

4. **R** What happens while the families are celebrating the first night of Hanukkah?
   I What effect does this occurrence have on their emotional states? What long-term effects might this event have on them?

Synthesizing

5. Has Anne changed during the time she has been in hiding? In what ways? Have others changed their opinions about Anne? Explain. What is your opinion of Anne? Has it changed since the beginning of the play?

Understanding Literature (Questions for Discussion)

1. **Suspense. Suspense** is a feeling of anxiousness or curiosity. Writers create suspense by raising questions in the reader's mind and by using details that create strong emotions. What is Anne's nightmare about? Why does Anne's nightmare create suspense?

2. **Dialogue. Dialogue** is conversation involving two or more people or characters. Dialogue lets readers understand characters better. What do you learn from dialogue about the relationship between Anne and her mother? between Anne and her father? between the Franks and the Van Daans? Does the dialogue seem "real" for the situation? Why, or why not?

Answers for Understanding Literature

Responses will vary. Possible responses are given.

1. **Suspense.** Anne's nightmare is about being discovered and taken away. Anne's nightmare creates suspense because the families live in daily fear of being discovered. Anne's nightmare is an intense display of that fear. It also contributes to the fear, because her screaming might give them away.

2. **Dialogue.** Anne and her mother disagree on a lot of things. Anne does not feel understood by her mother. Mrs. Frank wishes she were closer to Anne. Anne is much closer to her father. She is willing to share more with him. She is also more willing to do as he says. There is tension between the two families. Mrs. Van Daan tries to flirt with Mr. Frank. Mrs. Frank does not like the Van Daans. The dialogue is quite realistic.

Language Lab

Editing for Errors in Verbs

Verbs are a very important part of speech, so you should always edit your writing to make sure that you have not made a common verb error. If you edit your writing to make sure it is free of these errors, your work is more likely to impress its intended audience.

Subject/Verb Agreement

Make sure that your subject and your verb agree. A verb must be singular if its subject is singular. A verb must be plural if its subject is plural.

SINGULAR NOUNS	diary	family	thief
PLURAL NOUNS	diaries	families	thieves
SINGULAR VERBS	writes	hides	steals
PLURAL VERBS	write	hide	steal
SINGULAR SENTENCE	The **family hides** in the attic.		
PLURAL SENTENCE	The **families hide** in the attic.		

It may seem easy to remember that you should always use a singular verb with a singular subject, but sometimes this rule can be tricky. Look at the example below.

INCORRECT Mr. Dussel, among other people, **believe** that the Franks have gone to Switzerland.

CORRECT Mr. Dussel, among other people, **believes** that the Franks have gone to Switzerland.

Always make sure you have correctly determined the subject of a sentence before deciding whether to use a singular or a plural verb. In the above example, *Mr. Dussel* is the subject of the sentence, so a singular verb must be used.

LANGUAGE LAB

INTRODUCING THE SKILL

Inform students that verbs are an important part of speech. Have them identify verbs in sentences. Remind students that every sentence must contain a verb.

PREVIEWING THE SKILL

Have students read the material about editing for errors in verbs. Go over the examples with students.

PRACTICING THE SKILL

Have students complete the Try It Yourself exercise.

REVIEWING THE SKILL

Review the answers to the Try It Yourself exercise. If students need more practice, refer them to the exercises in the Language Arts Survey, 2.16, "Agreement of Subject and Verb"; 2.17, "Using Irregular Verbs"; and 2.18, "Avoiding Split Infinitives."

Irregular Verbs

Most of the time, the past tense of a verb is formed by adding *–ed, –d,* or sometimes *–t* to the base form of the verb.

PRESENT TENSE Miep **helps** the Franks and the Van Daans.
PAST TENSE Miep **helped** the Franks and the Van Daans.

Some verbs, however, are irregular, or the past tense of the verb is formed in a way other than by adding *–ed, –d,* or *–t.* The four principle parts of some common irregular verbs are listed below.

COMMON IRREGULAR VERBS

Infinitive	Past Tense	Present Participle	Past Participle
to bring	brought	[is] bringing	[has] brought
to drink	drank	[is] drinking	[has] drunk
to eat	ate	[is] eating	[has] eaten
to go	went	[is] going	[has] gone
to make	made	[is] making	[has] made
to say	said	[is] saying	[has] said
to see	saw	[is] seeing	[has] seen
to sell	sold	[is] selling	[has] sold
to write	wrote	[is] writing	[has] written

More irregular verbs are listed in the Language Arts Survey, 2.17, "Using Irregular Verbs."

Split Infinitives

One of the most common errors writers make when using verbs is splitting infinitives. Writers split infinitives when they insert adverbs or other parts of sentences between the word *to* and the base verb.

INCORRECT	Anne wanted *to* joyfully *sing* the Hanukkah song.
CORRECT	Anne wanted *to sing* joyfully the Hanukkah song.

While people sometimes split infinitives in their everyday speech, you should try to avoid split infinitives when writing.

Try It Yourself

Rewrite the following sentences, correcting errors in verb use as you find them. If a sentence does not contain errors in verb use, write *correct.*

EXAMPLE The three notebooks that made up Anne Frank's diary was published under the title *The Diary of a Young Girl.*

The three notebooks that made up Anne Frank's diary were published under the title *The Diary of a Young Girl.*

1. The Franks and the Van Daans hided in some rooms in the building where Mr. Frank had been in business.
2. The tiny space would have to eventually accommodate eight people.
3. Anne keeped a diary during their stay.
4. She writed about how it felt to live in hiding and about her dreams and fears.
5. One of Anne's dreams were about their hiding space being discovered.
6. During the day they have to be silent.
7. They were able to quietly walk about, but only when necessary.
8. When the day had ended and the workers had leaved, everyone breathed a sigh of relief.
9. One night they heared a noise from below.
10. They were afraid that they had been discovered, but nobody comed at that time.

ANSWERS FOR TRY IT YOURSELF

1. The Franks and the Van Daans hid in some rooms in the building where Mr. Frank had been in business.
2. The tiny space would eventually have to accommodate eight people.
3. Anne kept a diary during their stay.
4. She wrote about how it felt to live in hiding and about her dreams and fears.
5. One of Anne's dreams was about their hiding space being discovered.
6. During the day they had to be silent.
7. They were able to walk about quietly, but only when necessary.
8. When the day had ended and the workers had left, everyone breathed a sigh of relief.
9. One night they heard a noise from below.
10. They were afraid that they had been discovered, but nobody came at that time.

GOALS/OBJECTIVES

Studying this lesson will enable students to

- enjoy an adaptation of a Shakespearean comedy
- briefly explain when and why *A Midsummer Night's Dream* was written
- describe what rural Elizabethans believed about fairies
- define *character* and recognize similarities among characters
- write a dialogue

ADDITIONAL RESOURCES

Reader's Guide

- Selection Worksheet, 10.2

Assessment Portfolio

- Selection Check Test, 2.10.3
- Selection Test, 2.10.4

Pronunciation Exercise

- Grade 8 Audiocassette, Side B, Track 54

CROSS-CURRICULAR CONNECTIONS

World History

Students might enjoy one of the following activities:

- Students might research the Globe Theater. Students could then form groups and create models of the Globe Theater. Models may be as simple or as complex as students desire, but they should try to accurately represent the "wooden O" in which many of Shakespeare's dramas were first performed.
- Students might research the clothing and hairstyles of the Elizabethan Period. Encourage students to bring books which show Elizabethan costumes and hairstyles to class. Students should discuss how they imagine the appearance of each character in the play.

Prereading

A Midsummer Night's Dream

by William Shakespeare, retold by Charles and Mary Lamb

Cross-curricular Connection

World History. Most Shakespearean scholars agree that the comedy *A Midsummer Night's Dream* was written in 1595 or 1596, most likely for a wedding in a noble household. In Shakespeare's day, the term *comedy* referred to any literary work with a happy ending. In romantic comedies this happy ending typically took the form of one or more marriages. Shakespeare's *A Midsummer Night's Dream* focuses even more than most comedies on love leading to marriage, making the play quite appropriate for a noble wedding. Noble wedding ceremonies in Renaissance England were large and elaborate social events. Scholars have suggested that Queen Elizabeth I of England herself might have been expected at the wedding for which *A Midsummer Night's Dream* was written because there are some compliments to the queen in the play.

A Midsummer Night's Dream also reveals Shakespeare's love for rural England. The wood outside Athens in the play might well be based on the Forest of Arden, near Stratford-on-Avon, where Shakespeare grew up, and the fairies who exist in this wood have the names of common English insects and flowers. Belief in fairies was still common in rural England during Shakespeare's time. Fairies were seen as powerful creatures who could behave in a friendly manner toward humans but could also be mischievous or cruel.

The characters' confusion, the setting, and the supernatural fairies all create a dreamlike mood that is an essential part of *A Midsummer Night's Dream.* The relationship between dreams and reality was a source of fascination for Shakespeare. The title of the play reveals the importance of dreams in this comedy, and the ending suggests that the entire action of the story might be a dream. The version of *A Midsummer Night's Dream* that you are about to read is an adaptation.

As You Read

A Midsummer Night's Dream is full of characters who fall in love with the "wrong" characters before falling in love with the "right" ones. In your journal, make a chart like the one below. As you read, write down details about each character. If a character does not fall in love or change in any way, note that also.

Character	Wrong Beloved	Right Beloved	Details
Titania, Queen of Fairies	**Bottom**	**Oberon**	**does not want to give Oberon the changeling boy because his mother had been her friend**

AS YOU READ

Students might include the following details in their character chart: *Character*—Hermia, *Wrong Beloved*—Demetrius, *Right Beloved*—Lysander, *Details*—runs away to woods with Lysander to avoid losing her life or marrying Demetrius. *Character*—Helena, *Wrong Beloved*—Lysander, *Right Beloved*—Demetrius, *Details*—follows Demetrius into woods. *Character*—Lysander, *Wrong Beloved*—Helena, *Right Beloved*—Hermia, *Details*—temporarily falls in love with Helena because of fairies' potion. *Character*—Demetrius, *Wrong Beloved*—Hermia, *Right Beloved*—Helena, *Details*—realizes his love for Helena because of fairies' potion.

READER'S JOURNAL

What was the most fantastic dream you ever had? Where were you in your dream and what happened? Was there anything confusing or troubling about your dream? What parts of your dream seemed real? What parts seemed unreal? Write about these questions in your journal.

A Midsummer Night's Dream

WILLIAM SHAKESPEARE, RETOLD BY CHARLES AND MARY LAMB

Editor's note: The selection printed here is a prose adaptation of Shakespeare's A Midsummer Night's Dream. *In several places passages are reprinted from the original Shakespeare to give the reader an impression of the strength, humor, and beauty of Shakespeare's dramatic verse.*

There was a law in the ancient city of Athens which allowed fathers to force their daughters to marry men chosen by their parents. If a daughter refused to marry the man her father had chosen to be her husband, the father was allowed to have her put to death. Of course, fathers do not often want their own daughters to die, even if they are sometimes a little disobedient, so this law was seldom or never used. It is probable, however, that the young ladies of the city were often threatened by their parents with the terrors of it.

There was one time, however, when an old man called Egeus actually did come before Theseus, Duke of Athens, to complain of his daughter Hermia. He had ordered her to marry Demetrius, a young man of a noble Athenian family, but she refused to obey him because she loved another young Athenian who was called Lysander. Egeus demanded justice of Theseus and asked for this cruel law to be used against his daughter.

Hermia pleaded in excuse for her disobedience that Demetrius had previously said that he was in love with her best friend Helena and that Helena loved Demetrius to distraction. Although Hermia gave this good reason for not obeying her father, Egeus remained stern and unmoved.

Theseus, though a great and merciful prince, could not alter the laws of

❶ *What cruel law existed in Athens? For what purpose was it most often used? What "good reason" does Hermia have for not marrying Demetrius?*

WORDS FOR EVERYDAY USE

stern (stʉrn) *adj.,* unshakable, firm

READER'S JOURNAL

As an alternative activity, students might write about whether or not they believe that parents should have the right to choose the spouses of their children. Ask students what might be the benefits or the drawbacks of an arranged marriage.

SPELLING AND VOCABULARY WORDS FROM THE SELECTION

bower	extravagant
celestial	horrid
condemn	loathe
courtier	potent
courtship	reckon
coverlet	stern

ANSWER TO GUIDED READING QUESTION

❶ The cruel law said that if a daughter refused to marry the man her father had chosen to be her husband, the father was allowed to have her put to death. This law was most often used as a threat. Hermia does not want to marry Demetrius because he is in love with her best friend.

SUPPORT FOR LEP STUDENTS

PRONUNCIATIONS OF PROPER NOUNS AND ADJECTIVES

De • me • tri • us (də mē´trē us̀) n.
E • ge • us (ē´ jē us) n.
Ly • san • der (lī san´dər) n.
O • ber • on (ō´bər äǹ) n.
Ti • ta • ni • a (ti tā´nē ə) n.

ADDITIONAL VOCABULARY

distraction—great mental disturbance
meddling—interfering

VOCABULARY IN CONTEXT

• The judge was known for being stern and unmoving in his beliefs.

Answers to Guided Reading Questions

❶ The king and queen of the fairies are quarreling because Titania refuses to give Oberon a changeling boy. Their quarrel causes the countryside to be in an uproar.

❷ Hermia and Lysander decide to run away from Athens to Lysander's aunt's house where they will marry. They decide to meet in a wood outside Athens.

Historical Note

Students might mention that they find it strange that Egeus is willing to have his daughter put to death if she does not obey his wishes and marry Demetrius. Inform students that relationships between parents and children were more formal in Shakespeare's time than they are today. Children owed obedience and respect to their parents at all times, even in matters of choosing an occupation or a spouse. Because relationships between parents and children were so formal, it would not have been unusual for a father to have been outraged by his child's refusal to marry a particular person. However, Egeus's decision to have his daughter put to death for this disobedience would have seemed as extreme to Shakespeare's audience as it does to a modern audience.

❶ *What relationship presently exists between the king and queen of the fairies? Why? What is the effect of their quarrel on the countryside?*

❷ *What do Hermia and Lysander decide to do?*

his country. He could only give Hermia four days to consider and at the end of that time, if she still refused to marry Demetrius, she was to be put to death.

When Hermia was dismissed from the duke's presence, she went to see Lysander and told him of her danger—she must either give him up and marry Demetrius or lose her life in four days' time.

Lysander was very upset when he heard this terrible news. Remembering that he had an aunt who lived at some distance from Athens and that where she lived the cruel law could not be used against Hermia (this law did not apply outside the city), he suggested to Hermia that she should creep out of her father's house that night and run away with him to his aunt's house, where he would marry her. "I will meet you," Lysander said, "in the wood a few miles outside the city—the lovely wood where we once met Helena on the May morning."

Hermia joyfully agreed to the plan. She told no one about it except her friend Helena. Girls will do silly things for love and Helena, unkindly, decided to go and tell Demetrius. She didn't have any hope that betraying her friend's secret would do her any good apart from the poor pleasure of following her faithless lover to the wood, for she knew quite well that Demetrius would chase after Hermia.

The wood where Lysander and Hermia planned to meet was the favorite place of those creatures known as fairies. Oberon the king and Titania the queen of the fairies, with all their followers, held their midnight dances and parties in this wood.

The king and queen were at loggerheads[1] at this time. They never met by moonlight in the shady walks of this pleasant wood but they started quarrelling, till all the countryside itself was in an uproar. The reason for this unhappy disagreement was that Titania refused to give Oberon a little changeling[2] boy, whose mother had been Titania's friend. Upon her death, the fairy queen stole the child from its nurse and brought him up in the woods.

The night on which Hermia and Lysander planned to meet in this very wood, as Titania was walking with some of her maids of honor, she met Oberon attended by his train of fairy <u>courtiers</u>.

"How unfortunate to meet you in the moonlight, proud Titania," said the fairy king.

The queen replied, "What! Is that you, jealous Oberon? Fairies, skip away from here. I have promised myself to have nothing to do with him." "Stay, rash fairy!" said Oberon, "am I not your lord? Why does Titania cross her Oberon? Give me your little changeling boy to be my page."[3]

"Set your heart at rest," answered the queen, "your whole fairy kingdom would not buy the boy from me." She

1. **at loggerheads.** In disagreement
2. **changeling.** A child secretly exchanged for another by fairies
3. **page.** Young male attendant, especially one serving royalty

Words for Everyday Use

cour • ti • er (kôrťē ər) *n.,* attendant at a royal court

Vocabulary in Context

• The Russian Czar admired the kingdom of France, so he made all his <u>courtiers</u> learn French.

then left Oberon in great anger. "Well, go your way," said Oberon, "before the morning dawns I will punish you for this."

Oberon then sent for Puck, his chief favorite and helper.

Puck, or, as he was sometimes called, Robin Goodfellow, was a clever and mischievous sprite that used to play tricks in the neighboring villages—sometimes getting into the dairies and skimming the cream from the milk, sometimes hiding in the butterchurn so that the dairymaid would work without any success to change her cream into butter. The young men of the village didn't do any better; whenever Puck chose to play his tricks in the brewing vat, the ale was sure to be spoiled. When a few neighbors met for a sociable drink, Puck would jump into a tankard of ale in the likeness of a roasted crab apple and, just as some old woman was taking a sip, he would bob against her lips and spill the ale over her withered chin. When an old woman was about to sit down and tell her neighbors a sad story, Puck would disguise himself as a three-legged stool and slip out from under her. Down she toppled and all the old gossips would hold their sides and laugh at her, saying they never spent a merrier hour.

① *What are some of Puck's mischievous acts?*

"Come here, Puck," said Oberon to this merry wanderer of the night. "Fetch me the flower which girls call 'love in idleness.' If you put the juice of that little purple flower on the eyelids of someone who is asleep, it will make him fall in love with the first person he sees when he wakes up. I will drop some of that juice on the eyelids of my Titania when she is asleep and when she opens her eyes,

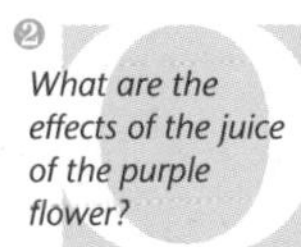

② *What are the effects of the juice of the purple flower?*

ANSWERS TO GUIDED READING QUESTIONS

① Puck causes people to spill beverages on themselves and disguises himself as a three-legged stool that slips out from under people.

② If the juice of the purple flower is put on the eyelids of someone who is sleeping, that person will fall in love with the first person he or she sees

LITERARY NOTE

Inform students that this story is a prose adaptation of Shakespeare's original dramatic verse. The adaptation is much shorter than Shakespeare's original play. Because the action of the play has been condensed, many of the details and subplots of Shakespeare's original play have been omitted, and the events in the adaptation are faster paced than in Shakespeare's original work. Due to the quick pacing of the story's action, some students may have difficulty following the plot of the story. Point out that the story's events are meant to be confusing to a certain degree, reflecting the confusion the couples experience in the wood outside Athens. Make sure students understand which characters are in love with other characters and whether this love is a matter of free choice or a result of the fairies' love charm.

You should also point out that the adapters of this work have changed Shakespeare's language to make it more understandable and contemporary. As an example of this type of adaptation, read students the original dialogue below and have them compare it to the dialogue in the adaptation.

Oberon: Ill met by moonlight, proud Titania.

Titania: What, jealous Oberon? Fairies skip hence—I have forsworn his . . . company.

Answers to Guided Reading Questions

❶ Oberon's plan is to charm Titania into falling in love with a strange creature and then to convince her to give him the changeling boy.

❷ Oberon's plan is to put the juice of the flower in Demetrius's eyes when he is near Helena so that when Demetrius wakes he will fall in love with her.

Additional Questions and Activities

Ask students the following questions: What power does the juice of the little purple flower have? On whom does Oberon wish to use the juice of this flower? Why does Oberon want to use the juice of the flower on these people?

Answers

The juice of the little purple flower when applied to the eyelids of someone who is asleep will make that person fall in love with the first person he or she sees when he or she wakes up. Oberon wishes to use the juice on Titania so that he will be able to convince her to give him the changeling boy. Oberon also wishes to use the juice on Demetrius because he overheard him arguing with Helena and he wishes to right the situation.

❶ *What is Oberon's plan to get the changeling boy?*

she will fall in love with whatever she sees even though it might be a lion or a bear, a meddling monkey or a busy ape. Before I take the charm from her sight, which I can do with another spell I know, I will make her give me the boy to be my page."

Puck, who loved mischief, was really pleased with this plan and ran to look for the flower. While Oberon was waiting for him to return, he noticed Demetrius and Helena enter the wood. He overheard Demetrius telling her off for following him and saying very unkind things. Helena reminded him how he used to love her and tell her how true he was to her. He then left her, as he said, to the mercy of the wild beasts and she ran after him as fast as she could.

The fairy king, who was always friendly to true lovers, felt very sorry for Helena.

❷ *What is Oberon's plan for Demetrius and Helena?*

When Puck returned with the little purple flower, Oberon said to him, "Take a part of this flower. A sweet Athenian lady, who is in love with a young man who doesn't care about her, has been here. If you find him sleeping, drop some of the love-juice in his eyes, but try to do it when she is near him so that she will be the first thing he sees when he wakes."SEE INSET Puck promised to manage this matter very skillfully.

Then without her noticing, Oberon went to Titania's <u>bower</u>, where she was preparing to sleep. Her fairy bower was a bank, covered with wild thyme, cowslips and sweet violets under a canopy of woodbine, musk-roses and eglantine. Titania always rested for a part of the night there. Her <u>coverlet</u> was the patterned skin of a snake, which, though small, was wide enough to wrap a fairy in.

He found Titania giving orders to her fairies of what they were to do while she slept. "Some of you," said Her Majesty, "must kill cankers in the musk-rose buds and some wage war with the bats for their leather wings to make my small elves coats, and some of you keep watch so that the noisy owl that nightly hoots does not come near me. First, sing me

FROM *A MIDSUMMER NIGHT'S DREAM*, ACT II, SCENE I BY WILLIAM SHAKESPEARE

Oberon I pray thee give it me.
I know a bank where the wild thyme blows,
Where oxlips and the nodding violet grows,
Quite over-canopied with luscious woodbine,
With sweet musk-roses, and with eglantine.
There sleeps Titania sometime of the night,
Lull'd in these flowers with dances and delight;
And there the snake throws her enamell'd skin,
Weed wide enough to wrap a fairy in;
And with the juice of this I'll streak her eyes,
And make her full of hateful fantasies.
Take thou some of it, and seek through this grove:
A sweet Athenian lady is in love
With a disdainful youth; anoint his eyes;
But do it when the next thing he espies
May be the lady. Thou shalt know the man
By the Athenian garments he hath on.
Effect it with some care, that he may prove
More fond of her than she upon her love:
And look thou meet me ere the first cock crow.

Words for Everyday Use

bow • er (bou´ər) *n.,* place enclosed by overhanging branches
cov • er • let (kuv´ər lit) *n.,* bedspread

Vocabulary in Context

- The children played in a <u>bower</u> formed by the overhanging tree branches.
- I use the handmade quilt my grandmother gave me as a <u>coverlet</u>.

to sleep." Then they began to sing this song:

You spotted snakes with double
tongue
Thorny hedgehogs, be not seen;
Newts and blind-worms, do no
wrong,
Come not near our fairy queen.
Philomel, with melody,
Sing in our sweet lullaby,
Lulla, lulla, lullaby; lulla, lulla,
lullaby:
Never harm,
Nor spell, nor charm,
Come our lovely lady nigh;
So good night with lullaby.

When the fairies had sung their queen to sleep with this pretty lullaby, they left her to get on with the important jobs she had given them. Oberon quietly approached Titania and dropped some of the love-juice on her eyelids, saying:

What thou seest when thou dost
wake,
Do it for thy true-love take.

Meanwhile, Hermia had made her escape from her father's house that night to avoid the death she was doomed to for refusing to marry Demetrius. When she entered the wood, she found her beloved Lysander waiting for her, to take her to his aunt's house. Before they had traveled halfway through the wood, Hermia was so tired that Lysander, who took great care of her, persuaded her to rest till the morning on a bank of soft moss. He lay down on the ground a little way off and they both soon fell fast asleep. Here they were found by Puck. He, seeing a handsome young man asleep and noting that his clothes were made in the Athenian fashion, and seeing a pretty young lady sleeping near him, assumed that this must be the couple whom Oberon had sent him to find. Naturally enough he reckoned that, as they were alone together, she must be the first he would see when he awoke. So without further delay, he poured some of the juice of the little purple flower on Lysander's eyelids. Unfortunately, just at the moment Lysander woke up, Helena, who had got lost while chasing Demetrius, came along. So Helena, not Hermia, was the first person Lysander saw when he opened his eyes. The love-charm was so powerful that all his love for Hermia vanished and Lysander instantly fell in love with Helena.

If he had seen Hermia first when he awoke, Puck's blunder would not have mattered for he could not love that faithful lady too well. For poor Lysander to be forced by a fairy love-charm to forget his own true Hermia and to run after another lady, leaving Hermia asleep quite alone in a wood at midnight, was a sad chance indeed.

1 *What mistake does Puck make?*

Words for Everyday Use

reck • on (rek´ən) *v.*, judge; consider; estimate

Answer to Guided Reading Question

1 Puck assumes that Lysander is Demetrius so he puts the juice of the flower on Lysander's eyelids. Helena then wanders along and Lysander wakes up, falling in love with Helena and forgetting his love for Hermia.

Additional Questions and Activities

Ask students the following questions: On whom does Puck use the juice of the flower? Why does Puck make this mistake? Who was the first person that Lysander saw when he opened his eyes? What does Lysander do to Hermia once he falls in love with Helena?

ANSWERS

Puck uses the juice of the flower on Lysander instead of on Demetrius. Puck makes this mistake because both men are wearing clothes in the Athenian fashion. Lysander sees Helena. Lysander leaves Hermia alone in the woods and runs after Helena.

Vocabulary in Context

- Jeremy glanced at all his I.O.U.s from his friend Soon and reckoned that Soon owed him fifteen dollars.

Answers to Guided Reading Questions

❶ Lysander gives up his love for Hermia because the love charm the fairies have placed on him is so potent.

❷ Helena is upset because she believes that the others are making fun of her. Hermia is upset because she does not understand why both Lysander and Demetrius, who were formerly in love with her, are now in love with Helena.

Additional Questions and Activities

Ask students the following questions: What does Helena think when Lysander proclaims his love for her? What does Hermia do when she wakes up alone in the wood? What does Oberon do when he learns of Puck's error? What happens as a result of Oberon's actions?

ANSWERS

Helena thinks that Lysander is making fun of her. Hermia wanders about searching for Demetrius. Oberon applies the love juice to Demetrius's eyelids. Demetrius falls in love with Helena.

This is what had happened. Helena tried to keep up with Demetrius when he so rudely ran away, but she could not. She soon lost sight of him and, as she was wandering about, miserable and lonely, she arrived at the place where Lysander was sleeping. "Ah!" she said, "this is Lysander lying on the ground. Is he dead or asleep?" Then, gently touching him, she said, "Good sir, if you are alive, wake up." Upon this Lysander opened his eyes and because the love-charm began to work, immediately spoke to her in terms of extravagant love and admiration. He told her that she was much more beautiful than Hermia as a dove is more beautiful than a raven. He said that he would run through fire for her and made many more such lover-like speeches. Helena, knowing Lysander was her friend and Hermia's lover and that he was solemnly engaged to marry her, was furious when she heard him. She thought (as well she might) that Lysander was making fun of her. "Oh!" she said, "why was I born to be mocked and scorned by everyone? Is it not enough, is it not enough, young man, that I can never get a gentle look or a kind word from Demetrius, but you, sir, must pretend in this mocking way to love me? I thought, Lysander, you were kinder than that." Enraged, she ran away and Lysander followed her, quite forgetting his own Hermia, who was still asleep.

❶ *Why does Lysander give up his love for Hermia?*

❷ *Why are both Helena and Hermia upset?*

When Hermia awoke all alone, she was frightened. She wandered about the wood, not knowing what had happened to Lysander or which way to go to find him. In the meantime, Demetrius, not being able to find Hermia and his rival Lysander and tired with his fruitless search, had fallen asleep. Oberon had learned from questioning Puck that he had applied the love-charm to the wrong person's eyes. Now, finding Demetrius, Oberon touched his eyelids with the love-juice. He woke up instantly and the first person he saw was—Helena. Just as Lysander had done before, Demetrius began telling her how much he loved her. At that moment, Lysander, followed by Hermia (for through Puck's unlucky mistake it was now Hermia's turn to run after her lover), came running up. Then Lysander and Demetrius, both speaking at the same time, told Helena how much they loved her. Both of them were under the influence of the same potent charm.

Poor Helena was astonished and thought that Demetrius, Lysander and her once best friend Hermia were all in plot together to make fun of her.

Hermia was as much surprised as Helena. She didn't know why Lysander and Demetrius, who both loved her before, were now in love with Helena. To Hermia the matter did not seem to be fun at all.

Hermia and Helena, who before had always been best friends, now started saying horrid things to each other.

"Unkind Hermia," said Helena, "you were the one who set Lysander on to

Words for Everyday Use

ex • trav • a • gant (ek strav´ə gənt) *adj.,* excessive or unrestrained

po • tent (pot´nt) *adj.,* effective or powerful in action

hor • rid (hôr´id) *adj.,* very bad, ugly, unpleasant

Vocabulary in Context

- Jenny thought that the many tears that Lucy shed at the film were extravagant because the film was not very moving.
- One of the most potent rulers of England and one of the most beloved by her people was Queen Elizabeth.
- Ray's singing voice is beautiful, but Herman's is horrid.

upset me with mock praises; and your other lover Demetrius, who used almost to kick me with his foot—you made him call me 'goddess,' 'nymph,' 'rare,' 'precious' and 'celestial.' He would not say these things to me, because he hates me, if you did not set him on to make fun of me. Unkind Hermia to join with men in scorning your poor friend. Have you forgotten the friendship of our schooldays? How often, Hermia, did the two of us used to sit on one cushion, both singing one song, with our needles embroidering the same flower on the same sampler, growing up together like twins? Hermia, it is neither friendly, nor lady-like to join with men in scorning your poor friend."

"I am amazed at your angry words," said Hermia. "I am not mocking you; it seems that you are mocking me."

"Oh, yes!" returned Helena. "Keep it up, pretend to look serious and then make faces at me when I turn my back; then wink at each other and keep the joke going. If you had any pity, grace or manners, you would not treat me like this."

While Helena and Hermia were speaking these angry words to each other, Demetrius and Lysander left them to fight each other over Helena.

When Helena and Hermia found the men had left them, they set off again and once more wandered wearily in the wood in search of their lovers.

As soon as they were gone, the fairy king, who, together with Puck, had been listening to their quarrels, said "Was all this a mistake, Puck, or did you play a trick?"

"Believe me, king of shadows," answered Puck, "it was a mistake. Didn't you tell me I should know the man by his Athenian clothes? However, I am not sorry it has happened, for I think their carryings-on are very funny."

"You heard," Oberon said, "that Demetrius and Lysander have gone to find a convenient place to fight. I order you to blanket the night with a thick fog and lead these quarrelsome lovers so far apart in the dark that they won't be able to find each other. Mimic their voices to each other and make it sound like they're daring each other, so that they follow you. Do this till they are so tired they can't go on. When they fall asleep, drop the juice of this other flower into Lysander's eyes. When he awakes, he will have forgotten his new love for Helena and return to his old love for Hermia. Then the two pretty girls will each be happy with the man she loves and they will think all that has happened was a bad dream. Get on with this quickly, Puck, and I will go and see what sweet love my Titania has found."

Titania was still sleeping. Near her, there was a workman, a weaver, who had lost his way in the wood and was also asleep. "This fellow," Oberon said, "shall be my Titania's true love." He magically fixed an ass's head over the weaver's; it seemed to fit him so well it might have grown upon his own shoulders. Although Oberon fixed on

❶ *What does Puck think of the confusion that he has caused?*

❷ ***What was the relationship between Hermia and Helena like in the past?***

❸ *What is Oberon's plan for setting things right again?*

WORDS FOR EVERYDAY USE

ce • les • tial (sə les´chəl) *adj.*, of the finest or highest kind, perfect

ANSWERS TO GUIDED READING QUESTIONS

❶ Puck finds the confusion he has caused to be very amusing.

❷ In the past, Hermia and Helena were good friends who grew up together like twins.

❸ Oberon's plan is to separate the quarreling couples until they fall asleep. Then Puck will drop the juice of another flower into Lysander's eyes so he will love for Hermia again.

QUOTABLES

"Confusion is a word that we have invented for an order which is not understood."

—Henry Miller

"In all chaos there is a cosmos, in all disorder a secret order."

—Henry Miller

LITERARY TECHNIQUE

CLIMAX

The **climax** is the point of highest interest and suspense in a literary work. Inform students that the action of *A Midsummer Night's Dream* reaches a climax on page 513 with the four main characters almost coming to blows. Point out that Shakespeare has brought the story of the four young people in the wood to its height of chaos and confusion. Ask students to predict how the author will resolve this confusion. How will the author make order of this disorder?

VOCABULARY IN CONTEXT

• Helen of Troy was renowned for her celestial beauty.

CROSS-CURRICULAR ACTIVITIES

ARTS AND HUMANITIES

You might ask students to form pairs and enact the scene between Titania and Bottom, the weaver. Students will better understand Shakespeare's language when it is spoken aloud. Encourage them to present their scenes in front of the class, making them as humorous or as dramatic as they wish.

the ass's[4] head very gently, it woke the weaver up, and unconscious of what Oberon had done to him, he wandered towards the bower where the fairy queen slept.

"Oh! What angel is that I see?" said Titania, opening her eyes. The juice of the little purple flower was beginning to take effect. "Are you as wise as you are handsome?"

"Why, madam," said the foolish weaver, "if I have enough brains to find the way out of this wood, I have as many as I want."

"Don't wish yourself out of the wood," said the love-struck queen. "I am not an ordinary spirit. I love you. Come with me and I will give you fairies to look after you." She then called four of her fairies. Their names were Peaseblossom, Cobweb, Moth and Mustardseed.SEE INSET

The queen said, "Look after this sweet gentleman. Hop in his walks and skip in his sight. Feed him with grapes and apricots and steal the honey-bags from the bees for him. "Come, sit with me," she said to the weaver, "and let me stroke your lovely hairy cheeks, my darling, and kiss your beautiful long ears."

"Where is Peaseblossom?" said the ass-headed man, not much impressed by the fairy queen's courtship but very proud of his new attendants.

"Here, sir," said Peaseblossom.

"Scratch my head," said the weaver, whose name was Bottom. "Where is Cobweb?"

4. **ass.** Donkey, burro, or any similar creature

WORDS FOR EVERYDAY USE

court • ship (kôrt´ship) *n.,* process of attempting to win someone's love

VOCABULARY IN CONTEXT

- The foreign prince's courtship of the country's princess was well known, and it was rumored that a wedding would be announced.

FROM *A MIDSUMMER NIGHT'S DREAM*, ACT II, SCENE I BY WILLIAM SHAKESPEARE

Titania I pray thee, gentle mortal, sing again:
Mine ear is much enamour'd of thy note;
So is mine eye enthralled to thy shape;
And thy fair virtue's force perforce doth move me
On the first view to say, to swear, I love thee.

Bottom Methinks, mistress, you should have little reason for that. And yet, to say the truth, reason and love keep little company together nowadays. The more the pity that some honest neighbors will not make them friends. Nay, I can gleek upon occasion.

Titania Thou art as wise as thou art beautiful.

Bottom Not so neither; but if I had wit enough to get out of this wood, I have enough to serve mine own turn.

Titania Out of this wood do not desire to go:
Thou shalt remain here, whether thou wilt or no.
I am a spirit of no common rate;
The summer still doth tend upon my state;
And I do love thee: therefore go with me.
I'll give thee fairies to attend on thee;
And they shall fetch thee jewels from the deep
And sing, while thou on pressed flowers dost sleep:
And I will purge thy mortal grossness so,
That thou shalt like an airy spirit go.
Peaseblossom! Cobweb! Moth! and Mustardseed!

"Here, sir," said Cobweb.

"Good Mr. Cobweb," said the foolish man, "bring me the honey-bag from the red humble-bee on the top of that thistle over there. Do not go for too much trouble, Mr. Cobweb, and take care that the honey-bag does not break. I should be sorry if you were drowned in honey. Where is Mustardseed?"

"Here, sir," said Mustardseed. "What can I do for you?"

"Nothing, good Mr. Mustardseed," said Bottom, "but help Mr. Peaseblossom to scratch. I must go to a barber's for a shave, Mr. Mustardseed, for I think I am astonishingly hairy about the face."

"My sweet love," said the queen, "what would you like to eat? I have a brave fairy who shall find the squirrel's hoard and fetch you some new nuts."

"I would rather have a handful of dried peas," said Bottom who had got an ass's appetite with his ass's head, "but, please, let none of your people disturb me, for I think I'd like a sleep."

"Sleep, then," said the queen, "and I will wrap my arms around you. O how I love you! How I adore you!"

When the fairy king saw the weaver sleeping in the arms of his queen, he came up to her and scolded her with having lavished her love upon an ass. She could not deny it, as the weaver was lying there asleep in her arms with his ass's head crowned by her with flowers. When Oberon had teased her for some time, he again asked her to give him the changeling boy and she did so.

Oberon, having obtained the little boy to be his page, took pity on the disgraceful situation. He poured some of the juice of the other flower onto Titania's eyelids and the fairy queen immediately recovered her senses. She was amazed at the sight of Bottom and said how she now loathed the sight of the strange monster.

Oberon ordered Puck to take the ass's head from Bottom and leave him to

WORDS FOR EVERYDAY USE

loathe (lōth) *v.*, feel intense dislike, disgust, or hatred for

LITERARY TECHNIQUE

RESOLUTION

The **resolution** is the point in a poem, story, or play in which the central conflict, or struggle, is ended. Ask students the following questions: In what way is the central conflict of this story resolved on pages 516 and 517? Who makes order of the confusion that the characters experienced? What do the main characters think about their experiences when they awaken?

ANSWERS

The central conflict is resolved when the fairies remove the charm from Lysander's eyes so that he falls in love with Hermia again. Puck makes order out of the confusion he initially created. The main characters believe that their experiences have been a dream.

VOCABULARY IN CONTEXT

- While my sister eats it with great delight, I have always loathed peanut butter.

ANSWER TO GUIDED READING QUESTION

❶ Hermia and Lysander wonder if their adventures really happened or if they were both dreaming the same dream.

LITERARY NOTE

Theseus's speech in act V, scene i, is one of Shakespeare's most famous speeches. You might read the speech aloud to the class. Ask students to discuss the idea of the lunatic, the lover, and the poet being of "imagination all compact." Ask them what these lines mean. What do these lines indicate about the four young people? about writing poetry?

finish his nap with his own fool's head upon his shoulders.

Oberon and Titania were now good friends again. He told her the story of the young lovers and their midnight quarrels and she agreed to go with him to see the end of their adventures.

The fairy king and queen found the four Athenians asleep on the grass quite near each other. Puck, to make up for his mistake, had worked hard to bring them all to the same place without anyone realizing the others were there. He had carefully removed the charm from Lysander's eyes with the juice the fairy king had given to him.

Hermia awoke first and, finding her lost Lysander asleep so near her, was looking at him and wondering at his strange unfaithfulness. Lysander opening his eyes and seeing his dear Hermia, came to his senses, his love for Hermia flooded back. They began to talk over the adventures of the night, wondering if these things had really happened or if they had both been dreaming the same bewildering dream.

❶ *What do Hermia and Lysander think of the adventures of the previous night?*

Helena and Demetrius were awake by this time. Sleep had calmed Helena's anger and she listened with delight when Demetrius told her again how much he loved her. To her surprise as well as her pleasure, she began to realize that he meant what he was saying.

The two girls, now no longer rivals, once more became best friends. All the unkind words they had said to each other were forgiven and they calmly discussed what was the best thing to do in their present situation. It was soon agreed that, as Demetrius had given up his claim to Hermia, he should try to persuade her father to take back the cruel sentence of death passed against her. Demetrius was preparing to return to Athens to do this, when they were all surprised by the sight of Egeus, Hermia's father, who came to the wood following his runaway daughter.

When Egeus understood that Demetrius no longer wanted to marry his daughter, he no longer opposed her marriage to Lysander. He agreed that they should be married in four days' time, that being the day when Hermia

FROM *A MIDSUMMER NIGHT'S DREAM,* ACT V, SCENE I
BY WILLIAM SHAKESPEARE

Hippolyta[1] 'Tis strange, my Theseus, that these lovers speak of.
Theseus More strange than true. I never may believe
These antique fables, nor these fairy toys.
Lovers and madmen have such seething brains,
Such shaping fantasies, that apprehend
More than cool reason ever comprehends.
The lunatic, the lover, and the poet
Are of imagination all compact:
One sees more devils than vast hell can hold;
That is the madman: the lover, all as frantic,
Sees Helen's beauty in a brow of Egypt:
The poet's eye, in a fine frenzy rolling,
Doth glance from heaven to earth, from earth to heaven;
And as imagination bodies forth
The forms of things unknown, the poet's pen
Turns them to shapes, and gives to airy nothing
A local habitation and a name.
Such tricks hath strong imagination,
That if it would but apprehend some joy,
It comprehends some bringer of that joy:
Or, in the night, imagining some fear,
How easy is a bush suppos'd a bear!

1. **Hippolyta.** Queen of the Amazons and betrothed to Theseus

had been condemned to lose her life. Helena joyfully agreed to marry her beloved and now faithful Demetrius on the same day.

The fairy king and queen, who were invisible spectators of this happy ending, were so much pleased that they decided to celebrate the wedding with sports and games throughout their fairy kingdom.SEE INSET (LEFT)

And now, if you are offended by this story of fairies and their pranks, just imagine that you have been asleep and dreaming. All these adventures were just visions you saw in your sleep. It was all a Midsummer Night's Dream.SEE INSET (RIGHT) ■

FROM A MIDSUMMER NIGHT'S DREAM, ACT V, SCENE I BY WILLIAM SHAKESPEARE

Puck. [*To the audience.*] If we shadows have offended,
Think but this, and all is mended,
That you have but slumber'd here
While these visions did appear.
And this weak and idle theme,
No more yielding but a dream,
Gentles, do not reprehend:
If you pardon, we will mend.
And, as I am an honest Puck,
If we have unearned luck
Now to 'scape the serpent's tongue,
We will make amends ere long;
Else the Puck a liar call.
So, goodnight unto you all.

About the Author

William Shakespeare (1564–1616) is considered by many to be the greatest poet in the English language and the finest dramatist the world has ever known. Shakespeare was born to middle-class parents in Stratford-on-Avon, England. He later lived in London and pursued a life in the theater, both as an actor and as a playwright. He wrote at least thirty-seven plays, including comedies, tragedies, histories, and romances. Shakespeare did not personally prepare his plays for publication, and no official collection of them appeared until after his death. Since that time his works have become widely produced and read in many different countries around the world.

Charles and Mary Lamb wrote *Tales from Shakespeare* in 1807, to introduce younger people to Shakespeare's works. Charles Lamb retold the tragedies, and his sister, Mary Lamb, retold the comedies, including *A Midsummer Night's Dream.*

WORDS FOR EVERYDAY USE

con • demn (kən dem´) *v.,* inflict a penalty on

SELECTION CHECK TEST WITH ANSWERS

EX. Where does this story take place?
The story takes place in and near Athens.

1. What does Egeus want Hermia to do? What does she want to do?
Egeus wants Hermia to marry Demetrius, but she wants to marry Lysander.

2. Who is Helena, and with whom is she in love?
Helena is a good friend of Hermia, and Helena is in love with Demetrius.

3. What does Puck do to Lysander to make him forget his love for Helena?
Puck puts the juice of a little purple flower on Lysander's eyelids, which causes him to fall in love with the first person he sees when he wakes up.

4. What does Helena think is happening when both Lysander and Demetrius claim that they love her?
Helena thinks that they are making fun of her.

5. What does Oberon get from Titania?
Oberon gets the little changeling boy.

VOCABULARY IN CONTEXT

- The judge condemned the defendant to ten years in prison.

RESPONDING TO THE SELECTION

Encourage students to talk about what elements of this story would be comic when represented on stage.

ANSWERS FOR REVIEWING THE SELECTION

RECALLING AND INTERPRETING

1. **Recalling.** Egeus asks Theseus to enforce the law that requires a daughter to marry the man her father chooses or be put to death. Hermia will not obey her father because she loves Lysander and because Demetrius had previously said that he loved Helena. Hermia and Lysander plan to run away and get married. **Interpreting.** Hermia seems to be strong-willed and determined.

2. **Recalling.** Oberon and Titania are arguing because Titania refuses to give Oberon a little changeling boy. **Interpreting.** Their disagreement disrupts the countryside. Students may think it unlikely that Titania will change her position because she seems very determined.

3. **Recalling.** Oberon puts on Titania's eyelids the juice of a flower that will cause her to love the first creature she sees when she wakes up. Puck mistakes Lysander for Demetrius and causes Lysander to fall in love with Helena. **Interpreting.** Helena believes that they are making fun of her because previously both Lysander and Demetrius were in love with Hermia. Puck is amused because the confusion causes the couples to behave in a ridiculous manner.

4. **Recalling.** Titania falls in love with a weaver with a donkey's head. Hermia marries Lysander and Helena marries Demetrius. **Interpreting.** Titania finally gives Oberon the boy because of the charm that makes her love the weaver. The mood is joyous and celebratory.

SYNTHESIZING

Responses will vary. Possible responses are given.

5. The confusion in the woods seems dreamlike. The events that occur in Theseus's court seem realistic. The dreamlike elements are associated with the wood outside Athens. Dreams might be associated with this place because it is removed from civilization and is ruled by fairies.

Responding to the Selection

What did you think of Lysander, Hermia, Helena, and Demetrius's actions in *A Midsummer Night's Dream?* Did the characters ever seem foolish or confused to you? Did any other characters seem foolish or confused? Why might foolish behavior and confusion be such an important part of this play?

Reviewing the Selection

RECALLING AND INTERPRETING

1. **R** What does Egeus ask Theseus to do in the beginning of this story? Why won't Hermia obey her father? What does she do instead?

   I Given what could happen to her, what do Hermia's actions reveal about her character?

2. **R** What is the reason for Oberon and Titania's disagreement?

   I What effect does their argument have on the countryside? Do you think that Titania will change her position? Why, or why not?

3. **R** What does Oberon do to Titania? What "blunder" do Puck and Oberon make when trying to get Demetrius and Helena together? What is the result of this error?

   I Why does Helena believe that Hermia, Lysander, and Demetrius are all making fun of her? Why does Puck find the situation so amusing?

4. **R** With whom does Titania fall in love? What does Oberon ask from Titania? What happens to Hermia, Helena, Lysander, and Demetrius at the end of the story?

   I Why does Titania give Oberon this thing so easily? What is the mood at the end of the story?

SYNTHESIZING

5. Dreams are an important part of this story. In the title, we are told that the story is a dream. At the end, we are told to imagine that the story was a dream. Which elements of this story seem particularly dreamlike? Which elements seem realistic? Do the dreamlike elements seem to be associated with any particular place? If so, where? Why might these elements be associated with this place?

Understanding Literature (Questions for Discussion)

Character. A **character** is a person or animal who takes part in the action of a literary work. Are there many major differences in the characters of Lysander, Demetrius, Hermia, and Helena, or do they all seem fairly similar? In what ways might their characters have affected Puck's blunder in mistaking Lysander for Demetrius? Why do you think that Shakespeare characterized these four characters in this way? What does Shakespeare seem to be saying about young people in love?

ANSWERS FOR UNDERSTANDING LITERATURE

Responses will vary. Possible responses are given.

Character. Students might say that the characters seem fairly similar. Their similarity in dress and actions might have led to Puck's blunder. Shakespeare might have intended to show that people who are in love act foolishly from time to time. Shakespeare seems to be saying that young people in love often act hastily and foolishly.

Writing Skills

Writing a Dialogue

Dialogue is conversation involving two or more people or characters. The dialogue in a story or a play is made up of the words spoken by its characters. The text of a drama consists of both dialogue and stage directions. Almost everything you learn about the characters and situation in a drama is revealed through the words of its characters. Dialogue also plays an essential role in most stories. The more believable a writer's dialogue is, the more his or her audience becomes involved with the writer's characters and their story.

Eve Marada

Alien Encounter

Ellen: This camping trip has been so boring. I haven't even seen one wild animal, so I guess I'll never be able to take interesting photos with my new camera. You would think we'd have seen a squirrel or a rabbit at least. I tell you, these woods aren't as wild as they're supposed to be. Here, Tonya, go pose over by that oak.

Tonya: (<u>annoyed.</u>) You've already taken two rolls of pictures of Amy and me. Could you just stop?

Ellen: I'm sorry. These woods are just making me nervous. They're so quiet.

Tonya: (<u>teasingly.</u>) Almost too quiet.

Amy: (<u>from offstage.</u>) Ahh, Ellen! Tonya! Come here, quick!

Ellen: Here we go again. That Amy! She probably found some rare wild flower or an odd shaped rock.

Tonya: Yeah. Remember when she got so excited when she saw that moss-covered bolder? She acted as if it were the find of the century.

Amy: (<u>from offstage.</u>) Ellen! Tonya! Hurry!

(<u>The two girls hurry in the direction of Amy's voice. Amy is standing near three small creatures.</u>)

Tonya: (<u>panting from running.</u>) What is it? What's wrong?

Amy: Don't move. Just look over there.

Tonya: Wow!

Ellen: What are they?

Try It Yourself

Write a dialogue between at least two characters. Your characters' dialogue should reveal something about themselves and their situation. If you must reveal something to your audience and it is impossible to do so in dialogue, you may use stage directions. Eve has decided to write her dialogue about some girls who discover alien creatures who are visiting Earth. She decides to use three characters—Ellen, Tonya, and Amy. The beginning of her dialogue is below.

Student Model

Writing Skills

Introducing the Skill

Inform students that if they were simply to transcribe a conversation, they would not have good written dialogue because conversations often rely on nonverbal communication and common frames of reference. To write good dialogue, students have to capture the rhythms of ordinary speech while providing enough information to keep the reader informed and interested.

Previewing the Skill

Have students read the model, "Alien Encounter." Point out that while the writer's dialogue seems like realistic speech, it also provides enough information for the reader to understand the action of the dialogue.

Prewriting and Drafting

Encourage students to listen to their friends' and family's conversations, asking themselves the following questions: What qualities of spoken dialogue might be capture in written dialogue? What additional information would have to be provided to make the conversation understandable to a reader?

Evaluating and Revising

Encourage students to read their dialogues aloud to discover places where the dialogue does not seem realistic.

Proofreading and Publishing

Some students might also be interested in expanding their dialogue to create a short one-act play.

ANSWERS FOR EXAMINING THE MODEL

1. The writer chose to write about a group of girls who discover three aliens while on a camping trip in the woods.

2. Through the dialogue, the reader learns that Amy is very interested in unusual things, is sensible and patient, and is good at coming up with plans. Ellen is talkative and likes to take pictures. Tonya is sensible and polite.

Tonya: They look just like little gray marshmallows with ears.

Ellen: And with sharp teeth! Look at those little fangs! Let me take a few photos of those little monsters! (pulls out her camera.)

Amy: Stop! You're scaring them. Look at how they're growling at you!

Tonya: Do you think they can talk?

Amy: I don't know yet. Let's ask them some questions.

Ellen: Do you speak English? Where are you from? What are you? Would you mind posing for the camera?

Amy: (To Ellen.) Wait. One question at a time. (To the creatures.) Do you speak English?

Largest Creature: Yes, we do. Who are you? What weapon is it that one of you keeps trying to aim at us?

Ellen: It's not a weapon, silly.

Tonya: We are humans, sir. Don't worry, that box Ellen is holding is not a weapon. It is just a device for taking photographs, a camera.

Amy: Where are you three from?

Largest Creature: We are from planet Ekeon, far away from your tiny solar system. We have come to learn more about your planet.

Amy: Can we do anything to help you?

Largest Creature: Yes, we would like to know more about your planet's culture.

Amy: I think we should bring them to a museum.

Largest Creature: We would like to go to this museum you speak of. Take us there.

Amy: We will.

Tonya: How will we sneak them in?

Amy: There's three of them and three of us. We can each put one of them in our backpacks.

Largest Creature: Good idea. Lead on, human!

[They exit]

Examining the Model

1. About what fictional event did this writer choose to write?
2. What does the dialogue tell you about each of the characters?

Prewriting and Drafting

1. Think of possible topics or story ideas for your dialogue. Read the Language Arts Survey, 1.13, "Gathering Ideas." Brainstorm for several minutes until you come up with a variety of ideas.
2. Decide who the characters in your dialogue will be. Make a cluster chart for each of the characters, listing words that describe them. Refer to the section on cluster charts in the Language Arts Survey, 1.5, "Finding a Topic."

3. Think about how you will use dialogue to help your readers get to know the characters as you described them in your cluster charts. How will you use dialogue to reveal your topic or story idea?
4. Write a first draft. Remember to refer to your prewriting notes as you begin your draft. Read the dialogue aloud as you write to make sure that it sounds natural.

Evaluating and Revising

1. Review the Language Arts Survey, 1.17, "Self-Evaluation," and 1.18, "Peer Evaluation." Exchange drafts with a classmate. Evaluate one another's work, focusing on the following questions:
   a. Is the dialogue centered around a particular topic, or story idea?
   b. Does the dialogue reveal something about each of the characters?
   c. Is the dialogue of each character distinctive, or do all the characters sound too similar?
   d. Does the dialogue sound like natural speech?
2. After carefully considering your classmate's comments, revise your draft. Follow the guidelines in the Language Arts Survey, 1.19, "Four Types of Revision."

Proofreading and Publishing

1. Proofread your revised manuscript. Make a clean copy and proofread it again. Refer to the Language Arts Survey, 1.22, "A Proofreading Checklist." Note that because dialogue follows the patterns of everyday speech, you may use sentence fragments and other informal irregularities in your dialogue that you would not use when writing other assignments in standard English.
2. Share your work with your classmates by reading your dialogue aloud. You may wish to read one of the parts in your dialogue and ask for volunteers to read the other parts.

Save your work in your writing portfolio.

ANALYTIC SCALE FOR WRITING SKILLS

Assign a score from 1 to 25 for each grading criterion below.

DIALOGUE

- **Content/Unity.** The dialogue reveals something about at least two characters and their situation.
- **Organization/Coherence.** The dialogue is easy to follow and is written in a sensible order.
- **Language/Style.** The dialogue uses vivid and precise nouns, verbs, and modifiers.
- **Conventions.** The dialogue avoids errors in spelling, grammar, usage, mechanics, and manuscript form.

PROJECT NOTE

Inform students that if they choose to design a set and costumes for *The Diary of Anne Frank,* they should pay close attention to the stage directions of the play, which describe certain necessary elements of the set. Using these guidelines as a starting point, students should use their imaginations to create the secret annex in Amsterdam.

If students choose to design a set and costumes for *A Midsummer Night's Dream*, they might research English Renaissance theater to create designs that represent what Shakespeare's audience might have seen when attending *A Midsummer Night's Dream.* Other students might be interested in creating more nontraditional sets and costumes like the ones described in the student model.

Unit Project

DESIGNING A SET AND COSTUMES

A set is the collection of objects on a stage that creates a scene. A set can include walls, furniture, painted backdrops, or trees. The costumes that actors wear can be elaborate, simple, or somewhere in between. In Shakespeare's time, theater sets were often simple. Sometimes sets would feature backdrops, furniture, and other items on stage. More often, signs were simply hung telling the audience where the action was taking place. Costumes were frequently the cast-off clothes of members of the aristocracy. In later years, sets and costumes grew very elaborate. Today, people often make creative setting and costume adjustments for plays. You might see a production of *Romeo and Juliet* in which the main characters wear T-shirts and blue jeans. You might see a production of *Hamlet* that takes place in the year 2048. Nontraditional productions of plays can be refreshing and interesting if they are done thoughtfully, and if they stay true to the ideas expressed in the original plays.

TRY IT YOURSELF

With two or three of your classmates, design the set for one scene from *The Diary of Anne Frank* or *A Midsummer Night's Dream.* You can design a traditional set, or you can design one that is highly unusual.

STUDENT MODEL

Gina and Lawrence are designing a set for the scene in *A Midsummer Night's Dream* in which Oberon and Titania meet by moonlight in the wood and quarrel. The two agree that they would like the scene to be set in the future on another planet. As Gina and Lawrence discuss items that might appear in the forest of a futuristic planet, they both take notes. They decide the wood will have narrow, swaying pink and purple trees; strange outcroppings of bolders; and green flowers. They both want to have a backdrop showing the nighttime sky. Because their scene will take place on a different planet, they want to put two moons rather than one in the sky. Gina decides that Titania should have flowing navy blue hair, pointy ears, and delicate green wings, and that she should wear a silver costume. Lawrence decides that Oberon should have a flowing navy blue beard, pointy ears, and gold-colored wings and that he should wear a silver costume and carry what appears to be a ray gun.

After Gina and Lawrence have made notes, they begin drawing the actual design for both the set and the costumes. They take four large sheets of white paper. On one, they sketch an outline of the stage. This first sketch shows how the stage looks if you are looking down on it. The next sketch shows what the audience sees as they are looking straight at the stage. They want to show both angles so people looking at their design will have a clearer idea of what should be on the stage and what the audience will be viewing. Gina and Lawrence are careful to label everything featured on stage. Then they draw Titania's costume on one sheet of paper and Oberon's on another. When Gina and Lawrence are finished, they share their designs with other members of their class. Then they take the design to a small, local theater group that often performs the plays of Shakespeare. Gina and Lawrence ask the theater group to consider their design if the group ever does a futuristic version of *A Midsummer Night's Dream.*

Examining the Model

1. What is the first step that Gina and Lawrence take in planning their design? What decisions do they make?
2. Why do Gina and Lawrence make two sketches of the set? What do they do with their sketches when they finish them?

Planning Your Set and Costumes

1. Form groups of two, three, or four. Flip through *The Diary of Anne Frank* or *A Midsummer Night's Dream* and choose a scene that everyone in your group likes.
2. Reread the scene and think about possible set designs and costume designs. People might want to talk about productions, set designs, and costumes that they have seen and liked in other plays or movies.
3. As you talk about possible set designs and costumes, keep the following questions in mind: Will you set the play in modern times? Will you use elaborate scenery and costumes, or will your stage have very little scenery and simple costumes? Will you have painted backdrops?
4. Decide on a set design and costume designs. Then make a list of the details. You will work from these notes as you draw your set design and your costume designs.

Making Your Set Design and Costume Designs

1. On two large pieces of paper or poster board, sketch two outlines of the same stage. One outline should show what someone would see if he or she were to look down on the stage. The other outline should show what the audience would see from their seats in front of the stage. You will also need a sheet of paper for each costume you have planned.
2. Look over the notes taken during your discussion. Everyone in the group should have a part in drawing your stage design and costume designs. Your drawings can be simple, but be sure to label everything.
3. You can make your designs as detailed and colorful as you'd like.

Sharing Your Set Design

1. Try to find people in a local theater group who might be interested in looking at set designs from your class. Ask if the group might consider performing a scene or two using your original set designs.
2. Hang your designs in your classroom or in your local library. Other students reading the play might be interested in seeing your designs. Compare your designs with those of other classmates. Would the play be interesting if you connected all of your set designs for one production?

Answers for Examining the Model

1. Gina and Lawrence decide on a scene for which they would like to create a set and costumes. They discuss elements of setting and costume and take notes. They decide that they wish to set the scene in the future on another planet.
2. Gina and Lawrence make two sketches of the set to show how it will look if you were looking down on it and to show what the audience will see. When they finish their sketches, they share them with the class and then bring them to a small, local theater group.

Analytic Scale for Project

Assign a score from 1 to 25 for each grading criterion below.

Designing a Set and Costumes

- **Organization.** The group set attainable goals and created a schedule or strategy for achieving those goals.
- **Cooperation.** The group assigned tasks fairly to each member, and each member cooperated toward achieving the group's goals.
- **Goal Achievement.** The group worked steadily toward its goals and did, in fact, achieve them.
- **Presentation.** The group presented a product of high quality that met the initial project description.

Vocabulary Check Test

Ask students to number their paper from one to ten. Have students complete each sentence with a word from the Vocabulary for the Unit in the Unit Review.

1. Because Michael had not had the chance to shop for his new apartment, it was sparsely furnished.
2. Giana wrote a note to her aunt to express gratitude for the thoughtful gift.
3. Alan was nervous, so he delivered the introduction of his speech falteringly.
4. From the grave expression on his brother's face, Jordan knew he had forgotten his birthday.
5. The skilled actor could mimic a variety of character types.
6. We thought Simone's rude behavior was intolerable.
7. Hank indignantly defended himself when his brother said that he never helped around the house.
8. The courtiers flattered the king to gain his favor.
9. Suzanne reckoned that she had saved enough money from babysitting to buy the chemistry set she wanted.
10. After a long weekend, many people loathe returning to work.

Unit Review

Summary

Literary Terms for the Unit

character, 518
dialogue, 502
suspense, 502

Vocabulary for the Unit

bower, 510
capitulation, 463
celestial, 513
coeducational, 477
condemn, 517
conspicuous, 464
courtier, 508
courtship, 514
coverlet, 510
extravagant, 473, 512
falteringly, 500
fatalist, 491
gratitude, 486
grave, 482
horrid, 512
improvise, 494
indignantly, 478
intolerable, 475
leisure, 465
loathe, 515
mercurial, 465
meticulous, 484
mimic, 479
ostentatiously, 496
pantomime, 471
portly, 464
potent, 512
quarrel, 478
reckon, 511
satchel, 494
scoffingly, 480
sparsely, 461
stern, 507
threadbare, 462
vile, 476

Questions for Writing, Discussion, and Research

1. The two selections in this unit are adaptations. What kinds of changes do you think the authors made to convert Anne Frank's *The Diary of a Young Girl* to the drama *The Diary of Anne Frank* or to convert William Shakespeare's *A Midsummer Night's Dream* from dramatic verse to a prose retelling?
2. What have you learned about the historical period in which *The Diary of Anne Frank* was set? How are aspects of history portrayed in dialogue, costume, and set?

For Your Reading List

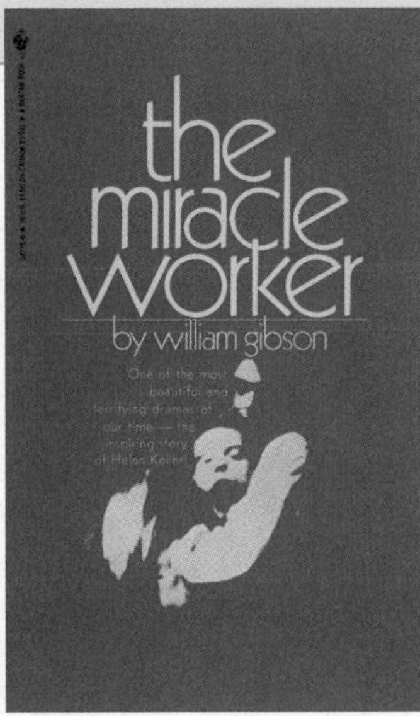

Christy Miller
Lewisburg Middle School
Lewisburg, Kentucky

The Miracle Worker
by William Gibson

I just read *The Miracle Worker* by William Gibson. It is a wonderful and inspiring drama based on the story of Helen Keller. This book tells the story of how Annie Sullivan, a half-blind teacher from Boston, tamed the wild five-year-old Helen Keller. In the beginning, young Helen rebels against every one of Annie's efforts to reach her. Annie requests two weeks alone with Helen in an old garden house to break through to Helen. When the two weeks have passed, Annie feels that she has not yet accomplished her mission. Then an unexpected turn for the better changes their lives. This excellent play is sure to catch the heart of anyone who reads it.

Spelling Check Test

Ask students to number their papers from one to ten. Read each word aloud. Then read aloud the sentence containing the word. Repeat the word. Ask students to write the word on their papers, spelling it correctly.

1. **portly**
Mr. Meyer is rather portly, and his wife, while also dignified, is rather slender.
2. **conspicuous**
Lisette's jeans were conspicuous at the semi-formal dance.
3. **quarreled**
Mick and Vick quarreled over who would sing first at the concert.
4. **indignantly**
"I never acted like a fool," said Niles indignantly.
5. **improvised**
We did not have enough chairs for everyone, so we improvised a bench with boxes and planks.
6. **satchel**
Kayla packed her books in her satchel in preparation for school the next day.
7. **reckoned**
Jeremy glanced at all his I.O.U.'s from his friend Soon and reckoned that Soon owed him fifteen dollars.
8. **bower**
The children played in a bower formed by the overhanging tree branches.
9. **courtship**
The foreign prince's courtship of the country's princess was well known, and it was rumored that a wedding would soon be announced.
10. **loathed**
While my sister eats it with great delight, I have always loathed

GOALS/OBJECTIVES

Studying this unit will enable students to
- appreciate autobiographies and biographies
- enjoy essays
- write a family history
- edit for errors in verbs
- present a slideshow biography
- discuss the theme of a selection
- recognize stereotypes
- identify figurative language
- recognize and explain examples of irony of situation
- understand analogies
- define *anecdote* and explain how anecdotes are used in writing

ADDITIONAL UNIT MATERIALS IN THE ASSESSMENT PORTFOLIO

- Vocabulary Worksheet 2.11.9
- Unit Test 2.11.10

See also the Additional Resources Box in the marginal notes accompanying each selection.

CROSS-CURRICULAR CONNECTIONS

- Mathematics, 562
- Physical Education, 530
- Science, 544, 544
- World History, 530

UNIT 11 NONFICTION

Fiesta. *Diego Rivera, 1928*

here is nothing so powerful as truth; and often nothing so strange.

—Daniel Webster

UNIT SKILLS OUTLINE

Literary Skills and Concepts

- Analogy, 569
- Anecdote, 569
- Autobiography, 540
- Biography, 551
- Figurative Language, 561
- Irony of Situation, 561
- Stereotype, 551
- Theme, 540

Other Language Arts Skills and Concepts

- Editing for Errors in Subject/Verb Agreement, 552
- Writing a Family History, 541

Additional Questions and Activities

Ask students if they enjoy reading nonfiction. Which types of nonfiction do they most like to read? In what ways does reading nonfiction differ from reading fiction?

Suggest that students read a biography or autobiography of somebody they admire. Then have students present reviews of the books they read.

Elements of Nonfiction

Nonfiction is writing that deals with actual events, people, places, things, and ideas. Types of nonfiction include histories, autobiographies, biographies, letters, diaries, speeches, contracts and political documents, and essays.

Nonfiction had its beginnings in the **oral tradition.** Before people could write things down, they passed information about heroes and historical events by word of mouth. When writing was developed, these accounts were written down and became the first **histories.** Also of historical importance are **speeches, contracts,** and other **legal and political writings.**

The desire to preserve information led to the creation of such nonfiction as **biographies** about the lives of others and **autobiographies** and **diaries** about the writer's own life. **Letters** and **journals** provide insight into people's lives. **Essays, articles,** and **reports** are also important forms of nonfiction writing. An essay is a brief piece of nonfiction prose that develops a single idea.

Other ways to classify nonfiction are by purpose or mode. A writer's **aim,** or **purpose,** is what he or she wants a work to accomplish. The first chart below shows the three main types of nonfiction classified by purpose.

A **mode** is a form of writing. The second chart below describes the four common modes of nonfiction writing.

TYPE OF NONFICTION	AIM	EXAMPLE
Expressive	**to express** personal feelings, attitudes, ideas, values, or beliefs	diary entry
Informative	**to inform** others about a subject	encyclopedia article
Persuasive	**to persuade** others to adopt some belief or take to take some course of action	editorial

MODE OF WRITING	DESCRIPTION
Narration	**Narration** relates events. Biographies, autobiographies, histories, and news reports rely heavily on narration.
Dialogue	**Dialogue** presents speech in the words the speakers actually used.
Description	**Description** portrays in words how things look, sound, smell, taste, or feel.
Exposition	**Exposition** presents facts or opinions in an organized manner. Types of exposition include classification, comparison, contrast, definition, and analysis.

Two Women. *Vincent van Gogh, 1882*

GOALS/OBJECTIVES

Studying this lesson will enable students to

- enjoy an autobiography
- discuss the subject of an autobiography
- explore the theme of a selection
- write a family history

ADDITIONAL RESOURCES

READER'S GUIDE

- Selection Worksheet, 11.1

ASSESSMENT PORTFOLIO

- Selection Check Test, 2.11.1
- Selection Test, 2.11.2

PRONUNCIATION EXERCISE

- Grade 8 Audiocassette, Side B, Track 55

CROSS-CURRICULAR CONNECTIONS

WORLD HISTORY AND PHYSICAL EDUCATION

If there are any rock climbers in your class, ask them to show their equipment and discuss the sport.

Have students consult climbing publications or speak with representatives at outdoor sporting shops about the equipment and instruction in this sport.

Prereading

AUTOBIOGRAPHY

from *Of Men and Mountains*
by William O. Douglas

Cross-curricular Connection

World History and Physical Education. Mountaineering, or mountain climbing, is a sport that has gained popularity in this century. In earlier times, mountains were usually climbed for practical purposes—to invade other lands or to make observations. Since 1786, when a French doctor earned a prize offered to the first person to scale Mont Blanc (the tallest peak in Europe at 15,771 feet), the practice of climbing mountains for pleasure and sport has grown immensely. Many of the world's highest and most difficult peaks have been scaled, including Mount Everest and K2, but mountaineers continue to seek the challenge of new and more difficult routes to the summit.

Mountaineering can be a dangerous sport for the untrained. While mountaineering is a term that can be applied to walking or hiking low mountains, it is more often used when referring to climbs that require greater skill and experience in dealing with extremely rugged terrain and challenging weather conditions. The three aspects of mountain climbing are hiking, rock climbing, and snow and ice work.

Hiking is often enjoyed as a sport on its own and may cover various types of terrain. It is an essential part of mountain climbing, as a great deal of time must be spent hiking the lower slopes of the mountain.

Rock climbing can also be enjoyed as a sport in itself. Rock climbers often learn and practice on small local cliffs or at climbing walls and rock gyms. Rock climbers use their hands and feet as key tools; feet are used for support, and hands, mostly for balance. Searching by sight and by touch is necessary for foot- and hand-holds.

Ice and snow present the climber with additional concerns and dangers, such as hidden crevasses and the possibility of avalanche. Special tools such as an ice ax and crampons are usually necessary for snow and ice climbing.

In all three aspects of mountain climbing, sound, informed judgment is crucial. Climbers should be physically prepared, properly equipped, and experienced for the conditions they are likely to face.

As You Read

In this selection from ***Of Men and Mountains,*** the narrator and his friend encounter several difficulties while mountain climbing. Make a chart like the one below. As you read, note the difficulties the climbers face and the solutions they find.

PROBLEM OR DIFFICULTY	SOLUTION
narrow ledges, precarious footwork	**took off shoes to make footwork easier**

AS YOU READ

Students might include the following difficulties and solutions in their charts: the ledge was narrow/they inched along with their stomachs pressed to the ledge; difficulty reaching ledge above/pulled up one knee at a time; reached a cul-de-sac/searched for a way up; no hand hold/jumped for a higher crevice; no toehold/Doug hoisted himself up with his arms alone; reached a cul-de-sac with no way out/forced to make their way back down; Doug could not make step to next ledge/on future climbs, person with longer legs would go first.

READER'S JOURNAL

Have you ever tried a dangerous activity? Have you ever forced yourself to your physical limits? Describe the situation. How did it feel? Would you like to experience this feeling again? Why, or why not?

FROM

Of Men and Mountains

WILLIAM O. DOUGLAS

It was in 1913 when Doug was 19 and I was not quite 15 that the two of us made this climb of Kloochman.[1] Walter Kohagen, Doug, and I were camped in the Tieton Basin at a soda spring. The basin was then in large part a vast rich bottomland. We were traveling light, one blanket each. The night, I recall, was so bitter cold that we took turns refueling the campfire so that we could keep our backs warm enough to sleep. We rose at the first show of dawn, and cooked frying pan bread and trout for breakfast. We had not planned to climb Kloochman, but somehow the challenge came to us as the sun touched her crest.

After breakfast we started circling the rock. There are fairly easy routes up Kloochman, but we shunned them. When we came to the southeast face (the one that never has been conquered, I believe) we chose it. Walter decided not to make the climb, but to wait at the base of the cliff for Doug and me. The July day was warm and cloudless. Doug led. The beginning was easy. For 100 feet or so we found ledges six to twelve inches wide we could follow to the left or right. Some ledges ran up the rock ten feet or more at a gentle grade. Others were merely steps to another ledge higher up. Thus by hugging the wall we could either ease ourselves upward or hoist ourselves from one ledge to another.

When we were about 100 feet up the wall, the ledges became narrower and footwork more precarious. Doug suggested we take off our shoes. This we did, tying them behind us on our belts. In stocking feet we wormed up the wall, clinging like flies to the dark rock. The pace was slow. We gingerly tested

1. **Kloochman.** Oval-shaped lava rock on the southern side of the Tieton Basin in the Cascade Mountains in the Northwest. The final third of the rock is a sheer cliff rising straight up 1,200 feet or more.

❶ *How do the conditions change during the first 100 feet of the climb?*

❷ *What is special about the route that the climbers choose?*

WORDS FOR EVERYDAY USE

grade (grād) *n.*, degree of rise or descent of a sloping surface

pre • car • i • ous (prē ker´ē əs) *adj.*, dependent on chance; risky

READER'S JOURNAL

If students have not had such an experience, have them describe an activity they would like to try or one they have watched others try.

SPELLING AND VOCABULARY WORDS FROM THE SELECTION

abyss	hurtle
appraise	inadequacy
bravado	laterally
buoyant	malice
composure	negotiate
crude	precarious
endeavor	respite
exert	tortuous
ford	treacherous
grade	ward

ANSWERS TO GUIDED READING QUESTIONS

❶ For the first one hundred feet, the ledges were about six to twelve inches wide and could easily be followed to the left or to the right. After one hundred feet, the ledges became narrower and more precarious.

❷ The climbers shunned the easy routes and chose to climb the southwest face, which had never been climbed.

SUPPORT FOR LEP STUDENTS

PRONUNCIATIONS OF PROPER NOUNS AND ADJECTIVES

Klooch • man (klo͞och´mən) n.
Tie • ton (tē´tän) n.

ADDITIONAL VOCABULARY

crabwise—move sideways like a crab
crevice—narrow crack
daredevil—bold, daring, and dangerous

VOCABULARY IN CONTEXT

- At first, we walked up gently sloping hills, but as we moved higher, the grade became steeper.
- Brenda got a ladder to help Basil from his precarious position at the top of the tree.

Answers to Guided Reading Questions

❶ Doug decides to try to jump for the handhold, although missing it would send him hurtling down six hundred feet onto the rocks.

❷ The author and Doug stop because they reach a cul-de-sac. There seems to be no place to go. Doug is unable to reach the next handhold. The author has longer legs and may have been able to reach the handhold, but he is behind Doug.

Additional Questions and Activities

What did Doug ask the narrator to do? Ask students how they would feel if they were the narrator and they were given such a message.

ANSWER

Doug asked the narrator to deliver a message to his family if he fell to his death. He asked the narrator to tell his family that he loved them, he did not suffer, he was proud of them, and he had lived a clean life and prayed for them.

each toehold and fingerhold for loose rock before putting our weight on it. At times we had to inch along sidewise, our stomachs pressed tightly against the rock, in order to gain a point where we could reach the ledge above us. If we got on a ledge that turned out to be a cul-de-sac,[2] the much more dangerous task of going down the rock wall would confront us. Hence we picked our route with care and weighed the advantages of several choices which frequently were given us. At times we could not climb easily from one ledge to another. The one above might be a foot or so high. Then we would have to reach it with one knee, slowly bring the other knee up, and then, delicately balancing on both knees on the upper ledge, come slowly to our feet by pressing close to the wall and getting such purchase[3] with our fingers as the lava rock permitted.

❶ *What important decision does Doug make?*

In that tortuous way we made perhaps 600 feet in two hours. It was late forenoon when we stopped to appraise our situation. We were in serious trouble. We had reached the feared cul-de-sac. The two- or three-inch ledge on which we stood ended. There seemed none above us within Doug's reach. I was longer-legged than Doug; so perhaps I could have reached some ledge with my fingers if I were ahead. But it was impossible to change positions on the wall. Doug was ahead and there he must stay. The problem was to find a way to get him up.

❷ *Why do the speaker and Doug stop? What makes their situation so difficult?*

Feeling along the wall, Doug discovered a tiny groove into which he could press the tips of the fingers of his left hand. It might help him maintain balance as his weight began to shift from the lower ledge to the upper one. But there was within reach not even a lip of rock for his right hand. Just out of reach, however, was a substantial crevice; one that would hold several men. How could Doug reach it? I could not boost him, for my own balance was insecure. Clearly, Doug would have to jump to reach it—and he would have but one jump. Since he was standing on a ledge only a few inches wide he could not expect to jump for his handhold, miss it, and land safely. A slip meant he would go hurtling down some 600 feet onto the rocks. After much discussion and indecision, Doug decided to take the chance and go up.

He asked me to do him a favor: If he failed and fell, I might still make it, since I was longer-legged; would I give certain messages to his family in that event? I nodded.

"Then listen carefully. Try to remember my exact words," he told me. "Tell Mother that I love her dearly. Tell her I think she is the most wonderful person in the world. Tell her not to worry—that I did not suffer. Tell Sister that I have been a mean little devil but I had no malice towards her. Tell her I love her too—that some day I wanted to marry a girl as wholesome and cheery and good as she.

2. **cul-de-sac.** Passage with only one way out
3. **purchase.** Firm hold

Words for Everyday Use

tor • tu • ous (tôr´cho͞o əs) *adj.*, full of twists, turns, curves, or windings
ap • praise (ə prāz´) *v.*, judge the quality or worth of
mal • ice (mal´is) *n.*, active ill will; spite

Vocabulary in Context

- The driver had difficulty navigating the bus along the tortuous mountain road.
- I asked the jeweler to appraise my mother's ring.
- Enoch pretended to be nice to Ivana, but underneath his pleasantries he was full of malice toward her.

"Tell Dad I was brave and died unafraid. Tell him about our climb in full detail. Tell Dad I have always been very proud of him, that some day I had planned to be a doctor too. Tell him I lived a clean life, that I never did anything to make him ashamed. . . . Tell Mother, Sister, and Dad I prayed for them."

Every word burned into me. My heart was sick, my lips quivered. I pressed my face against the rock so Doug could not see. I wept.

All was silent. A pebble fell from the ledge on which I squeezed. I counted seconds before it hit 600 feet below with a faint, faraway tinkling sound. Would Doug drop through the same space? Would I follow? When you fall 600 feet do you die before you hit the bottom? Closing my eyes, I asked God to help Doug up the wall.

In a second Doug said in a cheery voice, "Well, here goes."

A false bravado took hold of us. I said he could do it. He said he would. He wiped first one hand then the other on his trousers. He placed both palms against the wall, bent his knees slowly, paused a split second, and jumped straight up. It was not much of a jump—only six inches or so. But that jump by one pressed against a cliff 600 feet in the air had daredevil proportions. I held my breath; my heart pounded. The suspense was over.

Doug made the jump, and in a second was hanging by two hands from a strong, wide ledge. There was no toehold; he would have to hoist himself by his arms alone. He did just that. His body went slowly up as if pulled by some unseen winch.[4] Soon he had the weight of his body above the ledge and was resting on the palms of his hands. He then put his left knee on the ledge, rolled over on his side, and chuckled as he said, "Nothing to it."

A greater disappointment followed. Doug's exploration of the ledge showed he was in a final cul-de-sac. There was no way up. There was not even a higher ledge he could reach by

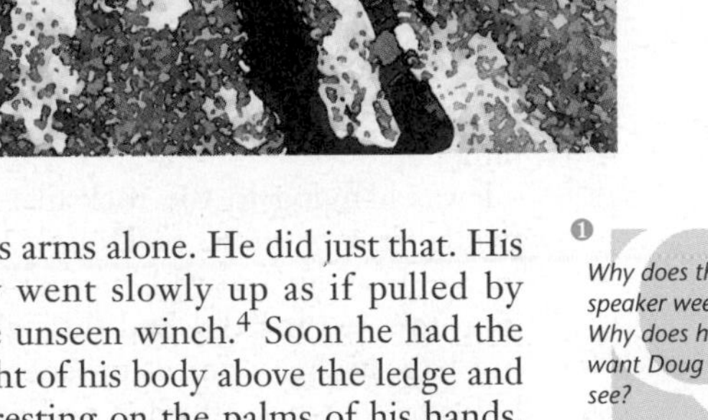

❶ *Why does the speaker weep? Why does he not want Doug to see?*

❷ *Do the climbers show their true feelings? Why, or why not?*

4. **winch.** Lifting mechanism

Words for Everyday Use

bra • va • do (brə vä´dō) *n.,* pretended courage or defiant confidence where there really is none

Answers to Guided Reading Questions

❶ The speaker weeps because he fears for Doug's life. He does not want Doug to see his fear.

❷ The climbers pretend to be cheerful and brave as they attempt the dangerous maneuver. They do not want to admit that Doug could die in the attempt.

Quotables

"There are only three sports—mountain climbing, bullfighting, and motor racing—all others being games."

—Ernest Hemingway

Vocabulary in Context

• "You can't push me around," Shaniqua told the bully with feigned bravado.

Answers to Guided Reading Questions

❶ The climbers are disappointed because the ledge Doug jumped to is a dead end. They are forced to go back down the way they came.

❷ Descent without ropes is often more difficult than ascent. The two climbers need to support, guide, and help one another down the mountain.

❸ The speaker imagines Doug plunging to his death because the speaker's strength gave out.

❶ *What disappointment do the climbers face? What do they decide to do as a result?*

jumping. We were now faced with the nightmare of going down the sheer rock wall. We could not go down frontwards because the ledges were too narrow and the wall too steep. We needed our toes, not our heels, on the rock; and we needed to have our stomachs pressed tightly against it. Then we could perhaps feel our way. But as every rock expert knows, descent of a cliff without ropes is often much more difficult than ascent.

❷ *What may be even more difficult than climbing to the top of a mountain? Can these climbers succeed separately?*

That difficulty was impressed on us by the first move. Doug had to leave the ledge he had reached by jumping. He dared not slide blindly to the skimpy ledge he had just left. I must help him. I must move up the wall and stand closer to him. Though I could not possibly hold his weight, I must exert sufficient pressure to slow up his descent and to direct his toe onto the narrow ledge from which he had just jumped.

I was hanging to the rock like a fly, twelve feet or more to Doug's left. I inched my way toward him, first dropping to a lower ledge and then climbing to a higher one, using such toeholds as the rock afforded and edging my way crabwise.

When I reached him I said, "Now I'll help."

Doug lowered himself and hung by his fingers full length. His feet were about six inches above the ledge from which he had jumped. He was now my responsibility. If he dropped without aid or direction he was gone. He could not catch and hold to the scanty ledge. I had little space for maneuvering. The surface on which I stood was not more than three inches wide. My left hand fortunately found an overhead crevice that gave a solid anchor in case my feet slipped.

I placed my right hand in the small of Doug's back and pressed upward with all my might. "Now you can come," I said.

He let go gently, and the full weight of his body came against my arm. My arm trembled under the tension. My left hand hung onto the crack in the rock like a grappling hook. My stomach pressed against the wall as if to find mucilage[5] in its pores. My toes dug in as I threw in every ounce of strength.

Down Doug came—a full inch. I couldn't help glancing down and seeing the rocks 600 feet below.

Down Doug moved another inch, then a third. My left hand seemed paralyzed. The muscles of my toes were aching. My right arm shook. I could not hold much longer.

❸ *What does the speaker imagine?*

Down came Doug a fourth inch. I thought he was headed for destruction. His feet would miss the only toehold within reach. I could not possibly hold him. He would plunge to his death because my arm was not strong enough to hold him. The messages he had given me for his family raced through my mind. And I saw myself, sick and ashamed, standing before

5. **mucilage.** Watery solution used as an adhesive

Words for Everyday Use

ex • ert (eg zurt´) *v.,* apply (oneself) with great energy or straining effort

Vocabulary in Context

• Paolo took a rest after exerting himself on the long hike.

them, testifying to my own inadequacy, repeating his last words.

"Steady, Doug. The ledge is a foot to your right." He pawed the wall with the toes of his foot, searching.

"I can't find it. Don't let go."

The crisis was on us. Even if I had been safely anchored, my cramped position would have kept me from helping him much more. I felt helpless. In a few seconds I would reach the physical breaking point and Doug would go hurtling off the cliff. I did not see how I could keep him from slipping and yet maintain my own balance.

I will never know how I did it. But I tapped some reserve and directed his right foot onto the ledge from which he had earlier jumped. I did it by standing for a moment on my left foot alone and then using my right leg as a rod to guide his right foot to the ledge his swinging feet had missed.

His toes grabbed the ledge as if they were the talons of a bird. My right leg swung back to my perch.

"Are you OK?" I asked:

"Yes," said Doug. "Good work."

My right arm fell from him, numb and useless. I shook from exhaustion and for the first time noticed that my face was wet with perspiration. We stood against the rock in silence for several minutes, relaxing and regaining our composure.

Doug said: "Let's throw our shoes down. It will be easier going." So we untied them from our belts and dropped them to Walter Kohagen, who was waiting at the rock field below us.

Our descent was painfully slow but uneventful. We went down backwards, weaving a strange pattern across the face of the cliff as we moved from one side to the other. It was perhaps midafternoon when we reached the bottom, retrieved our shoes and started around the other side of the rock. We left the southeast wall unconquered.

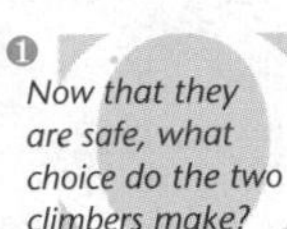

❶ *Now that they are safe, what choice do the two climbers make?*

But, being young, we were determined to climb the rock. So once more we started to circle. When we came to the northwest wall we selected it as our route.

Here, too, is a cliff rising 1,000 feet like some unfinished pyramid. But close examination shows numerous toe- and fingerholds that made the start at least fairly easy. So we set out with our shoes on.

Again it was fairly easy going for a hundred feet or so, when Doug, who was ahead, came to a ledge to which he could not step. On later climbs we would send the longer-legged chap ahead. And on other occasions Doug himself has used a rope to traverse this spot. But this day success of the climb depended at this point on Doug's short legs alone. The ledge to which he must move was up to his hips. There were few fingerholds overhead and none firm enough to carry his whole weight. Only a few tiny cracks were within reach to serve as purchase for him. But Doug would not give up.

❷ *What clue does the speaker give about the success of their attempt to climb the mountain?*

Words for Everyday Use

in • ad • e • qua • cy (in ad´i kwə sē) *n.,* state or quality of being not equal to what is required

hur • tle (hurt´'l) *v.,* move swiftly or with great force

com • po • sure (kəm pō´zhər) *n.,* calmness; tranquility

Answers to Guided Reading Questions

❶ The climbers choose to climb the rock from a different side.

❷ The speaker refers to other successful climbs that followed this climb.

Literary Technique

SIMILE

A simile is a comparison using *like* or *as*. Ask students to find the simile the author uses to describe Doug's landing on the ledge.

ANSWER

The author uses the simile "His toes grabbed the ledge as if they were the talons of a bird."

Additional Questions and Activities

Ask students if they have ever completed a physical task that they thought was beyond their abilities. What motivation did they have to succeed? Was there danger involved? How did they feel after meeting the challenge?

Vocabulary in Context

- The program was forced to shut down because of an inadequacy of funds.
- The bike hurtled down the hill at breakneck speed.
- Even in a crisis, Velma never loses her composure.

Answer to Guided Reading Question

❶ The speaker is careless and the ledge he is standing on gives way. He is left hanging by his fingers, unable to get a foothold.

Additional Questions and Activities

This selection is taken from William O. Douglas's autobiography. Ask students to think about one of their own adventures and write a chapter of their own autobiography about it. Students should write about the event and why it was significant in their life.

❶ *What causes the speaker's most difficult challenge?*

He hitched up his trousers, and grasped a tiny groove of rock with the tips of the fingers of his left hand, pressing his right hand flat against the smooth rock wall as if it had magical sticking power. Slowly he lifted his left knee until it was slightly over the ledge above him. To do so he had to stand tiptoe on his right foot. Pulling with his left hand, he brought his right knee up. Doug was now on both knees on the upper ledge. If he could find good purchase overhead for his hands, he was safe. His hands explored the wall above him. He moved them slowly over most of it without finding a hold. Then he reached straight above his head and cried out, "This is our lucky day."

He had found strong rough edges of rock, and on this quickly pulled himself up. His hands were on a ledge a foot wide. He lay down on it on his stomach and grasped my outstretched hand. The pull of his strong arm against the drop of 100 feet or more was as comforting an experience as any I can recall. In a jiffy I was at his side. We pounded each other on the shoulders and laughed.

My own most serious trouble was yet to come. For a while Doug and I were separated. I worked laterally along a ledge to the south, found easier going, and in a short time was 200 feet or more up the rock wall. I was above Doug, 25 feet or so, and 50 feet to his right. We had been extremely careful to test each toe- and fingerhold before putting our trust in it. Kloochman is full of treacherous rock. We often discovered thin ledges that crumbled under pressure and showered handfuls of rock and dust down below. Perhaps I was careless; but whatever the cause, the thin ledge on which I was standing gave way.

As I felt it slip, I grabbed for a hold above me. The crevasse[6] I seized was solid. But there I was, hanging by my hands 200 feet in the air, my feet pawing the rock. To make matters worse, my camera had swung between me and

6. **crevasse.** Deep crack

Words for Everyday Use

lat • er • al • ly (lat´ər əl lē) *adv.*, sideways

treach • er • ous (trech´ər əs) *adj.*, giving a false appearance of safety or reliability; insecure

Vocabulary in Context

- We moved laterally until we found a place where we could take a step up.
- The treacherous path was full of pitfalls.

the cliff when I slipped. It was a crude and clumsy instrument, a box type that I carried on a leather strap across my shoulders. Its hulk was actually pushing me from the cliff. I twisted in an endeavor to get rid of it, but it was firmly lodged between me and the wall.

I yelled to Doug for help. He at once started edging toward me. It seemed hours, though it was probably not over a few minutes. He shouted, "Hang on, I'll be there."

Hang on I did. My fingers ached beyond description. They were frozen to the rock. My exertion in pawing with my feet had added to the fatigue. The ache of my fingers extended to my wrists and then along my arms. I stopped thrashing around and hung like a sack, motionless. Every second seemed a minute, every minute an hour. I did not see how I could possibly hold.

I would slip, I thought, slip to sure death. I could not look down because of my position. But in my mind's eye I saw in sharp outline the jagged rocks that seemed to pull me toward them. The camera kept pushing my fingers from the ledge. I felt them move. They began to give way before the pull of a force too great for flesh to resist.

Fright grew in me. The idea of hanging helpless 200 feet above the abyss brought panic. I cried out to Doug but the words caught in my dry throat. I was like one in a nightmare who struggles to shout—who is then seized with a fear that promises to destroy him.

Then there flashed through my mind a family scene. Mother was sitting in the living room talking to me, telling me what a wonderful man Father was. She told me of his last illness and his death. She told me of his departure from Cleveland, Washington, to Portland, Oregon, for what proved to be a fatal operation. His last words to her were: "If I die it will be glory. If I live, it will be grace."

The panic passed. The memory of those words restored reason. Glory to die? I could not understand why it would be glory to die. It would be glory to live. But as Father said, it might take grace to live, grace from One more powerful than either Doug or I.

And so again that day I prayed. I asked God to save my life, to save me from destruction on this rock wall. I asked God to make my fingers strong, to give me strength to hang on. I asked God to give me courage, to make me unafraid. I asked God to give me guts, to give me power to do the impossible.

My fingers were as numb as flesh that is full of novocaine. They seemed detached from me, as if they belonged to someone else. My wrists, my shoulders, cried out for respite from the pain. It would be such welcome relief if they could be released from the weight that was on them.

Hang on? You can't hang on. You are a weakling. The weaklings die in the woods.

Weakling? I'll show you. How long must I hang on? All day? OK, all day

1 *What memory helps the speaker fight his fear?*

Answer to Guided Reading Question

1 The memory of his father facing his last illness and saying, "If I die it will be glory. If I live, it will be grace," helps the speaker fight his fear.

Words for Everyday Use

crude (krōōd) *adj.* primitive; not carefully made or done

en • deav • or (en dev´ər) *n.,* attempt; try

a • byss (ə bis´) *n.,* bottomless gulf; chasm

res • pite (res´pit) *n.,* interval of temporary relief or rest

Vocabulary in Context

- Alana did not have her tool box, so she used a rock as a crude hammer.
- Hard work turned Eben's endeavor into a success.
- There was no way to retrieve the fallen tools from the deep abyss.
- The shower offered a brief respite from the scorching sun.

ANSWERS TO GUIDED READING QUESTIONS

❶ The climbers seem to forget or ignore the dangers they faced in reaching the top of the mountain.

❷ The climbers have to make their way back to camp in the dark.

HISTORICAL NOTE

Mount Everest, the world's highest mountain, was successfully scaled in 1953 by Sir Edmund Hillary of New Zealand and Tenzing Norgay of Nepal. Attempts to climb the 29,028-foot mountain began in 1920 with the opening of the Tibetan route. Seven attempts to climb the Northeast Ridge and three attempts at the Southeast Ridge were unsuccessful because of extremely cold air, heavy winds, high altitude, and difficult terrain.

The 1953 expedition, sponsored by the Royal Geographical Society and the Joint Himalayan Committee of the Alpine Club, used special oxygen systems, insulated clothing, and radios. Eight camps were established en route. Hillary and Norgay reached the summit on May 29, 1953.

Since the first successful climb, many successful expeditions have been undertaken. Two Americans were the first to scale the West Ridge in 1963. They returned by a different route, thus completing the first transverse crossing. In 1975, Junko Tabei of Japan, with Ang Tsering of Nepal, became the first woman to reach the summit.

❶ *Does the climbers' pride in their accomplishment cloud their judgment about the danger on the Kloochman Rock? Explain.*

❷ *What challenges the climbers even after their climb is over?*

then. I'll hang on, I'll hang on. O, help me hang on!

I felt someone pushing my left foot upwards. It was Doug. As if through a dream his voice was saying, "Your feet are 18 inches below your toehold." Doug found those toeholds for my feet.

I felt my shoes resting in solid cracks, pulled myself up and leaned on my elbows on the ledge to which my hands had been glued. I flexed my fingers and bent my wrists to bring life back.

Doug came up abreast of me and said, "We're even Stephen now."

"Even Stephen?"

"Today each of us has saved the other's life."

It was shortly above the point where Doug saved my life that we discovered a classic path up Kloochman. It is a three-sided chimney chute,[7] a few feet wide, that leads almost to the top. There are several such chutes on Kloochman. In later years Cragg Gilbert and Louis Ulrich went up Devil's Chimney on the northeast face in a seven-hour nerve-wracking climb with ropes. Clarence Truitt and many others have gone up the chimney chute that Doug and I discovered. Then as now this chute was filled with loose rock that had to be cleared away. To negotiate the chute we took off our shoes and tied them to our belts. We climbed the chute in stocking feet, pressing our hands and feet against the opposing walls as we kept our backs to the abyss below us. This day we went up the chute with ease, stopping every eight feet or so to measure our progress.

The sun was setting when we reached the top. We were gay and buoyant. We talked about the glories of the scene in front of us. We bragged a bit about our skill in rock work—how we must be part mountain goat to have reached the top. We shouted and hallooed to the empty meadows far below us.

On Kloochman Rock that July afternoon both Doug and I valued life more because death had passed so close. It was wonderful to be alive, breathing, using our muscles, shouting, seeing.

We stayed briefly at the top. We went down as we came up, in stocking feet. We raced against darkness, propelled by the thought of spending the night on Kloochman's treacherous wall.

It was deep dusk when we rejoined Walter on the rock fields at the base. We put on our shoes and hurried on. We entered the woods at double-quick time, seeking the trail that led toward the South Fork of the Tieton. We saw the trail from the edge of a clearing as a faint, light streak in a pitch-black night. We had two ways of keeping on it. We had no matches or torch or flashlight. But we could feel the edges with our feet. And we could search out the strip of night sky over the path.

We finally decided that it would take too long to follow the trail to camp in

7. **chimney chute.** Deep, narrow crack in a cliff face

WORDS FOR EVERYDAY USE

ne • go • ti • ate (ni gō´shē āt') *v.*, succeed in crossing, surmounting or moving through

buoy • ant (boi´yənt) *adj.*, having or showing lightness of spirit; cheerfulness

VOCABULARY IN CONTEXT

- Vince had to negotiate the perilous path to get to the treasure.
- Magee's buoyant spirits kept everyone else's hope alive.

this groping way. We'd take a short cut to Westfall Rocks, whose formless shape we could see against the sky. We took to the brush on our right, and kept our hands out in front to ward off boughs and branches. We crossed a marshy bog where we went in up to our knees. We came to soft earth where we went in up to our hips.

There were animals in the brush. We could hear them in the thickets, disturbed by our approach, and going out ahead of us. Thinking they might be bear, we paused to listen. "Cattle," said Doug.

We reached the Tieton River, which we knew could not be forded in many places in that stretch. So we took off our pants, shoes, and shirts and rolled them in bundles which we held on our heads. We waded out into the dark, cold, swift river, Doug in the lead. We had by accident picked one of the few good fords in the Tieton. We were never in water over our waists.

Then we dressed and located the road leading back to camp. As we started along it Doug said: "You know, Bill, there is power in prayer."

That night I prayed again. I knelt on a bed of white fir boughs beside the embers of a campfire and thanked God for saving Doug's life and mine, for giving us the strength to save each other. ■

About the Author

William O. Douglas (1898–1980) was born in Maine, Minnesota, and raised in California and Washington. Douglas suffered a bout of polio in his childhood. In his personal exercise program of recovery, he developed what would become a lifelong love of the outdoors and rigorous outdoor activities. He taught school briefly, and then went to Columbia University Law School in New York. He worked for a year on Wall Street before returning to teach at Columbia for a year. Then he joined the law faculty at Yale University in Connecticut and taught there until 1936. Douglas was nominated to the Supreme Court by President Franklin Roosevelt in 1939, and joined the Court in 1940. Douglas fought fiercely against all forms of censorship. In 1974, Douglas suffered a stroke, and in 1975 he retired. Douglas wrote widely on a number of subjects. His books include *Of Men and Mountains* and *A Wilderness Bill of Rights*.

Words for Everyday Use

ward (wôrd) *v.*, turn aside; fend off

ford (fôrd) *v.*, cross at a shallow point in a river or stream

Cross-Curricular Activities

Social Studies

Have students research Hillary's expedition. They can locate Mount Everest on a map and trace Hillary's route. Discuss the equipment needed for the expedition. Students may also be interested in other climbing expeditions, such as those on K2, the second highest mountain in the world.

Selection Check Test with Answers

EX. How old was the author when the event he describes took place?
The author was fifteen.

1. Which face of Kloochman do Doug and the narrator first try to climb?
They first try to climb the southeast face.

2. How did Doug reach the crevice when they reached the cul-de-sac?
Doug had to jump to reach the crevice.

3. What did Doug discover when he made it to the ledge above the cul-de-sac?
He found another cul-de-sac.

4. Which face did the two climbers try in the afternoon?
They tried the northwest wall.

5. What difficulty did the climbers face when they reached the base of the rock after their climb?
They had to make their way back to camp in the dark without a light.

Vocabulary in Context

- Salvator put up his arm to ward off the blow.
- Inez could not find a place to ford the river, so she was forced to swim.

Responding to the Selection

Ask students to describe specific risks and challenges they have taken. Ask them why they chose to accept the risk or challenge and how facing it made them feel.

Answers for Reviewing the Selection

RECALLING AND INTERPRETING

1. **Recalling.** They chose to climb the treacherous southeast face of Kloochman Rock. **Interpreting.** *Responses will vary.* The climbers wanted the challenge of the dangerous climb that had never been done. They did not seem well prepared for the dangers of the climb.

2. **Recalling.** The climbers reached a cul-de-sac. They decided to try a risky jump to grab a handhold that was out of reach. **Interpreting.** *Responses will vary.* The climbers probably continued on their course because it provided the greatest challenge. They may have continued because it was dangerous and difficult to climb down.

3. **Recalling.** Doug had to lower himself slowly back down to the first foothold with the assistance of the narrator. **Interpreting.** *Responses will vary.* Often in situations of danger, people are able to do things they do not think they are physically able to do.

4. **Recalling.** They decided to climb the northwest wall, which they did successfully. **Interpreting.** *Responses will vary.* The pair decided to continue because they were young and determined and had little fear of the dangers of climbing the mountain. The dangers they faced made their success seem sweeter.

SYNTHESIZING

Responses will vary. Possible responses are given.

5. Mountain climbing showed the narrator how precious life is. It is a popular sport because many people enjoy taking risks and rising to challenges.

Responding to the Selection

"On Kloochman Rock that July afternoon both Doug and I valued life more because death had passed so close. It was wonderful to be alive, breathing, using our muscles, shouting, seeing." Is it wise to take risks and challenges like those described by the narrator? Is it necessary to take risks to appreciate life? Explain.

Reviewing the Selection

Recalling and Interpreting

1. **R** Which route did the narrator and Doug decided to take up Kloochman Rock?

   I Why did they choose this route? Were they prepared for this climb?

2. **R** What problem presented itself to the climbers in midafternoon? What did the climbers decide was the only solution?

   I Why do you think the climbers decided to continue on their current course despite the danger of their plan?

3. **R** What happened when Doug reached the next cul-de-sac?

   I What do you think allowed the narrator to hold on despite his feelings that he had no strength left?

4. **R** What did the climbers do after retracing their steps? Was this effort successful?

   I Why do you think they decided to continue? What effect did the new danger they encountered have on their feelings about the climb?

Synthesizing

5. What importance did mountain climbing play in the life of the author of this selection? Why do you think mountain climbing is a popular sport? What might people gain from mountain climbing?

Understanding Literature (Questions for Discussion)

1. **Autobiography.** An **autobiography** is the story of a person's life written by that person. What aspect of the author's life is captured in this selection? What do you learn about the beliefs, traits, and abilities of the author from this selection?
2. **Theme.** A **theme** is a central idea in a literary work. What idea about life does the author express in this selection? What specific aspects of this trip created strong feelings about life in the author?

Answers for Understanding Literature

Responses will vary. Possible responses are given.

1. **Autobiography.** The author's enjoyment of outdoor activities, especially mountain climbing, is captured in this selection. The reader learns that the author was strong, athletic, brave, and determined, and that he had a firm belief in God. The narrator valued life and grew to appreciate it more because of his experiences.

2. **Theme.** The author portrays life as a gift that is precious and uncertain. The three moments (when Doug jumped for the crevice, when the narrator was holding Doug up, and when the narrator was hanging from the crevice) of the climb when he thought either he or his friend was going to die created these feelings.

Writing Skills

Writing a Family History

In the selection from *Of Men and Mountains,* the author describes his exciting experiences. Have you ever talked to your parents or another relative about your great grandparents or great aunts and uncles or other relatives from the past? You may have discovered some interesting stories about their lives. These are all part of your family history. You can begin to trace your roots and learn about your heritage by talking to relatives.

Try It Yourself

Talk to your relatives about their lives and the lives of their parents and brothers and sisters. Ask them specific questions and ask them to relate some of their favorite family stories. Write a brief family history that captures the highlights of the information you gather.

Student Model

Francesca had always enjoyed listening to her Great Aunt Chiara, who was born in Italy, tell stories about her childhood. She decided she would find out as much as she could about her family and write a family history. Francesca decided that the easiest and most interesting way to gather information about her family would be to go to the source. She began interviewing family members, including her parents, her two living grandparents, her aunt, and her uncles, on what they could remember about their lives and the lives of other family members. These are the questions she asked each person:

1. Where and when were you born?
2. What is your earliest memory?
3. What is your favorite story about the family that you heard as you were growing up?
4. What is your favorite family story that you actually experienced?

CONTINUED

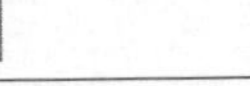

Writing Skills

Introducing the Skill

Everyone has some interesting stories, and most people enjoy sharing them. Tell students that learning the stories of others can be a valuable source of material for writing.

Previewing the Skill

Ask students to think about some of their favorite stories about their families. Have students share some of these stories if they wish.

Prewriting and Drafting

Ask students to freewrite about questions they have about people in their family. These questions may prompt students when they create their interview questions.

Evaluating and Revising

Remind students to be sensitive when evaluating each other's writing. Comments should be directed at the writing, not at the writer or subject.

Proofreading and Publishing

- Students might choose one episode or story from their family history to present at a family night. Students might invite relatives who live nearby to attend.
- Students may wish to assemble their family histories in a scrapbook or photo album. Suggest that students leave room to continue to add to their family histories.

ANSWERS FOR EXAMINING THE MODEL

1. She asked living members of her family to tell her about members who were no longer living.
2. Francesca left room at the back of her family history so that it could be continued.

Student Model (cont.)

5. What is your happiest memory? saddest? most exciting?
6. Describe the most memorable family gathering that you attended.
7. Describe your parents. What details (such as where they were born and how they met) do you know about their lives?
8. What about our family would you most like remembered?

At the end of each interview, Francesca collected a photograph of the person she interviewed. Sometimes she borrowed an old snapshot and sometimes she took a new one. Francesca kept notes from each interview on note cards. She labeled each card with the name of the person interviewed, and when applicable, the names of the people discussed. Francesca organized the information about each relative chronologically, in the order in which the events occurred.

When she was done, she wrote a family history that explained where her ancestors had come from, how her grandparents had met, and included stories about her family's trials and adventures, such as the time her great aunt Eva took a balloon ride and got caught in a tree or the time her great grandfather was attacked by a wild boar. She described family celebrations, including her grandparents' fiftieth anniversary and the family reunion that took place when she was seven. She illustrated her family history with photographs, maps showing important places for her family, and drawings she had made of special moments. Francesca put her family history into a scrapbook that had empty pages at the back so she or her grandchildren could continue the ongoing history of her family.

Examining the Model

1. How does Francesca learn about people in her family who are no longer living?
2. How does Francesca end her family history?

Prewriting and Drafting

Read the Language Arts Survey, 1.13, "Interviewing."

1. Decide whom you will interview. Make a list of possibilities. Include the names of family members you could interview either in person or on the phone.
2. Make a list of questions that would be appropriate for all interviews. Include question that ask basic facts and others that inquire about experiences. Refer to the sample questions asked by Francesca.

3. Contact the people on your list and interview them.
4. After interviewing and gathering as much information as possible, organize your notes chronologically, or in time order.
5. Begin with the earliest information you have and work forward through time until you come to yourself. Describe the people you are discussing as well as you can.

Evaluating and Revising

1. You may wish to ask an interested relative to be your first evaluator. Ask him or her to read your family history to detect any errors in dates or relationships.
2. Review the Language Arts Survey, 1.17, "Self-Evaluation," and 1.18, "Peer Evaluation." Exchange papers with a classmate. Read each other's family histories for clarity, continuity, and interest. Keeping these questions in mind:
   - Which stories do you like best?
   - Which people seem to come to life?
   - Which stories or people are not clearly described? Which do you have questions about?
3. Revise your draft, taking into account the suggestions of your classmate or relative. Follow the guidelines in the Language Arts Survey, 1.19, "Four Types of Revision," and 1.20, "A Revision Checklist."

Proofreading and Publishing

1. Proofread your revised manuscript. Then make a clean, final copy of it. Proofread it again.
2. Use photographs, drawings, maps, or other visual devices to accompany your stories. Display your family histories and share them with your classmates.
3. Make copies for interested relatives. It would make a special gift.

Save your work in your writing portfolio.

ANALYTIC SCALE FOR WRITING SKILLS

Assign a score from 1 to 25 for each grading criterion below.

FAMILY HISTORY

- **Content/Unity.** The family history contains stories and information about the author's family.
- **Organization/Coherence.** The history is organized in a logical way, for example in chronological order or by family member.
- **Language/Style.** The history uses vivid and precise nouns, verbs, and modifiers.
- **Conventions.** The history avoids errors in spelling, grammar, usage, mechanics, and manuscript form.

GOALS/OBJECTIVES

Studying this lesson will enable students to

- have a positive experience reading a biography
- briefly describe the type of work done by anthropologists
- define *stereotype* and explain why stereotypes are misleading
- define *biography* and explain some difficulties biographers encounter
- edit for errors in subject/verb agreement

ADDITIONAL RESOURCES

Reader's Guide

- Selection Worksheet, 11.2

Assessment Portfolio

- Selection Check Test, 2.11.3
- Selection Test, 2.11.4

Pronunciation Exercise

- Grade 8 Audiocassette, Side B, Track 56

CROSS-CURRICULAR CONNECTIONS

Science

Students might form small groups and research the lives of different anthropologists. Possible subjects include Franz Boas, Alfred Kroeber, Margaret Mead, Ruth Benedict, or Edward Sapir. Students might then present what they have learned about the anthropologists to the class. Students should focus on the cultures that the anthropologists studied, and on their fieldwork.

Prereading

Biography

from *Ishi in Two Worlds*
by Theodora Kroeber

Cross-curricular Connection

Science. Anthropology is the scientific study of humans and human culture. Anthropologists focus their study on the ways that people live in social groups, including all of the rules and beliefs that the members of a social group learn and share. Anthropologists also study the ways that different humans adapt to different environments. One study approach is to compare various groups of people around the world to find the similarities and differences among them.

Anthropology differs from psychology in that anthropologists typically focus on the qualities of a particular population as a group, not on the individual minds of that population. Unlike historians, anthropologists try to use direct observations of people within their culture rather than documentary accounts of a culture. Sometimes, anthropologists will conduct fieldwork, which can involve living in close contact with the group that they are studying. Living with the people of a particular social group, speaking their language, and sharing in the practices of their daily life, anthropologists hope to learn how people in that social group view the world. Franz Boas, a German-born American, founded the cultural history school of anthropology that emphasized the necessity of fieldwork.

In general, the study of anthropology helps human beings to understand one another better. In the selection you are about to read, Ishi is the last member of a culture of the Pacific Northwest called the Yana. As such, Ishi particularly interested anthropologists who wished to know more about his people's way of life. T. T. Waterman and Alfred Kroeber were the anthropologists who recognized both Ishi's predicament and his value as the last of the southernmost Yana.

As You Read

The selection from ***Ishi in Two Worlds*** contains words that may not be familiar. Many of them describe parts of Native American culture. Others are standard English words that will be new. In your journal, make a chart like the one below. As you read, list all of the words that are unfamiliar to you, and write a definition for each. By using context clues, you should be able to figure out most of the definitions. If you remain uncertain about any definitions, look them up in the dictionary.

Unfamiliar Words	Definition
emaciated	**made thin from starvation**
Maidu, Wintu	**Native American languages**

AS YOU READ

Students might include the following unfamiliar words and definitions in their charts: corral—enclosed area; fatigue—exhaustion; padre—priest or chaplain; Shoshean—a Native American language; aboriginal—native; *tour de force*—skillful performance; Yana—a Native American people; *siwini*—Yana term for yellow pine; confidences—things told as personal secrets; induced—caused.

READER'S JOURNAL

Imagine that you are the last living person on Earth. Suddenly, you are taken captive by alien creatures. They take you away and lock you in a room. You do not understand a word they say. You are not familiar with the food or the clothing that they give you. How would you feel about your situation? What about your former way of life would you miss the most? What would you do to survive in your new world?

FROM

Ishi in Two Worlds

THEODORA KROEBER

Prologue: OUTSIDE THE SLAUGHTER HOUSE

The story of Ishi begins for us early in the morning of the twenty-ninth day of August in the year 1911 and in the corral of a slaughter house. It begins with the sharp barking of dogs which roused the sleeping butchers. In the dawn light they saw a man at bay, crouching against the corral fence—Ishi.

They called off the dogs. Then, in some considerable excitement, they telephoned the sheriff in Oroville two or three miles away to say that they were holding a wild man and would he please come and take him off their hands. Sheriff and deputies arrived shortly, approaching the corral with guns at the ready. The wild man made no move to resist capture, quietly allowing himself to be handcuffed.

The sheriff, J. B. Webber, saw that the man was an Indian, and that he was at the limit of exhaustion and fear. He could learn nothing further, since his prisoner understood no English. Not knowing what to do with him, he motioned the Indian into the wagon with himself and his deputies, drove him to the county jail in Oroville, and locked him up in the cell for the insane. There, Sheriff Webber reasoned, while he tried to discover something more about his captive he could at least protect him from the excited curiosity of the townspeople and the outsiders who were already pouring in from miles around to see the wild man.

The wild man was emaciated to starvation, his hair was burned off close to his head, he was naked except for a ragged scrap of ancient covered-wagon canvas which he wore around his

❶ *In what way did the "wild man" behave? Was he really a "wild man"? Why do you think his captors called him this?*

WORDS FOR EVERYDAY USE

rea • son (rē´zən) *v.,* think clearly and logically

READER'S JOURNAL

To understand better what they would miss most about their present ways of life, students might create cluster charts in which they write the words *present life* in the center circle. Students should then write details that show what they appreciate about their lives. Students might then refer to their cluster charts as they freewrite in their journals.

SPELLING AND VOCABULARY WORDS FROM THE SELECTION

adjacent	phonetically
badger	posterity
barrage	reason
dialect	skeletal
diffidence	specimen
fugitive	subsequent
hysteria	subtle
lurid	suppress
pantomime	tentative
patronize	unwonted

ANSWER TO GUIDED READING QUESTION

❶ The "wild man" behaved calmly, quietly, and passively. Students may say that the man does not behave like a "wild man" at all. His captors may have called him this because he was unable to communicate with them.

SUPPORT FOR LEP STUDENTS

PRONUNCIATIONS OF PROPER NOUNS AND ADJECTIVES

The • o • do • ra Kroe • ber (thē´ə dôr´ə krō´bər) n.
I • shi (ē´shi) n.
Ya • na (yä na) n.
O • ro • ville (ō´rō vil) n.

ADDITIONAL VOCABULARY

aboriginal—native

VOCABULARY IN CONTEXT

- Shana reasoned that if she practiced running every day, she would be able to make the track team in the spring.

Answer to Guided Reading Question

❶ Ishi may have suppressed his memories of the first few days of contact with white people because he was certain that he would be put to death or he may have thought it was unkind to recall suspicions that later proved groundless.

Literary Technique

NARRATOR

A narrator is a person or character who tells a story. The narrator of this biography often comments on actions and explains events to the reader. To encourage students to see this narrative voice, ask them the following questions: What does the narrator say about the sheriff's decision to lock up Ishi? What explanations does the narrator provide for the sheriff's actions? What explanations does the narrator provide for Ishi's never mentioning that he did not eat, drink, or sleep when first captured? What does the narrator say was "natural"? Does the narrator know for a fact why Ishi never mentioned his behavior when he was first captured?

ANSWERS

The narrator says that the sheriff's decision to lock up Ishi was "neither stupid nor brutal." The narrator says that the sheriff was protecting Ishi from the many people who came to stare at him. The narrator says that the first days of Ishi's contact with white people may have been so terrifying that he suppressed his memory of them, or he may have thought it unkind to mention his fears because they proved groundless. The narrator says that it was natural that Ishi expected to be killed by the white people. No, the narrator does not know this for a fact.

shoulders like a poncho. He was a man of middle height, the long bones, painfully apparent, were straight, strong, and not heavy, the skin color somewhat paler in tone than the full copper characteristic of most Indians. The black eyes were wary and guarded now, but were set wide in a broad face, the mouth was generous and agreeably molded. For the rest, the Indian's extreme fatigue and fright heightened a sensitiveness which was always there, while it masked the usual mobility and expressiveness of the features.

It should be said that the sheriff's action in locking Ishi up was neither stupid nor brutal given the circumstances. Until Sheriff Webber took the unwonted measure of keeping them out by force people filled the jail to gaze through the bars of his cell at the captive. Later, Ishi spoke with some diffidence of this, his first contact with white men. He said that he was put up in a fine house where he was kindly treated and well fed by a big chief. That he would eat nothing and drink nothing during his first days of captivity Ishi did not say. Such was the case; nor did he allow himself to sleep at first. Quite possibly it was a time of such strain and terror that he suppressed all memory of it. ❶ Or he may have felt that it was unkind to recall his suspicions which proved in the event groundless, for Ishi expected in those first days to be put to death. He knew of white men only that they were the murderers of his own people. It was natural that he should expect, once in their power, to be shot or hanged or killed by poisoning.

Why didn't Ishi ever say how he felt about his first contact with white people?

Meanwhile, local Indians and half-breeds as well as Mexicans and Spaniards tried to talk to the prisoner in Maidu, Wintu, and Spanish. Ishi listened patiently but uncomprehendingly, and when he spoke it was in a tongue which meant no more to the Indians there than to the whites.

The story of the capture of a wild Indian became headline news in the local valley papers, and reached the San Francisco dailies in forms more or less lurid and elaborated. The story in the *San Francisco Call* was accompanied by a picture, the first of many to come later. In another newspaper story, a Maidu Indian, Conway by name, "issued a statement" that he had conversed with the wild man. Conway's moment of publicity was brief since the wild man understood nothing of what he said.

These accounts were read by Professors Kroeber and Waterman, anthropologists at the University of California, who were at once alerted to the human drama behind the event and to its possible importance, the more particularly because it recalled to them an earlier episode on San Nicolas Island, one of the Channel Islands of the Pacific Ocean some seventy miles offshore from Santa Barbara.

In 1835, the padres of Mission Santa Barbara transferred the San Nicolas Indians to the mainland. A few minutes after the boat, which was carrying the Indians, had put off from the

Words for Everyday Use

un • wont • ed (un wän′tid) *adj.*, uncommon, rare

dif • fi • dence (dif′ə dəns) *n.*, shyness, lack of confidence in oneself

sup • press (sə pres′) *v.*, keep back; consciously dismiss from the mind

lu • rid (lo͝or′id) *adj.*, startling, sensational

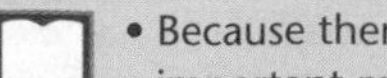

Vocabulary in Context

- Because there were unwonted security measures in town, Georgina assumed that someone very important must be arriving.
- Lionel spoke with diffidence about how difficult the first few weeks were in his new school.
- The lawyer suggested that the witness may have been suppressing her memories of the day in question.
- His parents told him that they did not want him reading such lurid comic books.

island, it was found that one baby had been left behind. It is not easy to land a boat on San Nicolas; the captain decided against returning for the baby; the baby's mother jumped overboard, and was last seen swimming toward the island. Half-hearted efforts made to find her in subsequent weeks were unsuccessful: it was believed that she had drowned in the rough surf. In 1853, eighteen years later, seal hunters in the Channel waters reported seeing a woman on San Nicolas, and a boatload of men from Santa Barbara went in search of her. They found her, a last survivor of her tribe. Her baby, as well as all her people who had been removed to the Mission, had died. She lived only a few months after her "rescue" and died without anyone having been able to communicate with her, leaving to posterity this skeletal outline of her grim story, and four words which someone remembered from her lost language and recorded as she said them. It so happens that these four words identify her language as having been Shoshonean, related to Indian languages of the Los Angeles area, not to those of Santa Barbara.

Another reason for the anthropologists' particular interest in the wild man was that three years earlier, in 1908, some surveyors working a few miles north of Oroville had surprised and routed a little band of Indians. After hearing of this incident, Waterman with two guides had spent several weeks in an unsuccessful search for the Indians: the wild man of Oroville might well be one of them.

On August 31, 1911, Kroeber sent the following telegram: "Sheriff Butte County. Newspapers report capture wild Indian speaking language other tribes totally unable understand. Please confirm or deny by collect telegram and if story correct hold Indian till arrival Professor State University who will take charge and be responsible for him. Matter important account aboriginal history."

The sheriff's office must have confirmed the report promptly: Waterman took the train to Oroville the same day. That he and Kroeber correctly "guessed" Ishi's tribe and language was no *tour de force* of intuition. The guess was based on field work with Indians all up and down California; they knew that Oroville was adjacent to country which formerly belonged to the Yana Indians; presumably the strange Indian would be a Yana. He might even be from the southernmost tribe of Yana, believed to be extinct. If this were true, neither they nor anyone so far as they knew could speak his language. But if he were a Northern or Central Yana, there were files of expertly recorded vocabularies for those dialects from two old Yanas, Batwi, called Sam, and Chidaimiya, called Betty Brown.

With a copy of Batwi's and Chidaimiya's vocabularies in his pocket, Waterman arrived in Oroville where he identified himself to Sheriff Webber and was taken to visit the

❶ *What did the woman on San Nicolas have in common with Ishi?*

❷ *How did Waterman and Kroeber guess the group to which Ishi belonged?*

Words for Everyday Use

sub • se • quent (sub´si kwənt) *adj.*, following

pos • ter • i • ty (päs ter´ə tē) *n.*, all succeeding generations

skel • e • tal (skel´ə t'l) *adj.*, meager, consisting of only the basic or general elements

ad • ja • cent (ə ja´sənt) *adj.*, near or close; adjoining

di • a • lect (dī ə lekt´) *n.*, differing form of speech within the broader framework of a single language

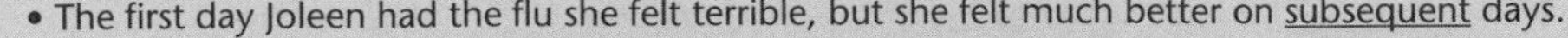

Answers to Guided Reading Questions

❶ Both Ishi and the woman on San Nicolas were the last surviving members of their people.

❷ They guessed Ishi's group because they knew from fieldwork that Oroville was adjacent to country that formerly belonged to the Yana.

Literary Note

If students are intrigued by the story of the woman of San Nicolas, you might encourage them to read the novel *Island of the Blue Dolphins* by Scott O'Dell. Although O'Dell's story is fictional, it was inspired by the story of the woman of San Nicolas.

Vocabulary in Context

- The first day Joleen had the flu she felt terrible, but she felt much better on subsequent days.
- The ancient Egyptians left enormous stone monuments to posterity, and succeeding generations have been awed by these works.
- The detective did not yet have a solution to the crime because he had such skeletal details from which to work.
- Because our yard is adjacent to the Johnson's, their children often come over to our yard to play.
- People could tell that he was originally from another state because of his dialect of English.

Answers to Guided Reading Questions

❶ Ishi's face lit up with recognition, and he and Waterman repeated the word over and over again, banging on the wood of the cot.

❷ Ishi asked Waterman if he was a Native American. Waterman said that he was, meaning that he was a friend.

Quotables

"All speech, written or spoken, is a dead language, until it finds a willing and prepared hearer."

—Robert Louis Stevenson

Additional Questions and Activities

Encourage students to discuss what they think it would be like to speak a language no one understands. How would they feel? Would they think of other ways to communicate? How would they feel if they finally found someone who could communicate with them?

Ishi, August 29, 1911

❶ *How did Ishi react when he first heard language he could understand?*

❷ *What did Ishi ask Waterman? How did Waterman respond?*

wild man. Waterman found a weary, badgered Indian sitting in his cell, wearing the butcher's apron he had been given at the slaughter house, courteously making what answer he could in his own language to a barrage of questions thrown at him in English, Spanish, and assorted Indian from a miscellaneous set of visitors.

Waterman sat down beside Ishi, and with his phonetically transcribed list of Northern and Central Yana words before him, began to read from it, repeating each word, pronouncing it as well as he knew how. Ishi was attentive but unresponding until, discouragingly far down the list, Waterman said *siwini* which means yellow pine, at the same time tapping the pine framework of the cot on which they sat. Recognition lighted up the Indian's face. Waterman said the magic word again; Ishi repeated it after him, correcting his pronunciation, and for the next moments the two of them banged at the wood of the cot, telling each other over and over, *siwini, siwini!*

With the difficult first sound recognition achieved, others followed. Ishi was indeed one of the lost tribe, a Yahi; in other words, he was from the southernmost Yana. Waterman was learning that the unknown Yahi dialect differed considerably but not to the point of unintelligibility from the two northern ones of his list. Together he and Ishi tried out more and more words and phrases: they were beginning to communicate. After a while Ishi ventured to ask Waterman, *I ne ma Yahi?* "Are you an Indian?" Waterman answered that he was. The hunted look left Ishi's eyes—here was a friend. He knew as well as did his friend that Waterman was not an Indian. The question was a tentative and subtle way of reassuring and being reassured, not an easy thing to do when the meaningful shared sounds are few. Between meetings with Ishi, Waterman wrote to Kroeber from Oroville:

> This man [Ishi] is undoubtedly wild. He has pieces of deer thong in place of ornaments in the lobes of his ears and a wooden plug in the septum of his nose. He recognizes most of my Yana words and a fair

Words for Everyday Use

badg • er (baj´ər) *v.,* annoy; pester

bar • rage (bə räzh´) *n.,* heavy attack of words

pho • net • i • cal • ly (fō net´ik lē) *adv.,* with respect to the spoken pronunciation of words

ten • ta • tive (ten´tə tiv) *adj.,* timid; hesitant; uncertain

sub • tle (sut´'l) *adj.,* not obvious or direct

Vocabulary in Context

- Carol's father told her not to badger him with questions.
- Simon could hardly catch his breath to respond to the lawyer's barrage of questions.
- The small child who was reading aloud struggledwith the phonetically spelled words.
- The kitten was tentative around strangers but quite rambunctious around people it knew well.
- Jenny was very subtle when trying to discover other people's secrets.

proportion of his own seem to be identical [with mine]. Some of his, however, are either quite different or else my pronunciation of them is very bad, because he doesn't respond to them except by pointing to his ears and asking to have them repeated. "No!" *k'u'i*—it is not—is one. "Yes!" *aha*, pleases him immensely. I think I get a few endings that don't occur in Northern Yana on nouns, for example. Phonetically, he has some of the prettiest cracked consonants I ever heard in my life. He will be a splendid informant, especially for phonetics, for he speaks very clearly. I have not communicated with him successfully enough to get his story, but what can I expect? He has a yarn to tell about his woman, who had a baby on her back and seems to have been drowned, except that he is so *cheerful* about it.

Waterman misunderstood. In the excitement and relief of having someone to talk to, Ishi poured out confidences and recollections which Waterman could by no means comprehend even with the aid of an elaborate pantomime. Ishi's seeming pleasure was not in the recollected event, but was rather a near hysteria induced by human interchange of speech and feelings too long denied.

Waterman's letters continue:

We had a lot of conversation this morning about deer hunting and making acorn soup, but I got as far as my list of words would take me. If I am not mistaken, he's full of religion—bathing at sunrise, putting out pinches of tobacco where the lightning strikes, etc. I'll try rattlesnake on him when I go back after lunch. It was a picnic to see him open his eyes when he heard Yana from me. And he looked over my shoulder at the paper in a most mystified way. He knew at once where I got my inspiration. . . . We showed him some arrows last night, and we could hardly get them away from him. He showed us how he flaked the points, singed the edges of the feathering, and put on the sinew wrappings.

Even before Waterman had established a thin line of communication with Ishi, the sheriff had become convinced that his prisoner was neither insane nor dangerous. There were no charges against him; he did not properly belong in jail. The question was, what in place of the shelter of the jail was there for him? Waterman offered to take him to San Francisco. Phones and telegraph wires were kept busy for the next forty-eight hours between Oroville and San Francisco, where the University's Museum of Anthropology then was, and between the museum and Washington, D.C.

While these negotiations were going forward, the sheriff, at Waterman's suggestion, sent a deputy to Redding to find and bring back with him the old man, Batwi, to act as interpreter-companion to Ishi. Batwi came, and although he patronized Ishi outrageously, he was for the present a help. He and Ishi could communicate in Yana, not without some difficulty, but

❶ *Where did they decide to bring Ishi?*

❷ *What did Waterman misunderstand?*

Words for Everyday Use

pan • to • mime (pan´tə mīm) *n.*, gestures without words as a means of expression

hys • te • ri • a (hi ster´ē ə) *n.*, outbreak of wild, uncontrolled excitement or feeling

pa • tron • ize (pā´ trən īz´) *v.*, act kind or helpful, but in a snobbish way

Answers to Guided Reading Questions

❶ They decided to bring Ishi to the University Museum of Anthropology in San Francisco.

❷ Waterman misunderstood Ishi's pleasure in communication. Ishi was merely excited about being able to communicate with another person at last.

Vocabulary in Context

- Because the shipwrecked man spoke a different language than his rescuers, he pantomimed to them that he was thirsty.
- Hank had claustrophobia, so being in that tiny enclosed attic brought him to the point of hysteria.
- Allison resented the way that Haley patronized her, because it made her feel incompetent.

Answer to Guided Reading Question

❶ Violence from other peoples, old age, and illness killed all the other members of Ishi's group.

Selection Check Test with Answers

EX. Who were T. T. Waterman and Alfred Kroeber?
They were anthropologists.

1. Where was Ishi discovered?
Ishi was discovered in the corral of a slaughterhouse.

2. Where was Ishi taken?
Ishi was taken to the county jail in Oroville.

3. Who was the first person to speak to Ishi that Ishi could understand? What was the word Ishi understood?
Waterman was the first person to speak to Ishi that Ishi could understand. The word was *siwini*, or yellow pine.

4. Who were Ishi's people? What happened to them?
Ishi's people were the Yahi, one of the southernmost Yana. They had all died.

5. Where did they decide to bring Ishi?
They decided to bring Ishi to the University Museum of Anthropology in San Francisco.

quite fully. Meanwhile, the Indian Bureau in Washington telegraphed permission for Ishi to go to the University's museum whose staff was to be responsible for him at least until there was opportunity for fuller investigation. The sheriff of Butte County was greatly relieved; he at once made out a receipt of release from the jail to the University. This remarkable document seems not to have survived the years of moving and storing in odd corners which has been the fate of the museum files and specimens.

In any case, Waterman, Batwi, and Ishi, with the release and government permission, left Oroville on Labor Day, September 4, arriving in San Francisco somewhat before midnight. There remained to Ishi four years and seven months of life, years which were to pass within the shelter of the museum walls at the Affiliated Colleges, or in the hospital next door when he was sick.

❶ What happened to the other members of Ishi's group?

Ishi was the last wild Indian in North America, a man of Stone Age culture subjected for the first time when he was past middle age to twentieth-century culture. He was content that it should be so, participating as fully as he could in the new life. Before examining more closely those astounding few years and what one Stone Age man contributed in so short a time to our understanding of man as such, let us go back to the years of childhood, young manhood, and middle age—almost a whole lifetime. These were years spent by him without experience or understanding of a way of life other than that of a tiny fugitive band of fewer than a dozen souls at most, opposing their ancient Yahi skills and beliefs to an unknown but hostile outside world.

There came the time—months, perhaps two or three years before August, 1911—when Ishi was the only one remaining of the little band, violence from without, old age and illness from within, having brought death to the others. ■

About the Author

Theodora Kroeber was the wife of famous American anthropologist Alfred Kroeber (1876–1960). Alfred Kroeber, who knew and studied Ishi, provided much of the information for his wife's biography of Ishi. Theodora Kroeber felt that it was her responsibility to write a biography of Ishi. After publishing the book in 1961, a year after her husband's death, Theodora Kroeber was overwhelmed by the number of emotional responses to Ishi's story. She called the outpouring in response to Ishi's story "the greatest human experience of my life."

Words for Everyday Use

spec • i • men (spes´ə mən) *n.*, sample used for study

fu • gi • tive (fyo͞o´ji tiv) *adj.*, having fled due to danger or repression

Vocabulary in Context

- The botanist kept several specimens of interesting plants in her home.
- The fugitive group fled from the authority of the tyrant who had oppressed them.

Responding to the Selection

What did you think about Ishi and his situation? If you were Ishi, what would your impression have been of American society in 1911? Would you have responded differently than Ishi did in this situation? Why, or why not?

Reviewing the Selection

Recalling and Interpreting

1. **R** What happened to Ishi in his first encounter with the "civilized" world?

   I Why do you think Ishi made no move to resist capture?

2. **R** What does the word *siwini* mean?

   I Why would such a simple, common word be so meaningful to Ishi in this context?

3. **R** What was one of the first questions Ishi asked Waterman? In what way did Waterman respond?

   I Why did Ishi ask Waterman this question? Why did Waterman respond as he did?

4. **R** Where did Ishi end up going?

   I What do you think about the decision to bring Ishi to this place?

Synthesizing

5. At the beginning of the selection, Ishi took a bold risk by stepping into the civilized world. Why do you think he took this risk? In what ways did Ishi's risk bring positive results? In what ways did his risk bring negative results? What was American society's attitude toward Ishi?

Understanding Literature (Questions for Discussion)

1. **Stereotype.** A **stereotype** is an unexamined, false idea about a type of person or group of people. In this selection, the men who first encountered Ishi said that they were holding a "wild man." In what ways was Ishi's behavior unlike this description? Why is this description a stereotype? Why do you think the men used this stereotype? In what way was the sheriff's view of Ishi different?
2. **Biography.** A **biography** is the story of a person's life, told by another person. What difficulties do you think you would encounter in trying to put together a biography of Ishi?

Responding to the Selection

Students might also discuss ways in which the townspeople and Waterman misinterpret Ishi.

Answers for Reviewing the Selection

RECALLING AND INTERPRETING

1. **Recalling.** In his first encounter, Ishi was found outside a slaughterhouse by some butchers and was taken into custody by the police. **Interpreting.** Ishi may have offered no resistance because of exhaustion, fear, or a submissive willingness to accept fate.

2. **Recalling.** The word *siwini* means "yellow pine." **Interpreting.** The word was meaningful to Ishi because it was the first verbal communication that Ishi was able to make in the "civilized" world. The ability to communicate, even at such a basic level, removed Ishi from total isolation.

3. **Recalling.** Ishi asked Waterman if he was a Native American, and Waterman replied that he was. **Interpreting.** Ishi asked this question because he wanted to know if Waterman was a friend. Waterman answered yes because he understood what Ishi was really asking.

4. **Recalling.** Ishi ended up going to the University Museum of Anthropology in San Francisco. **Interpreting.** Some students may say that placing Ishi in a museum, like a piece of art or an archaeological artifact, can be considered cruel and heartless. However, it is unclear what other options existed for the anthropologists.

SYNTHESIZING

Responses will vary. Possible responses are given.

5. Ishi probably took the step into the civilized world because of desperation, brought on by hunger and isolation. This was positive because modern anthropologists were able to learn much from Ishi and Ishi made friends. This was negative in that he was surrounded by an unfamiliar culture and by people who viewed him as an object of study or a curiosity. American society's reaction ranged from fear to wonder to genuine compassion and understanding.

Answers for Understanding Literature

Responses will vary. Possible responses are given.

1. **Stereotype.** Ishi was unlike this description because he was quiet and submissive, not wild, when captured by the sheriff and his deputies. The description is a stereotype because indigenous people have often been described as "wild" or "savage" despite civilized cultures and behavior that prove the contrary. The sheriff realizes that Ishi is not insane or dangerous.

2. **Biography.** The difficulty in communicating with Ishi must have made it especially difficult to piece together the story of his life, and because he was the last of his people, no other sources could be found for his history.

Language Lab

Introducing the Skill

Inform students that while they might think that words ending in *s* are plural, this rule does not hold true for verbs. Verbs that are in the present tense and that end in an *s* are always singular. Students will understand this concept more easily if you write examples of sentences on the chalkboard. For example: *The arrow flies. The arrows fly. The anthropologist observes. The anthropologists observe.*

Previewing the Skill

Have students review the teaching in the Language Lab. If they need more teaching, refer them to the Language Arts Survey, 2.16, "Agreement of Subject and Verb." Ask students to write examples of the following sentences: a sentence with a singular subject and verb, a sentence with a plural subject and verb, a sentence with *I* or *you* as a subject and a plural verb, a sentence with a compound subject and a plural verb, a sentence with a compound subject that names only one thing and takes a singular verb, and a sentence with a compound subject joined by *or* or *nor* and the appropriate verb.

Practicing the Skill

Once students seem familiar with the rules for subject/verb agreement, have them do the Try It Yourself exercises.

Reviewing the Skill

Some students might have difficulty with subject/verb agreement in compound sentences. If students need additional practice, have them do the Try It Yourself exercise in the Language Arts Survey, 2.16, "Agreement of Subject and Verb."

Language Lab

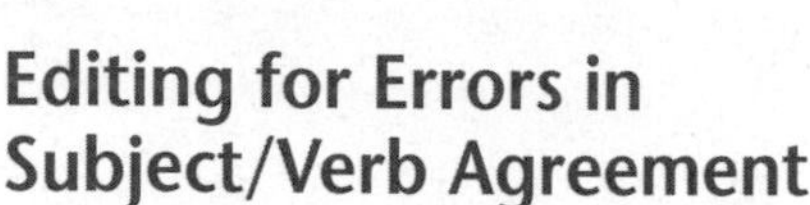

Editing for Errors in Subject/Verb Agreement

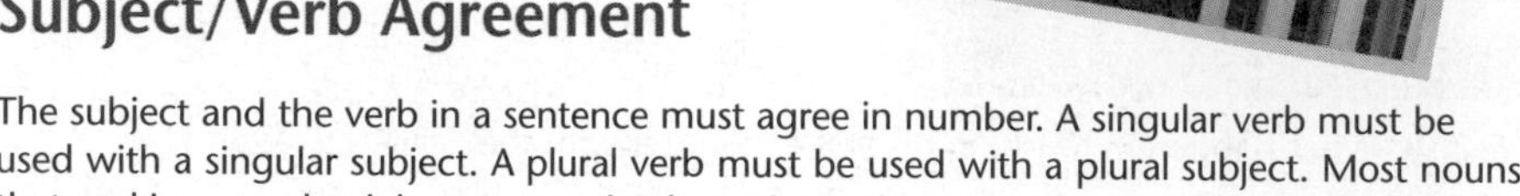

The subject and the verb in a sentence must agree in number. A singular verb must be used with a singular subject. A plural verb must be used with a plural subject. Most nouns that end in *s* are plural, but most verbs that refer to the present and end in *s* are singular.

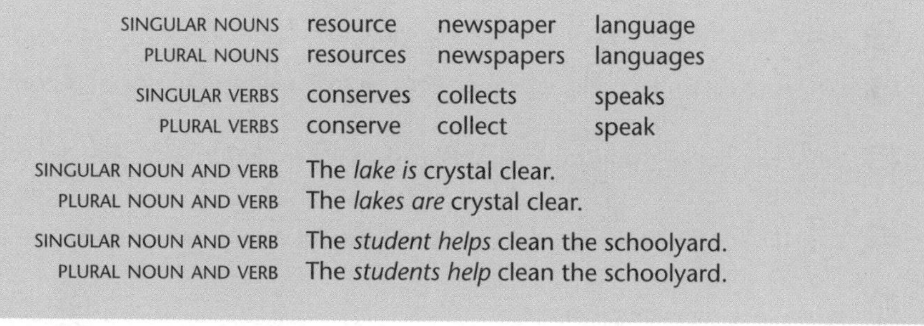

SINGULAR NOUNS	resource	newspaper	language
PLURAL NOUNS	resources	newspapers	languages
SINGULAR VERBS	conserves	collects	speaks
PLURAL VERBS	conserve	collect	speak
SINGULAR NOUN AND VERB	The *lake is* crystal clear.		
PLURAL NOUN AND VERB	The *lakes are* crystal clear.		
SINGULAR NOUN AND VERB	The *student helps* clean the schoolyard.		
PLURAL NOUN AND VERB	The *students help* clean the schoolyard.		

The pronouns *I* and *you* always take the plural form, except in *I am* and *I was*.

EXAMPLES *I recycle* the newspapers.
You recycle the aluminum cans.

Try It Yourself

Exercise A. Complete each sentence by choosing the correct form of the word in parentheses.

1. The students (is, are) learning to conserve and protect their environment.
2. Their teacher (explain, explains) the need for recycling and conservation.
3. Air pollution (causes, cause) problems in our atmosphere.
4. Deforestation (destroy, destroys) animal homes.
5. Will you (decides, decide) to help clean up our town?

CONTINUED

Agreement with Compound Subjects

A compound subject is formed by two or more nouns or pronouns that are joined by a conjunction and that share the same verb. A compound subject usually takes a plural verb.

EXAMPLE *Recycling* and *riding* your bike *help* protect our environment.

A compound subject takes a singular verb if the compound subject names only one person or thing, such as *peanut butter and jelly.* When a compound subject is joined by *or* or *nor,* use a verb that agrees in number with the subject nearer the verb.

EXAMPLES *His work and first love is* saving the environment.

Neither the botanist nor the other scientists are familiar with the unusual plant.

Try It Yourself

Exercise B. Complete the sentences by choosing the correct form of the verb in parentheses.

1. Oceans and rivers (contains, contain) a variety of living creatures.
2. Whales and dolphins (swims, swim) in the ocean.
3. Neither fish nor mammals (is, are) able to survive in polluted waters.
4. Noise pollution, air pollution, and water pollution (is, are) all dangerous to wildlife.
5. Children and adults (makes, make) a difference in keeping our precious environment clean.
6. Planting trees and recycling (demonstrates, demonstrate) your concern for the environment.
7. Neither governments nor the individual (is, are) solely responsible for our environment.
8. Acid rain and global warming (concerns, concern) people all over the world.
9. Pollution and deforestation (destroys, destroy) animal habitats.
10. Her pride and joy (is, are) the river she saved from pollution.

ANSWERS FOR TRY IT YOURSELF

EXERCISE A

1. are
2. explains
3. causes
4. destroys
5. decide

EXERCISE B

1. contain
2. swim
3. are
4. are
5. make
6. demonstrate
7. is
8. concern
9. destroy
10. is

GOALS/OBJECTIVES

Studying this lesson will enable students to

- analyze and appreciate an environmental essay
- understand the importance of a balanced environment
- identify and explain examples of irony of situation
- identify figurative language

ADDITIONAL RESOURCES

READER'S GUIDE

- Selection Worksheet, 11.3

ASSESSMENT PORTFOLIO

- Selection Check Test, 2.11.5
- Selection Test, 2.11.6

PRONUNCIATION EXERCISE

- Grade 8 Audiocassette, Side B, Track 57

See also Additional Resources Box in the marginal notes accompanying each selection.

CROSS-CURRICULAR CONNECTIONS

SCIENCE

Have students brainstorm a list of environmental problems that concern them. Students can work in small groups to research some of these problems. Have students present their findings in a skit, a poster, or an environmental newsletter.

Prereading

ESSAY

"Ships in the Desert" from *Earth in the Balance*

by Al Gore

Cross-curricular Connection

Science. A healthy environment is one where living things are adjusted to each other and to the surrounding conditions. Environmental scientists call this a balanced environment. If plants, animals, air, soil, and water are in a balanced relationship, then an environment can remain balanced and stay the same for several hundred years. Environmental change occurs when a new element appears and upsets the balance.

When this happens, an environment is said to become unbalanced. Elements that can unbalance an environment can be introduced either by nature or by humans. Examples of nature causing environmental change include a disease that wipes out a group of living things, a forest fire that destroys animal and plant habitats, or a climate change to which living things are unable to adapt. Examples of humans causing environmental change include urban expansion that destroys natural habitats, chemical wastes and industrial byproducts that pollute natural resources, and fuel emissions that poison the air.

One example of how the balance of nature is disturbed is illustrated by farmers who destroy chicken hawks. The chicken hawks, in addition to eating some of the farmers' chickens, also eat a great many field mice. Destroying the chicken hawks upsets the balance of nature because suddenly there are too many field mice. These tiny creatures can actually cause more damage to farmers' crops and supplies than chicken hawks do.

Another example is the use of fertilizers. Although fertilizers help crops grow, rain washes them into rivers and lakes, causing tiny algae in the water to grow. These algae continue to grow until they completely cover the lake. When this happens, food runs out, the algae die, and bacteria cause the dead algae to break down. In this unbalanced environment, the water begins to smell and causes some animals to die. Sometimes people make such errors because they are not aware of the long-term effects of their actions. Other times, they ignore the long-term effects for short-term gain.

As You Read

This selection from ***Earth in the Balance*** discusses a number of environmental problems in the world and the possible causes of those problems. In your journal, make a chart like the one below. As you read, make note of each environmental problem and its causes.

ENVIRONMENTAL PROBLEM	POSSIBLE CAUSE
several million starfish killed	**radioactive military waste in White Sea**

AS YOU READ

Students might include the following problems and possible causes in their charts: Aral Sea is dead/water is diverted for irrigation of cotton crops in the desert; dead dolphins washing up on the Riviera, dead dolphins along Gulf Coast in Texas/accumulated environmental stress, which made dolphins too weak to fight off a virus; dead birds and otters washing up on Prince William Sound/oil spill; polar ice cap might be thinning/global warming caused by rising levels of CO_2, which result from increased burning of coal and oil.

READER'S JOURNAL

Have you ever seen, firsthand, examples of nature being destroyed or polluted? If not, have you seen photographs or read books showing or describing the destruction of nature? What was being destroyed? What happened as a result of the destruction? How did these images make you feel? Write about these questions in your journal.

"Ships in the Desert"

AL GORE

I was standing in the sun on the hot steel deck of a fishing ship capable of processing a fifty-ton catch on a good day. But it wasn't a good day. We were anchored in what used to be the most productive fishing site in all of central Asia, but as I looked out over the bow, the prospects of a good catch looked bleak. Where there should have been gentle blue-green waves lapping against the side of the ship, there was nothing but hot dry sand—as far as I could see in all directions. The other ships of the fleet were also at rest in the sand, scattered in the dunes that stretched all the way to the horizon.

Oddly enough, it made me think of a fried egg I had seen back in the United States on television the week before. It was sizzling and popping the way a fried egg should in a pan, but it was in the middle of a sidewalk in downtown Phoenix. I guess it sprang to mind because, like the ship on which I was standing, there was nothing wrong with the egg itself. Instead, the world beneath it had changed in an unexpected way that made the egg seem—through no fault of its own—out of place. It was illustrating the newsworthy point that at the time Arizona wasn't having an especially good day, either, because for the second day in a row temperatures had reached a record 122 degrees.

As a camel walked by on the dead bottom of the Aral Sea, my thoughts returned to the unlikely ship of the desert on which I stood, which also seemed to be illustrating the point that its world had changed out from underneath it with sudden cruelty. Ten years ago the Aral was the fourth-largest inland sea in the world, comparable to the largest of North America's Great Lakes. Now it is disappearing because the water that used to feed it has been diverted in an ill-considered irrigation

1 *Why is it a bad fishing day? What is unusual about the location of the ship?*

WORDS FOR EVERYDAY USE

bleak (blēk) *adj.,* not promising or hopeful

di • vert (dī vʉrt′) *v.,* turn aside from a course or direction

READER'S JOURNAL

As an alternate activity, students might write about actions to protect the environment in which they have participated or that they have witnessed. Ask them to describe what happened, the purpose of the action, and how they felt about the action.

SPELLING AND VOCABULARY WORDS FROM THE SELECTION

aesthetic	peril
apparition	phenomenon
billow	proverbial
bleak	rendezvous
divert	spectral
eerily	speculative
indictment	translucent
inexorable	unprecedented

ANSWERS TO GUIDED READING QUESTIONS

1 It is a bad fishing day because although the ship is capable of processing a fifty-ton catch, no fish will be caught. The ship is anchored in the middle of a desert that used to be covered by ocean.

SUPPORT FOR LEP STUDENTS

PRONUNCIATIONS OF PROPER NOUNS AND ADJECTIVES

Ar • al (ar′əl) n.
Yab • lo • kov (yä′blə kôf′) n.
Muy • nak (ʉr′ nist) n.

ADDITIONAL VOCABULARY

irrigation—supply of water to an area, usually for crops
flotsam and jetsam—wreckage of ship and cargo floating in the sea
sonar—system used to determine depth based on the reflections of sound waves

VOCABULARY IN CONTEXT

- Our future will be bleak if we do not turn around ominous trends now.
- We must divert the coming apocalypse.

Answers to Guided Reading Questions

❶ Water that used to feed the Aral Sea has been diverted for irrigation of cotton crops in the desert. This has caused much of the Aral Sea to dry up. Fish canning continues, but the fish are shipped over a thousand miles to the cannery.

❷ The dead starfish are probably caused by radioactive military wastes. The dead dolphins probably suffered accumulated environmental stress that caused an immune deficiency. The otters and seabirds were killed by an oil spill. Each of these deaths represents one of the many problems faced by our environment. Each of these problems could be avoided. We should be concerned because the deaths are indications of serious problems in our world.

Cross-Curricular Activities

Social Studies and Science

The author of this selection visits many places to see the toll human actions are taking on the environment. Have students use a map or a globe to locate the different places the narrator describes.

Have students find articles in newspapers and magazines about environmental problems. Have students map the location of these problems. Students might use a large wall map to mark these points. Then, students can connect to each marker a card summarizing the article that explains the problem.

❶ *What has caused the change in the fishing industry?*

scheme to grow cotton in the desert. The new shoreline was almost forty kilometers across the sand from where the fishing fleet was now permanently docked. Meanwhile, in the nearby town of Muynak the people were still canning fish—brought not from the Aral Sea but shipped by rail through Siberia from the Pacific Ocean, more than a thousand miles away.

I had come to the Aral Sea in August 1990 to witness at first hand the destruction taking place there on an almost biblical[1] scale. But during the trip I encountered other images that also alarmed me. For example, the day I returned to Moscow from Muynak, my friend Alexei Yablokov, possibly the leading environmentalist in the Soviet Union, was returning from an emergency expedition to the White Sea, where he had investigated the mysterious and unprecedented death of several *million* starfish, washed up into a knee-deep mass covering many miles of beach. That night, in his apartment, he talked of what it was like for the residents to wade through the starfish in hip boots, trying to explain their death.

❷ *What explanations are offered for the dead starfish, dolphins, otters, and sea birds? Why should we be concerned by these deaths?*

Later investigations identified radioactive military waste as the likely culprit in the White Sea deaths. But what about all of the other mysterious mass deaths washing up on beaches around the world? French scientists recently concluded that the explanation for the growing number of dead dolphins washing up along the Riviera was accumulated environmental stress, which, over time, rendered the animals too weak to fight off a virus. This same phenomenon may also explain the sudden increase in dolphin deaths along the Gulf Coast in Texas as well as the mysterious deaths of 12,000 seals whose corpses washed up on the shores of the North Sea in the summer of 1988. Of course, the oil-covered otters and seabirds of Prince William Sound a year later presented less of a mystery to science, if no less an indictment of our civilization.

As soon as one of these troubling images fades, another takes its place, provoking new questions. What does it mean, for example, that children playing in the morning surf must now dodge not only the occasional jellyfish but the occasional hypodermic needle washing in with the waves? Needles, dead dolphins, and oil-soaked birds—are all these signs that the shores of our familiar world are fast eroding, that we are now standing on some new beach, facing dangers beyond the edge of what we are capable of imagining?

With our backs turned to the place in nature from which we came, we sense an unfamiliar tide rising and swirling around our ankles, pulling at the sand beneath our feet. Each time this strange new tide goes out, it leaves behind the flotsam and jetsam of some giant shipwreck far out at sea, startling images washed up on the sands of our time, each a fresh warning of hidden

1. **biblical.** Literally meaning of or like the Bible, but often used to describe something very large or widespread

Words for Everyday Use

un • prec • e • dent • ed (un pres´ ə den´tid) *adj.,* unheard of, new

phe • nom • e • non (fə näm´ ə nən´) *n.,* extremely unusual or extraordinary thing or occurrence

in • dict • ment (in dīt´ mənt) *n.,* accusation of wrongdoing, criminal charge

Vocabulary in Context

- An eighth grade student playing for the high school team was unprecedented.
- The aurora borealis is an interesting phenomenon.
- Joe received an indictment, but he was never found guilty of the crime.

dangers that lie ahead if we continue on our present course.

My search for the underlying causes of the environmental crisis has led me to travel around the world to examine and study many of these images of destruction. At the very bottom of the earth, high in the Trans-Antarctic Mountains, with the sun glaring at midnight through a hole in the sky, I stood in the unbelievable coldness and talked with a scientist in the late fall of 1988 about the tunnel he was digging through time. Slipping his parka back to reveal a badly burned face that was cracked and peeling, he pointed to the annual layers of ice in a core sample dug from the glacier on which we were standing. He moved his finger back in time to the ice of two decades ago. "Here's where the U.S. Congress passed the Clean Air Act," he said. At the bottom of the world, two continents away from Washington, D.C., even a small reduction in one country's emissions had changed the amount of pollution found in the remotest and least accessible place on earth.

But the most significant change thus far in the earth's atmosphere is the one that began with the industrial revolution early in the last century and has picked up speed ever since. Industry meant coal, and later oil, and we began to burn lots of it—bringing rising levels of carbon dioxide (CO_2), with its ability to trap more heat in the atmosphere and slowly warm the earth. Fewer than a hundred yards from the South Pole, upwind from the ice runway where the ski plane lands and keeps its engines running to prevent the metal parts from freeze-locking together, scientists monitor the air several times every day to chart the course of that inexorable change. During my visit, I watched one scientist draw the results of that day's measurements, pushing the end of a steep line still higher on the graph. He told me how easy it is—there at the end of the earth—to see that this enormous change in the global atmosphere is still picking up speed.

Two and a half years later I slept under the midnight sun at the other end of our planet, in a small tent pitched on a twelve-foot-thick slab of ice floating in the frigid Arctic Ocean. After a hearty breakfast, my companions and I traveled by snowmobiles a few miles farther north to a rendezvous point where the ice was thinner—only three and a half feet thick—and a nuclear submarine hovered in the water below. After it crashed through the ice, took on its new passengers, and resubmerged, I talked with scientists who were trying to measure more accurately the thickness of the polar ice cap, which many believe is thinning as a result of global warming. I had just negotiated an agreement between ice scientists and the U.S. Navy to secure the release of previously top secret data from submarine sonar tracks, data that could help them learn what is happening to the north polar cap. Now, I wanted to

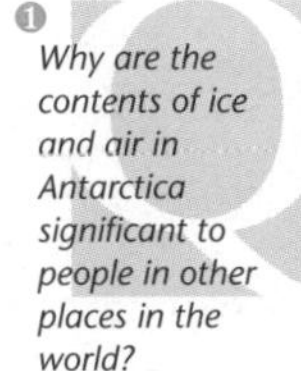

❶ *Why are the contents of ice and air in Antarctica significant to people in other places in the world?*

Words for Everyday Use

in • ex • o • ra • ble (in eks´ə rə bəl) *adj.,* that cannot be altered or checked

ren • dez • vous (rän´dā vo͞o´) *n.,* place designated for meeting or assembly

Answer to Guided Reading Question

❶ Air and water circulate over the globe, so pollution in one area affects another. Even in the South Pole the effects of pollution can be seen. For example, the ice core shows where Congress passed the Clean Air Act, which reduced the amount of pollution in the air.

Historical Note

The Industrial Revolution began in England in the late 1700s with the invention of machines for weaving. The Industrial Revolution included many technological changes including the use of new materials such as steel and iron; the use of new energy sources such as coal, steam engines, electricity, and petroleum; the invention of many machines; the development of factories; and the use of new methods of communication and transportation such as cars, airplanes, telegraphs, and radios. These changes have had an enormous impact on the environment.

Vocabulary in Context

- Li believes we can change our fate, but I believe our fate is inexorable.
- The rendezvous point is at Mr. Shaller's shop.

Quotables

"The sun, the moon, and the stars would have disappeared long ago, had they happened to be within reach of predatory human hands."

—Havelock Ellis

Additional Questions and Activities

Students can prepare a documentary on our vanishing wilderness. They might begin by brainstorming topics and then selecting the ones they wish to cover. Students should research the issues and prepare reports. Ask students to consider what visual aids or special effects they might include. If possible, have students videotape their production or present it to another class.

Answers to Guided Reading Questions

1. The rising levels of CO_2 cause temperatures to rise. As temperatures rise in the polar regions, the ice of the polar ice caps will thin. This could have a disastrous effect on weather patterns around the globe.

2. It is easy to ignore the plight of the Amazon rainforest, because the Amazon is far away and we do not directly see the lost species. The losses are signs of the further losses and destruction that will come if we do not heed the warning.

see the pole itself, and some eight hours after we met the submarine, we were crashing through that ice, surfacing, and then I was standing in an <u>eerily</u> beautiful snowscape, windswept and sparkling white, with the horizon defined by little hummocks, or "pressure ridges" of ice that are pushed up like tiny mountain ranges when separate sheets collide. But here too, CO_2 levels are rising just as rapidly, and ultimately temperatures will rise with them—indeed, global warming is expected to push temperatures up much more rapidly in the polar regions than in the rest of the world. As the polar air warms, the ice here will thin; and since the polar cap plays such a crucial role in the world's weather system, the consequences of a thinning cap could be disastrous.

> 1 *What effects might rising levels of CO_2 have?*

Considering such scenarios is not a purely <u>speculative</u> exercise. Six months after I returned from the North Pole, a team of scientists reported dramatic changes in the pattern of ice distribution in the Arctic, and a second team reported a still controversial claim (which a variety of data now suggest) that, overall, the north polar cap has thinned by 2 percent in just the last decade. Moreover, scientists established several years ago that in many land areas north of the Arctic Circle, the spring snowmelt now comes earlier every year, and deep in the tundra below, the temperature of the earth is steadily rising.

> 2 *Why is it easy to ignore the plight of the Amazon rainforest? Why is it imperative that we not ignore this plight?*

As it happens, some of the most disturbing images of environmental destruction can be found exactly halfway between the North and South poles—precisely at the equator in Brazil—where <u>billowing</u> clouds of smoke regularly blacken the sky above the immense but now threatened Amazon rain forest. Acre by acre, the rain forest is being burned to create fast pasture for fast-food beef; as I learned when I went there in early 1989, the fires are set earlier and earlier in the dry season now, with more than one Tennessee's worth of rain forest being slashed and burned each year. According to our guide, the biologist Tom Lovejoy, there are more different species of birds in each square mile of the Amazon than exist in all of North America—which means we are silencing thousands of songs we have never even heard.

But for most of us the Amazon is a distant place, and we scarcely notice the disappearance of these and other vulnerable species. We ignore these losses at our <u>peril</u>, however. They're like the <u>proverbial</u> miners' canaries, silent alarms whose message in this case is that living species of animals and plants are now vanishing around the world *one thousand times faster* than at any time in the past 65 million years (see illustration [on next page]).

To be sure, the deaths of some of the larger and more spectacular animal species now under siege do occasionally capture our attention. I have also visited another place along the equator,

Words for Everyday Use

ee • ri • ly (ir´ē lē) *adv.*, mysteriously, strangely

spec • u • la • tive (spek´ yo͞o lə tiv) *adj.*, theoretical, not practical

bil • low (bil´ō) *v.*, surge, swell or rise like a large wave

per • il (per´əl) *n.*, danger, exposure to harm

pro • ver • bi • al (prō vʉr´bē əl) *adj.*, well known because commonly referred to

Vocabulary in Context

- Alphonso shivered in fear as the wind moaned <u>eerily</u> around the house.
- Your <u>speculative</u> ideas are interesting, but they will not solve the problem.
- We had difficulty folding the blanket because it kept <u>billowing</u> in the wind.
- Maya put herself in great <u>peril</u> to save her cat from the rising floodwaters.
- Isabelle was drawn to Walter like the <u>proverbial</u> moth to the flame.

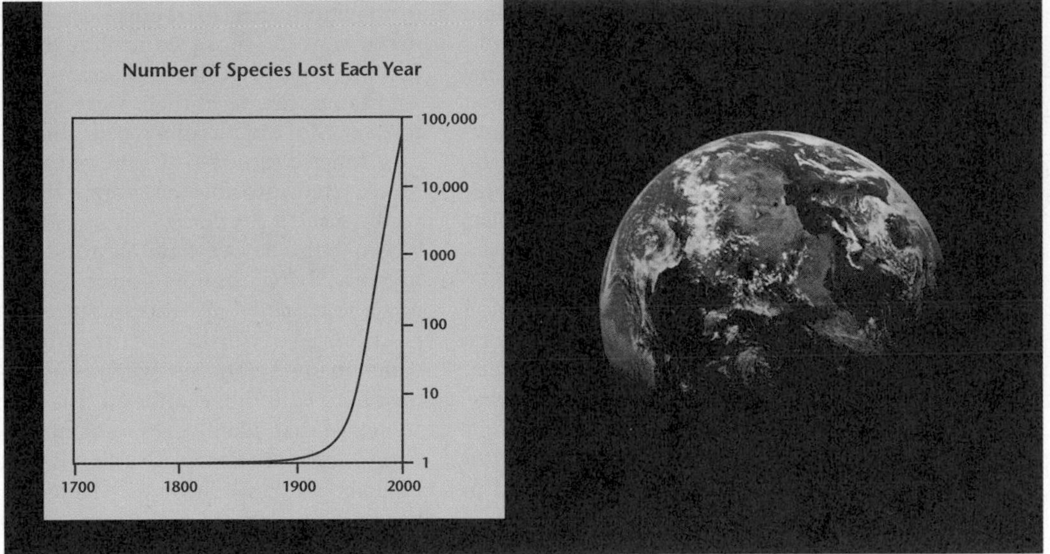

East Africa, where I encountered the grotesquely horrible image of a dead elephant, its head mutilated by poachers who had dug out its valuable tusks with chain saws. Clearly, we need to change our purely aesthetic consideration of ivory, since its source is now so threatened. To me, its translucent whiteness seems different now, like evidence of the ghostly presence of a troubled spirit, a beautiful but chill apparition, inspiring both wonder and dread.

A similar apparition lies just beneath the ocean. While scuba diving in the Caribbean, I have seen and touched the white bones of a dead coral reef. All over the earth, coral reefs have suddenly started to "bleach" as warmer ocean temperatures put unaccustomed stress on the tiny organisms that normally live in the skin of the coral and give the reef its natural coloration. As these organisms—nicknamed "zooks"—leave the membrane of the coral, the coral itself becomes transparent, allowing its white limestone skeleton to shine through—hence its bleached appearance. In the past, bleaching was almost always an occasional and temporary phenomenon, but repeated episodes can exhaust the coral. In the last few years, scientists have been shocked at the sudden occurrence of extensive worldwide bleaching episodes from which increasing numbers of coral reefs have failed to recover. Though dead, they shine more brightly than before, haunted perhaps by the same ghost that gives spectral light to an elephant's tusk.

1 *What problem does the bleaching of coral reefs indicate?*

Words for Everyday Use

aes • thet • ic (es thet´ ik) *adj.,* referring to beauty

trans • lu • cent (trans lo͞o´ sənt) *adj.,* partially transparent

ap • pa • ri • tion (ap´ə rish´ən) *n.,* anything that appears unexpectedly or in an extraordinary way; ghost

spec • tral (spek´trəl) *adj.,* like a ghost or phantom

Answer to Guided Reading Question

1 The bleaching of the coral reefs indicates warmer ocean temperatures. The warmer temperatures put stress on the organisms that live in the coral and give it its color. The fact that bleaching is becoming more and more common suggests that ocean temperatures are rising more extensively.

Cross-Curricular Activities

Mathematics and Science

Have students look at the chart on page 559. Ask them the following questions:

- Approximately how many species became extinct in 1900?
- Approximately how many species became extinct in 1950?
- Approximately how many species are likely to become extinct in 2000?

Students can research species that have become extinct within the last decade. Have students create a mural or bulletin board featuring plants and animals that have become extinct. Students might also wish to make an "Extinct Tomorrow?" section featuring endangered plants and animals.

Vocabulary in Context

- Although it was severely cold, Kyle chose not to wear a hat for aesthetic reasons.
- The translucent curtains allowed light into the room but blocked the view from outside.
- Fay was startled by the apparition as she walked down the lonely street.
- The fog had a spectral quality to it.

Answers to Guided Reading Questions

❶ The author sees acres of untouched forest being bulldozed to make room for buildings, parking lots, and streets. Wild creatures are forced to flee. In the process, deer are hit by cars and pheasants dart into yards.

❷ The animals inspire wonder and sadness in the author. They remind him that humans are creating a world that is hostile to wildness.

Selection Check Test with Answers

EX. Where is the ship that the author is standing on at the beginning of the selection?
The ship is in the middle of a desert that used to be the Aral Sea.

1. What washed up on the shores of the White Sea?
Millions of dead starfish washed up on the shores of the White Sea.

2. What became increasingly present in the atmosphere beginning with the Industrial Revolution?
Carbon dioxide became increasingly present.

3. Why is the Amazon rainforest being burned?
It is being burned to create pasture for fast-food beef.

4. What is happening to many coral reefs?
Many coral reefs are bleaching, or losing their color, because tiny organisms no longer live on the reefs.

5. What kind of world does the author say we are creating?
The author says we are creating a world that is hostile to wildness.

❶ *What destruction of nature does the author find close to home? What effect of this destruction does he see?*

❷ *What feelings do the animals in a zoo inspire in the author?*

But one doesn't have to travel around the world to witness humankind's assault on the earth. Images that signal the distress of our global environment are now commonly seen almost anywhere. A few miles from the Capitol, for example, I encountered another startling image of nature out of place. Driving in the Arlington, Virginia, neighborhood where my family and I live when the Senate is in session, I stepped on the brake to avoid hitting a large pheasant walking across the street. It darted between the parked cars, across the sidewalk, and into a neighbor's backyard. Then it was gone. But this apparition of wildness persisted in my memory as a puzzle: Why would a pheasant, let alone such a large and beautiful mature specimen, be out for a walk in my neighborhood? Was it a much wilder place than I had noticed? Were pheasants, like the trendy Vietnamese potbellied pigs, becoming the latest fashion in unusual pets? I didn't solve the mystery until weeks later, when I remembered that about three miles away, along the edge of the river, developers were bulldozing the last hundred acres of untouched forest in the entire area. As the woods fell to make way for more concrete, more buildings, parking lots, and streets, the wild things that lived there were forced to flee. Most of the deer were hit by cars; other creatures—like the pheasant that darted into my neighbor's backyard—made it a little farther.

Ironically, before I understood the mystery, I felt vaguely comforted to imagine that perhaps this urban environment, so similar to the one in which many Americans live, was not so hostile to wild things after all. I briefly supposed that, like the resourceful raccoons and possums and squirrels and pigeons, all of whom have adapted to life in the suburbs, creatures as wild as pheasants might have a fighting chance. Now I remember that pheasant when I take my children to the zoo and see an elephant or a rhinoceros. They too inspire wonder and sadness. They too remind me that we are creating a world that is hostile to wildness, that seems to prefer concrete to natural landscapes. We are encountering these creatures on a path we have paved—one that ultimately leads to their extinction. ■

About the Author

Al Gore (1948–) became the vice president of the United States in 1992, when William Clinton was elected the forty-second president. Before beginning a career in politics, Gore worked as a journalist for seven years. He then spent many years representing Tennessee in Congress. In 1976, he won a seat in the House of Representatives, and in 1984 he was elected to the Senate. Gore was a leader of environmental awareness in Congress and he has spent many years studying the global environment.

Responding to the Selection

After showing many vivid examples of an "unbalanced" environment, the author says, "We are creating a world that is hostile to wildness, that seems to prefer concrete to natural landscapes." Do you agree or disagree with this statement? Why? What examples from your own life can you draw upon to support your view?

Reviewing the Selection

RECALLING AND INTERPRETING

1. **R** What is said to be the cause of the disappearing Aral Sea ?

   I What impression of human planning does this create?

2. **R** What effect did passage of the Clean Air Act by the United States Congress have on ice core samples dug from polar glaciers?

   I What conclusions about air pollution can you draw from this evidence?

3. **R** In early 1989, the author discovered that the Amazonian rainforest was being destroyed at a rapid rate. How much of the rainforest was being burned each year?

   I Why is it a bad policy to destroy the rainforest in this way?

4. **R** What creature does the author discover crossing the street in his neighborhood one day?

   I Why does this discovery seem strange? What does the author realize as a result of this discovery?

SYNTHESIZING

5. From the examples given by the author, what conclusions can you draw about human beings' relationship to nature? What do you think would happen if the number of species lost each year continues at the current rate? What do you think can be done about this problem?

Understanding Literature (Questions for Discussion)

1. **Irony of Situation.** An event that contradicts the expectations of the characters, the reader, or the audience of a literary work is an example of **irony of situation.** The Aral Sea problem that the author describes involves an irony of situation. So does the sighting of the pheasant. What contradicts your expectations as a reader? What is the author's purpose in using these ironic situations?
2. **Figurative Language. Figurative language** is language that has more than a straightforward, literal meaning. In paragraph 7 of this section, what examples of figurative language can you identify? What words might the writer have used to describe the situation literally? What effect does the use of figurative language have on the description?

RESPONDING TO THE SELECTION

Ask students what benefits they see in maintaining wildness. Why are natural landscapes necessary?

ANSWERS FOR REVIEWING THE SELECTION

RECALLING AND INTERPRETING

1. **Recalling.** An ill-advised irrigation scheme drained the Aral Sea. **Interpreting.** *Responses will vary.* This example shows that in many cases humans plan projects without analyzing the effects they will have on the environment.
2. **Recalling.** The ice samples show lesser amounts of air pollution after the passage of the act. **Interpreting.** *Responses will vary.* You can conclude that air pollution is a global problem because the lessening of pollution in the United States led to a lessening of the pollution in the remote Arctic.
3. **Recalling.** In the Amazon rainforest, an area the size of Tennessee was burned each year. **Interpreting.** *Responses will vary.* The burning of vast tracts of forest have killed thousands of species.
4. **Recalling.** The author saw a large pheasant crossing the street. **Interpreting.** *Responses will vary.* The incident was strange because the pheasant is a wild bird. The author realized that even small-scale construction projects, like the one close to his house, could have dramatic effects on the surrounding environment.

SYNTHESIZING

Responses will vary. Possible responses are given.

5. The examples show that humans can have a destructive effect on nature and that humans often fail to appreciate the complex natural world in which they live. If the rate of loss of species continues, the ecosystem could collapse from the destruction of food chains. Global consensus should be reached on levels of environmental protection. Individual efforts, such as recycling, are also important.

ANSWERS FOR UNDERSTANDING LITERATURE

Responses will vary. Possible responses are given.

1. **Irony of Situation.** The images of a ship in the desert and of a large pheasant walking across a suburban street contradict the reader's expectations because both the ship and the pheasant are in strange settings. The author uses these ironic examples because he wants to stress how disturbed the ecossystem has become.
2. **Figurative Language.** The author uses the phrases "we sense an unfamiliar tide rising and swirling" and "it leaves behind the flotsam and jetsam of some giant shipwreck far out at sea." The author is using the language of the sea and of a shipwreck to describe the many environmental disasters we face.

GOALS/OBJECTIVES

Studying this lesson will enable students to

- have a positive experience reading an essay
- briefly explain the development of units of measurement
- define *analogy* and *anecdote* and identify these elements in a literary work

ADDITIONAL RESOURCES

READER'S GUIDE

- Selection Worksheet, 11.4

ASSESSMENT PORTFOLIO

- Selection Check Test, 2.11.7
- Selection Test, 2.11.8

PRONUNCIATION EXERCISE

- Grade 7 Audiocassette, Side B, Track 58

See also Additional Resources Box in the marginal notes accompanying selections.

CROSS-CURRICULAR CONNECTIONS

MATHEMATICS

Encourage students to debate whether or not United States citizens should start using the metric system. Students should state the benefits and the drawbacks of converting to the metric system. Ask students the following questions: Do the benefits of converting to the metric system outweigh the drawbacks? Why, or why not? What do you think people's reactions would be to this conversion?

Prereading

ESSAY

"The Size of Things" from *Red Giants and White Dwarfs*

by Robert Jastrow

Cross-curricular Connection

Mathematics. In the selection you are about to read, you will discover the challenge of talking about the measurement of size and distance of something as minute as the atom or as vast as the universe. Measurement is the process of finding out the extent, or dimensions, of something, especially by using a standard unit of measurement. Inches, meters, hours, ounces, kilograms, and degrees Kelvin, Celsius, or Fahrenheit are all standard units of measurement.

Ancient peoples developed the first systems for measuring length by comparing the length of one thing to the length of another. Many units of measurement were based on parts of the human body. The cubit used by ancient Egyptians, for example, represented the length of a person's forearm from the elbow to the tip of the middle finger. The Romans borrowed many Greek units of measurement, such as the uncia, which was the width of a thumb. Other Roman units of measurement include the ounce, the pound, and the mile. The Roman system of measurement was adopted throughout Europe and prevailed until France adopted the metric system in 1795. Today, most countries in the world use the metric system.

One of the problems in basing units of measurement on human body parts is that all humans are not the same size. Thus, nations had to develop measurement standards. In ancient Egypt, there was a royal master cubit made of black granite against which all cubit sticks in Egypt were checked.

The metric system is, for the most part, based on either natural or scientific standards. For example, the standard measurement for the second is set according to an atomic clock. This clock works by counting the vibrations made by atoms in the element cesium. These atoms vibrate 9,192,631,770 times per second.

As You Read

The selection from ***Red Giants and White Dwarfs*** presents information about the sizes of objects as well as the distances between objects. To help keep track of these details, make the following chart in your journal. As you read, record different objects in the left-hand column, and write a brief description of the item's size, weight, or distance from another object in the right-hand column.

KEEPING TRACK OF DETAILS

Item	Size, Weight, or Distance
electron	10,000 trillion trillion electrons per ounce

AS YOU READ

Students might include the following details in their charts: electron—10-trillionth of an inch; proton and neutron—1840 times heavier than electron; nucleus—one-trillionth of an inch; atom—one hundred-millionth of an inch; atom—ten thousand times size of nucleus; Earth—8000 miles in diameter; sun—weighs 700 times the combined weight of the planets; galaxy—diameter 100,000 light years; galaxy—average distance between one galaxy and another is one million light years.

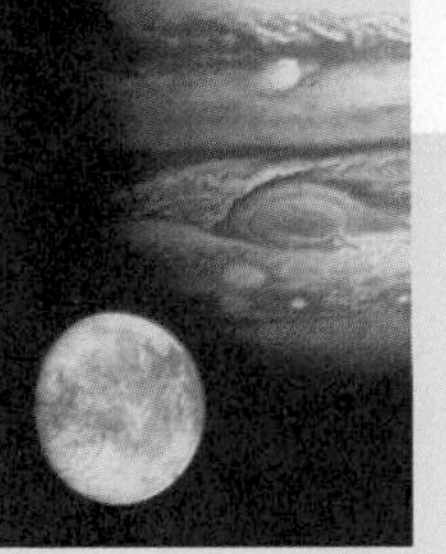

READER'S JOURNAL

Since ancient times, people have gazed into the sky at night and imagined traveling to distant planets or stars. What do you think it would be like to travel in space? How far away do you think other planets are? other stars? What do you think you would see as you traveled through space? What do you think some of the difficulties of space travel might be? Write about these questions in your journal.

"The Size of Things"

ROBERT JASTROW

I once had occasion to testify before the United States Senate Space and Aeronautics Committee on the scientific background of the space program; my talk dealt with the manner in which all substances in the universe are assembled out of neutrons, protons, and electrons as the basic building blocks. After I left the chamber a senior NASA official continued with a summary of the major space science achievements of the last year. Apparently my scholarly presentation had perplexed the senators, although they were anxious to understand the concepts I had presented. However, the NASA official's relaxed manner reassured them, and someone asked him: "How big is the electron? How much smaller is it than a speck of dust?" The NASA official correctly replied that the size of an electron is to a dust speck as the dust speck is to the entire earth.

The electron is indeed a tiny object. Its diameter is one 10-trillionth of an inch, a million times smaller than can be seen with the best electron microscope. Its weight is correspondingly small; 10,000 trillion trillion electrons make up one ounce. How can we be certain that such a small object exists? No one has ever picked up an electron with a pair of forceps[1] and said, "Here is one." The evidence for its existence is all indirect. During the 150 years from the late eighteenth century to the beginning of the twentieth century a great variety of experiments were carried out on the flow of electricity through liquids and gases. The existence of the electron was not proved conclusively by any single one of these experiments. However, the majority of them could be explained most easily if the physicist assumed

1. **forceps.** Tongs or pincers used for grasping, compressing, and pulling, most often by doctors and scientists

❶ *Why might people wonder if electrons exist?*

❷ *How much smaller is an electron than a speck of dust?*

WORDS FOR EVERYDAY USE

per • plex (pər pleks´) *v.,* confuse, puzzle

con • clu • sive • ly (kən klo͞o´siv lē) *adv.,* without a doubt, decisively

READER'S JOURNAL

As an alternative activity, you might ask students to freewrite about familiar objects to which they can compare something as small as an atom or as large as a galaxy.

SPELLING AND VOCABULARY WORDS FROM THE SELECTION

conclusively	luminous
conviction	minute
deduce	perplex
diffuse	scarcely

ANSWERS TO GUIDED READING QUESTIONS

❶ People might wonder if electrons exist because they are so small that people cannot see one or pick one up.

❷ An electron is to a speck of dust as the speck of dust is to the entire Earth.

SUPPORT FOR LEP STUDENTS

PRONUNCIATIONS OF PROPER NOUNS AND ADJECTIVES

Mil • li • kan (mil´i kən) n.
Hans Gei • ger (häns gī´gər) n.

ADDITIONAL VOCABULARY

atomizer—device used to shoot out a fine spray
inconceivably—in a manner that can hardly be thought of, understood, or imagined
macroscopic—visible to the naked eye
repulsion—mutual action by which bodies of matter tend to repel each other

VOCABULARY IN CONTEXT

- Hannah was perplexed by the events of World War I, until she went to her teacher for extra help.
- The scientist said that this experiment conclusively proved her theory.

ANSWER TO GUIDED READING QUESTION

❶ The writer compares the electrons that are attracted to a nucleus to the planets that circle around the sun.

ADDITIONAL QUESTIONS AND ACTIVITIES

Ask students the following questions: What are the "building blocks" from which all matter in the universe is constructed? What binds these tiny particles together? Of what is a nucleus composed? What do electrons do in relation to the nucleus? What do these particles form?

ANSWERS

Electrons, protons, and neutrons are the building blocks from which all matter in the universe is constructed. A strong force of attraction binds these particles together. A nucleus is composed of neutrons and protons that are attracted to each other. Electrons are attracted to the nucleus and they circle it, much as the planets circle the sun. These particles form an atom.

that the electricity was carried by a stream of small particles, each bearing its own electrical charge. Gradually physicists acquired a feeling, bordering on conviction, that the electron actually exists.

The question now was, how large is the electron, and how much electric charge does each electron carry? The clearest answer to this question came from an American physicist, Robert Millikan, who worked on the problem at the University of Chicago in the first decades of the twentieth century. Millikan arranged a device, clever for its simplicity, in which an atomizer created a mist of very fine droplets of oil just above a small hole in the top of a container. A small number of the droplets fell through the hole and slowly drifted to the bottom of the container. Millikan could see the motions of these droplets very clearly by illuminating them from the side with a strong light so that they appeared as bright spots against a dark background. Millikan discovered that some of these droplets carried a few extra electrons, which had been picked up in the atomizing process. By applying an electrical force to the droplets and studying their motions in response to this force, he could deduce the amount of electric charge carried by the electrons on each droplet. This charge turned out to be exceedingly minute. As a demonstration of its minuteness, it takes an electric current equivalent to a flow of one million trillion electrons every second to light a 10-watt bulb. All this happened rather recently in the history of science. Millikan's first accurate measurements were completed in 1914.

❶ *To what does the writer compare a nucleus and its electrons?*

The tiny electron, and two sister particles, are the building blocks out of which all matter in the world is constructed. The sister particles to the electron are the proton and the neutron. They were discovered even more recently than the electron; the proton was identified in 1920 and the neutron was first discovered in 1932. These two particles are massive in comparison with the electron—1840 times as heavy—but still inconceivably light by ordinary standards. The three particles combine in an amazingly simple way to form the objects we see and feel. A strong force of attraction binds neutrons and protons together to form a dense, compact body called the nucleus, whose size is somewhat less than one-trillionth of an inch. Electrons are attracted to the nucleus and circle around it as the planets circle around the sun, forming a solar system in miniature.

Together the electrons and the nucleus make up the atom.

The size of a typical atom is one hundred-millionth of an inch. To get a feeling for the smallness of the atom compared to a macroscopic object, imagine that you can see the individual atoms in a kitchen table, and that each atom is the size of a grain of sand. On this scale of enlargement the table will be 2000 miles long.

WORDS FOR EVERYDAY USE

con • vic • tion (kən vik´shən) *n.,* strong and firm belief

de • duce (dē do͞os´) *v.,* conclude from known facts or general principles

min • ute (mī no͞ot´) *adj.,* very small, tiny

VOCABULARY IN CONTEXT

- Gina had a strong conviction on almost every issue.
- From the clues left behind, the detective deduced the identity of the criminal.
- My sister said that she had left some juice for me in the refrigerator, but the amount that she left was minute.

The comparison of the atom with a grain of sand implies that the atom is a solid object. Actually, the atom consists largely of empty space. Each of the atoms that makes up the surface of a table consists of a number of electrons orbiting around a nucleus. The electrons form a diffuse shell around the nucleus, marking the outer boundary of the atom. The size of the atom is 10,000 times as great as the size of the nucleus at the center. If the outer shell of electrons in the atom were the size of the Astrodome that covers the Houston baseball stadium, the nucleus would be a ping-pong ball in the center of the stadium. That is the emptiness of the atom.

If most of the atom is empty space, why does a tabletop offer resistance when you push it with your finger? The reason is that the surface of the table consists of a wall of electrons, the electrons belonging to the outermost layer of atoms in the tabletop; the surface of your finger also consists of a wall of electrons; where they meet, strong forces of electrical repulsion prevent the electrons in your fingertip from pushing past the outermost electrons in the top of the table into the empty space within each atom. An atomic projectile such as a proton, accelerated to high speed in a cyclotron, could easily pass through these electrons, which are, after all, rather light and unable to hurl back a fast-moving object. But it would take more force than the pressure of the finger can produce to force them aside and penetrate the inner space of the atom.

The concept of the empty atom is a recent development. Isaac Newton described atoms as "solid, massy, hard, impenetrable, moveable particles." Through the nineteenth century, physicists continued to regard them as small, solid objects. Lord Rutherford, the greatest experimental physicist of his time, once said, "I was brought up to look at the atom as a nice hard fellow, red or grey in color, according to taste." At the beginning of the twentieth century, J. J. Thomson, a British physicist and one of the pioneers in the investigation of the structure of matter, believed that the atom was a spherical plum pudding of positive electric charge in which negatively charged electrons were embedded like raisins. No one knew that the mass of the atom, and its positive charge, were concentrated in a small, dense nucleus at the center, and that the electrons circled around this nucleus at a considerable distance. But in 1911 Rutherford, acting on a hunch, instructed his assistant, Hans Geiger, and a graduate student named Marsden, to fire a beam of alpha particles into a bit of thin gold foil. These alpha particles are extremely fast-moving atomic projectiles which should have penetrated the gold foil and emerged from the other side. Most of them did, but Geiger and Marsden found that in a very few cases the alpha particles came out of the foil on the same side they had entered. Rutherford said later, "It was quite the most incredible event that

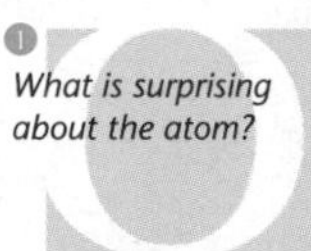

❶ *What is surprising about the atom?*

❷ *Why does a tabletop offer resistance to your finger even though it is composed of atoms which are mostly empty space?*

Words for Everyday Use

dif • fuse (di fyo͞os´) *adj.*, not concentrated, spread out

Answers to Guided Reading Questions

❶ The large amount of empty space in the atom is surprising.

❷ A tabletop offers resistance to your finger because both the surface of your finger and the surface of the table consist of a wall of electrons. When they meet they are electrically repelled.

CROSS-CURRICULAR ACTIVITIES

Science

Encourage students to draw two-dimensional or create three-dimensional models of the atom. Students should try to make their models as realistic as possible and to include all the parts of the atom.

Vocabulary in Context

• Population is highly concentrated in cities, but in rural areas population is more diffuse.

Additional Questions and Activities

Ask students the following questions: Why did Rutherford describe this experiment as the "most incredible event that has ever happened to me in my life"? To what does he compare his experiment? What did Rutherford determine because of this experiment? How many atoms are in a cubic inch of an ordinary solid substance?

ANSWERS

Rutherford described his experiment as incredible because all the alpha particles should have gone through the gold foil, but some came out on the same side that they had entered. He compares his experiment to firing "a 15-inch shell at a piece of tissue paper and having it come back and hit you." Rutherford determined that some of the alpha particles struck a small but massive object in the foil. He then determined that most of the mass of the atom is concentrated at its center, which he named the nucleus. There are a trillion trillion atoms in a cubic inch of an ordinary solid substance.

Jupiter and moons. *Photo courtesy of the National Aeronautics and Space Administration (NASA)*

has ever happened to me in my life. It was almost as incredible as if you fired a 15-inch shell at a piece of tissue paper and it came back and hit you."

Later Geiger told the story of the occasion on which Rutherford saw the meaning of the experiment. He relates: "One day [in 1911] Rutherford, obviously in the best of spirits, came into my room and told me that he now knew what the atom looked like and how to explain the large deflections of the alpha particles." What had occurred, Rutherford had decided, was that now and then an alpha particle hit a massive object in the foil, which bounced it straight back. He realized that the massive objects must be very small since the alpha particles hit them so rarely. He concluded that most of the mass of the atom is concentrated in a compact body at its center, which he named the nucleus. Rutherford's discovery opened the door to the nuclear era.

Let us continue with the description of the manner in which the universe is assembled out of its basic particles. Atoms are joined together in groups to form molecules, such as water, which consists of two atoms of hydrogen joined to one atom of oxygen. Large numbers of atoms or molecules cemented together form solid matter. There are a trillion trillion atoms in a cubic inch of an ordinary solid substance, which is roughly the same as the number of grains of sand in all the oceans of the earth.

The earth itself is an especially large collection of atoms bound together in a ball of rock and iron 8000 miles in diameter, weighing six billion trillion tons. It is one of nine planets, which are bound to the sun by the force of gravity. Together the sun and planets form the solar system. The largest of the planets is Jupiter, whose diameter is 86,000 miles; Mercury, the smallest, is 3100 miles across, one-third the size of the earth, and scarcely larger than the moon. All the planets are dwarfed by the sun, whose diameter is one million miles. The weight of the sun is 700 times greater than the combined weight of the nine planets. Like the atom, the solar system consists of a massive central body—the sun—surrounded by small, light objects—the planets—which revolve about it at great distances.

The sun is only one among 200 billion stars that are bound together by gravity into a large cluster of stars called the galaxy. The stars of the galaxy revolve about its center as the planets revolve about the sun. The sun itself participates in this rotating motion, completing one circuit around the galaxy in 250 million years.

The galaxy is flattened by its rotating motion into the shape of a disk, whose thickness is roughly one-fiftieth of its diameter. Most of the stars in the galaxy are in this disk, although some are located outside it. A relatively small, spherical cluster of stars, called the nucleus of the galaxy, bulges out of the disk at the center. The entire structure resembles a double sombrero[2] with the galactic nucleus as the crown and the disk as the brim. The sun is located in the brim of the sombrero about three-fifths of the way out from the center to the edge. When we look into the sky in the direction of the disk we see so many stars that they are not visible as separate points of light, but blend together into a luminous band stretching across the sky. This band is called Milky Way.

The stars within the galaxy are separated from one another by an average distance of about 36 trillion miles. In order to avoid the frequent repetition of such awkwardly large numbers, astronomical distances are usually expressed in units of the light year. A light year is defined as the distance covered in one year by a ray of light, which travels at 186,000 miles per second. The distance turns out to be six trillion miles; hence in these units the average distance between stars in the galaxy is five light years, and the diameter of the galaxy is 100,000 light years.

In spite of the enormous size of our galaxy, its boundaries do not mark the edge of the observable universe. The 200-inch telescope on Palomar Mountain[3] has within its range no less than 100 billion other galaxies, each

2. **sombrero.** Tall Mexican hat with a large brim
3. **Palomar Mountain.** Mountain is southwest California

❶ *What is the Milky Way?*

❷ *How many other stars are there in our galaxy?*

❸ *How many other galaxies have been observed?*

Words for Everyday Use

scarce • ly (skers le) *adv.*, only just, barely

lu • min • ous (lo͞o´mə nəs) *adj.*, shining, bright, giving off light

Answers to Guided Reading Questions

❶ The Milky Way is a band of stars so numerous that they are not visible as separate points of light, but blend together in a band of light.

❷ There are about two hundred billion other stars in the galaxy.

❸ About one hundred billion other galaxies have been observed.

Quotables

"I don't pretend to understand the universe, it is a great deal bigger than I am."

—Thomas Carlyle

"The eternal silence of those infinite spaces terrifies me."

—Blaise Pascal

"Today we can no more predict what use mankind may make of the Moon than could Columbus have imagined the future of the continent he had discovered."

—Arthur C. Clarke

Additional Questions and Activities

Students might discuss whether or not humans will ever travel to another solar system. What do students think are the chances of discovering life in another solar system? If we discovered life in another solar system, do students think that these forms of life would be similar to those on our planet or completely different?

Vocabulary in Context

- Antonio could scarcely see the tiny pinpoint of light in the distance.
- His new watch has a luminous face that makes it easy to read at night.

Answer to Guided Reading Question

❶ If the sun were the size of an orange, the closest star would be 1300 miles away.

Selection Check Test with Answers

EX. Before whom did the author of this selection testify?
The author testified before the United States Senate Space and Aeronautics Committee.

1. How small is an electron compared to a speck of dust.
The size of an electron is to a dust speck as a dust speck is to the entire Earth.

2. According to the author, which scientist gave the clearest answers about how large an electron is and how much charge it carries?
According to the author, Robert Millikan gave the clearest idea.

3. What is surprising about the atom?
It is surprising that the atom contains so much empty space.

4. How many other stars are there in our galaxy? How many other galaxies have been observed?
There are 200 billion stars in our galaxy, and 100 billion other galaxies have been observed.

5. If the sun were an orange, how big would the Earth be and how far would it be from the orange?
The Earth would be the size of a grain of sand and its orbit would be thirty feet away from the orange.

If the sun were the size of an orange, how far away would the closest star be?

comparable to our own in size and containing a similar number of stars. The average distance between these galaxies is one million light years. The extent of the visible universe, as it can be seen in the 200-inch telescope, is 15 billion light years.

An analogy will help to clarify the meaning of these enormous distances. Let the sun be the size of an orange; on that scale of sizes the earth is a grain of sand circling in orbit around the sun at a distance of 30 feet; the giant planet Jupiter, 11 times larger than the earth, is a cherry pit revolving at a distance of 200 feet or one city block; Saturn is another cherry pit two blocks from the sun; and Pluto, the outermost planet, is still another sand grain at a distance of ten city blocks from the sun.

❶ On the same scale the average distance between the stars is 2000 miles. The sun's nearest neighbor, a star called Alpha Centauri, is 1300 miles away. In the space between the sun and its neighbors there is nothing but a thin distribution of hydrogen atoms, forming a vacuum far better than any ever achieved on earth. The galaxy, on this scale, is a cluster of oranges separated by an average distance of 2000 miles, the entire cluster being 20 million miles in diameter.

An orange, a few grains of sand some feet away, and then some cherry pits circling slowly around the orange at a distance of a city block. Two thousand miles away is another orange, perhaps with a few specks of planetary matter circling around it. That is the void of space. ■

About the Author

Robert Jastrow has written several books on astronomy and space. He was one of the first members of NASA as well as the chairperson of NASA's Lunar Exploration Committee. Presently he is a professor of Earth Sciences at Dartmouth College. He has also appeared on many television programs on astronomy and space exploration.

Responding to the Selection

What did reading "The Size of Things" make you think about your size as a human being? In what ways are human beings simultaneously incredibly large and incredibly small? How did learning the facts presented about the size of objects in the universe make you feel?

Reviewing the Selection

Recalling and Interpreting

1. **R** According to the author, how big is an electron?
   I Why were scientists originally doubtful that such a particle existed?
2. **R** What particles make up the atom? What did people originally think atoms were like?
   I In what ways do atoms differ from early scientists' expectations? Why does a solid object offer resistance to another solid object?
3. **R** How large are the planets of the solar system in relation to the size of the sun?
   I Why does the author compare the solar system to the atom?
4. **R** How large is the visible universe as viewed from Earth through a 200-inch telescope?
   I What are the limitations of this estimate of the size of the universe?

Synthesizing

5. Why does the final line referring to "the void of space" seem like an appropriate description of the universe? In what ways are voids a part of both the smallest and the largest elements of the universe? What is your reaction to this idea of a void?

Understanding Literature (Questions for Discussion)

1. **Analogy.** An **analogy** is a comparison of things that are alike in some ways but different in others. What analogy is used to describe the size of an electron? the size of a typical atom? the size of the nucleus of an atom? the size of the sun and the planets, and the distance between them? Why do you think the author uses so many analogies?
2. **Anecdote.** An **anecdote** is a brief story, usually told to make a point. This essay begins with an anecdote. Why do you think the author chose to begin his essay with this particular anecdote?

RESPONDING TO THE SELECTION

Students might wish to talk about why thinking of such incredibly large and incredibly small things is difficult.

ANSWERS FOR REVIEWING THE SELECTION

RECALLING AND INTERPRETING

1. **Recalling.** An electron is one 10-trillionth of an inch in diameter, or relative to a dust speck as a dust speck is to the Earth. **Interpreting.** Scientists were doubtful that electrons existed because they could not see them or feel them.

2. **Recalling.** The electron, proton, and neutron make up the atom. Scientists originally believed that atoms were solid and hard. **Interpreting.** In contrast to earlier theories, scientists now believe the atom to be an almost completely hollow particle with a very small nucleus and a shell of electrons. The solid object offers resistance to another solid object because the two surfaces of the objects are electrically repelled from each other.

3. **Recalling.** All the planets are dwarfed by the sun, which weighs 700 times the weight of all the planets combined. **Interpreting.** The author compares the solar system to the atom because both contain particles that orbit around a central body, and great amounts of void.

4. **Recalling.** Through a 200-inch telescope, at least 100 billion other galaxies can be seen, each comparable to the size of our own. The average distance between these galaxies is one million light years. **Interpreting.** One limitation of this estimate is that since we can only see so far with today's telescopes, there is no way of telling how large the universe actually is.

SYNTHESIZING

Responses will vary. Possible responses are given.

5. The final line seems like an appropriate description because such great distances lie between stars and galaxies—the amount of matter in the universe is very small compared to the void that surrounds it. Voids are part of the picture we have of the universe and part of the picture we have of the inside of an atom.

ANSWERS FOR UNDERSTANDING LITERATURE

Responses will vary. Possible responses are given.

1. **Analogy.** The size of the electron is said to be to a speck of dust what a speck of dust is to the Earth; the size of the atom is said to be a grain of sand on a table 2000 miles long; the nucleus of the atom is said to be like a ping-pong ball placed in the middle of the Astrodome; the sun is described as an orange with the planets described as grains of sand and cherry pits circling the orange. The author uses many analogies to make the concepts he is talking about more understandable.

2. **Anecdote.** The author probably uses this anecdote to show that most people, even United States senators, are perplexed by the concepts discussed in the selection.

PROJECT NOTE

- Suggest to students that there are many interesting people in your school and community who would make fascinating subjects for slideshows.
- If they plan to interview the subjects of their slideshows, review the interviewing tips in the Language Arts Survey, 1.13, "Gathering Ideas."
- If students create slideshows about a person in the school or community, encourage them to invite the subjects to view the presentation.

Unit Project

PRESENTING A SLIDESHOW BIOGRAPHY

You may have heard the popular saying, "A picture is worth a thousand words." This idea prompts people to bring pictures and slideshows into meetings and presentations. When you are trying to share information or make an important point, a combination of words and pictures can be powerful. A slideshow is a series of images meant to emphasize important information. Slides, which are photographic transparencies shown with a special projector, are used to enrich a presentation or report.

TRY IT YOURSELF

Working with a partner, create a ten- to fifteen-minute "slideshow" biography. Using sketches, drawings, or photographs as your slides, present information about your subject. Present scenes and facts from the life of a friend, relative, historical figure, or celebrity.

STUDENT MODEL

Mario and Hannah are planning a slideshow biography for class. Through pictures, they will show the life of Ms. Rose Jordan, a favorite teacher who is retiring at the end of the school year. They choose her because most of their classmates know her and like her, and because they want to make sure she is remembered.

The two students interview Ms. Jordan one day after school. She tells them where she was born, what she studied in college, and about different jobs that she worked so that she could pay for college. She also tells them about some of her best moments as a teacher and a volunteer in the community. After the interview, Mario and Hannah organize their information on a sheet of paper. Then they find some large sheets of plain white paper and make a series of boxes on each page. Beside each box, they draw four or five lines. The pieces of paper will serve as their master plan for the slideshow. They will make rough sketches of the "slides" in the boxes, and they will describe each image in the lines drawn beside it. Most of the final "slides" will be drawings that Mario and Hannah create themselves and then mount on cardboard. Ms. Jordan does provide them with some photos, which they will also mount on cardboard.

Both Mario and Hannah work to turn their rough sketches into final "slides." Their opening image is a photograph of Ms. Jordan. They also use a photograph of the farmhouse where she lived as a child and a photograph of the first class she ever taught. Mario and Hannah include drawings of Ms. Jordan sitting at a desk studying and of her helping a child at one of her many volunteer jobs. They clip pictures of busy restaurants from magazines to show how hard she worked as a waitress to pay for college. Mario and Hannah create many interesting and original images. For each "slide," they also write notes on an index card.

Before giving the presentation, they number their images and their index cards and put them in order. They rehearse and time their slideshow, taking turns reading the index cards. When one person reads, the other holds up the slides. They give their presentation to their class and to Ms. Jordan's class, and they feel proud of their work when they see how honored Ms. Jordan feels.

Examining the Model

1. What did Mario and Hannah do to gather information for their report?
2. What steps did they take to organize their information and plan their slides?
3. What materials did they use to create slides?

Planning and Writing Your Slideshow

1. Get together with your partner and discuss possible subjects for your slide show. Choose a subject that interests you both. Write down your ideas.
2. Go to the library and collect some information about the person you chose. If you know your subject, try to arrange an interview with him or her. Write down important information.
3. Decide what you want to say in your slideshow. You will not have time to mention everything about a particular person. You can choose to present a general overview of a person's life, or you can choose to present a more detailed look at one event or period in a person's life.
4. Gather together your notes. Decide how you want to arrange your ideas. For biographies, information is usually arranged in chronological order. This means that events are arranged in order of the time when they happened.
5. To match the spoken part of your slideshow with the visual part, draw boxes with lines next to them on a blank sheet of paper. The blank boxes represent your slides. Make rough sketches in the boxes. Write information about each rough sketch on the lines beside it.

Making and Presenting Your Slideshow

1. Look over your sketches. Then create final drawings on sheets of paper. The drawings will be your slides, and you will hold them up as you talk about your subject. If you know your subject, he or she might provide you with photographs. If your subject is a historical figure or celebrity, you can look in magazines, newspapers, or books for photos to display during your show.
2. Take the information you wrote for each slide and rewrite it on an index card. Make one card for each slide and number the cards and slides. You and your partner should take turns reading the information from the cards during the show.
3. Present your slideshow to your teacher and your classmates. You might also invite other people in the school to the show. If you feel comfortable doing so, invite people to ask questions and to take closer looks at your slides when you have finished.

Answers for Examining the Model

1. Mario and Hannah interviewed Ms. Jordan.
2. They created a master plan on large sheets of paper. They made rough sketches of the slides in the order that they would appear and then they described the images.
3. They used some photographs borrowed from Ms. Jordan, pictures they drew, and pictures they cut from magazines. They mounted the "slides" on cardboard.

ANALYTIC SCALE FOR PROJECT

Assign a score from 1 to 25 for each grading criterion below.

Slideshow Biography

- **Organization.** The group set attainable goals and created a schedule or strategy for achieving those goals.
- **Cooperation.** The group assigned tasks fairly to each member, and each member cooperated toward achieving the group's goals.
- **Goal Achievement.** The group worked steadily toward its goals and did, in fact, achieve them.
- **Presentation.** The group presented a product of high quality that met the initial project description.

VOCABULARY CHECK TEST

Ask students to number their papers from one to ten. Have students complete each sentence with a word from the Vocabulary for the Unit in the Unit Review.

1. There was a new surprise waiting around every corner in the tortuous road.
2. Jasper lost his composure and broke down weeping at the ceremony.
3. Helen has a horseshoe over her door to ward off bad luck.
4. Natasha badgered Boris until he gave in to her pleas.
5. Uri pays attention to the big picture, but he often loses sight of minute details.
6. The door creaked open eerily as we approached.
7. Ned was fascinated by the lurid drawing on the cover of the book.
8. Pablo negotiated the difficult path with ease.
9. The antique vase was appraised at a much lower price than Vance expected.
10. There was a great chance that Imelda would slip and fall from her precarious footing.

Unit Review

SUMMARY

LITERARY TERMS FOR THE UNIT

analogy, 569
anecdote, 569
autobiography, 540
biography, 551
figurative language, 561
irony of situation, 561
stereotype, 551
theme, 540

VOCABULARY FOR THE UNIT

abyss, 537
adjacent, 547
aesthetic, 559
apparition, 559
appraise, 532
badger, 548
barrage, 548
billow, 558
bleak, 555
bravado, 533
buoyant, 538
composure, 535
conclusively, 563
conviction, 564
crude, 537
deduce, 564
dialect, 547
diffidence, 546
diffuse, 565
divert, 555
eerily, 558
endeavor, 537
exert, 534
ford, 539
fugitive, 550
grade, 531
hurtle, 535
hysteria, 549
inadequacy, 535
indictment, 556
inexorable, 557
laterally, 536
luminous, 567
lurid, 546
malice, 532
minute, 564
negotiate, 538
pantomime, 549
patronize, 549
peril, 558
perplex, 563
phenomenon, 556
phonetically, 548
posterity, 547
precarious, 531
proverbial, 558
reason, 545
rendezvous, 557
respite, 537
scarcely, 567
skeletal, 547
specimen, 550
spectral, 559
speculative, 558
subsequent, 547
subtle, 548
suppress, 546
tentative, 548
tortuous, 532
translucent, 559
treacherous, 536
unprecedented, 556
unwonted, 546
ward, 539

QUESTIONS FOR WRITING, DISCUSSION, AND RESEARCH

1. Define the following types of nonfiction: autobiography, biography, and essay. Describe the essential features of each with reference to selections in this unit.
2. Find examples of analogies and anecdotes used in the selections in this unit. What are the authors' purposes for including these analogies and anecdotes?

For Your Reading List

Elizabeth Vogtsberger
Bowling Green Junior High
Bowling Green, Ohio

I Know Why the Caged Bird Sings
by Maya Angelou

I Know Why the Caged Bird Sings by Maya Angelou is the story of her life as an African-American girl struggling to find her place amidst the segregation of the United States in the early 1940s. It tells of her experiences as a young girl with discrimination in Stamps, Arkansas and of her life in St. Louis where she was abused by her mother's boyfriend. Within the pages of this book, the author involves the reader with her family, friends and foes. Her brother Bailey, her Uncle Willie, her mother, her father, and her quick-thinking grandmother, Momma, are the foundations upon which she grows.

The style in which Maya Angelou narrates her life and describes her trials and tribulations moved me. This book helped me understand segregation and the power of the human spirit. Maya Angelou exposes her readers to the challenge of life and the discovery of its meaning. I hope *I Know Why the Caged Bird Sings* will move you as well.

Spelling Check Test

Ask students to number their papers from one to ten. Read each word aloud. Then read aloud the sentence containing the word. Repeat the word. Ask students to write the word on their papers, spelling it correctly.

bleak

1. Our future will be bleak if we do stop harmful trends now.

divert

2. We must divert the coming apocalypse.

scarcely

3. Antonio could scarcely see the tiny pinpoint of light in the distance.

luminous

4. His new watch has a luminous face that makes it easy to read at night.

unwonted

5. Because there were unwonted security measures in town, Georgina assumed that someone very important must be arriving.

diffidence

6. Lionel spoke with diffidence about how difficult the first few weeks were in his new school.

suppressing

7. The lawyer suggested that the witness may have been suppressing her memories of the day in question.

lurid

8. His parents told him that they did not want him reading such lurid comic books.

tortuous

9. The driver had difficulty navigating the bus along the tortuous mountain road.

appraise

10. I asked the jeweler to appraise my mother's ring.

GOALS/OBJECTIVES

Studying this unit will enable students to

- enjoy a classic science fiction novel
- understand the defining characteristics of science fiction, including its role in presenting critiques of the present and predictions or warnings about the future
- define and give examples of science fiction, subplot, allusion, and theme
- recognize and correct errors in pronoun usage
- use knowledge of the meanings of suffixes to determine the meanings of unfamiliar words
- use both general and specific encyclopedias for research
- apply interpersonal communication skills to speaking on the telephone and to holding conversations
- write a character sketch
- participate effectively in a debate

ADDITIONAL UNIT MATERIALS IN THE ASSESSMENT PORTFOLIO

- Vocabulary Worksheet 0.0.0
- Unit Test 0.0.0

See also the Additional Resources Box in the marginal notes accompanying each selection.

CROSS-CURRICULAR CONNECTIONS

- Science, 576
- Social Studies, 576

UNIT 12 THE NOVEL

Illustration by Rick Hudson

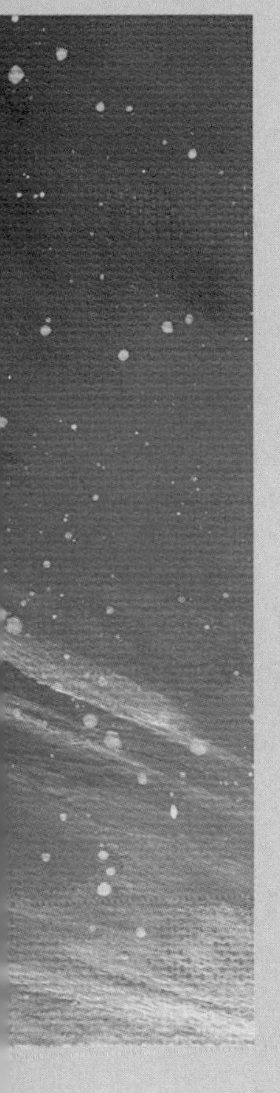

uman history becomes more and more a race between education and catastrophe.

—H. G. Wells

575

UNIT SKILLS OUTLINE

Literary Skills and Concepts

- Allusion, 660
- Science fiction, 659, 713
- Subplot, 660
- Theme, 660, 713

Other Language Arts Skills and Concepts

- Interpersonal Communication, 685
- Using Encyclopedias, 661
- Using Pronouns, 593
- Using Suffixes, 615
- Writing a Characer Sketch, 714

Art Note

The illustrations accompanying this novel were commissioned especially for this text. The opening illustrations shows one of H. G. Wells's Martian cylinders hurtling through space.

Biographical Note

More than most people, Wells understood the importance of education. He rose to great fame as a novelist and historian and even contributed to the founding of the United Nations, all on the strength of an intense program of self education that he undertook. That knowledge and learning can save us from catastrophe is a common theme in Wells's work.

GOALS/OBJECTIVES

Studying this lesson will enable students to

- enjoy the opening of one of the world's most popular works of science fiction
- learn basic facts about the planet Mars and relate these to a science fiction story
- describe a famous incident of mass hysteria from American history
- identify and correct common errors in pronoun usage

ADDITIONAL RESOURCES

READER'S GUIDE

- Selection Worksheet, 8.12

ASSESSMENT PORTFOLIO

- Selection Check Test, 2.12.1
- Selection Test, 2.12.2

PRONUNCIATION EXERCISE

- Grade 8 Audiocassette, Side B, Track 59

CROSS-CURRICULAR CONNECTIONS

SCIENCE

Choose a student to do a schematic drawing of our solar system on the chalkboard. Label the planets on this drawing. Discuss what students know about Mars, including the information provided on the prereading page. For extra credit, a student might go to the library and find a map of the Martian surface to share with the rest of the class.

SOCIAL STUDIES

Just for fun, you might choose to have students create their own radio dramatization based on the idea of an alien invasion.

Prereading

NOVEL

The War of the Worlds

by H. G. Wells

Cross-curricular Connections

Science. In H. G. Wells's pioneering science fiction novel *The War of the Worlds,* the Earth is attacked by invaders from Mars, a red planet named after the god of war whom the ancient Greeks called Ares, and the Romans, Mars. The fourth planet from the sun, Mars lies between the Earth and the giant planet Jupiter. It orbits the Sun at an average distance of 141 million miles. Because it lies about 48 million miles further away from the Sun than does the Earth, Mars is extremely cold. Even at midday, the average temperature does not rise above freezing, although temperatures at the equator at midsummer can rise as high as 60° Fahrenheit. About half the size of the Earth and twice the size of the Moon, Mars has two small, dark satellites of its own, Phobos and Deimos. In Greek mythology, these were sons of Ares whose names mean "fear" and "panic," respectively.

In 1877, the Italian astronomer Giovanni Schiaparelli made drawings of Mars based on telescopic observations. His drawings showed grooves that he called *caneli,* Italian for "channels." Members of the press and some other astronomers interpreted this word as a reference to canals. Canals are artificially constructed waterways used for transporting goods and people by boat and barge. The American astronomer Percival Lowell, founder of the Lowell Observatory in Arizona, became convinced that Mars was covered by canals made by intelligent creatures. In books such as *Mars* (1895), *Mars and Its Canals* (1906), and *Mars as an Abode of Life* (1909), Lowell described a dying planet, becoming increasingly colder, populated by advanced life forms that had built canals to irrigate frosty deserts. These ideas provided the background for H. G. Wells's extraordinary novel, which itself gave birth to the modern era of science fiction stories about visitations from outer space.

Social Studies. Orson Welles, a famous American actor, director, and writer, made history one night with his radio dramatization of *The War of the Worlds.* On October 30, 1938, Welles narrated a radio version of *The War of the Worlds* using the format of a pretend news broadcast. He announced an attack on New Jersey by aliens from Mars. Listeners, not realizing that the broadcast was fiction, went into panic. This particular show is most likely the most famous single radio show ever performed.

As You Read

The events of this novel begin with the launching from Mars, on August 12, 1894, of a mass of flaming gas. On the following evening, the narrator joins an astronomer named Ogilvy and watches another such event through a telescope. As you read, make a calendar of the events that take place. On your calendar, mark the dates and the major events that occur.

AS YOU READ

Students can do this activity simply by recording in a journal every reference to dates or number of days that appears in the novel. They can then use the information they have gathered to create a calendar of the novel's events. Explain that creating such a calendar is one way in which a novelist can plan what he or she wants to have happen in a work of fiction. The first few events to be included on such a calendar are as follows: August 12—mass of flaming gas released from Mars; August 13—narrator observes Mars with the astronomer Ogilvy; August 14–22—eight more cylinders released from Mars.

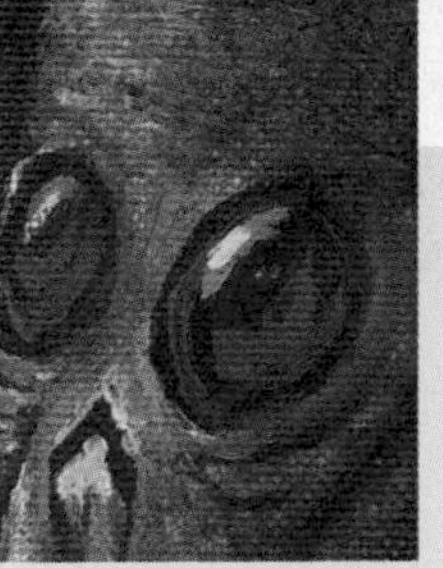

READER'S JOURNAL

Suppose that radio astronomers on Earth received a message from outer space—a series of mathematical equations, for example—that proved the existence of other intelligent creatures in the universe. How do you think people would react to this news? How would you react? Write about these questions in your journal.

The War of the Worlds

H. G. Wells

Book One: The Coming of the Martians

1 The Eve of the War

No one would have believed in the last years of the nineteenth century that this world was being watched keenly and closely by intelligences greater than man's and yet as mortal as his own; that as men busied themselves about their various concerns they were scrutinized and studied, perhaps almost as narrowly as a man with a microscope might scrutinize the transient creatures that swarm and multiply in a drop of water. With infinite complacency men went to and fro over this globe about their little affairs, serene in their assurance of their empire over matter. It is possible that the infusoria[1] under the microscope do the same. No one gave a thought to the older worlds of space as sources of human danger, or thought of them only to dismiss the idea of life upon them as impossible or improbable. It is curious to recall some of the mental habits of those departed days. At most, terrestrial men fancied there might be other men upon Mars, perhaps inferior to themselves and ready to welcome a missionary enterprise. Yet across the gulf of space, minds that are to our minds as ours are to those of the beasts that perish, intellects vast and cool and unsympathetic, regarded this Earth with envious eyes, and slowly and surely drew their plans against us. And early in the twentieth century came the great disillusionment.

❶ *Who is watching the Earth? To what are humans compared?*

The planet Mars, I scarcely need remind the reader, revolves about the sun at a mean distance of 140,000,000 miles, and the light and heat it receives from the sun is barely half of that received by this world. It must be, if the nebular hypothesis[2] has any truth, older than our world; and long before this Earth ceased to be

Chapter 1

1. **infusoria.** Microscopic animals
2. **nebular hypothesis.** Theory that says the solar system was once a nebula, or loose cloud of gas and dust, that condensed to form the sun and planets, sequentially, from the sun outward

Words for Everyday Use

scru • ti • nize (skrōōt´'n īz´) *v.*, look at very carefully; examine closely
tran • si • ent (tran´zē ənt) *adj.*, fleeting
com • pla • cen • cy (kəm plā´sən sē) *n.*, quiet satisfaction, often self-satisfaction or smugness
se • rene (sə rēn´) *adj.*, calm; peaceful
as • sur • ance (ə shoor´əns) *n.*, confidence
ter • res • tri • al (tə res´trē əl) *adj.*, of the earth

READER'S JOURNAL

As an alternative activity, you might ask students to list descriptions of space aliens from books, movies, and television programs. They can then share these in class and discuss the various shapes that the human imagination has taken with regard to this subject.

Answer to Guided Reading Question

❶ Intelligences greater than humankind's are watching the Earth. Humans are compared to creatures watched under a microscope.

SPELLING AND VOCABULARY WORDS FROM THE SELECTION

accost	incrustation
adjacent	inevitable
animated	insensible
aperture	intermittent
ascribe	intimation
assurance	irresolute
audible	jubilant
billowy	molten
calamity	multitude
cavity	pallid
circumference	palpitate
complacency	petrify
concussion	populous
consolation	projectile
contemplate	recede
deliberation	renew
derelict	rouse
derive	scoff
diameter	scrutinize
drone	scrutiny
dun	serene
eloquent	stupefy
embed	superficial
evident	tedious
excavation	terrestrial
fertility	tranquil
fluctuate	transient
impediment	transverse
impinge	tumult
impulse	unanimity
inanimate	undulate
inarticulate	velocity
incandescent	verge
incessant	vigil

Vocabulary in Context

- Scrutinize your papers carefully to find any spelling or punctuation errors.
- Joan's sickness was transient; after a few days, she felt much better.
- Hilbert's complacency kept him from doing anything to improve himself.
- Ms. Santori's serene expression made everyone else feel equally calm and peaceful.
- You have my assurance that the gymnasium will be cleaned up after the concert.
- Not all objects on Earth are terrestrial; for example, meteorites come from outer space.

ANSWER TO GUIDED READING QUESTION

1 Mars is cooling, its air is thin, and its oceans have shrunk. Earth is attractive because of its warmth, vegetation, water, and atmosphere.

molten, life upon its surface must have begun its course. The fact that it is scarcely one-seventh of the volume of the Earth must have accelerated its cooling to the temperature at which life could begin. It has air and water and all that is necessary for the support of animated existence.

Yet so vain is man and so blinded by his vanity, that no writer, up to the very end of the nineteenth century, expressed any idea that intelligent life might have developed there far, or indeed at all, beyond its earthly level. Nor was it generally understood that since Mars is older than our Earth, with scarcely a quarter of the superficial area and remoter from the sun, it necessarily follows that it is not only more distant from life's beginning but nearer its end.

The secular[3] cooling that must some day overtake our planet has already gone far indeed with our neighbor. Its physical condition is still largely a mystery, but we know now that even in its equatorial region[4] the mid-day temperature barely approaches that of our coldest winter. Its air is much more attenuated[5] than ours, its oceans have shrunk until they cover but a third of its surface, and as its slow seasons change huge snow caps gather and melt about either pole and periodically inundate[6] its temperate zones.[7] That last stage of exhaustion, which to us is still incredibly remote, has become a present-day problem for the inhabitants of Mars. The immediate pressure of necessity has brightened their intellects, enlarged their powers, and hardened their hearts. And looking across space with instruments and intelligences such as we have scarcely dreamed of, they see, at its nearest distance only 35,000,000 of miles sunward of them, a morning star of hope, our own warmer planet, green with vegetation and gray with water, with a cloudy atmosphere eloquent of fertility with glimpses through its drifting cloud-wisps of broad stretches of populous country and narrow, navy-crowded seas.

1 What has happened to Mars? Why do the Martians see the Earth as "a morning star of hope"?

And we men, the creatures who inhabit this Earth, must be to them at least as alien and lowly as are the monkeys and lemurs[8] to us. The intellectual side of man already admits that life is an incessant struggle for existence, and it would seem that this too is the belief of the minds upon Mars. Their world is far gone in its cooling and this world is still crowded with life, but crowded only with what they regard as inferior animals. To carry warfare sunward is, indeed, their only escape from the destruction that generation after generation creeps upon them.

And before we judge of them too harshly we must remember what ruthless and utter destruction our own species has wrought not only upon animals, such as the vanished bison and the dodo, but upon our own kind. The Tasmanians, for example, were entirely swept out of existence in a war of extermination waged by European immigrants, in the space of fifty years. Are we such apostles[9] of mercy as to complain if the Martians warred in the same spirit?

The Martians seem to have calculated their descent with amazing subtlety—their mathematical learning is evidently

3. **secular.** Continuing for a long time from age to age
4. **equatorial region.** Area surrounding the equator, or imaginary circle around the middle of a given planet
5. **attenuated.** Diluted or thinned
6. **inundate.** Engulf with a flood
7. **temperate zone.** Area between the polar caps and equatorial regions characterized by moderate climate
8. **lemurs.** Monkey-like animals
9. **apostles.** Persons sent on a special mission

WORDS FOR EVERYDAY USE

mol • ten (mōl´tən) *adj.*, melted or liquefied by heat
an • i • mat • ed (an´i māt´id) *adj.*, living
su • per • fi • cial (so͞o´pər fish´əl) *adj.*, of or being on the surface
el • o • quent (el´ə kwənt) *adj.*, expressive
fer • til • i • ty (fər til´ə tē) *n.*, state of being rich in resources or fruitful
pop • u • lous (päp´yo͞o ləs) *adj.*, full of people
in • ces • sant (in ses´ənt) *adj.*, constant

VOCABULARY IN CONTEXT

- Hot, molten lava flowed out of the crater at the top of the volcano.
- The characters in the animated film were so well drawn that they looked almost real.
- The child suffered a superficial scrape on his knee when he fell off his bicycle.
- The Reverend Martin Luther King, Jr., was one of the most eloquent speakers in American history.
- Because of its great fertility, the American prairie is known as the "breadbasket of the world."
- China is the most populous nation on the planet.
- The incessant yelling of the crowd in the stadium hurt my ears.

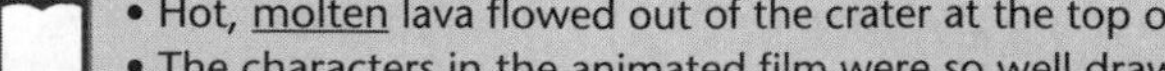

far in excess of ours—and to have carried out their preparations with a well-nigh perfect unanimity. Had our instruments permitted it, we might have seen the gathering trouble far back in the nineteenth century. Men like Schiaparelli[10] watched the red planet—it is odd, by-the-bye, that for countless centuries Mars has been the star of war—but failed to interpret the fluctuating appearances of the markings they mapped so well. All that time the Martians must have been getting ready.

During the opposition[11] of 1894 a great light was seen on the illuminated part of the disc, first at the Lick Observatory, then by Perrotin of Nice, and then by other observers. English readers heard of it first in the issue of *Nature* dated August 2nd. I am inclined to think that this blaze may have been the casting of the huge gun, in the vast pit sunk into their planet, from which their shots were fired at us. Peculiar markings, as yet unexplained, were seen near the site of that outbreak during the next two oppositions.

The storm burst upon us six years ago now. As Mars approached opposition, Lavelle of Java set the wires of the astronomical exchange palpitating with the amazing intelligence of a huge outbreak of incandescent gas upon the planet. It had occurred toward midnight of the 12th; and the spectroscope,[12] to which he had at once resorted, indicated a mass of flaming gas, chiefly hydrogen, moving with an enormous velocity toward this Earth. This jet of fire had become invisible about a quarter past twelve. He compared it to a colossal puff of flame suddenly and violently squirted out of the planet, "as flaming gases rushed out of a gun."

A singularly appropriate phrase it proved. Yet the next day there was nothing

of this in the papers except a little note in the *Daily Telegraph*, and the world went in ignorance of one of the gravest dangers that ever threatened the human race. I might not have heard of the eruption at all had I not met Ogilvy, the well-known astronomer, at Ottershaw. He was immensely excited at the news, and in the excess of his feelings invited me up to take a turn with him that night in a scrutiny of the red planet.

In spite of all that has happened since, I still remember that vigil very distinctly: the black and silent observatory, the shadowed lantern throwing a feeble glow upon

❶ *What is observed on Mars? What is the narrator's theory about this observation?*

❷ *About what is Ogilvy excited?*

s10. **Schiaparelli.** Giovanni Virginio Schiaparelli (1835–1910), astronomer

11. **opposition.** Circumstance in which two celestial bodies appear in opposite directions of the sky

12. **spectroscope.** Instrument used for forming and studying a spectrum, a series of colored bands arranged in the order of their respective wavelengths

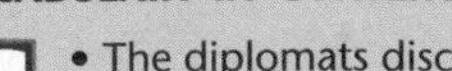

WORDS FOR EVERYDAY USE

u • na • nim • i • ty (yo͞o´nə nim´ə tē) *n.*, state of complete agreement

fluc • tu • ate (fluk´cho͞o āt´) *v.*, be continually changing or varying in an irregular way

pal • pi • tate (pal´pə tāt) *v.*, quiver; tremble; throb

in • can • des • cent (in´kən des´ənt) *adj.*, very bright; shining brilliantly

ve • loc • i • ty (və läs´ə tē) *n.*, speed

scru • ti • ny (skro͞ot´'n ē) *n.*, close examination

vig • il (vij´əl) *n.*, period of watchfulness

ANSWERS TO GUIDED READING QUESTIONS

❶ A blaze is observed on Mars. The narrator's theory is that the blaze might have been the casting of a huge gun.

❷ Ogilvy is excited about an eruption of flaming gas observed rushing from Mars toward Earth.

VOCABULARY IN CONTEXT

- The diplomats discussed the terms of the treaty until they reached complete agreement, or unanimity.
- Prices of stocks fluctuate, or move up and down, daily.
- If your heart starts to palpitate when you run, you should stop.
- Thomas Edison invented the first workable incandescent light bulb.
- The American tourists were impressed by the great velocity of the Japanese bullet train.
- The loving father kept a close vigil by his sick child's bed throughout the night.

ANSWERS TO GUIDED READING QUESTIONS

❶ Ogilvy is doubtful that Mars has inhabitants who are signaling the Earth.

❷ The narrator sees another jetting of gas from the planet.

the floor in the corner, the steady ticking of the clockwork of the telescope, the little slit in the roof—an oblong profundity[13] with the star-dust streaked across it. Ogilvy moved about, invisible but audible. Looking through the telescope, one saw a circle of deep blue and the little round planet swimming in the field. It seemed such a little thing, so bright and small and still, faintly marked with transverse stripes, and slightly flattened from the perfect round. But so little it was, so silvery warm—a pin's-head of light! It was as if it quivered, but really this was the telescope vibrating with the activity of the clockwork that kept the planet in view.

As I watched, the planet seemed to grow larger and smaller and to advance and recede, but that was simply that my eye was tired. Forty millions of miles it was from us—more than forty millions of miles of void. Few people realize the immensity of vacancy in which the dust of the material universe swims.

About what is Ogilvy doubtful? ❶

Near it in the field, I remember, were three faint points of light, three telescopic stars infinitely remote, and all around it was the unfathomable darkness of empty space. You know how that blackness looks on a frosty starlight night. In a telescope it seems far profounder. And invisible to me because it was so remote and small, flying swiftly and steadily toward me across that incredible distance, drawing nearer every minute by so many thousands of miles, came the Thing they were sending us, the Thing that was to bring so much struggle and calamity and death to the Earth. I never dreamed of it then as I watched; no one on Earth dreamed of that unerring missile.

What does the narrator see through the telescope? ❷

That night, too, there was another jetting out of gas from the distant planet. I saw it. A reddish flash at the edge, the slightest projection of the outline just as the chronometer[14] struck midnight; and at that I told Ogilvy and he took my place. The night was warm and I was thirsty, and I went, stretching my legs clumsily and feeling my way in the darkness, to the little table where the siphon[15] stood, while Ogilvy exclaimed at the streamer of gas that came out toward us.

That night another invisible missile started on its way to the Earth from Mars, just a second or so under twenty-four hours after the first one. I remember how I sat on the table there in the blackness, with patches of green and crimson swimming before my eyes, little suspecting the meaning of the minute gleam I had seen and all that it would presently bring me. Ogilvy watched till one, and then gave it up; and we lit the lantern and walked over to his house. Down below in the darkness were Ottershaw and Chertsey and all their hundreds of people, sleeping in peace.

He was full of speculation that night about the condition of Mars, and scoffed at the vulgar idea of its having inhabitants who were signaling us. His idea was that meteorites might be falling in a heavy shower upon the planet, or that a huge volcanic explosion was in progress. He pointed out to me how unlikely it was that organic evolution had taken the same direction in the two adjacent planets.

"The chances against anything man-like on Mars are a million to one," he said.

Hundreds of observers saw the flame that night and the night after, about midnight, and again the night after; and so for ten nights, a flame each night. Why the

13. **profundity.** Great depth
14. **chronometer.** Highly accurate clock
15. **siphon.** Soda siphon; bottle of carbonated water

WORDS FOR EVERYDAY USE

au • di • ble (ô´də bəl) *adj.,* that can be heard
trans • verse (trans vʉrs´) *adj.,* lying across
re • cede (ri sēd´) *v.,* go or move back; withdraw
ca • lam • i • ty (kə lam´ə tē) *n.,* deep trouble or misery
scoff (skôf) *v.,* show or express mocking contempt or ridicule
ad • ja • cent (ə jā´sənt) *adj.,* near or close

VOCABULARY IN CONTEXT

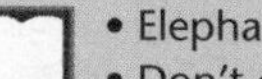

- Elephants communicate with sounds that are so low that they are not audible by humans.
- Don't go around the gym floor; a transverse course is quicker.
- The tide will recede at midday; at that time, we'll go look for starfish.
- The automobile accident on Route 128 was a terrible calamity.
- Most people scoff at stories about flying saucers.
- At night Philip could sometimes hear the radio of the person living in the adjacent apartment.

shots ceased after the tenth no one on Earth has attempted to explain. It may be the gases of the firing caused the Martians inconvenience. Dense clouds of smoke or dust, visible through a powerful telescope on Earth as little gray, fluctuating patches, spread through the clearness of the planet's atmosphere and obscured its more familiar features.

Even the daily papers woke up to the disturbances at last, and popular notes appeared here, there, and everywhere concerning the volcanoes upon Mars. The serio-comic periodical *Punch*, I remember, made a happy use of it in the political cartoon. And, all unsuspected, those missiles the Martians had fired at us drew Earthward, rushing now at a pace of many miles a second through the empty gulf of space, hour by hour and day by day, nearer and nearer. It seems to me now almost incredibly wonderful that, with that swift fate hanging over us, men could go about their petty concerns as they did. I remember how jubilant Markham was at securing a new photograph of the planet for the illustrated paper he edited in those days. People in these latter times scarcely realize the abundance and enterprise of our nineteenth-century papers. For my own part, I was much occupied in learning to ride the bicycle, and busy upon a series of papers discussing the probable developments of moral ideas as civilization progressed.

One night (the first missile then could scarcely have been 10,000,000 miles away) I went for a walk with my wife. It was starlight, and I explained the Signs of the Zodiac[16] to her, and pointed out Mars, a bright dot of light creeping zenithward,[17] toward which so many telescopes were pointed. It was a warm night. Coming home, a party of excursionists from Chertsey or Isleworth passed us singing and playing music. There were lights in the upper windows of the houses as the people went to bed. From the railway station in the distance came the sound of shunting trains, ringing and rumbling, softened almost into melody by the distance. My wife pointed out to me the brightness of the red, green, and yellow signal lights hanging in a framework against the sky. It seemed so safe and tranquil.

16. **Signs of the Zodiac.** Astrological signs that are assigned to a person according to his or her birthdate

17. **zenithward.** Toward the highest point

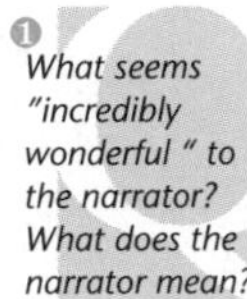

1 *What seems "incredibly wonderful" to the narrator? What does the narrator mean?*

Reviewing the Selection

Recalling and Interpreting

1. (R) What were "intelligences greater than ours" doing "in the last years of the nineteenth century"?

   (I) Why were these "intelligences" interested in Earth?

2. (R) What did Lavelle of Java observe toward midnight on August 12, 1894?

   (I) What was the real cause of the puffs of flame observed coming from Mars on ten consecutive nights?

Words for Everyday Use

ju • bi • lant (jo͞o´bə lənt) *adj.*, joyful and triumphant; rejoicing

tran • quil (tran´kwil) *adj.*, calm; peaceful

Answer to Guided Reading Question

1 It seems incredibly wonderful (in the sense of inspiring curiosity) that people should have gone about their everyday lives when a terrible fate was hanging over them. He is saying that people at the time did not realize what was in store for them.

Answers for Reviewing the Selection

RECALLING AND INTERPRETING

1. **Recalling.** They were scrutinizing the Earth. **Interpreting.** They were interested in Earth because their own planet was dying.

2. **Recalling.** He observed an outbreak of incandescent gas from the planet. **Interpreting.** The Martians are shooting projectiles, or missiles, toward the Earth.

Vocabulary in Context

- After winning the hockey tournament, the players were jubilant.
- The sea was so tranquil that the boat barely moved up or down.

Answers to Guided Reading Questions

❶ Ogilvy dimly perceives some evidence of design (of something that has been shaped, or made, by intelligent creatures).

❷ Ogilvy goes out to see what he believes will be a meteorite.

2
The Falling-Star

Then came the night of the first falling-star. It was seen early in the morning rushing over Winchester eastward, a line of flame high in the atmosphere. Hundreds must have seen it, and taken it for an ordinary falling-star. Albin described it as leaving a greenish streak behind it that glowed for some seconds. Denning, our greatest authority on meteorites, stated that the height of its first appearance was about ninety or one hundred miles. It seemed to him that it fell to Earth about one hundred miles east of him.

I was at home at that hour and writing in my study; and although my French windows face toward Ottershaw and the blind was up (for I loved in those days to look up at the night sky), I saw nothing of it. Yet this strangest of all things that ever came to Earth from outer space must have fallen while I was sitting there, visible to me had I only looked up as it passed. Some of those who saw its flight say it traveled with a hissing sound. I myself heard nothing of that. Many people in Berkshire, Surrey, and Middlesex must have seen the fall of it, and, at most, have thought that another meteorite had descended. No one seems to have troubled to look for the fallen mass that night.

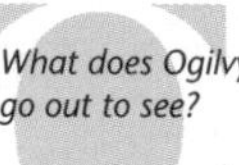

❶ *What does Ogilvy dimly perceive?*

❷ *What does Ogilvy go out to see?*

But very early in the morning poor Ogilvy, who had seen the shooting-star and who was persuaded that a meteorite lay somewhere on the common[1] between Horsell, Ottershaw, and Woking, rose early with the idea of finding it. Find it he did, soon after dawn, and not far from the sand-pits. An enormous hole had been made by the impact of the projectile, and the sand and gravel had been flung violently in every direction over the heath,[2] forming heaps visible a mile and a half away. The heather[3] was on fire eastward, and a thin blue smoke rose against the dawn.

The Thing itself lay almost entirely buried in sand, amidst the scattered splinters of a fir-tree it had shivered to fragments in its descent. The uncovered part had the appearance of a huge cylinder, caked over and its outline softened by a thick scaly dun-colored incrustation. It had a diameter of about thirty yards. He approached the mass, surprised at the size and more so at the shape, since most meteorites are rounded more or less completely. It was, however, still so hot from its flight through the air as to forbid his near approach. A stirring noise within its cylinder he ascribed to the unequal cooling of its surface; for at that time it had not occurred to him that it might be hollow.

He remained standing at the edge of the pit that the Thing had made for itself, staring at its strange appearance, astonished chiefly at its unusual shape and color, and dimly perceiving even then some evidence of design in its arrival. The early morning was wonderfully still, and the sun, just clearing the pine trees toward Weybridge, was already warm. He did not remember hearing any birds that morning, there was certainly no breeze stirring, and the only sounds were the faint movements from within the cindery cylinder. He was all alone on the common.

Chapter 2

1. **common.** Tract of land owned by no one and accessible to the public
2. **heath.** Open wasteland
3. **heather.** Low-growing plants with scalelike leaves and stalks of small purplish-pink flowers, common to the British Isles

Words for Everyday Use

pro • jec • tile (prō jek´tīl) *n.,* hurled object
dun (dun) *adj.,* dull grayish brown
in • crus • ta • tion (in´krus tā´shən) *n.,* hard coating or crust
di • am • e • ter (dī am´ət ər) *n.,* width of a circular object
as • cribe (ə skrīb´) *v.,* assign something to a supposed cause; attribute

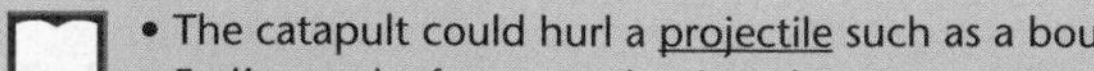

Vocabulary in Context

- The catapult could hurl a projectile such as a boulder several hundred yards.
- Earl's new loafers were dun in color.
- The workers were scraping an incrustation off the hull of the boat.
- The diameter of the basketball hoops at the circus was so small that no one could make a basket.
- Sara ascribed her exhaustion to working too many hours.

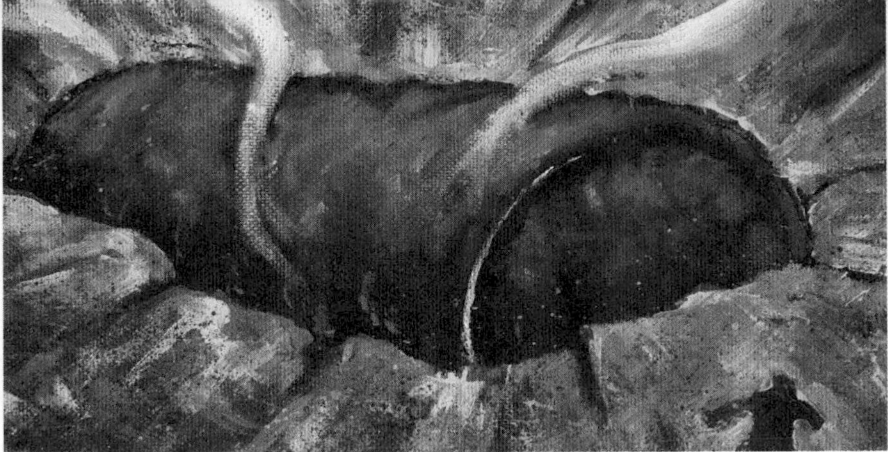

Then suddenly he noticed with a start that some of the gray clinker, the ashy incrustation that covered the meteorite, was falling off the circular edge of the end. It was dropping off in flakes and raining down upon the sand. A large piece suddenly came off and fell with a sharp noise that brought his heart into his mouth.

For a minute he scarcely realized what this meant, and, although the heat was excessive, he clambered down into the pit close to the bulk to see the Thing more clearly. He fancied even then that the cooling of the body might account for this, but what disturbed that idea was the fact that the ash was falling only from the end of the cylinder.

And then he perceived that, very slowly, the circular top of the cylinder was rotating on its body. It was such a gradual movement that he discovered it only through noticing that a black mark that had been near him five minutes ago was now at the other side of the circumference. Even then he scarcely understood what this indicated, until he heard a muffled grating sound and saw the black mark jerk forward an inch or so. Then the thing came upon him in a flash. The cylinder was artificial—hollow—with an end that screwed out! Something within the cylinder was unscrewing the top!

"Good heavens!" said Ogilvy. "There's a man in it—men in it! Half roasted to death! Trying to escape!"

At once, with a quick mental leap, he linked the Thing with the flash upon Mars.

The thought of the confined creature was so dreadful to him that he forgot the heat, and went forward to the cylinder to help turn. But luckily the dull radiation arrested him before he could burn his hands on the still glowing metal. At that he stood irresolute for a moment, then turned, scrambled out of the pit, and set off running wildly into Woking. The time then must have been somewhere about six o'clock. He met a waggoner and tried to make him understand, but the tale he told and his appearance were so wild—his hat had fallen off in the pit—that the man simply drove on. He was equally unsuccessful with the potman who was just unlocking the doors of the public-house by Horsell Bridge. The fellow thought he was a lunatic at large, and made an unsuccessful attempt to shut him into the tap-room.

❶ *How does Ogilvy feel at this point? Why?*

❷ *What thought is "dreadful" to Ogilvy? About what is he worried?*

Words for Everyday Use

cir • cum • fer • ence (sər kum´fər əns) *n.,* boundary of a circular object

ir • res • o • lute (ir rez´ ə lo͞ot´) *adj.,* wavering in purpose, decision, or opinion; indecisive

Answers to Guided Reading Questions

❶ Ogilvy is shocked because the movement indicates that there must be something alive inside the cylinder.

❷ Ogilvy is horrified at the possibility that some creature, trapped inside the cylinder, might come to harm.

Vocabulary in Context

- The circumference of a basketball is greater than that of a soccer ball.
- Andy continued to be irresolute; he couldn't decide whether he wanted to play soccer or football.

Answer to Guided Reading Question

❶ There has been no response to the rapping on the cylinder. That may be why the people have assumed that the creatures inside are dead.

Answers for Reviewing the Selection

RECALLING AND INTERPRETING

1. **Recalling.** He discovers a metal cylinder. **Interpreting.** He is surprised by its cylindrical shape and by its color.
2. **Recalling.** It moves. **Interpreting.** Ogilvy's conclusion is based on the fact that the top of the cylinder moves. This conclusion is not entirely justified, however, because the movement might be entirely mechanical.

That sobered him a little; and when he saw Henderson, the London journalist, in his garden, he called over the palings[4] and made himself understood.

"Henderson," he called, "you saw that shooting-star last night?"

"Well?" said Henderson.

"It's out on Horsell Common now."

"Good Lord!" said Henderson. "Fallen meteorite! That's good."

"But it's something more than a meteorite. It's a cylinder—an artificial cylinder, man! And there's something inside."

Henderson stood up with his spade in his hand.

"What's that?" he said. He was deaf in one ear.

Why might people think that the Martians are dead? ❶

Ogilvy told him all that he had seen. Henderson was a minute or so taking it in. Then he dropped his spade, snatched up his jacket, and came out into the road. The two men hurried back at once to the common, and found the cylinder still lying in the same position. But now the sounds inside had ceased, and a thin circle of bright metal showed between the top and the body of the cylinder. Air was either entering or escaping at the rim with a thin, sizzling sound.

They listened, rapped on the scaly burnt metal with a stick, and, meeting with no response, they both concluded the man or men inside must be insensible or dead.

Of course the two were quite unable to do anything. They shouted consolation and promises, and went off back to the town again to get help. One can imagine them, covered with sand, excited and disordered, running up the little street in the bright sunlight just as the shop folks were taking down their shutters and people were opening their bedroom windows. Henderson went into the railway station at once, in order to telegraph the news to London. The newspaper articles had prepared men's minds for the reception of the idea.

By eight o'clock a number of boys and unemployed men had already started for the common to see the "dead men from Mars." That was the form the story took. I heard of it first from my newspaper boy about a quarter to nine, when I went out to get my *Daily Chronicle.* I was naturally startled, and lost no time in going out and across the Ottershaw bridge to the sand-pits.

4. **palings.** Fence

Reviewing the Selection

Recalling and Interpreting

1. Ⓡ What does Ogilvy discover when he goes to the common between Horsell, Ottershaw, and Woking?

   Ⓘ What convinces Ogilvy that this Thing is not an ordinary meteorite?

2. Ⓡ What happens to the circular top of the Thing as Ogilvy watches it?

   Ⓘ Why might Ogilvy decide that "There's a man in it"? Is his conclusion justified? Why, or why not?

Words for Everyday Use

in • sen • si • ble (in sen´sə bəl) *adj.,* unconscious

con • so • la • tion (kän´sə lā´shən) *n.,* act of comforting or making less sad

Vocabulary in Context

- The driver of the car did not die, but he was knocked insensible when his head hit the steering wheel.
- Matthew offered his grandmother much consolation when his grandfather died.

3
On Horsell Common

I found a little crowd of perhaps twenty people surrounding the huge hole in which the cylinder lay. I have already described the appearance of that colossal bulk, embedded in the ground. The turf and gravel about it seemed charred as if by a sudden explosion. No doubt its impact had caused a flash of fire. Henderson and Ogilvy were not there. I think they perceived that nothing was to be done for the present, and had gone away to breakfast at Henderson's house.

There were four or five boys sitting on the edge of the pit, with their feet dangling, and amusing themselves—until I stopped them—by throwing stones at the giant mass. After I had spoken to them about it, they began playing at "touch" in and out of the group of bystanders.

Among these were a couple of cyclists, a jobbing gardener I employed sometimes, a girl carrying a baby, Gregg the butcher and his little boy, and two or three loafers and golf caddies who were accustomed to hang about the railway station. There was very little talking. Few of the common people in England had anything but the vaguest astronomical ideas in those days. Most of them were staring quietly at the big table-like end of the cylinder, which was still as Ogilvy and Henderson had left it. I fancy the popular expectation of a heap of charred corpses was disappointed at this inanimate bulk. Some went away while I was there, and other people came. I clambered into the pit and fancied I heard a faint movement under my feet. The top had certainly ceased to rotate.

It was only when I got thus close to it that the strangeness of this object was at all evident to me. At the first glance it was really no more exciting than an overturned carriage or a tree blown across the road. Not so much so, indeed. It looked like a rusty gas-float.[1] It required a certain amount of scientific education to perceive that the gray scale of the Thing was no common oxide, that the yellowish-white metal that gleamed in the crack between the lid and the cylinder had an unfamiliar hue. "Extraterrestrial" had no meaning for most of the onlookers.

At that time it was quite clear in my own mind that the Thing had come from the planet Mars, but I judged it improbable that it contained any living creature. I thought the unscrewing might be automatic. In spite of Ogilvy, I still believed that there were men in Mars. My mind ran fancifully on the possibilities of its containing manuscript, on the difficulties in translation that might arise, whether we should find coins and models in it, and so forth. Yet it was a little too large for assurance on this idea. I felt an impatience to see it opened. About eleven, as nothing seemed happening, I walked back, full of such thoughts, to my home in Maybury. But I found it difficult to get to work upon my abstract investigations.

In the afternoon the appearance of the common had altered very much. The early editions of the evening papers had startled London with enormous headlines:

A MESSAGE RECEIVED FROM MARS.
REMARKABLE STORY FROM WOKING,

and so forth. In addition, Ogilvy's wire to the Astronomical Exchange had roused every observatory in the three kingdoms.[2]

There were half a dozen flys[3] or more from the Woking station standing in the

❶ *What are the boys doing? Why does the narrator stop them?*

❷ *Why might the people gathered around the cylinder be disappointed?*

CHAPTER 3
1. **gas-float.** Ship used as a beacon or warning light
2. **three kingdoms.** England, Ireland, and Scotland
3. **fly.** Carriage for hire, or taxi

Words for Everyday Use

em • bed (em bed´) *v.*, set or fix firmly in a surrounding mass

in • an • i • mate (in an´ə mit) *adj.*, not moving; lifeless

ev • i • dent (ev´ə dənt) *adj.*, easy to see; obvious

rouse (rouz) *v.*, stir up; excite

Answers to Guided Reading Questions

❶ The boys are amusing themselves by throwing stones at the cylinder. The narrator probably stops them because there might be aliens inside, and if that is so, then what the boys are doing is not hospitable and could be dangerous.

❷ The narrator says that he believes the crowd to be disappointed that there are not charred alien corpses in the pit.

Vocabulary in Context

- The point of the arrow was embedded in the center of the target.
- The space probes sent to Mars did not discover life; all they found were inanimate rocks and dust.
- We were all impressed by the evident power of the rocket's engines.
- The announcer tried to rouse the expectations of the crowd by suggesting that a famous guest star would be appearing on stage before the show was over.

Answer to Guided Reading Question

❶ Previously, Ogilvy had been worried about the welfare of the creature or creatures inside the cylinder. The men are trying to excavate the cylinder, perhaps to save the creatures inside it.

road by the sand-pits, a basket-chaise from Chobham, and a rather lordly carriage. Besides that, there was quite a heap of bicycles. In addition, a large number of people must have walked, in spite of the heat of the day, from Woking and Chertsey, so that there was altogether quite a considerable crowd—one or two gaily dressed ladies among the others.

It was glaringly hot, not a cloud in the sky nor a breath of wind, and the only shadow was that of the few scattered pine trees. The burning heather had been extinguished, but the level ground toward Ottershaw was blackened as far as one could see, and still giving off vertical streamers of smoke. An enterprising sweet-stuff dealer in the Chobham Road had sent up his son with a barrow-load of green apples and ginger-beer.

What are the men trying to do? Why? ❶

Going to the edge of the pit, I found it occupied by a group of about half a dozen men—Henderson, Ogilvy, and a tall, fair-haired man that I afterwards learned was Stent, the Astronomer Royal, with several workmen wielding spades and pickaxes. Stent was giving directions in a clear, high-pitched voice. He was standing on the cylinder, which was now evidently much cooler; his face was crimson and streaming with perspiration, and something seemed to have irritated him.

A large portion of the cylinder had been uncovered, though its lower end was still embedded. As soon as Ogilvy saw me among the staring crowd on the edge of the pit he called to me to come down, and asked me if I would mind going over to see Lord Hilton, the lord of the manor.

The growing crowd, he said, was becoming a serious impediment to their excavations, especially the boys. They wanted a light railing put up, and help to keep the people back. He told me that a faint stirring was occasionally still audible within the case, but that the workmen had failed to unscrew the top, as it afforded no grip to them. The case appeared to be enormously thick, and it was possible that the faint sounds we heard represented a noisy tumult in the interior.

I was very glad to do as he asked, and so become one of the privileged spectators within the contemplated enclosure. I failed to find Lord Hilton at his house, but I was told he was expected from London by the six o'clock train from Waterloo; and as it was then about a quarter past five, I went home, had some tea, and walked up to the station to waylay him.

Reviewing the Selection

Recalling and Interpreting

1. **R** What are the boys sitting on the edge of the pit doing?

   I What reason might the narrator have for stopping the boys?

2. **R** What do Ogilvy and the other men attempt to do to the cylinder?

   I What reason do Ogilvy and the others have for their actions?

Words for Everyday Use

im • ped • i • ment (im ped´ə mənt) *n.*, something that bars or hinders a certain action, obstruction, or delay

ex • ca • va • tion (eks´kə vā´shən) *n.*, act of exposing by digging

tu • mult (to͞o´mult´) *n.*, noisy commotion; uproar

con • tem • plate (kän´təm plāt´) *v.*, have in mind as a possibility or plan

Vocabulary in Context

- The rain, the icy rocks, and the cold wind all were impediments to climbing the rest of the way up the mountain.
- Several children stood across the road, watching the excavation of a hole for the basement of the new house.
- When the Reds got a double play, a tremendous tumult arose from the crowd.
- Philosophers are people who contemplate basic questions such as "What can a person really know?"

4
The Cylinder Opens

When I returned to the common the sun was setting. Scattered groups were hurrying from the direction of Woking, and one or two persons were returning. The crowd about the pit had increased, and stood out black against the lemon-yellow of the sky—a couple of hundred people, perhaps. There were raised voices, and some sort of struggle appeared to be going on about the pit. Strange imaginings passed through my mind. As I drew nearer I heard Stent's voice:

"Keep back! Keep back!"

A boy came running toward me.

"It's a-movin'," he said to me as he passed—"a-screwin' and a-screwin' out. I don't like it. I'm a-goin' 'ome, I am."

I went on to the crowd. There were really, I should think, two or three hundred people elbowing and jostling one another, the one or two ladies there being by no means the least active.

"He's fallen in the pit!" cried someone.

"Keep back!" said several.

The crowd swayed a little, and I elbowed my way through. Everyone seemed greatly excited. I heard a peculiar humming sound from the pit.

"I say!" said Ogilvy; "help keep these idiots back. We don't know what's in the confounded thing, you know!"

I saw a young man, a shop assistant in Woking I believe he was, standing on the cylinder and trying to scramble out of the hole again. The crowd had pushed him in.

The end of the cylinder was being screwed out from within. Nearly two feet of shining screw projected. Somebody blundered against me, and I narrowly missed being pitched on to the top of the screw. I turned, and as I did so the screw must have come out, for the lid of the cylinder fell upon the gravel with a ringing concussion. I stuck my elbow into the person behind me, and turned my head toward the Thing again. For a moment that circular cavity seemed perfectly black. I had the sunset in my eyes.

I think everyone expected to see a man emerge—possibly something a little unlike us terrestrial men, but in all essentials a man. I know I did. But, looking, I presently saw something stirring within the shadow: grayish billowy movements, one above another, and then two luminous[1] discs—like eyes. Then something resembling a little gray snake, about the thickness of a walking-stick, coiled up out of the writhing[2] middle, and wriggled in the air toward me—and then another.

A sudden chill came over me. There was a loud shriek from a woman behind. I half turned, keeping my eyes fixed upon the cylinder still, from which other tentacles were now projecting, and began pushing my way back from the edge of the pit. I saw astonishment giving place to horror on the faces of the people about me. I heard inarticulate exclamations on all sides. There was a general movement backwards. I saw the shopman struggling still on the edge of the pit. I found myself alone, and saw the people on the other side of the pit running off, Stent among them. I looked again at the cylinder, and ungovernable terror gripped me. I stood petrified and staring.

A big grayish rounded bulk, the size, perhaps, of a bear, was rising slowly and painfully out of the cylinder. As it bulged

❶ *What did everyone expect?*

❷ *How do the people react to the emergence of the creature?*

❸ *What climbs out of the cylinder?*

Chapter 4

1. **luminous.** Brightly shining
2. **writhing.** Twisting; squirming

Words for Everyday Use

con • cus• sion (kən kush´ən) *n.,* violent shaking
cav • i • ty (kav´i tē) *n.,* hole or hollow place
bil • low • y (bil´ō ē) *adj.,* swelling in a large mass or surge
in • ar • tic • u • late (in´är tik´yo͞o lit) *adj.,* not able to speak understandably or coherently
pet • ri • fy (pe´tri fī´) *v.,* paralyze, stiffen as with fear

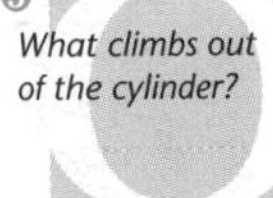

Answers to Guided Reading Questions

❶ Everyone expected to see something like a man.

❷ The people look with astonishment and then horror. They make exclamations and move backward. Some run off.

❸ A creature with a rounded, grayish bulk, roughly the size of a bear, climbs out.

Vocabulary in Context

- The concussion of the explosion of the chemistry experiment blew out three windows.
- The doll maker placed two beautiful brown eyes in the cavities of the face.
- The kite flew up so high that it seemed to touch the billowy clouds.
- Most one-year-olds are still inarticulate; by the age of three, however, most children are talking.
- The headlights of a car will petrify a deer, causing it to go rigid with fear.

up and caught the light, it glistened like wet leather.

Two large dark-colored eyes were regarding me steadfastly. The mass that framed them, the head of the thing, was rounded, and had, one might say, a face. There was a mouth under the eyes, the lipless brim of which quivered and panted, and dropped saliva. The whole creature heaved and pulsated convulsively. A lank tentacular appendage[3] gripped the edge of the cylinder, another swayed in the air.

Those who have never seen a living Martian can scarcely imagine the strange horror of its appearance. The peculiar V-shaped mouth with its pointed upper lip, the absence of brow ridges, the absence of a chin beneath the wedge-like lower lip, the incessant quivering of this mouth, the Gorgon groups of tentacles, the tumultuous breathing of the lungs in a strange atmosphere, the evident heaviness and painfulness of movement due to the greater gravitational energy of the Earth—above all, the extraordinary intensity of the immense eyes—were at once vital, intense, inhuman, crippled and monstrous. There was something fungoid in the oily brown skin, something in the clumsy deliberation of the tedious movements unspeakably nasty. Even at this first encounter, this first glimpse, I was overcome with disgust and dread.

Suddenly the monster vanished. It had toppled over the brim of the cylinder and fallen into the pit, with a thud like the fall of a great mass of leather. I heard it give a peculiar thick cry, and forthwith[4] another of these creatures appeared darkly in the deep shadow of the aperture.

3. **lank . . . appendage.** Long, slender, flexible part growing out of the main body

4. **forthwith.** Immediately; at once

Words for Everyday Use

de • lib • er • a • tion (dē lib´ər ā´shən) *n.*, slowness; carefulness
te • di • ous (tē´dē əs) *adj.*, tiresome; boring
ap • er • ture (ap´ər chər) *n.*, opening; hole; gap

Vocabulary in Context

- The tightrope walker had to move with great deliberation.
- Cleaning the hundreds of tiny blinds on the windows was a tedious job.
- The light comes into the camera through a tiny aperture.

I turned and, running madly, made for the first group of trees, perhaps a hundred yards away; but I ran slantingly and stumbling, for I could not avert my face from these things.

There, among some young pine trees and furze-bushes, I stopped, panting, and waited further developments. The common round the sand-pits was dotted with people, standing like myself in a half-fascinated terror, staring at these creatures, or rather at the heaped gravel at the edge of the pit in which they lay. And then, with a renewed horror, I saw a round, black object bobbing up and down on the edge of the pit. It was the head of the shopman who had fallen in, but showing as a little black object against the hot western sky. Now he got his shoulder and knee up, and again he seemed to slip back until only his head was visible. Suddenly he vanished, and I could have fancied a faint shriek had reached me. I had a momentary impulse to go back and help him that my fears overruled. ❶

Everything was then quite invisible, hidden by the deep pit and the heap of sand that the fall of the cylinder had made. Anyone coming along the road from Chobham or Woking would have been amazed at the sight—a dwindling multitude of perhaps a hundred people or more standing in a great irregular circle, in ditches, behind bushes, behind gates and hedges, saying little to one another and that in short, excited shouts, and staring, staring hard at a few heaps of sand. The barrow of ginger-beer stood, a queer derelict, black against the burning sky, and in the sand-pits was a row of deserted vehicles with their horses feeding out of nosebags or pawing the ground.

❶ *What do you think has happened to the shopman?*

Reviewing the Selection

Recalling and Interpreting

1. **R** What emerges from the cylinder? How does what emerges look?

   I What did you feel when you read the description of what emerges from the cylinder?

2. **R** What does the crowd do when the creatures start to appear?

   I What does the reaction of the crowd tell you about what the people are feeling?

3. **R** What happens to the shopman who fell into the pit?

   I What evidence does this chapter provide that the creatures might be dangerous?

Words for Everyday Use

re • new (ri n o͞o´) *v.*, make new or as if new again

im • pulse (im´puls´) *n.*, sudden inclination or desire to act

mul • ti • tude (mul´tə to͞od´) *n.*, large number of persons or things

der • e • lict (der´ə likt´) *n.*, property abandoned by its owner

Answer to Guided Reading Question

❶ The shopman may have been killed. What we know, for certain, is that he has vanished into the pit and has, the narrator fancies, shrieked.

Answers for Reviewing the Selection

Recalling and Interpreting

1. **Recalling.** A grayish creature about the size of a bear emerges from the cylinder. **Interpreting.** *Responses will vary.* Some readers may feel the same fears reported in the crowd.

2. **Recalling.** The crowd moves away. **Interpreting.** The crowd's reactions show fear.

3. **Recalling.** The shopman disappears, and the narrator fancies that he hears him scream. **Interpreting.** The shopman's scream indicates, perhaps, that the creatures have harmed him.

Vocabulary in Context

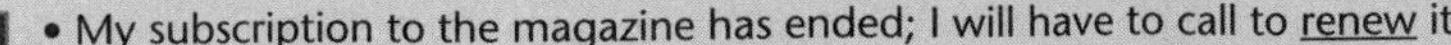

- My subscription to the magazine has ended; I will have to call to renew it.
- Please try to stifle the impulse to scream when the roller coaster enters the tunnel.
- A multitude of penguins stood around on the ice.
- An old car had been abandoned in the woods, and several animals were living in this derelict.

Answers to Guided Reading Questions

❶ The narrator is afraid of going back to the pit, but he wants to look into it.

❷ The Deputation wishes to signal that the humans gathered around are intelligent and mean no harm.

5
The Heat-Ray

After the glimpse I had had of the Martians emerging from the cylinder in which they had come to the Earth from their planet, a kind of fascination paralyzed my actions. I remained standing knee-deep in the heather, staring at the mound that hid them. I was a battle-ground of fear and curiosity.

❶ *What conflicting emotions does the narrator feel?*

I did not dare to go back toward the pit, but I felt a passionate longing to peer into it. I began walking, therefore, in a big curve, seeking some point of vantage and continually looking at the sand-heaps that hid these newcomers to our Earth. Once a leash of thin black whips, like the arms of an octopus, flashed across the sunset and was immediately withdrawn, and afterwards a thin rod rose up, joint by joint, bearing at its apex[1] a circular disc that spun with a wobbling motion. What could be going on there?

Most of the spectators had gathered in one or two groups—one a little crowd towards Woking, the other a knot of people in the direction of Chobham. Evidently they shared my mental conflict. There were few near me. One man I approached—he was, I perceived, a neighbor of mine, though I did not know his name—and accosted. But it was scarcely a time for articulate conversation.

"What ugly brutes!" he said. "Good God! What ugly brutes!" He repeated this over and over again.

"Did you see a man in the pit?" I said; but he made no answer to that. We became silent, and stood watching for a time side by side, deriving, I fancy, a certain comfort in one another's company. Then I shifted my position to a little knoll that gave me the advantage of a yard or more of elevation, and when I looked for him presently he was walking towards Woking.

The sunset faded to twilight before anything further happened. The crowd far away on the left, towards Woking, seemed to grow, and I heard now a faint murmur from it. The little knot of people towards Chobham dispersed. There was scarcely an intimation of movement from the pit.

It was this, as much as anything, that gave people courage, and I suppose the new arrivals from Woking also helped to restore confidence. At any rate, as the dusk came on a slow, intermittent movement upon the sand-pits began, a movement that seemed to gather force as the stillness of the evening about the cylinder remained unbroken. Vertical black figures in twos and threes would advance, stop, watch, and advance again, spreading out as they did so in a thin irregular crescent[2] that promised to enclose the pit in its attenuated horns. I, too, on my side began to move toward the pit.

Then I saw some cabmen and others had walked boldly into the sand-pits, and heard the clatter of hoofs and the gride of wheels. I saw a lad trundling off the barrow of apples. And then, within thirty yards of the pit, advancing from the direction of Horsell, I noted a little black knot of men, the foremost of whom was waving a white flag.

❷ *What does the Deputation mean to do?*

This was the Deputation. There had been a hasty consultation, and since the Martians were evidently, in spite of their repulsive forms, intelligent creatures, it had been resolved to show them, by approaching them with signals, that we too were intelligent.

Chapter 5

1. **apex.** Highest point; peak
2. **crescent.** Shape resembling a quarter moon, with both convex and concave edges

Words for Everyday Use

ac • cost (ə kôst´) *v.*, approach and speak to, often in an intrusive way
de • rive (dē rīv´) *v.*, get or receive
in • ti • ma • tion (in´tə mā´shən) *n.*, hint; suggestion
in • ter • mit • tent (in´tər mit´'nt) *adj.*, stopping and starting at intervals; pausing from time to time

Vocabulary in Context

- The newspaper boy would often accost people on the street, attempting to sell them his papers.
- Yolanda and I derive great enjoyment from listening to classical music.
- The walls of the room were white, with just the smallest intimation of lavender.
- From the direction of the bay, we could hear the intermittent sounds of a seagull crying.

Flutter, flutter, went the flag, first to the right, then to the left. It was too far for me to recognize anyone there, but afterwards I learned that Ogilvy, Stent, and Henderson were with others in this attempt at communication. This little group had in its advance dragged inward, so to speak, the circumference of the now almost complete circle of people, and a number of dim black figures followed it at discreet distances.

Suddenly there was a flash of light, and a quantity of luminous greenish smoke came out of the pit in three distinct puffs, which drove up, one after the other, straight into the still air.

This smoke (or flame, perhaps, would be the better word for it) was so bright that the deep blue sky overhead and the hazy stretches of brown common toward Chertsey, set with black pine trees, seemed to darken abruptly as these puffs arose, and to remain the darker after their dispersal. At the same time a faint hissing sound became audible.

Beyond the pit stood the little wedge of people with the white flag at its apex, arrested by these phenomena, a little knot of small vertical black shapes upon the black ground. As the green smoke rose, their faces flashed out pallid green, and faded again as it vanished. Then slowly the hissing passed into a humming, into a long, loud, droning noise. Slowly a humped shape rose out of the pit, and the ghost of a beam of light seemed to flicker out from it.

Forthwith flashes of actual flame, a bright glare leaping from one to another, sprang from the scattered group of men. It was as if some invisible jet impinged upon them and flashed into white flame. It was as if each man were suddenly and momentarily turned to fire.

Then, by the light of their own destruction, I saw them staggering and falling, and their supporters turning to run.

I stood staring, not as yet realizing that this was death leaping from man to man in that little distant crowd. All I felt was that it was something very strange. An almost noiseless and blinding flash of light, and a man fell headlong and lay still; and as the unseen shaft of heat passed over them, pine-trees burst into fire, and every dry furze-bush became with one dull thud a mass of flames. And far away toward Knaphill I saw the flashes of trees and hedges and wooden buildings suddenly set alight.

It was sweeping round swiftly and steadily, this flaming death, this invisible, inevitable sword of heat. I perceived it coming toward me by the flashing bushes it touched, and was too astounded and stupefied to stir. I heard the crackle of fire in the sand-pits and the sudden squeal of a horse that was as suddenly stilled. Then it was as if an invisible yet intensely heated finger were drawn through the heather between me and the Martians, and all along a curving line beyond the sand-pits the dark ground smoked and crackled. Something fell with a crash far away to the left where the road from Woking station opens out on the common. Forthwith the hissing and humming ceased, and the black, domelike object sank slowly out of sight into the pit.

All this had happened with such swiftness that I had stood motionless, dumbfounded and dazzled by the flashes of light. Had that death swept through a full circle, it must inevitably have slain me in my surprise. But it passed and spared me, and left the night about me suddenly dark and unfamiliar.

❶ *Why do the members of the Deputation carry a flag?*

❷ *What happens to the members of the Deputation?*

Words for Everyday Use

pal • lid (pal´id) *adj.*, faint in color; pale

drone (drōn) *v.*, make a continuous and monotonous humming or buzzing sound

im • pinge (im pinj´) *v.*, strike, hit, or dash

in • ev • i • ta • ble (in ev´i tə bəl) *adj.*, certain to happen; that cannot be avoided or evaded

stu • pe • fy (sto͞o´pə fī´) *v.*, stun

Answers to Guided Reading Questions

❶ The members of the Deputation are attempting to communicate with the flag. A white flag, symbolizes peaceful intentions.

❷ The members of the Deputation are destroyed by a sudden flash of flame.

Vocabulary in Context

- I could tell that Luke was sick because his normally rosy face was pallid.
- From the hive came the steady drone of innumerable bees.
- The ball impinged upon the backboard and rebounded to the court.
- That the Earth's supply of oil will eventually run out is inevitable.
- The opening of the ground at my feet during the earthquake was enough to stupefy me completely.

Answer to Guided Reading Question

① The narrator feels a "terrible astonishment" because he has just seen several people destroyed for no apparent reason.

Answers for Reviewing the Selection

RECALLING AND INTERPRETING

1. **Recalling.** They carry a white flag toward the pit. **Interpreting.** A white flag usually means surrender or that the carrier of the flag is of good will.

2. **Recalling.** They are destroyed by flames. **Interpreting.** The Martians kill the people who are attempting to communicate with them.

Selection Check Test with Answers

EX. With whom did the narrator observe the planet Mars through a telescope?
The narrator observed the planet Mars with the astronomer Ogilvy.

1. What is the shape of the thing that falls on the common?
It is shaped like a cylinder.

2. What do the boys at the edge of the pit amuse themselves by doing?
They throw stones at the cylinder.

3. What comes out of the cylinder?
A Martian comes out of the cylinder.

4. What do Ogilvy and the other members of the Deputation carry?
They carry a white flag.

5. What happens to Ogilvy and to the other members of the Deputation?
They are killed by a heat ray.

The undulating common seemed now dark almost to blackness, except where its roadways lay gray and pale under the deep-blue sky of the early night. It was dark, and suddenly void of men. Overhead the stars were mustering, and in the west the sky was still a pale, bright, almost greenish blue. The tops of the pine-trees and the roofs of Horsell came out sharp and black against the western afterglow. The Martians and their appliances were altogether invisible, save for that thin mast upon which their restless mirror wobbled. Patches of bush and isolated trees here and there smoked and glowed still, and the houses toward Woking station were sending up spires of flame into the stillness of the evening air.

Why does the narrator feel "a terrible astonishment"? ①

Nothing was changed save for that and a terrible astonishment. The little group of black specks with the flag of white had been swept out of existence, and the stillness of the evening, so it seemed to me, had scarcely been broken.

It came to me that I was upon this dark common, helpless, unprotected, and alone. Suddenly, like a thing falling upon me from without, came fear.

With an effort I turned and began a stumbling run through the heather.

The fear I felt was no rational fear, but a panic terror not only of the Martians but of the dusk and stillness all about me. Such an extraordinary effect in unmanning me it had that I ran weeping silently as a child might do. Once I had turned, I did not dare to look back.

I remember I felt an extraordinary persuasion that I was being played with, that presently, when I was upon the very verge of safety, this mysterious death—as swift as the passage of light—would leap after me from the pit about the cylinder and strike me down.

Reviewing the Selection

Recalling and Interpreting

1. (R) What do Ogilvy and the other members of the Deputation carry toward the pit?
   (I) What is the symbolic meaning of what they carry?

2. (R) What happens to Ogilvy and the other members of the Deputation?
   (I) What proof does this chapter provide that the Martians are not interested in peaceful communication with humans?

Words for Everyday Use

un • du • late (un´dyo͞o lāt´) *v.*, move as if in waves
verge (vurj) *n.*, edge, brink, or margin

Vocabulary in Context

- The tops of the stalks of wheat undulated in the breeze.
- The runner slipped and fell on the verge of reaching the finish line.

Language Lab

Editing for Errors in Pronoun Usage

When you revise your writing, check to be sure that you have avoided errors in pronoun usage. Pronouns are words, such as *I, me, who,* and *whom,* that are used in place of nouns. For more information about pronouns, see the Language Arts Survey, 2.3, "Types of Pronouns." The following guidelines will help you to avoid common pronoun errors:

Use the pronouns *I, he, she, it, they,* and *who* as subjects of sentences and after linking verbs such as *is, are, was,* and *were.*

AS SUBJECT	**He** told Ogilvy about the flash on the planet Mars.
AS SUBJECT	**Who** found the first cylinder?
AFTER LINKING VERB	The one who first saw the Martians close up was **I.**
AFTER LINKING VERB	The person who rented the dog cart to the narrator was **he.**

Use the pronouns *me, him, her, them,* and *whom* as objects of other verbs and as objects of prepositions. (Prepositions are connecting words such as *at, to, from, on, with, toward, between,* and *among* that are often used before nouns and pronouns.)

AS OBJECT OF VERB	Ogilvy handed **me** the white flag.
AS OBJECT OF VERB	He handed **whom** the white flag?
AS OBJECT OF PREPOSITION	I gave the white flag to **him.**
AS OBJECT OF PREPOSITION	From **whom** did the narrator first hear about the cylinder?

Occasionally, and especially in questions, the object of the verb appears before the verb. In such a situation, put the parts of the sentence in the usual subject-verb-object order. Then decide which pronoun is correct.

INCORRECT	**Who** did Ogilvy send to notify the authorities?
INCORRECT	He sent **who?**
CORRECT	He sent **whom?**
CORRECT	**Whom** did Ogilvy send to notify the authorities?

Language Lab

Introducing the Skill

Begin by reviewing with students what pronouns are. Define *pronoun* as "a word that is used in place of a noun," and have students give examples of pronouns and use them in sentences.

Previewing the Skill

Make two columns on the chalkboard. Label one "Subjects and After Linking Verbs" and the other "Objects of Verbs and of Prepositions." Write the pronouns *I* and *who* in the first column and the pronouns *me* and *whom* in the second column. Ask students to give example sentences using these pronouns in the ways listed in the column headings.

Practicing the Skill

In class, have students read through the teaching and examples on page 593 and at the top of page 594. Ask students to suggest additional examples. Then assign Try It Yourself exercise A.

Reviewing the Skill

Correct Try It Yourself exercise A orally in class. Then assign exercise B. For additional practice, refer students to the lessons on pronoun usage in the Language Arts Survey and to the corresponding worksheet in the Essential Skills Practice Book: Language.

ANSWERS FOR TRY IT YOURSELF

EXERCISE A

1. Paul and I did our report on science fiction stories about gigantic, destructive creatures.
2. The subject was quite interesting to Paul and me.
3. It was I who thought up the idea after seeing the movie *Godzilla*.
4. Who created the sci-fi genre of movies about gigantic, destructive creatures? It was the Japanese.
5. It was they who created the genre after the destruction of Hiroshima and Nagasaki by atomic bombs.
6. It seems obvious to Paul and me that the destruction of Tokyo by Godzilla and the actual destruction of Hiroshima and Nagasaki are related.
7. It bothered Paul and me that this idea of total destruction should have become so much a part of Japanese popular culture.
8. Who can imagine what it would be like to have such an example of total destruction actually occur?

EXERCISE B

1. Have you read anything by Rebecca West? She and H. G. Wells admired one another tremendously.
2. I've read that there was a close relationship between Wells and her.
3. Whom did she describe as an extremely talented, heroic man?
4. Correct.
5. The oral report on Wells's life will be done by Paul, Chandra, Juan, and me.

Make sure to use the right form of the pronoun when a pronoun is joined with another word using the conjunction *and*. To find the right form of the pronoun, try using the pronoun by itself in the sentence.

INCORRECT	Ogilvy and me decided to approach the Martians, carrying a white flag.
INCORRECT	Me decided to approach the Martians, carrying a white flag.
CORRECT	I decided to approach the Martians, carrying a white flag.
CORRECT	Ogilvy and I decided to approach the Martians, carrying a white flag.

Try It Yourself

Exercise A. On your own paper, write the correct pronoun from those given in parentheses.

EXAMPLE Lettie and (she, her) did an oral report on science fiction stories about invasions from outer space.

she

1. Paul and (I, me) did our report on science fiction stories about gigantic, destructive creatures.
2. The subject was quite interesting to Paul and (I, me).
3. It was (I, me) who thought up the idea after seeing the movie *Godzilla*.
4. (Who, Whom) created the sci-fi genre of movies about gigantic, destructive creatures? It was the Japanese.
5. It was (them, they) who created the genre after the destruction of Hiroshima and Nagasaki by atomic bombs.
6. It seems obvious to Paul and (me, I) that the destruction of Tokyo by Godzilla and the actual destruction of Hiroshima and Nagasaki are related.
7. It bothered Paul and (I, me) that this idea of total destruction should have become so much a part of Japanese popular culture.
8. (Who, Whom) can imagine what it would be like to have such an example of total destruction actually occur?

Exercise B. Identify the errors in pronoun usage in the following sentences. If a sentence contains an error, rewrite it on your own paper, correcting that error. If the sentence does not contain an error, write *Correct*.

EXAMPLE The novelist ———— called H. G. Wells a genius; her and Wells were very good friends.

The novelist ———— called H. G. Wells a genius; she and Wells were very good friends.

1. Have you read anything by ————? Her and H. G. Wells admired one another tremendously.
2. I've read that there was a close relationship between Wells and she.
3. Who did she describe as an extremely talented, heroic man?
4. To whom did Wells dedicate his book?
5. The oral report on Wells's life will be done by Paul, Chandra, Juan, and I.

READER'S JOURNAL

If you had been present to see what happened to the men of the Deputation in the previous chapter, how would you have reacted? What would you have done? Write about these questions in your journal.

6
The Heat-Ray in the Chobham Road

It is still a matter of wonder how the Martians are able to slay men so swiftly and so silently. Many think that in some way they are able to generate an intense heat in a chamber of practically absolute non-conductivity. This intense heat they project in a parallel beam against any object they choose by means of a polished parabolic mirror[1] of unknown composition, much as the parabolic mirror of a lighthouse projects a beam of light. But no one has absolutely proved these details. However it is done, it is certain that a beam of heat is the essence of the matter. Heat, and invisible, instead of visible light. Whatever is combustible flashes into flame at its touch, lead runs like water, it softens iron, cracks and melts glass, and when it falls upon water, incontinently that explodes into steam.

That night nearly forty people lay under the starlight about the pit, charred and distorted beyond recognition, and all night long the common from Horsell to Maybury was deserted and brightly ablaze.

The news of the massacre probably reached Chobham, Woking, and Ottershaw about the same time. In Woking the shops had closed when the tragedy happened, and a number of people, shop-people and so forth, attracted by the stories they had heard, were walking over the Horsell Bridge and along the road between the hedges that runs out at last upon the common. You may imagine the young people brushed up after the labors of the day, and making this novelty, as they would make any novelty, the excuse for walking together and enjoying a trivial flirtation. You may figure to yourself the hum of voices along the road in the gloaming. . . .

As yet, of course, few people in Woking even knew that the cylinder had opened, though poor Henderson had sent a messenger on a bicycle to the post office with a special wire to an evening paper.

As these folks came out by twos and threes upon the open, they found little knots of people talking excitedly and peering at the spinning mirror over the sand-pits, and the newcomers were, no doubt, soon infected by the excitement of the occasion.

By half-past eight, when the Deputation was destroyed, there may have been a crowd of three hundred people or more at this place, besides those who had left the road to approach the Martians nearer. There were three policemen too, one of

Chapter 6

1. **parabolic mirror.** Mirror that is bowl-shaped

❶ *How does the Martian Heat-Ray work?*

Words for Everyday Use

com • po • si • tion (käm´pə zish´ən) *n.,* makeup of a thing or person

com • bus • ti • ble (kəm bus´tə bəl) *adj.,* flammable, that catches fire and burns easily

in • con • ti • nent • ly (in kän´tə nənt lē) *adv.,* without being able to restrain or stop something

triv • i • al (triv´ē əl) *adj.,* insignificant; unimportant

READER'S JOURNAL

As an alternative activity, you might ask students to role play being government ministers faced with this situation. The ministers should meet and debate the best possible course of action for the government to take.

SPELLING AND VOCABULARY WORDS FROM THE SELECTION

acuteness	haze
albeit	immemorial
allay	imminent
apparition	incongruity
avail	incontinently
bawl	indefatigable
belligerent	indiscriminate
bevy	indisputably
canard	inert
clamor	insensate
colossus	invigorate
combustible	lassitude
commend	lethargy
composition	lurid
conflagration	minute
consume	smite
contagion	obscurity
conveyance	perplexed
cowl	perplexingly
deploy	pinnacle
desist	ply
desolate	precipitate
detachment	reins
deter	repugnance
detonation	reverberation
disgorge	scintillate
dispense	sentinel
ejaculatory	silhouette
exertion	smite
exultant	torpor
foreboding	torrent
furtively	timidity
fusillade	trench
gaunt	trivial
haggard	ultimatum

VOCABULARY IN CONTEXT

- The geologist studied the composition of the rocks brought back from Mars.
- Old rags, placed in a cupboard, can be quite combustible.
- The excited fans incontinently shouted the names of the rock stars.
- A good boss does not allow herself to be distracted by trivial matters.

ANSWER TO GUIDED READING QUESTION

❶ Great heat is produced in a non-conductive chamber and then projected by means of a mirror.

Answer to Guided Reading Question

❶ They sent for troops to protect the Martians from the crowd. Ironically, it is the crowd that needs protection from the Martians.

whom was mounted,[2] doing their best, under instructions from Stent, to keep the people back and <u>deter</u> them from approaching the cylinder. There was some booing from those more thoughtless and excitable souls to whom a crowd is always an occasion for noise and horseplay.

Why did Stent and Ogilvy send for troops? What is ironic about this? ❶

Stent and Ogilvy, anticipating some possibilities of a collision, had telegraphed from Horsell to the barracks as soon as the Martians emerged, for the help of a company of soldiers to protect these strange creatures from violence. After that they returned to lead that ill-fated advance. The description of their death, as it was seen by the crowd, tallies very closely with my own impressions: the three puffs of green smoke, the deep humming note, and the flashes of flame.

But that crowd of people had a far narrower escape than mine. Only the fact that a hummock of heathery sand intercepted the lower part of the Heat-Ray saved them. Had the elevation of the parabolic mirror been a few yards higher, none could have lived to tell the tale. They saw the flashes and the men falling, and an invisible hand, as it were, lit the bushes as it hurried toward them through the twilight. Then, with a whistling note that rose above the droning of the pit, the beam swung close over their heads, lighting the tops of the beech trees that line the road, and splitting the bricks, smashing the windows, firing the window-frames, and bringing down in crumbling ruin a portion of the gable[3] of the house nearest the corner.

In the sudden thud, hiss, and glare of the igniting trees, the panic-stricken crowd seems to have swayed hesitatingly for some moments. Sparks and burning twigs began to fall into the road, and single leaves like puffs of flame. Hats and dresses caught fire. Then came a crying from the common. There were shrieks and shouts, and suddenly a mounted policeman came galloping through the confusion with his hands clasped over his head, screaming.

"They're coming!" a woman shrieked, and incontinently every one was turning and pushing at those behind, in order to clear their way to Woking again. They must have bolted as blindly as a flock of sheep. Where the road grows narrow and black between the high banks the crowd jammed, and a desperate struggle occurred. All that crowd did not escape; three persons at least, two women and a little boy, were crushed and trampled there, and left to die amid the terror and the darkness.

2. **mounted.** Upon a horse
3. **gable.** Triangular wall of a building enclosed by the sloping ends of a ridged roof

Words for Everyday Use

de • ter (dē tʉr´) *v.,* keep or discourage someone or something from an action

Vocabulary in Context

• The Great Wall of China was built to <u>deter</u> invasion.

Reviewing the Selection

RECALLING AND INTERPRETING

1. **R** What weapon do the Martians use on the crowd?

   I What modern invention, unknown in Wells's time, is similar to the Martians' weapon?

2. **R** Why do Stent and Ogilvy send for soldiers?

   I In what way did Stent and Ogilvy misread the Martians? Was theirs a sensible reaction to the situation? Explain.

7
How I Reached Home

For my own part, I remember nothing of my flight except the stress of blundering against trees and stumbling through the heather. All about me gathered the invisible terrors of the Martians; that pitiless sword of heat seemed whirling to and fro, flourishing overhead before it descended and smote me out of life. I came into the road between the cross-roads and Horsell, and ran along this to the cross-roads.

At last I could go no farther; I was exhausted with the violence of my emotion and of my flight, and I staggered and fell by the wayside. That was near the bridge that crosses the canal by the gasworks. I fell and lay still.

I must have remained there some time.

I sat up, strangely perplexed. For a moment, perhaps, I could not clearly understand how I came there. My terror had fallen from me like a garment. My hat had gone, and my collar had burst away from its fastener. A few minutes before there had only been three real things before me—the immensity of the night and space and nature, my own feebleness and anguish, and the near approach of death. Now it was as if something turned over, and the point of view altered abruptly. There was no sensible transition from one state of mind to the other. I was immediately the self of every day again—a decent, ordinary citizen. The silent common, the impulse of my flight, the starting flames, were as if they had been in a dream. I asked myself had these latter things indeed happened? I could not credit it.

1 *What can the narrator hardly believe?*

I rose and walked unsteadily up the steep incline of the bridge. My mind was blank wonder. My muscles and nerves seemed drained of their strength. I dare say I staggered drunkenly. A head rose over the arch, and the figure of a workman carrying a basket appeared. Beside him ran a little boy. He passed me, wishing me goodnight. I was minded to speak to him, but did not. I answered his greeting with a meaningless mumble and went on over the bridge.

Over the Maybury arch a train, a billowing tumult of white, firelit smoke, and a long caterpillar of lighted windows, went flying

WORDS FOR EVERYDAY USE

smite (smīt) *v.*, hit or strike hard

per • plexed (pər plekst´) *adj.*, puzzled, full of doubt or uncertainty

Answers for Reviewing the Selection

RECALLING AND INTERPRETING

1. **Recalling.** The Martians use a heat ray on the crowd. **Interpreting.** The laser, unknown in Wells's day, is similar to Wells's heat ray.

2. **Recalling.** They send for soliders to protect the Martians from the crowd. **Interpreting.** Stent and Ogilvy misread the Martians by assuming that these creatures are friendly. Responses will vary with regard to whether the men's actions were sensible.

Answer to Guided Reading Question

1 The narrator can hardly believe all that has happened—the appearance of the Martians, the killing of the members of the Deputation, the use of the heat ray on the crowd, and so on.

Vocabulary in Context

- You can get your aggression and anger out by using this tennis racket to smite that pillow.
- The perplexed driver thought he must have taken a wrong turn.

Answers to Guided Reading Questions

❶ The narrator says that the Martians are sluggish and will not be able to get out of the pit.

❷ The narrator's wife is worried that the Martians might come to the town where her home is.

❸ According to Ogilvy, the gravity of the Earth is three times that of Mars, making the Martians three times heavier than they are used to being. Based on this fact, Ogilvy concluded that the Martians could not establish themselves on Earth.

south—clatter, clatter, clap, rap, and it had gone. A dim group of people talked in the gate of one of the houses in the pretty little row of gables that was called Oriental Terrace. It was all so real and so familiar. And that behind me! It was frantic, fantastic! Such things, I told myself, could not be.

❶ *What reason for not fearing the Martians does the narrator give?*

Perhaps I am a man of exceptional moods. I do not know how far my experience is common. At times I suffer from the strangest sense of detachment from myself and the world about me; I seem to watch it all from the outside, from somewhere inconceivably remote, out of time, out of space, out of the stress and tragedy of it all. This feeling was very strong upon me that night. Here was another side to my dream.

❷ *About what is the narrator's wife worried?*

But the trouble was the blank incongruity of this serenity and the swift death flying yonder, not two miles away. There was a noise of business from the gasworks, and the electric lamps were all alight. I stopped at the group of people.

"What news from the common?" said I.

There were two men and a woman at the gate.

"Eh?" said one of the men, turning.

"What news from the common?" I said.

"Ain't yer just *been* there?" asked the men.

❸ *Why are the Martians heavier on Earth than on Mars? What conclusion did Ogilvy draw from this fact?*

"People seem fair silly about the common," said the woman over the gate. "What's it all abart?"

"Haven't you heard of the men from Mars?" said I— "the creatures from Mars?"

"Quite enough," said the woman over the gate. "Thenks"; and all three of them laughed.

I felt foolish and angry. I tried and found I could not tell them what I had seen. They laughed again at my broken sentences.

"You'll hear more yet," I said, and went on to my home.

I startled my wife at the doorway, so haggard was I. I went into the dining room, sat down, . . . and so soon as I could collect myself sufficiently I told her the things I had seen. The dinner, which was a cold one, had already been served, and remained neglected on the table while I told my story.

"There is one thing," I said, to allay the fears I had aroused—"they are the most sluggish things I ever saw crawl. They may keep the pit and kill people who come near them, but they cannot get out of it. . . . But the horror of them!"

"Don't, dear!" said my wife, knitting her brows and putting her hand on mine.

"Poor Ogilvy!" I said. "To think he may be lying dead there!"

My wife at least did not find my experience incredible. When I saw how deadly white her face was, I ceased abruptly.

"They may come here," she said again and again.

I . . . tried to reassure her.

"They can scarcely move," I said.

I began to comfort her and myself by repeating all that Ogilvy had told me of the impossibility of the Martians establishing themselves on the earth. In particular I laid stress on the gravitational difficulty. On the surface of the earth the force of gravity is three times what it is on the surface of Mars. A Martian, therefore, would weigh three times more than on Mars, albeit his muscular strength would be the same. His own body would be a cope[1] of lead to him. That, indeed, was the general opinion. Both the *Times* and the *Daily Telegraph*, for instance, insisted on it the next morning, and both over-

CHAPTER 7

1. **cope.** Large cape worn by priests at certain ceremonies

Words for Everyday Use

de • tach • ment (dē tach´mənt) *n.*, separation; disengagement

in • con • gru • i • ty (in´kan grōō´ i tē) *n.*, condition or quality of having a lack of harmony or agreement

hag • gard (hag´ərd) *adj.*, having a wild, wasted, worn look

al • lay (a lā´) *v.*, lessen: relieve

al • be • it (ôl bē´it) *conj.*, even though; although

Vocabulary in Context

- Try not to be overly concerned about the outcome; instead, cultivate a little detachment.
- I couldn't get over the incongruity between Mr. Smyth's small build and his deep, booming voice.
- After fighting that fire all night, the volunteers looked quite haggard.
- This ointment will allay the pain of the burn.
- This band is quite popular in Europe, albeit they are not yet well known in the United States.

looked, just as I did, two obvious modifying influences.

The atmosphere of the earth, we now know, contains far more oxygen or far less argon (whichever way one likes to put it) than does Mars. The invigorating influences of this excess of oxygen upon the Martians indisputably did much to counterbalance the increased weight of their bodies. And, in the second place, we all overlooked the fact that such mechanical intelligence as the Martian possessed was quite able to dispense with muscular exertion at a pinch.

But I did not consider these points at the time, and so my reasoning was dead against the chances of the invaders. With . . .food, the confidence of my own table, and the necessity of reassuring my wife, I grew by insensible degrees courageous and secure.

"They have done a foolish thing," said I . . . . "They are dangerous because, no doubt, they are mad with terror. Perhaps they expected to find no living things—certainly no intelligent living things.

"A shell in the pit," said I, "if the worst comes to the worst, will kill them all."

The intense excitement of the events had no doubt left my perceptive powers in a state of erethism.[2] I remember that dinner table with extraordinary vividness even now. My dear wife's sweet, anxious face peering at me from under the pink lampshade, the white cloth with its silver and glass table furniture—for in those days even philosophical writers had many little luxuries—. . . are photographically distinct. At the end of it I sat, . . . regretting Ogilvy's rashness, and denouncing the short-sighted timidity of the Martians.

So some respectable dodo in the Mauritius might have lorded it in his nest, and discussed the arrival of that shipful of pitiless sailors in want of animal food. "We will peck them to death to-morrow, my dear."

I did not know it, but that was the last civilized dinner I was to eat for very many strange and terrible days.

1. **erethism.** Abnormal, extreme sensitivity

❶ *Why does the narrator think that the Martians have acted foolishly?*

❷ *To what does the narrator compare humans? What is the point of this comparison?*

WORDS FOR EVERYDAY USE

in • vig • or • ate (in vig´ər āt´) *v.*, energize

in • dis • put • a • bly (in dis´ pyo͞ot´ə blē) *adv.*, unquestionably; undoubtedly

dis • pense (di spens´) *v.*, do away with; get rid of

ex • er • tion (eg zʉr´shən) *n.*, energetic activity

ti • mid • i • ty (tə mid´ə tē) *n.*, state of shyness or hesitancy

ANSWERS TO GUIDED READING QUESTIONS

❶ The narrator believes that dropping a shell on the pit will kill all the Martians.

❷ The narrator compares humans to dodos, the extinct birds of Mauritius. The point of the comparison is that, at the time, the narrator and other humans have no more understanding of the Martians than dodos had with regard to the sailors who drove them to extinction.

VOCABULARY IN CONTEXT

- A little rest and some fresh air will invigorate you.
- Albert Einstein was, indisputably, the greatest scientist of the twentieth century.
- Please dispense with formality and call me by my first name.
- The cyclist was tired from the exertion of cycling up the enormous hill.
- The piano player overcame his natural timidity and performed for the crowd at the party.

Answers for Reviewing the Selection

RECALLING AND INTERPRETING

1. **Recalling.** The narrator says that the Martians are too sluggish to be able to move from the pit. **Interpreting.** The narrator and the newspapers underestimate the Martians because they do not yet know much about them. They fail to realize that the Martians, being intelligent enough to travel to the Earth, are probably intelligent enough to get out of the pit.

2. **Recalling.** He believes that the Martians could be killed by shelling the pit. **Interpreting.** The narrator believes that the Martians have acted out of terror and may well have spelled their own doom. The comparison to the dodo and the indication that the narrator was not to have a civilized meal for very many days both suggest that something terrible is about to happen, that the Martians are not, in fact, powerless.

Answers to Guided Reading Questions

❶ The most extraordinary thing about their actions is that people behave in ordinary, commonplace, habitual ways.

❷ For the most part, people continue their usual routines.

Reviewing the Selection

Recalling and Interpreting

1. **R** What does the narrator tell his wife about the Martians' ability to move?
   I In what way did the narrator and the newspapers underestimate the Martians? Why do you think they made such a mistake?

2. **R** In what way does the narrator expect that the Martians might be killed?
   I Why does the narrator say that the Martians "have done a foolish thing"? What lines at the end of the chapter suggest that the narrator was misreading the situation?

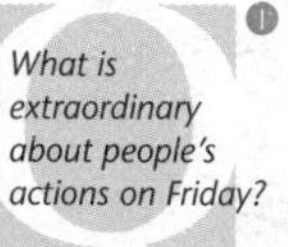

8
Friday Night

❶ What is extraordinary about people's actions on Friday?

The most extraordinary thing to my mind, of all the strange and wonderful things that happened upon that Friday, was the dovetailing of the commonplace habits of our social order with the first beginnings of the series of events that was to topple that social order headlong. If on Friday night you had taken a pair of compasses and drawn a circle with a radius of five miles round the Woking sand-pits, I doubt if you would have had one human being outside it, unless it were some relation of Stent or of the three or four cyclists or London people lying dead on the common, whose emotions or habits were at all affected by the newcomers. Many people had heard of the cylinder, of course, and talked about it in their leisure, but it certainly did not make the sensation that an ultimatum to Germany would have done.

In London that night poor Henderson's telegram describing the gradual unscrewing of the shot was judged to be a canard, and his evening paper, after wiring for authentication from him and receiving no reply—the man was killed—decided not to print a special edition.

Even within the five-mile circle the great majority of people were inert. I have already described the behavior of the men and women to whom I spoke. All over the district people were dining and supping; working-men were gardening after the labors of the day, children were being put to bed, young people were wandering through the lanes love-making, students sat over their books.

❷ What do people do "for the most part"?

Maybe there was a murmur in the village streets, a novel and dominant topic in the public-houses, and here and there a messenger, or even an eyewitness of the later occurrences, caused a whirl of excitement, a shouting, and a running to and fro; but for the most part the daily routine of working, eating, drinking, sleeping, went on as it had done for countless years—as though no planet Mars existed in the sky. Even at Woking station and Horsell and Chobham that was the case.

In Woking junction, until a late hour, trains were stopping and going on, others were shunting on the sidings, passengers were alighting and waiting, and everything was proceeding in the most ordinary way.

Words for Everyday Use

ul • ti • ma • tum (ul´tə māt´əm) *n.*, final offer or demand

ca • nard (kə närd´) *n.*, false report that has been fabricated with the intention of doing harm

in • ert (in ʉrt´) *adj.*, tending to be physically or mentally inactive

Vocabulary in Context

- The emperor gave his enemies an ultimatum: surrender or fight.
- The travel agent said, "You do not really believe that canard about the dangers of travel in our country, do you?"
- People were gathered around the python's cage, waiting for it to move, but the large snake remained inert.

A boy from the town, trenching on Smith's monopoly, was selling papers with the afternoon's news. The ringing impact of trucks, the sharp whistle of the engines from the junction, mingled with their shouts of "Men from Mars!" Excited men came into the station about nine o'clock with incredible tidings, and caused no more disturbance than drunkards might have done. People rattling Londonwards peered into the darkness outside the carriage windows and saw only a rare, flickering, vanishing spark dance up from the direction of Horsell, a red glow and a thin veil of smoke driving across the stars, and thought that nothing more serious than a heath fire was happening. It was only round the edge of the common that any disturbance was perceptible. There were half a dozen villas burning on the Woking border. There were lights in all the houses on the common side of the three villages, and the people there kept awake till dawn.

A curious crowd lingered restlessly, people coming and going but the crowd remaining, both on the Chobham and Horsell bridges. One or two adventurous souls, it was afterwards found, went into the darkness and crawled quite near the Martians; but they never returned, for now and again a light-ray, like the beam of a warship's searchlight, swept the common, and the Heat-Ray was ready to follow. Save for such, that big area of common was silent and desolate, and the charred bodies lay about on it all night under the stars, and all the next day. A noise of hammering from the pit was heard by many people.

So you have the state of things on Friday night. In the center, sticking into the skin of our old planet Earth like a poisoned dart, was this cylinder. But the poison was scarcely working yet. Around it was a patch of silent common, smouldering in places, and with a few dark, dimly seen objects lying in contorted attitudes here and there. Here and there was a burning bush or tree. Beyond was a fringe of excitement, and farther than that fringe the inflammation had not crept as yet. In the rest of the world the stream of life still flowed as it had flowed for immemorial years. The fever of war that would presently clog vein and artery, deaden nerve and destroy brain, had still to develop.

All night long the Martians were hammering and stirring, sleepless, indefatigable, at work upon the machines they were making ready, and ever and again a puff of greenish-white smoke whirled up to the starlit sky.

❶ *What are the Martians doing?*

About eleven a company of soldiers came through Horsell, and deployed along the edge of the common to form a cordon.[1] Later a second company marched through Chobham to deploy on the north side of the common. Several officers from the Inkerman barracks had been on the common earlier in the day, and one, Major Eden, was reported to be missing. The colonel of the regiment came to the Chobham bridge and was busy questioning the crowd at midnight. The military authorities were certainly alive to the seriousness of the business. About eleven, the next morning's papers were able to say, a squadron of hussars,[2] two Maxims, and about four hundred men of the Cardigan regiment started from Aldershot.

A few seconds after midnight the crowd in the Chertsey road, Woking, saw a star fall from heaven into the pine woods to the northwest. It had a greenish color and caused a silent brightness like summer lightning. This was the second cylinder.

❷ *To what does the narrator compare the cylinder?*

CHAPTER 8

1. **cordon.** Line of guards, police officers, or soldiers placed around an area in order to protect it

2. **hussars.** Members of the light calvary

WORDS FOR EVERYDAY USE

trench (trench) *v.*, infringe upon another's rights

des • o • late (deś ə lit) *adj.*, uninhabited, deserted

im • me • mo • ri • al (im´me môr´ē əl) *n.*, extending back beyond memory or record, ancient

in • de • fat • i • ga • ble (in´di fat´i gə bəl) *adj.*, untiring, not yielding to fatigue

de • ploy (dē ploi´) *v.*, spread out or place military troops

ANSWERS TO GUIDED READING QUESTIONS

❶ The narrator compares the cylinder to a poisoned dart, stuck into Earth.

❷ The Martians are building machines.

VOCABULARY IN CONTEXT

- "Do not trench on my territory," one flower seller said to another.
- Death Valley is known as the most desolate place in America.
- The young man told us that the Navajo had been in the Americas from time immemorial.
- The indefatigable runner completed the marathon in record time and then jogged up to the reviewing stand to receive her prize.
- The president has the authority to deploy troops, but only Congress can declare war.

Answers for Reviewing the Selection

RECALLING AND INTERPRETING

1. **Recalling.** Surprisingly, they go about their normal routines. **Interpreting.** *Responses will vary.* Some will feel that the people's reactions are believable because people tend to act habitually and not to believe the extremely bizarre until they are confronted with it directly. Others will feel that the people's reactions are unbelievable because the appearance of extraterrestrials on Earth would be an epoch-making event.

2. **Recalling.** Another cylinder falls into the pine woods. **Interpreting.** There may be many more of the cylinders on the way, indicating a full-scale invasion from Mars.

Reviewing the Selection

Recalling and Interpreting

1. **R** How do the people who live near the common react to the presence of the Martians?

   I Do you consider this description of the people's reactions believable? Why, or why not?

2. **R** What falls into the pine woods to the northwest?

   I Why might the falling of this object be a cause for alarm?

9
The Fighting Begins

Saturday lives in my memory as a day of suspense. It was a day of lassitude too, hot and close, with, I am told, a rapidly fluctuating barometer.[1] I had slept but little, though my wife had succeeded in sleeping, and I rose early. I went into my garden before breakfast and stood listening, but toward the common there was nothing stirring but a lark.

The milkman came as usual. I heard the rattle of his chariot, and I went round to the side gate to ask the latest news. He told me that during the night the Martians had been surrounded by troops, and that guns were expected. Then—a familiar, reassuring note—I heard a train running toward Woking.

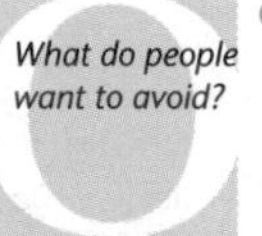

What do people want to avoid?

"They aren't to be killed," said the milkman, "if that can possibly be avoided."

I saw my neighbor gardening, chatted with him for a time, and then strolled in to breakfast. It was a most unexceptional morning. My neighbour was of opinion that the troops would be able to capture or to destroy the Martians during the day.

"It's a pity they make themselves so unapproachable," he said. "It would be curious to know how they live on another planet; we might learn a thing or two."

He came up to the fence and extended a handful of strawberries, for his gardening was as generous as it was enthusiastic. At the same time he told me of the burning of the pine woods about the Byfleet Golf Links.

"They say," said he, "that there's another of those blessed things fallen there—number two. But one's enough, surely. This lot'll cost the insurance people a pretty penny before everything's settled." He laughed with an air of the greatest good humor as he said this. The woods, he said, were still burning, and pointed out a haze of smoke to me. "They will be hot underfoot for days, on account of the thick soil of pine needles and turf," he said, and then grew serious over "poor Ogilvy."

After breakfast, instead of working, I decided to walk down toward the common. Under the railway bridge I found a group of

Chapter 9

1. **barometer.** Instrument used to measure atmospheric pressure that can be used to predict the weather

Words for Everyday Use

las • si • tude (las´i to͞od) *n.*, weariness, feeling of being tired and listless

haze (hāz) *n.*, dispersion of smoke or dust in the air that reduces visibility, fog

Vocabulary in Context

- At this time of year, the heat is so intense that people in this part of the country give themselves over to lassitude.
- The smokestacks created a haze over the city.

soldiers—sappers,[2] I think, men in small round caps, dirty red jackets unbuttoned, and showing their blue shirts, dark trousers, and boots coming to the calf. They told me no one was allowed over the canal, and, looking along the road toward the bridge, I saw one of the Cardigan men standing sentinel there. I talked with these soldiers for a time; I told them of my sight of the Martians on the previous evening. None of them had seen the Martians, and they had but the vaguest ideas of them, so that they plied me with questions. They said that they did not know who had authorized the movements of the troops; their idea was that a dispute had arisen at the Horse Guards. The ordinary sapper is a great deal better educated than the common soldier, and they discussed the peculiar conditions of the possible fight with some acuteness. I described the Heat-Ray to them, and they began to argue among themselves.

"Crawl up under cover and rush 'em, say I," said one.

"Get aht!" said another. "What's cover against this 'ere 'eat? Sticks to cook yer! What we got to do is to go as near as the ground'll let us, and then drive a trench."

"Blow yer trenches! You always want trenches; you ought to ha' been born a rabbit, Snippy."

"Ain't they got any necks, then?" said a third, abruptly—a little, contemplative, dark man, smoking a pipe.

I repeated my description.

"Octopuses," said he, "that's what I calls 'em. Talk about fishers of men—fighters of fish it is this time!"

"It ain't no murder killing beasts like that," said the first speaker.

"Why not shell the darned things strite off and finish 'em?" said the little dark man. "You carn tell what they might do."

"Where's your shells?" said the first speaker. "There ain't no time. Do it in a rush, that's my tip, and do it at once."

So they discussed it. After a while I left them, and went on to the railway station to get as many morning papers as I could.

But I will not weary the reader with a description of that long morning and of the longer afternoon. I did not succeed in getting a glimpse of the common, for even Horsell and Chobham church towers were in the hands of the military authorities. The soldiers I addressed didn't know anything; the officers were mysterious as well as busy. I found people in the town quite secure again in the presence of the military, and I heard for the first time from Marshall, the tobacconist, that his son was among the dead on the common. The soldiers had made the people on the outskirts of Horsell lock up and leave their houses.

I got back to lunch about two, very tired, for, as I have said, the day was extremely hot and dull; and in order to refresh myself I took a cold bath in the afternoon. About half-past four I went up to the railway station to get an evening paper, for the morning papers had contained only a very inaccurate description of the killing of Stent, Henderson, Ogilvy, and the others. But there was little I didn't know. The Martians did not show an inch of themselves. They seemed busy in their pit, and there was a sound of hammering and an almost continuous streamer of smoke. Apparently they were busy getting ready for a struggle. "Fresh attempts have been made to signal, but without success," was the stereotyped formula of the papers. A sapper told me it was done by a man in a ditch with a flag

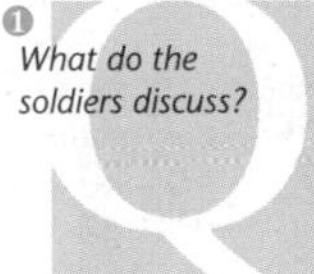

❶ *What do the soldiers discuss?*

2. **sappers.** Soldiers employed in acts such as digging ditches and laying mines

Words for Everyday Use

sen • ti • nel (sen´ti nəl) *n.,* guard

ply (plī) *v.,* address someone urgently and constantly

a • cute • ness (ə kyo͞ot´nəs) *n.,* quality of having a keen or quick mind

Answer to Guided Reading Question

❶ The soldiers discuss possible approaches to fighting the Martians.

Vocabulary in Context

- The sentinel on top of the tower spotted the invading ships as they entered the harbor.
- Reporters plied the defense attorney with questions about the case.
- Misha answered all of the quiz bowl questions correctly, impressing us all with his acuteness.

Answer to Guided Reading Question

❶ The Martians take no notice of attempts to communicate with them. Given the preceding events, their failure to respond might indicate a hostile intention.

❶ *Of what do the Martians take no notice? What might explain their failure to respond?*

on a long pole. The Martians took as much notice of such advances as we should of the lowing of a cow.

I must confess the sight of all this armament, all this preparation, greatly excited me. My imagination became belligerent, and defeated the invaders in a dozen striking ways; something of my schoolboy dreams of battle and heroism came back. It hardly seemed a fair fight to me at that time. They seemed very helpless in that pit of theirs.

About three o'clock there began the thud of a gun at measured intervals from Chertsey or Addlestone. I learned that the smoldering pine wood into which the second cylinder had fallen was being shelled, in the hope of destroying that object before it opened. It was only about five, however, that a field gun reached Chobham for use against the first body of Martians.

About six in the evening, as I sat at tea with my wife in the summer-house talking

Words for Everyday Use

bel • lig • er • ent (bə lij´ər ənt) *adj.,* seeking war, warlike

Vocabulary in Context

• The peacemaker tried to bring the belligerent parties to the negotiating table.

vigorously about the battle that was lowering upon us, I heard a muffled detonation from the common, and immediately after a gust of firing. Close on the heels of that came a violent, rattling crash quite close to us, that shook the ground; and, starting out upon the lawn, I saw the tops of the trees about the Oriental College burst into smoky red flame, and the tower of the little church beside it slide down into ruin. The pinnacle of the mosque[3] had vanished, and the roof-line of the college itself looked as if a hundred-ton gun had been at work upon it. One of our chimneys cracked as if a shot had hit it, flew, and a piece of it came clattering down the tiles and made a heap of broken red fragments upon the flowerbed by my study window.

I and my wife stood amazed. Then I realised that the crest of Maybury Hill must be within range of the Martians' Heat-Ray now that the college was cleared out of the way.

At that I gripped my wife's arm, and without ceremony ran her out into the road. Then I fetched out the servant, telling her I would go upstairs myself for the box she was clamoring for.

"We can't possibly stay here," I said; and as I spoke the firing reopened for a moment upon the common.

"But where are we to go?" said my wife in terror.

I thought, perplexed. Then I remembered her cousins at Leatherhead.

"Leatherhead!" I shouted above the sudden noise.

She looked away from me downhill. The people were coming out of their houses astonished.

"How are we to get to Leatherhead?" she said.

Down the hill I saw a bevy of hussars ride under the railway bridge; three galloped through the open gates of the Oriental College; two others dismounted, and began running from house to house. The sun, shining through the smoke that drove up from the tops of the trees, seemed blood-red, and threw an unfamiliar lurid light upon everything.

"Stop here," said I; "you are safe here;" and I started off at once for the Spotted Dog, for I knew the landlord had a horse and dog-cart. I ran, for I perceived that in a moment every one upon this side of the hill would be moving. I found him in his bar, quite unaware of what was going on behind his house. A man stood with his back to me, talking to him.

"I must have a pound," said the landlord, "and I've no one to drive it."

"I'll give you two," said I, over the stranger's shoulder.

"What for?"

"And I'll bring it back by midnight," I said.

"Lord!" said the landlord; "what's the hurry? I'm selling my bit of a pig. Two pounds, and you bring it back? What's going on now?"

I explained hastily that I had to leave my home, and so secured the dog-cart. At the time it did not seem to me nearly so urgent that the landlord should leave his. I took care to have the cart there and then, drove it off down the road, and, leaving it in charge of my wife and servant, rushed into my house and packed a few valuables, such plate as we had, and so forth. The beech trees below the house were burning while I did this, and the palings up the

1 *Why is the landlord surprised?*

2 *Why can't the narrator and his wife stay where they are?*

3. **mosque.** Muslim place of worship

WORDS FOR EVERYDAY USE

det • o • na • tion (det´'n ā´shən) *n.* explosion

pin • na • cle (pin´ə kəl) *n.*, highest point, culmination

clam • or (klam´ər) *v.*, cry out; complain; demand

bev • y (bev´ē) *n.*, any group or collection

lur • id (lo͝or´id) *adj.*, glowing through a haze

ANSWERS TO GUIDED READING QUESTIONS

1 The landlord is surprised that the narrator is willing to offer so much money for the rental of the cart.

2 The narrator and his wife cannot stay where they are because the Martians are heading toward them.

VOCABULARY IN CONTEXT

- The detonation of the land mine could be heard for several miles.
- The hikers planted a flag at the pinnacle of the mountain.
- From the exit I could hear the crowd clamor for another encore.
- A bevy of quail was hidden in the brush.
- I could see the outlines of the fire fighters through the lurid smoke that rose from the remains of the burned-down building.

Answer to Guided Reading Question

➊ The Martians are setting fire to everything within range of their heat ray.

Answers for Reviewing the Selection

RECALLING AND INTERPRETING

1. **Recalling.** The soldiers are discussing how best to deal with the Martian threat. **Interpreting.** *Responses will vary.* The soldiers probably do not understand the technological superiority of the Martians.

2. **Recalling.** A field gun appears on the scene for use against the Martians. **Interpreting.** The military has no real plan, does not get equipment to the scene quickly, and does not have an effective means of countering the Martians' major weapon, the heat ray.

road glowed red. While I was occupied in this way, one of the dismounted hussars came running up. He was going from house to house, warning people to leave. He was going on as I came out of my front-door, lugging my treasures, done up in a tablecloth. I shouted after him:

"What news?"

He turned, stared, bawled something about "crawling out in a thing like a dish cover," and ran on to the gate of the house at the crest. A sudden whirl of black smoke driving across the road hid him for a moment. I ran to my neighbor's door and rapped to satisfy myself of what I already knew, that his wife had gone to London with him and had locked up their house. I went in again, according to my promise, to get my servant's box, lugged it out, clapped it beside her on the tail of the dog-cart, and then caught the reins and jumped up into the driver's seat beside my wife. In another moment we were clear of the smoke and noise, and spanking down the opposite slope of Maybury Hill toward Old Woking.

What are the Martians doing? ➊

In front was a quiet, sunny landscape, a wheatfield ahead on either side of the road, and the Maybury Inn with its swinging sign. I saw the doctor's cart ahead of me. At the bottom of the hill I turned my head to look at the hillside I was leaving. Thick streamers of black smoke shot with threads of red fire were driving up into the still air, and throwing dark shadows upon the green treetops eastward. The smoke already extended far away to the east and west—to the Byfleet pine woods eastward, and to Woking on the west. The road was dotted with people running toward us.

And very faint now, but very distinct through the hot, quiet air, one heard the whirr of a machine-gun that was presently stilled, and an intermittent cracking of rifles. Apparently the Martians were setting fire to everything within range of their Heat-Ray.

I am not an expert driver, and I had immediately to turn my attention to the horse. When I looked back again the second hill had hidden the black smoke. I slashed the horse with the whip, and gave him a loose rein until Woking and Send lay between us and that quivering tumult. I overtook and passed the doctor between Woking and Send.

Reviewing the Selection

Recalling and Interpreting

1. **R** What subject is being discussed by the soldiers under the railway bridge?

   I Do you think that the soldiers have a clear idea about what they are up against? Why, or why not?

2. **R** What does not appear on the scene until five o'clock?

   I What evidence does this chapter present that the military is not prepared to deal adequately with this emergency?

Words for Everyday Use

bawl (bôl) *v.*, shout or call out noisily; yell

reins (rāns) *n.*, means of guiding or controlling, especially a horse

Vocabulary in Context

- When the baby dropped her bottle, she began to bawl.
- If you pull back on the reins, the horse will stop.

10
IN THE STORM

Leatherhead is about twelve miles from Maybury Hill. The scent of hay was in the air through the lush meadows beyond Pyrford, and the hedges on either side were sweet and gay with multitudes of dog-roses. The heavy firing that had broken out while we were driving down Maybury Hill ceased as abruptly as it began, leaving the evening very peaceful and still. We got to Leatherhead without misadventure about nine o'clock, and the horse had an hour's rest while I took supper with my cousins and commended my wife to their care.

My wife was curiously silent throughout the drive, and seemed oppressed with forebodings of evil. I talked to her reassuringly, pointing out that the Martians were tied to the pit by sheer heaviness, and at the utmost could but crawl a little out of it; but she answered only in monosyllables.[1] Had it not been for my promise to the innkeeper, she would, I think, have urged me to stay in Leatherhead that night. Would that I had! Her face, I remember, was very white as we parted.

For my own part, I had been feverishly excited all day. Something very like the war fever that occasionally runs through a civilized community had got into my blood, and in my heart I was not so very sorry that I had to return to Maybury that night. I was even afraid that that last fusillade I had heard might mean the extermination of our invaders from Mars. I can best express my state of mind by saying that I wanted to be in at the death.

It was nearly eleven when I started to return. The night was unexpectedly dark; to me, walking out of the lighted passage of my cousins' house, it seemed indeed black, and it was as hot and close as the day. Overhead the clouds were driving fast, albeit not a breath stirred the shrubs about us. My cousins' man lit both lamps. Happily, I knew the road intimately. My wife stood in the light of the doorway, and watched me until I jumped up into the dog-cart. Then abruptly she turned and went in, leaving my cousins side by side wishing me good hap.

I was a little depressed at first with the contagion of my wife's fears, but very soon my thoughts reverted to the Martians. At that time I was absolutely in the dark as to the course of the evening's fighting. I did not know even the circumstances that had precipitated the conflict. As I came through Ockham (for that was the way I returned, and not through Send and Old Woking) I saw along the western horizon a blood-red glow, which, as I drew nearer, crept slowly up the sky. The driving clouds of the gathering thunderstorm mingled there with masses of black and red smoke.

Ripley Street was deserted, and except for a lighted window or so the village showed not a sign of life; but I narrowly escaped an accident at the corner of the road to Pyrford, where a knot of people stood with their backs to me. They said nothing to me as I passed. I do not know what they knew of the things happening beyond the hill, nor do I know if the silent houses I passed on my way were sleeping securely, or deserted and empty, or harassed and watching against the terror of the night.

From Ripley until I came through Pyrford I was in the valley of the Wey, and the red glare was hidden from me. As I ascended the little hill beyond Pyrford

❶ *What promise does the narrator intend to keep? Do you think that he is doing the right thing? Why, or why not?*

CHAPTER 10

1. **monosyllables.** Words or utterances with only one syllable

WORDS FOR EVERYDAY USE

com • mend (kə mend) *v.*, put in the care of another, entrust
fore • bod • ing (fôr bōd´iŋ) *n.*, prediction of something bad or harmful
fu • sil • lade (fyo͞o´sə läd´) *n.*, simultaneous or rapid and continuous discharge of many firearms
con • ta • gion (kən tā´jən) *n.*, spreading of emotions, ideas, or customs from one person to another
pre • cip • i • tate (prē sip´ə tāt) *v.*, cause to happen before expected

ANSWER TO GUIDED READING QUESTION

❶ The narrator intends to return the cart. Obviously, since the narrator has promised to return the cart, he should try to do so. Some students may feel, however, that the danger of the present situation is sufficient to nullify such a promise. After all, a cart is not worth risking one's life.

VOCABULARY IN CONTEXT

- The principal would like to commend you for making the honor roll.
- The fog and the wailing of the sirens in the distance filled Marco with a sense of foreboding.
- The soldiers hunkered down in their trenches when the fusillade began.
- When the plague broke out in the city, Newton left to avoid contagion.
- News of the oncoming snowstorm precipitated a rush to the grocery stores to buy supplies.

Answer to Guided Reading Question

➊ The narrator sees a large, moving mass of machinery on a tripod stand. Inside this enormous war machine is a Martian.

Church the glare came into view again, and the trees about me shivered with the first intimation of the storm that was upon me. Then I heard midnight pealing out from Pyrford Church behind me, and then came the silhouette of Maybury Hill, with its treetops and roofs black and sharp against the red.

Even as I beheld this a lurid green glare lit the road about me and showed the distant woods toward Addlestone. I felt a tug at the reins. I saw that the driving clouds had been pierced as it were by a thread of green fire, suddenly lighting their confusion and falling into the field to my left. It was the Third Falling-Star!

What does the narrator see? ➊

Close on its apparition, and blindingly violet by contrast, danced out the first lightning of the gathering storm, and the thunder burst like a rocket overhead. The horse took the bit between his teeth and bolted.

A moderate incline runs toward the foot of Maybury Hill, and down this we clattered. Once the lightning had begun, it went on in as rapid a succession of flashes as I have ever seen. The thunder-claps, treading one on the heels of another and with a strange crackling accompaniment, sounded more like the working of a gigantic electric machine than the usual detonating reverberations. The flickering light was blinding and confusing, and a thin hail smote gustily at my face as I drove down the slope.

At first I regarded little but the road before me, and then abruptly my attention was arrested by something that was moving rapidly down the opposite slope of Maybury Hill. At first I took it for the wet roof of a house, but one flash following another showed it to be in swift rolling movement. It was an elusive vision—a moment of bewildering darkness, and then, in a flash like daylight, the red masses of the Orphanage near the crest of the hill, the green tops of the pine trees, and this problematical object came out clear and sharp and bright.

And this Thing I saw! How can I describe it? A monstrous tripod,[2] higher than many houses, striding over the young pine-trees, and smashing them aside in its career; a walking engine of glittering metal, striding now across the heather; articulate ropes of steel dangling from it, and the clattering tumult of its passage mingling with the riot of the thunder. A flash, and it came out vividly, heeling over one way with two feet in the air, to vanish and reappear almost instantly as it seemed, with the next flash, a hundred yards nearer. Can you imagine a milking-stool tilted and bowled violently along the ground? That was the impression those instant flashes gave. But instead of a milking-stool imagine it a great body of machinery on a tripod stand.

Then suddenly the trees in the pine wood ahead of me were parted, as brittle reeds are parted by a man thrusting through them; they were snapped off and driven headlong, and a second huge tripod appeared, rushing, as it seemed, headlong toward me. And I was galloping hard to meet it! At the sight of the second monster my nerve went altogether. Not stopping to look again, I wrenched the horse's head hard round to the right, and in another moment the dog-cart had heeled over upon the horse; the shafts smashed noisily, and I was flung sideways and fell heavily into a shallow pool of water.

I crawled out almost immediately, and crouched, my feet still in the water, under

2. **tripod.** Three-legged stand or support

Words for Everyday Use

sil • hou • ette (sil´o͞o et´) *n.,* any dark shape or figure seen against a light background

ap • pa • ri • tion (ap´ə rish´ən) *n.,* anything that appears unexpectedly or in an extraordinary way

re • ver • ber • a • tion (ri vʉr´bə rā´shən) *n.,* reechoed sound

Vocabulary in Context

- I could see the silhouettes of three people cast upon the shade drawn over the window.
- In the movie, someone moves into a new house and then starts seeing apparitions in the basement at night.
- Calling across the canyon, Wendy could her the reverberation of her voice off the sides of the cliffs.

a clump of furze. The horse lay motionless (his neck was broken, poor brute!) and by the lightning flashes I saw the black bulk of the overturned dog-cart and the silhouette of the wheel still spinning slowly. In another moment the colossal mechanism went striding by me, and passed uphill toward Pyrford.

Seen nearer, the Thing was incredibly strange, for it was no mere insensate machine driving on its way. Machine it was, with a ringing metallic pace, and long, flexible, glittering tentacles (one of which gripped a young pine tree) swinging and rattling about its strange body. It picked its road as it went striding along, and the brazen hood that surmounted it moved to and fro with the inevitable suggestion of a head looking about. Behind the main body was a huge mass of white metal like a gigantic fisherman's basket, and puffs of green smoke squirted out from the joints of the limbs as the monster swept by me. And in an instant it was gone.

So much I saw then, all vaguely for the flickering of the lightning, in blinding high lights and dense black shadows.

As it passed it set up an exultant deafening howl that drowned the thunder—"Aloo! aloo!"—and in another minute it was with its companion, half a mile away, stooping over something in the field. I have no doubt this Thing in the field was the third of the ten cylinders they had fired at us from Mars.

For some minutes I lay there in the rain and darkness watching, by the intermittent light, these monstrous beings of metal moving about in the distance over the hedge-tops. A thin hail was now beginning, and as it came and went their figures grew misty and then flashed into clearness again. Now and then came a gap in the lightning, and the night swallowed them up.

I was soaked with hail above and puddle-water below. It was some time before my blank astonishment would let me struggle up the bank to a drier position, or think at all of my imminent peril.

Not far from me was a little one-roomed squatter's hut of wood, surrounded by a patch of potato-garden. I struggled to my feet at last, and, crouching and making use of every chance of cover, I made a run for this. I hammered at the door, but I could not make the people hear (if there were any people inside), and after a time I desisted, and, availing myself of a ditch for the greater part of the way, succeeded in crawling, unobserved by these monstrous machines, into the pine wood toward Maybury.

Under cover of this I pushed on, wet and shivering now, toward my own house. I walked among the trees trying to find the footpath. It was very dark indeed in the wood, for the lightning was now becoming infrequent, and the hail, which was pouring down in a torrent, fell in columns through the gaps in the heavy foliage.

If I had fully realized the meaning of all the things I had seen I should have immediately worked my way round through Byfleet to Street Cobham, and so gone back to rejoin my wife at Leatherhead. But that night the strangeness of things about me, and my physical wretchedness, prevented me, for I was bruised, weary, wet to the skin, deafened and blinded by the storm.

I had a vague idea of going on to my own house, and that was as much motive as I had. I staggered through the trees, fell into a ditch and bruised my knees against a plank, and finally splashed out into the lane that ran down from the College Arms. I say

1 *What is behind the main body of the Martian machine?*

2 *What does the narrator fail to realize?*

Words for Everyday Use

in • sen• sate (in sen´) *adj.,* not capable of feeling sensation
ex • ult • ant (eg zult´´nt) *adj.,* triumphant
im • mi • nent (im´ə nənt) *adj.,* likely to happen without delay; impending
de • sist (di zist´) *v.,* stop; abstain
a • vail (ə vāl) *v.,* take advantage of; use; utilize
tor • rent (tôr´ənt) *n.,* very heavy fall of rain

Answers to Guided Reading Questions

1 Behind the machine is a huge mass of white metal like a gigantic fisherman's basket.

2 The narrator fails to realize the meaning of all the things that he has seen.

Vocabulary in Context

- After Will's accident, the nerves in his lower legs were insensate.
- After scoring a touchdown, the quarterback gave out an exultant yell.
- The security guards were anticipating the imminent arrival of the president.
- Please desist from littering on the sidewalk!
- Our attempts to coax the cat down from the tree were to no avail.
- The storm clouds released a torrent that washed away much of the top soil.

Answer to Guided Reading Question

❶ The narrator sees the landlord of the Spotted Dog—the person from whom he had borrowed the cart. The landlord is dead.

Answers for Reviewing the Selection

RECALLING AND INTERPRETING

1. **Recalling.** He wishes to return the cart belonging to the landlord of the Spotted Dog. **Interpreting.** Responses will vary. Some students may feel that the narrator acts sensibly because a promise is a promise. Others may feel that by attempting to return the cart, the narrator puts himself in great danger.
2. **Recalling.** The narrator sees the gigantic tripods used by the Martians. The tripods support a mass of machinery. Tentacles extend from the machine. At the back of one of the tripods is a basket. **Interpreting.** Responses will vary.

splashed, for the storm water was sweeping the sand down the hill in a muddy torrent. There in the darkness a man blundered into me and sent me reeling back.

He gave a cry of terror, sprang sideways, and rushed on before I could gather my wits sufficiently to speak to him. So heavy was the stress of the storm just at this place that I had the hardest task to win my way up the hill. I went close up to the fence on the left and worked my way along its palings.

Near the top I stumbled upon something soft, and, by a flash of lightning, saw between my feet a heap of black broadcloth and a pair of boots. Before I could distinguish clearly how the man lay, the flicker of light had passed. I stood over him waiting for the next flash. When it came, I saw that he was a sturdy man, cheaply but not shabbily dressed; his head was bent under his body, and he lay crumpled up close to the fence, as though he had been flung violently against it.

Whom does the narrator see? What has happened to this person? ❶

Overcoming the repugnance natural to one who had never before touched a dead body, I stooped and turned him over to feel for his heart. He was quite dead. Apparently his neck had been broken. The lightning flashed for a third time, and his face leaped upon me. I sprang to my feet. It was the landlord of the Spotted Dog, whose conveyance I had taken.

I stepped over him gingerly and pushed on up the hill. I made my way by the police station and the College Arms toward my own house. Nothing was burning on the hillside, though from the common there still came a red glare and a rolling tumult of ruddy smoke beating up against the drenching hail. So far as I could see by the flashes, the houses about me were mostly uninjured. By the College Arms a dark heap lay in the road.

Down the road toward Maybury Bridge there were voices and the sound of feet, but I had not the courage to shout or to go to them. I let myself in with my latch-key, closed, locked and bolted the door, staggered to the foot of the staircase, and sat down. My imagination was full of those striding metallic monsters, and of the dead body smashed against the fence.

I crouched at the foot of the staircase with my back to the wall, shivering violently.

Reviewing the Selection

Recalling and Interpreting

1. (R) Why does the narrator leave his wife to return to Woking?
   (I) Is the narrator's action an understandable thing to do under these circumstances? Why, or why not?
2. (R) What does the narrator see on Maybury Hill? What do they look like?
   (I) What would you do if you were the narrator and encountered these things?

Words for Everyday Use

re • pug • nance (ri pug´nəns) *n.,* extreme dislike or distaste, aversion

con • vey • ance (kən vā´əns) *n.,* vehicle; means for carrying or transporting

Vocabulary in Context

- Philip felt great repugnance for violent films and television programs.
- Airplanes, automobiles, trains, and trucks are all common modern conveyances.

11
At the Window

I have already said that my storms of emotion have a trick of exhausting themselves. After a time I discovered that I was cold and wet, and with little pools of water about me on the stair-carpet. I got up almost mechanically, and then I was moved to change my clothes.

After I had done that I went upstairs to my study, but why I did so I do not know. The window of my study looks over the trees and the railway toward Horsell Common. In the hurry of our departure this window had been left open. The passage was dark, and, by contrast with the picture the window-frame enclosed, the side of the room seemed impenetrably dark. I stopped short in the doorway.

The thunderstorm had passed. The towers of the Oriental College and the pine trees about it had gone, and very far away, lit by a vivid red glare, the common about the sand-pits was visible. Across the light, huge black shapes, grotesque and strange, moved busily to and fro.

It seemed indeed as if the whole country in that direction was on fire—a broad hillside set with minute tongues of flame, swaying and writhing with the gusts of the dying storm, and throwing a red reflection upon the cloud-scud above. Every now and then a haze of smoke from some nearer conflagration drove across the window and hid the Martian shapes. I could not see what they were doing, nor the clear form of them, nor recognize the black objects they were busied upon. Neither could I see the nearer fire, though the reflections of it danced on the wall and ceiling of the study. A sharp, resinous tang of burning was in the air.

I closed the door noiselessly and crept toward the window. As I did so, the view opened out until, on the one hand, it reached to the houses about Woking station, and on the other to the charred and blackened pine woods of Byfleet. There was a light down below the hill, on the railway, near the arch, and several of the houses along the Maybury road and the streets near the station were glowing ruins. The light upon the railway puzzled me at first; there were a black heap and a vivid glare, and to the right of that a row of yellow oblongs. Then I perceived this was a wrecked train, the forepart smashed and on fire, the hinder carriages still upon the rails.

❶ *What are the Martians doing to the trains? Why might they be doing this?*

Between these three main centers of light, the houses, the train, and the burning country toward Chobham, stretched irregular patches of dark country, broken here and there by intervals of dimly glowing and smoking ground. It was the strangest spectacle, that black expanse set with fire. It reminded me, more than anything else, of the Potteries at night. At first I could distinguish no people at all, though I peered intently for them. Later I saw against the light of Woking station a number of black figures hurrying one after the other across the line.

And this was the little world in which I had been living securely for years, this fiery chaos! What had happened in the last seven hours I still did not know; nor did I know, though I was beginning to guess, the relation between these mechanical colossi and the sluggish lumps I had seen disgorged from the cylinder. With a queer feeling of impersonal interest I turned my desk chair to the window,

❷ *What has happened to the narrator's world?*

Words for Everyday Use

mi • nute (mī no͞ot´) *adj.*, small

con • fla • gra • tion (kän´flə grā´shən) *n.*, large, destructive fire

co • los • sus (kə läs´əs) *n.*, huge or important person or thing

dis • gorge (dis gôrj´) *v.*, pour forth the contents of

Answers to Guided Reading Questions

❶ The Martians are destroying the trains. They are probably doing so in order to stop the movement of people and supplies, including military personnel and equipment.

❷ The narrator's world has changed from one of security to one of fiery chaos.

Vocabulary in Context

- Yolanda and the other science students used a microscrope to study the minute amoebae.
- A terrible conflagration once destroyed much of the city of Chicago.
- In front of the museum stood a colossus—a gigantic statue of Moses.
- The train stopped at Mission Station to disgorge its passengers.

Answer to Guided Reading Question

1 The narrator wonders whether the mechanisms are intelligent or whether a Martian sits within each mechanism, directing its movements.

sat down, and stared at the blackened country, and particularly at the three gigantic black things that were going to and fro in the glare about the sand-pits.

What does the narrator wonder about the mechanisms? 1

They seemed amazingly busy. I began to ask myself what they could be. Were they intelligent mechanisms? Such a thing I felt was impossible. Or did a Martian sit within each, ruling, directing, using, much as a man's brain sits and rules in his body? I began to compare the things to human machines, to ask myself for the first time in my life how an iron-clad[1] or a steam-engine[2] would seem to an intelligent lower animal.

The storm had left the sky clear, and over the smoke of the burning land the little fading pinpoint of Mars was dropping into the west, when a soldier came into my garden. I heard a slight scraping at the fence, and rousing myself from the lethargy that had fallen upon me, I looked down and saw him dimly, clambering over the palings. At the sight of another human being my torpor passed, and I leaned out of the window eagerly.

"Hist!" said I, in a whisper.

He stopped astride of the fence in doubt. Then he came over and across the lawn to the corner of the house. He bent down and stepped softly.

"Who's there?" he said, also whispering, standing under the window and peering up.

"Where are you going?" I asked.

"God knows."

"Are you trying to hide?"

"That's it."

"Come into the house," I said.

I went down, unfastened the door, and let him in, and locked the door again. I could not see his face. He was hatless, and his coat was unbuttoned.

"My God!" he said, as I drew him in.

"What has happened?" I asked.

"What hasn't?" In the obscurity I could see he made a gesture of despair. "They wiped us out—simply wiped us out," he repeated again and again.

He followed me, almost mechanically, into the dining room.

Abruptly he sat down before the table, put his head on his arms, and began to sob and weep like a little boy, in a perfect passion of emotion, while I, with a curious forgetfulness of my own recent despair, stood beside him, wondering.

It was a long time before he could steady his nerves to answer my questions, and then he answered perplexingly and brokenly. He was a driver in the artillery,[3] and had only come into action about seven. At that time firing was going on across the common, and it was said the first party of Martians were crawling slowly toward their second cylinder under cover of a metal shield.

Later this shield staggered up on tripod legs and became the first of the fighting-machines I had seen. The gun he drove had been unlimbered[4] near Horsell, in order to command the sand-pits, and its arrival it was that had precipitated the action. As the limber gunners went to the rear, his horse trod in a rabbit-hole and came down, throwing him into a depression of the ground. At the same moment the gun exploded behind him, the ammunition blew up, there was fire all about him, and he found himself lying under a heap of charred dead men and dead horses.

Chapter 11

1. **iron-clad.** Ship built with and covered by metal
2. **steam-engine.** Railroad train powered by steam energy
3. **artillery.** Division of an army in charge of firing the heavy guns
4. **unlimbered.** Prepared for firing by removing the front part of the gun carriage

Words for Everyday Use

leth • ar • gy (leth´ər jē) *n.,* great lack of energy; sluggishness

tor • por (tôr´pər) *n.,* state of being inactive

ob • scu • ri • ty (əb skyo͞or´ə tē) *n.,* condition or quality of being dim or lacking light

per • plex • ing • ly (pər pleks iŋ lē) *adv.,* with confusion or hesitancy

Vocabulary in Context

- Overcome by lethargy because of the heat, the hikers paused to rest.
- The hikers were roused from their torpor by the sudden appearance of a brown bear.
- Out of the obscurity of the fog came a young man on a bicycle.
- The crossword puzzle was perplexingly difficult.

"I lay still," he said, "scared out of my wits, with the forequarter of a horse atop of me. We'd been wiped out. And the smell—good God! Like burnt meat! I was hurt across the back by the fall of the horse, and there I had to lie until I felt better. Just like a parade it had been a minute before—then stumble, bang, swish!

"Wiped out!" he said.

He had hid under the dead horse for a long time, peeping out furtively across the common. The Cardigan men had tried a rush, in skirmishing order,[5] at the pit, simply to be swept out of existence. Then the monster had risen to its feet, and had begun to walk leisurely to and fro across the common among the few fugitives, with its headlike hood turning about exactly like the head of a cowled human being. A kind of arm carried a complicated metallic case, about which green flashes scintillated, and out of the funnel of this there smote the Heat-Ray.

In a few minutes there was, so far as the soldier could see, not a living thing left upon the common, and every bush and tree upon it that was not already a blackened skeleton was burning. The hussar had been on the road beyond the curvature of the ground, and he saw nothing of them. He heard the Maxims rattle for a time and then become still. The giant saved Woking station and its cluster of houses until the last; then in a moment the Heat-Ray was brought to bear, and the town became a heap of fiery ruins. Then the Thing shut off the Heat-Ray, and, turning its back upon the artilleryman, began to waddle away toward the smoldering pine woods that sheltered the second cylinder. As it did so a second glittering Titan built itself up out of the pit.

The second monster followed the first, and at that the artilleryman began to crawl very cautiously across the hot heather ash toward Horsell. He managed to get alive into the ditch by the side of the road, and so escaped to Woking. There his story became ejaculatory. The place was impassable. It seems there were a few people alive there, frantic for the most part, and many burned and scalded. He was turned aside by the fire, and hid among some almost scorching heaps of broken wall as one of the Martian giants returned. He saw this one pursue a man, catch him up in one of its steely tentacles, and knock his head against the trunk of a pine tree. At last, after nightfall, the artilleryman made a rush for it and got over the railway embankment.

Since then he had been skulking along toward Maybury, in the hope of getting

❶ *What happened to the soldiers? What does this event reveal about the narrator's theory that humans will wipe out the Martians?*

❷ *What did the artilleryman see?*

5. **skirmishing order.** Military formation in which the soldiers are grouped tightly together

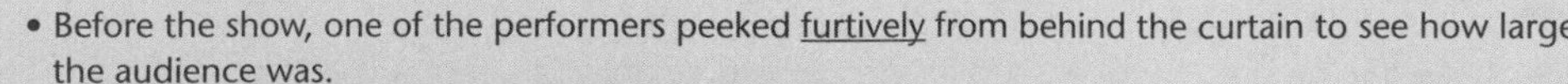

WORDS FOR EVERYDAY USE

fur • tive • ly (fur´tiv lē) *adv.,* stealthily; in a sneaky manner as if to avoid observation

cowl (ko͞ol) *v.,* put on a hood

scin • til • late (sint´'l āt´) *v.,* flash, sparkle

e • jac • u • la • to • ry (ē jak´yo͞o lə tôr ē) *adj.,* exclamatory

ANSWERS TO GUIDED READING QUESTIONS

❶ The soldiers are wiped out by the Martians. The narrator's theory is completely wrong.

❷ The artilleryman saw a Martian machine grab a man and kill him.

VOCABULARY IN CONTEXT

- Before the show, one of the performers peeked furtively from behind the curtain to see how large the audience was.
- The monks cowled their heads as they left the church.
- The lights of the supercomputer scintillated in the dark room.
- Do you enjoy the ejaculatory comments that sports announcers make during games?

Answer to Guided Reading Question

➊ The Martians make war indiscriminately (that is, on everyone) and universally (that is, on everything in their range).

Answers for Reviewing the Selection

RECALLING AND INTERPRETING

1. **Recalling.** The narrator views the scene with impersonal interest. **Interpreting.** Responses will vary. The narrator may simply be overwhelmed by the recent events, which may be what causes him to feel an impersonal detachment.
2. **Recalling.** The other soliders were all killed. **Interpreting.** One might draw the conclusion that the soldiers of Earth are no match for the Martian war machines.

Selection Check Test with Answers

EX. What weapon do the Martians use on the Chobham Road?
They use a heat ray.

1. When the narrator gets back home, what does he tell his wife about how the Martians might be destroyed?
He says that they might be destroyed by a shell in the pit.
2. Who stands around discussing ways to destroy the Martians at the beginning of Chapter 9?
A group of soldiers stands around discussing ways to destroy the Martians.
3. What does the narrator compare to a "milking-stool tilted and bowled violently along the ground"?
The narrator compares a Martian tripod to a milking stool.
4. From what place does the narrator observe the fiery chaos into which his world has been thrown?
He observes this from the window of his home.
5. Who survives a Martian attack by lying in a depression beneath dead horses and men?
The artilleryman does.

out of danger Londonward. People were hiding in trenches and cellars, and many of the survivors had made off toward Woking village and Send. He had been consumed with thirst until he found one of the water mains near the railway arch smashed, and the water bubbling out like a spring upon the road.

That was the story I got from him, bit by bit. He grew calmer telling me and trying to make me see the things he had seen. He had eaten no food since mid-day, he told me early in his narrative, and I found some mutton[6] and bread in the pantry and brought it into the room. We lit no lamp for fear of attracting the Martians, and ever and again our hands would touch upon bread or meat. As he talked, things about us came darkly out of the darkness, and the trampled bushes and broken rose-trees outside the window grew distinct. It would seem that a number of men or animals had rushed across the lawn. I began to see his face, blackened and haggard, as no doubt mine was also.

When we had finished eating we went softly upstairs to my study, and I looked again out of the open window. In one night the valley had become a valley of ashes. The fires had dwindled now. Where flames had been there were now streamers of smoke; but the countless ruins of shattered and gutted houses and blasted and blackened trees that the night had hidden stood out now gaunt and terrible in the pitiless light of dawn. Yet here and there some object had had the luck to escape—a white railway signal here, the end of a green-house there, white and fresh amid the wreckage. Never before in the history of warfare had destruction been so indiscriminate and so universal. ➊ And shining with the growing light of the east, three of the metallic giants stood about the pit, their cowls rotating as though they were surveying the desolation they had made.

➊ What is different about the kind of war waged by the Martians?

It seemed to me that the pit had been enlarged, and ever and again puffs of vivid green vapour streamed up out of it toward the brightening dawn—streamed up, whirled, broke, and vanished.

Beyond were the pillars of fire about Chobham. They became pillars of blood-shot smoke at the first touch of day.

6. **mutton.** Meat of an adult sheep

Reviewing the Selection

Recalling and Interpreting

1. Ⓡ What is the narrator's reaction to the view that he sees from his study window?
   Ⓘ Would you have the same reaction in a similar circumstance? What is unusual about this narrator?
2. Ⓡ What happened to the other soldiers who were on the common with the artilleryman?
   Ⓘ What conclusions might be drawn based on this first skirmish between the Martians and the Earthlings?

Words for Everyday Use

con • sume (kən so͞om) *v.,* overtake, absorb completely
gaunt (gônt) *adj.,* looking grim, forbidding, or desolate
in • dis • crim • in • ate (in´di skrim´i nit) *adj.,* random; not based on careful selection

Vocabulary in Context

- The hungry customer consumed three plates of spaghetti.
- A gaunt scarecrow, with sticks for arms, was propped up in the middle of the field.
- Do not be indiscriminate in your television viewing; instead, carefully select the programs that you will watch.

Vocabulary Skills

Suffixes

A **suffix** is a group of letters added to the end of a base word to change its meaning and, often, its part of speech. Knowing the meanings of suffixes can help you to understand unfamiliar words that you encounter in your reading. The following chart explains the meanings of some common suffixes.

COMMON SUFFIXES

Suffix	Meaning	Example	Meaning
–able	capable of	inflatable	capable of being inflated
–fold	multiplied by	fourfold	multiplied by four
–ful	full of	joyful	full of joy
	amount that would fill	cupful	amount that would fill a cup
	showing the quality of	helpful	showing the quality of helping
–less	not having	friendless	not having friends
–logy, –ology	science of	zoology	the science of living creatures

SUFFIXES THAT CREATE NOUNS

Suffix	Examples
–er, –or	create (verb) + –or = creator (noun)
	paint (verb) + –er = painter (noun)
–ism	Romantic (adjective) + –ism = Romanticism (noun)
	natural (adjective) + –ism = naturalism (noun)

CONTINUED

LANGUAGE LAB

INTRODUCING THE SKILL

Review the following terms with your students: *base word* (a word to which a prefix or suffix is added), *prefix* (a word part added to the beginning of a word), and *suffix* (a word part added to the end of a word).

PREVIEWING THE SKILL

Write the example words from the charts on the chalkboard. Have students come to the board and draw lines to separate the suffix of each word from its base. Then ask each student to tell what the suffix means.

PRACTICING THE SKILL

Assign the Try It Yourself exercise.

REVIEWING THE SKILL

Go over students' work with them. Try to identify the words that they find most difficult to spell. Ask them to use these words in sentences.

Answers for Try It Yourself

Exercise

1. removeable, able to be removed
2. eightfold, multiplied by eight
3. teaspoonful, amount that would fill a teaspoon
4. sorrowful, full of sorrow
5. regretful, showing the quality of regret
6. psychology, the study of the psyche, or mind
7. regretable, capable of being regretted
8. expressionless, not having expression
9. twelvefold, multiplied by twelve
10. toneless, not having tone

Suffix	Examples
–ist	final (adjective) + –ist = finalist (noun)
–ment	govern (verb) + –ment = government (noun) entitle (verb) + –ment = entitlement (noun)
–ness	green (adjective) + –ness = greenness (noun) greedy (adjective) + –ness = greediness

SUFFIXES THAT CREATE ADJECTIVES

Suffix	Examples
–al	nature (noun) + –al = natural (adjective) series (noun) + –al = serial (adjective)
–istic	future (noun) + istic = futuristic (adjective) natural (noun) + istic = naturalistic (adjective)

When you use a suffix in your writing, check a dictionary, if necessary, to see how the word is spelled.

Try It Yourself

Exercise. Create new words by joining together each pair of base words and suffixes given below. Tell what each new word means.

EXAMPLE master + ful
masterful, showing the quality of mastery

1. remove + able
2. eight + fold
3. teaspoon + ful
4. sorrow + ful
5. regret + ful
6. psyche + ology
7. regret + able
8. expression + less
9. twelve + fold
10. tone + less

READER'S JOURNAL

If you were the Prime Minister of England facing the events described up to this point, how would you react? What measures would you take to meet the challenge of the Martian invasion? Consider such matters as military action, the maintenance of public order, and the handling of refugees from the war zone. Write about these questions in your journal.

12
What I Saw of the Destruction of Weybridge and Shepperton

As the dawn grew brighter we withdrew from the window from which we had watched the Martians, and went very quietly downstairs.

The artilleryman agreed with me that the house was no place to stay in. He proposed, he said, to make his way Londonward, and thence rejoin his battery—No. 12, of the Horse Artillery. My plan was to return at once to Leatherhead; and so greatly had the strength of the Martians impressed me that I had determined to take my wife to Newhaven, and go with her out of the country forthwith. For I already perceived clearly that the country about London must inevitably be the scene of a disastrous struggle before such creatures as these could be destroyed.

Between us and Leatherhead, however, lay the Third Cylinder, with its guarding giants. Had I been alone, I think I should have taken my chance and struck across country. But the artilleryman dissuaded me: "It's no kindness to the right sort of wife," he said, "to make her a widow"; and in the end I agreed to go with him, under cover of the woods, northward as far as Street Cobham before I parted with him. Thence I would make a big detour by Epsom to reach Leatherhead.

I should have started at once, but my companion had been in active service and he knew better than that. He made me ransack the house for a flask, which he filled; and we lined every available pocket with packets of biscuits and slices of meat. Then we crept out of the house, and ran as quickly as we could down the ill-made road by which I had come overnight. The houses seemed deserted. In the road lay a group of three charred bodies close together, struck dead by the Heat-Ray; and here and there were things that people had dropped—a clock, a slipper, a silver spoon, and the like poor valuables. At the corner turning up toward the post-office a little cart, filled with boxes and furniture, and horseless, heeled over on a broken wheel. A cash-box had been hastily smashed open and thrown under the debris.

Except the lodge at the Orphanage, which was still on fire, none of the houses had suffered very greatly here. The Heat-Ray had shaved the chimney tops and passed. Yet, save ourselves, there did not seem to be a living soul on Maybury Hill. The majority of the inhabitants had escaped, I suppose, by way of the Old Woking road—the road I had taken when I drove to Leatherhead—or they had hidden.

❶ *What does the narrator perceive clearly already?*

❷ *What does the artilleryman talk the narrator out of doing? What reason does the artilleryman give?*

Words for Everyday Use

bat • ter • y (bat´ər ē) *n.,* basic unit of military personnel

dis • suade (di swād´) *v.,* persuade not to do something

Vocabulary in Context

- A battery of loyalist soldiers moved into place near the rebel camp.
- Ms. Markham tried to dissuade her daughter from getting another puppy.

READER'S JOURNAL

As an alternative activity, you might ask students to describe what might be the proper response of other countries, such as the United States and France, to the events occurring in England.

Answers to Guided Reading Questions

❶ He perceives that there will be a disastrous struggle with the Martians.

❷ The artilleryman talks the narrator out of heading to Leatherhead to rejoin his wife. The artilleryman argues that the narrator would be doing no kindness to his wife if he risked his life.

SPELLING AND VOCABULARY WORDS FROM THE SELECTION

allusion	dissuade
annihilate	dubiously
apathy	eddy
arcade	estuary
ascertain	exempt
assiduously	exhort
battery	exorbitant
blight	expend
brevity	expostulate
broach	extent
cannonade	exultation
cleft	facade
coherency	flaxen
confluence	formidable
congested	froth
conical	furtive
conspicuously	galvanize
copse	gesticulate
counsel	gout
darkling	gradient
decapitate	granary
delusive	hearsay
demented	impassable
detail	impetus
dilated	impotent
din	inarticulately
dispatched	inaudibly
disseminated	incapacity

(cont.)

Answer to Guided Reading Question

❶ The lieutenant says that the description is "confounded nonsense." He says this because the description is of something quite unusual and therefore quite unbelievable.

SPELLING AND VOCABULARY WORDS FROM THE SELECTION

incessant	promenaders
insoluble	prosecute
interminable	prostrate
intermittently	provisions
intricate	proximity
invulnerable	pugilistic
jaded	pungent
lass	quasi-proclamation
leviathan	raiment
liquefaction	reiterate
loiter	remnant
lurid	resolute
magnitude	ricochet
menagerie	rouse
methodically	rout
mettle	sack
multitudinous	sallow
network	sally
nocturnal	siege
nomadic	spasmodic
obliquely	staccato
oblivious	stippled
officiate	terminus
ominous	terminus
onslaught	tocsin
opaque	treble
palpable	ulation
parapet	unkempt
parboil	utterly
parody	vehement
paroxysm	ventilator
patent	vicar
pier	vigilant
placard	volition
pluckily	volley
portmanteau	wretch
precipitation	

We went down the lane, by the body of the man in black, sodden now from the overnight hail, and broke into the woods at the foot of the hill. We pushed through these toward the railway without meeting a soul. The woods across the line were but the scarred and blackened ruins of woods; for the most part the trees had fallen, but a certain proportion still stood, dismal gray stems, with dark-brown foliage instead of green.

❶ What does the lieutenant think of the artilleryman's description? Why?

On our side the fire had done no more than scorch the nearer trees; it had failed to secure its footing. In one place the woodmen had been at work on Saturday; trees, felled and freshly trimmed, lay in a clearing, with heaps of sawdust by the sawing-machine and its engine. Hard by was a temporary hut, deserted. There was not a breath of wind this morning, and everything was strangely still. Even the birds were hushed, and as we hurried along I and the artilleryman talked in whispers and looked now and again over our shoulders. Once or twice we stopped to listen.

After a time we drew near the road, and as we did so we heard the clatter of hoofs and saw through the tree stems three cavalry soldiers riding slowly toward Woking. We hailed them, and they halted while we hurried toward them. It was a lieutenant and a couple of privates of the 8th Hussars, with a stand like a theodolite,[1] which the artilleryman told me was a heliograph.[2]

"You are the first men I've seen coming this way this morning," said the lieutenant. "What's brewing?"

His voice and face were eager. The men behind him stared curiously. The artilleryman jumped down the bank into the road and saluted.

"Gun destroyed last night, sir. Have been hiding. Trying to rejoin battery, sir. You'll come in sight of the Martians, I expect, about half a mile along this road."

"What the dickens are they like?" asked the lieutenant.

"Giants in armor, sir. Hundred feet high. Three legs and a body like 'luminium,[3] with a mighty great head in a hood, sir."

"Get out!" said the lieutenant. "What confounded nonsense!"

"You'll see, sir. They carry a kind of box, sir, that shoots fire and strikes you dead."

"What d'ye mean—a gun?"

"No, sir," and the artilleryman began a vivid account of the Heat-Ray. Halfway through, the lieutenant interrupted him and looked up at me. I was still standing on the bank by the side of the road.

"Did you see it?" said the lieutenant.

"It's perfectly true," I said.

"Well," said the lieutenant, "I suppose it's my business to see it too. Look here"—to the artilleryman—"we're detailed here clearing people out of their houses. You'd better go along and report yourself to Brigadier-General Marvin, and tell him all you know. He's at Weybridge. Know the way?"

"I do," I said; and he turned his horse southward again.

"Half a mile, you say?" said he.

"At most," I answered, and pointed over the treetops southward. He thanked me and rode on, and we saw them no more.

Farther along we came upon a group of three women and two children in the road, busy clearing out a laborer's cottage. They

Chapter 12

1. **theodolite.** Surveying instrument used to measure angles
2. **heliograph.** Device used for signaling by flashing the sun's rays with a mirror
3. **'luminium.** Slang for the metal aluminum

Words for Everyday Use

de • tail (dē tāl´) *v.,* choose for a particular task

Vocabulary in Context

- Several players on the football team were detailed to clean up the field.

had got hold of a little hand truck, and were piling it up with unclean-looking bundles and shabby furniture. They were all too assiduously engaged to talk to us as we passed.

By Byfleet station we emerged from the pine trees, and found the country calm and peaceful under the morning sunlight. We were far beyond the range of the Heat-Ray there, and had it not been for the silent desertion of some of the houses, the stirring movement of packing in others, and the knot of soldiers standing on the bridge over the railway and staring down the line toward Woking, the day would have seemed very like any other Sunday.

Several farm wagons and carts were moving creakily along the road to Addlestone, and suddenly through the gate of a field we saw, across a stretch of flat meadow, six twelve-pounders, standing neatly at equal distances pointing toward Woking. The gunners stood by the guns waiting, and the ammunition wagons were at a businesslike distance. The men stood almost as if under inspection.

"That's good!" said I. "They will get one fair shot, at any rate."

The artilleryman hesitated at the gate.

"I shall go on," he said.

Farther on toward Weybridge, just over the bridge, there were a number of men in white fatigue jackets throwing up a long rampart,[4] and more guns behind.

"It's bows and arrows against the lightning, anyhow," said the artilleryman. "They 'aven't seen that fire-beam yet."

The officers who were not actively engaged stood and stared over the treetops southwestward, and the men digging would stop every now and again to stare in the same direction.

Byfleet was in a tumult; people packing, and a score of hussars, some of them dismounted, some on horseback, were hunting them about. Three or four black government wagons, with crosses in white circles, and an old omnibus, among other vehicles, were being loaded in the village street. There were scores of people, most of them sufficiently sabbatical[5] to have assumed their best clothes. The soldiers were having the greatest difficulty in making them realize the gravity of their position. We saw one shriveled old fellow with a huge box and a score or more of flowerpots containing orchids, angrily expostulating with the corporal who would leave them behind. I stopped and gripped his arm.

"Do you know what's over there?" I said, pointing at the pine-tops that hid the Martians.

"Eh?" said he, turning. "I was explainin' these is vallyble."

"Death!" I shouted. "Death is coming! Death!" and leaving him to digest that if he could, I hurried on after the artilleryman. At the corner I looked back. The soldier had left him, and he was still standing by his box, with the pots of orchids on the lid of it, and staring vaguely over the trees.

No one in Weybridge could tell us where the headquarters were established, the whole place was in such confusion as I had never seen in any town before. Carts, carriages everywhere, the most astonishing miscellany of conveyances and horseflesh. The respectable inhabitants of the place, men in golf and boating costumes, wives prettily dressed, were packing; river-

4. **rampart.** Embankment for defense against attack

5. **sabbatical.** Relating to the Sabbath, the day of rest and worship in the Jewish and Christian religions

❶ *What does the narrator try to make the older man understand?*

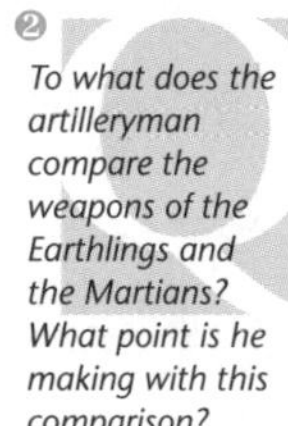

❷ *To what does the artilleryman compare the weapons of the Earthlings and the Martians? What point is he making with this comparison?*

Words for Everyday Use

as • sid • u • ous • ly (ə sij´o͞o əs lē) *adv.*, with constant and careful attention

ex • pos • tu • late (eks päs´ chə lāt´) *v.*, demand vehemently

Answers to Guided Reading Questions

❶ The narrator tries to make the older man understand that he and the others are in great danger and that this is no time to be worrying about matters as trivial as the welfare of a few plants.

❷ The artilleryman says that in comparison to the Martians' weaponry, that of the Earthlings is like bows and arrows against lightning.

Vocabulary in Context

- The baker worked assiduously all morning to finish the wedding cake.
- The soldiers knew better than to expostulate with their drill sergeant.

side loafers energetically helping, children excited, and, for the most part, highly delighted at this astonishing variation of their Sunday experiences. In the midst of it all the worthy vicar was very pluckily holding an early celebration, and his bell was jangling out above the excitement.

I and the artilleryman, seated on the step of the drinking fountain, made a very passable meal upon what we had brought with us. Patrols of soldiers—here no longer hussars, but grenadiers[6] in white—were warning people to move now or to take refuge in their cellars as soon as the firing began. We saw as we crossed the railway bridge that a growing crowd of people had assembled in and about the railway station, and the swarming platform was piled with boxes and packages. The ordinary traffic had been stopped, I believe, in order to allow of the passage of troops and guns to Chertsey, and I have heard since that a savage struggle occurred for places in the special trains that were put on at a later hour.

We remained at Weybridge until midday, and at that hour we found ourselves at the place near Shepperton Lock where the Wey and Thames join. Part of the time we spent helping two old women to pack a little cart. The Wey has a treble mouth, and at this point boats are to be hired, and there was a ferry across the river. On the Shepperton side was an inn with a lawn, and beyond that the tower of Shepperton Church—it has been replaced by a spire—rose above the trees.

Here we found an excited and noisy crowd of fugitives. As yet the flight had not grown to a panic, but there were already far more people than all the boats going to and fro could enable to cross. People came panting along under heavy burdens; one husband and wife were even carrying a small outhouse door between them, with some of their household goods piled thereon. One man told us he meant to try to get away from Shepperton station.

There was a lot of shouting, and one man was even jesting. The idea people seemed to have here was that the Martians were simply formidable human beings, who might attack and sack the town, to be certainly destroyed in the end. Every now and then people would glance nervously across the Wey, at the meadows toward Chertsey, but everything over there was still.

Across the Thames, except just where the boats landed, everything was quiet, in vivid contrast to the Surrey side. The people who landed there from the boats went tramping off down the lane. The big ferryboat had just made a journey. Three or four soldiers stood on the lawn of the inn, staring and jesting at the fugitives, without offering to help. The inn was closed, as it was now within prohibited hours.

"What's that?" cried a boatman, and "Shut up, you fool!" said a man near me to a yelping dog. Then the sound came again, this time from the direction of Chertsey, a muffled thud—the sound of a gun.

The fighting was beginning. Almost immediately unseen batteries across the river to our right, unseen because of the trees, took up the chorus, firing heavily one after the other. A woman screamed. Everyone stood arrested by the sudden stir of battle, near us and yet invisible to us. Nothing was to be seen save flat meadows, cows feeding unconcernedly for the most part, and silvery pollard[7] willows motionless in the warm sunlight.

---

6. **grenadiers.** Special force of soldiers attached to the royal household

7. **pollard.** Plant or tree with no limbs

Words for Everyday Use

vicar (vik´ər) *n.* a parish priest

pluck • i • ly (pluk´i lē) *adv.*, bravely, spiritedly

treb • le (treb´əl) *adj.*, threefold; triple

for • mi • da • ble (fôr´mə də bəl) *adj.*, causing fear or dread

sack (sak) *v.*, loot; plunder

Vocabulary in Context

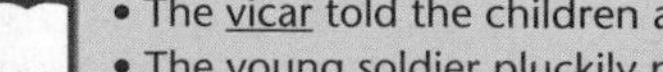

- The vicar told the children a story from the Bible.
- The young soldier pluckily picked up the flag and carried it under fire back to friendly territory.
- Under the treble leadership of the principal, the assistant principal, and the head speech coach, we got the new debate program underway.
- Great Britain found out that the American colonies were a formidable opponent.
- The Viking raiders sacked several cities along the coast of England.

"The sojers'll stop 'em," said a woman beside me, doubtfully. A haziness rose over the tree-tops.

Then suddenly we saw a rush of smoke far away up the river, a puff of smoke that jerked up into the air and hung; and forthwith the ground heaved underfoot and a heavy explosion shook the air, smashing two or three windows in the houses near, and leaving us astonished.

"Here they are!" shouted a man in a blue jersey. "Yonder! D'yer see them? Yonder!"

Quickly, one after the other, one, two, three, four of the armored Martians appeared, far away over the little trees, across the flat meadows that stretch toward Chertsey, and striding hurriedly toward the river. Little cowled figures they seemed at first, going with a rolling motion and as fast as flying birds.

Then, advancing obliquely toward us, came a fifth. Their armored bodies glittered in the sun as they swept swiftly forward upon the guns, growing rapidly larger as they drew nearer. One on the extreme left, the remotest that is, flourished a huge case high in the air, and the ghostly, terrible Heat-Ray I had already seen on Friday night smote toward Chertsey and struck the town.

At sight of these strange, swift, and terrible creatures the crowd near the water's edge seemed to me to be for a moment horror-struck. There was no screaming or shouting, but a silence. Then a hoarse murmur and a movement of feet—a splashing from the water. A man, too frightened to drop the portmanteau he carried on his shoulder, swung round and sent me staggering with a blow from the corner of his burden. A woman thrust at me with her

❶ *In what manner do the Martian mechanisms move?*

Words for Everyday Use

ob • lique • ly (ə blēk´ lē) *adv.*, with a change of direction of approximately 45 degrees

port • man • teau (pôrt man´ tō´) *n.*, suitcase; travel case or bag

Answer to Guided Reading Question

❶ They move in a rolling motion and are as fast as flying birds.

Vocabulary in Context

- The teacher drew a line, obliquely, from the upper left corner of the chalkboard to the lower right corner of it.
- The traveling salesperson took three suits from her portmanteau.

Answers to Guided Reading Questions

① The narrator wants to get underwater to escape being burned.

② The Martian machine is destroyed, along with the Martian within it. This shows that the Martians are not invincible.

③ The steam and the huge wave are caused by the heat ray hitting the water.

① *Why does the narrator want to get underwater?*

② *What happens to the Martian machine? Are the Martians invincible?*

③ *What causes the steam and the huge wave?*

hand and rushed past me. I turned, with the rush of the people, but I was not too terrified for thought. The terrible Heat-Ray was in my mind. To get underwater! That was it!

"Get underwater!" I shouted, unheeded.

I faced about again, and rushed toward the approaching Martian, rushed right down the gravelly beach and headlong into the water. Others did the same. A boatload of people putting back came leaping out as I rushed past. The stones under my feet were muddy and slippery, and the river was so low that I ran perhaps twenty feet scarcely waist-deep. Then, as the Martian towered overhead scarcely a couple of hundred yards away, I flung myself forward under the surface. The splashes of the people in the boats leaping into the river sounded like thunderclaps in my ears. People were landing hastily on both sides of the river.

But the Martian machine took no more notice for the moment of the people running this way and that than a man would of the confusion of ants in a nest against which his foot has kicked. When, half-suffocated, I raised my head above water, the Martian's hood pointed at the batteries that were still firing across the river, and as it advanced it swung loose what must have been the generator of the Heat-Ray.

In another moment it was on the bank, and in a stride wading halfway across. The knees of its foremost legs bent at the farther bank, and in another moment it had raised itself to its full height again, close to the village of Shepperton. Forthwith the six guns which, unknown to anyone on the right bank, had been hidden behind the outskirts of that village, fired simultaneously. The sudden near concussions, the last close upon the first, made my heart jump. The monster was already raising the case generating the Heat-Ray as the first shell burst six yards above the hood.

I gave a cry of astonishment. I saw and thought nothing of the other four Martian monsters; my attention was riveted upon the nearer incident. Simultaneously two other shells burst in the air near the body as the hood twisted round in time to receive, but not in time to dodge, the fourth shell.

The shell burst clean in the face of the Thing. The hood bulged, flashed, was whirled off in a dozen tattered fragments of red flesh and glittering metal.

"Hit!" shouted I, with something between a scream and a cheer.

I heard answering shouts from the people in the water about me. I could have leaped out of the water with that momentary <u>exultation</u>.

The <u>decapitated</u> colossus reeled like a drunken giant; but it did not fall over. It recovered its balance by a miracle, and, no longer heeding its steps and with the camera that fired the Heat-Ray now rigidly upheld, it reeled swiftly upon Shepperton. The living intelligence, the Martian within the hood, was slain and splashed to the four winds of heaven, and the Thing was now but a mere <u>intricate</u> device of metal whirling to destruction. It drove along in a straight line, incapable of guidance. It struck the tower of Shepperton Church, smashing it down as the impact of a battering-ram might have done, swerved aside, blundered on, and collapsed with tremendous force into the river out of my sight.

A violent explosion shook the air, and a spout of water, steam, mud, and shattered metal shot far up into the sky. As the camera of the Heat-Ray hit the water, the latter had immediately flashed into steam. In another moment a huge wave, like a

Words for Everyday Use

ex • ul • ta • tion (eg´zul tā´ shən) *n.,* rejoicing; jubilation
de • cap • i • tate (dē kap´ə tāt) *v.,* behead
in • tri • cate (in´tri kit) *adj.,* full of elaborate detail

Vocabulary in Context

- There was much <u>exultation</u> in Mudville when the hometown team won the tournament.
- The Red Queen told her soldiers to <u>decapitate</u> the Cheshire Cat.
- Macolm admires the <u>intricate</u> designs found in Islamic art.

muddy tidal bore[8] but almost scaldingly hot, came sweeping round the bend upstream. I saw people struggling shorewards, and heard their screaming and shouting faintly above the seething and roar of the Martian's collapse.

For the moment I heeded nothing of the heat, forgot the patent need of self-preservation. I splashed through the tumultuous water, pushing aside a man in black to do so, until I could see round the bend. Half a dozen deserted boats pitched aimlessly upon the confusion of the waves. The fallen Martian came into sight downstream, lying across the river, and for the most part submerged.

Thick clouds of steam were pouring off the wreckage, and through the tumultuously whirling wisps I could see, intermittently and vaguely, the gigantic limbs churning the water and flinging a splash and spray of mud and froth into the air. The tentacles swayed and struck like living arms, and, save for the helpless purposelessness of these movements, it was as if some wounded thing were struggling for its life amid the waves. Enormous quantities of a ruddy-brown fluid were spurting up in noisy jets out of the machine.

My attention was diverted from this death flurry by a furious yelling, like that of the thing called a siren in our manufacturing towns. A man, knee-deep near the towing-path, shouted inaudibly to me and pointed. Looking back, I saw the other Martians advancing with gigantic strides down the riverbank from the direction of Chertsey. The Shepperton guns spoke this time unavailingly.

At that I ducked at once underwater, and, holding my breath until movement was an agony, blundered painfully ahead under the surface as long as I could. The water was in a tumult about me, and rapidly growing hotter.

When for a moment I raised my head to take breath and throw the hair and water from my eyes, the steam was rising in a whirling white fog that at first hid the Martians altogether. The noise was deafening. Then I saw them dimly, colossal figures of gray, magnified by the mist. They had passed by me, and two were stooping over the frothing, tumultuous ruins of their comrade.

The third and fourth stood beside him in the water, one perhaps two hundred yards from me, the other toward Laleham. The generators of the Heat-Rays waved high, and the hissing beams smote down this way and that.

The air was full of sound, a deafening and confusing conflict of noises—the clangorous din of the Martians, the crash of falling houses, the thud of trees, fences, sheds flashing into flame, and the crackling and roaring of fire. Dense black smoke was leaping up to mingle with the steam from the river, and as the Heat-Ray went to and fro over Weybridge its impact was marked by flashes of incandescent white, that gave place at once to a smoky dance of lurid flames. The nearer houses still stood intact, awaiting their fate, shadowy, faint, and pallid in the steam, with the fire behind them going to and fro.

For a moment perhaps I stood there, breast-high in the almost boiling water, dumbfounded at my position, hopeless of escape. Through the reek I could see the people who had been with me in the river scrambling out of the water through the reeds, like little frogs hurrying through grass from the advance of a

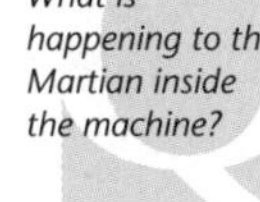

1 *What is happening to the Martian inside the machine?*

8. **tidal bore.** Large wave

WORDS FOR EVERYDAY USE	
	pat • ent (pat´nt) *adj.* obvious; plain; evident
	in • ter • mit • tent • ly (in´tər mit´´nt lē) *adv.*, periodically
	froth (frôth) *n.*, foam
	in •au • di • bly (in ôd´ ə blē) *adj.*, not able to be heard

ANSWER TO GUIDED READING QUESTION

1 The Martian inside the machine might be dying.

VOCABULARY IN CONTEXT

- Kiki thinks that astrology is patent nonsense.
- Throughout the night, the sirens blared intermittently.
- According to Greek myth, the goddess Aphrodite was born from the froth of the waves.
- The submarine was able to move inaudibly, that is, without making a sound.

ANSWER TO GUIDED READING QUESTION

❶ The foot of a Martian comes down within "a score of yards" (twenty yards) of the narrator's head.

ANSWERS FOR REVIEWING THE SELECTION

RECALLING AND INTERPRETING

1. **Recalling.** The artilleryman says that the Earthlngs' weapons are like bows and arrows against lightning. **Interpreting.** *Responses will vary.*
2. **Recalling.** The old fellow wants to take his expensive orchids with him. The corporal wants to leave them behind. **Interpreting.** The shriveled old fellow does not understand that at any moment the Martians could be there and they could all be dead.
3. **Recalling.** The first of the "Martian monsters" is destroyed by a shell that goes off in its face. **Interpreting.** The destruction of this one Martian machine shows that they are not invincible.
4. **Recalling.** A Martian sits inside the machine and guides it. **Interpreting.** Very little is known about the Martians at this point. The reader does know something of their physical appearance (brownish gray, about the size of a bear). The reader also knows that these creatures have superior weapons that they use freely. Thus, the creatures are very intelligent and unsympathetic.

man, or running to and fro in utter dismay on the towing-path.[9]

How close do the Martians get to the narrator? ❶

Then suddenly the white flashes of the Heat-Ray came leaping toward me. The houses caved in as they dissolved at its touch, and darted out flames; the trees changed to fire with a roar. The Ray flickered up and down the towing-path, licking off the people who ran this way and that, and came down to the water's edge not fifty yards from where I stood. It swept across the river to Shepperton, and the water in its track rose in a boiling weal crested with steam. I turned shoreward.

In another moment the huge wave, well-nigh at the boiling point, had rushed upon me. I screamed aloud, and scalded, half-blinded, agonized, I staggered through the leaping, hissing water toward the shore. Had my foot stumbled, it would have been the end. I fell helplessly, in full sight of the Martians, upon the broad, bare gravelly spit that runs down to mark the angle of the Wey and Thames. I expected nothing but death.

I have a dim memory of the foot of a Martian coming down within a score of yards of my head, driving straight into the loose gravel, whirling it this way and that, and lifting again; of a long suspense, and then of the four carrying the debris of their comrade between them, now clear and then presently faint through a veil of smoke, receding interminably, as it seemed to me, across a vast space of river and meadow. And then, very slowly, I realized that by a miracle I had escaped.

9. **towing-path.** Path alongside a canal, used by men or animals towing boats

Reviewing the Selection

RECALLING AND INTERPRETING

1. Ⓡ What description does the artilleryman give of the relative strength of the Martians and the Earthlings?

   Ⓘ Does the artilleryman's description seem to you a reasonable summary of the situation?

2. Ⓡ Why does the "shriveled old fellow" argue with the corporal?

   Ⓘ What doesn't the "shriveled old fellow" understand?

3. Ⓡ What happens to the first of the "Martian monsters"?

   Ⓘ Are the Martians invincible? How do you know?

4. Ⓡ What controls the machines on the gigantic tripods?

   Ⓘ What do you know of the Martians at this point in the novel? In the first chapter, the Martians are described as having "intellects vast and cool and unsympathetic." Do later events in the novel bear out this description? Explain.

13
How I Fell In with the Curate

After getting this sudden lesson in the power of terrestrial weapons, the Martians retreated to their original position upon Horsell Common; and in their haste, and encumbered with the debris of their smashed companion, they no doubt overlooked many such a stray and negligible victim as myself. Had they left their comrade and pushed on forthwith, there was nothing at that time between them and London but batteries of twelve-pounder guns, and they would certainly have reached the capital in advance of the tidings of their approach; as sudden, dreadful, and destructive their advent would have been as the earthquake that destroyed Lisbon a century ago.[1]

But they were in no hurry. Cylinder followed cylinder on its interplanetary flight; every twenty-four hours brought them reinforcement. And meanwhile the military and naval authorities, now fully alive to the tremendous power of their antagonists, worked with furious energy. Every minute a fresh gun came into position until, before twilight, every copse, every row of suburban villas on the hilly slopes about Kingston and Richmond, masked an expectant black muzzle. And through the charred and desolated area—perhaps twenty square miles altogether—that encircled the Martian encampment on Horsell Common, through charred and ruined villages among the green trees, through the blackened and smoking arcades that had been but a day ago pine spinneys,[2] crawled the devoted scouts with the heliographs that were presently to warn the gunners of the Martian approach. But the Martians now understood our command of artillery and the danger of human proximity, and not a man ventured within a mile of either cylinder, save at the price of his life.

It would seem that these giants spent the earlier part of the afternoon in going to and fro, transferring everything from the second and third cylinders—the second in Addlestone Golf Links and the third at Pyrford—to their original pit on Horsell Common. Over that, above the blackened heather and ruined buildings that stretched far and wide, stood one as sentinel, while the rest abandoned their vast fighting-machines and descended into the pit. They were hard at work there far into the night, and the towering pillar of dense green smoke that rose therefrom could be seen from the hills about Merrow, and even, it is said, from Banstead and Epsom Downs.

And while the Martians behind me were thus preparing for their next sally, and in front of me Humanity gathered for the battle, I made my way with infinite pains and labor from the fire and smoke of burning Weybridge toward London.

1 *What are the Martians doing? What are the humans doing?*

I saw an abandoned boat, very small and remote, drifting down-stream; and throwing off the most of my sodden clothes, I went after it, gained it, and so escaped out of that destruction. There were no oars in the boat, but I contrived to paddle, as well as my parboiled hands would allow, down the river toward Halliford and Walton, going very tediously and continually looking behind me, as you may well understand. I followed the river, because I considered that the water gave me my best chance of escape should these giants return.

Chapter 13

1. **Lisbon a century ago.** Lisbon, the capital of Portugal, was nearly destroyed by an earthquake in 1755
2. **spinneys.** Small wooded areas

Words for Everyday Use

copse (käps) *n.*, thicket of small trees or shrubs
ar • cade (är kād′) *n.*, passageway
prox • im • i • ty (präks im′ə tē) *n.*, state or quality of being near
sal • ly (sal′ē) *n.*, attack; sudden rushing forth
par • boil (pär′boil) *adj.*, partly cooked in a boiling liquid

Answer to Guided Reading Question

1 The Martians are preparing for their next sally, or forward assault. The humans are preparing for battle.

Vocabulary in Context

- The filtration of light through the trees gave a cathedral-like quality to the copse of white pine.
- They played video games in the arcade until closing time.
- The proximity of the suburban town to San Francisco made it a convenient commute.
- The platoon sallied forth to attack the enemy.
- Meg parboiled the potatoes before placing them in the roasting pan with the meat.

Answer to Guided Reading Question

❶ The narrator's irrational anger comes from his frustration. There is no real, legitimate reason for being angry with his wife.

❶ *What might be the reason for the narrator's being angry with his wife? Why is this "a curious thing"?*

The hot water from the Martian's overthrow drifted downstream with me, so that for the best part of a mile I could see little of either bank. Once, however, I made out a string of black figures hurrying across the meadows from the direction of Weybridge. Halliford, it seemed, was deserted, and several of the houses facing the river were on fire. It was strange to see the place quite tranquil, quite desolate under the hot, blue sky, with the smoke and little threads of flame going straight up into the heat of the afternoon. Never before had I seen houses burning without the accompaniment of an obstructive crowd. A little farther on the dry reeds up the bank were smoking and glowing, and a line of fire inland was marching steadily across a late field of hay.

For a long time I drifted, so painful and weary was I after the violence I had been through, and so intense the heat upon the water. Then my fears got the better of me again, and I resumed my paddling. The sun scorched my bare back. At last, as the bridge at Walton was coming into sight round the bend, my fever and faintness overcame my fears, and I landed on the Middlesex bank and lay down, deadly sick, amid the long grass. I suppose the time was then about four or five o'clock. I got up presently, walked perhaps half a mile without meeting a soul, and then lay down again in the shadow of a hedge. I seem to remember talking, wanderingly, to myself during that last spurt. I was also very thirsty, and bitterly regretful I had drunk no more water. It is a curious thing that I felt angry with my wife; I cannot account for it, but my impotent desire to reach Leatherhead worried me excessively.

I do not clearly remember the arrival of the curate,[3] so that probably I dozed. I became aware of him as a seated figure in soot-smudged shirt-sleeves, and with his upturned, cleanshaven face staring at a faint flickering that danced over the sky. The sky was what is called a mackerel sky—rows and rows of faint down-plumes of cloud, just tinted with the midsummer sunset.

I sat up, and at the rustle of my motion he looked at me quickly.

"Have you any water?" I asked abruptly.

He shook his head.

3. **curate.** Member of the clergy

Words for Everyday Use

im • po • tent (im´pə tənt) *adj.*, ineffective; powerless

Vocabulary in Context

• We were amused by her impotent attempts to coax the cat out of the closet.

"You have been asking for water for the last hour," he said.

For a moment we were silent, taking stock of each other. I dare say he found me a strange enough figure, naked save for my water-soaked trousers and socks, scalded, and my face and shoulders blackened by the smoke. His face was a fair weakness, his chin retreated, and his hair lay in crisp, almost flaxen curls on his low forehead; his eyes were rather large, pale blue, and blankly staring. He spoke abruptly, looking vacantly away from me.

"What does it mean?" he said. "What do these things mean?"

I stared at him and made no answer.

He extended a thin white hand and spoke in almost a complaining tone.

"Why are these things permitted? What sins have we done? The morning service was over, I was walking through the roads to clear my brain for the afternoon, and then—fire, earthquake, death! As if it were Sodom and Gomorrah![4] All our work undone, all the work—What are these Martians?"

"What are we?" I answered, clearing my throat.

He gripped his knees and turned to look at me again. For half a minute, perhaps, he stared silently.

"I was walking through the roads to clear my brain," he said. "And suddenly—fire, earthquake, death!"

He relapsed into silence, with his chin now sunken almost to his knees.

Presently he began waving his hand.

"All the work—all the Sunday schools—What have we done—what has Weybridge done? Everything gone—everything destroyed. The church! We rebuilt it only three years ago. Gone!—swept out of existence! Why?"

Another pause, and he broke out again like one demented.

"The smoke of her burning goeth up for ever and ever!" he shouted.

His eyes flamed, and he pointed a lean finger in the direction of Weybridge.

By this time I was beginning to take his measure. The tremendous tragedy in which he had been involved—it was evident he was a fugitive from Weybridge—had driven him to the very verge of his reason.

"Are we far from Sunbury?" I said, in a matter-of-fact tone.

"What are we to do?" he asked. "Are these creatures everywhere? Has the earth been given over to them?"

"Are we far from Sunbury?"

"Only this morning I officiated at early celebration—"

"Things have changed," I said, quietly. "You must keep your head. There is still hope."

"Hope!"

"Yes. Plentiful hope—for all this destruction!"

I began to explain my view of our position. He listened at first, but as I went on the dawning interest in his eyes gave place to their former stare, and his regard wandered from me.

"This must be the beginning of the end," he said, interrupting me. "The end! The great and terrible day of the Lord! When men shall call upon the mountains and the rocks to fall upon them and hide them—hide them from the face of Him that sitteth upon the throne!"

I began to understand the position. I ceased my labored reasoning, struggled to my feet, and, standing over him, laid my hand on his shoulder.

4. **Sodom and Gomorrah.** Biblical cities destroyed by fire because of sinfulness

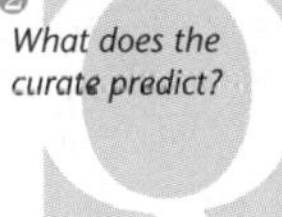

❶ *To what cause does the curate attribute the coming of the Martians?*

❷ *What does the curate predict?*

Words for Everyday Use

flax • en (flak´sən) *adj.,* pale yellow; straw-colored
de • ment • ed (dē ment´id) *adj.,* insane; mentally deranged
of • fi • ci • ate (ə fish´ē āt´) *v.,* perform function of a priest or minister at a religious ceremony

Answers to Guided Reading Questions

❶ The curate is blaming the coming of the Martians on the sinfulness of humans.

❷ The curate predicts the end of the world, the "great and terrible day of the Lord," when "men shall call upon the mountains and the rocks to fall upon them and hide them."

Vocabulary in Context

- She allowed her flaxen hair to blow freely in the wind.
- The villagers locked their doors in fear because a demented patient had escaped from the hospital.
- Father John officiated at the wedding of his niece.

Answers to Guided Reading Questions

❶ The narrator tries to bring the curate back to his senses by telling him that religion should not collapse under adversity.

❷ The Martians are not invulnerable because, as we have seen, they can be killed.

❸ Since the Martians act mercilessly and randomly, it really does not make sense to view them as the curate does.

Answers for Reviewing the Selection

RECALLING AND INTERPRETING

1. **Recalling.** A new cylinder lands every twenty-four hours. **Interpreting.** The Martians intend to launch a full-scale invasion of Earth.

2. **Recalling.** The narrator meets the curate. **Interpreting.** The curate is a hysterical person. The narrator, in contrast, is able to remain somewhat calm and collected in the face of adversity.

❶ *In what ways does the narrator try to bring the curate to his senses?*

❷ *Are the Martians, in fact, invulnerable?*

❸ *Does it make sense to view the Martians as "God's ministers"?*

"Be a man!" said I. "You are scared out of your wits! What good is religion if it collapses under calamity? Think of what earthquakes and floods, wars and volcanoes, have done before to men! Did you think God had exempted Weybridge? He is not an insurance agent."

For a time he sat in blank silence.

"But how can we escape?" he asked, suddenly. "They are invulnerable, they are pitiless."

"Neither the one nor, perhaps, the other," I answered. "And the mightier they are the more sane and wary should we be. One of them was killed yonder not three hours ago."

"Killed!" he said, staring about him. "How can God's ministers be killed?"

"I saw it happen." I proceeded to tell him. "We have chanced to come in for the thick of it," said I, "and that is all."

"What is that flicker in the sky?" he asked, abruptly.

I told him it was the heliograph signaling—that it was the sign of human help and effort in the sky.

"We are in the midst of it," I said, "quiet as it is. That flicker in the sky tells of the gathering storm. Yonder, I take it, are the Martians, and Londonward, where those hills rise about Richmond and Kingston and the trees give cover, earthworks are being thrown up and guns are being placed. Presently the Martians will be coming this way again."

And even as I spoke he sprang to his feet and stopped me by a gesture.

"Listen!" he said.

From beyond the low hills across the water came the dull resonance of distant guns and a remote, weird crying. Then everything was still. A cockchafer[5] came droning over the hedge and past us. High in the west the crescent moon hung faint and pale above the smoke of Weybridge and Shepperton and the hot, still splendor of the sunset.

"We had better follow this path," I said, "northward."

5. **cockchafer.** Large beetle found usually in Europe

Reviewing the Selection

Recalling and Interpreting

1. (R) What happens every twenty-four hours?

   (I) What do you think the Martians' intentions are? Explain.

2. (R) Whom does the narrator meet in this chapter?

   (I) How would you describe this person's general attitude and personality? How does this person differ from the narrator?

Words for Everyday Use

ex • empt (eg zempt´) *v.,* not subject to a situation or rule that applies to others

in • vul • ner • a • ble (in vul´nər ə bəl) *adj.,* that cannot be wounded or injured

Vocabulary in Context

- We will exempt Tasha from washing dishes tonight.
- The fortress was invulnerable to attack.

14
In London

My younger brother was in London when the Martians fell at Woking. He was a medical student, working for an imminent examination, and he heard nothing of the arrival until Saturday morning. The morning papers on Saturday contained, in addition to lengthy special articles on the planet Mars, on life in the planets, and so forth, a brief and vaguely worded telegram, all the more striking for its brevity.

The Martians, alarmed by the approach of a crowd, had killed a number of people with a quick-firing gun, so the story ran. The telegram concluded with the words: "Formidable as they seem to be, the Martians have not moved from the pit into which they have fallen, and, indeed, seem incapable of doing so. Probably this is due to the relative strength of the Earth's gravitational energy." On that last text their leader-writer expanded very comfortingly.

Of course all the students in the crammer's biology class,[1] to which my brother went that day, were intensely interested, but there were no signs of any unusual excitement in the streets. The afternoon papers puffed scraps of news under big headlines. They had nothing to tell beyond the movements of troops about the common, and the burning of the pine woods between Woking and Weybridge, until eight. Then the *St. James's Gazette*, in an extra special edition, announced the bare fact of the interruption of telegraphic communication. This was thought to be due to the falling of burning pine trees across the line. Nothing more of the fighting was known that night, the night of my drive to Leatherhead and back.

My brother felt no anxiety about us, as he knew from the description in the papers that the cylinder was a good two miles from my house. He made up his mind to run down that night to me, in order, as he says, to see the Things before they were killed. He dispatched a telegram, which never reached me, about four o'clock, and spent the evening at a music hall.

In London, also, on Saturday night there was a thunderstorm, and my brother reached Waterloo in a cab. On the platform from which the midnight train usually starts he learned, after some waiting, that an accident prevented trains from reaching Woking that night. The nature of the accident he could not ascertain; indeed, the railway authorities did not clearly know at that time. There was very little excitement in the station, as the officials, failing to realize that anything further than a breakdown between Byfleet and Woking junction had occurred, were running the theater trains which usually passed through Woking, round by Virginia Water or Guildford. They were busy making the necessary arrangements to alter the route of the Southampton and Portsmouth Sunday League excursions. A nocturnal newspaper reporter, mistaking my brother for the traffic manager, to whom he bears a slight resemblance, waylaid and tried to interview him. Few people, excepting the railway officials, connected the breakdown with the Martians.

I have read, in another account of these events, that on Sunday morning "all London was electrified by the news from

❶ *Why isn't the brother worried?*

❷ *Why might the Martians have interrupted telegraphic communication?*

Chapter 14

1. **crammer's biology class.** Preparatory class for the University of London's biology examinations

Words for Everyday Use

brev • i • ty (brev´ə tē) *n.,* shortness; quality of being concise

dis • patch (di spach´) *v.,* send off promptly

as • cer • tain (as´ər tān´) *v.,* find out without doubt

noc • tur • nal (näk tur´nəl) *adj.,* functioning or active during the night

Answers to Guided Reading Questions

❶ The brother is not worried because the cylinder is two miles from the narrator's house, and the brother seems to think that the Martians will be readily destroyed.

❷ Interrupting communication is a common military tactic. Doing this keeps the opposition from being able to communicate the orders necessary to mount its military strategy.

Quotables

"Nothing could have been more obvious to the people of the early twentieth century than the rapidity with which war was becoming impossible. And as certainly they did not see it. They did not see it until the atomic bombs burst in their fumbling hands."

—H. G. Wells

Vocabulary in Context

- The hungry students were grateful for the brevity of his speech.
- He dispatched a messenger to her hotel with the urgent news.
- She looked in her rear-view mirror frantically trying to ascertain the direction of the approaching siren.
- Owls are nocturnal hunters.

Answers to Guided Reading Questions

❶ Londoners are not distressed because they are used to being personally secure and because they commonly read remarkable stories in the newspapers.

❷ The trains are not showing up on time because the Martians have interfered with them.

Woking." As a matter of fact, there was nothing to justify that very extravagant phrase. Plenty of Londoners did not hear of the Martians until the panic of Monday morning. Those who did took some time to realize all that the hastily worded telegrams in the Sunday papers conveyed. The majority of people in London do not read Sunday papers.

Why aren't Londoners distressed by the news of the Martians? ❶

The habit of personal security, moreover, is so deeply fixed in the Londoner's mind, and startling intelligence so much a matter of course in the papers, that they could read without any personal tremors: "About seven o'clock last night the Martians came out of the cylinder, and, moving about under an armor of metallic shields, have completely wrecked Woking station with the adjacent houses, and massacred an entire battalion of the Cardigan Regiment. No details are known. Maxims have been absolutely useless against their armor; the field guns have been disabled by them. Flying hussars have been galloping into Chertsey. The Martians appear to be moving slowly toward Chertsey or Windsor. Great anxiety prevails in West Surrey, and earthworks are being thrown up to check the advance Londonward." That was how the Sunday *Sun* put it, and a clever and remarkably prompt "hand-book" article in the *Referee* compared the affair to a menagerie suddenly let loose in a village.

No one in London knew positively of the nature of the armored Martians, and there was still a fixed idea that these monsters must be sluggish: "crawling," "creeping painfully"—such expressions occurred in almost all the earlier reports. None of the telegrams could have been written by an eyewitness of their advance. The Sunday papers printed separate editions as further news came to hand, some even in default of it. But there was practically nothing more to tell people until late in the afternoon, when the authorities gave the press agencies the news in their possession. It was stated that the people of Walton and Weybridge, and all that district, were pouring along the roads Londonward, and that was all.

My brother went to church at the Foundling Hospital in the morning, still in ignorance of what had happened on the previous night. There he heard allusions made to the invasion, and a special prayer for peace. Coming out, he bought a *Referee*. He became alarmed at the news in this, and went again to Waterloo station to find out if communication were restored. The omnibuses, carriages, cyclists, and innumerable people walking in their best clothes seemed scarcely affected by the strange intelligence that the news vendors were disseminating. People were interested, or, if alarmed, alarmed only on account of the local residents. At the station he heard for the first time that the Windsor and Chertsey lines were now interrupted. The porters told him that several remarkable telegrams had been received in the morning from Byfleet and Chertsey stations, but that these had abruptly ceased. My brother could get very little precise detail out of them. "There's fighting going on about Weybridge" was the extent of their information.

Why are the trains not showing up on time? ❷

The train service was now very much disorganized. Quite a number of people who had been expecting friends from places on the South-Western network were standing about the station. One gray-headed old gentleman came and abused the South-Western Company bitterly to my brother. "It wants showing up," he said.

Words for Everyday Use

me • nag • er • ie (mə naj´ər ə) *n.,* collection of wild animals caged for exhibition

al • lu • sion (ə lo͞o´zhən) *n.,* indirect reference

dis • sem • i • nate (di sem´ə nāt´) *v.,* scatter far and wide, spread abroad

ex • tent (ek stent´) *n.,* range or limit; scope

net • work (net´wurk´) *n.,* system, as of roads, rails, canals

Vocabulary in Context

- The child has a menagerie of stuffed animals on her bed.
- His unconscious allusion to that time brought back unhappy memories for her.
- The wildflower seeds were disseminated randomly over the field.
- A scraped elbow and a bad bruise on the knee were the extent of his injuries.
- The office computers are linked together in a network.

One or two trains came in from Richmond, Putney, and Kingston, containing people who had gone out for a day's boating and found the locks closed and a feeling of panic in the air. A man in a blue-and-white blazer addressed my brother, full of strange tidings.

"There's hosts of people driving into Kingston in traps[2] and carts and things, with boxes of valuables and all that," he said. "They come from Molesey and Weybridge and Walton, and they say there's been guns heard at Chertsey, heavy firing, and that mounted soldiers have told them to get off at once because the Martians are coming. We heard guns firing at Hampton Court station, but we thought it was thunder. What the dickens does it all mean? The Martians can't get out of their pit, can they?"

My brother could not tell him.

Afterwards he found that the vague feeling of alarm had spread to the clients of the underground railway, and that the Sunday excursionists began to return from all over the southwestern "lungs"[3]—Barnes, Wimbledon, Richmond Park, Kew, and so forth—at unnaturally early hours; but not a soul had anything more than vague hearsay to tell of. Everyone connected with the terminus seemed ill-tempered.

About five o'clock the gathering crowd in the station was immensely excited by the opening of the line of communication, which is almost invariably closed, between the South-Eastern and the South-Western stations, and the passage of carriage-trucks bearing huge guns and carriages crammed with soldiers. These were the guns that were brought up from Woolwich and Chatham to cover Kingston. There was an exchange of pleasantries: "You'll get eaten!" "We're the beast-tamers!" and so forth. A little while after that a squad of police came into the station and began to clear the public off the platforms, and my brother went out into the street again.

The church bells were ringing for evensong,[4] and a squad of Salvation Army lasses came singing down Waterloo Road. On the bridge a number of loafers were watching a curious brown scum that came drifting down the stream in patches. The sun was just setting, and the Clock Tower and the Houses of Parliament rose against one of the most peaceful skies it is possible to imagine, a sky of gold, barred with long transverse stripes of reddish-purple cloud. There was talk of a floating body. One of the men there, a reservist he said he was, told my brother he had seen the heliograph flickering in the west.

In Wellington Street my brother met a couple of sturdy roughs who had just rushed out of Fleet Street with still wet newspapers and staring placards. "Dreadful catastrophe!" they bawled one to the other down Wellington Street. "Fighting at Weybridge! Full description! Repulse of the Martians! London in Danger!" He had to give threepence for a copy of that paper.

Then it was, and then only, that he realized something of the full power and terror of these monsters. He learned that they were not merely a handful of small sluggish creatures, but that they were minds swaying vast mechanical bodies; and that they could move swiftly and smite with such power that even the mightiest guns could not stand against them.

They were described as "vast spider-like machines, nearly a hundred feet high,

❶ *In what way do the man's comments reveal that Londoners are in the dark about what is happening?*

❷ *When does the brother realize the danger that people face?*

2. **traps.** Light, two-wheeled carriage
3. **lungs.** Open spaces around London
4. **evensong.** Worship service during the evening hours

Words for Everyday Use

hear • say (hir´sā´) *n.,* rumor; gossip
ter • mi • nus (tʉr´mə nəs) *n.,* station at the end of a railway line
lass (las) *n.,* young woman; girl
pla • card (plak´ärd) *n.,* notice for display in a public place; poster

Answers to Guided Reading Questions

❶ The man seems to believe, as the narrator once did, that the Martians cannot get out of the pit. He is going on old misinformation.

❷ The brother realizes the danger when he gets a copy of a paper being sold on Wellington Street. The paper describes the fighting at Weybridge.

Vocabulary in Context

- His conviction was based on hearsay evidence.
- The terminus is a busy place at rush hour with commuters hurrying to catch their trains.
- The lass had her father's freckles and her mother's dark blue eyes.
- Placards advertising the new Broadway show were seen all over Manhattan.

Answers to Guided Reading Questions

❶ *Responses will vary.* Students will for the most part agree that these assurances are not justified, for the government has not yet been able to stop the Martian advance.

❷ If people were to panic, the situation would get even worse. Panic would make an orderly evacuation impossible.

❶ *Are the assurances of the authorities justified? Why, or why not?*

❷ *Why would the authorities want people not to panic?*

capable of the speed of an express train, and able to shoot out a beam of intense heat." Masked batteries, chiefly of field guns, had been planted in the country about Horsell Common, and especially between the Woking district and London. Five of the machines had been seen moving toward the Thames, and one, by a happy chance, had been destroyed. In the other cases the shells had missed, and the batteries had been at once annihilated by the Heat-Rays. Heavy losses of soldiers were mentioned, but the tone of the despatch was optimistic.

The Martians had been repulsed; they were not invulnerable. They had retreated to their triangle of cylinders again, in the circle about Woking. Signallers with heliographs were pushing forward upon them from all sides. Guns were in rapid transit from Windsor, Portsmouth, Aldershot, Woolwich—even from the north; among others, long wire guns of ninety-five tons from Woolwich. Altogether one hundred and sixteen were in position or being hastily placed, chiefly covering London. Never before in England had there been such a vast or rapid concentration of military material.

Any further cylinders that fell, it was hoped, could be destroyed at once by high explosives, which were being rapidly manufactured and distributed. No doubt, ran the report, the situation was of the strangest and gravest description, but the public was exhorted to avoid and discourage panic. No doubt the Martians were strange and terrible in the extreme, but at the outside there could not be more than twenty of them against our millions.

The authorities had reason to suppose, from the size of the cylinders, that at the outside there could not be more than five in each cylinder—fifteen altogether. And one at least was disposed of—perhaps more. The public would be fairly warned of the approach of danger, and elaborate measures were being taken for the protection of the people in the threatened southwestern suburbs. And so, with reiterated assurances of the safety of London and the ability of the authorities to cope with the difficulty, this quasi-proclamation closed.

This was printed in enormous type on paper so fresh that it was still wet, and there had been no time to add a word of comment. It was curious, my brother said, to see how ruthlessly the usual contents of the paper had been hacked and taken out to give this place.

All down Wellington Street people could be seen fluttering out the pink sheets and reading, and the Strand was suddenly noisy with the voices of an army of hawkers following these pioneers. Men came scrambling off buses to secure copies. Certainly this news excited people intensely, whatever their previous apathy. The shutters of a map shop in the Strand were being taken down, my brother said, and a man in his Sunday raiment, lemon-yellow gloves even, was visible inside the window hastily fastening maps of Surrey[6] to the glass.

Going on along the Strand to Trafalgar Square,[7] the paper in his hand, my brother saw some of the fugitives from West Surrey. There was a man with his wife and two boys and some articles of furniture in a cart such as greengrocers[8] use. He was driving from the direction of Westminster

6. **Surrey.** English county southeast of London
7. **Strand . . . Trafalgar Square.** Sections of London
8. **greengrocers.** Retailers of fresh fruits and vegetables

Words for Everyday Use

an • ni • hi • late (ə nī´ ə lāt´) *v.,* destroy completely
ex • hort (eg zôrt´) *v.,* urge earnestly by advice or warning
re • it • er • ate (rē it´ ə rāt´) *v.,* repeat
qua • si - proc • la • ma • tion (kwā´zē präk´ lə mā´shən) *n.,* seemingly official announcement
ap • a • thy (ap´ə thē) *n.,* lack of interest; unconcern
rai• ment (rā´mənt) *n.,* clothing; apparel

Vocabulary in Context

- Nuclear weapons have the power to annihilate the human race.
- During the air raid the public was exhorted to proceed calmly and quickly to the shelters.
- The authorities reiterated the warning to remain calm.
- To cut down on litter in the city streets, the mayor issued a quasi-proclamation that all citizens found littering would be fined one hundred dollars.
- City dwellers are notorious for their apathy toward street crime.
- The children were dressed in their best raiment for the party.

Bridge; and close behind him came a hay wagon with five or six respectable-looking people in it, and some boxes and bundles. The faces of these people were haggard, and their entire appearance contrasted conspicuously with the Sabbath-best appearance of the people on the omnibuses. People in fashionable clothing peeped at them out of cabs. They stopped at the Square as if undecided which way to take, and finally turned eastward along the Strand. Some way behind these came a man in workday clothes, riding one of those old-fashioned tricycles with a small front wheel. He was dirty and white in the face.

My brother turned down toward Victoria, and met a number of such people. He had a vague idea that he might see something of me. He noticed an unusual number of police regulating the traffic. Some of the refugees were exchanging news with the people on the omnibuses. One was professing to have seen the Martians. "Boilers on stilts, I tell you, striding along like men." Most of them

① *What do the Martian machines look like, according to the refugee?*

WORDS FOR EVERYDAY USE

con • spic • u • ous • ly (kən spik´yo͞o əs lē) *adv.*, unusually strikingly; obviously

ANSWER TO GUIDED READING QUESTION

① The refugee says that the machines look like boilers on stilts.

VOCABULARY IN CONTEXT

• The black dog contrasted conspicuously with the white snow.

Answer to Guided Reading Question

➊ The brother fears that the worst has happened to the narrator.

were excited and animated by their strange experience.

Beyond Victoria the public-houses[9] were doing a lively trade with these arrivals. At all the street corners groups of people were reading papers, talking excitedly, or staring at these unusual Sunday visitors. They seemed to increase as night drew on, until at last the roads, my brother said, were like Epsom High Street on a Derby Day. My brother addressed several of these fugitives and got unsatisfactory answers from most.

None of them could tell him any news of Woking except one man, who assured him that Woking had been entirely destroyed on the previous night.

What does the brother fear? ➊

"I come from Byfleet," he said; "a man on a bicycle came through the place in the early morning, and ran from door to door warning us to come away. Then came soldiers. We went out to look, and there were clouds of smoke to the south—nothing but smoke, and not a soul coming that way. Then we heard the guns at Chertsey, and folks coming from Weybridge. So I've locked up my house and come on."

At that time there was a strong feeling in the streets that the authorities were to blame for their incapacity to dispose of the invaders without all this inconvenience.

About eight o'clock a noise of heavy firing was distinctly audible all over the south of London. My brother could not hear it for the traffic in the main thoroughfares, but by striking through the quiet back streets to the river he was able to distinguish it quite plainly.

He walked from Westminster to his apartments near Regent's Park, about ten. He was now very anxious on my account, and disturbed at the evident magnitude of the trouble. His mind was inclined to run, even as mine had run on Saturday, on military details. He thought of all those silent, expectant guns, of the suddenly nomadic countryside; he tried to imagine "boilers on stilts" a hundred feet high.

There were one or two cartloads of refugees passing along Oxford Street, and several in the Marylebone Road, but so slowly was the news spreading that Regent Street and Portland Place were full of their usual Sunday-night promenaders, albeit they talked in groups, and along the edge of Regent's Park there were as many silent couples "walking out" together under the scattered gas-lamps as ever there had been. The night was warm and still, and a little oppressive; the sound of guns continued intermittently, and after midnight there seemed to be sheet lightning[10] in the south.

He read and reread the paper, fearing the worst had happened to me. He was restless, and after supper prowled out again aimlessly. He returned and tried in vain to divert his attention to his examination notes. He went to bed a little after midnight, and was awakened from lurid dreams in the small hours of Monday by the sound of doorknockers, feet running in the street, distant drumming, and a clamor of bells. Red reflections danced on the ceiling. For a moment he lay astonished, wondering whether day had come or the world gone mad. Then he jumped out of bed and ran to the window.

His room was an attic; and as he thrust his head out, up and down the street there were a dozen echoes to the noise of his window sash, and heads in every kind of

9. **public-houses.** Taverns

10. **sheet lightning.** General illumination caused by lightning reflected by clouds

Words for Everyday Use

in • ca • pac • i • ty (in′kə pas′i tē) *n.,* lack of ability or power

mag • ni• tude (mag′nə tood′) *n.,* greatness of extent

no • mad • ic (nō mad′ik) *adj.,* characterized by the lifestyle of wandering peoples

prom • e • nad • er (präm′ə nād′ər) *n.,* person who is walking leisurely

lu • rid (loor′id) *adj.,* vividly harsh or shocking

Vocabulary in Context

- The old man's incapacity to forgive alienated his children all their lives.
- She was frightened by the magnitude of his ambition.
- As a freelance photojournalist traveling constantly on assignment, she led a very nomadic life.
- The promenaders strolled along the boardwalk.
- The lurid headlines jumped out at him from the newsstand.

night disarray appeared. Inquiries were being shouted. "They are coming!" bawled a policeman, hammering at the door; "the Martians are coming!" and hurried to the next door.

The sound of drumming and trumpeting came from the Albany Street Barracks, and every church within earshot was hard at work killing sleep with a vehement disorderly tocsin. There was a noise of doors opening, and window after window in the houses opposite flashed from darkness into yellow illumination.

Up the street came galloping a closed carriage, bursting abruptly into noise at the corner, rising to a clattering climax under the window, and dying away slowly in the distance. Close on the rear of this came a couple of cabs, the forerunners of a long procession of flying vehicles, going for the most part to Chalk Farm station, where the North-Western special trains were loading up, instead of coming down the gradient into Euston.

For a long time my brother stared out of the window in blank astonishment, watching the policemen hammering at door after door, and delivering their incomprehensible message. Then the door behind him opened, and the man who lodged across the landing came in, dressed only in shirt, trousers, and slippers, his braces[11] loose about his waist, his hair disordered from his pillow.

"What the devil is it?" he asked. "A fire? What a devil of a row!"

They both craned their heads out of the window, straining to hear what the policemen were shouting. People were coming out of the side streets, and standing in groups at the corners talking.

"What the devil is it all about?" said my brother's fellow lodger.

My brother answered him vaguely and began to dress, running with each garment to the window in order to miss nothing of the growing excitement. And presently men selling unnaturally early newspapers came bawling into the street:

"London in danger of suffocation! The Kingston and Richmond defenses forced! Fearful massacres in the Thames Valley!"

And all about him—in the rooms below, in the houses on each side and across the road, and behind in the Park Terraces and in the hundred other streets of that part of Marylebone, and the Westbourne Park district and St. Pancras, and westward and northward in Kilburn and St. John's Wood and Hampstead, and eastward in Shoreditch and Highbury and Haggerston and Hoxton, and, indeed, through all the vastness of London from Ealing to East Ham—people were rubbing their eyes, and opening windows to stare out and ask aimless questions, and dressing hastily as the first breath of the coming storm of Fear blew through the streets. It was the dawn of the great panic. London, which had gone to bed on Sunday night oblivious and inert, was awakened in the small hours of Monday morning to a vivid sense of danger.

Unable from his window to learn what was happening, my brother went down and out into the street, just as the sky between the parapets of the houses grew pink with the early dawn. The flying people on foot and in vehicles grew more numerous every moment. "Black Smoke!" he heard people crying, and again "Black Smoke!" The contagion of such a unanimous fear was inevitable. As my brother hesitated on the doorstep, he saw another news vendor approaching him, and got a

11. **braces.** Suspenders

1 *Of what do the policemen warn?*

2 *What makes the policemen's message "incomprehensible"?*

Answers to Guided Reading Questions

1 The police warn the people about the coming of the Martians.

2 The coming of Martians is such a bizarre thing that it it is difficult to comprehend.

Words for Everyday Use

ve • he • ment (vē ə mənt) *adj.*, acting or moving with great force

toc • sin (täk´sin) *n.*, alarm bell

gra • di • ent (grā´dē ənt) *n.*, slope of a road or railway

ob • liv • i • ous (ə bliv´ē əs) *adj.*, unmindful; unaware

par • a • pet (par´ə pet´) *n.*, low wall or railing

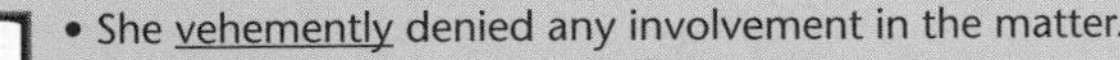

Vocabulary in Context

- She vehemently denied any involvement in the matter.
- A tocsin was rung to warn the citizens of the fire.
- He shifted into low gear to accomodate the steep gradient of the hill.
- The young lovers were oblivious to anything or anyone else around them.
- Connie could see an approaching thunderstorm from the parapet of the house.

Answers to Guided Reading Questions

❶ The dispatch is "catastrophic" because it admits that the Martians cannot be stopped.

❷ The people react by evacuating—pouring en masse northward.

Answers for Reviewing the Selection

RECALLING AND INTERPRETING

1. **Recalling.** The Londoners are not particularly alarmed by the first reports. **Interpreting.** The first reports are misleading because they indicate that the Martians cannot leave their pit.

2. **Recalling.** The narrator's brother first realizes the extent of the danger when he reads about the attack on Weybridge in a newspaper that he buys on the street. The new weapon being used by the Martians is the black vapor. **Interpreting.** It is difficult to imagine six million people moving out of a city without there being some chaos, confusion, panic, and danger.

paper forthwith. The man was running away with the rest, and selling his papers for a shilling each as he ran—a grotesque mingling of profit and panic.

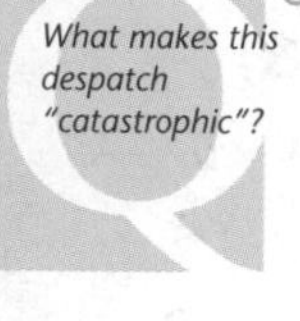

❶ *What makes this despatch "catastrophic"?*

And from this paper my brother read that catastrophic despatch of the Commander-in-Chief:

"The Martians are able to discharge enormous clouds of a black and poisonous vapor by means of rockets. They have smothered our batteries, destroyed Richmond, Kingston, and Wimbledon, and are advancing slowly toward London, destroying everything on the way. It is impossible to stop them. There is no safety from the Black Smoke but in instant flight."

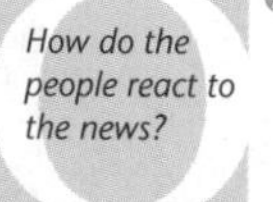

❷ *How do the people react to the news?*

That was all, but it was enough. The whole population of the great six-million city was stirring, slipping, running; presently it would be pouring en masse northward.

"Black Smoke!" the voices cried. "Fire!"

The bells of the neighboring church made a jangling tumult, a cart carelessly driven smashed, amid shrieks and curses, against the water trough up the street. Sickly yellow light went to and fro in the houses, and some of the passing cabs flaunted unextinguished lamps. And overhead the dawn was growing brighter, clear and steady and calm.

He heard footsteps running to and fro in the rooms, and up and down stairs behind him. His landlady came to the door, loosely wrapped in dressing gown and shawl; her husband followed. . . .

As my brother began to realize the import of all these things, he turned hastily to his own room, put all his available money—some ten pounds[15] altogether—into his pockets, and went out again into the streets.

15. **pound.** British monetary unit similar to the dollar

Reviewing the Selection

RECALLING AND INTERPRETING

1. **R** How do Londoners react to the first reports of the Martians?

   I What is misleading about these reports?

2. **R** When does the narrator's brother first realize the extent of the danger? What new weapon is described by the people fleeing the Martian attacks in the Thames Valley?

   I What do you think will happen when people start trying to get out of the city?

15
What Had Happened in Surrey

It was while the curate had sat and talked so wildly to me under the hedge in the flat meadows near Halliford, and while my brother was watching the fugitives stream over Westminster Bridge, that the Martians had resumed the offensive. So far as one can ascertain from the conflicting accounts that have been put forth, the majority of them remained busied with preparations in the Horsell pit until nine that night, hurrying on some operation that disengaged huge volumes of green smoke.

But three certainly came out about eight o'clock, and, advancing slowly and cautiously, made their way through Byfleet and Pyrford toward Ripley and Weybridge, and so came in sight of the expectant batteries against the setting sun. These Martians did not advance in a body, but in a line, each perhaps a mile and a half from his nearest fellow. They communicated with one another by means of siren-like howls, running up and down the scale from one note to another.

It was this howling and the firing of the guns at Ripley and St. George's Hill that we had heard at Upper Halliford. The Ripley gunners, unseasoned artillery volunteers who ought never to have been placed in such a position, fired one wild, premature, ineffectual volley, and bolted on horse and foot through the deserted village, while the Martian without using his Heat-Ray, walked serenely over their guns, stepped gingerly among them, passed in front of them, and so came unexpectedly upon the guns in Painshill Park, which he destroyed.

The St. George's Hill men, however, were better led or of a better mettle. Hidden by a pine wood as they were, they seem to have been quite unsuspected by the Martian nearest to them. They laid their guns as deliberately as if they had been on parade, and fired at about a thousand yards' range.

The shells flashed all round him, and he was seen to advance a few paces, stagger, and go down. Everybody yelled together, and the guns were reloaded in frantic haste. The overthrown Martian set up a prolonged ululation, and immediately a second glittering giant, answering him, appeared over the trees to the south. It would seem that a leg of the tripod had been smashed by one of the shells. The whole of the second volley flew wide of the Martian on the ground, and, simultaneously, both his companions brought their Heat-Rays to bear on the battery. The ammunition blew up, the pine trees all about the guns flashed into fire, and only one or two of the men who were already running over the crest of the hill escaped.

> ❶ *What happens to one of the Martians? Who comes to the Martian's rescue?*

After this it would seem that the three took counsel together and halted, and the scouts who were watching them report that they remained absolutely stationary for the next half-hour. The Martian who had been overthrown crawled tediously out of his hood, a small brown figure, oddly suggestive from that distance of a speck of blight, and apparently engaged in the repair of his support. About nine he had finished, for his cowl was then seen above the trees again.

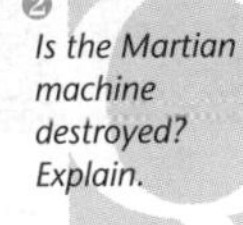

> ❷ *Is the Martian machine destroyed? Explain.*

It was a few minutes past nine that night when these three sentinels were joined by four other Martians, each carrying a thick black tube. A similar tube was handed to each of the three, and the seven proceeded to distribute themselves at equal distances

Words for Everyday Use

vol • ley (väl´ē) *n.*, simultaneous discharge of a number of firearms

met • tle (met´'l) *n.*, quality of character

ul • u • la • tion (yo͞ol´yoo lā´shən) *n.*, loud howling or hooting

coun • sel (koun´səl) *n.*, discussion and deliberation

blight (blīt) *n.*, plant disease, such as mildew or rust

Answers to Guided Reading Questions

❶ One of the Martians is knocked down by the shelling. Two other Martians come to the rescue of the first.

❷ The machine is not completely destroyed. The Martian inside it is able to climb out, repair the machine, and be back in operation shortly thereafter.

Vocabulary in Context

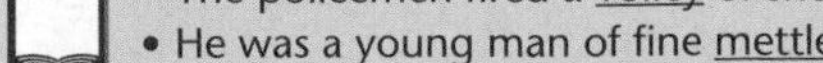

- The policemen fired a volley of shots overhead to honor their fellow officer.
- He was a young man of fine mettle.
- There was a ulalation of disapproval from the crowd at the referee's ruling.
- They took counsel together and decided the best course of action.
- She sprayed her rose bushes for blight.

ANSWER TO GUIDED READING QUESTION

❶ The Martians can move much faster than humans. It is safer to hide from them.

QUOTABLES

"Human history becomes more and more a race between education and catastrophe."

—H. G. Wells

Why is it "no good running from the Martian"?

❶ along a curved line between St. George's Hill, Weybridge, and the village of Send, southwest of Ripley.

A dozen rockets sprang out of the hills before them so soon as they began to move, and warned the waiting batteries about Ditton and Esher. At the same time four of their fighting-machines, similarly armed with tubes, crossed the river, and two of them, black against the western sky, came into sight of myself and the curate as we hurried wearily and painfully along the road that runs northward out of Halliford. They moved, as it seemed to us, upon a cloud, for a milky mist covered the fields and rose to a third of their height.

At this sight the curate cried faintly in his throat, and began running; but I knew it was no good running from a Martian, and I turned aside and crawled through dewy nettles and brambles into the broad ditch by the side of the road. He looked back, saw what I was doing, and turned to join me.

The two halted, the nearer to us standing and facing Sunbury, the remoter being a gray indistinctness toward the evening star, away toward Staines.

The occasional howling of the Martians had ceased; they took up their positions in the huge crescent about their cylinders in absolute silence. It was a crescent with twelve miles between its horns. Never since the devising of gunpowder was the beginning of a battle so still. To us and to an observer about Ripley it would have had precisely the same effect—the Martians seemed in solitary possession of the darkling night, lit only as it was by the slender moon, the stars, the afterglow of the daylight, and the ruddy glare from St. George's Hill and the woods of Painshill.

But facing that crescent everywhere—at Staines, Hounslow, Ditton, Esher, Ockham, behind hills and woods south of the river, and across the flat grass meadows to the north of it, wherever a cluster of trees or village houses gave sufficient cover—the guns were waiting. The signal rockets burst and rained their sparks through the night and vanished, and the

WORDS FOR EVERYDAY USE

dark • ling (därk´liŋ) *adj.,* dark; dim

VOCABULARY IN CONTEXT

• The fairies and wood sprites ruled the darkling midsummer night.

spirit of all those watching batteries rose to a tense expectation. The Martians had but to advance into the line of fire, and instantly those motionless black forms of men, those guns glittering so darkly in the early night, would explode into a thunderous fury of battle.

No doubt the thought that was uppermost in a thousand of those vigilant minds, even as it was uppermost in mine, was the riddle—how much they understood of us. Did they grasp that we in our millions were organized, disciplined, working together? Or did they interpret our spurts of fire, the sudden stinging of our shells, our steady investment of their encampment, as we should the furious unanimity of onslaught in a disturbed hive of bees? Did they dream they might exterminate us? (At that time no one knew what food they needed.) A hundred such questions struggled together in my mind as I watched that vast sentinel shape. And in the back of my mind was the sense of all the huge unknown and hidden forces Londonward. Had they prepared pitfalls? Were the powder mills at Hounslow ready as a snare? Would the Londoners have the heart and courage to make a greater Moscow[1] of their mighty province of houses?

Then, after an interminable time, as it seemed to us, crouching and peering through the hedge, came a sound like the distant concussion of a gun. Another nearer, and then another. And then the Martian beside us raised his tube on high and discharged it, gunwise, with a heavy report that made the ground heave. The one toward Staines answered him. There was no flash, no smoke, simply that loaded detonation.

I was so excited by these heavy minute guns following one another that I so far forgot my personal safety and my scalded hands as to clamber up into the hedge and stare toward Sunbury. As I did so a second report followed, and a big projectile hurtled overhead toward Hounslow. I expected at least to see smoke or fire, or some such evidence of its work. But all I saw was the deep-blue sky above, with one solitary star, and the white mist spreading wide and low beneath. And there had been no crash, no answering explosion. The silence was restored; the minute lengthened to three.

"What has happened?" said the curate, standing up beside me.

"Heaven knows!" said I.

A bat flickered by and vanished. A distant tumult of shouting began and ceased. I looked again at the Martian, and saw he was now moving eastward along the riverbank, with a swift, rolling motion.

Every moment I expected the fire of some hidden battery to spring upon him; but the evening calm was unbroken. The figure of the Martian grew smaller as he receded, and presently the mist and the gathering night had swallowed him up. By a common impulse we clambered higher. Toward Sunbury was a dark appearance, as though a conical hill had suddenly come into being there, hiding our view of the farther country; and then, remoter across the river, over Walton, we saw another such summit. These hill like forms grew lower and broader even as we stared.

Moved by a sudden thought, I looked northward, and there I perceived a third of these cloudy black kopjes[2] arisen.

Everything had suddenly become very still. Far away to the southeast, marking

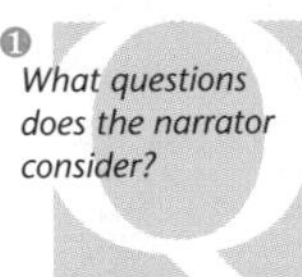

❶ *What questions does the narrator consider?*

CHAPTER 15

1. **Moscow.** In 1812, Russians destroyed their own city of Moscow so that Napoleon could not capture it
2. **kopjes.** Small hills

WORDS FOR EVERYDAY USE

vig • i • lant (vij´ə lənt) *adj.*, watchful and alert to danger or trouble

on • slaught (än´ slôt´) *n.*, violent, intense attack

in • ter • mi • na • ble (in tʉr´ mi nə bəl) *adj.*, without end

con • i • cal (kän´i kəl) *adj.*, resembling or shaped like a cone

ANSWER TO GUIDED READING QUESTION

❶ The narrator wonders whether the Martians think of the human opposition as organized and intelligent or simply as reflexive and automatic, like the movement of disturbed bees. The narrator also wonders whether the Martians will exterminate people.

VOCABULARY IN CONTEXT

- The faithful old dog stood vigilant guard as his master slept.
- They were unprepared for the onslaught of the epidemic.
- The monthly meeting seemed interminable.
- The boy wore a conically shaped hat.

Answers to Guided Reading Questions

❶ The artillery doesn't fire on the Martians because the soldiers in the artillery are dead.

❷ The new weapon is a cloud of deadly gas.

❸ *Answers will vary.* Some students will consider the mood of this passage somewhat sinister and ominous.

Why doesn't the artillery fire on the Martians? ❶

What new weapon is being used by the Martians? How does it work? ❷

What mood is created by this description? ❸

the quiet, we heard the Martians hooting to one another, and then the air quivered again with the distant thud of their guns. But the earthly artillery made no reply.

Now at the time we could not understand these things, but later I was to learn the meaning of these ominous kopjes that gathered in the twilight. Each of the Martians, standing in the great crescent I have described, had discharged, by means of the gunlike tube he carried, a huge canister over whatever hill, copse, cluster of houses, or other possible cover for guns, chanced to be in front of him. Some fired only one of these, some two—as in the case of the one we had seen; the one at Ripley is said to have discharged no fewer than five at that time. These canisters smashed on striking the ground—they did not explode—and incontinently disengaged an enormous volume of heavy, inky vapor, coiling and pouring upward in a huge and ebony cumulus cloud, a gaseous hill that sank and spread itself slowly over the surrounding country. And the touch of that vapor, the inhaling of its pungent wisps, was death to all that breathes.

It was heavy, this vapor, heavier than the densest smoke, so that, after the first tumultuous uprush and outflow of its impact, it sank down through the air and poured over the ground in a manner rather liquid than gaseous, abandoning the hills, and streaming into the valleys and ditches and watercourses even as I have heard the carbonic-acid gas[3] that pours from volcanic clefts is wont to do. And where it came upon water some chemical action occurred, and the surface would be instantly covered with a powdery scum that sank slowly and made way for more. The scum was absolutely insoluble and it is a strange thing, seeing the instant effect of the gas that one could drink without hurt the water from which it had been strained. The vapor did not diffuse as a true gas would do. It hung together in banks, flowing sluggishly down the slope of the land and driving reluctantly before the wind, and very slowly it combined with the mist and moisture of the air, and sank to the earth in the form of dust. Save that an unknown element giving a group of four lines in the blue of the spectrum is concerned, we are still entirely ignorant of the nature of this substance.

Once the tumultuous upheaval of its dispersion was over, the black smoke clung so closely to the ground, even before its precipitation that fifty feet up in the air, on the roofs and upper stories of high houses and on great trees, there was a chance of escaping its poison altogether, as was proved even that night at Street Cobham and Ditton.

The man who escaped at the former place tells a wonderful story of the strangeness of its coiling flow, and how he looked down from the church spire and saw the houses of the village rising like ghosts out of its inky nothingness. For a day and a half he remained there, weary, starving and sun-scorched, the earth under the blue sky and against the prospect of the distant hills a velvet-black expanse, with red roofs, green trees, and, later, black-veiled shrubs and gates, barns, outhouses, and walls, rising here and there into the sunlight.

But that was at Street Cobham, where the black vapor was allowed to remain until it sank of its own accord into the ground. As a rule the Martians, when it

3. **carbonic-acid gas.** Weak, colorless acid formed by the solution of carbon dioxide in water

Words for Everyday Use

om • i • nous (äm´ə nəs) *adj.,* threatening; serving as a bad sign or omen

pun • gent (pun´ jənt) *adj.,* producing a sharp sensation of taste and smell

cleft (kleft) *n.,* crack, crevice

in • sol • u • ble (in säl´yo͞o bəl) *adj.,* that cannot be dissolved

pre • cip • i • ta • tion (prē sip´ə tā´shən) *n.,* discharging of a substance, usually said of rain or snow from a cloud

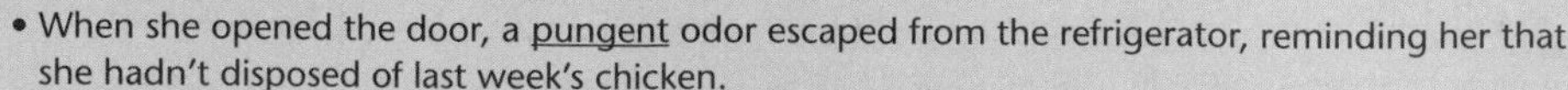

Vocabulary in Context

- An ominous rumble of thunder was heard in the distance.
- When she opened the door, a pungent odor escaped from the refrigerator, reminding her that she hadn't disposed of last week's chicken.
- A tiny wildflower had taken root in the cleft of the rock.
- Oil-based paint is insoluble in water.
- The meteorologist reported a 40 percent chance of precipitation.

had served its purpose, cleared the air of it again by wading into it and directing a jet of steam upon it.

This they did with the vapor banks near us, as we saw in the starlight from the window of a deserted house at Upper Halliford, whither we had returned. From there we could see the searchlights on Richmond Hill and Kingston Hill going to and fro, and about eleven the windows rattled, and we heard the sound of the huge siege guns that had been put in position there. These continued intermittently for the space of a quarter of an hour, sending chance shots at the invisible Martians at Hampton and Ditton, and then the pale beams of the electric light vanished, and were replaced by a bright red glow.

Then the fourth cylinder fell—a brilliant green meteor—as I learned afterwards, in Bushey Park. Before the guns on the Richmond and Kingston line of hills began, there was a fitful cannonade far away in the southwest, due, I believe, to guns being fired haphazard before the black vapor could overwhelm the gunners.

So, setting about it as methodically as men might smoke out a wasps' nest, the Martians spread this strange stifling vapor over the Londonward country. The horns of the crescent slowly moved apart, until at last they formed a line from Hanwell to Coombe and Malden. All night through their destructive tubes advanced. Never once, after the Martian at St. George's Hill was brought down, did they give the artillery the ghost of a chance against them. Wherever there was a possibility of guns being laid for them unseen, a fresh canister of the black vapor was discharged, and where the guns were openly displayed the Heat-Ray was brought to bear.

By midnight the blazing trees along the slopes of Richmond Park and the glare of Kingston Hill threw their light upon a network of black smoke, blotting out the whole Valley of the Thames and extending as far as the eye could reach. And through this two Martians slowly waded, and turned their hissing steam-jets this way and that.

They were sparing of the Heat-Ray that night, either because they had but a limited supply of material for its production or because they did not wish to destroy the country but only to crush and overawe the opposition they had aroused. In the latter aim they certainly succeeded. Sunday night was the end of the organized opposition to their movements. After that no body of men would stand against them, so hopeless was the enterprise. Even the crews of the torpedo boats and destroyers that had brought their quick-firers up the Thames refused to stop, mutinied, and went down again. The only offensive operation men ventured upon after that night was the preparation of mines and pitfalls, and even in that their energies were frantic and spasmodic.

One has to imagine, as well as one may, the fate of those batteries toward Esher, waiting so tensely in the twilight. Survivors there were none. One may picture the orderly expectation, the officers alert and watchful, the gunners ready, the ammunition piled to hand, the limber gunners with their horses and wagons, the groups of civilian spectators standing as near as they were permitted, the evening stillness, the ambulances and hospital tents with the burned and wounded from Weybridge; then the dull resonance of the shots the Martians fired, and the clumsy projectile whirling over the trees and houses and smashing amid the neighboring fields.

❶ *Of what was Sunday night the end? What possibility do people have of overcoming the Martians by force?*

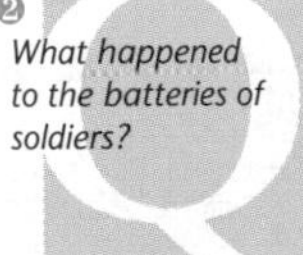

❷ *What happened to the batteries of soldiers?*

Words for Everyday Use

siege (sēj) *adj.,* blockade or bombardment

can • non • ade (kan′ən ād´) *n.,* continuous firing of artillery

me • thod • i • cal • ly (mə thäd´i kəl lē) *adv.,* orderly; systematically

spas • mod • ic (spaz mäd´ik) *adj.,* fitful; intermittent

Answers to Guided Reading Questions

❶ Sunday night was the end of organized opposition to the Martians. People have no possibility of overcoming the Martians by force.

❷ The batteries of soldiers were destroyed.

Vocabulary in Context

- No supplies could reach the city, which was under siege.
- The cannonade continued all that night and into the next morning.
- She methodically set about preparing dinner.
- He had spasmodic muscle contractions in his leg.

Answer to Guided Reading Question

❶ The government is trying to organize the evacuation of London.

Answers for Reviewing the Selection

RECALLING AND INTERPRETING

1. **Recalling.** The soldier on St. George's Hill killed a Martian with a shell. **Interpreting.** In retaliation, the Martians use the black vapor to destroy batteries of soldiers.
2. **Recalling.** The black smoke is released from canisters. It spreads and poisons all whom it touches. **Interpreting.** The black smoke kills all the soldiers so that they cannot fire their guns.

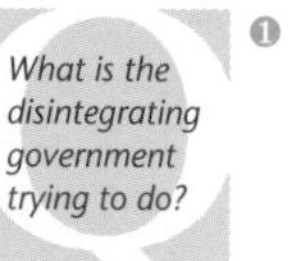

What is the disintegrating government trying to do? ❶

One may picture, too, the sudden shifting of the attention, the swiftly spreading coils and bellyings of that blackness advancing headlong, towering heavenward, turning the twilight to a palpable darkness, a strange and horrible antagonist of vapor—striding upon its victims, men and horses near it seen dimly, running, shrieking, falling headlong, shouts of dismay, the guns suddenly abandoned, men choking and writhing on the ground, and the swift broadening out of the opaque cone of smoke. And then night and extinction—nothing but a silent mass of impenetrable vapor hiding its dead.

Before dawn the black vapor was pouring through the streets of Richmond, and the disintegrating organism of government was, with a last expiring effort, rousing the population of London to the neccessity of flight.

Reviewing the Selection

Recalling and Interpreting

1. (R) What do the soldiers on St. George's Hill do?
   (I) How do the Martians retaliate?

2. (R) How does the black smoke work?
   (I) What makes this black smoke a particularly effective weapon against batteries of guns?

Words for Everyday Use

pal • pa • ble (pal´pə bəl) *adj.,* easily perceived; that can be felt
o •paque (ō pāk´) *adj.,* not letting light through; obscuring

Vocabulary in Context

- The fact that Johnny was not a very good ballplayer was palpable to all the spectators.
- The opaque glass windows of the basement created a gloomy atmosphere.

16
The Exodus from London

So you understand the roaring wave of fear that swept through the greatest city in the world just as Monday was dawning—the stream of flight rising swiftly to a torrent, lashing in a foaming tumult round the railway stations, banked up into a horrible struggle about the shipping in the Thames, and hurrying by every available channel northward and eastward. By ten o'clock the police organization, and by midday even the railway organizations, were losing coherency, losing shape and efficiency, guttering, softening, running at last in that swift liquefaction of the social body.

All the railway lines north of the Thames and the South-Eastern people at Cannon Street had been warned by midnight on Sunday, and trains were being filled. People were fighting savagely for standing room in the carriages even at two o'clock. By three, people were being trampled and crushed even in Bishopsgate Street, a couple of hundred yards or more from Liverpool Street station; revolvers were fired, people stabbed, and the policemen who had been sent to direct the traffic, exhausted and infuriated, were breaking the heads of the people they were called out to protect.

And as the day advanced and the engine drivers and stokers refused to return to London, the pressure of the flight drove the people in an ever-thickening multitude away from the stations and along the northward-running roads. By midday a Martian had been seen at Barnes, and a cloud of slowly sinking black vapor drove along the Thames and across the flats of Lambeth, cutting off all escape over the bridges in its sluggish advance. Another bank drove over Ealing, and surrounded a little island of survivors on Castle Hill, alive, but unable to escape.

After a fruitless struggle to get aboard a North-Western train at Chalk Farm—the engines of the trains that had loaded in the goods yard there *ploughed* through shrieking people, and a dozen stalwart men fought to keep the crowd from crushing the driver against his furnace—my brother emerged upon the Chalk Farm road, dodged across through a hurrying swarm of vehicles, and had the luck to be foremost in the sack of a cycle shop. The front tire of the machine he got was punctured in dragging it through the window, but he got up and off, notwithstanding, with no further injury than a cut wrist. The steep foot of Haverstock Hill was impassable owing to several overturned horses, and my brother struck into Belsize Road.

So he got out of the fury of the panic, and, skirting the Edgware Road, reached Edgware about seven, fasting and wearied, but well ahead of the crowd. Along the road people were standing in the roadway, curious, wondering. He was passed by a number of cyclists, some horsemen, and two motorcars. A mile from Edgware the rim of the wheel broke, and the machine became unridable. He left it by the roadside and trudged through the village. There were shops half-opened in the main street of the place, and people crowded on the pavement and in the doorways and windows, staring astonished at this extraordinary procession of fugitives that was beginning. He succeeded in getting some food at an inn.

For a time he remained in Edgware not knowing what next to do. The flying

❶ *What has happened to public order in the city?*

Words for Everyday Use

co • her • en • cy (kō hir´ən sē´) *n.*, quality of being logically integrated or consistent

liq • ue • fac • tion (lik´wi fak´shən) *n.*, changing into liquid

im • pas • sa • ble (im pas´ə bəl) *adj.*, cannot be crossed or traveled over

Answer to Guided Reading Question

❶ Public order in the city has broken down. There is savage fighting and rioting.

Vocabulary in Context

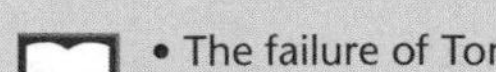

- The failure of Tommy's campaign for class president was blamed on his lack of coherency on the issues.
- Liquefaction of the metal is an early part of the recycling process.
- Due to the avalanche, Jean's favorite ski trail was clearly impassable.

Answer to Guided Reading Question

❶ The brother immediately grasps that the men are attempting to steal the ladies' conveyance.

people increased in number. Many of them, like my brother, seemed inclined to loiter in the place. There was no fresh news of the invaders from Mars.

At that time the road was crowded, but as yet far from congested. Most of the fugitives at that hour were mounted on cycles, but there were soon motorcars, hansom cabs,[1] and carriages hurrying along, and the dust hung in heavy clouds along the road to St. Albans.

It was perhaps a vague idea of making his way to Chelmsford, where some friends of his lived, that at last induced my brother to strike into a quiet lane running eastward. Presently he came upon a stile,[2] and, crossing it, followed a footpath northeastward. He passed near several farmhouses and some little places whose names he did not learn. He saw few fugitives until, in a grass lane toward High Barnet, he happened upon the two ladies who became his fellow travelers. He came upon them just in time to save them.

He heard their screams, and, hurrying round the corner, saw a couple of men struggling to drag them out of the little pony-chaise[3] in which they had been driving, while a third with difficulty held the frightened pony's head. One of the ladies, a short woman dressed in white, was simply screaming; the other, a dark, slender figure, slashed at the man who gripped her arm with a whip she held in her disengaged hand.

What situation does the brother immediately grasp? ❶

My brother immediately grasped the situation, shouted, and hurried toward the struggle. One of the men desisted and turned toward him, and my brother, realizing from his antagonist's face that a fight was unavoidable, and being an expert boxer, went into him forthwith and sent him down against the wheel of the chaise.

It was no time for pugilistic chivalry, and my brother laid him quiet with a kick, and gripped the collar of the man who pulled at the slender lady's arm. He heard the clatter of hoofs, the whip stung across his face, a third antagonist struck him between the eyes, and the man he held wrenched himself free and made off down the lane in the direction from which he had come.

Partly stunned, he found himself facing the man who had held the horse's head, and became aware of the chaise receding from him down the lane, swaying from side to side, and with the women in it looking back. The man before him, a burly rough, tried to close, and he stopped him with a blow in the face. Then, realizing that he was deserted, he dodged round and made off down the lane after the chaise, with the sturdy man close behind him, and the fugitive, who had turned now, following remotely.

Suddenly he stumbled and fell; his immediate pursuer went headlong, and he rose to his feet to find himself with a couple of antagonists again. He would have had little chance against them had not the slender lady very pluckily pulled up and returned to his help. It seems she had had a revolver all this time, but it had been under the seat when she and her companion were attacked. She fired at six yards' distance, narrowly missing my brother. The less courageous of the robbers made off, and his companion followed him, cursing his cowardice. They both stopped in sight down the lane where the third man lay insensible.

Chapter 16

1. **hansom cab.** Two-wheeled, horse-drawn carriage for two passengers; the driver is seated above and behind the cab.
2. **stile.** Set of steps used to climb over a fence or wall
3. **pony-chaise.** Carriage pulled by one or two ponies

Words for Everyday Use

loi • ter (loit´ər) *v.*, spend time idly; linger
con • ges • ted (kən jest´id) *adj.*, clogged; overcrowded
pu • gil • is • tic (pyo͞o´jil iz´ tik) *adj.*, fighting

Vocabulary in Context

- The security guard repeatedly warned the teenagers not to loiter in front of the store.
- The congested highway guarunteed that Beth would once again be late to work.
- After getting into three fights in a month, Bill's parents decided that his pugilistic attitude had to stop.

"Take this!" said the slender lady, and she gave my brother her revolver.

"Go back to the chaise," said my brother, wiping the blood from his split lip.

She turned without a word—they were both panting—and they went back to where the lady in white struggled to hold back the frightened pony.

The robbers had evidently had enough of it. When my brother looked again they were retreating.

"I'll sit here," said my brother, "if I may"; and he got upon the empty front seat. The lady looked over her shoulder.

"Give me the reins," she said, and laid the whip along the pony's side. In another moment a bend in the road hid the three men from my brother's eyes.

So, quite unexpectedly, my brother found himself, panting, with a cut mouth, a bruised jaw, and blood-stained knuckles, driving along an unknown lane with these two women.

He learned they were the wife and the younger sister of a surgeon living at Stanmore, who had come in the small hours from a dangerous case at Pinner, and heard at some railway station on his way of the Martian advance. He had hurried home, roused the women—their servant had left them two days before—packed some provisions, put his revolver under the seat—luckily for my brother—and told them to drive on to Edgware, with the idea of getting a train there. He stopped behind to tell the neighbors. He would overtake them, he said, at about half-past four in the morning, and now it was nearly nine and they had seen nothing of him. They could not stop in Edgware because of the growing traffic through the place, and so they had come into this side lane.

That was the story they told my brother in fragments when presently they stopped again, nearer to New Barnet. He promised to stay with them, at least until they could determine what to do, or until the missing man arrived, and professed to be an expert shot with the revolver—a weapon strange to him—in order to give them confidence.

They made a sort of encampment by the wayside, and the pony became happy in the hedge. He told them of his own escape out of London, and all that he knew of these Martians and their ways. The sun crept higher in the sky, and after a time their talk died out and gave place to an uneasy state of anticipation. Several wayfarers came along the lane, and of these my brother gathered such news as he could. Every broken answer he had deepened his impression of the great disaster that had come on humanity, deepened his persuasion of the immediate necessity for prosecuting this flight. He urged the matter upon them.

"We have money," said the slender woman, and hesitated.

Her eyes met my brother's, and her hesitation ended.

"So have I," said my brother.

She explained that they had as much as thirty pounds in gold, besides a five-pound note, and suggested that with that they might get upon a train at St. Albans or New Barnet. My brother thought that was hopeless, seeing the fury of the Londoners to crowd upon the trains, and broached his own idea of striking across Essex toward Harwich and thence escaping from the country altogether.

Mrs. Elphinstone—that was the name of the woman in white—would listen to no

❶ *What might have become of the surgeon?*

Words for Everyday Use

rouse (rouz) *v.*, awaken

pro • vi • sions (prō vizh´ənz) *n.*, stock of food and other supplies assembled for future needs

pros • e • cute (präs´ i kyo͞ot´) *v.*, pursue

broach (brōch) *v.*, bring up; introduce

Answer to Guided Reading Question

❶ The surgeon might have been killed by the Martians.

Vocabulary in Context

- The sound of the screaming drill sergeant roused the troops.
- Before setting out on the hiking trip, Lisa and Raul checked that they had enough provisions for the long journey.
- Erika knew she had to go to medical school if she wanted to prosecute her dreams of becoming a doctor.
- Although he knew it would not be easy, Frank felt he must broach the subject of the money Hank owed him.

Answer to Guided Reading Question

❶ The man in evening dress has been driven to madness by his anger.

reasoning, and kept calling upon "George"; but her sister-in-law was astonishingly quiet and deliberate, and at last agreed to my brother's suggestion. So designing to cross the Great North Road, they went on toward Barnet, my brother leading the pony to save it as much as possible.

As the sun crept up the sky the day became excessively hot, and underfoot a thick, whitish sand grew burning and blinding, so that they traveled only very slowly. The hedges were gray with dust. And as they advanced toward Barnet a tumultuous murmuring grew stronger.

❶ *What is the man in evening dress experiencing?*

They began to meet more people. For the most part these were staring before them, murmuring indistinct questions, jaded, haggard, unclean. One man in evening dress passed them on foot, his eyes on the ground. They heard his voice, and, looking back at him, saw one hand clutched in his hair and the other beating invisible things. His paroxysm of rage over, he went on his way without once looking back.

As my brother's party went on toward the crossroads to the south of Barnet they saw a woman approaching the road across some fields on their left, carrying a child and with two other children; and then passed a man in dirty black, with a thick stick in one hand and a small portmanteau in the other. Then round the corner of the lane, from between the villas that guarded it at its confluence with the highroad, came a little cart drawn by a sweating black pony and driven by a sallow youth in a bowler hat[4] gray with dust. There were three girls, East End factory girls, and a couple of little children crowded in the cart.

"This'll tike us rahnd Edgware?" asked the driver, wild-eyed, white-faced; and when my brother told him it would if he turned to the left, he whipped up at once without the formality of thanks.

My brother noticed a pale gray smoke or haze rising among the houses in front of them, and veiling the white façade of a terrace beyond the road that appeared between the backs of the villas. Mrs. Elphinstone suddenly cried out at a number of tongues of smoky red flame leaping up above the houses in front of them against the hot, blue sky. The tumultuous noise resolved itself now into the disorderly mingling of many voices, the gride[5] of many wheels, the creaking of wagons, and the staccato of hoofs. The lane came round sharply, not fifty yards from the crossroads.

"Good heavens!" cried Mrs. Elphinstone. "What is this you are driving us into?"

My brother stopped.

For the main road was a boiling stream of people, a torrent of human beings rushing northward, one pressing on another. A great bank of dust, white and luminous in the blaze of the sun, made everything within twenty feet of the ground gray and indistinct, and was perpetually renewed by the hurrying feet of a dense crowd of horses and of men and women on foot, and by the wheels of vehicles of every description.

"Way!" my brother heard voices crying. "Make way!"

It was like riding into the smoke of a fire to approach the meeting-point of the lane and road; the crowd roared like a fire, and the dust was hot and pungent. And, indeed, a little way up the road a villa was burning and sending rolling masses of black smoke across the road to add to the confusion.

4. **bowler hat.** Stiff felt hat with a round crown and a curved brim

5. **gride.** Harsh, rasping sound made by scraping or grating

Words for Everyday Use

jad • ed (jād´id) *adj.*, tired; worn out

par • ox • ysm (par´əks iz´əm) *n.*, sudden outburst or fit

con• flu • ence (kän´flo͞o əns) *n.*, place where two things join

sal • low (sal´ō) *adj.*, sickly-looking

fa • çade (fə säd´) *n.*, front

stac • ca • to (stə kät´ō) *n.*, sound broken up into abrupt, distinct elements

Vocabulary in Context

- After the long trip, we were all dirty and jaded.
- Linda's paroxysm about the outcome of the auditions embarassed her fellow actors.
- The confluence of the rivers was a favorite place for fishing.
- Tisha looked sallow and worn down as she entered the nurse's office.
- The façade of the car was only slightly damaged in the accident.
- The bird's shrill staccato woke up the sleeping campers.

Two men came past them. Then a dirty woman, carrying a heavy bundle and weeping. A lost retriever dog, with hanging tongue, circled dubiously round them, scared and wretched, and fled at my brother's threat.

So much as they could see of the road Londonward between the houses to the right was a tumultuous stream of dirty, hurrying people, pent in between the villas on either side; the black heads, the crowded forms, grew into distinctness as they rushed toward the corner, hurried past, and merged their individuality again in a receding multitude that was swallowed up at last in a cloud of dust.

"Go on! Go on!" cried the voices. "Way! Way!"

One man's hands pressed on the back of another. My brother stood at the pony's head. Irresistibly attracted, he advanced slowly, pace by pace, down the lane.

Edgware had been a scene of confusion, Chalk Farm a riotous tumult, but this was a whole population in movement. It is hard to imagine that host. It had no character of its own. The figures poured out past the corner, and receded with their backs to the group in the lane. Along the margin came those who were on foot, threatened by the wheels, stumbling in the ditches, blundering into one another.

The carts and carriages crowded close upon one another, making little way for those swifter and more impatient vehicles that darted forward every now and then when an opportunity showed itself of doing so, sending the people scattering against the fences and gates of the villas.

❶ *Why aren't people driving cautiously and courteously?*

Words for Everyday Use

du • bi • ous • ly (do͞o bē äs´lē) *adv.*, outcome undecided or hanging in the balance

Answer to Guided Reading Question

❶ The people are impatient to get out of the city and to safety.

Vocabulary in Context

• The result of the elections still dubiously unknown, the Senator was pacing nervously.

"Push on!" was the cry. "Push on! They are coming!"

In one cart stood a blind man in the uniform of the Salvation Army, gesticulating with his crooked fingers and bawling, "Eternity! eternity!" His voice was hoarse and very loud, so that my brother could hear him long after he was lost to sight in the dust. Some of the people who crowded in the carts whipped stupidly at their horses and quarreled with other drivers; some sat motionless, staring at nothing with miserable eyes; some gnawed their hands with thirst, or lay prostrate in the bottoms of their conveyances. The horses' bits were covered with foam, their eyes bloodshot.

There were cabs, carriages, shop-carts, wagons, beyond counting; a mailcart, a road-cleaner's cart marked "Vestry of St. Pancras," a huge timber-wagon crowded with roughs. A brewer's dray[6] rumbled by with its two near wheels splashed with fresh blood.

"Clear the way!" cried the voices. "Clear the way!"

"Eter-nity! eter-nity!" came echoing down the road.

There were sad, haggard women tramping by, well dressed, with children that cried and stumbled, their dainty clothes smothered in dust, their weary faces smeared with tears. With many of these came men, sometimes helpful, sometimes lowering and savage. Fighting side by side with them pushed some weary street outcast in faded black rags, wide-eyed, loud-voiced, and foul-mouthed. There were sturdy workmen thrusting their way along, wretched, unkempt men, clothed like clerks or shop-men, struggling spasmodically; a wounded soldier my brother noticed, men dressed in the clothes of railway porters, one wretched creature in a nightshirt with a coat thrown over it.

But varied as its composition was, certain things all that host had in common. There were fear and pain on their faces, and fear behind them. A tumult up the road, a quarrel for a place in a wagon, sent the whole host of them quickening their pace; even a man so scared and broken that his knees bent under him was galvanized for a moment into renewed activity. The heat and dust had already been at work upon this multitude. Their skins were dry, their lips black and cracked. They were all thirsty, weary, and footsore. And amid the various cries one heard disputes, reproaches, groans of weariness and fatigue; the voices of most of them were hoarse and weak. Through it all ran a refrain:

"Way! way! The Martians are coming!"

Few stopped and came aside from that flood. The lane opened slantingly into the main road with a narrow opening, and had a delusive appearance of coming from the direction of London. Yet a kind of eddy of people drove into its mouth; weaklings elbowed out of the stream, who for the most part rested but a moment before plunging into it again. A little way down the lane, with two friends bending over him, lay a man with a bare leg, wrapped about with bloody rags. He was a lucky man to have friends.

A little old man, with a gray military moustache and a filthy black frock coat, limped out and sat down beside the trap, removed his boot—his sock was blood-stained—shook out a pebble, and hobbled on again; and then a little girl of eight or nine, all alone, threw herself

6. **dray.** Low, sturdily built cart with detachable sides used to carry heavy loads

Words for Everyday Use

ges • tic • u • late (jes tik´ yo͞o lāt´) *v.* make movements, as with hands or arms

pros • trate (präs´ trāt´) *adj.*, flat, face down

un • kempt (un kempt´) *adj.*, not tidy or neat

gal • va • nize (gal´ və nīz´) *v.*, rouse or stir as if by electric shock

de • lus • ive (di lo͞os´iv) *adj.*, misleading

ed • dy (ed´ē) *n.*, whirlwind or whirlpool

Vocabulary in Context

- If you gesticulate wildly, people are likely to stare.
- In order to rest his back, the doctor told Charles to lie prostrate on the sidelines.
- The interviewer was noticeably unimpressed by John's unkempt appearance.
- The sound of gunfire galvanized the soldiers into action.
- The congressperson felt the conclusions of the report were very delusive.
- The nature of the rock formations created a small eddy at one point on the river.

under the hedge close by my brother, weeping.

"I can't go on! I can't go on!"

My brother woke from his torpor of astonishment and lifted her up, speaking gently to her, and carried her to Miss Elphinstone. So soon as my brother touched her she became quite still, as if frightened.

"Ellen!" shrieked a woman in the crowd, with tears in her voice—"Ellen!" And the child suddenly darted away from my brother, crying "Mother!"

"They are coming," said a man on horseback, riding past along the lane.

"Out of the way, there!" bawled a coachman, towering high; and my brother saw a closed carriage turning into the lane.

The people crushed back on one another to avoid the horse. My brother pushed the pony and chaise back into the hedge, and the man drove by and stopped at the turn of the way. It was a carriage, with a pole for a pair of horses, but only one was in the traces. My brother saw dimly through the dust that two men lifted out something on a white stretcher and put it gently on the grass beneath the privet hedge.[7]

One of the men came running to my brother.

"Where is there any water?" he said. "He is dying fast, and very thirsty. It is Lord Garrick."

"Lord Garrick!" said my brother—"the Chief Justice?"

"The water?" he said.

"There may be a tap," said my brother, "in some of the houses. We have no water. I dare not leave my people."

The man pushed against the crowd toward the gate of the corner house.

"Go on!" said the people, thrusting at him. "They are coming! Go on!"

Then my brother's attention was distracted by a bearded, eagle-faced man lugging a small handbag, which split even as my brother's eyes rested on it and disgorged a mass of sovereigns[8] that seemed to break up into separate coins as it struck the ground. They rolled hither and thither among the struggling feet of men and horses. The man stopped and looked stupidly at the heap, and the shaft of a cab struck his shoulder and sent him reeling. He gave a shriek and dodged back, and a cart-wheel shaved him narrowly.

"Way!" cried the men all about him. "Make way!"

So soon as the cab had passed, he flung himself, with both hands open, upon the heap of coins, and began thrusting handfuls in his pocket. A horse rose close upon him, and in another moment, half rising, he had been borne down under the horse's hoofs.

"Stop!" screamed my brother, and pushing a woman out of his way, tried to clutch the bit of the horse.

Before he could get to it, he heard a scream under the wheels, and saw through the dust the rim passing over the poor <u>wretch's</u> back. The driver of the cart slashed his whip at my brother, who ran round behind the cart. The <u>multitudinous</u> shouting confused his ears. The man was writhing in the dust among his scattered money, unable to rise, for the wheel had broken his back, and his lower limbs lay limp and dead. My brother stood up and yelled at the next driver, and a man on a black horse came to his assistance.

"Get him out of the road," said he; and, clutching the man's collar with his free hand, my brother lugged him sideways.

7. **privet hedge.** Hedge made up of shrubs or trees of the olive family

8. **sovereigns.** British gold coins

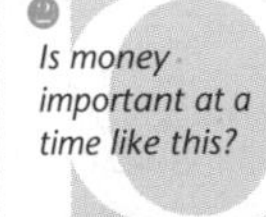

❶ *What has happened to the little girl and her mother?*

❷ *Is money important at a time like this?*

Words for Everyday Use

wretch (rech) *n.*, miserable or unhappy person, person in deep distress or misfortune

mul • ti • tu • di •nous (mul´tə to͞od´´n əs) *adj.*, very great, made up of many parts

Answers to Guided Reading Questions

❶ The little girl has been separated from her mother.

❷ This passage reveals the absurdity of caring about money at a time like this. Without life and safety, money is, of course, meaningless.

Vocabulary in Context

- After losing his fortune, the once rich man was now a <u>wretch</u>.
- The <u>multitudinous</u> number of parts in the engine made it impossible for Maura to put it back together.

Answers to Guided Reading Questions

❶ The girl proved her quality by standing up to the men.

❷ The man behind will back off if he is in danger of losing his horse, which is his means of escape from the Martians.

How did the girl prove her quality the first time? ❶

Why does the brother say to point the revolver at the horse? ❷

But he still clutched after his money, and regarded my brother fiercely, hammering at his arm with a handful of gold. "Go on! Go on!" shouted angry voices behind. "Way! Way!"

There was a smash as the pole of a carriage crashed into the cart that the man on horseback stopped. My brother looked up, and the man with the gold twisted his head round and bit the wrist that held his collar. There was a concussion and the black horse came staggering sideways, and the cart-horse pushed beside it. A hoof missed my brother's foot by a hair's breadth. He released his grip on the fallen man and jumped back. He saw anger change to terror on the face of the poor wretch on the ground, and in a moment he was hidden and my brother was borne backward and carried past the entrance of the lane, and had to fight hard in the torrent to recover it.

He saw Miss Elphinstone covering her eyes, and a little child, with all a child's want of sympathetic imagination, staring with dilated eyes at a dusty something that lay black and still, ground and crushed under the rolling wheels. "Let us go back!" he shouted, and began turning the pony round. "We cannot cross this—hell," he said; and they went back a hundred yards the way they had come, until the fighting crowd was hidden. As they passed the bend in the lane my brother saw the face of the dying man in the ditch under the privet, deadly white and drawn, and shining with perspiration. The two women sat silent, crouching in their seats and shivering.

Then beyond the bend my brother stopped again. Miss Elphinstone was white and pale, and her sister-in-law sat weeping, too wretched even to call upon "George." My brother was horrified and perplexed. So soon as they had retreated he realized how urgent and unavoidable it was to attempt this crossing. He turned to Miss Elphinstone, suddenly resolute.

"We must go that way," he said, and led the pony round again.

For the second time that day this girl proved her quality. To force their way into the torrent of people, my brother plunged into the traffic and held back a cab-horse, while she drove the pony across its head. A wagon locked wheels for a moment and ripped a long splinter from the chaise. In another moment they were caught and swept forward by the stream. My brother, with the cabman's whipmarks red across his face and hands, scrambled into the chaise and took the reins from her.

"Point the revolver at the man behind," he said, giving it to her, "if he presses us too hard. No!—point it at his horse."

Then he began to look out for a chance of edging to the right across the road. But once in the stream he seemed to lose volition, to become a part of that dusty rout. They swept through Chipping Barnet with the torrent; they were nearly a mile beyond the center of the town before they had fought across to the opposite side of the way. It was din and confusion indescribable; but in and beyond the town the road forks repeatedly, and this to some extent relieved the stress.

They struck eastward through Hadley, and there on either side of the road, and at another place farther on they came upon a great multitude of people drinking at the stream, some fighting to come at the water. And farther on, from a hill near East Barnet, they saw two trains running slowly one after the other without signal or order—trains swarming with people, with men even among the coals behind

Words for Everyday Use

di • lated (dī lāt´id) *adj.*, enlarged or widened

res • o • lute (rez´ə lo͞ot´) *adj.*, determined; having or showing firm purpose

vo • li • tion (vō lish´ən) *n.*, power or faculty of using one's will

rout (rout) *n.*, disorderly crowd; noisy mob

din (din) *n.*, loud, continuous noise or confused clamor

Vocabulary in Context

- After seeing the optometrist, Hiren's pupils were dilated.
- The man was resolute that the watch was indeed his.
- The two boys decided to leave school on their own volition, although they said the third boy was the reason they had gone.
- After the concert was canceled, the fans quickly turned into an angry rout.
- The unceasing din of the party next door forced the neighbors to call the police.

the engines—going northward along the Great Northern Railway. My brother supposes they must have filled outside London, for at that time the furious terror of the people had rendered the central termini impossible.

Near this place they halted for the rest of the afternoon, for the violence of the day had already utterly exhausted all three of them. They began to suffer the beginnings of hunger; the night was cold, and none of them dared to sleep. And in the evening many people came hurrying along the road near by their stopping place, fleeing from unknown dangers before them, and going in the direction from which my brother had come.

Reviewing the Selection

Recalling and Interpreting

1. (R) Whom does the narrator's brother rescue?

   (I) Why do you think that the men were attempting to take the chaise? Why do you think that they chose to attack a chaise belonging to two women?

2. (R) What finally scares off the robbers?

   (I) How does Mrs. Elphinstone differ from her companion? Which is the more admirable character? Why?

Words for Everyday Use

ter • mi • nus (tur´mə nəs) *n.,* train station
ut • ter • ly (ut´ər lē) *adv.,* completely; totally

Answers for Reviewing the Selection

RECALLING AND INTERPRETING

1. **Recalling.** The narrator's brother rescues the two women who are being robbed of their carriage. **Interpreting.** The men are attempting to take the chaise so that they will have a quick way out of the city. They have chosen to take a vehicle belonging to people who are less physically powerful than they are.

2. **Recalling.** The sound of the revolver finally scares off the robbers. **Interpreting.** Mrs. Elphinstone is unreasonable and hysterical. Her sister-in-law, in contrast, is quiet and deliberate—a much more admirable character in such adverse circumstances, for she can be depended on to do what is necessary in order to survive.

Vocabulary in Context

- Realizing he would be reunited with his family, Jacques anxiously awaited the sight of the terminus.
- Ken was utterly confused by the new Algebra lesson.

Answers to Guided Reading Questions

❶ If they had wished to do so, they could have annihilated the entire population of London on Monday.

❷ Their intent seems to be not to destroy everyone but to demoralize everyone and to end any opposition.

❸ The narrator claims that such a large-scale movement of human beings had never before occurred.

17
The *Thunder Child*

❶ *What might the Martians have done on Monday?*

Had the Martians aimed only at destruction, they might on Monday have annihilated the entire population of London, as it spread itself slowly through the home counties. Not only along the road through Barnet, but also through Edgware and Waltham Abbey, and along the roads eastward to Southend and Shoeburyness, and south of the Thames to Deal and Broadstairs, poured the same frantic rout. If one could have hung that June morning in a balloon in the blazing blue above London, every northward and eastward road running out of the tangled maze of streets would have seemed stippled black with the streaming fugitives, each dot a human agony of terror and physical distress. I have set forth at length in the last chapter my brother's account of the road through Chipping Barnet, in order that my readers may realize how that swarming of black dots appeared to one of those concerned. Never before in the history of the world had such a mass of human beings moved and suffered together. The legendary hosts of Goths and Huns, the hugest armies Asia has ever seen, would have been but a drop in that current. And this was no disciplined march; it was a stampede—a stampede gigantic and terrible—without order and without a goal, six million people, unarmed and unprovisioned, driving headlong. It was the beginning of the rout of civilization of the massacre of mankind.

❷ *What seems to be the Martians' real intent?*

❸ *What had never before occurred on such a large scale?*

Directly below him the balloonist would have seen the network of streets far and wide, houses, churches, squares, crescents, gardens—already derelict—spread out like a huge map, and in the southward *blotted.* Over Ealing, Richmond, Wimbledon, it would have seemed as if some monstrous pen had flung ink upon the chart. Steadily, incessantly, each black splash grew and spread, shooting out ramifications this way and that, now banking itself against rising ground, now pouring swiftly over a crest into a newfound valley, exactly as a gout of ink would spread itself upon blotting-paper.

And beyond, over the blue hills that rise southward of the river, the glittering Martians went to and fro, calmly and methodically spreading their poison-cloud over this patch of country and then over that, laying it again with their steam-jets when it had served its purpose, and taking possession of the conquered country. They do not seem to have aimed at extermination so much as at complete demoralization and the destruction of any opposition. They exploded any stores of powder they came upon, cut every telegraph, and wrecked the railways here and there. They were hamstringing mankind. They seemed in no hurry to extend the field of their operations, and did not come beyond the central part of London all that day. It is possible that a very considerable number of people in London stuck to their houses through Monday morning. Certain it is that many died at home, suffocated by the Black Smoke.

Until about midday the Pool of London was an astonishing scene. Steamboats and shipping of all sorts lay there, tempted by the enormous sums of money offered by fugitives, and it is said that many who swam out to these vessels were thrust off with boathooks and drowned. About one o'clock in the afternoon the thinning remnant of a cloud of the black vapor appeared between the arches of Blackfriars

Words for Everyday Use

stip • pled (stip´əld) *adj.,* covered or marked with dots

in • ces • sant • ly (in ses´ənt lē) *adv.,* continually; constantly

gout (gout) *n.,* large splash or clot

rem • nant (rem´nənt) *n.,* remainder; residue

Vocabulary in Context

- Rhonda's stippled face confirmed he had chicken pox.
- Although few cared what he said, the candidate spoke incessantly about his ideas.
- The gout of sauce on his white pants was the first sign that the evening would be a disaster.
- Only a small remnant of the original cake was there when Rebecca finally reached the dessert table.

Bridge. At that the Pool became a scene of mad confusion, fighting, and collision, and for some time a multitude of boats and barges jammed in the northern arch of the Tower Bridge, and the sailors and lightermen[1] had to fight savagely against the people who swarmed upon them from the riverfront. People were actually clambering down the piers of the bridge from above.

When, an hour later, a Martian appeared beyond the Clock Tower and waded down the river, nothing but wreckage floated above Limehouse.

Of the falling of the fifth cylinder I have presently to tell. The sixth star fell at Wimbledon. My brother, keeping watch beside the women in the chaise in a meadow, saw the green flash of it far beyond the hills. On Tuesday the little party, still set upon getting across the sea, made its way through the swarming country toward Colchester. The news that the Martians were now in possession of the whole of London was confirmed. They had been seen at Highgate, and even, it was said, at Neasden. But they did not come into my brother's view until the morrow.

That day the scattered multitudes began to realize the urgent need of provisions. As they grew hungry the rights of property ceased to be regarded. Farmers were out to defend their cattlesheds, granaries, and ripening root crops with arms in their hands. A number of people now, like my brother, had their faces eastward, and there were some desperate souls even going back toward London to get food. These were chiefly people from the northern suburbs, whose knowledge of the Black Smoke came by hearsay. He heard that about half the members of the government had gathered at Birmingham, and that enormous quantities of high explosives were being prepared to be used in automatic mines across the Midland counties.

He was also told that the Midland Railway Company had replaced the desertions of the first day's panic, had resumed traffic, and was running northward trains from St. Albans to relieve the congestion of the home counties. There was also a placard in Chipping Ongar announcing that large stores of flour were available in the northern towns, and that within twenty-four hours bread would be distributed among the starving people in the neighborhood. But this intelligence did not deter him from the plan of escape he had formed, and the three pressed eastward all day, and heard no more of the bread distribution than this promise. Nor, as a matter of fact, did anyone else hear more of it. That night fell the seventh star, falling upon Primrose Hill. It fell while Miss Elphinstone was watching, for she took that duty alternately with my brother. She saw it.

On Wednesday the three fugitives—they had passed the night in a field of unripe wheat—reached Chelmsford, and there a body of the inhabitants, calling itself the Committee of Public Supply, seized the pony as provisions, and would give nothing in exchange for it but the promise of a share in it the next day. Here there were rumors of Martians at Epping, and news of the destruction of Waltham Abbey Powder Mills in a vain attempt to blow up one of the invaders.

People were watching for Martians here from the church towers. My brother, very

CHAPTER 17

1. **lightermen.** Operators of lighters, barges that lighten ships of their cargo

❶ *Of what are the Martians in possession?*

❷ *What happens to the pony belonging to the two women?*

WORDS FOR EVERYDAY USE

pier (pir) *n.,* heavy structure supporting a bridge
gran • a • ry (gran´ə rē) *n.,* building for storing grain

ANSWERS TO GUIDED READING QUESTIONS

❶ The Martians are in possession of all of London.

❷ The pony is seized as provisions.

VOCABULARY IN CONTEXT

- The two brothers often enjoyed fishing together off the local pier.
- As the drought continued, the granaries became increasingly bare.

Answer to Guided Reading Question

❶ Mrs. Elphinstone readily gives herself over to hysteria. Her sister-in-law, in contrast, is cool and self-possessed.

luckily for him as it chanced, preferred to push on at once to the coast rather than wait for food, although all three of them were very hungry. By midday they passed through Tillingham, which, strangely enough, seemed to be quite silent and deserted, save for a few furtive plunderers hunting for food. Near Tillingham they suddenly came in sight of the sea, and the most amazing crowd of shipping of all sorts that it is possible to imagine.

❶ *How would you characterize Mrs. Elphinstone? How does she differ from her sister-in-law?*

For after the sailors could no longer come up the Thames, they came on to the Essex coast, to Harwich and Walton and Clacton, and afterwards to Foulness and Shoebury, to bring off the people. They lay in a huge sickle-shaped curve that vanished into mist at last toward the Naze. Close inshore was a multitude of fishing-smacks[2]—English, Scotch, French, Dutch, and Swedish; steam- launches from the Thames, yachts, electric boats; and beyond were ships of large burden, a multitude of filthy colliers,[3] trim merchantmen, cattle ships, passenger-boats, petroleum tanks, ocean tramps,[4] an old white transport[5] even, neat white and gray liners from Southampton and Hamburg; and along the blue coast across the Blackwater my brother could make out dimly a dense swarm of boats chaffering[6] with the people on the beach, a swarm which also extended up the Blackwater almost to Maldon.

About a couple of miles out lay an ironclad, very low in the water, almost, to my brother's perception, like a water-logged ship. This was the ram *Thunder Child.* It was the only warship in sight, but far away to the right over the smooth surface of the sea—for that day there was a dead calm—lay a serpent of black smoke to mark the next ironclads of the Channel Fleet, which hovered in an extended line, steam up and ready for action, across the Thames estuary during the course of the Martian conquest, vigilant and yet powerless to prevent it.

At the sight of the sea, Mrs. Elphinstone, in spite of the assurances of her sister-in-law, gave way to panic. She had never been out of England before, she would rather die than trust herself friendless in a foreign country, and so forth. She seemed, poor woman, to imagine that the French and the Martians might prove

2. **fishing-smacks.** Fishing boats
3. **colliers.** Ships used to carry coal
4. **tramps.** Freight ships
5. **transport.** Ship used to transport people or goods
6. **chaffering.** Chat or discussion, often negotiating a price

Words for Everyday Use

fur • tive (fur´tiv) *adj.*, done or acting in a stealthy manner

es • tu • ar • y (es´tyo͞o er ē) *n.*, inlet of the sea

Vocabulary in Context

- Knowing that his mother was just around the corner, Paul made sure to be furtive in his mission to get some cookies.
- The small estuary was a favorite place for fishing.

very similar. She had been growing increasingly hysterical, fearful, and depressed during the two days' journeyings. Her great idea was to return to Stanmore. Things had been always well and safe at Stanmore. They would find George at Stanmore.

It was with the greatest difficulty they could get her down to the beach, where presently my brother succeeded in attracting the attention of some men on a paddle steamer from the Thames. They sent a boat and drove a bargain for thirty-six pounds for the three. The steamer was going, these men said, to Ostend.

It was about two o'clock when my brother, having paid their fares at the gangway, found himself safely aboard the steamboat with his charges. There was food aboard, albeit at exorbitant prices, and the three of them contrived to eat a meal on one of the seats forward.

There were already a couple of score of passengers aboard, some of whom had expended their last money in securing a passage, but the captain lay off the Blackwater until five in the afternoon, picking up passengers until the seated decks were even dangerously crowded. He would probably have remained longer had it not been for the sound of guns that began about that hour in the south. As if in answer, the ironclad seaward fired a small gun and hoisted a string of flags. A jet of smoke sprang out of her funnels.[7]

Some of the passengers were of opinion that this firing came from Shoeburyness, until it was noticed that it was growing louder. At the same time, far away in the southeast the masts and upper works of three ironclads rose one after the other out of the sea, beneath clouds of black smoke. But my brother's attention speedily reverted to the distant firing in the south. He fancied he saw a column of smoke rising out of the distant gray haze.

The little steamer was already flapping her way eastward of the big crescent of shipping, and the low Essex coast was growing blue and hazy, when a Martian appeared, small and faint in the remote distance, advancing along the muddy coast from the direction of Foulness. At that the captain on the bridge swore at the top of his voice with fear and anger at his own delay, and the paddles seemed infected with his terror. Every soul aboard stood at the bulwarks[8] or on the seats of the steamer and stared at that distant shape, higher than the trees or church towers inland, and advancing with a leisurely parody of a human stride.

It was the first Martian my brother had seen, and he stood, more amazed than terrified, watching this Titan advancing deliberately toward the shipping, wading farther and farther into the water as the coast fell away. Then, far away beyond the Crouch, came another, striding over some stunted trees, and then yet another, still farther off, wading deeply through a shiny mudflat that seemed to hang halfway up between sea and sky. They were all stalking seaward, as if to intercept the escape of the multitudinous vessels that were crowded between Foulness and the Naze. In spite of the throbbing exertions of the engines of the little paddleboat, and the pouring foam that her wheels flung behind her, she receded with terrifying slowness from this ominous advance.

❶ Why are the Martians walking into the sea?

Glancing northwestward, my brother saw the large crescent of shipping already

7. **funnels.** Smokestacks of the ship
8. **bulwarks.** Part of a ship's side above the deck

WORDS FOR EVERYDAY USE

- **ex • or • bi • tant** (eg zor´bi tənt) *adj.,* excessive, extravagant
- **ex • pend** (ek spend´) *v.,* consume by using
- **hoist** (hoist) *v.,* raise aloft
- **par • o • dy** (par´ə dē) *n.,* imitation, often humorous

ANSWER TO GUIDED READING QUESTION

❶ The Martians are walking into the sea as if to intercept the escape of the vessels crowded offshore.

VOCABULARY IN CONTEXT

- The exorbitant lifestyle of the Smiths led to their financial troubles.
- The athletes were very tired after expending so much energy during the game.
- The sailors hoisted the other sails in order to gain speed.
- Bonnie's parody of her teacher got her sent to the principal's office.

Answer to Guided Reading Question

➊ The *Thunder Child* is able to get close to the Martians because the Martians do not know what to make of her.

➊ *What enables* the Thunder Child *to get so close to the Martians?*

writhing with the approaching terror; one ship passing behind another, another coming round from broadside to end on, steamships whistling and giving off volumes of steam, sails being let out, launches rushing hither and thither. He was so fascinated by this and by the creeping danger away to the left that he had no eyes for anything seaward. And then a swift movement of the steamboat (she had suddenly come round to avoid being run down) flung him headlong from the seat upon which he was standing. There was a shouting all about him, a trampling of feet, and a cheer that seemed to be answered faintly. The steamboat lurched and rolled him over upon his hands.

He sprang to his feet and saw to starboard[9] and not a hundred yards from their heeling[10] pitching boat, a vast iron bulk like the blade of a plough tearing through the water, tossing it on either side in huge waves of foam that leaped toward the steamer, flinging her paddles helplessly in the air, and then sucking her deck down almost to the waterline.

A douche[11] of spray blinded my brother for a moment. When his eyes were clear again he saw the monster had passed and was rushing landward. Big iron upperworks rose out of this headlong structure, and from that twin funnels projected and spat a smoking blast shot with fire. It was the torpedo-ram, *Thunder Child*, steaming headlong coming to the rescue of the threatened shipping.

Keeping his footing on the heaving deck by clutching the bulwarks, my brother looked past this charging leviathan at the Martians again, and he saw the three of them now close together, and standing so far out to sea that their tripod supports were almost entirely submerged. Thus sunken, and seen in remote perspective, they appeared far less formidable than the huge iron bulk in whose wake the steamer was pitching so helplessly. It would seem they were regarding this new antagonist with astonishment. To their intelligence, it may be, the giant was even such another as themselves. The *Thunder Child* fired no gun, but simply drove full speed toward them. It was probably her not firing that enabled her to get so near the enemy as she did. They did not know what to make of her. One shell, and they would have sent her to the bottom forthwith with the Heat-Ray.

She was steaming at such a pace that in a minute she seemed halfway between the steamboat and the Martians—a diminishing black bulk against the receding horizontal expanse of the Essex coast.

Suddenly the foremost Martian lowered his tube and discharged a canister of the black gas at the ironclad. It hit her larboard[12] side and glanced off in an inky jet that rolled away to seaward, an unfolding torrent of Black Smoke, from which the ironclad drove clear. To the watchers from the steamer, low in the water and with the sun in their eyes, it seemed as though she were already among the Martians.

They saw the gaunt figures separating and rising out of the water as they retreated shoreward, and one of them raised the camera-like generator of the Heat-Ray. He held it pointing obliquely downward, and a bank of steam sprang from the water at its touch. It must have driven through the iron of the ship's side like a white-hot iron rod through paper.

9. **starboard.** Right side of the ship as one is standing forward
10. **heeling.** Following closely behind
11. **douche.** Jet of liquid
12. **larboard.** Left side of the ship as one is facing forward

Words for Everyday Use

le • vi • a • than (lə vī´ə thən) *n.,* anything huge or very powerful

Vocabulary in Context

• The wave was a leviathan compared to the small rowboat.

A flicker of flame went up through the rising steam, and then the Martian reeled and staggered. In another moment he was cut down, and a great body of water and steam shot high in the air. The guns of the *Thunder Child* sounded through the reek, going off one after the other, and one shot splashed the water high close by the steamer, ricochetted toward the other flying ships to the north, and smashed a smack to matchwood.

But no one heeded that very much. At the sight of the Martian's collapse the captain on the bridge yelled inarticulately, and all the crowding passengers on the steamer's stern shouted together. And then they yelled again. For, surging out beyond the white tumult drove something long and black, the flames streaming from its middle parts, its ventilators and funnels spouting fire.

She was alive still; the steering gear, it seems, was intact and her engines working. She headed straight for a second Martian, and was within a hundred yards of him when the Heat-Ray came to bear. Then with a violent thud, a blinding flash, her decks, her funnels, leaped upward. The Martian staggered with the violence of her explosion, and in another moment the flaming wreckage, still driving forward with the impetus of its pace, had struck him and crumpled him up like a thing of cardboard. My brother shouted involuntarily. A boiling tumult of steam hid everything again

"Two!" yelled the captain.

Everyone was shouting. The whole steamer from end to end rang with frantic cheering that was taken up first by one and then by all in the crowding multitude of ships and boats that was driving out to sea.

The steam hung upon the water for many minutes, hiding the third Martian and the coast altogether. And all this time the boat was paddling steadily out to sea and away from the fight; and when at last the confusion cleared, the drifting bank of black vapor intervened, and nothing of the *Thunder Child* could be made out, nor could the third Martian be seen. But the ironclads to seaward were now quite close and standing in toward shore past the steamboat.

The little vessel continued to beat its way seaward, and the ironclads receded slowly toward the coast, which was hidden still by a marbled bank of vapor, part steam, part black gas, eddying and combining in the strangest ways. The fleet of refugees was scattering to the northeast; several smacks were sailing between the ironclads and the steamboat. After a time, and before they reached the sinking cloud-bank, the warships turned northward, and then abruptly went about and passed into the thickening haze of evening southward. The coast grew faint, and at last indistinguishable amid the low banks of clouds that were gathering about the sinking sun.

Then suddenly out of the golden haze of the sunset came the vibration of guns, and a form of black shadows moving. Every one struggled to the rail of the steamer and peered into the blinding furnace of the west, but nothing was to be distinguished clearly. A mass of smoke rose slantingly and barred the face of the sun. The steamboat throbbed on its way through an interminable suspense.

The sun sank into gray clouds, the sky flushed and darkened, the evening star trembled into sight. It was deep twilight when the captain cried out and pointed.

1 *What happens to the two Martians?*

Words for Everyday Use

ric • o • chet (rik´ə shā) *v.,* make an oblique rebound after hitting something at an angle

in • ar • tic • u • lat • ly (in´är tik´yo͞o lit lē) *adv.,* not understandably; unintelligibly

ven • ti • la • tor (vent´'l āt´ər) *n.,* device used to circulate air

im • pet • us (im´pə təs) *n.,* force with which a body moves against resistence

Answer to Guided Reading Question

1 They are destroyed by the *Thunder Child.*

Vocabulary in Context

- The ball ricochetted off the wall and hit Mrs. Skinner in the head.
- The man explained his predicament to the police inarticulately.
- Tim wanted a ventilator in his office because he needed fresher air.
- Juan's desire to succeed was the impetus by which he broke through the defensive line.

ANSWER TO GUIDED READING QUESTION

❶ The Martians have a flying machine.

SELECTION CHECK TEST WITH ANSWERS

EX. Why does the narrator, at one point, jump underwater?
He jumps underwater to escape the heat ray.

1. What causes the water to boil?
A Martian, with its heat ray, falls into the water.

2. Who believes that the Martian attack is part of the end of the world?
The curate believes that the Martian attack is part of the end of the world.

3. What false belief did the narrator's brother have about the Martians that was corrected by the account in the newspaper that he bought on Wellington Street?
The narrator's brother believed that the Martians were not able to move from their pit.

4. What new weapon is used by the Martians against the batteries of guns?
They use the black vapor, which kills people on contact.

5. What is the name of the boat that destroys the two Martian machines?
The boat is called the *Thunder Child.*

❶ What technological ability do the Martians have that is unknown to people of the time when this story takes place?

My brother strained his eyes. Something rushed up into the sky out of the grayness—rushed slantingly upward and very swiftly into the luminous clearness above the clouds in the western sky; something flat and broad and very large, that swept round in a vast curve, grew smaller, sank slowly, and vanished again into the gray mystery of the night. And as it flew it rained down darkness upon the land.[13]

13. **rained . . . land.** Biblical reference to Genesis 19:24 and Exodus 10:21

Responding to the Selection

In the final chapter of Book One, the narrator describes the stampede from London as being "the beginning of the rout of civilization, of the massacre of mankind." Extreme circumstances test people's characters, bringing out the best and the worst in people. Of the characters encountered so far in the novel, which seem most attractive to you? Why? Which seem least attractive? Why? Discuss these questions with your classmates.

Reviewing the Selection

Recalling and Interpreting

1. R According to the narrator, what might a balloonist have seen from the air above Ealing, Richmond, and Wimbledon?

   I What makes "blotted" a particularly good adjective for describing the destruction?

2. R What is the *Thunder Child*?

   I Why would the *Thunder Child* be able to destroy two Martians when other means had failed?

3. R What does the captain of the steamboat see in the deep twilight?

   I What new danger is suggested by the last sentence of Book One?

Synthesizing

4. At this point in the novel, how would you sum up the situation of the Earthlings? Do they have reason for hope? How would you feel at this point if you were the narrator or the narrator's brother? Explain.

Understanding Literature (Questions for Discussion)

1. **Science Fiction. Science fiction** is imaginative literature based on scientific principles, discoveries, or laws.

   Science fiction reflects the state of scientific knowledge at the time when it is written. Review the Cross-curricular Connection on page 000. How does Wells's story reflect the scientific beliefs about Mars current in his day? What do we now know about Mars that contradicts parts of Wells's story?

   Science fiction often makes predictions about the future. In *The War of the Worlds,* H. G. Wells made many predictions about technological advances that later came true. What aspects of modern technology that have since come true were predicted by Book One of this novel?

   Science fiction usually warns people about alarming possibilities in the near or distant future. Of what does Wells warn in this novel? Is Wells's warning something that we should take seriously today? Explain.

RESPONDING TO THE SELECTION

As an alternate activity, you might give students a hypothetical situation and have them explain how various characters would react to it. Example: On a tour, a boy falls off a bridge into deep running water. What would the narrator do? Mrs. Elphinstone? Mrs. Elphinstone's sister-in-law? the curate?

ANSWERS FOR REVIEWING THE SELECTION

RECALLING AND INTERPRETING

1. **Recalling.** One would have seen on every road a mass of streaming fugitives. Ealing, Richmond, and Wimbledon would have appeared blotted out, as if a pen had flung ink on them. **Interpreting.** The black vapor looks like ink.

2. **Recalling.** The *Thunder Child* is a type of boat known as a ram. **Interpreting.** The Martians do not know what to make of the *Thunder Child.* By the time they figure it out, the *Thunder Child* has already destroyed two of them.

3. **Recalling.** He sees a flying ship. **Interpreting.** A flying ship would be able to drop things, such as canisters of black vapor, onto the ground.

SYNTHESIZING

Responses will vary. Possible responses are given.

4. At this point the Earthlings seem to have little reason for hope.

ANSWERS FOR UNDERSTANDING LITERATURE

Responses will vary. Possible responses are given.

1. **Science Fiction.** In Wells's day, people still believed that Mars had canals and, possibly, intelligent life on it. Today we believe, based on investigations by space probes, that Mars is devoid of life. Some inventions predicted by Book One of this novel include lasers (the heat ray), chemical warfare (the black vapor), space travel (the cylinders), war machines (the tripods), and flight. Wells's novel warns about possible invasion from outer space. Opinions about the existence of life elsewhere in space differ. Many scientists today believe that there is good reason to expect that life exists elsewhere in the universe but that the distances to be traveled from one place to another preclude visitations and invasions.

(cont.)

Understanding Literature (Questions for Discussion)

2. **Subplot.** A **subplot** is a story told in addition to the main story in a work of fiction. The main plot in this novel is the story of the adventures of the narrator. What is the subplot? What part of the invasion story does the author use this subplot to tell?
3. **Allusion.** An **allusion** is a reference in a literary work to something famous. In Genesis 19:24, fire and brimstone are described as raining out of the sky onto the cities of Sodom and Gomorrah. In Exodus 10:21, there is darkness over the land of Egypt that lasts for three days. The last line of Book One is an allusion to these and other passages from the Bible. What mood, or emotion, is created by these allusions? Why do you think Wells chose to end Book One with such an allusion?
4. **Theme.** A **theme** is a main idea in a literary work. In the first paragraph of this novel, people are described as being "complacent," or self-satisfied, and as being "serene in their assurance of their empire over matter." What danger does Wells see in humans' feeling too complacent or sure of their own power and control?

   In Chapter 1, the narrator describes how the Tasmanians were "entirely swept out of existence in a war of extermination waged by European immigrants." How does this extermination parallel what the Martians do? What lesson does the narrator want us to draw from thinking about the Martians' actions and our own?

ANSWERS FOR UNDERSTANDING LITERATURE (CONT.)

Responses will vary. Possible responses are given.

2. **Subplot.** The subplot of this novel tells the story of the adventures of the narrator's brother in London and en route out of London.

3. **Allusion.** The allusions to the Bible at the end of Book One create a dark mood, one that is catastrophic or apocalyptic. These allusions help to raise suspense and thus to get the reader to turn to the rest of the novel.

4. **Theme.** Wells believes that people should not be complacent, that they should realize the tentativeness of their position. The narrator wants the reader to realize that might does not make right, that possession of superior power does not make a culture superior or give it the right to behave colonially.

Study and Research Skills

Using Encyclopedias

In the eighteenth century, a group of French scholars led by Denis Diderot had a brilliant idea. They decided to publish a single work that would be a complete guide to knowledge. This guide would be organized alphabetically, like a dictionary, and would contain essays on every field of human thought and endeavor. The result of their work was the first **encyclopedia**, considered by many to be the greatest literary achievement of the eighteenth-century "Age of Reason."

General and Specified Encyclopedias

There are two main types of encyclopedias. **General encyclopedias,** such as the *Encyclopædia Britannica, Compton's Encyclopedia,* and the *World Book Encyclopedia,* attempt to survey the whole of human knowledge. They contain information on a wide variety of topics. Specialized encyclopedias, such as *The Encyclopedia of World War II,* also cover a wide variety of topics, but these topics are all related to some specific subject area. The *Encyclopædia Britannica,* a multivolume encyclopedia, is divided into two parts. The first part, called the *Micropædia,* contains short articles on many subjects. The second part, called the *Macropædia,* contains long, in-depth articles on a few major subjects.

Encyclopedias on Computer

Today most of the major general encyclopedias are published electronically on CD/ROM, on diskettes, or on-line via computer services that can be reached by modem. The chief advantage offered by such computerized encyclopedias is that you can easily search for information by typing in or selecting subjects or key words.

Finding Information in an Encyclopedia

As mentioned above, most encyclopedias contain alphabetically organized articles on many subjects. Some encyclopedias come in a single volume. Most take up many volumes. To find information on a subject, you can often simply look the subject up alphabetically. Sometimes, however, an encyclopedia will not contain an article on the specific subject that you are researching. In such cases, look up your subject in the **index** to the encyclopedia to find articles that deal with it. The index is simply an alphabetical list of subjects touched upon or covered by articles in the main body of the encyclopedia. In one-volume encyclopedias, the index is usually located at the back of the book. In multivolume encyclopedias, the index may appear in one or more separate books.

STUDY AND RESEARCH SKILLS

INTRODUCING THE SKILL

Most students will already be familiar with general encyclopedias. You may wish to take them to the library to show them a variety of specialized encyclopedias in the reference section.

PREVIEWING THE SKILL

Have students read the teaching on page 661 and study the points in the chart on page 662.

PRACTICING THE SKILL

Assign the Try It Yourself exercise on page 662.

REVIEWING THE SKILL

You may wish to have your students use encyclopedias for an "Information Scavenger Hunt." The game is played as follows: Divide the class up into several teams. Have each team do research in specialized encyclopedias to come up with five questions and their answers. Then compile the questions and have the teams compete to see who can answer all the questions first.

Answers for Try It Yourself

1. Wells was born in the town of Bromley, in the county of Kent, in England.
2. The *Outline of History* was written from 1919 to 1920.
3. The Soviet probe *Mars 3* placed an instrumented capsule on Mars in 1971, but this capsule lasted only twenty seconds. The *Viking 1* lander touched down in June of 1976.
4. There are no canals on Mars, but there are some channels.
5. The father of Mars was Jupiter (Zeus). His wife was Venus (Aphrodite).
6. The River Thames runs through Surrey.
7. London is the capital of England, and approximately nine million people live there.
8. A laser is a beam of amplified light somewhat similar to Wells's heat ray.
9. The first sustained, powered, controlled airplane flight was that of Orville and Wilbur Wright in 1903.
10. Chemical warfare was first used by the Germans in World War I, from 1915 to 1918.

Here are some additional guidelines for using encyclopedias:

GUIDELINES FOR USING ENCYCLOPEDIAS

- Remember that information on your subject may be found in several different articles. Therefore, it usually pays to check the encyclopedia's index.
- In many areas of human thought and research, such as science and technology, knowledge is continually expanding. Older ideas are revised as new discoveries are made or as new theories emerge. Therefore, make sure that the encyclopedia that you use is current. Many encyclopedias list the year in which they were created on their title pages and on their covers or spines. In any case, you can find out when the encyclopedia was published and revised by looking at the copyright page, on the back of the title page.
- Many publishers of encyclopedias also publish, yearly, books of updated information called yearbooks or annuals. Check yearbooks or annuals for information on current topics such as recent world events or discoveries.
- For the most part, encyclopedias are accurate. Occasionally, however, errors do creep into them. Therefore, always check your facts in more than one source.
- When using ideas or quotations from an encyclopedia in a piece of writing, credit the source of your information. (For more information on giving credit to sources, see the Language Arts Survey, 4.18, "Documenting Sources.")

Try It Yourself

Use encyclopedias in your school or community library to answer the following questions.

1. Where was H. G. Wells born?
2. When did H. G. Wells write his *Outline of History*?
3. What was the name of the spacecraft that first landed on Mars?
4. Are there actually canals on Mars?
5. According to Roman mythology, who were the wife and father of the god Mars?
6. Through what part of England does the River Thames run?
7. Of what country is London the capital, and how many people live there?
8. What is a laser, and how is it similar to the Martian heat ray in Wells's *The War of the Worlds*?
9. When did human beings invent flight?
10. When was chemical warfare, such as the black smoke described by Wells, first used by humans in war?

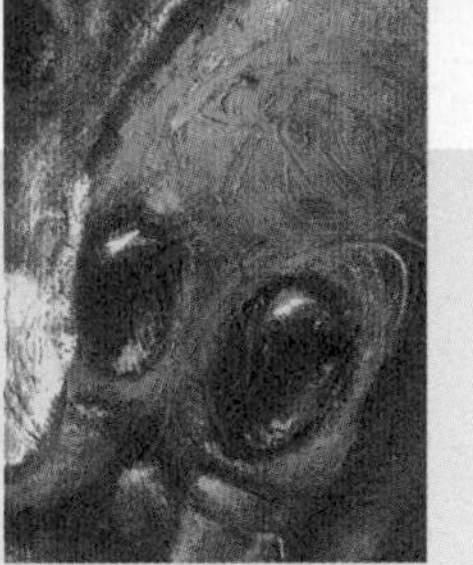

READER'S JOURNAL

What qualities are most important in people in times of crisis? What sort of people would you like to have around you during a terrible disaster such as a military invasion, an epidemic, or a hurricane? Write about these questions in your journal.

Book 2: The Earth under the Martians
1
Under Foot

In the first book I have wandered so much from my own adventures to tell of the experiences of my brother that all through the last two chapters I and the curate have been lurking in the empty house at Halliford whither[1] we fled to escape the Black Smoke. There I will resume. We stopped there all Sunday night and all the next day—the day of the panic—in a little island of daylight, cut off by the Black Smoke from the rest of the world. We could do nothing but wait in an aching inactivity during those two weary days.

My mind was occupied by anxiety for my wife. I figured her at Leatherhead, terrified, in danger, mourning me already as a dead man. I paced the rooms and cried aloud when I thought of how I was cut off from her, of all that might happen to her in my absence. My cousin I knew was brave enough for any emergency, but he was not the sort of man to realize danger quickly, to rise promptly. What was needed now was not bravery, but circumspection. My only consolation was to believe that the Martians were moving Londonward and away from her. Such vague anxieties keep the mind sensitive and painful. I grew very weary and irritable with the curate's . . .; I tired of the sight of his selfish despair. After some ineffectual remonstrance I kept away from him, staying in a room—evidently a children's schoolroom—containing globes, forms, and copybooks. When he followed me thither,[2] I went to a box-room at the top of the house and, in order to be alone with my aching miseries, locked myself in.

We were hopelessly hemmed in by the Black Smoke all that day and the morning of the next. There were signs of people in the next house on Sunday evening—a face at a window and moving lights, and later the slamming of a door. But I do not know who these people were, nor what became of them. We saw nothing of them next day. The Black Smoke drifted slowly riverward all through Monday morning, creeping nearer and nearer to us, driving at last along the roadway outside the house that hid us.

A Martian came across the fields about mid-day, laying the stuff with a jet of superheated steam that hissed against the walls,

❶ *What worries lie heavily on the narrator?*

Chapter 1
1. **whither.** Where
2. **thither.** There

Words for Everyday Use

cir • cum • spec • tion (sʉr´kəm spekt´shən) *n.*, act of carefully considering all the facts before acting

re • mon • strance (ri män´strəns) *n.*, protest

hem (hem) *v.*, confine; surround

Vocabulary in Context

- After a great deal of circumspection, the jury found the defendant not guilty.
- Judy and Frederick planned a remonstrance against the killing of whales.
- After a half hour, Glenn finally hemmed in his dog, Ralphie.

READER'S JOURNAL

As an alternative activity, have students make a list of people whom they admire and tell why they admire these people.

Answer to Guided Reading Question

❶ The narrator is worried about his wife, whom he imagines to be both in danger and mourning him as a dead man.

SPELLING AND VOCABULARY WORDS FROM THE SELECTION

acute
aghast
agile
allude
anemic
aperture
ashen
aspect
atrocity
cajole
cardinal
caricature
circumspection
contrivance
convulsive
copiously
credible
culminate
decorum
defunct
despondent
dexterous
discriminating
ebb
efficacious
elemental
emit
endeavor
enigma
expedient
facetious
fluctuation
forethought
frond
gesticulation
hem
heterogeneous
impart
implore
importunity
inconclusive
incur
instantaneous
intermediation
intermittent
intolerable
lethargic
manifest
masonry
modulation
morbidity
oscillate
oust
paradoxical
parch
phantasm
physiological
polarize
radiate
rampart
reconcile
remonstrance
rendering
rout
rudimentary
salient
scullery
sham
spatulate
sumptuous
supersede
timorous
traverse
tussle
vehemence
vestige
vitiate

Answer to Guided Reading Question

➊ The curate and the narrator argue about whether they should leave. The narrator is more sensible, for if the two men stay where there are, they are likely to be discovered and killed.

smashed all the windows it touched, and scalded the curate's hand as he fled out of the front room. When at last we crept across the sodden rooms and looked out again, the country northward was as though a black snowstorm had passed over it. Looking towards the river, we were astonished to see an unaccountable redness mingling with the black of the scorched meadows.

For a time we did not see how this change affected our position, save that we were relieved of our fear of the Black Smoke. But later I perceived that we were no longer hemmed in, that now we might get away. So soon as I realized that the way of escape was open, my dream of action returned. But the curate was lethargic, unreasonable.

"We are safe here," he repeated; "safe here."

I resolved to leave him—would that I had! Wiser now for the artilleryman's teaching, I sought out food and drink. I had found oil and rags for my burns, and I also took a hat and a flannel shirt that I found in one of the bedrooms. When it was clear to him that I meant to go alone—had reconciled myself to going alone—he suddenly roused himself to come. And all being quiet throughout the afternoon, we started about five o'clock, as I should judge, along the blackened road to Sunbury.

What disagreement do the curate and the narrator have? Who is the more sensible of the two? ➊

In Sunbury, and at intervals along the road, were dead bodies lying in contorted attitudes, horses as well as men, overturned carts and luggage, all covered thickly with black dust. That pall of cindery powder made me think of what I had read of the destruction of Pompeii.[3] We got to Hampton Court without misadventure, our minds full of strange and unfamiliar appearances, and at Hampton Court our eyes were relieved to find a patch of green that had escaped the suffocating drift. We went through Bushey Park, with its deer going to and fro under the chestnuts, and some men and women hurrying in the distance toward Hampton, and so we came to Twickenham. These were the first people we saw.

Away across the road the woods beyond Ham and Petersham were still afire. Twickenham was uninjured by either Heat-Ray or Black Smoke, and there were more people about here, though none could give us news. For the most part they were like ourselves, taking advantage of a lull to shift their quarters. I have an impression that many of the houses here were still occupied by scared inhabitants, too frightened even for flight. Here, too, the evidence of a hasty rout was abundant along the road. I remember most vividly three smashed bicycles in a heap, pounded into the road by the wheels of subsequent carts. We crossed Richmond Bridge about half-past eight. We hurried across the exposed bridge, of course, but I noticed floating down the stream a number of red masses, some many feet across. I did not know what these were—there was no time for scrutiny—and I put a more horrible interpretation on them than they deserved. Here again on the Surrey side, were black dust that had once been smoke, and dead bodies—a heap near the approach to the station; but we had no glimpse of the Martians until we were some way toward Barnes.

We saw in the blackened distance a group of three people running down a side street towards the river, but otherwise it seemed deserted. Up the hill Richmond

3. **destruction of Pompeii.** The ancient Italian city of Pompeii was completely destroyed by the eruption of Mt. Vesuvius in AD 79.

Words for Everyday Use

le • thar • gic (li thär´jik) *adj.,* having extreme apathy or great lack of energy

rec • on • cile (rek´ən sīl´) *v.,* make content or agreeable

rout (rout) *n.,* disorderly flight or retreat

Vocabulary in Context

- Rick's parents were concerned because he was very lethargic and asked him to get a summer job.
- The mediator proposed a compromise and reconciled the two parties.
- During the battle, one army suddenly fled the battlefield in a rout.

town was burning briskly; outside the town of Richmond there was no trace of the Black Smoke.

Then, suddenly, as we approached Kew, came a number of people running, and the upper-works of a Martian fighting-machine loomed in sight over the housetops, not a hundred yards away from us. We stood aghast at our danger, and had the Martian looked down we must immediately have perished. We were so terrified that we dared not go on, but turned aside and hid in a shed in a garden. There the curate crouched, weeping silently, and refusing to stir again.

But my fixed idea of reaching Leatherhead would not let me rest, and in the twilight I ventured out again. I went through a shrubbery, and along a passage beside a big house standing in its own grounds, and so emerged upon the road toward Kew. The curate I left in the shed, but he came hurrying after me.

That second start was the most foolhardy thing I ever did. For it was manifest the Martians were about us. No sooner had the curate overtaken me than we saw either the fighting-machine we had seen before or another, far away across the meadows in the direction of Kew Lodge. Four or five little black figures hurried before it across the green-gray of the field, and in a moment it was evident this Martian pursued them. In three strides he was among them, and they ran radiating from his feet in all directions. He used no Heat-Ray to destroy them, but picked them up one by one. Apparently he tossed them into the great metallic carrier which projected behind him, much as a workman's basket hangs over his shoulder.

It was the first time I realized that the Martians might have any other purpose than destruction with defeated humanity. We stood for a moment petrified, then turned and fled through a gate behind us into a walled garden, fell into, rather than found, a fortunate ditch, and lay there, scarce daring to whisper to each other until the stars were out.

❶ *What purpose other than destruction might the Martians have in mind for humans?*

I suppose it was nearly eleven o'clock before we gathered courage to start again, no longer venturing into the road, but sneaking along hedgerows and through plantations, and watching keenly through the darkness, he on the right and I on the left, for the Martians, who seemed to be all about us. In one place we blundered upon a scorched and blackened area, now cooling and ashen, and a number of scattered dead bodies of men, burned horribly about the heads and trunks but with their legs and boots mostly intact; and of dead horses, fifty feet, perhaps, behind a line of four ripped guns and smashed gun-carriages.

Sheen, it seemed, had escaped destruction, but the place was silent and deserted. Here we happened on no dead, though the night was too dark for us to see into the side roads of the place. In Sheen my companion suddenly complained of faintness and thirst, and we decided to try one of the houses.

The first house we entered, after a little difficulty with the window, was a small semi-detached villa, and I found nothing eatable left in the place but some mouldy cheese. There was, however, water to drink; and I took a hatchet, which promised to be useful in our next house-breaking.

We then crossed to a place where the road turns toward Mortlake. Here there stood a white house within a walled garden, and in the pantry of this domicile we found a store of food—two loaves of bread

WORDS FOR EVERYDAY USE

a • ghast (ə gast´) *adj.*, terrified; horrified
man • i • fest (man´ ə fest´) *adj.*, clear; obvious
ra • di • ate (rā´ dē āt´) *v.*, branch out in lines from a center
ash • en (ash´ən) *adj.*, made up of ashes

ANSWER TO GUIDED READING QUESTION

❶ The Martians plan to use humans for food.

QUOTABLES

"New and stirring ideas are belittled, because if they are not belittled the humiliating question arises, 'Why then are you not taking part in them?'"

—H. G. Wells

VOCABULARY IN CONTEXT

- After seeing the result of the children's food fight, Mrs. Hudson was aghast.
- The point Manuel was making in his oral presentation was manifest to all of us.
- The heat radiated from the stove and soon the cabin was cozy.
- The house was an ashen pile after the fire.

Answer to Guided Reading Question

❶ There is a terrible explosion, and parts of the house are destroyed. (The reader will later learn that a Martian cylinder has landed just outside the house.)

in a pan, an uncooked steak, and the half of a ham. I give this catalogue so precisely because, as it happened, we were destined to subsist upon this store for the next fortnight. There were two bags of haricot beans and some limp lettuces. This pantry opened into a kind of wash-up kitchen, and in this was firewood; there was also a cupboard, in which we found tinned soups and salmon and two tins of biscuits.

We sat in the adjacent kitchen in the dark—for we dared not strike a light—and ate bread and ham. The curate, who was still timorous and restless, was now, oddly enough, for pushing on, and I was urging him to keep up his strength by eating when the thing happened that was to imprison us.

What happens to the house in which the narrator and the curate are hiding? ❶

"It can't be midnight yet," I said, and then came a blinding glare of vivid green light. Everything in the kitchen leaped out, clearly visible in green and black, and vanished again. And then followed such a concussion as I have never heard before or since. So close on the heels of this as to seem instantaneous came a thud behind me, a clash of glass, a crash and rattle of falling masonry all about us, and the plaster of the ceiling came down upon us, smashing into a multitude of fragments upon our heads. I was knocked headlong across the floor against the oven handle and stunned. I was insensible for a long time, the curate told me, and when I came to we were in darkness again, and he, with a face wet, as I found afterwards, with blood from a cut forehead, was dabbing water over me.

For some time I could not recollect what had happened. Then things came to me slowly. A bruise on my temple asserted itself.

"Are you better?" asked the curate, in a whisper.

At last I answered him. I sat up.

"Don't move," he said. "The floor is covered with smashed crockery from the dresser. You can't possibly move without making a noise, and I fancy *they* are outside."

We both sat quite silent, so that we could scarcely hear each other breathing. Everything seemed deadly still, but once something near us, some plaster or broken brick-work slid down with a rumbling sound. Outside and very near was an intermittent, metallic rattle.

"That!" said the curate, when presently it happened again.

"Yes," I said. "But what is it?"

"A Martian!" said the curate.

I listened again.

"It was not like the Heat-Ray," I said, and for a time I was inclined to think one of the great fighting-machines had stumbled against the house, as I had seen one stumble against the tower of Shepperton Church.

Our situation was so strange and incomprehensible that for three or four hours, until the dawn came, we scarcely moved. And then the light filtered in, not through the window which remained black, but through a triangular aperture between a beam and a heap of broken bricks in the wall behind us. The interior of the kitchen we now saw grayly for the first time.

The window had been burst in by a mass of garden mold, which flowed over the table upon which we had been sitting and lay about our feet. Outside, the soil was banked high against the house. At the top of the window-frame we could see an uprooted drain-pipe. The floor was littered with smashed hardware; the end of the kitchen toward the house was broken into, and since the daylight shone in there,

Words for Everyday Use

tim • or • ous (tim´ər əs) *adj.,* timid; full of or subject to fear

in • stan • ta • ne • ous (in´stən tā´nē əs) *adj.,* done, made, or happening in an instant

ma • son • ry (mā´sən rē) *n.,* something built by a person using stone, brick, etc.

in • ter • mit • tent (in´tər mit´´nt) *adj.,* periodic

ap • er • ture (ap´ər chər) *n.,* opening; hole; gap

Vocabulary in Context

- The captured raccoon appeared scared and timorous.
- The collision was instantaneous after the car ran the red light.
- The masonry of the fireplace was beautifully arranged.
- Hector and John watched the birds fly into the feeder at intermittent times.
- The plumber came to patch the aperture in the pipes.

it was evident the greater part of the house had collapsed. Contrasting vividly with this ruin was the neat dresser, stained in the fashion, pale green, and with a number of copper and tin vessels below it, the wallpaper imitating blue and white tiles, and a couple of colored supplements[4] fluttering from the walls above the kitchen range.

As the dawn grew clearer, we saw through the gap in the wall the body of a Martian, standing sentinel, I suppose, over the still glowing cylinder. At the sight of that we crawled as circumspectly as possible out of the twilight of the kitchen into the darkness of the scullery.

Abruptly the right interpretation dawned upon my mind.

"The fifth cylinder," I whispered, "the fifth shot from Mars, has struck this house and buried us under the ruins!"

For a time the curate was silent, and then he whispered:

"God have mercy upon us!"

I heard him presently whimpering to himself.

4. **colored supplements.** Newspaper circulars

❶ *What explanation does the narrator give for the explosion of the previous evening?*

WORDS FOR EVERYDAY USE

scul • ler • y (skul´ər ē) *n.,* room next to kitchen where the dirtier kitchen work is done

ANSWER TO GUIDED READING QUESTION

❶ The fifth cylinder struck the house and buried it.

VOCABULARY IN CONTEXT

• After dinner Peggy and Rick had to clean the dishes in the scullery.

Answer to Guided Reading Question

❶ The Martians seem to be building something.

Answers for Reviewing the Selection

RECALLING AND INTERPRETING

1. **Recalling.** The Martian puts a man into the carrier. **Interpreting.** The Martians plan to use them for food.
2. **Recalling.** The house is hit by a cylinder from Mars. **Interpreting.** The narrator and the curate might be discovered by the Martians and killed.

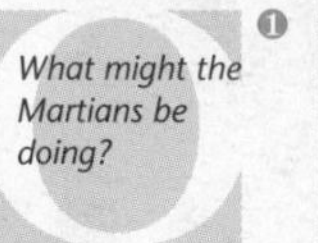

❶ *What might the Martians be doing?*

Save for that sound we lay quite still in the scullery; I for my part scarce dared breathe, and sat with my eyes fixed on the faint light of the kitchen door. I could just see the curate's face, a dim, oval shape, and his collar and cuffs. Outside there began a metallic hammering, then a violent hooting, and then again, after a quiet interval, a hissing like the hissing of an engine. These noises, for the most part problematical, continued intermittently, and seemed if anything to increase in number as time wore on. Presently a measured thudding and a vibration that made everything about us quiver and the vessels in the pantry ring and shift, began and continued. Once the light was eclipsed, and the ghostly kitchen doorway became absolutely dark. For many hours we must have crouched there, silent and shivering, until our tired attention failed. . . .

At last I found myself awake and very hungry. I am inclined to believe we must have spent the greater portion of a day before that awakening. My hunger was at a stride so insistent that it moved me to action. I told the curate I was going to seek food, and felt my way toward the pantry. He made no answer, but so soon as I began eating the faint noise I made stirred him up and I heard him crawling after me.

Reviewing the Selection

Recalling and Interpreting

1. Ⓡ What does the Martian put into the "great metallic carrier which projected behind him"?

   Ⓘ Why might the Martians be collecting people in this manner?

2. Ⓡ What happens to the house in which the narrator and the curate take shelter?

   Ⓘ What dangers do the narrator and the curate face?

2
What We Saw from the Ruined House

After eating we crept back to the scullery, and there I must have dozed again, for when presently I looked round I was alone. The thudding vibration continued with wearisome persistence. I whispered for the curate several times, and at last felt my way to the door of the kitchen. It was still daylight, and I perceived him across the room, lying against the triangular hole that looked out upon the Martians. His shoulders were hunched, so that his head was hidden from me.

I could hear a number of noises almost like those in an engine-shed, and the place rocked with that beating thud. Through the aperture in the wall I could see the top of a tree touched with gold, and the warm blue of a tranquil evening sky. For a minute or so I remained watching the curate, and then I advanced, crouching and stepping with extreme care amid the broken crockery that littered the floor.

I touched the curate's leg, and he started so violently that a mass of plaster went sliding down outside and fell with a loud impact. I gripped his arm, fearing he might cry out, and for a long time we crouched motionless. Then I turned to see how much of our rampart remained. The detachment of the plaster had left a vertical slit open in the debris, and by raising myself cautiously across a beam I was able to see out of this gap into what had been overnight a quiet suburban roadway. Vast, indeed, was the change that we beheld.

The fifth cylinder must have fallen right into the midst of the house we had first visited. The building had vanished, completely smashed, pulverized, and dispersed by the blow. The cylinder lay now far beneath the original foundations—deep in a hole, already vastly larger than the pit I had looked into at Woking. The earth all round it had splashed under that tremendous impact—"splashed" is the only word—and lay in heaped piles that hid the masses of the adjacent houses. It had behaved exactly like mud under the violent blow of a hammer. Our house had collapsed backward; the front portion, even on the ground floor, had been destroyed completely; by a chance the kitchen and scullery had escaped, and stood buried now under soil and ruins, closed in by tons of earth on every side save towards the cylinder. Over that aspect we hung now on the very edge of the great circular pit the Martians were engaged in making. The heavy beating sound was evidently just behind us, and ever and again a bright green vapor drove up like a veil across our peephole.

❶ *What has happened to the earth around the cylinder?*

The cylinder was already opened in the center of the pit, and on the farther edge of the pit, amid the smashed and gravel-heaped shrubbery, one of the great fighting-machines, deserted by its occupant, stood stiff and tall against the evening sky. At first I scarcely noticed the pit and the cylinder, although it has been convenient to describe them first, on account of the extraordinary glittering mechanism I saw busy in the excavation, and on account of the strange creatures that were crawling slowly and painfully across the heaped mold near it.

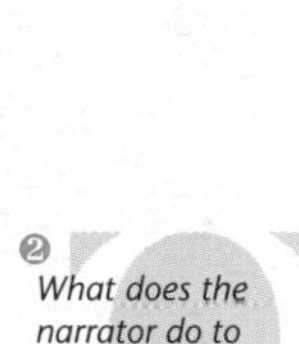

❷ *What does the narrator do to keep the curate from crying out? Why is it important that the curate not cry out?*

The mechanism it certainly was that held my attention first. It was one of those complicated fabrics that have since been called handling-machines, and the study of which has already given such an enormous

Words for Everyday Use

ram • part (ram´pärt´) *n.,* embankment for defense against attack

as • pect (as´pect´) *n.,* view

Answers to Guided Reading Questions

❶ The earth around the cylinder has been splashed like mud under the blow of a hammer.

❷ The narrator grips the curate's arm to keep him from crying out. It is important that the curate not cry about because the Martians would probably kill them if they discovered them.

Vocabulary in Context

- The soldiers prepared the rampart for the inevitable attack.
- The professor admitted he had never thought about that aspect of the issue.

Answers to Guided Reading Questions

❶ The Martian machine moves swiftly, complexly, and perfectly.

❷ The machine seems like a living creature and the Martian inside it like the cerebral portion of that creature.

❶ What is extraordinary about the Martian machine?

❷ To what does the narrator compare the machine? the Martian?

impetus to terrestrial invention. As it dawned upon me first it presented a sort of metallic spider with five jointed, agile legs, and with an extraordinary number of jointed levers, bars, and reaching and clutching tentacles about its body. Most of its arms were retracted, but with three long tentacles it was fishing out a number of rods, plates, and bars which lined the covering and apparently strengthened the walls, of the cylinder. These, as it extracted them, were lifted out and deposited upon a level surface of earth behind it.

Its motion was so swift, complex, and perfect that at first I did not see it as a machine, in spite of its metallic glitter. The fighting-machines were coordinated and animated to an extraordinary pitch, but nothing to compare with this. People who have never seen these structures, and have only the ill-imagined efforts of artists or the imperfect descriptions of such eye-witnesses as myself to go upon, scarcely realize that living quality.

I recall particularly the illustration of one of the first pamphlets to give a consecutive account of the war. The artist had evidently made a hasty study of one of the fighting-machines, and there his knowledge ended. He presented them as tilted, stiff tripods, without either flexibility or subtlety, and with an altogether misleading monotony of effect. The pamphlet containing these renderings had a considerable vogue, and I mention them here simply to warn the reader against the impression they may have created. They were no more like the Martians I saw in action than a Dutch doll is like a human being. To my mind, the pamphlet would have been much better without them.

At first, I say, the handling-machine did not impress me as a machine, but as a crab-like creature with a glittering integument,[1] the controlling Martian whose delicate tentacles actuated its movements seeming to be simply the equivalent of the crab's cerebral portion. But then I perceived the resemblance of its gray-brown, shiny, leathery integument to that of the other sprawling bodies beyond, and the true nature of this dexterous workman dawned upon me. With that realization

Chapter 2

1. **integument.** Natural outer covering of the body or of a plant, such as skin, shell, or husk

Words for Everyday Use

a • gile (aj´əl) *adj.,* quick and easy of movement
ren • der • ing (ren´dər iŋ) *n.,* drawing
dex • ter• ous (deks´tər əs) *adj.,* having or showing skillful use of the hands or body

Vocabulary in Context

- The fox was too agile for the hound to cartch.
- Hank drew a rendering of his aunt's farm.
- The martial artist was extremely quick and dexterous.

my interest shifted to those other creatures, the real Martians. Already I had had a transient impression of these, and the first nausea no longer obscured my observation. Moreover, I was concealed and motionless, and under no urgency of action.

They were, I now saw, the most unearthly creatures it is possible to conceive. They were huge round bodies—or, rather, heads—about four feet in diameter, each body having in front of it a face. This face had no nostrils—indeed, the Martians do not seem to have had any sense of smell—but it had a pair of very large, dark-colored eyes, and just beneath this a kind of fleshy beak. In the back of this head or body—I scarcely know how to speak of it—was the single tight tympanic[2] surface, since known to be anatomically an ear, though it must have been almost useless in our denser air. In a group round the mouth were sixteen slender, almost whip-like tentacles, arranged in two bunches of eight each. These bunches have since been named rather aptly, by that distinguished anatomist, Professor Howes, the *hands*. Even as I saw these Martians for the first time they seemed to be endeavoring to raise themselves on these hands, but of course, with the increased weight of terrestrial conditions, this was impossible. There is reason to suppose that on Mars they may have progressed upon them with some facility.

The internal anatomy, I may remark here, as dissection has since shown, was almost equally simple. The greater part of the structure was the brain, sending enormous nerves to the eyes, ear, and tactile tentacles. Besides this were the bulky lungs, into which the mouth opened, and the heart and its vessels. The pulmonary distress caused by the denser atmosphere and greater gravitational attraction was only too evident in the convulsive movements of the outer skin.

And this was the sum of the Martian organs. Strange as it may seem to a human being, all the complex apparatus of digestion, which makes up the bulk of our bodies, did not exist in the Martians. They were heads—merely heads. Entrails they had none. They did not eat, much less digest. Instead, they took the fresh, living blood of other creatures, and *injected* it into their own veins. I have myself seen this being done, as I shall mention in its place. But, squeamish as I may seem, I cannot bring myself to describe what I could not endure even to continue watching. Let it suffice to say, blood obtained from a still living animal, in most cases from a human being, was run directly by means of a little pipette into the recipient canal. . . .

The bare idea of this is no doubt horribly repulsive to us, but at the same time I think that we should remember how repulsive our carnivorous habits would seem to an intelligent rabbit.

The physiological advantages of the practice of injection are undeniable, if one thinks of the tremendous waste of human time and energy occasioned by eating and the digestive process. Our bodies are half made up of glands and tubes and organs, occupied in turning heterogeneous food into blood. The digestive processes and their reaction upon the nervous system sap our strength and color our minds. Men go happy or miserable as they have healthy or unhealthy livers, or sound gastric glands.[3] But the Martians were lifted

2. **tympanic.** Of or like a drum
3. **gastric glands.** Organs near and including the stomach

❶ *How does Martian anatomy differ from human anatomy?*

❷ *What use do Martians have for humans?*

Words for Everyday Use

en • deav • or (en dev´ər) *v.*, make a serious attempt, strive
con • vul • sive (kən vul´siv) *adj.*, having the nature of involuntary spasms
phys • i • o • log • i • cal (fiz´ē ō läj´i kəl) *adj.*, relating to the workings of the body
het • er • o • ge • ne • ous (het´ər ō´jē´nē əs) *adj.*, different; dissimilar

Answers to Guided Reading Questions

❶ The Martians are mere heads, without digestive tracts.

❷ The Martians inject blood from victims directly into themselves.

Vocabulary in Context

- Marcus endeavored to win the science award at the fair.
- Due to nervousness, Ron could not stop the convulsive shaking of his hands.
- The doctor assured Mary her problem was psychological not physiological.
- There were heterogeneous types of birds in the park.

Answers to Guided Reading Questions

❶ Martians bud off from their parents like polyps.

❷ The Martian domestic animals look like humans.

❸ Sleep is unnecessary for the Martians because they have no extensive muscular mechanism that needs to recuperate.

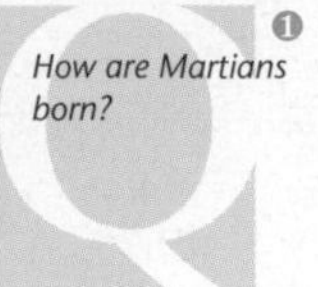

❶ *How are Martians born?*

❷ *What do the Martian domestic animals look like?*

❸ *Why is sleep unnecessary for the Martians?*

above all these organic fluctuations of mood and emotion.

Their undeniable preference for men as their source of nourishment is partly explained by the nature of the remains of the victims they had brought with them as provisions from Mars. These creatures, to judge from the shriveled remains that have fallen into human hands, were bipeds with flimsy, silicious skeletons (almost like those of the silicious sponges) and feeble musculature, standing about six feet high and having round, erect heads, and large eyes in flinty sockets. Two or three of these seem to have been brought in each cylinder, and all were killed before Earth was reached. It was just as well for them, for the mere attempt to stand upright upon our planet would have broken every bone in their bodies.

And while I am engaged in this description, I may add in this place certain further details which, although they were not all evident to us at the time, will enable the reader who is unacquainted with them to form a clearer picture of these offensive creatures.

In three other points their physiology differed strangely from ours. Their organisms did not sleep, any more than the heart of man sleeps. Since they had no extensive muscular mechanism to recuperate, that periodical extinction was unknown to them. They had little or no sense of fatigue, it would seem. On Earth they could never have moved without effort, yet even to the last they kept in action. In twenty-four hours they did twenty-four hours of work, as even on Earth is perhaps the case with the ants.

In the next place, wonderful as it seems in a sexual world, the Martians were absolutely without sex, and therefore without any of the tumultuous emotions that arise from that difference among men. A young Martian, there can now be no dispute, was really born upon Earth during the war, and it was found attached to its parent, partially *budded* off, just as young lily-bulbs bud off, or like the young animals in the freshwater polyp.[4]

In man, in all the higher terrestrial animals, such a method of increase has disappeared; but even on this Earth it was certainly the primitive method. Among the lower animals, up even to those first cousins of the vertebrated animals, the Tunicates,[5] the two processes occur side by side, but finally the sexual method superseded its competitor altogether. On Mars, however, just the reverse has apparently been the case.

It is worthy of remark that a certain speculative writer of quasi-scientific repute, writing long before the Martian invasion, did forecast for man a final structure not unlike the actual Martian condition. His prophesy, I remember, appeared in November or December, 1893, in a long-defunct publication, the *Pall Mall Budget*, and I recall a caricature of it in a pre-Martian periodical called *Punch*. He pointed out—writing in a foolish, facetious tone—that the perfection of mechanical appliances must ultimately supersede limbs; the perfection of chemical devices, digestion; that such organs as hair, external nose, teeth, ears, and chin were no longer essential parts of the human being, and that the tendency of natural selection would lie in the direction of their steady diminution through

4. **freshwater polyp.** Water organism having many small, slender stringing tentacles

5. **Tunicates.** Family of sea chordates having a sac-like body enclosed by a thick shell

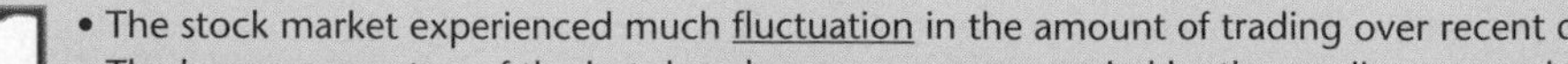

Words for Everyday Use

fluc • tu • a • tion (fluc´cho͞o ā shən) *n.*, continual, irregular changes

su • per • sede (so͞o´pər sēd´) *v.*, cause to be dropped from use as inferior or obsolete

de • funct (dē fuŋkt´) *adj.*, out of existence

car • i • ca • ture (kar´i kə chər) *n.*, exaggerated imitation of someone or something used to mock

fa • ce • tious (fə sē shəs) *adj.*, joking, inappropriate

Vocabulary in Context

- The stock market experienced much fluctuation in the amount of trading over recent days.
- The larger computers of the last decade were soon superseded by the smaller personal computers.
- Due to fishing, many species of whales were almost made defunct.
- Jill was upset at the caricature of her drawn by Jenny.
- While almost everyone at the meeting took Peter seriously, I knew he was only being facetious.

the coming ages. The brain alone remained a cardinal necessity. Only one other part of the body had a strong case for survival, and that was the hand, "teacher and agent of the brain." While the rest of the body dwindled, the hands would grow larger.

There is many a true word written in jest, and here in the Martians we have beyond dispute the actual accomplishment of such a suppression of the animal side of the organism by the intelligence. To me it is quite credible that the Martians may be descended from beings not unlike ourselves, by a gradual development of brain and hands (the latter giving rise to the two bunches of delicate tentacles at last) at the expense of the rest of the body. Without the body the brain would, of course, become a mere selfish intelligence, without any of the emotional substratum[6] of the human being.

The last salient point in which the systems of these creatures differed from ours was in what one might have thought a very trivial particular. Micro-organisms, which cause so much disease and pain on earth, have either never appeared upon Mars or Martian sanitary science eliminated them ages ago. A hundred diseases, all the fevers and contagions of human life, consumption, cancers, tumors and such morbidities, never enter the scheme of their life. And speaking of the differences between the life on Mars and terrestrial life, I may allude here to the curious suggestions of the red weed.

Apparently the vegetable kingdom in Mars, instead of having green for a dominant color, is of a vivid blood-red tint. At any rate, the seeds which the Martians (intentionally or accidentally) brought with them gave rise in all cases to red-colored growths. Only that known popularly as the red weed, however, gained any footing in competition with terrestrial forms. The red creeper was quite a transitory growth, and few people have seen it growing. For a time, however, the red weed grew with astonishing vigor and luxuriance. It spread up the sides of the pit by the third or fourth day of our imprisonment, and its cactus-like branches formed a carmine[7] fringe to the edges of our triangular window. And afterwards I found it broadcast throughout the country, and especially wherever there was a stream of water.

The Martians had what appears to have been an auditory organ, a single round drum at the back of the head-body, and eyes with a visual range not very different from ours except that, according to Philips, blue and violet were as black to them. It is commonly supposed that they communicated by sounds and tentacular gesticulations; this is asserted, for instance, in the able but hastily compiled pamphlet (written evidently by someone not an eyewitness of Martian actions) to which I have already alluded, and which, so far, has been the chief source of information concerning them. Now no surviving human being saw so much of the Martians in action as I did. I take no credit to myself for an accident, but the fact is so. And I assert that I watched them closely time after time, and that I have seen four, five, and (once) six of them sluggishly performing the most elaborately complicated operations together without either sound or gesture. Their peculiar hooting invariably preceded feeding; it had no modulation, and was, I believe, in no sense a signal, but merely

6. **substratum.** Foundation
7. **carmine.** Red or purplish-red, crimson

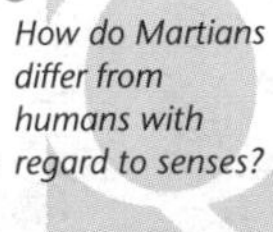
❶ *How do Martians differ from humans with regard to senses?*

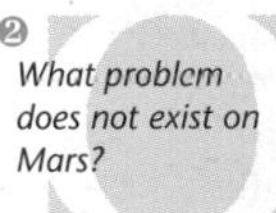
❷ *What problem does not exist on Mars?*

Words for Everyday Use

- **car • di • nal** (kärd´'n əl) *adj.*, principal
- **cred • i • ble** (kred´ə bəl) *adj.*, believeable
- **sa • lient** (sāl´yənt) *adj.*, noticeable; prominent
- **mor • bid • i • ty** (môr bid´ə tē) *n.*, something relating to death or disease
- **al • lude** (ə lo͞od´) *v.*, refer in an indirect way
- **ges • tic • u • la • tion** (jes tik´ yo͞o lā´shən) *n.*, energetic movement
- **mod • u • la • tion** (mäj´ə lā shən) *n.*, variation in stress or pitch

Answers to Guided Reading Questions

❶ The Martians have an auditory organ, and their visual range is much like that of humans, except that both blue and violet look like black to them.

❷ Microorganisms that cause disease or pain either never appeared on Mars or were all destroyed long ago.

Vocabulary in Context

- The cardinal rule when writing is "Do not plagiarize."
- All the jurors felt the expert witness was credible.
- The most salient player on the team was the star catcher, Tammy.
- Many people dislike hospitals because of their association with morbidity.
- Although everyone was congratulating Rona, Fran alluded to the fact that she also received an A on the exam.
- The leader spoke with great fire and gesticulation.
- The modulation of the song was soothing and subtle.

Answers to Guided Reading Questions

❶ The hooting is not a signal but rather an expiration of air in preparation for the suction that they do when feeding.

❷ The narrator believes that the Martians communicate by telepathy.

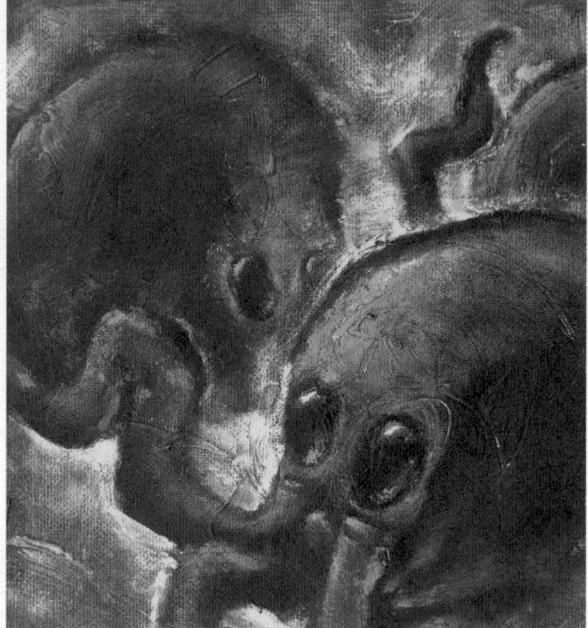

What is the narrator's explanation of the Martians' hooting?

How do the Martians communicate?

❶ the expiration of air preparatory to the suctional operation. I have a certain claim to at least an elementary knowledge of psychology, and in this matter I am convinced—as firmly as I am convinced of anything—that the Martians interchanged thoughts without any physical intermediation. ❷ And I have been convinced of this in spite of strong preconceptions. Before the Martian invasion, as an occasional reader here or there may remember, I had written with some little vehemence against the telepathic theory.[8]

The Martians wore no clothing. Their conceptions of ornament and decorum were necessarily different from ours; and not only were they evidently much less sensible of changes of temperature than we are, but changes of pressure do not seem to have affected their health at all seriously. Yet though they wore no clothing, it was in the other artificial additions to their bodily resources, that their great superiority over man lay. We men, with our bicycles and road-skates, our Lilienthal soaring-machines,[9] our guns and sticks and so forth, are just in the beginning of the evolution that the Martians have worked out. They have become practically mere brains, wearing different bodies according to their needs just as men wear suits of clothes and take a bicycle in a hurry or an umbrella in the wet. And of their appliances, perhaps nothing is more wonderful to a man than the curious fact that what is the dominant feature of almost all human devices in mechanism is absent—the *wheel* is absent; among all the things they brought to earth there is no trace or suggestion of their use of wheels. One would have at least expected it in locomotion. And in this connection it is curious to remark that even on this Earth Nature has never hit upon the wheel, or has preferred other expedients to its development. And not only did the Martians either not know of (which is incredible), or abstain from, the wheel, but in their apparatus singularly little use is made of the fixed pivot, or relatively fixed pivot, with circular motions thereabout confined to one plane. Almost all the joints of the machinery present a complicated system of sliding parts moving over small but beautifully curved friction bearings. And while upon this matter of detail, it is remarkable that the long leverages of their machines are in most

8. **telepathic theory.** Idea that communication through thoughts is possible

9. **Lilienthal soaring-mechanisms.** Early gliders produced by Otto Lilienthal

Words for Everyday Use

in • ter • me • di • a • tion (in′tər mē′dē ā′shən) *n.*, happening or means in between

ve • he • mence (vē′ə məns) *n.*, state of having intense feeling or passion

de • cor • um (di kôr′əm) *n.*, propriety and good taste in behavior or appearance

ex • pe • di • ent (ek spē′dē ənt) *adj.*, something useful for attaining a particular result

Vocabulary in Context

- The intermediation to the two halves of the football game was a perfomance by a marching band.
- Paul argued with the teacher in favor of less homework with great vehemence.
- Knowing little about proper etiquette, Jim entered the party with little decorum.
- The dried leaves around the campsite were good expedients to lighting the fire.

cases actuated by a sort of sham musculature of discs in an elastic sheath; these discs become polarized and drawn closely and powerfully together when traversed by a current of electricity. In this way the curious parallelism to animal motions, which was so striking and disturbing to the human beholder, was attained. Such quasimuscles abounded in the crab-like handling-machine which, on my first peeping out of the slit, I watched unpacking the cylinder. It seemed infinitely more alive than the actual Martians lying beyond it in the sunset light, panting, stirring ineffectual tentacles, and moving feebly after their vast journey across space.

While I was still watching their sluggish motions in the sunlight, and noting each strange detail of their form, the curate reminded me of his presence by pulling violently at my arm. I turned to a scowling face, and silent, eloquent lips. He wanted the slit, which permitted only one of us to peep through; and so I had to forego watching them for a time while he enjoyed that privilege.

When I looked again, the busy handling-machine had already put together several of the pieces of apparatus it had taken out of the cylinder into a shape having an unmistakable likeness to its own; and down on the left a busy little digging mechanism had come into view, emitting jets of green vapor and working its way round the pit, excavating and embanking in a methodical and discriminating manner. This it was which had caused the regular beating noise, and the rhythmic shocks that had kept our ruinous refuge quivering. It piped and whistled as it worked. So far as I could see, the thing was without a directing Martian at all.

Reviewing the Selection

Recalling and Interpreting

1. **R** What machines does the narrator see from his peephole?

   I What is extraordinary about the machines that the narrator sees?

2. **R** What further description of the physical appearance of the Martians does the narrator give? For what are the "tympanic surface" and the "whip-like tentacles" used? What has happened to the Martians' brains and digestive tracts over time?

   I How might the present appearance of the Martians have come about?

3. **R** How do the Martians communicate with one another?

   I What indication does the speaker give that belief in telepathy has not been scientifically respectable?

Words for Everyday Use

sham (sham) *n.*, imitation; artificial
po • lar • ize (pō´lər īz´) *v.*, separate into opposing groups
tra • verse (trə vurs´) *v.*, cross or pass through
e • mit (ē mit´) *v.*, send out; give forth
dis • crim • i • nat • ing (dis krim´ə nāt´iŋ) *adj.*, making fine distinctions; distinguishing

Answers for Reviewing the Selection

RECALLING AND INTERPRETING

1. **Recalling.** The narrator sees the elaborate, delicate handling machine and a digging mechanism. **Interpreting.** The machines are very lifelike.

2. **Recalling.** The Martians are round heads, about four feet in diameter, with large, dark eyes, a fleshy beak, a tympanic surface, and tentacles bunched around a mouth. The tympanic surface is an organ of hearing. The tentacles are used for movement. **Interpreting.** The appearance might have come about through the gradual development of the brain and hands at the expense of the rest of the body.

3. **Recalling.** The Martians communicate by means of telepathy. **Interpreting.** The speaker says that he himself had strong preconceptions against the idea and had written to that effect.

Vocabulary in Context

- It turns out the rare painting Rico bought was a sham.
- The decision whether to go to the zoo or the museum for a field trip polarized the student body.
- The hikers traversed the dangerous mountain ridge with no trouble.
- The air conditioner emitted cool air into the humid room.
- Paula chose between the slices of pie in a careful and discriminating manner.

ANSWER TO GUIDED READING QUESTION

❶ The narrator does not think much of the curate. He uses the following adjectives in his description of him: *incompatible, helpless, stupid, endless, spoiled,* and *weak.*

3

THE DAYS OF IMPRISONMENT

The arrival of a second fighting-machine drove us from our peephole into the scullery, for we feared that from his elevation the Martian might see down upon us behind our barrier. At a later date we began to feel less in danger of their eyes, for to an eye in the dazzle of the sunlight outside, our refuge must have been blank blackness, but at first the slightest suggestion of approach drove us into the scullery in heart-throbbing retreat. Yet terrible as was the danger we incurred, the attraction of peeping was for both of us irresistible. And I recall now with a sort of wonder that, in spite of the infinite danger in which we were between starvation and a still more terrible death, we could yet struggle bitterly for that horrible privilege of sight. We would race across the kitchen in a grotesque way between eagerness and the dread of making a noise, and strike each other, and thrust and kick, within a few inches of exposure.

What does the narrator think of the curate? What adjectives does the narrator use to describe him? ❶

The fact is that we had absolutely incompatible dispositions and habits of thought and action, and our danger and isolation only accentuated the incompatibility. At Halliford I had already come to hate the curate's trick of helpless exclamation, his stupid rigidity of mind. His endless muttering monologue vitiated every effort I made to think out a line of action, and drove me at times, thus pent up and intensified, almost to the verge of craziness. He was lacking in restraint. He would weep for hours together, and I verily believe that to the very end this spoiled child of life thought his weak tears in some way efficacious. And I would sit in the darkness unable to keep my mind off him by reason of his importunities. He ate more than I did, and it was in vain I pointed out that our only chance of life was to stop in the house until the Martians had done with their pit, that in that long patience a time might presently come when we should need food. He ate and drank impulsively in heavy meals at long intervals. He slept little.

As the days wore on, his utter carelessness of any consideration so intensified our distress and danger that I had, much as I loathed doing it, to resort to threats, and at last to blows. That brought him to reason for a time. But he was one of those weak creatures, void of pride, timorous, anemic, hateful souls, full of shifty cunning who face neither God nor man, who face not even themselves.

It is disagreeable for me to recall and write these things, but I set them down that my story may lack nothing. Those who have escaped the dark and terrible aspects of life will find my brutality, my flash of rage in our final tragedy, easy enough to blame; for they know what is wrong as well as any, but not what is possible to tortured men. But those who have been under the shadow, who have gone down at last to elemental things, will have a wider charity.

And while within we fought out our dark, dim contest of whispers, snatched food and drink, and gripping hands and blows, without, in the pitiless sunlight of that terrible June, was the strange wonder, the unfamiliar routine of the Martians in the pit. Let me return to those first new experiences of mine. After a long time I ventured back to the peephole, to find that the newcomers had been reinforced by the occupants of no fewer than three of the fighting-machines. These last had brought

WORDS FOR EVERYDAY USE

in • cur (in kur´) *v.,* become subject to through one's own actions
vi • ti • ate (vish´ē āt´) *v.,* spoil; weaken
ef • fi • ca • cious (ef´i kā shəs) *adj.,* effective
im • por • tu • ni • ty (im´pôr to͞on´i tē) *n.,* persistent urgent demands
a • ne • mic (ə nē´mik) *adj.,* lacking vitality
el • e • men• tal (el´ə ment´'l) *adj.,* most basic

VOCABULARY IN CONTEXT

- By skipping the family picnic, Bill incurred the wrath of his father.
- The repeated running plays by the football team vitiated the other team's defense.
- Hadi's, for his efficacious attempt to save the cat during the fire, was rewarded with a medal from the mayor.
- Mr. Rockwell's importunities for better perfomance on the students' homework eventually resulted in better test grades.
- After a long day of riding their bikes, the group as a whole was anemic.
- Addition and subtraction are the elemental parts of advanced mathematics.

with them certain fresh appliances that stood in an orderly manner about the cylinder. The second handling- machine was now completed, and was busied in serving one of the novel contrivances the big machine had brought. This was a body resembling a milk can in its general form, above which oscillated a pear-shaped receptacle, and from which a stream of white powder flowed into a circular basin below.

The oscillatory motion was imparted to this by one tentacle of the handling-machine. With two spatulate hands the handling-machine was digging out and flinging masses of clay into the pear-shaped receptacle above, while with another arm it periodically opened a door and removed rusty and blackened clinkers[1] from the middle part of the machine. Another steely tentacle directed the powder from the basin along a ribbed channel toward some receiver that was hidden from me by the mound of bluish dust. From this unseen receiver a little thread of green smoke rose vertically into the quiet air. As I looked, the handling-machine, with a faint and musical clinking, extended, telescopic fashion, a tentacle that had been a moment before a mere blunt projection, until its end was hidden behind the mound of clay. In another second it had lifted a bar of white aluminum into sight, untarnished as yet and shining dazzlingly, and deposited it in a growing stack of bars that stood at the side of the pit. Between sunset and starlight this dexterous machine must have made more than a hundred such bars out of the crude clay, and the mound of bluish dust rose steadily until it topped the side of the pit.

The contrast between the swift and complex movements of these contrivances and the inert, panting clumsiness of their masters was acute, and for days I had to tell myself repeatedly that these latter were indeed the living of the two things.

The curate had possession of the slit when the first men were brought to the pit. I was sitting below, huddled up, listening with all my ears. He made a sudden

❶ *What are the Martians making? Why might they be doing this?*

CHAPTER 3

1. **clinkers.** Hard mass of fused stony matter formed in a furnace

WORDS FOR EVERYDAY USE

con • triv • ance (kən trī´vəns) *n.*, something ingeniously constructed; invention

os • cil • late (äs´ə lāt´) *v.*, swing or move regularly back and forth

im • part (im pärt´) *v.*, give

spat • u • late (spach´ə lāt´) *adj.*, of or like a cooking utensil, the spatula

a • cute (ə kyo͞ot´) *adj.*, severe; sharp

ANSWER TO GUIDED READING QUESTION

❶ The Martians are making aluminum. They may be planning to use this material to build other machines.

VOCABULARY IN CONTEXT

- Antonio's contrivance won first prize at the science fair.
- The children oscillated on the swing set out back.
- Uncle Robert always imparts great gifts to the children during the holidays.
- Rufus removed the snow from his driver with his spatulate shovel.
- The pain in his leg after he fell off the tree was acute.

Answers to Guided Reading Questions

❶ The well-dressed man is eaten by the Martians.

❷ The "atrocity" is the use of human beings for food.

What happens to the well-dressed man? ❶

What is the "atrocity" that robs the curate "of all vestiges of reason"? ❶

movement backward, and I, fearful that we were observed, crouched in a spasm of terror. He came sliding down the rubbish and crept beside me in the darkness, inarticulate, gesticulating, and for a moment I shared his panic. His gesture suggested a resignation of the slit, and after a little while my curiosity gave me courage, and I rose up, stepped across him, and clambered up to it. At first I could see no reason for his frantic behavior. The twilight had now come, the stars were little and faint, but the pit was illuminated by the flickering green fire that came from the aluminum-making. The whole picture was a flickering scheme of green gleams and shifting rusty black shadows, strangely trying to the eyes. Over and through it all went the bats, heeding it not at all. The sprawling Martians were no longer to be seen, the mound of blue-green powder had risen to cover them from sight, and a fighting-machine, with its legs contracted, crumpled, and abbreviated, stood across the corner of the pit. And then, amid the clangor of the machinery, came a drifting suspicion of human voices, that I entertained at first only to dismiss.

I crouched, watching this fighting-machine closely, satisfying myself now for the first time that the hood did indeed contain a Martian. As the green flames lifted I could see the oily gleam of his integument and the brightness of his eyes. And suddenly I heard a yell, and saw a long tentacle reaching over the shoulder of the machine to the little cage that hunched upon its back. Then something—something struggling violently—was lifted high against the sky, a black, vague enigma against the starlight; and as this black object came down again, I saw by the green brightness that it was a man. For an instant he was clearly visible. He was a stout, ruddy, middle-aged man, well dressed; three days before he must have been walking the world, a man of considerable consequence. I could see his staring eyes and gleams of light on his studs and watch-chain. He vanished behind the mound, and for a moment there was silence. And then began a shrieking and a sustained and cheerful hooting from the Martians.

I slid down the rubbish, struggled to my feet, clapped my hands over my ears, and bolted into the scullery. The curate, who had been crouching silently with his arms over his head, looked up as I passed, cried out quite loudly at my desertion of him, and came running after me.

That night, as we lurked in the scullery balanced between our horror and the terrible fascination this peeping had, although I felt an urgent need of action I tried in vain to conceive some plan of escape; but afterwards, during the second day, I was able to consider our position with great clearness. The curate, I found, was quite incapable of discussion; this new and culminating atrocity had robbed him of all vestiges of reason or forethought. Practically he had already sunk to the level of an animal. But, as the saying goes, I gripped myself with both hands. It grew upon my mind, once I could face the facts, that, terrible as our position was, there was as yet no justification for absolute despair. Our chief chance lay in the possibility of the Martians making the pit nothing more than a temporary encampment. Or even if they kept it permanently, they might not consider it necessary to guard it, and a chance of escape might be afforded us. I also weighed very carefully the possibility of our digging a way out in

Words for Everyday Use

e • nig • ma (i nig´mə) *n.*, perplexing, baffling person or matter

cul • mi • nate (kul´mə nāt´) *v.*, reach the highest point or climax

a • troc • i • ty (ə träs´ə tē) *n.*, very cruel, evil, or brutal act

ves • tige (ves´tij) *n.*, trace

fore • thought (fôr´thôt´) *n.*, thinking or planning beforehand

Vocabulary in Context

- How John was left off the baseball team was an enigma to all the players.
- The Friday evening culminated with a hot fudge sundae.
- The killing of the animals in the lab was seen by many as an atrocity.
- After the fire had been put out, there was nothing but a vestige of the house left.
- The decision to skip the movies and go to the miniature golf course instead was a forethought.

a direction away from the pit, but the chances of our emerging within sight of some sentinel fighting-machine seemed at first too great. And I should have had to do all the digging myself. The curate would certainly have failed me.

It was on the third day, if my memory serves me right, that I saw the lad killed. It was the only occasion on which I actually saw the Martians feed. After that experience I avoided the hole in the wall for the better part of a day. I went into the scullery, removed the door, and spent some hours digging with my hatchet as silently as possible; but when I had made a hole about a couple of feet deep the loose earth collapsed noisily, and I did not dare continue. I lost heart, and lay down on the scullery floor for a long time, having no spirit even to move. And after that I abandoned altogether the idea of escaping by excavation.

It says much for the impression the Martians had made upon me that at first I entertained little or no hope of our escape being brought about by their overthrow through any human effort. But on the fourth or fifth night I heard a sound like heavy guns.

It was very late in the night, and the moon was shining brightly. The Martians had taken away the excavating-machine, and, save for a fighting-machine that stood on the remoter bank of the pit and a handling-machine that was busied out of my sight in a corner of the pit immediately beneath my peephole, the place was deserted by them. Except for the pale glow from the handling-machine and the bars and patches of white moonlight, the pit was in darkness, and, except for the clinking of the handling-machine, quite still. That night was a beautiful serenity; save for one planet, the moon seemed to have the sky to herself. I heard a dog howling, and that familiar sound it was that made me listen. Then I heard quite distinctly a booming exactly like the sound of great guns. Six distinct reports I counted, and after a long interval six again. And that was all.

❶ *Why does the narrator not want to go back to the peephole?*

Reviewing the Selection

Recalling and Interpreting

1. **R** What does the Martian machine make out of clay?

   I Why might the Martians be making these things out of clay? What purpose might they serve?

2. **R** On what do the Martians feed, and how?

   I What causes the narrator to stay away from the peephole "for the better part of a day"?

Answer to Guided Reading Question

❶ The narrator does not want to go back because he is so horrified by what he has witnessed.

Answers for Reviewing the Selection

RECALLING AND INTERPRETING

1. **Recalling.** The Martian machine makes aluminum bars. **Interpreting.** The Martians may be making these materials for use in building machines.

2. **Recalling.** The Martians feed on people by sucking their blood. **Interpreting.** The narrator stays away for the better part of a day after seeing a boy killed.

Answer to Guided Reading Question

❶ The curate is sorry for having preached acceptable folly, for having held his peace while the poor were trodden into the dust.

4
THE DEATH OF THE CURATE

It was on the sixth day of our imprisonment that I peeped for the last time, and presently found myself alone. Instead of keeping close to me and trying to oust me from the slit, the curate had gone back into the scullery. I was struck by a sudden thought. I went back quickly and quietly into the scullery. In the darkness I heard the curate.

For a few minutes there was a tussle. I desisted and rose. We stood panting, threatening each other. In the end I planted myself between him and the food, and told him of my determination to begin a discipline. I divided the food in the pantry into rations to last us ten days. I would not let him eat any more that day. In the afternoon he made a feeble effort to get at the food. I had been dozing, but in an instant I was awake. All day and all night we sat face to face, I weary but resolute, and he weeping and complaining of his immediate hunger. It was, I know, a night and a day, but to me it seemed—it seems now—an interminable length of time.

Q ❶ *For what is the curate sorry?*

And so our widened incompatibility ended at last in open conflict. For two vast days we struggled in undertones and wrestling contests. There were times when I beat and kicked him madly, times when I cajoled and persuaded him, and once I tried to bribe him, for there was a rainwater pump from which I could get water. But neither force nor kindness availed; he was indeed beyond reason. He would neither desist from his attacks on the food nor from his noisy babbling to himself. The rudimentary precautions to keep our imprisonment endurable he would not observe. Slowly I began to realize the complete overthrow of his intelligence, to perceive that my sole companion in this close and sickly darkness was a man insane.

From certain vague memories I am inclined to think my own mind wandered at times. I had strange and hideous dreams whenever I slept. It sounds paradoxical, but I am inclined to think that the weakness and insanity of the curate warned me, braced me, and kept me a sane man.

On the eighth day he began to talk aloud instead of whispering, and nothing I could do would moderate his speech.

"It is just, O God!" he would say, over and over again. "It is just. On me and mine be the punishment laid. We have sinned, we have fallen short. There was poverty, sorrow; the poor were trodden in the dust, and I held my peace. I preached acceptable folly—my God, what folly!—when I should have stood up, though I died for it, and called upon them to repent—repent! . . . Oppressors of the poor and needy! . . . The wine-press of God!"

Then he would suddenly revert to the matter of the food I withheld from him, praying, begging, weeping, at last threatening. He began to raise his voice—I prayed him not to. He perceived a hold on me—he threatened he would shout and bring the Martians upon us. For a time that scared me; but any concession would have shortened our chance of escape beyond estimating. I defied him, although I felt no assurance that he might not do this thing. But that day, at any rate, he did not. He talked, with his voice rising slowly, through the greater part of the eighth and ninth days—threats, entreaties, mingled with a torrent of half-sane and always frothy repentance for his vacant

Words for Everyday Use

oust (oust) *v.*, force or drive out
tus • sle (tus´əl) *n.*, vigorous struggle; scuffle
ca • jole (kə jōl´) *v.*, coax or persuade with flattery
ru • di • men • ta • ry (ro͞o´də men´tər ē) *adj.*, basic; fundamental
par • a • dox • i • cal (par´ə daks´i kəl) *adj.*, seemingly full of contradictions

Vocabulary in Context

- George's mother ousted the dirty dog from the new living room.
- The brother and sister were involved in a tussle over the last candy bar.
- The dentist cajoled the child to open her mouth.
- The ability to throw a ball is a rudimentary skill in baseball.
- How the seemingly untalented Jays won the Little League championship was paradoxical.

sham of God's service, such as made me pity him. Then he slept awhile, and began again with renewed strength, so loudly that I must needs make him desist.

"Be still!" I implored.

He rose to his knees, for he had been sitting in the darkness near the copper.

"I have been still too long," he said, in a tone that must have reached the pit, "and now I must bear my witness. Woe unto this unfaithful city! Woe! woe! Woe! woe! woe! to the inhabitants of the Earth by reason of the other voices of the trumpet—"

"Shut up!" I said, rising to my feet, and in a terror lest the Martians should hear us. "For God's sake—"

"Nay!" shouted the curate, at the top of his voice, standing likewise and extending his arms. "Speak! The word of the Lord is upon me!"

In three strides he was at the door leading into the kitchen.

"I must bear my witness! I go! It has already been too long delayed."

I put out my hand and felt the meat-chopper hanging to the wall. In a flash I was after him. I was fierce with fear. Before he was halfway across the kitchen I had overtaken him. With one last touch of humanity I turned the blade back and struck him with the butt. He went headlong forward and lay stretched on the ground. I stumbled over him and stood panting. He lay still.

Suddenly I heard a noise without, the run and smash of slipping plaster, and the triangular aperture in the wall was darkened. I looked up and saw the lower surface of a handling-machine coming slowly across the hole. One of its gripping limbs curled amid the debris; another limb appeared, feeling its way over the fallen beams. I stood petrified, staring. Then I saw through a sort of glass plate near the edge of the body the face, as we may call it, and the large dark eyes of a Martian, peering, and then a long metallic snake of tentacle came feeling slowly through the hole.

I turned by an effort, stumbled over the curate, and stopped at the scullery door. The tentacle was now some way, two yards or more, in the room, and twisting and turning, with queer sudden movements, this way and that. For a while I stood fascinated by that slow, fitful advance. Then, with a faint, hoarse cry, I forced myself across the scullery. I trembled violently; I could scarcely stand upright. I opened the door of the coal-cellar, and stood there in the darkness staring at the faintly lit doorway into the kitchen, and listening. Had the Martian seen me? What was it doing now?

Something was moving to and fro there, very quietly; every now and then it tapped against the wall, or started on its movements with a faint metallic ringing, like the movement of keys on a split-ring. Then a heavy body—I knew too well what—was dragged across the floor of the kitchen towards the opening. Irresistibly attracted, I crept to the door and peeped into the kitchen. In the triangle of bright outer sunlight I saw the Martian, in its Briareus[1] of a handling-machine, scrutinizing the curate's head. I thought at once that it would infer my presence from the mark of the blow I had given him.

I crept back to the coal-cellar, shut the door, and began to cover myself up as much as I could, and as noiselessly as

❶ *What does the narrator fear?*

❷ *What does the narrator do? Is this action justified? Why, or why not?*

CHAPTER 4

1. **Briareus.** Many-armed, many-headed monster in Greek mythology

WORDS FOR EVERYDAY USE

im • plore (im plôr´) *v.*, ask or beg earnestly for

ANSWERS TO GUIDED READING QUESTIONS

❶ The narrator fears that the Martians will hear the curate.

❷ The narrator strikes the curate, killing him, in order to stop him from making their presence known to the Martians.

VOCABULARY IN CONTEXT

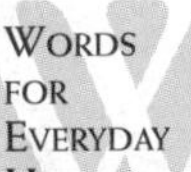

• The driver implored the officer not to give him a ticket.

Answer to Guided Reading Question

❶ The narrator is on the verge of screaming because the Martian tentacle is very close. In fact, it even touches the heel of the narrator's boot.

Answers for Reviewing the Selection

RECALLING AND INTERPRETING

1. **Recalling.** The narrator and the curate quarrel over food and drink. **Interpreting.** It is important to ration the food and drink so that the two people will not run out before they are able to leave their hiding place.

2. **Recalling.** The curate threatens to "bear witness," making himself known to the Martians. The narrator responds by hitting the curate with the back end of a cleaver. **Interpreting.** *Responses will vary.* Certainly, the narrator probably saved his own life by acting as he did, and the curate would probably have been dead in any case.

possible in the darkness, among the firewood and coal therein. Every now and then I paused, rigid, to hear if the Martian had thrust its tentacle through the opening again.

Then the faint metallic jingle returned. I traced it slowly feeling over the kitchen. Presently I heard it nearer—in the scullery, as I judged. I thought that its length might be insufficient to reach me. I prayed copiously. It passed, scraping faintly across the cellar door. An age of almost intolerable suspense intervened; then I heard it fumbling at the latch. It had found the door! The Martians understood doors!

It worried at the catch for a minute, perhaps, and then the door opened.

In the darkness I could just see the thing—like an elephant's trunk more than anything else—waving towards me and touching and examining the wall, coals, wood, and ceiling. It was like a black worm swaying its blind head to and fro.

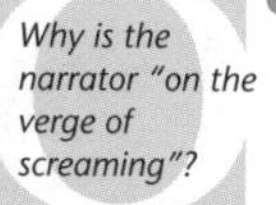

Why is the narrator "on the verge of screaming"? ❶

Once, even, it touched the heel of my boot. I was on the verge of screaming; I bit my hand. For a time the tentacle was silent. I could have fancied it had been withdrawn. Presently, with an abrupt click, it gripped something—I thought it had me!—and seemed to go out of the cellar again. For a minute I was not sure. Apparently it had taken a lump of coal to examine.

I seized the opportunity of slightly shifting my position, which had become cramped, and then listened. I whispered passionate prayers for safety.

Then I heard the slow, deliberate sound creeping towards me again. Slowly, slowly it drew near, scratching against the walls and tapping the furniture.

While I was still doubtful, it rapped smartly against the cellar door and closed it. I heard it go into the pantry, and the biscuit-tins rattled and a bottle smashed, and then came a heavy bump against the cellar door. Then silence, that passed into an infinity of suspense.

Had it gone?

At last I decided that it had.

It came into the scullery no more; but I lay all the tenth day in the close darkness, buried among coals and firewood, not daring even to crawl out for the drink for which I craved. It was the eleventh day before I ventured so far from my security.

Reviewing the Selection

Recalling and Interpreting

1. Ⓡ Over what do the narrator and the curate quarrel?

   Ⓘ Why is it important not to eat too much of the food at once?

2. Ⓡ What does the curate threaten to do just before his death? How does the narrator respond?

   Ⓘ Do you think that the narrator was justified in his actions? Why, or why not?

Words for Everyday Use

co • pi • ous • ly (kō´pē əs lē) *adv.,* with many words; profusely

in • tol • er • a • ble (in täl´ər ə bəl) *adj.,* unbearable, too severe to be endured

Vocabulary in Context

- The speaker spoke copiously at the banquet.
- The heat was intolerable on the ballfield and Charlie decided to go inside.

5
The Stillness

My first act before I went into the pantry was to fasten the door between the kitchen and the scullery. But the pantry was empty; every scrap of food had gone. Apparently, the Martian had taken it all on the previous day. At that discovery I despaired for the first time. I took no food, or no drink either, on the eleventh or the twelfth day.

At first my mouth and throat were parched, and my strength ebbed sensibly. I sat about in the darkness of the scullery, in a state of despondent wretchedness. My mind ran on eating. I thought I had become deaf, for the noises of movement I had been accustomed to hear from the pit had ceased absolutely. I did not feel strong enough to crawl noiselessly to the peep-hole, or I would have gone there.

On the twelfth day my throat was so painful that, taking the chance of alarming the Martians, I attacked the creaking rain-water pump that stood by the sink, and got a couple of glassfuls of blackened and tainted rainwater. I was greatly refreshed by this, and emboldened by the fact that no inquiring tentacle followed the noise of my pumping.

During these days, in a rambling, inconclusive way, I thought much of the curate and of the manner of his death.

On the thirteenth day I drank some more water, and dozed and thought disjointedly of eating and of vague impossible plans of escape. Whenever I dozed I dreamt of horrible phantasms, of the death of the curate, or of sumptuous dinners; but, asleep or awake, I felt a keen pain that urged me to drink again and again. The light that came into the scullery was no longer gray, but red. To my disordered imagination it seemed the color of blood.

On the fourteenth day I went into the kitchen, and I was surprised to find that the fronds of the red weed had grown right across the hole in the wall, turning the half-light of the place into a crimson-colored obscurity.

It was early on the fifteenth day that I heard a curious, familiar sequence of sounds in the kitchen, and, listening, identified it as the snuffing and scratching of a dog. Going into the kitchen, I saw a dog's nose peering in through a break among the ruddy fronds. This greatly surprised me. At the scent of me he barked shortly.

I thought if I could induce him to come into the place quietly I should be able, perhaps, to kill and eat him; and, in any case, it would be advisable to kill him, lest his actions attracted the attention of the Martians.

❶ *Why does the narrator call the dog? Do you think he is justified in his actions?*

I crept forward, saying "Good dog!" very softly; but he suddenly withdrew his head and disappeared.

I listened—I was not deaf—but certainly the pit was still. I heard a sound like the flutter of a bird's wings, and a hoarse croaking, but that was all.

For a long while I lay close to the peep-hole, but not daring to move aside the red plants that obscured it. Once or twice I heard a faint pitter-patter like the feet of the dog going hither and thither on the sand far below me, and there were more birdlike sounds, but that was all. At length, encouraged by the silence, I looked out.

Except in the corner, where a multitude of crows hopped and fought over the skeletons of the dead the Martians had consumed, there was not a living thing in the pit.

Words for Everyday Use

parch (pärch) *v.*, make very thirsty or dry
ebb (eb) *v.*, weaken; decline
de • spond • ent (di spän´dənt) *adj.*, filled with loss of hope or courage
in • con • clu • sive (in´kən klo͞o siv) *adj.*, not leading to a definite result
phan • tasm (fan´ taz´əm) *n.*, ghost; specter
sump • tu • ous (sump´cho͞o əs) *adj.*, magnificent or splendid
frond (fränd) *n.*, leaf of a fern or palm

Answer to Guided Reading Question

❶ The narrator calls the dog because he hopes to kill and eat it. In any case, it is advisable to kill the dog so that its actions will not reveal the narrator's whereabouts.

Vocabulary in Context

- Marc parched his shirt in the sun so he could wear it that night.
- James ebbed the flow of water out ofthe pipes by patching it with some duct tape.
- After the loss in the championship tennis match, Julie was despondent.
- The findings of Jamal's report on global warming were inconclusive.
- Neighborhood kids had heard rumors that a phantasm was haunting the old abandoned mill.
- The chocolate cake at Marcia's party was sumptuous.
- On the beach, Ruben relaxed and fanned himself with a frond.

Answers to Guided Reading Questions

❶ A red Martian plant has grown all over the ground.

❷ The day seems bright because the narrator has been confined for a long time in the darkness of the buried house.

Answers for Reviewing the Selection

RECALLING AND INTERPRETING

1. **Recalling.** The narrator runs out of food and water. **Interpreting.** The narrator must find a means of escape because if he does not, then he will die of thirst or hunger.
2. **Recalling.** A red Martian plant is growing up the pit and in the roofless rooms of houses. **Interpreting.** The red color might be due to the characteristic red vegetation of the planet.

Selection Check Test with Answers

EX. With whom is the narrator trapped in the house?
The narrator is trapped with the curate.

1. Why do the Martians collect people?
The Martians collect people in order to ingest their blood.
2. What has a fleshy beak and a tympanic surface?
A Martian does.
3. What cause of disease and pain does not exist on Mars?
There are no microorganisms on Mars.
4. How does the curate die?
The narrator kills him.
5. What does the narrator find growing everywhere when he finally leaves the buried house?
He finds a red Martian weed growing everywhere.

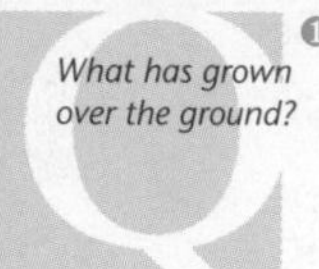

❶ *What has grown over the ground?*

❷ *Why does the day seem dazzlingly bright?*

I stared about me, scarcely believing my eyes. All the machinery had gone. Save for the big mound of grayish-blue powder in one corner, certain bars of aluminum in another, the black birds, and the skeletons of the killed, the place was merely an empty circular pit in the sand.

Slowly I thrust myself out through the red weed, and stood upon the mound of rubble. I could see in any direction save behind me, to the north, and neither Martians nor sign of Martians were to be seen. The pit dropped sheerly from my feet, but a little way along the rubbish afforded a practicable slope to the summit of the ruins. My chance of escape had come. I began to tremble.

I hesitated for some time, and then, in a gust of desperate resolution, and with a heart that throbbed violently, I scrambled to the top of the mound in which I had been buried so long.

I looked about again. To the northward, too, no Martian was visible.

When I had last seen this part of Sheen in the daylight it had been a straggling street of comfortable white and red houses, interspersed with abundant shady trees. Now I stood on a mound of smashed brickwork, clay, and gravel, over which spread a multitude of red cactus-shaped plants, knee-high, without a solitary terrestrial growth to dispute their footing. The trees near me were dead and brown, but further a network of red threads scaled the still living stems.

The neighboring houses had all been wrecked, but none had been burned; their walls stood, sometimes to the second story, with smashed windows and shattered doors. The red weed grew tumultuously in their roofless rooms. Below me was the great pit, with the crows struggling for its refuse. A number of other birds hopped about among the ruins. Far away I saw a gaunt cat slink crouchingly along a wall, but traces of men there were none.

The day seemed, by contrast with my recent confinement, dazzlingly bright, the sky a glowing blue. A gentle breeze kept the red weed that covered every scrap of unoccupied ground gently swaying. And oh! the sweetness of the air!

Reviewing the Selection

Recalling and Interpreting

1. Ⓡ What happens to the narrator's food and water?
   Ⓘ Why must the narrator find a means of escape from his hiding place?
2. Ⓡ What is growing up the pit and in the roofless rooms of houses?
   Ⓘ What does this novel suggest might be the cause of the red color of the planet Mars as viewed through a telescope?

Speaking and Listening Skills

Interpersonal Communication

Wells's Martians know that, without effective communication, the social order breaks down and confusion results. There are many methods of **interpersonal communication.**

Talking on the telephone and holding face-to-face conversations are the most common situations involving interpersonal communication. The guidelines below will help you to communicate effectively in such situations.

GUIDELINES FOR SPEAKING ON THE TELEPHONE

- When answering the telephone, begin by saying "Hello." Then identify your household or your place of business by saying something like "Perez residence" or "Dewey Middle School. Camilla Perez speaking. How may I help you?"
- When making a telephone call, wait for the person on the other end of the line to answer before speaking. Then identify yourself and ask for the person to whom you wish to speak.
- If you call a wrong number, or if someone calls you by mistake, do not simply hang up the telephone. Instead, say something like, "Sorry, I (or you, as the case may be) must have the wrong number."
- When receiving a call for someone who is not in, ask the caller if he or she would like to leave a message. If so, write down the name of the caller, the time of the call, whether the caller wishes his or her call returned, and any additional message that the caller wishes to leave.
- Before making a business call, think through clearly what you want to say and to whom. At the end of a business call, thank the person to whom you are speaking.

Try It Yourself

Exercise A. Read the following telephone conversation. Then, on your own paper, explain the ways in which the conversation violates the guidelines given above.

Caller: Hi. This is Bob. Let me speak to Mike.
Receptionist: Hello? Acton Tools, Yolanda Jones speaking. May I help you?

SPEAKING AND LISTENING SKILLS

INTRODUCING THE SKILL

Explain that interpersonal communication is simply communication between people in ordinary, everyday situations. Ask your students to suggest examples of interpersonal communication. Speaking on the telephone and face-to-face conversation are, of course, two of the most common.

PREVIEWING THE SKILL

Orally, in class, go over the guidelines in the boxes on pages 685 and 686. Ask students to come up with examples of interchanges that would violate each guideline.

PRACTICING THE SKILL

Assign Try It Yourself exercises A and B.

REVIEWING THE SKILL

Have students meet in small groups to discuss their responses to the exercises.

Answers for Try It Yourself

Exercise A

The caller violates the listed guidelines in the following ways:

- The caller does not wait for the person answering the telephone to speak first.
- The caller does not begin by saying, "Hello."
- The caller does not clearly identify the person to whom he wishes to speak.
- The caller does not thank the person to whom he is speaking.

In addition, the caller fails to use polite, formal language appropriate for a business call.

Exercise B

Responses will vary.

Try It Yourself (cont.)

Caller:	Yeah. This is Bob. Mike there?
Receptionist:	Do you mean Mr. Williams, sir?
Caller:	Yeah. Mike. Lemme speak to him.
Receptionist:	One moment, sir, and I'll connect you.
Caller:	Right.
Receptionist:	Mr. Williams is not in. May I take a message?
Caller:	Naw. Forget it.
Receptionist:	OK. Thank you, sir, and have a nice day.
Caller:	Great. Just great. (Caller hangs up.)

Guidelines for Holding Conversations

- Do not monopolize the conversation. Allow the other person ample time to speak and to respond, and be willing to discuss subjects of interest to the other person.
- When the other person is speaking, listen to what he or she is saying, and show by means of eye contact, facial expressions, and body language that you are listening.
- To ensure that you understand what the other person is saying, practice listening and reflecting. To do this, repeat back what the other person has said using your own words. For example, you might say, "So you mean that _______." If you have misunderstood the other person, he or she will then have an opportunity to correct the misunderstanding.
- Keep your emotions under control. If you find yourself becoming very emotional, pause to get your emotions under control. If doing so is not possible, suggest that you continue the conversation at a later time.
- Be conscious of what you are communicating by means of your tone, facial expressions, gestures, body language, and proximity (distance from the person to whom you are speaking).
- Do not change the subject until the discussion of that subject reaches a natural end.
- Use language appropriate to the relationship that you have with the other person. When speaking with people whom you do not know well, maintain an appropriate degree of formality. With older persons, use forms of address such as *Mr.* and *Ms.*

Try It Yourself

Exercise B. Pair up with a classmate and discuss your answers to the Guided Reading questions in the margins of chapters 1–5 of Book 2 of *The War of the Worlds.* As you discuss your answers, practice Rogerian listening. Then meet with your class as a whole to discuss the effectiveness of this listening technique.

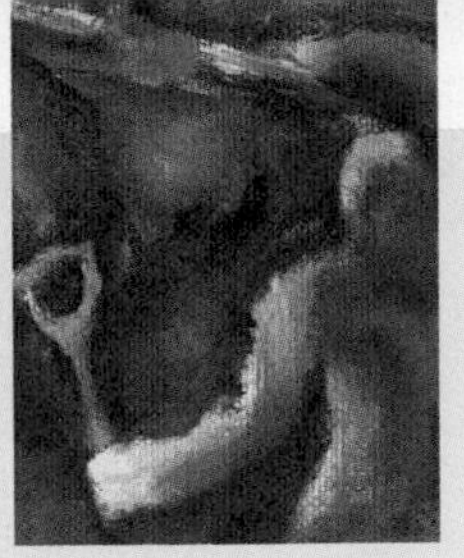

READER'S JOURNAL

Suppose that you were one of the survivors of the Martian invasion and had met other survivors and were living, secretly, somewhere in the wilderness as the Martians established their dominion over the Earth. What would you suggest that your small group of survivors do? What practical measures would you take? What long-range plans would you consider? Write about these questions in your journal.

6
The Work of Fifteen Days

For some time I stood tottering on the mound regardless of my safety. Within that noisome den from which I had emerged I had thought with a narrow intensity only of our immediate security. I had not realized what had been happening to the world, had not anticipated this startling vision of unfamiliar things. I had expected to see Sheen in ruins—I found about me the landscape, weird and lurid, of another planet.

For that moment I touched an emotion beyond the common range of men, yet one that the poor brutes we dominate know only too well. I felt as a rabbit might feel returning to his burrow and suddenly confronted by the work of a dozen busy navvies digging the foundations of a house. I felt the first inkling of a thing that presently grew quite clear in my mind, that oppressed me for many days, a sense of dethronement, a persuasion that I was no longer a master, but an animal among the animals, under the Martian heel. With us it would be as with them, to lurk and watch, to run and hide; the fear and empire of man had passed away.

But so soon as this strangeness had been realized it passed, and my dominant motive became the hunger of my long and dismal fast. In the direction away from the pit I saw beyond a red-covered wall, a patch of garden ground unburied. This gave me a hint, and I went knee-deep, and sometimes neck-deep, in the red weed. The density of the weed gave me a reassuring sense of hiding. The wall was some six feet high, and when I attempted to clamber it I found I could not lift my feet to the crest. So I went along by the side of it, and came to a corner and a rockwork that enabled me to get to the top and tumble into the garden I coveted. Here I found some young onions, a couple of gladiolus[1] bulbs, and a quantity of immature carrots, all of which I secured, and, scrambling over a ruined wall, went on my way through scarlet and crimson trees toward Kew—it was like walking through an avenue of gigantic blood-drops—possessed with two ideas: to get more food, and to limp, as soon and as far as my strength permitted, out of this accursed unearthly region of the pit.

Some way farther, in a grassy place, was a group of mushrooms which also I devoured, and then I came upon a broad sheet of flowing shallow water, where meadows used to be. These fragments of

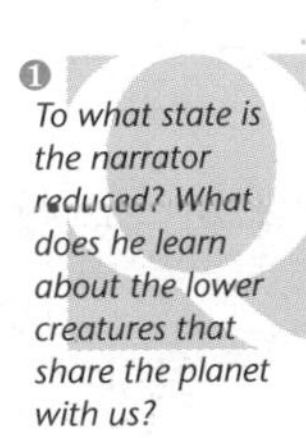

❶ *To what state is the narrator reduced? What does he learn about the lower creatures that share the planet with us?*

Chapter 6

1. **gladiolus.** Any of the plants in the iris family, with swordlike leaves and tall spikes of funnel-shaped flowers

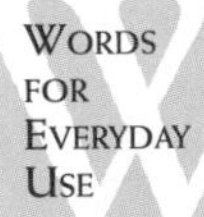

Words for Everyday Use

tot • ter (tät´ər) *v.*, rock or shake as if about to fall
noi • some (noi´səm) *adj.*, harmful to health
lu • rid (lo͞or´id) *adj.*, vivid in a harsh way
dom • i • nate (däm´ə nāt´) *v.*, rule or control by superior power or influence
de • throne • ment (dē thrōn´mənt) *n.*, act of ousting from any high position
cov • et (kuv´it) *v.*, long for with envy

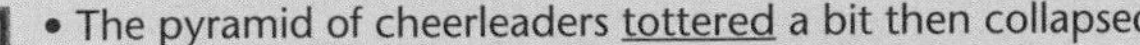

Reader's Journal

As an alternative activity, you might ask students to tell how they would end the novel if they were Wells and had reached this point in the story.

Answer to Guided Reading Question

❶ The narrator is reduced to the state of an animal. He learns what it is like to lurk and watch, to run and hide, in the face of a superior force that has no compassion.

Spelling and Vocabulary Words from the Selection

appalling, circuitously, countervailing, covet, culvert, cumbersome, cutlass, dethronement, devise, dominate, exuberance, fetish, fluorescent, formulate, impede, kinetic, languid, lurid, noisome, ornamental, piety, precipitate, reconnoiter, remorse, revulsion, singularly, somber, stout, succumb, taint, totter, unawares, vestige, vitality, whet

Vocabulary in Context

- The pyramid of cheerleaders tottered a bit then collapsed.
- The presence of asbestos in the walls has been shown to be noisome.
- The critics' reviews of the new novel were especially lurid.
- The defendiing champions dominated the challengers in the final game of the season.
- The dethronement of the captain was the result of a mutiny.
- All the neighbors coveted Mr. Johnson's new riding mower.

ANSWER TO GUIDED READING QUESTION

❶ The red weed dies due to some bacterial disease.

nourishment served only to whet my hunger. At first I was surprised at this flood in a hot, dry summer, but afterwards I discovered that it was caused by the tropical exuberance of the red weed. Directly this extraordinary growth encountered water it straightway became gigantic and of unparalleled fecundity.[2] Its seeds were simply poured down into the waters of the Wey and Thames, and its swiftly growing and Titanic water fronds speedily choked both those rivers.

At Putney, as I afterwards saw, the bridge was almost lost in a tangle of this weed, and at Richmond, too, the Thames waters poured in a broad and shallow stream across the meadows of Hampton and Twickenham. As the waters spread the weed followed them, until the ruined villas of the Thames Valley were for a time lost in this red swamp, whose margin I explored, and much of the desolation the Martians had caused was concealed.

❶ What happens to the red weed?

In the end the red weed succumbed almost as quickly as it had spread. A cankering[3] disease, due, it is believed, to the action of certain bacteria, presently seized upon it. Now by the action of natural selection, all terrestrial plants have acquired a resisting power against bacterial diseases—they never succumb without a severe struggle, but the red weed rotted like a thing already dead. The fronds became bleached, and then shriveled and brittle. They broke off at the least touch, and the waters that had stimulated their early growth carried their last vestiges out to sea.

My first act on coming to this water was, of course, to slake my thirst. I drank a great deal of it, and, moved by an impulse, gnawed some fronds of red weed; but they were watery, and had a sickly, metallic taste. I found the water was sufficiently shallow for me to wade securely, although the red weed impeded my feet a little; but the flood evidently got deeper toward the river, and I turned back to Mortlake. I managed to make out the road by means of occasional ruins of its villas and fences and lamps, and so presently I got out of this spate[4] and made my way to the hill going up toward Roehampton and came out on Putney Common.

Here the scenery changed from the strange and unfamiliar to the wreckage of the familiar: patches of ground exhibited the devastation of a cyclone, and in a few score yards I would come upon perfectly undisturbed spaces, houses with their blinds trimly drawn and doors closed, as if they had been left for a day by the owners, or as if their inhabitants slept within. The red weed was less abundant; the tall trees along the lane were free from the red creeper. I hunted for food among the trees, finding nothing, and I also raided a couple of silent houses, but they had already been broken into and ransacked. I rested for the remainder of the daylight in a shrubbery, being, in my enfeebled condition, too fatigued to push on.

All this time I saw no human beings, and no signs of the Martians. I encountered a couple of hungry-looking dogs but both hurried circuitously away from the advances I made them. Near Roehampton I had seen two human skeletons—not bodies, but skeletons, picked clean—and in the wood by me I found the crushed and scattered bones of several cats and rabbits and the skull of a sheep. But though I

2. **fecundity.** State of fertility or fruitfulness
3. **cankering.** Canker is a plant disease that causes decay
4. **spate.** Flash flood

WORDS FOR EVERYDAY USE

whet (wet) *v.,* stimulate
ex • u • ber • ance (eg zo͞o´bər əns) *n.,* great abundance; luxuriance
suc • cumb (sə kum´) *v.,* yield; submit; give way
ves • tige (ves´tij) *n.,* trace; bit
im • pede (im pēd´) *v.,* obstruct; delay
cir • cu • i • tous • ly (sər kyo͞o´ət əs lē) *adv.,* in a roundabout, indirect, or devious manner

VOCABULARY IN CONTEXT

- The smell of popcorn in the movie theater whetted Jacob's appetite.
- Although the king had great exuberance, he could not buy happiness.
- The two thieves were forced to succumb to the police when the realized they were surrounded.
- The two children picked up the last vestiges of toys left on the ground.
- The beaver dam impeded the flow of water down the river.
- Kurt told his parents about the broken lamp circuitously.

gnawed parts of these in my mouth, there was nothing to be got from them.

After sunset I struggled on along the road toward Putney, where I think the Heat-Ray must have been used for some reason. And in a garden beyond Roehampton I got a quantity of immature potatoes, sufficient to stay my hunger. From this garden one looked down upon Putney and the river. The aspect of the place in the dusk was singularly desolate: blackened trees, blackened, desolate ruins, and down the hill the sheets of the flooded river, red-tinged with the weed. And over all—silence. It filled me with indescribable terror to think how swiftly that desolating change had come.

For a time I believed that mankind had been swept out of existence, and that I stood there alone, the last man left alive. Hard by the top of Putney Hill I came upon another skeleton, with the arms dislocated and removed several yards from the rest of the body. As I proceeded I became more and more convinced that the extermination of mankind was, save for such stragglers as myself, already accomplished in this part of the world. The Martians, I thought, had gone on and left the country desolated, seeking food elsewhere. Perhaps even now they were destroying Berlin or Paris, or it might be they had gone northward.

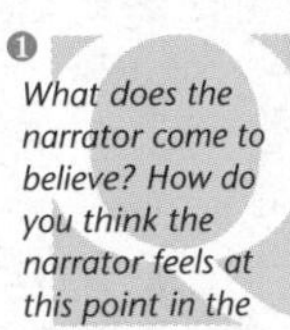

❶ *What does the narrator come to believe? How do you think the narrator feels at this point in the story?*

Reviewing the Selection

Recalling and Interpreting

1. Ⓡ What causes the red weed to die?

   Ⓘ Why is the red weed not immune to Earthly diseases?

2. Ⓡ What does the narrator feel as he stands on top of Putney Hill?

   Ⓘ Why might the narrator feel as he does? At this point in the novel, what do you think the narrator's expectations are for humanity as a whole?

Words for Everyday Use

sin • gu • lar • ly (siŋ´gyə lər lē) *adv.*, uniquely; exceptionally

Answer to Guided Reading Question

❶ The narrator comes to believe that human beings have been swept out of existence. There is a peculiar, shocked, numb feeling to the narrator's monologue at this point in the story.

Answers for Reviewing the Selection

RECALLING AND INTERPRETING

1. **Recalling.** A bacterial infection causes the red weed to die. **Interpreting.** The red weed is not immune to Earthly diseases because it is not native to Earth and has not been exposed to these diseases and built up antibodies to them.
2. **Recalling.** The narrator feels as though he were one of the last people left alive in this part of the world. **Interpreting.** The narrator has seen so much horror, so much helplessness from humans, and so much power on the part of the Martians that his expectations for humanity as a whole are quite low.

Vocabulary in Context

- The sky that night seemed singularly filled with stars.

Answers to Guided Reading Questions

❶ The narrator stands trial in the sense that, alone, he presents what he has done to God, the ultimate judge. The narrator decides that there was an inevitability to what happened and that he himself did not act criminally, for he did not foresee what would happen, and "crime is to foresee and do."

❷ The narrator thinks about the killing of the curate, the whereabouts of the Martians, and the fate of his wife.

7
The Man on Putney Hill

❶ *In what sense does the narrator stand trial? For what?*

❷ *About what three things does the narrator think?*

I spent that night in the inn that stands at the top of Putney Hill, sleeping in a made bed for the first time since my flight to Leatherhead. I will not tell the needless trouble I had breaking into that house—afterwards I found the front door was on the latch—nor how I ransacked every room for food, until, just on the verge of despair, in what seemed to me to be a servant's bedroom, I found a rat-gnawed crust and two tins of pineapple. The place had been already searched and emptied. In the bar I afterwards found some biscuits and sandwiches that had been overlooked. The latter I could not eat, they were too rotten, but the former not only stayed my hunger, but filled my pockets. I lit no lamps, fearing some Martian might come beating that part of London for food in the night. Before I went to bed I had an interval of restlessness, and prowled from window to window, peering out for some sign of these monsters. I slept little. As I lay in bed I found myself thinking consecutively—a thing I do not remember to have done since my last argument with the curate. During all the intervening time my mental condition had been a hurrying succession of vague emotional states or a sort of stupid receptivity. But in the night my brain, reinforced, I suppose, by the food I had eaten, grew clear again, and I thought.

Three things struggled for possession of my mind: the killing of the curate, the whereabouts of the Martians, and the possible fate of my wife. The former gave me no sensation of horror or remorse to recall; I saw it simply as a thing done, a memory infinitely disagreeable but quite without the quality of remorse. I saw myself then as I see myself now, driven step by step toward that hasty blow, the creature of a sequence of accidents leading inevitably to that. I felt no condemnation; yet the memory, static, unprogressive, haunted me. In the silence of the night, with that sense of the nearness of God that sometimes comes into the stillness and the darkness, I stood my trial, my only trial, for that moment of wrath and fear. I retraced every step of our conversation from the moment when I had found him crouching beside me, heedless of my thirst, and pointing to the fire and smoke that streamed up from the ruins of Weybridge. We had been incapable of cooperation—grim chance had taken no heed of that. Had I foreseen, I should have left him at Halliford. But I did not foresee; and crime is to foresee and do. And I set this down as I have set all this story down, as it was. There were no witnesses—all these things I might have concealed. But I set it down, and the reader must form his judgment as he will.

And when, by an effort, I had set aside that picture of a prostrate body, I faced the problem of the Martians and the fate of my wife. For the former I had no data; I could imagine a hundred things, and so, unhappily, I could for the latter. And suddenly that night became terrible. I found myself sitting up in bed, staring at the dark. I found myself praying that the Heat-Ray might have suddenly and painlessly struck her out of being. Since the night of my return from Leatherhead I had not prayed. I had uttered prayers, fetish prayers, had prayed as heathens mutter charms when I was in extremity; but now I prayed indeed, pleading steadfastly and sanely, face to face

Words for Everyday Use

re • morse (ri môrs´) *n.,* deep, torturing sense of guilt

fet • ish (fet´ish) *adj.,* having devotion that is too strong

Vocabulary in Context

- Billy felt great remorse that his friend Alex did not make the team.
- Anna's fetish belief that she would get an A on the test was crushed when the results were posted.

with the darkness of God. Strange night! strangest in this, that so soon as dawn had come, I, who had talked with God, crept out of the house like a rat leaving its hiding-place—a creature scarcely larger, an inferior animal, a thing that for any passing whim of our masters might be hunted and killed. Perhaps they also prayed confidently to God. Surely, if we have learned nothing else, this war has taught us pity—pity for those witless souls that suffer our dominion.

The morning was bright and fine, and the eastern sky glowed pink, and was fretted with little golden clouds. In the road that runs from the top of Putney Hill to Wimbledon was a number of poor vestiges of the panic torrent that must have poured Londonward on the Sunday night after the fighting began. There was a little two-wheeled cart inscribed with the name of Thomas Lobb, Greengrocer, New Malden, with a smashed wheel and an abandoned tin trunk; there was a straw hat trampled into the now hardened mud, and at the top of West Hill a lot of blood-stained glass about the overturned water-trough. My movements were languid, my plans of the vaguest. I had an idea of going to Leatherhead, though I knew that there I had the poorest chance of finding my wife. Certainly, unless death had overtaken them suddenly, my cousins and she would have fled thence; but it seemed to me I might find or learn there whither the Surrey people had fled. I knew I wanted to find my wife, that my heart ached for her and the world of men, but I had no clear idea how the finding might be done. I was also sharply aware now of my intense loneliness. From the corner I went, under cover of a thicket

1 *What does the narrator believe that people should have learned from the war with the Martians?*

Words for Everyday Use

lan • guid (laŋ´gwid) *adj.,* weak; without interest

Answer to Guided Reading Question

1 The narrator believes that this war should have taught people "pity for those witless souls that suffer our dominion" (i.e., for animals).

Quotables

"The crazy combative patriotism that plainly threatens to destroy civilization is very largely begotten by the schoolmaster and the schoolmistress in their history lessons. They take the growing mind at a naturally barbaric phase and they inflame and fix its barbarism."

—H. G. Wells

Vocabulary in Context

- The interest of the students in today's lesson was languid.

Answers to Guided Reading Questions

❶ The man on the hill is the artilleryman with whom the narrator spoke earlier.

❷ The man on the hill lays claim to all the hill down to the river, back to Clapham, and up to the edge of the common.

of trees and bushes, to the edge of Wimbledon Common, stretching wide and far.

That dark expanse was lit in patches by yellow gorse and broom;[1] there was no red weed to be seen, and as I prowled, hesitating, on the verge of the open, the sun rose, flooding it all with light and vitality. I came upon a busy swarm of little frogs in a swampy place among the trees. I stopped to look at them, drawing a lesson from their stout resolve to live. And presently, turning suddenly, with an odd feeling of being watched, I beheld something crouching amid a clump of bushes. I stood regarding this. I made a step toward it, and it rose up and became a man armed with a cutlass. I approached him slowly. He stood silent and motionless, regarding me.

❶ *Who is the man on the hill?*

As I drew nearer I perceived he was dressed in clothes as dusty and filthy as my own; he looked, indeed, as though he had been dragged through a culvert. Nearer, I distinguished the green slime of ditches mixing with the pale drab of dried clay and shiny, coaly patches. His black hair fell over his eyes, and his face was dark and dirty and sunken, so that at first I did not recognize him. There was a red cut across the lower part of his face.

"Stop!" he cried, when I was within ten yards of him, and I stopped. His voice was hoarse. "Where do you come from?" he said.

I thought, surveying him.

"I come from Mortlake," I said. "I was buried near the pit the Martians made about their cylinder. I have worked my way out and escaped."

❷ *To what does the man on the hill lay claim? Why? To what state has political order fallen?*

"There is no food about here," he said. "This is my country. All this hill down to the river, and back to Clapham, and up to the edge of the common. There is only food for one. Which way are you going?"

I answered slowly.

"I don't know," I said. "I have been buried in the ruins of a house thirteen or fourteen days. I don't know what has happened."

He looked at me doubtfully, then started, and looked with a changed expression.

"I've no wish to stop about here," said I. "I think I shall go to Leatherhead, for my wife was there."

He shot out a pointing finger.

"It is you," said he—"the man from Woking. And you weren't killed at Weybridge?"

I recognized him at the same moment.

"You are the artilleryman who came into my garden."

"Good luck!" he said. "We are lucky ones! Fancy *you*!" He put out a hand, and I took it. "I crawled up a drain," he said. "But they didn't kill everyone. And after they went away I got off toward Walton across the fields. But—It's not sixteen days altogether—and your hair is gray." He looked over his shoulder suddenly. "Only a rook," he said. "One gets to know that birds have shadows these days. This *is* a bit open. Let us crawl under those bushes and talk."

"Have you seen any Martians?" I said. "Since I crawled out—"

"They've gone away across London," he said. "I guess they've got a bigger camp there. Of a night, all over there, Hampstead way, the sky is alive with their lights. It's like a great city, and in the glare you can just see them moving. By daylight you can't. But nearer—I haven't seen them—" (he counted on his fingers) "five days. Then I saw a couple across Hammersmith way carrying something big. And the

Chapter 7

1. **gorse and broom.** Types of shrubs

Words for Everyday Use

vi • tal • i • ty (vī tal´ə tē) *n.*, power to live

stout (stout) *adj.*, powerful; forceful

cut • lass (kut´ləs) *n.*, short, thick, curving sword with a single cutting edge

cul • vert (kul´vərt) *n.*, drain that passes under a road

Vocabulary in Context

- Ever since she began eating right and exercising, Donna has had tremendous vitality.
- Paul's desire to learn how to play the oboe was strong and stout.
- Pretending to be a pirate, little Peter held his stick up in the air as if it were a cutlass.
- A blockage in the culvert created flooding in the streets.

night before last"—he stopped and spoke impressively—"it was just a matter of lights, but it was something up in the air. I believe they've built a flying-machine, and are learning to fly."

I stopped, on hands and knees, for we had come to the bushes.

"Fly!"

"Yes," he said, "fly."

I went on into a little bower, and sat down.

"It is all over with humanity," I said. "If they can do that they will simply go round the world."

He nodded.

"They will. But—It will relieve things over here a bit. And besides—" He looked at me. "Aren't you satisfied it *is* up with humanity? I am. We're down; we're beat."

I stared. Strange as it may seem, I had not arrived at this fact—a fact perfectly obvious so soon as he spoke. I had still held a vague hope; rather, I had kept a lifelong habit of mind. He repeated his words, "We're beat." They carried absolute conviction.

"It's all over," he said. "They've lost *one*—just *one*. And they've made their footing good and crippled the greatest power in the world. They've walked over us. The death of that one at Weybridge was an accident. And these are only pioneers. They keep on coming. These green stars—I've seen none these five or six days, but I've no doubt they're falling somewhere every night. Nothing's to be done. We're under! We're beat!"

I made him no answer. I sat staring before me, trying in vain to devise some countervailing thought.

"This isn't a war," said the artilleryman. "It never was a war, any more than there's war between men and ants."

Suddenly I recalled the night in the observatory.

"After the tenth shot they fired no more—at least, until the first cylinder came."

"How do you know?" said the artilleryman. I explained. He thought. "Something wrong with the gun," he said. "But what if there is? They'll get it right again. And even if there's a delay, how can it alter the end? It's just men and ants. There's the ants build their cities, live their lives, have wars, revolutions, until the men want them out of the way, and then they go out of the way. That's what we are now—just ants. Only—"

"Yes," I said.

"We're eatable ants."

We sat looking at each other.

"And what will they do with us?" I said.

"That's what I've been thinking," he said—"that's what I've been thinking. After Weybridge I went south—thinking. I saw what was up. Most of the people were hard at it squealing and exciting themselves. But I'm not so fond of squealing. I've been in sight of death once or twice; I'm not an ornamental soldier, and at the best and worst, death—it's just death. And it's the man that keeps on thinking comes through. I saw everyone tracking away south. Says I, "Food won't last this way," and I turned right back. I went for the Martians like a sparrow goes for man. All round"—he waved a hand to the horizon—"they're starving in heaps, bolting, treading on each other."

He saw my face, and halted awkwardly.

"No doubt lots who had money have gone away to France," he said. He seemed to hesitate whether to apologize, met my eyes, and went on: "There's food all about here. Canned things in shops; wines, spirits,

❶ *On what do the two men agree?*

❷ *In what sense was there never a war?*

Words for Everyday Use

de • vise (di vīz´) *v.,* create by thinking; plan

coun • ter • vail • ing (kount´ər vāl´iŋ) *adj.,* compensating; counteracting

or • na • men • tal (ôr´nə ment´'l) *adj.,* serving as an ornament; decorative

Answers to Guided Reading Questions

❶ They agree that it is all over for humanity.

❷ There never was a war in the sense that a real war requires combatants with somewhat similar strength, not ones as unequal as men and ants.

Vocabulary in Context

- The general devised a plan to overtake the enemy.
- Most students thought school would be canceled; however, the countervailing opinion among the teachers was that school would be open.
- The ornamental posters seemed to give new life to the classroom.

Answers to Guided Reading Questions

➊ The artilleryman doesn't seem to think much of upper-class manners. He expects these to be of no further use.

➋ The Martians will start picking the best people and storing them in cages.

➌ He considers the artilleryman "a man, indeed" because this man has a plan for regaining control from the Martians. The artilleryman is considering ways to make the defeated condition of humans temporary.

➊ *What does the artilleryman think of upper-class manners?*

➋ *What does the artilleryman think that the Martians will do after they are in full control?*

➌ *Why does the narrator think the artilleryman "a man, indeed"?*

mineral waters; and the water mains and drains are empty. Well, I was telling you what I was thinking. 'Here's intelligent things,' I said, 'and it seems they want us for food. First, they'll smash us up—ships, machines, guns, cities, all the order and organization. All that will go. If we were the size of ants we might pull through. But we're not. It's all too bulky to stop. That's the first certainty.' Eh?"

I assented.

"It is; I've thought it out. Very well, then—next; at present we're caught as we're wanted. A Martian has only to go a few miles to get a crowd on the run. And I saw one, one day, out by Wandsworth, picking houses to pieces and routing among the wreckage. But they won't keep on doing that. So soon as they've settled all our guns and ships, and smashed our railways, and done all the things they are doing over there, they will begin catching us systematic, picking the best and storing us in cages and things. That's what they will start doing in a bit. Lord! they haven't begun on us yet. Don't you see that?"

"Not begun!" I exclaimed.

"Not begun. All that's happened so far is through our not having the sense to keep quiet—worrying them with guns and such foolery. And losing our heads, and rushing off in crowds to where there wasn't any more safety than where we were. They don't want to bother us yet. They're making their things—making all the things they couldn't bring with them, getting things ready for the rest of their people. Very likely that's why the cylinders have stopped for a bit, for fear of hitting those who are here. And instead of our rushing about blind, on the howl, or getting dynamite on the chance of busting them up, we've got to fix ourselves up according to the new state of affairs. That's how I figure it out. It isn't quite according to what a man wants for his species, but it's about what the facts point to. And that's the principle I acted upon. Cities, nations, civilization, progress—it's all over. That game's up. We're beat."

"But if that is so, what is there to live for?"

The artilleryman looked at me for a moment.

"There won't be any more blessed concerts for a million years or so; there won't be any Royal Academy of Arts, and no nice little feeds at restaurants. If it's amusement you're after, I reckon the game is up. If you've got any drawing-room manners or a dislike to eating peas with a knife or dropping aitches, you'd better chuck 'em away. They ain't no further use."

"You mean—"

"I mean that men like me are going on living—for the sake of the breed. I tell you, I'm grim set on living. And if I'm not mistaken, you'll show what insides *you've* got, too, before long. We aren't going to be exterminated. And I don't mean to be caught, either, and tamed and fattened and bred like a thundering ox. Ugh! Fancy those brown creepers!"

"You don't mean to say—"

"I do. I'm going on. Under their feet. I've got it planned; I've thought it out. We men are beat. We don't know enough. We've got to learn before we've got a chance. And we've got to live and keep independent while we learn. See! That's what has to be done."

I stared, astonished, and stirred profoundly by the man's resolution.

"Great God!" cried I. "But you are a man, indeed!" And suddenly I gripped his hand.

"Eh!" he said, with his eyes shining. "I've thought it out, eh?"

"Go on," I said.

"Well, those who mean to escape their catching must get ready. I'm getting ready. Mind you, it isn't all of us that are made for wild beasts; and that's what it's got to be. That's why I watched you. I had my doubts. You're slender. I didn't know that it was you, you see, or just how you'd been buried. All these—the sort of people that lived in these houses, and all those damn little clerks that used to live down that way—they'd be no good. They haven't any spirit in them—no proud dreams and no proud lusts; and a man who hasn't one or the other—Lord! what is he but funk[2] and precautions? They just used to skedaddle[3] off to work—I've seen hundreds of 'em, bit of breakfast in hand, running wild and shining to catch their little season-ticket train, for fear they'd get dismissed if they didn't; working at businesses they were afraid to take the trouble to understand; skedaddling back for fear they wouldn't be in time for dinner; keeping indoors after dinner for fear of the black streets, and sleeping with the wives they married, not because they wanted them, but because they had a bit of money that would make for safety in their one little miserable skedaddle through the world. Lives insured and a bit invested for fear of accidents. And on Sundays—fear of the hereafter. As if hell was built for rabbits! Well, the Martians will just be a godsend to these. Nice roomy cages, fattening food, careful breeding, no worry. After a week or so chasing about the fields and lands on empty stomachs, they'll come and be caught cheerful. They'll be quite glad after a bit. They'll wonder what people did before there were Martians to take care of them. And the bar-loafers, and mashers, and singers—I can imagine them. I can imagine them," he said, with a sort of somber gratification. "There'll be any amount of sentiment and religion loose among them. There's hundreds of things I saw with my eyes that I've only begun to see clearly these last few days. There's lots will take things as they are—fat and stupid; and lots will be worried by a sort of feeling that it's all wrong, and that they ought to be doing something. Now whenever things are so that a lot of people feel they ought to be doing something, the weak, and those who go weak with a lot of complicated thinking, always make for a sort of do-nothing religion, very pious and superior, and submit to persecution and the will of the Lord. Very likely you've seen the same thing. It's energy in a gale of funk, and turned clean inside out. These cages will be full of psalms and hymns and piety. And those of a less simple sort will work in a bit of—what is it?—eroticism."

He paused.

"Very likely these Martians will make pets of some of them; train them to do tricks—who knows?—get sentimental over the pet boy who grew up and had to be killed. And some, maybe, they will train to hunt us."

"No," I cried, "that's impossible! No human being—"

"What's the good of going on with such lies?" said the artilleryman. "There's men who'd do it cheerful. What nonsense to pretend there isn't!"

And I succumbed to his conviction.

"If they come after me," he said—"Lord! if they come after me!" and subsided into a grim meditation.

I sat contemplating these things. I could find nothing to bring against this man's reasoning. In the days before the invasion no one would have questioned my intellectual superiority to his—I, a professed and recognized writer on philosophical themes, and he, a common soldier; and yet he had already formulated a situation that I had scarcely realized.

2. **funk.** Fear
3. **skedaddle.** Informal term meaning to run or scurry away

❶ *To what creatures does the artilleryman compare the average person? Why will the Martians, in his view, "be a godsend" to such people?*

❷ *What does the narrator admire about the artilleryman?*

WORDS FOR EVERYDAY USE

som • ber (säm´bər) *adj.*, dark and gloomy or dull
pi • e • ty (pī´ə tē) *n.*, devotion to religious duties and practices
for • mu • late (fôr´myo͞o lāt´) *v.*, work out in one's mind; develop

ANSWERS TO GUIDED READING QUESTIONS

❶ The artilleryman compares the average person to rabbits. The Martians will "be a godsend" to such people because they will have everything taken care of for them.

❷ The artilleryman has already formulated a situation that the narrator, a professional writer on philosophical themes, has scarcely realized.

VOCABULARY IN CONTEXT

- The somber mood of the family told Henrietta that something was wrong.
- In many ancient societies, piety was required of its members.
- The night before the big match, Rita formulated how she would beat her opponent.

Answers to Guided Reading Questions

❶ The artilleryman proposes to live underground.

❷ The artilleryman's long-range plan is to learn everything the Martians know and to use the Martians' own knowlege against them.

"What are you doing?" I said, presently. "What plans have you made?"

He hesitated.

"Well, it's like this," he said. "What have we to do? We have to invent a sort of life where men can live and breed, and be sufficiently secure to bring the children up. Yes—wait a bit, and I'll make it clearer what I think ought to be done. The tame ones will go like all tame beasts; in a few generations they'll be big, beautiful, rich-blooded, stupid—rubbish! The risk is that we who keep wild will go savage—degenerate into a sort of big, savage rat. . . . You see, how I mean to live is underground. I've been thinking about the drains. Of course, those who don't know drains think horrible things; but under this London are miles and miles—hundreds of miles—and a few days' rain and London empty will leave them sweet and clean. The main drains are big enough and airy enough for anyone. Then there's cellars, vaults, stores, from which bolting passages may be made to the drains. And the railway tunnels and subways. Eh? You begin to see? And we form a band—able-bodied, clean-minded men. We're not going to pick up any rubbish that drifts in. Weaklings go out again."

Where does the artilleryman propose to live? ❶

"As you meant me to go?"

"Well—I parleyed, didn't I?"

"We won't quarrel about that. Go on."

"Those who stop obey orders. Able-bodied, clean-minded women we want also—mothers and teachers. No lackadaisical ladies—no blasted rolling eyes. We can't have any weak or silly. Life is real again, and the useless and cumbersome and mischievous have to die. They ought to die. They ought to be willing to die. It's a sort of disloyalty, after all, to live and taint the race. And they can't be happy. Moreover, dying's none so dreadful; it's the funking makes it bad. And in all those places we shall gather. Our district will be London. And we may even be able to keep a watch, and run about in the open when the Martians keep away. Play cricket, perhaps. That's how we shall save the race. Eh? It's a possible thing? But saving the race is nothing in itself. As I say, that's only being rats. It's saving our knowledge and adding to it is the thing. There men like you come in. There's books, there's models. We must make great safe places down deep, and get all the books we can; not novels and poetry swipes,[4] but ideas, science books. That's where men like you come in. We must go to the British Museum and pick all those books through. Especially we must keep up our science—learn more. We must watch these Martians. Some of us must go as spies. When it's all working, perhaps I will. Get caught, I mean. And the great thing is, we must leave the Martians alone. We mustn't even steal. If we get in their way, we clear out. We must show them we mean no harm. Yes, I know. But they're intelligent things, and they won't hunt us down if they have all they want, and think we're just harmless vermin."

What is the artilleryman's long-range plan? ❷

The artilleryman paused and laid a brown hand upon my arm

"After all, it may not be so much we may have to learn before—Just imagine this: Four or five of their fighting-machines suddenly starting off—Heat-Rays right and left, and not a Martian in 'em. Not a Martian in 'em, but men—men who have learned the way how. It may be in my time, even—those men. Fancy having one of them lovely things, with its Heat-Ray

4. **swipes.** Implying that poetry books are thin and useless

Words for Everyday Use

cum • ber • some (kum´bər səm) *adj.*, hard to handle because of size or weight; clumsy; burdensome

taint (tānt) *v.*, poison; corrupt; stain

Vocabulary in Context

- The old refrigerator was cumbersome and difficult to move out of the house.
- The EPA investigates landfills which could possibly taint the local water supply.

wide and free! Fancy having it in control! What would it matter if you smashed to smithereens at the end of the run, after a bust like that? I reckon the Martians'll open their beautiful eyes! Can't you see them, man? Can't you see them hurrying, hurrying—puffing and blowing and hooting to their other mechanical affairs? Something out of gear in every case. And swish, bang, rattle, swish! just as they are fumbling over it, *swish* comes the Heat-Ray, and, behold! man has come back to his own."

For a while the imaginative daring of the artilleryman, and the tone of assurance and courage he assumed, completely dominated my mind. I believed unhesitatingly both in his forecast of human destiny and in the practicability of his astonishing scheme, and the reader who thinks me susceptible and foolish must contrast his position, reading steadily with all his thoughts about his subject, and mine, crouching fearfully in the bushes and listening, distracted by apprehension. We talked in this manner through the early morning time, and later crept out of the bushes, and, after scanning the sky for Martians, hurried precipitately to the house on Putney Hill where he had made his lair. It was the coal-cellar of the place, and when I saw the work he had spent a week upon—it was a burrow scarcely ten yards long, which he designed to reach to the main drain on Putney Hill—I had my first inkling of the gulf between his dreams and his powers. Such a hole I could have dug in a day. But I believed in him sufficiently to work with him all that morning until past mid-day at his digging. We had a garden-barrow and shot the earth we removed against the kitchen range. We refreshed ourselves with a tin of mock-turtle soup and wine from the neighboring pantry. I found a curious relief from the aching strangeness of the world in this steady labor. As we worked, I turned his project over in my mind, and presently objections and doubts began to arise; but I worked there all the morning, so glad was I to find myself with a purpose again. After working an hour I began to speculate on the distance one had to go before the cloaca[5] was reached, the chances we had of missing it altogether. My immediate trouble was why we should dig this long tunnel, when it was possible to get into the drain at once down one of the manholes, and work back to the house. It seemed to me, too, that the house was inconveniently chosen, and required a needless length of tunnel. And just as I was beginning to face these things, the artilleryman stopped digging, and looked at me.

❶ *In what does the narrator believe?*

❷ *What causes the narrator to begin to doubt the artilleryman?*

5. **cloaca.** Sewer or cesspool

Words for Everyday Use

pre • cip • i • tate • ly (prē sip´ə tit lē) *adv.*, very suddenly

Answers to Guided Reading Questions

❶ The narrator believes unhesitatingly in the artilleryman's forecast of human destiny and in the pratical nature of the artilleryman's scheme for human survival.

❷ The narrator begins to doubt the artilleryman when he sees how little has already been dug of the tunnel that would take them to the main drain on Putney Hill.

Vocabulary in Context

• The dog precipitately began barking at the darkness.

Answer to Guided Reading Question

❶ The narrator is beginning to understand that the artilleryman is a big talker but not a big doer. In short, the artilleryman is lazy.

"We're working well," he said. He put down his spade. "Let us knock off a bit," he said. "I think it's time we reconnoitered from the roof of the house."

I was for going on, and after a little hesitation he resumed his spade; and then suddenly I was struck by a thought. I stopped, and so did he at once.

"Why were you walking about the Common," I said, "instead of being here?"

"Taking the air," he said. "I was coming back. It's safer by night."

"But the work?"

"Oh, one can't always work," he said, and in a flash I saw the man plain. He hesitated, holding his spade. "We ought to reconnoiter now," he said, "because if any come near they may hear the spades and drop upon us unawares."

I was no longer disposed to object. We went together to the roof and stood on a ladder peeping out of the roof door. No Martians were to be seen, and we ventured out on the tiles, and slipped down under shelter of the parapet.

What is the narrator beginning to understand about the artilleryman? ❶

From this position a shrubbery hid the greater portion of Putney, but we could see the river below, a bubbly mass of red weed, and the low parts of Lambeth flooded and red. The red creeper swarmed up the trees about the old palace, and their branches stretched gaunt and dead, and set with shriveled leaves, from amid its clusters. It was strange how entirely dependent both these things were upon flowing water for their propagation. About us neither had gained a footing; laburnums, pink mays, snowballs, and trees of arborvitae, rose out of laurels and hydrangeas, green and brilliant into the sunlight. Beyond Kensington dense smoke was rising, and that and a blue haze hid the northward hills.

The artilleryman began to tell me of the sort of people who still remained in London.

"One night last week," he said, "some fools got the electric light in order, and there was all Regent's Street and the Circus ablaze, crowded with painted and ragged drunkards, men and women, dancing and shouting till dawn. A man who was there told me. And as the day came they became aware of a fighting-machine standing near by the Langham and looking down at them. Heaven knows how long he had been there. It must have given some of them a nasty turn. He came down the road toward them, and picked up nearly a hundred too drunk or frightened to run away."

Grotesque gleam of a time no history will ever fully describe!

From that, in answer to my questions, he came round to his grandiose plans again. He grew enthusiastic. He talked so eloquently of the possibility of capturing a fighting-machine that I more than half believed in him again. But now that I was beginning to understand something of his quality, I could divine the stress he laid on doing nothing precipitately. And I noted that now there was no question that he personally was to capture and fight the great machine.

After a time we went down to the cellar. Neither of us seemed disposed to resume digging, and when he suggested a meal, I was nothing loath.[6] He became suddenly very generous and was inclined to regard my coming as a great occasion. . . .

And pursuant to this idea of a holiday, he insisted upon playing cards after we had eaten. He taught me euchre,[7] and after dividing London between us, I tak-

6. **nothing loath.** Not reluctant
7. **euchre.** Card game

Words for Everyday Use

rec • on • noi • ter (rek´ə noit´ ər) *v.,* examine or spy on an area
un • a • wares (un ə werz´) *adv.,* unexpectedly; suddenly; by surprise

Vocabulary in Context

- The soldier was sent to reconnoiter the position of the enemy camp.
- Tori was afraid that Heath might come upon her unawares while she was typing.

ing the northern side and he the southern, we played for parish points.[8] Grotesque and foolish as this will seem to the sober reader, it is absolutely true, and, what is more remarkable, I found the card game and several others we played extremely interesting.

Strange mind of man! that, with our species upon the edge of extermination or appalling degradation, with no clear prospect before us but the chance of a horrible death, we could sit following the chance of this painted pasteboard, and playing the "joker"[9] with vivid delight. Afterwards he taught me poker, and I beat him at three tough chess games. When dark came we decided to take the risk, and lit a lamp.

After an interminable string of games, we supped. The artilleryman was no longer the energetic regenerator of his species I had encountered in the morning. He was still optimistic, but it was a less kinetic, a more thoughtful optimism. I remember he wound up with my health, proposed in a speech of small variety and considerable intermittence. I went upstairs to look at the lights of which he had spoken, that blazed so greenly along the Highgate hills.

At first I stared unintelligently across the London valley. The northern hills were shrouded in darkness; the fires near Kensington glowed redly, and now and then an orange-red tongue of flame flashed up and vanished in the deep blue night. All the rest of London was black. Then, nearer, I perceived a strange light, a pale, violet-purple fluorescent glow, quivering under the night breeze. For a space I could not understand it, and then I knew that it must be the red weed from which this faint irradiation proceeded. With that realization my dormant sense of wonder, my sense of the proportion of things, awoke again. I glanced from that to Mars, red and clear, glowing high in the west, and then gazed long and earnestly at the darkness of Hampstead and Highgate.

I remained a very long time upon the roof, wondering at the grotesque changes of the day. I recalled my mental states from the midnight prayer to the foolish card-playing. I had a violent revulsion of feeling. My folly came to me with glaring exaggeration. I seemed a traitor to my wife and to my kind; I was filled with remorse. I resolved to leave this strange undisciplined dreamer of great things to his drink and gluttony, and to go on into London. There, it seemed to me, I had the best chance of learning what the Martians and my fellow-men were doing. I was still upon the roof when the late moon rose.

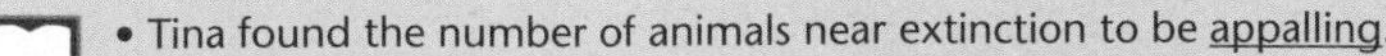

8. **parish points.** The stakes were London parishes or districts, not money

9. **joker.** The high card in euchre.

❶ *What is "grotesque and foolish" about the card game?*

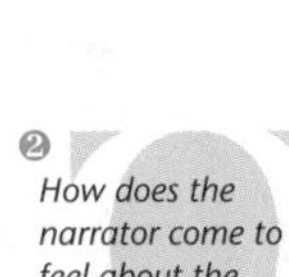

❷ *How does the narrator come to feel about the artilleryman? Why?*

WORDS FOR EVERYDAY USE

ap • pall • ing (ə pôl´iŋ) *adj.* causing horror or shock

ki • net • ic (ki net´ik) *adj.*, energetic or dynamic

flu • o • res • cent (flo͞o´ə res´ənt) *adj.*, producing light when acted on by radiation

re • vul • sion (ri vul´shən) *n.*, sudden, complete and violent change

Answers to Guided Reading Questions

❶ It is grotesque and foolish that the two men should make so light of the current situation as to play a card game based on it.

❷ The narrator comes to feel that the artilleryman is simply a hedonistic dreamer.

Vocabulary in Context

- Tina found the number of animals near extinction to be appalling.
- The kinetic performance of the dancers was inspiring.
- The fluorescent lamp lit up the whole basement.
- Nick was at first opposed to the idea, but apparently had a revulsion of opinion.

ANSWERS FOR REVIEWING THE SELECTION

RECALLING AND INTERPRETING

1. **Recalling.** The narrator meets the artilleryman. **Interpreting.** This person is claiming ownership of the surrounding land and its resources.

2. **Recalling.** The artilleryman plans to hide out with other people under the city, to learn about the Martian ways, and eventually to mount an insurrection. The artilleryman has not gone far toward carrying out his plans. **Interpreting.** The narrator recognizes that the artilleryman likes to talk big but does not like to work.

ANSWER TO GUIDED READING QUESTION

❶ The black dust is left over from the black vapor.

Reviewing the Selection

RECALLING AND INTERPRETING

1. Ⓡ Whom does the narrator meet on top of Putney Hill?

   Ⓘ Why does the person on top of Putney Hill challenge the narrator on first meeting him?

2. Ⓡ What dreams for the future does the artilleryman have? How far has the artilleryman gotten in carrying out his plans?

   Ⓘ What causes the narrator's feelings toward the artilleryman to change?

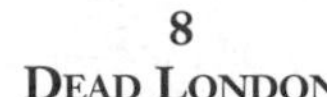

8
DEAD LONDON

After I had parted from the artilleryman, I went down the hill, and by the High Street across the bridge to Fulham. The red weed was tumultuous at that time, and nearly choked the bridge roadway; but its fronds were already whitened in patches by the spreading disease that presently removed it so swiftly.

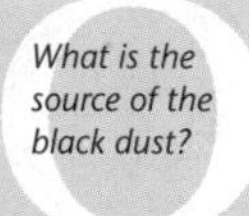

What is the source of the black dust? ❶

At the corner of the lane that runs to Putney Bridge station I found a man lying. He was as black as a sweep with the black dust. I could get nothing from him but curses and furious lunges at my head. I think I should have stayed by him but for the brutal expression of his face.

There was black dust along the roadway from the bridge onwards, and it grew thicker in Fulham. The streets were horribly quiet. I got food—sour, hard, and moldy, but quite eatable—in a baker's shop here. Some way toward Walham Green the streets became clear of powder, and I passed a white terrace of houses on fire; the noise of the burning was an absolute relief. Going on toward Brompton, the streets were quiet again.

Here I came once more upon the black powder in the streets and upon dead bodies. I saw altogether about a dozen in the length of the Fulham Road. They had been dead many days, so that I hurried quickly past them. The black powder covered them over, and softened their outlines. One or two had been disturbed by dogs.

Where there was no black powder, it was curiously like a Sunday in the City, with the closed shops, the houses locked up and the blinds drawn, the desertion, and the stillness. In some places plunderers had been at work, but rarely at other than the provision shops. A jeweler's window had been broken open in one place, but apparently the thief had been disturbed, and a number of gold chains and a watch were scattered on the pavement. I did not trouble to touch them. Farther on was a tattered woman in a heap on a doorstep; the hand that hung over her knee was gashed and bled down her rusty brown dress. She seemed asleep, but she was dead.

The farther I penetrated into London, the profounder grew the stillness. But it was not so much the stillness of death—it was the stillness of suspense, of expectation. At any time the destruction that had already singed the northwestern borders of the metropolis, and had annihilated Ealing and Kilburn, might strike among these houses and leave them smoking ruins. It was a city condemned and derelict. . . .

In South Kensington the streets were cleared of dead and of black powder. It was near South Kensington that I first heard the howling. It crept almost imperceptibly upon my senses. It was a sobbing alternation of two notes, "Ulla, ulla, ulla, ulla," keeping on perpetually. When I passed streets that ran northward it grew in volume, and houses and buildings seemed to deaden and cut it off again. It came in a full tide down Exhibition Road. I stopped, staring toward Kensington Gardens, wondering at this strange, remote wailing. It was as if that mighty desert of houses had found a voice for its fear and solitude.

"Ulla, ulla, ulla, ulla," wailed that superhuman note—great waves of sound sweeping down the broad, sunlit roadway, between the tall buildings on each side. I turned northward, marveling, toward the iron gates of Hyde Park. I had half a mind to break into the Natural History Museum and find my way up to the summits of the towers, in order to see across the park. But I decided to keep to the ground, where quick hiding was possible, and so went on up the Exhibition Road. All the large mansions on each side of the road were empty and still, and my footsteps echoed against the sides of the houses. At the top, near the park gate, I came upon a strange sight—a bus overturned, and the skeleton of a horse picked clean. I puzzled over this for a time, and then went on to the bridge over the Serpentine. The voice grew stronger and stronger, though I could see nothing above the housetops on the north side of the park, save a haze of smoke to the northwest.

"Ulla, ulla, ulla, ulla," cried the voice, coming, as it seemed to me, from the district about Regent's Park. The desolating cry worked upon my mind. The mood that had sustained me passed. The wailing took possession of me. I found I was intensely weary, footsore, and now again hungry and thirsty.

It was already past noon. Why was I wandering alone in this city of the dead? Why was I alone when all London was lying in state, and in its black shroud? I felt intolerably lonely. My mind ran on old friends that I had forgotten for years. I thought of the poisons in the chemists' shops, of the liquors the wine-merchants stored; I recalled the two sodden creatures of despair who, so far as I knew, shared the city with myself. . . .

I came into Oxford Street by the Marble Arch, and here again were black powder and several bodies, and an evil, ominous smell from the gratings of the cellars of some of the houses. I grew very thirsty after the heat of my long walk. With infinite trouble I managed to break into a public-house and get food and drink. I was weary after eating, and went into the parlor behind the bar, and slept on a black horsehair sofa I found there.

I awoke to find that dismal howling still in my ears, "Ulla, ulla, ulla, ulla." It was now dusk, and after I had routed out some biscuits and a cheese in the bar—there was a meat-safe, but it contained nothing but maggots—I wandered on through the silent residential squares to Baker Street—Portman Square is the only one I can name—and so came out at last upon Regent's Park. And as I emerged from the top of Baker Street, I saw far away over the

1 *What does the narrator hear? What words does he use to describe this sound?*

Words for Everyday Use

in • tol • er • a • bly (in täl´ər ə blē) *adv.*, unbearably; painfully

Answer to Guided Reading Question

1 The narrator hears a cry. He describes this cry as *wailing,* as a *desolating cry,* and as a *dismal howling.*

Vocabulary in Context

• Martha felt intolerably anxious before the chess match.

Answers to Guided Reading Questions

❶ The Martian machine seems to have driven blindly straight at a house and to have been overthrown. The narrator thinks that perhaps the machine has escaped from the guidance of its Martian.

❷ The narrator wants to know what the reason is for the strange crying sound that he is hearing.

❶ *What happened to the Martian? What theory does the narrator have to explain this?*

❷ *What does the narrator want to know?*

trees in the clearness of the sunset the hood of the Martian giant from which this howling proceeded. I was not terrified. I came upon him as if it were a matter of course. I watched him for some time, but he did not move. He appeared to be standing and yelling, for no reason that I could discover.

I tried to formulate a plan of action. That perpetual sound of "Ulla, ulla, ulla, ulla," confused my mind. Perhaps I was too tired to be very fearful. Certainly I was more curious to know the reason of this monotonous crying than afraid. I turned back away from the park and struck into Park Road, intending to skirt the park, went along under shelter of the terraces, and got a view of this stationary, howling Martian from the direction of St. John's Wood. A couple of hundred yards out of Baker Street I heard a yelping chorus, and saw, first a dog with a piece of putrescent red meat in his jaws coming headlong toward me, and then a pack of starving mongrels in pursuit of him. He made a wide curve to avoid me, as though he feared I might prove a fresh competitor. As the yelping died away down the silent road, the wailing sound of "Ulla, ulla, ulla, ulla," reasserted itself.

I came upon the wrecked handling-machine halfway to St. John's Wood station. At first I thought a house had fallen across the road. It was only as I clambered among the ruins that I saw, with a start, this mechanical Samson lying, with its tentacles bent and smashed and twisted, among the ruins it had made. The forepart was shattered. It seemed as if it had driven blindly straight at the house, and had been overwhelmed in its overthrow. It seemed to me then that this might have happened by a handling-machine escaping from the guidance of its Martian. I could not clamber among the ruins to see it, and the twilight was now so far advanced that the blood with which its seat was smeared, and the gnawed gristle of the Martian that the dogs had left, were invisible to me.

Wondering still more at all that I had seen, I pushed on toward Primrose Hill. Far away, through a gap in the trees, I saw a second Martian, as motionless as the first, standing in the park toward the Zoological Gardens, and silent. A little beyond the ruins about the smashed handling-machine I came upon the red weed again, and found the Regent's Canal a spongy mass of dark-red vegetation.

As I crossed the bridge, the sound of "Ulla, ulla, ulla, ulla," ceased. It was, as it were, cut off. The silence came like a thunder-clap.

The dusky houses about me stood faint and tall and dim; the trees toward the park were growing black. All about me the red weed clambered among the ruins, writhing to get above me in the dimness. Night, the mother of fear and mystery, was coming upon me. But while that voice sounded, the solitude, the desolation, had been endurable; by virtue of it London had still seemed alive, and the sense of life about me had upheld me. Then suddenly a change, the passing of something—I knew not what—and then a stillness that could be felt. Nothing but this gaunt quiet.

London about me gazed at me spectrally. The windows in the white houses were like the eye-sockets of skulls. About me my imagination found a thousand noiseless enemies moving. Terror seized me, a horror of my temerity. In front of me the road became pitchy black as though it was tarred, and I saw a con-

Words for Everyday Use

pu • tres • cent (pyo͞o tres´ənt) *adj.*, rotting
spec • tral • ly (spek´trəl lē) *adv.*, like a ghost
te • mer • i • ty (tə mer´ə tē) *n.*, recklessness; foolish or rash boldness

Vocabulary in Context

- The smell was found to be coming from the putrescent fruit which was left on the counter.
- The old man spectrally approached the trespassing children.
- Myles and William were scolded for their temerity.

torted shape lying across the pathway. I could not bring myself to go on. I turned down St. John's Wood Road, and ran headlong from this unendurable stillness toward Kilburn. I hid from the night and the silence, until long after midnight, in a cabmen's shelter in Harrow Road. But before the dawn my courage returned, and while the stars were still in the sky I turned once more toward Regent's Park. I missed my way among the streets, and presently saw down a long avenue, in the half-light of the early dawn, the curve of Primrose Hill. On the summit, towering up to the fading stars, was a third Martian, erect and motionless like the others.

An insane resolve possessed me. I would die and end it. And I would save myself even the trouble of killing myself. I marched on recklessly toward this Titan, and then, as I drew nearer and the light grew, I saw that a multitude of black birds was circling and clustering about the hood. At that my heart gave a bound, and I began running along the road.

I hurried through the red weed that choked St. Edmund's Terrace (I waded breast-high across a torrent of water that was rushing down from the water-works toward the Albert Road), and emerged upon the grass before the rising of the sun. Great mounds had been heaped about the crest of the hill, making a huge redoubt of it—it was the final and largest place the Martians had made—and from behind these heaps there rose a thin smoke against the sky. Against the skyline an eager dog ran and disappeared. The thought that had flashed into my mind grew real, grew credible. I felt no fear, only a wild, trembling exultation, as I ran up the hill toward the motionless monster. Out of the hood hung

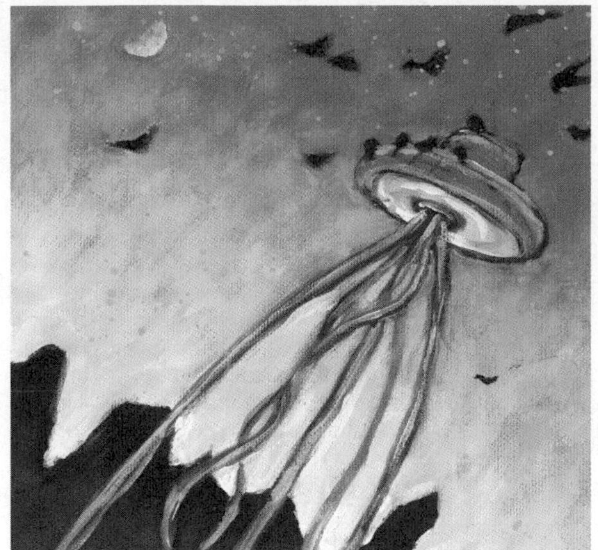

lank shreds of brown, at which the hungry birds pecked and tore.

In another moment I had scrambled up the earthen rampart and stood upon its crest, and the interior of the redoubt was below me. A mighty space it was, with gigantic machines here and there within it, huge mounds of material and strange shelter-places. And scattered about it, some in their overturned war-machines, some in the now rigid handling-machines, and a dozen of them stark and silent and laid in a row, were the Martians—*dead!*—slain by the putrefactive and disease bacteria against which their systems were unprepared; slain as the red weed was being slain; slain, after all man's devices had failed, by the humblest things that God, in his wisdom, has put upon this Earth.

For so it had come about, as indeed I and many men might have foreseen had

❶ *What has happened to the Martians?*

❷ *Why does the narrator's heart give "a bound"?*

❸ *What is ironic about the death of these creatures?*

WORDS FOR EVERYDAY USE

re • doubt (ri dout´) *n.*, stronghold; fortification

pu • tre • fac • tive (pyo͞o´trə fak´tiv) *adj.*, rotting; decomposing

ANSWERS TO GUIDED READING QUESTIONS

❶ The Martians have died. Animals are picking at their remains.

❷ The narrator's heart gives a "bound" because he sees that the Martians are dead.

❸ These Martians, who are so powerful that they have overcome the might of humankind, have been destroyed by the humblest of creatures—by bacteria.

VOCABULARY IN CONTEXT

- The city prepared a large redoubt in expectation of the invasion.
- The putrefactive food had been left in the heat all day.

Answer to Guided Reading Question

❶ Humans have developed immunities to bacteria over the centuries.

not terror and disaster blinded our minds. These germs of disease have taken toll of humanity since the beginning of things—taken toll of our prehuman ancestors since life began here. But by virtue of this natural selection of our kind we have developed resisting power; to no germs do we succumb without a struggle, and to many—those that cause putrefaction in dead matter, for instance—our living frames are altogether immune. But there are no bacteria in Mars, and directly these invaders arrived, directly they drank and fed, our microscopic allies began to work their overthrow. ❶ Already when I watched them they were irrevocably doomed, dying and rotting even as they went to and fro. It was inevitable. By the toll of a billion deaths man has bought his birthright of the Earth, and it is his against all comers; it would still be his were the Martians ten times as mighty as they are. For neither do men live nor die in vain.

What keeps humans from being destroyed by bacteria?

Here and there they were scattered, nearly fifty altogether, in that great gulf they had made, overtaken by a death that must have seemed to them as incomprehensible as any death could be. To me also at that time this death was incomprehensible. All I knew was that these things that had been alive and so terrible to men were dead. For a moment I believed that the destruction of Sennacherib[1] had been repeated, that God had repented, that the Angel of Death had slain them in the night.

I stood staring into the pit, and my heart lightened gloriously, even as the rising sun struck the world to fire about me with his rays. The pit was still in darkness; the mighty engines, so great and wonderful in their power and complexity, so unearthly in their tortuous forms, rose weird and vague and strange out of the shadows toward the light. A multitude of dogs, I could hear, fought over the bodies that lay darkly in the depth of the pit, far below me. Across the pit on its farther lip, flat and vast and strange, lay the great flying-machine with which they had been experimenting upon our denser atmosphere when decay and death arrested them. Death had come not a day too soon. At the sound of a cawing overhead I looked up at the huge fighting-machine that would fight no more forever, at the tattered red shreds of flesh that dripped down upon the overturned seats on the summit of Primrose Hill.

I turned and looked down the slope of the hill to where, enhaloed now in birds, stood those other two Martians that I had seen overnight, just as death had overtaken them. The one had died, even as it had been crying to its companions; perhaps it was the last to die, and its voice had gone on perpetually until the force of its machinery was exhausted. They glittered now, harmless tripod towers of shining metal, in the brightness of the rising sun.

All about the pit, and saved as by a miracle from everlasting destruction, stretched the great Mother of Cities. Those who have only seen London veiled in her somber robes of smoke can scarcely imagine the naked clearness and beauty of the silent wilderness of houses.

Eastward, over the blackened ruins of the Albert Terrace and the splintered spire of the church, the sun blazed dazzling in a clear sky, and here and there some facet in the great wilderness of roofs caught the light and glared with a white intensity.

Northward were Kilburn and Hampstead, blue and crowded with houses; westward the great city was dimmed; and

Chapter 8

1. **Sennacherib.** King of Assyria, 705–681 BC

Words for Everyday Use

ir • rev • o • ca • bly (ir rev´ə kə blē) *adv.,* in a way that cannot be changed or undone

Vocabulary in Context

• The nightline of the city was irrevocably altered by the new skyscraper.

southward, beyond the Martians, the green wash of Regent's Park, the Langham Hotel, the dome of the Albert Hall, the Imperial Institute, and the giant mansions of the Brompton Road came out clear and little in the sunrise, the jagged ruins of Westminster rising hazily beyond. Far away and blue were the Surrey hills, and the towers of the Crystal Palace[2] glittered like two silver rods. The dome of St. Paul's[3] was dark against the sunrise, and injured, I saw for the first time, by a huge gaping cavity on its western side.

And as I looked at this wide expanse of houses and factories and churches, silent and abandoned; as I thought of the multitudinous hopes and efforts, the innumerable hosts of lives that had gone to build this human reef, and of the swift and ruthless destruction that had hung over it all; when I realized that the shadow had been rolled back, and that men might still live in the streets, and this dear vast dead city of mine be once more alive and powerful, I felt a wave of emotion that was near akin to tears.

The torment was over. Even that day the healing would begin. The survivors of the people scattered over the country—leaderless, lawless, foodless, like sheep without a shepherd—the thousands who had fled by sea, would begin to return; the pulse of life, growing stronger and stronger, would beat again in the empty streets and pour across the vacant squares. Whatever destruction was done, the hand of the destroyer was stayed. All the gaunt wrecks, the blackened skeletons of houses that stared so dismally at the sunlit grass of the hill, would presently be echoing with the hammers of the restorers and ringing with the tapping of their <u>trowels</u>. At the thought I extended my hands toward the sky and began thanking God. In a year, thought I—in a year . . .

With overwhelming force, came the thought of myself, of my wife, and the old life of hope and tender helpfulness that had ceased forever.

❶ What does the narrator believe will be true in a year?

2. **Crystal Palace.** Exhibition hall in London, built in 1857 and destroyed by fire in 1936
3. **St. Paul's.** Cathedral in London, built in the late 1600s and still standing today

Reviewing the Selection

Recalling and Interpreting

1. **R** What sound does the narrator hear as he walks through the deserted streets of London? What does the narrator resolve to do about his situation?

   I Do you consider the narrator's resolution to be a sane response to the circumstances?

2. **R** What kills the Martians?

   I In what sense has humanity "bought his birthright of the Earth" by means of "a billion deaths"?

Words for Everyday Use

trow • el (trou′əl) *n.*, small, hand tool used for smoothing plaster or concrete

Answer to Guided Reading Question

❶ The narrator believes that within a year things will be restored to normal.

Answers for Reviewing the Selection

RECALLING AND INTERPRETING

1. **Recalling.** He hears a strange crying. The narrator resolves to end it all by rushing toward one of the Martians. **Interpreting.** The narrator's response is not a sane one. He is obviously at some extremity. That his is not a sane response is evident from the fact that he is ready to throw everything away at the very time when human beings are achieving success in their battle against the invaders.
2. **Recalling.** The Martians are killed by bacteria. **Interpreting.** Human beings have throughout the centuries developed immunities to many diseases that would kill outsiders.

Vocabulary in Context

• Martin, <u>trowel</u> in hand, set off to plaster the walls of the bathroom.

ANSWERS TO GUIDED READING QUESTIONS

❶ The narrator has been told that Leatherhead has been destroyed, along with every soul in it. This is important to him because his wife is there.

❷ The other people of the world send supplies to help the English. Their doing so shows solidarity and concern.

9
WRECKAGE

And now comes the strangest thing in my story. Yet, perhaps, it is not altogether strange. I remember, clearly and coldly and vividly, all that I did that day until the time that I stood weeping and praising God upon the summit of Primrose Hill. And then I forget.

Of the next three days I know nothing. I have learned since that, so far from my being the first discoverer of the Martian overthrow, several such wanderers as myself had already discovered this on the previous night. One man—the first—had gone to St. Martin's-le-Grand, and, while I sheltered in the cabmen's hut, had contrived to telegraph to Paris. Thence the joyful news had flashed all over the world; a thousand cities, chilled by ghastly apprehensions, suddenly flashed into frantic illuminations; they knew of it in Dublin, Edinburgh, Manchester, Birmingham, at the time when I stood upon the verge of the pit. Already men, weeping with joy, as I have heard, shouting and staying their work to shake hands and shout, were making up trains, even as near as Crewe, to descend upon London. The church bells that had ceased a fortnight since suddenly caught the news, until all England was bell-ringing. Men on cycles, lean-faced, unkempt, scorched along every country lane shouting of unhoped deliverance, shouting to gaunt, staring figures of despair. And for the food! Across the Channel, across the Irish Sea, across the Atlantic, corn, bread, and meat were tearing to our relief. All the shipping in the world seemed going Londonward in those days. But of all this I have no memory. I drifted—a demented man. I found myself in a house of kindly people, who had found me on the third day wandering, weeping, and raving through the streets of St. John's Wood. They have told me since that I was singing some inane doggerel about "The Last Man Left Alive! Hurrah! The Last Man Left Alive!" Troubled as they were with their own affairs, these people, whose name, much as I would like to express my gratitude to them, I may not even give here, nevertheless cumbered themselves with me, sheltered me, and protected me from myself. Apparently they had learned something of my story from me during the days of my lapse.

❶ *What has the narrator been told about the fate of Leatherhead? Why is this important to him?*

Very gently, when my mind was assured again, did they break to me what they had learned of the fate of Leatherhead. Two days after I was imprisoned it had been destroyed, with every soul in it, by a Martian. He had swept it out of existence, as it seemed, without any provocation, as a boy might crush an anthill, in the mere wantonness of power.

❷ *What do other people in the world do for the English? What does this reveal about them?*

I was a lonely man, and they were very kind to me. I was a lonely man and a sad one, and they bore with me. I remained with them four days after my recovery. All that time I felt a vague, a growing craving to look once more on whatever remained of the little life that seemed so happy and bright in my past. It was a mere hopeless desire to feast upon my misery. They dissuaded me. They did all they could to divert me from this morbidity. But at last I could resist the impulse no longer, and, promising faithfully to return to them, and parting, as I will confess, from these four-day friends with tears, I went out again into the streets that had lately been so dark and strange and empty.

Already they were busy with returning people; in places even there were shops

WORDS FOR EVERYDAY USE

in • ane (in ān´) *adj.,* lacking sense or meaning
cum • ber (kum´bər) *v.,* burden in a troublesome way
lapse (laps) *n.,* slipping into a worse condition
prov • o • ca • tion (präv´ə kā´shən) *n.,* act of exciting into action or angering
wan • ton • ness (wän´tən nes) *n.,* senseless cruelty

VOCABULARY IN CONTEXT

- The speaker's inane speech bored the audience.
- While Keith was happy to go to the park with Fred and his family, he made sure not to cumber them unnecessarily.
- After scoring well in her math tests all quarter, Halle had a lapse with the most recent exam.
- The bulls charged the ranch hands without any provocation.
- The boy teased the young girl out of sheer wantoness.

open, and I saw a drinking-fountain running water.

I remember how mockingly bright the day seemed as I went back on my melancholy pilgrimage to the little house at Woking, how busy the streets and vivid the moving life about me. So many people were abroad everywhere, busied in a thousand activities, that it seemed incredible that any great proportion of the population could have been slain. But then I noticed how yellow were the skins of the people I met, how shaggy the hair of the men, how large and bright their eyes, and that every other man still wore his dirty rags. Their faces seemed all with one of two expressions—a leaping exultation and energy or a grim resolution. Save for the expression of the faces, London seemed a city of tramps. The vestries[1] were indiscriminately distributing bread sent us by the French government. The ribs of the few horses showed dismally. Haggard special constables with white badges stood at the corners of every street. I saw little of the mischief wrought by the Martians until I reached Wellington Street, and there I saw the red weed clambering over the buttresses of Waterloo Bridge.

At the corner of the bridge, too, I saw one of the common contrasts of that grotesque time—a sheet of paper flaunting against a thicket of the red weed, trans-

CHAPTER 9

1. **vestries.** Group of church members who manage the affairs of the church

❶ *Why might people have these two expressions?*

WORDS FOR EVERYDAY USE

in • dis • crim • i • nate • ly (in´di skrim´i nit lē) *adv.,* randomly; not carefully chosen

ANSWER TO GUIDED READING QUESTION

❶ The people either have expressions of leaping exultation or grim resolution. The former expression could result from having survived or having discovered that loved ones have survived. The latter expression could result from deciding to continue in the face of great loss.

VOCABULARY IN CONTEXT

• The storm indiscriminately blew down several buildings in the town.

Answers to Guided Reading Questions

❶ Among other things, the Martian mechanisms have revealed the secret of flying.

❷ The narrator has a quick flash of hope that his wife will be OK.

❶ *What have people learned by studying the Martian mechanisms?*

❷ *Why does the narrator suddenly have hope?*

fixed by a stick that kept it in place. It was the placard of the first newspaper to resume publication—the *Daily Mail.* I bought a copy for a blackened shilling I found in my pocket. Most of it was in blank, but the solitary compositor who did the thing had amused himself by making a grotesque scheme of advertisement stereo on the back page. The matter he printed was emotional; the news organization had not as yet found its way back. I learned nothing fresh except that already in one week the examination of the Martian mechanisms had yielded astonishing results. Among other things, the article assured me what I did not believe at the time, that the "Secret of Flying" was discovered. At Waterloo I found the free trains that were taking people to their homes. The first rush was already over. There were few people in the train, and I was in no mood for casual conversation. I got a compartment to myself, and sat with folded arms, looking grayly at the sunlit devastation that flowed past the windows. And just outside the terminus the train jolted over temporary rails, and on either side of the railway the houses were blackened ruins. To Clapham Junction the face of London was grimy with powder of the Black Smoke, in spite of two days of thunderstorms and rain, and at Clapham Junction the line had been wrecked again; there were hundreds of out-of-work clerks and shopmen working side by side with the customary navvies, and we were jolted over a hasty relaying.

All down the line from there the aspect of the country was gaunt and unfamiliar; Wimbledon particularly had suffered. Walton, by virtue of its unburned pine woods, seemed the least hurt of any place along the line. The Wandle, the Mole, every little stream, was a heaped mass of red weed, in appearance between butcher's meat and pickled cabbage. The Surrey pine woods were too dry, however, for the festoons of the red climber. Beyond Wimbledon, within sight of the line, in certain nursery grounds, were the heaped masses of earth about the sixth cylinder. A number of people were standing about it, and some sappers were busy in the midst of it. Over it flaunted a Union Jack, flapping cheerfully in the morning breeze. The nursery grounds were everywhere crimson with the weed, a wide expanse of livid color cut with purple shadows, and very painful to the eye. One's gaze went with infinite relief from the scorched grays and sullen reds of the foreground to the blue-green softness of the eastward hills.

The line on the London side of Woking station was still undergoing repair, so I descended at Byfleet station and took the road to Maybury, past the place where I and the artilleryman had talked to the hussars, and on by the spot where the Martian had appeared to me in the thunderstorm. Here, moved by curiosity, I turned aside to find, among a tangle of red fronds, the warped and broken dog-cart with the whitened bones of the horse, scattered and gnawed. For a time I stood regarding these vestiges. . . .

Then I returned through the pine wood, neck-high with red weed here and there, to find the landlord of the Spotted Dog had already found burial, and so came home past the College Arms. A man standing at an open cottage door greeted me by name as I passed.

I looked at my house with a quick flash of hope that faded immediately. The door had been forced; it was unfastened, and was opening slowly as I approached.

Words for Everyday Use

fes • toon (fes to͞on´) *n.,* wreath or garland of flowers

liv • id (liv´id) *adj.,* red

Vocabulary in Context

- During the holidays many houses hang colorful festoons on their doors.
- The livid-roofed house stood out among all the other houses in the town.

It slammed again. The curtains of my study fluttered out of the open window from which I and the artilleryman had watched the dawn. No one had closed it since. The smashed bushes were just as I had left them nearly four weeks ago. I stumbled into the hall, and the house felt empty. The stair-carpet was ruffled and discolored where I had crouched, soaked to the skin from the thunderstorm the night of the catastrophe. Our muddy foot-steps I saw still went up the stairs.

I followed them to my study, and found lying on my writing table still, with the selenite[3] paperweight upon it, the sheet of work I had left on the afternoon of the opening of the cylinder. For a space I stood reading over my abandoned arguments. It was a paper on the probable development of Moral Ideas with the development of the civilizing process; and the last sentence was the opening of a prophecy: "In about two hundred years," I had written, "we may expect—" The sentence ended abruptly. I remembered my inability to fix my mind that morning, scarcely a month gone by, and how I had broken off to get my *Daily Chronicle* from the newsboy. I remembered how I went down to the garden gate as he came along, and how I had listened to his odd story of "Men from Mars."

I came down and went into the dining room. There were the mutton and the bread, both far gone now in decay, and a beer bottle overturned, just as I and the artilleryman had left them. My home was desolate. I perceived the folly of the faint hope I had cherished so long. And then a strange thing occurred. "It is no use," said a voice. "The house is deserted. No one has been here these ten days. Do not stay here to torment yourself. No one escaped but you."

I was startled. Had I spoken my thought aloud? I turned, and the French window was open behind me. I made a step to it, and stood looking out.

And there, amazed and afraid, even as I stood amazed and afraid, were my cousin and my wife—my wife white and tearless. She gave a faint cry.

"I came," she said, "I knew—knew—"

She put her hand to her throat—swayed. I made a step forward, and caught her in my arms.

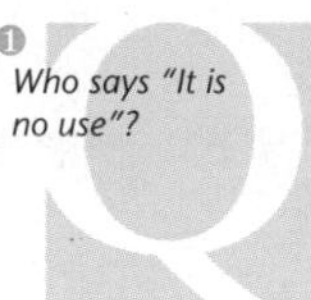

1 *Who says "It is no use"?*

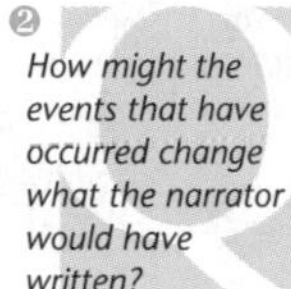

2 *How might the events that have occurred change what the narrator would have written?*

3. **selenite.** Kind of gypsum found in transparent crystals

Reviewing the Selection

Recalling and Interpreting

1. **R** What happens to the narrator in the days following his experience on Primrose Hill?
   I Why might this have happened to the narrator?
2. **R** What do the people who take in the narrator try to persuade him not to do?
   I Is the narrator right in wanting to go back to his home to see what is left? Why, or why not?
3. **R** Whom does the narrator meet when he returns to his house?
   I At the end of the chapter, the narrator's wife says, "I knew—knew—." What did she know?

Answers to Guided Reading Questions

1 The cousin says this.

2 *Responses will vary.* It is difficult to imagine that the narrator would have written anything with as much optimism as in the past.

Answers for Reviewing the Selection

Recalling and Interpreting

1. **Recalling.** The narrator wanders about in a daze, doing he knows not what, for he has no memory of that time. **Interpreting.** The narrator has suffered a breakdown due to extreme mental and physical exhaustion.

2. **Recalling.** The people try to persuade the narrator not to go back to Woking. **Interpreting.** As it turns out, the narrator proves to be right in wanting to go back to check, for he finds his wife safe and sound.

3. **Recalling.** He meets his wife and his cousin. **Interpreting.** She knew that her husband was alive.

Answers to Guided Reading Questions

❶ It is "by no means a proven conclusion" that bacteria killed the Martians, although it is highly probable.

❷ The Martians might have gone to Venus.

Quotables

"In England we have come to rely upon a comfortable time-lag of fifty years or a century intervening between the perception that something ought to be done and a serious attempt to do it."

—H. G. Wells

10
The Epilogue

I cannot but regret, now that I am concluding my story, how little I am able to contribute to the discussion of the many debatable questions which are still unsettled. In one respect I shall certainly provoke criticism. My particular province is speculative philosophy. My knowledge of comparative physiology is confined to a book or two, but it seems to me that Carver's suggestions as to the reason of the rapid death of the Martians is so probable as to be regarded almost as a proven conclusion. I have assumed that in the body of my narrative.

❶ *What is "by no means a proven conclusion"?*

At any rate, in all the bodies of the Martians that were examined after the war, no bacteria except those already known as terrestrial species were found. That they did not bury any of their dead, and the reckless slaughter they perpetrated, point also to an entire ignorance of the putrefactive process. But probable as this seems, it is by no means a proven conclusion.

Neither is the composition of the Black Smoke known, which the Martians used with such deadly effect, and the generator of the Heat-Ray remains a puzzle. The terrible disasters at the Ealing and South Kensington laboratories have disinclined analysts for further investigations upon the latter. Spectrum analysis of the black powder points unmistakably to the presence of an unknown element with a brilliant group of three lines in the green, and it is possible that it combines with argon to form a compound which acts at once with deadly effect upon some constituent in the blood. But such unproven speculations will scarcely be of interest to the general reader, to whom this story is addressed. None of the brown scum that drifted down the Thames after the destruction of Shepperton was examined at the time, and now none is forthcoming.

The results of an anatomical examination of the Martians, so far as the prowling dogs had left such an examination possible, I have already given. But everyone is familiar with the magnificent and almost complete specimen in spirits at the Natural History Museum, and the countless drawings that have been made from it; and beyond that the interest of their physiology and structure is purely scientific.

A question of graver and universal interest is the possibility of another attack from the Martians. I do not think that nearly enough attention is being given to this aspect of the matter. At present the planet Mars is in conjunction,[1] but with every return to opposition I, for one, anticipate a renewal of their adventure. In any case, we should be prepared. It seems to me that it should be possible to define the position of the gun from which the shots are discharged, to keep a sustained watch upon this part of the planet, and to anticipate the arrival of the next attack.

In that case the cylinder might be destroyed with dynamite or artillery before it was sufficiently cool for the Martians to emerge, or they might be butchered by means of guns so soon as the screw opened. It seems to me that they have lost a vast advantage in the failure of their first surprise. Possibly they see it in the same light.

❷ *Where might the Martians have gone?*

Lessing has advanced excellent reasons for supposing that the Martians have actually succeeded in effecting a landing on the planet Venus. Seven months ago now, Venus and Mars were in alignment with the sun; that is to say, Mars was in opposition from the point of view of an observer on Venus. Subsequently a peculiar luminous and sinuous marking[2] appeared on the unillumined half of the inner planet,

Chapter 10

1. **conjunction.** When the Sun is directly between Mars and Earth

2. **sinuous marking.** Apparently, the Martians signaled home to Mars

and almost simultaneously a faint dark mark[3] of a similar sinuous character was detected upon a photograph of the Martian disc. One needs to see the drawings of these appearances in order to appreciate fully their remarkable resemblance in character.

At any rate, whether we expect another invasion or not, our views of the human future must be greatly modified by these events. We have learned now that we cannot regard this planet as being fenced in and a secure abiding place for Man; we can never anticipate the unseen good or evil that may come upon us suddenly out of space. It may be that in the larger design of the universe this invasion from Mars is not without its ultimate benefit for men; it has robbed us of that serene confidence in the future which is the most fruitful source of decadence, the gifts to human science it has brought are enormous, and it has done much to promote the conception of the commonweal[4] of mankind. It may be that across the immensity of space the Martians have watched the fate of these pioneers of theirs and learned their lesson, and that on the planet Venus they have found a securer settlement. Be that as it may, for many years yet there will certainly be no relaxation of the eager scrutiny of the Martian disc, and those fiery darts of the sky, the shooting stars, will bring with them as they fall an unavoidable apprehension to all the sons of men.

The broadening of men's views that has resulted can scarcely be exaggerated. Before the cylinder fell there was a general persuasion that through all the deep of space no life existed beyond the petty surface of our minute sphere. Now we see further. If the Martians can reach Venus, there is no reason to suppose that the thing is impossible for men, and when the slow cooling of the sun makes this Earth uninhabitable, as at last it must do, it may be that the thread of life that has begun here will have streamed out and caught our sister planet within its toils.

Dim and wonderful is the vision I have conjured up in my mind of life spreading slowly from this little seed-bed of the solar system throughout the inanimate vastness of sidereal[5] space. But that is a remote dream. It may be, on the other hand, that the destruction of the Martians is only a reprieve. To them, and not to us, perhaps, is the future ordained.

I must confess the stress and danger of the time have left an abiding sense of doubt and insecurity in my mind. I sit in my study writing by lamplight, and suddenly I see again the healing valley below set with writhing flames, and feel the house behind and about me empty and desolate. I go out into the Byfleet Road, and vehicles pass me, a butcher-boy in a cart, a cabful of visitors, a workman on a bicycle, children going to school, and suddenly they become vague and unreal, and I hurry again with the artilleryman through the hot, brooding silence. Of a night I see the black powder darkening the silent streets, and the contorted bodies shrouded in that layer; they rise upon me tattered and dog-bitten. They gibber and grow fiercer, paler, uglier, mad distortions of humanity at last, and I wake, cold and wretched, in the darkness of the night.

I go to London and see the busy multitudes in Fleet Street and the Strand, and it comes across my mind that they are but

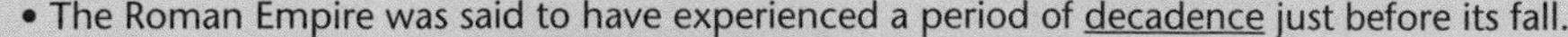

3. **faint dark mark.** The flare of the light on Mars looks dark on a photograph of Mars
4. **commonweal.** Public good
5. **sidereal.** Of or pertaining to the stars

❶ *What positive effects has the Martian invasion had?*

Words for Everyday Use

dec • a • dence (dek´ə dəns) *n.,* process, condition, or period of moral and cultural decline

re • prieve (ri prēv´) *n.,* temporary relief or escape

or • dain (ôr dān´) *v.,* command; decree

gib • ber (jib´ər) *v.,* speak or utter incoherently

Answer to Guided Reading Question

❶ The Martian invasion has improved terrestrial science and technology, and it has made people of different nations feel as though they had something in common—the larger public good.

Vocabulary in Context

- The Roman Empire was said to have experienced a period of decadence just before its fall.
- The children got a temporary reprieve because their mother had not yet discovered the spill.
- The king ordained the festival to begin.
- In a state of panic, Hector gibbered quickly the events of the story to the officer.

ANSWER TO GUIDED READING QUESTION

❶ It seems strange because he had once believed himself to be separated from her forever.

BIOGRAPHICAL NOTE

H. G. Wells is a fine example of the so-called "self-made" person—of a person who rises to high rank or station as a result of his or her own hard work and skill. Key to Wells's success was his intense desire to learn. His program of self-education, founded on reading classics by Plato, Swift, Voltaire, Gibbon, and others, led him to be able to attend college and, importantly, to spin off many creative ideas that combined his reading with his scientific research.

SELECTION CHECK TEST WITH ANSWERS

EX. Through what deserted city does the narrator wander?
He wanders through London.

1. What makes the crying sound that the narrator hears?
The Martians make the crying sound.

2. What is the source of the red meat being carried by the dog?
It comes from a Martian.

3. Who decides to end it all and run toward the Martians?
The narrator does.

4. What kills the Martians?
Microorganisms kill the Martians.

5. With whom is the narrator reunited at the end of the novel?
The narrator is reunited with his wife.

the ghosts of the past, haunting the streets that I have seen silent and wretched, going to and fro, phantasms in a dead city, the mockery of life in a galvanized body. And strange, too, it is to stand on Primrose Hill, as I did but a day before writing this last chapter, to see the great province of houses, dim and blue through the haze of the smoke and mist, vanishing at last into the vague lower sky, to see the people walking to and fro among the flowerbeds on the hill, to see the sightseers about the Martian machine that stands there still, to hear the tumult of playing children, and to recall the time when I saw it all bright and clear-cut, hard and silent, under the dawn of that last great day. . . .

❶ *Why does it seem strange to the narrator to hold his wife's hand again?*

And strangest of all is it to hold my wife's hand again, and to think that I have counted her, and that she has counted me, among the dead. ■

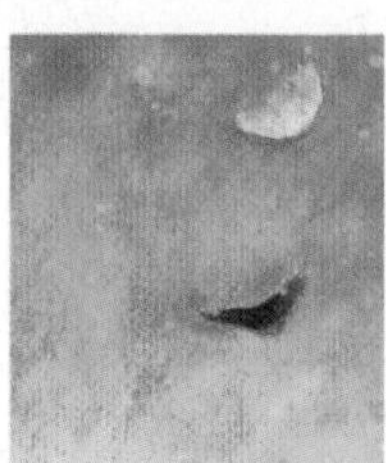

About the Author

Herbert George (H. G.) Wells (1866–1946), along with Jules Verne, is considered the creator of modern science fiction. As a young man, Wells struggled with poverty and ill health but managed to make his own way in the world by a rigorous program of self-education. He graduated from the Normal School of Science in London, England, where he studied under the famous biologist T. H. Huxley. After teaching school for a time, he turned to writing. Then, in less than a decade, he wrote the great science fiction tales that were to bring him fame: *The Time Machine* (1895), *The Island of Dr. Moreau* (1896), *The Invisible Man* (1897), *The War of the Worlds* (1898), *The First Men in the Moon* (1901), *The Food of the Gods* (1904), and *How It Came to Earth* (1904). In his later years, Wells turned his enormous energies toward social and political concerns. His mammoth *Outline of History* (1920), more than a million words long, became a best-seller. Before World War II, Wells warned of the consequences of global warfare in a novel with a title that gave a new phrase to the English language, *The Shape of Things to Come* (1933). Wells interviewed both Joseph Stalin and Franklin Delano Roosevelt and was part of the intellectual movement that led to the founding of the United Nations. Besides creating many of the plots that would become common for science fiction writers in days to come, in his fiction Wells predicted many future developments, including lasers, flying machines, robots, chemical warfare, and space travel.

Responding to the Selection

The narrator says that as a result of the experience of the Martian invasion, there has been a "broadening of men's views." Has reading this novel broadened your views in any way? What questions has the novel raised in your mind about outer space, other life forms, and the future? Has the novel changed your ideas about society or our treatment of other people or of animals? Explain.

Reviewing the Selection

Recalling and Interpreting

1. **R** What evidence points to the conclusion that the Martians were killed by terrestrial bacteria?

   I Can human beings share any of the glory for overcoming the Martians and ending their invasion? What does this novel teach about the relative power of human beings and of nature?

2. **R** What possibility does the narrator suggest for human beings after "the slow cooling of the Sun" has made "this Earth uninhabitable"?

   I Scientists now know that long before the Sun cools to become a white dwarf, it will first expand, becoming a red giant that engulfs the inner planets, including the Earth. In what respect was Wells's narrator mistaken about the future of the Sun and the Earth? Does his suggestion for the future of humanity make sense anyway? Explain.

3. **R** What effects have the events of the novel had on the narrator's state of mind?

   I How have the events of the novel changed the narrator? What negative and positive effects have these events had on him?

Synthesizing

4. Do you think that events like those described in this novel could actually occur? Why, or why not?

Understanding Literature (Questions for Discussion)

1. **Science Fiction. Science fiction** is imaginative literature based on scientific principles, discoveries, or laws. Science fiction often makes predictions about the future. In *The War of the Worlds,* H. G. Wells made many predictions about technological advances that later came true. What aspects of modern technology that have since come true were predicted in Book 2 of this novel?
2. **Theme.** A **theme** is a central idea in a work of literature. What does the ending of this novel teach about taking the blessings of our lives for granted? What does the novel as a whole teach about human pride? What does it teach about our relationships toward life forms that we think of as "lower" than humans?

Responding to the Selection

The prompt consists of several very open-ended questions. Encourage students to share their thoughts and feelings related to reading this novel, without censure or evaluation. Here are some additional questions that you might pose: Should people be fearful in their attitude toward extraterrestrial life? Should people actively seek to establish communication with intelligent extraterrestrials (as we are doing through the SETI project)?

Answers for Reviewing the Selection

RECALLING AND INTERPRETING

1. **Recalling.** There are not microorgnisms on Mars. The Martians did not take care of disposal of their dead. **Interpreting.** Human beings were powerless to overcome the Martians. The novel teaches that nature is more powerful than people are.

2. **Recalling.** It may be that people will stream out from earth and populate Venus. **Interpreting.** Wells seems to think that the sun will simply burn down and that the Earth will therefore get cooler.

3. **Recalling.** The narrator is haunted by the events that he has seen to the extent that often the ordinary sights around him seem unreal. The narrator now has an abiding sense of doubt and insecurity. **Interpreting.** The narrator's doubt and insecurity are both negative, but the narrator's new knowledge of the depth of his love for his wife is positive.

SYNTHESIZING

Responses will vary. Possible responses are given.

4. Some students may feel that the possibility of contact with aliens from outer space is remote. However, scientists on Earth seem to think the idea probable enough to merit spending research funds on programs to make such contacts.

Answers for Understanding Literature

Responses will vary. Possible responses are given.

1. **Science Fiction.** Flight and human travel to other planets have both come true since the writing of the novel.

2. **Theme.** The novel teaches us not to take for granted the many wonderful parts of our lives, such as shelter and food and the company of loved ones. The novel teaches that humans are too prideful, and it teaches that we should treat lower life forms with kindness and respect.

Writing Skills

Introducing the Skill

Explain that a character sketch simply brings a character alive in a reader's mind. Have students think about and share with the rest of the class interesting descriptions of characters that they can remember from their reading or television or movie viewing.

Previewing the Skill

Have students read aloud the student model, "How I Lost a Cat and Found a Friend."

Prewriting and Drafting

Have students share their character-detail charts with one another and suggest additional details that will contribute to an overall dominant effect.

Evaluating and Revising

Stress the importance of the bulleted evaluation questions.

Proofreading and Publishing

Some students may wish to develop their sketches into full-fledged short stories.

Writing Skills

Writing a Character Sketch

A character sketch is a short essay that describes a person. The descriptions of the curate and the artilleryman in *The War of the Worlds* are examples of fictional character sketches. The object of a character sketch is to make someone come alive in the reader's mind, to give the reader an impression of what the living, breathing person is like. To do this, the writer of a character sketch must use lots of vivid, concrete details. The writer must also choose among available details to find ones that will create a single dominant impression.

Try It Yourself

Write a character sketch that is four to six paragraphs long describing someone whom you know and admire.

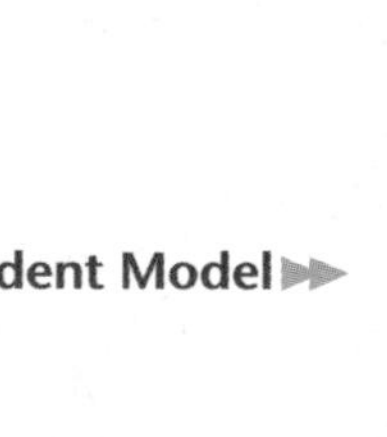

Student Model

Jill Gatto

Grade 8

"How I Lost a Cat and Found a Friend"

At first glance, one wonders which is shabbiest, Mr. Freedman or the shop that he keeps. Day after day, Mr. Freedman sits in a chair pulled up against the letters on the shop window that spell out, backward, "Freedman's Used Books Cheap." There he reads and waits for customers. The revolving fan beside him swirls the dust from the old books around in the light that streams through the window. The light falls on the elderly man, with his rumpled white hair and rumpled white shirt and tie thirty years out of date. It falls, as well, on the book that he reads. An old man with his old books—at first I wanted nothing to do with either of them.

I showed up at Mr. Freedman's in late May. I had lost my cat and was going around the neighborhood hanging up fliers. When I opened the door to the bookshop, a little bell tinkled, and Mr. Freedman rose, slowly, as though in pain. I stood in the middle of the floor, waiting and looking around, casually, at the mess in the shop—the shelves and shelves of wormy old volumes, the papers piled among old coffee cups on the desk in the corner. "You are looking for a book, maybe?" Mr. Freedman said.

"No, actually, I'm looking for a cat," I answered, showing him the flier and asking if I could post it in the window. "If you wish," he replied. "To lose a cat is a terrible thing. You can wait for a moment? There is a book about it." Mr. Freedman disappeared behind a bookshelf without waiting for my reply. I could hear him rummaging around. He came back with a dirty paperback. "This novelist, he writes about an old man, like me, very old, who has a kitten given him, from his daughter. The old man, he pretends not to like the kitten, and about it he says horrible things. Of rats and mosquitoes you would speak more kindly. One day, this kitten she sneaks through a hole in the kitchen wall and crawls under the floorboards of the man's apartment, and suddenly the man, he is like a crazy person with grief and loss, tearing up the floorboards and walls to rescue his cat."

"Well, does he find it?" I asked.

"This you must learn for yourself when you buy the book," Mr. Freedman answered, winking.

After passing out the rest of my fliers, I went back to the shop to buy the book. Perhaps it would bring me luck. Mr. Freedman asked if I lived in the neighborhood and would like a job, coming in for a couple of afternoons to straighten up. "My wife," he said, "always she is after me to do this."

So that's how I started coming into Mr. Freedman's shop. Over the next few weeks, I spent a lot of afternoons in there, pretending to help out, though Mr. Freedman didn't really want the place cleaned up. What he did want was the company, which I found myself glad to give. I learned a little in return about bookselling and a lot of crazy stories that were stored up in Mr. Freedman's memory as they were stored up on his shelves. A few times a day, a customer would wander in, and, whatever interested that person, Mr. Freedman knew a book about it, a strange and curious book that like him might have been overlooked. Never, for the weeks that I was there, did the bookseller fail to ask me if my cat had come back. My new cat likes to come sit on my textbooks when I'm doing homework. The cat likes books. I call him Freedman.

Examining the Model

1. What physical description does Jill give of Mr. Freedman? What concrete details help the reader to picture him?
2. What anecdotes, or very brief stories, does Jill tell about Mr. Freedman? What do these details reveal about him?
3. What is the significance of the closing of the character sketch? What detail reveals Jill's affection for Mr. Freedman?

Answers for Examining the Model

1. She says that he is elderly, has rumpled white hair and a rumpled white shirt, and wears a tie thirty years out of date.
2. She tells the anecdote about meeting him and hearing him tell about the cat book.
3. The fact that she names her cat Freedman suggests that she is very fond of the elderly man.

Analytic Scale for Writing Skills

Assign a score from 1 to 25 for each grading criterion below.

Character Sketch

- **Content/Unity.** The character sketch communicates a single main idea through related concrete details.
- **Organization/Coherence.** The character sketch has an introduction, a body, and a conclusion.
- **Language/Style.** The character sketch uses vivid and precise nouns, verbs, and modifiers.
- **Conventions.** The character sketch avoids errors in spelling, grammar, usage, mechanics, and manuscript form.

Prewriting and Drafting

1. Choose a person about whom you would like to write your character sketch. Your subject can be a real person or it can be a person you have imagined.
2. Make a chart like the following to collect details for your sketch:

CHARACTER DETAILS
Name of character:
Main idea to be conveyed about this character:
Character's background:
Character's appearance:
Character's personality:
Character's habits:
Character's hobbies or interests:
Interesting or revealing anecdotes about the character:

3. Make a rough outline of your essay. The outline should include an introduction, a body, and a conclusion. Read the Language Arts Survey, 1.15, "Outlining," for more information.
4. Review the Language Arts Survey, 1.16, "Drafting." Using your outline and your chart of details about the character, write a rough draft of your character sketch, incorporating as many vivid details as you can in four to six paragraphs.

Evaluating and Revising

1. Review the Language Arts Survey, 1.17, "Self-Evaluation," and 1.18, "Peer Evaluation." Exchange papers with a classmate and evaluate one another's work. Keep the following questions in mind:
   - Does the sketch have an introduction, body, and conclusion?
   - Does it communicate a single main idea about the character?
   - Does it use concrete details to make the character come alive?

   After reviewing your classmate's comments, evaluate your own paper following the same guidelines that you used for the peer evaluation.
2. Revise your character sketch, following the guidelines for revision in the Language Arts Survey, 1.19, "Four Types of Revision," and 1.20, "A Revision Checklist."

Proofreading and Publishing

1. Proofread your revised draft. Make a clean copy and proofread it again. Refer to the Language Arts Survey, 1.21, "Using Proofreader's Marks," 1.22, "A Proofreading Checklist," and 1.23, "Proper Manuscript Form."
2. Share your character sketch in one of the following ways:
   a. Collect all the papers in the class and mix them up. Redistribute them so that each student has one other student's paper to read and evaluate.
   b. Create a class book of character sketches. You may illustrate the book with photographs or drawings of the subjects. Display your work in the classroom.

Save your work in your writer's portfolio.

PROJECT NOTE

Familiarize students with the structure of a debate by having them read the student model. Make sure that they understand the meanings of the terms *constructive speeches, rebuttal speeches, affirmative, negative,* and *proposition.*

Unit Project

HOLDING A DEBATE

Since the early days of science fiction stories by H. G. Wells and Jules Verne, people have wondered about whether life exists on planets other than our own. A large scientific literature has grown up around the subject, and government projects have been set up specifically to find out whether we are alone in the universe.

TRY IT YOURSELF

In class, hold a debate on the subject of the existence of life on other planets. Your debate proposition—the statement that you will argue for or against—will be "There is good reason to believe that life exists on planets other than Earth." In a debate, two teams argue for or against the proposition. Teams take turns presenting their ideas in their opening speeches, called constructive speeches. When the constructive speeches are completed, both teams have a chance to argue the constructive speeches with rebuttal speeches. Organize your debate in this way.

STUDENT MODEL

Mr. Willis's class is holding a debate on the proposition "Emerson Middle School should make foreign language instruction required at all grade levels." The class divides into teams of two debaters each. Each team is assigned to argue in favor of the proposition (in the affirmative) or against the proposition (in the negative). Sara and Chandra are on an affirmative team. Mark and Myron are on a negative team. Sara and Chandra's team is chosen to debate Mark and Myron's team.

Sara chooses to give the constructive speech for her team. In a brief (one-minute) speech, she gives the following reasons in favor of the proposition:

- mass communications have made the world much smaller, and people today have more contact with people from other parts of the globe, thus making learning a foreign language important
- many jobs today require knowledge of foreign languages
- to learn a foreign language, a person must study the language over a period of years, not simply for one year, as currently required at the school
- learning a foreign language teaches people about other cultures in which that language is spoken, making them more tolerant

Myron gives the constructive speech for his team. His main arguments are these:

- adding new foreign language classes would be very expensive
- most students have schedules that are already too full
- many adults find that they can get along just fine speaking and writing only English

Chandra and Mark then give the rebuttal speeches for their teams. In their rebuttal speeches, each student attacks the arguments given by the opposing speaker in his or her constructive speech.

The rest of the class listens to the debate and judges who they think won on the basis of the persuasiveness of the arguments presented.

Examining the Model

1. What is the debate proposition?
2. What is a rebuttal speech?
3. Who judges the debate?

Planning Your Debate

1. Write the debate proposition on the board.
2. Choose a partner and pick, at random, which two-person teams will debate the affirmative and which will debate the negative.
3. Do research in the library to gather evidence to support your team's side of the debate proposition. Make a list of arguments in favor of your side.
4. Think ahead to any arguments that you think the opposing team might present. Come up with arguments to use in rebuttal. Make a list of your rebuttal arguments.

Holding Your Debate

Surface of Mars. Photo courtesy of the National Aeronautics and Space Administration (NASA)

1. Choose at random which teams will debate in what order.
2. As each team debates, the rest of the class should listen and judge the teams on the basis of the soundness of the arguments presented and the persuasiveness of the speakers.
3. Once all the debates are over, take a class vote to see where everyone in the class actually stands on this question. Discuss the reasons behind your positions (that is, the most powerful arguments presented in the debates).

Answers for Examining the Model

1. The debate proposition is *There is good reason to believe that life exists on planets other than Earth.*
2. A rebuttal speech is one in which a debater attacks the constructive arguments of the opposing team.
3. The debate is judged by the rest of the class.

Analytic Scale for Project

Assign a score from 1 to 25 for each grading criterion below.

Debate

- **Organization.** The group set attainable goals and created a schedule or strategy for achieving those goals.
- **Cooperation.** The group assigned tasks fairly to each member, and each member cooperated toward achieving the group's goals.
- **Goal Achievement.** The group worked steadily toward its goals and did, in fact, achieve them.
- **Presentation.** The group presented a product of high quality that met the initial project description.

VOCABULARY CHECK TEST

Ask students to number their paper from one to ten. Have students complete each sentence with a word from the Vocabulary for the Unit in the Unit Review.

1. After the car accident, we were relieved albeit shaken
2. We got our feet wet walking near the estuary.
3. Old newspapers left in an attic can be combustible.
4. The rodent poked furtively at the pile of crumbs.
5. Because of his apathy, the project fell apart.
6. Wanda becomes rude and belligerent when she is tired.
7. The mayor would like to commend you for your hard work.
8. The sun was shining through a small aperature in the wall.
9. I have not been able to broach the subject with my boss.
10. His excitement was evident in his face.

Unit Review

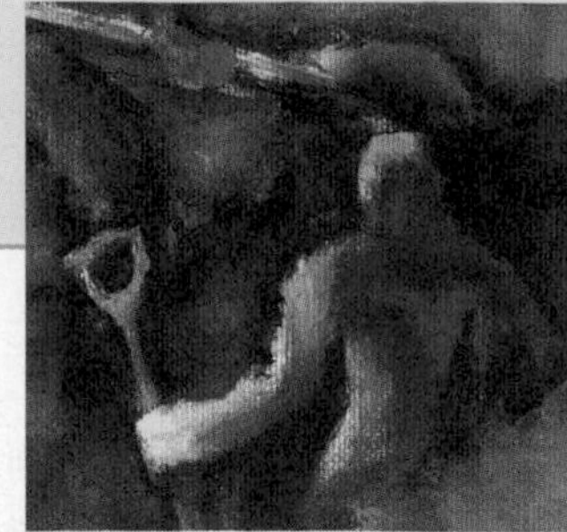

SUMMARY

allusion, 660
science fiction, 659, 713
subplot, 660
theme, 660, 713

VOCABULARY FOR THE UNIT

accost, 590
acuteness, 603
adjacent, 580
albeit, 598
allay, 598
allusion, 630
animated, 578
annihilate, 632
apathy, 632
aperture, 588
appalling, 699
apparition, 608
arcade, 625
ascertain, 629
ascribe, 582
assiduously, 619
assurance, 577
audible, 580
avail, 609
battery, 617
bawl, 606
belligerent, 604
bevy, 605
billowy, 587
blight, 637
brevity, 629
broach, 645
calamity, 580
canard, 600
cannonade, 641
cavity, 587
circuitously, 688
circumference, 583
clamor, 605
cleft, 640
coherency, 643
colossus, 611
combustible, 595
commend, 607
complacency, 577
composition, 595
concussion, 587
conflagration, 611
confluence, 646
congested, 644
conical, 639
consolation, 584
conspicuously, 633
consume, 614
contagion, 607
contemplate, 586
conveyance, 610
copse, 625
counsel, 637
countervailing, 693
cowl, 613
culvert, 692
cumber, 706
cumbersome, 696
cutlass, 692
darkling, 638
decadence, 711
decapitate, 622
deliberation, 588
delusive, 648
demented, 627
deploy, 601
derelict, 589
derive, 590
desist, 609
desolate, 601
detachment, 598
detail, 618
deter, 596
detonation, 605
devise, 693
diameter, 582
dilated, 650
din, 650
disgorge, 611
dispatch, 629
dispense, 599
disseminate, 630
dissuade, 617
drone, 591
dubiously, 647
dun, 582
eddy, 649
ejaculatory, 613
eloquent, 578
embed, 585
estuary, 654
evident, 585
excavation, 586
exempt, 628
exertion, 599
exhort, 632
exorbitant, 655
expend, 655
expostulate, 619
extent, 630
exultant, 609
exultation, 622
façade, 646
fertility, 578
festoon, 708
fetish, 690
flaxen, 627
fluctuate, 579
fluorescent, 699
foreboding, 607
formidable, 620
formulate, 695
furtive, 654
furtively, 613
fusillade, 607

Vocabulary for the Unit

galvanize, 649
gaunt, 614
gesticulate, 648
gibber, 711
gout, 652
gradient, 635
granary, 653
haggard, 598
haze, 602
hearsay, 631
heterogeneous, 671
hoist, 655
immemorial, 601
imminent, 609
impassable, 643
impediment, 586
impinge, 591
impotent, 626
impulse, 589
inaudibly, 623
inane, 706
inanimate, 585
inarticulate, 587
incandescent, 579
incapacity, 634
incessant, 578
incessantly, 652
incongruity, 598
incontinently, 595
incrustation, 582
indefatigable, 601
indiscriminate, 614
indiscriminately, 707
indisputably, 599
inert, 600
inevitable, 591
insensate, 609
insensible, 584
insoluble, 640
interminable, 639
intermittent, 590
intermittently, 623
intimation, 590
intolerable, 682
intolerably, 701
intricate, 622
invigorate, 599
invulnerable, 628
irresolute, 583
irrevocably, 704
jaded, 646
jubilant, 581
kinetic, 699
languid, 691
lapse, 706
lass, 631
lassitude, 602
lethargy, 612
liquefaction, 643
livid, 708
loiter, 644
lurid, 605
magnitude, 634
menagerie, 630
methodically, 641
mettle, 637
minute, 611
molten, 578
multitude, 589
multitudinous, 649
network, 630
nocturnal, 629
nomadic, 634
obliquely, 621
oblivious, 635
obscurity, 612
officiate, 627
ominous, 640
onslaught, 639
opaque, 642
ordain, 711
ornamental, 693
pallid, 591
palpable, 642
palpitate, 579
parapet, 635
parboil, 625
parody, 655
paroxysm, 646
patent, 623
perplexed, 597
perplexingly, 612
petrify, 587
pier, 653
piety, 695
pinnacle, 605
placard, 631
pluckily, 620
ply, 603
populous, 578
portmanteau, 621
precipitate, 607
precipitately, 697
precipitation, 640
projectile, 582
promenader, 634
prosecute, 645
prostrate, 649
provisions, 645
provocation, 706
proximity, 625
pugilistic, 644
pungent, 640
putrefactive, 703
putrescent, 702
quasi-proclamation, 632
raiment, 632
recede, 580
reconnoiter, 698
redoubt, 703
reins, 606
reiterate, 632
remnant, 652
remonstrance
remorse, 690
renew, 589
reprieve, 711
repugnance, 610
resolute, 650
reverberation, 608
revulsion, 699
rouse, 585
rout, 650
sack, 620
sallow, 646

Vocabulary for the Unit

sally, 625
scintillate, 613
scoff, 580
scrutinize, 577
scrutiny, 579
sentinel, 603
serene, 577
siege, 641
silhouette, 608
smite, 597
somber, 695
spasmodic, 641
spectrally, 702
staccato, 646
stippled, 652
stout, 692
stupefy, 591
superficial, 578
taint, 696
tedious, 588
temerity, 702
terminus, 631
terrestrial, 577
timidity, 599
tocsin, 635
torpor, 612
torrent, 609
tranquil, 581
transient, 577
transverse, 580
treble, 620
trench, 601
trivial, 595
trowel, 705
tumult, 586
ultimatum, 600
ululation, 637
unanimity, 579
unawares, 698
undulate, 592
unkempt, 649
utterly, 651
vehement, 635
velocity, 579
verge, 592
vicar, 620
vigil, 579
vigilant, 639
vitality, 692
volition, 650
volley, 637
wantonness, 706
wretch, 649

Questions for Writing, Discussion, and Research

1. "It may be that in the larger design of the universe this invasion from Mars is not without its ultimate benefit for men." Explain this quotation from the novel. What positive effects has the invasion had on humankind? on the narrator?
2. What does this novel teach about society and humankind's perceptions of itself and other life forms? Explain your response using details from the story.

Spelling Check Test

Ask students to number their papers from one to ten. Read each word aloud. Then read aloud the sentence containing the word. Repeat the word. Ask students to write the word on their papers, spelling it correctly.

1. **complacency**

Hilbert's complacency kept him from doing anything to improve himself.

2. **populous**

China is the most populous nation on the planet.

3. **vigil**

The loving father kept a close vigil by his sick child's bed throughout the night.

4. **scoff**

Most people scoff at stories about flying saucers.

5. **jubilant**

After winning the hockey tournament, the players were jubilant.

6. **deliberation**

The tightrope walker had to move with great deliberation.

7. **derive**

Yolanda and I derive great enjoyment from listening to classical music.

8. **pallid**

I could tell that Luke was sick because his normally rosy face was pallid.

9. **composition**

The geologist studied the composition of the rocks brought back from Mars.

10. **beckoned**

The fortress was invulnerable to attack.

For Your Reading List

Karla Nockleby
Roseville Middle School
Roseville, Minnesota

The House of Dies Drear
by Virginia Hamilton

By the time I got to the second chapter of Virginia Hamilton's mystery, *The House of Dies Drear,* I was hooked. I didn't notice time passing as I sprawled across the couch, wide-eyed and anxiously awaiting the story's outcome.

The book begins when the Small family moves from their southern home to an old house in Ohio. Mr. Small, a Civil War–history professor, buys the house, not minding the fact that it had been empty for one hundred years and that Dies Drear and two slaves had been murdered in the house. Mr. Small hopes to learn more about the Underground Railroad from living in the house, and perhaps even find uncharted passageways below. Thomas, Mr. Small's son, can't get off his mind the legend of Dies Drear roaming the old house, especially when eerie things begin to happen. Thomas is frightened by nightly unexplained events—the cries of twin babies after Thomas pushes a hidden button, a haunting moan from the walls, strange triangles on bedroom door frames, and the night visitor who wears a black cape and only Thomas sees.

If you'd like a riveting story about the Underground Railroad packed inside a mystery, you'll love *The House of Dies Drear.*

724 LANGUAGE ARTS SURVEY

LANGUAGE ARTS SURVEY

1. *Essential Skills: Writing*
   - Introduction to Writing
   - Understanding the Writing Process
2. *Essential Skills: Language*
   - The Parts of Speech
   - Using Sentences
   - Editing for Grammar and Usage Errors
   - Editing for Punctuation Errors
   - Editing for Capitalization Errors
   - Editing for Spelling Errors
   - Developing Your Vocabulary
   - Varieties of English
3. *Essential Skills: Speaking and Listening*
4. *Essential Skills: Study and Research*
   - Study Skills
   - Test-taking Skills
   - Research Skills
   - Thinking Skills
5. *Essential Skills: Applied English*

Essential Skills: *Writing*

INTRODUCTION TO WRITING

1.1 The Writing Process

We live in an information society that depends on communication in every facet of its existence. Imagine what a busy airport would be like without an advanced communication system. Businesses are dependent upon good communication among their employers, employees, and clients. Good communication among governments is crucial for world peace. Even the success of our interpersonal relationships hinges on our ability to communicate with others.

While much of our communication is oral, learning how to communicate in writing is a vital skill for anyone living in today's world. Back in 1682, John Sheffield said, "Of all those arts in which the wise excel,/Nature's chief masterpiece is writing well." The most important action that you can take to shape a successful future for yourself is to learn how to write clearly and effectively.

Almost anyone can learn to write well by learning about the **writing process.** The writing process is simply the steps a person takes to put together a piece of writing.

SIX STAGES IN THE PROCESS OF WRITING	
1. Prewriting	In this stage, you plan your writing; choose a topic, audience, purpose, and form; gather ideas; and arrange them logically.
2. Drafting	In this stage, you get your ideas down on paper without worrying about getting everything just right.
3. Peer and Self-Evaluation	*Evaluation* is the act of judging something. In this stage, you judge your writing to see how it might be improved. When a classmate judges your writing, that is called **peer evaluation.** When you judge your own writing, that is called **self-evaluation.**
4. Revising	In this stage, you work to improve the content, organization, and expression of your ideas.
5. Proofreading	In this stage, you check your writing for errors in spelling, grammar, capitalization, and punctuation. After correcting these errors, you make a final copy of your paper and proofread it again.
6. Publishing and Presenting	In this stage, you share your work with an audience.

Try It Yourself 1.1

Choose one of the following scenes and write a paragraph describing it. Try to make your description accurate, vivid, and detailed so that the picture your reader forms in his or her mind will closely match what you observed.

the crowd at a football game or at a rally
your neighborhood after a heavy thunderstorm or snowstorm
snorkeling in a clear lake
a house fire

1.2 Keeping a Journal

Benjamin Franklin stated that "The next thing most like living one's life over again seems to be a recollection of that life, and to make that recollection as durable as possible by putting it down in writing." A **journal** is a special notebook for putting down in writing your thoughts, experiences, ideas, and dreams. Any type of notebook can be used for a journal, or you may wish to keep your journal on computer.

Keeping a journal can help you see the direction of your life and give you a better perspective on the events of your life. Looking over old journals gives you an appreciation of how much you have matured (and may be good for a few laughs!)

IDEAS FOR JOURNALS	
Use your journal as	
A Diary, or Day-to-day Record of Your Life	July 9, 1999. Today is a sad day—our last day here before we move to Michigan, almost 1,000 miles away. I have grown up in this house and I can't imagine any other house being home. All my friends are here, and I know I'll never find such good friends anywhere else. I've already saved up $60 to be able to fly back here for a visit next summer. Maybe one of my friends could fly out to Michigan to see me. Hey, how about over winter break? I wonder if there is good skiing in Michigan?
A Reader Response Journal	All my life I've read or seen stories about aliens visiting from outer space. There must be a million stories like that. It amazes me to think that H. G. Wells came up with the idea first. His book The War of the Worlds has to be one of the most original things ever written. Way back at the end of the last century, before space travel was even invented, he dreamed up Martians that travel through space and invade the earth. What an imagination he had!
A Commonplace Book, or Book of Quotations	"Mistakes are the usual bridge between inexperience and wisdom." —Phyllis Theroux "A gentle answer turns away wrath, but a harsh word stirs up anger." —Proverbs 15:1

CONTINUED

ANALYTIC SCALE FOR WRITING SKILLS 1.1

Assign a score from 1 to 25 for each grading criterion below.

Descriptive Paragraph

- **Content/Unity.** The descriptive paragraph describes a scene in detail.
- **Organization/Coherence.** The descriptive paragraph is written in a sensible order.
- **Language/Style.** The descriptive paragraph uses vivid and precise nouns, verbs, and modifiers.
- **Conventions.** The descriptive paragraph avoids errors in spelling, grammar, usage, mechanics, and manuscript form.

ANSWERS FOR TRY IT YOURSELF 1.2

Encourage students to experiment with the different types of journals to see which type is right for them. Inform students that they need not confine themselves to one type of journal, but can combine types to match their moods and ideas.

A Writer's Lab, or Collection of Ideas for Writing	Story Idea: What if there were gateways into other dimensions so that we could go into other worlds? Suppose I am the main character telling the story from my viewpoint. I'm torn between the two worlds—I want the adventure of the new dimension, but I'm afraid of leaving my world behind.
A Learning Log, or Record of What You Have Learned	Science: Today we saw a film clip of the Tacoma Narrows Bridge, a suspension bridge that collapsed only four months after it was finished. High winds made the bridge start swaying, and then the whole thing was twisting and rippling until finally it just snapped. It was incredible to see such a huge thing self-destruct. We learned about different kinds of bridges. They are pretty amazing things.
A List of Questions About the World	How do animals hibernate? How is glass made? How do antibiotics work?
A Daily Organizer	Things to do tomorrow: • Find library book about Alaska • Band practice after school • Call Lila about surprise party for Kellie • Write thank-you note to Grandma

Try It Yourself 1.2

Start keeping a journal. Begin by choosing a notebook in which to keep your journal or by setting up a file on your computer. Set aside a time every day for writing in your journal. This might be in the morning, in the evening, during homeroom, or during a study period. Try to write at least one of each of the kinds of journal entries listed in the "Ideas for Journals" chart.

1.3 YOUR WRITING PORTFOLIO

A **writing portfolio** is a place to keep your writing. A portfolio may be simply a file folder with your name on it, or you may design or buy a fancy portfolio. Your teacher may ask you to keep a **complete portfolio,** one that includes all the pieces of writing that you do. Another possibility is that your teacher will ask you to keep a **selected portfolio,** one that has in it your very best pieces of writing.

When you put a piece of writing in your portfolio, make sure that it is labeled clearly with your name and the date. Also, attach to the back of the piece of writing any notes or earlier versions of the writing that you have.

From time to time, you and your teacher will meet for a **student-teacher conference** to **evaluate,** or examine, your portfolio. Your teacher will help you to find strengths and weaknesses in your writing. He or she will also help you to make plans for improving your writing in the future.

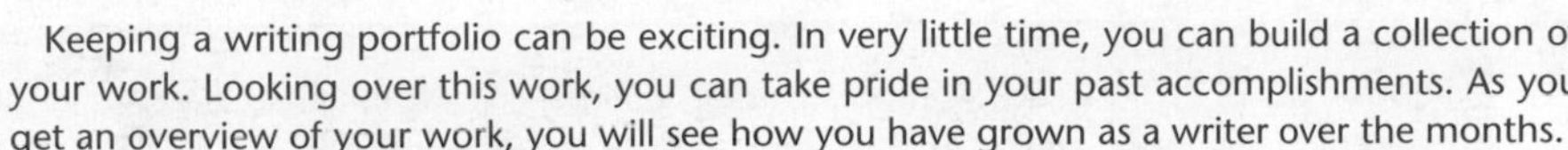

Keeping a writing portfolio can be exciting. In very little time, you can build a collection of your work. Looking over this work, you can take pride in your past accomplishments. As you get an overview of your work, you will see how you have grown as a writer over the months.

ANSWERS FOR TRY IT YOURSELF 1.3

Decide whether you would like students to keep complete portfolios or selected portfolios. Inform students that the purpose of the student-teacher conference will be to review their writing and together to think of ways of improving it.

Try It Yourself 1.3

Create a writing portfolio. Follow the directions given by your teacher.

UNDERSTANDING THE WRITING PROCESS

1.4 MAKING A WRITING PLAN

In the **prewriting stage** of the writing process, you make a plan. You decide on a topic, purpose, audience, and form. You also gather ideas and organize them.

THE PARTS OF A WRITING PLAN	
Topic	A **topic** is simply something to write about. For example, you might write about the life of Ludwig von Beethoven or about your volunteer work in a soup kitchen.
Purpose	A **purpose,** or **aim,** is the goal that you want your writing to accomplish. For example, you might write to express your feelings, to provide information, to persuade, or to entertain.
Audience	An **audience** is the person or group of people for whom you will write. For example, you might write for yourself, for a friend, or for members of your community.
Form	A **form** is a kind of writing. For example, you might write a paragraph, an editorial, a poem, a letter, or a research report.

1.5 FINDING A TOPIC

You might sometimes have trouble deciding on a topic for writing. Here are some steps you can take to come up with interesting writing topics:

WAYS TO FIND A WRITING TOPIC	
Check your journal	Search through your journal for ideas that you jotted down in the past. Many professional writers get their ideas from their journals.
Think about your experiences	Think about people, places, or events that affected you strongly. Recall experiences that taught you important lessons or that created strong feelings in you.

CONTINUED

Look at reference works	Reference works, such as dictionaries, atlases, almanacs, and encyclopedias, are rich sources of information about almost any topic. Many reference works are available both in printed and in computerized form.
Browse in a library	Libraries are treasure houses of information and ideas. Simply looking around in the stacks of a library can suggest lots of good writing ideas.
Use the mass media	Mass media include newspapers, magazines, radio, television, and films, any one of which can suggest good writing topics. For example, a newsmagazine might suggest interesting current events topics.
Talk to people	Friends, relatives, teachers, and other people you know make great sources for writing topics.
Do some freewriting	Simply put your pen or pencil down on a piece of paper and write about whatever pops into your mind. Write for two to five minutes without pausing to worry about whether your writing is perfect. Then look back over what you have written to see if you can find any good topics there.
Ask "What if" questions	Ask questions beginning with "What if" to come up with topics for creative writing. For example, you might ask, "What if I could be transported back in time? What time period would I choose to visit?"
Make a cluster chart	Write some general subject such as Japan or amphibians in the middle of a piece of paper. Circle this subject. Then, around it, write other ideas that come into your mind as you think about the subject. Circle these and draw lines to connect the outer circles to the inner one.

Student Model: Siobbhan needed to come up with a topic for a paper for science class. She thought she might want to write about something related to oceanography, so she made a cluster chart.

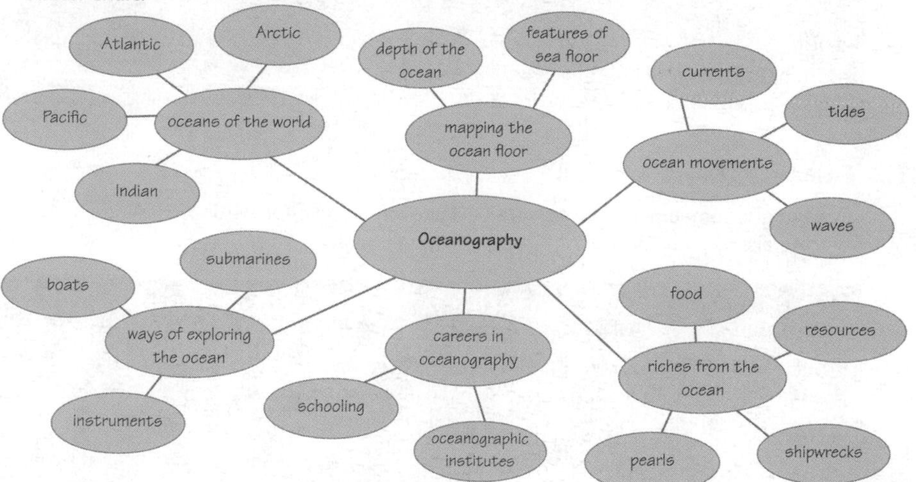

She decided to find out where the deepest point in the ocean is located and to write her paper on what is known about the ocean at that depth.

Try It Yourself 1.5

Use three of the techniques discussed above to come up with three different possible topics for essays.

1.6 Focusing a Topic

Sometimes a topic is too broad to be treated in a short piece of writing. When you have a topic that is too large, you must **focus,** or limit, the topic.

WAYS TO FOCUS A WRITING TOPIC	
Break the topic into parts	For example, the topic "weather" could be broken down into clouds, precipitation, wind, temperature, storms, forecasting, and so on.
Ask questions about the topic	Begin your questions with the words *who, what, where, when, why,* and *how.*
Make a cluster chart or do some freewriting	(For information on these techniques, see the Language Arts Survey, 1.5, "Finding a Topic," and 1.13, "Gathering Ideas.")

Student Model: William chose the topic "railroads" for a paper for his American history class. He realized, however, that the topic was too large for a short paper. Therefore, he wrote some questions about that topic:

What are some of the challenges of laying railroad track?
When and where was the first railroad in the United States built?
How does a locomotive work?
How did railroads affect westward expansion?
How did railroads affect business in the United States?

He decided to write about the first transcontinental railroad—how it was built and the impact it had on the development of America.

Try It Yourself 1.6

Choose one of the topics that you came up with in Try It Yourself 1.5. Using the techniques described above, focus one of the general topics to come up with a good topic for a brief paragraph.

Answers for Try It Yourself 1.5

Students should use any three of the techniques to come up with three different topics. Discuss as a class which topics are most likely to lead to interesting essays.

Answers for Try It Yourself 1.6

Students should narrow one of the topics that they came up with in Try It Yourself 1.5 by breaking it into parts, asking questions about the topic, making a cluster chart, or freewriting. Stress to students that they should always try to focus on a topic before writing. Point out that when students choose a topic that is too broad or general, it will be difficult to discuss adequately all aspects of the topic in their essay. Focused topics lead to interesting, well-organized essays.

Answers for Try It Yourself 1.7

Students' chosen audiences should be appropriate to their topic. Ask students what reasons led them to choose a particular audience.

1.7 Choosing an Audience

Your writing will be most effective if you have a specific audience in mind. Knowing the audience you are targeting will help you to make important decisions about your work regarding the purpose, the form, the vocabulary, and so on. For example, if you are writing for young children, you will use simple words and ideas that they will understand. Keep the following questions in mind when choosing and thinking about your audience.

THINKING ABOUT YOUR AUDIENCE

- What people would most appreciate the kind of writing that I am doing or be most interested in my topic?
- How much does the audience that I am considering already know about the topic?
- How much background information do I need to provide?
- What words, phrases, or concepts in my writing will my audience not understand? For which will I have to provide explanations?
- What can I do at the beginning of my writing to capture my audience's attention and interest?

Try It Yourself 1.7

Choose an audience for a brief paragraph about the topic that you focused in Try it Yourself 1.6. Your audience can be anyone from a brother or sister to the queen of England. Answer each of the questions above about your audience.

1.8 Choosing a Form

Another important decision that a writer needs to make is what form his or her writing will take. The following chart lists some types of writing that you might want to consider.

FORMS OF WRITING		
Advertisement	Calendar	Diary
Adventure	Caption	Directions
Advice column	Cartoon	Dream report
Agenda	Character sketch	Editorial
Apology	Cheer	Epitaph
Appeal	Children's story	Essay
Autobiography	Comedy	Eulogy
Biography	Consumer report	Experiment
Book review	Debate	Fable
Brochure	Detective story	Family history
Bulletin board	Dialogue	Fantasy

CONTINUED

Fortune cookie insert	Mystery	Résumé
Greeting card	Myth	Schedule
Headline	Narrative	Science fiction
History	Newspaper article	Short story
Human interest story	Obituary	Sign
Instructions	Parable	Skit
Interview questions	Paragraph	Slide show
Introduction	Paraphrase	Slogan
Invitation	Petition	Song lyric
Itinerary	Play	Speech
Joke	Police/Accident report	Sports story
Journal entry	Poster	Statement of belief
Letter	Proposal	Summary
Magazine article	Radio or TV spot	Tall tale
Memorandum	Rap	Thank-you note
Menu	Recipe	Tour guide
Minutes	Recommendation	Want ad
Movie review	Research report	Wish list

Try It Yourself 1.8

Imagine that you are an advice columnist. Choose a question that a teenager might ask, then write a paragraph answering the question. Keep in mind who your audience is, and make your answer helpful, to the point, and suitable for a newspaper advice column.

1.9 Purpose: Writing to Express Yourself

One very important reason for writing is to come to understand yourself better. The best way to clarify what you really think about something is to write it down. Writing helps you to sort out your thoughts, air your feelings, and formulate your hopes and plans for the future. Getting your own thoughts and feelings on paper is called **expressive writing.** Expressive writing is done primarily for oneself, not for a reader. Expressive writing can take many forms, but its most common form is the journal or diary entry. For more information about journal writing, see the Language Arts Survey, 1.2, "Keeping a Journal."

Try It Yourself 1.9

Think of a recent experience that stirred strong emotions in you, whether positive or negative. Write a journal entry describing this experience and expressing how you feel about it. Try to identify clearly how it affected you. A few days later, read over what you have written and see if your perspective has changed.

ANALYTIC SCALE FOR WRITING SKILLS 1.8

Assign a score from 1 to 25 for each grading criterion below.

Advice Column

- **Content/Unity.** The advice column provides a helpful, brief answer to a question that a teenager might ask.
- **Organization/Coherence.** The advice column presents advice in a logical order.
- **Language/Style.** The advice column uses vivid and precise nouns, verbs, and modifiers.
- **Conventions.** The advice column avoids errors in spelling, grammar, usage, mechanics, and manuscript form.

ANALYTIC SCALE FOR WRITING SKILLS 1.9

Assign a score from 1 to 25 for each grading criterion below.

Journal Entry

- **Content/Unity.** The journal entry describes a recent experience that stirred strong emotions in the writer.
- **Organization/Coherence.** The journal entry is written in a sensible order.
- **Language/Style.** The journal entry uses vivid and precise nouns, verbs, and modifiers.
- **Conventions.** The journal entry avoids errors in spelling, grammar, usage, mechanics, and manuscript form.

Analytic Scale for Writing Skills 1.10

Assign a score from 1 to 25 for each grading criterion below.

Informative Essay

- **Content/Unity.** The informative essay provides information on a specific topic.
- **Organization/Coherence.** The informative essay is written in a logical order and contains an introduction, a body, and a conclusion.
- **Language/Style.** The informative essay uses vivid and precise nouns, verbs, and modifiers.
- **Conventions.** The informative essay avoids errors in spelling, grammar, usage, mechanics, and manuscript form.

Analytic Scale for Writing Skills 1.11

Assign a score from 1 to 25 for each grading criterion below.

Persuasive Letter

- **Content/Unity.** The persuasive letter describes and provides reasons for changes that should be made in a school.
- **Organization/Coherence.** The persuasive letter is written in a sensible order and reasons are provided as support for opinions.
- **Language/Style.** The persuasive letter uses vivid and precise nouns, verbs, and modifiers.
- **Conventions.** The persuasive letter avoids errors in spelling, grammar, usage, mechanics, and manuscript form.

1.10 Purpose: Writing to Inform

You will often need to write to convey information to someone else. Communication of facts is called **informative writing.** In addition to many of the essays and reports that you will write for school, informative writing includes news reports, memoranda, scientific and technical reports, directions, recipes, and encyclopedia articles. Whether you are taking a telephone message for a family member or writing a technical report on an environmental issue, you need to make your communication clear and accurate. Be sure to get your facts straight, and back up any opinions with solid facts. For more information on fact and opinion, see the Language Arts Survey, 4.22, "Fact or Opinion?"

Try It Yourself 1.10

Choose one of the following topics and write a brief informative essay on it. Do some research on your topic to gather information. Write the body of your paper. Then write an introduction and conclusion. Make sure to include all the facts that your reader will need to know.

Preparing to go camping, Tuning up a car, Cooking a complete meal, Caring for a pet

What causes tsunamis, Why birds fly south in winter, What events led to World War I, What caused the *Challenger* explosion

1.11 Purpose: Writing to Persuade

The purpose of **persuasive writing** is to convince others to believe or to do something. Common types of persuasive writing include editorials, sales letters, advertising copy, and political speeches. When writing persuasively, you attempt to get your reader to adopt your views and/or to take some action. You need to have solid reasons for your position that your readers will be able to accept. You should also appeal to your readers' feelings—perhaps their sense of justice or their sympathy. Be sure to support your position with facts, and try to identify those arguments and emotional appeals to which your readers would most likely respond. Remember, however, that people can sense when they are being manipulated, so try to be persuasive without being manipulative.

Try It Yourself 1.11

Think of a way that you feel your school could be improved. Perhaps you would like to see some changes in the curriculum or the schedule, or maybe there is an elective course that you think should be offered. Write a letter to your principal or school board describing your suggestions. Back up your opinion with strong reasons, and identify at least one emotion to which you could appeal. For information on proper letter form, see the Language Arts Survey, 5.4, "Writing a Business Letter."

1.12 Purpose: Creative Writing

Creative writing can take many forms, including stories, poems, novels, cartoons, plays, or letters. Creative writing attempts to amuse, thrill, delight, anger, or scare the readers. To come up with an idea for a piece of creative writing, pay attention to your own thoughts and to things happening around you. Then let your imagination go. Feel free to let your imagination take you down different paths until you hit upon an idea you would like to pursue.

Try It Yourself 1.12

One good way to get your imagination working is to ask "What if" questions. Make a list of four "What if" questions that could be used as ideas for nature stories, human interest stories, or adventure stories. Record these questions in your journal for future use.

1.13 Gathering Ideas

Have you ever been faced with a writing assignment and had no idea where to start? This section of the Language Arts Survey will give you suggestions about specific actions you can take to come up with ideas and begin to put them together.

Freewriting

Your own mind is a rich source of ideas. The trick is to be able to pull out those ideas when you need them. **Freewriting** can help you to discover ideas and begin to assemble them. Freewriting is simply the act of taking a pencil and paper and writing whatever comes into your mind. Try to write for several minutes without stopping and without worrying about spelling, grammar, usage, or mechanics. If you get stuck, just repeat the last few words until something new pops into your mind.

Student Model: Bruce needed to write a personal essay for English class, but was having trouble coming up with a topic. He tried freewriting to get the ideas flowing.

My life is boring. How can I come up with an interesting topic? Same routine every day—get up, go to school, come home, have a snack, do homework, deliver meals, eat dinner, more homework, go to bed. Well, sometimes I do other things too, like soccer practice or researching the new computer we want to get or hanging out. I'm getting tired of delivering meals for the old people—having to go to the elderly housing, get the bag, pick up the meals from the restaurant, then take them back. I'll be glad when this semester of Life Skills is over and we don't have to do our service projects any more. My sister says I have a bad attitude. I say let her do it. I suppose it is easier for me to trudge through the snow and rain than it is for the old people. Mrs. Klein couldn't do it at all, being in a wheelchair and all. She's a pretty nice lady. It must be a real drag to be cooped up all day. She seems to like seeing me. Maybe I could talk with her for a minute some day.

Bruce decided to write about his experience delivering meals to the elderly.

Answers for Try It Yourself 1.12

Students should list four thought-provoking "What if" questions that could be used for nature stories, human interest stories, or adventure stories.

ANSWERS FOR TRY IT YOURSELF 1.13a

Students should focus their freewriting on things they did not want to do but had to do. They should be able to choose one idea that they would like to write about from their freewriting.

ANSWERS FOR TRY IT YOURSELF 1.13b

Students should create cluster charts on a specific topic. The charts should contain subtopics that are related to their main topic.

To gather ideas about a specific topic, you might want to try **focused freewriting.** In a focused freewrite, you still write nonstop for a few minutes, but you stick with one topic and write whatever comes to mind as you think about that topic.

Try It Yourself 1.13a

Imagine that you have been assigned to write a personal essay about something you didn't want to do but had to do. Do a focused freewrite for five minutes to come up with as many ideas as possible in this category. Then choose the one idea you would most like to write about.

Clustering

Another way to draw upon what you already know is to make a **cluster chart.** To make such a chart, draw a circle in the center of your paper and in it write a topic you want to explore. Branching out from your center circle, draw more circles and fill them with subtopics related to your main topic. See the sample cluster chart in the Language Arts Survey, 1.5, "Finding a Topic."

Try It Yourself 1.13b

Choose one of the following topics or a topic of your own and make a cluster chart about it.

winter sports and activities	money and possessions
being in the hospital	sleep
the human brain	art

Questioning

Another excellent technique for generating ideas is **questioning.** Try asking the familiar **reporting questions** *who? what? where? when? why?* and *how?* This approach is especially useful for gathering information about an event or for planning a story.

If you are doing expressive or creative writing, try asking questions that begin with the words *what if.* "What if" questions can spark your imagination and lead you down unexpected and interesting paths. Here are some examples:

EXAMPLES

What if you could shrink to one inch in height? How would you use this ability? What would be the dangers?

What if your friend got hurt while the two of you were hiking together? Would you stay with your friend? Would you go for help?

What if a house by the sea were haunted by the ghosts of seventeenth-century pirates? What if a family with children moved in? What would the pirates do?

Try It Yourself 1.13c

Choose three of the following types of stories. For each one, write a "What if" question and some follow-up questions that might be developed into a plot for that kind of story. Follow the models shown above.

adventure story	mystery
children's story	science fiction
human interest story	tall tale

Analyzing

To **analyze** is to examine the parts of something in order to understand its essential features. Analyzing is a way to sort out and categorize information about a topic. An **analysis chart** can help you to list the elements and to describe each one. The technique of analysis can be used to study an object, a process, a phenomenon, or a piece of writing. Here is an example of chart created by a student to analyze the process of sewing an item of clothing:

ANALYSIS OF SEWING A GARMENT

STEP	DESCRIPTION
Select	Choose pattern, fabric, thread, accessories (zippers, buttons, snaps, etc.)
Prepare	Assemble all necessary items: table, sewing machine, scissors, pins, pattern, fabric, thread, accessories, iron
Cut	Lay out pattern on fabric and cut out pieces
Sew	Pin pieces together and sew according to instructions in pattern
Finish	Sew on buttons, tack facings, sew hem, press

Try It Yourself 1.13d

Choose an activity or process with which you are familiar (for example, making a sculpture, playing "Capture the Flag," or resolving a conflict). Create an analysis chart describing the different elements of that process.

Sensory Detail Charts

Your body has five different **senses** through which you receive information about the world. The more of these senses you use to observe something, the more you will notice about that thing. A **sensory detail chart** can help you to collect information about something so that you can describe it thoroughly. To make a sensory detail chart, begin by writing your subject at the top of the page. Then make columns for each of the five senses: sight, sound, touch, taste, and smell. In the column under each heading, list details about your subject that you learn from that sense.

ANSWERS FOR TRY IT YOURSELF 1.13c

Students should write at least one "What if" question for each type of story listed. The follow-up questions should provide a focus on the "What if" questions that could be used to develop a story.

ANSWERS FOR TRY IT YOURSELF 1.13d

Students' analysis charts should break an activity or process into parts or elements. The information should be organized in chart form.

ANSWERS FOR TRY IT YOURSELF 1.13e

Students should record sensory details from all five senses.

ANSWERS FOR TRY IT YOURSELF 1.13f

Students' time lines should show dates at equal divisions. At least ten events in students' immediate families, or in preceding generations, should be listed.

Student Model: Naomi had to write a descriptive paragraph for English class. She decided to write about going to the train station to meet her cousin. She made a sensory detail chart to help her recall the impressions she had received from her different senses.

OBSERVATIONS: TRAIN STATION				
Sight	Hearing	Touch	Taste	Smell
trains barreling into station black smoke pouring from train	clatter of wheels on tracks screech of brakes	sitting on hard bench jostling against other people	sweet soda hot dog stale popcorn	smoke fuel and oil food and coffee

Try It Yourself 1.13e

Go to a public place in your community, such as a mall, park, airport, restaurant, or beach, and observe your surroundings for a half-hour. Create a sensory detail chart to record observations that you make there.

Time Lines

A **time line** gives you an overview of the sequence of events during a particular time period. It can be useful when you are planning a story or a historical account. To make a time line, draw a line on a piece of paper and divide it into equal parts. Label each part with a date or a time. Then add key events at the right places along the time line.

Landmark Events in the History of the Civil Rights Movement (1950–1975)

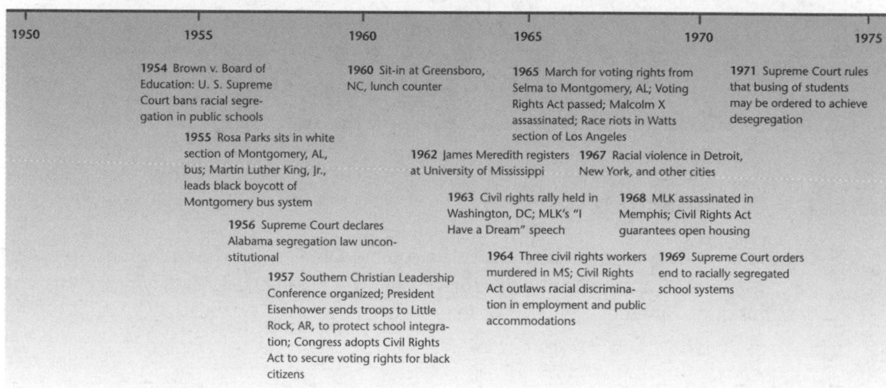

Try It Yourself 1.13f

Make a time line of your family history. Talk to older family members to find out some key dates and events. You may do a time line just for your immediate family, or, if you prefer, you may go back through several generations. Include at least ten events on your time line.

Story Maps

A **story map** is a chart that shows the various elements of a work of fiction. Most story maps include the elements shown in the chart below.

ELEMENT	DESCRIPTION
Setting	The time and place in which the story occurs
Characters	The people (or sometimes animals) who play roles in the story
Plot	The series of events taking place in the story
Conflict	A struggle between two forces in the story
Mood	The emotion created in the reader by the story
Theme	The main idea of the story

Here is a story map created for O. Henry's short story "A Retrieved Reformation":

STORY MAP	
ELEMENT	DESCRIPTION
Setting	Nineteenth-century United States, Midwest and South
Characters	Jimmy Valentine, a burglar; Ben Price, a detective; Annabel Adams, Jimmy's girlfriend
Plot	After being released from prison, Jimmy Valentine returns to his burglary profession. Then he falls in love with Annabel Adams and must decide what to do with his life. Meanwhile, Ben Price is pursuing Jimmy to get him back in jail.
Conflict	Between Jimmy Valentine and Ben Price, who is trying to capture Jimmy and put him behind bars; within Jimmy, whether to continue in his life of crime
Mood	Curiosity, humor, irony, anticipation, suspense
Theme	Love can transform a person.

Try It Yourself 1.13g

Choose a fairy tale that you might retell for a children's story book. Make a story map to describe the parts of the story.

Pro and Con Charts

A **pro and con chart** shows arguments for and against a particular position on some issue. This technique can be useful when you need to think through a decision or take sides on an issue. To create a pro and con chart, begin by writing a **proposition** at the top of a piece of paper. A proposition is an idea to be considered, a statement to be proved, or a policy to be debated. Under the proposition, make two columns, one labeled *Pro* and the other, *Con.* In the pro column, list arguments in favor of the proposition. In the con column, list arguments against the proposition.

ANSWERS FOR TRY IT YOURSELF 1.13g

Students' story maps should describe the following elements of a fairy tale: setting, characters, plot, conflict, mood, and theme.

Answers for Try It Yourself 1.13h

Students should describe the proposition and list reasons for and against this proposition. Most students will probably list more reasons against this proposition than for it.

ANALYTIC SCALE FOR WRITING SKILLS 1.13i

Assign a score from 1 to 25 for each grading criterion below.

Essay

- **Content/Unity.** The essay describes what the writer learned about the foreign country from the writer's interview with a subject.
- **Organization/Coherence.** The essay is written in a sensible order.
- **Language/Style.** The essay uses vivid and precise nouns, verbs, and modifiers.
- **Conventions.** The essay avoids errors in spelling, grammar, usage, mechanics, and manuscript form.

Proposition: Athletes should not be allowed to compete professionally until age 18.

Pro	Con
—Professional competition is too stressful on young people; early burnout can occur	—Decision should be up to the athlete and his or her family
—Easy for a teenager to give in to lure of money, drugs, fame	—In some sports, athletes are at their peak in their teen years
—Rigorous training can be damaging to a developing body	—Unfair to deny the right to compete to someone who is qualified
—Young athlete may neglect school and not prepare for a career after sports	

Try It Yourself 1.13h

Imagine that your town is experiencing a rise in juvenile crime and is considering imposing a 9:00 P.M. curfew on all people under eighteen. Create a pro and con chart to explore this idea. List as many reasons on both sides as you can.

Interviewing

In an **interview**, you meet with someone and ask him or her questions. Interviewing experts is an excellent way to gain information about a particular topic. For example, if you are interested in becoming a florist, you might interview the owner of a greenhouse.

When planning an interview, you should put some thought into the questions you would like to ask. The reporting questions *who? what? where? when? why?* and *how?* are very useful for interviewing. Write out a list of questions, including some about the person's background as well as about your topic. Other questions might occur to you as the interview proceeds. Here are some more tips for interviewing:

- If possible, tape-record the interview. Then you can review the tape at your leisure.
- If you do not have access to a tape recorder, take notes on a notepad. Write down the main points and some key words to help you remember details. Record the person's most important statements word for word.
- Be sure to get the correct spelling of the person's name and to ask permission to print his or her statements.

Try It Yourself 1.13i

Find someone who has lived in a foreign country—perhaps a friend, a relative, or a neighbor. Ask if you may interview him or her to find out what it was like to live there. Before you meet with the person, do some background research on the country and write out some questions to ask. As you conduct the interview, listen carefully and take good notes. Then write a short essay telling what you have learned.

Using Reference Works

No matter what subject you wish to explore, you can probably find information about it in a reference work. **Reference works** include encyclopedias, dictionaries, almanacs, atlases, indexes, and more. Every library has a section of reference books, and some libraries have access to reference material on computer. Ask your librarian for help in finding the sources you need. For additional information about reference materials and how to find them, see the Language Arts Survey, 4.17, "Using Reference Works."

Whenever you use someone else's writing to help you in your own writing, you need to take good notes and document your sources. You should have a system for recording information about your subject. You should also keep track of where you find your information. For tips about taking notes, see the Language Arts Survey, 4.20, "Formal Note-taking."

Try It Yourself 1.13j

Use reference works in your library to find answers to the following questions. Follow the tips provided in parentheses.

1. What countries border Switzerland? (Consult a world atlas.)
2. What was Edwin Land's most famous invention? (Consult an encyclopedia.)
3. Who said "As for me, give me liberty or give me death!"? (Consult an index of quotations.)
4. What is the meaning of the word *egregious*? (Consult a dictionary.)
5. Find four synonyms for the word *big*. (Consult a thesaurus.)
6. Who won the Nobel Peace Prize in 1995? (Consult an almanac.)

1.14 Organizing Ideas

Once you have gathered ideas for a piece of writing, the next step is to organize these ideas in a sensible and interesting way. Stories are usually written in **chronological order** (that is, in the order in which events occur). Other types of writing will follow different formats.

Writing a Thesis Statement

If you are writing an essay, the first step is to identify the major idea that you want to communicate. Write a **thesis statement** expressing this major theme.

Main Ideas and Supporting Details

Next you must select several **main ideas** related to your thesis statement. Review your notes and pick out several main ideas you would like to present. For each main idea, list several **supporting details**—statements, facts, examples, and illustrations that more fully explain or demonstrate your main idea. Here is an example of details organized according to thesis statement, main ideas, and supporting details.

Answers for Try It Yourself 1.13j

1. Switzerland is bordered by France, Italy, Austria, and Germany.
2. Edwin Land invented the Polaroid camera.
3. Patrick Henry said, "As for me, give me liberty or give me death!"
4. *Egregious* means "outstanding for undesirable qualities; remarkably bad."
5. *Responses will vary.*
6. Daw Oung San Suii Kyi of Burma won the Nobel Peace Prize in 1995.

"The Consequences of the Martian Invasion in H. G. Wells's *The War of the Worlds*"

Thesis statement: In H. G. Wells's *The War of the Worlds,* the Martian invasion teaches human beings many lessons.

Main idea: The invasion teaches human beings not to be so proud.

—Supporting idea: After the invasion, humans know that they are not the only intelligent life form in the universe.

—Supporting idea: After the invasion, humans know that they narrowly escaped being wiped out.

—Supporting idea: After the invasion, humans know that they were not able, on their own, to defeat the Martians.

Main idea: The invasion teaches human beings to be more respectful of life.

—Supporting idea: The invasion teaches human beings to be respectful of the so-called "lower forms of life" on which they depend for food, for humans themselves have experienced being treated by the Martians as lower forms of life.

—Supporting idea: The invasion teaches human beings to be respectful of cultures for they have seen the consequences of the Martians' lack of respect for human culture.

Main idea: The invasion teaches human beings much new science and technology.

—Supporting idea: The narrator says in the Epilogue that studying the machines brought by the Martians has been a boon to science on Earth.

—Supporting idea: One such new invention, which humans learn about from Martian technology, is flight.

Another way of organizing your writing is to choose some overall guiding organizational principle. The following chart describes some common ways in which writers organize ideas:

METHOD OF ORGANIZATION	DESCRIPTION
Chronological Order	Give events in the order in which they happen or should be done; connect events by using transitions such as *first, second, next, then,* and *finally.*
Spatial Order	Describe parts in order of their location in space, for example, from back to front, left to right, or top to bottom; connect your descriptions with transitions such as *next to, beside, above, below, beyond,* and *around.*
Order of Importance	List details from least important to most important or from most important to least important; connect your details with transitions such as *more important, less important, most important,* and *least important.*

Try It Yourself 1.14

For a short piece of writing, such as a paragraph, you will have one main idea and several supporting details. Write an informative paragraph about a topic of your choice, including a main idea and at least three supporting details. Underline your main idea and put brackets around each of your supporting details.

1.15 Outlining

An **outline** is a framework for highlighting main ideas and related ideas. Outlining is an excellent way to sketch out your plans for a piece of writing. There are two main types of outlines commonly used by writers.

Rough Outlines

To begin ordering your ideas, start with a **rough outline.** To create a rough outline, simply list your main ideas or topics in some logical order. Under each main idea, list the supporting details set off by dashes.

Student Model: Roger's family went to New York City over school vacation, and he decided to do his American history paper on the Statue of Liberty. He collected information when they visited the statue, and he did further research in the library. Then he organized his notes into the following rough outline:

The Statue of Liberty

Why it was built

—Gift from France, proposed during centennial celebration of Declaration of Independence

—To commemorate alliance of 1778 between France and United States and their lasting friendship

—To symbolize freedom

How it was built

—Designed by Fredéric Auguste Bartholdi

—Made of hammered copper, about 1/8 inch thick

—Statue is hollow, supported upon steel frame anchored in pedestal (underpinnings in pedestal designed by Alexander Eiffel)

—Statue was erected in Paris, presented to United States on July 4, 1884

—Dismantled and shipped to New York, reassembled on Liberty Island in New York Harbor (1884–1886)

Facts about its structure

—Liberty portrayed as a woman: burning torch in right hand, book of law in left hand, broken shackles at her feet

—Weighs 225 tons; stands 152 feet in height; tip of torch is 305 feet above sea level

—Width of face = 10 feet; width of eyes = 2 feet, 6 inches; length of arm = 42 feet

Formal Outlines

A **formal outline** has headings and subheadings identified by numbers and letters. One type of formal outline is the **topic outline.** Such an outline has entries that are words or phrases rather than complete sentences.

Analytic Scale for Writing Skills 1.14

Assign a score from 1 to 25 for each grading criterion below.

Informative Paragraph

- **Content/Unity.** The informative paragraph presents one main idea and at least three supporting details on a specific topic.
- **Organization/Coherence.** The paragraph presents the main idea and then provides the supporting details.
- **Language/Style.** The informative paragraph uses vivid and precise nouns, verbs, and modifiers.
- **Conventions.** The informative paragraph avoids errors in spelling, grammar, usage, mechanics, and manuscript form.

Answers for Try It Yourself 1.15

Responses will vary. Possible responses are given.

Antarctica

Location and description of **Antarctica:**

—Antarctica is the area at the southern extremity of the Earth, centered approximately around the South Pole

—Antarctica is a frozen continent surrounded by ocean filled with icebergs

—An icecap with estimated average thickness of two miles covers the continent

—Major indentations of shoreline are Ross Sea and Weddell Sea

Animal life in Antarctica:

—Antarctica has no land vertebrates

—Land invertebrates include ticks, mites, lice, and wingless flies

—Krill (shrimplike crustaceans) live in sea

—Birds include penguins, terns, and cormorants

—Whales and seals are abundant in surrounding waters

Early expeditions to Antarctica:

—Sir Ernest Shackleton's expedition of 1908 climbed Mount Erebus (12,448 ft.) and came within one hundred miles of pole

—South Pole first reached by Roald Amundsen in 1911

—Robert F. Scott reached the South Pole thirty-four days after Amundsen; his whole party died on the return

—Admiral Richard E. Byrd led four expeditions (1928–1946)

Student model: Shanaz is preparing an Earth Day presentation about pollution in her community. Here is a formal outline covering the topics she plans to present:

Pollution in our Community

I. The problems
  A. Litter
    1. On school grounds
    2. On public beach
    3. Along Route 17
  B. Air pollution
    1. Tomato canning factory
    2. Automobile emissions
  C. Water pollution
    1. Tomato canning factory
    2. Sewage treatment plant

II. The solutions
  A. Education
    1. K–12 environmental awareness program
      a. Stress civic responsibility
      b. Warn of threats to our future
      c. Emphasize conservation
    2. Informative radio spots enlisting community help
  B. Action
    1. Organize student clean-up brigades
    2. Adopt-a-Highway program
    3. Increase recycling efforts
  C. Political action
    1. Lobby for stricter standards for factory and sewage plant
    2. Tighter enforcement of automobile inspection
    3. Boycott canned tomatoes

Try It Yourself 1.15

Here are three main headings for a paper about Antarctica:

Location and description of Antarctica
Animal life in Antarctica
Early expeditions to Antarctica

Organize the supporting details below under the three main headings to create a rough outline for the paper.

—Land invertebrates include ticks, mites, lice, and a wingless fly
—South Pole first reached by Roald Amundsen in 1911
—Birds include penguins, terns, and cormorants
—An icecap with estimated average thickness of two miles covers the continent
—Sir Ernest Shackleton's expedition of 1908 climbed Mount Erebus (12,448 ft.) and came within one hundred miles of pole
—Antarctica is the area at the southern extremity of the earth, centered approximately around the South Pole
—Whales and seals are abundant in surrounding waters
—Antarctica is a frozen continent surrounded by ocean filled with icebergs
—Krill (shrimplike crustaceans) live in sea
—Admiral Richard E. Byrd led four expeditions (1928–1946)
—Antarctica has no land vertebrates
—Robert F. Scott reached South Pole thirty-four days after Amundsen; his whole party died on the return
—Major indentations of shoreline are Ross Sea and Weddell Sea

1.16 Drafting

After you have gathered and organized your information, the next step in writing is to produce a **draft.** A draft is simply an early attempt at a piece of writing. Some writers prefer to start with a **discovery draft,** getting all their ideas down on paper quickly without worrying about spelling, grammar, and mechanics. The draft is then reworked as many times as necessary to polish it. Other writers prefer to write a **careful draft,** working slowly and carefully to perfect each part as they go. Either approach can produce great writing.

Try It Yourself 1.16

Write either a discovery draft or a careful draft for a paragraph on one of the following topics. If you choose to do a discovery draft, write quickly. Get all your ideas on paper. Then go back and rewrite the paragraph, polishing it as you go. If you choose to write a careful draft, work on each sentence until it is just how you want it.

the person you respect most
a dangerous experience
a big mistake you made
a beautiful scene

1.17 Self-Evaluation

When you **evaluate** something, you examine it carefully to find its strengths and weaknesses. Evaluating your own writing is called **self-evaluation.** After producing a rough draft of a piece of writing, the next step is to do an evaluation of that draft to find out what you need to improve. You may wish to wait a day or two before doing your self-evaluation so that you are able to experience the piece more as a first-time reader would.

A good self-evaluation practice is to read through the piece of writing three times:

First, check for content. Make sure that you have said all that you want to say, that you have not left out important details, and that you have not included unnecessary details.

Second, check for organization. Make sure that your ideas are presented in a reasonable order.

Third, check the style and language that you have used. Make sure that your language is appropriately formal or informal, that your tone is appropriate to your message, and that you have defined any key or unfamiliar terms.

As you check your writing, make notes about what you need to revise, or change. See the Language Arts Survey, 1.20, "A Revision Checklist," for a further guide to what to look for as you evaluate your writing.

Try It Yourself 1.17

Do a self-evaluation of the piece of writing that you did for Try It Yourself 1.16. Follow the guidelines given above, and use the revision checklist on page 748.

1.18 Peer Evaluation

A **peer evaluation** is an evaluation of a piece of writing done by a classmate, or peer. The following are some guidelines for peer evaluation:

Answers for Try It Yourself 1.16

Students should either write a discovery draft or a careful draft on one of the given topics. Inform students that in a draft they do not have to worry about spelling, grammar, usage, and punctuation. Students will edit these types of errors in the proofreading stage. Students' main concern should be to present their ideas in a sensible order.

Answers for Try It Yourself 1.17

Students should evaluate the draft they did for Try It Yourself, 1.16, focusing on content, organization, style, and language.

ANSWERS FOR TRY IT YOURSELF 1.18

Encourage students to provide constructive criticism. Point out that it is positive and helpful to say, "I think you might add a few more details to support this idea." It is negative and not very helpful to say, "You did not support any of your ideas at all." Tell students that they must, however, note both strengths and ways in which the paper can be improved when evaluating one another's work.

For the Writer

- Mention to your evaluator any aspects of the writing that you are particularly concerned about. For example, if you are wondering whether something you have said is clear, ask the reader if he or she understands that part of what you have written.
- Feel free to ask questions to clarify comments that your peer evaluator makes.
- Accept your peer evaluator's comments graciously. Remember that criticisms can help you to identify weaknesses and so produce a better piece through revision. Do not take the criticisms personally.

For the Evaluator

- Be focused. Concentrate on content, organization, and style. Refer to the Language Arts Survey, 1.20, "A Revision Checklist." At this point do not worry about proofreading matters, such as spelling and punctuation, that can be fixed later.
- Be positive. Let the writer know what he or she has done right. Show how the paper could be improved by making the changes that you are suggesting.
- Be specific. Give the writer concrete ideas for improving his or her work. For example, if you find a sentence that is weak or unnecessary, you can suggest that it be deleted or offer an idea for replacing it.
- Be tactful. Consider the other person's feelings and use a pleasant tone of voice. Do not criticize the writer. Instead, focus on the writing itself and how it can be made better.

Try It Yourself 1.18

Team up with a classmate and exchange the pieces of writing that you did in Try It Yourself 1.16. Evaluate one another's papers, noting both strengths of the papers and ways in which they might be improved. Follow the guidelines given above.

1.19 FOUR TYPES OF REVISION

After identifying weaknesses in a draft through self-evaluation and peer evaluation, the next step is to **revise** the draft, to make changes for the purpose of improving it. Here are four basic techniques that you can use when doing a revision:

Adding

Sometimes a piece of writing can be improved by adding details, examples, or transitions to connect ideas. Often a single added adjective, for example, can make a piece of writing clearer or more vivid.

UNREVISED SENTENCE	The jeep made its way up the mountain road.
REVISED SENTENCE	The jeep made its way up the treacherous mountain road.

Cutting

A piece of writing can be improved by cutting material that is unnecessary or unrelated.

UNREVISED SENTENCE	Janelle was excited and thrilled about her new little sister.
REVISED SENTENCE	Janelle was thrilled about her new little sister.

Replacing

Weak parts of a piece of writing can be replaced with parts that are stronger, more concrete, more vivid, or more precise.

UNREVISED SENTENCE	The workmen threw their stuff into the truck.
REVISED SENTENCE	The landscapers threw their tools into the old pickup.

Moving

Often you can improve the organization of a piece of writing by moving part of it so that related ideas appear near one another.

UNREVISED SENTENCES	The cherry trees were in full bloom. The sunlight splashed on the river and drenched the people strolling along it. The trees sprouted little boys in their branches.
REVISED SENTENCES	The cherry trees were in full bloom, sprouting little boys in their branches. The sunlight splashed on the river and drenched the people strolling along it.

When you mark a piece of writing for revisions, use the standard proofreading symbols. The symbols for adding, cutting, replacing, and moving are the first four symbols in the chart on page 748.

Try It Yourself 1.19

Revise these sentences, following the suggestions given in parentheses.

1. Gabrielle felt cold and achy and sore all over after her first day on the slopes. (Cut the words that are unnecessary.)
2. She flopped down by the fire in the lodge. (Add adjectives to describe the fire and the lodge.)
3. Slowly she thawed out. The warmth of the fire began to penetrate into her bones. Life came back into her fingers and toes. (Move the sentences to make a more logical order. Combine the first and third sentences.)
4. When her muscles would move again, she went to the snack bar and bought a bunch of stuff. (Replace the phrase *a bunch of stuff* with specific items.)

ANSWERS FOR TRY IT YOURSELF 1.19

Responses will vary. Possible responses are given.

1. Gabrielle felt cold and sore after her first day on the slopes.
2. She flopped down by the roaring fire in the cozy lodge.
3. Slowly she thawed out, and life came back into her fingers and toes. The warmth of the fire began to penetrate her bones.
4. When her muscles would move again, she went to the snack bar and bought hot cider and muffins.

ANSWERS FOR TRY IT YOURSELF 1.20

Students should read through their work three times and make notes about what needs to be revised, using the Revision Checklist.

1.20 A REVISION CHECKLIST

The following chart lists some questions to ask yourself whenever you are revising a piece of writing. If your answer to any of these questions is *no,* then you need to revise your work. Continue revising until you can answer *yes.*

REVISION CHECKLIST: CONTENT
1. Does the writing achieve its purpose?
2. Are the main ideas clearly stated and supported by details?
REVISION CHECKLIST: ORGANIZATION
1. Are the ideas arranged in a sensible order?
2. Are the ideas connected to one another within paragraphs and between paragraphs?
REVISION CHECKLIST: STYLE
1. Is the language appropriate to the audience and purpose?
2. Is the mood appropriate to the purpose of the writing?

Try It Yourself 1.20

Choose a piece of writing you have done previously. Read it through three times, using the checklist above to note what needs to be revised.

1.21 USING PROOFREADER'S MARKS

When you **proofread** your writing, you read it through to look for errors and mark corrections. When you mark corrections to your writing, use the standard proofreading symbols. With just a little practice you'll find them very easy and convenient.

PROOFREADER'S SYMBOLS	
Symbol and Example	**Meaning of Symbol**
The ~~very~~ first time	Delete (cut) this material.
cat^s cradle	Insert (add) something that is missing.
Geor~~z~~e (g)	Replace this letter or word.
All the horses (king's)	Move this word to where the arrow points.
french toast	Capitalize this letter.

Symbol and Example	Meaning of Symbol
the vice-President	Lowercase this letter.
housse	Take out this letter and close up space.
book keeper	Close up space.
gebril	Change the order of these letters.
end. "Watch out," she yelled.	Begin a new paragraph.
Love conquers all	Put a period here.
Welcome friends.	Put a comma here.
Getthe stopwatch	Put a space here.
Dear Madam	Put a colon here.
She walked he rode.	Put a semicolon here.
name brand products	Put a hyphen here.
cats meow	Put an apostrophe here.
cat's cradle (stet)	Let it stand. (Leave as it is.)

1.22 A Proofreading Checklist

After you have revised your draft, make a clean copy of it and proofread it for errors in spelling, grammar, and punctuation. Use the following proofreading checklist.

PROOFREADING CHECKLIST	
Spelling	• Are all words, including names, spelled correctly?
Grammar	• Does each verb agree with its subject? • Are verb tenses consistent and correct? • Are irregular verbs formed correctly? • Are there any sentence fragments or run-ons? • Have double negatives been avoided? • Have frequently confused words, such as *affect* and *effect*, been used correctly?
Punctuation	• Does every sentence end with an end mark? • Are commas used correctly? • Do all proper nouns and proper adjectives begin with capital letters?

Answers for Try It Yourself 1.22

On July 24 1911, an enthusiastic young Yale graduat named Hiram Bingham discovered the ruins of Machu Picchu, high in the Andes Mountains of Peru. his discovery of the lost city of the Incas were the results of intense curiousity, feirce dedication, mountaineering skill, and phenominal luck.

Bingham has visited Peru in 1909 fora tour of Inca ceremonial sites. He was deeply effected by seing such magnificent ruins. He resolved to return and serch for the last fortress of the Incas, where they had fleed to escape the Spanish conquistadores. The citadel had manajed to escape discovery for nearly four cenchuries.

Bingham and his companians had to trek deep withinthe Andean jungle, along danjerous cliffs, and up a steep mountain paths. it is all worth it when they layed eyes on the lost city, choked with weeds but still clothed with majesty

Try It Yourself 1.22

There are twenty-five mistakes in spelling, grammar, usage, and punctuation in the following paragraph. Find these mistakes and correct them on your own paper.

On July 24 1911, an enthusiastic young Yale graduat named Hiram Bingham discovered the ruins of Machu Picchu, high in the Andes Mountains of Peru. his discovery of the lost city of the Incas were the results of intense curiousity, feirce dedication, mountaineering skill, and phenominal luck.

Bingham has visited Peru in 1909 fora tour of Inca ceremonial sites. He was deeply effected by seing such magnificent ruins. He resolved to return and serch for the last fortress of the Incas, where they had fleed to escape the Spanish conquistadores. The citadel had manajed to escape discovery for nearly four cenchuries.

Bingham and his companians had to trek deep withinthe Andean jungle, along danjerous cliffs, and up a steep mountain paths. it is all worth it when they layed eyes on the lost city, choked with weeds but still clothed with majesty

1.23 Proper Manuscript Form

After proofreading your draft, you will want to prepare your final manuscript. Follow the guidelines given by your teacher or the guidelines given here:

GUIDELINES FOR PREPARING A MANUSCRIPT

1. Keyboard your manuscript using a typewriter or word processor, or write it out neatly using blue or black ink.
2. Double-space your paper. Leave one blank line between every line of text.
3. Use one side of the paper.
4. Leave one-inch margins on all sides of the text.
5. Indent the first line of each paragraph.
6. In the upper right-hand corner of the first page, put your name, class, and date. On every page after the first, include the page number in this heading, as follows:
   Alejandro Fernandez
   English 8
   October 17, 1999
   p. 2
7. Make a cover sheet listing the title of the work, your name, the date, and the class.

After preparing a final manuscript according to these guidelines, proofread it one last time for keyboarding or copying errors.

Try It Yourself 1.23

Find five errors in manuscript form in the following passage from the second page of a student report.

English 8
Leo Wibberley
p. 2

Another of the Wonders of the Ancient World was the Colossus of Rhodes. It was a huge bronze sculpture of the sun god Helios. It stood over one hundred feet in height, straddling the harbor of the Greek island of Rhodes. It was so big that ships could sail between its legs. It took twelve years to build and was completed about 280 BC. Less than sixty years later it was leveled by an earthquake.

1.24 Publishing or Presenting Your Work

Some writing, such as in a journal, is done just for oneself. Most writing, however, is meant to be shared with others. There are many ways in which to share your work. Here are several ways in which you can publish your writing or present it to others:

- Find a local publication that will accept such work (a school literary magazine, a school newspaper, or a community newspaper are possibilities).
- Submit the work to a regional or national publication. Check a reference work such as *Writer's Market* to find information on types of manuscripts accepted, manuscript form, methods and amounts of payment, and so on.
- Enter the work in a contest. Your teacher may be able to tell you about writing contests for students. You can also find out about such contests by looking for announcements in writers' magazines and literary magazines.
- Read your work aloud to classmates, friends, or family members.
- Obtain permission to read your work aloud over the school's public address system.
- Work with other students to prepare a publication—a brochure, literary magazine, anthology, or newspaper.
- Prepare a poster or bulletin board, perhaps in collaboration with other students, to display your writing.
- Make your own book by typing or word processing the pages and binding them together in some way. Another possibility is to copy your work into a blank book.
- Hold a recital of student writing as a class or schoolwide project.
- Share your writing with other students in a small writers' group that meets periodically to discuss students' recent work. (Members of the group should receive the work to be discussed beforehand so they can read it and make notes on it.)
- If the work is dramatic in nature, work with other students to present a performance of it, either as straight drama or as reader's theater. If the work is poetry, fiction, or nonfiction, work with others to present it as an oral interpretation. (One possibility is to pair with another student, exchange pieces, and then coach each other in oral interpretations of the pieces.)

Answers for Try It Yourself 1.23

1. Student's name should come before the class name.
2. Student should include the date.
3. Heading should be on the right-hand corner of the page.
4. The text should be double-spaced.
5. The first line of each paragraph should be indented.

ESSENTIAL SKILLS: *Language*

THE PARTS OF SPEECH

2.1 THE PARTS OF SPEECH

There are eight parts of speech. Each part of speech is identified in the chart below.

DEFINITION	EXAMPLE(S)
Noun. A **noun** names a person, place, thing, or idea.	Tonya, Langston Hughes, glacier, peace, theory, song, sailboat
Verb. A **verb** expresses action or a state of being.	imagine, write, fly, hope, paint, climb, is, are, were
Pronoun. A **pronoun** is used in place of a noun.	Give the computer disk to **Chandra,** and ask **Chandra** to print the file. Give the computer disk to **Chandra,** and ask **her** to print the file.
Adjective. An **adjective** modifies, or changes the meaning of, a noun or pronoun.	**strange** situation, **noble** action, **perfect** sphere, **translucent** film, **blue** water
Adverb. An **adverb** modifies, or changes the meaning of, a verb, an adjective, or another adverb.	Andrea **finally** finished her report on *War of the Worlds.* She planned her paper **very carefully.**
Preposition. A **preposition** is used to show how a noun or a pronoun is related to other words in the sentence. Common prepositions are *in, after, among, at, behind, beside, off, through, until, upon,* and *with.*	The submarine sank **beneath** the waves. **On** the roof **of** the house **at** the corner **of** the street was a tiny kitten.
Conjunction. A **conjunction** is used to join words or groups of words. Common conjunctions are *and, but, for, nor, or, so,* and *yet.*	Live **and** let live. Act practically, **but** remember your dreams.

CONTINUED

Interjection. An **interjection** is a word used to express emotion. Common interjections are *oh, ah, well, say,* and *wow.*	**Wow!** Those dinomation creatures look real! **Yikes!** There's a snake in the water.

Try It Yourself 2.1

"THE WAR OF THE WALL," PAGE 118

On your own paper, identify the part of speech of each underlined word in the following passage.

EXAMPLE The twin with the red ribbons was hugging a jug of cloudy lemonade. **adjective**

[1] "Good evening," [2] Side Pocket said in his best ain't-I-fine voice. But the painter lady was moving from the milk crate to the step stool to the ladder, moving up and down [3] fast, scribbling all over the wall like a [4] crazy person. [5] We looked [6] at Side Pocket. He looked at the twins. The twins [7] looked at us. The painter lady was giving a show. It was like those old-timey music movies where the dancer [8] taps on the table top and then starts jumping all over the furniture, kicking chairs over, [9] and not skipping a beat. She didn't even look where she was stepping. And for a minute there, hanging on the ladder to reach a far spot, she looked like she was going to tip right over. [10] "Ahh," Side Pocket cleared his throat and moved fast to catch the ladder.

2.2 Types of Nouns

A **noun** is a person, place, thing, or idea.

EXAMPLES Ibrahim (person), Nigeria (place), mountain (thing), freedom (idea)

A **compound noun** is a noun made up of two or more words. Some compound nouns are written as one word, some as two words, and some as hyphenated words.

COMPOUND NOUNS sister-in-law, lemon tree, Valentine's Day, grandfather, New York, editor-in-chief

A **common noun** names any person, place, thing, or idea.
A **proper noun** names a specific person, place, or thing and begins with a capital letter.

COMMON NOUNS ocean, nation, holiday, writer, religion
PROPER NOUNS Indian Ocean, Kenya, Thanksgiving, Maya Angelou, Islam

ESSENTIAL SKILLS: LANGUAGE

Answers for Try It Yourself 2.1

1. adjective
2. noun
3. adverb
4. adjective
5. pronoun
6. preposition
7. verb
8. verb
9. conjunction
10. interjection

ANSWERS FOR TRY IT YOURSELF 2.2

1. proper; concrete
2. common; concrete; rain|coats
3. common; abstract
4. common; abstract; self-|confidence
5. common; concrete; class|mates
6. proper; concrete; United|States
7. common; abstract
8. common; abstract
9. common; concrete
10. common; abstract

A **concrete noun** names a thing that can be touched, seen, heard, smelled, or tasted—something that can be perceived with any of your five senses.

An **abstract noun** names an idea, a theory, a concept, or a feeling—something that cannot be touched or seen.

CONCRETE NOUNS	burrow, face, plum, lamp
ABSTRACT NOUNS	integrity, psychology, Romanticism, hope

Try It Yourself 2.2

"THE FAN CLUB," PAGE 154

Write whether each underlined noun is common or proper. Then tell whether it is concrete or abstract. If a noun is compound, draw a line between its two parts.

EXAMPLE Laura gave a speech about how we must overcome prejudice.
common; abstract

1. Laura disliked school because of the mean-spirited people in her class.
2. All the popular students seemed to have the same fashion sense and wore mohair sweaters, madras shirts, and pea-green raincoats.
3. Rachel Horton desperately wanted companionship and tried to befriend Laura.
4. Laura's work was well-respected by her teachers, and she had more self-confidence than Rachel had.
5. Rachel was less mature than her classmates and suffered from intense embarrassment at school.
6. Laura believed that the United States could not really be a democracy when prejudice continued to exist.
7. Rachel's presentation of shells did not go well; the other students responded with ridicule.
8. Laura did not enjoy Rachel's suffering, but she was glad not to be in Rachel's shoes.
9. The other students made cards saying "Hortensky's Fan Club" to mock Rachel.
10. Laura betrayed her own principles by joining the others in their cruel joke.

2.3 TYPES OF PRONOUNS

A **pronoun** is used in place of a noun. The word a pronoun stands for is its **antecedent**. In the following sentence, *Clem* is the antecedent of the pronoun *his*.

EXAMPLE **Clem** waved **his** scarf to stop the bus.

A **personal pronoun** is used in place of the name of a person or thing. Personal pronouns are *I, me, my, mine, we, us, our, ours, you, your, yours, he, him, his, she, her, hers, it, its, they, them, their,* and *theirs*. Use pronouns to refer to yourself, to refer to people to whom you are talking, and to refer to other people, places, and things.

PERSONAL PRONOUNS THAT REFER TO YOURSELF	**I** cannot help wanting **my** teacher to choose **me.** **We** laughed **ourselves** silly.
PERSONAL PRONOUNS THAT REFER TO A PERSON TO WHOM YOU ARE SPEAKING	**You** can take **your** flowers and go home. **Yours** is not to reason why.
PERSONAL PRONOUNS THAT REFER TO OTHER PEOPLE, PLACES, OR THINGS	Candice wore **her** helmet when **she** rode. **They** don't want **their** names in the article. The raccoon washed **its** fruit before eating.

An **interrogative pronoun** is used to ask a question. Some interrogative pronouns are *who, whose, what, whom,* and *which.*

INTERROGATIVE PRONOUNS	**What** do you like most about horses? **Which** guitar do you play? **Who** would like to paint?

An **indefinite pronoun** is a pronoun that points out a person, place, or thing, but not a particular one. Some of the most common indefinite pronouns are *some, someone, somebody, something, any, anyone, anybody, anything, everyone, everybody, everything, other, another, either, neither, all, many, few, each, both, one, none, nobody,* and *nothing.*

INDEFINITE PRONOUNS	**Nobody** knows why that man never speaks. **Either** piece of music would be appropriate.

A **relative pronoun** is a pronoun that connects a group of words with an antecedent. In the examples below, *Leily* is the antecedent of the relative pronoun *who,* and *sweater* is the antecedent of the relative pronoun *that.*

RELATIVE PRONOUNS	Leily is the teacher **who** has the most students. Would you hand me **that** sweater, please.

Try It Yourself 2.3

"HUMANS ARE DIFFERENT," PAGE 188

On your own paper, name the pronouns in the following sentences. Hint: Some sentences have more than one pronoun.

EXAMPLE The narrator in the story says that humans are his business. **his**

1. In the first paragraph, he reveals that he is a robot.
2. The robots read their history books and learned that humans came from the planet Earth.

CONTINUED

ANSWERS FOR TRY IT YOURSELF 2.3

1. he; he
2. their
3. their
4. they; any; they
5. he; his
6. who; he; no one; whom
7. He
8. him; he; him
9. he; nothing
10. he

Try It Yourself 2.3 (cont.)

3. Robots knew that humans traveled from planet to planet, leaving their representatives behind.
4. However, they never returned to any of the planets they settled.
5. The robot seems to regret that he and his kind do not have the "divine flame" that humans have.
6. The narrator met the last human, who had forgotten how to talk because he had no one with whom to communicate.
7. He befriended the human, but one day the human developed a fever.
8. The robot "turned him off" and was surprised that he could not turn him on again.
9. Eventually, the human disintegrated until he was nothing but bones.
10. The robot decided after this experience that he did not understand humans.

2.4 Types of Verbs

A **verb** expresses action or a state of being.

VERBS THAT EXPRESS ACTION	sing, save, smile Mother Teresa **saves** people's lives daily.
VERBS THAT EXPRESS A STATE OF BEING	is, are, were, being, am, was, be, been seem, feel, sound, look, taste Carlos **seems** happiest when he is with Maria.

ACTION VERB	Sylvia **built** a studio.

An **action verb** expresses physical or mental activity.

A **linking verb** connects a noun with another noun, a pronoun, or an adjective that describes it or identifies it. Common linking verbs include *am, are, is, was,* and *been*. Other words that can be used as linking verbs include *seem, sound, look, stay, feel, remain*, and *become*.

LINKING VERBS	Soledad **remains** convinced of his innocence. Would everyone **be** quiet?

A **helping verb** helps a main verb to express action or a state of being. Common helping verbs are *can, could, may, might, must, shall, should, will, would,* and forms of the verbs *to be, to have,* and *to do.*

SENTENCE	VERBS
Karen **is painting.** Larry **will call.** Shane **has arrived.**	is (helping verb); painting (main verb) will (helping verb); call (main verb) has (helping verb); arrived (main verb)

The **direct object** of a verb is a noun or a pronoun that names the person or thing upon which the verb acts. Verbs that must have direct objects are **transitive verbs.** Verbs that do not need direct objects are **intransitive verbs.** Some verbs are both transitive and intransitive. A linking verb is a special type of intransitive verb.

TRANSITIVE VERBS Seri **paid** Lisa the money she owed her.
INTRANSITIVE VERBS Susan **thought** and **wrote.**

An **infinitive** is a verb form that usually begins with the word *to.* An infinitive may be used as a noun, an adjective, or an adverb.

INFINITIVES Would you like **to follow** me?
Whether **to be** or not **to be** was Hamlet's question.

Try It Yourself 2.4

"Zoo," PAGE 192

Name the verbs in the following sentences. Tell whether they are action verbs, linking verbs, or helping verbs. If a verb is a helping verb, identify both the main verb and the helping verb. If a verb is an action verb, identify it as transitive or intransitive.

EXAMPLE Children on Earth behaved very well during the month of August.
behaved, action verb, Intransitive

1. People in the Chicago area expected Professor Hugo and his zoo to arrive.
2. Thousands gathered near the parking area and paid a dollar to see the strange creatures from other planets.
3. Professor Hugo had brought three-legged creatures from Venus and shown tall, thin men from Mars.
4. The audience watched as the ship's sides rose to reveal the barred cages.
5. The creatures they saw were insectlike horses who chattered like monkeys.
6. Professor Hugo wore a rainbow cape and top hat like a ringmaster, and he called through a microphone.
7. He warned that his ship would stay for only six hours.
8. After he left Chicago, the professor planned to travel to New York, London, Paris, Rome, Hong Kong, and Tokyo.
9. When the ship arrived on Kaan again, the horse spiders ran to tell their relatives about all they had seen.
10. They raved that the zoo was worth the fee they had paid to make the trip.

Answers for Try It Yourself 2.4

1. expected (action; transitive); arrive (action; intransitive)
2. gathered (action; intransitive); paid (action; transitive); see (action; transitive)
3. had (helping verb); brought (main verb; action verb; transitive); shown (action verb; transitive)
4. watched (action verb; transitive); rose (action; intransitive); reveal (action; transitive)
5. saw (action verb; transitive); were (linking verb); chattered (action verb; intransitive)
6. wore (action; transitive); called (action; intransitive)
7. warned (action; intransitive); would (helping verb); stay (linking verb)
8. left (action; transitive); planned (action; intransitive); travel (action; intransitive)
9. arrived (action; intransitive); ran (action; intransitive); tell (action; transitive); had (helping verb); seen (main verb; action verb; transitive)
10. raved (action; intransitive); was (linking verb); had (helping verb); paid (main verb; action verb; transitive); make (action verb; transitive)

Answers for Try It Yourself 2.5

1. white, adjective; mares, noun; hind, adjective; legs, noun
2. green, adjective; doors, noun; porcelain, adjective; doors, noun; remote, adjective; Heavens, noun
3. milky, adjective; dust, noun
4. tiger, adjective; sun, noun
5. one, adjective; lick, noun; vermilion, adjective; tongue, noun
6. hazel, adjective; wood, noun
7. white, adjective; moths, noun
8. glimmering, adjective; girl, noun
9. apple, adjective; blossom, noun
10. silver, adjective; apples, noun; golden, adjective; apples, noun

2.5 Adjectives and Articles

An **adjective** modifies, or changes the meaning of, a noun or a pronoun.

ADJECTIVES **clear** eyes, **shy** manner, **spicy** carrots, **late** arrival

The adjectives *a, an,* and *the* are called **articles**. Use the article *a* before words that begin with consonant sounds. Use the article *an* before words that begin with vowel sounds.

ARTICLES **a** peel, **an** article, **the** fire

Try It Yourself 2.5

Unit 3, page 94

On your own paper, identify the adjectives in each of the following phrases from the poems in unit 3. Then name the nouns that they modify. Do not worry about identifying articles.

EXAMPLE Night Clouds/ golden hoofs
Night, adjective; Clouds, noun; golden, adjective; hoofs, noun

1. The white mares of the moon are all standing on their hind legs
2. Pawing at the green porcelain doors of the remote Heavens
3. Scatter the milky dust of stars
4. Or the tiger sun will leap upon you and destroy you
5. With one lick of his vermilion tongue
6. I went out to the hazel wood
7. And when white moths were on the wing
8. It had become a glimmering girl
9. With apple blossom in her hair
10. The silver apples of the moon,/ The golden apples of the sun.

2.6 Adverbs

An **adverb** modifies, or changes the meaning of a verb, an adjective, or another adverb.

ADVERBS Send for me **quickly** if you need me.
The cup was **strangely** beautiful.
Clarissa danced **extremely** well.

Try It Yourself 2.6

"The Medicine Bag," page 162

Identify the adverbs in each of the following phrases and sentences from "The Medicine Bag." Then name the verbs, adjectives, or adverbs that they modify.

EXAMPLE Our friends who had always lived in the city
always, adverb; lived, verb

1. but they usually barked singly from the safety of their own yards
2. Now it sounded as if a whole pack of mutts were barking together in one place.
3. "Grandpa," I said and felt pretty dumb when my voice cracked.
4. "Hau, Takoza, Grandchild," he greeted me formally in Sioux.
5. Besides, he admitted sheepishly, he was lonesome after we left.
6. I was so proud of him and amazed at how respectfully quiet my buddies were.
7. But too many of the young men were filled with despair and hatred.
8. His shoulders were shaking with quiet sobs, and I looked away until he began to speak again.
9. Wearily he leaned his head against the pillow.
10. I stood alone on the lonely prairie of the reservation and put the sacred sage in my medicine bag.

2.7 Prepositions, Conjunctions, and Interjections

Preposition. A **preposition** is used to show how a noun or a pronoun is related to other words in the sentence. Common prepositions are *in, on, after, among, at, behind, beside, off, through, until, upon,* and *with.*

PREPOSITIONS **After** lunch, let's go for a walk.
Once **upon** a time, there was a boy whose best friend was a computer.

Conjunction. A **conjunction** is a word used to join words or groups of words. The main coordinating conjunctions are *and, but, for, nor, or, so,* and *yet.*

CONJUNCTIONS Clark **and** Lois don't really know each other.
Walk toward the corner, **but** stop when you see me.

Interjection. An **interjection** is a word used to express emotion. Common interjections are *oh, ah, well, say,* and *wow.*

INTERJECTIONS **Ah,** the air smells delicious.
Well, I used to be able to do three cartwheels in a row.

Answers for Try It Yourself 2.6

1. usually, adverb; barked, verb; singly, adverb; barked, verb
2. together, adverb; barking, verb
3. pretty, adverb; dumb, adjective
4. formally, adverb; greeted, verb
5. sheepishly, adverb; admitted, verb
6. respectfully, adverb; quiet, adjective
7. too, adverb; many, adjective
8. away, adverb; looked, verb; again, adverb; speak, verb
9. Wearily, adverb; leaned, verb
10. alone, adverb; stood, verb

Answers for Try It Yourself 2.7

1. preposition
2. conjunction
3. preposition
4. conjunction
5. preposition
6. preposition
7. conjunction
8. interjection
9. preposition
10. interjection

Try It Yourself 2.7

"Yemoja, Queen of the Seas," page 294

On your own paper, identify the underlined word as either a preposition, a conjunction, or an interjection.

EXAMPLE The Yoruba are a people who live in West Africa. **preposition**

1. Once upon a time, in a remote village by the sea in West Africa, there lived an eleven-year-old boy named Tunde.
2. One day Tunde went to the riverbank to swim and play with his friends.
3. He picked up a little rock and aimed carefully at a frog on a tree about twenty yards away.
4. Tunde felt dizzy, for he knew he had offended the Maker of that little creature, the same One who made him.
5. He did not even hear the sound of his friends running away.
6. The sound of the great bembe drum announced the arrival of the most wonderful queen.
7. She was unbelievably beautiful and queenly yet she had the kindest face Tunde had ever seen.
8. "So, Tunde, it is right for you to expect that any deed will have its fitting consequences."
9. Well, after reading about Tunde, I see that this story has a moral to teach.
10. Gosh, I wonder if spirits of the dead really could come back as other creatures.

2.8 Using Colorful Nouns, Verbs, and Modifiers

When you are writing, try to choose nouns that tell your reader exactly what you mean. Precise and colorful nouns make your writing come alive for your reader.

EXAMPLES Maeve **said** that she was **tired.**
Maeve **complained** that she was **exhausted.**

Colorful verbs also help to create a clear picture in a reader's mind. Use verbs that tell the reader exactly what you mean.

EXAMPLES Thomas **walked** to the train station and **got** on the train.
Thomas **strolled** to the train station and **jumped** on the train.

A **modifier** is a word that modifies—that is, changes or explains—the meaning of another word. Adjectives and adverbs are modifiers. Colorful modifiers can turn dull reading into dynamic reading.

EXAMPLES The **cold** wind blew **hard.**
The **frigid** wind blew **furiously.**

Try It Yourself 2.8

"Ode to My Socks," page 422

In each of the following sentences, choose from the words and phrases in parentheses the most colorful and precise noun, verb, or modifier. Write your answer on your paper.

EXAMPLE The speaker in Pablo Neruda's poem (worshipped, liked) a gift of socks. **worshipped**

1. He looked at his feet and saw them as (glimmering, shiny) fish.
2. In another (picture, vision) he sees them as a pair of hunters.
3. The speaker appreciates the (cozy, warm) woolen socks.
4. The Pied Piper (lured, brought) the rats out of Hamelin town.
5. The mayor and council (quaked, shook) with fear when the town threatened to fire them.
6. The piper's (sharp, clear) eyes were bright blue.
7. He wore a red and yellow coat and had (loose, long) pale hair.
8. His fingers seemed (ready, eager) to play the pipe.
9. The mayor promised a reward, and the piper's sharp eyes (twinkled, shined).
10. When the mayor broke his promise, the piper (charmed, took) the children away.

Answers for Try It Yourself 2.8

1. glimmering
2. vision
3. cozy
4. lured
5. quaked
6. sharp
7. loose
8. eager
9. twinkled
10. charmed

ESSENTIAL SKILLS: LANGUAGE

USING SENTENCES

2.9 Functions of Sentences

A **sentence** is a group of words that expresses a complete thought. There are four different types of sentences. They are **declarative**, **imperative**, **interrogative**, and **exclamatory.**

A **declarative sentence** tells something. It makes a statement and is followed by a period.

DECLARATIVE SENTENCES	Claire jumped when she saw the lizard. The baby had black, curly hair.

An **imperative sentence** gives a command or an order or makes a request.

IMPERATIVE SENTENCES	Give me the monkey wrench! Clap when the performer bows.

An **interrogative sentence** asks a question. It ends with a question mark.

INTERROGATIVE SENTENCES	Will you hold my coat? Did you enjoy the Steinbeck story?

Answers for Try It Yourself 2.9

1. imperative
2. interrogative
3. declarative
4. declarative
5. declarative
6. interrogative
7. imperative
8. declarative
9. interrogative
10. exclamatory

An **exclamatory sentence** expresses a strong feeling, such as joy, surprise, excitement, or anger. It ends with an exclamation point.

EXCLAMATORY SENTENCES We had four feet of snow in two days**!**
What a coincidence**!**

Try It Yourself 2.9

FROM *THE DIARY OF ANNE FRANK,* PAGE 460

On your own paper, identify each of the following sentences as declarative, imperative, interrogative, or exclamatory.

EXAMPLE The setting of Anne Frank's diary is the top floor of a warehouse and office building in Amsterdam. **declarative**

1. Know that the diary begins on Monday, the sixth of July, nineteen hundred and forty-two.
2. Can you imagine being trapped in an attic, living in fear for years?
3. They could only move around for a few hours in the evening.
4. Anne did not want to burn her Star of David.
5. No one can lock up your mind.
6. Why does Anne tease Peter so much?
7. Think about how lucky you are.
8. Learning was very important to Anne's father.
9. Why did Anne talk so much?
10. She must have been terrified most of the time!

2.10 Types of Sentences

In a complete sentence, every verb has a subject. A complete sentence can stand alone. In the examples below, *s* indicates a subject and *v* indicates a verb.

EXAMPLES The snow (s) fell (v).
Arnie (s) played (v).
A mountain (s) loomed (v).

A **simple sentence** has one subject and one verb.

SIMPLE SENTENCE Ed (s) travels (v).

An **independent clause** presents a complete thought and can stand alone as a sentence. A **compound sentence** is made up of two or more independent clauses. The clauses are usually combined by a coordinating conjunction. A **coordinating conjunction** is a connecting word such as *and, but, for, nor, or,* or *yet*. A comma is usually placed before the connecting word in a compound sentence.

COMPOUND SENTENCES Sonya called Martin, **but** he wasn't home.

A **subordinate clause** does not present a complete thought and cannot stand alone as a sentence. A **complex sentence** contains one independent clause and at least one subordinate clause. The clauses are joined by a subordinating conjunction. A **subordinating conjunction** is a word or group of words that connects a subordinate clause to an independent clause. Some subordinating conjunctions are *after, although, as, because, before, if, since, that, unless, until, when,* and *while.*

COMPLEX SENTENCES Don't open your umbrella **until** you get outside.
Because the earth is tilted, Brazil is cold when New York is warm.

Try It Yourself 2.10

FROM *OF MEN AND MOUNTAINS,* PAGE 530

Identify each of the following sentences as simple, compound, or complex.

EXAMPLE Doug and the narrator chose the most difficult climb. **simple**

1. When the sun rose to its zenith, they took the challenge.
2. The first one hundred feet were easy, but then the ledges became narrower.
3. They took off their shoes.
4. Unless they kept their stomachs pressed against the cliff, they might have lost their balance.
5. They climbed six hundred feet in two hours, and then they stopped to evaluate the situation.
6. Since Doug was short, he would have to jump to the next crevice.
7. Doug asked the narrator to remember a message for his family.
8. Doug made the crevice, but there was nowhere to go from there.
9. While Doug hung by his fingers full-length, the narrator supported him with one arm.
10. The narrator prayed at the end of the day and thanked God for saving his life and the life of his friend.

ESSENTIAL SKILLS: LANGUAGE

Answers for Try It Yourself 2.10

1. complex
2. compound
3. simple
4. complex
5. compound
6. complex
7. simple
8. compound
9. complex
10. simple

Answers for Try It Yourself 2.11

1. Goha returned his neighbor's pot along with another, smaller pot.
2. He said that the big pot had given birth to the smaller pot overnight.
3. Soon afterward, Goha borrowed two pots from his generous neighbor.
4. Not too long afterward, his optimistic neighbor decided to loan Goha all of his pots.
5. When a few months later Goha had still not returned the pots, the neighbor began to worry.
6. The neighbor went to visit Goha because he wanted to retrieve his pots.
7. Goha apologized to his neighbor, saying that the pots had died.
8. The neighbor became angry and said that pots don't die.
9. Goha scolded his neighbor, reminding him that he had believed that pots give birth.
10. Goha had a point, and his neighbor probably had to agree.

2.11 Combining Sentences

If you use several short sentences in a paragraph, your writing might sound choppy, and your reader might have trouble understanding how ideas are connected. You can often combine two sentences that deal with the same main idea. If you are able to combine short sentences, your writing will sound smooth and clear. The reader will see how ideas are connected to one another.

One way of combining sentences is to take a word or phrase from one sentence and insert it into another sentence. You might need to change the form of the word.

GIVEN SENTENCES	A horse tripped on the rock. The rock was sharp.
COMBINED SENTENCE	A horse tripped on the **sharp** rock.
GIVEN SENTENCES	Last Chance Gulch was the name of Helena, Montana. It was the original name.
COMBINED SENTENCE	Last Chance Gulch was the **original** name of Helena, Montana.

Another way of combining sentences is to take two related sentences and combine them into one sentence that states both ideas. Your two sentences can be combined with a comma and a conjunction.

GIVEN SENTENCES	Sage looked on in disbelief. Martin juggled sixteen tangerines.
COMBINED SENTENCE	**As** Martin juggled sixteen tangerines, Sage looked on in disbelief.
GIVEN SENTENCES	It snowed on the day of the class picnic. We postponed it to the following weekend.
COMBINED SENTENCE	**Because** it snowed on the day of the class picnic, we postponed it to the following weekend.

Try It Yourself 2.11

"Goha and the Pot," page 288

On your own paper, combine the sentences below. Use the hints provided in parentheses.

EXAMPLE Goha wanted to make a meal for his family. He did not have a pot. (Use *but.*)
Goha wanted to make a meal for his family, but he did not have a pot.

1. Goha returned his neighbor's pot. He brought with it another, smaller pot. (Use *along.*)
2. He said that the big pot had given birth to the smaller pot. This had occurred *overnight.* (Use the word in italics in the first sentence.)
3. Soon afterward, Goha borrowed two pots from his neighbor. His neighbor was *generous.* (Use the word in italics in the first sentence.)
4. Not too long afterward, his neighbor decided to loan Goha all of his pots. The neighbor was *optimistic.* (Use the word in italics in the first sentence.)

continued

Try It Yourself 2.11 (cont.)

5. A few months later, Goha had still not returned the pots. The neighbor began to worry. (Use the word *when.*)
6. The neighbor went to visit Goha. He wanted to retrieve his pots. (Use the word *because.*)
7. Goha apologized to his neighbor. He said that the pots had died. (Use the word *saying.*)
8. The neighbor became angry. He said that pots don't die. (Use the word *and.*)
9. Goha scolded his neighbor. He reminded him that he had believed that pots give birth. (Use the word *reminding.*)
10. Goha had a point. His neighbor probably had to agree. (Use the word *and.*)

2.12 Correcting Sentence Fragments

A sentence contains a subject and a verb and should express a complete thought. A **sentence fragment** is a phrase or clause that does not express a complete thought but has been punctuated as though it did.

SENTENCE FRAGMENT	Robin put on her snowpants. **So she could make angels in the snow.**
COMPLETE SENTENCE	Robin put on her snowpants so she could make angels in the snow.
SENTENCE FRAGMENT	The baritone sang the melody. **While the sopranos trilled in the background.**
COMPLETE SENTENCE	The baritones sang the melody while the sopranos trilled in the background.

Try It Yourself 2.12

"The Sniper," page 364

Correct the sentence fragments below by adding words to them or attaching them to complete sentences. Some of the sentences below are already complete. When you come across a complete sentence, simply write *complete* on your paper.

EXAMPLE Alone, on the rooftop. The sniper waited.
Alone, on the rooftop, the sniper waited.

1. Dublin could not rest in darkness. With the guns roaring in Four Courts.
2. Republicans wanted Ireland to be completely independent.
3. The sniper shot his enemy. When he raised his head above the turret.
4. Shot in the arm. The sniper had to dress his own wound.
5. At first the sniper was thrilled to see his enemy fall.

CONTINUED

Answers for Try It Yourself 2.12

1. Dublin could not rest in darkness with the guns roaring in Four Courts.
2. Complete.
3. The sniper shot his enemy when he raised his head above the turret.
4. Shot in the arm, the sniper had to dress his own wound.
5. Complete.
6. Overcome with the horror of war, the sniper threw down his gun.
7. The sniper laughed when his own revolver fired and just missed him.
8. Complete.
9. On the way, he decided to find out whom he had killed.
10. He saw the dead face of his brother when he turned the corpse over.

Answers for Try It Yourself 2.13

1. The narrator could not find the fox. He held back his tears.
2. The narrator's father claims that the fox will be an egg stealer. The boys argue that he was only "pranking" as a youngster when he did that.
3. It was cold that year. The fire was always burning in the stove.
4. The fox doesn't hibernate in winter. It hunts in the woods.
5. Colin made a frame out of cardboard. Then he started to draw his picture.
6. The narrator and his mother protect Colin. He is delicate and artistic.
7. Colin and Bandit had been very close. The boy saved the cub after the creature's mother was killed.
8. The fox allowed the boy to put his arm around him. Then he went back to his mate.
9. The farmers got together to hunt down the fox. He was stealing chickens from them.
10. Bandit outsmarted the dogs all day. Finally, he was shot by a chance hunter.

Try It Yourself 2.12 (cont.)

6. Overcome with the horror of war.
7. Laughing when his own revolver fired and just missed him.
8. He recovered his spirits and headed for his company commander.
9. On the way. He decided to find out whom he had killed.
10. He saw the dead face of his brother. When he turned the corpse over.

2.13 Correcting Run-ons

A **run-on** is made up of two or more sentences that have been run together as if they were one complete thought. You can fix a run-on by dividing it into two separate sentences. Mark the end of each idea with a period, question mark, or exclamation point. Capitalize the first word of each new sentence.

RUN-ON	Maika was born in poverty, she had no roof over her head.
TWO SENTENCES	Maika was born in poverty. She had no roof over her head.
RUN-ON	All children deserve a home, would you argue with that?
TWO SENTENCES	All children deserve a home. Would you argue with that?

Try It Yourself 2.13

"Last Cover," page 384

Correct each run-on by making it into two separate sentences. Mark the end of each idea with a period, question mark, or exclamation point. If a sentence is correct, simply write *correct* on your paper.

EXAMPLE "Last Cover" is a story about a boy, the boy is an artist who loved a fox.
"Last Cover" is a story about a boy**.** The boy is an artist who loved a fox.

1. The narrator could not find the fox, he held back his tears.
2. The narrator's father claims that the fox will be an egg stealer, the boys argue that he was only "pranking" as a youngster when he did that.
3. It was cold that year, the fire was always burning in the stove.
4. The fox doesn't hibernate in winter, it hunts in the woods.
5. Colin made a frame out of cardboard, then he started to draw his picture.
6. The narrator and his mother protect Colin, he is delicate and artistic.
7. Colin and Bandit had been very close, the boy saved the cub after the creature's mother was killed.
8. The fox allowed the boy to put his arm around him, then he went back to his mate.
9. The farmers got together to hunt down the fox, he was stealing chickens from them.
10. Bandit outsmarted the dogs all day, finally, he was shot by a chance hunter.

2.14 Correcting Wordy Sentences

As you write, try to use only words that you need to get your meaning across to a reader. Edit your sentences so that they are not wordy and complicated. Replace complicated or unclear words with simple and clear words.

WORDY	Joan Baez sings earthy folksongs in a light, airy, celestial voice that seems better suited to opera.
CLEAR AND DIRECT	Joan Baez sings earthy songs in a celestial voice.
WORDY	In the 1970s California, the golden state, was a place of individual independence and personal freedom to a huge extent.
CLEAR AND DIRECT	In the 1970s California was a place of great personal freedom.

Try It Yourself 2.14

"Tears of Autumn," page 126

On your own paper, revise the following sentences to make them less wordy. As you do this exercise, think about what each sentence is really saying. How might it be rewritten to be shorter and clearer?

EXAMPLE Hana Omiya looked out and stared at the sea through her dark, deep eyes and wished and longed to be home again in Oka Village, the place where she was from.

Hana Omiya stared at the sea and longed to be home again in Oka Village.

1. She felt that her body was lifeless and dead as though it were an empty shell or vehicle carrying her and transporting her to America, the United States.
2. Hana blamed herself and knew she was responsible for her own situation and the fate that awaited her.
3. She had wanted more than to be a farmer's wife, the spouse of a man who worked in the rice paddies, and more than a life of hard, physical labor in which she would burden her body.
4. She was curious about life in America and wanted an adventure and an opportunity to travel and see a place very different from Japan.
5. She had learned and knew that in the United States women were given more respect than they were given in Japan and also that American people married for love and affection rather than only for practical, logical reasons.
6. At first and before she had gotten accustomed to the idea, Hana's mother refused to allow and denied her the right to go to America to marry this man.
7. Eventually, in due course, Hana's mother gave her consent and agreed to pursue the marriage agreement or contract with Taro Takeda.
8. As the boat approached San Francisco, Hana became anxious and nervous about the prospect of meeting for the first time her husband-to-be.
9. When she first saw and set eyes on Taro, she was surprised and disappointed to see that he was bald, had very little hair on his head.
10. She was able to laugh and find humor in her situation when Taro himself laughed and promised her that the boat ride across the bay would be a short one, no more than twenty minutes.

Answers for Try It Yourself 2.14

1. She felt lifeless, as though her body were an empty shell carrying her to the United States.
2. Hana blamed herself for her situation and her fate.
3. She had wanted to be more than a farmer's wife with a life of physical labor.
4. She was curious about America and wanted an opportunity to see a place very different from Japan.
5. She knew that in the United States women were given more respect than in Japan and that American people married for love.
6. At first, Hana's mother refused her the right to go to America to marry this man.
7. Eventually, Hana's mother gave her consent to pursue the marriage contract with Taro Takeda.
8. As the boat approached San Francisco, Hana became nervous about meeting her husband-to-be.
9. When she first saw Taro, she was disappointed to see that he was bald.
10. She was able to laugh when Taro laughed and promised her that the boat ride across the bay would be a short one.

Answers for Try It Yourself 2.15

1. Mr. Frank remembered the wartime tragedies.
2. active
3. The Nazis forced Anne's father out of business.
4. Anne teased Peter because he was shy and reserved.
5. Miep will get some ration books on the other side of town for the Franks.
6. Peter had seen Anne at school, but Anne had not seen Peter.
7. Peter burnt his Star of David.
8. The Nazis forced him to wear the emblem.
9. Every time Mrs. Frank hears the door buzzer, she feels as though her heart stops.
10. The hidden families light the Hanukkah candles.

2.15 Correcting Passive Sentences

A verb is in the **active voice** when the subject of the verb performs the action. It is in the **passive voice** when the subject of the verb receives the action.

ACTIVE Shala's stories sent the audience into storms of laughter.
PASSIVE The audience was sent into storms of laughter.

A common characteristic of poor writing is overuse of the passive voice. Keep your verbs in the active voice unless you have a good reason for using the passive voice. In the examples that follow, note how the action verbs make the writing more natural and interesting.

WITH PASSIVE VERBS **Rats!**
Dogs were fought by, and cats were killed by,
Babies in the cradles were bit by,
Cheese out of the vats was eaten by,
Soup from the cook's own ladles was licked by

WITH ACTIVE VERBS **Rats!**
They fought the dogs and killed the cats,
And bit the babies in the cradles,
And ate the cheese out of the vats,
And licked the soup from the cook's own ladles

—Robert Browning,"The Pied Piper of Hamelin"

Try It Yourself 2.15

FROM *THE DIARY OF ANNE FRANK,* PAGE 460

On your own paper, change each passive sentence into an active sentence. If a sentence is already in the active voice, write *active.*

EXAMPLE Mr. Frank was asked by Miep if he was all right.
Miep asked Mr. Frank if he was all right.

1. The wartime tragedies are remembered by Mr. Frank.
2. He nearly refuses to take the diary of Anne with him.
3. Anne's father was forced out of business by the Nazis.
4. Peter was teased by Anne because he was shy and reserved.
5. Some ration books will be gotten by Miep on the other side of town for the Franks.
6. Anne had been seen by Peter at school, but Peter had not been seen by Anne.
7. His Star of David was burnt by Peter.

CONTINUED

Try It Yourself 2.15 (cont.)

8. He had been forced to wear the emblem by the Nazis.
9. Every time the door buzzer is heard by Mrs. Frank, she feels as though her heart stops.
10. The Hanukkah candles are lit by the hidden families.

EDITING FOR GRAMMAR AND USAGE ERRORS

2.16 Agreement of Subject and Verb

A word that describes or stands for one person, place, thing, or idea is **singular.** A word that describes or stands for more than one person, place, thing, or idea is **plural.**

SINGULAR NOUNS	boy, letter, smile
PLURAL NOUNS	boys, letters, smiles

In a sentence, a verb must be singular if its subject is singular and plural if its subject is plural. In other words, a verb must **agree in number** with its subject.

SINGULAR	**Ralphie knows** how to play chess.
PLURAL	**They know** how to play chess.
SINGULAR	**Joanne paints** stencil designs.
PLURAL	My **friends paint** stencil designs.

Some verbs have special forms. The verb forms *is* and *was* are singular. The forms *are* and *were* are plural. The verb form *has* is singular. The verb form *have* is plural.

SINGULAR	Karl **is** here.
PLURAL	Karl and Jack **are** here.
SINGULAR	Sandra **has** long braids.
PLURAL	Sandra and Joan **have** long braids.

The pronouns *I* and *you* almost always take verb forms that look plural.

EXAMPLES	I **look** for the first blooms.
	You **bake** very well.

ESSENTIAL SKILLS: LANGUAGE

ANSWERS FOR TRY IT YOURSELF 2.16

1. digs
2. sees
3. nestles
4. rests
5. boasts
6. drinks
7. straightens
8. nicks
9. awake
10. digs

Try It Yourself 2.16

"DIGGING," PAGE 430

Read the following sentences and identify the subject. Then, on your own paper, identify the form of the verb in parentheses that agrees with the subject.

EXAMPLE The speaker in Heaney's poem (hold, holds) a pen as though it were a gun. **speaker; holds**

1. His father, below his window, (dig, digs) in the gravelly ground.
2. The speaker (see, sees) the father bending among the flowers.
3. The father's boot (nestle, nestles) on the shaft of the spade.
4. The shaft (rest, rests) against his father's knee.
5. The speaker (boast, boasts) that his grandfather was a champion turf cutter.
6. He remembers that his grandfather, in the midst of cutting, (drink, drinks) a bottle of milk in one gulp.
7. His grandfather (straighten, straightens) up to drink the milk and then bends down again immediately to dig.
8. He remembers his grandfather (nick, nicks) and slices at the sod.
9. The speaker feels the roots of peat (awake, awakes) in his head.
10. The speaker says that he (dig, digs) with his pen.

2.17 USING IRREGULAR VERBS

When you want to write about something that happened in the past, you have to use the **past tense** forms of verbs. Make the past tense form of a regular verb by adding *–ed* or *–d* to the verb's **base form**.

EXAMPLES The housekeeper loved the river. **love (base form) + ed**
The adventurer sailed to Polynesia. **sail (base form) + ed**

Some verbs are **irregular.** The past tense forms of irregular verbs are not formed by simply adding *–ed* or *–d.* They often have a different spelling. The following chart lists some of the most common irregular verbs.

IRREGULAR VERBS

Base Form	Past Tense	Base Form	Past Tense	Base Form	Past Tense
begin	began	fall	fell	make	made
bring	brought	feel	felt	ride	rode
burst	burst	fly	flew	run	ran
choose	chose	give	gave	see	saw
come	came	go	went	sing	sang
cut	cut	grow	grew	take	took
do	did	have	had	take	took

CONTINUED

IRREGULAR VERBS (CONT.)					
Base Form	Past Tense	Base Form	Past Tense	Base Form	Past Tense
draw	drew	hurt	hurt	teach	taught
drink	drank	know	knew	wear	wore
eat	ate	lay	laid	write	wrote

Try It Yourself 2.17

"THE SNIPER," PAGE 364

For each of the following sentences, name on your own paper the correct past tense form of the italicized verb.

EXAMPLE Republicans in the city of Dublin have *feel* that Ireland should be completely independent of Britain. **felt**

1. Free Staters *choose* to be a British dominion that is self-governing.
2. In "The Sniper," Liam O'Flaherty *write* about a Republican soldier firing from the roof of a Dublin building.
3. He *drink* water from a flask as he watches the street below.
4. Then he *see* an enemy soldier firing from the turret of an armored car.
5. After he was shot, he *cut* open his sleeve to see what damage had been done to his arm.
6. He *make* it appear that he was dead and *draw* the enemy out into the open.
7. He *lay* his broken arm over the side of the building.
8. Although his arm *hurt,* he steadied it so that he could aim his revolver.
9. After the enemy soldier died, the sniper *feel* depressed and angry about the war.
10. When he turned the soldier over, he *know* that he had killed his own brother.

2.18 Avoiding Split Infinitives

In the English language, the infinitive is often in the form of two words, *to* and the base word.

EXAMPLES to walk, to hug, to sing

Under traditional rules of grammar, the infinitive should not be "split." In other words, adverbs or other sentence components should not come between *to* and the base word.

NONSTANDARD Sukie decided to enthusiastically hug the child.
STANDARD Sukie decided to hug the child enthusiastically.

Answers for Try It Yourself 2.17

1. chose
2. wrote
3. drank
4. saw
5. cut
6. made; drew
7. laid
8. hurt
9. felt
10. knew

ANSWERS FOR TRY IT YOURSELF 2.18

1. He would only have to stay impatiently in prison for a very short time.
2. With all his connections in high places, Jimmy Valentine only had to request quietly what he wanted.
3. After being released from prison, Jimmy wanted to go quickly and have a good meal.
4. Then he returned to his place and began to pack his belongings carefully.
5. Jimmy continued to practice his art skillfully.
6. His nemesis, Ben Price, began regularly to recognize Jimmy's style in bank robberies.
7. One day, Jimmy arrived in a small town and cunningly began to scope out the possibility of robbing its bank.
8. Once he saw the banker's daughter, though, his thoughts began to move swiftly in a different direction.
9. After a year, he was happily engaged to marry the woman of his dreams.
10. Then, suddenly, he reluctantly had to reveal his past because his skills were needed to save the life of a child quickly.

Try It Yourself 2.18

"A RETRIEVED REFORMATION," PAGE 372

Each of the following sentences contains a split infinitive. Rewrite the sentences on your own paper, correcting the split infinitive.

EXAMPLE It was said that to properly cut the hair of a prisoner like Jimmy Valentine was hardly worth the trouble.
It was said that to cut the hair of a prisoner like Jimmy Valentine was hardly worth the trouble.

1. He would only have to impatiently stay in prison for a very short time.
2. With all his connections in high places, Jimmy Valentine only had to quietly request what he wanted.
3. After being released from prison, Jimmy wanted to quickly go and have a good meal.
4. Then he returned to his place and began to carefully pack his belongings.
5. Jimmy continued to skillfully practice his art.
6. His nemesis, Ben Price, began to regularly recognize Jimmy's style in bank robberies.
7. One day, Jimmy arrived in a small town and began to cunningly scope out the possibility of robbing its bank.
8. Once he saw the banker's daughter, though, his thoughts began to swiftly move in a different direction.
9. After a year, he was engaged to happily marry the woman of his dreams.
10. Then, suddenly, he had to reluctantly reveal his past because his skills were needed to quickly save the life of a child.

2.19 USING *I* AND *ME*

Before you use the words *I* and *me* in a sentence, remember that *I* is always the subject of a verb and *me* is always the object of a verb or of a preposition.

EXAMPLES **I** want to help orphans.
Claire and **I** want to help orphans.

I is the subject in both of these sentences.

EXAMPLES Eva gave **me** a poem she wrote.
Eva gave Bryce and **me** a poem she wrote.

In both sentences, *me* is the object of the verb *gave.*

If you are not sure which pronoun to use, try each part of your sentence separately.

EXAMPLE Chloe and (I, me) called the doctor.
INCORRECT Me called the doctor.
CORRECT I called the doctor. (So the correct choice would be, **Chloe and I called the doctor.**)

EXAMPLE Can you bring some paper for Raoul and (I, me)?
INCORRECT Can you bring some paper for I?
CORRECT Can you bring some paper for me? (So the correct choice would be **Can you bring some paper for Raoul and me?**)

Try It Yourself 2.19

FROM *ISHI IN TWO WORLDS*, PAGE 544

Decide if you need to use the pronoun *I* or the pronoun *me* in order to complete each of the following sentences correctly. List the correct pronouns on your paper.

EXAMPLE (I, Me) believe that people react strongly to Ishi's story. **I**

1. The story of Ishi meant a lot to (I, me).
2. To imagine the early part of his life, (I, me) had to put from out of mind thousands of years of human civilization.
3. To (I, me) the treatment of Ishi by the scientists and legal professionals seemed cruel.
4. If someone like (I, me) were kept confined in a museum for years, he or she would die young also.
5. It seems to (I, me) that the last representative of the Stone Age should have been treated with more respect.
6. To live through the loss of one's entire community, (I, me) believe, is a huge trauma.
7. If the Bureau of Indian Affairs had asked (I, me) to keep Ishi in a university museum, I would have refused.
8. (I, Me) see it as no surprise that Ishi lived less than five years under these circumstances.
9. Couldn't he have been given the same freedom in San Francisco as people like you and (I, me) would have?
10. If you or (I, me) ends up the sole survivor of our culture, let's hope we're treated more fairly.

2.20 USING *WHO* AND *WHOM*

The pronoun *who* has two different forms. *Who* is the form used as a subject of a sentence. *Whom* is the form used as the direct object of a verb or of a preposition.

ANSWERS FOR TRY IT YOURSELF 2.19

1. me
2. I
3. me
4. I
5. me
6. I
7. me
8. I
9. I
10. I

Answers for Try It Yourself 2.20

1. who, subject
2. who, subject
3. who, subject
4. who, subject
5. who, subject
6. whom, object of a preposition
7. whom, direct object
8. who, subject
9. whom, subject
10. whom, object of a preposition

SUBJECT	**Who** picked the roses?
SUBJECT	Where is the girl **who** won the race?
DIRECT OBJECT	**Whom** did you call about the leak?
DIRECT OBJECT	The boy **whom** I invited is named Craig.
OBJECT OF PREPOSITION	Of **whom** is she dreaming?
OBJECT OF PREPOSITION	About **whom** was the book written?

Try It Yourself 2.20

"The War of the Wall," page 118

Decide if you need to use the pronoun who or the pronoun whom in order to complete each sentence correctly. On your own paper, name the correct pronoun, then identify the pronoun as a subject, a direct object, or an object of a preposition.

EXAMPLE The narrator and Lou did not know (who, whom) the painter lady was.
who, subject

1. She was painting the wall at the end of their street, but (who, whom) gave her permission?
2. Jimmy Lyons, whose name was on the wall, was the veteran (who, whom) had not returned from the Vietnam War.
3. The narrator believes that the people of Taliaferro Street are the only ones (who, whom) should touch the wall.
4. The painter is from New York, and people (who, whom) are from the North are known to be rude.
5. Toni Cade Bambara, (who, whom) wrote this story, was an African American from New York and New Jersey.
6. For (who, whom) was she painting the wall anyway?
7. The painter lady will paint (who, whom) on the wall?
8. The narrator, (who, whom) had planned to destroy the painter's work was shocked by the finished mural.
9. The narrator recognized those (who, whom) were illustrated on the wall.
10. The faces, one of (who, whom) was the narrator, were beautiful.

2.21 Agreement of Pronouns with Antecedents

When you use pronouns in your writing, be sure that they agree with their antecedents in **number** and **gender. Number** refers to singular and plural. If the antecedent is singular, the pronoun must also be singular; if the antecedent is plural, the pronoun must also be plural.

INCORRECT NUMBER	**Everyone** must explain to **their** parents.
CORRECT NUMBER	**Everyone** must explain to **his or her** parents.
	All children must explain to **their** parents.

Gender is the form a word takes to show whether it is masculine, feminine, or neuter (neither masculine nor feminine). The pronoun must match its antecedent in terms of gender.

INCORRECT GENDER	The queen was displeased with his son's behavior.
CORRECT GENDER	The queen was displeased with **her** son's behavior.

Try It Yourself 2.21

"NIGHT CLOUDS," PAGE 48

For each sentence choose the pronoun in parentheses that agrees with its antecedent in number and gender. Write your answer on your own paper.

EXAMPLE Amy Lowell wrote a poem (he, she) called "Night Clouds." **she**

1. The poem describes white mares that "rush along the sky/Beating (their, her) golden hoofs."
2. The speaker uses the mares as (her, their) symbol for clouds.
3. The white mares come from the moon, and each stands on (her, their) hind legs.
4. They paw at the green porcelain doors and strain (her, their) utmost.
5. The speaker tells (them, her) to "Fly, Mares!"
6. Then they "scatter the milky dust of stars" on (their, her) way.
7. The speaker warns that the "tiger sun will leap upon" them with (his, their) "vermilion tongue."
8. In the poem, the sun is the enemy of the clouds because of (his, their) fire.
9. Because the mares are "of the moon," the reader might visualize (them, her) as night beings.
10. Amy Lowell uses beautiful imagery in (her, his) poem.

2.22 Avoiding Double Negatives

A **negative** is a "no" word. Using two negatives in a sentence when only one is needed is called using a **double negative.** Check your writing to be sure that you have not used a negative word such as *not, nobody, none, nothing, hardly, barely, can't, doesn't, won't, isn't,* or *aren't* with another negative word. Change double negatives by replacing one of the negative words in the sentence with a positive word.

DOUBLE NEGATIVE	Stay here and **don't** answer the door for **no one.**
SINGLE NEGATIVES	Stay here and **don't** answer the door for anyone.
	Stay here and answer the door for **no one.**
DOUBLE NEGATIVE	**Don't** ask **nothing.**
SINGLE NEGATIVES	**Don't** ask anything.
	Ask **nothing.**
DOUBLE NEGATIVE	**Don't** bring **no** sweets.
SINGLE NEGATIVES	**Don't** bring any sweets.
	Bring **no** sweets.

Answers for Try It Yourself 2.21

1. their
2. her
3. her
4. their
5. them
6. their
7. his
8. his
9. them
10. her

ANSWERS FOR TRY IT YOURSELF 2.22

1. anything
2. anyone
3. would
4. ever
5. anyone
6. ever
7. will
8. will
9. ever
10. wouldn't

Try It Yourself 2.22

"THE CLEVELAND WRECKING YARD," PAGE 80

Number your paper 1–10. For each sentence list the correct word from the words in parentheses.

EXAMPLE Richard Brautigan's novel *Trout Fishing in America* doesn't contain (any, no) realistic trout fishing stories. **any**

1. In "The Cleveland Wrecking Yard," the signs on the store don't say (anything, nothing) typical of signs.
2. The narrator doesn't want (anyone, no one) to come with him to see the merchandise.
3. We (would, wouldn't) scarcely think of trout streams as something for sale in a retail shop.
4. The salesman says he won't (never, ever) give the waterfalls up for free.
5. The salesman says he wouldn't want (no one, anyone) to think he would sell a muddy trout stream.
6. He says they have not (ever, never) damaged a trout stream while moving it from its original location.
7. He also says no one (won't, will) know how good the fishing will be in any one part of the stream.
8. The salesman implies that the narrator (won't, will) never find a better deal on a trout stream.
9. The narrator said he had not (ever, never) seen so many doors before in his life.
10. There was a canvas top on the bird cage so that the birds (would, wouldn't) get any of their feathers wet.

2.23 OTHER PROBLEMS WITH MODIFIERS

The pronoun *them* is a personal pronoun. The pronoun *those* is a demonstrative pronoun, which means it is used to point out a particular person, place, or thing. Try not to confuse the two words in your writing.

NONSTANDARD **Them** children are lost.
STANDARD **Those** children are lost.

The words *bad* and *badly* often confuse writers. *Bad* should be used as an adjective, and *badly* should be used as an adverb. The adjective *bad* should follow a linking verb such as *feel, see, smell, sound,* or *taste.*

NONSTANDARD Marsha felt **badly** about the accident.
STANDARD Marsha felt **bad** about the accident.
NONSTANDARD Scott ran **bad** with his sprained ankle.
STANDARD Scott ran **badly** with his sprained ankle.

The words *good* and *well* also tend to confuse writers. *Good* is an adjective and should only be used to modify a person, place, thing, or idea. *Good* should not be used to modify an action verb. *Well* can be used as an adverb meaning "successfully" or "skillfully" or as an adjective meaning "healthy" or "of a satisfactory condition."

NONSTANDARD Kevin rides **good.**
STANDARD Kevin rides **well.**
Kevin is a **good** rider.
Kevin is healthy again; he feels **well.**

Try It Yourself 2.23

"For My Sister Molly Who in the Fifties," page 104

For each sentence choose the correct word from the words in parentheses. Write your answers on your own paper.

EXAMPLE Alice Walker wrote a poem for her sister Molly who sculpted (well, good) with mashed potatoes. **well**

1. The speaker in the poem grew up in (them, those) days when many people lived in rural areas.
2. Molly knew that some children spoke (bad, badly) but did not want her siblings to be among them.
3. The speaker learned that some words were no longer (well, good).
4. Molly knew Hamlet (well, good).
5. She read the children (them, those) African songs.
6. Molly smelled as (well, good) as the flowers she picked.
7. She felt (bad, badly) when someone was bitten by a wasp.
8. She told stories very (well, good) and made the children laugh.
9. Molly felt (well, good) when the children asked her questions.
10. She knew (them, those) endings of stories the narrator had forgotten.

2.24 Common Usage Problems I

Sections 2.24 and 2.25 of the Language Arts Survey list and explain some words that are commonly confused. Watch for these words as you edit your own writing.

accept, except. To *accept* is to "welcome something" or to "receive something willingly." To *except* is to "exclude or leave something out." *Except* is also used as a preposition meaning "but."

EXAMPLES Susan **accepts** people's differences.
Don't **except** me from any house rules.
All the trees **except** one had turned yellow.

Answers for Try It Yourself 2.23

1. those
2. badly
3. good
4. well
5. those
6. good
7. bad
8. well
9. good
10. those

Answers for Try It Yourself 2.24

1. Between
2. can
3. fewer
4. advice
5. can
6. except
7. altogether
8. may
9. all together
10. less

advice, advise. *Advice* is a noun meaning "guidance or recommendation regarding a decision." To *advise* is to "recommend or inform."

EXAMPLES My **advice** is not to waste time on that movie.
Will you **advise** Billy about how to stay warm on the mountain?

altogether, all together. *Altogether* is an adverb meaning "thoroughly." Something done *all together* is done as a group or mass.

EXAMPLES Shantal is wearing **altogether** too much makeup.
Let's sing **all together** as loud as we can.

among, between. The word *between* should be used when you are talking about two people or things at a time. The word *among* should be used when you are talking about a group of three or more.

EXAMPLES Nat and I had no secrets **between** us.
The friendship **among** the four sisters lasted all their lives.

can, may. The word *can* means "able to do something." The word *may* is used to ask or give permission.

EXAMPLES Mandy **can** jump rope faster than anyone.
You **may** have another cookie.
May we come in?

fewer, less. *Fewer* refers to the number of units of something. *Less* refers to bulk quantity.

EXAMPLES We have **fewer** birds this year than last.
There is **less** snow at the seashore.

Try It Yourself 2.24

"Lose Now, Pay Later" page 196

For each sentence, choose the correct word from the words in parentheses. Write your answers on your own paper.

EXAMPLE The narrator in "Lose Now, Pay Later" finds it difficult to (accept, except) that something desirable is free. **accept**

1. (Among, Between) Trinja and the narrator, they decide to go into the shop.
2. They realize they (can, may) get one of the Swoodies.
3. By the time they leave the store, they have had no (fewer, less) than a dozen Swoodies.

CONTINUED

Try It Yourself 2.24 (cont.)

4. Trinja's (advice, advise) to other people was to go ahead and try the Swoodies.
5. The Health Brigade Corp said that they were safe enough so that we (can, may) eat them without fear of illness.
6. Everyone (accept, except) the narrator's brother thinks Swoodies and Slimmers are wonderful.
7. The situation seems (altogether, all together) too suspicious for him.
8. He believes that if we give permission so that the slimmers (can, may) take our fat, aliens could use the fat for their own purposes.
9. He says that when there are (altogether, all together) too many marks on someone's arm, he or she may be "culled from the flock."
10. Nobody could be (less, fewer) suspicious than Trinja and the narrator, however.

2.25 Common Usage Problems II

in, into. The word *in* is a preposition used to indicate location. The preposition *into* indicates the direction of motion, from the outside to the inside.

EXAMPLES All the raisins are **in** the bread.
The wolf cannot get **into** the rabbit den.

lay, lie. *Lay* is a transitive verb meaning to "put" or to "place." It always takes a direct object. *Lie* is an intransitive verb meaning to "rest" or to "be in a lying position." *Lie* never takes a direct object. (Note that the past tense of *lie* is *lay.*)

EXAMPLES Just **lay** your sweater on the couch.
Paul **laid** his books down on the desk.
The baby can **lie** on a pillow.
The sheep **lay** in the meadow.

like, as. *Like* is a preposition meaning "similar to." *Like* usually introduces a phrase. *As* should be used as a conjunction. *As* usually introduces a clause that has a subject and a verb.

NONSTANDARD Children need respect just **like** we do.
STANDARD Children need respect just **as** we do.

NONSTANDARD Lorene looks **as** her mother.
STANDARD Lorene looks **like** her mother.

Answers for Try It Yourself 2.25

1. There
2. too
3. as
4. lie
5. into
6. like
7. your
8. to
9. to
10. as

their, they're, there. The word *their* is a possessive pronoun. The word *they're* is the contracted form of *they are*. The word *there* refers to a place.

EXAMPLES Clarissa and Tory made **their** famous fruit salad.
They're the best figure skaters on the team.
The sun will set over **there.**

to, too. *To* is a preposition that can mean "in the direction of." *Too* is an adverb that means both "extremely, overly" and "also."

EXAMPLES Let's go **to** the movies.
There's **too** much pepper in the soup.
I like Robin **too.**

your, you're. *Your* is a possessive pronoun. *You're* is the contracted form of *you are*.

EXAMPLES This is **your** birthday gift.
You're looking beautiful.

Try It Yourself 2.25

"Harrison Bergeron," page 204

For each sentence, choose the correct word from the words in parentheses. Write your answers on your own paper.

EXAMPLE In the year 2081, everyone is finally (like, as) everyone else. **like**

1. (Their, They're, There) is no one who is smarter, better looking, or stronger than anyone else.
2. When the H-G men took George and Hazel Bergeron's fourteen-year-old son away, they couldn't feel (to, too) upset because they couldn't concentrate very well.
3. A buzzer went off in George's head periodically, just (like, as) the Handicapper General had expected it to do.
4. When a twenty-one-gun salute went off in George's ear, two out of the eight ballerinas dancing on the television had to (lay, lie) down on the studio floor.
5. George was afraid that if he let some of the lead balls out of his bag, he would have to go (in, into) prison.
6. He also did not want his era to be (like, as) the dark ages of competition.
7. When sirens are going off in (your, you're) head, it is difficult to think very long about one thing.
8. On the television, George saw his son, Harrison, and he saw ballerinas, technicians, musicians, and announcers on their knees expecting (to, too) die.

CONTINUED

Try It Yourself 2.25 (cont.)

9. Harrison chose his empress from among the ballerinas, and he and she listened (to, too) the music he requested.
10. After Harrison and the ballerina were killed, Hazel looked confused (like, as) usual.

EDITING FOR PUNCTUATION ERRORS

2.26 End Marks

End marks tell the reader where a sentence ends. An end mark also shows the purpose of the sentence. The three end marks are the **period,** the **question mark**, and the **exclamation point.**

A declarative sentence ends with a **period.**

DECLARATIVE Orange is a good color for Janine.
Martin took the dog for a walk**.**

An interrogative sentence ends with a **question mark.**

QUESTION What do you want**?**
Why is Diego laughing**?**

An exclamatory sentence ends with an **exclamation point.**

EXCLAMATION Look out for that bus**!**
I dare you to get on the horse**!**

Try It Yourself 2.26

THE GEOGRAPHY, HISTORY, AND ORAL LITERATURES OF AFRICA, PAGE 278

Read the following sentences, and name an appropriate end mark for each one. Write your answers on your own paper.

EXAMPLE Would you have guessed that *Africa* was a Roman name **question mark**

1. The people of Europe were living in the Stone Age when the great Egyptian culture thrived
2. Look into your history books to see how advanced Egyptian civilization was
3. Other African empires were the Kush and the Meroë
4. Axum became the Christian Empire of Ethiopia
5. Who began the African slave trade in the fifteenth century

CONTINUED

Answers for Try It Yourself 2.26

1. period
2. period
3. period
4. period
5. question mark
6. period
7. period
8. question mark
9. period
10. period

Try It Yourself 2.26 (cont.)

6. The Portuguese began the slave trade that resulted in the stealing of ten million human beings from their homes
7. The European nations, during the late 1800s, divided Africa into colonies
8. What do you think was the purpose of the colonies
9. It was to enrich the colonizing countries at the cost of the indigenous people
10. Not until 1994 was the last government by white minority rule, that of South Africa, finally ended

2.27 Commas

A **comma** separates words or groups of words within a sentence. Commas tell the reader to pause at certain spots in the sentence. These pauses help keep the reader from running certain words and phrases together when these phrases should be kept apart. Following is a list of the most common ways commas should be used.

RULE	EXAMPLES
Use commas to separate items in a series. Three or more words make a series.	The puppy growls, yips, and barks. Would you like your eggs scrambled, poached, or fried?
Use commas when you combine sentences using *and, but, or, nor, yet, so,* or *for.* Place the comma before these words.	Some toddlers take naps. Others do not. Some toddlers take naps, but others do not. You could take the bus here. I could pick you up after school. You could take the bus here, or I could pick you up after school.
Use a comma to set off words or phrases that interrupt sentences. Use two commas if the word or phrase falls in the middle of the sentence. Use one comma if the word or phrase comes at the beginning or at the end of a sentence.	Lou's brother, the emergency medical technician, knows CPR. When the tide comes in, we'll go swimming. Caitlin, can you bring the volleyball?
Use commas to separate the parts of a date. Do not use a comma between the month and the year.	Pearl Harbor was bombed on December 7, 1941. The recital will be on Tuesday, April 4.
Use commas to separate items in addresses. Do not put a comma between the state and the ZIP code.	Robin was born in Lima, Peru. They live at 2529 Randolph Drive, Chicago, Illinois 60501.

Try It Yourself 2.27

"THE SIZE OF THINGS," PAGE 562

Copy the sentences below, adding commas where they are necessary.

EXAMPLE Everything in the universe is made up of protons, neutrons, and electrons.
Everything in the universe is made up of protons, neutrons, and electrons.

1. Amazingly the size of an electron is to a speck of dust as the speck of dust is to the earth.
2. Although no one has ever picked up an electron with a pair of forceps we know that the electron exists.
3. Robert Millikan who did research at the University of Chicago was the first to measure the amount of electrical charge carried by electrons.
4. The University of Chicago is in Hyde Park Chicago.
5. Millikan's first accurate measurements were complete in 1914 so they would have been available by December 31 1914.
6. If an atom were the size of a grain of sand on a kitchen table then the table would be two thousand miles long.
7. Lord Rutherford was the first to discover the nucleus of the atom the dense center of the body.
8. Like the sun with the planets orbiting around it the nucleus with electrons orbiting around it is much larger and denser than its satellites.
9. The average distance between stars is five light-years equal to about thirty trillion miles.
10. The diameter of the galaxy believe it or not is one hundred thousand light-years.

2.28 Semicolons

You have seen how two related sentences can be combined into one using a conjunction such as *and, but, so,* and *or*. Another way to join two related sentences into one is to use a **semicolon**. The semicolon can be used in place of the comma and the conjunction.

EXAMPLES Marilyn has a nasty cold, so she took an afternoon nap.
Marilyn has a nasty cold; she took an afternoon nap.
There was lead paint in the old home, and we had to remove it.
There was lead paint in the old home; we had to remove it.

Answers for Try It Yourself 2.27

1. Amazingly, the size of an electron is to a speck of dust as the speck of dust is to the earth.
2. Although no one has ever picked up an electron with a pair of forceps, we know that the electron exists.
3. Robert Millikan, who did research at the University of Chicago, was the first to measure the amount of electrical charge carried by electrons.
4. The University of Chicago is in Hyde Park, Chicago.
5. Millikan's first accurate measurements were complete in 1914, so they would have been available by December 31, 1914.
6. If an atom were the size of a grain of sand on a kitchen table, then the table would be two thousand miles long.
7. Lord Rutherford was the first to discover the nucleus of the atom, the dense center of the body.
8. Like the sun with the planets orbiting around it, the nucleus with electrons orbiting around it is much larger and denser than its satellites.
9. The average distance between stars is five light-years, equal to about thirty trillion miles.
10. The diameter of the galaxy, believe it or not, is one hundred thousand light-years.

Answers for Try It Yourself 2.28

1. Alexei Yablokov investigated the sudden death of several million starfish; later, scientists concluded that radioactive military waste had been the cause of their deaths.
2. Environmental stress may be responsible for the deaths of dolphins along the Riviera; it may also explain the deaths of twelve thousand seals along the shores of the North Sea.
3. A scientist in Antarctica dug through a glacier to look at ice that had been on the surface of the Earth at various times in history; he considered the effect of the Clean Air Act and the beginning of the Industrial Revolution.
4. Scientists measure the thickness of the polar ice cap; it may be thinning because of global warming.
5. Global warming is expected to raise temperatures faster in the polar regions than in other parts of the earth; when the temperature rises the ice thins and weather systems around the globe will be affected.
6. One team reported that the north polar cap has thinned by 2 percent in the last decade; scientists also believe that spring snowmelt comes earlier every year in the Arctic Circle.
7. In Brazil, the rainforest is being destroyed; a section of forest the size of Tennessee is disappearing each year.
8. In each square mile of the Amazon, there are more species of birds than in all of North America; living species of all animals and plants are vanishing at a rate a thousand times faster than at any time in the past sixty-five million years.
9. Elephants are being destroyed for their tusks in East Africa; their mutilated skulls are left to dry in the burning sun.
10. Coral is being bleached white in the Caribbean; the warmer ocean temperatures are destroying the life forms that give it its color.

Try It Yourself 2.28

"Ships in the Desert" page 554

Rewrite the following sentences using semicolons. If two sentences are already joined with a conjunction, replace the comma and the conjunction with a semicolon. If the two sentences are separate, combine them and insert a semicolon as needed.

EXAMPLE In Al Gore's essay, he describes a sea that is now a desert. The Aral Sea is disappearing because its feeder rivers have been diverted for irrigation.

In Al Gore's essay, he describes a sea that is now a desert**;** the Aral Sea is disappearing because its feeder rivers have been diverted for irrigation.

1. Alexei Yablokov investigated the sudden death of several million starfish, and later, scientists concluded that radioactive military waste had been the cause of their deaths.
2. Environmental stress may be responsible for the deaths of dolphins along the Riviera. It may also explain the deaths of twelve thousand seals along the shores of the North Sea.
3. A scientist in Antarctica dug through a glacier to look at ice that had been on the surface of the Earth at various times in history. He considered the effect of the Clean Air Act and of the beginning of the Industrial Revolution.
4. Scientists measure the thickness of the polar ice cap. It may be thinning because of global warming.
5. Global warming is expected to raise temperatures faster in the polar regions than in other parts of the earth. When the temperature rises the ice thins and weather systems around the globe will be affected.
6. One team reported that the north polar cap has thinned by 2 percent in the last decade. Scientists also believe that spring snowmelt comes earlier every year in the Arctic Circle.
7. In Brazil, the rainforest is being destroyed. A section of forest the size of Tennessee is disappearing each year.
8. In each square mile of the Amazon, there are more species of birds than in all of North America. Living species of all animals and plants are vanishing at a rate a thousand times faster than at any time in the past sixty-five million years.
9. Elephants are being destroyed for their tusks in East Africa. Their mutilated skulls are left to dry in the burning sun.
10. Coral is being bleached white in the Caribbean. The warmer ocean temperatures are destroying the life forms that give it its color.

2.29 Colons

Use a **colon** to introduce a list of items.

EXAMPLES Here are the people who are coming: Scott, Randy, Claire, and Julia.
Most children get the following illnesses: chicken pox, ear infections, and stomach flu.

You should also use a colon between numbers that tell hours and minutes.

EXAMPLES 10:14 A.M 5:00 P.M. 12:35 A.M.

A colon is often used after the greeting in a business letter.

EXAMPLES Dear Sirs: Dear Sir or Madam: Dear Ms. Pitt:

Try It Yourself 2.29

VARIOUS SELECTIONS

Copy the sentences, adding colons where they are necessary.

EXAMPLE Rita Dove's speaker writes the following "Open it."
Rita Dove's speaker writes the following: "Open it."

1. She also says this "It's not like it's the end of the world—/just the world as you think/you know it."
2. Eve Merriam says that a poem has none of the following core, stem, rind, pit, seed, or skin.
3. I read Ms. Merriam's poem this afternoon at 5 41.
4. If I wrote her a letter about that poem, I'd write "Dear Generous Hostess."
5. Malcolm X admitted that he was once nearly illiterate he could not understand most of what he read.
6. Malcolm X said, "Let me tell you something from then until I left that prison, in every free moment I had, if I was not reading in the library, I was reading in my bunk."
7. He said the following "I never had been so truly free in my life."
8. Saki is the pen name of this man Hector Hugh Munro.
9. The little girl in the story won these medals one for obedience, one for punctuality, and one for good behavior.
10. The children wrote thank-you notes to the stranger and began them "Dear Sir."

2.30 Apostrophes

An **apostrophe** is used to form the possessive of nouns. To form the possessive of a singular noun, you should add an apostrophe and an *s* to the end of the word.

EXAMPLES Karl**'s** Saturday job is in a restaurant. (Karl + **'s** = Karl**'s**)
Mr. Poloni**'s** hair is getting white. (Poloni + **'s** = Poloni**'s**)

ESSENTIAL SKILLS: LANGUAGE

Answers for Try It Yourself 2.29

1. She also says this: "It's not like it's the end of the world—/just the world as you think/you know it."
2. Eve Merriam says that a poem has none of the following: core, stem, rind, pit, seed, or skin.
3. I read Ms. Merriam's poem this afternoon at 5:41.
4. If I wrote her a letter about that poem, I'd write "Dear Generous Hostess:"
5. Malcolm X admitted that he was once nearly illiterate: he could not understand most of what he read.
6. Malcolm X said, "Let me tell you something: from then until I left that prison, in every free moment I had, if I was not reading in the library, I was reading in my bunk."
7. He said the following: "I never had been so truly free in my whole life."
8. Saki is the pen name of this man: Hector Hugh Munro.
9. The little girl in the story won these medals: one for obedience, one for punctuality, and one for good behavior.
10. The children wrote thank-you notes to the stranger and began them "Dear Sir:"

Answers for Try It Yourself 2.30

1. The speaker says that the city's bridges "quake with fear."
2. He describes the houses' lights as moving from one house to another.
3. According to the poem, trains' windows shine "like a smile full of teeth."
4. New York's smells and sounds are not sweet, but to me they are not hostile either.
5. Just as a different species' way of life seems foreign to humans, the city organism seems alien to someone from the wilderness.
6. The poem's speaker says he sees "machines eating houses."
7. Builder's equipment could be leveling houses to prepare for new construction.
8. The speaker says "stairways walk by themselves," but he must be referring to an escalator's motion.
9. He says "people disappear" behind the elevator's doors.
10. To me an urban center's constant change, motion, and noise is exciting, not frightening.

The possessive of a plural noun is formed two different ways. If the plural noun does not end in *s*, you add an apostrophe and an *s* to the end of the word. If the plural noun ends with an s, add only an apostrophe.

EXAMPLES Children's noses grow faster than the other parts of their faces. (Children + 's = Children's)
The nurses' job is to care for the patient. (nurses + ' + nurses')

There are some words that end in *s* and are singular, such as *species* or *Jesus,* that have an irregular possessive form. Form the possessive of these words by adding only an apostrophe.

EXAMPLES Jesus' words
species' characteristics

Try It Yourself 2.30

"The City Is So Big," page 52

Copy the sentences, adding apostrophes where they are necessary.

EXAMPLE Richard Garcias poem "The City Is So Big" describes a frightening vision of urban machines.
Richard Garcia's poem "The City Is So Big" describes a frightening vision of urban machines.

1. The speaker says that the citys bridges "quake with fear."
2. He describes the houses lights as moving from one house to another.
3. According to the poem, trains windows shine "like a smile full of teeth."
4. New Yorks smells and sounds are not sweet, but to me they are not hostile either.
5. Just as a different species way of life seems foreign to humans, the city organism seems alien to someone from the wilderness.
6. The poems speaker says he sees "machines eating houses."
7. Builders equipment could be leveling houses to prepare for new construction.
8. The speaker says "stairways walk by themselves," but he must be referring to an escalators motion.
9. He says "people disappear" behind the elevators doors.
10. To me an urban centers constant change, motion, and noise is exciting, not frightening.

2.31 Underlining and Italics

Italics are a type of slanted printing used to make a word or phrase stand out. In handwritten documents, or in forms of printing in which italics are not available, **underlining** is used. You should underline or italicize the titles of books, magazines, works of art, movies, and plays.

BOOKS	*Huckleberry Finn, Katherine* or <u>Huckleberry Finn</u>, <u>Katherine</u>
MAGAZINES	*Time, People* or <u>Time</u>, <u>People</u>
WORKS OF ART	*The Blue Boy, The Pietà* or <u>The Blue Boy</u>, <u>The Pietà</u>
MOVIES	*Jumangi, Little Women* or <u>Jumangi</u>, <u>Little Women</u>
PLAYS	*Romeo and Juliet, The Importance of Being Earnest* or <u>Romeo and Juliet</u>, <u>The Importance of Being Earnest</u>

Try It Yourself 2.31

VARIOUS SELECTIONS

Copy the following sentences, adding underlines (or italics) where they are necessary.

EXAMPLE In The Autobiography of Malcolm X, the African-American leader describes his transformation in prison.
In *The Autobiography of Malcolm X,* the African-American leader describes his transformation in prison.

1. While waiting for my doctor to see me for an annual checkup, I read Newsweek magazine from cover to cover.
2. When I first saw Michelangelo's sculpture David, I did not realize how beautiful it was.
3. My parents always watch the film It's a Wonderful Life during the holidays.
4. The best theatrical production I have ever seen is an outdoor performance of Shakespeare's A Midsummer Night's Dream.
5. Did you know that John Kennedy, Jr. publishes a magazine called George?
6. One of the most famous paintings is one by Leonardo da Vinci called The Mona Lisa.
7. The movie Little Women dramatizes Louisa May Alcott's book beautifully.
8. I believe Cats is now the longest-running play on Broadway.
9. Theodora Kroeber, in her biography Ishi in Two Worlds, tells the story of a Stone Age man who was studied by scientists in the early part of the twentieth century.
10. The magazine with the widest circulation is TV Guide.

2.32 Quotation Marks

When you use a person's exact words in your writing, you are using a **direct quotation.** Enclose the words of a direct quotation in **quotation marks.**

EXAMPLES "Could you take the reins?" asked Margaret.
"Yes, I'd love to," Carlos replied.

Answers for Try It Yourself 2.31

1. While waiting for my doctor to see me for an annual checkup, I read *Newsweek* magazine from cover to cover.
2. When I first saw Michelangelo's sculpture *David*, I did not realize how beautiful it was.
3. My parents always watch the film *It's a Wonderful Life* during the holidays.
4. The best theatrical production I have ever seen is an outdoor performance of Shakespeare's *A Midsummer Night's Dream.*
5. Did you know that John Kennedy, Jr. publishes a magazine called *George?*
6. One of the most famous paintings is one by Leonardo da Vinci called *The Mona Lisa.*
7. The movie *Little Women* dramatizes Louisa May Alcott's book beautifully.
8. I believe *Cats* is now the longest-running play on Broadway.
9. Theodora Kroeber, in her biography *Ishi in Two Worlds*, tells the story of a Stone Age man who was studied by scientists in the early part of the twentieth century.
10. The magazine with the widest circulation is *TV Guide.*

Answers for Try It Yourself 2.32

1. "The Cleveland Wrecking Yard" is a disturbing chapter of the novel *Trout Fishing in America.*
2. One of the sweetest folk songs, "Spoon River," counsels peace between friends after the Civil War.
3. I read an article on the *Boston Globe's* editorial page called "Investment in the China Trade."
4. The first chapter in H. G. Wells's *The War of the Worlds* is called "The Eve of the War."
5. "How did you feel when you found out what happened to Anne Frank in the end?" Tony asked Raoul.
6. "The War of the Wall" is a very effective short story about the power of visual art.
7. As she expressed clearly in her poem "The Brain—is wider than the Sky," Emily Dickinson revered imagination.
8. To welcome the new students from Mexico, we sang Woody Guthrie's "This Land is Your Land."
9. Chapter 12 of *The War of the Worlds* is called "What I Saw of the Destruction of Weybridge and Shepperton."
10. Pablo Neruda's poem "Ode to My Socks" illustrates the idea that a poem's subject can be anything.

A direct quotation should always begin with a capital letter. Separate a direct quotation from the rest of the sentence with a comma, question mark, or exclamation point. Do not separate the direct quotation from the rest of the sentence with a period. All punctuation marks that belong to the direct quotation itself should be placed inside the quotation marks.

EXAMPLES "**L**ook out for the rocks**,**" yelled Isis.
Martin crooned**,** "**S**he's so gorgeous**.**"
Maggie asked**,** "**D**o these have sugar in them**?**"
"**T**ell me about yourself**,**" invited Pedro.

Use quotation marks to enclose the titles of short works such as short stories, poems, songs, articles, and parts of books.

SHORT STORIES	"A Day's Wait," "The Fan Club"
POEMS	"Jabberwocky", "Inner City"
SONGS	"Alice's Restaurant", "Battle Hymn of the Republic"
ARTICLES, ESSAYS	"An Essay on Man", "Self-Reliance"
PARTS OF BOOKS	"The Shop of the Gods"

Try It Yourself 2.32

VARIOUS SELECTIONS

Copy the sentences, adding quotation marks where they are necessary.

EXAMPLE In the eighth grade, Suzanna read Amy Lowell's poem Night Clouds.
In the eighth grade, Suzanna read Amy Lowell's poem "Night Clouds."

1. The Cleveland Wrecking Yard is a chapter in the novel *Trout Fishing in America.*
2. One of the sweetest folk songs, Spoon River, counsels peace between friends after the Civil War.
3. I read an article on the *Boston Globe's* editorial page called Investment in the China Trade.
4. The first chapter in H. G. Wells's *The War of the Worlds* is called The Eve of the War.
5. How did you feel when you found out what happened to Anne Frank in the end? Tony asked Raoul.
6. The War of the Wall is a very effective short story about the power of visual art.
7. As she expressed clearly in her poem The Brain—is wider than the Sky, Emily Dickinson revered imagination.
8. To welcome the new students from Mexico, we sang Woody Guthrie's This Land Is Your Land.
9. Chapter 12 of *The War of the Worlds* is called What I Saw of the Destruction of Weybridge and Shepperton.
10. Pablo Neruda's poem Ode to My Socks illustrates the idea that a poem's subject can be anything.

2.33 Hyphens and Dashes

A **hyphen** is used to make a compound word.

EXAMPLES come-as-you-are party, brother-in-law, eighth-grade girl, happy-go-lucky, vice-president

A **dash** is used to show a sudden break or change in thought.

EXAMPLE A hurricane moves everything—and everyone—in its path.

Try It Yourself 2.33

The War of the Worlds, page 576

On your own paper, rewrite the sentences, inserting hyphens and dashes where they are needed.

EXAMPLE Scientists around the turn of the century believed that Mars was a life sustaining planet.
Scientists around the turn of the century believed that Mars was a life-sustaining planet.

1. The two satellites of Mars Phobos and Deimos have names that mean "fear" and "panic," respectively.
2. H. G. Wells some say the father of extraterrestrials wrote *The War of the Worlds*, an adventure story about Martians invading Earth.
3. The planet Mars is a cold, dry rocky place under a salmon colored sky.
4. In the story, the Martians saw Earth a warmer and more fertile planet as a place to colonize a new home for themselves and their families.
5. Wells's Martians are advanced beings who see Earthlings as learning disabled newcomers to the galaxy.
6. Most Americans especially those who are descended from European colonists have no reason to criticize the Martians for their dreams of exploitation.
7. European immigrants have destroyed many indigenous cultures Mayan, Incan, and Tazmanian to name but a few.
8. For thousands of years by the way Mars has been known as the star of war.
9. An attack quick, burning, and silent by one of Wells's Martians resulted in immediate disintegration of the victim.
10. Wells gave the Martians one disadvantage in the story they were extremely slow moving creatures.

EDITING FOR CAPITALIZATION ERRORS

2.34 Proper Nouns and Adjectives

Using capital letters is called **capitalization**. Always capitalize **proper nouns** and **adjectives.** A proper noun names a specific person, place, or thing. A proper adjective is an adjective formed from a proper noun.

Answers for Try It Yourself 2.33

1. The two satellites of Mars—Phobos and Deimos—have names that mean "fear" and "panic," respectively.
2. H. G. Wells—some say the father of extraterrestrials—wrote *The War of the Worlds*, an adventure story about Martians invading Earth.
3. The planet Mars is a cold, dry rocky place under a salmon-colored sky.
4. In the story, the Martians saw Earth—a warmer and more fertile planet—as a place to colonize a new home for themselves and their families.
5. Wells's Martians are advanced beings who see Earthlings as learning-disabled newcomers to the galaxy.
6. Most Americans—especially those who are descended from European colonists—have no reason to criticize the Martians for their dreams of exploitation.
7. European immigrants have destroyed many indigenous cultures—Mayan, Incan, and Tazmanian to name but a few.
8. For thousands of years—by the way—Mars has been known as the star of war.
9. An attack—quick, burning, and silent—by one of Wells's Martians resulted in immediate disintegration of the victim.
10. Wells gave the Martians one disadvantage in the story—they were extremely slow-moving creatures.

Answers for Try It Yourself 2.34

1. After crossing the Annisquam River Bridge, you will be on an island.
2. My favorite poet is Wallace Stevens, who was actually an insurance executive in Hartford, Connecticut.
3. On January 28, 1986, the *Challenger* exploded, and all seven astronauts on board, including a teacher from New Hampshire named Christa MacAuliffe, were killed.
4. From the top of the Sears Tower in Chicago, you can see a huge metropolitan area.
5. A Jewish scholar knows how to read Hebrew and has memorized much of the Torah.
6. The National Basketball Association evaluated the Chicago Bulls after they won the championship.
7. My father, Dr. Arnold Chelew, is the president of the Monterey Chamber of Commerce.
8. The senior class trip for River Dell Regional High School was to the Grand Canyon in Arizona.
9. People who practice Confucianism use a book of sacred writings called the *I Ching,* or book of changes.
10. Charlie belonged to a soccer team called The Monument, and this weekend they are playing in Sunshine, Florida.

PROPER NOUNS Bosnia, Queen Victoria, Freud
PROPER ADJECTIVES Bosnian, Victorian, Freudian

Capitalize the names of people and pets.

PEOPLE AND PETS Christopher Reeve, Bill Clinton, Spot

There are many different kinds of proper nouns. The chart on the next page should help you to recognize some of them.

PROPER NOUNS	
Titles Used with Names	Ms. Montalra, Dr. Axelrod, Mr. Shepherd
Months, Days, Holidays	February, Monday, Valentine's Day
Religions	Taoism, Judaism, Jansenism
Sacred Writings	Torah, I Ching, New Testament
Cities, States, Countries	Guatemala, Paris, Oregon
Nationalities	Chinese, Australian, Brazilian
Streets, Bridges	Granite Street, Bay Bridge
Buildings, Monuments	Chrysler Building
Clubs, Organizations, Businesses	Girl Scouts of America, Masons, Hewlett Packard

Try It Yourself 2.34

Rewrite the following sentences, changing lowercase letters to capital letters wherever necessary.

EXAMPLE Because Clara's mother was in the navy, she has lived in germany, panama, and the philippines.
Because Clara's mother was in the Navy, she has lived in Germany, Panama, and the Philippines.

1. After crossing the annisquam river bridge, you will be on an island.
2. My favorite poet is wallace stevens, who was actually an insurance executive in hartford, connecticut.
3. On january 28, 1986, the *challenger* exploded, and all seven astronauts on board, including a teacher from new hampshire named christa macAuliffe, were killed.
4. From the top of the sears tower in chicago, you can see a huge metropolitan area.
5. A jewish scholar knows how to read hebrew and has memorized much of the torah.

CONTINUED

Try It Yourself 2.34 (cont.)

6. The national basketball association evaluated the chicago bulls after they won the championship.
7. My father, dr. arnold chelew, is the president of the monterey chamber of commerce.
8. The senior class trip for river dell regional high school was to the grand canyon in arizona.
9. People who practice confucianism use a book of sacred readings called the *i ching,* or book of changes.
10. Charlie belonged to a soccer team called the monument, and this weekend they are playing in sunshine, florida.

2.35 *I* and First Words

Capitalize the first word of every sentence.

EXAMPLES **I**s football too violent?
All the children danced.

Capitalize the word *I* whenever it appears.

EXAMPLES Next Sunday, **I** will be thirteen.
Sri and **I** participated in a pledge walk to help hungry children.

Try It Yourself 2.35

"The Flying Machine," page 68

On your own paper, rewrite the following sentences, changing lowercase letters to capital letters wherever necessary.

EXAMPLE the story "The Flying Machine" takes place about sixteen hundred years ago.
The story "The Flying Machine" takes place about sixteen hundred years ago.

1. if i were the emperor, i'm not sure i could have destroyed the machine and its inventor.
2. the emperor is afraid that an evil person will use a flying machine to destroy The Great Wall of China.
3. if The Great Wall were destroyed, the enemies of the emperor's people could attack them.
4. as far as i can see, however, the emperor is a rather simple-minded man.
5. he doesn't realize that the flying machine could expand his little world.
6. on the other hand, i suppose, he is right that peace is very valuable.

CONTINUED

Answers for Try It Yourself 2.35

1. If I were the emperor, I'm not sure I could have destroyed the machine and its inventor.
2. The emperor is afraid that an evil person will use a flying machine to destroy The Great Wall of China.
3. If The Great Wall were destroyed, the enemies of the emperor's people could attack them.
4. As far as I can see, however, the emperor is a rather simple-minded man.
5. He doesn't realize that the flying machine could expand his little world.
6. On the other hand, I suppose, he is right that peace is very valuable.
7. He assumes that no one else will invent the flying machine and that he can terrorize the servant and the farmer into keeping the secret to themselves.
8. His idea is that he must protect the simple miracles of life that he and his people already have.
9. Tea, the rising sun, and the sweet air are all the miracles he wants to see.
10. He warns the servant who wants to show him the flying machine, "I must have time to prepare myself for the sight."

Answers for Try It Yourself 2.36

1. In the story, "The Flying Machine," Emperor Yuan destroys a fantastic invention.
2. Malcolm X was a leader of African Americans.
3. Of all my older relatives, Uncle Bob is probably my favorite.
4. A rabbit has a dream that he becomes a king and can laugh at the tiny cat.
5. The boy Colin in "Last Cover" was an artist, and his father was puzzled by him.
6. Ngolela Dibinga wrote a story about a common man who married a princess.
7. In "The Sniper," a street soldier plans a strategy to ambush and kill his enemy.
8. *Earth in the Balance,* a book about threats to life on Earth, was written by the vice president of the United States.
9. The mayor of Hamelin was foolish to refuse to pay the Pied Piper after he had rid the town of rats.
10. In the play *A Midsummer Night's Dream,* Titania is queen of the fairies.

Try It Yourself 2.35 (cont.)

7. he assumes that no one else will invent the flying machine and that he can terrorize the servant and the farmer into keeping the secret to themselves.
8. his idea is that he must protect the simple miracles of the life that he and his people already have.
9. tea, the rising sun, and the sweet air are all the miracles he wants to see.
10. he warns the servant who wants to show him the flying machine, "i must have time to prepare myself for the sight."

2.36 Family Relationships and Titles of Persons

A word for a family relation such as *Mom, Dad,* or *Grandpa* should be capitalized if it is used as the name or part of the name of a particular person. Do not capitalize a word for a family relation if a modifier such as *the, a, my,* or *your* comes before it.

CAPITALIZED When they were younger, **A**unt **P**eggy, **U**ncle **J**im, and **U**ncle **F**rank lived in **S**outh **B**oston.

NOT CAPITALIZED My **g**randpa was a baker and a nephew to **B**uffalo **B**ill **C**ody.

Capitalize the official title of a person when it is followed by the person's name or when it is used instead of a name in direct address.

EXAMPLES Princess **D**iana, **Q**ueen **I**sabella, the **D**alai **L**ama
Welcome, **M**r. **P**resident.

Do not capitalize references to occupations.

EXAMPLES the artist, the teacher, the boat captain, the comedian, the scientist, the journalist, the writer

Try It Yourself 2.36

VARIOUS SELECTIONS

On your own paper, rewrite the following sentences, changing lowercase letters to capital letters and capital letters to lowercase letters wherever necessary. If a sentence contains no errors, write *correct.*

EXAMPLE In the story "Harrison Bergeron," handicapper general Diana Moon Glampers restricts people's talents.
In the story "Harrison Bergeron," **H**andicapper **G**eneral Diana Moon Glampers restricts people's talents.

1. In the story, "The Flying Machine," emperor Yuan destroys a fantastic invention.
2. Malcolm X was a Leader of African Americans.

CONTINUED

Try It Yourself 2.36 (cont.)

3. Of all my older relatives, uncle Bob is probably my favorite.
4. A rabbit has a dream that he becomes a King and can laugh at the tiny cat.
5. The boy Colin in "Last Cover" was an artist, and his Father was puzzled by him.
6. Ngolela Dibinga wrote a story about a common man who married a Princess.
7. In "The Sniper," a Street Soldier plans a strategy to ambush and kill his enemy.
8. *Earth in the Balance,* a book about threats to life on earth, was written by the Vice President of the United States.
9. The Mayor of Hamelin was foolish to refuse to pay the Pied Piper after he had rid the town of rats.
10. In the play *A Midsummer Night's Dream,* Titania is Queen of the fairies.

2.37 Geographical Names, Directions, and Historical Names

Capitalize the names of specific places, including terms such as *lake, mountain, river,* or *valley* if they are used as part of a name.

BODIES OF WATER	Mississippi River, Pacific Ocean
CITIES AND TOWNS	San Jose, St. Louis
COUNTIES	Bergen County, Orange County
COUNTRIES	New Zealand, Argentina
ISLANDS	Guam, Mozambique
MOUNTAINS	Mount Shasta, Mount Monadnock
STATES	California, Tennessee
STREETS AND HIGHWAYS	Granite Street, Route 66

Do not capitalize general names for places.

EXAMPLES	Along the ocean road grew pink and purple ice plant. The river is my favorite place to think.

Capitalize geographical directions if they are part of a specific name or a commonly recognized region. Do not capitalize words such as *east(ern), west(ern), north(ern),* and *south(ern)* if they are used only to indicate direction.

CAPITALIZED	West Africa, Southern Europe, Southeast Asia, the South
NOT CAPITALIZED	east of Salinas, northern tip of the island, southern part of the state, western regions

Answers for Try It Yourself 2.37

1. William Shakespeare lived most of his life in southern England.
2. Along Taliaferro Street, most people felt like part of a big family.
3. One clean river where fishing was once banned is the Hudson River.
4. "Rip Van Winkle" is a story that takes place in the Catskill Mountains of New York.
5. "The Sniper" takes place in Dublin near the Liffey River.
6. When astronomers first saw the deep grooves on Mars, they thought they were canals built by living beings.
7. On Mount Rushmore are stone carvings of the faces of four U.S. presidents.
8. Scientists can detect changes in the polar icecaps that reflect air and water pollution since the beginning of the Industrial Age.
9. In County Galway is the town of Connemara, a beautiful town on the western coast of Ireland.
10. At the North Pole, scientists measure the density of the ice at various levels to see the impact of environmental changes that have taken place over time.

Capitalize historical events, special events, and recognized periods of time.

HISTORICAL EVENTS	**R**econstruction, **B**oer **W**ar
HISTORICAL PERIODS	**S**tone **A**ge, **R**enaissance
SPECIAL EVENTS	**O**lympics, **W**orld's **F**air

Try It Yourself 2.37

VARIOUS SELECTIONS

Rewrite the following sentences, changing lowercase letters to capital letters wherever necessary.

EXAMPLE Richard Brautigan traveled around Northern Montana and southern Washington.
Richard Brautigan traveled around **n**orthern Montana and southern Washington.

1. William Shakespeare lived much of his life in Southern England.
2. Along taliaferro street, most people felt like part of a big family.
3. One clean river where fishing was once banned is the hudson river.
4. "Rip Van Winkle" is a story that takes place in the catskill mountains of New York.
5. "The Sniper" takes place in Dublin near the liffey river.
6. When astronomers first saw the deep grooves on mars, they thought they were canals built by living beings.
7. On mount rushmore are stone carvings of the faces of four U.S. presidents.
8. Scientists can detect changes in the polar icecaps that reflect air and water pollution since the beginning of the industrial age.
9. In county galway is the town of connemara, a beautiful town on the western coast of ireland.
10. At the north pole, scientists measure the density of the ice at various levels to see the impact of environmental changes that have taken place over time.

2.38 Titles of Art Works and Literary Works

Apply **title capitalization** to titles of art works and literary works. In title capitalization, capitalize the first word, the last word, and all other words except articles (*a, an,* and *the*) and prepositions.

EXAMPLES Grant Wood's *American Gothic;* Winslow Homer's *Young Soldier;* Jullian Gatto's *Mother Moon, Sister Crow;* Richard Brautigan's *Trout Fishing in America;* Malcolm X's *The Autobiography of Malcolm X;* Alice Walker's *The Color Purple*

Try It Yourself 2.38

VARIOUS SELECTIONS

On your own paper, rewrite the following sentences, changing small letters to capital letters or capital letters to small letters wherever necessary.

EXAMPLE Ray Bradbury's *fahrenheit 451* is entitled for the temperature at which paper, and therefore books, will burn.
Ray Bradbury's *Fahrenheit 451* is entitled for the temperature at which paper, and therefore books, will burn.

1. Richard Garcia's poem "the city is so big" expresses fear and alienation.
2. When Alice Walker wrote "for my sister molly who in the fifties," she may have been describing her own early life.
3. The phrase "a raisin in the sun" from Langston Hughes's poem "a dream deferred" later became the title of a play by Lorraine Hansberry.
4. Toni Cade Bambara's story "the war of the wall" describes a community conflict about a tribute to a family member who is gone.
5. William Butler Yeats wrote a poem called "the song of wandering aengus."
6. Sandra Cisneros's poem "Bums In The Attic" is about someone who knows the sorrow of being without a home and vows never to forget it.
7. The title of a myth from Egypt, "the secret name of ra," refers to the name of the Egyptian sun god.
8. In "tears of autumn," Yoshiko Uchida describes the frightening experience of leaving one's home to travel to an unknown future.
9. The narrator in Alan Bloch's "humans are different" is a robot.
10. Luis Omar Salinas writes a tribute to his father called "my father is a simple man."

EDITING FOR SPELLING ERRORS

2.39 Using Spelling Rules I

Always check your writing for spelling errors, and try to recognize the words that give you more trouble than others. Adding prefixes and suffixes often causes spelling errors. A **prefix** is a letter or a group of letters added to the beginning of a word to change its meaning. When adding a prefix, do not change the spelling of the word itself.

EXAMPLES dis + illusioned = disillusioned
un + acceptable = unacceptable

A **suffix** is a letter or group of letters added to the end of a word to change its meaning. The spelling of most words is not changed when the suffix *–ness* or *–ly* is added.

EXAMPLES kind + ness = kindness
real + ly = really

Answers for Try It Yourself 2.38

1. Richard Garcia's poem "The City Is So Big" expresses fear and alienation.
2. When Alice Walker wrote "For My Sister Molly Who in the Fifties," she may have been describing her own early life.
3. The phrase "a raisin in the sun" from Langston Hughes's poem "A Dream Deferred" later became the title of a play by Lorraine Hansberry.
4. Toni Cade Bambara's story "The War of the Wall" describes a community conflict about a tribute to a family member who is gone.
5. William Butler Yeats wrote a poem called "The Song of Wandering Aengus."
6. Sandra Cisneros's poem "Bums in the Attic" is about someone who knows the sorrow of being without a home and vows never to forget it.
7. The title of a myth from Egypt, "The Secret Name of Ra," refers to the name of the Egyptian sun god.
8. In "Tears of Autumn," Yoshiko Uchida describes the frightening experience of leaving one's home to travel to an unknown future.
9. The narrator in Alan Bloch's "Humans Are Different" is a robot.
10. Luis Omar Salinas write a tribute to his father called "My Father Is a Simple Man."

Answers for Try It Yourself 2.39

1. circling; realizing
2. going
3. really
4. insecurity; encouragement
5. wholesome; cheery
6. quivering; carefully
7. exploration
8. glancing
9. possibly; picturing; explaining
10. foreshadowing; suffering

If you are adding a suffix to a word that ends with *y*, and that *y* follows a vowel, you should usually leave the *y* in place. (**Vowels** are the letters *a, e, i, o,* and *u.*)

EXAMPLES coy + ly = coyly; say + ing = saying; pray + ing = praying; bay + ed = bayed

If you are adding a suffix to a word that ends with *y*, and that *y* follows a consonant, you should usually change the *y* to *i.* (**Consonants** are all letters that are not vowels.)

EXAMPLES soggy + est = soggiest; dry + ed = dried; lazy + ness = laziness; airy + ly = airily

If you are adding a suffix that begins with a vowel to a word that ends with a silent *e*, you should usually drop the *e.*

EXAMPLES close + ing = closing; bone + y = bony; due + ly = duly; brake + ing = braking

If you are adding a suffix that begins with a consonant to a word that ends with a silent *e*, you should usually leave the *e* in place.

EXAMPLES time + less = timeless; hate + ful = hateful; fortunate + ly = fortunately; close + ness = closeness

Try It Yourself 2.39

"Of Men and Mountains," page 98

Find the misspelled words in the following sentences. Spell them correctly on your own paper. Some of the quoted material may contain misspellings.

EXAMPLE The story by William Douglas is about experienceing danger and challengeing the wilderness with a friend. **experiencing**

1. Doug and the narrator begin circleing the rock they plan to climb, realizing that it has never been climbed before.
2. One of the more dangerous parts of the journey was goeing down the rock wall.
3. At one point, they saw a realy large crevice, but there seemed to be no way Doug could reach it.
4. The narrator had to hide his insecureity to give Doug as much encouragment as possible.

CONTINUED

Try It Yourself 2.39 (cont.)

5. Doug, thinking he might die, asks the narrator to tell his mother that he had "wanted to marry a girl as wholsome and cheerey and good as she."
6. As he heard his friend's words, the narrator's lips were quivereing, but he carfully put his face against the rock so that Doug would not see.
7. Doug made the jump, but further exploreation showed that there was no way up from that cul-de-sac.
8. Sometimes they couldn't help glanceing down, even though they knew it was unwise.
9. At one point, the narrator thinks he cannot possibley hold onto Doug, but picture-ing himself explaineing Doug's death to Doug's family gives him additional strength.
10. About halfway through the story, an example of foreshadoweing—"on later climbs we would"—relieves some of the suspense the reader has been suffereing.

2.40 Using Spelling Rules II

When a word is spelled with the letters *i* and *e* and has the long *e* sound, it is spelled *ie* except after the letter *c*.

EXAMPLES grief, brief, relief
friend, believe, pier

The only word in the English language that ends in *–sede* is *supersede*. Only the following three words end in *–ceed*: *exceed, proceed,* and *succeed.* Every other word that ends with the "seed" sound is spelled *cede*.

EXAMPLES precede, recede, concede, accede

Most noun plurals are formed by simply adding *–s* to the end of the word.

EXAMPLES rocks, kittens, riverboats, rabbits

The plurals of nouns that end in *o, s, x, z, ch,* or *sh* should be formed by adding *–es*.

EXAMPLES potatoes, messes, sixes, fezes, couches, sashes

Answers for Try It Yourself 2.40

1. cities
2. potatoes
3. autobiographies
4. supersede
5. sixes
6. solos
7. fiendish
8. succeeds
9. believes
10. cries

An exception to the rule above is that musical terms (and certain other words that end in *o*) are usually pluralized by adding *–s*.

EXAMPLES pianos, solos, concertos, sopranos, banjos, radios

Form the plurals of nouns that end in *y* following a vowel by adding *–s*.

EXAMPLES boy + *s* = boys monkey + *s* = monkeys
Saturday + *s* = Saturdays day + *s* = days

Form the plurals of nouns that end in *y* following a consonant by changing the *y* to an *i* and adding *–es*.

EXAMPLES bunnies, cries, buddies, ladies

Try It Yourself 2.40

VARIOUS SELECTIONS

Find the misspelled words in the following sentences. Spell them correctly on your own paper.

EXAMPLE In his greif after the loss of his family, Mr. Frank almost loses Anne's diary.
grief

1. Richard Garcia probably doesn't like citys.
2. The twins in "The War of the Wall" carry a dinner of sweet potatos, ham, and gravy to the painter lady.
3. My favorite of the autobiographys I have read is Malcolm X's.
4. Desire to protect one's climbing partner must supercede desire to protect oneself.
5. Rip Van Winkle was all at sixs and sevens when he awakened after a twenty-year sleep.
6. The Pied Paper played soloes on his flute to get the rats to follow him away from Hamelin.
7. In *A Midsummer Night's Dream,* Oberon tries to play a feindish trick on his wife, Titania.
8. In the end, the painter lady succedes in winning the approval of the families on Taliaferro Street.
9. Emily Dickinson beleives that the brain is larger than the sky.
10. Sometimes George Bergeron lets out tiny crys when a loud sound goes off in his ear to keep him from thinking.

2.41 Common Spelling Errors

Some English words are often misspelled. The following box contains a list of 150 commonly misspelled words. If you master this list, you will avoid many errors in your spelling.

COMMONLY MISSPELLED ENGLISH WORDS		
absence	colossal	judgment
abundant	column	league
academically	committee	leisure
accessible	conceivable	license
accidentally	conscientious	lightning
accommodate	conscious	liquefy
accurate	consistency	magnificent
acknowledgment	deceitful	manageable
acquaintance	descendant	maneuver
adequately	desirable	meadow
adolescent	disastrous	mediocre
advantageous	discipline	miniature
advisable	efficiency	mischievous
ancient	eighth	misspell
annihilate	embarrass	mortgage
anonymous	enormous	mysterious
answer	enthusiastically	naive
apparent	environment	necessity
article	exhaust	nickel
attendance	existence	niece
bankruptcy	fascinating	noticeable
beautiful	finally	nucleus
beggar	forfeit	nuisance
beginning	fulfill	nutritious
behavior	guidance	obedience
biscuit	guerrilla	occasionally
breathe	hindrance	occurrence
business	hypocrite	orchestra
calendar	independent	outrageous
camouflage	influential	pageant
catastrophe	ingenious	parallel
cellar	institution	pastime
cemetery	interference	peasant
changeable	irrelevant	permanent
clothes	irresistible	persistent

CONTINUED

ANSWERS FOR TRY IT YOURSELF 2.41

1. outrageous
2. persistent
3. beggar
4. judgment
5. weird
6. responsibility
7. ingenious
8. camouflages
9. accidentally
10. maneuvered

phenomenon	rhythm	transparent
physician	schedule	twelfth
pneumonia	seize	undoubtedly
prestige	separate	unmistakable
privilege	sergeant	unnecessary
procedure	siege	vacuum
prophesy	significance	vehicle
prove	souvenir	vengeance
receipt	sponsor	villain
referred	succeed	vinegar
rehearsal	surprise	weird
relieve	symbol	whistle
resistance	synonymous	withhold
resources	temperature	yacht
responsibility	tomorrow	yield

Try It Yourself 2.41

VARIOUS SELECTIONS

Find the misspelled words in the following sentences. Spell them correctly on your own paper.

EXAMPLE The idea of intelligent life on Mars is an unrealistic but fassinating one. **fascinating**

1. Richard Brautigan's premise for "The Cleveland Wrecking Yard" is outragous and terrifying.
2. The painter lady in "War of the Wall" was so persisstent that she did not even stop painting to eat a meal.
3. In "Bums in the Attic," the narrator doesn't want to go with her family to look at the houses on the hill because she doesn't want to look like a begger.
4. In Vice President Gore's judgement, we need to start protecting wildlife now.
5. The idea of eating a poem seems a little wierd, although good writing should offer a sensory experience.
6. The sister in Alice Walker's poem felt that it was her responseability to teach the other children to speak well and to use their imaginations.
7. The ingeneous invention of a flying machine is not valued by the emperor in Bradbury's story.
8. A Republican soldier camoflages himself on a rooftop to hide from his enemies.
9. The robot accedentelly kills the human in "Humans Are Different."
10. The climbers manuevered carefully up to the ledge.

DEVELOPING YOUR VOCABULARY

2.42 Using Context Clues

There will be times when you will be reading and a dictionary will not be available to you. If you come across an unfamiliar word in this situation, you can often figure out the meaning of a word by using **context clues.**

One type of context clue is **restatement.** The author may tell you the meaning of the word you do not know by using different words to express the same idea in another sentence.

EXAMPLE Sister Marguerite seemed almost **clairvoyant** in her **insights** about people's characters.

A reader can figure out from the restatement that *clairvoyant* means able to see what cannot be seen.

Another type of context clue is **apposition.** An apposition is renaming something in different words. Look for a word or phrase that has been placed in the sentence to clarify the word you do not know.

EXAMPLE Nancy's chilblains, sores on her fingers, got worse in the winter.

Examples given in a sentence can also be used as context clues.

EXAMPLE All of these marsupials—koalas, kangaroos, and wombats—are native to Australia.

The examples given show that a marsupial is an animal that carries its young in a pouch.

Try It Yourself 2.42

The War of the Worlds, page 576

On your own paper, define the underlined words by using the context clues provided.

EXAMPLE I he people were disappointed at the inanimate, motionless, mound.
inanimate = not moving; lifeless

1. The cylinder was <u>embedded</u> in the ground, and the onlookers gazed downward at it buried in the sand.
2. The multitude of hundreds of people began to <u>dwindle</u> when the cylinder remained still.
3. A line of white flame <u>impinged</u> upon each man, and after the attack the men turned to fire.
4. Whatever is <u>combustible</u>, wood, paper, oily rags, will burst into flame when the Martian flashes hit.
5. The Martians were <u>invigorated</u>, refreshed, by the high content of oxygen in the atmosphere.

CONTINUED

Answers for Try It Yourself 2.42

1. embedded = buried
2. dwindle = grow less
3. impinge = struck
4. combustible = able to be set aflame
5. invigorated = refreshed
6. indefatigable = tireless
7. disgorged = poured forth
8. ascertain = find out
9. exhorted = advised strongly
10. coherency = organization

Try It Yourself 2.42 (cont.)

6. They worked all night long, seeming indefatigable.
7. The narrator began to suspect that the slow lumps disgorged from the cylinder were Martians or their machines.
8. Although the narrator's brother knew that there was an accident on the trainline between London and Woking, he could not ascertain the nature of the accident.
9. The public was exhorted, or advised strongly, to resist panic.
10. Eventually, the governmental bodies and police began to lose coherency, become disconnected and disorganized.

2.43 Base Words, Prefixes, and Suffixes

You can build your vocabulary if you start to notice how certain words are created. Many words are formed by adding **prefixes** or **suffixes** to **base words.** (See the Language Arts Survey, 2.39, "Using Spelling Rules I.") If you are unfamiliar with a word that is formed with a prefix or a suffix, check to see if you recognize the meaning of the base word and the meaning of its prefix or the suffix. For example, you might not know the meaning of the word *maladjusted.* However, you might recognize the meaning of the base word *adjusted.* You know from words such as *malfunction, malnutrition,* and *malpractice* that the prefix *mal–* means "badly" or "poor." The following charts show other examples.

PREFIX	MEANING	EXAMPLE	MEANING
anti–	"against"	antibacterial	against bacteria
dis–	"not, opposite"	disagreeable	not agreeable
hyper–	"over, excessively"	hyperactive	excessively active
im–, un–	"not"	unusual	not usual
post–	"after"	postseason	after the season
re–	"again"	reprint	print again

SUFFIX	MEANING	EXAMPLE	MEANING
–er, –or	"one who"	narrator	one who narrates
–ful	"full of"	graceful	full of grace
–ish	"like"	childish	like a child
–ity, –ty	"state of, quality"	captivity	state of being captive
–less	"without"	fearless	without fear
–ment	"act of, state of"	achievement	act of achieving

Try It Yourself 2.43

VARIOUS SELECTIONS

Using your knowledge of base words, prefixes, and suffixes, as well as the clues in the sentences below, define the underlined words on your own paper.

EXAMPLE Aphrodite was a vengeful goddess who always punished her enemies severely.
vengeful = full of vengeance

1. The primary instigater of this mischief is bound to be Oliver, but he no doubt had help from Claire.
2. The speaker in Sandra Cisneros's "Bums in the Attic" decides to postpone her enjoyment of grand houses until she has one of her own.
3. Edward Hoch's story "Zoo" is fanciful but also chilling, because it doesn't seem impossible.
4. In her bereavement over the loss of her country, the speaker in "Tears of Autumn" does not enjoy her ocean voyage.
5. The speaker in "The Fan Club" views her classmates' behavior as immoral, but she joins them in the end.
6. Julianne is hypersensitive to criticism, so she might get angry if I tell her that her slip is showing.
7. We saw an antiwar demonstration when we visited Ireland.
8. In the world described by Kurt Vonnegut in "Harrison Bergeron," there is perfect equality.
9. What a thankless job that inventor had in Bradbury's "The Flying Machine."
10. In many of Ray Bradbury's stories, the enemy is the establishment.

2.44 Word Origins

The English language gains new words from many different sources. One source is the **names of people and places.**

WORD	ORIGIN
hamburger	Originally known as "Hamburg steak," the hamburger takes its name from the city of Hamburg, Germany.
marathon	A footrace covering 26 miles, 385 yards; in 490 BC, a Greek runner ran from the battlefield of Marathon to Athens. *Marathon* has come to mean any event requiring exceptional endurance.
scrooge	The main character in Charles Dickens's *A Christmas Carol* was so miserly that his name has come to mean "a stingy or greedy person."
spoonerism	A slip of the tongue whereby the beginning sounds of words are switched; named after Rev. William A. Spooner, who was noted for such slips. For example, after officiating at a wedding, he told the groom, "It is kisstomary to cuss the bride."

ESSENTIAL SKILLS: LANGUAGE

Answers for Try It Yourself 2.43

1. mischief = harm, damage or injury
2. postpone = put off until later or after another event
3. fanciful = full of fancy, imagination
4. bereavement = state of being sad and bereaved
5. immoral = not moral
6. hypersensitive = excessively sensitive
7. antiwar = against war
8. equality = state of being equal
9. thankless = without thanks, not thankful
10. establishment = act of establishing

Answers for Try It Yourself 2.44

1. lycra: spandex fiber or fabric, an Americanism
2. pampas: extensive treeless plains of Argentina, borrowed from Spanish
3. SWAT: Special Weapons and Tactics law enforcement agency, an Americanism
4. violin: stringed instrument played with a bow, borrowed from Italian *violino*
5. yang: in Chinese philosophy, the positive force and source of light and heat, from Mandarin Chinese
6. zydeco: heavily syncopated dance music (blues mixed with Cajun music) that originated among the African Americans of southern Louisiana
7. PERT chart: Program Evaluation and Review Technique; a system of planning, scheduling, controlling and reviewing events to efficiently complete a project, an Americanism
8. enchilada: a tortilla with meat inside, an American Spanish word
9. catharsis: a purging or purifying experience, borrowed from Greek
10. indigo: a blue dye, borrowed from Indian language

Another source of words in the English language is **acronyms.** Acronyms are words formed from the first letter or letters of the major parts of terms.

EXAMPLES **sonar,** from **so**und **n**avigation **r**anging; **NATO,** from **N**orth **A**tlantic **T**reaty **O**rganization; **NASA,** from **N**ational **A**eronautic and **S**pace **A**dministration

Some words in the English language are **borrowed** from other languages.

EXAMPLES **deluxe** (French), **Gesundheit** (German), **kayak** (Eskimo), **maestro** (Italian), **mañana** (Spanish), **samurai** (Japanese)

Many words are formed by shortening longer words.

EXAMPLES **ad,** from *advertisement;* **auto,** from *automobile;* **lab,** from *laboratory;* **memo,** from *memorandum;* **phone,** from *telephone;* **stereo,** from *stereophonic*

Brand names are often taken into the English language. People begin to use these words as common nouns, even though most of them are still brand names.

EXAMPLES Scotch tape, Xerox, Rollerblade, Levis

Try It Yourself 2.44

Read the following list of ten words. Then look each word up in a good dictionary. Write the definition of the word, and then describe the word's source. Is the word borrowed from another language? Is it an acronym? Has it evolved from the name of a particular person, place, or product? See the Language Arts Survey 4.15, "Using a Dictionary," for more information.

EXAMPLE espionage: the act of spying; borrowed from French

1. Lycra
2. pampas
3. SWAT
4. violin
5. yang
6. zydeco
7. PERT chart
8. enchilada
9. catharsis
10. indigo

VARIETIES OF ENGLISH

2.45 Formal and Informal English

You may use both formal English and informal English when you speak or write. It all depends on the situation. You would use formal English for school essays, oral or written reports, or test answers. You would use informal English when you speak with a friend or write personal letters or notes. There are two types of informal English.

A **colloquialism** is a word or phrase used in everyday conversation.

EXAMPLES You **guys** must be **sick of** doing the same thing day after day.
He was totally **turned off** by the movie.

Slang is a form of speech made up of invented words or old words that have changed in meaning.

EXAMPLES You better **chill out** for a while—you're too angry to face him now.
She has a real **hang-up** about riding in red cars.

Try It Yourself 2.45

VARIOUS SELECTIONS

Each sentence below contains informal words or phrases that have been underlined. Replace the underlined items with more formal words and phrases.

EXAMPLE The speaker's sister Molly, in Alice Walker's poem, pitched in doing things a parent would normally do for the family.

The speaker's sister Molly, in Alice Walker's poem, contributed doing things a parent would normally do for the family.

1. Richard Garcia's speaker in "The City Is So Big" was a little freaked out about urban centers.
2. The rabbit in Wallace Stevens poem spaces out and dreams what life would be like if he didn't have to be afraid.
3. I was so bummed out when I learned what Fahrenheit 451 is.
4. What a trip it must be to have someone assign you a new name.
5. It would be so cool if we could paint a mural of all our neighbors on our street.
6. What a drag to have no way to make your dreams come true.
7. Diana Moon Glampers was such a twisted lady, wasn't she?
8. It is so depressing to have other kids rag on you the way the kids in "The Fan Club" did.
9. The robot is totally in the dark about human anatomy when he tries to revive the human.
10. Rip Van Winkle has been taking a very long snooze.

2.46 Tone and Voice

Tone is a writer's or speaker's attitude toward a subject. The tone of a piece should match the meaning of the piece. The writer shapes the tone of a piece of writing by carefully choosing words and phrases.

ESSENTIAL SKILLS: LANGUAGE

Answers for Try It Yourself 2.45

1. Richard Garcia's speaker in "The City Is So Big" was a little frightened of urban centers.
2. The rabbit in Wallace Stevens' poem uses his imagination and dreams what life would be like if he didn't have to be afraid.
3. I was so disappointed when I learned what *Fahrenheit 451* is.
4. What an unusual experience it must be to have someone assign you a new name.
5. It would be interesting and fun if we could paint a mural of all our neighbors on our street.
6. It is difficult and sad to have no way to make your dreams come true.
7. Diana Moon Glampers was such an odd lady, wasn't she?
8. It is so depressing to have other kids teasing you the way the kids in "The Fan Club" did.
9. The robot is totally ignorant about human anatomy when he tries to revive the human.
10. Rip Van Winkle has been taking a very long rest.

Answers for Try It Yourself 2.46

1. boredom
2. suspense, questioning
3. curiosity, wonder
4. fear
5. amazement, excitement
6. melancholy
7. anxiety
8. joy
9. enjoyment
10. deep sadness, hurt

The following examples give two different descriptions of the same scene. One scene is described in a tone of fear, and the other is described in a tone of awe. If you were writing a story about someone who was afraid of the ocean, you would probably use the more negative description. If you were writing about someone who enjoyed the ocean, you would probably use the more positive description.

TONE OF FEAR Menacing black waves rolled in relentlessly, crashing down upon the rocks and threatening to sweep everything in their path out to sea. Mountainous and savage, the waves pounded the shore with a fury that sent a chill of dread through my soul.

TONE OF AWE Powerful breakers were rolling in majestically, splashing against the rocks and sending fountains of spray high into the air. I stood in awe of this force so mighty that it could be stopped by no man.

Try It Yourself 2.46

VARIOUS SELECTIONS

Tone expresses emotions and attitudes. Read the following sentences taken from selections in your textbook. On your own paper, identify what emotion or attitude is being expressed in each sentence.

EXAMPLE Fortunately, right outside my door was a corridor light that cast a glow into my room. The glow was enough to read by, once my eyes adjusted to it. So when "lights out" came, I would sit on the floor where I could continue reading in that glow.
hopefulness

1. The children moved listlessly toward the aunt's end of the carriage. Evidently her reputation as a story-teller did not rank high in their estimation.
2. Whistling, he let the escalator waft him into the still night air. He walked toward the corner, thinking little at all about nothing in particular. Before he reached the corner, however, he slowed as if a wind had sprung up from nowhere, as if someone had called his name.
3. "Yes," said the Emperor sadly, "I know it must be true. For I felt my heart move with you in the air and I wondered: What is it like? How does it feel? How do the distant pools look from so high? And how my houses and servants? Like ants? And how the distant towns not yet awake?"
4. The early morning mist had become a light chilling rain, and on the pier black umbrellas bobbed here and there, making the task of recognition even harder. Hana searched desperately for a face that resembled the photo she had studied so long and hard. Suppose he hadn't come. What would she do then?
5. Then Lou gasped and dropped the paint bag and ran forward, running his hands over a rainbow. He had to tiptoe and stretch to do it, it was so high. I couldn't breathe either. The painter lady had found the chisel marks and had painted Jimmy Lyons's name in a rainbow.
6. I never thought that Grandpa would be lonely after our visits, and none of us noticed how old and weak he had become. But Grandpa knew, and so he came to us. He had ridden on buses for two and a half days. When he arrived in the city, tired and stiff from sitting so long, he set out, walking, to find us.
7. School. It loomed before her now, massive and dark against the sky. In a few minutes, she would have to face them again—Diane Goddard with her sleek blonde

CONTINUED

Try It Yourself 2.46 (cont.)

hair and Terri Pierce in her candy-pink sweater. And Carol and Steve and Bill and Nancy. . . . there were so many of them, so exclusive as they stood in their tight little groups laughing and joking.

8. In one house, the she-creature was happy to see the return of her mate and off-spring. She babbled a greeting in the strange tongue and hurried to embrace them. "It was a long time you were gone. Was it good?"
9. Do you know that wonderful spurt of air that rushes out when you first open an expensive box of candy? The inside of that store smelled just like the inside of one of those boxes. For a few seconds we just stood there sniffing and grinning. My salivary glands started swimming.
10. My chest felt hollow. I wanted to cry like Colin over our lost fox, but at fourteen a boy doesn't cry. Colin had squatted down on the floor and got out his small hammer and nails to start another new frame for a new picture. Maybe then he'd make a drawing for the frame and be able to forget his misery. It had been that way with him since he was five.

2.47 Dialects of English

A **dialect** is a version of a language spoken by people of a particular place, time, or group. Dialects are usually based on social differences (upper class, middle class, and lower class) or on regional differences. (In the United States, the major regional dialects are northern, southern, midland, and western.) The dialect used by the most powerful social class is usually considered the standard, and other dialects are considered nonstandard. All dialects, however, serve the most important purpose of language—communicating.

Try It Yourself 2.47

The following lines of dialogue are spoken in nonstandard dialects. Try to rewrite them in standard English.

EXAMPLE My gran said the tay was waik enuf ta bay aninted.
My grandmother said the tea was weak enough to be anointed.

1. Mind the chilring, woncha?
2. Set a spell and eat yur vittles.
3. That lil rooster got his come-uppance when he tried to order Gussie around.
4. Cut me some slack, pal.
5. I'll just tidy up a bit in the parlor before himself gets home.
6. Let's hear it for Ralphie on the skins.
7. Thay's a meetin' house up yonder.
8. Swab the decks, maty.
9. Cheez it, the cops!
10. Maht as well; cain't dance, and it's too wet to plow.

Answers for Try It Yourself 2.47

1. Watch the children, would you?
2. Sit down for awhile and eat you meal.
3. That little rooster got what he deserved when he tried to order Gussie around.
4. Don't be so hard on me; I am trying my best.
5. I'll just clean up the parlor a little before he comes home.
6. Could we have a round of applause for our drum player, Ralphie?
7. There is a meeting house over there.
8. Mop the decks, sailor.
9. Let's get out of here, the cops are coming!
10. I might as well; I can not dance and it is too wet to plow.

Essential Skills: *Speaking and Listening*

3.1 Verbal and Nonverbal Communication

When a person expresses meaning through words, he or she is using **verbal communication.** When a person expresses meaning in other ways, by waving or by bowing, for example, he or she is using **nonverbal communication.**

ELEMENTS OF VERBAL COMMUNICATION		
Element	**Description**	**Guidelines for Speakers**
Volume	Loudness or softness	Vary your volume, but make sure that you can be heard.
Melody, Pitch	Highness or lowness	Vary your pitch. Avoid speaking in a **monotone** (at a single pitch).
Pace	Speed	Vary the speed of your delivery to suit what you are saying. Excitement, for example, can be communicated by a fast pace, and seriousness can be communicated by slowing down and saying something forcefully.
Tone	Emotional quality	Suit your tone to your message, and vary it appropriately as you speak. For example, you might use a light tone for a happy message and a heavier one for a sad message.
Enunciation	Clearness with which words are spoken	When speaking before a group, pronounce your words more precisely than is common in ordinary conversation.

ELEMENTS OF NONVERBAL COMMUNICATION		
Element	**Description**	**Guidelines for Speakers**
Eye Contact	Looking audience members in the eye	Make eye contact regularly with people in your audience.
Facial Expression	Using your face to show emotion	Use your facial expression to emphasize your message—raised eyebrows for a question, pursed lips for concentration, eyebrows lowered for anger, and so on.
Gesture	Meaningful motions of the arms and hands	Use gestures to emphasize points. Be careful, however, not to overuse gestures. Too many can be distracting.
Posture/Body	Position of the body	Keep your spine straight and head high. Stand with your arms and legs slightly open, except when adopting other postures to express particular emotions.
Proximity	Distance from the audience	Maintain a comfortable distance, not too close for comfort, but not so far away as to hamper communication.

Try It Yourself 3.1

Exercise A. Select a short poem or part of a story from your textbook, one you would like to read aloud to your classmates. Make a copy of this selection. Write notes in the margins to show places where you might increase or decrease your volume or pace. Look up any unfamiliar words in a dictionary and make sure that you can pronounce them clearly. Also make notes on the tone with which each part of the poem should be read. Finally, practice reading the poem aloud, varying your volume, pitch, pace, and tone.

Exercise B. In a small group, practice communicating various emotions nonverbally. Take turns adopting various facial expressions, gestures, and postures to communicate emotions such as anticipation, anger, happiness, relief, fear, love, sadness, and disappointment. Discuss the various ways in which each of these emotions can be expressed without saying a word. Make a chart of your findings. On the chart, list emotions and the ways in which they can be communicated nonverbally. Follow this example:

EXAMPLE	**Emotion**	**Method of Expression**
	Sadness	Downturned mouth
		Hunched shoulders

Answers for Try It Yourself 3.1

Exercise A

Students should be prepared to present a poem. Presentations should exhibit changes of pace, tone, and volume. Pronunciation of all words should be correct, and enunciation should be clear.

Exercise B

Responses will vary.

3.2 Listening Actively

Learning to listen well is essential not only for success in personal life but also for success in school and, later, on the job. The mind of a good listener is continually active during the listening process. In other words, he or she is an **active listener.**

Listening to a Lecture or Demonstration

- As you listen, maintain eye contact with the speaker. Remember that in a lecture or demonstration, as in a conversation, the speaker depends on you for positive **feedback,** or response.
- Take notes as you listen. Note main ideas and related details. Do not try to write down what the speaker says word for word. Instead, use phrases, symbols, and abbreviations, such as *w/* for *with, Amer.* for *American,* and & or + for *and.* (For more information on taking notes, see section 4.7 of the Language Arts Survey.)
- Check your understanding of what the speaker is saying by putting it into your own words, in your head, as you listen.
- When you do not understand something that the speaker is saying, make a note. Save questions and comments for an appropriate time, usually when the speaker pauses or when he or she invites questions. Then raise your hand before asking your question or making your comment.

Listening in Conversations

- Do not monopolize the conversation. Give the other person plenty of opportunities to speak.
- When the other person is speaking, attend to what he or she is saying. Show through eye contact, body language, and facial expressions that you are interested and attentive.
- Ask the other person questions. Asking questions is a good way to start a conversation, to keep the conversation going, and to show the other person that you are really listening. The best questions are usually ones that directly relate to what the speaker has been saying.
- When you speak, respond to what the other person has been saying. Relate what you say to what he or she has said.
- Take time to think about what the other speaker has said before responding. Do not be afraid of a lull in the conversation while you think about what has been said and about your response.
- If you find yourself becoming overly emotional during a conversation, stop, take a breath, and bring your emotions under control before continuing. If controlling your emotions seems too difficult, consider continuing the conversation at a later time.

Listening to the Media

- Avoid being a couch potato. Television, movies, and radio programs can be powerful manipulators. As you watch or listen, think critically about what you are seeing and hearing.
- When watching or listening to news programs or commercial advertisements, make sure to distinguish **facts** from **opinions.** Facts are statements that can be proved by checking a reference work or making observations. Opinions are **statements of value** or **statements of policy.** A statement of value expresses

positive or negative attitudes. A statement of policy says what should or should not be done. When you hear an opinion, ask yourself whether it is supported by the facts.

- When watching or listening to an entertainment program, think about the quality of the program. Consider the quality of the acting, the directing, and the writing. Also consider the production qualities of the program—the lighting, sound effects, staging, camera work, costuming, properties, and music.
- Think about what message or messages are being delivered by the program and whether you agree or disagree with them.
- Set standards about what you will watch or listen to. Learn to turn off a program or to switch to another program when something does not meet your standards.
- Limit the time that you spend watching or listening to the broadcast media. Remember that there is much more that you might be doing with your life, such as reading, learning a new hobby or skill, writing in your journal, exercising, interacting with other people, creating works of art, or simply thinking.

Try It Yourself 3.2

Exercise A. For a period of two weeks, keep a detailed record of the time that you spend watching or listening to entertainment programs on broadcast media. List dates, times, and program titles. After each entry, write two or three comments evaluating the program.

Exercise B. Watch a television news program. Make a list of three facts and three opinions expressed in the course of the program. Note, especially, when opinions are presented as facts by reporters of the news.

Exercise C. Imagine that a friend of yours has come to you with a problem that he or she would like to discuss. Make a list of responses, both verbal and nonverbal, that you should make to show that you are actively listening to your friend. Discuss possible responses with your classmates and rate their effectiveness.

3.3 Communicating with Others

The ordinary interactions that take place between people in daily life involve a great deal of **interpersonal communication.** The following guidelines will help you to communicate effectively in such daily interactions.

- Make eye contact with your listener and maintain a relaxed posture.
- Provide feedback as you listen.

  Smile or nod to show understanding and/or agreement.

  Ask questions or make comments when the speaker pauses for feedback.

  Try not to interrupt or to finish the speaker's sentences for him or her.

- Reflect back what the speaker has said to make sure that you understand him or her.

  For example, suppose that the speaker says, "The ancient Sumerians first began recording their literature in writing over 4,500 years ago." You could reflect back, "So, Sumerians developed literature that long ago? That's interesting. In what way do you think their literature was similar to and different from our own?"

Answers for Try It Yourself 3.2

Exercise A

Responses will vary but should include comments reflecting conscious evaluation of the programs.

Exercise B

Responses will vary. Students should be able to distinguish between fact and opinion.

Exercise C

Responses will vary. Students may wish to complete this activity as a role play. The problem discussed should be hypothetical.

Answers for Try It Yourself 3.3

Responses will vary, but discussions should be polite, rational, and fair. Students should answer the questions accurately.

- Think before you speak.

  Thinking first can make your communication clearer and more efficient. It also shows respect for your listener.

- Control your emotions.

  If you become angry while listening to someone, take a deep breath and count to ten. Make sure you haven't misunderstood the speaker by reflecting back the statement that angered you. If you can contain your anger, express your objections calmly. If you cannot contain your anger, end your conversation and say that you would like to continue it at another time.

Try It Yourself 3.3

With a partner, role play a conversation about a problem you are having with a friend or family member. (For this exercise, the problem selected should be an imaginary one.) Take turns being the speaker and the listener and using the communication guidelines described above. Make sure each of you gets equal time speaking and listening. Carry on each discussion for about ten minutes. Make notes afterward about your discussions. Answer these questions: Did you make eye contact and remain relaxed? What feedback did you give? What feedback did you get? Did either party monopolize the conversation or interrupt? Did either party reflect back what the other said? Did both parties control their emotions?

3.4 Collaborative Learning and Discussion

Collaboration is the act of working with one or more other people to achieve a goal. Many common learning situations involve collaboration.

- Participating in a small-group discussion
- Doing a small-group project
- Doing peer evaluation
- Tutoring another student or being tutored

GUIDELINES FOR DISCUSSION

- Listen actively during the discussion. Maintain eye contact with the speakers. Make notes on what they say. Mentally translate what they say into your own words. Think critically about whether you agree or disagree with each speaker and why.
- Be polite. Wait for your turn to speak. Do not interrupt others. If your discussion has a group leader, ask to be recognized before speaking by raising your hand.
- Participate in the discussion. At appropriate times, make your own comments or ask questions of other speakers.
- Stick to the discussion topic. Do not introduce unrelated or irrelevant ideas.
- For **formal discussions,** choose a **group leader** to guide the discussion and a **secretary** to record the **minutes** (the main ideas and proposals made by group members). Also draw up an **agenda,** before the discussion, listing items to be discussed.

GUIDELINES FOR PROJECTS

- Choose a group leader to conduct the meetings of your project group.
- Set a goal for the group, some specific outcome or set of outcomes that you want to bring about.
- Make a list of tasks that need to be performed.
- Make a schedule for completing the tasks, including dates and times for completion of each task.
- Make an assignment sheet. Assign particular tasks to particular group members. Be fair in distributing the work to be done.
- Set times for future meetings. You might want to schedule meetings to evaluate your progress toward your goal as well as meetings to actually carry out specific tasks.
- When the project is completed, meet to evaluate your overall success and the individual contributions of group members.

GUIDELINES FOR TUTORING

- Find out where the other student stands and what he or she needs to learn.
- Break down your teaching into steps that can be followed easily.
- Review basic concepts, terms, and processes. Encourage the other student to explain these to you in his or her own words.
- Give the other student practice activities or exercises and help him or her to do these.
- Be patient. Give the person time to respond, to make mistakes, and to ask questions.
- Be encouraging and supportive. Remember that your job is to help someone else to learn, not to display your own knowledge.

GUIDELINES FOR BEING TUTORED

- Bring with you to the tutorial all materials that you will need, such as your textbook, study guides, notes, worksheets, pencils, and paper.
- Explain as clearly as you can what you need help with. You will find it useful to prepare questions beforehand.
- Ask questions about anything that you do not understand. Remember that no question is silly if it is sincere.
- Be patient. Learning takes time.
- Do not give up if you do not understand immediately. Practice makes perfect.
- Be polite and thank your tutor for his or her help.

For information on peer evaluation, see the Language Arts Survey, 1.18, "Peer Evaluation."

ANSWERS FOR TRY IT YOURSELF 3.4

See the Analytic Scale for Project that accompanies the project in each unit.

Try It Yourself 3.4

Follow the guidelines for projects given above while completing one of the unit projects listed in the table of contents in this textbook. When the project is finished, meet to discuss how well your group followed the guidelines.

3.5 GIVING A SPEECH

The fear of speaking in public, though quite common and quite strong in some people, can easily be overcome by preparing a speech thoroughly and practicing positive thinking and relaxation. Learning how to give a speech is a valuable skill, one that you will most likely find much opportunity to use in the future.

The following are the three main types of speeches:

- **Impromptu speech.** This is a speech given without any preparation. For example, if you were surprised by a gift or an award, you might be called upon to give a brief speech.
- **Memorized speech.** This is a speech that has been written out and memorized word for word. Your teacher may ask you to prepare a memorized speech on a topic you are studying at school.
- **Extemporaneous speech.** This is a speech in which the speaker refers to notes occasionally. Most professional speakers prefer to deliver extemporaneous speeches because they combine the liveliness of an impromptu speech with the careful preparation of a memorized speech. While the speaker does not plan what he or she will say word for word, the speaker does create an overall plan for the speech and records important points on cards.

When you write a speech, you should always include a beginning, a middle, and an end. The beginning, or introduction, should spark the audience's interest and present your main idea. The middle, or body, of your speech should expand upon your main idea. The end, or conclusion, of your speech should be memorable and should give your audience a sense of completion.

STEPS IN PREPARING AN EXTEMPORANEOUS SPEECH

1. Do prewriting.
2. Do research.
3. Prepare note cards. Make notes about verbal and nonverbal methods you might use. Plan your introduction and your conclusion carefully.
4. Rehearse with your note cards, using a mirror or a recording device.
5. Deliver your speech.

Try It Yourself 3.5

Prepare note cards for an extemporaneous speech on one of the topics below or on a topic of your own choosing. Make sure your speech has an introduction, a body, and a conclusion. You may want to include brief stories and quotations to make your speech more entertaining and memorable.

- Why a particular hobby or sport is both fun and interesting
- How to think critically about television commercials
- Why protecting the environment is important

3.6 Oral Interpretation

Oral interpretation is the art of presenting a literary work aloud to an audience. It differs from theater in that the performer, known as an **interpreter,** does not move around the stage. One type of oral interpretation is the dramatic interpretation of poetry or prose. In the past, people often entertained one another by reading aloud. This practice can be lots of fun, provided that the people doing the interpreting follow a few basic guidelines to ensure the quality of their performances.

Interpreting Poetry

Types of Selections. The way in which you prepare your dramatic interpretation will depend on the type of selection that you will be interpreting. Three basic types of poetry are the lyric poem, the narrative poem, and the dramatic poem.

A **lyric poem** has a single speaker who reports his or her own emotions.

A **narrative poem** tells a story. Usually a narrative poem has lines belonging to a **narrator,** or person who is telling the story. The narrator may or may not take part in the action of the poem.

A **dramatic poem** is one that contains characters who speak. A dramatic poem may be a lyric, in which characters simply report emotions, or a narrative, which tells a story. A **dramatic monologue** presents a single speaker at a moment of crisis or self-revelation and is usually narrative.

Before attempting to interpret any poem, first read through the poem carefully several times. Make sure that you understand it well. An excellent way to check your understanding of a poem is to try to paraphrase it, or restate its ideas, line by line, in your own words.

Analyzing the Speaker of a Lyric Poem. When interpreting a lyric poem or a dramatic lyric, think about the poem's speaker. Ask yourself these questions:

- Who is the speaker?
- How old is the speaker?
- Is the speaker male or female?
- What is the situation in which the speaker finds himself or herself?
- How does the speaker feel about his or her situation?

Answers for Try It Yourself 3.5

Responses will vary. Speeches should include an introduction, a body, and a conclusion. Students should have prepared for this speech, but they should not read the speech. Instead, they should refer to note cards. Students should make eye contact with their audience.

- What does the speaker think about his or her situation?
- What values, opinions, beliefs, wishes, or needs does the speaker have?
- Is the speaker fully aware of the implications of what he or she is saying, or does the reader know more than the speaker does?

Try to form a clear image of the speaker in your mind. Think about how such a person might sound, feeling and thinking as he or she does.

Analyzing the Narrator and Characters of a Narrative or Dramatic Poem. When analyzing a narrative or dramatic poem, ask about the narrator and the characters the same questions that you would ask about the speaker of a lyric poem. In addition, ask yourself how the narrator and the characters are related to one another. In what ways are they similar? In what ways are they dissimilar? Is there anything that the narrator understands that one or more of the characters do not?

List the narrator and each of the characters in the poem, along with his or her characteristics. Then try to form in your mind a clear image of each one. Again, think about how each might sound, feeling and thinking as he or she does. If the poem is a narrative, think of the role that each character plays in the story.

Interpreting Prose

Prose is all writing that is not drama or poetry. Common types of prose that make for good oral interpretations include short stories, fairy tales, fables, and myths. Prose almost always has a narrator, or person who is telling the story. This narrator sometimes takes part in the action of the selection. Prose usually also contains characters who speak.

Analyzing the Narrator and Characters of Prose. When analyzing prose, follow the guidelines given above for analyzing the narrator and characters of a narrative or dramatic poem. List the characteristics of the narrator and of each of the characters in the selection, trying to form a clear image of each in your mind. Think about the relationships between characters and the ways in which characters react to certain situations. Also think about the manner of speech of each different character.

Using Elements of Verbal and Nonverbal Communication

After analyzing the speaker (in the case of a lyric poem) or the narrator and characters (in the case of a narrative poem, dramatic poem, or prose selection), make a copy of the selection and mark it to show

- the different voices that you will use when reading
- the emotions that you will express
- the places where you will increase or decrease your pace
- the places where you will raise or lower your volume
- the gestures and facial expressions that you will use to communicate emotions

When a selection contains more than one voice, such as the voices of a narrator and of characters, strive to make each sound different from the others. Excellent ways to distinguish voices when reading include changing your tone (the emotion expressed) and pitch (the highness or lowness of your voice) and looking in a different direction each time you change voices.

Memorizing the Selection

To memorize your selection, work line by line or sentence by sentence. Look at one line or sentence. Look away and repeat it. Then check to see that you got it right. Once you get that line right, add a second line or sentence. Look away and repeat both. Then check them. Continue in this manner until the entire selection is memorized. You may wish to have someone else check a copy of the selection while you recite it aloud. This second person can prompt you when you forget a line. Memorize the selection thoroughly before you begin working on the qualities of your reading. If you have not thoroughly memorized the lines, you will not be able to concentrate on how you sound.

Rehearsing and Presenting Your Interpretation

Rehearse your interpretation using a tape recorder or a video recorder. You might also want to rehearse in front of a mirror so that you can view your facial expressions and gestures. Before actually presenting your interpretation, relax and adopt a confident attitude. If you begin to feel stage fright, try to concentrate on the selection and on the audience, not on yourself.

Try It Yourself 3.6

Choose a poem or prose selection from this text, or any other selection that you enjoy and that is suitable for presentation in class. Prepare a dramatic interpretation of your selection, following the guidelines given above.

3.7 Understanding a Film Script

To get the most out of a film, or movie, it is helpful to know something about **scripts,** the written works from which films are created. A film script is like a script for a play in that it contains both dialogue and stage directions.

Typically, the first step taken toward the creation of a film script is the writing of a **synopsis,** or summary, of the film's main idea. Then, an outline, sometimes called a **treatment,** is written to provide more detail about the film. Finally, a script is produced. Often the script goes through several revisions, called **rewrites,** before the final version is completed. Often the rewriting of a script continues well into the filming of the movie. Sometimes, the script may even be rewritten after the filming is done, during the editing of the final film. The version of the script that is used by directors, camera operators, and others during the filming is called the **shooting script**. Shooting scripts contain extensive information about camera angles, special effects, and other details related to the filming. Sometimes, shooting scripts are arranged in the order that scenes will be filmed, not in the order in which they will appear in the film itself. This is because all scenes involving the same set and the same actors are typically shot at the same time.

Answers for Try It Yourself 3.6

Responses will vary. Students should present a selection using appropriate changes in pace, volume, and voice and appropriate gestures and facial features.

Answers for Try It Yourself 3.7

EXT.—exterior shot; Angle on—camera angle that includes a particular object or person, here a farmer in a field; SFX—sound effects, here rumbling; CU—close up, here on the shaking earth; tight shot—shot of subject, here farmer's torso, and little else; SFX—sound effects, here of violent tearing; POV—point-of-view shot, from a point in the middle of the field; cut to—quick change to a new shot; SFX—sound effects, here of a whirring sound; cut to—quick change to a new shot.

TERMS AND ABBREVIATIONS IN FILM SCRIPTS

TERM	DESCRIPTION
ANGLE ON	A camera angle that includes a particular object or person
CU	Close-up
CUT TO	Quick change to a new shot
ECU	Extreme close-up
EXT	Exterior shot (outside)
INT	Interior shot (inside)
PAN	Movement of camera from right to left or from left to right
POV SHOT	Point-of-view shot, taken from the point of view of a character
PULL BACK	Movement of camera away from subject
SFX	Sound effect
SUPER	Superimposed; letters or graphics appearing over a picture, often as a caption
TIGHT SHOT	Shot of subject and little or nothing else
V/O	Voice-over; a voice heard without an accompanying picture of the speaker
ZOOM IN	Movement of camera toward the subject
ZOOM OUT	Movement of camera away from the subject

Since 1920, more than half of all fiction films have been adapted from plays and novels. Because a film typically runs from an hour and a half to two hours, much of the dialogue or narration of the original novel or play inevitably gets cut. Good film script writers try to compensate for what is cut from a novel or play by writing concise scenes and dialogue and by making economical use of sounds and of visuals.

Try It Yourself 3.7

Read the following selection from a film script. Explain the meanings of all the underlined terms used in this selection.

ACT ONE

(MUSIC: *Shaker hymn "Simple Gifts"*)

(<u>EXT.</u> DAY: <u>*Angle on*</u> *a* FARMER *plowing a field in Iowa*)

CONTINUED

Try It Yourself 3.7 (cont.)

(SFX: *Rumbling*)

(CU: *Earth shaking*)

(TIGHT SHOT: *of* FARMER*'s torso, head, arms, and hands on plow. Plow begins to shake violently like a jackhammer.*)

FARMER. What the heck?

(SFX: *Sound as of a violent tearing*)

(POV: *shot down length of plow to earth being thrown up violently from a point in center of field. Screen fills with mud as farmer screams.*)

(CUT TO *long shot of enormous crater with person-high lip of mud around it. Two state police vehicles parked on periphery of the crater.* OFFICERS *climb lip of crater and peer down into it.*)

OFFICER 1. What do ya think this is all about, Jim?

OFFICER 2. Beats me. I've never seen anything like it. I mean, a sinkhole's one thing, but this . . . .

OFFICER 1. Can you see the bottom? It doesn't seem to have a bottom. Want to go have a look?

OFFICER 2. Not me, buddy. I think we ought to call someone over from the university to have a look at this. A geologist, maybe.

(SFX: *Whirring sound. Bright green light from center of crater.*)

(CUT TO: *Int. biological laboratory.* DR. SARA CHANG *is giving a group of students a tour.*)

DR. CHANG. And what do you think is the largest form of life on the earth?

STUDENT 1. Elephant. The African elephant.

STUDENT 2. No way. Whales. Blue whales.

STUDENT 3. Sequoia trees are bigger than whales.

DR. CHANG. Yes, those are all very large creatures—elephants, whales, sequoias. But the largest creature on the planet is this. (*She holds up a piece of mushroom with a tong.*)

STUDENT 1. That's just a little piece of mushroom.

DR. CHANG. This little piece of mushroom is a part of one enormous mushroom found in a forest in northern Wisconsin. The entire mushroom, which grew beneath forest leaves, is estimated to cover approximately four and one half square kilometers and to weigh over three tons.

3.8 Reviewing a Film Critically

A good film is thought-provoking. It will make you think in new ways about other people, other places, other situations, and yourself. Many films, however, are created simply to make money. Such films rely on trite, overused gimmicks. Although you may not be able, on your own, to influence the types of films that are made, you can control the types of films that you view. The following guidelines will help you to become a more discriminating consumer of films:

- Plan which films you will watch and when you will watch them. Rather than choosing to view any movie that happens to be playing at your local theater or on television, look at a guide and choose the movies you are truly interested in seeing. Rather than attending a movie you never planned on seeing simply because you cannot think of something better to do, read a book, enjoy the company of friends, exercise, write your own stories, or practice one of your hobbies. Attend a film only when it is one that you would truly like to see and have planned on seeing. Read film reviews before you decide on seeing a new film.
- Question what you see and hear in a film. Be critical of dialogue and story-lines. If a movie you are watching seems cliché and predictable, it probably is. Many films recycle conventional story lines and dialogue. Many also contain violent or otherwise sensationalistic scenes included simply to provoke audiences. Sometimes these scenes serve no other purpose. They do not, for example, advance the story line or themes of the film. Learn to be a critical movie-goer, and discuss your criticisms with others.
- Be aware that previews of coming attractions are designed to encourage you to see particular films. These previews can make a film seem better, funnier, or more exciting than it really is by showing you only the best lines of dialogue and the best action clips.
- Try viewing a film that is much different from the type of film that you usually see. In this way, you can broaden your movie-going horizons. If you normally watch action movies, try watching a drama, a classic film, a foreign film, a documentary, a historical drama, or a romantic comedy.
- Never see a film adaptation of a literary work instead of reading the work itself. While seeing such an adaptation can be a good introduction to a literary work or an interesting activity after you have read the work, a film seldom captures all the richness of the original. Adaptations can leave out much of the dialogue and the plot. Also, some film adaptations are drastically different from the original works. One

reason why film adaptations fail to portray literary works adequately is that film scripts are much shorter than most novels and plays. Films also present other people's interpretations of literary works. First the screenwriter interprets the work to produce a script. Then the script is interpreted by the director, the camera operators, the makeup artists, the set designers, the costumers, the actors, the film editors, and others. When you read a work of literature, you can form your own interpretations. Interpretations that you see in film adaptations, in contrast, come second, third, or fourth hand.

Try It Yourself 3.8

Read several movie reviews in local or national newspapers. Then try your hand at writing a review for your classmates of a film that you have recently seen. Begin your review by stating the name of the film, the name of the director, and the names of the film's leading actors. In the first paragraph of your review, make a general judgment about the quality of the film. Then, in subsequent paragraphs, back up your judgment with criticisms of the film's script, direction, camera work, acting, costumes, and sets. Share your review with other students in a small group.

ANALYTIC SCALE FOR WRITING SKILLS 3.8

Assign a score from 1 to 25 for each grading criterion below.

Movie Review

- **Content/Unity.** The review presents an opinion about a movie and then offers supporting evidence for the opinion.
- **Organization/Coherence.** The review begins with general information about the film, including title, director, and leading actors, and the reviewer's opinion. The review is organized in a logical manner.
- **Language/Style.** The review uses vivid and precise nouns, verbs, and modifiers.
- **Conventions.** The review avoids errors in spelling, grammar, usage, mechanics, and manuscript form.

Essential Skills: *Study and Research*

STUDY SKILLS

4.1 Developing Good Study Habits

Success in a future career depends largely on success in school. No matter what your experience in school so far, you can improve your performance enormously by developing good study habits. Doing so will make learning easier and more enjoyable.

Finding a place to work. Homework is best done in a special study area. Follow these guidelines for picking an appropriate place to study:

- Choose a quiet location, away from distractions such as conversation, television, or loud music.
- Choose a place that is well lighted and comfortable. Adequate lighting will help you to avoid eyestrain and headaches.
- Choose a study area that is available at regular times. Set aside a specific time each day for study.
- Have all the tools that you will need, such as paper, pencils, textbooks, handouts, and reference works, ready and at hand.

Keeping an assignment notebook. Keeping track of assignments in your head can be dangerous because of the possibility of forgetting important details. Try, instead, to write all your assignments down in a special assignment notebook. For each assignment, record the following information:

- The name of the subject
- Details of the assignment, including what, precisely, is to be done
- The date of the assignment
- The date when the assignment is due

Making a study plan. Many of your assignments will be due on the following day. Others will be long-term projects. At the end of each school day, make a habit of looking over your assignment notebook. Decide what tasks you need to complete for the following day. Break longer assignments down into specific steps that need to be completed by specific times. Record all of these assignments on a calendar, or study plan. Suppose, for example, that you have been given an assignment to write a five-page report on a novel for your English class. Your study plan for a two-week period might look like this:

M	T	W	T	F	S
Read chapters 1-3 of novel	Read chapters 4-6 of novel	Band practice	Finish reading; begin science project	Do prewriting for paper on novel	Do library research for paper on novel
Gather and organize notes	Write rough draft; finish science project	Band practice	Simone's birthday party; study for math test	Revise rough draft	Proofread and type final paper

Try It Yourself 4.1

If you are not already doing so, start keeping an assignment notebook. Use information from this notebook to make a study plan for a two-week period. On your study plan, record daily assignments and steps required for completing longer assignments.

4.2 Understanding the Assignment

Following spoken directions. Often teachers give assignments orally. When listening to spoken assignments, follow these guidelines:

FOLLOWING SPOKEN DIRECTIONS

1. Listen carefully. Write down the directions as you hear them.
2. Notice what steps are involved in the assignment. Also notice the order of these steps.
3. Listen for the key word in each step. A key word is one that tells you what to do. Examples are *read, write, organize,* and *memorize.*
4. If you do not understand the directions, ask your teacher to explain them.

Following written directions. Directions for tests are usually written down. Assignment directions also sometimes appear in written form on chalkboards, overhead transparencies, or handouts. When reading written directions, follow these guidelines:

Answers for Try It Yourself 4.1

Study plans should include all daily assignments as well as a plan for completing long-term assignments.

Answers for Try It Yourself 4.2

Key words: *Select, analyze, make, design, draw* or *cut, collect, write.*

FOLLOWING WRITTEN DIRECTIONS
1. Read all the directions completely before you begin the assignment.
2. Ask questions to clarify any points not covered in the directions.
3. Divide the assignment into steps. Put these steps in a logical order.
4. Decide what materials you will need, and assemble them before you begin.
5. Reread each step before you actually do it.

Try It Yourself 4.2

Read the directions given below for a short story project. Identify the key words in each step.

Select one story in each of the following categories: science fiction, mystery, and fantasy.
Analyze each story using the skills you have learned in class.
Make a notebook for your stories and analyses.
    Design a cover for your notebook.
    For each story, draw your own illustrations or cut out pictures from magazines.
    Collect your stories in the notebook and write a table of contents for it.

4.3 Studying an Assignment

One excellent way to study is to use the **SQ3R method.** SQ3R stands for **S**urvey, **Q**uestion, **R**ead, **R**ecite, and **R**eview. The chart below describes the SQ3R study method:

USING SQ3R	
Survey	Look over the material to get a general idea of what you will be reading. Read the introduction and also the summary, if there is one. Check the titles and headings. Look at any illustrations.
Question	Prepare a set of questions. Decide what questions you should be able to answer at the end of your reading. Use any study questions presented in the book or provided by your teacher. You can also make up your own questions based on titles, pictures, or charts.
Read	Read carefully and look for the answers to your questions as you read. Also identify the main ideas in each section.
Recite	After you finish your careful reading, recite in your own words the answers to your questions. Make notes on the answers. Make sure you understand any other important points of the selection.
Review	Quickly read over your notes. Look over the main ideas in the book so that you will remember them. Look up the answers to any questions you could not answer in the previous step.

Try It Yourself 4.3

Read the Language Arts Survey, 3.2, "Listening Actively." Use the SQ3R method to learn and remember the key points in this material.

4.4 Types of Reading

People read in different ways for different purposes. Three types of reading that you can use are scanning, skimming, and slow and careful reading.

When you **scan,** you look through written material very quickly to locate particular information. Scanning is useful, for example, when you want to find an entry in an index or a definition in a textbook chapter. To scan, simply run your eye down the page, looking for a key word. When you find the key word, slow down and read carefully.

When you **skim,** you glance through material quickly to get a general idea of what it is about. Skimming is an excellent way to get a quick overview of material. It is useful for previewing a chapter in a textbook, for surveying material to see if it contains information that will be useful to you, and for reviewing material for a test or essay. When skimming, look at titles, headings, and words that appear in boldface or colored type. Also read any summaries, first and last paragraphs of sections, and topic sentences of paragraphs. In addition, glance at any illustrations, photographs, charts, maps, or other graphics.

When you read **slowly** and **carefully,** you look at each sentence, taking the time to absorb its meaning before going on. Slow and careful reading is appropriate when reading for pleasure or when studying a textbook chapter for the first time. If you encounter words that you do not understand, try to figure them out from context or look them up in a dictionary, and write them down in a notebook. The act of writing down a word will help you to remember it later. When reading for school, it is a good idea to take notes using a rough outline form. Again, writing down the material will help you to remember it. (For more information on slow and careful reading, see the Language Arts Survey, 4.6, "Reading Actively.")

READING TECHNIQUES

Technique	Purpose	Tips
Scanning	Finding specific information quickly	Look for key words; look at chapter and part headings.
Skimming	Getting a general idea of the content of a piece	Ask questions; look at introductions; look at chapter and part headings.
Slow and careful reading	Learning and enjoyment	Read actively.

Answers for Try It Yourself 4.3

Students should follow the outlined steps to learn and remember the key points. You may wish to quiz them on this material.

ANSWERS FOR TRY IT YOURSELF 4.4

EXERCISE A

Responses will vary. Students should identify the main point of the article and list several questions that might be answered by the article.

EXERCISE B

Rita Dove was born in 1952. Her books include *Thomas and Beulah, The Yellow House on the Corner, Grace Notes, Fifth Sunday,* and *Through the Ivory Gate.*

ANSWERS FOR TRY IT YOURSELF 4.5a

Responses will vary.

Try It Yourself 4.4

Exercise A. Skim a long magazine article about a subject that interests you. Based on that skimming, make some notes about the main idea of the article and write some questions that might be answered by reading the article carefully.

Exercise B. Scan the biography of Rita Dove on page 6 to find the date of her birth and the titles of two works that she wrote.

4.5 PREVIEWING YOUR READING

In a movie theater, the previews of coming attractions give you information about what new movies are about. Similarly, previewing a work before you read it will help you to understand what that work is about. Previewing is an excellent way to form some general ideas about a subject before tackling its details. Use previewing when reading materials for your classes.

PREVIEWING ACTIVITIES	
1. **Read** the title.	**Ask:** What is the piece about?
2. **Skim** the first paragraph(s).	**Ask:** What is the main point, or thesis, of the piece?
3. **Read** the headings.	**Ask:** What are the main points?
4. **Skim** the last paragraph(s) (but not if the piece to be read is a work of literature).	**Ask:** What is the author's conclusion?

Try It Yourself 4.5a

Preview a chapter that you have not yet read from one of your textbooks. Answer the previewing questions from the chart above.

The parts of a book. When previewing an entire book, you might want to glance at all of its parts. Every book will have some or all of the following parts:

THE PARTS OF A BOOK	
Title page	Gives the title, author, and publisher
Copyright page	Gives information regarding the publication of the book and the copyrights protecting it from being copied or sold illegally
Table of contents	Lists the units, chapters, and/or subjects of the book and the page numbers where they are found
Preface, introduction, or foreword	Introduces the book
Text	Main part of the book
Afterword or epilogue	Gives concluding thoughts about the book or tells what happened later
Appendix	Gives additional information about subjects covered in the book, often in chart or table form
Glossary	Lists key words used in the book and their definitions
Bibliography	Lists sources used in writing the book or sources for further study
Index	Lists in alphabetical order the subjects mentioned in the book and pages where these subjects are treated

Try It Yourself 4.5b

Suppose you are reading a book about the history and civilization of ancient China. In which parts of the book would you most likely find each of the following?

1. information about the page where Chinese mythology is discussed
2. a list of rulers of ancient China and the dates of their reigns
3. the complete title of the book and the name of the author
4. the definition of yin-yang
5. a list of other books you might consult about Chinese history

4.6 Reading Actively

Reading actively means *thinking* about what you are reading as you are reading it. Here are some important strategies for reading actively:

Ask questions as you read. Some questions that you might ask yourself when reading a literary work include the following:

- How does what I am reading make me feel?
- What is the setting of this work? How do things look, sound, taste, feel, or smell?

Answers for Try It Yourself 4.5b

1. index
2. appendix
3. title page
4. glossary
5. bibliography

ANSWERS FOR TRY IT YOURSELF 4.6

Responses will vary.

- How do I feel about this character? Do I identify with him or her? Do I like or dislike the character? Why?
- Does what I am reading involve some conflict? If so, what is that conflict? How might it be resolved?
- What main images, ideas, symbols, or themes appear in the work?
- What can be learned from the experiences of these characters?

Make predictions as you read. While reading, think often about what will come next. When reading a work of literature, think about how situations might turn out, what characters might do, what you would do if you were in their place, what the author might have in store, and so on.

Summarize parts as you read them. Especially when reading longer works, it is a good idea to stop from time to time to put what you have read so far into your own words. Doing so will help you to follow and remember complicated material.

Try It Yourself 4.6

Choose any selection from this book and read it. As you read, write down at least four questions and two predictions about the selection. Use the questions above to guide you.

4.7 TAKING NOTES

When taking notes in class or on your reading, use a rough outline, or modified outline, form. Write main ideas, capitalizing the first letter of the first word and all proper nouns and proper adjectives. Beneath the main ideas, write related subordinate ideas, preceded by dashes.

Felipe Salazar
Social Studies
Dec. 19, 1999

Location of Ancient Egyptian Civilization
—Northeastern Africa
—Along Nile River
Periods in Egyptian History
—Archaic Period
–3100 BC–2575 BC
–two kingdoms united
—Old Kingdom
–2575 BC–2040 BC
–great pyramids built
—Middle Kingdom
–2040 BC–1550 BC
–cult of god Osiris developed
—New Kingdom or Golden Age
–1532 BC–1070 BC
–empire extended into Mesopotamia

When taking notes, use abbreviations and symbols to save time. The following chart lists a few of the many that might be used.

SYMBOLS AND ABBREVIATIONS FOR NOTE-TAKING					
Amer.	America	**def**	definition	>	more, greater than
Eng.	England	**ex**	example	~	approximately, about
&	and	–	not, minus	Δ	change
w/	with	<	less, less than	∴	therefore, conclusion

Try It Yourself 4.7

Read the prereading page that introduces H. G. Wells's *The War of the Worlds* on page 576. Take notes for yourself on this material, following a rough outline form.

4.8 Using Graphic Aids

Graphic aids are pictures, maps, illustrations, graphs, charts, and other visual materials that present information. Two common types of graphic aids are pie charts and bar graphs.

Pie charts. A **pie chart** is a circle that stands for a whole group or set. The circle is divided into parts to show the divisions of the whole. When you look at a pie chart, you can see the relationships of the parts to one another and to the whole.

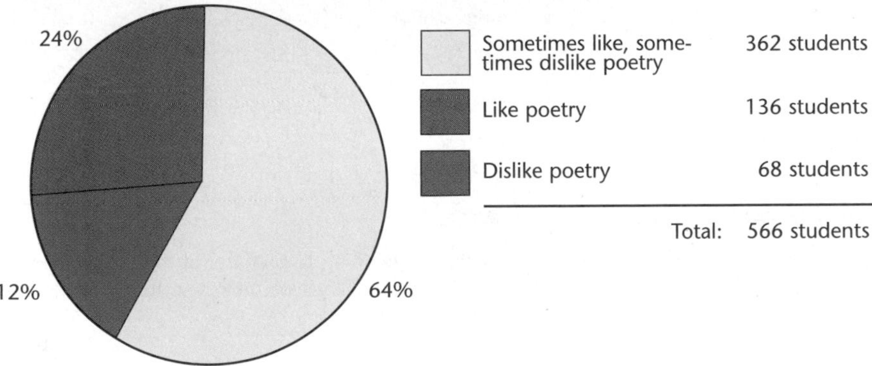

Answers for Try It Yourself 4.7

Responses will vary. Notes should include the following information:

—Mars
—red planet
—fourth from Sun
—named for god of war
—size: half of earth/twice of moon
—channels discovered by Giovanni Schiaparelli
—Percival Lowell believes in intelligent life on Mars

—"The War of the Worlds" (radio)
—Oct. 30, 1938, Orson Welles' radio dramatization
—pretend newscast
—listeners panicked

—*The War of the Worlds* (novel)
—science fiction
—based on beliefs of intelligent life on Mars
—Aug. 12, 1894, gas launched from Mars
—narrator and Ogilvy watch next night

Answers for Try It Yourself 4.8

1. 12%
2. 36%
3. 88%
4. Jamestown donated more.
5. Zion made the second highest donation. The community donated just over $600 worth of goods.

Bar graphs. A **bar graph** compares amounts of something by representing the amounts as bars of different lengths. In the bar graph below, each bar represents the value in dollars of canned goods donated by several communities to a food drive. To read the graph, simply draw in your imagination a line from the edge of the bar through the bottom of the graph. Then read the number. For example, the following graph shows that the community of Russell Springs donated just under $600 worth of goods during the food drive.

DOLLAR VALUE OF DONATED GOODS TO CANNED FOOD DRIVE

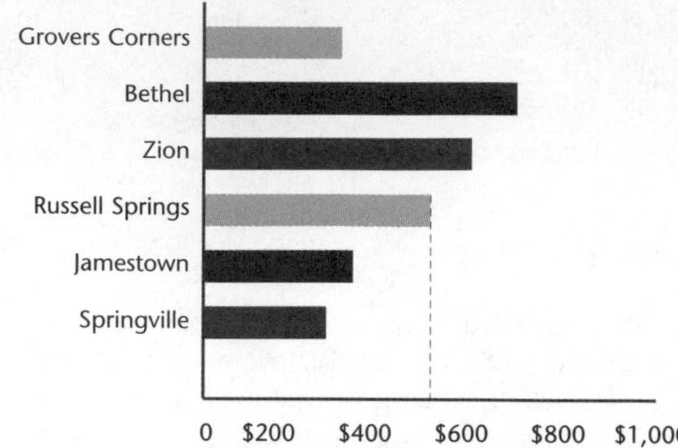

Try It Yourself 4.8

Study the pie chart and the bar graph above and answer the following questions:

1. What percentage of students said that they dislike poetry?
2. What percentage of students said they either like or dislike poetry?
3. How many students did not express a dislike for all poetry?
4. Which community donated more to the canned food drive, Grovers Corners or Jamestown?
5. Which community made the second highest donation to the canned food drive? How much did that community donate?

TEST-TAKING SKILLS

4.9 Preparing for Tests

Tests are a common part of school life, and learning to prepare for them can make being a student a lot more enjoyable. The following guidelines will help you to get ready to take a test.

PREPARING FOR A TEST

1. Know exactly what you will be tested on. If you have questions, ask your teacher.
2. Make a study plan to allow yourself time to go over all the material. Avoid last-minute, late-night cramming.
3. Review the subject matter. Use your notes, your SQ3R questions, and any study questions given by your teacher.
4. Make lists of important names, dates, definitions, or events. Ask a friend or family member to quiz you on them.
5. Try to predict questions that may be on the test. Make sure you can answer them.
6. Get plenty of sleep the night before the test. Eat a nutritious breakfast on the morning of the test.

Knowing what to do before a test is important. So is knowing what to do during a test. The following tips will help you to use your test-taking time wisely.

TAKING A TEST

1. Survey the test. Look over the whole test to see how long it is and what types of questions are included.
2. Read all directions and questions carefully. Make sure that you know exactly what you are supposed to do.
3. Plan your time. Answer the easiest questions first. Allow extra time for long or complicated questions. If a question seems too difficult, skip it and go back to it later. Work quickly, but do not rush.
4. Save time for review. Once you have finished, look back over the test. Make sure that you have answered all the questions. Double-check your answers, but do not change answers too often. Your first ideas are often the correct ones.

For guidelines on taking specific types of tests, see the next three sections.

Try It Yourself 4.9

Make a study guide for a test that you will have to take soon. As you review the material, make a list of important facts to memorize. Also make a list of questions that you predict will be on the test.

ANSWERS FOR TRY IT YOURSELF 4.9

Responses will vary.

4.10 Taking Objective Tests

Objective tests require simple right-or-wrong answers. This chart describes the kinds of questions you may see on objective tests.

QUESTIONS FOUND ON OBJECTIVE TESTS	
Description	**Guidelines**
True/False. You are given a statement and asked to tell whether the statement is true or false.	1. If any part of a statement is false, then the statement is false. 2. Words like *all, always, never,* and *everyone* often appear in false statements. 3. Words like *some, usually, often,* and *most* often appear in true statements. 4. If you do not know the answer, try to guess. You have a 50/50 chance of being right.
Matching. You are asked to match items in one column with items in another column.	1. Check the directions. See if each item is used only once. Also check to see if some are not used at all. 2. Read all items before starting. 3. Match those you know first. 4. Cross out items as you match them.
Multiple-choice. You are asked to choose the best answer from a group of answers given.	1. Read *all* choices first. 2. Rule out incorrect answers. 3. Choose the answer that is most complete or accurate. 4. Pay particular attention to choices such as *none of the above* or *all of the above.*
Short Answer. You are asked to answer the question with a word, a phrase, or a sentence.	1. Read the directions to find out if you are required to answer in complete sentences. 2. Use correct spelling, grammar, punctuation, and capitalization. 3. If you cannot think of the answer, move on. Something in another question might remind you of the answer.

Try It Yourself 4.10

Read each question below and identify what kind of question it is (true/false, matching, multiple-choice, or short answer).

1. The invaders in H. G. Wells's novel came from ________________.
2. T F Wells studied under the biologist T. H. Huxley.
3. ____ 1. Martians — a. killed by narrator
   ____ 2. curate — b. killed by bacteria
   ____ 3. Ogilvy — c. not killed
   ____ 4. artilleryman — d. killed by Martians
4. Which one of the following people dies in *The War of the Worlds?*
   (A) the narrator
   (B) artilleryman
   (C) the curate
   (D) the narrator's wife

ANSWERS FOR TRY IT YOURSELF 4.10

1. short answer
2. true/false
3. matching
4. multiple-choice

4.11 TAKING ESSAY TESTS

An **essay** is a short piece of writing that expresses the writer's thoughts about a particular subject. To answer an essay question, you will need to write one or more paragraphs.

Analyzing the question. One key to writing good answers to essay questions is to take time to analyze, or study, each question. Once you understand clearly what you have to do, you will be able to organize and write more effective essays in the time available.

First read the *entire* question carefully. Look for key words in the question that tell you what is expected. Underline these words or write them on your own note paper. Then make sure to answer *all* parts of the question.

UNDERSTANDING AN ESSAY QUESTION

Type of Essay Question	Tasks of Essay
analyze	break into parts and describe the parts and their relationships
compare; compare and contrast	identify and describe similarities and differences
describe; explain	tell the steps in a process; identify causes and effects
define; describe; identify	classify and tell the features of
interpret	tell the meaning and significance of
summarize	retell very briefly, stating only the main points
argue; prove; show	tell and evaluate reasons for believing a statement

Answers for Try It Yourself 4.11

1. *Compare and contrast*
2. *Define* and *give examples*

Organizing your answer. Determining how you will spend the time available is an important part of planning an essay. Allow time for planning, writing, and reviewing.

Before you begin writing, make a rough outline of the main points you will make. Include main points and key details. Later, if you find yourself running out of time, try at least to state your remaining main points and to add a conclusion.

Write a clear introduction. This will help to keep you on track as you write each paragraph. Your introduction should state the thesis, or main idea, of your essay and should *briefly* answer the question. In the rest of the essay, you can elaborate on your answer, providing evidence to support it.

Reviewing your answer. Before you turn in your completed essay, take time to review and polish it. The guidelines in the chart will help you.

QUESTIONS FOR REVIEWING AN ANSWER TO AN ESSAY QUESTION

- Does the essay answer all parts of the question?
- Does the introduction state clearly the main idea of the essay?
- Does the body of the essay provide evidence to support the main idea?
- Does the essay cover all the points in your rough outline?
- Are there any points that could be made more strongly or clearly?
- Is every word in the essay easily readable?
- Is the essay free of mistakes in spelling, grammar, punctuation, and capitalization?

Try It Yourself 4.11

Read the essay questions below. For each question, identify the key words that tell you what to do.

1. Compare and contrast Rita Dove's "The First Book" and Eve Merriam's "How to Eat a Poem" in terms of theme, style, and literary techniques.
2. Define the term *imagery* and give two examples of metaphors from Unit 9.

4.12 Taking Standardized Tests

Standardized tests are tests given to many students in a school district, a state, or a country. You may already have taken a standardized test, such as the Iowa Test of Basic Skills, and you certainly will take more during your school career. Some standardized tests, such as the Scholastic Aptitude Test, or SAT, are used to determine entrance to colleges and universities. Others must be passed to enter certain vocations or professions. A standardized test measures overall ability, or achievement over a period of time. Learning how to take standardized tests well can help you to achieve your academic and career goals.

Marking your answers. Most standardized tests are multiple-choice. You mark your answer by filling in a circle on an answer sheet that can be read and graded by a computer. When taking one of these tests, use the type of pencil specified by the test monitor. Be sure to fill in the circles *completely* and *neatly.* Each time you answer a question, make sure that the number you are marking is the same as the number of the question you are answering.

Not good	Not good: incomplete	Not good: stray marks	Good

Choosing your answers. When selecting an answer on a standardized test, remember these points: If you do not know the answer, try to rule out some choices and then guess from those remaining. If a question seems too difficult, skip it and go back to it later. Be aware, however, that most tests do not allow you to return to a previous section. You can go back to questions only within a section. Always follow the instructions of the test monitor.

Analogy questions. Analogy questions ask you to find the relationship between a given pair of words and then to recognize a similar relationship between another pair of words. In an analogy question, the symbols : and :: mean "is to" and "as," respectively. The example below would be "Mare is to horse as . . ." when read aloud. To answer an analogy question, you must examine *all* of the answers. If more than one answer seems correct, choose the *best* answer.

EXAMPLE MARE : HORSE ::

(A) lamb : sheep (C) boy : girl (E) doe : deer
(B) man : woman (D) bee : wasp

The answer is E.

To answer an analogy question, think of a sentence that relates the two words. For example, you might think of the sentence "A *mare* is a female *horse.*" Then look for another pair of words that would make sense in that sentence: "A *doe* is a female *deer.*"

Reading comprehension questions. Reading comprehension questions give you a short piece of writing and then ask you several questions about it. The questions may ask you to figure out something based on information in the passage. Use the following strategies when answering reading comprehension questions:

STEPS IN ANSWERING READING COMPREHENSION QUESTIONS

1. Read all the questions quickly.
2. Read the passage with the questions in mind.
3. Reread the first question carefully.
4. Scan the passage, looking for key words related to the question. When you find a key word, slow down and read carefully.
5. Answer the first question.
6. Repeat this process to answer the rest of the questions.

Answers for Try It Yourself 4.12

Exercise A

1. D
2. B

Exercise B

1. C
2. D
3. C

Exercise C

1. C
2. C

Synonym and antonym questions. A synonym or antonym question gives you a word and asks you to select the word that has the same meaning (for a synonym) or the opposite meaning (for an antonym). You must select the *best* answer, even if none is exactly correct. For this type of question, you should try all the choices to see which one works best. Always keep in mind whether you are looking for a synonym or an antonym, because you will usually find both among the answers.

EXAMPLE Write the letter of the word that is most nearly the *opposite* in meaning to the word in capital letters.

1. AMIABLE

(A) capable (B) friendly (C) hostile (D) lovely (E) soulful

The answer is C.

Try It Yourself 4.12

Exercise A. Answer the following analogy questions.

1. daisy : flower ::

(A) flower : tree (C) day : night
(B) stem : daisy (D) apple : fruit

2. hour : day ::

(A) time : minute (C) clock : time
(B) chapter : book (D) foot : inch

Exercise B. Read the Cross-curricular Connection about North Africa on page 284 of Unit 7 and answer the following reading comprehension questions:

1. Which of the following countries is *not* part of North Africa?

(A) Tunisia (C) Zimbabwe
(B) Morocco (D) Libya

2. The exports of the region include

(A) oil (C) cotton
(B) phosphates (D) all of the above

3. Algeria achieved its independence in

(A) 1862
(B) 1892
(C) 1962
(D) 1992

Exercise C. Answer the following synonym and antonym questions.

1. Write the letter of the word that is most nearly the *same* in meaning as the word in capital letters.

   ANTAGONISTIC

   (A) antipathy (C) hostile

   (B) angry (D) friendly

2. Write the letter of the word that is most nearly *opposite* in meaning to the word in capital letters.

   LUMINOUS

   (A) dim (C) bright

   (B) gloomy (D) lovely

RESEARCH SKILLS

Learning is a lifelong process, one that extends far beyond school. Both in school and on your own, it is important to remember that your learning and growth are up to you. One good way to become an independent lifelong learner is to master research skills. **Research** is the process of gathering ideas and information. One of the best resources for research is the library.

4.13 How Library Materials Are Organized

Books are classified into two major groups: fiction and nonfiction. **Fiction** books contain stories that authors have imagined or invented. They are arranged on shelves alphabetically by authors' last names. **Nonfiction** books are true and factual. They are arranged on shelves by subject.

The Dewey Decimal System. The **Dewey Decimal System** is used for classifying nonfiction books in most school and public libraries. This system classifies books by number in one of ten major categories. Each book is given its own special number called a **call number.** This number, printed on the **spine,** or edge, of the book, is used to classify the book. The Dewey system also helps the library to keep track of its books. The chart below shows the main divisions of the Dewey Decimal System.

THE DEWEY DECIMAL SYSTEM

Call Numbers	Subjects
000–099	Reference and General Works
100–199	Philosophy, Psychology
200–299	Religion
300–399	Social Studies
400–499	Language

CONTINUED

500–599	Science, Mathematics
600–699	Technology
700–799	Arts
800–899	Literature
900–999	History, Geography, Biography[1]

1. Biographies (920s) are arranged alphabetically by the name of the person whose life is treated in each biography.

Locating materials in the library. If you know the call number of a book or the subject classification number you want, you can usually go to the bookshelves, or **stacks,** to obtain the book. Use the signs at the ends of the rows to locate the section you need. Then find the particular shelf that contains call numbers close to the one you want.

Library collections include many other types of publications besides books, including magazines, newspapers, audio and video recordings, and government documents. Ask a librarian to tell you where to find the materials you need.

Interlibrary loans. Many libraries are part of larger library networks. In these libraries, the computerized catalog covers the collections of several libraries. If you want a book from a different library, you will need to request the book, which then will be shipped to your library.

COMPUTERIZED CATALOG SEARCHES		
Search by . . .	**Example**	**Hints**
author	gould, stephen j	Type last name first. Type as much of the name as you know.
title	mismeasure of man	Omit articles such as *a, an,* or *the* at the beginning of titles.
subject	intelligence tests; ability—testing	Use the list of subjects provided by the library.
key words	darwin; intelligence; craniology	Use related topics if you can't find anything in your subject.

Computer-assisted research. Using a computer, you can connect to various sources of information that are available electronically. If you, your school, or your library subscribes to an online service, you may be able to get news, encyclopedias, homework assistance, and research services. You may also be able to use the service to connect to the Internet, which links you to universities, libraries, businesses, government agencies, and individuals around the world. Your school may be connected to a special education network, such as TENET (Texas Education Network). Find out from your school or public librarian what services are available.

A CD/ROM database works just like an on-line database except that you get the information directly from a CD instead of through a network. Your library may have a collection of CDs that can be used with computers.

Try It Yourself 4.13

Give the call numbers of the section in the Dewey Decimal System in which each of the following topics would be found.

1. the life of Anne Frank
2. dramatists of the English Renaissance
3. the parts of the atom
4. Shintoism
5. the Ainu of Japan

4.14 Using Catalogs

To find the call numbers of books that will help you with your research, use the library's **catalog.** The catalog lists all the books in the library (or a group of libraries if it is part of a larger system).

Computerized catalogs. Many libraries today use **computerized catalogs**. Systems differ from library to library, but most involve using a computer terminal to search through the library's collection. You can usually search by **author, title, subject,** or **key word.** If your library has a computerized catalog, you will need to learn how to use your library's particular system. A librarian can help you to master the system. Here is a sample book entry screen from a computerized catalog.

Author	Wallace, David Rains, 1945-
Title	The Quetzal and the Macaw: The Story of Costa Rica's National Parks
Publication info.	Sierra Club Books, 1992
No. of pages/size	xvi, 222p. : maps : 24 cm.
ISBN	ISBN 0-87156-585-4
Subjects	National Parks and reserves—Costa Rica—History
	Costa Rica. Servicio de Parques Nacionales—History
	Nature conservation—Costa Rica—History
Dewey call number	333.78

Card catalogs. Like a computerized catalog, a **card catalog** contains basic information about each book in the library. In a card catalog, the information is typed on paper cards, and the cards are arranged alphabetically in drawers. For each book, there is a **title card**, one **author**

Answers for Try It Yourself 4.13

1. 920
2. 800–899
3. 500–599
4. 200–299
5. 300–399

Answers for Try It Yourself 4.14

1. The title is *The Uses of Error.*
2. The call number is 809. It is in the 800s, Literature, because it is literary criticism.
3. The book was first published in 1991.
4. You could look under Literature—History and Criticism.

card for each author, and at least one **subject card.** All of these cards show the book's title, author, and call number, so you can search for a book by title, author, or subject. The following illustration shows a typical subject card.

A SUBJECT CARD

```
              CRITICISM
809     Kermode, Frank.
          The uses of error.--Cambridge
        MA: Harvard Univ. Press. c1991
          xiii. 432 p.  :24cm.

          1. Criticism.  2. Literature--
        History and criticism. I. Title

        0674931521 (alk. paper)   90-47100
```

When you find the cards for the books you want, write down the call number of each book and then go to the shelves (see the Language Arts Survey, 4.13, "How Library Materials Are Organized"). If you cannot find a particular book you need in the card catalog, ask the librarian if your library can request books from another library through an interlibrary loan.

Try It Yourself 4.14

Use the sample card catalog card above to answer these questions:

1. What is the title of the book of criticism written by Frank Kermode?
2. What is the call number of this book? Why is it in the 800s?
3. In what year was this book first published?
4. Under what subject heading in the card catalog could you look to find more books about this topic?

4.15 Using a Dictionary

The entries in a dictionary provide much more information about words than just their spellings and definitions, as shown in the sample entry.

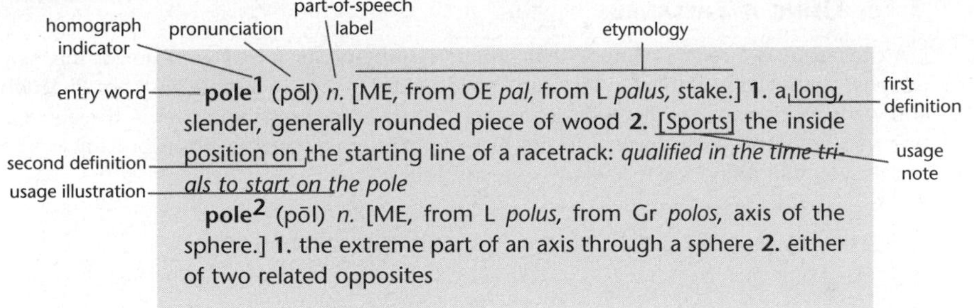

The **pronunciation** is given immediately after the entry word, usually in parentheses. You can find a complete key to pronunciation symbols by looking in the dictionary's table of contents. In some dictionaries, a simplified key is provided at the bottom of each page.

An abbreviation of the **part of speech** usually follows the pronunciation. This label tells the ways in which a word can be used (see the Language Arts Survey, 2.1–2.8, "The Parts of Speech"). In the example, the *n.* shows that the word is used as a noun. If a word can be used in more than one way, definitions in the entry are grouped by part of speech.

An **etymology** is the history of a word. In the first entry, the word *pole* can be traced back through Middle English (ME) and Old English (OE) to the Latin (L) word *palus,* which means "stake." In the second entry, the word *pole* can be traced back through Middle English to the Latin word *polus,* which comes from the Greek word *polos,* meaning "axis of the sphere."

Each **definition** in the entry gives a different meaning of the word. When a word has more than one meaning, the different definitions are numbered. The first definition in an entry is the most common meaning of the word.

Sometimes the entry will include a list of **synonyms.** The entry may also include an **illustration of usage,** which is an example of how the word is used.

Try It Yourself 4.15

Use a dictionary to answer the following questions. You may have to check more than one dictionary.

1. What part of speech is the word *inure?*
2. What is the origin of the word *malaria?*
3. What is a *paramecium?* What is the plural form of the word *paramecium?*
4. What are three different meanings for the word *bank?*
5. What does the word *limpid* mean? What are some synonyms for this word?

Answers for Try It Yourself 4.15

1. verb
2. It comes from the Italian *mala aria,* meaning bad air.
3. A paramecium is a one-celled organism that moves by means of cilia. The plural is *paramecia.*
4. Meanings include an establishment for receiving, keeping, or lending money; a place for collecting goods, such as blood, organs, or food for distribution; long mound or heap; sloping of an airplane to avoid slipping on a turn; to shoot a basketball so that it bounces off the backboard into the basket; shore; bench for rowers; row of keys on a keyboard; subheads under a newspaper headline.
5. *Limpid* means perfectly clear. Synonyms include *transparent, lucid,* and *clear.*

ANSWERS FOR TRY IT YOURSELF 4.16

Responses will vary. Possible responses are given.

1. foe, adversary, opponent
2. stroll, saunter, march
3. wrath, rage, fury

4.16 Using a Thesaurus

A **thesaurus** is a reference book that groups **synonyms,** or words with similar meanings. Suppose that you are writing an essay and have a word that means almost but not quite what you want, or perhaps you find yourself using the same word over and over. A thesaurus can give you fresh and precise words to use. For example, if you look up the word *say* in a thesaurus, you might find the following synonyms listed:

say (v.) speak, remark, utter, express, voice, declare, pronounce

Try It Yourself 4.16

Use a thesaurus to find three synonyms for each of the following words.

1. enemy
2. walk
3. anger

4.17 Using Reference Works

Most libraries have an assortment of **reference works** in which knowledge is collected and organized so that you can find it easily. Usually, reference works cannot be checked out of the library.

Almanacs and yearbooks. Almanacs and yearbooks are published each year. An **almanac** provides statistics and lists, often related to recent events. In an almanac you can find facts about current events, countries of the world, famous people, sports, entertainment, and many other subjects. An overview of the events of the year can be found in a **yearbook.**

Some of the more widely used almanacs and yearbooks are *The Guinness Book of World Records;* the *Information Please Almanac, Atlas, and Yearbook;* the *World Almanac and Book of Facts;* and the *World Book Yearbook of Events.*

Atlases. An **atlas** is a collection of maps and other geographical information. Some atlases show natural features, such as mountains and rivers; others show political features, such as countries and cities. If you need to locate a particular feature on a map in an atlas, refer to the **gazetteer,** an index that lists every item shown on a map.

Biographical references. A biographical reference contains information on the lives of famous people. Examples include *Who's Who,* the *Dictionary of American Biography,* and *Contemporary Authors.*

Encyclopedias. Encyclopedias provide a survey of knowledge. **General encyclopedias,** such as *World Book,* contain information on many different subjects. **Specialized encyclopedias,** such as the *LaRousse Encyclopedia of Mythology,* contain information on one particular area of knowledge.

The topics in an encyclopedia are treated in **articles,** which are usually arranged in alphabetical order. If you look up a topic and do not find it, check the **index** (usually in the last volume). The index will tell you where in the encyclopedia your topic is covered.

Periodicals. A **periodical** is a publication that comes out regularly, usually once a week, once a month, or four times a year. **Magazines** and **newspapers** are periodicals. Because they are published frequently and quickly, periodicals are an excellent source for the latest news and information, but they may not be as accurate as some other sources.

Try It Yourself 4.17

Go to the reference section of your school library or local library and find the answers to the questions below. Note the type of source you used to find each answer.

1. What are the titles of three of Ivan Turgenev's novels?
2. Who won the Nobel Prize for literature in 1994?
3. What are the major rivers in China?
4. What is one news item that made national headlines last week?
5. When did Queen Elizabeth I of England rule?

4.18 Documenting Sources

Plagiarism is taking someone else's words or thoughts and pretending that they are your own. Plagiarism is a very serious problem and has been the downfall of many students and even famous people. Whenever you use someone else's writing to help you with a paper or a speech, you must be very careful either to put the ideas in your own words or to use quotation marks. In either case, you must give credit to the person whose ideas you are using. Giving such credit to others is called **documenting your sources.**

Bibliographies. If you are writing a research paper, your teacher will ask you to include a bibliography to tell where you got your information. A **bibliography** is a list of sources that you used for your writing. A **source** is a book, a magazine, a film, or any other written or audio-visual material that you use to get information. As you work on your paper, you should be writing down on note cards the information for each source that you use. (See the Language Arts Survey, 4.20, "Formal Note-taking.") The chart below shows the correct form for different types of bibliography entries.

FORMS FOR BIBLIOGRAPHY ENTRIES

A. A book

Douglass, Frederick. Escape from Slavery: The Boyhood of Frederick Douglass in His Own Words. New York: Alfred A. Knopf, 1994.

B. A magazine article

Reston, James, Jr. "Orion: Where Stars Are Born." National Geographic. December 1995: 90-101.

C. An encyclopedia entry

"Lewis and Clark Expedition." Encyclopedia Americana. Jackson, Donald. 1995 ed.

D. An interview

Campbell, Silas. Personal interview. 6 February 1997.

Bibliography cards. For each source that you use, you should prepare an index card with complete bibliographical information. Include all of the information in the following chart when preparing your cards. A sample bibliography card is shown after the chart.

ANSWERS FOR TRY IT YOURSELF 4.17

Sources used will vary. Possible sources are given.

1. *Rudin, Home of the Gentry, On the Eve,* and *Fathers and Sons.* (encyclopedia)
2. Kenzabura Oe (almanac)
3. Huang Ho, or Yellow River, and the Yangtze River (atlas)
4. *Responses will vary.* (periodical)
5. She ruled from 1558–1603. (biographical reference, encyclopedia)

Answers for Try It Yourself 4.18

Exercise A

Responses will vary. The paragraph should be rewritten in the student's own words. Any material taken directly from the source should be properly quoted.

Exercise B

Wallace, David Rains.

The Quetzal and the Macaw: The Story of Costa Rica's National Parks

San Francisco: Sierra Club, 1992

333.78

Missing information includes the number of the card and the library where the book was found.

INFORMATION TO INCLUDE ON A BIBLIOGRAPHY CARD	
Author(s)	Write the complete name(s) of all author(s), editor(s), and translator(s).
Title	Write the complete title. If the piece is contained in a larger work, include the title of the larger work. (For example, write the name of the encyclopedia as well as the name of the article you used.)
Publisher	Write exactly as it appears on the title page.
Place and date of publication	Copy this information from the title page or copyright page of a book. For a magazine, write the date of the issue that you used.
Location and call number	Note where you found the book. If it is in a library collection, write the call number.
Card number	Give each bibliography card that you prepare a number. Write that number in the top right-hand corner of the card and circle it. When you take notes from the source, include this number on each note card so that you will be able to identify the source of the note later on.

```
Van Lawick-Goodall,Jane.
        In the Shadow of Man

          Boston: Houghton, 1971.

        Peabody Institute Library

599.8
```

Try It Yourself 4.18

Exercise A. The paragraph below is plagiarized from the Cross-curricular Connection on intelligence on page 204 of Unit 5. Rewrite the paragraph to correct the plagiarism. Use your own words or use quotation marks. Give credit to the source.

Intelligence is difficult to define, but it involves the speed and ability to understand ideas and use them to solve problems and create new ideas. Traditionally, logical/mathematical abilities and verbal/linguistic abilities have been used to measure intelligence, but intelligence also involves abilities such as how quickly you can do a math problem, how well you understand what you read, what structures you can build, or how easy it is for you to play a musical instrument. Today, many scientists believe that humans have more than just these two types of intelligences. Other types of intelligence include visual/spatial, or the ability to understand and manipulate space and objects; bodily/kinesthetic, or the ability to use the body in motion; musical/rhythmic, or the ability to work with pitch and rhythm; and interpersonal and intrapersonal, or the ability to understand oneself and work with other people.

Try It Yourself 4.18 (cont.)

Exercise B. Below is some information collected by a student for a paper about Costa Rica. Organize this material on an index card, following the format given in the sample bibliography card.

The Quetzal and the Macaw:
The Story of Costa Rica's National Parks
by David Rains Wallace
published by Sierra Club Books of San Francisco in 1992
call number 333.78

4.19 Paraphrasing and Summarizing

Often, when writing a paper for school, you will want to put ideas from your sources into your own words. There are two ways to do this. If you repeat the ideas of the source in different words, you are **paraphrasing.** If you repeat only the main ideas from your source, putting them into *fewer* words of your own choosing, then you are **summarizing.**

Here is an example of paraphrasing:

SOURCE To thine own self be true.
PARAPHRASE Be true to yourself.

Notice that the paraphrase is about as long as the source.

Here is an example of a summary:

SOURCE In 1900, most of the population of the United States lived on farms and in rural areas. However, the history of the nation shows a steady population shift away from rural, farm-based life. For example, in 1861, 90 percent of the population of southern states lived in rural areas. By 1920, only 49 percent of the population of the United States was rural.

SUMMARY The percentage of the United States population living in rural areas has steadily dropped over time; for example, it dropped from 90 percent to 49 percent between 1861 and 1920.

Notice that the summary is significantly shorter than the source. Only those ideas that are of central importance to the original are retained.

ANSWERS FOR TRY IT YOURSELF 4.19

EXERCISE A

Responses will vary. Possible responses are given.

1. A book is good if the reader is good.
2. You can only understand life by looking back upon it, but you must live it first.

EXERCISE B

Responses will vary.

Try It Yourself 4.19

Exercise A. Paraphrase the following statements.

1. 'Tis the good reader that makes the good book. —Ralph Waldo Emerson
2. Life can only be understood backwards, but it must be lived forwards. —Søren Kierkegaard

Exercise B. Read the Cross-curricular Connection on page 126. Write a one-paragraph summary of the main ideas of that essay.

4.20 FORMAL NOTE-TAKING

Use **formal note-taking** whenever you need to tell where you found your information, as when you are writing a research paper. In formal note-taking, you write each quotation or piece of information on a separate index card, along with the source where you found it. This method will help you to organize your paper because you can easily put your note cards in the order you want. Some of the kinds of notes you can take are described below.

Quoting. Sometimes you will want to quote directly from your source. **Quoted** words are those borrowed exactly from someone else. Copy the quotation word for word, put quotation marks around it, and be sure to tell who said it.

Paraphrasing. Paraphrasing is telling someone else's ideas in your own words. Paraphrasing is still a form of borrowing, so be sure to give credit to the source of those ideas.

Summarizing. To **summarize** is to simplify a piece of writing into a short statement of the main ideas. You might use a note card to summarize the main points of a newspaper article, for example.

Outlining. An **outline** lays out a framework for a report, showing how the ideas should be arranged. Outlining is a good way to organize your ideas.

Follow the guidelines in the chart below when preparing individual note cards. A sample note card with a quotation is shown after the chart.

PREPARING NOTE CARDS

1. Identify the source at the top right corner of the card. (Use the source numbers from your bibliography cards.)
2. Identify the subject or topic of the note on the top line of the card. (This will make it easier to organize the cards later.)
3. Use a separate card for each fact or quotation. (This will make it easier to organize the cards later.)
4. Write the page number or numbers after the note.

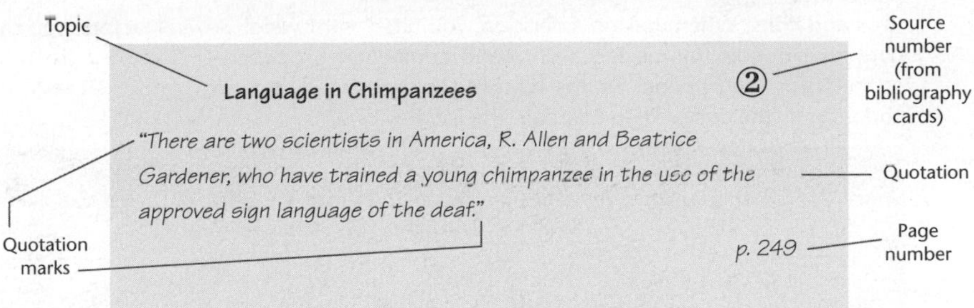

Try It Yourself 4.20

Following is some information collected by a student preparing a paper. Organize the material on a note card, using the format above.

"Washoe was asked (in sign language) 'Who is that?' as she was looking into a mirror. Washoe . . . signaled back, 'Me, Washoe.'"

"This is . . . scientific proof . . . that . . . the chimpanzee has a primitive awareness of self." (pp. 250–51)

THINKING SKILLS

Everyone thinks, but not everyone realizes that thinking—like hitting a baseball or playing the piano—is a skill that you can improve by learning and practicing. This section gives you some tips that can greatly improve your ability to learn, to solve problems, and to make decisions.

4.21 Making Decisions and Solving Problems

Decision Making

When you have a decision to make, the best approach is to weigh the alternatives available to you. You can do this by making a **criteria analysis chart.** To make such a chart, list the results that you want to achieve down the left side of the chart. List your choices across the top of the chart. Then, assign points from 1 to 5 to each choice, with 1 being the lowest and 5 being the highest. Add up the points for each choice to see which one is best.

CRITERIA ANALYSIS CHART

Transportation for Family Vacation	Bus	Plane
1. Comfort	2	4
2. Low cost	5	1
3. Speed	2	5
4. Convenience	3	3
TOTAL	12	13

Answers for Try It Yourself 4.20

Responses will vary. Students should arrange the material in the proper form.

Pros and cons. When making a decision, you often must weigh several factors. You can compare your options by making a **pros and cons** chart on paper. First make a list of all your options. For each option, list the reasons for choosing it (the *pros*) and the reasons for not choosing it (the *cons*). Then compare the lists.

PROS AND CONS			
What to Buy Sister for Birthday			
	Clothing	**Toys**	**Books**
Pros	could use a new sweater enjoys new clothes	loves stuffed animals not too expensive	likes Louise Fitzhugh's novels not too expensive
Cons	expensive not sure of correct size	not sure what kind to buy	not sure which novels she has already read

Problem Solving

There are many ways to solve problems. To solve a complex problem, you will probably need to use more than one strategy. Here are three approaches you can try:

Trial and error. Sometimes when you have to solve a problem, you just make a guess and see if it works. For example, if you are in a house of mirrors at an amusement park, you try one path and if it leads to a dead end, you go back and try another. You may not have realized that you were using a thinking strategy known as **trial and error.** In a trial and error approach, you try one possible solution and if it doesn't work you try another. You might use trial and error if you are trying to decide which of your keys works in a specific lock. If you don't know how to solve a particular math problem, you could guess the answer, plug it back into the problem, then revise your answer as necessary.

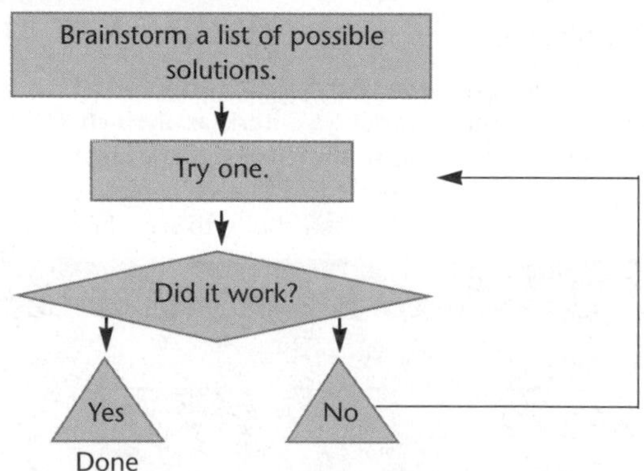

Divide and conquer. Another strategy for problem solving is to divide the problem into parts and then solve each part one at a time in a logical sequence. Here is an example:

WERS FOR
YOURSELF 4.23

*will vary. Possible
e given.*

n instruments: bells, cymbals, drums, xylo-

ed instruments: cello, fid-
p, lute, lyre, violin

oard instruments: harpsi-
, organ, piano

nd instruments: clarinet, flute,
e, saxophone, trombone,
mpet

ANALYTIC SCALE FOR WRITING SKILLS 4.24

Assign a score from 1 to 25 for each grading criterion below.

Comparison/contrast Essay

- **Content/Unity.** The essay compares and contrasts the styles of two authors.
- **Organization/Coherence.** The essay is organized in a logical manner.
- **Language/Style.** The account uses vivid and precise nouns, verbs, and modifiers.
- **Conventions.** The account avoids errors in spelling, grammar, usage, mechanics, and manuscript form.

The key step in classifying is choosing categories that fit your purpose. Make sure that your categories are clearly defined.

Try It Yourself 4.23

Below is a list of musical instruments. Read the list and decide how you might group the items into logical categories. Make a heading for each category you choose, and list each item under the proper heading.

bells	flute	piano
castanets	harp	saxophone
cello	harpsichord	trombone
clarinet	lute	trumpet
cymbals	lyre	violin
drums	oboe	xylophone
fiddle	organ	

4.24 Comparing and Contrasting

Comparing and contrasting are closely related processes. When you **compare** one thing to another, you describe similarities between the two things. When **contrasting,** you describe differences between the two things.

To compare and contrast, begin by listing the features of each subject. Then go down both lists and check whether each feature is shared or not. Choose the most interesting similarities and differences.

Try It Yourself 4.24

Read any two poems or short stories by different authors in this book and write a paper comparing and contrasting the author's styles.

4.25 Analyzing

When you **analyze** something, you break it down into parts and then think about how the parts are related to each other and to the whole. For example, you might analyze a painting by describing its composition, shapes, lines, colors, and subject. You might analyze a short story by describing its conflict, plot, characters, setting, and theme. You might analyze a movie by describing its acting, directing, writing, settings, and costumes.

Problem	It is your friend's birthday on Saturday, and you are in charge of planning a surprise party for him or her.
Strategy Solution	Break the job down into small, manageable goals: (1) Decide where to hold the party and how to decorate. (2) Send invitations with instructions not to inform your friend of the surprise. (3) Decide upon easy-to-prepare refreshments and divide up the preparations among your friends. (4) Choose music for the party.

Try It Yourself 4.21

Exercise A. Choose a product that you would like to own, such as a mountain bike or a new coat. Do some comparative shopping and make a criteria analysis chart to compare various brands.

Exercise B. Imagine that you are on a student committee that must plan a dance to take place on a Saturday evening in the school gymnasium. Use the divide-and-conquer method to create a strategy for making the dance a success.

4.22 Fact or Opinion?

What is the difference between the following statements?

The first people to create a written literature, over 4,500 years ago, were the Sumerians.

Sumerian literature is the best in the entire world.

The first statement expresses a **fact.** You can prove this fact by looking in a reference book. The second statement expresses an **opinion.** It is the kind of statement that can be supported but not proved.

A fact is a statement that, at least in principle, could be proved by direct observation. Every statement of fact is either true or false. The following statements are examples of facts:

H. G. Wells wrote *The War of the Worlds.* (This statement can be proved by getting a copy of the book and looking at the title page to see who the author is.)

The soil of Mars is reddish-orange in color. (Proving this statement by direct observation is, of course, impossible for most people. However, space probes have landed on Mars and have taken pictures that can be seen by looking up Mars in a science book or an encyclopedia.)

Answers for Try It Yourself 4.21

Exercise A

Responses will vary. Charts should reflect the criteria students have chosen and students' ratings of different brands based on those criteria.

Exercise B

Responses will vary. Students should present a reasonable strategy for planning a successful dance.

An opinion is a statement that expresses not a fact about the world but rather an attitude or desire. Three common types of opinions are **statements of value, statements of policy,** and certain types of **predictions.**

A statement of value expresses an attitude toward something. Such statements often include judgment words such as the following:

attractive	good	treasure
awesome	honest	ugly
beautiful	junk	unattractive
cheap	kind	valuable
dishonest	mean	wonderful
excellent	nice	worthless
fine	petty	worthwhile

Examples of statements of value include the following:

Ancient Egypt produced some beautiful and inspiring myths.
Rock and roll music is just terrible.

A statement of policy, also known as a **statement of obligation,** tells not what is but what someone believes should be. Such statements usually include words such as *should, should not, ought to, ought not, must,* or *must not.* Examples of statements of policy include the following:

The president should (or should not) veto the bill.
You must (must not) see that new movie.

Closely related to statements of policy are **requests** and **commands:**

Reelect the president.
Do not see that new movie.

A **prediction** makes a statement about the future. Because the future is unpredictable, most such statements can be considered opinions:

We will find the cures for many diseases in the future.
We will have a blizzard next week.

Evaluating facts and opinions. When evaluating a fact, ask yourself whether it can be proved through direct observation or by checking a reliable source such as a reference work or an unbiased expert. An opinion is as good as the facts that support it. Some opinions are well supported by facts and can be trusted. Others are not supported by facts and cannot be trusted. The opinion that Sumerian literature is the best literature on Earth is supported by the fact that it is of great interest to scholars because it is a very early form of literature. However, others might argue that modern literature is more relevant to most readers. Of course, no list of facts would conclusively prove or disprove the opinion.

When you write and speak, express opinions sparingly. Usually, you can make a stronger case by substituting related facts for opinions. For example, instead of saying, "This was a wonderful day," you could say something like, "Today the sun was shining, it was 74° outside, I got an A on my math test," and so on. When you express an opinion, especially in writing, include facts to back up or support that opinion.

When reading or listening, be critical about the statements that you encounter. Ask yourself, is this a fact or an opinion? If it is a statement of fact, consider whether it can be proved or seems likely. If it is an opinion, consider whether it is supported by facts.

Try It Yourself 4.22

Exercise A. Read each of the following statements of fact. For each statement, tell how you might go about proving or disproving it.

1. Albert Camus won the Nobel Prize for Literature in 1957.
2. Jupiter has sixteen moons.
3. The tomato is a type of fruit.
4. The woolly mammoth is an extinct species.

Exercise B. Tell whether each of the following opinions is a statement of value, a statement of policy, or a prediction.

1. No place on Earth is quite as wonderful as Weeki Wachee Springs.
2. You should definitely go there.
3. Undoubtedly, you will see many marvelous things in the future.
4. Nothing that you will see, however, will ever be better than the world's only live underwater mermaid show.

Exercise C. Look through some recent magazine articles and find examples of four statements of fact and four statements of opinion.

Exercise D. Write two opinions about which you feel strongly. For each opinion, list two or three facts that support it.

4.23 Classifying

To **classify** is to put into classes or categories. Items in the same category should share one or more characteristics. For example, whales are classified by their method of eating as baleen or toothed whales.

Exercise B

1. statement o
2. statement of
3. prediction
4. statement of valu

Exercise C

Responses will vary.

Exercise D

Responses will vary.

Try It Yourself 4.25

Choose a short story from this textbook. Read the story. On your own paper, provide the following information to describe each part.

Setting:

Main Character:

Central Conflict:

Major Events in Plot:

Theme:

Then answer these questions about the relationships between the parts of the story:

1. What effect, if any, does the setting have on the central conflict and the main character?
2. How does the main character come to be involved in this central conflict?
3. What plot events develop and then resolve the central conflict?
4. How is the theme of the story related to the setting, the main character, and the central conflict?

ANSWERS FOR TRY IT YOURSELF 4.25

Responses will vary. Students should identify the setting, main character, central conflict, major plot events, and theme of the story. Students should be able to identify relationships in the story and answer the questions.

4.26 GENERALIZING

To **generalize** is to make a broad statement based on one or more particular observations. For example, suppose that you and your friend Casey-Lou both just got a pair of in-line skates. One day when you and Casey-Lou are talking, you discover that you both have fallen quite often while learning to skate. You might make a generalization, based on this discovery, that "people who are learning to skate fall down quite often." Such generalizations are also called **inferences.** Most of what people know about the world—from obvious facts such as "rain is wet" to less obvious ones such as "people who are learning to skate fall down quite often"—they have learned by making generalizations based on their experiences.

Generalization is therefore an extremely important thinking tool. Unfortunately, it is not a perfect one. The problem with generalizations is that they can be proved false quite easily by a new and different experience. All it takes is getting to know a single person who could instantly skate with ease to falsify, or prove false, the generalization discussed above.

Since most of what we know is based on generalizations, and since generalizations can easily be proved false by new experience, it is important to recognize that much of our knowledge has to be considered tentative. It pays to keep an open mind and to be willing to revise one's ideas about the world.

Overgeneralizations. A generalization based on too little evidence is called an **overgeneralization**. Suppose, for example, that Lori has never listened to classical music. One evening, she hears a single piece by Stravinski on a classical music station, and she dislikes it intensely. She might conclude, on that basis, that she dislikes classical music. That conclusion, however, would be an overgeneralization because there are many different types of classical music, and most of them sound nothing at all like Stravinski. One way to correct an overgeneralization is to use a **qualifier** such as *some, a few,* or *many* instead of *all* or *none.* Instead of saying "I dislike all classical music," for example, Lori could say, "I dislike some classical music," which would be truer to the actual experience that she has had.

Answers for Try It Yourself 4.26

Exercise A

Responses will vary. Responses should support the generalizations.

Exercise B

Responses will vary. Possible responses are given.

1. Most people love rock and roll music.
2. Many wild animals are dangerous.
3. Many novels deal with characters who are growing up.
4. Few people listen to classical music these days.

Stereotypes. An overgeneralization about a group of people is known as a **stereotype.** Stereotypes are one of the most dangerous of all overgeneralizations. Remember that the differences among people within a single race or ethnic background are greater than the average differences between races or ethnic groups as a whole. Stereotyping is always based on lack of knowledge or experience. It is the basis of prejudice and is unacceptable in a civilized society.

Try It Yourself 4.26

Exercise A. Give two examples that support each of these generalizations.

1. Many of the Nobel Prizes for literature have been given to French citizens.
2. Science fiction contains fantastic elements based on scientific principles, discoveries, or laws.

Exercise B. Rewrite each overgeneralization, using qualifiers to correct each statement.

1. Everyone loves rock and roll music.
2. All wild animals are dangerous.
3. Novels deal with characters who are growing up.
4. No one listens to classical music these days.

4.27 Avoiding False Arguments and Propaganda

Another very important thinking skill is learning to use good logic. Life is a process of trying to learn what is true and then to live according to what you believe to be true. Not only do you need good facts, but you also need to know how to put those facts together to come up with the right conclusions. Learning how to think clearly will enable you to avoid errors in logic and to arrive at true conclusions. It will also help you to recognize faulty thinking in others who might be trying to persuade you of something (especially advertisers). The intentional use of false arguments to persuade others is called **propaganda.** Here are some of the many faulty arguments of which you should be aware:

Unsound opinions. A **fact** is a statement that can be proven. An **opinion** is a statement that cannot be proven. An opinion is someone's personal idea of what is right, and may or may not be true. A **sound opinion** is one that can be supported by facts. An **unsound opinion** is one that cannot be supported by facts. Always be sure that you make a clear distinction between facts and opinions, and that you can back up your opinions with facts.

FACT	*One Flew over the Cuckoo's Nest* won several Academy Awards in 1975.
OPINION	*One Flew over the Cuckoo's Nest* was the best film of 1975.
ANALYSIS	This statement that "*One Flew over the Cuckoo's Nest* was the best film" is someone's personal feeling about the film. However, it is probably a sound opinion because it is backed up by the fact that the film received several Academy Awards in 1975.

Circular reasoning. Circular reasoning is the error of trying to support an opinion by restating it in different words. You can avoid circular reasoning by always backing up your opinions with facts.

EXAMPLE That mystery story was thrilling because it was full of excitement.

ANALYSIS The "reason" the speaker gives for saying that the book was thrilling is really just another way of saying it was thrilling. He or she should mention some specific examples to show what makes the story thrilling.

Loaded words. In trying to argue for or against something, people will often use **loaded words,** words that stir up strong feelings, whether positive or negative. You should be careful not to let your feelings interfere with your understanding of the facts.

EXAMPLE Senator Applecake is just another greedy, worthless politician.

ANALYSIS This statement is an emotional attack on the senator using loaded words that will stir up feelings against him or her. It is not a reasonable evaluation of his or her policies or actions in office.

Bandwagon. Sometimes you may worry about being left out or feeling different from others; you want to fit in with the crowd, not stand out as being different. When you think this way, you run the risk of falling for the **bandwagon** appeal. The bandwagon technique appeals to your desire to be part of the crowd—to be like everyone else and to do what everyone else is doing. Beware of advertisements or arguments that try to get you to think or act like everyone else. Just because "everybody" believes or does something does not make it good or right for you.

EXAMPLE Intelligent and discriminating people drink Sparkly Springs Special Mineral Water.

ANALYSIS This statement suggests that you aren't really part of the "in" crowd of intelligent and discriminating people unless you drink this brand of mineral water. It does not prove, or even *say,* anything about the quality of the mineral water.

Try It Yourself 4.27

Listen to some television commercials and read some advertisements in newspapers and magazines. Collect examples of circular reasoning, loaded words, and bandwagon appeal. Share these with other students in your class.

ANSWERS FOR TRY IT YOURSELF 4.27

Responses will vary. Students should be able to identify which type of faulty argument is being used in each example.

ESSENTIAL SKILLS: *Applied English*

5.1 FILLING OUT FORMS AND APPLICATIONS

Forms and applications are a necessary evil of modern life. Entering a new school, going to a new doctor, requesting credit or insurance, applying for a job—these are but a few of the thousands of activities that involve filling out forms and applications. The following guidelines will help you to complete a form or an application in a way that will make a good impression.

GUIDELINES FOR COMPLETING FORMS AND APPLICATIONS

- Get an extra copy or make a photocopy of the form or application, so that you can complete a practice form or application.
- Read through the directions and the form or application itself.
- Gather the information you will need to complete the form or application. This information may include former addresses, dates of events, or a social security number.
- Complete the form or application neatly. Avoid smudges or cross-outs. Use the writing implement requested. Most forms and applications request that you either type or use black or blue ink.
- Do not leave any lines blank. Use N.A. for "not applicable" if a request for information does not apply to you. For example, if you have always lived at the same address, you would write N.A. in the blank following "Previous Addresses."
- Proofread the form or application for errors in punctuation, spelling, or grammar. Make sure your information is correct.
- Submit the form or application to the appropriate person or address. Use an envelope or folder to keep the form or application neat and clean.
- It is a good idea to keep a copy of the form or application for your own records.

Try It Yourself 5.1

Below is an application for a volunteer position at a local hospital. On your own paper, make a copy of the form and then complete it.

APPLICATION FOR VOLUNTEER EMPLOYMENT AT HOPKINS HOSPITAL

Type of work desired (circle one):
- reading aloud to children
- delivering flowers, books, and magazines to patients
- helping organize hospital functions

Personal Data

Applicant's Name: ______________________________
Last Name First Name Middle Initial

Address: ______________________________
Street City State ZIP

Phone: ______________ Date of Birth: ______________

Previous Work or Volunteer Experience

Location: ______________________________

Type of Job: ______________________________

Description: ______________________________

Employment Period: ______________________________

Education

School Name ______________ Address ______________

5.2 WRITING INSTRUCTIONS

Every day people all over the world face the challenge of doing something they have never done before. Despite their inexperience, many succeed because they either receive or read clear, precise instructions. You have probably read instructions before, such as the manual for a computer or the playing rules for a game. Sometimes in life, it is necessary to give instructions to others. You may have to tell your parents how to program the VCR or teach a younger sibling how to play a sport, tie a shoe, or add numbers. Later in life, you may have to write instructions for a more complex procedure or process for a coworker. The following guidelines will help you to write and give clear, precise instructions that others will be able to follow.

ANSWERS FOR TRY IT YOURSELF 5.1

Students should fill out the form neatly in blue or black ink with the correct information, avoiding smudges or cross-outs. Students should not leave any lines blank, and the application should be free of errors in punctuation, spelling, and grammar.

ANALYTIC SCALE FOR WRITING SKILLS 5.2

Assign a score from 1 to 25 for each grading criterion below.

INSTRUCTIONS

- **Content/Unity.** The instructions explain how to perform a specific procedure. All necessary tools and equipment are listed.
- **Organization/Coherence.** The instructions are broken into a number of short, simple, easy-to-follow steps.
- **Language/Style.** The instructions use vivid and precise nouns, verbs, and modifiers. The instructions use simple language and the second-person imperative.
- **Conventions.** The instructions avoid errors in spelling, grammar, usage, mechanics, and manuscript form.

GUIDELINES FOR WRITING INSTRUCTIONS

1. First, make sure that you are very familiar with the procedure you will be teaching.
2. Completely think through the instructions for this procedure, from start to finish, before you begin to write.
3. List any tools or equipment needed to complete the task.
4. Break the task you are trying to describe into a series of short, simple steps.
5. Write each step in the order in which it should be taken.
6. Do not include any unnecessary steps.
7. Use simple language that can easily be understood.
8. Use the second person imperative. Write "Press the enter key," not "The user should press the enter key."
9. If appropriate, draw pictures and diagrams.
10. Proofread your instructions to make sure they are easy to follow.
11. Ask someone who isn't familiar with the procedure to follow the instructions.

Try It Yourself 5.2

Write a set of instructions for one of the following procedures, or choose a procedure on your own that you wish to explain. Follow the guidelines given above.

a. how to program a VCR
b. how to play a video game
c. how to play a favorite board game
d. how to do long division
e. how to send e-mail

5.3 WRITING A PERSONAL LETTER

In the days before telephones, people communicated over long distances by letter. Even today, letters continue to be an important way for people to keep in touch with one another. Letters help friends, relatives, and acquaintances maintain their bonds.

Telephoning has one clear advantage. Calling someone on the telephone allows for immediate, two-way communication. Still, letters have much to recommend them. When you write a letter, you can take the time to think through carefully what you want to say. For this reason, and because you can rewrite and revise, a letter gives you a better chance than telephoning does to communicate precisely what you think and feel. A letter can be more entertaining and interesting than a telephone call. In addition, a letter can be kept as a reminder of someone who is significant in your life.

Here are some tips for reviving in your own life what is often called "the lost art of letter writing":

GUIDELINES FOR WRITING PERSONAL LETTERS	
Keep your reader in mind as you write.	In personal letters, use informal language. The better you know the person to whom you are writing, the more informal, familiar, expansive, and personal your letter can be. If you are answering a letter that you have received, refer to the letter and its contents in your response. You might want to keep a copy of the previous letter in front of you as you write. Your reader will appreciate your thoughtfulness in this regard. Write about subjects that will interest your reader. You may wish to refer to experiences that you and your reader have shared.
Avoid vague, clichéd language.	Too many letters read like this: "How are you? I am well. I hope you are fine. It was nice seeing you. I look forward to getting together again really soon. Well, I've got to go. So, take care." Instead, strive for originality in your expression, and fill your letter with lots of vivid, concrete details.
Vary your subjects.	People often fill their personal letters with vague one-liners about their recent experiences, such as "I went to a concert with Bill last Saturday. Today we're going to the beach." Personal experiences are interesting to write about, but they become much more interesting if you include significant details or share whole stories that have a point to them. Other possibilities include: • descriptions of books, stories, poems, movies, plays, or sporting events from your recent life • your ideas and opinions about recent events • your plans or goals for the future • stories from your current life or from your past • expressions of gratitude or appreciation
Vary the mode of your writing.	Often people stick to a single mode when writing a personal letter, informing others about what they have been doing. In a personal letter, however, variety is often a plus. Feel free to include expressive writing, informative writing, persuasive writing, creative writing, and even dialogue. Figures of speech such as metaphors, similes, and personifications will often brighten up a dull letter. See the Handbook of Literary Terms for more information.

The preceding guidelines will help you to improve the content of your personal letters. It is also important to follow the proper form when writing a personal letter. A personal letter typically has the following parts:

PARTS OF A PERSONAL LETTER

1. a **return address,** including the writer's address and the date when the letter was written;
2. a **salutation,** or greeting, followed by a comma;
3. the **body,** or text, of the letter;
4. an appropriate **closing,** followed by a comma;
5. a **signature**; and
6. an optional **postscript**, or additional, final comment, preceded by the abbreviation *P. S.*

Student Model: Antonia wrote the following personal letter to thank her uncle for allowing her to stay at his ranch in Montana for a vacation.

137 Tremont St. ①
Miami, FL 11113
July 19, 1999

Dear Uncle Randy, ②

I just can't thank you enough for having me stay with you at the ranch for the first two weeks of July. If you were down here in this heat wave that we have been having, you would better understand how cool and soothing the weather up in Montana seems to a Floridian! I loved riding your horses and milking the cows in the morning. Despite your many skeptical predictions to the contrary, I must remind you that only one bucket of milk was spilled and I never got kicked in the head, so maybe there's a future for me in your business! (Don't tell the cows yet—they might complain!) I was truly impressed when you took me to see the Rocky Mountains. You are both an excellent host and an extraordinary tour guide. You're a pretty good uncle as well. ③

Thanks again, and visit us in Miami soon so that I can play tour guide for you.

Your niece, ④

Antonia ⑤

P. S. Give Snowball an apple for me. ⑥

Try It Yourself 5.3

Write a personal letter to an adult you know—perhaps a relative, a friend of the family, or a teacher—thanking him or her for some gift, favor, or assistance. Use the proper form for personal letters.

5.4 Writing a Business Letter

A business letter is usually addressed to someone you do not know personally or with whom you do not have a personal relationship. Therefore, a formal tone is appropriate for such a letter.

Following appropriate form is especially important when writing business letters. If you follow the correct form, write well, and avoid errors in spelling, grammar, usage, and mechanics, your letter will sound professional and make a good impression.

A business letter includes the same parts as a personal letter. In addition, an **inside address** appears above the salutation. The inside address includes the name and title of the person to whom you are writing and the name and address of that person's company or organization (see the model on the following page).

One common form for a business letter is the **block form.** In the block form, each part of the letter begins at the left margin. The parts are separated by line spaces.

Begin the salutation with the word *Dear,* followed by the courtesy or professional title used in the inside address, such as *Ms., Mr.,* or *Dr.* If you are not writing to a specific person, you may use a general salutation such as *Dear Sir or Madam.*

In the body of your letter, use a polite, formal tone and standard English. Make your points clearly, in as few words as possible.

End with a standard closing such as *Sincerely, Yours truly,* or *Respectfully yours.* Capitalize only the first word of the closing. Type your full name below the closing, leaving three or four blank lines for your signature. Sign your name below the closing in blue or black ink (never in red or green). Proofread your letter before you send it. Poor spelling, grammar, or punctuation can ruin an otherwise well-written business letter.

GUIDELINES FOR WRITING A BUSINESS LETTER

- Outline your main points before you begin writing.
- Keyboard your letter, if at all possible. Type or print it on clean 8 1/2 x 11" white or off-white paper. Use one side of the paper only.
- Use the block form or another standard business letter form.
- Single space, leaving a blank line between each part, including paragraphs.
- Use a standard salutation and a standard closing.
- Stick to the subject. State your main idea clearly at the beginning of the letter. Keep the letter brief and informative.
- Check your spelling, grammar, usage, and punctuation carefully.

ANALYTIC SCALE FOR WRITING SKILLS 5.3

Assign a score from 1 to 25 for each grading criterion below.

Personal Letter

- **Content/Unity.** The personal letter thanks an adult for something.
- **Organization/Coherence.** The personal letter is written in a sensible order.
- **Language/Style.** The personal letter uses vivid and precise nouns, verbs, and modifiers.
- **Conventions.** The personal letter avoids errors in spelling, grammar, usage, mechanics, and manuscript form.

ANALYTIC SCALE FOR WRITING SKILLS 5.4

Assign a score from 1 to 25 for each grading criterion below.

BUSINESS LETTER

- **Content/Unity.** The business letter expresses the student's interest in a summer job as a camp counselor.
- **Organization/Coherence.** The business letter is written in a sensible order.
- **Language/Style.** The business letter uses vivid and precise nouns, verbs, and modifiers. The letter is brief and informative.
- **Conventions.** The business letter avoids errors in spelling, grammar, usage, mechanics, and manuscript form.

Student Model: Nils loves deep-sea fishing and would like to get a summer job working part time on a deep-sea fishing boat that takes tourists on day trips. This is a copy of the letter that he sent to the captain of such a boat.

271 Cockle Cove Rd.
Seaview, SC 89900
May 17, 1998

Ms. Elaine Goodweather
Captain of the *Banshee*
800 Babbling Brook Dr.
Seaview, SC 89900

Dear Ms. Goodweather:

Please consider me for a position as a member of your crew on the *Banshee* for the coming summer. I understand that in the summer your business increases considerably and that you might have the need for a responsible, hard-working individual. I bring to my application considerable knowledge of deep-sea fishing, fishing equipment, and boating. I also have experience working with the public in a bait-and-tackle shop.

I will be available to work three days per week between July 1 and August 30. I am enclosing a résumé and references. Please contact me if you wish to set up an interview.

Sincerely,

Nils Sandpiper
Nils Sandpiper

Try It Yourself 5.4

Imagine that you have just learned about a summer camp that is looking for counselors for the upcoming season. The camp features a variety of activities for younger children—everything from sailing, baseball, and mountain-climbing to drama, writing, and painting. You know that you would be an excellent counselor for the camp. Write a letter to Ms. Julianne Finkle, Director of Camp White Mountain, at 300 Main Street, Greenville, WI 77740. Express your interest in the position of a counselor at this camp, briefly explain why you are qualified for this position, mention that you have enclosed a résumé, and express your interest in speaking further with Ms. Finkle. Follow the proper form for a business letter.

5.5 WRITING A MEMO

In businesses, schools, and other organizations, employees, students, and others often communicate by means of memoranda, or memo. For example, the captain of a school volleyball team might write a memo to the editor of the student newspaper announcing tryouts for the team.

Some memos will be more informal than others. If you know the person to whom you are writing well or if the memo has only a social function, such as announcing a staff party, the tone will be fairly informal. Most memos, however, have a fairly formal tone.

A memo begins with a **header.** Often this header contains the word *memorandum* (the singular form of *memoranda*) and the following words and abbreviations:

TO	RE (meaning *regarding*)
FR (meaning *from*)	C (meaning *copy*)
DT (meaning *date*)	

Student Model: Alicia McNorton, the captain of the volleyball team at Wilson Middle School, wishes to have the upcoming tryouts for her team announced in the school newspaper. She decides to write a memo to the editor of the paper, Annie Clayton.

MEMORANDUM

TO: Annie Clayton
FR: Alicia McNorton   **C:** Ms. Wise
RE: Tryouts for the volleyball team
DT: February 12, 1999

Please include the following announcement in the upcoming issue of the *Wilson Gazette:* Tryouts for the Wilson volleyball team will be held on Friday, February 26, at 3:00 P.M., in the Wilson Middle School Gymnasium. Students interested in trying out for the team should come to the gymnasium at that time, wearing gym clothes. For additional information, please contact Ms. Wise, the team's coach, or any member of the volleyball team.

Thank you.

Try It Yourself 5.5

Think of a new club or organization that you would like to start at your school. Perhaps you would like to start a literary magazine or a video games enthusiasts' club. Write a memo to your school principal requesting that such a club be sponsored by the school and telling why you think this club would be an excellent addition to the extracurricular activities that your school now offers. Follow proper memo form.

ANALYTIC SCALE FOR WRITING SKILLS 5.5

Assign a score from 1 to 25 for each grading criterion below.

MEMO

- **Content/Unity.** The memo requests sponsorship of a club and explains why the club would be a good addition.
- **Organization/Coherence.** The memo is written in a sensible order.
- **Language/Style.** The memo uses vivid and precise nouns, verbs, and modifiers.
- **Conventions.** The memo avoids errors in spelling, grammar, usage, mechanics, and manuscript form.

HANDBOOK OF *Literary Terms*

ABSTRACT An **abstract** word, like *hope* or *pride,* names something that cannot be directly seen, touched, tasted, heard, or smelled. See *concrete.*

ACCENT See *stress.*

ACRONYM (ak´rə nim´) An **acronym** is a word made from the first letters of a group of words. The word *laser* is an acronym. Many organizations, such as SADD, have names that are acronyms spelling out words in English.

Laser=	**SADD =**
Light-	*Students*
Amplification by	*Against*
Stimulated	*Drunk*
Emission	*Driving*
Radiation	

ACROSTIC An **acrostic** is a poem in which the first or last letters of each line spell out something. This poem is an acrostic:

Black and sharp winged, it
Arcs through caves and down chimneys
Take care of your hair; it's a bat.

ACT An **act** is a major part of a play. Long plays are often divided into several acts. Sometimes acts are divided into scenes.

ACTOR An **actor** is someone who plays a character. Actors perform in theater, television, and films. They also do readings and storytelling. Today, the word *actor* is used to speak about both male and female performers.

ADAGE See *proverb.*

AIM A writer's **aim** is his or her purpose, or goal. People may write to express themselves (expressive writing), to inform others (informative writing), to persuade others (persuasive writing), or to create a literary work (literary writing). Here are examples of the four categories of aim:

Expressive writing
part of a diary, a personal letter

Persuasive writing
a campaign speech, a television commercial

Informative writing
an encyclopedia article, an accident report

Literary writing
a poem, a play, or a short story

ALLEGORY An **allegory** is a literary work in which each part stands for, or symbolizes, something else. "The Song of Wandering Aengus," in Unit 2, can be read as an allegory of the stages in life. Each stanza represents a different stage, transforming the speaker from youth to middle age to old age.

ALLITERATION **Alliteration** is the repetition of consonant sounds at the beginnings of syllables, as in *bats in the belfry* or *dead as a doornail.* The repetition of the *l* and *h* sounds in the following lines are examples of alliteration:

When a Man Hath No Freedom to Fight for at Home

When a man hath no freedom to fight for at home,
Let him combat for that of his neighbors;
Let him think of the glories of Greece and of Rome,
And get knocked on the head for his labors.

To do good to mankind is the chivalrous plan,
And is always nobly requited;
Then battle for freedom wherever you can,
And, if not shot or hanged, you'll get knighted.

—George Gordon, Lord Byron

ALLUSION An **allusion** is a reference in a literary work to something famous. The thing referred to may be a person, an object, an event, a work of art, a literary work, or anything else that is well known. The following lines from Alice Walker's "For My Sister Molly Who in the Fifties," in Unit 3, contain an allusion to a poem by Robert Service called "The Cremation of Sam McGee":

Who read from *Prose and Poetry*
And loved to read "Sam McGee from Tennessee"
On nights the fire was burning low

ANALOGY An **analogy** is a comparison of things that are alike in some ways but different in others. The following passage makes an analogy between reading a book and taking a journey:

Imagine that you have taken a journey. You have hiked up a mountainside in Peru or have wandered through the Valley of the Kings in Egypt. You have gone shopping in the Ginza district of Tokyo or have bounced in a spacesuit over the surface of the moon. After such an experience, you return home a different person. You think about the experience and what it meant to you.

A work of literature is an opportunity to take just such an exotic journey. Using your imagination, you take the writer's trip. You have an experience. Then you reflect on the experience you had. You think about what you thought and felt, about what the experience meant to you. That reflection is called reader response.

ANALYSIS **Analysis** is the act of dividing a subject into parts and then thinking about how the parts are related. For example, an analysis of a short story might consider these parts: the plot, the setting, the characters, and the theme, or main idea.

ANAPEST, ANAPESTIC See *meter.*

ANECDOTE (ăn´ik dōt´) An **anecdote** is a brief story, usually told to make a point. The following anecdote from Robert Jastrow's "The Size of Things," in Unit 11, is used to introduce an essay that deals with the *physical* size of objects in space:

I once had occasion to testify before the United States Senate Space and Aeronautics Committee on the scientific background of the space program; my talk dealt with the manner in which all substances in the universe are assembled out of neutrons, protons, and electrons as the basic building blocks. After I left the chamber a senior NASA official continued with a summary of the major space science achievements of the last year. Apparently my scholarly presentation had perplexed the senators, although they were anxious to understand the concepts I had presented. However, the NASA official's relaxed manner reassured them, and someone asked him: "How big is the electron? How much smaller is it than a speck of dust?" The NASA official correctly replied that the size of an electron is to a dust speck as the dust speck is to the entire earth.

ANTAGONIST In a story, a character who struggles with the main character is called an **antagonist.** For example, in "Harrison Bergeron," in Unit 5, the Handicapper General, Diana Moon Glampers, is the antagonist who destroys the main character, Harrison Bergeron.

APHORISM An **aphorism** is a short saying. An example of an aphorism is the Nigerian saying "If a child washes his hands, he can eat with kings."

APOSTROPHE An **apostrophe** is a poem that addresses an object or person directly. "The First book" and "How to Eat a Poem," in Unit 1, are apostrophes.

APPOSITION An **apposition** is a renaming of something in different words. The following sentence includes an apposition for the name Gilgamesh:

> Gilgamesh, the Sumerian hero, had to confront the reality of death.

ARCHAIC LANGUAGE **Archaic language** is language that is old-fashioned.

ARTICLE An **article** is a brief nonfiction work on a specific topic. Encyclopedia entries and nonfiction magazine pieces are examples of articles.

ASIDE An **aside** is a statement made by a character in a play, meant to be heard by the audience but not by the other characters.

ASSONANCE **Assonance** is the repetition of vowel sounds in stressed syllables that end in different consonant sounds, as in *lime light.*

ATMOSPHERE See *mood.*

AUTOBIOGRAPHY An **autobiography** is the story of a person's life, written by that person. *Of Men and Mountains,* excerpted in Unit 11, is a autobiographical work by Supreme Court Justice William O. Douglas.

BACKGROUND INFORMATION **Background information** is information provided in a literary work, often at the beginning, to explain the situation to the reader. A writer may include background information to explain the central conflict, the relationships between the characters, the setting, or any other part of his or her work. The following background information, from the beginning of Alan Bloch's story "Humans are Different," in Unit 5, gives the reader clues suggesting that the story is set in the far future, long after the passing of humans:

> I'm an archeologist, and Humans are my business. Just the same I wonder if we'll ever find out what made Humans different from us Robots—by digging around on the dead planets.

BALLAD A **ballad** is a simple poem that tells a story. Most ballads have four-line stanzas that have the rhyme scheme *abcb.* Sometimes the last line of a stanza is repeated. The following lines are from the American folk ballad "Barbara Allen":

> In Scarlet Town, long time ago,
> There was a fair maid dwellin',
> And all the boys from miles around
> Came to call on Barbara Allen.

BIBLIOGRAPHY A **bibliography** is a list of books, magazines, or other sources of information. A writer may include a bibliography at the end of his or her work to show where he or she got the information that appears in the work. A complete bibliography entry for a book gives its author, its title, its place of publication, its publisher, and its date of publication:

> Lester, Julius. *To Be a Slave.* New York: Scholastic, 1968.

For more information on bibliographies, see the Language Arts Survey, 4.18, "Documenting Sources."

BIOGRAPHY A **biography** is the story of a person's life, told by another person. Theodora Kroeber's *Ishi in Two Worlds,* a selection from which appears in Unit 11, is a biography about a Native American who is the last surviving member of his tribe.

BLEND A **blend,** or **portmanteau,** is a new word created by joining together two old ones, as in *smog,* from the words *smoke* and *fog;* or *pixel,* which is a dot on a computer screen, from the words *picture* and *element.*

CATASTROPHE (kə tas´trə fē) A **catastrophe** is the part of a plot in which the main character meets a tragic end.

CENTRAL CONFLICT A **central conflict** is the main problem or struggle in the plot of a poem, story, or play. In Rona Maynard's short story, "The Fan Club," in Unit 4, the central conflict is between the main character's desire to be free of prejudice and her wish to be accepted by the "in crowd" at her school. See *conflict* and *plot.*

CHARACTER A **character** is a person or animal who takes part in the action of a literary work. The main character is called the protagonist. A character who struggles against the main character is called an antagonist.

Characters can also be classified as major characters or minor characters. Major characters are ones who play important roles in a work. Minor characters are ones who play less important roles.

A one-dimensional character, flat character, or caricature is one who exhibits a single quality, or character trait. A three-dimensional, full, or rounded character is one who seems to have all the complexities of an actual human being.

CHARACTERIZATION **Characterization** is the act of creating or describing a character. Writers use three major techniques to create a character: direct description, portraying the character's behavior, and presenting the thoughts and emotions of the character. Direct description allows the reader to learn about such matters as the character's appearance, habits, dress, background, personality, and motivations through the comments of a speaker, a narrator, or another character. The writer might present the actions and speech of the character, allowing the reader to draw his or her own conclusions from what the character says or does. The writer might also reveal the character's private thoughts and emotions. See *character.*

CHRONOLOGICAL ORDER Events arranged in order of the time when they happened are said to be in **chronological order.** This method of organization is used in most stories, whether they are fiction or nonfiction. Chronological order is also used in informative nonfiction writing that describes processes and cause-and-effect relationships.

CLICHÉ (klē shā′) A **cliché** is an overused expression such as *happy as a lark* or *time is money.* Most clichés begin as vivid, colorful expressions but become uninteresting because of overuse.

CLIMAX The **climax** is the point of highest interest and suspense in a literary work. The climax sometimes signals the *turning point* of the action in a story or play. In "Harrison Bergeron," in Unit 5, the climax occurs when Harrison removes his handicaps and those of a ballerina and together they dance a wonderful dance. See *plot.*

COHERENCE **Coherence** is the logical arrangement of ideas in speech or writing. Writers achieve coherence by presenting their ideas in a logical order and by using transitions to show how their ideas are connected to one another. See *transition.*

COINED WORDS **Coined words** are ones that are intentionally created, often from already existing words or word parts. Examples of recently coined words include *modem, sit-com,* and *videophone.*

COMIC RELIEF Comic relief is the use of a funny scene in a serious work to relieve the intensity felt by the reader or audience.

CONCRETE A **concrete** word, like *cloud* or *airplane,* names something that can be directly seen, tasted, touched, heard, or smelled. *Piano, fish, grape* and *notebook* are examples of concrete terms. See *abstract.*

CONCRETE POEM A **concrete poem,** or **shape poem,** is one with a shape that suggests its subject. The following is an example of a concrete poem:

o o
ball n

CONFLICT A **conflict** is a struggle between two people or things in a literary work. A plot is formed around conflict. A conflict can be internal or external. A struggle that takes place between a character and some outside force such as another character, society, or nature is called an external conflict. In H. G. Wells's *The War of the Worlds,* in Unit 12, humans are engaged in a struggle against Martians, an external force. A struggle that takes place within a character is called an internal conflict. In "The Fan Club," in Unit 4, the main character experiences a struggle between her desire to remain free of prejudice and her desire to be accepted by the "in crowd." See *central conflict* and *plot.*

CONNOTATION A **connotation** is an emotional association attached to a word or statement. For example, the word *unique* has positive emotional associations, while the word *strange* has negative ones, even though the two words denote, or refer to, something highly unusual. See *denotation.*

CONSONANCE **Consonance** is the use of different vowel sounds followed by the same consonant sound, as in *flim flam*. In "The Garden," in Unit 9, the following line makes use of consonance:

In between the diamonds, ol' man Simon

COUPLET See *stanza.*

CRISIS The **crisis,** or turning point, is the point in a plot when something happens to determine the future course of events and the eventual fate of the main character. The crisis in "The Medicine Bag," in Unit 4, occurs when Martin's friends finally meet his great-grandfather. See *plot.*

CRITICISM **Criticism** is the act of explaining or judging a literary work.

DACTYL, DACTYLIC See *meter.*

DEFINITION A **definition** is an explanation of the meaning of a word or phrase. A dictionary definition often contains two parts, the genus and differentia. The genus tells the group or class to which the thing belongs. The differentia tells the differences between the thing and other members of its group or class.

DENOTATION A **denotation** is the basic meaning, or dictionary definition, of a word. See *connotation.*

DESCRIPTION A **description** gives a picture in words of a character, object, or scene. Descriptions make use of sensory details—words and phrases that describe how things look, sound, smell, taste, or feel. Eve Merriam's poem, "How to Eat a Poem," Unit 1, appeals to the senses of sight, touch, and taste.

DIALECT A **dialect** is a version of a language spoken by people of a particular place, time, or group. Writers often use dialect to give their works a realistic flavor. The following dialogue from Washington Irving's "Rip Van Winkle," in Unit 8, is written in a dialect spoken in America shortly before the American Revolution:

Poor Wolf, . . . thy mistress leads thee a dog's life of it; but never mind, my lad, whilst I live thou shalt never want a friend to stand by thee!

DIALOGUE **Dialogue** is conversation involving two or more people or characters. Plays are made up of dialogue and stage directions. Fictional works are made up of dialogue, narration, and description. In a play, dialogue appears after the names of characters:

MR. FRANK. Burn them.

MIEP. But, Mr. Frank, there are letters, notes . . .

MR. FRANK. Burn them. All of them.

—Frances Goodrich and Albert Hackett,
The Diary of Anne Frank

In fiction, dialogue is enclosed in quotation marks ("") and is often accompanied by tag lines, words and phrases such as *he said* or *she replied* that tell who is speaking:

"Me?" said Jimmy, in surprise.
"Why, I never cracked a safe in my life."

—O. Henry, "A Retrieved Reformation"

DIARY A **diary** is a day-to-day record of a person's life, thoughts, or feelings. *The Diary of a Young Girl,* by Anne Frank is one of the most famous diaries ever written. It was composed by an eleven-year-old girl, who later died in a Nazi concentration camp. The play *The Diary of Anne Frank,* in Unit 10, is based on that diary.

DRAMA A **drama,** or play, is a story told through characters played by actors. The script of a drama typically consists of characters' names, dialogue spoken by the characters, and stage directions. Drama is meant to be read or performed before an audience. When a person reads a drama, he or she should imagine what it would be like to see and hear the action. Drama is different from other types of literature because of the importance played in it by the spectacle. The spectacle of a drama includes everything that the audience sees and hears, such as lighting, costumes, makeup, properties, set pieces, music, sound effects, and the movements and expressions of actors. Drama also differs from other types of literature in being a collaborative effort involving the author as well as a director, actors, and others involved in the production. Frances Goodrich and Albert Hackett's *The Diary of Anne Frank,* in Unit 10, is an example of a drama.

DRAMATIC IRONY **Dramatic irony** happens when something is known by the reader or audience of a literary work but is not known by the characters. An example of dramatic irony occurs in O. Henry's "A Retrieved Reformation." The reader is aware that Ralph Spencer was once a safe-cracking burglar, while the characters think he is an upstanding citizen.

EDITORIAL An **editorial** is a short piece of persuasive writing that appears in a newspaper, magazine, or similar work. The following is an example of an editorial:

> The staff of the Emerson Middle School *Herald* urges the school administration to consider keeping the language lab open after school hours and on weekends. Learning another language, such as Spanish or French, takes lots of practice, and the best kind of practice is to spend time listening to the language and responding in the language. The language lab makes such practice possible, but many students do not have free time during the school day to spend in the language lab. If the lab were open after school or on weekends, students would be able to come during their free time to get the extra practice that they need.

ESSAY An **essay** is a short nonfiction work on a single subject. A good essay develops a single idea, or thesis, and is organized into an introduction, a body, and a conclusion. Al Gore's essay from *Earth in the Balance,* in Unit 11, is a narrative essay. A narrative essay tells a true story to make some point. Persuasive essays are written to advance an opinion. The introduction to Unit 7 is an informative essay, one written to communicate facts.

EUPHEMISM A **euphemism** is a less emotionally powerful word or phrase used in place of one that might be offensive. For example, some people use the euphemism *deceased* instead of the more direct and powerful word *dead.* The phrase *pre-owned vehicle,* used in place of *used car,* is an example from advertising.

EXPOSITION The exposition is the part of a plot that introduces the setting and the major characters. Here is part of the exposition from the short story "The Flying Machine" in Unit 2.

> In the year AD 400, the Emperor Yuan held his throne by the Great Wall of China, and the land was green with rain, readying itself toward the harvest, at peace, the people in his dominion neither too happy nor too sad.

EXTERNAL CONFLICT An **external conflict** is a struggle that takes place between a character and something outside that character. The struggle between the fox and the hunters is the external conflict in "Last Cover," in Unit 8.

FABLE A **fable** is a brief story with animal characters and a moral. Famous fables include those of Æsop and La Fontaine. "Why the Frog Croaks," in Unit 7, is an example of a fable.

FAIRY TALE A **fairy tale** is a type of European folk tale containing supernatural events and often imaginary creatures such as elves, giants, and fairies. Fairy tales often use medieval settings. "Cinderella," "The White Snake," and "The Little Mermaid" are famous examples.

FANTASY A **fantasy** is a very unrealistic or imaginative story. Fantasy is often contrasted with *science fiction,* in which the unreal elements are given a scientific or pseudoscientific basis. Wallace Stevens's "A Rabbit as King of the Ghosts," in Unit 2, is an example of fantasy.

FICTION **Fiction** is prose writing about imagined events or characters. The primary forms of fiction are the short story and the novel. Saki's "The Story-Teller," in Unit 1, is an example of a short story. Ray Bradbury's *Fahrenheit 451,* excerpted in Unit 1, and H. G. Wells's *The War of the Worlds* , in Unit 12, are examples of novels. See *novel.*

FIGURE OF SPEECH **A figure of speech** is a statement that has more than a straightforward, literal meaning. Pablo Neruda uses a figure of speech when he says:

> my feet became,
> two wooden
> fish.

Hyperbole, metaphor, personification, and simile are all figures of speech. See *hyperbole, metaphor, personification,* and *simile.*

FIRST-PERSON POINT OF VIEW In a story told from the **first-person point of view,** the narrator takes a part in the action and refers to himself or herself using words such as *I* and *we.* The selection from Richard Brautigan's *Trout Fishing in America,* in Unit 2, is told from the first-person point of view:

> My own experience with the Cleveland Wrecking Yard began two days ago when I heard about a used trout stream they had on sale out at the Yard. So I caught the Number 15 bus on Columbus Avenue and went out there for the first time . . .

FLASHBACK A **flashback** is a part of a story, poem, or play that presents events that happened at an earlier time. Writers use flashbacks for many purposes. One common technique is to begin a work with a final event and then to tell the rest of the story as a flashback that explains how that event came about. Another common technique is to begin a story in the middle of the action and then to use a flashback to fill in the events that occurred before the opening of the story. "Tears of Autumn," in Unit 3, begins with the main character traveling by ship to America. The author, however, later experiences a flashback that explains the events that led up to the main character's journey.

FOLK SONG A **folk song** is an anonymous song originally passed from singer to singer without being written down. Examples include the ballad "Bonny Barbara Allan," the sea chantey "Blow the Man Down," the children's song "Row, Row, Row Your Boat," the spiritual "Go Down, Moses," the railroad song "Casey Jones," and the cowboy song "The Streets of Laredo." The term *folk song* is sometimes used for works composed in imitation of true folk songs. Modern composers of songs in the folk tradition include Bob Dylan, Paul Simon, Joan Baez, and the Indigo Girls. See *ballad.*

FOLK TALE A **folk tale** is a story passed by word of mouth from generation to generation. Famous collections of folk tales include the fairy tales collected by the Brothers Grimm and Zora Neale Hurston's collection of African-American folk tales and other folklore materials, *Mules and Men.* An example of a folk tale from this text is "Goha and the Donkey," in Unit 7.

FOOT In poetry, a **foot** is a unit of rhythm containing strongly and weakly stressed syllables. See *meter* and *stress.*

FORESHADOWING **Foreshadowing** is the act of hinting at events that will happen later in a poem, story, or play. In the following lines from "The Sniper," in Unit 8, the writer foreshadows that the enemy sniper will turn out to be someone that the main character knows.

> When the sniper reached the laneway on the street level, he felt a sudden curiosity as to the identity of the enemy sniper whom he had killed. He decided that he was a good shot, whoever he was. He wondered did he know him. Perhaps he had been in his own company before the split in the army. He decided to risk going over to have a look at him.

FREE VERSE **Free verse** is poetry that does not use regular rhyme, rhythm, meter, or division into stanzas. The poems "How to Eat a Poem," in Unit 1, and "The City is So Big," in Unit 2, are examples of free verse.

GENRE A **genre** (zhän´rə) is a type of literary work. Some terms used to name literary genres include *autobiography, biography, drama, essay, novel, poetry, short story,* and *tragedy.* Literary works are sometimes classified into genres based on subject matter. Such a classification might describe *detective stories, mysteries, adventure stories, romances, westerns,* and *science fiction* as different genres of fiction.

HAIKU (hī´ko͞o) A **haiku** is a traditional Japanese three-line poem. It has five syllables in the first line, seven in the second, and five in the third. A traditional haiku presents an image in order to arouse in the reader a specific emotional state. Contemporary writers have adapted the form for other purposes.

HALF RHYME See *slant rhyme.*

HYPERBOLE A **hyperbole** (hī pur´bə lē) is an exaggeration made for effect. Emily Dickinson uses hyperbole in "The Brain—is wider than the sky—" in the lines "The Brain—is wider than the sky—" and "The Brain is deeper than the sea—."

IAMB, IAMBIC See *meter.*

IMAGE An **image** is language that describes something that can be seen, heard, touched, tasted, or smelled. The images in a literary work are referred to, when considered altogether, as the work's *imagery*. These lines from Seamus Heaney's "Digging," in Unit 9, contain images of sight, sound, and touch.

Between my finger and my thumb
The squat pen rests; snug as a gun.
Under my window, a clean rasping sound
When the spade sinks into gravelly ground:
My father, digging. I look down

IMAGERY Taken together, the images in a poem or passage are called its **imagery**. See *image*.

INCITING INCIDENT The **inciting incident** is the event that introduces the central conflict, or struggle, in a poem, story, or play. In the short story "The Medicine Bag," in Unit 4, the arrival of Martin's great-grandfather is the inciting incident. This arrival leads to the basic conflict between Martin's embarrassment and his love and respect for his great-grandfather.

INFORMATIVE WRITING See *aim*.

INTERNAL CONFLICT An **internal conflict** is a struggle that takes place inside the mind of a character. In "Tears of Autumn," in Unit 3, the main character experiences an internal conflict between her fears of going to a new country and marrying a stranger and her desire to escape from her family and future life in Japan. See *conflict*.

IRONY **Irony** is a difference between appearance and reality. In "The Fan Club," in Unit 4, the main character decides to join the "in" group by making fun of another character. It is ironic that the main character does so because earlier in the story she gave a speech about the need to overcome prejudice and to tolerate others regardless of their differences.

IRONY OF SITUATION An event that contradicts the expectations of the characters, the reader, or the audience of a literary work is an example of **irony of situation.** In Liam O'Flaherty's "The Sniper," in Unit 8, the revelation that the sniper killed his own brother is an example of irony of situation. See *irony*.

JOURNAL A **journal,** like a diary, is a day-to-day record of a person's life, thoughts, or feelings.

LEGEND A **legend** is a story based on important real events or characters, often from the distant past. Some people believe that "The Epic of Gilgamesh," in Unit 6, is based upon stories about a real king who lived thousands of years ago in Mesopotamia.

LIGHT VERSE **Light verse** is poetry meant to be humorous. "The Garden," by Shel Silverstein, in Unit 9, is an example.

LIMERICK A **limerick** is a five-line light verse. The first, second, and fifth lines end with one rhyme. The third and fourth lines end with another. The rhyme scheme is *aabba.* See *light verse.*

There was an old man who supposed
That the street door was partially closed;
But some very large rats
Ate his coats and his hats,
While that futile old gentleman dozed.

—Edward Lear

LIMITED POINT OF VIEW A story is written from a **limited point of view** if everything is seen through the eyes of a single character. The short story "Humans Are Different," in Unit 5, is written from a limited point of view—that of a robot who studies humans.

LIST OF WORKS CITED A **list of works cited** is a bibliography that lists works used or referred to by an author. A standard feature of a research paper, the list of works cited appears at the end of the paper and is arranged in alphabetical order. See *bibliography*.

LITERARY WRITING See *aim.*

LYRIC POEM A **lyric poem** is a verse that tells the emotions of a speaker and does not tell a story. Lyric poems are often contrasted with narrative poems, which have telling a story as their main purpose. Examples of lyric poems in this text include "The First Book," by Rita Dove, in Unit 1; Wallace Stevens's "A Rabbit as King of the Ghosts," in Unit 2; and William Butler Yeats's "The Stolen Child," in Unit 9.

MAIN CHARACTER A **main character** is the most important figure in a literary work. See *character.*

MAJOR CHARACTER A **major character** is one who plays an important role in a literary work. See *character.*

METAPHOR A **metaphor** is a figure of speech in which one thing is spoken or written about as if it were another. This figure of speech invites the reader to make a comparison between the two things. Eve Merriam's poem "How to Eat a Poem," in Unit 1, describes a poem as if it were a fruit. A metaphor works because the things to be compared have one or more qualities in common. In Merriam's poem, for example, both a poem and a fruit are the result of someone's hard work and cultivation. Both can also bring pleasure to others.

METER The **meter** of a poem is its overall rhythm, or pattern of beats. In the following lines from Yeats's "The Stolen Child," in Unit 9, every other syllable has a strong stress:

 ˘ / ˘ / ˘ / ˘
Where dips the rocky highland

An **iamb** is a weakly stressed syllable followed by a strongly stressed syllable. A **trochee** is a strongly stressed syllable followed by a weakly stressed syllable. An **anapest** is two weakly stressed syllables followed by one strongly stressed syllable. A **dactyl** is a strongly stressed syllable followed by two weakly stressed syllables. See *stress.*

MOOD **Mood,** or **atmosphere,** is the emotion created in the reader by a piece of writing. A writer creates a mood by using concrete details. Notice the uneasy, frightened mood created in the first stanza of "The City is So Big," in Unit 2:

The city is so big,
Its bridges quake with fear
I know, I have seen at night

MOTIF A **motif** is anything that appears repeatedly in one or more works of literature, art, or music. In the novel *Trout Fishing in America,* from which the selection in Unit 2 was taken, the search for a stream full of trout is a recurring motif.

MOTIVATION A **motivation** is a force that moves a character to think, feel, or behave in a certain way.

MOTIVE A **motive** is a reason for acting in a certain way. For example, in "The Story-Teller," in Unit 1, the bachelor's motives for telling the children a story are to quiet them down and to show the aunt something about good storytelling.

MYTH A **myth** is a story that explains the beginnings of things in the natural world. These natural objects or events are explained as the result of the action of some supernatural force or being. "Why the Sky Is Far Away from the Earth," in Unit 7, explains why people can no longer touch the sky. "Why the Frog Croaks," in Unit 7, explains how the frog's voice became hoarse .

NARRATION **Narration** is writing that tells a story. The story is made up of occurrences, or events.

NARRATIVE POEM A **narrative poem** is a verse that tells a story. "The Pied Piper of Hamelin," in Unit 9, is an example of a narrative poem. See *ballad.*

NARRATOR A **narrator** is a person or character who tells a story. Works of fiction almost always have a narrator. The narrator in a work of fiction may be a major or minor character or simply someone who witnessed or heard about the events being related. In Sandra Cisneros's "Bums in the Attic," in Unit 2, the narrator is the main character. In Saki's short story "The Story-Teller," in Unit 1, the narrator is not a character but an omniscient, or all-knowing, observer, who knows everything about the characters and events that take place in the story. See *point of view.*

NONFICTION **Nonfiction** is writing about real people, places, things, and events. Essays, autobiographies, biographies, and news stories are all types of nonfiction. See *prose.*

NONSENSE VERSE **Nonsense verse** is light verse with parts that are meant to be silly, contradictory, or meaningless. The following lines by Lewis Carroll are an example of nonsense verse:

They roused him with muffins—
They roused him with ice—
They roused him with mustard and cress—
They roused him with jam and judicious
  advice—
They set him conundrums to guess.

See *light verse.*

NOVEL A **novel** is a long work of prose fiction. Often novels have involved plots; many characters, both major and minor; and numerous settings. H. G. Wells's novel *The War of the Worlds* appears in Unit 12.

OMNISCIENT POINT OF VIEW A story is written from an **omniscient point of view** if the narrator, or storyteller, knows everything and can see into the minds of all the characters. Edward Hoch's "Zoo," in Unit 5, is written from an omniscient point of view. See *point of view.*

ONOMATOPOEIA (än´ō mat´ō pē´ ə) **Onomatopoeia** is the use of words or phrases like *meow* or *beep* that sound like what they name.

ORAL TRADITION An **oral tradition** is works, ideas, or customs that are passed by word of mouth from generation to generation. Works found in the oral traditions of peoples around the world include folk tales, fables, fairy tales, tall tales, nursery rhymes, proverbs, legends, myths, parables, riddles, charms, spells, and ballads. Mesopotamian, Egyptian, Indian, Chinese, Japanese, and African myths, legends, and folk tales in Units 6 and 7 are examples of works from the oral tradition.

OXYMORON An **oxymoron** is a statement that contradicts itself, such as *bittersweet.*

PARABLE A **parable** is a story told to communicate a moral.

PARADOX A **paradox** is an apparent contradiction.

PARALLELISM **Parallelism** is the expression of similar ideas in a similar way. Eve Merriam uses parallelism in the closing lines of her poem "How to Eat a Poem," in Unit 1. Each line is made up of the conjunction *or* followed by a noun.

PARAPHRASE A **paraphrase** is a rewriting of a passage in different words. Consider the following example:

> The Hindus worship a number of deities, but all are viewed as manifestations of the one deity named Brahma.

Paraphrase:

> The many gods of the Hindu religion are considered aspects of one god called Brahma.

See *summary.*

PARODY A **parody** is a humorous imitation of a literary work.

PENTAMETER In poetry, a **pentameter** line is one that contains five feet. The following line, which describes the beautiful Helen of Troy, is an example of iambic pentameter:

> ˘ / ˘ / ˘ / ˘ / ˘ /
> Is this | the face | that launched | a thou | sand ships?
> —Christopher Marlowe

See *foot.*

PERIODICAL A **periodical** is a newspaper, magazine, or newsletter that is published regularly (once a month, for example).

PERSONAL ESSAY A **personal essay** is a short nonfiction work on a single topic related to the life of the writer. A personal essay is written from the author's point of view, using the pronouns *I* and *me.* See *essay.*

PERSONIFICATION **Personification** is a figure of speech in which something not human is described as if it were human. Wallace Stevens personifies a rabbit in his poem "A Rabbit as King of the Ghosts." He describes the rabbit as if it had the power to think as humans do.

PERSUASIVE WRITING See *aim.*

PLAGIARISM **Plagiarism** is the act of presenting someone else's work as if it were your own. To avoid plagiarism, always give credit to a source from which you have taken information. In addition, use quotation marks around material picked up word for word from a source.

PLOT A **plot** is a series of events related to a central conflict, or struggle. A plot usually involves the introduction of a conflict, its development, and its eventual resolution. The following terms are used to describe the parts of a plot:

- The **exposition**, or **introduction**, sets the tone or mood, introduces the characters and the setting, and provides necessary background information.
- The **inciting incident** is the event that introduces the central conflict.
- The **climax** is the high point of interest or suspense in the plot.
- The **crisis**, or **turning point**, often the same event as the climax, is the point in the plot where something happens to decide the future course of events and the eventual working out of the conflict.
- The **resolution** is the point at which the central conflict is ended, or resolved.

- The **dénouement** is any material that follows the resolution and that ties up loose ends.

Some plots do not contain all of these parts. See *conflict*.

POETRY **Poetry** is language used in special ways so that its sound reflects its meaning more powerfully than in ordinary speech and writing. Many of the poems that you will read are lyric poems. A lyric poem is a verse that reveals a speaker's feelings in a musical way. William Butler Yeats's "The Song of Wandering Aengus," in Unit 2, and Countee Cullen's "If You Should Go," in Unit 3, are examples of lyric poems.

A narrative poem is one that tells a story. Robert Browning's, "The Pied Piper of Hamelin," in Unit 9, is an example.

POINT OF VIEW **Point of view** is the vantage point from which a story is told. If a story is told from the first-person point of view, the narrator uses the pronouns *I* and *we* and is a part of or a witness to the action. *The War of the Worlds*, by H. G. Wells, is told from the first-person point of view:

> In spite of all that has happened since, I shall remember that vigil very distinctly: the black and silent observatory; the shadowed lantern throwing a feeble glow upon the floor in the corner, the steady ticking of the clockwork of the telescope.

When a story is told from a third-person point of view, the narrator is outside the action; uses words such as *he, she, it,* and *they;* and avoids the use of *I* and *we*. Ray Bradbury's *Farhenheit 451,* excerpted in Unit 1, is told from the third-person point of view:

> With his symbolic helmet numbered 451 on his stolid head, and his eyes all orange flame with the thought of what came next, he flicked the igniter and the house jumped up in a gorging fire that buried the evening sky red and yellow and black. He strode in a swarm of fireflies.

PROSE **Prose** is the word used to describe all writing that is not drama or poetry. Prose includes fiction and nonfiction. Types of prose writing include novels, short stories, essays, and news stories. Most biographies, autobiographies, and letters are written in prose. See *fiction*.

PROTAGONIST A **protagonist** is the main character in a story. The protagonist faces a struggle or conflict. The protagonist in "The Epic of Gilgamesh" is Gilgamesh, King of Uruk. He struggles against many opponents and to find everlasting life.

PROVERB A **proverb,** or **adage,** is a traditional saying. Examples of proverbs include "Beauty is only skin deep" and "You can lead a horse to water, but you can't make it drink." Another word for *proverb* is *aphorism.*

PSEUDONYM (so͞o´də nim´) A **pseudonym** is a name used by a writer instead of his or her real name. O. Henry is the pseudonym of William Sydney Porter. Paul Annixter is the pseudonym of Howard Sturtzel.

PUN A **pun** is a play on words that makes use of a double meaning.

PURPOSE See *aim.*

QUATRAIN See *stanza.*

RAP A **rap** is an improvised rhymed verse that is chanted or sung, often to music.

REALISM **Realism** is the attempt to present in art or literature an accurate picture of reality.

REFRAIN A **refrain** is one or more lines repeated in a poem or song. In Alice Walker's poem "For My Sister Molly Who in the Fifties," in Unit 3, the title of the poem is also a refrain that appears several times throughout the poem.

REPETITION **Repetition** is the use, again, of a sound, word, or group of words. Norman Russell uses repetition in his poem "My Father's Hands Held Mine," in Unit 3. He repeats the word *hands* throughout the poem.

RESOLUTION The **resolution** is the point in a poem, story, or play in which the central conflict, or struggle, is ended. In "How the Common Man Married the Princess," in Unit 7, the resolution occurs when Malu solves the king's riddle and wins his respect, and the king decides that Malu can marry his daughter. See *plot*.

REVIEW A **review** is a piece of writing that describes and judges a work of art, a performance, or a literary work.

RHYME **Rhyme** is the repetition of sounds at the ends of words. Notice the rhyming words that end the first and third lines and the second and fourth line in William Butler Yeats's "The Stolen Child," in Unit 9:

Where dips the rocky highland
of Sleuth Wood in the lake,
There lies a leafy island
Where flapping herons wake.

RHYTHM **Rhythm** is the pattern of beats in a line of poetry or prose. See *meter* and *stress.*

RIDDLE A **riddle** is a word game in which something is described in an unusual way and the reader or listener must guess what that something is. Here is a riddle:

This man is my father, but I am not his son. Who am I?

Answer: his daughter

SATIRE **Satire** is humorous writing that points out errors or failings in people, things, or ideas. John Hall Wheelock's poem "Earth," in Unit 5, satirizes the idea that warfare and destructive powers are a mark of an intelligent civilization.

SCENE A **scene** is a short section of a literary work, one that happens in a single place and time. Act I of *The Diary of Anne Frank,* in Unit 10, consists of five scenes. All the scenes take place in the Franks' hiding place in Amsterdam, Holland.

SCIENCE FICTION **Science fiction** is imaginative literature based on scientific principles, discoveries, or laws. It is similar to fantasy in that it deals with imaginary worlds, but differs from fantasy in having a scientific basis. Often science fiction deals with the future, the distant past, or with worlds other than our own. Science fiction stories often take place on distant planets, in parallel universes, or in worlds beneath the ground or the sea. An example of science fiction in this text includes Carol Farley's "Lose Now, Pay Later," in Unit 5. See *fantasy.*

SET A **set** is the collection of objects on a stage that create a scene.

SETTING The **setting** of a literary work is the time and place in which it happens. Writers create settings in many different ways. In drama, the setting is usually made plain by the stage set and the costumes. In fiction, setting is most often revealed by means of descriptions of landscape, scenery, buildings, furniture, clothing, the weather, and the season. It can also be revealed by how characters talk and behave. The setting of the *Diary of Anne Frank,* in Unit 10, helps to create a mood, or a particular feeling of tension and anxiety.

The three rooms of the top floor and a small attic space above are exposed to our view . . . . The rooms are sparsely furnished with a few chairs, cots, a table or two. The windows are painted over, or covered with a makeshift blackout curtains . . . . The room on the left is hardly more than a closet . . . . Directly under the room is a small steep stairwell, with steps leading down to a door. This is the only entrance from the building below. When the door is opened we see that is has been concealed on the outer side by a bookcase attached to it.

SIMILE A **simile** is a comparison using *like* or *as.* Pablo Neruda uses a simile in "Ode to My Socks."

I slipped my feet into them as if into jewel
cases

The simile compares the socks to jewels cases.

SLANT RHYME A **slant rhyme,** or **half rhyme,** is one that is almost but not completely exact, as in *step* and *stop* or *mud hut.*

SPEAKER The **speaker** is the voice that speaks, or narrates, a poem. The speaker and the writer of a poem are not necessarily the same person. In Kujo Takeka's poem "I do not consider . . .," the speaker expresses two contradictory feelings:

I do not consider myself worth counting,
but sometimes even for me
heaven and earth are too small.

STAGE A **stage** is an area where a play is performed.

STAGE DIRECTIONS **Stage directions** are notes included in a play to describe how something should look, sound, or be performed. Stage directions describe setting, lighting, music, sound effects, entrances and exits, properties, and the movements of characters. They are usually printed in italics and enclosed in brackets or parentheses. Here is an example of stage directions from the play *The Diary of Anne Frank,* in Unit 10:

> [*She stops as she hears someone coming. They all watch the door tensely.* MR. FRANK *comes quietly in.* ANNE *rushes to him, holding him tight.*]

STANZA A **stanza** is a group of lines in a poem. Stanzas are usually separated by spaces from other groups of lines. A couplet is a two-line stanza. A tercet is a three-line stanza. A quatrain is a four-line stanza. Emily Dickinson's poem "The Brain—is wider than the Sky—," in Unit 9, is divided into four-line stanzas, or quatrains:

> The Brain—is wider than the sky—
> For—put them side by side—
> The one the other will contain
> With ease—and You—beside—

STEREOTYPE A **stereotype** is an unexamined, false idea about a type of person or group of people. The idea that all teenagers love to shop at malls is a stereotype.

STRESS **Stress,** or **accent,** is the amount of emphasis given to a syllable. The pattern of stresses in a poem determines its rhythm. Some syllables are described as being strongly or weakly stressed, and accented or unaccented. When you read a line of poetry, a strongly stressed syllable receives a strong emphasis and a weakly stressed syllable receives a weak one. In the following lines from "The Pied Piper of Hamelin," the strongly stressed syllables are marked with a slash mark (/).

```
/
Rats!
         /          /           /         /
They fought the dogs and killed the cats,
        /        /             /
And bit the babies in the cradles,
        /           /    /           /
And ate the cheeses out of the vats
        /           /               /            /
And licked the soup from the  cooks' own ladles.
```

SUMMARY A **summary** is a rewriting of a passage in different and fewer words. See *paraphrase.*

SUSPENSE **Suspense** is a feeling of anxiousness or curiosity. Writers create suspense by raising questions in the reader's mind and by using details that create strong emotions. In Liam O'Flaherty's "The Sniper," the author builds suspense by causing the reader to wonder at first if the main character will survive and later if the main character will recognize the man he killed.

> He rolled over the roof to a chimney stack in fear, and slowly drew himself up behind it, until his eyes were level with the top of the parapet. There was nothing to be seen—just the dim outline of the opposite housetop against the blue sky. His enemy was under cover.
>
> Just then an armored car came across the bridge and advanced slowly up the street. It stopped on the opposite side of the street, fifty yards ahead. The sniper could hear the dull panting of the motor. His heart beat faster. It was an enemy car. He wanted to fire, but he knew it was useless.

SYMBOL A **symbol** is a thing that stands for or represents both itself and something else. Some traditional symbols include doves for peace; the color green for jealousy; the color purple for royalty; winter, evening, or night for old age; roses for beauty; roads or paths for the journey through life; and owls for wisdom. The books burnt in *Fahrenheit 451,* excerpted in Unit 1, symbolize freedom, knowledge, and creativity.

TAG LINE A **tag line** is a phrase like "she said" used in a story to tell who is speaking. See *dialogue.*

TALL TALE A **tall tale** is a lighthearted or humorous story with many exaggerated elements. There are many tall tales about Paul Bunyan and Pecos Bill.

TERCET See *stanza.*

TETRAMETER See *foot.*

THEME A **theme** is a central idea in a literary work. One theme in Toni Cade Bambara's "The War of the Wall" is that people derive their sense of identity from their communities.

THESIS A **thesis** is a main idea in a work of nonfiction such as an essay. The thesis of Robert Jastrow's essay "The Size of Things," in Unit 11, is that it is very difficult to form a conception of something as small as the atom or something as large as the universe.

THIRD-PERSON POINT OF VIEW In a story told from the **third-person point of view,** the narrator does not take part in the action and tells the story using words such as *he* and *she* and avoiding the use of *I* and *we*. O. Henry's "A Retrieved Reformation, in Unit 8, is written from the third-person point of view. See *point of view.*

TONE **Tone** is a writer or speaker's attitude toward the subject. Joseph Campbell expresses a sense of wonder and appreciation in "Indra and the Carpenter."

TRANSITION A **transition** is a word, phrase, sentence, or paragraph used to connect ideas and to show relationships between them. Here are some common transitions:

TRANSITIONS	
To show chronological order	at, finally, first, next, second, soon, then, third
To show spatial order	above, around, behind, beneath, beside, beyond, next to, on top of, to the left, to the right
To show order of importance	least important, less important, more important, most important
To show cause and effect	as a consequence, as a result, one cause, therefore
To introduce a summary	as a consequence, as a result, finally, in conclusion, in short, in summary, therefore

TROCHEE, TROCHAIC See *meter.*

TURNING POINT See *crisis.*

UNDERSTATEMENT An **understatement** is a statement that treats something important as though it were not important. In "Digging," in Unit 9, the speaker's feelings of love and awe for his father and grandfather are understated in the following lines:

By God, the old man could handle a spade.
Just like his old man.

UNITY **Unity** is the use in a piece of writing of details related to the main idea, or theme. An essay with unity, for example, is one in which all the parts help to support the thesis statement, or main idea. See *essay.*

VERBAL IRONY A statement that says one thing but means the opposite is an example of **verbal irony**. For example, if someone pushes to the front of a line, and someone else says, "What polite behavior," that is an example of verbal irony. See *irony.*

Glossary

OF WORDS FOR EVERYDAY USE

PRONUNCIATION KEY

VOWEL SOUNDS

a	hat	i	sit	o͞o	blue, stew	ə	extra
ā	play	ī	my	oi	boy		under
ä	star	ō	go	ou	wow		civil
e	then	ô	paw, born	u	up		honor
ē	me	o͝o	book, put	ʉ	burn		bogus

CONSONANT SOUNDS

b	but	j	jump	p	pop	*th*	the
ch	watch	k	brick	r	rod	v	valley
d	do	l	lip	s	see	w	work
f	fudge	m	money	sh	she	y	yell
g	go	n	on	t	sit	z	pleasure
h	hot	ŋ	song, sink	th	with		

A

a • brupt • ly (ə brupt´lē) *adv.,* suddenly, unexpectedly

ab • sorb (ab sôrb´) *v.,* soak up; take in

a • byss (ə bis´) *n.,* anything too deep for measurement; ocean depths; bottomless gulf, chasm

a • cute (ə kyo͞ot´) *adj.,* severe; sharp

a • ghast (ə gast´) *adj.,* terrified; horrified

a • lac • ri • ty (ə lak´rə tē) *n.,* eager willingness or readiness

a • ne • mic (ə nē´mik) *adj.,* lacking vitality

a • troc • i • ty (ə träs´ə tē) *n.,* very cruel, evil, or brutal act

a • ver • sion (ə vʉr´zhən) *n.,* definite dislike

ac • quire (ə kwīr´) *v.,* get or gain by one's own effort

ad • dle (ad´'l) *v.,* make muddled or confused

ad • her • ent (ad hir´ənt) *n.,* supporter or follower

ad • ja • cent (ə ja´sənt) *adj.,* near or close; adjoining

aes • the • tic (es thet ´ ik) *adj.,* referring to beauty

af • flu • ence (af´lo͞o əns) *n.,* abundance of riches, wealth

a • gile (aj´əl) *adj.,* quick and easy of movement

al • lude (ə lo͞od´) *v.,* refer in an indirect way

al • lu • sion (ə lo͞o´zhən) *n.,* indirect reference

an • ni • hi • late (ə nī´ə lāt´) *v.,* destroy completely

ap • a • thy (ap´ə thē) *n.,* lack of interest; unconcern

ap • er • ture (ap´ər chər) *n.,* opening; hole; gap

ap • pall • ing (ə pôl´iŋ) *adj.,* causing horror or shock

ap • pro • ba • tion (ap´rə bā shən) *n.,* official approval or sanction

ap • pa • ri • tion (ap´ə rish´ən) *n.,* anything that appears unexpectedly or in an extraordinary way; ghost

ap • praise (ə prāz´) *v.,* judge the quality or worth of

ar • cade (är kād´) *n.,* passageway

ar • tic • u • late (är tik´yo͞o lit) *adj.*, expressing oneself easily and clearly

as • cend (ə send´) *v.*, move upward, rise

as • cer • tain (as´ər tān´) *v.*, find out without doubt

as • cet • ic (ə set´ik) *adj.*, characteristic of anyone who lives with strict self-discipline

as • pect (as´pect') *n.*, view

as • sail (ə sāl´) *v.*, attack with arguments

as • sid • u • ous • ly (ə sij´o͞o əs lē) *adv.*, with constant and careful attention

as • ton • ish • ing (ə stän´ish iŋ) *adj.*, amazing, wonderful

ash • en (ash´ən) *adj.*, made up of ashes

au • da • cious (ô dā´shəs) *adj.*, bold or daring

au • gust (ô gust´) *adj.*, worthy of respect

aus • tere (ô stir´) *adj.*, severe; forbidding

awe (ô) *n.*, feeling of fear and wonder

az • ure (azh´ər) *adj.*, blue colored

B

bab • ble (bab´əl) *v.*, talk foolishly or too much

badg • er (baj´ər) *v.*, annoy; pester

ba • rom • e • ter (bə räm´ət ər) *n.*, instrument that forecasts changes in weather

bar • rage (bə räzh´) *n.*, heavy attack of words

bas • in (bās´ən) *n.*, round, shallow container for holding water

bat • ter • y (bat´ər ē) *n.*, basic unit of military personnel

beck • on (bek´'n) *v.*, call or summon by a silent gesture

be • lea • guer (bē lē´gər) *v.*, beset with difficulties

bel • low (bel´ō) *v.*, utter loudly or powerfully

be • reave (bē rēv´) *v.*, rob, deprive

be • tray (bē trā´) *v.*, disclose secret information

be • wil • der • ment (bē wil´dər mənt) *n.*, condition of being hopelessly confused

bil • low (bil´ō) *v.*, surge; swell or rise like a large wave

binge (binj) *v.*, spree of unrestrained eating

bleak (blēk) *adj.*, not promising or hopeful

blight (blīt) *n.*, plant disease, such as mildew or rust

bou • le • vard (bo͞ol´ə värd´) *n.*, broad, well-made street

bow • er (bou´ər) *n.*, place enclosed by overhanging branches

bra • va • do (brə vä´dō) *n.*, pretended courage or defiant confidence where there really is none

brev • i • ty (brev´ə tē) *n.*, shortness; quality of being concise

broach (brōch) *v.*, bring up; introduce

brook (bro͞ok) *v.*, put up with

buoyant (boi´yənt) *adj.*, having or showing lightness of spirit; cheerfulness

bush • el (bo͞osh´əl) *n.*, unit of measure for grain or fruit

C

ca • jole (kə jōl´) *v.*, coax or persuade with flattery

can • non • ade (kan´ən ād´) *n.*, continuous firing of artillery

ca • pit • u • la • tion (kə pich´yoo lā´shən) *n.*, conditional surrender, act of giving up under prearranged terms

car • di • nal (kärd´'n əl) *adj.*, principal

car • i • ca • ture (kar´i kə chər) *n.*, exaggerated imitation of someone or something used to mock

cav • ern (kav´ərn) *n.*, large cave

ce • les • tial (sə les´chəl) *adj.*, of the finest or highest kind, perfect

chat • ter (chat´ər) *v.*, talk fast

cir • cu • i • tous • ly (sər kyo͞o´ət əs lē) *adv.*, in a roundabout, indirect, or devious manner

cir • cum • spec • tion (sʉr´kəm spek´shən) *n.*, act of carefully considering all the facts before acting

cleft (kleft) *n.*, crack, crevice

clem • en • cy (klem´ən sē) *n.*, forgiveness; leniency

clench (klench) *v.*, grip tightly

co • ed • u • ca • tion • al (kō´ej ə kā´shən əl) *adj.,* having students of both sexes attend classes together

co • her • en • cy (kō hir´ən sē´) *n.,* quality of being logically integrated or consistent

come • ly (kum´lē) *adj.,* attractive

com • mo • tion (kə mō´shən) *n.,* noisy rushing about

com • pressed (kəm prest´) *adj.,* made more compact

com • po • sure (kəm pō´zhər) *n.,* calmness; tranquility

con • cus • sion (kən kush´ən) *n.,* shock from impact

con • demn (kən dem´) *v.,* inflict a penalty on

con • fed • er • ate (kən fed´ər it) *n.,* partner, accomplice

con • fine (kän´ fīn) *n.,* limit or boundary

con• flu • ence (kän´flo͞o əns) *n.,* place where two things join

con • found (kən found´) *v.,* confuse; bewilder

con • ges • ted (kən jest´id) *adj.,* clogged; overcrowded

con • i • cal (kän´i kəl) *adj.,* resembling or shaped like a cone

con • sent (kən sent´) *v.,* give permission or approval

con • spic • u • ous (kən spik´ yo͞o əs) *adj.,* obvious; attracting attention by being unusual or unexpected

con • spic • u • ous • ly (kən spik´yo͞o əs lē) *adv.,* unusually strikingly; obviously

con • stel • la • tion (kän´stə lā´shən) *n.,* cluster; gathering

con • ster • na • tion (kän´ster na´shən) *n.,* great fear or shock

con • sump • tion (kən sump´shən) *n.,* act of eating and drinking

con • triv • ance (kən trī´vəns) *n.,* something ingeniously constructed; invention

con • vey (kən vā´) *v.,* make known, communicate

con • vic • tion (kən vik´shən) *n.,* strong and firm belief

con • vul • sion (kən vul´shən) *n.,* violent, involuntary spasm of the muscles

con • vul • sive (kən vul´siv) *adj.,* having the nature of involuntary spasms

con • clu • sive • ly (kən klo͞o´siv lē) *adv.,* without a doubt, decisively

co • pi • ous • ly (kō´pē əs lē) *adv.,* with many words; profusely

copse (käps) *n.,* thicket of small trees or shrubs

cor • rob • o • rate (kə räb´ə rāt´) *v.,* confirm, bolster, support

cos • mic (käz´mik) *adj.,* relating to the universe as a whole

coun • sel (koun´səl) *n.,* discussion and deliberation

coun • te • nance (koun´tə nəns) *n.,* face

coun • ter • vail • ing (kount´ər vāl´iŋ) *adj.,* compensating; counter-acting

cour • ti • er (kôrt´e ər) *n.,* attendant at a royal court

court • ship (kôrt´ship) *n.,* process of attempting to win someone's love

cov • er • let (kuv´ər lit) *n.,* bedspread

cov • et (kuv´it) *v.,* long for with envy

cow • er (kou´ər) *v.,* crouch or huddle, as from fear

cred • i • ble (kred´ə bəl) *adj.,* believeable

cro • ny (krō´nē) *n.,* close companion

crotch • et • y (kräch´it ē) *adj.,* grouchy; stubborn

crude (kro͞od) *adj.* primitive; not carefully made or done

cu • bi • cle (kyo͞o´ bi kəl) *n.,* small compartment

cul • mi •nate (kul´mə nāt´) *v.,* reach the highest point or climax

cul • vert (kul´vərt) *n.,* drain that passes under a road

cum • ber (kum´bər) *v.,* burden in a troublesome way

cum • ber • some (kum´bər səm) *adj.*, hard to handle because of size or weight; clumsy; burdensome

cun •ning (kun´iŋ) *adj.*, clever; sly; crafty

cut • lass (kut´ləs) *n.*, short, thick, curving sword with a single cutting edge

cy • ni • cal (sin´i kəl) *adj.*, sarcastic; sneering

D

dark • ling (därk´liŋ) *adj.*, dark; dim

daunt (dônt) *v.*, make afraid; discourage

dec • a • dence (dek´ə dəns) *n.*, process, condition, or period of moral and cultural decline

de • cap • i • tate (dē kap´ə tāt) *v.*, behead

de • cor • um (di kôr´əm) *n.*, propriety and good taste in behavior or appearance

de • duce (de do͞os´) *v.*, conclude from known facts or general principles

de • funct (dē fuŋkt´) *adj.*, out of existence

de • grade (dē grād´) *v.*, bring into dishonor or contempt; lower in rank or status

de • i • ty (dē´ə tē) *n.*, god or goddess

de • lus • ive (di lo͞os´iv) *adj.*, misleading

de • ment • ed (dē ment´id) *adj.*, insane; mentally deranged

de • mur (dē mʉr´) *v.*, hesitate because of doubts

de • scend • ant (dē sen´dənt) *n.*, immediate or remote offspring of a person

de • spond • ent (di spän´dənt) *adj.*, filled with loss of hope or courage

de • tail (dē tāl´) *v.*, choose for a particular task

de • throne • ment (dē thrōn´mənt) *n.*, act of ousting from any high position

de • vise (di vīz´) *v.*, create by thinking; plan

dex • ter • ous (deks´tər əs) *adj.*, having or showing skillful use of the hands or body

di • a • lect (dī ə lekt´) *n.*, differing form of speech within the broader framework of a single language

dif • fi • dence (dif´ə dəns) *n.*, shyness, lack of confidence in oneself

dif • fuse (di fyo͞os´) *adj.*, not concentrated, spread out

di • lated (dī lāt´id) *adj.*, enlarged or widened

din (din) *n.*, loud, continuous noise or confused clamor

din • gy (din´je) *adj.*, not bright or clean; shabby

disc (disk) *n.*, circle-shaped object

dis • crim • i • nat • ing (dis krim´ə nāt´iŋ) *adj.*, making fine distinctions; distinguishing

dis • il • lu • sion (dis´i lo͞o´zhen) *v.*, disappointed

dis • patch (di spach´) *v.*, send off promptly

dis • po • si • tion (dis'pə zish´ən) *n.*, temperament; general frame of mind

dis • pu • ta • tious (dis'pyo͞o tā´shəs) *adj.*, fond of arguing

dis • sem • i • nate (di sem´ə nāt´) *v.*, scatter far and wide, spread abroad

dis • sen • tient (di sen´shent) *adj.*, going against a majority opinion

dis • suade (di swād´) *v.*, persuade not to do something

dis • trib • u • tive (di strib´yo͞o tiv) *adj.*, administered; furnished

dit • ty (dit´ē) *n.*, short, simple song

di • vert (dī vʉrt') *v.*, turn aside from a course or direction

dom • i • nate (däm´ə nāt´) *v.*, rule or control by superior power or influence

draught (draft) *n.*, drink

drawl (drôl) *v.*, speak in a slow way, drawing out the syllables

dri • ly (drī´lē) *adv.*, without emotion, in a matter-of-fact way

driv • el (driv´əl) *v.*, drool

drought (drout) *n.*, period of dry weather; lack of rain

du • bi • ous • ly (do͞o bē äs´lē) *adv.*, outcome undecided or hanging in the balance

dwell (dwel) *v.*, live; make one's home

E

ebb (eb) *v.*, flow back; recede; weaken; decline

ed • dy (ed´ē) *n.*, whirlwind or whirlpool

ee • ri • ly (ir´ē lē) *adv.*, mysteriously, strangely

ef • fi • ca • cious (ef´i kā shəs) *adj.*, effective

el • e • men• tal (el´ə ment´'l) *adj.*, most basic

el • o • quence (el´ə kwəns) *n.*, speech that is powerful, vivid, and persuasive

e • merge (ē murj´) *v.*, come forth; develop

em • i • grate (em´i grāt) *v.*, leave one country to live in another

em • i • nent (em´ə nənt) *adj.*, renowned; distinguished

e • mit (ē mit´) *v.*, send out; give forth

em • pha • sis (em´fə sis) *n.*, special attention given to something

em • u • late (em´yo͞o lāt´) *v.*, imitate, copy

en • deav • or (en dev´ər) *n.*, earnest attempt or effort; strive

en • deav • or (en dev´ər) *v.*, attempt; try

en • gross (en grōs´) *v.*, take entire attention of, occupy wholly

e • nig • ma (i nig´mə) *n.*, perplexing, baffling person or matter

en • vi • ous (en´ve əs) *adj.*, showing or feeling discontent and ill will because of another's advantages or possessions

en • voy (än´voi´) *n.*, messenger

en • vy (en´vē) *n.*, ill will or discontent because of another's advantage

es • tu • ar • y (es´tyo͞o er ē) *n.*, inlet of the sea

e • ter • ni • ty (ē tur´nə tē) *n.*, time without beginning or end

e • vince (ē vins´) *v.*, show plainly

ex • alt (eg zôlt´) *v.*, praise; glorify; worship

ex • empt (eg zempt´) *v.*, not subject to a situation or rule that applies to others

ex • hort (eg zôrt´) *v.*, urge earnestly by advice or warning

ex • or • bi • tant (eg zor´bi tənt) *adj.*, excessive, extravagant

ex • panse (ek spans´) *n.*, large, open area

ex • pe • di • ent (ek spē´dē ənt) *adj.*, something useful for attaining a particular result

ex • pend (ek spend´) *v.*, consume by using

ex • pos • tu • late (eks päs´chə lāt´) *v.*, demand vehemently

ex • tent (ek stent´) *n.*, range or limit; scope

ex • trav • a • gant (ek strav´ə gənt) *adj.*, excessive or unrestrained; beyond reasonable limits

ex • u • ber • ance (eg zo͞o´bər əns) *n.*, great abundance; luxuriance

ex • ul • ta • tion (eg´zul tā´shən) *n.*, rejoicing; jubilation

ex • ert (eg zurt´) *v.*, apply (oneself) with great energy or straining effort

F

fa • çade (fə säd´) *n.*, front

fa • ce • tious (fə sē shəs) *adj.*, joking, inappropriate

fain (fān) *adj.*, glad

fal • ter • ing • ly (fôl´tər iŋ lē) *adv.*, unsteadily; uncertainly; haltingly

fa • nat • ic (fə nat´ik) *n.*, person who holds extreme and unreasonable views; zealot

fan • cy (fan´sē) *n.*, imagination

fa • tal • ist (fat´'l ist) *n.*, one who believes all events are determined by fate and are therefore inevitable

fa • tigue (fə tēg´) *n.*, extreme weariness or exhaustion

fat • u • ous • ly (fach´o͞o əs lē) *adv.*, foolishly; stupidly

feign (fān) *v.*, make a false show of, imitate, simulate

fe • roc • i • ty (fə räs´ə tē) *n.*, quality of being fierce or savage

fes • ter (fes´tər) *v.*, form pus, become infected; grow bitter; decay

fes • toon (fes to͞on´) *n.*, wreath or garland of flowers

fet • ish (fet´ish) *adj.*, having devotion that is too strong

flag • on (flag´ən) *n.,* container for liquids with a handle, narrow neck, spout, and sometimes a lid

flax • en (flak´sən) *adj.,* pale yellow; straw-colored

fluc • tu • a • tion (fluc´cho͞o ā shən) *n.,* continual, irregular changes

flue (flo͞o) *n.,* pipe, tube, or shaft

flu • o • res • cent (flo͞o´ə res´ənt) *adj.,* producing light when acted on by radiation

ford (fôrd) *v.,* cross at a shallow point in a river or stream

fore • thought (fôr´thôt´) *n.,* thinking or planning beforehand

for • lorn (fôr lôrn´) *adj.,* abandoned; in pitiful condition

for • mi • da • ble (fôr´mə də bəl) *adj.,* causing fear or dread

for • mu • late (fôr´myo͞o lāt´) *v.,* work out in one's mind; develop

frol • ic (fräl´ik) *n.,* lively party or game

frond (fränd) *n.,* leaf of a fern or palm

froth (frôth) *n.,* foam

fu • gi • tive (fyo͞o´ji tiv) *adj.,* having fled due to danger or repression

func • tion • al (fuŋk´ shə nəl) *adj.,* able to perform a task well enough to serve its purpose

fur • tive (fʉr´tiv) *adj.,* done or acting in a stealthy manner

G

gal • va • nize (gal´və nīz´) *v.,* rouse or stir as if by electric shock

gam • bol (gam´bəl) *v.,* jump and skip about in play, frolic

gar • ment (gär´mənt) *n.,* any article of clothing

gaud • y (gôd´ē) *adj.,* bright and showy, but lacking in good taste

gen • i • al • ly (jēn´yəl ē) *adv.,* cheerfully

ges • tic • u • late (jes tik´yo͞o lāt´) *v.* make movements, as with hands or arms

ges • tic • u • la • tion (jes tik´ yo͞o lā´shən) *n.,* energetic movement

ges • ture (jes´chər) *v.,* express or emphasize ideas and emotions with physical movement

gib • ber (jib´ər) *v.,* speak or utter incoherently

glim • mer • ing • ly (glim´ər ing lē) *adv.,* faintly, dimly

gorge (gôrj´) *v.,* swallow greedily

gout (gout) *n.,* large splash or clot

grade (grād) *n.,* degree of rise or descent of a sloping surface

gra • di • ent (grā´dē ənt) *n.,* slope of a road or railway

gran • a • ry (gran´ə rē) *n.,* building for storing grain

gran • di • ose (gran´dē ōs´) *adj.,* magnificent; grand

grat • i • tude (grat´i to͞od´) *n.,* feeling of appreciation; thankfulness

grave (grāv) *adj.,* somber; serious

grave • ly (grāv lē) *adj.,* seriously, solemnly; with dignity

gul • li • ble (gul´ə bəl) *adj.,* easily cheated or tricked

H

hav • oc (hav´ək) *n.,* great destruction and devastation

hear • say (hir´sā´) *n.,* rumor; gossip

heft (heft) *v.,* lift; try to determine the weight of by lifting

hem (hem) *v.,* confine; surround

het • er • o • ge • ne • ous (het´ər ō´jē´nē əs) *adj.,* different; dissimilar

hind • drance (hin´drəns) *n.,* obstacle

hoard (hôrd) *v.,* hide or keep away

hoist (hoist) *v.,* raise aloft

hor • rid (hôr´id) *adj.,* very bad, ugly, unpleasant

hue (hyo͞o) *n.,* color

hunch (hunch) *v.,* push, shove

hur • tle (hʉrt´'l) *v.,* move swiftly or with great force

hyp • no • tize (hip´nə tīz´) *v.,* put into a trance

hys • ter • i • a (hi ster´ē ə) *n.*, outbreak of wild, uncontrolled excitement or feeling

hys • ter • i • cal (hi ster´i kəl) *adj.*, wild, uncontrolled

I

il • lu • mi • na • tion (i lo͞o´mə nā´shən) *n.*, highest spiritual understanding

im • part (im pärt´) *v.*, give

im • pas • sa • ble (im pas´ə bəl) *adj.*, cannot be crossed or traveled over

im • pede (im pēd´) *v.*, obstruct; delay

im • ped • i • ment (im ped´ə mənt) *n.*, something that delays or obstructs

im • per • cep • ti • bly (im´pər sep´tə bəl lē) *adv.*, unnoticeably

im • pe • tus (im´pə təs) *n.*, force with which a body moves against resistence

im • plore (im plôr´) *v.*, ask or beg earnestly for

im • por • tu • ni • ty (im´pôr to͞on´ i tē) *n.*, persistent urgent demands

im • po • tent (im´pə tənt) *adj.*, ineffective; powerless

im • pro • vise (im´prə viz´) *v.*, make with the materials at hand, usually to fill an unforeseen need

im • pulse (im´puls´) *n.*, sudden force or action

im • pu • ni • ty (im pyo͞o´ni tē) *n.*, freedom from punishment or penalty

in • ad • e • qua • cy (in ad´i kwə sē) *n.*, state or quality of being not equal to what is required

in • ane (in ān´) *adj.*, lacking sense or meaning

in • ar • tic • u • late • ly (in´är tik´yo͞o lit lē) *adv.*, not understandably; unintelligibly

in • au • di • bly (in ôd´ ə blē) *adj.*, not able to be heard

in • ca • pac • i • ty (in´kə pas´i tē) *n.*, lack of ability or power

in • ces • sant • ly (in ses´ənt lē) *adv.*, continually; constantly

in • con • clu • sive (in´kən klo͞o siv) *adj.*, not leading to a definite result

in • cred • u • lous (in krej´o͞o ləs) *adj.*, skeptical, unwilling or unable to believe

in • cur (in kur´) *v.*, become subject to through one's own actions

in • dict • ment (in dīt ´ mənt) *n.*, accusation of wrongdoing, criminal charge

in • dig • nant • ly (in dig´nənt lē) *adv.*, angrily; scornfully

in • dis • crim • i • nate • ly (in´di skrim´i nit lē) *adv.*, randomly; not carefully chosen

in • ev • i • ta • ble (in´ev´i tə bəl) *adj.*, certain to happen

in • ex • or • a • ble (in eks´ə rə bəl) *adj.*, that cannot be altered or checked

in • fi • nite (in´fə nit) *adj.*, endless

in • fi • nite • ly (in´fə nit lē) *adv.*, beyond measure or comprehension

in • sol • u • ble (in säl´yo͞o bəl) *adj.*, that cannot be dissolved

in • stan • ta • ne • ous (in´stən tā´nē əs) *adj.*, done, made, or happening in an instant

in • tact (in takt´) *adj.*, whole and uninjured

in • ter • me • di • a • tion (in´tər mē´dē ā´shən) *n.*, happening or means in between

in • ter • mi • na • ble (in tʉr´ mi nə bəl) *adj.*, without end

in • ter • mit • tent (in´tər mit´'nt) *adj.*, periodic

in • ter • mit • tent • ly (in´tər mit´'nt lē) *adv.*, periodically

in • tol • er • a • ble (in täl´ər ə bəl) *adj.*, unbearable, too severe to be endured

in • tol • er • a • bly (in täl´ər ə blē) *adv.*, unbearably; painfully

in • tri • cate (in´tri kit) *adj.*, full of elaborate detail

in • val • id (in´və lid) *n.*, weak, sickly person

in • vul • ner • a • ble (in vul´nər ə bəl) *adj.*, that cannot be wounded or injured

ir • ra • tion • al (ir rash´ə nəl) *adj.*, lacking the power to reason; absurd

ir • rev • o • ca • bly (ir rev´ə kə blē) *adv.*, in a way that cannot be changed or undone

i • so • la • tion (ī´so la´shən) *n.,* aloneness, solitude

J

jad • ed (jād´id) *adj.,* tired; worn out

jos • tling (jäs´liŋ) *adj.,* roughly pushing

K

ki • net • ic (ki net´ik) *adj.,* energetic or dynamic

L

lan • guid (laŋ´gwid) *adj.,* weak; without interest

lap • is (lā´pis) *n.,* blue, semiprecious stone

lapse (laps) *n.,* slipping into a worse condition

lass (las) *n.,* young woman; girl

lat • er • al • ly (lat´ər əl lē) *adv.,* sideways

lav • ish (lav´ish) *v.,* give or spend generously or liberally

lei • sure (lē´zhər) *n.,* free, unoccupied time

le • thar • gic (li thär´jik) *adj.,* having extreme apathy or great lack of energy

le • vi • a • than (lə vī´ə thən) *n.,* anything huge or very powerful

liq • ue • fac • tion (lik´wi fak´shən) *n.,* changing into liquid

liv • id (liv´id) *adj.,* red

loathe (lōth) *v.,* feel intense dislike, disgust, or hatred for

loi • ter (loit´ər) *v.,* spend time idly; linger

low (lō) *v.,* moo; make the sound of a cow

lu • bri • cat • ed (lo͞o´bri kāt´id) *adj.,* smooth or slippery

lu • mi • nous (lo͞o´mə nəs) *adj.,* giving off light; shining; bright; clear, readily understood

lu • rid (lo͞or´id) *adj.,* vivid in a harsh way; shocking; startling, sensational

M

mag • ni• tude (mag´nə to͞od´) *n.,* greatness of extent

mal • ice (mal´is) *n.,* active ill will; spite

mam • moth (mam´əth) *adj.,* very big

man • i • fest (man´ə fest´) *adj.,* clear; obvious

man • i • fes • ta • tion (man´ə fes tā´shən) *n.,* example, instance

ma • son • ry (mā´sən rē) *n.,* something built by a person using stone, brick, etc.

mea • ger (mē´gər) *adj.,* of poor quality or small amount

me • di • ate (mē´dē āt') *v.,* be the medium for bring about an agreement, result, or solution between disputing parties

med • i • tate (med´ə tāt´) *v.,* think deeply

me • nag • er • ie (mə naj´ər ə) *n.,* collection of wild animals caged for exhibition

mer • cu • ri • al (mər kyo͞or´ē əl) *adj.,* volatile; frequently and unexpectedly changing

met • a • mor • phose (met´ə môr´ fōs´) *v.,* change

me • thod • i • cal • ly (mə thäd´i kəl lē) *adv.,* orderly; systematically

me • tic • u • lous (mə tik´yo͞o ləs) *adj.,* extremely careful about details

met • tle (met´'l) *n.,* quality of character

mim • ic (mim´ik) *v.,* imitate in speech or action

mi • nute (mī no͞ot´) *adj.,* very small, tiny

mirth (murth) *n.,* joyfulness, merriment

mis • sion (mish´ən) *n.,* belief or purpose

mod • u • la • tion (mäj´ə lā shən) *n.,* variation in stress or pitch

mor • bid • i • ty (môr bid´ə tē) *n.,* something relating to death or disease

mul • ti • tu • di • nous (mul´tə to͞od´'n əs) *adj.,* very great, made up of many parts

N

ne • go • ti • ate (ni gō´shē āt') *v.,* succeed in crossing, surmounting or moving through

net • work (net´wurk´) *n.,* system, as of roads, rails, canals

neu • tral • ize (no͞o´trə liz´) *v.,* make ineffective

noc • tur • nal (näk tʉr´nəl) *adj.,* functioning or active during the night

noi • some (noi´səm) *adj.,* harmful to health

O

o • bese (ō bēs´) *adj.,* very fat

ob • lique • ly (ə blēk´ lē) *adv.,* with a change of direction of approximately 45 degrees

ob • liv • i • ous (ə bliv´ē əs) *adj.,* unmindful; unaware

ob • se • qui • ous (əb sē´kwē əs) *adj.,* showing too great a willingness to serve or obey

ode (ōd) *n.,* poem or song

of • fi • ci • ate (ə fish´ē āt´) *v.,* perform function of a priest or minister at a religious ceremony

om • i • nous (äm´ə nəs) *adj.,* threatening; serving as a bad sign or omen

on • slaught (än´slôt´) *n.,* violent, intense attack

o • paque (ō pāk´) *adj.,* not letting light through; obscuring

op • press (ə pres´) *v.,* keep down by cruel or unjust use or power

or • dain (ôr dān´) *v.,* command; decree

or • na • men • tal (ôr´nə ment´'l) *adj.,* serving as an ornament; decorative

os • cil • late (äs´ə lāt´) *v.,* swing or move regularly back and forth

os • ten • ta • tious • ly (äs´tən tā´shəs lē) *adv.,* with a showy display; obviously proud or boastful

oust (oust) *v.,* force or drive out

P

pal • pa • ble (pal´pə bəl) *adj.,* easily perceived; that can be felt

pan • to • mime (pan´tə mīm´) *n.,* dramatic presentation given without words, using only action and gestures

par • a • dox • i • cal (par´ə daks´i kəl) *adj.,* seemingly full of contradictions

par • a • pet (par´ə pet´) *n.,* low wall or railing

par • boil (pär´boil) *adj.,* partly cooked in a boiling liquid

parch (pärch) *v.,* make very thirsty or dry

par • o • dy (par´ə dē) *n.,* imitation, often humorous

par • ox • ysm (par´əks iz´əm) *n.,* sudden attack, convulsion, outburst or fit

pat • ent (pat´nt) *adj.* obvious; plain; evident

pa • tron • ize (pā´trən īz´) *v.,* act kind or helpful, but in a snobbish way

paunch (pônch) *n.,* large, protruding belly; potbelly

pe • des • tri • an (pi des´trēən) *n.,* walker, one who moves on foot

per • il (per´əl) *n.,* danger, exposure to harm

per • pet • u • al (pər pech´o͞o əl) *adj.,* continual

per • pet • u •ate (pər pech´ o͞o āt') *v.,* cause to continue or be remembered

per • plex (pər pleks´) *v.,* confuse, puzzle

per • se • cu • tion (pʉr´si kyo͞o´shən) *n.,* affliction or constant harassing

per • sist • ent (pər sist´ənt) *adj.,* continuing in the face of opposition; unrelenting

pes • ti • lent (pes´tə lənt) *adj.,* annoying; troublesome

phan • tasm (fan´taz´əm) *n.,* ghost; specter

phe • nom • e • non (fə näm´ ə nən´) *n.,* extremely unusual or extraordinary thing or occurrence

pho • net • i • cal • ly (fō net´ik lē) *adv.,* with respect to the spoken pronunciation of words

phys • i • o • log • i • cal (fiz´ē ō läj´i kəl) *adj.,* relating to the workings of the body

pier (pir) *n.,* heavy structure supporting a bridge

pi • e • ty (pī´ə tē) *n.,* devotion to religious duties and practices

pla • card (plak´ärd) *n.,* notice for display in a public place; poster

plat • form (plat´fôrm) *n.,* statement of principles, usually by a political party or candidate

pluck • i • ly (pluk´i l ē) *adv.,* bravely, spiritedly

po • lar • ize (pō´lər īz´) *v.,* separate into opposing groups

por • tal (pôrt´'l) *n.*, doorway, gate, or entrance

port • ly (pôrt´lē) *adj.*, large and heavy in a dignified way

port • man • teau (pôrt man´tō´) *n.*, suitcase; travel case or bag

pos • ter • i • ty (päs ter´ə tē) *n.*, all succeeding generations

po • tent (pot´nt) *adj.*, effective or powerful in action

pre • car • i • ous (prē ker´ē əs) *adj.*, dependent on chance; risky

prec • i • pice (pres´i pis) *n.*, steep cliff

pre • cip • i • tate • ly (prē sip´ə tit lē) *adv.*, very suddenly

pre • cip • i • ta • tion (prē sip´ə tā shən) *n.*, rush; haste; discharging of a substance, usually said of rain or snow from a cloud

prin • ci • pal • ly (prin´sə pəl lē) *adv.*, most importantly or significantly

priv • i • lege (priv´ə lij) *n.*, right or favor

pros • e • cute (präs´i kyo͞ot´) *v.*, pursue

pros • trate (präs´trāt´) *adj.*, flat, face down

prov • ince (präv´ins) *n.*, territorial district

pro • vi • sions (prō vizh´ənz) *n.*, stock of food and other supplies assembled for future needs

pro • ver • bi • al (prō vʉr´bē əl) *adj.*, well known because commonly referred to

prov • o • ca • tion (präv´ə kā´shən) *n.*, act of exciting into action or angering

prox • im • i • ty (präks im´ə tē) *n.*, state or quality of being near

pu • gil • is • tic (pyo͞o´jil iz´tik) *adj.*, fighting

pu • ri • fy • ing (pyo͞or´ə fī´ŋ) *adj.*, cleansing

pu • tre • fac • tive (pyo͞o´trə fak´tiv) *adj.*, rotting; decomposing

pu • tres • cent (pyo͞o tres´ənt) *adj.*, rotting

pun • gent (pun´jənt) *adj.*, producing a sharp sensation of taste and smell

Q

quaff (kwäf) *v.*, drink heartily in a thirsty way

quar • rel (kwôr´əl) *v.*, fight; dispute heatedly

qua • si - proc • la • ma • tion (kwä´zē präk´ lə mā´shən) *n.*, seemingly official announcement

qui • ver (kwiv´ər) *v.*, shake or tremble

R

ra • di • ant • ly (rā´dē ənt lē) *adv.*, brightly

ra • di • ate (rā´dē āt´) *v.*, branch out in lines from a center

rai • ment (rā´mənt) *n.*, clothing; apparel

ram • part (ram´pärt´) *n.*, embankment for defense against attack

rav • age (rav´ij) *v.*, destroy violently

reason (re´zən) *v.*, think clearly and logically

re • cip • ro • cate (ri sip´rə kāt´) *v.*, return

reck • on (rek´ən) *v.*, judge; consider; estimate

rec • on • cile (rek´ən sīl´) *v.*, make content or agreeable

rec • on • noi • ter (rek´ə noit´ər) *v.*, examine or spy on an area

re • doubt (ri dout´) *n.*, stronghold; fortification

re • fract (ri frakt´) *v.*, cause a wave of light or sound to bend

re • ha • bil • i • ta • tion (rē´hə bil´ə tā´shən) *n.*, process of restoring physical or mental health; preparation for employment

re • in • force (rē´in fôrs´) *v.*, strengthen

re • it • er • ate (rē it´ə rāt´) *v.*, repeat

re • luc • tant • ly (ri luk´tənt lē) *adv.*, unwillingly

rem • nant (rem´nənt) *n.*, remainder; residue

re • mon • strance (ri män´strəns) *n.*, protest

re • morse (ri môrs´) *n.,* deep sense of guilt over a wrong that one has done

ren • der • ing (ren´dər iŋ) *n.,* drawing

ren • dez • vous (rän´dā vo͞o´) *n.,* place designated for meeting or assembly

re • plen • ish (ri plen´ish) *v.,* make full or complete again; resupply

re • prieve (ri prēv´) *n.,* temporary relief or escape

res • o • lute (rez´ə lo͞ot´) *adj.,* determined; having or showing firm purpose

re • solve (ri zälv´) *n.,* firm determination; fixed purpose

res • pite (res´pit) *n.,* interval of temporary relief or rest

retch (rech) *v.,* become ill; vomit

ret • ri • bu • tion (re´trə byo͞o´shən) *n.,* punishment for a specific act

re • vul • sion (ri vul´shən) *n.,* sudden, complete and violent change

rib • ald (rib´əld) *n.,* person characterized by coarse or vulgar joking or mocking

ric • o • chet (rik´ə shā) *v.,* make an oblique rebound after hitting something at an angle

rif • fle (rif´əl) *v.,* leaf or look rapidly through something such as a book

rouse (rouz) *v.,* awaken; stir up to flight; cause to rise from cover

rout (rout) *n.,* disorderly crowd; noisy mob; disorderly flight or retreat

ru • di • men • ta • ry (ro͞o´də men´tər ē) *adj.,* basic; fundamental

ruse (ro͞oz) *n.,* trick

S

sack (sak) *v.,* loot; plunder

sa • cred (sā´krid) *adj.,* holy or special

sa • lient (sāl´yənt) *adj.,* noticeable; prominent

sal • low (sal´ō) *adj.,* sickly-looking

sal • ly (sal´ē) *n.,* attack; sudden rushing forth

sanc • tion (saŋk´shən) *v.,* support, permit, authorize

sanc • tu • ar • y (saŋk´cho͞o er´ē) *n.,* place of refuge or protection, asylum

satch • el (sach´əl) *n.,* small bag for carrying belongings, especially clothes or books

scarce (skers) *adv.,* hardly

scarce • ly (skers le) *adv.,* only just, barely

scarf (skärf) *v.,* consume greedily; eat quickly

scheme (skēm) *v.,* plan in a deceitful way, plot

scoff (skôf) *v.,* mock; show contempt

scoff • ing • ly (skäf´iŋ lē) *adv.,* making fun of; in mockery of

scul • ler • y (skul´ər ē) *n.,* room next to kitchen where the dirtier kitchen work is done

scur • ry (skʉr´ē) *v.,* run quickly

sham (sham) *n.,* imitation; artificial

sheep • ish • ly (shēp´ish lē) *adv.,* in an awkwardly shy or embarrassed manner

siege (sēj) *adj.,* blockade or bombardment

singe (sinj) *v.,* burn slightly or superficially

sin • gu • lar • ly (siŋ´gyə lər lē) *adv.,* uniquely; exceptionally

skel • e • tal (skel´ə t'l) *adj.,* meager, consisting of only the basic or general elements

smite (smīt) *v.,* hit or strike hard

sole (sōl) *adj.,* only

sol • emn (säl´əm) *adj.,* serious

som • ber (säm´bər) *adj.,* dark and gloomy or dull

sparse • ly (spärs´lē) *adv.,* thinly; not densely

spas • mod • ic (spaz mäd´ik) *adj.,* fitful; intermittent

spas • mod • i • cal • ly (spaz mäd´ ik lē) *adv.,* suddenly, violently, and intermittently

spat • u • late (spach´ə lāt´) *adj.,* of or like a cooking utensil, the spatula

spe • ci • men (spes´ə mən) *n.,* sample used for study

spec • tral (spek´trəl) *adj.,* like a ghost or phantom

spec • tral • ly (spek´trəl lē) *adv.,* like a ghost

spec • u • la • tive (spek´ yo͞o lə tiv) adj., theoretical, not practical

spy (spī) *v.,* see; catch sight of; perceive

stac • ca • to (stə kät´ō) *n.,* sound broken up into abrupt, distinct elements

stark (stärk) *adj.,* bleak; desolate; barren

state • ly (stāt´lē) *adj.,* dignified

stern (stʉrn) *adj.,* unshakable, firm

stip • pled (stip´əld) *adj.,* covered or marked with dots

stol • id (stäl´id) *adj.,* having or showing little or no emotion or sensitivity

stout (stout) *adj.,* brave; courageous; powerful; forceful

strewn (stro͞on) *adj.,* sprinkled; scattered

sub • con • scious (sub kän´shəs) *adj.,* occurring without full knowledge or perception

sub • se • quent (sub´si kwənt) *adj.,* following

sub • ter • ra • ne • ous (sub´tə rā´nē əs) *adj.,* underground

subt • le (sut´'l) *adj.,* not obvious or direct

suc • cumb (sə kum´) *v.,* yield; submit; give way

sul • try (sul´trē) *adj.,* humid, excessively hot and moist

sum • mon (sum´ən) *v.,* call together; order to appear

sump • tu • ous (sump´cho͞o əs) *adj.,* magnificent or splendid

sup • press (sə pres´) *v.,* keep back; consciously dismiss from the mind

su • per •sede (so͞o´pər sēd´) *v.,* cause to be dropped from use as inferior or obsolete

sur • mount (sər mount´) *v.,* be at the top of

swarth • y (swôr´thē) *adj.,* having a dark complexion

sym • bol • ic (sim bäl´ik) *adj.,* serving as a representation or suggestion of another thing

sym • me • try (sim´ə tre) *n.,* balance, proportion

syn • chro • nize (sing´krə niz´) *v.,* cause to agree in time or rate of speed

T

taint (tānt) *v.,* poison; corrupt; stain

te • mer • i • ty (tə mer´ə tē) *n.,* recklessness; foolish or rash boldness

tem • pes • tu • ous (tem pes´cho͞o əs) *adj.,* violent; stormy

ten • ta • tive (ten´tə tiv) *adj.,* timid; hesitant; uncertain

ter • ma • gant (tʉr mə gənt) *adj.,* quarrelsome

ter • mi • nus (tʉr´mə nəs) *n.,* station at the end of a railway line

thick • et (thik´it) *n.,* thick growth of shrubs, underbrush, or small trees

thong (thôŋ) *n.,* narrow strip of leather

thread • bare (thred´ber´) *adj.,* worn down so that the threads show

throng (thrôŋ) *v.,* crowd; press upon in large numbers

tim • or • ous (tim´ər əs) *adj.,* timid; full of or subject to fear

toc • sin (täk´sin) *n.,* alarm bell

tor • tu • ous (tôr´cho͞o əs) *adj.,* full of twists, turns, curves, or windings

tot • ter (tät´ər) *v.,* rock or shake as if about to fall

tran • quil • i • ty (tran kwil´ə tē) *n.*, calmness

tran • si • ent (tran´zē ənt) *adj.*, temporary; passing quickly

trans • form (trans fôrm´) *v.*, change nature or character of

trans • gres • sor (trans gres´sər) *n.*, one who breaks a law or commandment

trans • lu • cent (trans lo͞o´sant) *adj.*, partially transparent

tra • verse (trə vʉrś) *v.*, cross or pass through

treach • er • ous (trech´ər əs) *adj.*, giving a false appearance of safety or reliability; insecure

treb • le (treb´əl) *adj.*, threefold; triple

trow • el (trou´əl) *n.*, small, hand tool used for smoothing plaster or concrete

tur • bu • lent (tʉr´byo͞o lənt) *adj.*, marked by wildly irregular motion

tus • sle (tus´əl) *n.*, vigorous struggle; scuffle

U

ul • u • la • tion (yo͞ol´yo͞o lā´shən) *n.*, loud howling or hooting

un • a • wares (un ə werz´) *adv.*, unexpectedly; suddenly; by surprise

un • ceas • ing (un sēs´ŋ) *adj.*, not ending

un • kempt (un kempt´) *adj.*, not tidy or neat

un • nerve (un nʉrv´) *v.*, cause to lose one's courage or self-confidence

un • ob • tru • sive • ly (un əb tro͞o´siv lē) *adv.*, without calling attention to oneself

un • pre • ce • den • ted (un pres´ ə den´tid) *adj.*, unheard of, new

un • seem • ly (un sēm´lē) *adj.*, not decent or proper

un • won • ted (un wän´tid) *adj.*, uncommon, rare

ut • ter • ly (ut´ər lē) *adv.*, completely; totally

V

vague (vāg) *adj.*, not sharp, certain or precise in thought, feeling or expression

vain (vān) *adj.*, without force or effect

ve • he • mence (vē´ə məns) *n.*, state of having intense feeling or passion

ve • he • ment (vē ə mənt) *adj.*, acting or moving with great force

ven • om • ous (ven´əm əs) *adj.*, poisonous

ven • ti • la • tor (vent´'l āt´ər) *n.*, device used to circulate air

ver • min (vʉr´mən) *n.*, various insects or small animals seen as pests

ves • tige (ves´tij) *n.*, trace; bit

vi • car (vik´ər) *n.* a parish priest

vig • i • lance (vij´ə ləns) *n.*, the quality of being watchful and alert to danger and trouble

vig • i • lant (vij´ə lənt) *adj.*, watchful and alert to danger or trouble

vile (vīl) *adj.*, disgusting; repulsive

vi • ra • go (vi rā´gō) *n.*, quarrelsome woman

vir • ile (vir´əl) *adj.*, having stength; forceful

vis • age (viz´ij) *n.*, face

vi • tal • i • ty (vī tal´ə tē) *n.*, power to live

vi • ti • ate (vish´ē āt´) *v.*, spoil; weaken

vo • li • tion (vō lish´ən) *n.*, power or faculty of using one's will

vol • ley (väl´ē) *n.*, simultaneous discharge of a number of firearms

W

waft (wäft) *v.*, transport as if through the air

wan • ton • ness (wän´tən nes) *n.*, senseless cruelty

ward (wôrd) *v.*, turn aside; fend off

weath • er (weth´ər) *v.,* become discolored or disintegrated from exposure to the elements

whet (wet) *v.,* stimulate

wince (wins) *v.,* shrink or draw back slightly, usually with a grimace

wrest (rest´) *v.,* pull or force away violently with a twisting motion

wretch (rech) *n.,* miserable or unhappy person, person in deep distress or misfortune

Index of Titles and Authors

Index of Skills

Language

Speaking and Listening

Study and Research

Applied English

Index of Fine Art

Art Acknowledgments

Canoe in Rapids. Winslow Homer, 1897. Watercolor over graphite on white paper, 343 mm X 529 mm. Courtesy of Fogg Art Museum, Harvard University Art Museums, Louise E. Bettens Fund, **cover**; Le Moulin de la Galette. Auguste Renoir, 1876, **2**; The Home Lesson. Albert Anker, **6**; Still Life—Fruit. Vincent van Gogh, **10**; Artist's Father. Edward Hopper, 1900, **17**; Archive Photo, NY, **26**; Starry Night. Vincent van Gogh, 1889, **46**; Rick Hudson, **50**; Mark Jernstrom, **71, 73, 74**; The Annointing. Bonnie Auten, 1995, **98**; The Contribution of the Negro to Democracy in America, 1943. Charles White. Egg tempera (fresco secco), 11′ 9″ X 17′ 3″. Hampton University Museum, Hampton, VA, **122**; The Problem We All Live With. Norman Rockwell. Printed by permission of the Norman Rockwell Family Trust. Copyright © 1995 by the Norman Rockwell Family Trust. Photo courtesy of the Norman Rockwell Museum at Stockbridge, **142**; Rooftops (No. 1, This is Harlem). Jacob Lawrence. Hirshhorn Museum and Sculpture Garden, Smithsonian Institution, Gift of Joseph H. Hirshhorn, 1966, photo by Ricardo Blanc, **146**; Grandpa Stones. Marvin Toddy, oil on canvas, 18″ by 24″. Tanner's Indian Arts, Gallup, NM, **165**; Colter Bay Indian Arts Museum, Grand Teton National Park, Wyoming, **168**; Lemons. Diego Rivera, 1916, **180**; Courtesy of National Aeronautics and Space Administration (NASA), **184**; Rick Hudson, **190**; Sherberts. Tamayo, 1938, **200**; Reed E. Brewer, **206, 209**; Landscapes. Pieter Brueghel the Elder, **218**; Roman Temple. Bellotto D. Canaletto, **220**; Kevin K. Knight, **242, 244**; Sara Day, **262**; David W. Ferreira, **268**; Oyo Gallery, Photo by Phil Leo, **286, 288, 296, 302, 329**; Mexican Landscape. Velasco, 1885, **338**; Taxeria. Anonymous, 1834, **340**; Landscape with Peacocks. Paul Gauguin, **343**; Hills. Edward Hopper, 1930, **349**; The Return of Rip Van Winkle. John Quidor, c. 1849. Andrew W. Mellon Collection, © Board of Trustees, National Gallery of Art, Washington, **352**; Rodney Busch, **389**; Apples in a Tin Pail. Levi Wells Prentice, 1892. Charles H. Hayden Fund, Courtesy of Museum of Fine Arts, Boston, **400**; Rake. Vincent van Gogh, 1889, **402**; Allan Williams, **409**; Rick Hudson, **413, 414, 424**; Portrait Woman. Diego Rivera, 1927, **436**; Don Mathias, Jr., **440, 442, 445, 447, 448**; The Cliff Walk, Claude Monet, **456**; Fields. Vincent van Gogh, 1884, **459**; Archive Photo, NY, **467, 472, 479, 492**; Fiesta. Diego Rivera, 1928, **526**; Two Women. Vincent van Gogh, 1882, **529**; Courtesy of John H. Quinn, **548**; Photo courtesy of the National Aeronautics and Space Administration (NASA), **566**; Rick Hudson, **574, 579, 583, 588, 599, 604, 612, 621, 626, 633, 642, 647, 651, 654, 658, 667, 668, 670, 674, 677, 689, 691, 697, 703, 707**.

Additional Photos and Illustrations

Courtesy of Correl Professional Photos: 54, 78, 83, 102, 107, 114, 128, 131, 150, 231, 250, 281, 282, 285, 309, 366, 377, 420, 533, 536; **Courtesy of Sol Graphic Design:** 60, 64, 509, 514; **Courtesy of Photodisc:** 28, 315, 432; **Courtesy of Planet Art:** 280, 283, 321; **Author Illustrations:** All author illustrations by Sara Day, except: Library of Archive Photo, NY, 28; The Library of Congress, 38, 60, 74, 146, 359, 410, 517; Wole Alade, 298, 303, 315, 323, 330; Wellesley College Library, Special Collections, 448.

Literary Acknowledgments *(continued from copyright page)*

This page constitutes an extension of the copyright page. We have made every effort to trace the ownership of all copyrighted material and to secure permission from copyright holders. In the event of any question arising as to the use of any material, we will be pleased to make the necessary corrections in future printings. Thanks are due to the following authors, publishers, and agents for permission to use the materials indicated.

King-Size Publications, Inc. "Zoo," by Edward D. Hoch. Copyright © 1958 by King-Size Publications, Inc. © renewed 1986 by Edward D. Hoch. Reprinted by permission of the author. **Houghton Mifflin Company/Seymour Lawrence.** Excerpt from *Trout Fishing in America,* by Richard Brautigan. Copyright © 1968 by Richard Brautigan. Reprinted by permission of Houghton Mifflin Company/Seymour Lawrence. All rights reserved. **Houghton Mifflin Company.** Excerpt from *Earth in the Balance—Ecology and the Human Spirit,* by Al Gore [pp. 19–26]. Copyright © 1992 by Senator Al Gore. Reprinted by permission of Houghton Mifflin Company. All rights reserved. "Night Clouds," from *The Complete Poetical Works of Amy Lowell.* Copyright © 1955 by Houghton Mifflin Company. Copyright © renewed © 1983 by Houghton Mifflin Company, Brinton P. Roberts and G. D'Andelot Belin, Esq. Reprinted by permission of Houghton Mifflin Co. All rights reserved. **Fitzgerald Iyamabo.** "Yemoja, Queen of the Seas" and "Why the Sky Is Far Away from the Earth," retold by Fitzgerald Iyamabo. Reprinted with permission of the author. **Little, Brown and Company.** Poem "The Brain—is wider than the Sky," by Emily Dickinson from *The Complete Poems of Emily Dickinson,* edited by Thomas H. Johnson. Copyright 1960 by Mary L. Hampton, © 1961 by Little, Brown and Company. Reprinted by permission of the publisher. **Longmeadow Press.** "A Midsummer Night's Dream," from *Illustrated Tales from Shakespeare, a Modern Adaptation from the Charles and Mary Lamb Classic,* pp. 18–22, 24–29. Copyright © 1992 Aventinum. Reprinted by permission of Longmeadow Press, a division of Waldenbooks. **Marian Reiner.** "How to Eat a Poem," from *A Sky Full of Poems,* by Eve Merriam. Copyright © 1964, 1970, 1973, 1986 by Eve Merriam. Copyright © renewed 1992 Eve Merriam. Reprinted by permission of Marian Reiner. **Rona Maynard.** "The Fan Club," by Rona Maynard. **Mahmoud Ibrahim Mostafa.** "Goha and His Donkey" and "Goha and the Pot," retold by Mahmoud Ibrahim Mostafa. Reprinted with permission of the author. **New Directions.** Enomoto Seifu-Jo. Poem "Everyone is asleep . . ." from *Women Poets of Japan,* translated and edited by Kenneth Rexroth and Ikuko Atsumi. Copyright © 1977 by Kenneth Rexroth and Ikuko Atsumi. Reprinted by permission of New Directions. Kujō Takeko. Poem "I do not consider . . ." from *Women Poets of Japan,* translated and edited by Kenneth Rexroth and Ikuko Atsumi. Copyright © 1977 by Kenneth Rexroth and Ikuko Atsumi. Reprinted by permission of New Directions. **Jandiwe Njobe.** "Dingane the Brave Warrior," retold by Jandiwe Njobe. Reprinted with permission of the author. **Liam O'Flaherty.** "The Sniper," from *Spring Sowing,* by Liam O'Flaherty, 1926. Harcourt Brace and Company. **Peter Bedrick Books.** "The Secret Name of Ra," from *Gods & Pharaohs from Egyptian Mythology,* by Geraldine Harris. Copyright © 1981 by Eurobook Limited. Reprinted by permission of Peter Bedrick Books, New York. **Poolbeg Press, Ltd.** Excerpt "Amaterasu," from "The Sun, the Looking-Glass, and the Dragon, retold by Carolyn Swift from *World Myths and Tales.* Copyright © 1993 by Carolyn Swift. Reprinted by permission of Poolbeg Press, Ltd. **John H. Quinn.** Excerpt from *Ishi in Two Worlds, a Biography of the Last Wild Indian in North America,* by Theodora Kroeber. Copyright © 1961 Theodora Kroeber. Reprinted by permission of John H. Quinn. **Random House, Inc.** From *The Diary of Anne Frank,* by Frances Goodrich and Albert Hackett, copyright © 1954, 1956 as an unpublished work. Copyright © 1956 by Albert Hackett, Frances Goodrich, and Otto Frank. Reprinted by permission of Random House, Inc. Excerpt from *The Autobiography of Malcolm X,* by Alex Haley and Malcolm X. Copyright © 1964 by Alex Haley and Malcolm X. Copyright © 1965 by Alex Haley and Betty Shabazz. Reprinted by permission of Random House, Inc. **The Regents of the University of California.** "Ode to My Socks," by Pablo Neruda, translated from the Spanish by Margaret Sayers Peden, from *Selected Odes of Pablo Neruda.* Copyright © 1990 by The Regents of the University of California. Reprinted by permission of the publisher. **Nightingale Rukuba-Ngaiza.** "Why the Frog Croaks," retold by Nightingale Rukuba-Ngaiza. Reprinted with permission of the author. **Norman H. Russell.** "My Father's Hands Held Mine," by Norman H. Russell. Copyright © by Norman H. Russell. Reprinted by permission of the author. **Luis Omar Salinas.** "My Father Is a Simple Man," from *The Sadness of Days: Selected and New Poems,* by Luis Omar Salinas. Copyright © 1987 by Luis Omar Salinas. Reprinted by permission of the author. **Saki (H. H. Munro).** "The Story-Teller," from *The Complete Short Stories of Saki (H.H. Munro).* The Viking Press, Inc. **Simon & Schuster.** "The Stolen Child" and "The Song of Wandering Aengus," by W. B. Yeats. Reprinted with permission of Simon & Schuster from *The Poems of W. B. Yeats: A New Edition,* edited by Richard J. Finneran (New York: Macmillan, 1983). **Yoshiko Uchida.** "Tears of Autumn," from *The Forbidden Stitch,* by Yoshiko Uchida. Copyright © 1989 by Yoshiko Uchida. Reprinted by permission of the author's estate. **Vintage Books.** "Bums in the Attic," from *The House on Mango Street,* by Sandra Cisneros. Copyright © 1984 by Sandra Cisneros. Published by Vintage Books, a division of Random House, Inc., and in hardcover by Alfred A. Knopf in 1994. Reprinted by permission of Susan Bergholz Literary Services, New York. **Virginia Driving Hawk Sneve.** "Medicine Bag," by Virginia Driving Hawk Sneve, published in *Boy's Life,* March 1975. Copyright © 1975 by Virginia Driving Hawk Sneve. Reprinted by permission of the author. **H. G. Wells.** *The War of the Worlds* by H. G. Wells. **John Hall Wheelock.** "Earth." Reprinted by permission of Scribner, a Division of Simon & Schuster from *The Gardener and Other Poems,* by John Hall Wheelock. p. 46. Copyright © 1961 by John Hall Wheelock. Renewed 1989 by Sally Wheelock Brayton. **William Morrow & Company.** "The Rebel," from *I Am a Black Woman,* by Mari Evans, published by William Morrow & Company, 1970. Reprinted by permission of the author. **W. W. Norton & Company, Inc.** Excerpt from *Red Giants and White Dwarfs,* by Robert Jastrow, pp. 8–11, 13–15. Copyright © 1990 Reader's Library, Inc. Reprinted by permission of W. W. Norton & Company, Inc.